THE LIFE AND LETTERS OF ST. FRANCIS XAVIER

THE LIFE AND LETTERS OF ST. FRANCIS XAVIER

HENRY JAMES COLERIDGE

(OF THE SOCIETY OF JESUS)

SECOND EDITION

IN TWO VOLUMES

VOL I

GYAN

Published by

Gyan Publishing House
5, Ansari Road
Daryaganj, New Delhi-110002
Phone: 011-47034999, 9811692060
E-mail: books@gyanbooks.com

Distribution Network
gyanbooks.com
India, USA, Canada, UK, Australia, France

ISBN : 978-81-212-3709-3 (Set)
ISBN : 978-81-212-4997-3 (PB)
First Published, 1874

2nd Impression 2020

Printed at: Gyan Press, Delhi.

The Life and Letters of St. Francis Xavier
Author: Henry James Coleridge

✠

AETERNE · RERUM · OMNIUM · EFFECTOR · DEUS
MEMENTO · ABS · TE · ANIMAS · INFIDELIUM · PROCREATAS
EASQUE · AD · IMAGINEM · ET · SIMILITUDINEM · TUAM
CONDITAS
ECCE · DOMINE · IN · OPPROBRIUM · TUUM
HIS · IPSIS · INFERNUS · IMPLETUR
MEMENTO · JESUM · FILIUM · TUUM
PRO · ILLORUM · SALUTE · ATROCISSIMAM · SUBIISSE · NECEM
NOLI · QUAESO · DOMINE · ULTRA · PERMITTERE
UT · FILIUS · TUUS · AB · INFIDELIBUS · CONTEMNATUR
SED · PRECIBUS · SANCTORUM · ELECTORUM · TUORUM
ET · ECCLESIAE · SANCTISSIMAE · SPONSAE · FILII · TUI
PLACATUS
RECORDARE · MISERICORDIAE · TUAE
ET · OBLITUS · IDOLOLATRIAE · ET · INFIDELITATIS · EORUM
EFFICE · UT · ET · IPSI · ALIQUANDO · AGNOSCANT · QUEM
MISISTI
DOMINUM · JESUM · CHRISTUM
IN · QUO · EST · SALUS · VITA · ET · RESURRECTIO · NOSTRA
PER · QUEM · SALVATI · ET · LIBERATI · SUMUS
CUI · SIT · GLORIA · PER · INFINITA · SAECULA
SAECULORUM.
AMEN.

PREFACE.[1]

ALTHOUGH several beautiful Lives of St. Francis Xavier exist—some of them in our own language—I do not think that any excuse will be required for the attempt made in the present work to produce a new Life, which may satisfy in some sort the legitimate requirements of our own time. We are accustomed to set a higher value than men of former generations on those indications of personal character, in the case of great men and conspicuous Saints, which are to be found in their own words, in their letters, in anecdotes which set them familiarly before our eyes, and the like. The Catholics of the sixteenth and seventeenth centuries would take the letter of a Saint, for instance, of St. Teresa or St. Francis Xavier, and cut it to pieces for the sake of making up a signature out of letters from separate words, or forming some holy text in the Saint's handwriting in the same way. Many valued such relics as these, without caring much for the actual words and thoughts of the Saint, which they were often content to have in a translation, or a paraphrase which preserved the general sense, but not the peculiar colouring and incommunicable character of the mind from which the words proceeded; we, on the other hand, value above all things the minute traits of character and

[1] To the First Edition.

shades of feeling which can only be discerned by close and faithful study of the mind and heart of some one in whose history we are interested, and we set the highest store on such biographies as make this study most easy to us, by putting before us in its native simplicity whatever comes to us most immediately from such a heart and mind.

There can be no doubt, that if St. Francis Xavier had lived within the present century, the first thought of his biographers would have been to collect every detail within reach, even as to the external circumstances and scenery of his career, and that, in particular, every scrap of writing that ever proceeded from his pen would have been religiously preserved and examined, even if it had not been published. Such was not the way in which biographies were written in the generation which succeeded that of Francis Xavier and Ignatius, and the lives which that generation and subsequent generations produced differ in proportion from those which we require. At this distance of time, and under all the circumstances of the case, it might be impossible, even for one with far greater opportunities than it is my lot to possess, to supply fully what is to us a sort of deficiency in earlier lives of the Saint. A very large number of his letters have perished altogether. Those which remain to us exist chiefly in a Latin translation, which appears to have the merit of conscientious fidelity, but which must certainly fail to give us much of the fire, much of the delicate grace, much of the intense tenderness, which must have breathed in every line of the originals. Moreover, a great many collateral facts, which would render the letters more complete as an integral portion of his biography, have certainly been lost to us. There are other accessories which might be supplied, even at the present day, but which I am painfully aware are wanting in the present work. A knowledge of India and the East, including Japan, an acquaintance with the scenes of his labours, with the living effects which still remain of his preaching, notably in the south of India, with the unchanged and unchangeable aspects of nature in the gorgeous world of the Eastern Isles, with the half civilized and half savage tribes to whom he preached, and of whose manners he has given so striking an account—these and other similar qualifications would have enabled me not only to render the picture more full and attractive, but to supply many an absolute deficiency, and explain much that is now hardly free from obscurity.

No one will rejoice more heartily than myself should any future writer, possessed of such qualifications, undertake to write a more complete life of the Saint than this can pretend to be. In the mean time, it may serve to the glory of God and the honour of St. Francis to have done that which has been now attempted: that is, to give a clear narrative of his life as it stands in the ordinary biographies, and to use the whole of the letters and fragments which have survived to us, in the form in which we possess them, to illustrate the life and to speak to us of his character for themselves. The only former biographer of St. Francis who has made much direct use of the letters is Père Bouhours, whose work is known in England from its translation by Dryden. But our acquaintance with the letters has been increased since his time, and he did not use those which he had as fully as might be wished. He had the advantage, which is shared by the excellent Italian writer Massei, over the earlier biographers, Turselline and Lucena, of writing after the Processes had been completed and largely used by Bartoli, who, in his *Asia*, has really furnished the storehouse from which all subsequent authors have supplied themselves. Massei, who wrote at Rome, where the documents on which the Processes were founded exist, tells us that he consulted them independently, and that he has here and there added details from them which Bartoli had passed over. But in the main the last named author has furnished the materials, derived mainly from the Processes and the letters to Rome from the East, on which our knowledge of the life of St. Francis Xavier has been founded. Bartoli is very full, accurate, and industrious, but the letters were less perfectly known to him than to us. We have the great advantage of the very useful though unostentatious labours of Father Menchacha, who at the end of the last century, and during the suppression of the Society, published the letters in two volumes at Bologna, summing up at the same time, in his Prolegomena, all that can be said about them, and going through them carefully in the 'Chronotaxis' which forms a part of those Prolegomena, with a view to their arrangement and connexion with the life of St. Francis. Father Menchacha once or twice expresses a hope that a Life may some day be written which may give to the letters their due weight in illustrating the history. No one could have been more fit than himself, from his devotion to the Saint and his intimate knowledge of all that remains to us concerning him, to have undertaken such a task; but he has been content to make it possible for others.

Father Menchacha's collection of the letters has existed for some years in French, having been admirably translated by M. Léon Pagès, who has prefixed to his translation a succinct life of St. Francis, which, if it had been fuller, and if the letters had been incorporated with it, would have made superfluous the work which is now laid before the reader. I feel bound to say that, unpretending as this memoir is, I have found it of the very greatest service, as it adds dates and details in a number of places where they were wanting before; and I have so generally found these additions correct as to have learnt to give almost implicit confidence to any statement of M. Léon Pagès, even unsupported by a reference. M. Léon Pagès is now engaged on a work on the history of Christianity in Japan, and I should be extremely glad to know that the volume which relates to St. Francis Xavier's labours in that country would appear in time for use in the second volume of this work. I fear, however, that such will hardly be the case.

The earlier biographers of St. Francis must not be undervalued in comparison with their successors. Turselline appears to me to have much of that charm which hangs about such books as Ribadeneyra's Lives of the Saints—a sort of quaint unction, a simple Catholic spirit, uncritical, not so much in the sense of over credulity and want of due examination, as in that of an absolute freedom from fear and hesitation in dwelling on the religious and supernatural aspect of the subjects treated of, and in supposing in the mind of the reader the same loving piety and glow of devotion with which the writers themselves were kindled. I have been fortunate enough to meet with an old English version of Turselline, which has enabled me to put some of the wellknown facts of the history before the reader in language corresponding to his own in this respect. Lucena's *Vida da San Francesco* is a grand work, possessing the same merit which I have attributed to Turselline, and, moreover, based upon an accurate knowledge of documents and of the history of the Portuguese in the East. It is a large work, here and there diffuse, but it professes to be more than a history of the personal exertions of St. Francis Xavier. I have also used the Portuguese writer Faria y Sousa, who published the annals of Portuguese Asia, *Asia Portuguesa*, at Lisbon in 1655.[2] He was a voluminous and industrious writer, and his facts may be thoroughly depended on. He appears to have consulted a very large number of authorities in the compilation of his history. His style is rather curt and pretentious, and he dwells entirely upon the military and political side of history. I have found him frequently confirm the statements of the biographers of St. Francis, of whom he always speaks with a veneration which seems to reflect the high honour which was always paid to the Saint by the Portuguese officers and governors of India, with a few notable exceptions.

There is every reason for believing that, to speak in general, the history of St. Francis Xavier rests upon human evidence of the very highest kind. All the marvellous actions and incidents with which it is illustrated are supported by sworn witnesses, who came forward when the Processes were formed in the East by the order of the King of Portugal. The documents at the disposal of Bartoli and Massei contained the depositions of the witnesses in each case—depositions as carefully and conscientiously drawn as any that pass current in legal investigations. Bartoli very frequently gives the exact words of the witnesses. It was not the custom in his time to add footnotes and references: the story flows on from page to

[2] His works seem to have been published both in Portuguese and Spanish. The copy used in this work is in Spanish.

page in his grand folios without interruption or the anticipation of questioning, much as the narratives of Herodotus or Thucydides. In our days, no doubt, he would add the names of the witnesses and the like: but to have done it then would have been an anachronism. I have not myself consulted the immense mass of the documents which still exist at Rome, but I have had the advantage of using a manuscript *Relatio super Sanctitate et Miraculis Francisci Xaverii*, drawn up before the canonization of the Saint by three distinguished Roman theologians, auditors of the Rota in the time of Paul V., men of the very highest character, who had examined the evidence formally as its judges, and who made their report to the Pope in this *Relatio*, upon which it seems very clear that the Bull of Canonization was founded. In this document there is a full account of the Processes, and each piece of testimony which is adduced is attributed to its proper author, and it is stated whether he was an eyewitness, or merely one who heard others speak of what had been done. I hope in the second volume to find room at least for an abstract of this very interesting document, which is full of consummate theological and ascetical learning.[3]

I may be allowed to add, that I have made it the chief object of this work to draw out the character of St. Francis Xavier from his own words and actions, rather than to accumulate all the materials that are at the disposal of his biographers. When the letters are added to the narrative of a life such as his, short comparatively though it was, the work becomes almost too large, unless some points are treated con-

[3] This hope had to be abandoned, on account of the great amount of matter which had to be contained in the second volume. *Note to Second Edition.*

cisely. Thus, now and then an anecdote is omitted, or placed in a note, not from the slightest wish to slur it over, but to economize space where the reader was already familiar with the trait of character or the evidence of power which the anecdote might illustrate. I can only pray that the perusal of these pages may have to others the charm which their composition has had to myself—that of making them seem to understand more familiarly the workings of a noble, tender, and most affectionate heart, on fire with the love of God and zeal for souls, and borne, under the guidance of the holy spirit of charity, along a path of heroic enterprize and selfsacrifice by the side of which the achievements of the great ones of the world look poor and unfruitful indeed.

H. J. C.

London, Feast of St. Antony Abbot, 1872.

CONTENTS.

BOOK I.

FROM THE BIRTH OF FRANCIS TO HIS SAILING FOR INDIA.

1506-1541.

CHAPTER I.

Francis Xavier at the University of Paris.

CHAPTER II.

Labours in Italy and Rome.

CHAPTER III.

Francis in Lisbon.

NOTES TO BOOK I.

BOOK II.

From the Sailing of Francis for India to his first Voyage to the Farther East.

1541-1545.

CHAPTER I.

Voyage to India, and first Labours at Goa.

CHAPTER II.

Francis Xavier among the Paravas.

CHAPTER III.

The Fishery Coast and Travancore.

CHAPTER IV.

Manaar, Jafanapatam, and Meliapor.

NOTES TO BOOK II.

BOOK III.

From the first Voyage of Francis to the Eastern Archipelago to his Return to India.

1545-1548.

CHAPTER I.

Francis at Malacca.

CHAPTER II.

The Moluccas.

CHAPTER III.

Four more Months in Malacca.

BOOK I.

FROM THE BIRTH OF FRANCIS TO HIS SAILING FOR INDIA.

1506-1541.

CHAPTER I.

Francis Xavier at the University of Paris.

IN His last discourse to His Apostles, before He went forth to the Garden of Gethsemani on the night of the Passion, our Blessed Lord told them that their election to their high mission in the Church and all their fruitfulness in it depended on Himself. 'You have not chosen Me, but I have chosen you, and have appointed you that you should go and should bring forth fruit, and that your fruit should remain.'[1] This truth necessarily holds good of all who, in any way or degree, have been called in the history of the Church to a work or mission like to that of the Apostles: their original vocation and their preparation for their office, the power which has been with them in carrying it out, and the success and permanence of their work, all have come from our Lord. But as the manner in which He called or prepared the Apostles was so various, as Andrew and John were led to follow Him while they were disciples of the Baptist, as He called Matthew from the receipt of custom, and St. Paul on his way to persecute the Christians at Damascus, so it has been since. The manifold diversity of the vocations of later Saints, of the methods by which they have been attracted, and of the places or occupations in which the Divine Voice has made itself heard by them, is as wonderful as the rich multiformity of their graces and the teeming fertility of their labours. The three canonized Saints of the first generation of the Society of Jesus illustrate this remark, for St. Ignatius was called to God on a bed of convalescence, St. Francis Borgia in the midst of active political services, and St. Francis Xavier from a career of honourable study. It is with the call of the last-named Saint that we have now to do.

[1] St. John xv. 16.

It is perhaps not easy for us to understand fully how important to the Church, in the middle ages and the centuries which immediately followed them, were the great Universities of Europe, or the influence which they exercised on the intellectual life of the time. The universality of printing and reading has to some extent dispersed and distributed that power over the general thought which formerly was, as it were, stored up in the great centres of learning. Again, the effect of the movement of the sixteenth century has been to dissolve Christendom into separate and hostile, though outwardly Christian, nationalities, and one part of this process of disintegration has been the enfeebling of the attraction which drew students to the great Universities without distinction of race or country. The highest idea of a University is now that which represents it as a national institution. Famous and influential as it may be within the shores or the frontiers of a particular country, no University now aspires to be European. Rome alone, in our time, has gathered within her halls the Catholic students of every clime and race, and that she did so was, humanly speaking, one of the supports of that power which the enemies of the Church are striving to root up by the destruction of the Temporal and independent Princedom of the Supreme Pontiff. Moreover, the creation of clerical seminaries in the several dioceses, which was one of the results of the Council of Trent, though it may as yet have been only partially carried out in more than one Catholic country, has tended to dry up the supply of students in philosophy and theology in Universities strictly so called. For these and other causes, and notably on account of the comparative fewness in number of the students now to be found collected at any one spot, no modern University can be considered as an adequate reproduction of the University of Paris in the days of which we are about to speak—when it numbered among its scholars St. Ignatius, St. Francis Xavier, and their companions, and became the providential mother and nurse of the Society of Jesus.

It is not, however, difficult to see the fitness of the place for the work which was to be brought to its first maturity within its walls. Englishmen, at least, can well understand, from the ecclesiastical history of their country during the last forty years, how important it must always be for a religious movement that aims at gaining any permanent hold on the intelligent and educated classes, to seize on a great seat of learning as its own centre. The movement towards Catholicism within the pale of the Anglican Establishment would never have exercised so wide or so rapid an influence over the nation if it had not risen up in the very heart of English cultivation. Elsewhere it would have crept along in the dark, and it would have grown slowly and by fits—if it had not been crushed out before it had the time to grow: at Oxford it placed itself at once in the full light of day, and attained a vigorous manhood when, in point of years, it was still in its infancy. Tractarianism sank into a pietistic decrepitude as soon as it had run through that portion of its career towards Catholic Unity which lay logically and consistently within the limits of obedience to Anglican authorities, of maintenance of Anglican tests of doctrine, and of adherence to the partial compromise on which the Establishment rests. When its intellectual principles led its true followers beyond these bounds, its onward course was necessarily and violently separated from the place which had witnessed its birth: but it left behind it seeds of mental activity and a thirst for truth and progress which have still their effect upon the University, which, under many and great disadvantages, has been raised by these and other influences from the comparative degradation which had characterized it, with almost unbroken uniformity, from the days of the Reformation to our own.

We are not about to compare two things in themselves so different in principle and in history as what is called the Oxford movement of our own time and the formation of the Society of Jesus. Both, however, illustrate the importance of securing, as the startingpoint of a powerful movement, some great centre of intellectual activity, some stronghold of learning frequented by large numbers and successive generations of students in the opening prime of life and in the first vigour of mental energy. Every great movement, and, in particular, every great religious movement, depends, as far as human means are concerned, on the force with which it may draw to itself a larger or smaller proportion of the rich growth of generous, intelligent, and powerful minds with which each generation of a healthy Christian community may be assumed to teem; and the place where such minds are collected, where they flourish and develope under a congenial air, and under the influence of their own mutual attraction and collision, is generally to be found in the Universities. Both of the movements of which we speak illustrate, though not to an equal degree, the manner in which minds which begin with a simple thirst for knowledge for its own sake may become the most fitting and powerful instruments for ends far higher than those which they at first set before themselves. Such minds are naturally to be found at Universities, and when they are taken captive by some revelation of the glories and beauties of the ancient Church, of the noble end for which man was created, and of the importance of salvation and perfection, they are often formed into the mightiest weapons of the armoury of the Church. They are 'not incredulous to the heavenly vision,' and their devotion of themselves to its behests is the welfare of thousands of souls. And those who have inherited the benefits of the connection of the later movement with the great seat of learned education in England may well linger with pleasure over the thought of those few years, in the first half of the sixteenth century, when a little band of students in the University of Paris found themselves united together under the spiritual leadership of Ignatius of Loyola, for the purpose of following a rule of life founded upon the Exercises, and with the determination to spend their lives simply in work for the greater glory of God, and when the Society of Jesus issued from their union.

When, in February 1528, Ignatius arrived in Paris, he was already of middle age.[2] Seven years, full of events in his personal and spiritual history, had passed since his conversion to God by the reading of Ludolph of Saxony's *Life of Jesus Christ*

[2] He was in his thirty-seventh year.

and the *Lives of the Saints*, as he lay on his sickbed, slowly recovering from the effects of the wound which he had received in the breach at Pampeluna. They had been years of rare favours and lights received from God, of deep spiritual experience, and of the most unquestionable fruits of the highest sanctity in the souls of others whom he had laboured to win to God. They had seen him in his seclusion at Manresa, and in his voyage and visit to that Holy Land which left such ineffaceable marks upon his memory, and which drew to itself the first deliberate choice of his apostolic zeal. Early in this time he had composed his book of the *Spiritual Exercises*, and had had distinctly revealed to him the outline and plan of the Order which he was to found upon them in the Church. He had lived with the reputation of a saint at Barcelona, at Alcala, and at Salamanca; everywhere persecution, the shadow of sanctity, as well as the admiration of good Christians, had waited upon him. At Barcelona he had been assaulted and left for dead by the agents of some gay cavaliers who could not brook the return to strictness and cloistral observances which he had introduced into a convent of nuns with whom they were acquainted. At Alcala he had been imprisoned on account of the imprudent devotion of some noble ladies whom he had converted, and who had set off alone and without money upon a long pilgrimage; and at Salamanca also he had been imprisoned, on suspicion of being an unauthorized teacher of new doctrines. In all these cases, the violence or the injustice with which he had been treated had redounded to his greater credit and attracted to him still greater veneration, and the inquiries that had been made into his life and conversation had issued in the fullest and most formal declaration of his innocence, and even of his sanctity. But he had as yet made no progress towards the formation of that body of men who were to be his associates and children in the great work for the glory of God, which was the one engrossing object of his life. His first companions, men who had known him at Barcelona, had gone with him to Alcala, and who had shared his persecutions there, had fallen away from him; he had met some who were afterwards to be among the most eminent of his spiritual children—Martin Olave had given him alms, and Francis Borgia, then a brilliant young noble of seventeen, had seen him led through the streets of the same city between two officers of justice. We shall find that some of his future companions were afterwards attracted to Paris by the reputation he had left behind him in Spain. Still, when he came to the French capital he was alone. Even his first converts in Paris afterwards fell off—Juan de Castro, Peralta, and another, whom he had nevertheless admitted to those Exercises which he often long delayed in the case of souls from whom he hoped much, and who, as a proof of their sincerity, had sold their property, given it to the poor, and taken up their abode at St. Jacques de l'Hôpital, living upon alms.

After his return from the Holy Land, we see nothing more in Ignatius of that overpowering love of solitude and seclusion which had characterized him in his earlier fervour in the cave of Manresa; henceforth his time was to be given to the great centres of life, as if in obedience to that characteristic love of such scenes of action which was afterwards impressed on his Society, and which is commemorated in the well-known Latin distich, which we may thus paraphrase—

In sheltered valleys Bernard loved to dwell,
St. Bennet chose the mountain's lonely crest,
In towns St. Francis fixed his peaceful cell,
But mighty cities pleased Ignatius best.[3]

But it was not every great city, nor even every University, that could be the nursing mother of such an Order as that which he was called to found. The severe orthodoxy of the Spanish seats of learning saved them from the invasions of heretical teachers and dangerous opinions, but they lacked also the stir of mind and conflict of argument which accompany such invasions, and some experience of which may be requisite in those who are to meet falsehood most successfully.

[3] Bernardus valles, montes Benedictus amabat,
Oppida Franciscus, magnas Ignatius urbes.

Perhaps the Society, composed as it was at first in great measure of Spaniards, would have been too exclusively national in character, if Alcala or Salamanca, instead of Paris, had been the place of its birth. At all events, Ignatius failed if he really attempted to found it in Spain. But his long-deferred success came at last. The two first, and in some sense the two greatest, of his spiritual disciples were awaiting him in Paris at the College of St. Barbara, where they had already for some years been intimate friends, sharing even the same room.[4] These two were Peter Favre, a native of Villaret, in the diocese of Geneva, and Francis Xavier, a native of Navarre, born fifteen years[5] after Ignatius himself, at the Castle of Xavier, a few leagues distant from Pampeluna.

Our main business is with the last and most famous of these two, but the beautiful and winning character of Peter

[4] There were at that time a great number of Colleges at Paris. A short account of more than forty will be found in F. Prat's *Maldonat et l'Université de Paris au seizième Siècle*, p. 527, Paris, 1856. These are said to be the 'principal' Colleges. The whole of the city on the south bank of the Seine was occupied by the University. The foundation of the College Royale by Francis I., which gave an impulse to the studies at the same time that it aroused the jealousies of the University, took place in 1531—at the very time, therefore, when Ignatius and his companions were students. The influence of the new College was favourable to innovations of every kind, and naturally gave umbrage to the orthodox. Calvin had studied at the College Montaigu, where Ignatius attended the classes of 'humanities,' a few years before his arrival, and he returned from Bourges to Paris to disseminate heresy in 1534. Ramus, another great innovator, came to Paris in 1523, and began by attaching himself as servant to a rich student at the College of Navarre. He took his degree as Master of Arts in 1536, two years after Ignatius. The Colleges were originally the places of residence of the scholars, many of whom lived on 'burses' attached to the foundation. They were under the care of a 'regent,' who took them to the public lectures of the University. Afterwards the teaching was carried on in the Colleges themselves, as at the English Universities at the present day. St. Ignatius did not proceed to the College of St. Barbara till after he had spent nearly a year in Paris, during which he appears, as has been said, to have studied 'humanities.' It is asserted that there were between twelve and sixteen thousand students in Paris at this period.

[5] The earlier biographers of St. Francis gave the year 1497 as that of his birth. (St. Ignatius was born in 1491.) But Poussines, a later, and in some respects a more accurate writer, gives good reason for supposing that so early a date is an error, and quotes an old register of the family, in which April 7th, 1506, is fixed as the day of his birth. It was the Tuesday in Holy Week.

Favre tempts us to linger over the first mention of his name. When Ignatius arrived in Paris, Peter Favre was in his twenty-second year, and already far advanced in his studies in philosophy. Piety and simplicity were combined in him with a singular love of study and a remarkable appreciation of the value of intellectual gifts. His parents, though not wealthy, had made great efforts to support him as a student, and this he accounted as one of the great blessings of his life. At the age of ten, when tending his father's sheep, he had been inspired with a very ardent desire of knowledge, and had begged most earnestly from his parents the privilege of a good education. They consented, and placed him under the charge of a master, Pierre Veillard, of whom he always spoke with the most intense gratitude, and whom after his death he used to invoke as a saint. Veillard's means raised him above the necessity of teaching for gain, but he kept school for the love of imparting knowledge, and he took care to season his lessons with instructions in piety. Peter Favre said of him that he had a way of making the profane authors whom he taught speak the language of the Gospel. The possibility of this will be denied by no one who is acquainted with the spirit in which the Catholic Church has, from the first, sanctioned the use of the great masters of Greek and Roman literature in the education of her own children. The classics are dangerous if taught in any other spirit, but when they are used in accordance with this, they are not only harmless, but full of beauties and fruitful in advantages which can be found nowhere else. After two years of study under a master of this kind, we find the young Peter Favre solemnly consecrating himself to God by a vow of chastity; and he has left it on record that his fondness for study helped him greatly to keep his vow, as well as to escape numerous temptations and to make progress in virtue. At the age of eighteen he went to the University of Paris, and began his philosophical studies under Juan Peña, at the College of St. Barbara. He became at once the most distinguished and favourite pupil of his master, and when Ignatius presented himself for the same purpose, and took up his abode in the same room with Peter Favre and Francis Xavier, Peter was selected by Peña to 'repeat' the lectures on philosophy to the new student, with whom he soon became very intimate.

Francis Xavier, with whom Ignatius was thus brought into contact at the same time as with Peter Favre, was of a different character from the gentle and simple Savoyard, though like him in the purity of his life, in the excellence of his intellectual gifts, and in his devotion to study. The youngest son of a large and very noble family, he had early surprised his relatives by preferring the pursuit of letters to that of war. The name of his family came from his mother, the sole heiress of the houses of Azpilqueta and Xavier. His father, Juan de Jasso,[6] was also of noble and ancient family, but he was a man of the robe and the pen, high in employment with the King of Aragon, and he was not sorry to see Francis inclined to a career more like his own than that of a soldier; so he made the effort that was required to send his son to Paris without reluctance, though not without difficulty. It is disappointing that we should be left so very much to our imagination if we would form a picture of the earlier years of one who became afterwards so singularly attractive as well as so wonderfully

[6] The account given by Turselline, the earliest biographer of St. Francis, is as follows. (We quote an old English translation, to which we shall often have recourse.) Juan de Jasso, he says, was 'a man noble both for antiquity of his family and wealth, but especially for his learning and prudence, as being the chosen Privy Councillor to King John of Navarre. He now having, through the persuasion of his father in law, removed his dwelling from the Castle Jasso, the ancient seat of his ancestors, to Xavier, his wife's jointure, and having more fortunate success in marriage than his said father in law had—[Martin Azpilqueta was the father in law, who had married Jane Xavier, and had no child but Mary, the sole heiress of the two families, and the mother of our saint]—provided better for the family of the Xaviers than for his own. For having by Mary many children, whereof this our Francis was one, he began to take great care how he might keep up two of the most ancient families of Navarre, which were now somewhat in declining. Whereupon he resolved to leave the name of his own family, although it were neither mean nor obscure, and to give his children and posterity the name of his wife's kindred, so as some of them were called Azpilquetas, others Xaviers.' The same use of two family names seems to have been common in Spain. St. Teresa was the issue of the marriage of a Cepeda and a Ahumada, and the children divided the names. She was Teresa de Ahumada, her brother Lorenzo de Cepeda, and so on.

holy. But no one has preserved for us any childish anecdote of St. Francis which may be placed by the side of St. Teresa's youthful attempt at martyrdom, when she set out with her little brother to seek it at the hands of the Moors. We are left to infer his sweetness of disposition, his high and quick spirit, his generosity and courage, as a boy or a youth, from the evidence of these qualities which meet us in him in after years. We can draw no picture on which we can rely of the family group at the Castle of Xavier. There was the highborn tender mother, who may have loved him specially as the youngest of her children, and whom in after years he was to pass by unvisited on his road to the Indies, not only, perhaps, that he might fulfil to the letter the injunction of our Lord,[7] but also because it might have cost him too much to expose her and himself to the sorrows of a parting interview. The father, the man of business, skilled in the management of affairs, and the trusted servant of his Sovereign, would be of a different character, while the many sons probably despised their father's profession, and considered that Francis had made a strange choice in giving himself to letters. There was one of the sisters, Maddalena, who might have trained him in saintly ways, as she became herself renowned for sanctity, but she probably left her home early to hold a post at the Court of Queen Isabella, before she renounced the world to become the famous Abbess of the Poor Clares at Gandia.

The scanty account which we have of Francis Xavier as a boy represent him as piously brought up, and carefully trained even in such booklearning as was then given to youth. 'He was of an excellent constitution and comeliness of person, of a great and sharp wit, given more to his book than usually children are. None more innocent, none more pleasant, none more affable than he: which made him beloved of all, both at home and abroad.'[8] His purity was remarkable at this early age, and he preserved it unsullied to the end of his life. 'His chastity,' continues the same author, 'as is the nature thereof, sharpened his wit, and prepared his mind as a most pure soil to

7 *Neminem per viam salutaveritis* (St. Luke x. 4).

8 Turselline, lib. i. c. 1.

receive the seeds of wisdom. Therefore, making no account of his brothers' words, who went about by warlike discourses to draw him to be a man of arms (the ancient ornament of their ancestors), he stuck close to his resolution, and whether stirred up by the late example of his father, or drawn by the delight of knowledge, or moved by divine instinct, he preferred the glory of learning before warlike praises.' But he still preserved 'the desire of honour, and was of a high and lofty spirit.' Both these qualities of purity and nobility of aim were needed when, in the eighteenth year of his age, he was sent by his father to the University of Paris, where he was already well-known and highly distinguished when, four years later, Ignatius followed him thither. He finished his earlier studies, and was made Master of Arts in 1530. He then lectured for some time on the logic, metaphysics, and physics of Aristotle, at the College Beauvais. The University was at that time neither perfect in discipline nor immaculate in morals, or even in orthodoxy. The multitudes of young men who flocked thither from all parts were probably exposed to as great temptations as are now incurred by the students of any Continental University, and on account of the entire absence of moral supervision, to greater than are to be met with, as an ordinary rule, under the collegiate system of Oxford and Cambridge. Francis was brilliant and industrious, and his whole character and bearing breathed a singular purity—a virtue against which many snares were sure to be laid in an atmosphere like that of Paris, and which the scanty discipline and independent life of the students did not do much to protect. That he lived pure is a sign that he could not have been eaten up by pride, vanity, and ambition; but at the time of which we are speaking he enjoyed his own great reputation and success, and the perfection of Christian humility and love of contempt had not conquered in his heart the high thoughts of opening manhood and the native haughtiness of his race. He had a heart capable of the largest devotion and the fullest selfsacrifice, a vigour of will that could never have stopped short of success in any career to which he had once given himself, a mind above the world, and yet—

because the light from heaven which was to guide him to the high sanctity to which he was destined had not yet shone upon it—inclined for the moment to occupy itself with such glories as that of a great teacher of philosophy, a renowned doctor, or a brilliant Prelate. He himself tells us, in the first of his letters, that he had not escaped exposure to the danger of the corrupt doctrines which were insidiously disseminated among the youth of the University. He had been too ready to trust the fair appearances of some men of his own age, of ready wit and great accomplishments, who were infected by heresy, and who might in time have led him astray after them. From this danger he was saved by means of the greatest of all the blessings he received at Paris—the friendship of Ignatius.

Yet, strange to say, Francis Xavier was by no means easily won to accept this friendship as a blessing, and his case is not altogether uncommon or unintelligible. There is often an air of sadness and a reserve about men of lofty minds and large intellectual powers who have not yet been ennobled by a great religious vocation, as if they, most of all men, felt instinctively the little that the world can ask them to do and the emptiness of its rewards, and yet were not awake to the opportunities of mighty work and of glorious crowns which are open to those whom God calls to His service. When their own vocation becomes manifest to them, their trial corresponds exactly to that of the young man in the Gospel, whose eagerness in asking his question as to perfection was a proof of the uneasiness with which his soul was secretly consumed. *Quid adhuc mihi deest?* are the words of one who feels a want he does not know how to supply. Then comes the revelation of the truth which tests their hearts to the very core—*Si vis perfectus esse, vade, et vende omnia quæ possides, et da pauperibus, et habebis thesaurum in cælo, et veni, sequere Me!*: and when those who have been more faithful to so gracious though so severe an invitation than he to whom it was first given, look back on their state before their surrender to grace,—whether that surrender be made at once or only after an internal struggle,—they are often inclined to accuse themselves of pride, of vanity, of a contempt of littleness and humility, which certainly at the time were not conscious and deliberate faults. Another characteristic of minds as yet in a state of struggle and uncertainty is a sort of instinctive fear of, and shrinking from, the persons or things which seem either to rebuke their hesitation or to have the power of forcing upon them a clearer and keener light as to the will of God. They feel themselves in the presence of a master whose eye is reading their soul, and they often take occasion, from any mistakes that may be made in the manner of dealing with them, or even from personal and accidental circumstances of birth, or condition, or character, or antecedents, in those who approach them, to recoil from advances made to them, or interest and kindness displayed towards them. 'The word of God is living and effectual, and more piercing than any two-edged sword, and reaching unto the division of the soul and the spirit, of the joints also and the marrow, and is a discerner of the thoughts and intents of the heart.'[9] The presence of those who have the gift of making us read our own characters and vocations more clearly than before is often felt by human nature as that of a sword pointed at our hearts.

Peter Favre and Francis Xavier stand by themselves at the head of the famous six men who formed with Ignatius the first members of the Society of Jesus. The other four had high qualities enough to interest us intensely if they were not somewhat cast into the shade by those two. We must mention them very briefly, in order to pass on to matters more immediately belonging to our subject. Simon Rodriguez of Azevedo was the first in order of time to form acquaintance with Ignatius. He was a Portuguese, born at Vinzella. Both his father's family —he was a Gonsalvez—and his mother's, whose name Simon took, are illustrious in the annals of the Society. He was a child in arms when his father died, and the good Gonsalvez had commended him prophetically to the special care of his mother as one for whom God intended a great destiny in the Church. The King of Portugal had at his own expense sent him to Paris to study, and his devotion had inspired him with

[9] Heb. iv. 12.

designs somewhat like those formed by Ignatius himself, of an apostolic life in the Holy Land. When, therefore, he made acquaintance with Ignatius, he was easily disposed to join him and put himself under his guidance. We have a special debt of gratitude to Simon Rodriguez, as he alone of the first disciples of Ignatius has left us in writing an account of the early years of the Society. After Simon, we find James Laynez, Alfonsus Salmeron, and Nicolas Bobadilla, joining the silently formed company; silently, indeed, for each one was unaware of the thoughts and intentions of the rest, and supposed himself to be the only friend and associate of Ignatius.

Laynez was about the same age as Peter Favre and Francis Xavier; Salmeron was younger still—but little more than eighteen—but he was already known as a prodigy of learning. These two men, who of all the first companions of Ignatius were the most learned, and were destined to become the most conspicuous as theologians, were yet attracted to Paris, as we are assured, from Alcala, where they had made their studies, less by an esteem for the advantages of the great University than by their desire to make the acquaintance of Ignatius, of whose sanctity they had heard so much in the very place where he had been persecuted and imprisoned. We are told that Ignatius chanced to pass as they were dismounting from their horses on their arrival at Paris, and that Laynez at once felt sure that it was he of whom he had heard so much, and went up to speak to him. Theology, properly so called, was the study in which Laynez particularly excelled; Salmeron was famous for his knowledge of the ancient languages, including Hebrew. Salmeron's character is stamped for us on the admirable and copious commentaries on the New Testament which he has left behind him, which combine to a degree uncommon even among Catholic and religious commentators the qualities of solidity, clearness, piety, and the soundest judgment. Salmeron was also a great, fluent, and very effective preacher, and it is this perhaps which gives their peculiar character to his commentaries, which sometimes seem about to glide into sermons. They may be considered, indeed, in many respects as furnishing the type for those *Lectiones Sacræ*, or Lectures on Scripture in the form of Sermons, which afterwards became an institution in the Society and in the Church, and which have often been published in books of great value. The splendid career of Laynez as a theologian at the Council of Trent, his succeeding Ignatius as the second General of his Order, and the design seriously entertained by a large number of the Cardinals to raise him to the Pontifical throne after the death of Paul IV., are too well known to be dwelt upon in detail here. He left behind him, we believe, several treatises of theology in manuscript, and we can hardly imagine a more valuable monument of the soundest theology of the age of the Council of Trent. But, though the manuscript exists, the handwriting is said to be absolutely illegible. Nicolas Bobadilla completes the inner circle of Parisian students around St. Ignatius. He had studied 'humanities' at Valladolid, and had come to Paris to study philosophy. Ignatius was already well enough known to be continually supplied with alms for his own support, and these were even more abundant than his necessities required. The Spanish merchants in the Low Countries, and still more those in England, gave liberally to him. He was thus able to pursue his studies without interruption, and also to help other students like himself. Nicolas was poor and unknown, and became the friend of Ignatius in the first instance by being the receiver of his charitable aid. He was a man of great ability and devotion, more fitted, however, to be guided than to guide, and whose zeal in after years not unfrequently overcame his prudence. It is strange to remember that he it was of the first companions of Ignatius who, if the arrangement first made had been carried out, would have had the great work assigned to him which was accomplished by Francis Xavier. Providence overruled the plan, by keeping Bobadilla on a bed of sickness until the time had passed for the Father demanded by the King of Portugal to set out from Rome, and so Francis Xavier was sent instead. Useful as Bobadilla might have been, we can hardly think that the Indies lost by the exchange.

It takes but a short time to run through the few particular details which require notice as to the seven years (1528—1535) which were passed by Ignatius in Paris, and which witnessed the quiet and deliberate formation of the first Fathers of the Society. We catch glimpses of his visit to Flanders and England for the purpose of obtaining alms, of the widespread influence which he exercised in Paris over many besides those who became his intimate companions, of the opposition which a character and a work like his was certain to meet with, of heroic acts of charity and mortification, of persecution and public suspicion, and of one or two attempts at violence against him. It cannot surprise us to hear of his failure in some cases to win the souls to which he laid siege. Many must have turned away from him sorrowfully, and it seems certain that if the results of his labour for souls at the University were to be measured by the actual numbers of those whom he induced to join his Society, he might to human eyes have appeared to have toiled almost in vain. But, in fact, his apostleship was far too wide in its influence to be estimated by this test, and he was himself too clearsighted, too prudent, and too single-minded to wish to shape all the souls that came under his influence in the particular mould and form which characterized the men of the Society. The anecdotes which remain to us of this time show us how he was perpetually on the watch to do good in any form or degree. His charity was remarkable for its refined ingenuity. He brought the victim of a criminal passion of the worst kind to abandon the occasion of sin, by placing himself up to his neck in water under a bridge, over which the man had to pass in his evening visits to his mistress, and calling out to him that he was there to do penance for him. He won back to strictness of life a lax religious, by making a general confession of the whole of his own life to him with the greatest compunction and exactness. He converted a Prelate of expensive habits and worldly life, by accepting his challenge at a game of chance, at which he happened to find him playing, on condition that the loser should become the servant of the winner for a month. By the side of records of opposition, persecution, and deafness to his influence, we find the most indisputable evidence of the deep general respect in which Ignatius was held, and we are told of the very large numbers whom he induced to lead a more perfect life, or to enter the religious state in various institutions. For his own body he gained a few noble and devoted souls, and we cannot doubt that his chief care was their gradual training and formation. One greater than any of the saints, One Whom Ignatius constantly set before himself as his Pattern and Master, had spent three years of the most active apostolical life, made luminous to the whole world by a perfect constellation of the most marvellous miracles, and at the end of that term the visible fruit of His labours seemed to be confined to a dozen intimate followers—not strong enough to stand by Him in the hour of trial—a few devout women, and some scores of less matured disciples. Yet the Church was formed in the formation of the band of the Apostles, and in her the great instrument of the regeneration of the world was brought to perfection. It may be that there is often this analogy between the most real and lasting work of the great saints, and the secret, quiet, and almost invisible labour of the Incarnate Son of God in the hearts and souls of His Apostles. Certainly, in respect of the point of which we are speaking, as the solid foundations of the Church were laid in our Lord's three years' ministry, so the seven years which passed between the arrival of Ignatius in Paris and the departure of the first Jesuits from that capital on their way to Venice, embrace the time during which the founder of the Society of Jesus stamped with indelible characters the essential features of his institute on the souls of his companions, and moulded them into that spiritual form which they ever afterwards retained. At a later time, he had no leisure for this work. After this time he became the ruler, the prudent guide, the administrator of the affairs of the body, and its representative before authorities, secular and ecclesiastical, and before the world at large. At this stage he was, as it were, the master of novices, the patient cultivator of a few chosen souls, who was hereafter to reap the fruit of his prayers and penances and continual watchfulness in seeing his children serving the Church in her great Council, restoring the use of the long-neglected Sacraments, staving off the ruin of tottering orthodoxy in Germany, reforming the courtiers of Spain, Portugal, or Austria, beginning that internecine war with heresy and infidelity which has ever been the chosen service of their successors, or bearing across the Atlantic, or to the newly-opened worlds of India and the farthest East, the treasure of that Catholic faith which was being spurned by so many nations who had formerly been among the most devoted handmaids of the Church.

Peter Favre, the first of the disciples of Ignatius, is perhaps that one of them all as to his dealings with whom we have the most detailed account. Peter was tormented with scruples, as well as with temptations against the angelical virtue which he had so early in his life vowed to God to preserve unto the end, and this interior misery seems to have driven him for the first time to open his heart to his friend, who seemed to possess a serenity and peace of mind, and a gift of discernment as remarkable as the purity of his life and his zeal for souls. Ignatius, without at once teaching Peter to meditate on the great mysteries, or initiating him into the Exercises, taught him great watchfulness over himself, and some of the methods of what is called the 'discernment of spirits.' He further recommended him to make a general confession, and to adopt the then unusual practice of weekly confession and communion. He taught him also the use of the 'particular examen,' for the purpose, first, of overcoming one by one the faults that he discovered in his own character, taking the most predominant first, and then of acquiring in the same manner virtue after virtue, continuing the exercise as to each till he had acquired the habit of it. He continued him in this simple method for two years, the term afterwards fixed in the Society for the duration of the noviceship. It was not till after Peter Favre had made very great progress under his direction, and had resolved on placing himself in his hands for the whole of his life, to live after the example of the Apostles in poverty and labours for the glory of God, and not till after he had revisited his home to bid it farewell, and had returned to Paris, that Ignatius allowed him to go through the Spiritual Exercises in the midst of a very cold winter, which gave his penitent an opportunity of practising the severest mortification by exposing himself to the cold, as well as by prolonging his fast for several days. This fast cured him of a troublesome inclination to over-eating with which he had been beset. Thus Ignatius prepared him for receiving the priesthood—first of all the Society. In the summer of the same year Peter Favre celebrated his first mass on the Feast of St. Mary Magdalene, and, nearly a month later, it was he who said the mass at the church of our Lady at Montmartre, when all his associates received Communion at his hands, and, for the first time, made their vows of poverty and chastity. It was the Feast of the Assumption, 1534.

It is remarkable that at this moment, from which may be dated the birth of the Society of Jesus, there was but one other of the little band of the followers of Ignatius who had not yet passed through the Spiritual Exercises, which had been so long delayed in the case of Peter Favre. That one was Francis Xavier. That it should have been so shows the singular patience and caution of Ignatius in dealing with this great and heroic soul, though it appears that a secondary reason for the delay existed in the occupation of Francis as a lecturer in philosophy. Yet it seems hardly likely that this alone would have caused him to wait. It is not impossible that Ignatius, who afterwards put off the celebration of his own first mass for so many months after his ordination as priest,[10] may in many cases have refrained from giving the Exercises to souls in whom he hoped after a time to see the most perfect possible dispositions for so great a spiritual act, the fruits of which must always depend in considerable measure upon the fervour with which it is entered upon. He often used the Exercises, or some part of them, for the awakening and conversion of persons who were

[10] F. Genelli remarks that St. Ignatius 'resolved to devote a whole year to his preparation for saying his first Mass, and afterwards added six other months to the time, owing perhaps to his not having yet given up all hope of going to Jerusalem, and celebrating for the first time the Holy Sacrifice on Calvary, or in Bethlehem, at the shrine of the Holy Nativity.' (Eng. Tr. p. 138.)

leading lives below their Christian profession; but they were also, in his hands, the frequent means by which a sacrifice and consecration of self to God which had already been carried very far might be consummated according to the requirements of the sublimest perfection. The truths of the Exercises, like certain graces of the Sacraments, will produce some of their most marvellous effects upon the souls which receive them most worthily.

We have already remarked that Francis Xavier was at first somewhat inclined to turn away from Ignatius, from whom he shrank with a sort of fear, which readily disguised itself under the mask of contempt for the gentleman of noble lineage who had demeaned himself so lowly as to beg for alms and lead the life of a pauper. We can hardly help seeing a prudent care in dealing with such souls as that of Xavier in the celebrated remonstrance with the rector of the College which Ignatius made in the early beginning of his own philosophical studies, against a public chastisement to which it was intended to expose him on account of the influence which he was exercising over a large number of young men, whom he seemed to be withdrawing from their proper pursuits as students for the sake of giving their time to exercises of piety. His conversation on divine things was irresistibly attractive, and it may well have been that in many cases the bounds of discretion were passed by his scholars. The voluntary disputations held on feastdays in the College were neglected, and the time was spent in church instead of in the schools. The professor, Peña, a worthy man in his way, was displeased; he remonstrated in vain, and at length laid the matter before the rector, Andrew Govea, who determined to inflict on Ignatius the ignominious form of punishment known as a public 'hall.' This punishment was a lasting disgrace. All the masters and students were called together by the sound of the bell into the public hall, where the disputations were usually held. The masters had rods in their hands, and with these they touched the shoulders of the culprit, who was considered ever afterwards as a person to be shunned and avoided.

The reader of any one of the numerous lives of St. Ignatius will remember the oft-repeated story, how he at first recoiled from the idea of submitting to so great an indignity, then how he overcame the risings of pride by the love of the Cross and of humility; and how, after he had presented himself as usual at the College, after the gates were closed behind him, and the students assembled by the sound of the bell to be witnesses of the chastisement which was to degrade him for ever in the eyes of the University, he sought an interview with the rector, and, in a few gentle and earnest words, set before him the dishonour that would be done to God if any one were punished publicly whose only crime was, in substance, a burning desire and zeal to make others love and serve better His Divine Majesty. Govea, the rector, was converted on the spot, and, taking the hand of Ignatius, led him into the hall, where the members of the College were assembled in expectation, and there threw himself at the feet of the saint, acknowledging his own error, and bearing the most honourable witness to his goodness and sanctity. If the scene which had been prepared by the enemies of Ignatius might have been calculated most seriously to injure him in the yet wavering mind of Francis Xavier, we can hardly imagine anything more likely to force on him a true estimate, not only of Ignatius himself, but of the cause of which he was the representative and the advocate, than the very different scene which actually took place. Here was something higher, better, nobler than the applause which waited upon the ordinary triumphs of the University. Francis was at that time teaching philosophy with great success, and his biographers have all related how earnestly Ignatius set himself to win that noble heart, praising him to himself and others, and doing all in his power to increase the number of his pupils. It appears, too, from the first letter in our collection—the earliest which remains to us from the pen of Francis Xavier—that Ignatius also supplied him with money during some part of his career at Paris. By so many various means did he seek to secure the confidence and the respect of Francis, and when these were gained he used them to open to himself the opportunity of conversing with his friend and disciple on spiritual subjects, and of sounding in his ears the maxim of Jesus Christ—'What shall it profit a man if he gain the whole world and suffer the loss of his own soul?' We may judge of the state of mind in which Francis then found himself from his own famous letter about the doctors of the University, written several years later, when he was in the midst of his career as the Apostle of the Indies. 'They labour night and day to acquire knowledge, and they give all diligence to mastering the subjects of their studies, but if they would spend as much trouble in that which is the solid fruit of learning and in teaching the ignorant those things which are necessary unto salvation, they would certainly be far better prepared to meet their Lord when He says to them, "Give an account of your stewardship." I fear very much that those who spend so many years in our Universities in studying the liberal arts, do so rather with a view to empty honours and ecclesiastical titles, than to the duties and the burthens which are connected with those distinctions. It has come to this pass, I perceive, that those who are the most diligent in their studies of higher literature, make open profession that their object in doing this is to gain a reputation for learning, and so obtain some ecclesiastical dignity through which to serve our Lord and His Church. Miserable mistake! it is their own profit, not the profit of the public, that they are seeking by their studies. *They are afraid that God will not choose what their own desires point to, and so they are unwilling to commit the whole matter* [of their vocation] *entirely to the will of God.*'[11] These may well be the words of one who had had intimate experience of the struggle which is inevitable when the soul that wishes to serve God has conceived desires of its own as to the manner in which it is to serve Him; and we can understand how the conversation of a saintly friend, persistently harping on the great maxims of Christian perfection, must have caused sorrow and disturbance in a generous mind until the moment came when the battle was won.

Spiritual conversation, indeed, was, both now and at other

[11] See below, Book ii. ch. 2.

times, the great weapon of Ignatius. We hear of his preaching in Spain and even elsewhere, but his sermons probably derived their power far more from the fervour of his charity and the authority of his example than from any gift of eloquence, native or acquired. But the art of winning souls to God by holy conversation may almost be called one of the incommunicable privileges of true sanctity, and it was this that made Ignatius a power in the University of Paris, as a similar gift had made Socrates so powerful with the thinking portion of his countrymen at Athens. It was this that gathered round him the small circle of immediate disciples of whom we are now speaking; it was this that bound them to him by so intense and solid a devotion, and that gave him so wonderful an influence over a far wider circle among the companions of their studies. As we have seen, Peter Favre was made his disciple by this means alone, and, in the same way, it was by this that his empire over the soul of Francis Xavier was gradually gained.

The remaining obstacles to the perfect adhesion of Francis to the plans of Ignatius, came, as has often been related, from without. His father had put himself to considerable expense for the sake of supporting him at the University of Paris, and he thought of sending for him to his own country, where, of course, his chance of ecclesiastical preferment, to which the father naturally looked as the fruit of all his own sacrifices, would be the greatest. Indeed, we hear of the offer of a canonry at Pampeluna made to Francis just before he finally left Paris. At an earlier period, when his theological studies were as yet far from complete, and when his ideas of what became his birth had made him spend rather more money than was convenient to Don Juan, his father is said to have been deterred from recalling him only by the intercession of his own daughter already mentioned—the holy nun in the Convent of St. Clare at Gandia —who wrote to tell him that God had chosen her brother for a great work in the Church. We shall never know, in this world, how much this saintly and heroic soul, who died about the time of the final conversion of her brother in 1533, had to do with the secret formation of his great sanctity. She died a death of terrible suffering, which she prayed might be hers instead of that of another religious of the same Convent. Another effort to hinder his onward course was made by a dependent of Xavier's, who attempted to assassinate Ignatius, when he saw the ascendancy which he was acquiring over his patron. We are not told of the exact moment at which Francis took his final and irrevocable resolution to give up the world. Such designs often mature very gradually in hearts like his.

When we consider the work actually performed by the religious body of which these immediate followers of Ignatius became the nucleus, and compare it with the designs which they had conceived at the time of their first solemn consecration of themselves to God in the church of Montmartre, we are inclined to be surprised at the discrepancy between the issue and the intention. The Holy Land was the great object of their ambition—not merely that they might visit it as pilgrims, as Ignatius had done, but that they might obtain leave to remain and to preach there. Even at the outset, however, they seem to have understood that this design might never be fulfilled. Still, it was the original plan of the whole body. They were to wait a year at Venice for the opportunity of passing to the East, and only when that space of time had been passed in fruitless expectation were they to proceed to Rome to place themselves absolutely at the disposal of the Supreme Pontiff. And yet it is known that Ignatius had had the whole outline and plan of the Society which he was to form set before him at Manresa. Can it be that, but for the war between the Venetians and Solyman, the Society of Jesus would have pursued so very different a career from that which has actually been its portion? Would it have left heresy unopposed in Europe, would it never have undertaken the renovation of Christian education and the reformation of manners at home, would its name never have been heard of in the schools and its services never rendered to literature in every branch from theology and philosophy down to physical science and grammar? The answer is surely to be found in the character of the men whom Ignatius had gathered round him, and in the importance which he invariably and at so much cost attached, both in his own case and in that of others, to intellectual cultivation and deep theological learning. His object was in the first instance to form them in the true Apostolical spirit after the model of our Lord, to detach them perfectly from all earthly things, and inflame them to the utmost with the fire of the love of God. It was his object in the second place to arm them in the most complete intellectual and theological panoply that could be acquired anywhere in Christendom, and so to fit them to carry on the Apostolical work in any region whatever of the world, civilized or uncivilized, Christian and Pagan, with those full resources even of human learning of the use of which we see so marked an instance in the career of St. Paul. We may judge of the universality of his aim from the large range of acquirements, spiritual and intellectual, with which he sought to store his followers—content, with such an end in view, to wait for so many precious years before he launched them on the world.

If it appears to us that Palestine might have been no fitting field for the labours of men of this stamp, it may be that we have too long accustomed ourselves to accept the present state of things in the East as something to be acquiesced in without an effort, something which the sober judgment of Christian men is to consider as beyond the hope of change. Palestine was not to be the providential scene of the labours of the companions of Ignatius, but we cannot conclude from this that the very greatest results, even for Europe, might not have issued from their enterprize if it had been the will of God that it should be carried out. The East is nearer to us than India, China, Japan, or the New World. Whenever the day of regeneration shall dawn for the East, for Syria, Asia Minor, Egypt, and the region of the Euphrates and the Caspian, then a blow will have been struck at the power which hinders the progress of God's Kingdom upon earth such as it has never yet felt. That region is the very heart of the world, and its conquest to the Church would even now, humanly speaking, ensure the accomplishment of that great work which has been for so many centuries prevented by the Greek schism and the dominion of Islam—the work of the Christianization of Asia. But great as this blow would be even now, it may be said that its consequences would have been far greater then, when the Turks were still a power which kept Europe in awe by sea and by land, when Lepanto had not been fought, nor Malta besieged, nor the flood of barbarian invasion rolled back from the walls of Vienna, and when the colossal power of Russia had not yet risen up to aid by its strength the schism of Constantinople. We shall follow Francis Xavier in his labours in the still farther East—labours the fruits of which it cost the Church incredible efforts to keep up and develope for more than two centuries by supplies from Europe, supplies which always depended in great measure upon the goodwill of politicians, and which were at last dried up, almost entirely, by the triumph of the Bourbon Courts in the suppression of the Society. The evangelizing of the far East, bright and grand as its history is, might have had annals far brighter and grander if the work had been begun in Palestine, and had advanced steadily eastwards. We shall find Francis, at the very end of his short career, renewing in some sense the design with which he began, in his intention to preach westward from China until he came again to the shores of the Mediterranean. Such are the dreams of saints. But we must not measure them by our narrow views of expediency or possibility, and we may feel assured that, if Ignatius and his companions had really been sent by Providence to Palestine, they might not have done the less in their own persons and in those of their followers in the battle against heresy or worldliness or ignorance in the Catholic countries of Europe. At all events, Ignatius never changed his mind about the importance of the Holy Land, nor laid aside his wish that the Society which he had founded might be allowed to fix one of its chief seats at Jerusalem, the one place of Christian pilgrimage which can never lose its attraction, under whatever external circumstances of disadvantage, as long as this world lasts, and which is so obviously fitted to be the centre from which all good influences may flow over the whole of the long-desolate Eastern world. In the very last year of his life, we find Ignatius refusing to give up his hopes. Don Pedro de Zarata de Bermeo, a knight of the Holy Sepulchre, obtained in 1554 a bull from Pope Julius III. for the foundation of three Colleges of the Society in the East—in Jerusalem, in Constantinople, and in Cyprus. Ignatius made many efforts to bring about the accomplishment of this design; but he was always thwarted by the apathy of the persons to whom he addressed himself, or other causes. Even before the bull was actually obtained, he had sent Simon Rodriguez—mindful of that early attraction to the Holy Land which had first brought them together—as far as Venice on his way to Jerusalem, where he was to wait for a suitable opportunity of establishing the College. But Rodriguez fell so ill at Venice that he was unable to go farther. Still, when in 1556 the Franciscans urged him to renounce the right which the bull of Pope Julius had given him, Ignatius declined to do so, saying that he did not think he could do so with a clean conscience, even though it might seem unlikely that the design could be carried out in his own lifetime.[12]

We must pass rapidly over the time—a space of two years and three months—which passed between the first happy meeting of the companions of Ignatius in the crypt at Montmartre, where they pronounced their vows and received communion

[12] The history of this plan of Zarata's is related at length by F. Genelli in the fifth chapter of his second part of his *Life of St. Ignatius* (Eng. Tr. pp. 260-263). The Bollandists give the letter, which is quoted by F. Genelli, in which Ignatius refused to renounce his right. 'As we do not know,' he says, 'what God our Lord may be pleased to do through the poor instrumentality of this little Society, it does not seem to me to be right, or conformable to the Spirit of God, to consent to the closing of the prospect of having a College in the Holy Land. *And even were I to renounce it, this act would not bind the Society in any future time.* And I do not think I can consent with a free conscience to a renunciation of this kind, even though it should appear unlikely that we should found a College there during my lifetime. It is of course quite possible that this design may never be carried into execution, but we must not engage ourselves by a promise that it shall not be done.' We may add, that our own days may very possibly see a great change in the state of affairs in the East, one of the results of which may well be the accomplishment of the long-cherished designs of St. Ignatius for the benefit of its peoples.

from the hands of Peter Favre, to the 15th of November 1536, when they finally left Paris on their road to Venice, there to attempt the accomplishment of their design of passing to the Holy Land. We are not told at what exact point in his academical career Francis Xavier left off the teaching of philosophy and devoted himself to the study of theology, but we know that the completion of their theological studies was the chief reason for the delay resolved upon by Ignatius. It would take us too long, also, to follow Francis through the Exercises, which he made some time after the day of the first vows. The rules of the little Society were few and simple. They were unable to live in common, but they met on Sundays and feasts, were as much in one another's company as possible, and, for the purpose of fostering charity and of that immense spiritual profit which comes from intercourse with congenial souls on fire with the love of God, they invited one another to their simple meals, and thus renewed the 'Love-feasts' of the early Christians. Ignatius himself was with them only till the end of March in the year following the meeting at Montmartre. He went to Spain, partly for his health, and partly also that he might arrange the private affairs of some of the little body, Francis Xavier, Laynez, and Salmeron, who thought it more prudent not to revisit their homes for such a purpose. The vow of poverty which they had made at Montmartre consisted in the renouncement of all possessions and dignities in this world, and as this renouncement could not be carried out while they remained in France as students, they had fixed a time at which it was to be formally effected. This was the business which Ignatius was to perform for them at their homes. One more associate, Claude Le Jay, of Geneva, had been added to the little Society before Ignatius left. Two more, who raised the number of the original Fathers to ten, John Codurius and Paschase Brouet, were gathered in after his departure, when Peter Favre was a sort of father and superior to the rest in the place of Ignatius. They practised weekly confession and communion, daily meditation and examination of conscience, and spiritual reading in the Bible and the *Imitation of Christ.* The rest of their time was given to study and to such good works as lay within the sphere of students such as they were.

It takes but a few lines thus to describe the life led by Francis Xavier and his friends during their last years at the University. But the happiest, the brightest, the most peaceful stages of our lives, those which influence the remainder of our course because they have been the seedtimes of our minds and souls, those which mould and develope our affections, and to which our memories turn back with the fondest thankfulness, are often those which can thus easily be summed up. Tranquil times have little history, but they are yet the times of growth and of maturing life. 'So is the kingdom of God, as if a man should cast seed into the earth, and should sleep and rise, night and day, and the seed should spring, and grow up whilst he knoweth not. For the earth of itself bringeth forth fruit, first the blade, then the ear, afterwards the full corn in the ear. And when the fruit is brought forth, immediately he putteth in the sickle, because the harvest is come.'[13] The harvest was to come in its time for Xavier and the rest. Meanwhile their life was steady, uniform, obscure. They passed from their rooms to the schools or to the church, from the schools and the church to the meadows and walks on the banks of the Seine, to Montmartre and its quarries, or on some hidden errand of mercy or charity. Ignatius had so formed each one that his presence was not needed to guide them at every moment, or to retain them in their unity of purpose, or to prevent them from falling asunder. They enjoyed the highest of Christian delights in their own mutual love and confidence, at the same time that they were adding daily to their stores of intellectual and spiritual wisdom. They were never again to be so much together, so much at peace and at rest. But wherever they went in after years, in the Old World or the New World, to Court or Council or Bishop or King, among Catholics or heretics or the heathen, they would retain their affection for one another, their brotherhood of spiritual form-

[13] St. Mark iv. 26-29.

ation, and the intellectual development and the theological learning which they had so patiently acquired within the bosom of the great University.

The journey of Ignatius to Spain, which we have already mentioned, gave occasion to the first letter of Francis Xavier which remains to us. It is addressed to his elder brother, and contains a kind of vindication of himself, as well as the strongest possible recommendation of Ignatius. Its style has still much of the formality and stateliness of the Spanish nobleman about it, and in this respect contrasts strongly with the later letters we possess from the same hand.

(1.) *To the Captain of Azpilqueta, his eldest brother.*

My good Lord,

I have lately written to you more than once by different hands. I had several powerful reasons for doing so, the first and strongest of which was the tie of natural duty which binds me to you, and that feeling of pious respect which, next to the love of my parents, is due in the highest degree from me a younger to you an elder brother, the firstborn of our family. Beside this there was the gratitude I feel for your great and manifold kindnesses to me. These have been indeed so many and of such a kind that I fear I shall never be able to repay them as they deserve, and that I must expect to appear ungrateful in the eyes of those who judge of my will only from my deeds.

I am therefore most anxious to find all possible ways of showing you what I think and feel with all the strength of the most sincere and earnest attachment, in order, if possible, to make you some return for your charity towards me, which is ever showing itself by the most conspicuous proofs. Often, indeed, to my great sorrow and trouble, I fail to find any such ways, and I feel often compelled, in the anxious disquiet of my love for you, to suspect that those many letters which I spare no pains to send to you, as witnesses of my tender and respectful affection, by the hand of every one who leaves this for your parts, are not all faithfully conveyed to you, more particularly when I consider the immense extent of country and the almost insurmountable difficulties of communication between Paris and Obaños.

It is most probably on account of some cause of the same kind that I receive answers from you less frequently than I desire. I feel sure that it is not that you have given up correspondence so delightful and so longed for by me, but that either the faithfulness, the industry, or the good fortune of your messengers has failed to be answerable to the efforts of your unwearied care concerning me. For, indeed, the accounts of our friends, and other proofs no less certain, have fully convinced me that you have a cordial sympathy for the sufferings to which my labours as a student and my dwelling in a foreign land expose me, and that in your residence at Obaños, with every comfort round you, you feel the troubles of my watchings, and the difficulties with which I have to contend, as much as I feel them myself in Paris, where I am often without the necessaries of life, for no other reason, I feel certain, than that your unfailing readiness to come to my aid has not been sufficiently informed as to the numberless wants which I suffer,—wants, the particulars of which sound, for the most part, minute and insignificant when spoken of, but which are yet very hard to bear. The only thing that keeps me up in the midst of them all is the hope that I have in that kindness of yours which I have so often experienced, and this hope makes me confident that as soon as you know what and how much I want, you will abundantly supply all that is required, and that the straits in which I now find myself will be at once turned into abundance by a large outpouring of your liberality.

A few days ago I had a long talk with the Rev. Father Vear, who has lately come to the University. He spoke long and most pleasantly concerning you all, and then took occasion gradually to let me know plainly that grave complaints of me had been made to you by some persons who bear me ill will. At my request he told me openly every particular. If you will do me the favour to believe my solemn declaration that these charges have absolutely no foundation, and that they are maliciously laid to the score of your innocent brother, I am sure that you will share my grief at them, and understand the sharp pain which calumnies of such a kind must have given one who is conscious of being entirely undeserving of these reproaches. And yet I tell you the simplest truth, when I say that I felt more patient as to the undeserved loss of my own reputation than as to the grief which these reports must have caused you. When Father Vear was telling me about this, I felt each word before he uttered it; for I could easily understand, without being told it, knowing as I do the warmth of your love for me, how much this wicked accusation must of necessity have wounded you to the heart.

But it seems that these same detestable sycophants have not been afraid to associate with me in their calumnies the most innocent and the holiest of men, Master Don Ignatius. As for this charge, you will see a first proof of the innocence of his life and the purity of his conduct in the step he has, of his own accord, taken of going to visit you in your own house and to deliver into your own hands, in private, this letter which I have charged him to convey to you. Were he indeed what the false colours of calumny have painted him, were he not, on the contrary, full of the greatest confidence in his own conscious integrity, he would certainly not venture, unarmed and alone, to place himself in the power of persons whom he would remember to have grievously injured, and whom he would also know to be perfectly aware that he had so injured them.

But that you, my lord and elder brother, so worthy of my tenderest reverence, may well understand clearly what a signal grace of God our Lord it has been for me to have for a friend a man so perfect as Master Don Ignatius, I hereby solemnly declare, as if this was a duly signed document, certified with all the sacred obligations of an oath, that the services which this friend has rendered me infinitely outweigh all that the most devoted gratitude from me during the course of my whole life could either repay or answer to, even in part.

For, in the first place, in the serious private inconvenience which the distance that separates me from you has often occasioned, he has always come opportunely to my aid, both by putting at my disposal the funds which I needed, and by assisting me in a thousand other ways, either by his own means or by the intervention of his friends. And, in the second place, what is of infinitely greater importance, he has preserved the thoughtlessness of my youth from the deadly danger of forming friendships with men strongly inclined to heresy, numbers of whom are to be met with in the present day in this University of Paris; persons of my own age, who craftily hid under the specious veil of attractive gifts of cultivation and talent their corruption as to faith and as to morals. Ignatius alone has preserved my too yielding inexperience from engaging myself in these pernicious friendships, by showing me the mischief of wiles of which I was quite ignorant. So great was the evil from which I was saved by this kindness of his, that I should never have thought the whole world too dear a price to pay for such deliverance if it had been in my power to pay it. And were this the only good that Master Don Ignatius has done me, it would still be of such a kind that I do not know how or when I could repay it worthily, or be grateful enough for it. For certainly, but for his intervention, I should never have escaped falling into intimacy with those young men, good in outward appearance, but inwardly corrupted with vice and heresy, as their own deeds and the event afterwards made clear. I beg and entreat of you, therefore, by the ties of kindred and by the share that your brotherly love for me prompts you to take in my feelings, my wishes, and my obligations, do all that is in your power, as you would if I were present to make the request, to omit nothing as regards assistance and attention to make welcome the one person of all the world to whom I profess and acknowledge myself most deeply indebted for the inestimable services he has rendered me.

After having made this earnest request in the interest of Don Ignatius, I will add another on your own account. I pray you to take advantage of the opportunity now offered to you to enjoy the conversation and familiarity of a man of the highest wisdom, whom God has adorned with singular gifts. Trust my experience, you will gather abundant spiritual fruits and the greatest consolation from his earnest admonitions and prudent counsel. Open to him with confidence all the troubles that afflict your mind; set before him any doubts you may have. Listen to his advice and obey his counsel. You will find by your own experience the truth of my promises as to the incredible advantages you will gain from knowing and conversing with a man so filled with the Spirit of God. He will give you, moreover, the fullest information you can desire, and all that it is so much my interest that you should have, about myself and the present state of my affairs here. And I beg of you to have the same confidence in his statements that you would have in mine if I were with you. He is, in fact, most thoroughly acquainted with my heart. He knows most accurately and minutely all the particulars of my private concerns, and he knows, I may almost say, better than myself, the nature and extent of my needs and of the assistance I require from you.

After what he tells you shall have explained my necessity, if, as I feel sure you will, you intend to come to my assistance, I beg of you to make him the medium of your favours. It is true, he is not returning here so as to be able to bring to me in Paris what he has received from you; but he has at his command a very safe means of sending anything to me. There is here a young man from Almazan,[14] a friend of mine, who is following the same course of study: he receives from his family the sums necessary for his maintenance by regular remittances which never fail. This young man, when Don Ignatius left, gave him letters for his father, with a commission to act for him in a certain business, and for this purpose Don Ignatius must, on leaving you, pass through Almazan. I will ask you, therefore, to intrust to him when he leaves you whatever money you wish to send me. He will faithfully place the whole in the hands of the worthy gentleman of Almazan, the father of my fellow student, who will send the pension you intend for me by the same means and in the same money (so as to have as little

[14] This was, of course, Laynez.

loss as possible in exchange), as the yearly allowance which he transmits for his son's expenses. His son, at my desire, has asked him to do this in the letter which he has now sent him. I once more earnestly entreat you that, now that you have so favourable an opportunity of sending me some funds, you will not let me any longer grow old in such wretched destitution.

As to our family concerns here, I have nothing particular to tell you worth the writing, except our good cousin's disappearance from this University. The news came to me late, and I got a carriage and followed the boy for some time, hoping to catch him and bring him back if I could. My labour was in vain, for, after pursuing him, with the fastest horses I could get, for as much as twenty-four leagues from Paris to Notre Dame de Cléry, I was obliged to give it up in despair and turn back. Pray do not forget to let me know by the first opportunity whether the runaway has turned up in Navarre. I have great fears about the recovery of a character so headlong in its bent to evil. You will hear, much better than I can tell you, from Master Don Ignatius how Church matters stand here, and the direction in which our lately threatened heresies have begun to break out, and I shall therefore say nothing about this. And so I end, my dear lord, by kissing a thousand times, as well as I can at such a distance, your dear hands and those of my sister, your lady wife, and I pray God to preserve you both and crown you with all prosperity and happiness of life, and to give you good fortune for many years, according to the desires of your pious and generous hearts. God grant it! Such is my prayer.

Your most devoted servant and younger brother,

FRANCIS XAVIER.

Paris, March 24th, 1535.

It is not very easy to imagine what the calumnies can have been from which Francis here clears himself, unless they related to his manner of life. They possibly involved the charge of novelty in doctrine, which may have been regarded as bringing disgrace on the family. Whatever the charges were, they were shared by Ignatius. The strong petition for help in money may have been prompted by the necessities of his position at Paris, where he was yet to remain for a year and a half after the letter was written. Many things in the letter seem to imply that Don Juan de Jasso, the father of the saint, was dead, but as to this we have no certain information. The eldest brother may have settled at Obaños on his marriage as the representative of the Azpilqueta family, and come into possession of the corresponding portion of his mother's property. He may thus have been independent of his father, and so able to help Francis.

CHAPTER II.

Labours in Italy and Rome.

FRANCIS XAVIER was in his thirty-first year when he left Paris (November 15th, 1536) with his companions for the purpose of joining Ignatius at Venice at the beginning of the ensuing year. He had spent twelve years in the University, and was on the point of taking the degree of Doctor in Divinity, the usual crown of studies such as his. He was never again to spend any great length of time in a single place; and we shall see from his letters how much the University had moulded his character, and how frequently his thoughts recurred to the place which, longer than any other, had been his earthly home. Paris had done for him what it could, and he was certainly not an ungrateful son. It would seem that he and his companions, especially Peter Favre, were highly valued in the University. Great opposition was made to their departure. Simon Rodriguez tells us that they consulted two learned and pious doctors as to their plans, which were approved, while they were at the same time warned that their execution would be full of difficulty. Another theologian came to Favre, and told him that he thought he was forsaking a sphere of great and certain usefulness for one of much hazard and uncertainty, and that he could not do so without incurring the guilt of mortal sin. At the same time Francis Xavier received from Spain the news that he had been nominated to a canonry at Pampeluna.

Nothing of this sort could shake their resolution. But how were the companions to get to Venice? They were mostly Spaniards, and war was now raging between Charles V. and

Francis I.[1] They determined to take a long and circuitous route for the sake of safety, though it was certain, especially during winter, to be a cause of much inconvenience and many sufferings. They would pass from Paris eastwards into Lorraine, the Duke of which country was at peace with both the belligerents. Then they would make their way to Basle and Constance, and so, probably through the Tyrol, to Venice. They provided as well as they could against the dangerous questions which their appearance was sure to occasion. They wore the long dress and hat of the Parisian students. Each one had his pilgrim's staff, his leather satchel on his shoulders—in which he had a Bible, a Breviary, and his manuscripts containing his theological notes taken while at Paris—and his rosary round his neck. They gave their money to the poor on leaving Paris; but it was afterwards agreed that they should accept as alms and carry with them a sufficient sum of money for their journey, as they might otherwise be involved in inextricable difficulties in the heretical countries through which they were to pass. As long as they were in French territory the Frenchmen among them were to answer, in the name of all, the questions which might be addressed to them, and if the Spaniards were asked about themselves, they were to say that they were students of Paris on a pilgrimage. There was a famous shrine of St. Nicolas on the German border of Lorraine, beyond Metz, which lay on their road, and they were to be pilgrims to this shrine until they reached it. After this

[1] In this war Charles V. had invaded the south-eastern provinces of France (in July), and had found the frontiers unprepared for attack. Francis I. had ordered the devastation of the whole country between the sea and the Durance, the Alps and the Rhone; Arles, Tarascon, and Marseilles alone were to be defended: even the towns, and Aix itself, the capital of Provence, were destroyed, in order to hinder the invasion. The Dauphin died on August 10, with suspicion of poison, which was attributed to the Emperor: but there seems to have been sufficient natural cause for his sudden death. Charles laid siege to Marseilles, but was forced to retreat with loss, on account of want of food and disease among the troops, in September. The northern frontiers of France were also invaded from the Low Countries. There would have been, therefore, the greatest exasperation everywhere against Spaniards, and the whole of the south of France must have been miserable as well as hostile enough to make our travellers choose the route by Lorraine.

they would pass into German territory, and here the Spaniards were to come forward in the name of all, and the Frenchmen, if they were separately questioned, were to give the same answers which the Spaniards had given before, only that it was to be the Holy House of Loreto to which their pilgrimage was directed. Each day they spent a considerable time in united prayer, morning and evening, before they left their resting place for the night, and on their arrival. Those that were priests said mass every morning whenever they could, and the others received holy communion. The whole day was so arranged that prayer, meditation, and spiritual conversation, occupied them during the journey.

The perils and adventures with which they met on their way were neither few nor trifling, and Simon Rodriguez, as we have mentioned, wrote down his reminiscences concerning them many years later, at the request of the General, Everard Mercurian. At the very outset of the pilgrimage, Francis Xavier seemed to be in danger of his life. He had bound cords round his arms and thighs in a spirit of penance, having to reproach himself—as we are told—with a certain amount of vanity and selfsatisfaction in which he had formerly indulged on the score of his agility, activity, and nimbleness in running and leaping in the games played by the scholars at Paris. These cords he had not removed on starting, and, notwithstanding the severe pain which they must have caused him, he persevered until his strength entirely gave way. It was found that the cords had buried themselves deeply in his flesh, which had swollen round them so that they were hardly visible, and the surgeons who were called in despaired of being able to cut them. His companions betook themselves to prayer, and the next morning the cords were found to have broken of themselves, and the swelling had passed away.

The first stage of the travellers was Meaux. Two or three days' journey beyond the town they were pursued and overtaken by friends from Paris, urging them, in vain, to return. The hostels along the route were full of heretics, to whom the devotions which were openly practised by the pilgrims on arriving and setting forth were the subject of frequent remark, either of amusement or astonishment. The companions always avowed their creed, and had many controversial discussions with any more learned men of the Lutheran party who might be called in to the aid of the more ordinary disputants. On arriving at the frontier of France towards Lorraine, they all went solemnly to confession and communion—as it were, to bid goodbye to France, says Simon Rodriguez. Lorraine was at first more dangerous to them. It was full of French soldiers returning from a raid into the Low Countries, and, as was usual in those days, treating the inhabitants of the neutral country not much better than if they had been enemies. Metz was shut against these freebooters as against a hostile army, and it was with the greatest possible difficulty that our travellers obtained admission, along with some poor country folk who were flying from the soldiers.

They spent several weary weeks in their journey from Lorraine into Italy. Once in Germany, they had a new difficulty to encounter in their ignorance of the language of the country. They were thus unable to ask the way, and frequently lost it for hours together. It was winter, and the country was covered with snow. The narrative of Rodriguez shows us incidentally the miserable moral and religious state of the towns through which they passed. They stopped three days at Basle—which was openly heretical, and in which Carlstadt[2] then resided. Here they had many disputes for the faith. Another time they wandered by chance into a village, which was keeping high holiday for the marriage of its parish priest. A short time before they reached Constance they were challenged to controversy by another parish priest, who was already married and had a large family of children. He invited them to supper, but they declined to eat at the same table with him. After some further dispute, he was reduced to silence, and then threatened to have them imprisoned and punished. Early the next morning they were roused by a 'fair and gracious young

[2] His real name was Bodenstein, but he is more commonly known from the place of his birth.

man of about thirty,' who guided them along paths quite covered with snow for some miles, and then left them after pointing out the road along which they were to proceed. Constance, like Basle, had apostatized from Catholicism: mass was only allowed in a church outside the walls of the town, and all who assisted at it had to pay a certain fine. A little further on, at a place whose name Simon forgot, they came upon a hospital, at the door of which an old woman met them, who began to genuflect, kiss their rosaries, and cry out in German that she was an old Catholic, delighted to see men who were still faithful to the Church. She ran in, and brought out a lapful of rosaries, legs, arms, and other fragments of sacred statues, and the like, which were all venerated by the Fathers, much to the old dame's delight, who began to scold the people of the hospital who had told her that all the world had become heretical like themselves.

These few incidents paint for us the hardships and difficulties of the journey to Venice, at which city the band of companions arrived about the Epiphany 1537. Ignatius was there to await his spiritual children, and their joy at meeting him may easily be imagined. Ignatius had arrived at Venice a few days only before his companions. He had sailed from Valencia to Genoa, and the vessel in which he was had nearly been lost in a storm. 'While the other passengers abandoned themselves to terror and alarm, Ignatius spent the time in calmly examining his conscience, which only reproached him with not having corresponded to the graces he had received as faithfully as he deemed he ought to have done.'[3] He had other troubles by land. He had made his way from Genoa to Venice by Bologna on foot, and had suffered very greatly from the weather, the bad roads, and absolute destitution. Several months were to pass before they could sail to Jerusalem, and it was determined to spend a part of this time among the poor in the hospitals at Venice, and the rest in a journey to Rome to obtain the blessing of the Pope. We thus find these first Fathers of the Society practised at once in the 'experiments' which were afterwards

[3] *Genelli*, Eng. Trans. p. 132.

insisted on in the case of those who joined themselves to the body, when its rules and constitutions had been put into shape. Francis Xavier was one of those appointed to the Hospital of the Incurables. He was to be the servant of all there, to wait upon the sick, dress their wounds, sores, or ulcers, make their beds, prepare their food, sweep the room, and the like, and he was also to take care of their souls, instructing them, consoling them, preparing them for the last sacraments, and after their death carrying them forth for burial. It was here in Venice that he won the grace, never to find any wound or ulcer, however loathsome in itself, a cause of horror or disgust to him. The grace, however, was won by a signal victory over his natural delicacy, when, finding a great and sickening repugnance rising in him on having to dress an ulcerous wound of the most disgusting kind, he forced himself to lick it and suck it to the very last drop of the nauseous matter of which it had been full.[4]

After nine or ten weeks thus spent in Venice, the little company of the disciples of Ignatius set out on foot for Rome. There were prudential reasons why Ignatius himself should not accompany them. Somehow he had incurred the hostility of the newly made Cardinal Carafa, who had lately helped St.

[4] This is the account given by Turselline, who is quoted in the abstract of the Processes made for the canonization of St. Francis. Turselline, like all the writers of his time, does not give his authority. The valuable account of this period drawn up many years after by Simon Rodriguez at the desire of Everard Mercurian does not mention the incident, at least does not mention it in exactly the same form, and it appears from internal evidence that Simon was one of the companions of Francis at the Hospital of the Incurables. He seldom mentions names, but he speaks of 'one of the Fathers.' A man covered with what seemed to be leprosy called this Father to him and asked him to rub his back. Then the feeling of nausea came on, as well as the fear of contagion, and Francis first scraped the ulcerous sores with his fingers, and then put them into his mouth, licked and sucked them. He told his companion of it the next day, saying that the night before he had dreamt that the leprous matter had stuck to his mouth, and that he had in vain tried to cough it away. It is quite possible that this may be another anecdote, but it seems almost certainly to refer to Francis Xavier, who was very intimate with Simon, and told him such things as his dreams more than once. Simon adds another similar anecdote, which is probably of himself. One of the companions begged the infirmarian to place in his bed a beggar

Cajetan in founding the Theatine Order, and was afterwards Pope Paul IV. Carafa may perhaps have disliked the notion of the Order which Ignatius seemed to be trying to found, as being so very like his own. At a later time he wished the Theatines to be fused with the Society, but Ignatius declined. Ignatius was also afraid of finding an enemy in Pedro Ortiz, the representative of the Emperor at the Papal Court, who was one of those who had denounced him to the Inquisition in Paris. His expectations, however, were very happily disappointed in the case of Ortiz. The journey of the nine companions occupied several weeks, and gave them an occasion of continued and immense suffering. It was determined that they should practise the strictest poverty—another of the experiments of the Society—and this precluded them from taking with them any provisions or money whatever. It was Lent, and they would not seek any dispensation from the strict law of fasting. They were a large body to support themselves all at once by begging, as well as to find lodgings from charity. The roads were extremely bad, the rains incessant, the country in many parts flooded. From Venice they begged their way to Ravenna by land, thence they embarked for Ancona, and then passed on through Loreto and Tolentino, across the Apennines to Foligno and Spoleto, and thence, as it appears, by Terni and Narni to

---

covered with leprosy, whose application for admission had been refused on the ground that there was no room for him in the Hospital. On rising the next morning he found himself covered with leprosy; but the next day he was entirely and suddenly cured. This narrative of Simon's, which here adds other particulars like those which we have now quoted, has been used by Mariani, the best Italian writer of a Life of St. Ignatius. This Life has been translated in the Oratorian Series. Mariani inserts the anecdote from Turselline, given above in the text, as well as that contained in this note; but he gives no references. Simon's narrative was printed at Rome in 1869. (*De Origine et Progressu Societatis Jesu* usque ad ejus confirmationem. Commentarium P. Simonis Rodriguez, qui fuit e novem sociis S. Ignatii Patris: Romæ, 1869.) The passage we have been quoting is at pp. 34, 35. Simon tells us a little further on that when the Fathers first entered Italy, the practice of confession and communion had become so rare, that any one who approached these sacraments once a week was talked of everywhere, and his doing so was mentioned in letters as an extraordinary piece of news.

Rome. The first part of the journey was the most trying. The people were afraid of them, supposing that they must be men who had formed part of the army which, under the Constable Bourbon, had some years before taken and sacked Rome, and were now on their way, in a pilgrimage of penance, to obtain pardon at the shrine of the Apostles.

Whenever they obtained admission to the hospitals, which seem at this time to have generally served as the 'night-refuges' of mendicant travellers, they edified every one by their patience and humility, and the piety and zeal with which they instructed and exhorted the poor sufferers who were the permanent inmates of these charitable resting places. But they had often no shelter at all for the night, and were sometimes whole days without food except the cones of pine trees. The simple tale of Simon Rodriguez draws a touching picture of their sufferings, and of the self-reproach which some of them felt at having wasted their strength by an excess of mortification as to food while they were sojourning at Venice. Often only the worst and foulest beds in the hospitals were offered them; the ferrymen at the rivers refused to take them across without payment; they had sometimes to give their shirts or their inkstands in lieu of coin. At Ancona they were not allowed to land because they could not pay the fare, and one had to get leave to go into the town and pawn his breviary to deliver the rest. Simon gives us a scene in the marketplace of Ancona, describing one of his companions, who seems to have been Francis Xavier. He was barefooted, his robe tucked up to his knees, going about among the market women, humbly begging from one an apple, from another a radish, or some other vegetable; and this was the young noble, the glory of the University of Paris for his learning and mental gifts! The market people at Ancona were liberal, and that day, Simon says, they had enough for a joyous and frugal repast to satisfy their hunger, as well as for the redemption of the breviary. Loreto consoled them, as it has consoled thousands of saints before and after them. They spent two or three days in prayer at that sweet and beautiful sanctuary.

At Rome each one went to the Hospital of his own nation. They were at first thought to have come to seek some benefices at the hands of the Curia, or, as before, to have come for pardon for great crimes, or to get rid of the vows of some religious order to which they belonged. But they were soon found out, and were all taken into the great Hospital of San Giacomo, that of the Spanish nation. Pedro Ortiz himself presented them to the Pope, Paul the Third. When the Pope heard that they were theologians from Paris, he desired them to dispute before him with some of the Roman Doctors during his dinner, and was delighted at the combination of so much learning with so much humility. He gave them the leave which they desired to go to Jerusalem, adding, however, that he feared they would not have the opportunity of accomplishing their purpose. He already knew that war was brewing between Venice and the Turks. He gave them, also, leave to receive sacred orders on three consecutive feast days without the usual 'interstices,' at the hand of any Bishop they might choose. Their learning was to be instead of the required 'patrimony.' Paul III. gave them, moreover, a considerable alms to enable them to pay their passage to the Holy Land—conscious as he was that the voyage would never take place—and this sum was increased by the contributions of some pious Spaniards in Rome to the amount of 210 ducats. It was sent by letter of exchange to merchants at Venice, and was afterwards duly returned by Ignatius and his companions when their design of going to the Holy Land was finally abandoned.

The party of pilgrims returned to Venice after a short sojourn at Rome, and resumed their labours of charity at the hospitals. Their next step was to avail themselves of the Pope's permission to receive sacred orders. Before doing this, they renewed their vows of poverty and chastity in the hands of Monsignor Girolamo Veralli, Archbishop of Rossano, who was residing in Venice as Nuncio from the Pope. Their ordination followed in a few days. The sacred rite was administered by Monsignor Vincenzo Nigusanti, Bishop of Arba, on the Feast of St. John the Baptist, June 24, 1537. Meanwhile the approaching war between the Turks and Venice, which the Pope had been able to forecast, seemed to become a certainty, and there could be no opportunity of sailing to the Holy Land for that year. It was determined that another year should be passed before any further step was taken, that they might not lose any possible opportunity of fulfilling their vow.

The companions now resolved to disperse themselves in the neighbourhood of Venice, and prepare themselves solemnly and as perfectly as possible for the great act of the first celebration of holy mass. Vicenza, Treviso, Bassano, and Monselice—not far from Padua—were pointed out to them as places which they might find suited for their purpose of spending some time in quiet contemplation and the exercises of penance. Two, Bobadilla and Brouet, went to Verona; two others, Laynez and Favre, accompanied Ignatius to Vicenza; Le Jay and Simon Rodriguez went to Bassano; Codurius and Hozès (a new addition to their number, who was, as it turned out, the first of all to die) went to Treviso; and Salmeron and Xavier to Monselice. These were all places within the Venetian dominion. The Nuncio had given them, soon after their ordination, faculties in writing to say mass, administer the sacraments, preach, explain Scripture, and absolve from reserved cases, within the states of the Republic.

In the arrangements now made among themselves, we again find the object of practising the religious rule steadily kept in view. It is probable that the number of the companions would have been too large for them to establish themselves anywhere, as yet, as one religious community, and such a step would at once have caused enquiry as to their Institute, which had not yet received any approbation, either written or verbal, from authority. This may have been another reason for their dispersion. But the little parties of two or three began now to practise obedience regularly, though the vow on this subject had been omitted when they originally made their vows, and when they renewed them before Monsignor Veralli. Each one was Superior for a week, and then in his turn obeyed his companion. When afterwards they went to reside in Rome, this system was continued, the period of authority being extended to a month. It was thus that obedience and discipline were practised among them until the formal election of a General in the person of Ignatius. Up to that time, he had taken his turn with the rest, although he was always respected and honoured by them all in a singular manner.

The austerities of the Fathers at this time were almost excessive, and their sufferings from weakness, poverty and bad lodging were very great. Ignatius and Simon Rodriguez fell ill, but recovered. After a time, Ignatius collected them all in the old ruined monastery at Vicenza where he had taken up his quarters, and thus it happened that several of them, and among them Francis Xavier, said their first mass at that place. It was then determined, probably because the hopes of Palestine had grown visibly fainter,[5] that after finishing their appointed time of retirement they should disperse, until the year of waiting was out, into some of the chief cities of Italy, in order to labour for the good of souls. Ignatius and his two companions of Vicenza were to go to Rome itself, Salmeron and Brouet to Siena, Xavier and Bobadilla to Bologna, Le Jay and Rodriguez to Ferrara, and Codurius and Hozès to Padua. It was agreed that they were to continue the same rule of life and the same exercises of charity and zeal as before. Ignatius told them that when they were asked who they were, they were to say that they belonged to the Compañia, or band, of Jesus.

While these arrangements were being made at Vicenza, Xavier, with one of his companions—perhaps Rodriguez—had fallen ill, and had been moved to the Hospital of Incurables in the town, that they might be somewhat better tended than was possible in the old ruin already mentioned. They had, however, only one bed between them; and as the one required as much warmth as possible, and the other was at the

[5] F. Genelli remarks (p. 139, Eng. Trans.) that on account of the war 'it was impossible to cross the sea to Syria during the whole of that time during which Ignatius and his companions had made a vow to wait; and it was exactly after this time had elapsed, and after they had given up the intention of their pilgrimage, that the war ceased and the sea was again open for the passage.'

height of a raging fever, it was not easy for both to enjoy at once the little comfort that might otherwise have been at their command. It was here that Francis Xavier had a vision in which St. Jerome, to whom he had a great devotion, appeared to him and consoled him, promising him at the same time a far severer cross at Bologna, to which city he was to be sent, and naming at the same times the several cities in which his companions were to labour.

In the choice made by Ignatius and his associates of the cities in which they were to place themselves, it is not difficult to see the same love for large centres of population, especially when such cities were also seats of intellectual activity, which we have already remarked upon. Bologna, the first scene of Francis Xavier's priestly labours, seems to have received him with special affection, and to have gained a place of peculiar regard in his heart. He was forced by the importunities of Jerome Casalini, a Canon of St. Petronio and Rector of the church of Santa Lucia, to accept a lodging in his house instead of in the common hospital; but Francis would never consent to live upon anything but the alms he collected himself. The Canon's sister, Isabella, had been attracted by the extraordinary fervour and devotion with which Francis celebrated mass at the tomb of St. Dominic. His time was spent in preaching in the public piazzas, in hearing confessions, visiting the prisons and hospitals, and catechizing children. He spared himself so little that he soon fell ill of a dangerous quartan ague, which was the cross predicted to him by St. Jerome. He had nearly recovered, when he was summoned by Ignatius to Rome, towards the end of winter.

Ignatius, with his two companions, Laynez and Favre, had arrived in Rome, it seems, in the course of November 1537. The Pope received him graciously, and appointed Favre to lecture in positive theology, Laynez in scholastic theology, in the University of the Sapienza. Ignatius occupied himself chiefly in giving the Spiritual Exercises, and many men of distinction placed themselves in his hands for this purpose. Among these was Ortiz himself, who took Ignatius with him to Monte Cassino,[6] where he went through the Exercises with the utmost fervour, offering himself, at the end of his retreat, as a member of the new Society. Ignatius, however, dissuaded him on the ground of his age and the importance of the business with which he was charged by the Emperor, whose representative he was in the matter of the divorce sued for by Henry VIII. from Catharine of Aragon. At Monte Cassino, while hearing Mass, Ignatius was made suddenly aware of the happy death of Hozès, his lately acquired associate, who fell a victim to his own zeal at Padua.

The ordinary abode of the little party was in a vineyard near the Trinità di Monti, but when about Easter the remainder of the companions were summoned to join the three already at Rome, they removed into the heart of the city, to the Torre del Melangolo in the Piazza Margana, near the present convent of Sta. Catarina dei Funari. As soon as they were all assembled, Ignatius submitted to them his thoughts concerning the erection of the Society into a religious order. It cannot be doubted that this had been all along his intention, and indeed it was well known in after years that the whole plan of the Society had been set before him at Manresa. But it was the method of Ignatius to proceed in all things with the fullest deliberation, and to let every onward step in the accomplishment of his plan be the issue of prayer and the workings of the Holy Ghost on the hearts of those who were concerned. Alcazar has preserved to us the address in which he expressed his thoughts.[7] The purport was that they had not indeed been able to pass to Palestine according to their vow, but that in Italy, the centre of Christendom, they had seen with their eyes and tested by their own experience how vast a field God had laid open to their apostolic labours, and how plentiful a

[6] We are told by Alcazar (*Chrono-Historia de la Compañia de Jesus en la Provincia de Toledo*, 1 Part. Lib. Prelim. c. vii.) that one of St. Ignatius' favourite means of doing good was to give away spiritual books, and that he gave each monk at Monte Cassino a copy of the book *de Contemptu Mundi*, i.e. the *Imitation of Christ*, which Spanish writers of that time, such as Louis of Grenada, call by that name.

[7] See Alcazar, at the place quoted above, § 4.

harvest He had enabled them to reap in their efforts for the conversion and reformation of souls. This, then, was the enterprize to which God now invited them, and with His aid they might hope to carry on the work begun by the Apostles, to 'root up and plant,' combat heresy and vice, and extend the faith of Jesus Christ over the whole earth. The means of doing this most surely was to bind themselves by a permanent bond, under one head, adding the vow of obedience to the vows of poverty and chastity, which they had already taken. They would thus perpetuate, beyond the span of their own lives, the bond of charity which united them, erecting their Company into a religious Order which might multiply itself in all countries and last until the end of time. This new bond of union would alter nothing, it would only strengthen themselves and ennoble the designs which they had conceived. God seemed to show that this was His design by the great fruits which they had already reaped, and by the men of ability who were daily brought to them as fresh companions. There would be no guarantee for such in the future unless the body were made permanent. However, Ignatius added, he did not insist on an immediate answer to his proposals, he would have them all take time, reflect, and pray that God would make known to them His most holy Will, that their final determination might result in His own greater glory, which was and always had been the rule and end of their desires.

In the May of this year 1538, Paul III. went to Nice to meet Charles V. and Francis I., in hope of bringing about a peace between these two inveterate rivals. Cardinal Carafa was left as Legate at Rome, and he gave Ignatius and his companions the leave to preach and hear confessions which they so much desired. The two professors at the Sapienza continued their courses, but took their turns in preaching as well, Favre assisting Francis Xavier in the church of San Lorenzo in Damaso, and Salmeron preaching in that of Santa Lucia del Gonfalone. Ignatius himself preached in Spanish at the Spanish church, Santa Maria in Monserrato (the rest preached in Italian), Laynez in the church of San Salvatore in Lauro, Le

Jay at San Luigi dei Francesi, Rodriguez at Sant' Angelo in Pescheria, and Bobadilla at SS. Celso e Guiliano ai Banchi.

They had little reason to expect great success. Ignatius speaks, even after this time, of the soil of Rome as 'sterile of good fruits and fertile of bad fruits.' They had already many enemies who were industriously spreading evil reports against them, and who delayed for a time the issue of their faculties by the Legate there. It was also unusual for preachers to appear in the pulpits except during the sacred seasons of Advent and Lent, and the population was accustomed, after the effort required for the performance of their Easter duties, to relapse into enjoyment, if not into sin. Moreover, they thought, as Ignatius says, that they had but little elegance or attractiveness to draw audiences to them. Nevertheless, the fruit was great, the Sacraments began to be frequented more regularly, and a striking reformation of manners was the result.

It could hardly be otherwise, considering the evident sanctity and fervour of the preachers, their holy and austere lives, and the high character which their learning gave to them. But the new association was to be tried by persecution. Our Lord had appeared, we are told, to Ignatius when he reached the little village of La Storta, so well known to travellers as the last stage before Rome is reached, on the roads from Florence or Loreto, and He had promised him His protection in the famous words, *Ego vobis Romæ propitius ero.* The favour thus promised was to be purchased and secured by a heavy cross. Many writers have told the history of the accusation made against Ignatius and his companions, of its prompt refutation, of the delay on the part of the Legate and the Governor of Rome to give a distinct sentence in their favour on account of the high standing of some of the persons concerned in the propagation of the calumny, of the persistence of Ignatius in demanding a full trial and public decision, and of the providential presence in the Holy City of so many persons of authority who could bear witness to his past career,—Juan Figueroa, the Vicar-General, who had imprisoned him at Alcala, Gaspar de Doctis, the official of the Legate at Venice, who had inquired into their lives and doctrine before they first began to preach in the dominion of the Republic, the Inquisitor of Paris, Ori, who had also examined him there, and the Bishop of Vicenza, in whose diocese some of the companions had preached and laboured. The story belongs rather to the history of the Society, or to the life of Ignatius, than to that of Francis Xavier, but it must have had, with all else that passed during these two years at Rome, an effect upon the full formation of his Apostolic character. The Pope's return to his States in the autumn saved Ignatius and his companions from the blight which would have fallen on their reputation if the calumnies had been allowed to linger on without positive condemnation from authority. Ignatius had a long interview with Paul III. at Frascati, before the time of the villegiatura was ended, and the result was a peremptory order to the Governor Conversini, to bring the affair to an issue. Paul had now come under the influence of that peculiar charm which the sanctity and noble simplicity of Ignatius enabled him to exercise on all who conversed with him intimately. The Pope spoke openly in favour of the companions, even in their own presence—for they were admitted once a fortnight to dispute on theology in his presence during his meal. The deferred sentence bears date November 18, 1538. In a letter written about a month after this time,[8] Ignatius mentions that they had then been allowed a further liberty in instructing children in schools—one of the works of the Christian ministry on which he set the highest value.

The winter which succeeded this first year of the labours of the companions now in Rome gave them another opportunity of winning for themselves the esteem and love which always, in the long run, find out true devotion and ardent charity. A severe famine fell upon the city, and thousands would have perished from hunger or disease consequent upon privation, but for the exertions of this handful of strangers, who had but just been

[8] To Elisabeth Roser in Spain, Dec. 19, 1538; Menchacha, *Ep. S. Ign.* l. i. ep. 8.

vindicated from charges which represented them as the most worthless of men. Very soon they had under their charge in one large building four hundred poor, for whom they begged food, clothing, bedding, and all other necessaries, and of whose souls they took care after they had cared for their bodies. A great movement of charity was the natural result of their noble example, and the poor were supported by large contributions until the spring had set in.

Meanwhile, several men of distinction were applying for admission into the Company, and Ignatius had also been requested to send some of his labourers to other cities in Italy. He had been unable to receive recruits, because one of the charges brought against him and his friends had been that they were endeavouring to found a new religious order without leave from the Holy See. It had also seemed inexpedient that they should separate, although they did not yet live what is called a strict 'community life,' without first determining on many essential points. In fact, several months in the year 1539 (the last of Francis Xavier's life in Rome and as a companion of Ignatius) were spent in prayer, deliberation, and consultation as to the future of the Company. They laboured in their works of charity by day, and spent part of the night in their consultations. We have an account of these deliberations from Ignatius himself,[9] and it shows how slowly and prudently the plan of the Society was matured. If the date given by Alcazar of the proposals submitted to the companions on their first assembly in Rome be correct, a whole year must have elapsed before the vital question of obedience under one head, in which the whole existence of the Society as an order was involved, was finally determined. There were difficulties internal and external. The chief difficulty as to the formation of a body under one head seems to have consisted in the intention of the

[9] The original of this most interesting document is, or was, in the Archivium of the Society at Rome, in Latin, in the handwriting of St. Ignatius. Alcazar l(. c.) gives an exact translation in Spanish. The deliberations began after Easter 1539 ('after Lent was passed'). Easter-day fell that year on April 6th. The paper mentioned a little further on was signed on Tuesday, April 15th.

companions to offer themselves unreservedly to the Pope. If the Pope were to send them hither and thither, were they to keep up as before their mutual relations one to another? There were also great external difficulties which had, in fact, to be overcome, and which it cost Ignatius many prayers and sacrifices to dispose of. The religious orders at that time were in so bad a state generally, that there were thoughts in high places either of abolishing them altogether, or of reducing them very greatly in number. The idea of a new order would hardly be tolerated; a new order, moreover, which, as the companions were fully conscious, would require the permission on the part of the Holy See to depart in some very essential particulars from any existing type.

The question as to the retention at all costs of the union in which they had found so much happiness and profit was resolved unanimously in the affirmative. The question as to the obedience to one head cost much deliberation; and it was at one time thought that it would be expedient for them to retire for some such space as forty days into absolute solitude, spending their time entirely in prayer and austerities, in order to solve it. This idea was abandoned, partly from fear of the scandal that might follow if they seemed to disperse or to leave Rome. Ignatius gives us the reasons which were urged on both sides. The decision, however, was at last unanimous in favour of the addition of a third vow of obedience to the vow of poverty and chastity; and a document was drawn up, and signed by all the companions on the 15th of April 1539, which pledged them all to enter the Society as soon as it was approved by the Pope. The fourth vow, which is now taken by the Professed of the Society, to go on any mission on which the Pope shall send them, whether among Christians or among the heathen, was decided on the 4th of May. Other arrangements as to the teaching of children, the duration of the Generalate, and the 'experiments' to which those who wished to enter the Society were to be subjected, were added, and the whole plan was then put on paper and submitted by Ignatius to the Pope. The Pope gave it for consideration to the Master of the Sacred Palace,—

the great order of St. Dominic being made, as it were, to stand sponsor for the original constitution of the Society founded by Ignatius. Father Badia returned it to the Pope with great commendations, and it was finally approved, but only verbally, by Paul III. on Sept. 3, 1539, at Tivoli. The formal approbation, as to which the Pope at first hesitated, and which at one time seemed extremely improbable, on account of the strenuous and obstinate opposition of Cardinal Guidiccioni, who had taken up strongly the opinion that all religious orders ought to be reduced to four, was not granted till more than a year later, when, on the Feast of SS. Cosmas and Damian, Sept. 27, 1540, Paul III. signed the bull *Regimini militantis Ecclesiæ*. Before that time Francis Xavier had left Rome and the side of Ignatius for ever. The bull was not formally promulgated till the spring of 1541.

Soon after the last points submitted for deliberation had been settled, the dispersion of the members of the future Society had begun. In May, Simon Rodriguez and Brouet had been sent to Siena, along with Francis Strada, a young Spaniard whom Ignatius had fallen in with more than a year before, on his return from Monte Cassino. The object of the Pope in sending the Fathers to Siena was the restoration of discipline in a certain convent, but the benefit of their presence was soon felt in the whole town. Codurius preached in the summer at Velletri, and in the following Advent at Tivoli. Laynez and Favre were sent to accompany the Cardinal of St. Angelo in his Legation to Parma, where Jerome Domenech and some other valuable recruits were gained to the Society. Laynez laboured also at Piacenza and Reggio; Bobadilla went to help in reviving religion, and indeed civil peace and order itself, in Ischia, and preached with much fruit in Naples itself. Meanwhile Salmeron continued his lectures at Rome, and preached and heard confessions also: Codurius, Le Jay, Ignatius himself, and Francis Xavier made up the little company. Francis Xavier was the secretary, and kept up the correspondence with the absent members. He thus began to be the chief letter writer of the Society—but unfortunately those first Fathers were too busy and too frequently changing their abodes to keep letters. Thus the months passed on, until on the 15th of March 1540, Ignatius called him to his room, and told him that it was his lot to leave Rome the next day in company with the Portuguese ambassador, Pedro de Mascareñas, to join Simon Rodriguez, who had already sailed for Lisbon from Civita Vecchia, in the first missionary expedition of the Society to the East Indies.

It was one of those providential arrangements which seem the result of simple chance. Govea, the Superior of the College of St. Barbara at Paris, who had been so nearly betrayed into an act of so much hostility and unfairness to Ignatius as the infliction upon him of a public flogging, and who had been converted to a better mind by the interview which the Saint sought with him, was now the trusted adviser of John III., King of Portugal, a zealous Christian Prince, most desirous of doing all in his power to further the spread of the Gospel truth in the new empire which had fallen into his hands in the extreme East. Govea had written to Ignatius about the great wants of the Indies, and he had recommended the King to apply for several of the companions of Ignatius as missionaries to the heathen there. The King ordered Mascareñas to make the request. The ambassador asked for six, Ignatius would only give two, and the Pope declined to force him to do more. Ignatius named Simon Rodriguez, naturally acceptable to the King, as he was himself a Portuguese of noble family, and Bobadilla, who was still labouring in the kingdom of Naples. Rodriguez sailed, as we have said, at once: he had but just returned from Siena, and was troubled with a quartan ague; but nothing could stop him. He took with him as a companion Father Paul of Camerino, who had lately joined the companions, and of whom we shall hear more in the letters of Francis Xavier. The second, or rather the third, of the missionaries was to travel to Portugal by land with Mascareñas. But Bobadilla only reached Rome just before the time appointed for the departure of the ambassador, and when he arrived he fell so ill as to be unable to travel. The ambassador could not wait, and would not go without the promised missionary. A substitute had to be found at the last moment, and Ignatius gave to the Indian mission his very right hand, his secretary, the man for whose conversion he had laboured so industriously and so perseveringly at Paris. Xavier had just time to receive the parting blessing of Paul III., and then he embraced Ignatius for the last time, and set forth on the long journey, or series of journeys, which was to end twelve years and a half later on the little island of San Chan within sight of the shores of China.

CHAPTER III.

Francis in Lisbon.

THE appointment of Francis Xavier to the mission of the Indies appears, as we have said, to have been brought about by chance, and was certainly a variation from the original intention of Ignatius. It is nevertheless true that it was not unexpected by Francis himself. He had heard of the wonderful field opened to Apostolic labourers in the Indies by the establishment of the Portuguese dominion in those countries, and of the miserable darkness which involved so many millions of souls redeemed by the Blood of Jesus Christ. He had longed to offer himself for such labours, and those who knew him most intimately had heard him utter strange words concerning them. Laynez used to relate afterwards how, when he was sleeping in the same room with Francis, he had sometimes been awakened by hearing him cry out as if under the strain of a great burthen, and how Francis had afterwards confessed that he had seemed to have been carrying on his shoulders an Indian, the weight of whom had seemed almost to crush him, and how he had found himself perfectly exhausted by his exertions. Simon Rodriguez, whom he was once nursing during an illness, had heard him cry out in his dreams, 'More! more!' and when Francis parted from him on his own voyage to the East, he told him as a last secret that he had then had represented to him a vast scene of toil—labours, dangers, and sufferings which he was to undergo—and how God had given him the courage to desire that the sufferings might be even increased. These things show how much his mind was turned in that direction, as well as the magnanimous courage with which he was ready to encounter the career of toil now opened to him.

The Society was not yet approved by the Holy Father

except by word of mouth. The conclusion of the affair was expected daily, but it did not really take place till half a year after the time when Xavier left Rome. He placed in Laynez's hands a letter to be used when the time came for the members of the Society to give their suffrages. It contained three declarations. First of all, he declared that he accepted beforehand all the rules and constitutions which should be made by those of the Society who might be conveniently assembled at Rome, as soon as his Holiness granted his approbation to their plan. He knew that the companions would soon be dispersed into various countries, and he promised acquiescence in the arrangements of those who might be assembled, if only two or three or whoever they might be. This he signed with his name. A second part contained his suffrage for the election of Superior. He declared that he thought it right, in his conscience, that their old and true Father, Master Ignatius, who had brought them together with so much labour, should be their Superior. 'He will know best how to preserve us, guide us, and urge us on to better things, because he thoroughly knows every one of us.' After his death, Master Peter Favre should, he thought, be chosen. A third declaration is added, in which he promises 'now for then, when the Society shall have been collected, and a Superior chosen, perpetual poverty, chastity, and obedience therein.' He adjures Laynez, his dearest Father in Christ, to offer these his vows for him to the Superior who shall be elected.[1]

It was late in Lent when Francis left Rome. The account of his journey to Portugal, which lasted till nearly the end of June, is chiefly derived from his own letters, though they naturally omit certain details as to himself which he was very unlikely to have mentioned. He reached Bologna soon after Easter, having passed through Loreto, where he paid his devotions, again, and for the last time, in the Holy House of Nazareth. At Bologna he was received with enthusiasm, for the memory of his labours there two years before had not died away. On the first day of his arrival the church of Santa

[1] We print this letter in the Notes to this Book.

Lucia, where he was to say mass, was full, two hours before day, of people who desired to assist at it, and he spent a great deal of time in hearing confessions and seeing old friends.[2] He had a long interview with the Cardinal Legate, who promised his favour to the Society. The following letter, in answer to one which he had received from Ignatius, gives a short account of his proceedings, thus far, and it is full of that tender feeling of personal affection which made his apostolical exile from his friends a sacrifice of peculiar intensity to him.

(II.) *To my brothers in our Lord Jesus Christ, Don Ignatius and Don Peter Codacio,*[3] *at the Torre Melangolo, at the house of Signor Antonio Freripani.*[4]

May the grace and love of our Lord Jesus Christ be ever with us, to help and favour us! Amen.

On Easter Day I received your letter which came with the despatches of my Lord Ambassador; and I cannot express all the joy and consolation which it has caused me—God our Lord alone knows it. For what is left of this life, I am well assured, it will be by letter only that we shall hold intercourse—in the other life, we shall be *facie ad faciem*[5] and embrace one

[2] Some years after this, the church of Santa Lucia itself was given to the Society.

[3] Codacio was a priest, a native of Lodi, of a good family and considerable wealth (sacerdos honestus et clarus e Pontificiâ familiâ—of the Pope's household—nec parvis Ecclesiæ opibus ac facultatibus præditus) says Orlandini (ii. 66), who was the first Italian to enter the Society, and had begged to be allowed to act as its Procurator in temporal matters. Orlandini tells us that he was so useful to it that some people called it Codacio's Society.

[4] The original of this letter was preserved at Bologna, in the College of St. Lucia, and Father Menchacha, the very careful editor of the Epistles of St. Francis, says that he copied it out from the Spanish. (Proleg. p. liv.) It appears, however, somewhat altered in his text, as that part of his book had been printed before he made the comparison. We follow the original in our translation.

[5] P. Poussines, who published a large collection of the Letters of St. Francis in 1666, tells us in his *Prolegomena*, that whenever the Saint, writing in Spanish or Portuguese, puts in a few words in Latin, either as a quotation or otherwise, he has left them in italics in his own text. We shall insert them either in the text or in notes. See Menchacha, Ep. S. Francisci, t. i. p. xxxviii.

another perpetually. So what remains to us is that for this little time which we have still to pass in our mortal exile, we should take frequent looks at one another by means of letters, and for my part, I mean to do just as you bid me in this matter, and to keep the rule which little girls observe of writing constantly to their mothers.

'I have had a long, leisurely, and perfectly open conversation with my Lord Cardinal of Ivrea,[6] as you commissioned me in your letter. He received me in the kindest way, offering with great earnestness to favour us in everything that lies in his power. The good old man embraced me when I left him and kissed his hand: and while he was talking, I could not help throwing myself at his feet, and kissing his hand in the name of all our Society. As far as I could judge from his answers to me, he highly approves our way of going on.

The Lord Ambassador heaps so many favours and attentions upon me that I should never finish if I were to tell you all, and I don't know how I could ever have consented to accept them, if I did not reflect, and were not convinced, that in India I shall pay for them at the cost of my life and nothing less. On Palm Sunday I heard his confession in the Church of our Lady at Loreto, and gave him holy communion. I did the same to a number of his people. I said mass in the Chapel of our Lady, and the good ambassador got all the people of his suite to receive holy communion with him in that Holy House. Again on Easter Day I heard his confession, gave him absolution, and afterwards communion, as well as to other good and religious persons of his household. His domestic Chaplain commends himself very much to all your prayers. He has promised to go with us to the Indies.

Please, my dearest brother Don Pedro, to give my salutations to Donna Faustina Ancolini, and remind her in my name, if it is not too much for you to do, to keep her promise to me that she would go to confession and communion. Tell her also, if you please, to write and let me know that she has done so, and how often. Tell her that I have said one mass

[6] Philibert Ferreri, Bishop of Ivrea, Cardinal Legate of Bologna.

for her and my dear Vincenzo, and that to-morrow I shall say one for herself. She may be quite sure, moreover, that I shall never forget her, even when I am in India. And tell her from me that if she wishes to do a thing that will give real pleasure to her and my dear Vincenzo, she will forgive those who killed her son, for Vincenzo certainly prays a great deal for them in heaven. Here in Bologna I have more to do hearing confessions than I had lately in Rome at San Luigi. My tenderest love to all of you; if I do not mention each one by name, it is not, you may be quite sure, that I forget any one.

Your Brother and Servant in Jesus Christ,

FRANCIS.

Bologna, March 31st, 1540.

We must suppose that the lady here spoken of had lost her son in one of the quarrels so frequent among the young men of the time, and had been consoled by Francis before his departure.

The next letter which we possess is written from Lisbon some time after his arrival there.

(III.) *To the Fathers and Brothers of the Society of Jesus at Rome.*

May the grace and love of Christ our Lord be always our support and help! Amen.

We have received from Christ our Lord many and continual favours all through our journey from Rome into Portugal, which has taken us three months. That all that distance and time, through so many difficulties and toils, my Lord Ambassador and all his suite, from the highest to the lowest, should never have ceased to enjoy perfect health, is a matter for which we ought certainly to give great thanks and praise to Christ our Lord, especially as over and above ordinary helps He has held a hand of particular protection over us to deliver us from all dangers, and was also pleased to inspire my Lord Ambassador with wisdom and prudence to keep all his people in so holy an order, that they have seemed to be rather a religious community than a secular household. He managed this by himself frequenting the sacraments of penance and holy communion : his servants consequently did the same of their own accord, induced by so noble an example; and this they did so often and in such large numbers, that often as we went along it was easy to foresee that when we got to our hostel we should have far too little time and too scanty convenience for satisfying the wants of so many; and so I was obliged now and then to turn aside from the road and dismount and find a convenient place, so as to hear a part of the retinue beforehand.

We had not yet got out of Italy when our Lord was pleased to show His power in a manner quite miraculous, on one of our company, a servant of my Lord Ambassador. It was the same man whom you saw at Rome first put off, through weakness and cowardice, the design he had formed of embracing the religious life, and afterwards abandon it altogether. We came on a large river, and no one knew whether or where there was a ford. This poor man was urged by his own rashness to try to find it, though we all cried out to him not to do it; all in vain, for he rode on into the channel of the stream, though he knew nothing of its depth. He had not gone far, when the force of the current overpowered his horse, and carried it away together with its rider. We all looked on in heartfelt pity. The stream bore him down in a moment, quite as far as the distance from your house at Rome to San Luigi's. And then our Lord God vouchsafed to hear the ardent prayers which His servant, my Lord Ambassador, poured forth at that pitiable sight, praying, and all his servants with him, *non sine lacrymis*, for what was in all human appearance the desperate case of that poor fellow. Our Lord heard their prayers, and saved him from the very jaws of destruction by a manifest miracle. The man was Master of the Horse in my Lord's household. No doubt when he was being carried along by the whirling stream he would much have preferred the inside of a monastery to his present case. And his greatest trouble at this time, as he told me himself afterwards, was the memory of the opportunity he had refused, and which then he would have willingly regained at any price whatsoever. He told me that he was much less overwhelmed by horror at the danger he was in at that dreadful moment than by the sting of his conscience, which keenly reproached him with having led a careless life without making provision for death, and he added, that at that critical juncture he was tormented above all by tardy repentance for having put off his entrance into religion, to which he had felt that God certainly called him. He was so full of these thoughts when we recovered him that he fell to exhorting the whole company not to sin in the same way. His face and countenance were all changed, pale beyond expression, and marked with the sense of the danger he had run; he seemed a man come back from hell, and all this gave great weight to his words. He discoursed long and pathetically upon the torments of the damned, like a man who had experienced them: and he said over and over again that it was very true indeed, that a man who during life had not thought of preparing for death, had no time to remember God when the necessity of death was upon him. Such was the discourse of this good man, discourse not gathered from reading books, or from studious meditation, but dictated by his own experience. And when I think this over, I am deeply moved at the very similar carelessness of many whom in various ways we have made acquaintance with and known as friends, whom I see putting off in the same way the execution of good plans and holy desires to serve God, which they acknowledge to have felt. And I fear very much that they, too, may find themselves some day surprised by a time when they may most ardently desire to accomplish what they had determined and will then have no power of accomplishing.

[The lives of Francis Xavier are unanimous in attributing the miraculous rescue of the poor man here mentioned to the prayers of the Saint. It needs but little acquaintance with the manner of speaking and writing of matters in which they themselves are concerned which is common to great servants of God, to see through the veil which his humility has here thrown over his own part in the affair, as well as over his influence in producing the marvellous piety and regularity which prevailed in the whole company during the journey. Two other instances of his charity and its preternatural reward are mentioned in the same histories. In the first case he is said to have risked his own life to save the secretary of the ambassador, who had fallen over a precipice in the Alps into a deep cavity in the snow, and in the second to have saved another of the party who had ridden on in advance and fallen under his horse in a very dangerous manner.

Francis also makes no mention of an incident on the journey which has often been mentioned as an instance of that close adherence to the words of our Lord and to the spirit of an Apostolical vocation which is characteristic of men such as he. The road through Spain passed at no great distance from the Castle of Xavier, where his mother, of whom he was the youngest and perhaps the darling son, was still living. The ambassador knew this, and was expecting Francis to apply to him for leave to turn aside for a short time, in order to visit his mother for the last time. When Francis said nothing, Mascareñas began to urge him to take the opportunity, and to offer to make arrangements for his convenience. But he only answered that they would meet with all the greater joy in heaven for having taken no leave of one another on earth. As Francis only knew of his destination for India the day before he left Rome, and travelled quite as fast as an ordinary messenger could have travelled, it is certain that he could not have apprized his family of his journey, and that therefore they would not have expected him. The pain of foregoing a last tender interview was all his own.

The letter, which we have for a moment interrupted, continues as follows :]

On the very day of our arrival in Lisbon I fell in with Master Simon, who was expecting the access of a quartan fever, which, as was thought, was due at that very time. But he was so extremely glad to see me—not more glad than I was to see and to embrace him—that his joy sent away his fever and all its effects, and neither that day, nor ever since, has he felt anything of the kind, though it is now a month since our arrival. He is perfectly reestablished in health, and labours hard in our Lord's vineyard, not without gathering in much fruit.

The number of persons here who are friendly and well disposed towards us is very great, indeed so great that I am much concerned not to be able, on account of their multitude, to return to all of them, one by one, all due observance in the way of salutations and visits, which it would certainly be a duty to return, if time allowed us to fulfil the obligation, on account of the honourable and conspicuous dignity of the greater part of these persons. I have also observed a great many who are inclined to good things, and desirous of serving God, to whom it would be a most salutary thing to give some of the Spiritual Exercises, in order to help them to form the resolutions of executing at once what they go on putting off *de die in diem.* For whatever haste men may make to execute what they know they ought to do, it is not easy for them to escape having something to answer for to God on the ground of overmuch delay, and thus it is well to use great attention in putting to flight the excuses which occur for continuing to temporize. The full knowledge of this obligation puts very salutary spurs to many men's sides, which make them feel as if they were roused from a sort of lethargy, so as to see that where there is no peace to be found they will never find it—those men especially I speak of, who against all reason try to draw God whither they wish, and refuse to go where He calls them, allowing themselves to be moved more by their own disordered affections than by the good desires which He breathes into their hearts. Far more worthy, certainly, of pity than envy! All those whom we see straining themselves to climb up a path so steep and rugged, toiling up hill with continual labour, are seeking after all nothing but the risk of a headlong fall, or rather the certain catastrophe of a miserable ruin.

After we had been in this royal city three or four days, the King sent for us, and received us with the utmost kindness. He was alone, in his cabinet, with the Queen.[7] We remained with him for an hour, or a little more. Their Highnesses asked us many questions, particularly about our Institute, how long ago and in what manner we had come to know one another and unite ourselves in a body, then what had been the scope of our first plans, and lastly about the persecutions we had suffered. They were delighted with our account of the manner in which the truth had at last been discovered, and praised us in particular for having carried the matter on with constancy and courage to the extreme issue of a judicial sentence. The King expressed a desire to see with his own eyes the sentence by which we were absolved. It is certainly the general opinion of all that we acted both piously and wisely in never letting anything persuade us to desist from urging on the cause to the final publication of the sentence. Most people here go so far in praising us for this, as to say that they cannot help expressing the opinion that if we had not done what we did, it appears to them that we should never have been in a position to reap any fruit from our ministrations. So, as I said, they are never tired of praising our constancy in braving it out intrepidly on to the final issue of the sentence which at length put the truth forward in full light. To return to the King and Queen, they were much pleased with all the details which they heard from us of the form and system of our houses, and of the object and scope of our ministrations, and of the whole Institute. During our audience, the King sent for the Infanta, his daughter, and the Prince Royal his son, that we might see them, and told us in the kindest manner how many sons and daughters the Lord had given him, and who of them were dead and who living.

Both their Highnesses, King and Queen alike, have showed us great affection. The King urged us with much earnestness, on the very day of our first interview, to hear the confessions of the pages of his household. For he has ordered that all

[7] The Queen was Catharine of Austria, sister of the Emperor Charles V.

the young noblemen who frequent the Court should go to confession once a week, and he has seriously charged us to look to the execution of this order and to have our eyes on all these youths. He gave the following reason for his care in this respect, that he considered that if young men in this position were accustomed from their childhood to know and serve God, they would grow up in later life good and virtuous men.[8] Then if the nobles are what they ought to be, the common people will doubtless form itself after their example, and thus the hopes of restoring good morals among all the seculars of the kingdom turn upon the good education of the youth of the upper classes. For it certainly is beyond doubt that if that first order in the kingdom were conspicuous for holiness, a large part of the remainder would be drawn to follow their example.

We have certainly great reason to praise God for the religious disposition and the zeal of this excellent King for the promotion of the Divine glory, and for the great piety with which he is inclined to everything that is good and holy; and we of the Society of Jesus in particular are very much his debtors, for his extreme kindness to all of us, to you at Rome as well as to us who are here. The ambassador, who has had a conversation with the King since our audience, told me that he had said that he should be greatly delighted if he could collect and have near him all those who have as yet entered the Society, even though the cost of feeding them and furnishing them with necessaries were to consume a large part of the revenues of the Crown.

We know that a great number of our friends here are making efforts to oppose our departure for India, because they think that here we should reap greater fruits by hearing confessions, by familiar instructions, by giving the Spiritual Exercises, and by exhorting all the faithful to make frequent confessions and communions; in short by working diligently in that same sort of teaching which we mean to adopt in the Indies. Among

[8] One of these young nobles was Miguel de Souza, who entered the Society, and was a man of conspicuous virtue.

the persons who think this are the Confessor and the Preacher of the King, who both urge him to keep us here in the hope oι more abundant fruit. Certain others hold different language, and talk wonderfully about the results that may be expected from our ministry in India. Those who speak thus are men of authority on such subjects, having lived many years in the Indies. They say that they have remarked that the native tribes are very well disposed to accept the religion of our Lord Jesus Christ, if it be offered them by representatives and teachers such as we are—they mean whose way of proceeding is far removed from all appearance of avarice. If therefore we retain out there also what we show here, the same abstention from and contempt of worldly convenience and gain, they say that without any doubt we shall in a few years convert two or three kingdoms of idolaters to the faith of Jesus Christ, and that the people will not hesitate to believe us and trust us, as soon as they have found out for certain that we seek nothing but the salvation of souls. These assurances, given us by persons of such character, who have had experience on the spot, and who have, as I have said, passed many years in India, beget in us a great confidence of reaping in that country most abundant fruits for the glory of God.

Here we are taking great pains to find out priests who, setting before themselves no reward but that of serving God and helping the salvation of souls, may be willing to go with us to India, and indeed we can see nothing by which we can, at this moment, do more service or give greater pleasure to our Lord than by gaining such associates. For if we could but gather together a band of only as many as twelve such priests, who would be willing to unite themselves to us with one heart in these plans and purposes, it is unquestionable that we should find it well worth our labour. And already some such offer themselves to us. We have fallen in with a priest whom we knew in Paris, and who has promised us to come and remain with us until death, sharing our manner of life and all our designs. We think ourselves certain enough of him, for he has given us fair proofs and pledges of constancy of will. There is also another, a subdeacon, who will soon be a priest, who offers himself for the same object with great fervour. And further, a certain Doctor of Medicine, who was at one time a familiar acquaintance of ours at Paris, has promised to sail with us to India, and that there he will avail himself of his medical knowledge, as far as shall be expedient, for the good of souls, and to draw them to the saving knowledge of their Creator, without seeking any temporal reward by his services. This one thing above all we keep in view always, that those whom we take as companions should be entirely free from all desire of gain. Nor will this in itself be enough, unless we are also altogether free from even the most distant appearance of it, so that neither in ourselves nor in those who have near relations with us, shall there be seen anything at all which may give rise to the slightest suspicion that we have come there to seek and acquire temporal rather than spiritual goods.

His Highness has spoken to the Bishop, who is our friend, and also to his own Confessor, about using us as public preachers in the sacred pulpit. But as we desired to begin with more lowly offices, we at first put the matter off and showed our wish not to occupy ourselves in preaching, although those who know us are very desirous to hear us in the pulpits in the churches. But one day the King sent for us, and, after many other things, told us that it would gratify him if we were to preach. So then we offered ourselves for the work with the greatest readiness, not only on account of our eagerness, and indeed our duty, to follow the injunctions of his Highness, but also on account of our hope, founded on the help of Christ our Lord accompanying our efforts, of spending our labours with some useful profit for souls. We shall begin next Sunday week; and the special goodwill which is shown to us on all sides by the inhabitants of this city forbids us to doubt of a favourable reception. What we implore of our Lord with repeated prayers is this, that He will be pleased to increase the faith of those who charitably hope for some good from us.[9] And this good opinion concerning us which has got abroad so happily in

[9] *ut augeat eorum fidem qui de nobis aliquam expectationem habent.* (Orig.)

these parts will, we hope, be an occasion to God, out of His immense goodness, in which alone we trust, of imparting to us, if not for our own sakes, at least for the sake of the people here who show so much faith and devotion in listening to us, such knowledge and grace that we may be able to console them, and to speak to them the things that are necessary or useful to them for the salvation of their souls.[10]

To all of you, my dearest in Christ,

FRANCIS.

Lisbon, July 3d, 1540.

The sanguine hopefulness which was always characteristic of Francis Xavier, and which is so often allied with that great affectionateness of heart which became in him, as in St. Paul, the foundation of many of the distinctively Apostolical graces which he received, is hardly more conspicuous in this letter than the strong feeling, almost of indignation mingled with alarm and pity, with which he regarded the case of so many who seemed to him to be resisting or trifling with a high vocation offered to them in the counsels of God. He will be content with a band of only twelve priests, who were to live the same sort of life with himself and have the same single aim in the preaching of the Gospel. It does not appear that he meant them necessarily to become members of the Society. We shall find that these moderate expectations were to turn out to be very far in excess of what the future reserved for him in the way of companionship. We cannot tell whether the priest from Paris persevered in his desire of entering the Company, but he did not sail for India. The subdeacon, if he were Francis Mancias, who Xavier afterwards says was not yet in any holy orders, went to India, and though he did not always remain with St. Francis, we owe much to him for having preserved to us a large number of the letters of his Apostolical Superior. Nor do we hear anything more of the Doctor of Medicine. Francis Xavier might have been disconcerted if he had known,

[10] *ut possimus consolari eos, et quæ vel necessaria vel utilia sunt ad animarum salutem dicere.* (Latin words in the original.)

too, that Simon Rodriguez, his own intimate friend, was to remain in Portugal, and that he was himself to be the only one of the original companions who took the voyage to the East. But, as we shall see, there was at one time great danger lest the Eastern mission should be abandoned altogether, as far as Francis and his companions were concerned. All of the first disciples of Ignatius seem to have been endowed in some high degree with that charming attractiveness which is one of the prerogatives of great holiness, and which sometimes is imparted in a measure even to those who have had much intercourse with men who have the gift in its perfection. Certainly of all these Francis Xavier and Simon Rodriguez were not the least likely pair to win to themselves the hearts of those among whom they moved. Their manner of life was humble and mortified. They lodged in the Hospital, though an apartment had been prepared for them in the Palace, and they lived on alms which they collected for themselves daily. After a time, however, their spiritual labours increased so much and required so much time, that they judged it expedient to beg alms only once or twice a week, as an exercise of humility and mortification, and they lived on the food sent to them from the Palace, or rather on a portion of it. The rest they gave to the poor. Shortly after their arrival, the prisoners of the Inquisition were placed under their spiritual charge by the Cardinal, Don Henry. Their conversation and character drew all to them, and the King began to consider that they might do less good in the distant East than in the capital of his own States. The question thus raised is mentioned in the following letter, written before the end of July, about three weeks after the preceding. We shall see that Francis, even after so short an interval, speaks much more moderately as to his hopes of companions for India.

(IV.) *To the Father Master Ignatius of Loyola.*

May the grace and love of Christ our Lord ever help and favour us! Amen.

After I had written the other day at great length about affairs here, certain points have occurred to me which I then omitted. Here are some. If the Brief which concerns the whole Society is as yet published, send us, I beseech you, a copy. The King and all our friends in Portugal will be glad to see it, as well as the sentence of the Governor of Rome, when we were declared innocent. The King has asked for the book of the *Exercises*, wishing to see it. If you think proper to send us also one of the corrected copies, it would give his Highness much pleasure. This great Prince is, in fact, wonderfully well disposed towards the whole Society, and it seems as if nothing that we can do for him would be too much in the way of gratitude for the singular and very great love which he bears us. I have received two letters from you, both very short: one dated the 8th June, the other the 1st May. It will gratify my Lord Ambassador very much to receive a letter from you. You would hardly believe how carefully he keeps that one which you did write to him, and which he received on our journey from Rome into Portugal; he preserves it with the greatest care. If you cannot write to him yourself, manage at least that the letters which we receive from Strada may be such as we can show him.

At this moment we are preparing to give the Exercises to two licentiates in theology, one of whom is a very famous preacher, and the other preceptor to the King's brother, the Infant, Don Henry. We are striving also to make other persons of distinction desire to have them, for we are convinced that the more earnestly they wish for them the more abundant fruit will they reap from them. There is really great reason for praising God our Lord, when we see the number of persons here who frequent the sacraments of penance and holy communion.

Determine what you think best to do with Francis Strada, whether you will like to send him to the University of Coimbra. In that University neither he nor others will want the resources necessary for their studies, if we may judge from the fact that people there are very well inclined to all that is pious and good. Hence we do not doubt that before long some kind of a College of ours will be founded in that University. When an opportunity offers we shall not fail to treat with the King about getting up a College of Students: but for this we shall want to be told what your mind is as to the form of such an establishment, and the method of life to be followed in it, the person who is to rule the community, and the discipline under which the members are to live, in order that they may grow in spirit more than in letters.[11] We want this, that when we speak with the King, we may explain to him the kind of life which is to be led by those who study in our Colleges. On all this subject, then, I wish very much that you would write at good length. It does not seem as if anything would prevent our having a house built there for receiving our Masters and Scholars, or indeed other houses of our Institute. People here would very willingly build houses for us, if there were any persons to inhabit them.

Our friend, the Bishop, has told us that the King has not yet made up his mind whether he will send us to India, because he thinks we should serve our Lord as well in Portugal as there; but two Bishops, who judge differently, have urged that we ought on no account to be kept here, but by all means be sent to India, because they think that in that case some Indian King will be converted. We keep ourselves intent upon aggregating companions, and I think, as things become gradually more clear and definite, we shall not fail to find some. If we remain here, we shall found several houses. It will be easier to find people who will join us to remain in this country, than to go to India; but if we go there, and if God our Lord grant us some years of life, we will found with His help some houses in India and Ethiopia.

11 *ut crescant magis in spiritu quam in literis.* (Orig.)

If the Brief about our whole Society is not yet issued, at any rate I entreat you to see that we have powers granted us to found houses of the Institute among the heathen. But whether we are to remain established here or to sail for India, I beg of you, for the sake of the love and service of God our Lord, to write to us the method and order which we should observe in receiving new members into our Society, and to do this *multum ad longum*, for you know well enough how very little cleverness we have; so that if you don't help us, an occasion of promoting the greater service of our Lord God may be lost on account of our want of experience in managing such business. Farewell.

Your holy Charity's least son in Christ,

FRANCIS.

Lisbon, July 26, 1540.

It is in such private letters as this last—for the former must have been meant to be passed from hand to hand—that the beautiful humility and self-diffidence of Francis Xavier most frequently break out, especially when he is addressing his most tenderly loved father, Ignatius. The mention of the University of Coimbra in this letter shows us that the mind of Francis was much occupied with the desire of seeing the Society permanently established in the great seat of learning in Portugal. The Constitutions of the Society were, of course, not yet in existence, and there was the greatest need of some definite plan on which such foundations as that contemplated in the letter should be framed. Francis had an uncle at Coimbra, the celebrated Master of Azpilqueta, called Navarrus, or the Doctor of Navarre. He appears to have earnestly desired to see Francis, and even to have requested the King to send him to Coimbra. He offered to give two courses of lectures more than he was obliged to give if the King would consent, and at a later time offered himself to go to India, but Francis told him that a man of his age and acquirements was better employed at home. We have two letters from Francis to Doctor Martin, which may be here inserted.

(v.) *To the very Reverend my Lord the Doctor of Azpilqueta, at Coimbra.*

Very Reverend Sir,

Since I have been in this city, I have received two letters from you full of tenderness and charity towards me.[12] May our Lord Jesus Christ, the love of Whom moved you to write to me, reward you duly for your so great kindness! for I, wish it as much as I may, am unable to discharge the debt for myself, or to answer as I ought to your extreme benevolence to one so unworthy and so poor. So I must acknowledge and confess my inability in this respect, and understanding as I do by the mercy of God,[13] Whose singular gift it is that we know ourselves, how useless I am for everything good,[14] I shall make some little effort, such as I may, to discharge this duty, and then I have determined to place all my hope and confidence in God, seeing that I am unable to return to any one favour for favour in equal measure, and in truth I find great consolation in the thought that God is able to return to that holy soul of yours and to others like you a most abundant recompense on my behalf.[15]

With regard to the wish that you manifest of knowing of my affairs, and especially of my rule of life,[16] it would be a great joy to me if we could have an opportunity of meeting, for no one could be readier than I am to tell you with the utmost fulness all that you desire to know in this respect. And I am not without hope that God our Lord, among the many favours with which His Divine Majesty most indulgently and mercifully loads me day by day, may add also this very special grace to

[12] *amoris ac pietatis erga me plenas.* (Orig.)

[13] *per Dei clementiam.* (Orig.)

[14] *quam inutilis ad omnia sim.* (Orig.)

[15] This is in Latin in the original: *studui spem omnem et fiduciam meam in Deo ponere, videns me nemini posse æquam gratiam referre; et hoc me plurimum solatur, quod potens est Deus sanctæ animæ tuæ et similibus retributionem amplissimam pro me dare.*

[16] *et præsertim de meæ vitæ instituto.* (Orig.)

all the rest, that I may see you for once in this life and talk with you at leisure, before my companion and I set sail for the Indies. There will be time for me to give you the most ample account of all things as to which you question me in your letter. There is too much of them for me to do it conveniently in writing. You add, that people talk a great deal, as men will talk, about our Institute. As to this, for the present I will only answer, It matters little, most excellent Doctor, how we are judged of by men, and especially by men who judge of matters before they understand them.[17]

Blas Lopez, who will give you this letter from me, wishes earnestly to place himself under your patronage and teaching. I love him very much, and he in return has a singular love for me, and for the sake of this bond between us, I beg of you to be good enough, if prayer of mine have any power with you—and so great is your goodness, that I know my prayers have no little such power[18]—accept kindly, as from me and on my recommendation, the great devotion which he offers you, wishing above all things to serve you as his good Patron, and to place himself under your teaching as a Master. So, I pray you, put him down as one of your own people, in which, besides that you will do, as I hope, a thing pleasing to our Lord God, you will also confer a singular favour on me. I shall indeed be obliged to you, as for a great and peculiar favour, if you will have the condescension to take charge of this good youth and to direct and help him in his studies. His intention and desire is to devote his youth to the careful study of those branches of learning in which you excel so much. You may well consider how much you owe to God, Who has enriched you with that rare talent of great learning—not certainly for your own benefit alone, but that you may be of assistance to many others besides yourself. But may God our

[17] Here also the original has the Latin sentences: *multa pro hominum consuetudine de nostro Instituto dici*—and again, *parum refert, Doctor egregie, ab hominibus judicari, præsertim ab iis qui priùs judicant quàm intelligant.*

[18] The original inserts the Latin words: *si preces meæ apud te quidpiam possunt* (*possunt autem multum per tuam humanitatem*).

Lord have us both alike and always in His holy keeping! Amen.

Your servant in Christ, while he lives,[19]

FRANCIS XAVIER.

Lisbon, Sept. 28, 1540.

(VI.) *To the Doctor Martin of Azpilqueta.*

The letter which you wrote to me on the 15th of October has caused me so much joy and consolation, that I find nothing gives me so much refreshment as to read it over, after having longed for it no very short time.[20] It lets me see all the piety that animates those holy labours and occupations in which you spend your time; for a work of great piety indeed it is to instruct in learning those who desire learning only for the sake of giving themselves wholly and singly to the service of Jesus Christ our Lord. And so I do not feel that pity for your Reverence which I really should feel if I thought that you did not use, as a faithful servant should use them, those very excellent gifts with which it has pleased Christ our Lord to adorn you, for I am quite sure that, however great and fatiguing may have been the toil by which the prize is won, very far greater will be the prize itself, when one who has been faithful in little shall be set over many things.[21] And if just at present you have to exert yourself particularly in giving a lecture or two more than is your wont, yet, after all, you ought to find fresh strength for this, so as to do it with the utmost willingness, in the thought that there may have been times when you have been less industrious than the excellent talent given you by God might require. And we certainly, who rejoice in all that is good for you, are delighted to see you work off old obligations in this way yourself, rather than leave them to be discharged by those who are to come after you. For there are many who suffer punishment in the next

[19] *Tuus in Christo, quoadusque vixerit.* (Orig.)

[20] *a me per multos jam dies optata.* (Orig.)

[21] *quando super multa erit constitutus, qui in modico fuit fidelis.* (Orig.)

world because they have trusted more than was right to the executors of their wills, and in this way it is a terrible thing to fall into the Hands of the Living God, and most especially in giving an account of our stewardship.[22]

May God, Who has so liberally given you such an abundance of learning that you have plenty to give to others, make you equally liberal in imparting it to those who desire only to know how to serve the Creator and Lord of all, setting before your eyes the glory of God and the increase thereof! Most certainly the Lord of all law and justice will grant to us that, if in this life we have been companions in His sufferings, in the next we shall be companions in consolation. So it will infallibly be, most excellent Doctor.[23] I won't say more at present, putting it off till the day when I may talk to you face to face. That day will come, though you do not think it will. That special love to me, which your letter shows me, makes it impossible that I should refuse to do as you wish in this matter. As for the love I bear to you, I say nothing of it. Our Lord, Who sees to the very bottom of the hearts of both of us, knows how dear you are to mine. Adieu, excellent Doctor, and keep me in your wonted love.[24]

Your humble servant in Christ,

FRANCIS XAVIER.

Lisbon, November 4, 1540.

We have no record of the meeting between uncle and nephew of which this last letter speaks as probable. Master Azpilqueta mentions that Francis wrote to him at his departure, in answer to his offer to go to India himself, comforting him for their separation with the hope of a speedy meeting in the Kingdom of Heaven. Neither have we any more detailed account of the life of Francis in Lisbon during the remainder

[22] *et ideo horrendum est incidere in manus Dei viventis, præscrtim in reddendâ villicationis ratione.* (Orig.)

[23] *dabit Dominus juris (et ita fiet, Doctor egregie) ut in aliâ vitâ socii consolationum simus, si in hâc fuerimus passionum comites.* (Orig.)

[24] *Ego vero meum erga te amoris vinculum taceo: Dominus novit, qui amborum mentem solus ipse rimat, quam mihi sis intimus corde. Vale, Doctor egregie, et me, ut soles, ama.* (Orig.)

of the year 1540, except such as is contained in the next hasty letter in our series, written some weeks earlier than the last to Dr. Azpilqueta. It appears that there was still some hesitation entertained by the Pope as to the Society, and that Ignatius had asked Francis to induce the King of Portugal to exert his influence for the furtherance of their interests. Ignatius had as yet not been able to give a distinct answer to the College at Coimbra.

(VII.) *To the Father Master Ignatius of Loyola and Peter Codacio, at Rome.*

May the grace and love of Christ our Lord always help and favour us! Amen.

The courier is ready to start and in a great hurry, and we are obliged to write these few lines as fast as we can. We can just tell you we are well, and are increasing. We are now six here, all acquaintances in old days in Paris, except two, Fathers Paul and Emanuel a Sancta Clara. Thus has it pleased our Lord to prosper our desires and exertions, by giving us these fellow labourers with us for the purpose of making His name great among the nations who know Him not.

We attribute the fruit which we here reap from our ministrations to the favour of God which you at Rome gain for us. This fruit far surpasses our capacity, learning or intelligence. Such numbers of persons, and persons of the highest rank, come to us to open their consciences in holy confession, that we have not time enough to satisfy them all. The Prince Don Henry, Grand Inquisitor of the Kingdom, and the King's brother, has often urged on us to take spiritual charge of the persons in the prisons of the Holy Inquisition. We visit them every day, and apply ourselves to make them understand how great a favour God has done them in placing them in this school of penance. Once a day we give them all together an exhortation, and we also give them the Exercises of the first weeks, to their great comfort and advantage. A large number of them tell us that they acknowledge it as a singular favour of God that they now hear as they do from us, what they have never heard before, so many truths, the knowledge of which is necessary for their salvation.

A few days ago we sent you letters from the King to the Holy Father and to his ambassador at Rome, in which he recommends the interests of our Society as if they were his own. To obtain recommendations of this kind from the Court here we have no longer need of any third person, we can do it all ourselves. And now too, if the King were not in great grief on account of the death of Prince Edward, he would have written again to his Holiness and to the Cardinal of the *Quattro Coronati*, as well as to other persons at Rome whose favour may be necessary or useful for our interests. But he is, as I say, so overwhelmed with grief, and so struck down by the death of the Prince his brother,[25] that he is shut up at home and receives no one. All business is suspended by this sad grief. We must allow a certain respite to such affectionate sorrow. In a few days, after the keenest pangs are past, we will obtain as many letters as you can wish to whoever you may name from this excellent King.

We have here living in community with us a person who has finished his course at Paris. Master Gonsalvo Medeiros is his name; he is not yet in orders. We beg of you from the service of our Lord God to obtain and send here a rescript of the Pope, by virtue of which he may be ordained *extra consueta tempora*, and may receive the sacred orders on three successive feasts, so that he may be ordained priest before we sail for India.[26] It might be necessary also that the privilege should be obtained, to be communicated to six clerics at our choice, of using the new Breviary.[27] This might be of some use in

[25] This brother was the Infant Edward, Duke of Guimaraens, the sixth son of Emanuel the Fortunate. He had two daughters, one of whom married the Duke of Braganza, whose grandson succeeded to the throne in 1640 as John IV., on the revolution which overthrew the Spanish domination in Portugal.

[26] This Father, however, remained in Portugal with Simon Rodriguez.

[27] This must have been the short Breviary arranged by Cardinal Quignon in 1536.

more readily inducing some to be willing to follow us to India. We conjure you, by the love of our Lord, to get the Brief under which we are to be sent to India forwarded to us as quickly as possible. The time for setting out is coming near. We have great hopes of plentiful fruit to follow from our voyage.

Let us know, we beseech you, as soon as possible, how we are to arrange as to those who have either been to Paris for their studies, or are going there. Give us also a clear answer as to what I wrote about Strada, and touching the plan of founding a house for our students in the University of Coimbra; for we can depend for this work and other pious works of the same sort upon the favour of the Princes and the liberality of rich men here. Let us know therefore at once what you have settled upon as to this, that according to what you may command we may endeavour to carry into effect what shall seem to be most expedient for the glory of God.[28] The man is snatching this out of my hands, reproaching me for keeping him so long. So what I have thus far written is to do duty for a letter of Master Simon as well as of my own; and he shall put his signature in the name of both of us, which is to stand for the seal.

In the name of both of us,

MASTER SIMON.

Lisbon, October 12th, 1540.

Before this letter was written, all doubt as to the Institute of the Society was removed by its confirmation by Paul III. on the 27th of September. A great number of masses and prayers had been offered by Ignatius and his brethren for the influential persons who opposed the approbation which the Pope was inclined to give, and these had their effect in the wonderful conversion of Cardinal Guidiccioni to the cause of the Society. He was a man of much weight from his learning and virtue, and had formed one of a commission a year or two before, ordered to examine into the abuses of the clergy, which had reported to the Pope that great scandals existed in monastic

[28] *magis expedire ad laudem Domini.* (Orig.)

houses. He was known to be strongly bent against the foundation of any new orders. Indeed, that commission had actually proposed to the Pope to extinguish all the orders by forbidding them to receive novices; after they had died out, a new generation might revive the primitive fervour. Guidiccioni had been appointed by the Pope one of the three Cardinals who were to examine the proposed plan of the Society; and St. Ignatius and his companions met his opposition by prayer. He would not at first look at the papers: but after a time he desired that they should be read to him, and then approved them entirely. There can be no doubt that this wonderful change in so important an opponent must have helped on the approval of the rule in a singular manner. The bull *Regimini militantis Ecclesiæ*, which gives a succinct account of the principles and objects of the Society, was, as we have said, not published till the April of 1541, just about the time of Francis Xavier's departure for the Indies from Lisbon. The only restriction placed upon the Society in this bull, a restriction afterwards removed in 1543, was that which limited the number of its professed members to sixty.

In the course of the autumn, however, the floating notions as to the retention of the two Fathers in Portugal, already briefly mentioned, took the form of serious negotiations, set on foot between the Courts of Portugal and Rome, which at one time seemed to threaten to prevent the enterprise on which our Saint's heart was now set. The great good done by the two companions in the Court and country of Portugal suggested naturally enough the idea that they should be retained there, and that other less distinguished missionaries might be sent to the Indies. Few words of our Blessed Lord have been more constantly and uniformly fulfilled in the history of the Church than those in which He declared that the harvest was plenteous, but the labourers few: and now that the King of Portugal had come to know the value of the two labourers whom he had obtained from Ignatius, it is not wonderful that he should have felt a scruple as to depriving himself, his capital, and the whole country over which he reigned, of spiritual advantages so singularly great. It was a time when no country in Christendom was well furnished with learned preachers, and even where the priesthood was in its best state it is probable that the number of priests who devoted themselves unremittingly to the more active duties of their calling was comparatively small. We have seen that even in Rome, when the companions of Ignatius began to preach, it was an unheard-of thing for a sermon to be given out of the more sacred seasons of Advent and Lent. To all who had the good of the people at heart, such workers as Francis and Simon were very precious. The question was argued in the Royal Council, and although the Cardinal Don Henry advocated the cause of the Indies with much earnestness, he was overruled, and a proposal was sent to Rome that the King should be authorized to retain Francis and Simon Rodriguez for the benefit of his subjects at home. It was a delicate thing then for the Pope or for Ignatius to refuse. The King had conferred very singular benefits on the Society. The mere fact of his coming forward unsolicited, the first of all Catholic Princes, to ask for several members of the new Order—not as yet sanctioned by the Pope—must have had much weight at Rome, even with the Pope himself, in favour of the Society, and he had at the same time, both by his ambassador and by his own letters, pleaded its cause directly and urgently. At the moment, he was the most powerful and valuable friend whom it possessed, and Ignatius was a man deeply and tenderly alive to the feeling of gratitude. He managed the affair, however, with his usual consummate prudence. The Pope gave it as his opinion that the two Fathers should be placed at the absolute disposal of the King, and letters to this effect were written from Rome. But Ignatius also sent a letter—it does not seem certain whether to Mascareñas, the former Ambassador, or to the Fathers themselves—saying that if the King wished to know his private opinion, he had thought of a middle course: that of sending Francis Xavier to the Indies, while Simon Rodriguez remained in Portugal, where he might be useful to the mission as well as to the kingdom itself by providing a seminary from which future missionaries might proceed to the East. This proposal was agreed to, and the decision was announced to Francis Xavier by the King himself.

As the time for sailing drew on, in the spring of 1541, John III. showed himself full of interest in the Society, and desirous to provide in every possible way for the success of the Indian mission and for the comfort of Francis and his companions. These were now reduced to two—two out of all the number on whom Francis had reckoned, and who had in various ways, as we see from the letters, offered their aid. His disappointment was very great, and we may observe how he feeds himself in the remaining letters written during this period on the hope of a speedy and numerous reinforcement. During the whole of his after career, the two greatest sorrows which he had to contend with were the hindrances put in the way of the Gospel preaching by the bad and tyrannical conduct of the Christian traders and officers, and, in the second place, the poor and sometimes very troublesome materials with which he had to work as his companions and subjects.

But we need not anticipate the troubles of which we shall hear enough by and bye. Only one of Francis' companions was a Priest, Father Paul of Camerino: the second was the Portuguese, Francis Mancias by name, simple, ignorant, dull, not yet in any holy orders, and with literary acquirements so scanty as to make Francis fear very much that he would break down in any examination to which he might be subjected as a condition of ordination. It is perhaps this that made him willing to put off his ordination till they reached India, where it was probable that the standard of learning was not very high, and that the Bishop might not be very particular. Such was the little band of missionaries destined to do so much among the poor Indians who had become the subjects of the Crown of Portugal.

Francis himself was laden with favours by the King. John III. had procured four Briefs from the Pope, two of which gave him the amplest possible spiritual faculties and jurisdiction, appointing him moreover the Apostolic Nuncio in the

Indies. The other two Briefs recommended him to the especial care and protection of all native Princes from the Cape of Good Hope eastwards, and especially to the Emperor of Ethiopia, of whose conversion to the Catholic faith some hopes were now entertained. The King also enjoined on Francis to write to him frequently and to give him an exact account of all that was done or required for the advancement of religion. Francis was to sail with the new Governor of the Indies, Don Martin Alfonso de Sousa, of whom he speaks in the highest terms in the letters which we shall presently translate. This officer had already distinguished himself greatly in the Indies, and the highest expectations were formed of the success of his new government. These expectations were not altogether fulfilled in the event, but Sousa was an upright, honourable man, and a zealous pious Christian, and desirous of showing every honour in his power to the missionaries who were to accompany him. But it was not easy to overcome Francis Xavier where his humility and love of poverty and suffering were concerned. The King had commanded the Conde de Castañeras, who held an office which we might call that of Purveyor-General for the Fleet, to provide Francis with everything that he desired for the voyage. The order was intimated to Francis, but the Conde waited in vain for a list of the articles which he was to provide. Francis, when questioned, said that he professed religious poverty and would rely only on the Providence of God. He could only be induced to accept a few books of devotion and some warmer clothing for the storms of the Cape of Good Hope. The Purveyor insisted—'at least he would have a servant allotted to him? It would not become the dignity of an Apostolic Nuncio to cook his own food and wash his own linen?' Then it was that St. Francis gave his memorable answer, his face burning with indignation, that as long as God gave him the use of hands and feet no one should wait on him but himself—that there was no occupation so lowly as that he would not glory in it in the sight of the whole world, that he would never fear for his dignity unless it should befal him to incur the mark of sin, and that this over attention to human wisdom, which was so opposed to the wisdom of God, was exactly the evil which had reduced the Church to so lamentable a state.

The two following letters, written on the same day, about three weeks before his embarkation, give us a picture of the warmth of his affection for the friends he was never to see again, his love for the Society, and his sanguine hopes as to the success of the mission he was about to undertake.

(VIII.) *To the Society at Rome.*

May the grace and love of Christ our Lord always help and favour us! Amen.

We have received your much longed for letter, and it has done our souls all that good which happy news of their mother ought to produce in the souls of children. We learn from it the healthy and flourishing state of the whole Society, the pious and holy works to which you are given up at Rome, the edifices, spiritual and material, that you are founding and building, thus providing for future generations as well as for the present, that both may be well furnished with the means for labouring in the Lord's vineyard,[29] and may be able to urge on and carry out to the end which we all desire that work which has now for some time been begun with so great a hope of giving extraordinary delight to our Lord God. I pray that our Lord may be pleased to help us also—so far absent from you in body though ever with you in heart, and never more so than now[30]—that we may imitate you, when He has shown to us also the way in which we are to serve Christ our Lord.

Now as to what may be good for you to know of matters here. The King, who greatly approves our way of life and conduct, and who, from his experience of the spiritual fruits which have already come from our labours, is induced to hope

[29] *subsidiis ad laborandum in vineâ Domini.* (Orig.)

[30] *absentes tantùm corpore, licet præsentes animo nunquam magis quàm nunc.* (Orig.)

for still greater advantage to souls if the number of our labourers be increased, has determined to found one College and one House of ours, that is of the Society of Jesus. Three of us are to remain here for these foundations, Master Simon, Master Gonsalez, and another priest well learned in canon law. Many others declare themselves day by day, and offer to enter the Society. This project of his Highness to build these two houses is no crude or passing idea, he is strongly bent upon it. For some time back, whenever we have been to him, he has, of his own accord, declared his intention, always being the first to introduce the matter, without any suggestion from us or from any friend, whom we might have asked. He has come into the plan of building these houses altogether of his own choice and judgment. The place where he intends to put them is the city of Evora. I believe he is writing to the Pope to send some one or more of the Society, to help Master Simon in the commencement. I must say that this good King, in his very great affection to our Society, the increase of which he desires as if he were one of ourselves,[31] doing all this out of the simple motive of his love and veneration to our Lord God, does really put us in truth under a very strict obligation of professing and affording to him unceasing service for the sake of God.[32] Nothing less than this is due to the thorough beneficence and constant good will which he has shown us, a good will which has by no means confined itself within the limits of an intention which costs nothing, but which has made him, without being asked, and with the utmost liberality, sedulously take every opportunity of deserving practically our greatest gratitude. And on this account, if we were not to acknowledge and publicly declare how much we owe to him, if we did not, by daily prayers and sacrifices, do what little lies in our poor power towards trying to repay the very great deserts of those who so signally distinguish themselves before God by helping and supporting us for His divine service, we should really contract a very serious fault, and should be ignominiously branded with the foul disgrace of extreme in-

[31] *tanquam unus ex nobis.* (Orig.) [32] *propter Deum.* (Orig.)

gratitude. And we should be unworthy of life itself, if any day were to come down to the very end of our lives, however long they may be, which could reproach us with having forgotten to keep in mind with the most affectionate and grateful service the name of King John of Portugal, our most liberal Patron and Benefactor.

Father Paul, another, who is a Portuguese, and myself, three in all, are to sail this week for India. We are full of great hopes, trusting in the merciful help of God our Lord that we shall there bring a large harvest into the garners of the Church. We think this from the wonderful things that we are told by good persons who have been eyewitnesses, having been many years in India, and who speak of the very favourable dispositions of those nations to listen to preachers of good, and to embrace the salvation of their souls when it is offered to them.

The King sends us away full and laden with favours of every kind from himself, and has also recommended us very particularly to the Governor whom he is sending this year to India. We are to sail with him in his own flagship. He has shown us much kindness, as far as to take upon himself the care of everything for our passage, and to forbid us or any one else to trouble himself about the preparations, or equipment necessary for us while we are at sea. He has already settled that we are to be his guests at table every day. This I mention, not so much to show off whatever honour or convenience for us this implies, as if we took pleasure in the advantage to ourselves,—which we would certainly rather go without,—but that you may understand, and in your zeal for God's glory may rejoice in, the good ground which we have in this great affection for us on the part of the supreme Governor of the Indies, for hoping for great assistance from him towards that on which our whole heart is set, the conversion of the heathen there, and may congratulate us on the favourable opportunity opened to us, of carrying the name of Jesus Christ before the native Kings of India, with whom, as every one knows, the authority and influence of the Portuguese Governor is supreme.

Our confidence is also strengthened by what we gather, partly from our own observation, partly from what we have been able up to this time to learn from others, of the sentiments, conduct, qualities, and aims of the Governor himself. In the first place he has great experience and familiarity with Indian affairs, and has spent many years in these countries with the highest reputation for integrity. You know how sharp and keen is the judgment of a Court as to the lives of men, and the Court here is agreed that he is a man of the highest virtue. According to good authorities, he is believed to be very much wished for in India, both by our own people and the natives. I had a friendly talk with him the day before yesterday, and he told me that there is an island in India peopled solely by heathen, without any mixture of Mahometans or Jews, and he added that he hoped there for great and speedy fruit from the preaching of the Gospel, and indeed, when he recollected what he had observed when there as to the direction in which men's minds were turned, and the strength of these tendencies, he had no doubt that the King of the country himself, and, after a little, the whole island with him, would openly embrace the religion of Jesus Christ.

The ground on which experienced persons of this sort think they may argue well of our success is, that they have thoroughly seen and approved the manner of our Institute and ministrations of which they have had satisfactory specimens here; and although we on our part are intimately conscious of our own slender stock of virtue and our great weakness, nevertheless we think that all these good wishes and auguries will not come to nothing, for we are animated by the belief that God is now going to take pity on the miserable blindness of all these nations who live destitute of all helps to salvation, and that it seems as if He would therefore make merciful use of the service which we, however weak and worthless servants we be, are most ready to render, that those nations who now know not God and worship devils instead of Him[33] may be recalled from the error and deplorable misery in which they

[33] *gentes quæ Deum ignorant et dæmonia colunt.* (Orig.)

now lie. And, to lay our most secret thoughts bare to you, it is only on this foundation of the hope we have of presumably very powerful and efficacious assistance which may probably be expected from God that our whole confidence in undertaking so great a work rests and is supported, and it is this that gives us courage and alacrity, this that feeds our hopes of a happy issue to our exertions, which we mean to strain to the utmost to give help to those most unhappy of men, to draw them to a true knowledge of our holy faith and religion, with no motive for our labours but to show love and do service to God our Lord, Whom we hold it for most certain that we shall please and serve in this work which we undertake.

And now we beseech of you in the strongest possible manner, to prepare for us in good time and at full leisure long and very particular instructions, which may be forwarded to us by the ships sailing from Lisbon for India in the March of next year. We desire and most humbly beg of you that they may contain directions written at full length by you and descending to all particulars, explaining minutely, what we are to do there, how we are to do it, with what precautions, and what rule of life and method of working we are to follow among the heathen. For although we are not without confidence that experience upon the spot will instruct and direct us to some extent in all this, still the chief hope we have of discerning what in the whole management of this matter is most pleasing to God, rests upon your suggestions and advice. We are persuaded that our Lord will inspire and guide you as to what He requires us to do, and to what extent, and that He will deign to declare to us His mind and the good pleasure of His Heart, as to the kind and manner of our life and ministry, by means of you whom He has hitherto made the interpreters of His will to us. And what moves me[34] again and again, and with all the urgency that you see, to beg this of you, is the fear that I have lest that should happen to us which so frequently happens to many in such positions to their very great hurt. I mean that, either by some negligence in considering and ex-

[34] The change of number to the singular is in the original.

amining all the circumstances of place, business, or of duties in which they find themselves, or again, from some pride which makes them trust themselves too much, and so not condescend to consult others in doubtful matters, and to follow the counsels of men wiser than themselves, they displease God, and are deservedly punished by being deprived by Him of many graces and much profitable knowledge, which He would mercifully have given them had they humbled their own minds and judgments, so far as to confess their own ignorance and weakness by asking the help and assistance of others, more especially of those by whose means God is wont to let us know in what and how He desires to be served by us. We beg of you therefore, dear Fathers, and implore you again and again in our Lord, by that tender and intimate union in Christ Jesus which binds us together,[35] do not think it too much trouble to write out for us diligently and at length, advice, orders, instructions which may teach us minutely and in particular, what is to be avoided, what followed, what to be guarded against, and what embraced, by men who wish what we wish with all our hearts, that is, in our whole life, and above all in the office of promoting the salvation of souls, to conform ourselves exactly to the will of God, which we are confident will be made known to us more by your hints and precepts than by anything else. And we trust also that your prayers will help us, weak as we are, to carry into execution whatever you shall so prescribe to us. And these prayers we beg you may be made for us in a very special way, besides the usual remembrance which we all make of one another.[36] And surely there is reason enough for this in our necessities, so far greater than usual, in the extraordinary dangers of our long voyage, and in what is to come after that, the continual intercourse we are to have with the heathen Indians, a race of men lost in vices of all sorts, the contagion of which may well hurt men so tepid and ignorant as we are; and that it may not do so we must

[35] *oramus ergo vos, Patres, et obsecramus iterum atque iterum in Domino, per illam nostram in Christo Jesu conjunctissimam amicitiam.* (Orig.)

[36] *ultra consuetam memoriam.* (Orig.)

strive and fight hard with all the most abundant grace and most efficacious helps from God which we can gain.

We shall write to you at full length from India by the first ships that sail after our arrival. Our letters will be on the same subject and in the same sense with those which we are to send to the King, in obedience to his Highness' commands. For when he bade us farewell for the last time before our departure, this good Prince most earnestly and strongly enjoined us, in the name of God our Lord and for His love, to inform him fully and exactly what appearance there may be in India of a disposition to the conversion of those miserable souls. He declared that he was burnt up and tormented with continual internal anguish at their unhappy lot, that his wish was, and that for the hope of this there was no price that he would not pay, to prevent the continuance of those offences against the Creator and Lord of all men on the part of His creatures, made after His own image and redeemed at such a cost, which have hitherto prevailed there. So ardent is the zeal for the glory of Christ our Lord and for the salvation of his neighbours which burns in the heart of this excellent King. For my part I feel incited to render endless praise and thanks to God for letting me see a King of immense power full of so much piety as to religious matters, and I must say with all truth, that unless I had had the evidence of my own senses to convince me, I could hardly have persuaded myself to believe that any secular person, especially one who as a Prince is at the very summit of worldly greatness, and amidst all the tumult of a great Court, could have a heart capable of such exquisite devotion and charity. I pray God that it may please Him to increase in the King these great gifts and multiply the days of his life into many long years—since he spends them in so holy a manner, and is so useful and so necessary unto his people.[37]

Thus much as to the King: now about the Court. No-

[37] *tam utilis et necessarius est populo suo.* (Orig.) Francis probably alludes to the traditional anecdote of the saying of St. Martin, '*Domine, si populo tuo adhuc sum necessarius, non recuso laborem.*'

thing can be more thoroughly well ordered--it is more like a religious community than a secular Court. There are so many who approach the holy sacraments of penance and communion weekly, that we unceasingly give great praise and thanks to God when we see and wonder at them. We have so many confessions to hear, that if there were twice as many of us, there would be plenty of work for all. We sit in the confessional whole days and part of the nights, and yet none but the people of the Court are allowed to come to us, all others are excluded. I recollect observing when the King was staying at Almerim how the people who came to the Court on business used to be surprised at what was to them a new custom, especially in followers of the Court, and how astonished they were to see so many of them going to communion every Sunday and on the Feast Days besides. A good many too of them imitated what they wondered at, purified their own souls by penance, and began to frequent holy communion. If there were here confessors enough to hear the whole crowd of people that usually come to the Court when it is in its progress, there would be hardly any one who comes to do business with his Highness who would not first settle his affairs with God. As it is, many who want to confess find no one to hear them, though, as I said, we do not spare ourselves, so little indeed, that we have been so constantly in the confessional that we have had no time for preaching. After due consideration we concluded that it was more for the service of God our Lord to give ourselves up to hearing confessions than to preach, because there is no lack of preachers in this Court, but considerable scarcity of practised confessors. So we have left the pulpit for the confessional.

And now we have nothing more to tell you, save that now that we are on the point of starting for India, we pray to our Lord God that in a better life He will vouchsafe to bring us together again with you from whom we are now separating ourselves for the sake of Him. In this life we can hardly hope to meet again, both on account of the immense distances of sea and land which divide Rome and India, as also because the abundant harvest which awaits us in those countries will probably shut us out from all thought or power of looking to other fields or spheres of labour, as offering to us opportunities of working with more fruit for the garners of the Lord of all, to whose service we have devoted ourselves. Whoever, therefore, of us may be the first to arrive at that Blessed Life, and there not to find the brother whom he loves in the Lord,[38] let him remember to make his prayer to Christ our King that He bring thither his brother also and make us all once more companions in His glory.

To all of you dear ones in our Lord at Rome,

FRANCIS XAVIER.

Lisbon, March 18th, 1541.

Francis wrote on the same day another letter to two of his first companions, Father Laynez and Father Le Jay, who at the time at which he wrote were labouring, the one at Parma, the other at Brescia, but were soon to be called to Rome for the election of the first General in the person of St. Ignatius. We have only a fragment left to us of this letter:

(IX.) *To the Fathers Le Jay and Laynez.*

With regard to the King and the alms that he intends for the building of the house,[39] I am writing to Peter Codacio what he ought to do at Rome. It seemed to me that just now, during this spring quarter that is beginning, the matter might present itself rather unseasonably, as it would be in the midst of the preparations which are making for a war which is said to be on the point of breaking out from the neighbouring coast of Africa. News comes frequently, and always to the same purport, that all the tribes of the Moors are in league,

[38] *non invenerit fratrem quem in Domino diligit.* (Orig.) The allusion is to St. Paul, 2 Cor. ii. 13.

[39] The Society had already taken possession of the church of Sta. Maria della Strada, which stood where the present church and house of the Gesù stand. It was Codacio who had got the church made over to the Society. The house for which alms were to have been sought from the King of Portugal was probably the house for the Fathers adjoining the church.

and threaten a formidable invasion of the Portuguese dominions.

When times are more quiet, it would help much for our business to gain at Rome the good offices of the Cardinals who stand best with the King, if they would be so very kind as to inform him accurately by letter how very profitably his Highness would spend his money on such a foundation. I think Cardinal Carpi is one of these Cardinals: I fancy this, because I know he is very intimate with Don Pedro (Mascareñas), and thus letters of recommendation coming from him, as well as from the Cardinal of the *Quattro Coronati* and others, whom you may know to be on good terms with his Highness, would be extremely useful to us. And if for any reason these Cardinals were to decline to write direct to the King, still I suppose they might, with no great difficulty, be induced, especially Cardinal Carpi, to write privately to Don Pedro to beg him to speak to the King and undertake the promotion of so excellent a work with his Highness. Besides, if the King's ambassador at Rome is well disposed towards the Society, it would be of the greatest service to obtain letters from him to the same effect, explaining to the King how much our interests at Rome are in need of the favour of his Highness.

Do not forget to write yourselves to Don Pedro de Mascareñas. I can't find words to tell you the pleasure he takes in your letters. Be quite sure that he loves you very much in the Lord;[40] he keeps with the greatest care the letters which he has from you, he reads every word in them over and over again with a pleasure and spiritual fruit which make his face shine with joy. Indeed, when I see by these clear proofs how devoted he is to you, I feel as if I ought to devote all my life to his service. We have been thinking here, saving better judgment,[41] that it would be well for you to write to the King to thank him for the desire he has shown of founding here a house or college for the Society. Good offices and observances of this sort are a frequent, established, and required

[40] *multum in Domino.* (Orig.) [41] *salvo meliori judicio.* (Orig.)

custom in the Court here, and I am certain, from what Don Pedro told me, that such a letter would please the King much. You should mention in it that you have been informed by us of the generous intentions expressed by his Highness of erecting a college or a house of our Society. This would be, as the proverb goes, to spur the willing steed, and would urge him all the more strongly to cut short all delay in the matter. Another thing I know, and I may as well tell it you,—you may be certain that the letters you write in the way I have suggested will pass through many hands and be read by many eyes.

Now let me tell you of Francesco Mancias. He is not yet in any sacred orders at all. There is a Bishop in India who, we trust in the Lord, will make no difficulty as to ordaining the good man, though it is certain he has a larger store of zeal, virtue, and simplicity, than of any extraordinary learning. Unless Master Paul can communicate to him some part of his own great knowledge, I am terribly afraid that without special aid from God he will hardly be found up to the mark in the examination which ought according to rule to precede the conferring of holy orders. If this were to happen it would upset our plans altogether. At all events, in the prospect of any such event, he would desire that you would get him letters from Rome excusing him from any very elaborate preparation for holy orders, and which might authorize him to receive *extra tempora* the three sacred orders, on three successive Feast days, on the title, as it were, of 'voluntary poverty and (very) sufficient' simplicity.[42] In order to obtain this favour, it may with truth be pleaded that in his case the deficiency of learning is supplied by much goodness and holy simplicity. In fact, if he had been as intimate with Bobadilla as he was with Cacerez,[43] he would, as so often hap-

[42] *ad titulum voluntariæ paupertatis et sufficientissimæ simplicitatis.* (Orig.) This is a play upon the formula used in ordinations, when the candidates are declared to be ordained, some 'titulo religionis,' others 'titulo beneficii,' and others 'sui sufficientis patrimonii.'

[43] This chance mention of Cacerez has hardly perhaps been noticed by the writers of the life of St. Ignatius. At the head of the list of signatures to the

pens, have got from the friction of daily familiar intercourse, something rather more like the erudition of the former than the ignorance of the latter, and we should not be in our present difficulty; in that case, we should certainly have had him moving at full sail over the vast ocean of the sacred Scriptures, and learning would burst from his lips spontaneously. Moreover, both Mancias and Don Paul would like to obtain from his Holiness the favour that every time they say mass, it may be as if at a 'privileged altar.'

The number of masses that we have already celebrated for Cardinal Guidiccioni amount to two hundred and fifty, from the time of our leaving Rome up to the present day. May God our Lord grant us grace to offer the rest in India! Indeed, when I think within myself what fruit and what spiritual joy I have always up to this time felt in offering sacrifice for this very reverend Prince of the Church, I feel drawn to recommend him to God our Lord in every mass that I shall say during the rest of my life.

[It appears that the news of the approval of the Institute, so long delayed by the opposition of Cardinal Guidiccioni, had now reached Portugal, and this accounts for the joyous burst of gratitude which the last quoted sentences of the letter contain. Francis had at least the consolation not to sail for the East before the good tidings reached him. His mind at once turns, as we see in the next paragraph, to those souls of whom he has already more than once spoken, who had thought of

paper drawn up in 1539, by Ignatius and his companions, about adding the vow of obedience to the other two vows, and, in fact, entering the Society as a religious body under a Superior, as soon as it was approved of by the Pope, appears the name of Cacres. It has always been a puzzle to the historians, as no such Father is elsewhere mentioned, and all the other signatures are those of the well-known 'Companions.' Two letters of St. Ignatius, written in 1536 to a nun in Spain, mention a Carceres or Cazeres as a friend of them both who has been giving her some instructions in spiritual matters. Cacerez may well have been one of those who dropped off after intending to join the Society. We gather from the present letter, which draws a playful picture both of Mancias and Bobadilla, that Cacerez was no great loss to the Society in point of learning. Where Mancias had fallen in with him, must be left to conjecture.

joining the Society, but could not muster up courage for the final step.]

We want much to know whether, now that our rule is confirmed, those persons to whom we used to say we were so largely in debt in the matter of mutual love on account of the very great and kind interest they voluntarily showed us in this business of ours, promoting it in every way and by every effort, whether these persons, I say, have either yet entered the Society or are on the point of doing so. I suspect there are some among them who would be glad to find peace to their souls, without undertaking this humble and painful life of ours. Whether they will find that peace I know not. It may well be that what they seek where they wish to find it, they will only find at last where they are afraid to seek it, if they ever manage to make up their minds to go there. I say this not only as to Francesco Zapata—I mean to include the worthy Licentiate, who, I imagine, won't know much of the quiet of a mind at rest while he haunts, as he does, the palaces of the great. As for the Doctor of Medicine, Ignatius Lopez, it seems to me that he will bring discredit on his own reputation and have to give up his profession altogether, if he withdraws without having perfectly cured the weak stomach of Father Ignatius and the deranged humours of Bobadilla. As to Diego Zappata and others like him,[44] I have nothing to say, except that it is very probable the world will find them useless, and so get rid of them, doomed to labour hard enough for the rest of their lives in a difficult search after any one who will care to have them.

I do not know how it is, but, since the King has settled that some of us are to remain here and others to go, I can't drive out of my mind an image that is continually presenting itself unbidden, the image of our dear brother Antonio Araoz, whom my prophetic mind sets before me as coming out by and bye to us in India, accompanied by six clerics at the least

[44] *et ei similibus.* (Orig.) The spelling of the name Zappata is different in the two places in this page.

and a fitting following of others; and if the men he brings us are not all prodigies of science, yet if they are well disposed to spend what remains of their life in the service of God our Lord, and are besides free from all appearance of avarice, we hope that their coming will be of the greatest use to us. And even if you should not send us any of this sort this year (that is to say, in the March of the year after this), but only two years hence, when you will have been able to receive letters from us in India, it would be no great inconvenience, so long as at the last date I have named we might have without fail the reinforcement of a certain number of good labourers sent out by you to us. We leave the whole of this affair to your wisdom: but we are most anxious that when you deliberate upon the point, you should seriously consider what I[45] assure you of most positively, that I am entirely convinced that the fruit of our labours in India will be by no means slight. Pray don't think that this is the mere guess of a mind that flatters itself. It is the constant assurance given us by men who have been there for many years that obliges us to hope it. How we find things on the spot you will learn from our letters, in which we mean diligently and fully to set forth from knowledge gained by our own eyes what is the true state and disposition of the country and its inhabitants, as far as concerns the affair of the salvation of souls, and the hopes and means of extending the Kingdom of Jesus Christ. We expect, as I said just now, that the singular favour of the Governor, which he manifests by doing every possible kind of service to us, will be of the very greatest and most universal help to insure the success of all the efforts we shall make of this kind, on account of the extremely high influence which he may well be expected to have with the kings and rulers of the countries who are allies of the King of Portugal, both on account of his own virtues, which are so well known of old in those parts, as well as on account of the new dignity with which he is now invested as the holder of the highest office in the government and as the representative of his Highness.

[45] The change of number is in the original.

If you think that any of the spiritual favours which can be got from the Pope would be useful to us by increasing the efficacy of our work out there, do as your charity and wisdom may suggest. One favour in particular we should like to obtain, and to have it sent to us in a regularly sealed diploma, as soon as may be, that is, the faculty granting by the authority of the Pope to ours in India, that they may receive sacred orders *extra tempora*, without patrimony or benefice, under the title of voluntary poverty which they have promised to God; with exemption when necessary from the canonical impediment resulting from illegitimate birth. Last of all, we implore you, when you write to us in India, not to do so by any means perfunctorily or shortly. We most earnestly wish you to tell us in particular about all and each of ours; what they are doing, how they are, what plans they have, what hopes of themselves, what fruit they produce. This ought not to seem a very severe task for you to undertake, since you will have no opportunity of writing to us except once and no more in each year. Do please manage to make your letters from Europe furnish us with abundant reading for a full week. We promise solemnly that we will do as much for you. Farewell.

In the name of all your dearest brothers here,

Lisbon, March 18th, 1541. FRANCIS XAVIER.

The bright and cheerful tone of this familiar letter to his old companions makes us wish that we had more such relics of the heart and hand of St. Francis. At the time at which this was written, the first Fathers of the Society were meeting in Rome for the purpose of electing their first General. When more than a fortnight later St. Francis set sail from Lisbon (on his thirty-fifth birthday, April 7; the Thursday in Passion Week), the election was actually proceeding, and his vote for St. Ignatius was counting with the rest.[46] Three others of

[46] Most of the suffrages are dated April 4, that of Ignatius himself April 5. Three days of prayer preceded the voting, and after the votes had been sealed up, three days more of prayer followed before they were opened. St. Ignatius, after much resistance on his own part, entered on his duties as General on the Easter Tuesday, April 19.

the original 'companions' were absent besides himself, Peter Favre, who was in Germany, Bobadilla, who was detained at Bisignano in the kingdom of Naples, and Simon Rodriguez, who accompanied him on board the Governor's ship, the *St. James*, to give and receive a last loving embrace. They were to meet no more in this world, and Francis was never to return to Europe. It was then that Francis revealed to Simon the secret of the words, 'Yet more, Lord, yet more,' which Simon had heard him utter in his dream in the sickroom at Rome, as well as another secret. Simon was again being nursed by him at night, and Francis had fallen asleep from fatigue at the foot of his patient's bed. Suddenly he had been seen to struggle violently in his sleep, and at last a quantity of blood burst from his mouth. Simon could never get him to tell him what had then passed, but now, in the openness of a soul that was wishing a dear friend goodbye, Francis avowed to him that by the grace of God he had never been stained by any, even the slightest, impurity, and that at that time an evil dream had tormented him, and his struggles in resisting it had been so violent that a small bloodvessel had been burst. It was solemnly attested after his death that this spotless purity of his had never been tarnished in the faintest degree. All the rest of his life was to be the fulfilment of the other vision. His brave, ardent, and most tender heart, which had then been endowed with so keen a thirst for more and more suffering, labours, and sorrows for the sake of the advancement of God's glory, was now to begin its career of sacrifice by a lifelong separation from the 'brethren whom he loved in the Lord.'

NOTES TO BOOK I.

(1.) *Suffrage of St. Francis Xavier in the election of a General for the Society of Jesus.*

The paper spoken of in p. 59 as having been left by St. Francis Xavier in Rome to be used when the occasion came for the election of a Superior for the Society, after its approval by the Holy Father, is considered by F. Menchacha to be rather a letter than a formal suffrage. The original, which was all in St. Francis' own handwriting, was inscribed on the outside, '*Esta es la Carta de Francisco para los de la Compañia*' (This is the letter of Francis for those of the Company). The proper word for 'paper' would have been 'papel' (Menchacha, *Epistolæ S. Fr. Xaverii*, t. ii. p. 501). The letter is printed by the Bollandists in the Life of St. Ignatius (*Acta Sanctorum* Julii, t. vii. in Comm. prævia de S. Ignatio Loyola, § 35, num. 360 seq.). It runs as follows:

1. I Francis say that, when his Holiness grants us our mode of life, I assent to all that the Society shall ordain concerning all our Constitutions, Rules, and manner of living, those Fathers being assembled at Rome who can be conveniently called together and assembled. And since his Holiness is sending many of us to different parts out of Italy, and all cannot come together, I declare by this letter and I promise that I will consider fair and good whatever those may ordain who are able to be present at the meeting, whether they are two or three, or whoever they may be. And so I declare by this present signed by my hand, and I promise that I will hold as binding all that they may do. Written at Rome in the year 1540, March 15. FRANCIS.

2. IHS. I Francis also declare and affirm that, in no manner persuaded by man, I judge that he who is to be elected as the Superior of our Society, to whom we are all to owe obedience,—as what seems to me just and speaking according to what my conscience dictates,—that our Superior should be our old and true Father Don Ignatius, who brought us all together

with so much labour. He,—not without labour also,—will know best how to keep us as we are, to govern us, and to make us advance from good to better, for he thoroughly knows every one of us. And after his death, speaking according to what my soul feels right, as if I were now at the point of death, I declare that Father Master Peter Favre should be chosen. And in this respect God is my witness that I say exactly what I think. In witness of which I subscribe this with my own hand. Done at Rome in the year 1540, March 15. FRANCIS.

3. In like manner, after the Society shall have been assembled and shall have chosen a Superior, I Francis promise, now for then, perpetual obedience, poverty, and chastity. And so, my dearest Father in Christ, Laynez, I beseech you for the service of our Lord God, in my absence to offer for me this my will with the three vows of Religion to the Superior, whom you and the rest shall have chosen. And from now, as from the day on which he shall be elected, I promise to observe them. In witness of which I have prepared this declaration signed with my own hand. Written at Rome in the year 1540, March 15. FRANCIS.

(2.) *Letter of St. Ignatius to his Nephew, recommending to him St. Francis Xavier and the Ambassador of the King of Portugal.*

The following letter, which we quote from Menchacha, *Epistolæ S. Ignatii* (l. 1, ep. xii.), shows, among other things, the great hurry in which our Saint left Rome for Portugal.

To Beltran, Lord of Loyola.

JESUS.

May our Lord ever help and favour us! Amen.

I am altogether prevented from writing to you at any length, as I would wish to do, by the great and extreme haste with which we are pressed at a moment's notice to send some of our Society to the Indies, some to Ireland, and others to different parts of Italy. The bearer of this is Master Francis Xavier, of Navarre, son of the Lord of Xavier, one of our Society. He is going [to India] by command of the Holy Father and at the request of the King of Portugal, as well as two others who are on their way to the King by sea. From the same Master Francis you will learn everything, and he will speak to you on any subject in my name, as if I myself were present. You should know that the ambassador of the King of Portugal, whom Master Francis accompanies, is allied to us by the bonds of the closest friendship, and that we owe him very much indeed, and that he hopes to be a great protector to us in matters which relate to the service of God with his King and with all others with whom he has influence. I beg you therefore, for the service of our Lord God, to receive him when he comes to your parts with the greatest honour and as splendidly as you can. If Araoz is with you, let him consider this letter as written to him. You may believe and rely on Master Francis in my name as much as on myself. I pray you commend me much to your lady wife, and to all your family. May our Lord ever help and favour you!

Your poor one in goodness,

INIGO.

Rome, March 16, 1540.

The third member of the Society who is here mentioned as having sailed with Simon Rodriguez for Portugal is evidently Father Paul of Camerino, who ultimately left for India along with Francis Xavier and Francis Mancias. It has been thought that the letter implies that St. Ignatius had not yet abandoned the idea of sending Bobadilla; but he could not be one of two who are mentioned as being already on their way by sea to Lisbon.

Antonio Araoz was a near relation of St. Ignatius, who had joined the Society the year before this letter was written, and was now in Spain. He afterwards became very celebrated among the earlier Fathers of the Society, was a great preacher, and filled many important offices. At this time he was not yet a Priest.

(3.) *Don Pedro Mascareñas.*

The Ambassador Mascareñas was one of the most distinguished servants of the Portuguese Crown. He had served in Africa with distinction, and had been a splendid ambassador at Brussels and at Rome. He was afterwards appointed tutor for a time to the Infante Don Juan, and ended his days, curiously enough, in India, where he was sent two years after the death of St. Francis, being himself seventy years of age, as Viceroy, much against his own will and the earnest entreaties to the King of his wife. The Portuguese annalist of India speaks of him in the highest terms of praise. 'It was believed that if he had continued in that government some years, he would have reestablished truth, justice, and honesty in India.—Don Pedro Mascareñas had such an awful presence and majestic deportment, that nobody before him durst do or say anything indecent.' One of the acts of his government in India was to send a Father and Brother of the Society to the Emperor of Ethiopia—'Prester John'—to induce him to become Catholic—'para persuadir al Preste Juan a que dexasse los ritos antiguos de la Christiandad profanada, que siguia.' See Faria y Sousa, *Asia Portuguesa*, t. ii. p. 2, cap. xi.

BOOK II.

FROM THE SAILING OF FRANCIS TO INDIA TO HIS FIRST VOYAGE TO THE FARTHER EAST.

1541-1545.

CHAPTER I.

Voyage to India, and first labours at Goa.

THE missionary of our own time usually embarks for India or China at Southampton or Marseilles in a large, swift, and well-appointed steamer, and finds himself, after a short experience of the Bay of Biscay or of the Mediterranean, at Gibraltar or at Malta, and then after another short interval at Alexandria, whence he mounts the Nile to Cairo and reaches Suez by a few hours of railway travelling, to find another steamer waiting for him which carries him to India in the space of not more than a few weeks. He has little in common, as far as the dangers and sufferings of the voyage are concerned, with St. Francis Xavier and his two companions on their long and weary sail to the Indian coast from Lisbon. Although the ships which in the sixteenth century were used for distant navigation were huge in size as compared with the ordinary vessels of the time, they were slow, unsafe, and of small accommodation when contrasted with passenger steamers or clippers of our own century, and, as they carried large freight in the way of merchandize and were also transports for soldiers, they were usually extremely crowded, with little space to spare, and the long time spent on board must always have been a period of suffering and confinement to all.[1] The voyage from Lisbon to Goa generally lasted about six months, and was considered in itself as an enterprise of no common danger. We are told that the seas about the Cape were particularly dreaded, and that passengers ordinarily provided themselves with a windingsheet, that their bodies might be committed to the waves, in case of their death, with some

1 Bartoli, in the first book of his *Asia* (p. 26-31, first ed. Rome, 1653), gives a long description of the ships used for these voyages, of the great dangers of the navigation, and of the virtues required in missionaries for India.

appearance of Christian decency. Before the storms at the Cape, there were the terrible calms off the Guinea coast, and the scurvy, the peculiar scourge of long and confined sea passages, not to speak of the very possible accidents of shipwreck and the like, as well as some which we should consider imaginary, such as the poisonous showers which were said to fall under the torrid zone, and the huge sea monsters which roamed the Indian Ocean, and could easily send a vessel to the bottom with a single stroke of their tails. The ships, which were dispatched only once a year, were crowded with inmates, and sailed in company. They carried a wild and motley multitude —merchants, soldiers, adventurers of every sort, as well as Government officials and an occasional missionary, and we are not surprised to learn that the confinement, hardships, and privations of the seafaring life, the enforced idleness, the bad food, the close lodging, the fierce climate to be passed through, as well as the excitement of anticipated adventures, the hopes of riches or advancement, and the recklessness produced in wild natures by the near neighbourhood of danger from the sea or from some sudden disaster, not to speak of warfare, worked rather upon the bad elements in that strange society than on the good, and made it more irreligious than ever instead of more pious. The restraints of ordinary life were thrown off, and the license which was the condition of existence in India was too often anticipated on the voyage.

The company in which Francis Xavier and his two associates sailed was to some extent exceptional. The Governor[2] was a thoroughly religious man, and the same may very likely have been the case with many of the officers; but we cannot expect the crew, the soldiers, and the adventurers, as a rule, to have been above the average. Francis was entirely in a new sphere. Hitherto he had lived either with students like himself, before he joined Ignatius, or with his own religious brethren. Even in the Court of Portugal he could have seen but little of

[2] Don Martin Alfonso Sousa is usually called Viceroy in the Lives of St. Francis, but he was one of the Governors of India who had not the additional title of Viceroy.

the rough selfish greed and brutal vice which so often characterize the class of men who seek their fortunes in a new world after having failed at home, and if he had known the lower strata of humanity as an active preacher and confessor in Italy, and in the prisons and hospitals which he had always made it his business to frequent, at least he had never been brought into that close contact with rude boisterous license of every kind which was inevitable to him now that he was cooped up for a six months' voyage within the planks of a galleon with nine hundred or more of his fellowbeings, whose reasons for the long and dangerous voyage which made them his companions were so very different from those by which he was moved. He was of a refined, delicate, even haughty, nature, and we see in his earlier letters some traces of what might be thought to have been severity of judgment as to even the ordinary secular life, if it were not so evidently the fruit of his own intense conviction of the reality of the maxims of faith,—perhaps also of the recollection of the struggle which it had once cost him to surrender himself to their guidance. We might have expected many men of the same character with St. Francis to shut themselves up in their cabin during the voyage, and hold as little intercourse as possible with the strange, wild, coarse, and violent world around them.

It was, however, on this voyage that Francis first began the practice of what has been called 'Apostolical conversation,' which he afterwards never intermitted for the rest of his life wherever he had occasion for it. It had been, as we have said, the great weapon of Ignatius: it had been the means by which Francis himself had been won to the pursuit of the greater glory of God. It was practised with the most careful and prayerful study by Peter Favre, as we find from his own notes, and it now became one of the most successful instruments of the salvation and improvement of others in the hands of his dear friend and brother to whom the Indies had been committed as the field of his Apostolate. Many years later, a Portuguese gentleman happened to find himself in the same vessel with Francis. He had long been desirous of knowing him, on account of his great reputation for sanctity: on asking which he was, he was shown a person standing in a group of men round a table where a game of chess was going on. He was talking with the soldiers, the crew, the merchants' clerks, and others, of whom the crowd was made up, at his ease with all, and all at their ease with him. The gentleman was scandalized, and declared to a friend that the Padre Santo, as he was called, was just like any other priest. At the end of the voyage, however, he sent a servant to follow and see what became of him. Francis went aside into a wood and began to pray, and the servant soon ran to call his master to see the Saint in an ecstasy lifted from the ground in his prayers.[3]

There was ample field for his zeal on board the ship in which he sailed—which carried, as we are told, very nearly a thousand persons. He mixed freely with all, especially with those who had most need of him—and it was soon found that he had won upon them so far that the habit of swearing was going out, and that many enmities had been made up. He began to hear confessions regularly and frequently. Under the Line the scurvy broke out so violently that it became a sort of plague: friends neglected friends, the sick were left to themselves, the medicine ran short, there was no one but Francis and his companions to tend the sufferers. Francis washed them and their linen, dressed their food, and fed them with his own hands. He had a little cabin of his own, but he gave it up to the sick. He had refused to take his meals at the Governor's table, but not to receive the daily portion of food which was sent him from it: this he divided among the sick. On Sundays he preached on deck, the Governor himself attending the sermon.

Francis himself appears to have suffered greatly from sickness in the first part of the voyage, which was lengthened beyond the usual time, probably by the calm which often detains vessels near the Equator. It was the custom of the Portuguese

[3] This anecdote will be found in Massei, l. ii. c. 15, p. 471. The gentleman was a famous Captain, Don Diego di Noroña, whose name often occurs in the *Asia Portuguesa* of Faria y Sousa. See t. ii. p. 2, ch. x.

navigators to sail at a distance round the Cape, so far southwards as to reach a latitude where the cold was sensibly felt. The ship did not reach Mozambique till late in August, at a time when under ordinary circumstances it would have been approaching Goa; and the lateness of the season as well as the prevalence of sickness determined the Governor to winter in the island. The letter which we are about to insert gives some account of the island,[4] and of the number of sick in the hospital where Francis took up his quarters. He makes no mention, however, of his own sufferings from a violent fever, which we learn from the testimony of others. He would not accept of the better lodging and care which were offered to him by many of the Portuguese inhabitants, and took his chance with the rest of the sick in the hospital. Indeed, the physician found him, in the height of his fever, visiting and instructing the others. On one occasion when he was ordered to bed, he is said to have answered humbly that he was anxious about the case of one, who had not made his peace with God, and that as soon as he had attended him, he would take rest himself. It was a poor sailor whom fever had already made delirious, and of whose recovery little hope could be entertained. Francis had him conveyed from the ship to his own bed: the next day the man was sensible enough to make his confession; but he died at night, after having received the sacraments, full of confidence in God. Francis then consented to be nursed himself, and was soon able to resume his usual labours. Another anecdote of his stay at Mozambique has been preserved to us. While he was attending the sick in the hospital, news was brought him of the sudden death of a boy who had sailed in the Governor's ship with him. Xavier asked whether he had attended the Christian doctrine—as the teaching of the Catechism is called among Catholics. He was filled with grief and selfreproach when he was told that the boy had apparently never had any instruction, and told the Governor, who strove to console him by saying that as he had never

[4] The Portuguese settlement was fixed in a small coral island close to the shore, which was well fortified, and contained large public buildings.

known of the lad's ignorant state he could not be responsible for it, that the simple fact that there should be any one in the same ship with him in need of instruction without his knowing it was a reproach to him.

We may leave the further details of the voyage to India to be gathered from the following letter, written from Goa some months after his arrival at that city.[5]

(x.) *To the Society at Rome.*

May the grace and love of Jesus Christ our Lord always help and favour us! Amen.

When on the point of sailing from Lisbon with Father Paul and Francis Mancias, I wrote to you a long letter about our voyage to India. And now, as you asked me to let you know of our arrival in India as soon as I should have leisure to do so, I send you this account of our voyage. We left Lisbon on the 7th April 1541, and reached India the 6th May of this the following year, having thus spent a year and more in the voyage, which is generally made in about six months. We sailed in the same vessel with the Governor, who treated us the whole time with great consideration: and we had all of us fair enough health. All the time there was no lack of confessions to hear, either of the sick, or others, and we never missed preaching on the Sundays. I count it a great favour from God that, while I was passing over the realm of fishes, I found men to whom to announce the Divine mysteries and to administer the sacrament of penance, quite as necessary on sea as on land.

In the course of the voyage we touched at an island called Mozambique, where we wintered for six months, together with the whole multitude of persons belonging to five large vessels. There are two cities in the island, one garrisoned by the Por-

[5] A close inspection of this and the other longer letters of Francis Xavier will enable the reader easily to detect that they were written at intervals, not all at once. Thus in the present letter he relates his arrival at Goa, and then goes back to Melinda and Socotra.

tuguese, the other occupied by friendly Mussulmans. While we were wintering there a great number of persons fell ill, and as many as eighty died. We quartered ourselves in the hospital all the time, employing ourselves in the service of the sick. Father Paul and Mancias waited on their bodily necessities, I attended to their souls also, hearing confessions continually and giving communion, but, alone as I was, I could not do all that was wanted for them. On Sundays I preached to a very large audience, as the Governor himself attended: and I was also often called away to hear confessions elsewhere. So that all the time we were at Mozambique we had always plenty to do. The Governor, his suite, and all the soldiers showed us great courtesy, and by the favour of God we spent those six months greatly to the satisfaction of all and with much spiritual profit.

Mozambique is about 900 leagues distant from India. The Governor was desirous of pursuing his voyage as soon as possible, but owing to the season there were still a great number of persons ill. So he asked that some of us might remain in the island to help the sick who were to be left there, and who could not at once continue the voyage on account of their health. As he thought it best, Father Paul and Mancias remained. I accompanied the Governor, who was himself by no means well, that I might hear his confession, in case his malady got worse and led to anything more serious. So it is now some time since I reached India in his company, and I am now daily expecting my companions by the vessels which generally arrive from Mozambique in September. We are now in the fifth month since we arrived at Goa, the capital of India. It is a fine-looking city, entirely in the hands of Christians. It has a convent of Franciscans, really very numerous, a magnificent cathedral with a large number of canons, and several other churches. There is good reason for thanking God that the Christian religion flourishes so much in this distant land in the midst of heathen.

Our voyage from Mozambique to Goa lasted two months and more. We stopped for a few days at Melinda, a port inhabited by Mussulmans who are friendly to the Portuguese, of whom there are some there, chiefly merchants. If any of them happen to end their days there, they are buried in large mounds, which are to be seen here and there with crosses over them which mark them out. The Portuguese have erected near the city a large and very handsome stone cross,[6] which is gilt all over. I cannot express to you what joy I felt in looking at it. It seemed like the might of the Cross appearing victorious in the midst of the dominion of the unbelievers.

The King of Melinda came on board our ship to compliment the Governor, and received him with kindness and friendliness. While I was at Melinda we celebrated the funeral of a man who had died on board our ship, and we had the full service for him, much to the approval of the Mussulmans, who admired our funeral ceremonies very much.

One of the principal Mahometan inhabitants of the city asked me whether our temples in which we go to pray were generally filled with Christian people, and how fervid and diligent Christians were in worshipping Christ; for, said he, all piety had long ago grown cold among his own people, and he wished to know whether the same was usual among Christian men. There were seventeen mosques at Melinda, but three only were attended and even those by very few. The good man was quite perplexed, and knew not what to make of it, having no idea how it was that his own people had lost all religion. He said it could only be on account of some great sin of their own. We had a great deal of conversation about this, and I told him that God, most Faithful and True, held the misbelievers and their prayers in abomination, and so willed that their worship, which He rejected altogether, should come to nought. My friend, who had very different notions from mine, was not satisfied with this, and then a Saracen Caciz—

[6] This erection of crosses seems to have been a practice among the Portuguese navigators. Vasco de Gama, in his celebrated voyage in 1497-99, when he first rounded the Cape of Good Hope and reached India, is said to have set up six crosses at different places, one of which, called after the Holy Ghost, was at Melinda, which town he was the first of his countrymen to visit. See *Asia Portuguesa*, by Faria y Sousa, Eng. Trans. t. i. p. 50, comp. 42.

a Caciz is a teacher of the Mahometan law—came up, a man of very eminent learning, and he declared that if Mahomet did not appear again on earth to visit them within two years, he himself should renounce that religion. One sees in such cases in what anxiety and despair the life of unbelievers and wicked men is so often passed: and indeed this in itself is a blessing sent them by God, that they may be thereby warned of their state and led to conversion.

After sailing from Melinda we touched at Socotra, an island about a hundred miles in circumference. It is a wild country with no produce, no corn, no rice, no millet, no wine, no fruit trees: in short, altogether sterile and arid, except that it has plenty of dates, out of which they make bread, and also abounds in cattle.[7] The island is exposed to great heat from the sun; the people are Christian in name rather than in reality, wonderfully ignorant and rude: they cannot read or write. They

[7] Socotra is here described with very fair accuracy. Its real length is 70 miles, by an average breadth of 15. The first Portuguese to visit it were Tristan de Cuña and others under his command in 1508. The old Portuguese account, Faria y Sousa, t. ii. p. 2, ch. i., says, 'Athwart the middle of it runs a ridge of hills as high as the clouds, yet not free from the sand of the shore, which is carried up to the very top by the north winds, and it is therefore barren, not only of plants but trees, only some small valleys that are under shelter of those winds. . . . Those valleys that are sheltered from the sand produce apple and palm trees, and the best aloes, which for its excellency is called Zocotorinos. The common food is maize, or Indian wheat, tamarinds, and milk. They are all Jacobite Christians, as the Ethiopians. The men use the names of the Apostles, the women chiefly that of Mary. They worship the Cross, which they wear on their clothes, and set up in their churches, where they pray thrice a day in the Chaldean language alternatively as in a choir: they receive but one wife, use circumcision, fasting and tithes. The men comely, the women so manly that they follow the war, and live like Amazons. . . . Their clothing, some cloth and skins, their habitation in caves, their weapons, stones and slings. . . . They were subject to the Arabian King of Caxem. Cuña found here an indifferent fort, not ill manned nor unprovided.' The writer then goes on to relate the brave feat of arms by which the fort was carried, and all the Moors put to death, except two. 'The natives, who had kept off, hearing of our success, came with their wives and children to thank our commander for delivering them from the heavy yoke of those infidels; and he, to their great satisfaction, received them under the protection of the King of Portugal. The mosque was cleared and made a church of our Lady of Victories, and many were there baptized.' This confirms the statement in the letter of St. Francis about the absence of baptism among these nominal Christians.

have consequently no records of any kind. Still they pride themselves on being Christians. They have churches, crosses, and lamps. Each village has its Caciz, who answers to the Parish Priest. These Caciz know no more of reading or writing than the rest; they have not even any books, and only know a few prayers by heart. They go to their churches four times a day—at midnight, at daybreak, in the afternoon, and in the evening. They use no bells; but wooden rattles, such as we use during Holy Week, serve to call the people together. Not even the Caciz themselves understand the prayers which they recite: which are in a foreign language (I think Chaldean). They render special honours to the Apostle St. Thomas, claiming to be descendants of the Christians begotten to Jesus Christ by that Apostle in these countries. In the prayers I have mentioned they often repeat a word which is like our alleluia. The Caciz never baptize any one, nor do they know the least what Baptism is. Whilst I was there I baptized a number of children, with the utmost goodwill of their parents. Most of them showed great eagerness to bring their children to me, and made such liberal offerings out of their poverty of what they had to give, that I should have been afraid to refuse the dates which they pressed upon me with such great goodwill. They also begged me over and over again to remain with them, promising that every single person in the island would be baptized. So I begged the Governor to let me remain where I found a harvest so ripe and ready to be gathered in. But as the island has no Portuguese garrison, and it is exposed to the ravages of the Mussulmans, the Governor would not hear of leaving me, fearing that I might be carried off as a slave. So he told me that I should soon be among other Christians who were not less, perhaps more, in need than the Socotrians of instruction and spiritual assistance, and amongst whom my work would be better spent.

One day I went to Vespers as recited by the Caciz; they lasted an hour. There was no end to their repetitions of prayers and of incensations: the churches are always full of incense. Though their Caciz have wives, they are extremely strict in regard to abstinence and fasting. When they fast they abstain not only from flesh meat and milk, but from fish also, of which they have a great supply. So strict is their rule that they would rather die than taste anything of the kind. They eat nothing but vegetables and palm dates. They have two Lents, during which they fast; one of these lasts two months. If any one is profane enough to eat meat during that time, he is not allowed to enter the church.

In a village in the island there was a Mussulman woman the mother of two young children. Not knowing that their father was a Mussulman, I was going to give them baptism, when they ran off, all of a sudden, to their mother to complain that I was trying to baptize them. The mother came to say that she would never let me baptize her children. She was a Mahometan, and would never have her children made Christians. Upon this the people of Socotra began to cry out that the Mussulmans were unworthy of so great a blessing; that they would not let them be baptized however much they desired it, and that they would never permit any Mussulman to become a Christian. Such is their hatred of Mussulmans.

We set sail from the island at the end of February, and the 6th of May, as I have told you, we arrived at Goa.

[The five vessels which we left at Mozambique sailed thence in March. One of these, the largest of all, and laden with valuable merchandise, was wrecked and lost. The crew were saved; the other four arrived safe.[8]]

Here at Goa I live in the Hospital, administering to the sick the Sacraments of confession and communion. But, be-

[8] These few lines must have been inserted in the letter by some copyist. St. Francis speaks a little further on of the arrival of F. Paul and Mancias, who must have been on board these vessels, as still expected by him. He is to leave for Cape Comorin, and the Governor promises to send them after him. The ship which was lost seems to have been the largest of the whole fleet, from which the Governor transferred himself and his suite on leaving Mozambique. It is said (see Massei, l. i. ch. iii. p. 58) that St. Francis always spoke of the ship as if she were destined to some great calamity. Predictions of this kind are frequent in his life.

sides the sick, such numbers of other persons want me to hear their confessions, that, if I could be in ten different places at once, I should never lack penitents. After attending to the sick, I gave my morning to hearing confessions: after midday I used to go to the prisons, and after giving the prisoners instructions as to making their confessions, I heard the confessions of their whole life. When I had got through this, I went to the Church of our Lady, which is near the Hospital, and there I began to teach the children—as many as three hundred were often present—their prayers, the Creed, and the Ten Commandments. Upon this the Bishop of Goa ordered the same to be done in the other churches, and it still continues to be practised. The fruits gained from it surpass all expectation, and have delighted the whole city.

Whilst I remained at our Lady's Church I used to preach in the morning on Sundays and holidays to the people promiscuously. In the afternoon I explained the articles of the Creed to the natives, and the crowd of hearers was so great that the church could hardly contain them. I afterwards taught them the Lord's Prayer, the *Hail Mary*, the Apostles' Creed, and the Ten Commandments of the Law of God. On Sundays I used to say mass for the lepers, whose hospital is close to the city, heard their confessions, and gave them communion. There was not one of them who did not approach the sacraments: and after the first sermon I preached to them they were all devoted to me.

I am now setting out by the Governor's order for a country where there is reason to hope that many will become Christians. Three students from the same country go with me, two of whom are deacons, fairly acquainted with Portuguese, as well as with their native tongue: the third has only received minor orders. I am in good hopes that my labours there may produce precious fruits for our holy religion. As soon as Fathers Paul and Mancias arrive from Mozambique, the Governor has promised to send them to join me. The place I speak of is called Cape Comorin, six hundred miles distant from Goa. I pray God, that for the sake of your prayers, He may be pleased to forget my sins and to grant me all the grace I am in need of, that I may do Him good service in those parts.

All the sufferings of the long voyage, all the charge of bearing the sins of others while one has to bear the weight of his own, the having to live a long time together among unbelievers, and the extreme heat of the sun in this climate—all these trials, if borne as they ought to be borne for the love of God, turn out to be very great consolations and the subject of many and intense spiritual delights. I am perfectly persuaded in my own mind that the lovers of the Cross of our Lord Christ consider a life of trials of this sort a blessed life, and that to fly from or to be without the Cross is death to them. For can there be a more cruel death than to live without Jesus Christ, after having once known Him, or to forsake Him for the sake of following our own desires? I assure you, dear friends, no cross is to be compared to such a cross as that. On the other hand, how blessed it is to live dying a daily death, breaking our own wills, that we may seek, not what is our own, but what belongs to Jesus Christ!

And now, dearest brothers, I entreat and conjure you by God to write to me about every single member of our Society, that as I have no hope that I shall see them in this life, as St. Paul says, *facie ad faciem*, I may at least see them *per ænigma*, in a dark manner, that is by means of your letters. Unworthy as I am, do not refuse me this boon. Remember that God has made you such, that I have the right to expect great consolation from you, and to receive it. Give me diligent instructions what method I should pursue in dealing with the heathen and the Mussulmans to whom I am sent, for I look forward to learning from God, through what you write to me, how I am to make them Christians without difficulty, and I expect to come to see, from your instructions, and so to correct, any blunders I may commit while I am waiting to hear from you. Meanwhile I don't despair, that by the merits and prayers of our holy Mother Church, on which I rely greatly, and through the prayers of you and others her living members, our Lord

Christ may deign to sow the seed of the Gospel by means of me, wicked servant though I am, in the land of the heathen, more especially since, as He uses so poor a creature as I am for so great a work, it will put to shame men who are born with capacities for great things, as well as be a spur to others of weak courage, when they see me who am but dust and ashes and the vilest of men made to bear witness from my own experience to the extreme scarcity which here exists of Apostolical labourers. Ah, how gladly would I make myself the slave during my whole life of any who would come out here and devote themselves to labour in the vineyard of the Lord of all!

And thus, then, I end my letter, imploring God, of His infinite mercy, to gather us all one day into that blessed joy of His for which we are made, and here in this life to increase our strength, so that we may labour in His service with the diligence which it deserves, and thus make ourselves entirely and altogether conformed unto His holy decrees and will.

Your useless brother in Jesus Christ,

FRANCIS XAVIER.

Goa, September 18th, 1542.

It may here be remarked that this letter, which is a fair specimen of those which Francis Xavier wrote from time to time during the remaining years of his life to his friends in Europe, leaves out, as might be expected, the circumstances most to his own personal credit. It is hardly necessary to repeat that nothing else could have been expected, not only from a person of singular holiness, but even from a person of ordinary modesty and good sense, and that few things can be more absurd than to question the many personal details which have been added to our knowledge by the companions and friends of St. Francis, on the ground that he himself makes no mention of them. We may add, also, that his life, even on board ship, and much more when he was once launched on his missionary career in India, was a life of extraordinary labour and active occupation, and that it is really wonderful that he should have found time to write letters so long and so full in detail as many that remain to us, which, however, represent only a percentage of the whole number which he is known to have written.

Before we proceed further, a few words may be added as to his efforts in favour of the inhabitants of Socotra. We do not possess the letter which Francis Xavier wrote to the King of Portugal concerning these islanders, but we know that he represented their case so strongly, that a Portuguese fleet was ordered to call there on its way to India, and the island conquered from the Mussulmans. At a later period, Xavier sent some members of the Society to preach to the people.[9]

It is not difficult to believe the deplorable accounts which are given us by the biographers of Xavier of the state of religion at Goa at the time of his arrival in that city. The circumstances of the case explain them and almost require them. The Portuguese were masters at Goa and in a number of other towns, chiefly along the coast, where their garrisons and factories were established, and the general supremacy of the Portuguese crown was recognized to a certain extent by many of the native Princes in the interior. Goa itself, the capital, was a city of much beauty and size, strong in its insular situation, possessing fine buildings and some handsome churches. But its population was a mixture of Portuguese, Mahometans, and native Indians. The Portuguese were comparatively few, though of course dominant, and a great number of them were adventurers of all sorts, merchants, soldiers, and the like, who had either left behind them in Europe, as it is too general for Europeans of all nations to leave behind them, even the semblance of outward religion and morality, or who had at all events become utterly corrupted by the temptations of their new position and the vices of their Mussulman neighbours, the influence of the climate, and the ease with which the Asiatics under their dominion lent themselves to be the instruments and victims of their profligacy. We shall find in the course of

[9] Turselline, lib. i. ch. xvi. But Bartoli, *Asia*, l. i. p. 439, does not mention the fleet, and puts the mission of the preachers after the death of Francis.

the narrative of the life of St. Francis many instances of highly religious officers and merchants, men really desirous of advancing the glory of God and the spiritual welfare of the native population, and willing to put themselves to great expenses and to incur severe dangers, for the purpose of aiding the Apostle in his works of charity and zeal. But the majority of the Portuguese, even after the reform introduced by him, and much more before that time, seem to have been such in their lives and conduct as to merit the severe language in which many writers speak of them. The Mussulmans, and some of the native heathens, were rich and powerful, important to the Portuguese Government on account of their numbers, influence, and the commerce which was kept up through them, and they made no pretence of hiding their religions or desisting from their most abominable practices even in Goa itself. The lower and poorer orders among them were even oppressed and persecuted if they showed any inclination to adopt Christianity, and indeed the lives of the majority of the Christians were such as to scandalize and revolt them. Many of the Portuguese led the most licentious lives, as too many of the European officers and officials in India do at the present time. Few Portuguese ladies could venture as far as India, and an almost recognised system of concubinage prevailed among the Europeans, who differed very little in this respect from the Mussulmans themselves. When marriages had been contracted the women had become Christians, but they were extremely ignorant of the religion which they had adopted, and their children were growing up almost entirely without instruction.

On the other hand, there were not wanting attempts at better things, which, however, had hitherto failed of success. The Bishop of Goa was an old Franciscan friar of the name of John Albuquerque, a good and holy man, but his jurisdiction was extremely extensive, embracing the whole of India and the Portuguese settlements in the East, and his activity was not equal to his piety and personal holiness. As a rule, the priests and religious to be found in Goa confined their labours to the Portuguese, and made few attempts at the conversion of the heathen. We must remember also, that in Europe itself, at the time of which we speak, the frequentation of the Sacraments had in many parts died out, and that, as we have mentioned above, even in Rome, it was strange to go often to Communion or for priests to preach except in Lent and Advent. A zealous Franciscan friar, Diego de Borba, a disciple of John of Avila, had been four years in Goa and had begun a good work in which he found many associates, for the benefit of the Indians. A College had been founded at Goa, through his exertions,[10] in which a large number of native boys from all parts of India were educated, with the intention that they should ultimately become Priests for their own countries, or at least interpreters and catechists for other missionaries. The College was endowed with an annual revenue by the Government out of funds which were taken away from the idolatrous priests. We shall hear more of the College, which was then called the College of Santa Fé, and afterwards of St. Paul. There was also a flourishing 'Confraternity of Mercy,' an institution to be found in most of the Portuguese settlements, devoted to works of active charity. These were elements of good among the Portuguese of Goa which only required the breath of Apostolic zeal to quicken them into life, and we read of no opposition offered to St. Francis when he began the work of reform.

On landing at Goa, he took up his abode, as usual, in the hospital—for a hospital answering, as we have already said, the purposes of 'poor house' as well, was sure to be found in every such city. He then went to the Bishop, and informed him of his mission from the Pope and the King—showing him his letters and faculties, including that which appointed him Apostolical Legate. At the same time he declared that he had no desire or intention of using the extraordinary powers conferred upon him, except so far as it seemed good and advisable to the Bishop himself. This absolute deference to the ordi-

[10] The chief founder of this College was the predecessor of Martin Alfonso Sousa as Governor, Don Estevan de Gama, a son of the famous Vasco de Gama.

nary ecclesiastical authority was a fixed principle with him during the whole of his missionary career, as it was also uniformly insisted upon by St. Ignatius in Europe. Francis adopted the principle not merely out of prudence, but in order that his work might have the blessing of obedience upon it as well as that of perfect union with the representatives of Divine authority in the Church.

We may also notice here, at the outset of his career in the East, other features of the method which he uniformly pursued, when it was possible, in the work of evangelizing the populations to whom he was sent. The practice of personal poverty, and of spending a large part of the night in prayer, while the day was given to active works of piety and charity, the devotion of his first care to those who most closely resembled our Lord in His suffering life, the sick, the lepers, and the prisoners, and a peculiar attention to the instruction of children and the most ignorant, are some of those features which are copied directly from the example and precepts of our Lord.

It is hardly necessary to add, that the good Bishop's heart was won at once by the humility and zeal of the new Apostle, and that from the first he became the fast friend of Francis. Indeed, the whole city was soon devoted to him, and in the space of five months a very great change for the better in matters of religion was the fruit of his labours. The particulars given in the letter last cited may serve as a summary of these happy results. A few details have been added by his biographers, gleaned from the memories of those who were at Goa at the time. The Governor, a pious and earnest man, as we have seen, took from Francis the custom of visiting the hospital and prison in person once a week, and this custom was afterwards recommended by the King to his successor. We are also told of Francis' manner of adapting himself to the character of the various persons, whom by private conversation he endeavoured to win to a more Christian life, sometimes admonishing them with the greatest gentleness and affability, at other times putting the great truths of eternity, of death, judgment and hell before them in the strongest and most terrible language. In this way a great number were induced to make their confession after a long period of disorderly life, to break off unlawful connections, or to render them lawful by marriage, as well as to make due restitution of unjust gains. The peculiar position of the Portuguese in India made the first of these kinds of disorders the most difficult to remedy in the majority of cases. Turselline, the first and in some respects the best biographer of St. Francis Xavier, has summed up so happily the tradition of his manner of dealing with these cases, that we may give it here in his words instead of in our own. 'Xavier,' he says, 'thinking within himself that he ought to apply some remedy to this great evil, began to dispose them with all the endeavour he could use. And first he went about to win them by all courteous means; then, as he met them in the streets, he would merely request them to invite a poor priest to their ordinary fare; which they willingly accepted of. He now sitting at table would before, or at, their repast, entreat his host to cause his children to be called; whereupon the little children coming presently at their father's call, Francis would take them up in his arms and hug them to his bosom, thanking God Who had given the father such children for the hope of his family, and withal would pray God to grant them a good and holy life. Then would he desire that their mother might be called (a thing which in another would have been temerity, but his sanctity easily excused it). When she was come, he would speak sweetly unto her, and commend her heartily to his host, thereby to draw him to take her to his wife, saying that doubtless she was of an excellent disposition and lovely countenance, so that she might well be accounted a Portuguese, that the children which he had by her were certainly worthy of a Portuguese to their father. Why therefore did he not marry her? What wife could he have better? And he should do well to provide with all speed for his children's credit and the woman's honesty.

'Which wholesome counsel of his proved not unprofitable. For by his words and authority without great difficulty he persuaded many of them to marry their mistresses, being himself witness thereof. But if by chance he lighted upon any one who had by some illfavoured Indian woman children like unto herself, then assuming great indignation thereat, he would cry out, Good God! what a monster have we here! Do you keep a devil in your house? Can you keep company with this ugly beast? Can you have children by her? Follow my counsel: drive this monster, this prodigious creature, presently out of your house, and seek you a wife worthy of yourself. So in putting away his mistress, he married a wife.'

We may add, to complete the picture, what the same writer adds of another practice of Francis Xavier: 'He, thirsting more after the salvation of souls than his own praise, was always thinking of some new ways how to help them, for the performance whereof there was nothing which he would not do. And amongst the rest he had one invention which, in such a man as he, gave an admirable example of Christian simplicity, and was also more profitable in effect, than fair to show. He being a man of grave years and authority, went up and down the highways and streets with a little bell in his hand (so far was he from thinking anything disgraceful to him that might be grateful to God, and profitable for man's salvation) to call the children and servants together to Christian Doctrine, at the corners of the streets and crossways, sometimes stirring up the inhabitants to piety with these or suchlike words: "*Faithful Christians, for the love which you bear to Christ, send your children and servants to the Christian Doctrine.*" Which new invention made infinite numbers of children, slaves, and others to run flocking unto him from all places: all whom, he himself marching before, he would lead into our Blessed Lady's Church, singing aloud the Catechism unto them, and teaching them the same, thereby to cause them the more willingly to come and hear him, and so the more easily to remember what was taught them in the manner of singing—both which proved afterwards to be so. And herein he used no less prudence than diligence. For knowing very well that his labour would then be profitably employed, if those things which ought to be learned were well understood, all that he sung he would explicate largely and clearly, according to the capacity of his auditors.

'To the ruder sort and to slaves he would purposely speak after a rude and homely manner, that their own fashion of speech might keep them more attentive and make deeper impression in their minds—which endeavour of his was neither fruitless nor in vain. For from hence arose that so worthy a custom of teaching and learning the Christian Doctrine which is at this day practised in India. And because men reaped more fruit by it than was expected, the Bishop caused the same to be practised by others in the other churches, so as, advancing himself in this new piety, those of the Society following Francis' institution, others stirred up thereunto partly by the Bishop's command, and partly by the example of the Society, it came at last to be a custom throughout all India, to the great advancement of the Christian cause. For this practice so spread itself abroad both in Goa and in other places, that everywhere in the schools, highways, streets, houses, fields, and ships, there were instead of vain and idle songs, sung and heard the principles of Christian faith with great delight. Wherefore it grew to a custom that children who could scarce speak did strive to sing most of those verses by heart. And in this exercise Xavier gave no less noble proof of his temperance and moderation, than of his industrious labours. For of all that was given to him under the title of alms, he received nothing to himself, but gave all to the sick and poor in the most private manner he could, to the end that human praise might not deprive him of any reward in the sight of God.'[11]

The work of teaching the Christian doctrine, or Catechism, to children and the ignorant was considered so essential by the first Fathers of the Society, that it had been proposed during their deliberations in Rome, when the form of the Institute was to be drawn up and submitted to the Pope, to join a clause relating to this duty to the fourth and distinctive vow of the Professed,—that, namely, which binds them to special

[11] Turselline, lib. i. c. 3.

obedience to the Pope as to any missions on which he may send them. This proposal was abandoned on account of the opposition of one only among the Fathers, Nicolas Bobadilla, but the fact shows the very high importance which Ignatius and his companions attached to the subject. Francis Xavier uniformly acted in the matter as if he had been bound by the proposed vow. The plan of setting the Christian doctrine to simple music, and teaching it in the way just mentioned by Turselline, was characteristic of his practical sense and joyous simplicity, and we find it specially mentioned as having been kept to throughout his career. In the Moluccas, the Processes tell us, he used to spend the day, after saying mass, in hearing confessions and teaching the rudiments of the faith to children and adults of both sexes in a church of our Lady, a great crowd attending his instructions; and from this the custom became general of the natives singing the prayers of the Doctrine as they were carrying their wares on board ship, and at night in their houses, 'which thing,' it is said, 'greatly moved all hearts to devotion. And not only there, and in Amboyna, and at Cape Comorin, but everywhere else where he taught, his prayers and teaching sank into their hearts as if they had been taught them by the Apostles themselves; and his Catechism was taught all over India, the children singing it as they went to and came from school; and in the streets at night the slaves and boys and girls as they passed about were heard to sing no other songs than his.'[12]

The last letter of St. Francis, which we have inserted above, makes mention of his approaching departure on his first missionary expedition, in aid of the recently converted Christians of the Fishery Coast. This coast and the neighbouring parts of Southern India formed the scene of his earliest labours in that kind of Apostolate which was to be his chief occupation for the remainder of his short life, and we are fortunate in possessing details of considerable importance concerning his method of action as well as the severe difficulties under which his work had to be carried on. There is some

[12] *Relatio super Sanctitate et Miraculis &c.* in cap. *de Fide.*

little uncertainty as to the length of his first stay at the Fishery Coast, as there is not perfect agreement between the different editors of his Letters as to the date of some of them which were written from Goa after his departure for the Coast, and which make it evident that he returned to that city after his first stay among the natives. But the question is not of any real importance, and we shall take the liberty of inverting the order in which these letters are usually printed, for the sake of afterwards considering at one glance, and without interruption, all that remains to us concerning the mission to the Fisheries.

The two following letters may probably, as we have hinted, have been written from Goa during a short visit paid by St. Francis to that city in the later months of 1543, after he had spent a year on the mission. They relate entirely to matters which concern the interests of religion in Goa, and were no doubt the fruit of many conferences between St. Francis and the Governor, Don Martin Alfonso de Sousa, over whom, as we have seen, he had acquired so excellent an influence. The second looks like a formal document, drawn up in such form as to be laid before the Pope or any of the authorities at Rome whom he might depute to consider whether the requests made in the name of the Governor could be granted. It asks for a plenary indulgence to be gained after confession and communion on the Feast of St. Thomas, the first Apostle of the Indies, and during his octave: for the same favour for the inmates of the hospitals of the city of Goa, and for those who wait upon them, every time they approach the sacraments, and also at the hour of death, and again for all the faithful on the feasts of our Blessed Lady, and for the members of the 'Confraternity of Mercy' and their wives, once a year and at the hour of death. Another demand is that on account of the very great distance between the various Portuguese settlements under the jurisdiction of the Bishop of Goa,—the Moluccas and Malacca in the far East, Ormuz on the Persian Gulf, Diu, Sofala on the African coast, and Mozambique—a distance which prevented the Bishop from visiting them regularly, he might be allowed to delegate to his vicars in those places the power which, under such circumstances, is sometimes committed to priests, of administering the sacrament of Confirmation. The last request strikes us as very strange, and is put forward with some appearance of hesitation as to the possibility of the concession. It is proposed that as the climate and seasons of India so far inverted the ordinary course of life for the Portuguese in the East as to occupy them in the active pursuits either of commerce or warfare during the spring, which is there also the hot season, and as this led to a general disregard of the observance of the Lenten fast, the Church should change her seasons to suit the convenience of her children, and transplant the fast of Lent to the months of June and July. The grounds for all these requests are formally given in the document which we shall presently quote.

The other letter which we shall place before that of which we have been speaking, is written with more freedom, though perhaps not with that entire abandonment of reserve which characterizes St. Francis when he is writing to St. Ignatius, with the certainty that he alone will see his letter. We see the warm and grateful interest which Francis felt towards the Governor de Sousa—a good and pious man, who afterwards proved, we are told, wanting in firmness in his arduous charge—and his ingenious charity in suggesting to Ignatius the little attentions which will go most nearly to the heart of Sousa. His sanguine desires as to the large supply of missionaries of the Society are put forward under the authority of the Governor. Francis had probably already begun to find out what was to be a very principal cross to him for the remainder of his life. The work at the centre of the Church is at some times so overwhelming that even the largest-hearted men at home are fain to shrink from the sacrifice involved in sending the best instruments at their disposal to a distance among the heathen. Later on we shall find Ignatius coming even to the conclusion that he must withdraw St. Francis himself from the East: and we may well imagine how the eager Apostle of the Indies felt at Goa, with the fine college of Santa Fé ready for his workmen, with so many new fields of labour opening out daily before him, as month after month passed without bringing him the long-desired reinforcements, or even a letter from his tenderly loved brethren in Europe to assure him of their sympathy.

(XI.) *To the Father Master Ignatius of Loyola.*

May the grace and love of our Lord Jesus Christ always help and favour us! Amen.

Some persons out here, guided, it is clear, by the inspiration of God, have lately founded a College at Goa, and no work could be named of which there was greater need in these parts. It increases daily, and we have great cause for giving thanks to God for the establishment of such a house for the instruction, I trust, of many converts and the conversion of many infidels. The building of the College is in the hands of men of great virtue and high position. The Governor himself favours the business greatly, and is so convinced that the design is one which tends to the advancement of the Christian religion, that it is chiefly with his funds and by means of him that the buildings destined for the purpose seem likely to be enlarged and finished in a short space of time. The church, which is close to the College, is of a very handsome design. The foundations were laid a long time ago, now the walls are finished, and they are putting on the roof. It will be consecrated next summer. If you want to know its size, it is twice as large as the church of the Sorbonne at Paris. The income allotted to the College is large enough to support easily a hundred students, and people think it will be further increased continually.[13] Indeed, we hope, with God's help, that in a few years many will go forth from this place who will do good service to religion in these countries, and extend far and wide the boundaries of holy Church.

Judging from these beginnings, I hope that by six years' time the students of the College will number quite three hun-

[13] The College was endowed originally with an annual sum of 800 crowns, which, as has been said, had formerly gone to the maintenance of pagan priests.

dred, youths of all races, nations, and tongues, and that by their labours the number of Christians will be very greatly increased. The Governor has promised that as soon as the heathen give him a little leisure (for he is constantly at war with them), he will get the College buildings rapidly finished. He has made up his mind that there is no work to be done in India more pious and holy than this, that the dedication of such houses to Christ has enabled him to win many and great victories which he has already won over the heathen, and he trusts with the help of God to win by and bye even greater. So I do beg of you over and over again, by Christ our Lord and His religion, to pray yourself for Don Martin Sousa, and have him commended to the prayers of the Society, that God may supply him abundantly with counsel and help from on high to govern well this immense province of India, so that he may so pass through things temporal as not to lose things eternal.[14]

And indeed, if I thought there was any room for recommendation from me, I should commend him to you as I would myself. His great virtue has rendered him so dear to me, that I do not love him less tenderly than he appears to love me, though all our affection and mutual services have the single object of the glory of Jesus Christ. Heaven forbid I should ever forget him. If I were to do so, I should expect to have to pay very severe penalties to God for so much ingratitude. The Governor is writing to the King about the College, that, if it seems well, his Highness may write to the Holy Father to urge him to send some of our Society to India, to be the future props of this College. Some people call it the College of the Conversion of St. Paul, others the College of the Holy Faith. This last name appears to me the best name for it, as its students seem to be educated for the purpose of sowing the seed of the Christian faith in the minds of the infidels.

The Governor has charged me to write to you at length about the College and its establishment, and I therefore do

[14] Latin words in the original: *ut sic transeat per bona temporalia, ut non amittat æterna.* The words are taken from a collect in the Missal.

so. The object of the institute is to bring up native boys of various nations in the Christian religion, who when sufficiently instructed may be sent home to teach their fellowcountrymen. I can find no words to tell you how much the Governor approves our Society and its institute. He considers that as you have been the means by which God has called us all into the Society of His Son, he owes it to his duty to God and his office to take care that you are informed by letter how very necessary it is that the youth of the College be instructed, in order that you may think of sending over here some of the Society for this purpose. He says that it is his business to finish the buildings of the College, and yours to provide it with competent teachers for the young men. He thinks also that it is important for the dignity of religion and the increase of piety in this country, that the Pope should be induced to grant to the high altar of this church the privilege of the liberation of a soul from Purgatory each time that mass is celebrated thereon for the dead, just as if it were at what is called a privileged altar at Rome. And that all question of gain to the priest who may wish to celebrate the mass there, may be excluded, he wishes the grant to be made out so as to contain the condition, that the privilege may only be gained when the priest says mass at this altar gratuitously, with no expectation of fee or human consideration, and when the person who gets it said goes to confession and receives communion at that mass. It is certainly quite fair that one who would set free the soul of another from Purgatory should first set his own free from hell and eternal damnation. The Governor's reason for wishing that some special Indulgence should be granted by the Pope to the priests who say mass at the altar, is that they may be attracted by such an advantage and be desirous of saying mass there; and he is very anxious that this Pontifical favour should be granted, in order to enhance the veneration for the shrine and increase the piety of the people. All these requests of his will be enough to make you understand the character of the good man, who feels so rightly about holy things and matters of piety, and is so painstaking about them.

I do not doubt that when you send some subjects out here, one or indeed many of them will be of approved virtue and constancy, as men should be who will have to administer a College like this, and to undergo all the many trials which this country is sure to afford. Sea and land alike will put their strength and virtue abundantly to the test. The work requires men of strong constitution and in vigorous health: young men will do better than old men, though we will not refuse the old, if they are hale and active. All who come will be welcomed with kindness and good will by the people here, and will be asked at once to hear confessions, to give pious meditations, and to preach. The harvest will be great and abundant. We have already more than sixty native children ready who are now being instructed by Diego de Borba, an excellent Franciscan friar. At the beginning of the summer they will move into the College. Most of them know how to read, several know how to write and are far enough on to be taught grammar. I tell you this that you may send us a good master for them, and, when he comes, he will find plenty of work in the discharge of his office.

His Excellency also hopes that, among those whom we expect from you, there may be one who is a Preacher, who may give instructions to the priests in things of necessity, lecturing on a part of the Scriptures, or the sacraments (for the generality of those who come out here are not overburthened with learning), and at the same time rouse them up to the love of God and devoted care of the salvation of men, as well by his example as by his teaching. I need not tell you that deeds are more persuasive than words. As for the rest of our people, he wishes them to be such as may labour with diligence in hearing confessions, administering the sacraments, and converting the heathen. This island itself may yield an abundant harvest in the conversion of heathen.[15] A great number of these lie utterly destitute of help in the darkness and night of super-

[15] He speaks of the island, or peninsula, in which Goa stood, which contained a large heathen population. The *Epistolæ Indicæ* of subsequent years speak of numerous conversions among them.

stition, ignorant altogether of the God Who made them and Who is their Lord. So the Governor expects you to send him three Priests and a Master of Humanities. He is also writing himself to the King, if I am not mistaken, to beg him to ask the Pope for four of our Society. He also asks for certain Indulgences, a list of which I send in a separate letter, so that when they have been granted, at the King's petition, our brothers who are to come out may bring them to India. I would have you thoroughly to understand that this service will win them the good will of all the Portuguese who are in India, and give them much consideration and authority, which will be found of the greatest value when they have to implant divine truths in the minds of these people. Of all the nations that I have seen, the Portuguese is the one which seems to me to go furthest in prizing Indulgences from Rome, and to be the most drawn to the frequentation of the sacraments by attractions of this kind. So I trust that, both to cherish this devotion of the nation that I mention, and also in consideration of their profound devotion to the Holy See, the Holy Father will be pleased to show himself very liberal in granting the request of children so obedient to him. Whatever graces of this sort may be obtained from the Holy Father you will take care to have sent to us with the documents in full form, that there may be the greater certainty and dignity about the concession.

His Excellency, I think, is writing to you himself. Though he has never seen you, he is devoted to you and to all the Society as well. Pray write to him and send him a couple of rosaries with the Papal Indulgences attached, as a present for himself and his wife. They will please him very much, both for the sake of the Indulgences and because they come from you. He begs you, moreover, because he has so much confidence in your influence and friendship, to obtain for him as a favour from the Pope, that every time he, his wife, or his children go to confession, they may gain all the Indulgences of the Seven Churches at Rome. If you do this for him, he will be greatly indebted to you. Moreover he will think that I have really some little influence with you, if you obtain these favours which I have mentioned from the Pope in consequence of this letter which I write to you in his name. But now I make an end, conjuring Jesus Christ our Lord, Who in His infinite mercy has united us under the same rule of life here, to be pleased to unite us after death in everlasting happiness.

The least of your sons, and the most distant from your presence,

FRANCIS.

Goa, Oct. 18, 1543.

(XII.) *To the Father Master Ignatius of Loyola.*

May the grace and love of our Lord Jesus Christ always assist and favour us! Amen.

The Governor of India, to whom we are all greatly indebted, both those of us who are here and who are at Rome, on account as well of his great zeal for the worship of God as of his especial love for our Society, has asked me to write to you concerning various spiritual wants of these countries. He is himself so much disposed to religion, and his requests are so conformable to piety and virtue, that I willingly undertake to make these petitions to you in his name.

In the first place, as the people of India honour with an especial worship the Apostle St. Thomas, the patron of India, the Governor, with a view to increase and honour this their veneration and worship, would wish that his Holiness should grant a Plenary Indulgence on the day of the Feast of that Apostle and seven days after, to those only who within that time shall duly go to confession and communion. He has named this condition, that the people may be induced to approach the sacraments, and that the feast day may be kept with due piety and observance, and this all the more because Lent falls in the summer in these countries, when everybody here is soldiering. The Indians are masters on the land, the Portuguese at sea. The consequence is that the holy season of Lent is spent in military occupations and in navigation, and thus the soldiers and the merchants have commonly no time to approach the sacraments of penance and holy communion.

The Governor therefore, that men may be attracted to the sacraments, asks the Holy Father to grant them the inducement of this Indulgence, which is likely to be a sort of Lent.

In the second place, he prays you to obtain from the Holy Father in favour of the hospitals of the city, that the sick and those who wait upon them may obtain a Plenary Indulgence as often as they go to confession and receive holy communion, and that the dying may receive the same Indulgence. He asks this in order that the sick may be induced to approach the sacraments more frequently, that the others may more willingly wait on the sick and give themselves to pious works with greater fervour, and that all, sick and strong, may worship God in purity and piety, and set a good example to the heathen among whom they live and dwell.

Again, his Excellency is remarkably devout to the Blessed Mother of God, and keeps her festivals most religiously. By far the greatest part of the year he spends at Goa with a large Court. Goa is a city in the island of the same name, about ten miles broad: and in this island there are several churches of our Lady, really very devotional and rich, well worth notice as to architectural beauty, vestments, sacred vessels, numbers of priests, and celebration of worship. As those churches keep each in their turn the festivals of our Lady with great magnificence, the Governor, in order to increase the number of worshippers and the true veneration of the Blessed Virgin, asks that any one who may visit these churches on those feast days after having been to confession and communion, may gain a Plenary Indulgence. Such graces are really more needed in India than elsewhere in Christian countries, because, the number of Christians being very large—for the Portuguese are very numerous, the Indian converts are numerous, and a large number are continually being received—still the number of priests is wonderfully small. They are quite unable to hear all the confessions in Lent. So the Governor, in order that no one out here may live without confession and communion, makes these requests to the Holy Father through you, in order that every one may have a wish to receive the sacraments, and that all may make use of these true treasures of grace left to us by our Blessed Lord for the attainment of eternal happiness.

Again, we have in this city, as well as in most other places where Christians have settled, a Confraternity of good men who undertake the relief of the poor among the inhabitants whether old Christians or converts. It is called the Confraternity of Mercy, and consists entirely of Portuguese. The ardour and perseverance with which these pious people serve God by relieving the poor is quite incredible. In order to kindle still more their charity, the Governor asks the Holy Father to grant them a Plenary Indulgence once a year, after confession and communion, and the same at the hour of death. As most of them are married, he would like these favours to be extended to the wives as well as the husbands.

The Portuguese are not only masters of the Indian sea, but they also occupy different places on the coast, where they reside with their wives and children. These places are very far apart. Thus, from Goa to the Moluccas,[16] where the King of Portugal has a fortress, is about 1000 leagues; to Malacca, a city where the Christians are very numerous, 500 leagues; to Ormuz, a famous city, much frequented by the Portuguese, 400 leagues; to Diu, 300 leagues; to Mozambique, 900 leagues; to Sofala, 1200 leagues. In each of these cities the Bishop of Goa has a Vicar-General, being unable to visit them regularly in person on account of the great distance. The Governor therefore, knowing how necessary the sacrament of Confirmation is to Christians living among savages and continually at war with the infidels, would ask the Holy Father, with the object of fortifying the Christian faith in India, to give the Bishop of Goa faculties to delegate to his Vicars the power of administering Confirmation, since a single Bishop could never satisfy the wants of places so far distant, let him be ever so willing to do so.

In these countries nature has so completely inverted the regular order of the seasons, that when on the other coast of India it is full summer, here on this side we are feeling the

[16] Francis speaks of 'Molucco' as a single place.

winter; and so on this, when they are under the winter colds, we are burnt up by the summer heats. And the heat in summer is something incredible. The sun is so hot, that fish begin to rot as soon as they die. So, during the hot season, when the sea on this side is navigated, it is shut on the other on account of tempests which frighten every one from sailing at that time. And, as I said before, in the season of Lent all the troops take arms and go on board the vessels for a sea campaign, and the merchants in like manner are in perpetual motion to and fro. For the Portuguese here, having greater command of sea than of land, are engaged in commerce, and support themselves and their families thereby. Thus, what with the excessive heat which I speak of, and what with the almost continual voyages of the Portuguese, Lent is disregarded and few persons observe the law of fasting. The Governor has charged me to lay all these facts carefully before you, and to beg of you in the name of God, that if such a thing be possible, you will get the Pope to change the time of Lent in these parts to the months of June and July, at which time of year the heat begins to relent, and there is much less navigation, on account of the roughness of the sea. So the milder temperature would make it easy for most people to fast, and the return of Lent at that time would be a sort of reminder, and they would then easily obey the precepts of the Church as to confession and communion. This measure is one which seems of the greatest importance for the service of God, unless you see any objection to it. The Governor entreats you earnestly not to let anything that can be done in this matter be left unattempted through any want of exertion on the part of his advocate. You will be rewarded for your trouble by the gratitude of all the inhabitants of these countries, and you will have a share in the fruits of the divine worship and the merits which will be acquired in consequence of all those graces. Adieu.

Goa, Oct. 20, 1543.

P.S. As I was leaving Lisbon, I wrote to you about a

College of the Society which the King was thinking of establishing at Coimbra, in the public University. He commissioned me to write and ask you for some of our Society for the purpose, and to offer his own assistance and favour for the buildings, as well as an endowment, for there is a great dearth in Portugal of men well fitted to instruct their heathen fellow-subjects,[17] separated from them as they are by such an immense distance, in the faith and precepts of our Lord Jesus Christ. Pray let me know as soon as possible what you have done in the matter.

Your child in Christ,

FRANCIS.

[17] *ethnicos populares suos.* The words are not quite free from ambiguity, but they seem to refer to the Indians; and the College of Coimbra, which Simon Rodriguez stayed in Portugal to found, was intended by St. Ignatius to feed the Indian mission.

CHAPTER II.

Francis Xavier among the Paravas.

It has already been mentioned that the first mission undertaken by St. Francis Xavier beyond the limits of the Portuguese city of Goa, was to the native Indians in the extreme south of the peninsula, dwelling along the coast which stretches eastwards from Cape Comorin as far as the point opposite the island which the old geographers called Rammanakoyel, at the northwestern extremity of the ridge of shoals known as Adam's Bridge, which reaches as far as Manaar close to the coast of Ceylon, and forms the boundary of the modern Gulf of Manaar. The whole of this coast derives its chief celebrity from the pearl fishery, which is carried on by the inhabitants, and which is probably the most famous in the world, though the Bahrein pearls are now said to be finer than those here obtained. The natives of the coast of which we speak, the Paravas, were low in caste, poor, and ill able to defend themselves against tyranny and aggression. When the Portuguese first came to India, and indeed down to a short time before the mission of St. Francis Xavier among them, they had been made subject by the Mussulmans—retaining, however, their own nominal chiefs—and the fisheries had been carried on by them for the benefit of their masters. A chance outrage, however, had opened the way alike to Portuguese influence and at least a superficial introduction of Christianity among them. At Tuticorin, a considerable town on the coast, about half way between the two extreme points, a Mussulman had wantonly torn an earring out of the ear of a Parava. This act was considered as the extremity of insult, and the Parava at once killed him. A conflict ensued, in which many Paravas lost their lives. They retaliated by collecting assistance from a number of their villages, and making a massacre of the Mussulmans.

But the Paravas were the weaker party, and this was perfectly well known to their own chiefs, who, in the accounts that remain to us, are called kings. These seem to have been frightened by the great preparations made by the Mussulmans, especially by sea, and hastened to make terms with them, undertaking, as it would seem, to punish their own subjects severely. The Paravas, an unwarlike and mild race, were in the greatest perplexity and alarm, and at the suggestion of a 'Christian Knight,' a converted native noble, who had gone to Portugal and been received with favour by the King, they applied for assistance from the Portuguese authorities at Cochin, sending a number of their Patangats, or Patangatins—officials somewhat answering, it appears, to the 'maires-de-village' in Europe—as ambassadors to plead their cause. The mixture of religion and policy in the advice of this Joam de Cruz is characteristic. 'He,' says Turselline, 'being a man both grave and pious, and hoping this fear of theirs might be an occasion to bring in the Gospel of Christ among them, so as at once they might be set free from the misery both of their war and their superstitions, told them his opinion was that in this extremity of danger they were to fly to extreme remedies; and seeing, contrary to all justice and equity, they were betrayed by their own kings, and hardly charged on all sides by their enemies' forces, they should implore aid of the Almighty King of Heaven and of the Portuguese their friends, who were His devoted and religious servants: that so, protected by the Portuguese and the Divine assistance, they might not only defend themselves, but also triumph over their enemies. For if they would yield themselves subjects to the Christian religion and to the Portuguese, they certainly would fight with all their forces for them, both from regard for religion, and because they were now become their subjects, and would also, by the help of God, carry the whole business with as good success as valour. And having conquered and overthrown the

Saracens, the deadly enemies of Christians, they might also perhaps give up the fishing of pearls (as taken from the Saracens by right of war) unto the Paravas, in respect they were become Christians, as a pledge of their religion.'[1] It appears that the Mussulmans had before this seized on the pearl fisheries, forcing the natives to work only for their profit. The advice of Joam de Cruz was taken, and the Patangatins who went as envoys to Cochin all received Baptism, and promised that their whole nation would do the same. The Portuguese accepted their terms, routed the Mussulman fleet, and gave the fisheries back to the Paravas. Some priests were also sent among them, the chief of whom was Miguel Vaz, the Bishop of Goa's Vicar, and the whole people was rapidly baptized.[2]

This wholesale conversion took place in 1532, ten years before the arrival of Francis in India. The work was not kept up in any way, and when St. Francis first heard of the Paravas from Miguel Vaz, who entreated him to go and evangelize them, they were entirely destitute of Priests, and very little seems to have been done after their first conversion to instruct them and maintain them in the faith. Francis found them ignorant of everything except that they were Christians. He left Goa late in the autumn of the year in which he arrived in India. We shall first give the letters in which he relates his mode of proceeding to St. Ignatius and his brothers at Rome, and then add what is known of his life at this period from other sources.

[1] Turselline, lib. ii. c. 5.

[2] Bartoli (*Asia*, t. i. lib. i. p. 49) tells us that the first Paravas who were baptized at Cochin were seventy in number. The Mussulmans, he adds, sent in alarm to Cochin to offer a large sum of money to the Portuguese, in hopes of buying them off, but the officer in command refused to traffic with the souls of the Paravas. After the defeat of the Mussulmans as many as twenty thousand, the inhabitants of thirty villages, became Christians.

(XIII.) *To the Reverend Father Ignatius, General of the Society, at Rome.*

May the grace and charity of Christ our Lord always help and favour us! Amen.

I wrote you a long letter from Goa about our voyage from Portugal to India. Now, because such is your wish, my best and sweetest Father, I will give you a little account of my expedition to Cape Comorin.

I set out with several native students from the Seminary at Goa, who have been under instruction, ever since their early youth, in the ceremonies of the Church, and are now in minor orders. We went through all the villages of the converts who were made Christians a few years ago. This country is too barren and poor for the Portuguese to live in, and the Christian inhabitants here have had no priests; they just know that they are Christians and nothing more. There is no one to say mass for them; no one to teach them the Creed, the Pater, the Ave Maria, and the Ten Commandments of God. So I have been incessantly occupied ever since I came here. I went diligently through the villages one after another, and baptized all the children who had not yet been baptized. In this way I have christened a multitude of children who, as the saying is, did not know their right hand from their left. Then the young boys would never let me say office, or eat, or sleep, till I had taught them some prayer. It made me understand for the first time that 'of such is the Kingdom of Heaven.'[3] Their petition was too pious for me to refuse it without impiety, so I began with the profession of belief in the Father, Son, and Holy Ghost,[4] and then taught them the Apostles' Creed, the Pater Noster, and the Ave Maria. I have found very great intelligence among them: and if they had any one to instruct them in religion, I doubt not they would turn out excellent Christians.

[3] Latin in the original: *talium esse regnum cœlorum.*

[4] That is, the sign of the Cross, with the words which usually accompany it.

One day I turned out of my road into a village of heathens, where no one was willing to become Christian, though all the neighbouring villages had been converted, because they said that the lord of their territory, a heathen, had forbidden his people to do so. There was there a woman with child, who had been three days in labour with so much difficulty, that many despaired of her life. Their prayers for her were not heard, for the prayer of the wicked is an abomination in the eyes of God, because the gods of the heathen are all devils.[5] I went, with one of my companions, to the sick woman's house, and began with confidence to call upon the Name of the Lord,[6] forgetting that I was in a strange land. I thought of that text, 'The earth is the Lord's and the fulness thereof, the compass of the world and all that dwell therein.'[7] So I began, through an interpreter, to explain to her the articles of our religion; and by the mercy of God, this woman believed what we taught her. At last I asked her whether she wished to be a Christian. She replied that she would, and gladly. Then I recited a Gospel over her—it was the first time, I suppose, that such words had been heard in those countries. I duly gave her Baptism. Not to make a long story, immediately after Baptism this good soul, who had put her hope in Christ,[8] and believed, was delivered of her child; and I afterwards baptized her husband, his children, the infant (on the day of its birth), and all the family. The whole village was soon full of the news of the miracle which God had wrought in that house. I went to the chiefs and bade them in the Name of God to acknowledge His Son Jesus Christ, in Whom alone the salvation of all mortals is placed. They said they could not venture to leave the religion of their ancestors without the permission of their master. Then I went to the steward of this chief, who happened to be there to exact some taxes due

[5] *quoniam omnes dii gentium dæmonia.* (Orig.)

[6] *invocare nomen Domini.* (Orig.)

[7] *Domini est terra et plenitudo ejus, orbis terrarum, et universi qui habitant in eo.* (Orig.)

[8] *quæ in Christo speravit et credidit.* (Orig.)

to his lord. When he had heard me speak about religion, he declared that he thought it a good thing to be a Christian, and that he gave leave to all who liked it to embrace the religion of Jesus Christ. But though he gave this good advice to others he did not practise it himself. However, the chief people of the place, with their whole households, were the first to embrace the faith, the rest followed their example, and so all, of every class and every age, received Baptism. This work done, we went straight to Tuticorin. The people there received us very kindly, and we have begun to hope that we shall reap an abundant harvest of souls in these parts.

The Governor is wonderfully fond of and kind to these converts, and not long ago gave them help against the Mussulmans who were annoying them. Most of them are fishermen living on the coast, and supporting themselves and their families by the fishery, chiefly of pearls. The Mussulmans had lately carried off the barks which they use in this fishery. When the Governor heard this, he attacked the Mussulmans with a strong squadron, defeated them with great slaughter, and took away all their ships.[9] He gave the richer converts their own barks back again, and made the poorer presents of the Mussulmans' boats, thus crowning his victory by a signal act of generosity. He himself had had experience of the assistance of God in his victory, and he wished to let the Chris-

[9] The Portuguese annals of India relate two expeditions of Martin Alfonso de Sousa, which may possibly have included this act of justice in favour of the Paravas, but the dates are not distinctly given. It was probably in 1542, the same year in which Francis Xavier first went among the Paravas, that the Governor with a large force went to Batecalà, a city in the territory of Canara, 'about 25 leagues from Goa' to the south (Baldæus), the queen of which was accused of refusing to pay her tribute and of harbouring pirates. The town was taken, and the Portuguese began to quarrel among themselves for the plunder. This encouraged the enemy, who put the Portuguese to flight, after which the Governor in revenge burnt the city and 'destroyed' the country. 'The city ran with the blood of all living creatures of both sexes and all ages, before it was burnt, and the country was laid waste and all the woods cut down' (Faria y Sousa, t. ii. p. i. ch. xi.). Later on, and probably in 1543 or 1544, the Governor must have sailed along the Malabar and Fishery Coasts with a fleet of 45 sail, with which he had intended to attack and plunder a famous Pagoda in the kingdom of Bisnaghur, not far from Meliapor, called Tremele. It is said

tians experience his own great kindness in their turn. The Mussulmans are quite cast down, and in a state of prostration. Not a man amongst them dares raise his eyes. Every one of their chiefs has been slain, and indeed every one else among them who seemed to be at all powerful. On account of all this the converts love the Governor as a father, and he on his side looks on them as his children. I can hardly tell you how earnestly he commended this newly planted vineyard of our Lord to my care. He has now got a grand plan in view which will be a matter for history to note as well as a great benefit to religion. He thinks of collecting all these native Christians who are now scattered at great distances from each other, of transplanting them to a certain island, and giving them a King to administer justice and look after their safety and interests. I am very sure that if the Holy Father only knew what great pains this Governor of India takes to advance religion, he would give him some mark of his approval for his very great diligence and exertions in the holy cause. So, if you think good, you might manage that the Holy Father should write to him to tell him how much he is delighted with his services. I do not mean that he should commend the converts to his care, for no one can have that matter more at heart than he has already, but rather that he should praise and thank this very

---

that this assault was ordered by the King of Portugal himself, in revenge for some ravages on territory friendly to him—it may be ravages such as those of the Badages, of whom we shall hear in the next chapter—but it is probable that the great richness of the heathen shrine was a part of the attraction. The attempt was abandoned, as the design was betrayed and discovered. Then, as Faria y Sousa tells us, the Governor was persuaded to plunder other pagodas instead of that which he had failed to surprize, and he actually despoiled a pagoda at Tebelicate near Calecoulan, which must have been in the territory of Travancore or one of the neighbouring kingdoms. A large sum of money taken from this pagoda was sent to Portugal, and afterwards restored by order of the King, who disapproved of the breach of faith. It is quite possible that in either of these expeditions Sousa may have taken the opportunity to humble the Mussulman oppressors of the Paravas in the way mentioned by St. Francis, and to do it would have cost him so little, as there is no mention of any Mussulman force on the spot, that it would hardly seem an exploit worthy of mention to the Portuguese annalists.

religious ruler as he deserves to be praised and thanked for taking so much care of the interests of the faith, and for watching so solicitously over the flock of Christ, lest any part of it be torn to pieces and destroyed by those wolves of heathen. And I would have you write to him yourself at all events, for I know how delightful your letter will be to him. And at the same time pray God for him, you and all the Society, that He may grant him His Divine assistance, and the grace of perseverance in his good beginnings. For it is not he who has begun well, but he who shall persevere to the end, who will be saved.[10]

As for myself, trusting in the infinite goodness of God and in your sacrifices and prayers as in those of all the Society, I hope that we shall see one another again, if not in this life, at least in that blessed life which is to come, whose joys far surpass all that we could have here.

Your child in Christ,

FRANCIS.

Tuticorin (in the Spring of 1543).[11]

The next letter, which is much fuller in its account of the mission among the Paravas, seems to have been written at the end of the same year (1543), after St. Francis had taken Francis Mancias back with him from Goa to help him in the

[10] *qui perseveraverit usque ad finem, hic salvus erit.* (Orig.)

[11] The date of this letter is differently given by the two authorities Turselline and Cutillas. It cannot have been written in October 1542, as Turselline states, as it is clear that the writer had been some months in the country—he says that he had spent four months in translating the Catechism, &c.—and Francis Xavier did not probably leave Goa before September 1542. Cutillas, who has altered a great many dates without giving his authority, gives for this date, May 23, 1543. He was a careful writer, and had many opportunities of ascertaining the truth, as there were several copies of the Letters, and in some cases, perhaps, the originals, at Madrid, where he wrote. In not giving his authority, as is now the custom, he only did what was usual in his time. If the letter was written towards the end of May, and the expedition of Martin Alfonso Sousa, mentioned in the last note, may be fixed for the year 1543, it would be very natural for St. Francis, writing at Tuticorin, to mention any act of protection to the Paravas which had taken place. He tells us himself above (p. 141) that the military expeditions usually took place in the time of Lent.

work. Francis probably had some occasion to go as far north as Cochin, whence the letter is dated.

(XIV.) *To the Society at Rome.*

May the grace and charity of Christ our Lord always help and favour us! Amen.

It is now the third year since I left Portugal. I am writing to you for the third time, having as yet received only one letter from you, dated February 1542. God is my witness what joy it caused me. I only received it two months ago—later than is usual for letters to reach India, because the vessel which brought it had passed the winter at Mozambique.

I and Francis Mancias are now living amongst the Christians of Comorin. They are very numerous, and increase largely every day. When I first came I asked them, if they knew anything about our Lord Jesus Christ? but when I came to the points of faith in detail and asked them what they thought of them, and what more they believed now than when they were Infidels, they only replied that they were Christians, but that as they are ignorant of Portuguese, they know nothing of the precepts and mysteries of our holy religion. We could not understand one another, as I spoke Castilian and they Malabar; so I picked out the most intelligent and well read of them, and then sought out with the greatest diligence men who knew both languages. We held meetings for several days, and by our joint efforts and with infinite difficulty we translated the Catechism into the Malabar tongue. This I learnt by heart, and then I began to go through all the villages of the coast, calling around me by the sound of a bell as many as I could, children and men. I assembled them twice a day and taught them the Christian doctrine: and thus, in the space of a month, the children had it well by heart. And all the time I kept telling them to go on teaching in their turn whatever they had learnt to their parents, family, and neighbours.

Every Sunday I collected them all, men and women, boys

and girls, in the church. They came with great readiness and with a great desire for instruction. Then, in the hearing of all, I began by calling on the name of the most holy Trinity, Father, Son, and Holy Ghost, and I recited aloud the Lord's Prayer, the *Hail Mary*, and the Creed in the language of the country: they all followed me in the same words, and delighted in it wonderfully. Then I repeated the Creed by myself, dwelling upon each article singly. Then I asked them as to each article, whether they believed it unhesitatingly; and all, with a loud voice and their hands crossed over their breasts, professed aloud that they truly believed it. I take care to make them repeat the Creed oftener than the other prayers; and I tell them that those who believe all that is contained therein are called Christians. After explaining the Creed I go on to the Commandments, teaching them that the Christian law is contained in those ten precepts, and that every one who observes them all faithfully is a good and true Christian and is certain of eternal salvation, and that, on the other hand, whoever neglects a single one of them is a bad Christian, and will be cast into hell unless he is truly penitent for his sin. Converts and heathen alike are astonished at all this, which shows them the holiness of the Christian law, its perfect consistency with itself, and its agreement with reason. After this I recite our principal prayers, as the *Our Father* and the *Hail Mary*, and they say them after me. Then we go back to the Creed, adding the *Our Father* and the *Hail Mary* after each article, with a short hymn; for, as soon as I have recited the first article, I sing in their language, '*Jesus, Son of the living God, grant us the grace to believe firmly this first article of your faith: and that we may obtain this from you, we offer you this prayer taught us by yourself.*' Then we add this second invocation: '*Holy Mary, Mother of our Lord Jesus Christ, obtain for us from your most sweet Son that we may believe without hesitation this article of the Christian faith.*' We do the same after all the other eleven articles.

We teach them the Commandments in the following way. After we have sung the first, which enjoins the love of God, we pray thus: '*Jesus Christ, Son of the living God, grant us the grace to love Thee above all things;*' and then we say for this intention the Lord's Prayer. Then we all sing together, '*Holy Mary, Mother of Jesus Christ, obtain for us from your Son the grace to observe perfectly the first of His Commandments;*' and then we say the *Hail Mary*. So we go on through the other nine, changing the words of our little invocation as occasion requires. Thus I accustom them to ask for these graces with the ordinary prayers of the Church, and I tell them at the same time that if they obtain them, they will have all other things that they can wish for more abundantly than they would be able to ask for them. I make them all, and particularly those who are to be baptized, repeat the form of general confession. These last I question after each article of the Creed as it is recited, whether they believe it firmly; and after they have answered yes, I give them an instruction in their own language explaining the chief heads of the Christian religion, and the duties necessary to salvation. Last of all, I admit them thus prepared to baptism. The instruction is ended by the *Salve Regina*, begging the aid and help of our Blessed Lady.

As to the numbers who become Christians, you may understand them from this, that it often happens to me to be hardly able to use my hands from the fatigue of baptizing: often in a single day I have baptized whole villages. Sometimes I have lost my voice and strength altogether with repeating again and again the Credo and the other forms.

The fruit that is reaped by the baptism of infants, as well as by the instruction of children and others, is quite incredible. These children, I trust heartily, by the grace of God, will be much better than their fathers. They show an ardent love for the Divine law, and an extraordinary zeal for learning our holy religion and imparting it to others. Their hatred for idolatry is marvellous. They get into feuds with the heathen about it, and whenever their own parents practise it, they reproach them and come off to tell me at once. Whenever I hear of any act of idolatrous worship, I go to the place with a large band of these children, who very soon load the devil with a greater amount of insult and abuse than he has lately received of honour and worship from their parents, relations, and acquaintances. The children run at the idols, upset them, dash them down, break them to pieces, spit on them, trample on them, kick them about, and in short heap on them every possible outrage.

I had been living for nearly four months in a Christian village, occupied in translating the Catechism. A great number of natives came from all parts to entreat me to take the trouble to go to their houses and call on God by the bedsides of their sick relatives. Such numbers also of sick made their own way to us, that I had enough to do to read a Gospel[12] over each of them. At the same time we kept on with our daily work, instructing the children, baptizing converts, translating the Catechism, answering difficulties, and burying the dead. For my part I desired to satisfy all, both the sick who came to me themselves, and those who came to beg on the part of others, lest if I did not, their confidence in, and zeal for, our holy religion should relax, and I thought it wrong not to do what I could in answer to their prayers. But the thing grew to such a pitch that it was impossible for me myself to satisfy all, and at the same time to avoid their quarrelling among themselves, every one striving to be the first to get me to his own house; so I hit on a way of serving all at once. As I could not go myself, I sent round children whom I could trust in my place. They went to the sick persons, assembled their families and neighbours, recited the Creed with them, and encouraged the sufferers to conceive a certain and wellfounded confidence of their restoration. Then after all this, they recited the prayers of the Church. To make my tale short, God was moved by

[12] 'to read a Gospel,' *i.e.* a passage from the Gospel, usually the passage from the first chapter of St. John, which is read at the end of mass (St. John i. 1-14). This it was and is customary to read over the sick, as a profession of faith in the Incarnation. Another custom of the same kind is the carrying about the person a copy of this passage of the Gospel, in the same way as an *Agnus Dei* or a scapular. The Ritual for the Visitation of the Sick contains a number of such portions of the Gospel, interspersed with appropriate prayers, which may be read over the sick; and St. Francis may probably mean any one of these when he speaks of 'a Gospel' in the text.

the faith and piety of these children and of the others, and restored to a great number of sick persons health both of body and soul. How good He was to them! He made the very disease of their bodies the occasion of calling them to salvation, and drew them to the Christian faith almost by force!

I have also charged these children to teach the rudiments of Christian doctrine to the ignorant in private houses, in the streets, and the crossways. As soon as I see that this has been well started in one village, I go on to another and give the same instructions and the same commission to the children, and so I go through in order the whole number of their villages. When I have done this and am going away, I leave in each place a copy of the Christian doctrine, and tell all those who know how to write to copy it out, and all the others are to learn it by heart and to recite it from memory every day. Every feast day I bid them meet in one place and sing all together the elements of the faith. For this purpose I have appointed in each of the thirty Christian villages men of intelligence and character who are to preside over these meetings, and the Governor, Don Martin Alfonso, who is so full of love for our Society and of zeal for religion, has been good enough at our request to allot a yearly revenue of 4000 gold *fanams* for the salary of these catechists. He has an immense friendship for ours, and desires with all his heart that some of them should be sent hither, for which he is always asking in his letters to the King.

There is now in these parts a very large number of persons who have only one reason for not becoming Christian, and that is that there is no one to make them Christians. It often comes into my mind to go round all the Universities of Europe, and especially that of Paris, crying out every where like a madman, and saying to all the learned men there whose learning is so much greater than their charity, '*Ah! what a multitude of souls is through your fault shut out of heaven and falling into hell!*'[13] Would to God that these men who labour so much

[13] In Latin in the original: *Heu, quam ingens animorum numerus vestro vitio exclusus cœlo deturbatur ad inferos!*

in gaining knowledge would give as much thought to the account they must one day give to God of the use they have made of their learning and of the talents entrusted to them! I am sure that many of them would be moved by such considerations, would exercise themselves in fitting meditations on Divine truths, so as to hear what God might say to them,[14] and then, renouncing their ambitions and desires, and all the things of the world, they would form themselves wholly according to God's desire and choice for them. They would exclaim from the bottom of their hearts: '*Lord, here am I; send me whithersoever it shall please Thee, even to India!*'[15] Good God! how much happier and how much safer they would be! With what far greater confidence in God's mercy would they meet their last hour, the supreme trial of that terrible judgment which no man can escape! They would then be able joyfully to use the words of the faithful servant in the Gospel: '*Lord, Thou gavest me five talents; behold, I have gained beside them other five!*'[16] They labour night and day in acquiring knowledge, and they are very diligent indeed in understanding the subjects which they study; but if they would spend as much time in that which is the fruit of all solid learning, and be as diligent in teaching to the ignorant the things necessary to salvation, they would be far better prepared to give an account of themselves to our Lord when He shall say to them: '*Give an account of thy stewardship.*'[17] I fear much that these men, who spend so many years in the Universities in studying the liberal arts, look more to the empty honours and dignities of the prelature than to the holy functions and obligations of which those honours are the trappings. It has come to this pass, as I see, that the men who are the most diligent in the higher branches of study, commonly make profession that they hope to gain some high post in the Church by their reputation for learning, therein to be able to serve our Lord and His Church. But all the time they deceive

[14] *ut audirent quid in eis loqueretur Dominus.* (Orig.)

[15] *Domine, ecce adsum; mitte me quocunque tibi cordi est, vel usque in Indiam.* (Orig.)

[16] St. Matt. xxv. 20.

[17] *Redde rationem villicationis tuæ.* (Orig.)

themselves miserably, for their studies are far more directed to their own advantage than to the common good. They are afraid that God may not second their ambition, and this is the reason why they will not leave the whole matter to His holy will. I declare to God that I had almost made up my mind, since I could not return to Europe myself, to write to the University of Paris, and especially to our worthy Professors Cornet and Picard, and to show them how many thousands of infidels might be made Christians without trouble, if we had only men here who would seek, not their own advantage, but the things of Jesus Christ. And therefore, dearest brothers, 'pray ye the Lord of the harvest that He send forth labourers into His harvest.'[18]

I wrote to you a year ago about the College which has been begun at Goa, and which is being built with dispatch. A considerable part of the building is already finished. A great number of pagan youths of different nations are taught there. Some learn Latin, others to read and write. Father Paul is their Superior as Rector of the College. He says mass for them every day, hears their confessions, and gives them religious instruction continually. The College is very large, it will hold as many as five hundred students, and has revenues enough for their support. Great sums of money are given to it as alms by many persons, and especially by the Governor. And well indeed may all Christians give thanks to God for this seminary, which is called the College of Santa Fé: for we hope that within a few years multitudes of heathens will by God's favour have become Christians, and that the pupils of this College will shortly be the means of extending the limits of the Church far and wide in the whole East.

We have in these parts a class of men among the pagans who are called Brahmins. They keep up the worship of the gods, the superstitious rites of religion, frequenting the temples and taking care of the idols. They are as perverse and wicked a set as can anywhere be found, and I always apply to them the words of holy David, '*from an unholy race and a wicked*

[18] *orate Dominum messis ut mittat operarios in messem suam.* (Orig.)

and crafty man deliver me, O Lord.'[19] They are liars and cheats to the very backbone. Their whole study is, how to deceive most cunningly the simplicity and ignorance of the people. They give out publicly that the gods command certain offerings to be made to their temples, which offerings are simply the things that the Brahmins themselves wish for, for their own maintenance and that of their wives, children, and servants. Thus they make the poor folk believe that the images of their gods eat and drink, dine and sup like men, and some devout persons are found who really offer to the idol twice a day, before dinner and supper, a certain sum of money. The Brahmins eat sumptuous meals to the sound of drums, and make the ignorant believe that the gods are banqueting. When they are in need of any supplies, and even before, they give out to the people that the gods are angry because the things they have asked for have not been sent, and that if the people do not take care, the gods will punish them by slaughter, disease, and the assaults of the devils. And the poor ignorant creatures, with the fear of the gods before them, obey them implicitly. These Brahmins have barely a tincture of literature, but they make up for their poverty in learning by cunning and malice. Those who belong to these parts are very indignant with me for exposing their tricks. Whenever they talk to me with no one by to hear them they acknowledge that they have no other patrimony but the idols, by their lies about which they procure their support from the people. They say that I, poor creature as I am, know more than all of them put together. They often send me a civil message and presents, and make a great complaint when I send them all back again. Their object is to bribe me to connive at their evil deeds. So they declare that they are convinced that there is only one God, and that they will pray to Him for me. And I, to return the favour, answer whatever occurs to me, and then lay bare, as far as I can, to the ignorant people whose blind superstitions have made them their slaves, their imposture and tricks, and this has induced many to leave the worship of the false gods, and

[19] Psalm xlii. 1.

eagerly become Christians. If it were not for the opposition of the Brahmins, we should have them all embracing the religion of Jesus Christ.

The heathen inhabitants of the country are commonly ignorant of letters, but by no means ignorant of wickedness. All the time I have been here in this country I have only converted one Brahmin, a virtuous young man, who has now undertaken to teach the Catechism to children. As I go through the Christian villages, I often pass by the temples of the Brahmins, which they call pagodas. One day lately, I happened to enter a pagoda where there were about two hundred of them, and most of them came to meet me. We had a long conversation, after which I asked them what their gods enjoined them in order to obtain the life of the blessed. There was a long discussion amongst them as to who should answer me. At last, by common consent, the commission was given to one of them, of greater age and experience than the rest, an old man, of more than eighty years. He asked me in return, what commands the God of the Christians laid on them. I saw the old man's perversity, and I refused to speak a word till he had first answered my question. So he was obliged to expose his ignorance, and replied that their gods required two duties of those who desired to go to them hereafter, one of which was to abstain from killing cows, because under that form the gods were adored; the other was to show kindness to the Brahmins, who were the worshippers of the gods.[20] This answer moved my indignation, for I could not but grieve intensely at the thought of the devils being worshipped instead of God by these blind heathen, and I asked them to listen to me in turn. Then I, in a loud voice, repeated the Apostles' Creed and the Ten Commandments. After this I gave in their own language a short explanation, and told them what Paradise is, and what Hell is, and also who they are who go to Heaven to join the company of the blessed, and who are to be sent to the eternal punishments of hell. Upon hearing these things they

[20] *primum, ut abstinerent cæde vaccarum, quarum specie dii colerentur; deinde, ut Brachmanis deorum cultoribus benigne facerent.* (Orig.)

all rose up and vied with one another in embracing me, and in confessing that the God of the Christians is the true God, as His laws are so agreeable to reason. Then they asked me if the souls of men like those of other animals perished together with the body.[21] God put into my mouth arguments of such a sort, and so suited to their ways of thinking, that to their great joy I was able to prove to them the immortality of the soul. I find, by the way, that the arguments which are to convince these ignorant people must by no means be subtle, such as those which are found in the books of learned schoolmen, but must be such as their minds can understand. They asked me again how the soul of a dying person goes out of the body, how it was, whether it was as happens to us in dreams, when we seem to be conversing with our friends and acquaintance? (Ah, how often this happens to me, dearest brothers, when I am dreaming of you!) Was this because the soul then leaves the body? And again, whether God was black or white?[22] For as there is so great a variety of colour among men, and the Indians being black themselves, consider their own colour the best, they believe that their gods are black. On this account the great majority of their idols are as black as black can be, and moreover are generally so rubbed over with oil as to smell detestably, and seem to be as dirty as they are ugly and horrible to look at. To all these questions I was able to reply so as to satisfy them entirely. But when I came to the point at last, and urged them to embrace the religion which they felt to be true, they made that same objection which we hear from many Christians when urged to change their life, —that they would set men talking about them if they altered their ways and their religion, and besides, they said that they should be afraid that, if they did so, they would have nothing to live on and support themselves by.

[21] *num animus hominum, item ut cæterorum animantium, simul cum corpore interisset.* (Orig.)

[22] *quà morientis animus exiret? qui fieret? ut in somnis cum amicis notisque versari nobis videamur? num quia animus exiliat a corpore? denique, albusne an ater sit Deus?* (Orig.)

I have found just one Brahmin and no more in all this coast who is a man of learning: he is said to have studied in a very famous Academy. Knowing this, I took measures to converse with him alone. He then told me at last, as a great secret, that the students of this Academy are at the outset made by their masters to take an oath not to reveal their mysteries,[23] but that, out of friendship for me, he would disclose them to me. One of these mysteries was that there only exists one God, the Creator and Lord of heaven and earth, whom men are bound to worship, for the idols are simply images of devils.[24] The Brahmins have certain books of sacred literature which contain, as they say, the laws of God. The masters teach in a learned tongue, as we do in Latin. He also explained to me these divine precepts one by one; but it would be a long business to write out his commentary, and indeed not worth the trouble. Their sages keep as a feast our Sunday. On this day they repeat at different hours this one prayer: 'I adore Thee, O God; and I implore Thy help for ever.'[25] They are bound by oath to repeat this prayer frequently, and in a low voice. My friend added, that the law of nature permitted them to have more wives than one, and their sacred books predicted that the time would come when all men should embrace the same religion.[26] After all this he asked me in my turn to explain the principal mysteries of the Christian religion, promising to keep them secret. I replied, that I would not tell him a word about them unless he promised beforehand to publish abroad what I should tell him of the religion of Jesus Christ. He made the promise, and then I carefully explained to him those words of Jesus Christ in which our religion is

[23] *primum omnium illius Academiæ discipulos a magistris adigi sacramento, ne ipsorum mysteria enuncient.* (Orig.)

[24] *unum esse Deum, cœli terræque conditorem ac dominum, illumque ab ipsis coli oportere; nam idola nihil aliud esse quam dæmonum simulacra.* (Orig.)

[25] *Veneror te, Deus, tuamque opem in perpetuum imploro.* (Orig.)

[26] *uxorum multitudinem ipsis naturæ lege permitti; atque in suis litterarum monumentis esse, tempus aliquando fore, cum mortales omnes unam religionem amplecterentur.* (Orig.)

summed up: 'He who believes and is baptized shall be saved.'[27] This text, with my commentary on it, which embraced the whole of the Apostles' Creed, he wrote down carefully, as well as the Commandments, on account of their close connection with the Creed. He told me also that one night he had dreamt that he had been made a Christian to his immense delight, and that he had become my brother and companion. He ended by begging me to make him a Christian secretly. But as he made certain conditions opposed to right and justice, I put off his baptism. I don't doubt but that by God's mercy he will one day be a Christian. I charged him to teach the ignorant and unlearned that there is only one God, Creator of heaven and earth;[28] but he pleaded the obligation of his oath, and said he could not do so, especially as he was much afraid that if he did it he should become possessed by an evil spirit.

And now I have nothing more to tell you except that so great is the intensity and abundance of the joy which God is accustomed to bestow upon those workmen of His vineyard who labour diligently in cultivating this barbarous part of the same, that for my part I do really believe that if there is in this life any true and solid happiness, it is here. It often happens to me to hear one whose lot it is to labour in this field cry out, '*O Lord, I beseech Thee overwhelm me not now in this life with so much delight, or at least, since in Thy boundless goodness and mercy Thou dost so overwhelm me, take me away to the abode of the blessed. For any one who has once known what it is to taste in his soul Thy ineffable sweetness must of necessity think it very bitter to live any longer without seeing Thee face to face.*'[29]

It is one of my greatest consolations, dearest brethren, to think often of you, and to call to mind that sweet and tender intercourse with you which God of His immense goodness vouchsafed to me of old. At the same time it makes me think

[27] *Qui crediderit et baptizatus fuerit salvus erit.* (Orig.)

[28] *unum esse Deum, cœli terræque procreatorem, regnantem in cœlo.* (Orig.)

[29] *Quæso te, Domine, noli me tanta lætitia perfundere in hac vita, aut certe quando pro tua infinita bonitate ac misericordia perfundis, transfer me in domicilium beatorum. Siquidem, qui tuam semel dulcedinem interiore gustavit sensu, vitam sine tuo aspectu acerbam putet, necesse est.* (Orig.)

over and feel very keenly, how much precious time I then spent uselessly, and gathered so little fruit from your holy example and conversation, and from your knowledge of the things of God. However, I owe it to your prayers for me that God has given me the blessing, absent as I am from you in the body, of having, by means of your care and intercession for me, the infinite number of my sins shown to me from God, and of having courage and strength given me to cultivate with all diligence the soil of heathendom. Endless thanks to God's goodness, and to your charity!

Among the many great blessings of my life past and present, and for which I have to thank the mercy of God, I count it as the greatest that I have heard the tidings of the approbation and confirmation of our Institute by the Holy Father. I give God endless thanks that He has now at last ordained to be publicly ratified by His Vicar, so as to be remembered by posterity for ever, that same rule of life which He Himself laid down in secret to His servant our Father Ignatius.

Here, then, I will leave off writing, begging of God that since in His goodness He has united us in a common way of life, and then has separated us so widely for the good of the Christian religion, so also He will be pleased to bring us together again in the abode and home of the Blessed. That He may grant us this grace, let us, if you will, plead the prayers, among others, of the infants and children whom I have baptized with my own hand, here, and whom God has called away to His mansions in heaven before they had lost their robe of innocence. They are, I think, more than a thousand in number, and I pray to them over and over again, begging that they will obtain for us from God that for what remains of this life, or rather of this time of exile, He will teach us to do His will, and to do it so completely as to accomplish all that He requires of us exactly as He Himself desires it to be done.

FRANCIS.

From Cochin, Dec. 31, 1543.

These two letters are all that remain to us from St. Francis himself as to what we may call the first period of his preaching among the native Indians. It appears that at first he had no one with him but the young students from the College of St. Paul or Santa Fé as his companions: Mancias and Father Paul of Camerino had not arrived from Mozambique at the time of his sailing for Tuticorin. He must probably have returned to Goa after some months among the Paravas, during which visit he might have written, at the request of the Governor, the letters given in the last chapter concerning the indulgences and other spiritual favours to be asked for from the Holy Father. He then returned to the Fishery Coast, taking with him Mancias, and leaving Father Paul of Camerino as Superior at the College. As the very interesting series of letters to Mancias which we shall have to give in the next chapter does not begin till the March of 1544, we must suppose that up to that time Mancias was his companion, and was being trained up for work by himself. He was not as yet a priest. The lives of St. Francis, which, as has been said, are derived from the processes taken in India and elsewhere with a view to his canonization,—processes which were begun almost as soon as his death was known in Europe,—now become our guides, giving us a great amount of information supplementary to that which the letters disclose either openly or by implication. A careful consideration indeed of the letters, if it be enlightened by a knowledge of the manner in which the chosen servants of God who are called to the Apostolic ministry are assisted by Him on the one hand, and are wont to imitate our Lord in casting a veil over their own great gifts on the other, will prove to us that there is hardly a single feature, however marvellous, in the narratives of other writers concerning this period of the life of St. Francis, which may not be traced in some way or degree in his own account of his proceedings given to his brethren at Rome and St. Ignatius, his father and Superior. The whole picture, when duly combined, gives us a very clear insight indeed into the conditions under which his ministry was carried on, and enables us to understand his marvellous success.

It must always be borne in mind that the natives to whom St. Francis was originally sent, the pearlfishers of the Comorin coast, were already nominally Christians. They had, as we have said, been baptized and very partially instructed some years before by Miguel Vaz and others; but the hardships and dangers of a life among them in a part of the country which was very poor and unhealthy, and where there were no Portuguese settlements or garrisons—except, it would seem, at Tuticorin and one or two other places—were too great for the courage of the ordinary Portuguese priests, who besides had plenty of occupation among their own countrymen in the garrisoned cities and forts along the coast. The work was preeminently a work which called for an Apostle, a man who would combine the heroic selfdevotion which was required for the full instruction of these poor natives, with the organizing power necessary for the establishment of a perfect system of religious teaching and administration of the sacraments among them, in so much completeness and fulness of growth as to stand by itself after he had left the spot for other fields of labour.

The beginnings, as the letters inform us, were toilsome and slow. The circumstances under which the Paravas had embraced Christianity naturally directed the attention of Francis Xavier to the children, in the first instance, as the best hopes for the future, and it was his principle, as we have seen in his work at Goa, to attach immense importance to elementary instruction, catechizing, and the like. His first occupation, however, was the simple act of charity to go about and baptize the infants who were as yet unbaptized; and to this, and to the care of the sick, the dying, and the dead, we find him afterwards recurring when he found himself from time to time unable to communicate with the people around him on account of ignorance of their language. Then came the great labour of translating the Catechism into the Malabar tongue, which he tells us occupied him and his catechists for as much as four months. The next step was to learn the new Catechism by heart, and to go from one village to another teaching the simple elements of Christian doctrine in the native language. We may well magine with what bright affectionateness and gentle condescension the Saint made his way to the hearts of the swarms of

Indian children who gathered around him, who soon began to take so important a share in his missionary work, and whose prayers he constantly solicited when about to incur any extraordinary danger. After a little time, as he tells St. Ignatius, the children would not leave him alone; he had no time after his daily rounds and course of teaching to say his office, take his slight repast of rice and water, or the scanty rest which he allowed himself.[30] They were never tired of learning prayers from his mouth. His evenings were also devoted to receiving visits of persons who had any questions to ask him or wished to consult him, and it was then too that he attended to such matters as bringing about reconciliations or rectifying irregular marriages.

The account given in the letters which we have last inserted of his method of catechizing tallies exactly with a paper drawn up by him for the instruction of the catechists of the Society in India, which was long preserved in the archives of the College at Goa. The catechist is to begin with the sign of the Cross, and two boys are to repeat in a loud clear voice the *Pater Noster* (in the native language) after him. Then he is to invite the people to profess their faith and make acts of the three great theological virtues—Faith, Hope, and Charity. The exercise of faith consists in the *Credo*, which is to be gone through, the people being asked whether they firmly believe each truth, and then praying to our Lord and His Blessed

[30] The Processes relate that St. Francis was in the habit of abstaining not only from flesh and wine, but even from wheaten bread, except when he was being entertained by others. (For this they quote the witnesses examined on oath at Goa and Bazain.) The same witnesses testify that he used to manage that what food he took was not well prepared—'insulse conditus.' He took food only once a day, and made no difference whether he was journeying or not. He usually went on foot, and without shoes, living only on roasted rice, which he begged as he went on. These facts are stated on the evidence taken at Cochin and Bazain. Massei tells us (also from the Processes) that on certain feasts he would have a cake made of rice, and exhort his companions to thank God for such delicacies, and take what was necessary to support them in their labours for souls. He seldom slept more than four hours, giving the rest of the night to prayer or to visiting the sick, and he slept on the ground with a stone under his head. These facts all rest on the same authority.

Mother to give and obtain for them the grace to do so, reciting the *Pater Noster* and *Ave Maria.* In the paper just mentioned the *Credo* is summarized, rather than simply repeated article by article, the truths about our Lord and the Incarnation being grouped together, and at the end, after the people had professed their belief in the existence of Hell, Paradise, Purgatory, the sacraments, and all that is taught by the Church, the catechist instructs them to pray to the Holy Ghost for His seven gifts, those especially which can help them to believe the Catholic faith. Then follow an act of hope and an act of love and contrition. After this preliminary service, the catechist is to proceed to the explanation of some particular truth, or of some virtue, or one of the sacraments, or the doctrine of prayer, and the like, speaking very plainly and simply, and adding an 'example,' or story, at the end to illustrate the argument. Then he is to recite with the boys the form of general confession, bidding the people meantime make interior acts of contrition or sorrow for sin for the love of God, then three *Ave Marias* are to be recited, one for the absent, the others for any particular intention.

There can be no doubt that this paper, which is printed among the Letters of St. Francis Xavier by Poussines and Menchacha, represents to us quite faithfully the Saint's way of proceeding at those meetings of the converts. Perhaps when he or any other priest was present the conclusion would be different. The form is drawn up for the use of meetings in which the catechist was a layman. He tells us himself that he had appointed some one in each village to look after the further instruction and catechizing, and had obtained an allowance from the Governor for the payment of these persons. It was his method, as we shall see from his letters to Mancias, to be liberal to these schoolmasters or catechists, to pay them a part of their salary in advance, to encourage them in every way, at the same time letting them feel that they were carefully watched and must be on their guard not to fail in their duty. They were to baptize newborn infants, publish marriages, preside at the prayers, and perform other offices of the same kind. The four thousand *fanams* which St. Francis tells us were allotted by the Governor for the payment of these catechists or Canacapoli, as we find them called, seem to have been taken out of a sum paid out of the revenues of India for the expenses of the wardrobe of the Queen of Portugal, and was supposed to keep her Highness in slippers. Francis wrote to her to say that the prayers of the poor Paravas would be the best sort of slippers for her to mount up to Paradise in.[31]

Francis tells us in the letter to his brethren at Rome, that he left a copy of the *Christian Doctrine*, or Catechism, in each of the villages when he departed, which was to be copied out and frequently recited. This may perhaps mean only the form of which we have been lately speaking. But we possess a rather long explanation of the Apostles' Creed, which he composed two or three years later for the people of the Moluccas, and if this was not the identical statement of Doctrine which he used when among the Paravas, it is at all events a fair specimen of his teaching under this head, and probably differs from what he may have drawn up on the Fishery Coast only in being somewhat more elaborate. In this document he goes through the whole Creed, giving a full doctrinal and historical commentary, which is pointed, as it were, at the errors most likely to beset those for whose benefit it was made. Thus he begins with the Creation, and he points out how the fact that

[31] M. Léon-Pagès (*Lettres de S. François Xavier*, t. i. p. 83) tells us that the *fanais*, *fanes*, or *fanams* were the Indian gold coins, much alloyed, equal in value to 12 *reals* (about halfacrown). Four thousand of these would make 500*l*. sterling, a very large sum for the sixteenth century. We are almost inclined to suspect that Turselline's statement is right; he makes the money four hundred crowns. It is also not quite certain that there were not two allowances: one by the Governor, a gift of a certain sum, and another, a continuation of the same gift as an annual contribution from the Queen. Turselline says, 'This said money was accustomed to be paid to Queen Catharine of Portugal, to buy her shoes and pantofles. Wherefore Francis wrote unto her Majesty, very pleasantly and piously, that she could have no fitter shoes or pantofles to climb to heaven than the Christian children of the Piscarian coast, and their instructions. Therefore he humbly entreated her to bestow her shoes and pantofles, as a tribute, unto their teachers and instructors, thereby to make herself a ladder to heaven, for she might be glad of such an occasion, than the which she could not perhaps have wished a better' (L. ii, c. 8, p. 140).

God gave one wife to Adam shows the unlawfulness of polygamy, as well as of that miserable system of concubinage in which so many Christians in those countries indulged. He also speaks strongly in the same place against idolatry, superstition, dealing with the devil, and suchlike evils. Each article of the Creed is attributed by him to one of the Apostles, the first to St. Peter, the second to St. Andrew, and so on in order, according to an old tradition of which many traces remain to us. The fall of the Angels and the seduction of man are related immediately after the first article. The actual accomplishment of the Incarnation in the fulness of time is attributed immediately to the prayer made by St. Michael and the holy Angels who had remained faithful to God when Lucifer and his companions fell. After the article in which the birth of our Lord is spoken of, a tolerably full account of His life is given as an introduction to the Passion. After this St. Francis gives a short description of Limbus, Purgatory, and Hell, before speaking of the descent of our Lord. The mystery of the most holy Trinity is shortly explained before the article on the Holy Ghost, in connection with the sign of the Cross. The sacraments are spoken of under the head of the Communion of Saints and the Remission of sins.

These documents, when put by the side of what we know of the laborious manner in which St. Francis devoted himself to catechetical instruction everywhere, and especially whenever he found himself among people so ignorant and simple as the Paravas of the Fishery Coast, enable us to understand what we are told by missionaries of a later date with respect to the thorough knowledge of the Catholic faith which these Christians were found to possess, as if its doctrines had been engrained in their minds. But they do not explain to us, nor does anything that St. Francis Xavier himself tells us explain to us, other facts such as those which are hinted at in the longer of the two letters now before us, as to the immense crowds which came to place themselves under instruction and to receive baptism, or as to the extent to which he was besieged by requests to go to visit and pray over the sick. It is clear from his own account that his ministry was by no means limited to the instruction of the Paravas who had already received baptism, and of their children. Thousands of heathen were baptized, and the presence of the Father was required on all sides. What was the attraction that brought so many to his feet? What was it that made them so ready to believe that his prayers and blessing could benefit the sick, and so eager to fetch him to the bedside of any of their own relatives who were in danger of death? His own words to St. Ignatius, in that private and familiar letter which seems to have been meant for him alone, his 'best and sweetest Father,' partly lift the veil, for he there speaks of the miracle wrought upon the heathen woman, who was so safely delivered of her child immediately after baptism, in language the purport of which can hardly be mistaken. He could write to his own intimate friend and guide of such a miracle, because it was so closely connected with the administration of the Sacrament of regeneration, and he could attribute it, as our Lord attributed His own miracles, to the faith of the person on whom it was wrought: but, we need hardly add, it would surprize us quite as much to find him giving in other and more public letters, or even in this, a long catalogue of miracles which had attended and confirmed his preaching, however true the facts might have been, quite as much as it would surprize us to be told that multitudes of persons of various nations flocked to his preaching and believed him to be a teacher sent from God, who had power to heal the maladies of the body as well as to enlighten the soul, without having had some tangible ground for supposing that this belief was true.

There is, in fact, every fair reason for believing that the life of Francis Xavier began at this time to be adorned by that very frequent and splendid exercise of the gift of miracles which is from time to time imparted to the Saints, especially to those who have the Apostolical mission. None of the great Saints of God are probably left altogether without gifts of this kind, but they seem to be especially frequent, as, so far as we can judge of such questions, they are also especially natural, in the case of great Apostolic preachers, and this not only among the heathen. Few lives contain more illustrious examples of this great gift than those of St. Bernard, St. Anthony of Padua, and St. Vincent Ferrer, all of them great preachers among Christian nations, and St. Bernard's most marvellous period was while he was on his mission through certain parts of Europe to organize a crusade. Like another great gift, of a more interior kind, of which we shall have to speak presently—that of immense consolation and spiritual joy amid external sufferings and dangers—the gift of miracles seems to find its natural place in the case of the Saints who have to do exactly what the Apostles were sent to do, at the time when the signs that were to 'follow those who believe' were promised by our Lord—to 'go into the whole world and preach the Gospel to every creature.'[32] The Processes which were carefully formed in India after the death of Francis Xavier are abundant in their evidence as to the magnitude and multitude of his miracles, and they often speak particularly of those which took place on the Fishery Coast during this period of his preaching. We shall follow his former biographers in mentioning a few of these; but it must be remembered that when the gift of miracles has really existed, no account which is made up merely of selections from those particular instances as to which ocular and sworn witnesses happened to be at hand some years later, can possibly give any but a very inadequate idea. It is probable that as St. John protests at the end of his Gospel, that our Lord did many other signs 'which are not written in this book,' and that 'if all that He had done were written, the world itself would not contain the books which should be written,' so also the most copious collection of evidence that the most diligent inquiry can furnish will never give us a true picture of the daily marvels with which the active Apostolic life of some of the more miraculous Saints have been illustrated.[33]

[32] St. Mark xvi. 15.

[33] There are traces of times in the history of the Apostles when miracles must have been of daily and almost hourly occurrence; as when 'the sick were brought into the streets and laid on couches, that when Peter came, his shadow

We may begin by that which, in the case of the Apostles themselves, was the 'beginning of signs,' that is, the gift of tongues. Many misconceptions may be current as to the nature of this gift as imparted to the Apostles and others who have had to tread in their footsteps. Nor is there any reason for supposing that it always took the same form with them or with their contemporaries. The 'gift of tongues,' indeed, of which St. Paul speaks to the Corinthians and elsewhere, was not always precisely that gift which enabled the Apostles on the day of Pentecost to make themselves understood by men of so many different nations at once. The natural interpretation of the words of St. Luke (Acts ii. 4, 6) seems to be, that while the Apostles spoke with 'divers tongues,' 'every man heard them speak in his own tongue,' and that the miracle must have been twofold,—in the possession of new languages by the Apostles, and in the hearing of the multitude that came together, on whose ears the same sound fell in many different languages at once. We may add that no one, as far as we know, has ever supposed that the Apostles and their companions became necessarily possessed of all the different dialects enumerated by the sacred historian in such a manner as to have them at their command for the ordinary purposes of life, so as to have been able to read or write them, to compose books or catechisms in them, or to be in any way independent, where the particular occasions for the miraculous gift ceased, of the ordinary difficulties in intercourse with persons of different nations which are the results of the confusion of tongues. No one has ever supposed that, because St. Peter or St. Paul raised Tabitha or Eutychus to life, either of those Apostles had the power of raising every dead person they met with, or of preserving themselves from the natural doom of death. Both these remarks are necessary for the illustration of the evidence which has

---

at the least might overshadow any of them, and they might be delivered from their infirmities' (Acts v. 15); and in the case of St. Paul when God wrought by his hand 'more than the common miracles (δυνάμεις οὐ τὰς τυχούσας), and persons were healed and delivered from devils by the touch of 'handkerchiefs' that had touched him (Acts xix. 11, 12).

reached us as to the possession of the gift of tongues by St. Francis Xavier. This evidence witnesses to his having had the power of speaking freely and clearly in the dialects of the numerous different tribes among whom he preached in the south of India, and those of Cape Comorin and the Coromandel coast are particularly named. The same statement is made as to the Moluccas, and as to Japan. Altogether it is supposed that he must have had to preach to as many as thirty different nations, a number which will not seem surprizing when we remember that the witnesses are here speaking of tribes, with dialects of their own, as separate nations. It is particularly stated in the evidence that his possession of this gift was notorious, and that it was considered by the natives themselves as a mark of his mission from God, and this illustrates the words of St. Paul, that 'tongues are for a sign, not to believers, but to unbelievers.'[34] People were led to hear him and receive the truths which he preached by finding a man who could never have learnt their language addressing himself to them with ease, and by observing that bystanders whose dialect differed from their own were as well able to understand him as themselves. The occasions on which this took place were when he preached to a crowd, and we do not find it stated that he could dispense with an interpreter for more familiar conversation; nor is it said that there were never times at which he did not possess the gift even for public instructions, which he was often in the habit of giving by means of such interpreters.

The gift of tongues, moreover, was but one of a number of marvellous powers imparted to Francis in the way and in the degree in which such powers are often bestowed upon the Saints. The number of his miracles on the Fishery Coast and in the adjacent parts was so great, that we are assured that they would of themselves fill a large volume. Some few of the more signal of these miracles may be rapidly mentioned. A beggar covered with sores and putrid wounds asked an alms

[34] 1 Cor. xiv. 22. We hope to give a short abstract of the results of the evidence as to the gift of tongues in the case of St. Francis further on (Book v. note 2).

of him, and Francis washed him with his own hands, drank some of the water, and sent him away perfectly cured and sound. He was about to say mass in a little church at Combutur, when a crowd entered with the corpse of a boy who had been drowned in a well. The mother threw herself at the feet of Francis Xavier, who had baptized her child, and implored him to restore him to life. After a short prayer, he took the dead child by the hand and bade him arise. The child rose up at once, and ran to his mother. One of two youths who accompanied him as catechists was bitten at night in the foot by a cobra da capello, and was found in the morning to be dead. Francis touched the foot with the saliva from his mouth, made the sign of the Cross over him, took him by the hand and bade him rise in the name of Jesus Christ. He rose at once, and was able to continue on their journey immediately, as if he had been simply asleep. There are other cases related of his raising the dead in this part of the country, and it is even stated in the Processes that one of the children whom he used to send about in his name to the sick raised two dead persons to life.

We have here touched upon another class of the prodigies wrought by Francis Xavier—those which were brought about by means of the Christian children. He mentions in his letter given above, that such things frequently took place, but he omits to add that the children usually armed themselves with something belonging to him, his rosary, or reliquary, or crucifix, and that after they had recited the prayers of the Church and asked the sick person whether he were ready to receive the Christian faith, they used to make the sign of the Cross over him, and that complete restoration to health ordinarily followed. The same method availed sometimes even for driving out devils. These children, as has been said, play quite an important part in this wonderful mission of the Fishery Coast. They instructed their own parents in the truths which they themselves had learnt at school, they witnessed against them fearlessly in case of their quarrelling or using bad language, they were keen after any one who made idols or got drunk, and their greatest delight of all was to assist at the demolition of the idols in the heathen temples.

The opposition which Francis everywhere met with from the Brahmins was natural and to be expected, and in the letter to his friends at Rome he speaks of them as he had found them. The Paravas, for whom he principally laboured, were of a low caste, and it is not likely that Francis had come across any very perfect information as to the extremely powerful influence which the system of castes exercises on Indian society. More than half a century was to elapse before the attempt made by the saintly Robert de' Nobili at Madura to convert the higher castes of the Indians, for which purpose he was obliged to separate himself entirely from the Portuguese, who, though still in unbroken power and empire in India, were held in abomination as men who ate beef, drank intoxicating drinks, and held communication with pariahs. The great ascendancy given to Francis Xavier by his character for sanctity, his miracles, his preternatural devotion to labours and sufferings of every kind for the benefit of others, is shown in the sort of deference which the Brahmins seemed to have felt obliged to pay him, if not from their own convictions, at least out of regard or fear for the popular opinion concerning him. He has spoken at some length concerning them, but he is entirely silent in the letters which we have as yet seen concerning another class of opponents, who were perhaps more mischievous to the cause of religion, and who were certainly causes to him of far more intense suffering. These foes were some of the Portuguese, and, among them, many officers in the service of the crown and in posts of authority along the coast, who treated the Indians in general, without making any exception in favour of the newly made Christians, with every kind of cruelty and injustice. If we were to judge only from the letters given above, comparing them with others which we shall presently have to translate, we might imagine that, in respect at least of any annoyance or opposition which might or might not have been met with from these representatives of a Catholic nation and sovereign, the first year of the preaching of Francis among the Fishers of

Cape Comorin was a time of peace and unchequered progress and victory in the cause of God. But the letters to Mancias, which we shall have to give in our next chapter, reveal a state of things the existence of which is not compatible with such a supposition. The miseries brought upon the Indian Christians from the misconduct and rapacity of the Portuguese are not there spoken of as anything new, but rather as old sores, which have long been festering, and which have almost determined St. Francis to give up his mission altogether.

We have now, perhaps, gone through the principal elements which must be combined and blended if we are to give ourselves some faint picture of the daily life of Francis Xavier at this period. It was a life of very great hardships, courted and even enhanced by his heroic spirit of mortification, and his ingenious love for poverty and humiliation. It was a life of incessant labour, toilsome service in waiting on the sick, instructing the ignorant and the children, burying the dead, settling disputes, listening to questions, and answering difficulties; but every pain and fatigue was sweetened and gilded by the intense charity which animated every action. It was, as we shall be able to show more fully in the next chapter, a life liable to frequent changes and interruptions, in which sudden dangers had to be met, great exertions were called for, consummate prudence, ready resolution, and rapid decision required to ensure safety and avert calamity, and, as will also be seen from the letters to Mancias, it was a life of great solitude in the midst of crowds and of the busiest occupation, if solitude is to be measured by the absence of true companionship and sympathy. It was a life beset by frequent risks and deadly hostility, and the darling aim of which was constantly and fatally thwarted by persons who ought to have been the first to further it with the utmost devotion. It was made splendid and luminous to the whole populations among whom Francis was moving by the habitual exercise of the gift of miracles, and by a repetition of the external wonders which had astonished and helped to convert the hearers of the Apostles. We are told that in Portugal the name of 'Apostle' clung to the members of the Society on account of the impression produced by the life and teaching of Francis and Simon Rodriguez. On the Fishery Coast Francis now came to be commonly spoken of as 'the Holy Father.'

A few more words complete what we know of this period. To all these features we must add another, to name which is to name that which to Francis himself was overwhelmingly predominant, and gave its own character to the whole tenour of his existence, and yet which it is given to few, and those only men like himself, even to understand in any perfect measure. More than once he bursts out in his letters about that which is usually the treasured secret of souls like his, but as to which either he was unable to keep silence, or he thought it well to speak for the glory of God and the encouragement of others to tread in the same path of devotion to the cause of the conversion of the heathen. This feature was the immense overpowering sweetness and consolation with which God so often flooded his whole soul—the joy which he felt too much for him here below, so that he was fain to pray that either that intense rapturous delight might be modified, or he might be taken away to see without interruption or veil the Face of God from Whom it came. The present reward of his share in Apostolical labours was a share also in the incommunicable consolations which are the peculiar privilege of such ministrations—consolations which none but those who have tasted them can ever distantly imagine, and which reflect, perhaps, in some faint degree the joy of the Good Shepherd Himself when 'He rejoiced in the Holy Ghost, and said, I confess to Thee, O Father, Lord of heaven and earth, because Thou hast hidden these things from the wise and prudent, and hast revealed them to little ones.'[35] When we consider that interior and sensible happiness of this kind was probably as habitual to Francis Xavier at this time as the gift of miracles, we are able to see in part how very faint an idea can be formed from without of the conditions and characteristics of an existence such as his.

[35] Luke x. 21.

CHAPTER III.

The Fishery Coast and Travancore.

WE have seen how, in his letters to Europe, Francis Xavier made no mention of two very important though very different elements which influenced in no slight degree, in their several ways, the life which he led at the time of which we are now speaking. He made no mention either of the multitude of constantly recurring miracles by which his mission was authenticated, or, on the other hand, of the frequent obstacles placed in the way of the advance of the Gospel by some of the Portuguese officers and traders who had dealings of various kinds with the natives, either Christian or heathen. Of this last element of annoyance, which probably in the end prevented him from attempting even more than he did attempt for the benefit of the various tribes and kingdoms in the south of India, we shall find abundant mention in the series of letters which remain to us to illustrate the second year of the labours of Francis in that part of the world, and we shall also find in the same documents a quantity of striking evidence as to another feature in his life at this time, which consisted in the comparative poorness of the tools with which he had to work, and the entire absence from his side of any one whom he could constantly look to as a companion and a brother, as had been his lot when he first began to labour in Italy for the good of souls.

It is indeed the almost inevitable lot of the great Saints who have to labour as Apostles in the Church of Christ, and especially of those whose vocation it is to bear the light and grace of the Gospel to heathen nations, that they should have to work in great loneliness, and find but little sympathy and few congenial hearts among such companions as may join themselves to them. It is almost a part of the character on which the great graces which are so often given to them are grounded, to be tender, sensitive, sympathetic, prodigal of affection to an extraordinary degree, and the quickness, largeness, warmth, and depth of their feelings are enhanced and intensified as divine charity more thoroughly penetrates and possesses them. But the hearts that are most ready to give love are also most eager for its return, and most poignantly disappointed by its absence. The hearts of the Saints approach more and more nearly the intense delicacy and tenderness of the Heart of the Saint of Saints. To one who practises attentive and thoughtful meditation on the life of our Lord, His own great loneliness will, perhaps, sometimes dawn in a fresh and more powerful light, as a feature in the history of which a cursory acquaintance with that history had given him a very inadequate idea, and we find the same feature in that picture of the mind and heart of the great Apostle of the Gentiles which has been drawn for us by himself in his Epistles, especially, for instance, in the second Epistle to the Corinthians, and in his Epistles to St. Timothy. The Cross of the Sacred Heart itself was wrought to a great extent by the coldness, dullness, and narrowness of those whom our Lord loved so tenderly, and in this respect even His friends and dearest Apostles had some share in the wounds which pierced It. One heart alone beat entirely and unceasingly in accordance with His own, and from that motherly heart He was often separated outwardly by the Providence which guided His steps on earth.

In the case of St. Francis Xavier it could hardly be otherwise. Almost every line of his letters shows his intense affectionateness. He had left the men who had been for so long his brothers in heart and life behind him in Europe, and before he set sail from Lisbon he had to abandon the hope of having even the single companionship of Simon Rodriguez in his labours in the East. His letters show us how he yearned with all his heart for marks of their sympathy from a distance, and how large a part of his thoughts and affections was ever occupied with them, and with that other and ever increasing band of brethren whom he had never seen in the flesh, but who were so closely linked to him by the spiritual ties which united all the members, living or dead, of his religious Society one to another. When one lonely heart is thus joined to many at a distance who have abundance of companionship to surround their daily life, it is but natural that the yearning for some sort of communication should be more deeply felt in the case of the first than in that of the last. So we may suppose it to have been here. While Francis was full of thoughts of his brethren, and writing to them at every opportunity, it would appear—not indeed that he was forgotten, for St. Ignatius, to speak of no other, was not a man to forget one who had entered so deeply into his heart as Francis Xavier—but that the multiplicity of their occupations and the immense distance between them made letters and communications to him from Europe few and far between. Other companions whom he hoped for and seemed to reckon upon in Portugal had failed him also. Those who went with him, Father Paul of Camerino and Francis Mancias, were good and zealous in their way, but we are sorry to find that they both gave him a good deal of trouble, nor were they men at all capable of repaying in kind the intense and watchful affection which he lavished upon them so freely. We shall have to make the same remark on some, at least, who joined him from Europe, for where there is a great scarcity of able workmen in the Church, and a great demand for the work of such men at home, it is almost inevitable that distant missions even of the highest importance should fare comparatively poorly, and have but little choice as to the men who are spared for their needs.

Francis had returned from the Fishery Coast to Goa, as has been said, towards the end of 1543.[1] He had some business to transact with the Governor, and was probably more open to him about the misconduct of the Portuguese than to his friends at Rome. He must at this time have arranged about the revenue to be allotted to the Canacopoli out of the

[1] Father Menchacha places it as early as September.

money which was usually paid for the shoes and slippers of Queen Catharine of Portugal. He found at Goa his two companions from Lisbon, Father Paul of Camerino and Francis Mancias, and, after settling that the former should govern the College of St. Paul for the Society, he returned to the Fishery Coast with the latter, as well as with two native priests, Francis Coelho and Joam de Lizana, with Joam d'Artiaga, a layman who had become attached to him after having been converted from a worldly life, and some other assistants of the same kind.[2]

We hear only occasionally of the greater part of this little band; but we may perhaps fairly suppose that Francis Mancias did not receive more of the attention of St. Francis than the rest, though we happen by a fortunate accident to hear a great deal about him. We have no accurate information as to the posts allotted to these different missionaries and catechists, and the names of places which occur in the letters which we are about to insert are in most cases names and nothing more. It is clear, however, that this little party was dispersed among the various villages of the Indians along the coast, each one having a small circuit of his own allotted to him, within which he was to keep passing from village to village. Mancias himself was probably the companion of Francis Xavier during the earlier months of the period of which we speak. After a time he was placed by himself, and was, most happily for us, in constant need of direction and encouragement, which he received from St. Francis in a series of letters, many of which are most fortunately preserved to us. Some of these letters are no more than short hasty notes. Francis sometimes wrote more than one on the same day, containing repetitions of instruction or advice, which he sent by different messengers so as to make the safe arrival of the contents more sure. The letters to which these were answers are not in our possession, but if they were, they would hardly, perhaps, add

[2] The letter to the Society, last inserted, was written from Cochin, which place Francis must have visited on some business after returning to the Fishery Coast.

very much to our knowledge of the character of Mancias himself, which is unconsciously pourtrayed by his correspondent. Mancias was not yet a priest when these letters were written (except the last). He did not ultimately persevere in the Society, and we can see traces in the correspondence of some of the faults of character which brought about his dismissal. But we are, as we have said, greatly his debtor for preserving to us this series of notes and letters, which make us, indeed, long for more records of the same sort, but which still throw a very great light upon the character of Francis Xavier. Most of these letters were unknown to his earlier biographers, and they have hardly been sufficiently used even by the later writers on his life. They come from his heart, and enable us to form a far more lively picture of the difficulties of his missionary career in India than if we possessed only a simple narrative of his labours. They certainly give us a great idea of his extreme activity in his correspondence with his fellow labourers and subordinates.

Among the difficulties with which St. Francis had to deal, we must in the first place reckon Mancias himself. He seems to have been hot tempered and violent, easily moved to anger and indignation, apt to have recourse to severity on every occasion, and at the same time—as is often the case with men of strong temper—easily disheartened, and wanting in energy and perseverance in his weary and apparently thankless work. This work was neither specious nor easy; it required strength, resolution, and immense patience. It was, as we have seen already, of the most elementary and laborious character. Francis Xavier had early learnt that the greatest hopes of the future Christian community, which was to be formed out of the native population, lay in the children. We have seen how, writing to his religious brethren in Rome, after having spent a year on the Malabar coast, he spoke of the intercession made in heaven for him and his friends by more than a thousand children whom he had baptized with his own hand, and who had died before attaining to the age of reason. He was always zealous to baptize and cause to be baptized all the newborn children that he and his fellow missionaries met with in the lately converted populations, and this was one of the charges which we find him most frequently repeating in the letters to Mancias. He had also made provision, as we have seen, for the constant teaching of the Catechism to all children of an age to learn, appointing native masters in all the villages, and securing them a salary. These men required continual supervision and encouragement, and it was very necessary to make them feel that a watchful eye was kept over them, and that their salaries might depend on the zeal with which their duties were performed. Then there were the meetings of the adults on Sundays and Feasts to be looked to. Men and women were to be assembled separately, to repeat the Creed, the Commandments, and the prayers which Francis had taught them. Besides this, there were the adults to be baptized as soon as they were sufficiently prepared and proved, the sick to be visited and prayed over, the poor to be attended to, and numberless affairs to be settled by the missionary, who was to be father and ruler to these ignorant and indolent people as well as religious teacher. His time could not be spent in any one place; he was to travel from village to village, baptizing, catechizing, visiting the sick, examining the schools and urging the catechists to their duty, and as soon as he had made his round through the circle of country committed to him, he was to begin again and again in the same way. This is what Francis himself had done during the first year of his work among the natives, and to this work he now had to keep Mancias.

The first letter of the series now before us shows that Francis already felt that his companion's courage was likely enough soon to give way. The Commandant mentioned in the second part of the letter must have been the Portuguese officer in command of the fort at Tuticorin, a certain Cosmo de Payva, of whom we shall hear more as a great thorn in the side of St. Francis.

(xv.) *To Francis Mancias, setting out for Comorin.*

May the grace and charity of Christ our Lord always help and favour us! Amen.

My dearest Brother,

I am most anxious to know what you are doing; and therefore I beg of you, for the love of Jesus Christ, to write to me accurately, taking plenty of time over your letter, everything that in any way concerns yourself and your companions in those parts. I will write to you as soon as ever I reach Munahpaud to tell you of my arrival.

Remember the instructions which I gave you in writing when we parted, and pray to God to strengthen you with great patience, the quality necessary above all others in dealing with the people you have to do with. Make up your mind that what you are to suffer among them is to be to you instead of your Purgatory, and that you are to pay now here and at once the penalty of your faults. And acknowledge how great a favour it is that God grants you, to be able while still breathing the breath of life to make atonement for the sins of your youth, while you have the opportunity of gaining grace by it (which could not be in Purgatory), and at the same time have so much less pain than you might have there.

You will tell Joam d'Artiaga that the Commandant writes me word that he has paid him ten gold crowns to be placed to my account, but that I have replied to the Commandant that neither you, nor Joam d'Artiaga, nor myself are in want of any money before his own return from the Fishery Coast, and that I have given orders to Joam d'Artiaga, to return this sum to him. Tell Artiaga from me to do this, unless this money, instead of being a gift, should be a payment which is owing to us, and to which we have a right, on some other account, which I have some reason to suspect. I have heard something to the effect that the Governor who furnishes us, by the King's orders, with what is necessary for our living and maintenance, has sent a bill for ten pardams to the Commandant here that he may get us an interpreter. It may be that the Commandant, not seeing any present opportunity or future hope of getting us an interpreter, and not wishing to keep other people's money in his hands to no purpose, has at once sent it on to those for whose use he knew it to be destined. If this is so, keep it by all means; if not, then let the Commandant have his money back at once, and I wish Artiaga to repay it immediately. I wish for you all the grace from heaven to enable you to serve God, that I desire and pray for for myself. Farewell.

From Punical, February 22, 1544.

I do not write to Joam d'Artiaga, because this letter is for him as well as for you.

Your most affectionate brother,

FRANCIS.

The next, ten days or so later, contains the same urgent entreaty—to which he adds a concession to the severity of Mancias, sending a beadle, or some officer of the kind, to punish drunken women.

(XVI.) *To Francis Mancias.*

My dearest Brother in Jesus Christ,

Your letter has given me great comfort. I implore you over and over again to deal with that poor degraded people as good fathers do with bad children. Don't let your courage give way, however many may be the depraved and wicked things you see them do: for God Himself, Whom they so grievously offend, nevertheless does not kill them, as He might by a single nod. He does not cease to supply them with what they need for their life and support, and yet, unless He were to keep His bountiful hand open to them, all these things would fail, and the poor wretches would perish for want, as indeed they deserve to perish. I would have you consider this example of God, and conform your mind to greater indulgence by it, casting aside all needless worry and distress of heart.

Your labours where you are are more fruitful than you think, and although you may not make all the way that you desire, still, take my word for it, you are doing very sufficient work, and work which you will never repent of. And, after all, whatever may be the success of your labours, you have a sure consolation in the fact that it was not your doing nor your fault in any way that it has been otherwise than could be wished. For the rest, as we have good precedents as well as good reason to show us that we may lawfully use the King's authority to break down the indomitable and stiffnecked obstinacy of a race over which he rules, I send you an officer whom I have asked of the Governor, who is commissioned to exact a fine of one *fanam* (two silver pieces) of any woman who continues to get tipsy on arrack, contrary to the edicts lately issued, and also to cast any one found guilty of such intemperance into prison for three days. And you must take care to have it published with all possible clearness throughout all your villages and dwellings, that this law will in future be inexorably enforced, and tell the Patangatins (the heads of the villages) that if after this any arrack is drunk in Punical, they must themselves expect severe punishment from me.

Exhort Matthew to behave to me like a good son; and say that, if he does this, I will give him far greater good things and advantages than he could ever have expected from his own parents. And just in this interval during which I am prevented from getting to you, as I am in haste to do, give some serious warnings to those Patangatins you speak of; tell them, if they are wise, to amend their bad ways, otherwise that I have made up my mind to use the power which the Governor has given me, and that all whom, when I come, I find still addicted to their favourite vices, I shall order to be taken in chains to Cochin; and they need not flatter themselves that they will soon get off with a light punishment. I have firmly resolved on what I now declare, that I will take good care that they shall never be allowed to return to Punical. It is as clear as it can be, that all the many crimes and wickednesses that are committed in their country are to be laid to the fault and charge of these Patangatins alone.

Mind to take the greatest care to baptize as soon as possible all newborn infants. And directly they are past infancy and are able to begin to be taught anything, begin as early as may be to teach them the rudiments of Christian doctrine, as you may remember that I enjoined you to do most earnestly. Every Sunday also you must give the Catechism to all the people together, men and women, boys and girls, training them well in the prayers and acts which it is my custom to teach them, as you know, and you should add to this a short sermon on some subject that may be practically useful. Watch with all diligence, even going so far as to visit and examine the workshops of the artisans, to prevent any one from carving or making idols. I hear that a letter has been sent directed to me, to where you are, from Alvarez Fogaza: do not send it here, but keep it for me till I come.

May our Lord God fill you, in this life and the next, with all those mighty consolations which I pray to Him to grant to myself. Farewell.

Your most affectionate brother in Jesus Christ,

FRANCIS.

From Munahpaud, March 14, 1544.

The Matthew here mentioned seems to have been a lad whom St. Francis had left with Mancias as an assistant, and the letters frequently speak of him in a playful way, as will be seen in our next extract. Mancias must have written, in the course of the same month, to tell Francis that he was well and enjoying great consolation and delight in his work. The answer is full of joy, sympathy, and, at the same time, warning.

(XVII.) *To Francis Mancias.*

My dearest Brother in Jesus Christ,

Your letter has given me incredible joy, and done my soul immense good, because it tells me that you are very happy in your mission and are visited by God with wonderful consolations. And now that you have had experience that God remembers you, do not let yourself ever forget Him. Beware of growing weary of your work, however ungrateful it may be, and don't let any kind of disgust weaken you so as to relax your keen and unconquerable perseverance in the good which you have begun. Keep always a humble and lowly spirit before God, with a meek feeling of internal thankfulness that He has chosen you for so lofty an office as that which you are discharging. You have the paper of injunctions that I gave you; I have nothing to add to them, nothing new to recommend. Remember me always, for I never forget to think of you. Tell Matthew to be my good child, and that he will find me a good father. I am always on the lookout for occasions of helping him on. Tell him also that I order him, on Sundays, when he repeats in church the answers to the Catechism, which you have taught him at home, to speak so loud that not only all the congregation may hear him, but that his voice may reach us here at Munahpaud. Let me know also about the Christians of Tuticorin, in what state they are, and whether the Portuguese who have stopped there give them any trouble; also what news there is about the Governor—whether he is to pass the winter at Cochin, or not.

Here we have an affair of great magnitude just beginning—one that promises a splendid opening for the service of God our Lord. I beg you to pray to Him very urgently that He may be pleased to bring the hopes which He has let us entertain to a prosperous issue, and ripen the good beginnings of the opportunity which we so much desire.

I entreat you to show continual marks of very great love to the whole of the people you are among, rulers and nobles, and also the lowest classes. The consequence will most certainly be that they will love you in return, and, if you once get to that, the ministry by which you are trying to lead them to the knowledge and worship of God our Lord will find its course more easy and its fruit more abundant. Accustom yourself to bear with great patience all their weaknesses and their slips from frailty, keeping up in your mind the merciful and charitable hope that though they are not yet good, they will one day become so. And, after all, if you can't make them advance quite as far as you intended, still don't repent of having tried, and take that little good which you have been able to beat out of them as a sufficient reward. For my part, this is the way I comfort myself in suchlike troubles.

May God be always with you, and give us grace that we may serve Him for ever! Farewell.

Your brother in Jesus Christ,

FRANCIS.

From Munahpaud, March 20th, 1544.

We here come for the first time upon a direct mention of the trouble caused by the Portuguese to the native Christians. There has probably never yet been a zealous European missionary in any part of the heathen world in which Christians from his own country have been settied, or which they have occasionally visited for purposes of commerce, who has not found among them the worst enemies to his work. No exception can be made as to this lamentable truth in favour of Catholic nations: Spaniards, Frenchmen, Portuguese, have as much to answer for in this respect as Dutchmen and Englishmen. Some Catholics, under such circumstances, have done infinitely more for religion than can be claimed for Protestants, and we shall find noble instances of this among the Portuguese merchants, as well as among the officers of the Crown, in the time of St. Francis. But many Catholics have done quite as much against religion as any others, and we shall now find this dark thread of the bad treatment of native Christians on the part of the Portuguese settlers, merchants, soldiers, and even officials, running through the whole of the story before us.

The letter also alludes to another plan which now occupied Francis. He had now fairly provided for the regular teaching of the converts on the Fishery Coast, and though the priests were few, it was quite possible for them, by frequent visits to the several villages, to administer the sacraments at stated intervals, while the ordinary instruction and the conferring of baptism in cases of necessity could be looked to by the catechists and Canacapoli. He was desirous of extending the range of his missionary action, and bringing yet more of the natives into the kingdom of Jesus Christ. On the western shores of the tongue of land which ends in Cape Comorin, and between the Fishery Coast itself and the Portuguese settlement at Cochin, lay the Kingdom of Travancore, and it was a part of the plan of the Saint to preach the Gospel to its inhabitants. It is not easy to settle with perfect clearness the exact relation which the Rajah of Travancore held towards other princes of the south of India, and it is probable that the relations between them were continually changing. At this time he seems to have been a potentate of considerable magnitude, though in the next century his successors had sunk into the lords of a small territory, tributary to the King or Rajah of Madura or Bisnaghur. At the time of St. Francis, he was known in his own country as the Maharajah or great Rajah, a name probably acquired by his success, shortly before, in bringing under his authority a number of petty princes, or, more properly speaking, nobles, who had up to that time ruled the country, each as the small tyrant of his own neighbourhood. These were the Pulas, or Polygars, of whom mention is made in the letter which will follow immediately; they dwelt in small castles or fastnesses on the high grounds, and kept the country round them in terror and subjection.[3] The position of a prince who had reduced this troublesome class to tacit submission may well be ima-

[3] We find these details in M. Léon Pagès' admirable French translation of the Letters of St. Francis (t. i. p. 100). He adds that the Mudaliars, whose name will occur further on, were a class on the Coromandel Coast, belonging to the Vaicyas (merchants and cultivators of the soil), the third caste among the Indians, who enjoyed great influence from the thirteenth to the sixteenth cen-

gined, and we can easily understand that the 'Great Rajah' of Travancore was anxious to secure the support of the Portuguese against these subordinate rajahs, who were certain to revolt as soon as it was in their power to do so with hopes of success, and who, moreover, might purchase for themselves the alliance of the Portuguese against him unless he anticipated them. How far these political reasons weighed with the Rajah of Travancore, Iniquitribirim,[4] cannot be known for certain; but he appears thus early in the year to have shown signs of a friendly disposition to St. Francis, even if the latter had not already, by his leave, preached in his country, which soon after this, at all events, became the scene of his most active labours, as well as of some most remarkable miracles. These facts explain to us the indignation which is expressed in the following letter at the thwarting of his plans by an act of unjustifiable violence on the part of some Portuguese adventurer.

(XVIII.) *To Francis Mancias.*

My dearest Brother in Jesus Christ,

No words could express the earnest desire which weighs upon me to get to you on the coast. I declare to you that it is the strict truth that if this very day I could find a ship that was leaving for those parts, I should at once embark in it.

Here are three nobles come to me from the Court of the Rajah of Travancore, complaining of a Portuguese who, they say, has arrested at Patanai a slave of their prince Iniquitribirim, and taken him in chains to Punical. They hear that the man boasts that he will take him to Tuticorin. Find out what the truth of the matter is, and write about it, I beg you, to the Commandant. And if it should be that the Portuguese be

---

tury. There are many ruins now to be seen of the fortresses built by them, and the common answer to an enquiry about a ruin in those parts is, that it was built by so and so, who was a Polygar, or a Mudaliar. A fact like this shows their importance, and the difficulty which the Rajah must have had in keeping them in order.

[4] The name is so given in the letters, but it is said to be hopelessly unlike any conceivable Hindoo name.

found there, whoever he may be, turn every stone that the poor prisoner be set free at once. If it be that he owes the Portuguese anything, let the complaint be laid before his own prince, who is sure to decide what is just, and who will maintain, as he always does, the rights of our people. This advice is no doubt given too late, for this is what they should have done in the beginning, and no subject of an allied prince ought to have been seized and taken out of a place in his dominions without his being consulted. How absurdly we use our strength! We spare our enemies and plunder our friends. This act of injustice shuts me out from access to the Rajah, who is otherwise well disposed, for it would be the unwisest thing in the world for me to present myself to an indignant Court, boiling over with the sense of so grave an insult lately received. I can well forgive their anger, which has a just cause to kindle it. For what can be more intolerable than that men who call themselves the allies of a Rajah should lay violent hands on the servant of one of his friends in his own dominions, without waiting for or asking his consent? an outrage never heard of even in the time of the Pulas, when they ruled in those parts in a manner that was simply tyrannical. As for me, I really don't know what line I shall take, so entirely are all my measures and precautions upset by the inconsiderate outbreak of this reckless miscreant. I feel strongly urged to be off and have done with it; for why should we waste more time here, among men who are utterly regardless of any considerations of justice, and who never care a straw at the cost of what damage to religion or to the State they indulge their own passions? above all, whose outrages are encouraged by impunity? Every one can see that if the men who were concerned in that shameless robbery of the myoparon[5] the other day had been punished as they deserved, we should not find the Portuguese now breaking out in outrages of the same sort. It will be a narrow escape for us now if the Rajah of Travan-

[5] A myoparon was a large flatbottomed boat—a sort of barge. We are without information as to the details of this outrage—one, probably, of a number that were constantly recurring.

core, irritated by so wanton an insult, do not take some severe measures against the Christians who are his subjects.[6]

I wish you to write and tell the Commandant how much I am distressed at this act of violence on the person of the Rajah of Travancore's slave, not only on account of the bad feeling which so scandalous a crime must produce, but also on account of the positive evils which threaten us in consequence of it. I myself have almost made up my mind never to write again on such matters, for these people want to do just what comes into their head, and they can't bear to be told what is disagreeable to hear. They seem to think that it is an injury and an insult to them if any one dares to open his mouth while they are trampling on rights of all kinds. If it should happen that you get certain information that the slave carried off by the Portuguese is at Tuticorin, then, I conjure you, by all the desire you have to please God, go yourself at once to the Commandant, and work upon him by all the means in your power to get the poor fellow set free at once. And let the Portuguese who had him arrested come here and make his claim or his complaint, and he will find all that consideration of his rights which is needed to give him full satisfaction.

I wonder whether the Portuguese would think it good if, when one of the natives happened to have a dispute with one of themselves, he was to seize the Portuguese by main force, put him in chains, and have him taken out of a place in our territory and carried up the country? Certainly not. The Indians must have the same feelings; why should we do to them what we don't wish to be done to ourselves? Why should we be astonished that they, like ourselves, are indignant when they are injured? There would be more to excuse the aggression if they denied us justice; but what plausible excuse can we plead now, when they undertake to do justice with the utmost faithfulness, observe exactly all the conditions of the

[6] This seems to show that the conversions in Travancore had already begun. But it would appear that the 'Great Rajah' had at least some authority at Munahpaud itself, whence Francis writes, and the whole Fishery Coast may have been under his suzerainty.

alliance, and when they keep the peace and deal with all the equity we could desire in their intercourse with us? Where can we possibly find a pretext to cover even speciously the shameful disgrace of our faithless breach of agreement? If any insurmountable obstacle should prevent you from going yourself at once to the Commandant, send Paul Vaz to him with a letter from you.

I declare once more that this news has disturbed me more than I can express by letter. May our Lord God give us the strength of mind that is needed for us to bear with becoming patience such reckless excesses as this! Though what I have said about the affair has been ascertained on good authority, still please not to think it too much trouble to write to me a thorough account of the whole matter, as far as you can find out on the spot. Is it true that a Portuguese has seized a slave of the Rajah of Travancore within the territory of the latter? If he has, what reason does he allege for it, and does he really intend to take the man to Tuticorin, and for what? I should be very glad to hear something at least which may diminish the atrocity of this detestable action, and prove that report had exaggerated it. If there is no way of lightening the ill feeling which has been caused, and if the facts really are what they are said to be, then I must give up my plan of going to see the Rajah, with whom I was going to treat of matters concerning the service of God. You well know how these people are incensed at these seizures of slaves, especially from territory of their own; and there can be no doubt that they must all be calling out for vengeance, and heaping reproaches upon the whole race of Portuguese, and even on the Christian religion. It would never be wise for me to expose myself to all this hostility. No, I shall have to think of going elsewhere. I have long thought of it, and now shall have to set myself to work to carry it out. I have long had the idea suggesting itself to my mind, and it really seems very attractive, of leaving India altogether, where so many obstacles are placed in the way of the advancement of the Gospel from quarters from which least of all such obstacles should arise, and going instead to Ethiopia, where there is a great and probable hope to invite us of advancing signally the glory of our Lord God by preaching the Gospel, and where there will be no Europeans to oppose us and pull down what we have built up. I cannot hide from you that I feel so strongly impelled that way, that it is not unlikely I shall embark at Munahpaud on one of the little country vessels,[7] of which there are plenty, and go to Goa at once to prepare all that is necessary for my departure for the dominions of Prester John.

May God grant us His help and grace! Amen.

Your most loving brother in Jesus Christ,

FRANCIS.

From Munahpaud, March 24th, 1544.

It may surprise the reader to hear Francis Xavier speak of going to Prester John. The Portuguese conquests on the coast of Africa, and their interference in the affairs of Abyssinia, had awakened in Europe a great interest in the almost nominal Christians of those countries. The famous expedition of Don Cristoval de Gama, who with 400 men marched with ease about the country which it cost an English army so many millions of pounds to penetrate a few years ago, took place in 1540. John III., five or six years later, asked for missionaries of the Society, and the negotiations issued in 1556 in the mission of Father Nuñez Barreto (as Patriarch) and several others, to Claudius King of Abyssinia, who occupied the place of the so-called Prester John. It may be feared that Francis Xavier would have found troubles enough in Abyssinia as well as in India.[8] At all events, his intention of setting off at once was not carried out. His next letter was written from the same spot, only a few days later. It mentions another outrage committed by the Portuguese, this time on the Christians.

7 *quos tonos vocant.* (Lat.) They seem to have been little more than row-boats, and a voyage to Goa in one of them would have been hazardous enough.

8 See Genelli's *Life of St. Ignatius* (Eng. Trans.), p. 267 seq.

(XIX.) *To Francis Mancias.*

I was delighted to learn what your letter tells me about you. I can see from it how great are the fruits of your zeal where you are. May our Lord Whom we serve prosper your diligence in the future also, and give you in His mercy sufficient strength to make you equal to a continuance of your exertions, so as to bring always to greater and greater perfection the good you have done, and, in short, to persevere courageously to the end, and so entirely overcome the obstacles and troubles which you may have to meet!

To hear as I do that our Christians are persecuted and oppressed both by the heathen and by the Portuguese, is a thing which wounds my heart to the very core, so atrocious and so mischievous is it. But I have had so much of this sort of thing, that if, as they say, the sting of such sorrows could be dulled by frequent practice, I ought long ago to have lost all feeling about it. Somehow I cannot find any relief or alleviation for this misery in the medicine of habit and lapse of time. It racks me with intense pain every time that I either see for myself or hear from others how these tender sucklings of the Church are exposed to every kind of violence and outrage from the very persons in whom such conduct is most shameful—how, new and fresh as they are in the faith, like infant children in the holy religion they have adopted, and when they ought to be indulgently cherished and nursed up by kindness on the part of their elder brothers, rather than left in neglect and contempt, or even subjected to violence and injury by them, they are cut to pieces and plundered by savage attacks, which no efforts we can make for their protection are able to delay, much less to avert. Wherever I go I carry this grief like a pain which eats out my heart. I heard three days ago from the Patangatins of a most wicked act of violence —the seizure of several slave girls—committed at Punical by certain Portuguese. As soon as I heard the miserable news

I wrote to the Bishop's vicars at Coulan[9] and Cochin, begging them earnestly to publish a threat of the major excommunication against the ravishers, and to make a public inquiry who they are, that their names may be known, their prey rescued from them, and the penalty enjoined by the law inflicted on them to warn others by their example.

[However, all his indignation against these Portuguese miscreants does not prevent him from descending to minute practical matters, such as the provision for the boy Matthew, of whom Mancias was probably frequently complaining—perhaps not without reason—and the correction of a mistake in the translation of the Credo made by Mancias himself.]

Do not forget to give Matthew all he wants for his clothing. And do all you can by showing him all the kindness of an indulgent father, to attach him to yourself. In that way you will make him willing to live with you. You know he is free and his own master, and he can be attached to our community only by the bonds of affection. When he was with me, I took all possible pains to keep his affection, by showing him almost the tenderness of a mother, and I should very much wish that you would do the same.

In your translation of the Apostles' Creed there is something which I think it well to tell you. It is not right to translate the words *Credo in Deum* by the word *Enaku-venum;* for in their dialect the word *venum* answers to *volo*, I will, I want. Thus you see at once that it won't do to say, *Volo in.* I think you should use the word *vichuam*[10] instead of *venum*. That word answers in the language of the country to the Latin word

[9] Coulan, now Quilon, lies about halfway between Cape Comorin and Cochin, on the western side of the peninsula, and consequently on the Travancore coast. There was a Portuguese station there, and it was the most important port south of Cochin. It was the scene, as we shall see, of one of Francis Xavier's most remarkable miracles.

[10] Baldæus, a Dutch writer of the next century, who was present at many of the battles in which this part of India was conquered by his countrymen from the Portuguese, and afterwards settled there as a Protestant pastor, gives a short account of the Malabar tongue, which includes the *Our Father* and *Creed* in that dialect. The word there used for 'I believe in' is written by him *vichu-*

Credo. Again, in that other article of the Creed where the Passion of Jesus Christ is spoken of, take care not to use the words *Vao pinale:* the people here use them generally in a sense which includes some notion of coercion. Now Jesus Christ did not suffer of necessity, but of His own accord and free will.

When any who are passing from the Fisheries come to where you are, lose no time in visiting the sick among them, and wherever you go take a boy with you as you go from cottage to cottage to recite over them the prayers which you find inserted in the written instructions I left you. After these prayers and the service content yourself by reading once the usual passage of the Gospel. For the rest, remember always to show great signs of charity in your intercourse with these people, making it a point of careful study to win them to love you in return. I should be very glad if you could tell me that none of them now drink arrack or carve idols, and that they all come on Sundays to recite the prayers. But if it should chance that we can't always have these things as we wish, we must not let our courage break down, but rather say to ourselves that if from the beginning of their conversion these poor wretched people had always had diligent teachers at hand to teach them what is necessary, as you are now doing, they would certainly have been infinitely better Christians than they are.

May our Lord grant you all the consolation in this life and glory in the next that I desire for myself! Farewell.

Your most affectionate brother in Jesus Christ,

FRANCIS.

Munahpaud, March 27, 1544.

We pass over a few pages, and we find St. Francis in comparative quiet and good hope. The report about the Travancore outrage must have died away, and he is expecting some communication from the Governor about the terms which he may offer to the Rajah of Travancore, who was seeking the

vadieren. His work exists in the third volume of the English collection of Churchill, *Collection of Voyages and Travels*, London, 1745. The Creed is given in Malabar at p. 600. The Tamil words in the text would, we believe, be written differently now.

Portuguese alliance to ensure himself against his insurgent vassals. But another trouble is upon him, in the instability of Joam d'Artiaga, who had been named in a former letter as companion to Mancias himself. He seems to have left his post, and then to have left St. Francis.

(xx.) *To Francis Mancias.*

My dearest Brother,

It is a wonderful joy to me to hear of your having gone to visit the Christians scattered over the country whom I recommended to your care, and I am still more rejoiced to learn from persons who have come hither from your parts, of the abundant fruits that your visit has produced for the gain of souls and of the Church.

I have been expecting today or tomorrow a message from the Governor, and if it brings the news which I hope, I shall not delay my journey to your mission, and I will turn out of the road as I go that I may meet you in passing wherever you may be. I long to see you extremely, though the eyes of my spirit are always upon you, even in absence.

Joam d'Artiaga has gone off, carried away by some disturbing imagination which left him no peace of mind, and which came, as far as appears, from the Evil Spirit. But this he neither sees himself, nor goes the right way to learn. He told me when he left that he was going to Combutur[11] to teach the people there. He said also that he chose a place not far from where you are on purpose to be near you. He may have wished this at the time, but whether he will persevere in it I know not. You know what an inconstant fellow he is, and how every wind turns him. However, whatever happens, if he comes to see you, I hardly think it will be worth your while to spend any length of time in talking with him.

[11] Some of the translations of the letters have identified the place with Coimbatoor, in the Carnatic. But Coimbatoor is far to the north, and inland. The place here spoken of is evidently, as we may gather from the Letters, on the coast, not very far from the place whence St. Francis writes (Munahpaud).

I have written to the Commandant to supply you with what you want. I have also begged Manuel da Cruz to lend you money as often as you want it, and he has very obligingly promised me to do so. Take great care of your health, for that is a necessary means in order for you to serve our Lord God so usefully. Tell Matthew it is my decided will that he should do what you tell him, and diligently obey you in all things. I wish him to understand clearly that I have often promised him to be as a father and mother to him, it will depend on your giving him a good character; but that otherwise, unless you can witness to me that you have found him perfectly good and obedient, I sha'n't think that I have any reason to take so much trouble about him, nor make his interests of so much importance. I wish you, on the other hand, to give him liberally whatever clothing he may require.

In your visitation of the scattered hamlets which you are now making, this is what I wish you to do. In each village that you come to, bid all the men assemble on one day, and on another all the women, and teach each of them separately all that they must know to escape sin; and don't think it enough that they can repeat by heart in those assemblies the prayers of the Church, which all Christians commonly know, but make them say the same prayers morning and evening at home, and give them diligent orders to do this. Also baptize all that have not yet received baptism, adults as well as children.

Meanwhile, that you may have no selfcomplacency in the fruits of your work which meet the eye, consider that if the mill has ground good wheat, all the glory is due to the great Master and Lord Who makes the stream flow which makes the millstone go round, and the whole machine move and work.

May God our Lord keep you, and guide you and help you on! Farewell.

Your most loving brother in Jesus Christ,

From Munahpaud, April 8th, 1544. FRANCIS.

There were the elements of a good deal of trouble in the wayward conduct of this Joam d'Artiaga, who was not a member of the Society and not strictly under regular obedience to Francis or any one else. He might get his friends into some conflict with the native authorities, and they were sure to have the credit of any eccentricities of which he might be guilty. We shall be glad to find further on that he seems to have come round again, won, probably, by the influence exercised upon him by Francis in some personal interview. The letter which has last been quoted was written on the Tuesday in Holy Week, and the provisions which it mentions for the support of Mancias seem to fall in with the conjecture that Francis was now meditating an excursion into some new part of the country. The next two letters are written from different spots, the exact position of which, as well as of the post at which Mancias himself was stationed, it is impossible to identify. Francis seems to have been moving about the country towards Travancore, and to have meant to meet Mancias on his way, then to have proceeded to Tuticorin, which, as we have said, was about the centre of the Fishery Coast opposite Ceylon, on account of some dissensions between the natives, which had to be settled for fear of their growing mischievous. With this short commentary, we must leave the three letters which follow to speak for themselves.

(XXI.) *To Francis Mancias.*

My dearest Brother in Jesus Christ,

I long immensely to see you, and I have reason to hope that God in His mercy will soon grant me my prayer. Meantime not a day passes that I do not watch you in spirit. I doubt not that it is the same with you, and that we continually enjoy the presence of one another in heart. Now, for the love you have to God, write, I pray, and tell me about yourself and all the Christians; how you are, what you are doing, how all your affairs are going on. And I wish you to tell me all minutely and precisely. Here I am, a whole week waiting for a Pula from Travancore. I don't think he will fail, for he wrote to say that he should come within that time. How am I myself, you ask? Well, my heart is strong with a lively confidence in the goodness of God, that something will come of this interview which will have somewhat to do with His own service and honour. Whatever comes of it, I will let you know at once, that you may give thanks to God our Lord. I am writing to the Patangatins to build the chapel of green branches. I used to think it a good plan to assemble the women in the church on Saturday morning, as they do at Munahpaud, and the men on Sunday. But I leave all to your discretion. When you want to write to the Commandant to supply any need that you have, do not wait till you are in extreme necessity, but give him notice in good time beforehand, so that if he requires some little space to provide what you want, you may not have to suffer the pangs of destitution meanwhile.

As to Joam d'Artiaga, I should be glad to hear from you where he is, and whether he is serving God. I am very much afraid that he will not persevere as the interests of God's kingdom and His greater glory require. You know how inconstant he is. The Father who is with me is quite well, and so am I. Tell the boy, I mean Matthew, from me, to go on being good, to speak up when he repeats at the catechism what you have taught him and to pronounce the words well. When I come to see you, I am going to bring him a little present which I know he will be delighted with. Write me word whether the children come regularly to say their prayers together at the appointed time, and how many of them can say them rightly by heart.

I want you never to spare words or paper in telling me about these things very particularly. And give your letters to the first person you come across, who is coming this way, to bring to me.

May the Lord be with you, as I pray that He may be with me!

Your most affectionate brother in Jesus Christ,

FRANCIS.

Livare, April 23d, 1544.

(XXII.) *To Francis Mancias.*

My dearest Brother in Jesus Christ,

To-day, the first of May, I have got your letters. I can't tell you on paper how much pleasure I have had in reading them. I have been ill the last four or five days with a burning and constant fever and have been bled twice. Now, by the grace of God, I am better. I have almost lost all recollection of the illness I have just gone through, in the joy of the good news you give me.

I hope with God's help to go to you at Punical next week. We thought the Pula of Travancore would be here today, at least tomorrow morning. When I am with you I will tell you what has passed with him. May our Lord God grant that something may result from it by which we may advance His service. Father Francis Coelho is sending you two umbrellas. As I shall so soon be able to see you I have no more to say now except my usual prayer that our Lord God may be pleased to help us with His grace, so that we may serve Him faithfully. Farewell.

Your most loving brother in Jesus Christ,

FRANCIS.

Nare, May 1st, 1544.

(XXIII.) *To Francis Mancias.*

My dearest Brother in Jesus Christ,

God, from Whom nothing is hidden, knows how much happier I should be spending a few days with you than to be kept for the same time at Tuticorin. But as it is necessary for me to remain here awhile, in order to settle certain quarrels which are setting the people here by the ears in a way that threatens danger, we must both of us be willing to postpone the consolation of seeing one another, which we have been longing for, to the great advantage which may be expected to the service of God from this peace which I hope to make, and we must rejoice that we are to be, not where we might wish to be, but where the most holy will of our Lord God and the interests of His kingdom and of His greater glory require. I must again and again pray you, do not get angry with these poor folk, however much their faults and frailties move your bile. I know what an extreme annoyance it is to be perpetually interrupted, when one is thoroughly absorbed in some work, by persons calling one away to attend to their own business, which is all they care for. Never mind, gulp down their importunities, keep a quiet mind all the time, and lend yourself tranquilly to the occupations which come of themselves to you from every side. Just do what you can do, and what you can't do now, let it go or put it off, and, when you cannot give them satisfaction in deed, take care to make it up in word, excusing yourself kindly, saying that you are not as able to help them as you could wish, and if you can't give them what they want, give them some hope of it in the future—a thing which generally softens people when they are disappointed as to getting what they desire. You owe great thanks to our Lord God, and I suppose you give them, for placing you where you can't be idle if you would, where so many affairs surround and besiege you at every moment with something to be done, one upon another, but where—what is the sweetest of all condiments to any toil, however great—everything of this kind which besets you is clearly a call which belongs to the service of God.

I send Peter to you, and do you send us Antonio in return, as soon as he is well, which we hope may be in six days or a week. I have sent to Manuel da Cruz a careful letter, pressing him both by entreaties and arguments to make haste about finishing the church.

Send me my little case[12] by the first boat that sets out for this place. I shall get through the work I have here on hand as soon as possible, and then be off to you; for in truth I long much more, I think, than you suppose, to stay and talk

[12] *Capsulam.* It may have been a satchel in which he carried what he wanted for the celebration of mass on his journeys.

with you for some days. Let me know by letter at once whatever you want either of help or advice. You will be sure of finding a messenger, there are so many going to and fro daily. Bear these people, as it were, on your shoulders, treat them with unwearied patience and longsuffering tolerance, keep them from evil and advance them in good as much as you can, and be content. And then, after all, if you find some whom you cannot win to their duty by indulgence and kindness, consider that the moment is come for that work of mercy which consists in the timely chastisement of those who deserve punishment, and who cannot be driven to good except by severity.

May God help you, as I pray that He may assist myself! Farewell.

Your most affectionate brother in Jesus Christ,

Tuticorin, May 14th, 1544. FRANCIS.

After this last letter the correspondence with Mancias is interrupted for more than a month (May 14—June 20), and there is a similar break later on, as we have no letter between September 29 and November 8. In fact, the letters are extremely irregular in their distribution; sometimes several are crowded together within a few days, at others, as we have said, long intervals separate them. When we consider the evident care with which Mancias has preserved what remains to us, it seems unlikely that he received many more. The probable solution of the apparent difficulty lies in remembering that the care of the Fishery Coast itself, which involved frequent correspondence with Mancias, Coelho, and the other assistants of Francis Xavier, was only a part, and even only an occasional part, of his occupation at this time, and that he was very frequently at a distance from Munahpaud, Punical, and Tuticorin, which seem to have been places where he had the appliances necessary for maintaining a correspondence, and that he wrote his letter to Mancias when he found himself at these spots, to which it is very possible that the answers and other communications to him would be addressed. Any one who reads cursorily over the series of letters on which we are now engaged might think that St. Francis was fixed on the Fishery Coast for nearly the whole of the year 1544. This, however, would be a mistaken conclusion, for his own letters to Europe, written early in the year 1545, and in which he speaks of the progress of the Gospel during the previous year, mention other parts, as the coast around Coulan, and the kingdom of Travancore, as the scene of numerous conversions, and we know in the same way that he visited Ceylon, and towards the end of the year sailed up the whole western coast of India to the extreme north, in order to meet the Governor at Cambaia, returning thence to Cochin, from which place the letters are written. The letters to Mancias, therefore, are strictly letters confined to the business of the moment as far as Mancias was himself concerned in it, and looked upon in this light, they give us an idea of the extreme activity of St. Francis at this time, when the affairs with which they deal formed but a part of his work. The biographers of Francis have not thought it necessary to dwell at any length on the letters now before us, probably for the reason already hinted at, that the more important labours of this year are not mentioned in them. These letters are valuable to us chiefly on account of the intimate knowledge which they afford us of the character of their writer, of which, indeed, in this respect, they form a monument almost unique. We must fill up the picture of the work of the year very mainly from other sources.

The most prominent part of that work was undoubtedly the conversion, in great measure, of the inhabitants of the kingdom of Travancore, of which we have already said something. It cannot be ascertained except conjecturally at what period of the year Francis first entered the kingdom, but we may perhaps place it conveniently at that point where the letters to Mancias break off for a month, without thereby implying that even at an earlier period Francis may not have preached in parts of Travancore. But the letters which we have already inserted show him to have been expecting some communication from the Court, and to have been inclined to defer a projected visit to the Rajah himself on account of the rumour about some Portuguese outrage. This visit to the royal residence may have been put off, and yet Francis may have preached in the country with the leave of the Prince. In a letter written early in the following year he mentions having baptized as many as ten thousand in the space of a month, and his giving this exact measure of time would fit in very well with the conjecture that the weeks between the middle of May and the middle of June were spent in this undertaking. The letter to which we refer gives also an account of his method of proceeding, which is almost the same with his method on the Fishery Coast, if we allow for the important difference, that in the case of the latter he had to do with people already nominally Christians. The people of Travancore were partly Mussulmans and partly idolaters. We must suppose, from an expression in a letter to the King of Portugal, in which the 'coasts of Coulan' are spoken of as being under his authority, that the Portuguese exercised some sort of power along the whole seaboard, and not only in their fortified settlements; but the whole country, except the fringe of land along the sea, was under the Rajah, who was an ally of Portugal. In accordance with his custom, Francis would endeavour to obtain, as St. Augustine asked from Ethelbert on his landing in England, the Rajah's acquiescence in his preaching to his subjects. This seems to have been readily given, and the conversions followed rapidly. No doubt the fame of the life and miracles of St. Francis had already spread far and wide through the whole coast of India: and the Processes assure us that neither the gift of tongues nor the other great signs of an Apostolate which had been seen on the Fishery Coast were wanting in Travancore. Village after village received him with joy; and after the instruction and baptism of the inhabitants, the heathen temples were pulled down and the idols broken to pieces. As he went on he left behind him everywhere a written abridgement of Christian doctrine, and made provision for its regular teaching to the children and in the weekly assemblies of the new converts. By the end of the year it is said that no less than forty-five infant churches had been founded in this way. He was accompanied in his mission for six months of the year by the Paul Vaz, mentioned a few pages above, who returned to Europe some years later, and whose report as to the method of life and preaching of Francis is preserved to us by Bartoli. He mentions the number just given, of forty-five churches founded in Travancore. Francis, he says, always went barefoot, with a poor torn cassock and a sort of cap of black stuff on his head. He was always called the Great Father, and the Rajah had issued an edict that his own brother the Great Father was to be obeyed as himself, and that any one was at liberty to become Christian. The Rajah gave him large sums of money, the whole of which he spent in the relief of the poor. He could speak the language excellently, though he had never learnt it, and the people flocked to hear him, five or six thousand at a time, so that he was obliged to preach from a tree in the open fields, where also he used to celebrate mass in the presence of multitudes, under a canopy made of the rails of the boats. When he left the country, it was in great part Christian.

This result, however, was of course not obtained within the short space of time of which we are now speaking. Not long after the middle of June we find St. Francis again on the Fishery Coast, just in time to hear of the ravages of the Vadhouger,[13] who are called in the translations of the letters and in the current lives of St. Francis, the Badages. These terrible brigands—for it seems most natural to call them by that name

[13] See Père Bertrand, *La Mission du Maduré* (Paris, 1548), t. ii. p. 2. The many various statements concerning them may not be really conflicting. They were a tribe from the north (Bisnaghur), settled in the interior of the kingdom of Madura, which lay east and northeast of Travancore and the Fishery Coast. At the time of which we speak, they had an independent territory—the state of Pandi—but the Naicker or Rajah of Madura was their immediate sovereign, and they were commissioned, or allowed by him, to collect tribute due to him from the neighbouring states under his supremacy. We have no absolute certainty as to the relations, in the time of St. Francis, between Madura and Travancore, which may often have shifted, and as Travancore seems to have been in an exceptional state of relative prosperity and influence, it may easily be supposed that these vassals of the Rajah of Madura may have been to some nominal extent under the authority of the Rajah of Travancore. Madura seems to have been

—were probably only too glad of so good an excuse for plundering the villages on the Fishery Coast as that which was afforded them by the fact that the inhabitants had become Christians, which in their eyes amounted to a desertion to the common enemies of all the independent natives of India—the Portuguese. They had fallen suddenly, a horde of well-armed horsemen, upon the feeble and defenceless natives, before they had time to collect in one spot to oppose force by force, and the issue is related in the following letter:

(XXIV.) *To Francis Mancias.*

My dearest Brother in Jesus Christ,

I arrived on Saturday evening at Munahpaud. On the road at Combutur I met with very sad news about the Christians at Cape Comorin, which has made me quite wretched. The Badages have fallen upon them with the sword, and driven them from their homes, plundered them, made a great number of them prisoners, and the rest have taken refuge in the caves of the rocks which run out into the sea, where they are perishing of hunger and thirst. I am going to their help as fast as I can, and set sail this very night with twenty tones from Munahpaud. Pray to God for these poor creatures and for us; and see above everything that the children pray to God for us.

At Combutur the inhabitants have promised me to build a church, and Manuel de Lima has promised to give a hundred

---

generally the more dominant state of the two. In 1609 the Paravas were tributaries of Madura (letter of F. A. Laerzio, quoted by Bertrand, l. c.). In 1700 we find Travancore also tributary to Madura (*Lettres Edifiantes*, t. x. p. 77), and the Vadhouger, or Badages, entering the territory of the former year after year to exact the tribute. F. Organtino, much nearer to the time of which we are speaking (1568), speaks of the Badages as people from Narsinga (a kingdom north of Madura, lying close to Bisnaghur), and calls them 'regiorum fermè vectigalium exactores' (Maffei, *Sel. Epist. ex Indiâ*, l. iv. p. 431). If we suppose these curious freebooters to have had a special hatred to everything Christian and Portuguese, we have exactly the conditions required to explain the whole story concerning them contained in the lives and letters of St. Francis.

fanams of his own money to help the building. Go over there and press on and arrange the work. You may set out on Thursday or Friday, and next week, God willing, you shall go to visit the Christians who are scattered up and down the country between Punical and Alendale; go into each cottage, baptize all whom you find who have not yet received baptism, and give to all the instructions and advice they want. Take particular and vigilant care to baptize everywhere the new-born infants. See to whether the persons who have to teach the children and to assemble them at appointed hours, do their duty.

Charge Manuel da Cruz, who is living at Combutur, to pay great attention to those two Christian villages of Careans, taking diligent care, in the first place, to extinguish at once any rising quarrels among them by reconciling the parties while the matter is yet in its infancy; and in the second place, to prevent any one from carving idols or getting drunk with arrack. Every Sunday let the people all be assembled to repeat their prayers and hear the Catechism; the men in the morning, the women in the evening.

If Francis Coelho be with you, tell him to come hither at once, and that this is my order.

May God keep you in His holy protection! Farewell.

Your most affectionate brother in Jesus Christ,

From Munahpaud, Monday,[14] June 16th, 1544. FRANCIS.

---

[41] It is necessary to suppose some of the dates of these letters to have become confused in transcription. The Latin date given for this letter is unusually precise, 'hâc feriâ secundâ, xii. Kal. Jul. (June 20) 1544.' St. Francis hardly ever gives the days of the week, but it is probable that the date of Monday is exact, as he would naturally set out to the relief of the Christians as soon as he could, and he arrived at Munahpaud on Saturday evening. But June 20th was on a Friday, not a Monday, so we must alter the date to June 16th. The letter (p. 212) dated June 30th speaks of his return to Munahpaud, after having failed to reach the Cape, and having been a week at sea, as 'last Tuesday'—that would be June 24th, and would just leave a week between the two letters. The intermediate letter dated Virandapatanam, June 22, would seem to have been written at a moment in the struggle to get along the coast where Francis may have put to land. The boats were sometimes towed along shore, so that he might easily be on shore to write a short note. This is evidently very hurried.

Francis Xavier seems to have set out at once for the Cape by sea, but to have failed in reaching it. The next two letters carry on the history.

(XXV.) *To Francis Mancias.*

My dearest Brother in Jesus Christ,

This to tell you that, by God's grace, I am very well. May He Who is pleased to give me health also grant that I may use it in His service!

Let me know daily how things are in your parts, how your affairs get on, what the Christians are about, and so on. Work as hard as you can to get the church built. Let me hear at once when it is finished. I send with this a letter to the Commandant, which please to put into the hands of a very trusty messenger. Again and again I beg of you to give your first attention to the education of the children. And I am also very anxious that you should take the greatest care to baptize yourself every newborn infant as soon as it is born, or as soon as possible, that Paradise may be peopled by their souls at least, most of which leave their little bodies before the age of reason, since we cannot get the grownup folk to go there, either by punishment or promises of good.

Greet Manuel da Cruz much for me. I exhort Matthew to persevere and to improve in all good. Take pains to show yourself kind and affable to the people, particularly to the magistrates and to the village chiefs—Adigares, as they are called. May our Lord be with you always Farewell.

Your most affectionate brother in Jesus Christ,

From Virandapatanam,[15] June 22, 1544. FRANCIS.

This conjecture would account for the unusual announcement that the writer was in good health—notwithstanding the sufferings to which he had been exposed. [It is as well to state that we here omit a letter inserted in the Latin collection. It is given in the notes.]

[15] Probably Viranda and Patanam—perhaps begun at one place and ended at the other—unless this was really a place combining the two names, Virandapatanam.

The next letter relates the issue of the unavailing attempt made by Francis to reach the Cape by sea.

(XXVI.) *To Francis Mancias.*

My dearest Brother in Jesus Christ,

On Tuesday last I came back to Munahpaud, and God our Lord knows what I have gone through in my voyage. I had set off with twenty tones to comfort the Christians whom the Badages have driven into flight, who, as I was told, were dying miserably of hunger and thirst amongst the rocks which bound the shores of Cape Comorin; but I met with strong winds from the opposite quarter, and neither by rowing nor by towing could we make head against the sea, and I was not able once to get a single vessel to the Cape. If these winds fall, I shall go there again to take what relief I can to these poor creatures in their extreme distress; for a man must be harder than iron if he could give up making all efforts in his power to relieve the miserable case of these people, who are our brethren in the worship of Christ—a case I really think the most calamitous that can be found anywhere. Many of the fugitives arrive every day at Munahpaud without clothing, nearly dead with hunger, and destitute of everything. I am writing to the Patangatins of Combutur, of Punical, and of Tuticorin, to collect for them some little alms, and get them sent to us: but bidding them, however, to exact nothing from the poor, but simply to ask the captains of vessels, and others who have some means, of their own free will to contribute to so pious a work. But though I have enjoined this, still, as I know what sort of persons the Patangatins are, I very much fear that they may make this an opportunity for extorting money from the poor.

I should like you to tell me how the building of the church at Combutur is getting on. Let me hear all particulars, and whether Manuel de Lima has yet paid the hundred fanams that he promised for the work. I should like you to give me at the same time a long and full account how your excursion through the villages and your instructions of the outlying farms went off, in what state you found the Christians, how you left them, whether the men whom we have appointed to instruct the children throughout the country everywhere do their duty well. I have been most faithful in paying them regularly the salary which was promised them, but I can't myself watch over their behaviour when I am away. So I wish you to let me know about this accurately, and also about yourself, how your health is, how you find your present abode, what is going on there, and how religion fares.

We were a whole week at sea, and you know by experience what it is to be on board a tone, especially with violent winds blowing in your teeth, as we had,—and we couldn't make our way against them by any skill or force whatever.

May God our Lord protect you ever! Farewell.

Your most affectionate brother in Jesus Christ,

FRANCIS.

From Munahpaud, June 30th, 1544.

After this letter the correspondence fails us again for a month, and we are therefore unable to trace the footsteps of Francis Xavier by its aid. He seems to have been out of reach of Mancias, and to have found letters from him when he himself returned to Munahpaud. We conjecture that they were out of reach of one another during this time, because the next letter which we shall insert, which is dated at the beginning of August, carries on the narrative of the relief of the Christians from the point at which the last leaves it, though several weeks passed between the two letters. We also suppose that during this interval Francis again plunged into the kingdom of Travancore.[16] Indeed, it is probable that we must fix upon this interval as the time for one of the most famous actions of the Saint in this country. The Vadhouger, or Badages, of whom we have already heard so much, seem to have either continued their raid westwards at some little distance inland, or to have

[16] In the next letter, where he speaks of the Christians to whose relief he had set out, he does not say that he had taken them to Munahpaud, but that he had provided for their being taken thither (*curavi deportandos*).

returned after a short interval and shown an intention of falling upon the villages on the western slopes of the mountains which end in Cape Comorin. About four leagues north of the Cape lay the city of Cotate, which a century and a half later than this time was of considerable size, but may in the time of St. Francis have been only a large village. A church, we believe, still exists on the plain a few miles north of Cotate, which commemorates the heroic action of which we speak. From the account given in Bartoli, it would appear that the invasion of Travancore was made by a more regular and formidable army than had been collected for the ravaging of the defenceless pearl fisheries along the south-eastern coast of the promontory. The Naicker of Madura was himself with them and in command, and the Rajah of Travancore himself was in motion with a considerable force of his own subjects to resist the aggressors. However this may have been, the attack was directed principally against the villages of new Christians, and Francis Xavier immediately flew to their assistance. When the Processes for his canonization came to be formed at Cochin, more than a dozen witnesses came forward to testify to the fact that the whole country was full of the story how, with a crucifix in his hand, he had gone forth alone to meet the invaders, and severely rebuked them in the name of God, how the front ranks stopped on their march before him, and how, when they were urged on by those behind them and encouraged by their leaders, the soldiers replied that they could go no further, because a man of great height, of terrible and majestic presence, in a black robe, overawed and frightened them, that no one could bear the fire that flashed from his face and eyes. The leaders themselves fell under the same overpowering influence, and the whole army turned upon its march and left the Christians in peace.[17]

[17] See Bartoli, *Asia*, t. i. l. i. p. 72. He is copied by Massei, *Vita de S. Francesco Xav.* l. ii. c. 2, and Bouhours, l. ii. Bartoli extracted his facts from the Processes; and the references, number and character of the witnesses, and other details are given in the *Relatio super sanctitate et miraculis F. Xaverii*, written at Rome by the Auditors of the Rota in the time of Paul V.

We shall hear more of these freebooters presently. Francis may probably have spent the greater part of July in preaching in Travancore, baptizing heathen, and instructing his converts. This country became the scene of a number of his most wonderful miracles. He is said to have raised four persons from the dead. In these cases no particulars are given. There are other instances of the same power in him, of which we have full details, and it may be worth while to relate them shortly in the words in which the evidence is summed up in the *Relatio*, prepared in the time of Paul V. The scene of the first of these miracles was Mutan, a town, as it seems, on the coast, where, as he was passing through the street one day, he met a funeral procession, as our Lord met that which was bearing to the grave the widow's son. The body was that of a youth who had died of a malignant fever, and had been kept twenty-four hours unburied in a shroud, 'as the manner is of that country,' says the writer before us. When Francis 'met the bier and saw the dead youth, led by the prayers of the parents and pitying their bereavement, he knelt down, and raising his eyes to heaven, prayed to God for the life of the lad; then he sprinkled the body with holy water and bade them cut open the funeral shroud, and when the body was seen, he made the sign of the Cross over it, and taking him by the hand, bade him in the name of Jesus to live, and at once the youth rose up alive, and he gave him sound and in good health to his parents.[18] And they that stood by,' he adds, 'marvelled, and held what had been done for a great miracle, praising the holiness of Francis, and in honour and memory of the deed erected a cross on the spot and held there a festival.'

The other miracle of the same kind took place at Coulan or Quilon on the coast. Francis had been for some time preaching there without producing much effect upon the peo-

[18] This miracle, as well as that which follows, has been selected by the Auditors of the Rota as resting upon incontrovertible evidence. It rests on the testimony of two witnesses whose names are given, Emanuel Gago and Joam Audicondam, who were present and saw what passed, one other who had heard of the miracle from the person himself who was raised from the dead, and several others who bore witness to the notoriety of the fact.

ple. Coulan was a seaport—a place in which men of all nations met for purposes of traffic, and where the Christian law was frequently and openly dishonoured by those who bore the Christian name. Francis felt himself baffled by the obstinacy of the hearts which he was trying to soften. He was in a church, for the Portuguese had a station there, and a man had been buried there the day before. He paused in his sermon, and prayed awhile silently with tears. Then he addressed his audience with burning words, telling them that God was pleased to raise the dead in order to convert them. He bade them open the tomb, take out the corpse, and tear open the shroud in which it was wrapped. Then he prayed again, and the dead man rose up to life. A large number were converted, praising and blessing God for the holiness and power He had given to His servant.[19]

We must take these miracles as but specimens—though no doubt splendid and remarkable in their kind—of the signs which waited upon the Apostolate of Francis Xavier in Travancore. His life at this time must have been extremely active, for we know him often to have been elsewhere, and yet we have seen that the fruits of his preaching during this year remained in the establishment of as many as forty-five Christian communities or villages in the country. Towards the end of July he is again on the Fishery Coast, and writes to Mancias a letter which continues the subject of his last.

(XXVII.) *To Francis Mancias.*

My dearest Brother in Jesus Christ,

May God our Lord be pleased to watch over and keep you ever, and grant you good health and great strength, that you may spend all for Him! Your last letter, which I have just received, gave me the greatest pleasure, inasmuch as it gave me manifest proofs of your great diligence in fortifying

[19] This miracle rests upon the testimony of Diego Fernandez, who was present and saw the whole, and of several other witnesses who testify to the notoriety of this fact.

and preparing the people against the invasion of the Badages, that they may not be suddenly taken by surprise by them.

I went off, after all, by land to the Cape, to visit those unhappy Christians who have survived the plundering and cruelties of the Badages. A more miserable sight could nowhere be seen; faces white with exhaustion, livid with hunger; the fields covered with dead and dying, the disfigured corpses which had had no burial, or the poor creatures who were at the point of death from wounds untended or sickness unrelieved. There were old men there utterly powerless from age or hunger, trying in vain to drag themselves along—there were women giving birth to children in the public roads, their husbands moving about them, but unable to help them, so universal and common to all was the very extremity of destitution. If you had seen this as I did, your heart would, I am sure, have been pierced with a pang of pity you would never have got over. I had all the poor taken to Munahpaud, where the greater part of this most afflicted people is now collected for us to take care of as well as we can. Pray to God that He may touch the hearts of the rich with some mercy for so many miserable creatures, pining away in the utmost distress.

I hope to go on Wednesday to Punical. Don't relax your watchfulness for the people, I entreat you, until it is well ascertained the Badages have gone back to their own territories. Tell Antonio Fernandez lo Grosso and the Patangatins of Old Chael that I expressly forbid the new colony to go and haunt the old place from which they came, that I will severely punish them if they attempt to do so. Take pains to tell Manuel da Cruz and Matthew also that I send them much love and all kinds of good wishes.

May our Lord be with you, and may He strengthen us by His grace, so that we may serve Him with all our might! Farewell.

Your brother in Jesus Christ,

From Munahpaud, August 1st, 1544. FRANCIS.

From the mention of the Badages in this letter it is clear

that the danger from them had by no means passed away, and indeed the subsequent letters are full of them. Early in the same month of August he writes to Mancias, who seems to have been himself in danger, and to have desired to retire from so arduous a post. He promises him that he would never himself rest until he had set him at liberty, if he should happen to be taken prisoner. He then tells him that he has sent a priest to warn the people in the parts where Mancias is, having received private information that the Badages are again on the move against them.

(XXVIII.) *To Francis Mancias.*

May God be with you ever!

My dear Brother in Jesus Christ,

The different kinds of news given me in your letter affected me each in its own way when I read it. I felt the greatest delight in that part of it which tells me how you have gone through your late visitation of the villages with very great spiritual fruit; but on the other hand, the mere mention of your being taken prisoner, which you tell me, and which, I see well enough, is possible, struck me with grief and raised a painful image before my mind. If that were to happen, I would never take a moment's rest until God gave you back, which I should think would be very soon. Some of us, as you know, have had the experience of troubles and dangers of the kind. May all things turn out to the honour and glory of our God, wonderful in goodness and in power!

I have sent one of our priests into your parts, who is to tell all the villages to get their boats ready and launch them all along the coast, so that they may all embark and get out to sea before these savage brigands come down on them, for I have good grounds for thinking that they will soon be pouring down upon this country, as I am informed that they are arming themselves and assembling their forces, in order to lay waste the whole coast down to the water's edge. So I am told by one of the principal Canacars,[20] a friend to the native Christians. I had sent to him a man with a letter addressed to the Rajah of Travancore, begging him to deliver it in person, and also to employ his favour with that prince, one of whose intimate friends he is, to get him to lay strict prohibitions on the Badages, forbidding them to molest our unhappy Christians, any harm done to whom the Governor of India would consider done to himself, and would avenge it.

I had reason to hope that he would do what I asked, for he is my friend, and as I have said, is well affected to the Christians, among whom he has several relations and connections. He came himself to see me, not only to pay his respects, but to help me, offering all the assistance in his power very earnestly. I wrote to him that if the Badages were so uncontrollable that the Rajah's authority was not enough to prevent their ravages, I begged that at least I might have timely notice given me of their intended invasion on the coast when it was about to take place, and so be able to send the Christians on board ship and get them out to sea, so as to escape by flight from massacre and spoliation by land. And now he has with great good faith given me notice that it is to be.

I have also written to the Commandant, begging him to send one of the larger craft ('catures') well armed, to serve as a protection for all the boats of the Christians, which are quite unarmed. And do you over and over again enjoin on the inhabitants, and especially those most distant from the sea, to set faithful and watchful sentinels at the proper points to report how things are hour by hour, that they may not be caught by a night attack of the horsemen before they are able to get to the boats, which they have made ready, and set in safety off the shore. But even when you have told them all this as urgently as you can, I would have you put but very little confidence in their doing what you tell them. I know too well their laziness and obstinate stupidity, and I quite expect they will grudge spending two fanams to pay the necessary expenses. So do you by yourself, and by means of persons whom you can

[20] The Canacars were native officials, probably collectors of revenue.

trust, undertake all the watching and all the care, urging them to get the women and children on board the boats, which are already launched; and take the opportunity of this time of calamity to require of them all, and especially of the weaker in sex and age, to have recourse to God by reciting their prayers. Fear is a grand teacher of prayer, especially when, as is the case with these poor folk, they have no one to look to for help but God alone.

I have no writingpaper here. I left a good deal at your place in a box, and I shall be glad if you can send me enough for present use by a messenger with great despatch. I shall expect a letter from you by the same hand, to tell me whether the boats are already at sea, and whether the poor furniture and slender properties of the families who are in danger on land have been placed in them, with the wives and children. If this has not been done, let it be seen to immediately. Go in my name to Antonio Fernandez lo Grosso, and conjure him by his friendship for me to pour out the whole of the love he bears to me in the work of saving these poor wretches, and to use his authority in hastening their flight, and even forcing them to it, as the only chance of saving their lives and not only their liberty. I say, their lives and lifeblood, because as to those who are better off than the rest, the greedy robbers may perhaps look for more gain by having them ransomed and bought off, and so may carry them away alive; but their avarice can expect nothing from the poor, and so these will be cruelly slaughtered. Again and again I insist, be sure to have sentinels on the watch, in many different places of the coast, all night, especially now that the moon is at the full and gives convenient light for any expedition by night.

May God keep you under His protection, the only protection worth trusting to! Farewell.

Your most loving brother in Jesus Christ,

From Munahpaud, August 3rd, 1544. FRANCIS.

A fortnight later we find him writing again most urgently to Mancias to do all in his power to relieve the misery of the

Christians. There was now danger in another quarter. Tuticorin, to the north, on the eastern coast of the extremity of the peninsula of India, has been threatened. There have been disturbances of some sort, in which we gather that it is only too probable that the Portuguese—a small garrison, apparently, holding a fortress of some strength, rather than the whole town—have had something to do. Francis is afraid that all this will make the case of the Christians harder than ever. Reports reach him that some Portuguese have been wounded, if not slain. Mancias must have been at Tuticorin, or nearer to it than Francis, for the letter requires him to let him know how things are. Then there is a postscript: he has just heard that the Christians had been plundered and chased into a forest by the Badages. 'We are overwhelmed with bad news from every side. God be praised always!'

(XXIX.) *To Francis Mancias.*

My dearest Brother in Jesus Christ,

I have another opportunity of writing, so I again urge upon you what I did this morning. I implore you again and again to relieve and console with every exertion in your power these unfortunate people in their deep distress; and also, what I shall count as the greatest kindness you can do me, in your charity to send me at once a faithful account of what has really taken place at Tuticorin.

I very much fear that these troubles at Tuticorin may somehow add fresh ruin and misery to our poor Christians, who have already miseries enough to bear. People here are in such consternation with anxiety about impending calamities that no words can describe it; I could not bear to think, and I hope no one else could, of our abandoning these people at this moment of uncertainty and affliction. So do not go with Joam Artiaga where he wishes to take you, as long as there is any danger at all from the Badages where you are; and when you have got any news about them, let me, I beseech you, have it from you at once.

The Rajah of Travancore is sending a Brahmin to them, who takes with him the interpreter of our Commandant to try and persuade them to peace. No one knows what will be the result. We have both the envoys here at Munahpaud just about to embark. I am very desirous to know what has been going on with the Portuguese at Tuticorin; and again and again I entreat you to write to me the whole story minutely and particularly, and to write at once; as soon as you have any news, write it down and send it off. I am in a perfect fever of anxiety and care and trouble, and nothing but letters from you can deliver me from it. There is a report here, that some Portuguese and Christians have been wounded or even killed; and whether it is true or not, whether anything has happened, and what and how, I am burning for you to tell me. As to your journey, we will either settle it when next we meet, or if the storm from the Badages should blow over first, I will write very soon and tell you what I think.

May our Lord be ever with you! Amen.

From Munahpaud, 19th August, 1544.

At this very moment I have a letter from Guarim, in which, my dearest brother, he sends me word that the Christians have fled into the forest, after having been stripped of everything by the Badages, who have wounded one of them, as well as a heathen native. Bad news comes pouring in on all sides. God our Lord be praised for ever and ever!

Your most loving brother in Jesus Christ,

FRANCIS.

The next day he writes, evidently in answer to a letter from Mancias, speaking very severely of the complicity in the misfortunes of the Christians of some one who ought to have been on their side—probably the Portuguese commandant. He is mentioned in a later letter as having been the cause of some homicides at Tuticorin, and as having extorted money from natives who were afterwards put to death. Mancias, like the Apostles in the Gospel, has been inclined to call down the vengeance of heaven on the offender.

(xxx.) *To Francis Mancias.*

May God be with you! Amen.

My dearest Brother,

Those words of our Lord, *He that is not with Me is against Me*, will make you understand how destitute we here are of any friends to aid us in bringing this people to Jesus Christ. But we must not despond, for God at the end will render unto each one according to his deserts, and it is very easy for Him, when He pleases, to accomplish by means of a few what seemed to require the work of many. I say again and again, I feel far more of compassion for those who fight against God, than of any desire to call down greater vengeance on their heads—they are already miserable enough in the mere fact that they do so fight. Why should we draw down on them God's vengeance, which will certainly not fail at its own time? And how severe are the punishments which God at last inflicts on His enemies, we see well enough, as often as we turn our mind's eye to the inextinguishable furnace of hell, whose fires are to rage throughout all eternity for so many miserable sinners.

The Brahmin I wrote to you about yesterday is going to you with the Rajah's message to the Badages: do your very best, I entreat you, that he may find a ship ready to take him safely and quickly to Tuticorin. I adjure you, as you love God, to write me word fully at once and diligently, what has happened and is happening there; I mean all about the Commandant, the Portuguese, the Christians of Tuticorin; tell me all most distinctly, if you care to relieve me from very painful anxiety.

Say a great many kind things to Joam d'Artiaga, and also to Manuel da Cruz, from me. Tell Matthew that he is not to think he is working in vain; I am getting ready for him a great many more good things than he expects or wishes for.

May our Lord be with you! Amen.

From Munahpaud, August 20th, 1544.

Pray, for the love of God, take care that the Brahmin meets with no delay in setting sail. Get the Commandant to receive him honourably, at least with kind words and looks.

Your most affectionate brother in Jesus Christ,

FRANCIS.

Again we have another letter on the following day. Mancias has been asking to be removed to a more secure spot. Francis tells him that he will send a priest in his stead as soon as his country is free from the alarm of the Badages: he is to go to Manaar, an island off Ceylon, of which we now hear for the first time, but which soon became famous in the Christian history of India. Francis himself is at Punical, where Mancias had been at first stationed. He has no interpreter, but finds work enough to do in baptizing children and taking care of the sick and poor. He is going off to Tala, to comfort the sufferers from the late raid; but the Badages have left his part of the coast free for the present. He hopes to reduce them to peace by the authority of the Rajah of Travancore. We give this letter, as well as another written on his return from Tala, which goes considerably into details as to his wish to visit the Rajah.

(XXXI.) *To Francis Mancias.*

May God be always with you! Amen.

My dearest Brother in Jesus Christ,

Your last letter gladdened my heart, giving me so much news that I was anxious to have, and which it will be of use for me to know. I am still expecting to hear again from you that your people and the country about you are entirely safe from the Badages, and I beg you to tell me of this as soon as ever you can do so with truth. Then you will be able without danger, and without giving your present people any ground of complaint, to go elsewhere, where, as you know, there is a bright hope and fair occasion of doing something good for the service of God. I shall then send you Father

Francis Coelho to take your present post. Thus you will be quite free, and will leave with the approval of all, and go where there is great expectation of fruitful labour for the glory of God, to baptize the natives of Careapatana, and work in other ways for the service of religion with the Carean people of Beadala and the ruler of those parts, whom they call the Mudaliar. The Governor of the province of Negapatam has great influence and favour with the Rajah of Jafanapatam, under whose dominion the isles of Manaar lie, and his disposition is such that we may well hope that he will protect them with his favour with his sovereign. As soon, therefore, as the people where you are are in perfect tranquillity, and entirely free from all fear of the Badages, you must send a messenger to let me know this, that I may send without further delay Francis Coelho with money, letters of introduction, where they are wanted, and written instructions, as to what I send you to Manaar to do, how it is to be done, and for how long.

I recommend our brother Joam d'Artiaga most particularly to your kindness; and write me word what he is in need of, that I may provide it duly for him. I am almost alone here, since Antonio has remained ill at Munahpaud, and what is very inconvenient, I am working in the midst of a people whose language I do not understand, and I have no interpreter. The only shifts for an interpreter that I have had are Rodriguez, who is here now, and Antonio when he was here. You can tell yourself how much they know of our language. So you can easily imagine how I live here, what sort of instructions I can give, when the persons who ought to explain to the people what I say don't understand me, nor I them. My only way of eloquence at present is that of signs. However, I am not without something to do, for I do not require an interpreter to baptize the little children just born, or those whom their parents bring to me for baptism, and when I see people without clothes or worn with hunger, the mere sight of them and their whole appearance tells me what they want. I am so well occupied in these two chief kinds of most useful work that I have no regret as to the time spent in them. The

Badages, who were infesting this coast, are all gone to Cabecate, leaving us free and without fear for the present; but those who were ranging through the interior of the country are still committing most cruel ravages there, nor will they cease from rapine and violence, until peace or a truce is made with them by the authority of the Rajah of Travancore. I told you we were trying to bring this about.

May our Lord be ever with you! Amen.

From Punical, August 21, 1544.

This night I sail for Tala, to comfort, if I can, the poor indigent folk who, I am told, are there in great numbers, suffering the utmost distress.

Your most affectionate brother in Jesus Christ,

FRANCIS.

It is important to notice the date of this last letter, as it makes it clear that as early as the August of 1544, Francis had received overtures from the inhabitants of the island of Manaar, who sent to him to beg for instruction and baptism. The fame of his miracles and sanctity had flown across the gulf which separates Ceylon and its little adjacent islands from the mainland of India. We shall presently have to relate the issue of this Manarese deputation, which came at a time when, as we shall see from the next letter in our series, Francis was very anxious to secure the work on which he had lately been engaged in Travancore from ruin by means of the protection of the (so called) 'Great King.' We have already spoken of the system adopted by Francis for the prosecution and increase of the faith among his converts on the Fishery Coast. Such system required considerable organization. The priests need not be very numerous; but there must be a building for religious meetings in each several village, and besides these, there must be persons appointed to take the lead at these meetings, to teach the Catechism to the children, to baptize newborn infants in cases of danger, to announce marriages, settle disputes, and the like; and the method adopted by Francis Xavier required that these should be well paid, and kept regularly to their work under the supervision of the missionaries, who were to move about from place to place, making several circuits in the course of the year. All this, together with the provision for the priests themselves, and the security of the new converts from the tyranny of their own local Adigares, as well as from the ever recurring danger of a raid from the Badages, had to be looked to, and it is evident that Francis was in hopes of inducing the Rajah himself to make arrangements for it. But so many demands required full exposition, and the personal influence of Francis himself to enforce them. The Rajah had already shown himself very favourable, as will be seen from the following letter, but there was still much to be done before the whole plan could be organized. We may reasonably suppose that it was this which had occupied Francis, and made him give up the thought of going himself to Manaar, while at the same time he was doubtful whether it would be prudent to venture to ask so much, as long as the Court of Travancore had just reason to feel indignant at the misconduct of the Portuguese.

(XXXII.) *To Francis Mancias.*

My dearest Brother in Jesus Christ,

The Prince who resides at Tala, and who is related to the Rajah of Travancore, is so friendly to us, that as soon as he heard of the wrongs done by the Adigares to the Christians of those parts, he sent at once one of his household in his own name with a letter for the Adigares, bidding them to permit free exportation of food and other necessaries from the continent to the islands where the Christians are, and to help them with every other kind of friendly assistance of which they are in need. He charged this officer to find out from the Christians the names of the Adigares, so as to communicate them to me, and bring him also a written list of them, that if he has occasion by and bye to go to visit the Rajah, he may be able to tell him the names of the men who holding the rank of Adigares have abused their authority to vex the

Christians, so that the Rajah, who shows us favour, may prevent them from such conduct in future.

I want you to arrange with the Patangatins that the person sent by the Prince to aid the Christians may be received by them with every mark of honour, that they may give him a present as a reward, paying him gratefully and well for the journey and trouble he has taken on their account. I cannot do it myself, nor can the people here, we are so poor just now. The Patangatins must not be afraid to spend in this useful and pious way a small sum out of the public money, which they very often spend so mischievously on dances, banquets, and other profane pleasures of the same kind. And do you yourself, out of your own poverty, give something to win the man's favour, that he may be softened by all these little presents, and discharge with greater alacrity and efficacy his commission, which is to make the Adigares afraid in future to annoy the Christians, as they have done up to the present time, to their great loss and suffering; and, on the contrary, to constrain them to show our people all those kindly offices which are to be expected from good and friendly neighbours in the thousand daily occasions of mutual intercourse and commerce.

I am most anxious to know what you have heard with certainty of the affair which has made so much noise here. It has been reported everywhere that a Portuguese had carried off one of the Rajah of Travancore's servants, and had taken him in fetters to Tuticorin. Now I know that rumour often reports things which are either without foundation, or much exaggerated by illwill. Tell me first whether the fact be true; then, if it be so, what right the Portuguese alleges on his own side, what occasion or pretext he would have had for such an act. I have already written to you at length touching this business and the reports which are current about it. It is the more necessary for me to know exactly how the truth is, as my plan of going to visit the Rajah depends on what I may hear. For if this crime has really been committed, and in the way report says, I think it will be better to put off the whole thing and not to go to that court, where the very sight of a European would be hateful, and where I should have to face the responsibility of so inexcusable an outrage. Any one can see how detestable the whole country and especially the Court itself must think it, that a foreigner should dare to lay violent hands on a servant of the Maharajah in a place under his dominion, especially when that prince is behaving so differently to us. Just lately he received Father Francis Coelho with wonderful courtesy, and granted him absolutely every favour that he asked for the Christians; indeed, he showed himself so very well inclined to benefit them on representations of this Father, that, to give him some striking proof of his regard, he, of his own accord, created four of our Munahpaud Christians Patangatins, and this without any fees from them, and without any cost to the people, for he formally forbade the exaction of any money on this occasion, as was formerly the custom in the time of the Pulas. Besides this, he has created three other Christian Patangatins in other places without any expense to the inhabitants, declaring with the greatest kindness that he did all this out of regard to Father Coelho, who had been to visit him, as I told you.

I conjure you, by the love you bear to God, write to the Commandant as precisely as possible in my name, to say that I entreat him over and over again that if he has any regard for me he will abstain during this whole month of September from any offence or violence whatever to the subjects of the Maharajah, and not permit any Portuguese to treat any of them injuriously during the same time. Give him as a reason, what is quite true, that we find this nation of the subjects of the Rajah of Travancore more easy to persuade and better disposed than any other in all that concerns the interests of religion and of the Christians. If the Commandant will only believe this, I cannot doubt that he would see most forcible reasons in it for granting my request that he will do no harm to people who deserve so well at our hands. You will easily see what I am at in making this compact for a kind of truce for this next month. You know that I am thinking, on account of important interests of religion, of going to the Rajah within the time I have named, and I should be annoyed and grieved beyond measure if my access to him were to be hindered by any new matter of complaint that might arise against our countrymen.

However, as I said, I have not positively settled whether I go or not. I am waiting to hear what plausible defence can be given as to this reported seizure of the Rajah's servant; and for this it is that I want you so much to write. If you can tell me what I wish, I shall set off without delay, embarking first for Cochin. But now mind that I wish this letter, on which my decision depends, should not be in your hand nor signed with your name. I remember that you gave me to understand that you had some things to tell me about this business which could only be told by word of mouth, when we were together. I can't help suspecting that there is something at the bottom about the Commandant himself, or the Portuguese, or possibly the native Christians, which it is well I should know, that I may remedy the evil, and well also that it should not be trusted to black and white, for if the letter were to chance to be intercepted, it might put you out with the persons among whom you live. I highly approve your caution, but, all the same, as just at this moment we cannot meet, and as my affairs are just at that turn when I can't do without this intelligence, I have made up my mind that you must let me know about the matter, whatever it is, by a letter written by some one else, and which, if it fall into any one's hands, may not be brought home to you by your handwriting or your signature. This letter send me by some very faithful messenger, and then, having had all information, I shall decide whether it is worth while for me to go to the Rajah. But I have already determined, if this crime by which the Rajah has been insulted is clearly proved, and as shameful and inexcusable as report makes it, I shall not go there at all.

May God our Lord always give us His aid and His grace!

Your most affectionate brother in Jesus Christ,

FRANCIS.

From Munahpaud, September 2, 1544.

The caution used by Mancias as to the information which he had to communicate concerning the outrage on the Travancorese noble throws considerable light on the conditions under which the missionary enterprize of Francis and his associates was carried on. They had not only to deal with the difficulties which consisted in the ignorance, idleness, and voluptuousness of the natives themselves, in their inveterate tendency to relapse into idolatry or superstition, to drink arrack, or revolt against the severity of the Christian law of chastity and monogamy. Nor did the external dangers to their faith or to their Christian practice lie only in the suspicion with which every convert, much more every convert community, must have been regarded by the remainder of the Indians, and by the Mussulmans and Jews, who were in great numbers and very influential in the country, in the tyranny of their own magistrates, or in the danger from foreign marauders. The Portuguese, as we have already said, were the great enemies of the converts, both directly, in the outrages which they so frequently committed upon them as well as upon the other inhabitants of the country indiscriminately, and indirectly in the odium which their outrages excited, and which fell upon all Christians, and notably upon these neophytes and their teachers. These last, as Francis Xavier seems to have felt, were particularly liable to be made responsible for the misdemeanours of their fellow countrymen, as they were undoubtedly in many cases the promoters, at least indirectly, of peace and alliance between the latter and the Portuguese, the good faith of which alliance was so frequently broken first on the Christian side. Their position is in some degree like that of the Catholic missionaries of our own time in North America, who often render great services to the Government of the United States by prevailing on the Indian tribes under their influence to accept terms of peace, which imply great concessions on their part, while all the time the Government is in truth unable to control the violence and wanton cruelty of its own settlers along the extreme frontiers of the civilized regions, whose barbarities sometimes exceed those of the unconverted Indians themselves, and very naturally place even the lives of the missionaries in danger. Francis Xavier may not have been exposed himself to this particular peril, but we see clearly how hopeless he felt it to be to struggle on for the free establishment of the Christian religion among these nations, with the enormous weight against him of the hostility so justly aroused by the wicked licentiousness and rapine of those Portuguese who looked upon India as a country in which their one business was to enrich themselves and indulge their own passions without regard to God or man, and who considered the Indians as hardly having the common rights of human beings when they came in the way of their own avarice or lust.

We have seen how Francis, in his last letter, was sanguine enough to hope that the Commandant of Tuticorin, Cosmo de Payva, would appreciate the force of the consideration he there urged in favour of peaceable conduct to the natives. There had as yet been no open breach between them, though the character of the man and the opinion of Francis concerning him are sufficiently indicated in the letter alluded to. It turned out, however, that nothing was to be hoped for in this quarter. We know Cosmo to have been one of the very worst of the bad Portuguese officers, of whom there were but too many in India, who on account of their own interests and the great opportunities which they possessed of furthering them with impunity at the expense of the cause of religion, became in fact more deadly enemies of the Gospel than the Badages themselves. He may have been led by his own guilty conscience to suspect that Francis had written to Goa to complain of him. At all events, he had written to Francis before his letter could reach Mancias, declaring that he would have nothing to do with his friendship, and loading him with reproaches and insults. It is quite clear that Francis must have crossed him unwittingly in some of the measures he had taken for the protection of the Christians, or to curb the aggressive and tyrannical violence of the Portuguese. But the poor man was soon an object of pity to all, as well as to the Saint. It would appear from one of two letters written only two days after the letter mentioned above, that he had in some way played into the hands of the Badages, instead of protecting the Christians, and had thus tried to purchase the friendship of the invaders for himself. His reward was that he shared the fate of the Christians of Tuticorin: his ship was burnt, as well as the building or fortress occupied by him on the shore, and he was driven like the Christians first of Cape Comorin, and then of Tuticorin, to take refuge on some barren islands off the coast to save his life. Francis was eager to help and save him. He urged Mancias to get provisions on board some boats—water to drink especially—and set off at once to his relief, and he wrote also to the native magistrates along the coast to do the same. He would go himself, he says, but he has just received the letter in which the Commandant renounces his friendship, and he would be sorry to pain him at such a time of extremity by the sight of one to whom he could use such language.

This calamity, which befell the Christians of Tuticorin, as we may suppose, the Christian natives living around that town, and the Commandant himself also, gave occasion to the two letters which next follow. We put that which relates to the Christian natives first.

(XXXIII.) *To Francis Mancias.*

May our Lord God always be with you with His aid! Amen.

My dearest Brother in Jesus Christ,

I am in much anxiety about the Christians of Tuticorin, who are in the greatest possible misery with no one to care for them. I beg and pray you, by the love you bear to God, use the utmost diligence to find out at once, and to let me know, the real truth of the matter and in what condition they are. If you think it would be for the service of God to go to them, then go at once with all the boats you can get at Combutur and Punical, and transport the poor wretched people from the barren isles where they now are, partly to Combutur, partly to Punical and Trinchandour. Set off at once, pray, and without delay, go as fast as possible with all the tones that you can find at Punical, and send them word at Combutur to follow you with all theirs.

I conjure you by our Lord never let it be that Beterbemali, the leader of these robber Badages, and all his horde of plundering ruffians, should have their hearts' desire fulfilled, that the remnant of this most afflicted people, who have been driven out of their homes and country by terror of them and their insolence, should perish of hunger and thirst because you were slow in succouring them. Fine watch indeed was kept over them by that Commandant of yours! It would certainly have been somewhat more reasonable for him to take care of the Christians committed to his ward and charge than to have chosen rather, as it appears he did, to make his own peace by presents with Beterbemali and his bloodthirsty horsemen, who fly all over the country, laying waste everything with fire and sword! I am writing to the Patangatins of Punical and Combutur, telling them to put themselves under your lead, and come at once with all the boats they have at hand to the succour of the Christians at Tuticorin, who are dying of hunger and thirst in those arid islands, destitute of all the necessaries of life, and to take them away at once.

The order I thus give you to go there is to be understood as depending on whether you think that your going is necessary to carry out the business effectively. If, when you have delivered my letter to the Patangatins, you see they are zealous enough and take up the thing heartily of themselves, that you can trust them to do what is necessary with thorough vigour without you, then by all means stay where you are, for I well know how much the need of your care on the spot may make you wish to stay at your work. You must therefore weigh in the scales of charity and balance duly one against the other the two claims on you, that of the extreme distress of the Tuticorinians on the one hand, and that of the good of the people amongst whom you are working on the other, and give the preference to the most urgent. If without your going there the death of so many poor creatures, who are already at their last gasp, cannot be prevented, then leave all else and go there as fast as possible. Settle yourself what is best, I leave the whole matter for your judgment to decide on the moment. What you must provide for is that, whether you go or whether you send some one else in your place, the boats go at once to these starving and thirsting wretches, and that they carry sufficient water and provisions to relieve as soon as ever they arrive the hunger and thirst of so many fellow creatures of every age and sex, who are dying on those inhospitable rocks.

May God our Lord be ever with you! Amen. Tell me as soon as you can whether Manuel da Cruz and Matthew have got the better of the state of grief in which they were when I last saw them. Farewell.

Your most affectionate brother in Jesus Christ,

FRANCIS.

September 5th, 1544.

It seems that just after writing this Francis received the news that the Commandant himself was in the same plight with the people whom he ought to have protected.

(XXXIV.) *To Francis Mancias.*

My dearest Brother in Jesus Christ,

I have the saddest possible news about the Commandant. His vessel has been burnt, and the whole of his residence on the shore has also been burnt, and he himself, ruined and in want, has taken refuge in the islands, where he is in extreme want and barely alive. Go at once to his aid, I beseech you, for the love of God. Get together as quickly as you can all the barques of the Punical people, as many as you can find, and put supplies on board, especially of water, and go yourself to the spot. It must be done with all despatch: his condition is as bad as it can be, and admits of no delay. I am writing most urgently to the Patangatins to aid you to the utmost in this most necessary work of assistance to the Commandant. I have told them to load as many barques as they can send off with all that can be of use in such a case, specially water to drink, as every one knows that the islands are entirely devoid of it: and I want the barques that are sent to be as many as possible, that there may be enough to bring back to the land the very large number of people of all ages and sexes who have been driven to take refuge on those inhospitable rocks by the same storm which has fallen on the Commandant.

I would go myself and leave you quiet at Punical, if I thought my presence would be pleasing to the Commandant, but quite lately he renounced all friendship with me in a letter full of the most atrocious charges. Among other things he said that he could not without grave scandal mention the evils which he felt that I had brought on him. God knows whether I have ever done him any harm, especially such as could not be mentioned without scandal. But this is no time for defending myself or making complaints; what is of present importance is that we understand that in his present state of feeling towards me, I should for his own sake avoid meeting him. The poor man's calamities are abundantly great as they are, and I might add to them some new annoyance if now at the moment of his deepest distress I were to force on him the sight of one whom he dislikes so much. It is this fear, chiefly, that prevents me from going to him, though there are many other reasons against my taking the journey. So do you, for God's sake, do all that I should do myself with the greatest diligence. I am writing to the Patangatins of Combutur and Bembare to get together immediately all the boats they can find everywhere, load them with food and water, and sail at once to the Commandant. And if you wish to please God, put your hand to the work with all vigour, and determine not to allow yourself ever to have the selfreproach of having left out anything that could be done in the way of the utmost exertion to relieve before it is too late the extreme distress of this Commandant, which calls on us for the greatest possible display of mercy and charity. And of course your care must extend itself to the numbers of unhappy Christians who have been struck by the same blows of fortune. The regard I have for them makes me more urgent, and again and again I pray you to leave nothing undone to supply with all haste, promptly and efficiently, the very urgent needs of so many unfortunate creatures.

May our Lord be ever with you! Amen.

Your most affectionate brother in Jesus Christ,

FRANCIS.

Alendale, September 5th, 1544.

It will seem almost hard to believe, but the very next letter of St. Francis, written two days later (September 7), speaks of a fresh provocation given on the part of the Portuguese, not to the Rajah of Travancore, who seems, as far as we can gather, not to have resented the injury already mentioned to his noble, but to the terrible Badages themselves in the person of their leader, Beterbemali. St. Francis had gone off, after giving directions to Mancias and others for the relief of the Commandant, to visit some Christian settlements on the western side of Cape Comorin, and was proceeding on his road, when he was arrested by the news that some Portuguese had seized and carried off the brother in law of Beterbemali himself. The act may perhaps have been one of reprisal. The Portuguese were generally safe enough in their vessels or their fortresses, though the late calamity at Tuticorin may have warned them not to be too secure even there, and they may have had little fear of any revenge that the Badages might take. That revenge would be taken on the defenceless native population, who had placed themselves in so questionable a position in the eyes of their fellow countrymen by becoming Christians—a position which gave them the character of friends of the foreigner without ensuring to them protection from him. They were like the Catholics in England after the attempt of the Catholic King to overthrow Queen Elizabeth had failed, save that these had more claim on the forbearance of their countrymen on account of their own tried loyalty. It was easy work for the unscrupulous men who formed these garrisons to commit outrage upon outrage, for which the native Christians were to pay, and this abundantly explains their aggressiveness, and the position of St. Francis with regard to them. The Christian populations were nothing to them and all to him, and he had not only to convert the heathen, form the new converts into Christian communities, and then secure them at least liberty and toleration from their natural rulers, but also to meet storm after storm which swept over them in consequence of the depredations and outrages of the Portuguese.

In the case before us we have a letter of unusual length, in which he explains to Mancias what steps he has taken. The Badages had sworn vengeance against everything bearing the Christian name, but they were pretty sure to confine their revenge to those Christians who were at their mercy. The whole of the Christian population of the Comorin coast was in danger of the fate which had already befallen them once before, and which now was befalling the people of Tuticorin. Coelho, the secular priest already named, seems to have been left in Travancore by St. Francis in the course of his preaching there, and he is now sent to protect the Christians on the spot, and to use the name of Francis to pacify them. He hopes also in future to secure for the converts an asylum, not under the illusory protection of the Portuguese, but in the territories of this heathen king, who had become his friend, and who had also political reasons for hoping some advantage to himself from the friendship of the Governor. We give the letter in question, which shows how confidently St. Francis could speak of his own influence.

(xxxv.) *To Francis Mancias.*

My dearest Brother in Jesus Christ,

May it please God to grant us His most holy grace! For in this world truly we have no help but in Him alone. I was at Trinchandour and on the point of setting off for Virandapatanam to visit the Christians there, as I had done at Alendale, Pudicurim, and Trinchandour. I had found plenty to do everywhere, and to convince me how necessary such visits are. Well, as I said, I was in the act of setting off again, when a number of messengers from all parts came to tell me in the greatest alarm that the whole savage race of the Badages was in excitement and all but up in arms. The cause of their fury is that the Portuguese have seized and taken prisoner a near relation of Beterbemali, their leader, in fact his wife's own brother. The Badages, exasperated by this affront, were all vowing to exterminate everything Christian throughout the whole coast of Comorin.

As soon as I heard all this, I wrote at once to Father Francis Coelho that immediately on receiving my letter he was to hasten to the place where the Christians of Comorin have taken refuge, to protect as far as may be by my influence these unfortunate people, and preserve them from the terrible disasters which threaten them on this occasion. I know that amongst the Badages there is a great deal of talk about my credit with Iniquitribirim, whom they call their Rajah, though they are far from obeying him implicitly, and indeed some of them, who follow Beterbemali, have openly shaken off his authority. But the greater part have still a certain respect for the Rajah's name, so I hope that Father Coelho, as sent by me, and representing, as he does, me, may find some respect paid him, and be able to protect these cruelly used people. I have all the more hope of this, as I learn from Father Coelho's letter that it is not only the rebel Badages that are incensed at the capture of Beterbemali's brother in law, but that the rest of the nation is being roused to arms against the people of Comorin by a relation of Iniquitribirim, Rajah of Travancore, who has lately gone among them. Now with this chief a recommendation from me seemed likely to be of some use in preventing him from using violence against the Christians, because he knows that I am in some sort of account and honour with his Rajah. My hope was strengthened by news which Coelho gives me in the same letter, written quite lately, that the Rajah of Travancore had sent three or four of his principal courtiers to see me, who would have been here already if the fatigues of the journey had not made them halt at Munahpaud to take some repose. They are the bearers of a letter from the Rajah, in which he begs me not to think it too much trouble to come to him, and not to delay, for that he has to communicate some business of very great moment, which it is of much importance both to him and to us that he should talk over with me. As far as I can fathom the matter at this distance, I think I see reason for supposing that the Rajah takes this line because he feels himself in much need of the protection of the Governor of India. Current reports say that the subordinate chiefs who are not loyal to him, the Pulas of whom we have heard so much in these parts, have grown very powerful and become very rich from long prosperity, so that the Rajah has some reason to fear that they may make large presents to the Portuguese Governor, and get him on their side, so as to help them with some troops.

Knowing all this of the state of Iniquitribirim's affairs, I am the more ready to believe the letter which I have this moment received from him. In this he promises me, in the strongest and plainest terms, that he will show all favour to the Christians, whom he even invites into his dominions, answering for it that they shall live in perfect security and tranquillity. So I shall go to him with all speed, and intend to leave this tonight. My chief motive is the anxiety which I feel so strongly to do something at once for our unfortunate Christians who have been driven out of Tuticorin and Bembare, and to secure for them a fixed and safe place of settlement in the dominions of the Maharajah. The first thing that I shall settle with Iniquitribirim, and with the utmost diligence, will be to get him to assign a certain territory where these most miserable exiles may dwell unhurt and in peace.

Meanwhile I wish you to use every means that occurs to you with all diligence to get them over from the desert islands, where they are being killed by want, to Combutur and Punical; and see that they are hospitably entertained there until, as I said before, I can provide for them. Remember to write to me fully and minutely about the affairs and conditions of the Christians, especially the Commandant and the Portuguese, how each one is, and how their affairs get on. I should like you also, if you can steal so much of time from your more urgent occupations, to make an excursion to visit the Christians at Combutur, as well as the Careans on the Fishery Coast and those who live in the village where Thomas de Motta is head of affairs, and lastly, those who live near Patanam. It would delight me very much if you found leisure to visit them all, for I know the need they have of such lookings up. Would that I had time myself to go there now! I should like nothing better than to inspect all those places and make an accurate visitation of them all.

I beg of you, therefore, do all this for me, and inquire particularly how the instruction of the children is getting on everywhere, and whether it is faithfully performed. You know that in all these places I have established schoolmasters. For the salary which I have promised them you can take a hundred fanams, which is deposited for this purpose with your friend Manuel da Cruz, who lives at Punical. You must spend this sum in paying the schoolmasters and catechists their salary, each one will tell you how much I usually give him. Don't think that any money or time can be better employed, and rely upon it you will do a great deal for the special service of God our Lord, if you take pains and care to have this instruction of the young, a thing more necessary than any other, assiduously and diligently carried on. The man who is going to your parts, and to whom I have given this letter for you, appears very good, and inspired with great desire to serve God. Receive him kindly, and keep him with you till I return from Iniquitribirim; or, if you think it advantageous for the service of God, and if he would like it also, leave him at Combutur, he may do what he can in the building of the church. I hear a report that a certain barber is setting out from where you are. I shall very likely meet him on the road I am going, so pray write by him a full account of everything. I am very uneasy as to how things are, both with the Portuguese and Christians.

May our Lord grant us in the next life more tranquillity and consolation than we find in this! Farewell.

Your most loving brother in Jesus Christ,

FRANCIS.

From Trinchandour, September 7, 1544.

In the next letter, a few days later, he speaks of other concessions which he hopes to gain.

(XXXVI.) *To Francis Mancias.*

My dearest Brother in Jesus Christ,

I could not tell you if I tried the heartfelt joy your letter gives me. It has taken away that wearing, burning anxiety of heart which I felt about the Commandant and the others who, like him, were driven from house and home by the late storm. May God our Lord dwell with them all, as I pray that He may be with myself!

On Tuesday, about two hours before daybreak, I sent Father Francis Coelho to the Prince, the Rajah of Travancore's relation, who is now staying at Tala, about two leagues from Munahpaud. Father Coelho was most graciously received by him. I sent him in hopes of thus giving peace to all this country, which is now in suspense, disquiet, fear, and indeed in perfect consternation at the threatened inroad of the Badages. I should like, before I go away from this, to leave these afflicted people, if not at perfect peace, at least with some truce to their miseries. The Prince told Coelho that Beterbemali was making great haste to meet the Maharajah by sea, with the intention of giving him battle. Another reason for my sending Coelho was to obtain letters from the Prince to the Adigares, commanding them to allow the exportation of rice and other useful articles of food. On the afternoon of the same Tuesday I got your letter, I immediately sent off a safe person to Father Coelho, with a letter which he was to deliver from me to the Prince. In this letter I have begged him to write to the Adigares of your country not to oppose, as they have hitherto done, the importation of provisions to Punical, nor to continue to vex the Christians, but rather to treat them with kindness. In short, I am doing all I can so as to leave this coast in some sort of tranquillity before setting out on my journey to Iniquitribirim. I hope to return armed with more effectual powers under the royal authority itself to resist the injustice of these Adigares.

Tomorrow morning I shall write to the Commandant: I can't write now, for the messenger is in such a hurry to set off. I am expecting Francis Coelho tonight. Tomorrow morning I shall send you a farther letter. For the present remember me most kindly to Paul Vaz, and tell Matthew that I am writing to Manuel da Cruz to pay him the twelve fanams which he asked me for his father and for that sister of his who is so poor. Francis Coelho will bring me news enough, enough to fill a longer letter, as I have promised. May our Lord be pleased to bring us together in His kingdom! Amen.

Your most affectionate brother in Jesus Christ,

FRANCIS.

From Munahpaud, September 10th, 1544.

The next very short letter is important as giving us a clue to the movements of the writer after it was sent. Francis had made up his mind, it seems, to go to the Rajah, and he begs the prayers of the children for the success of his undertaking and the safety of his journey.

(XXXVII.) *To Francis Mancias.*

My dearest Brother in Jesus Christ,

Antonio is ill in bed, and can do nothing for us. Send me immediately to Munahpaud Antonio the Parava to act as servant to us. Write to me, I beseech you, and tell me whether those poor afflicted people are well treated. My anxiety for them accompanies me everywhere, and leaves me no rest, and the only thing that comforts me is to have from time to time news of how they are going on.

As soon as I get to the Rajah of Travancore, I will take care to have orders dispatched by him, and I will send them to you, commanding all the Adigares throughout the country to treat the Christians well. Pray to God for me, and tell all the children to remember to commend me to God in their prayers. I have addressed a bill of exchange to Manuel da Cruz, on account of which he will give you 100 fanams to pay for the instruction of the children. I send it to you with this letter.

May our Lord ever assist you with His help and favour! Amen.

Your most affectionate brother in Jesus Christ,

FRANCIS.

From Tuticorin, September 20th, 1544.

How exactly Francis fared in his journey to the Rajah of Travancore, we have no precise information; but we can gather a good deal from incidental expressions in subsequent letters, as well as from the details afterwards gathered on the spot. We find him not long after this writing to St. Ignatius as to the sort of persons who are fitted to be missionaries in the countries in which he has been labouring; and when he speaks of the strength and courage which are required, he mentions that there are sometimes occasions when life itself has to be risked in the cause of God. We may well understand that in proportion to the hold which his character and miracles gave him upon the people would be the hatred with which he was regarded by the Brahmins and the teachers of the false religions which he overthrew. He never made any compromise with them, and one of the first steps which he took after baptizing the inhabitants of a village was to destroy the idols and their pagodas. It is natural enough that frequent attempts should have been made on his life. The cottages in which he rested were burnt down, sometimes three or four in one day. Once he was saved, like Charles II., in the thick branches of a tree, around the stem of which his enemies were seeking him to slay him. He always had a desire for martyrdom, and was almost reckless in exposing himself to danger. From a letter of the next year to Mancias we find that the Rajah had given him a sum of money for the purpose of building churches for the converts, and from this we may conjecture that a considerable part of the concessions which Francis desired to obtain from him was granted on occasion of this visit. It is certain that religion took deep root and flourished in Travancore from this time.

CHAPTER IV.

Manaar, Jafanapatam, and Meliapor.

We have already mentioned the little island of Manaar, which gives its name to the gulf between Ceylon and the Fishery Coast, in which the pearl fishery, of which we have heard so much, was carried on. Manaar lies a little off the northwestern coast of Ceylon, separated from the larger island by a narrow but deep and turbulent channel, the remaining and far larger width of the belt of sea which lies between the continent of India and the two islands being at that point crossed by the remarkable ridge of shoals which goes by the name of Adam's Bridge, which almost connects Manaar with the island of Rameserum lying just off the mainland. Manaar is described as a sandy and not very fertile island, with one good port and a considerable traffic. It was greatly inferior in all material and natural richness to its beautiful neighbour Ceylon, called by its own inhabitants the Land of Delights, and traditionally regarded as the site of the terrestrial Paradise. Manaar was subject to one of the several small kingdoms into which Ceylon was divided—that of Jafanapatam. We are not told precisely at what point of the preaching of St. Francis on the Fishery Coast and in Travancore it was that the inhabitants of this little island sent to request him to come to instruct and baptize them, nor do we know whether, in their case as in the case of the Paravas, there were any motives of policy to help in inclining them to desire to receive the faith. They proved the sincerity of their conversion, after it had taken place, in the noblest manner. Francis wished himself to go in answer to the invitation, but the affairs of the Travancore mission were then at a critical point, and he had also to provide for the protection of the Christians of the Fisheries. He sent therefore, in his place, one of the secular priests who had accompanied him from Goa, and in a short time received the news of the instruction and baptism of a considerable number of the Manarese.

The position of the Portuguese in India was at that time such that it was quite natural for any of the native princes, either on the mainland or in Ceylon, to look upon the conversion of their subjects in any numbers as an act of dangerous rebellion on their part, and as involving further aggression and a further advance in power on that of the formidable strangers from Europe. The Rajah of Jafanapatam immediately took the alarm, and treated the Manarese with the utmost severity. He was a bigoted heathen, hating everything Christian, all the more because he was obliged from motives of fear to pretend to be a friend to the Portuguese. The insular position of Manaar might make it very easy for the Portuguese to seize it under the pretext of protecting the new converts. Moreover, the Rajah was an usurper, and his elder brother, whom he had dethroned, was still alive. All these motives for fear made him act at once, and endeavour to tread out the new faith before it had made further progress. A considerable force was sent into the island, and the new Christians, after having been commanded and having refused to renounce their religion, were put to death. The number of men, women, and children who thus suffered is given as six hundred.

Some writers continue the story of the persecution in Manaar by connecting it with the conversion of a young prince of one of the kingdoms of Ceylon which happened at this time, but which appears more likely to have taken place at Candy than at Jafanapatam.[1] It is characteristic of the times and of

[1] Bartoli, who is followed by Massei and others, tells us that this prince was the eldest son of the Rajah of Jafanapatam himself. This is hardly consistent with the way in which Francis Xavier speaks of him in a letter which will follow soon. Lucena, a very careful and sagacious writer, thinks it must have been the Prince of Candy, as Don Joam de Castro afterwards put that kingdom, as well as that of Jafanapatam, into the hands of a fugitive prince who had come to Goa, and been made a Christian. This would just suit the case of the cousin of the youth of whom we are now speaking. See Lucena, *Vida de S. Francisco de Xavier*, liv. ii. c. 19.

the Portuguese character that we should find that it was not unfrequent for the merchants who traded at the various heathen ports in the East to take on themselves the part of missionaries of the Gospel, enlarging on the beauty and blessings of the Christian faith to those with whom they dealt. One of these merchants had come to be received with great favour at the Court of Candy, and had made so much way with the eldest son of the Rajah as to persuade him to receive instruction as a preparation for baptism. The Rajah heard of it, and the youth was at once put to death by his order.[2] His body was left naked and exposed on the ground; but the Christian merchant buried it in the night. In the morning the earth was found to have opened itself over the corpse in the shape of a wellformed cross, and this prodigy was repeated in spite of the efforts of the heathen to fill up the cross again and again. Moreover, a cross of red light was seen by multitudes in the air over the grave: a great number of converts were made, many of whom were put to death, others flying the country to escape the fury of the Rajah. Among these fugitives were two young princes, the brother and the cousin of the youth who had been martyred.[3] The mother of one of these princes, the aunt of the other, appears to have connived at their conversion, and she sent them secretly out of the country to preserve their lives. They were placed under the protection of the Portuguese, and came to Francis in Travancore on their way to Goa. At the same time the brother of the Rajah of Jafanapatam, already mentioned, seems to have found fresh reason for feeling himself unsafe while within reach of his brother. He made his way with some adherents to Negapatam, a port on the eastern side of the Indian peninsula, at the very southern extremity of the long sweep of coast which forms the shore of the great bay of Bengal. From Negapatam he passed overland to Goa, where he placed him-

[2] Lucena speaks of him as baptized in his own blood.

[3] The historians tell us that the latter of the two was the heir to the throne, it being the custom in India for the Rajahs to be succeeded by the children of their sisters, rather than by their own, real or supposed, it being thought that the royal line was more certainly secured in that way.

self under instruction, undertaking, if his kingdom were restored to him, to make it Christian as well as tributary to the Portuguese crown.

All these affairs, of which St. Francis speaks summarily in one of the letters which we shall have presently to insert, turned his thoughts at this time to a journey and voyage northwards, that he might confer concerning them with the Governor of India, who, if he did not need any one to urge him to punish the Rajah of Jafanapatam for his cruelty to the new Christians, might perhaps require advice and influence that might induce him not to carry matters too far or with too high a hand.[4] We see also in the letters some hint of arrangements to be made with him on the part of the Rajah of Travancore. The two following letters of the series which Mancias has preserved to us speak of the intention of Francis Xavier to go and see the Governor. He seems to have supposed that Sousa might be at Cochin, though it turned out that he had sailed as far to the north beyond Goa itself as Cambaia. The considerable interval which separates the letters at this point may be accounted for either by the absence of Francis in Travancore, from which country he never seems to have written, or by the certain fact that at some period of the later autumn Mancias was his companion in an expedition to Ceylon itself, of the circumstances of which we have no details.

The two following letters were written, as it seems, at the same date, and in fact are very similar in their contents. It has been thought that they are but different forms of the same letter; but as each contains much that is wanting in the other, it is well to print them both, especially as the latter gives us an insight, not very clear, it is true, into another of the troubles which beset the native Christians at this time. The earlier paragraphs of the first letter are almost a repetition of former admonitions given to Mancias, to urge on him the forbearance and patience necessary for his arduous duties among the natives.

[4] Francis says in his letter on the subject that he had to exert himself to prevent the Governor from taking too severe a revenge. See below, p. 282.

(XXXVIII.) *To Francis Mancias.*

I beg and entreat you most earnestly, my dearest brother, to show the people you are with, and especially the grown-up men and old men, very great kindness and charity, and to aim at making yourself beloved by them in return. Be quite sure that if you are beloved by them, you will be able to turn their hearts whatever way you wish. So bear with moderation and wisdom all their weaknesses and infirmities, and say to yourself that if they are not yet all that you desire, in time at least they will become so. If you cannot get out of them all the good you ask, take what you can get. You know this is my way. You should make up your mind to be to them what a good father is to bad children, and never give up caring and providing for them, though you see them all the time covered with many vices. God Himself, though often offended by them and by us, does not cease to heap His benefits upon us. He might most justly destroy us, but in His mercy He very often seems blind to our sins, and helps us in our difficulties, that He may overcome evil by good.[5] And so you, if you cannot do all you wish, be glad to do what you can, since it is not your fault that all the progress which you might desire has not been made. If you sometimes find yourself so distracted by a number of duties that you cannot manage them all, do as much as you can and be content with that, and even give thanks to God for the particular blessing that He has led you to work in a place where there are so many sacred duties to be performed that you cannot be idle, however much you might wish it, for this is in truth one of the greatest blessings that God bestows. Imagine yourself in Purgatory, making satisfaction for your sins; you will think yourself very happily dealt with in that God gives you the troubles of this life instead of the torments of the fires of Purgatory. But if, perchance, men turn out so wicked that you can do nothing with them by gentleness, then sometimes use

[5] *ut vincat in bono malum.* (Orig.)

severity; for, after all, it is a work of mercy to correct those who are wrong, and be sure that it is a great sin not to chastise sinners, especially when they cause scandal to others.

Nevertheless, I do not think you should give these people up now that they are in so much trouble, or indeed ever. At this time more than ever you must bid the children whom you have under instruction to ask of God to defend and help us, for in these countries we have no protection at all, except the protection of God. For if that saying of Him Who is the Truth be true—'He who is not with Me is against Me'[6]—any one can see how destitute we are of all human aid when we have so few who are with us to convert these people to the faith of Jesus Christ. But we must not lose heart: God will reward every one according to his merits; He can bring about wonders however great by means of a few, as well as by means of many. I am much more inclined to grieve for the lot of those who are against God, than to call down punishment upon them. God Himself, of His own accord, will take terrible vengeance by and by on His enemies, as we see plainly enough in the case of those who are undergoing the eternal pains and punishments of hell.

I am going to Travancore to meet the Governor. I shall go by land, at least as far as Cape Comorin, and visit the Christian villages as I go, and baptize the infants. I want you to pray much to God for me, and to get the young children you are instructing in the Christian doctrine to pray also. Their prayers will be a defence and guard to me, with which I shall make light of the dangers with which my friends try to deter me from this land journey; telling me that I shall have to pass through a country that hates everything Christian, and me in particular. But I tell you plainly, I am sometimes weary of my life, and think I had better rather die for religion than live in the sight of so many and such grievous outrages upon the majesty of God, especially when I cannot help seeing them and yet cannot prevent them. Rather than see and hear them,

[6] *Qui non est mecum contra me est.* (Orig.)

I would go to Ethiopia or into the dominions of Prester John, where one might work very hard and well for God with no one to oppose. Nothing gives me so much pain as to have been wanting in sharp resistance to those whom I see outraging His Heavenly Majesty. May God in His infinite goodness be pleased to forgive them; and I pray and beseech Him to abide with you always and to accompany my steps! Farewell.

Your most loving brother in Jesus Christ,

FRANCIS.

From Munahpaud, November 8th, 1544.

The first part of the next letter is full of references to matters with which we can only be imperfectly acquainted. It seems that the Governor Sousa had sent a Portuguese officer, a relation of his own, to treat with the Pulas or subordinate princes or nobles of Travancore, who, as the reader may remember, are mentioned in a former letter as not unlikely to attempt to negotiate on their own part with the Portuguese, with a view of rendering themselves independent of the king of their country. The negotiation would seem to have failed, and the officer was displeased with the Pulas. The second paragraph relates to some tyrannical proceedings at Tuticorin, of which we have no other account. It would almost seem as if some sort of legal persecution had been raised against the Christian converts on the part of powerful heathen or Mussulmans, who had been supported by the Portuguese authorities, turned the Christians out of their homes, and found others more pliant, who occupied them on some terms derogatory to their religion. This at least is what we gather from the language of the letter, which orders that the new tenants shall not be permitted to take part in the pearl fishery, and adds a severe reprimand and warning to a certain Nicolas Barbosa, who was probably a Portuguese who farmed some crown rights, or employed the divers on his own account.

(XXXIX.) *To Francis Mancias.*

My dearest Brother in Jesus Christ,

I had arrived at Munahpaud, and was on the point of going to meet Alexis de Sousa when two Nairs[7] met me, bringing me a letter from a Portuguese, in which he informed me that urgent affairs detained him at Bearim, that he had for me a letter from the King's Treasurer, and other commissions which he was charged with for me, but that he could only give them to me or explain them to me in person. He could only tell me that his commissions were such as to make it necessary for me to see Iniquitribirim again. Alexis de Sousa has gone to Coulan. It is said he went away very much irritated against the Pulas. Whether this is an unfounded report I cannot as yet well make out. I am now going hence by land from the Cape, to visit as I pass the Christian villages which lie on my way, and to baptize the newborn infants and any adults that I find sufficiently disposed.

I wish that next Monday, unless you prefer another day (which I leave to your discretion), you would visit the Christians who have been expelled from Tuticorin, and as in the new and temporary dwellings where they now are they have no place to meet in, collect them outside the enclosure of their huts in the open field, and then give them instructions and administer the sacraments. I beg of you strictly to charge Nicolas Barbosa not to summon to the pearl fishery any of the people at Tuticorin who have established themselves in the dwellings of those who are now in exile. The King and the Governor have given me a certain authority in this matter, and I will not have it that Christians in revolt and rebellion, or to call things by the right name, apostates, should partake in the fruits of the sea which belongs to us. It may be allowed to the people of Punical; and if any of them are disposed to go and dive off the isles of Tuticorin to bring up the mother of

[7] The Nairs were a high caste, the members of which generally embraced the profession of arms. *Léon Pagès.*

pearl shells from the bottom of the sea, they have my leave. So Barbosa may employ them to work for his profit. If he show himself inclined to resist this, give him a stern admonition from me,—that he had better take very great care on his own account not to be guilty of any fresh fault, for he has committed a very great number of transgressions in times past, of which many are quite as mindful as himself.

I rely much, for the aid of God to help me in the hazards of my journey and in the doubtful issue of the affairs I have to manage, on your prayers for me and those of the children where you are, and I beg of you not to let my request for them be in vain. They will be an assistance and a shield to me, and I shall go with head erect and heart undaunted to confront all the terrors which the Christians vie with one another to frighten me with, insisting on it that for me to undertake a journey by land through those countries is to run into almost certain destruction, because they think that the barbarous tribes who inhabit them will certainly pour forth all their burning hatred for our holy religion on my head as on its principal support. But, to tell you the inmost thoughts of my heart, I am so weary of my life that the very thing which they make an objection of in order to frighten me from the journey is an attraction to me the other way; I really think it a thousand times better for me to be killed out of hatred to our holy faith than to live on and witness so many sins against God, committed every day under our very eyes, which we try to prevent and cannot. It is the real truth; nothing in myself has disappointed me more than that. I have been unable to oppose the men who—you know whom I mean—who are guilty of offences so enormous against God. May our Lord help and favour you for ever! Amen.

From Munahpaud, November 10th, 1544.

I am just starting for Pudicar. Father Francis Coelho is going to visit the Christians who are at Atanapatanam.

Your most loving brother in Jesus Christ,

FRANCIS.

After this letter we hear no more of Francis Xavier till the middle of the following month of December, when he arrived at Cochin. He had thus spent more than a month on his road, and had no doubt lingered in many places for the sake of instructing and baptizing converts. What dangers he may have run during this month we cannot tell, but we may be sure that it was a time of great consolation to him, as he found himself alone and far from all his usual annoyances, preaching to the fishers scattered along the coast of Travancore. On arriving at Cochin he found that the Governor was not there, but, as has been said, far to the north at Cambaia. But a very dear friend met him at Cochin; no other than Miguel Vaz, the vicar of the Bishop of Goa, who had been the first to suggest to him to undertake the instruction of the Paravas, and who could thoroughly sympathize with all his desires, and all the anxieties regarding the position of the native converts in India. The conversations which they had together ended in important steps for the benefit of the Indian Christians, of which we shall presently speak. But another great pleasure was awaiting him at Cochin. That year's ships from Portugal had arrived at Goa in time for the letters, and the news which they brought, to be sent on to Cochin before he reached it, and he was thus greeted with many pieces of happy intelligence, as well as with a bundle of correspondence which filled his affectionate heart with joyous and tender thoughts of the friends who had sent it.

Miguel Vaz, as has been said, was entirely of the same mind with Francis Xavier as to the miserable influence on the native Christians of the example and conduct of the Portuguese, and as to the many abuses which needed severe and immediate correction at the hands of the government at home. Some of the more crying evils in the state of things at Goa itself had been corrected by the preaching of St. Francis; at least, many Portuguese had given up their practice of concubinage; the neglect of the sacraments, which in men who led such lives as the majority of the Europeans had been looked upon as the only mark left in them of the fear of God, had ceased; and the diminution of scandalous vice had probably occasioned a proportionate falling off in the quarrels and assassinations which naturally resulted from the general licentiousness of manners.[8] There were still remaining other great scandals, which had more particular reference to the honour due to religion, and the support which the true faith ought to receive from a Christian government. The first of these scandals was the open toleration of idolatrous worship, even in Goa, while in the towns around it there was no attempt made to check either idolatry or the superstitious customs and immoralities with which it was connected. Then again, the public offices under the Crown were sold, and Mussulmans frequently allowed to hold them, while the native Christians, on account of their poverty, were excluded. The Paravas on the pearl coast, who had to pay a certain royalty to the Crown out of their gains, were thus brought under the power of officials, often Mussulmans, who forced them to sell their pearls at so low a price as to render the transaction a simple robbery. Christian converts, also, were frequently sold as slaves to Mussulmans or heathens. At Cochin itself, the second city in Portuguese India, and entirely at the command of the Christian government, the native Rajah was in the habit of confiscating the property of any of his subjects who became Christians, and this abuse was allowed to go on without even a remonstrance. As the two friends talked over these scandals and bewailed their evil influence on the souls for which both were so anxious, Miguel Vaz offered of his own accord to go to Portugal and lay them in person before the King. The abuses in themselves were not beyond the reach of cure, though it is likely enough that neither Martin Alfonso Sousa, nor any other Governor, could have dealt with them satisfactorily single-handed. But they implied a state of things which nothing but

[8] Bartoli, *Asia*, t. i. p. 43, enumerates among the abuses prevalent in Goa before the arrival of Francis Xavier, the practice of the Portuguese of the purchase or seizure of slave girls who were made to carry on the most infamous traffic and pay their masters a certain sum out of their earnings, and the selling of justice in the courts to the highest bidder. The mention of these abuses illustrates some of the letters which we have lately given, in which similar practices on the part of the Portuguese on the Fishery Coast are alluded to.

a very radical change in the whole Portuguese population in India could have set right. They were exposed to unusual temptations, and a higher standard of public morality would have cut the evil at its root. The government might certainly do something by precepts and injunctions, but who was there to carry them out and insure their general observance? St. Francis, as we shall see, hit upon the best possible expedient when he proposed to the King to send out an independent minister with full authority, whose one business it should be to protect the interests of religion; but it may be questioned whether if such an official had been appointed, he might not have been himself carried away by the current of corruption all around him, or at least have been intimidated by the union of influences of all kinds which would have joined to resist him in the execution of his duty. However, Miguel Vaz and Francis Xavier did their best for India when they resolved that one of them should go in person to plead the cause of religion with the King.

The letters from Europe which Francis found at Cochin were full of interesting news. The Society was flourishing and increasing: the limitation at first imposed by the Pope as to the number of the professed Fathers, who were not to exceed sixty, had been taken away; many pious works, which remain to the present day, had been started by Ignatius in Rome, and progress had been made towards the building and completion of the permanent house of the Society, which is now the Gesù, close to the little church of Sta. Maria a Strata. Peter Favre and Bobadilla were active in Germany and in the Low Countries, Laynez had done much in Venice, and Salmeron in Modena. Many distinguished recruits had joined the Order—among others, the pure, brilliant, and candid youth who was afterwards known as Peter Canisius. Perhaps the brightest part of the news, at least to St. Francis, was the great advance of the Society in Portugal, where the College at Coimbra was being built by the King, the establishment being already at work in a temporary dwelling, where there were as many as sixty students of the Society. All this gave good hope for the future of the

Indian mission, and the heart of its great Apostle was swelling with thankfulness and hope when he wrote from Cochin, almost immediately after his arrival, to Mancias, telling him that he was to be ordained priest, and to take charge at once of the mission of Travancore. Francis himself was to set sail at once for Cambaia, to arrange with the Governor about the affair of Jafanapatam.

(XL.) *To Francis Mancias.*

My dearest Brother in Jesus Christ,

The day before yesterday, the 16th of December, I arrived at Cochin. Before I got there I had baptized all I could reach of the Matchuas,[9] a race of fishermen who live in the kingdom of Travancore. God, Who sees our inmost heart, knows how gladly I would have returned thither at once to baptize the people of another tribe which lives there, who are not ill disposed to embrace the yoke of Jesus Christ. But the Vicar-general, Don Miguel Vaz, thinks that it is now of importance, for the greater service of our Lord, that I should go to the Governor, to arrange with him about the affair of Jafanapatam. So in two or three days I shall sail for Cambaia in a well appointed barque,[10] soon, I hope, to return with the affair settled as we could wish—as the interests of religion and of the glory of God require.

His Lordship the Bishop is not coming to Cochin this year, but the Vicar-general will sail by the first vessel for Portugal. He will very soon come back to us, as I hope from the goodness of God, knowing how important to the service of God it is that he should do so. Diego, who is at Goa in the College of St. Paul, is burning to come here. Father Master Diego and Master Paul and all the College are in good health. I have received a great number of letters from Portugal, which have lately arrived at Goa. Among them is a rescript to authorize you to receive the holy priesthood without producing

[9] Matchoua is the Sanskrit name for the caste of fishermen.

[10] A *cature*—apparently a large, swift, undecked boat.

the usual proofs of having sufficient patrimony or title or the revenues of an ecclesiastical benefice sufficient for your maintenance; but I think you have no occasion to use this faculty, since the Bishop is ready to pass over all such requirements and ordain you priest, as he has lately ordained Father Manuel and Father Gaspar, who are now here with us at Cochin, and who will soon set out to gather fruit in the same part of our Lord's vineyard with you. The letters I speak of say that two of our brothers had set sail from Portugal hither, and I am very uneasy about them, because they have not yet arrived. I fear much they may either be wintering at Mozambique, or have been forced to turn back to Portugal by adverse seas and tempests. They tell me one is Portuguese by birth, the other an Italian; and the King in his letter to me sounds their praises loudly. May God be pleased to bring both of them to us safe and sound! I know neither of them, for they are not any of those we left at Lisbon. More than sixty young men of our Society are now studying in the University of Coimbra, and the accounts we get of them, their religious character, their modesty, and their abilities, give great reason for praising and thanking God for them as much as possible. They are nearly all Portuguese, of which I am exceedingly glad. There is also very joyful news about our brethren in Italy. I will not say more of all this now, because I hope in less than a month to be with you, and then you shall have all these letters from Europe to read.

And now for yourself. As soon as you get this, I most earnestly entreat you again and again, as you love God our Lord, and desire to please Him, set out at once to visit those newly made Christians whom I lately baptized in great numbers on the coast of the kingdom of Travancore. Set up a school in each village, where the young children capable of instruction may assemble every day under the direction of a master, and appoint one to teach them. For his salary and any school expenses, you may take, I should think, 150 fanams of the money reserved for this purpose. This sum you will divide among the masters of the different village schools, as soon as you see that they have begun their work and got it into order; and don't go away from any place without giving the master at least a part of his salary, so that they may work on more zealously, and look forward to proving how well they have done, by having some progress on the part of the children to show when we go there again, as well as have the hopes of future pay. Don't leave a single hamlet, in all the district right up to the Great Fishery, in which you have not yourself been present at these daily assemblies of the children, and also provided aright for their continuance after your departure. For your own support get money from the Commandant.

At Munahpaud get a boat to take you to Careapatana; but before you get there, turn aside to Monchur. It is a village of Matchuas not yet baptized, not much more than a league from the extreme point of Cape Comorin. Baptize them, for they are sufficiently prepared for it, and have often shown that they desire it, by sending some of their people to entreat me to have the kindness to go and baptize them all. I was willing enough to satisfy their pious desire; but though I have often attempted to get there, I have always been detained by more urgent affairs. Antonio Fernandez, one of the Malabar Christians, is soon to follow you, and may probably join you very soon, being on board a very light and swift boat. You must take him with you everywhere, as a companion and adviser in all that you do on this coast, until you have baptized all the inhabitants. He is a very good man, burning with zeal for the glory of God. He knows by experience the ways of the people, in what manner and with what precautions they are to be dealt with; so do whatever he thinks good, and never disagree with him nor prevent him from doing good. He is a man that one can well trust. I always trusted him when in those parts, and never repented of it. So that I not only advise you to defer to his advice and let him manage everything, but I pray and beseech you to do so.

Take with you Matthew and the royal officer who used to go with me from Viranda to Patanam; also your servant lads and a Canacapole who knows how to write, and who can transcribe for you the prayers which the children and other catechumens are to be taught by heart by the care and diligence of the teachers of Christian doctrine who are appointed, copies of which you can leave behind you everywhere. Employ the same secretary to write the letters you want to send anywhere as you think well, and also to read and help you to understand all those that are addressed to you from time to time from different parts of the country. Pay the Canacapole's salary, not out of the money set apart for the instruction of the children, but out of that which the King has ordered to be paid for our use and maintenance, which the Commandant will give you in the regular instalments.

On leaving where you are, intrust the work which you have been doing, of baptizing and instructing the people of the Comorin district, to the good priest Joam de Lizana. Francis Mendez, who is to take this letter to you, is ready to start, and in such a hurry that for the present I can write no more.

May our Lord be always your helper, as much as I pray that He may be my own!

Your most affectionate brother in Jesus Christ,

FRANCIS.

From Cochin, December 18th, 1544.

As soon as this letter was dispatched, St. Francis embarked for Cambaia,[11] where the Governor Sousa was to be found. This northward voyage gave him the opportunity for one of those beautiful conquests of charity which were so frequent

[11] In some old maps of India the peninsula of Gujerat is called Cambaia; but the name is at present limited to the city of Cambay, at the head of the gulf of the same name, which separates Gujerat on the south-east from the mainland. The Portuguese had a fortress at Diu, a town on the southern coast of the peninsula, and disputes were now arising concerning the observance of the terms of a treaty of peace made some years before by the Viceroy, Don Garcia da Noroña, which had permitted a native prince to build a wall between the fort and the part of the town inhabited by the Mussulmans. This wall was being made a fortification, and there was a league among the Indian princes to attack and take the fort. This and other matters mentioned by Faria y Sousa, *Asia Portuguesa*, t. ii. p. 1. c. xiv., probably occasioned the presence of the Governor in those parts.

during his life in the East, where his constant passages from place to place brought him across so many wild and rough characters, in whose hearts the seeds of faith had not been altogether destroyed even by a career of licentiousness. On this voyage he found himself the chance companion of a man of rank and high office, whose impiety and wicked life were so notorious as to be a cause of scandal even to the heathen. Francis made himself his familiar friend, and at last endeavoured to lead him to converse on matters of religion. He made very little way with him, however; and when he asked him about going to confession, the other broke out into blasphemous language, declaring that nothing should ever induce him to do it. So matters went on, day after day, St. Francis always paying him great attention, and seeming to court his friendship, until they arrived at Cananor, a port on their route, and, as the vessel stayed there for a few hours, the two friends landed and walked together into a palm grove that was near the shore. Then Francis Xavier threw himself on his knees, laid his shoulders bare, and began to scourge himself cruelly with a discipline, until the ground was red with his blood and the whole grove sounded with the noise of the blows. Then he began to tell the man that it was for him that he was doing this penance, and he had cost far more than this to his Saviour Jesus Christ, Whom he implored to look upon the price of His own Blood, to send His light into that poor soul, and stretch out His hand to save him. The other was overwhelmed, and cried out in his turn that Francis had conquered him, begging him to hear his confession and reconcile him to God at once; and so great was his sorrow that Francis was able to receive his confession and absolve him before they returned to the boat.[12]

[12] We have another anecdote of this visit to Cananor preserved to us, which, like all the incidental information that exists as to this period of the life of Francis Xavier, bears witness to the esteem in which he was universally held, and the common opinion of his sanctity. A good Christian father came to him to bewail his own wretched lot, on account of the bad behaviour of a son of his, as yet a lad. Francis consoled him, by saying that age would probably bring with it an improvement; and then, after a few moments of recollection, he

Francis had little difficulty in persuading the Governor of India to undertake the punishment of the usurping Rajah of Jafanapatam for the cruelty with which he had treated his Christian subjects. Martin Alfonso had lately terrified him into a sort of submission to the supremacy of the Portuguese Crown by the payment of an annual tribute of 4000 ducats;[13] and he was ready enough to order immediately an expedition against Jafanapatam which would show to all the princes of India and Ceylon that it would not be permitted them with impunity to persecute Christians. The subordinate officers along the coast received orders to collect their forces in men and ships, and Negapatam was named as the place at which the armament was to rendezvous. When we remember the severe way in which Batecala had been treated by this same Governor, it is not surprising that St. Francis should have been anxious rather to mitigate his wrath than to inflame it. The fact that the execution of the punishment was to be committed to the local commandants, whose character Francis had already had so many occasions of learning, was not a very favourable omen; and he seems to have readily fallen in with the suggestion that he should be on the spot when the armament sailed. Indeed, a part of the Governor's order was, that the offending Rajah should be placed at his disposal; an arrangement which, if the expedition had succeeded, would probably have saved his life if he had been made prisoner.

It appears from a passage in a letter to Simon Rodriguez, written by Francis after his return from Cambaia, that he stop-

---

seized the hand of his friend with great signs of joy, and told him to be of good heart, for his son would become a Franciscan friar, and be renowned both for learning and holiness. The prophecy turned out true: the youth grew up to enter the Franciscan Order, became famous for learning and virtue, and died a martyr's death in Ceylon, whither he was sent to preach.

[13] See Faria y Sousa, *Asia Portuguesa*, t. ii. p. 1. c. xiii. § 5. This was at the time of the expedition spoken of above, when the pagoda of Tebilicaré was plundered. At the same time, the writer informs us that the King 'called "Grande" at Comorin' made the Governor a large present out of fear. This was probably the Maharajah of Travancore, whom we know from the letters of St. Francis to have been desirous of conciliating the Portuguese.

ped for a short time at Goa before proceeding to find the Governor. He does not seem to have lingered there on his return, as we find him again at Cochin in the middle of January 1545, from which place he wrote several letters to be sent to Europe by the same ships which were to take Miguel Vaz on his embassy of charity. Perhaps Miguel himself may have been still at Cochin.[14] Three of these letters must now be inserted. The first was addressed to King John of Portugal, recommending Miguel to the favour and attention of the King, and insisting, with true apostolical liberty, on the duty incumbent on his Highness' conscience of providing for the advancement of religion in India, and in particular of punishing by something more forcible than a mere reprimand or expression of his will the officers under the Crown who did so much mischief by their violence and cruelty towards the new converts. The other letters which remain to us are to the Society at Rome and to Simon Rodriguez in Portugal, who was also to read the letter to Rome before it was sent on.

[14] We find another of St. Francis' occasional prophecies connected with his stay at Cochin. His great friend, Cosmo Añez, one of the benefactors of the College of Santa Fé, who held some office like that of Treasurer under the Crown, had bought a very valuable diamond for the King, on his own responsibility, and sent it to Portugal. Francis asked him which ship it was in, and when the ship was named, said he would rather have heard him say any other. This frightened Añez, who begged him to pray for the safety of the vessel. Some days after, he was again at table with Añez, who was anxious about his jewel, and then Francis turned to him, and told him to give thanks to God, because the diamond was safe in the hands of the Queen. It turned out afterwards that the ship had been in great danger from a large leak which had suddenly appeared, and which made the captain think of running her on shore, and trying to save the crew and cargo; but the leak had been stopped, as suddenly as it appeared, without any one being able to explain the favourable turn of the matter. This anecdote, taken by Bartoli from the Processes, will be found in Massei, *Vita di S. Francesco*, t. ii. c. vi. Cosmo Añez was the friend who challenged Francis about the miracle at Mutan, related above. Francis cried out, 'Jesus! how can you believe that a man so miserable as I am could raise the dead!' and confessed that the young man was 'found to be alive,' and that the people 'imagined' a miracle.

(XLI.) *To John III. King of Portugal.*

Sire,

I would fain that your Highness may be fully convinced, and that the reflections of your own heart may continually tell you, that God our Lord has given to your Highness, before all other Christian princes of the earth, the empire of the Indies, in order that He might therein test your virtue, and prove with what faithfulness you discharge the work committed to you, and with what active gratitude you answer to His benefits: and that God's purpose in this was not so much to enrich your royal treasury with the profits of precious fruits from distant lands and the influx of wealth from abroad, as rather to present to you occasions of heroic labours and afford your intense and religious devotion the means of making themselves pleasing to Himself, in bringing, by your own burning zeal, and by the work of skilful ministers employed by you, the unbelievers of these countries to the knowledge of Him, the Creator and the Saviour of the world.

Justly and rightly, therefore, does your Highness recommend to those servants of yours whom you send hither to exert themselves much in propagating widely our holy faith, and in the advancement of religion. Since your Highness well understands that God will require of you an account of the salvation of so many nations, who are ready to follow the better path if any one will show them it, but meanwhile, for want of a teacher, lie in blind darkness and the filth of most grievous sins, offending continually their Creator, and casting their own souls headlong into the misery of eternal death.

Your Highness will receive a report from Don Miguel Vaz, who has been the Vicar-general of the Bishop of Goa, and is now leaving us for Portugal, as to what his experience has been of the readiness of these nations to be taught the faith, and of the other openings which present themselves here for the good progress of religion. He has left among them so great an amount of regret at his departure, that his return at the end of a year is very advisable for their consolation and protection; though there is quite reason enough for his return in your Highness' own interests. I mean that you may thus confide to a servant so entirely competent and industrious the grave duty which is urgent upon you of advancing the glory of God in India. If you set this faithful and experienced steward over this business, you may rest in full security, for you may rely on his eminent virtue, proved by so many years' experience, and which has won for him the veneration of the whole population here, for losing no opportunity of defending or advancing religion.

Again and again I entreat and conjure your Highness, that if you wish to provide well for the service of God and the interests of the Church, if you have any regard for all the good well reputed persons who live here in India, for the Christians lately converted to our holy faith, and I may add, if you wish to do me a real kindness once in this life, order Don Miguel Vaz, who is now leaving us, to come back again. I have no other reason for begging this than the service of God, the increase of our holy faith, and the discharge of the conscience of your Highness. God our Lord is witness that I say the truth. I know how much a man like that is regretted here, and how useful he is. And so, to fulfil my duty and to discharge my own conscience as well as yours, I declare and protest to your Highness, that it is quite essential, if you desire that our holy faith should be promoted and spread abroad here in India, and if you wish those who are already gathered into the Church not to be torn from her and to fall back into their old superstitions, scandalized and scared away by the many grievous injuries and vexations which they suffer—and especially from your Highness' own servants—that you send hither again Don Miguel Vaz, who has so brave a heart and so constant a courage in resisting those who persecute the Christians.

Although the Bishop is a prelate of all that consummate virtue which he in truth possesses, yet, as your Highness is aware, he is now bent down with old age, and has besides so much to suffer from diseases, as no longer to possess bodily strength sufficient to undergo the very great labours which are required for the exact discharge of all the duties of the Episcopate out here, however much he abounds in vigour of mind, and, indeed, increases in it daily. There is a reward which God is wont to grant to those who have persevered for many years in His service, spending all their life and prime in undergoing great labours for His sake, until they have attained to an almost entire victory over the rebellion of their body against the spirit. To such men God gives in their late old age this victory as a fruit of their continual struggles, and that others their subjects may see their example and imitate their perseverance, that they feel themselves as it were growing young again in the renewal of spiritual strength just at the time when nature gives way under the weight of all the troubles of decrepitude and old age. They have spent their lives in the practice of virtue, and, as strength gradually fails them, the earthly body is changed into a heavenly spirit. So it is with our good Bishop, and the time has come when he needs assistance for the labours which his office lays upon him.

I entreat you, my lord King, and conjure you for the sake of God's service, that, as I write what follows with the purest intention and in the most perfectly sincere truthfulness, so also your Highness may be pleased to receive what I suggest with like kindness, favour, and goodwill. It is indeed with the single motive of advancing the service and honour of God, and out of the desire which I feel to deliver your royal conscience from a heavy burthen, that I entreat and beseech you not to be content with recommending to your servants here the interests of religion by letter, but also to make your recommendation authoritative and weighty by letting men see examples of just retribution in the punishment of those who have failed in their duty in this respect. For there is danger that when our Lord God calls your Highness to His judgment —which will be when it is least expected, and there will be no hope or method of avoiding it—there is danger, I say, that your Highness may hear angry words from God, 'Why didst thou not punish those who owned thy authority and were thy subjects, and who were enemies to Me in India? Thou wouldst surely have been severe in punishing them, if they had been found negligent in their care of taxes due to thee and in matters of thy revenue.' Nor do I know, Sire, what weight in excusing you at that moment will be allowed to the answer you may make, and say, 'Every year when I wrote to my ministers, Lord, I recommended to them the interests of Thy divine service.' For the answer will come at once, 'But those who altogether trampled upon those solemn commandments thou didst allow to do so unpunished, and at the same time those whom thou didst find unfaithful and remiss as to their attention to thy own interests, thou didst duly chastise.'

Again, Sire, by all the zeal which burns in you for the glory of God, and by the very great care which I am sure you have to discharge before God the obligations of your royal office, and to keep your conscience free from burthen, I conjure and beseech your Highness to send to India a special and competent minister, armed with all due authority, whose single office it may be to provide for the salvation of the countless souls here which are now in danger of being lost. And let him have for his discharge of this duty powers from you quite independent of all authority or command of your officers whose duty it is to attend to the revenue and management of your government. In this way the troubles and scandals may be avoided which have hitherto so grievously and so frequently disturbed the progress of religion.

I would have your Highness take an exact account, and add up the full sum of all the revenues and temporal advantages which, by the goodness of God, you receive from India. Then deduct what you spend here for the service of God and the cause of religion. And then, when all has been fairly reckoned up, make such a division of profits between what is to go to your royal purse and what is to be given to God and His heavenly kingdom as shall seem just and good to your grateful and religious heart, taking care that the Creator of all things may never seem to be repaid poorly and charily by your Highness by too small a portion of the gifts which He has poured so lavishly into your bosom. And let your Highness do this without any delay or procrastination, for, however quickly it be done, it will always be later than it ought. What urges me to write is the true and burning charity of my heart towards you; for, in truth, I seem to hear voices rising to heaven from these countries against your Highness, complaining, on the part of India, that she is dealt with in a niggardly way by your Highness, since while your treasury is being enriched by immense revenues from her, you barely give in return so very small a pittance in aid of the relief of her most grievous spiritual necessities.

It will not, I think, be unpleasant to your Highness, on whom lies this duty of providing for the salvation of souls in this your people of India, to know how the affairs of that salvation stand at present. In Jafanapatam and on the coast of Coulan it may well be that before the end of the year more than a hundred thousand souls will have been added to the Church of Christ. I do not speak of Ceylon. Would to God that the Rajah of that island were at all softened by the great favour your Highness shows him, so as not to be so cruelly adverse to admitting our Lord Jesus Christ into any part of his territories!

Send out to us, Sire, as many labourers as possible of our Society, that there may be enough not only to baptize and instruct in the Christian doctrine the great numbers who are led to embrace our holy faith here, but also some who may be spared to be sent to Malacca and the countries near that city, where there are many converts.

Father Master Diego and Don Paul are at the College of Santa Fé. As they are now writing at full length to your Highness about that holy College, I will say nothing of it at present except that I beg as a special favour that your Highness will be at the trouble to write to Cosmo Añez, that as he began and has carried on the foundation of the College, he is not to give up completing it and bringing it to full perfection, nor by any means to be conquered by this labour, for that he will certainly have a worthy reward for so good a work, first from God, and then from your Highness.

Francesco Mancias and myself live on the promontory of Comorin, among the Christians converted by Don Miguel Vaz, the Vicar-general of India. I have now with me three priests, natives of the country. The College of Cranganor,[15] which is the work of Fra Vincenzo, makes great progress, and will advance from good to better if your Highness continues to favour it as heretofore. There is really the truest reason for giving constant thanks to God for the great fruit to the service of Christ our Lord which has arisen from that holy College. There is a very probable hope that it will send forth religious men who may make the whole of Malabar, which is now sunk in vice and error, feel a saving shame at its own state of misery, and may bring the light of our Lord Jesus Christ to the benighted minds of the people, and make His Holy Name manifest among them all, by the work and ministrations of the disciples of Fra Vincenzo. I beseech and implore your Highness, for the sake of God, to vouchsafe to show him favour, both by other proofs of your royal goodwill and also by granting him the alms which he asks of you. As I expect to die in these Indian regions and never to see your Highness again in this life, I beg you, my lord, to help me with your prayers, that we may see one another again in the next world, where we shall certainly have more rest than here; asking for me of our Lord God what I in return ask for your Highness—that is, that He may give you the grace so to think and act now as at the hour of your death you would be glad to have thought and to have acted.

Your Highness' servant,

FRANCIS.

Cochin, January 20th, 1545.

---

[15] Brother Vincent de Lagos, a Franciscan friar, accompanied to India, in 1538, Don Joam Albuquerque. Great fruits resulted from his labours at Goa and Cranganor. He founded, in 1540, a College in the lastmentioned city, under the name of St. James, and taught there during ten years. He converted a great number of Greek and Armenian schismatics in the kingdom ot Tanor. He died in 1550. (*Léon Pagès.*)

We can hardly account for the very great anxiety with which Francis urges on the King to send back Miguel Vaz; an anxiety which shows itself also in the letter to Simon Rodriguez which was written at the same time. Perhaps it was merely that Miguel was the one person he had met with in India who most thoroughly sympathized with him in his zeal for the native Christians, as he was apparently the single person in high position whose voice was always sure to be lifted in their defence. It may be, however, that this very quality in the Vicar-general made him odious to some of the Portuguese in India, who would not augur any good to themselves from his presence at the Court, and who might be very willing to see him detained in Portugal rather than sent back with powers for the protection of the natives. The next letter is to St. Ignatius.

(XLII.) *To the Reverend Father Ignatius of Loyola, General of the Society of Jesus, at Rome.*

May the grace and charity of our Lord Jesus Christ always help and favour us! Amen.

If you would do what is greatly desired by all who take an interest in the College of Santa Fé, and especially the Governor, the most devoted of them all, I do beseech and conjure you, by our Lord, to send us, at least if it can be done, the faculties that have been asked of you; I mean what they wanted you to get for them from the Holy Father, that the high altar of this College may be privileged for one soul as often as mass is said on it, on the conditions that I wrote you two years ago in the name of the Governor. We are also waiting for the other graces about which I wrote to you at the same time by his order.

Any of our Society who are not fit for hearing confessions or preaching, or for discharging the other functions of the Society, would be of great use here after having been duly practised in meditation and spending some months in humble and abject services, if they had good strength of body and virtue of mind. For here, among the heathen, great learning is not needed. It is enough if they are not altogether uneducated, so as to know how to teach children and ignorant persons the usual prayers of the Church; and to go round the towns and villages to baptize newborn infants. Many of these die without baptism, because we cannot be at so many places, so distant, too, from one another. So any men that you may come across of this sort, who, not well adapted for our Society in Europe, and whom you see to be fit for going about here to baptize newborn children and teach the Catechism to the ignorant, send them out to us, for here they will do a very great deal of good. I want them to be thoroughly strong in body, and well able to bear fatigue. This is a most trying and fatiguing country, both from the excessive heat, the scarcity of wholesome water, and also the poorness of the food. Rice, fish, and milk are what we live on and nothing else; no bread, no wine, none of the other things that you have plenty of. So I want young men and hale men, not weak and old men, that they may bear the fatigue of continual baptizing, teaching, and going about, as they will often have to do, not only to baptize newborn children, but to protect the Christians from the fury and rage of the heathen. Sometimes God gives us here the singular blessing of being obliged to risk our lives for His sake, and of having no way of avoiding the risk without breaking the law of charity. They must remember that we are born mortal, and that for a Christian nothing can be more desirable than to suffer death for Christ. So they must be armed with a brave heart and strength from above.

And as I, who have none of this courage and virtue, am now setting off for countries where I shall have the very greatest need of heavenly aid, I conjure you, by God and His holy religion, to remember me by name in your holy sacrifices, and also take diligent care that I may have the protection of the prayers of the whole Society. I am quite persuaded that I have already been delivered by God from many and great dangers by your intercessions and that of the Society. I write this to you that you may understand what sort of men we want.

However, if you find any strong enough to bear all the labours and inconveniences of which I have spoken, but not very ready or eager to risk their lives, I would have you send them still, for there are many regions here where they may work for religion without any danger of death. Remember always that to catch these heathen there is no need of great learning. Men, such as I speak of, after they have been a few years in these countries, will have added to them from Heaven strength and courage for greater works. You may also send us men capable of hearing confessions and of giving the Spiritual Exercises, even if they are not able to bear harder work; for they will reside at Goa or at Cochin, in which towns they will be able greatly to serve religion, and have plenty of everything themselves, just as in Portugal. For these towns are full of Portuguese families, and there will be no lack of what is wanted to relieve them in case of delicate health or illness; in both places there are plenty of physicians and plenty of medicines. In other places where the Portuguese do not live, such as those which we are now going through in our missions, there is no provision or help for the sick. But in both the cities I have named great good may be done by teaching the inhabitants the practice of the Spiritual Exercises.

It is four years since we sailed from Portugal, and during this interval I have received from you one letter and no more. I have had two from Father Simon, from Portugal, and I long very much, my Father, to hear something at least once a year about you and our other brothers. I do not doubt that you write to me every year, as I do to you; but I fear that the letters on both sides miscarry, and that you desiderate mine as I yours. Two of ours were coming to India this year, but their vessel has not yet reached Goa. Whether it has returned to Portugal or passed the winter at Mozambique, as Portuguese vessels often do, I know not in the least.

I should like to hear whether our old friend still goes about upon a mule. If he does, as he did when I left, he must be very infirm not to have recovered the use of his feet, after so many physicians and so many remedies. I have no other news to tell you, only that you are to send here as many as you can, for we are in extreme dearth of workers for God. I pray God that if we are never to see one another again in this life, at all events we may do so in that blessed life which is to come, where there will be so much more peace than we can enjoy now.

Cochin, January 22d, 1545.

This letter seems to begin abruptly, and we might suspect that its first paragraph, as well as the signature at the end, may have perished under the hands of the relic hunters, who have certainly destroyed for us a great number of the letters of the Saints. But it is clearly meant for St. Ignatius alone, and may have been a note to him of the things which St. Francis wished to suggest, particularly as to the sort of subjects to be sent out to India, and so may have been written originally as we have it. We may remark that it contains the first allusion to the intention of St. Francis to proceed to the further East—at least we may so interpret his words about his own great need of the protection of prayer. The passage about the old friend and the mule is probably an allusion to some domestic joke current among the early companions of St. Ignatius; and it shows us that Francis had received a budget of personal details in the letters from Rome, which he is answering. We subjoin the letter written at the same time to Simon Rodriguez, who seems to have been expressing a desire to come out to India himself. The Fernandez mentioned in the second paragraph was a friend of Simon's, who seems to have had some idea of entering religion in India. The letter contains the strongest possible denunciation of the conduct and maxims of the Portuguese officials, as well as an earnest entreaty to Simon to use his influence with the King to prevent any hindrance being put in the way of Miguel Vaz's return. We may add to this letter another written to the Society at Rome without further comment.

(XLIII.) *To Master Simon Rodriguez, of the Society of Jesus.*

May the grace and love of Jesus Christ our Lord always favour and help us! Amen.

The letters that I write to Rome I send open to you, that you may read them through first and become acquainted with the state of things out here, and so be stirred up to send us out every year as many as possible to labour in the preaching of the Gospel. However many may come, they will find abundant scope for great work in the service of God. As to your coming hither yourself, for my part, if I could feel sure that your strength and powers of body were equal to the vigour of your mind, I should have been the first to invite you, and should have prayed you very much to be so very good as to come, supposing, that is, that our Father Ignatius approved and had himself suggested the idea to you. For he is our Father, and we must obey him, and it would be wrong to move hand or foot without his orders.

Now I must tell you of Diego Fernandez. I saw him at Goa in excellent health about a month ago. He lives very happily and quite to his own taste in the College of Santa Fé with Master Diego de Borba and Don Paul. He works hard and strenuously in the service of God, and is so happy in it, that he does not regret living there nor working as he does. He told me he was writing you a long letter, and I should be strongly for your answering him, as he loves you very much and is much influenced by you. A letter from you would give him incredible pleasure, especially if you tell him that you approve of his living in the College of Goa where he now is.

Francis Mancias and I commend ourselves to your fervent prayers and to those of all our brothers. We are here in these countries at an immense distance, poor clients and dependents of yours, and we cling to your help and protection as what are to provide for all our hopes and interests. It is a work well worthy of your charity,—and here I address my letter to all of you together and to each one in particular,—it is a worthy work for your goodness and piety to plead our cause with God most earnestly with prayers and sacrifices kindled by a holy sense of duty, and to obtain for us the many helps and blessings for body and soul which we so urgently need, and to get for the same intention the prayers of others under your spiritual direction. I also beg you very much and I pray you for the love of God, write to me; or if you cannot do it yourself, bid some other of our Society to write, but you must all of you write at good length; not giving me only heads and general facts, but particulars and minute details, telling me of all and each of our brothers who are in Portugal, at Rome or elsewhere. I assure you that we have nothing left in this life which does our souls more good than what we get from such letters when the ships come in from Portugal. The letter that I am now writing to our brothers at Rome, if it is not too much trouble, show to our excellent friend Pedro Carvalho, and tell him from me that as I look on him as one of our brothers at Rome and in Portugal, I consider the letters I address to them as belonging also to him, and that therefore I have not written to him separately. And I should be glad if you would make all our brothers who are with you at Lisbon understand the same, that so great is my true love for each one of them that I should have written separately to each, if I had not felt confident that each would consider this one letter as entirely his own, and that so it would supply the place of many. This saving of time is a benefit to them and a necessity to me.

A long time ago, at the request of the Governor, I took measures to have certain graces and indulgences asked for from Rome, for the great benefit of these countries, and I am writing concerning them this year to his Highness. I entreat you, by all the desire you have for the consolation and spiritual progress of the people out here, and by all the care you have to please and do service to our Lord God, see that his Highness does not forget them, and that he may please to have the dispatch of these graces urged by his ambassador at Rome. I wrote some years ago now, and I have written again this year to our Father Ignatius to obtain from the Pope in favour of the high altar of the church at Goa, which serves for the members of the College of Santa Fé, a privilege like that with which several altars at Rome are distinguished, namely, that every time a priest offers the holy sacrifice there he delivers a soul from the flames of Purgatory. And if you can yourself in any way contribute to the accomplishment of this wish, you will do a thing very pleasing to the Governor, who earnestly solicits the favour, and all this venerable College and its founders, who so well deserve to have their hopes gratified.

Send us all the subjects you can into India. The greater the number the wider will be the extension of the limits of holy Church. I have learnt by experience the mischief occasioned here from the want of men on fire with zeal for the increase of the holy faith and religion of Jesus Christ our Lord, and this is why I so often urge the request that labourers may be sent into the field which is already white for the harvest. God, who sees the inmost recesses of the soul, knows how I long to see you. It would be an incredible joy to me to press you to my heart and talk with you face to face. It cannot be otherwise, considering your virtues and the other gifts that God has so abundantly shed abroad in your soul. The hope of reaping the fruit of these by real and actual intercourse makes me desire so very intensely to see you again. If it were in accordance with the greater advantage, or even the equal advantage, of the service of God, that we should be together again, how I should be penetrated with the sweetest possible joy, and how I should delight in having you here to wait upon, God alone, who sees all the secrets of our hearts, can truly understand.

Do not allow any of your friends to be sent to India with the charge of looking after the finances and affairs of the King. To such persons we may most truly apply which is written—'Let them be blotted out of the book of the living, and let their name not be written among the just.'[16] However great may be your confidence in any one whom you know and love, trust my experience and oppose him on this point, and fight to the last to prevent him from being exposed to this greatest of dangers. Otherwise, unless he be confirmed in grace as were the Apostles, do not expect to see him persevere in his duty or remain constant in innocency. There is here a power, which I may call irresistible, to thrust men headlong into the abyss, when beside the seductions of gain, and the easy opportunities of plunder, their appetite for greed will have been sharpened by having tasted it, and there will be a whole torrent of bad examples and evil customs to overwhelm and sweep them away. Robbery is so public and common that it hurts no one's character, and is hardly counted a fault: people scarcely hesitate to think that, what is done with impunity, it cannot be bad to do. Everywhere, and at all times, it is rapine, hoarding, and robbery. No one thinks of making restitution of what he has once taken. The devices by which men steal, the various pretexts under which it is done, who can count? I never cease wondering at the number of new inflexions, which, in addition to all the usual forms, have been added, in this new lingo of avarice, to the conjugation of that illomened verb 'to rob.' And when, in the midst of it all, these unhappy men are called out of this world, it is wretched to see in what a miserable state of utter neglect and desperate confusion, as to all that relates to their hopes of salvation, their poor souls have to present themselves before the inexorable tribunal.

Miguel Vaz, who has been Vicar of the Bishop here, is going to Lisbon. You could hardly find a man more burningly and zealously devoted to the glory and service of God. I have no doubt that you will see him and talk with him; and I am sure that, from the peace and joyfulness of soul which you will remark in him, united with so vehement a desire for the glory of God, you will gather a knowledge and a just estimate of his virtues and merits. You may trust entirely to all he says,

[16] Psalm lxviii. 29. *Deleantur de libro viventium, et cum justis non scribantur.* (Orig.)

and I am sure he will give you a full and ample account of everything here. I am writing to the King about him, urging him as strongly as I can, for the relief of my own conscience and that of his Highness, to send him back as soon as possible. He is a man needed here more than can be told, for he it is who defends the lambs of Jesus Christ against the violence and snares of wolves whom nothing will satisfy. Miguel Vaz is a brave intrepid man; nothing ever prevents him from raising his voice against the persecutors and despoilers of the new converts to the religion of Christ. If the King were to think of sending some one else here in his place, where—to speak of the very least of his merits—could his Highness find a person equally experienced in Indian affairs, which during the last twelve years he has not only taken part in, but actually directed? Where would he find any one as much beloved by the good, and as much feared by the bad? Depend upon it, if the King looks out for any one else, whatever pains he may take in his choice, he will run a great risk of failing to attain the object he desires. So pray work, I entreat you, with much earnestness upon his Highness to send back Miguel Vaz and no one else. Farewell.

Your true and most loving brother in Jesus Christ,

FRANCIS.

From Cochin, January 22d, 1545.

(XLIV.) *To the Society, at Rome.*

May the grace and love of Christ our Lord always help and favour us! Amen.

God knows, my dear brothers, how much more happy I should be to see you, than to write you this letter, which must run its chance as to reaching you on account of the distance which divides us. For in truth the Providence which has put our bodies with an almost infinite space between them, while our minds are all the time most closely united, has not loosened the tie of affection which binds us together. It is true, we are no longer living together as we used to live, but we are almost perpetually looking on one another with the eyes of the mind. Such is the power of true and genuine friendship, that absent friends are present to each other, and enjoy one another's presence and conversation in heart. I know that I am always thinking of you all, my brethren, and that I do this is a blessing for which I am indebted to you rather than to myself; for your prayers and holy sacrifices which you continually offer for me, a miserable sinner, awake in me all this tender remembrance and longing for you. It is you, my beloved brothers, it is you who stamp on my heart your own images; and if I am so mindful of you, I am ready to confess that you are still more mindful of me. May God reward you as you deserve; for I can give you no other satisfaction than to confess that I can in no way repay your deserts, for I see very clearly how much I owe to every one and all of the Society.

Now to speak of what I know you are most anxious to hear about—the state of religion in India. In this region of Travancore, where I now am, God has drawn very many to the faith of His Son Jesus Christ. In the space of one month I made Christians of more than ten thousand. This is the method I have followed. As soon as I arrived in any heathen village where they had sent for me to give baptism, I gave orders for all, men, women, and children, to be collected in one place. Then, beginning with the first elements of the Christian faith, I taught them there is one God—Father, Son, and Holy Ghost; and at the same time, calling on The three divine Persons and One God, I made them each make three times the sign of the Cross; then, putting on a surplice, I began to recite in a loud voice and in their own language the form of general Confession, the Apostles' Creed, the ten Commandments, the Lord's Prayer, the *Ave Maria*, and the *Salve Regina*. Two years ago I translated all these prayers into the language of the country, and learned them by heart. I recited them so that all of every age and condition followed me in them. Then I began to explain shortly the articles of the Creed and the ten Commandments in the language of the country. Where the people appeared to me sufficiently instructed to receive baptism, I ordered them all to ask God's pardon publicly for the sins of their past life, and to do this with a loud voice and in the presence of their neighbours still hostile to the Christian religion, in order to touch the hearts of the heathen and confirm the faith of the good. All the heathen are filled with admiration at the holiness of the law of God, and express the greatest shame at having lived so long in ignorance of the true God. They willingly hear about the mysteries and rules of the Christian religion, and treat me, poor sinner as I am, with the greatest respect. Many, however, put away from them with hardness of heart the truth which they well know. When I have done my instruction, I ask one by one all those who desire baptism if they believe without hesitation in each of the articles of the faith. All immediately, holding their arms in the form of the Cross, declare with one voice that they believe all entirely. Then at last I baptize them in due form, and I give to each his name written on a ticket. After their baptism the new Christians go back to their houses and bring me their wives and families for baptism. When all are baptized I order all the temples of their false gods to be destroyed and all the idols to be broken in pieces. I can give you no idea of the joy I feel in seeing this done, witnessing the destruction of the idols by the very people who but lately adored them. In all the towns and villages I leave the Christian doctrine in writing in the language of the country, and I prescribe at the same time the manner in which it is to be taught in the morning and evening schools. When I have done all this in one place, I pass to another, and so on successively to the rest. In this way I go all round the country, bringing the natives into the fold of Jesus Christ, and the joy that I feel in this is far too great to be expressed in a letter, or even by word of mouth.

The island of Manaar is about 150 miles from this place. Its inhabitants sent me some of their people to beg me to go there to baptize them, as they had determined to become Christians. I was occupied on affairs of the greatest importance, relating to the interests of religion, and so could not go myself; but I persuaded a certain priest to go instead of me and baptize as many as possible. He had already baptized a great number, when the Rajah of Jafanapatam, under whose dominion the island lies, most cruelly put to death a large number of the converts, simply because they had become Christians. Let us give thanks to our Lord Jesus Christ that even in our time He does not let us lack martyrs, and that while He sees so few souls avail themselves of all His divine mercy and indulgence to work out their salvation, He permits, in the mystery of His Providence, that human barbarity should fill up the destined ranks and number of the blessed.

I have already written you word how great a friend the Governor of India is to me and to all the Society. He was so angry and indignant at the horrible slaughter of the converts, that as soon as I began to speak to him about it, he ordered a powerful fleet to be fitted out for the destruction of the tyrant, and I was obliged myself to restrain the warmth of his most righteous indignation. This same Rajah who has put the Christians to death has a brother, the legitimate heir to the crown, who lives in exile for fear of his brother's cruelty. This prince has promised that, if he is put in possession of his dominions by the Governor, he will become Christian as well as the principal persons of his kingdom. The Governor has given orders to his officers to restore him to the throne if he embrace the Christian religion, and to put to death the Rajah who persecuted the converts, or to treat him as I shall think proper. I do not doubt that the prayers of the converts whom he has rendered martyrs may win for him the grace to acknowledge his wickedness and blindness, and that after doing a wholesome penance he may obtain pardon from God for so much crime and barbarity.

The island of Ceylon, whither I lately went with Francis Mancias, is about 120 miles distant from the Indian continent; there a prince, son of one of the Rajahs, had resolved to become Christian. When the Rajah heard of his intention he had him put to death. The persons present at his execution declare that they saw a cross of fire in the heavens, and that on the spot where he was slain the earth opened in the form of a cross. They add, that many of the inhabitants at the sight of these prodigies became disposed to embrace the Christian faith. A brother of the prince I have mentioned, touched by these marvellous events, persuaded a certain priest to give him baptism. He has now taken refuge with the Governor of India in order to ask his assistance against the Rajah who killed his brother. I met and talked with this prince in the course of his journey, and I have great hope, from what he said, of seeing that kingdom before long embrace the faith of Jesus Christ. The people are strongly moved by the prodigies and signs which have taken place; and the prince who has lately become a Christian is the heir to the throne.

In the kingdom of Macazar, about 500 leagues distant from Travancore, three of the chief princes and many of the other inhabitants came into the Church of Jesus Christ eight months ago. They have sent messengers to Malacca, a city belonging to the King of Portugal, to ask for persons able to instruct them in the law of God; and have declared that, having lived hitherto like animals without reason, they intend for the future to live like men, as soon as they shall have received the knowledge and religion of the true God. The Commandant of Malacca has sent them some priests who are to instruct them. You may judge from this alone, my very dear brothers, what great and what fertile harvests this uncultivated field promises to produce. This part of the world is so ready, so teeming with shooting corn, as I may say, that I hope within this very year to make as many as a hundred thousand Christians. *Pray the Lord of the harvest that He send forth labourers into His harvest.*[17] If any persons come to these countries, where the fields are already white unto the harvest,[18] in the desire of extending the worship of God and propagating religion, they will be received not only courteously but with real affection by the Portuguese, so that they will have all necessaries supplied them in abundance. The Portuguese nation is in fact so desirous of the extension of the Christian

[17] *rogate Dominum messis, ut mittat operarios in messem suam.* (Orig.)
[18] *ubi campi jam sunt albi ad messem.* (Orig.)

faith, that if there was no other motive, this pious zeal of theirs and their great friendliness to our Society ought certainly to draw many of you hither. And now what ought you to do when you see the minds of these people so well prepared to receive the seed of the Gospel? May God make known to you His most holy will, and give you at the same time strength and courage to carry it out; and may He in His Providence send as many as possible of you into this country!

The least and most lonely of your brothers,

FRANCIS.

From Cochin, January 27th, 1545.

We need hardly make much commentary on the earlier paragraphs of this last letter. There is the same immense overflowing tenderness of heart in the passage in which St. Francis speaks of his constant memory of his distant brethren. The account of the work in Travancore shows us that he kept to his usual and most laborious method in evangelizing that new tract of country, and we may fairly gather from it that the work was almost complete, at least as to the foundation of the new Churches. The affairs of Manaar and Ceylon have already been specially mentioned. The last paragraph of the letter, however, refers to some events which had a very great influence on the course of St. Francis' labours in the East, and the thoughts which they suggested to him as the direction of his future career had been now for some time working in his mind. The whole story, like that of the expedition against Jafanapatam, is thoroughly characteristic of the times and of the proceedings of the Portuguese in the East, and deserves to be given almost as we find it in the old annalists of their empire.

The island that Francis Xavier calls Macazar is that which is now known generally by the name of Celebes, Macazar or Macassar being the name of one of many small kingdoms or territories into which it was divided. Portuguese traders had for some years visited it for purposes of traffic, the sandalwood and other productions of the island being much in request among them. St. Francis mentions eight months before the date of his letter as the time at which the conversions of which he speaks took place. They were brought about by a captain named Antonio de Payva, who was in charge of a ship belonging to Rodrigo Vaz Pereira. It appears that Payva had some time before made the acquaintance of the petty King of Sian, which is called by some one of the territories of Macazar, by others a separate island,[19] and had begun to talk with him on matters of religion. But he had to sail away without having finished the King's conversion. On a later voyage he came to Supa, a port of Celebes, the capital of another small kingdom. The King of Supa was an old man of seventy, who came down to the sea to meet the Portuguese merchant, with a youth the heir to his throne and a court of thirty ladies, splendidly dressed and loaded with jewels. Payva accepted his hospitality, and before long began to talk about religion, a subject very much discussed in those parts at that time, as the Mussulmans of Java were endeavouring to induce the Malay princes to adopt the creed of Mahomet. The King asked Payva why the Christians hated the Mussulmans so much, and received in answer an instruction on the filthy sensuality of the Mahometan law, and the purity and holiness of the Gospel.

Payva then left the old King half persuaded, and sailed away to his former friend at Sian. Here, as we are told, he had a long discussion, first as to what was meant by holiness, and then as to what was a lie. Payva's speech on this latter question is singularly characteristic. He told the King that he would tell him the truth with all the openness and sincerity which were due to the sublime nature of the religious subjects on which they were discoursing, and also to a prince so highly gifted with good qualities as himself. To lie to a King, who represented God on earth, was to lie to God, and God would not so far abandon him as to let him do this. He would speak out of obedience and a sense of duty—only, let the King promise him one thing,—that if he made him angry by what he should say, that anger might fall on himself and not on his innocent companions. He might freely risk his own life, but

[19] There is an island, Siao, not far to the northeast of Celebes.

not theirs, although they would all die gloriously in an attempt to bring about the salvation of the King and his people. After receiving the pledge he required, Payva said boldly that the best instance of a lie which he could name was the religion which the King and his subjects professed, in which devils, the authors of all evil since the beginning of the world, were worshipped instead of the true God, the sacrifices and rites of which were abominable, as well as false, the doctrine more fabulous than the merest dream, and the manners taught by which were more fit for wild beasts than for men; and all the while they had no knowledge of Jesus Christ, the Son of the living God, the Way, the Truth, and the Life; and their whole existence was so encompassed and penetrated with lying, that they asked what it was, as a thing which they knew not. Jesus Christ was the Truth, and the King's religion was a lie. It seems that at the time of Payva's visit the island was in want of rain, after a long drought, and while he was speaking the sky became overclouded, and one of the violent rainstorms of the tropics, with thunder and lightning, came on. It was looked on as a sign from heaven that Payva's words were true.

While the King was still hesitating, a fleet arrived in the harbour, which at first caused some alarm, as it was well armed and numerous: but it turned out to be the fleet of the King of Supa, who had come with a large court to seek for Payva. He asked whether the King of Sian had been baptized, and was told that he had taken time to consider. A thing so important as the salvation of the soul, he answered, was not to be put off, and he asked himself to be baptized at once. The Portuguese had no priest with them, so the oldest man baptized him by the name of Don Luis: his queen followed his example, with a large number of the nobles and soldiers in her train; and the ceremony of baptism was accompanied by the discharge of all the artillery, by music, and all the other resources of oriental feast-keeping. The example of the court of Supa was irresistible to that of Sian, and the King with a large following was baptized, taking the name of Don Juan or Joam, after the King of Portugal. 'So,' says Faria y Sousa, 'two Courts and two Kings at the same time placed their necks, untamed throughout so many centuries, under the sweet yoke of Christ, by one of the most rare and unexpected means which that divine husbandry ever made gain by. So did Antonio de Payva, passing from his profane trafficking to a so illus trious and abundant merchandise, come to make himself the fellow of the sacred Evangelist Matthew, who had the wit from being a man of trade to change himself to an Apostle.'[20]

The newly converted princes sent, as St. Francis tells us, to the Governor of Malacca for priests to instruct them, and the tidings of this application had reached Xavier some time, as it appears, after his arrival at Cochin on his way to meet the Governor at Cambaia. These tidings seem to have fallen upon him with the weight of a providential intimation that it was for him to undertake the farther conversion and instruction of the people of Macazar—a work which had many attractions in itself, as the natives of Celebes were Malays, and there was as yet no mixture of false religions among them, Mahometanism not having as yet taken root; moreover, there seemed, as we shall find farther on, a chance that the good done by the missionary would not be frustrated and spoiled by the misconduct of any Portuguese officials. The coming of the new Fathers from Europe gave him an opportunity of supplying the missions of Travancore and the Fishery Coast with priests, so that his own presence was no longer absolutely necessary. Perhaps, too, he felt that until Miguel Vaz should return and bring with him the strict injunctions and measures of retribution which were so urgently needed, he himself would labour with little hope of effecting permanent good in the continent of India. When we look at the remainder of his Apostolate in the East, we can see how his voyage to Malacca and his designs on Macazar led him on in the end to Japan and to the

[20] *Asia Portuguesa*, t. ii. p. 1. cap. 13. Bartoli, *Asia*, t. i. p. 88, tells the story rather differently from Faria y Sousa, but the substance is the same. In his account the speech about lying is addressed to the King of Supa, and Payva, in his last discourse to the King of Sian, dwells particularly on the beauty of Christian works of mercy. The rainstorm, also, is omitted by Bartoli.

coast of China, and how the news of the success of Antonio de Payva was, in fact, a turning point in his career. But the matter as yet presented itself to him only as an uncertain prompting, and it was long before the light fully dawned on his soul which made it clear to him that it was the will of God that he should now proceed farther eastward.

Francis sailed for Negapatam, taking Ceylon, Manaar, and a small island called De las Vaccas, near Manaar, in his way, not long after the date of the letter which we have last inserted. The voyage to Ceylon was signalized by another wonderful conversion. This time it was the pilot of the vessel; a man who had for years led a licentious life, neglecting in consequence the sacraments; he had two mistresses on board the ship during this very voyage. Francis won his heart by kind familiar conversation, talking to him on the subjects connected with his business, the weather, the stars, and the like, leaving the poor man himself to begin to speak on religion. At last the pilot opened his heart to him, and told him how long he had been without confession, promising to approach the sacraments as soon as they got to land. When the time came—it is not certain whether it was at Colombo or at Galle—he repented of his promise, and avoided the sight of the Father. He met him, however, by chance, on the shore, and rather out of shame than any better feeling, asked him when he would hear his confession. Francis told him to begin at once, and they paced up and down for a time, while the pilot confessed some of his sins in a perfunctory way, without, however, being interrupted or reproved. Grace meanwhile was working in his heart, and he began to be pierced with true contrition. Then Francis led him aside into a little chapel, brought him a cushion or mat to kneel upon, and helped him to make a thorough and perfect confession, which led to an entire change of his life.[21]

[21] The Processes relate two celebrated miracles of St. Francis at this time. He raised a child to life on the island De las Vaccas. When he landed at Manaar a pestilence was raging, and about a hundred died every day. The people came to beg him to pray for them. He retired for three days, which he spent in prayer, after which the pestilence ceased.

When he arrived at Negapatam, Francis found the Portuguese armament almost ready to sail, but the expedition was put an end to by a strange accident. A Portuguese vessel, richly laden with merchandise from Pegu, ran ashore on the coast of Jafanapatam, and was at once seized by the Rajah. The Portuguese officers at Negapatam were either interested themselves in the cargo or had friends whose money had been staked in it, and they thought of nothing for the moment but of recovering it from the Rajah by negotiations. He was probably glad enough to buy them off so easily; at all events, the expedition was abandoned. It is probable that the unpopularity of the Governor, of which we hear much in the annalists, and the want of real Christian zeal on the part of many of the officers, had much to do with the failure of the enterprize.

It does not seem to have been finally abandoned when the following letter — the last of the series to Mancias, now a priest in charge of the Travancore mission—was written from Negapatam.

(XLV.) *To Father Francis Mancias.*

My dearest Father and Brother,

God, the witness and judge of my inmost feelings, knows how far rather I would talk with you face to face than write to you from a distance, for so I could more fully and diligently give you by word of mouth the form and method which you should use in your work and your conduct in the country where you are, so as duly to discharge the grave duties incumbent upon you of doing service to our Lord God by the right administration of that newly founded Church, and by watchfully keeping guard on every side and in every way over the tender flock of Christians newly gathered into the fold of Christ which is committed to your care. But now I mean to give you hints about all this in a few words, in the best manner that I can, for I am quite uncertain what is before me, and so I am bound to snatch whatever opportunity I can get of giving you counsel.

May our Lord grant us soon what we so ardently desire, and have been long waiting for—some certain indication of His most holy will as to the work and the place in which He desires that I should employ myself with the greatest usefulness to the interests of His divine service! We hang upon His nod, and by His grace are entirely disposed to follow out at once what and whatsoever it may be to which He may show that His will inclines. He has sometimes wonderful means of manifesting His will,—secret touches, which pierce the depths of the soul and flood it with light from heaven, so that the soul which is struck by these divine beams can feel no doubt at all where God desires it to go and what work to undertake. It has been most truly said of mortals such as we are in this life, that, in order to acquit themselves of what is required of their state and condition, they ought to be as strangers and travellers, who are entangled by no attachment to place or thing which might prevent them from flitting freely hither or thither, and starting up in all readiness at a moment's notice whithersoever the purpose of their journey and the object in which their hopes are summed up may invite. Just in this way we, first of all, ought to have our minds prepared, to be standing with girt loins, glowing with alacrity for either of different and even contrary occupations or scenes of labour, equally disposed to obey any yet uncertain command, and to fly whithersoever we may be directed by the indication of the will of Him Who sends us. East, west, north, or south, all are the same: the single thing in all that has to be noticed as making any difference in our choice being the consideration which we see of more or less opportunity promised us of advancing God's honour most usefully and most conspicuously.

I learn from certain information that a great door is opened to the Gospel in the neighbourhood of Malacca, and that a field is there to be found in which it seems that any industry of ours may give itself full course, with the most probable hope of seeing great rewards for its labour in the service of God. They say the harvest is ripe and only wants reapers; that it is certain that the only reason why great numbers out there do not adopt the religion of Jesus Christ is because no one calls them to it. I confess the opportunity of increasing the kingdom of Jesus Christ and extending the boundaries of the Church has a most fascinating attraction for me; but I am detained here by this affair of Jafanapatam, the issue of which still hangs in doubt. This is the only difficulty which prevents my making up my mind to go to Malacca, and if time shall settle it—I was in hopes it would be settled in the course of this next May—I shall go thither at once, and if then I can see for certain that God wishes to use my work in the island of Macazar,—where it is said that many persons have lately become Christians, and as letters inform us, the king of the place himself has asked for preachers of the Gospel from Malacca, whom I am afraid he may not have been able to get, for I think there are no fit persons to be found there,—I say, if I make up my mind before the end of May to go to Malacca, I shall not sail without having dispatched a message to my Lord Governor, to let him know my resolution, and to ask for letters of introduction to the Commandant of Malacca, ordering him to assist and further our work in whatever way we want his help in serving God our Lord in the conversion of those nations. If these things fall out as I have arranged, and it should be necessary for me to sail to Macazar, I shall still not embark without writing to you from Malacca, and informing you of the whole matter.

Meantime I beg you not to lose heart or to let your courage be worn out, and never slacken your efforts in the long and toilsome work of cultivating those poor ignorant people where you are. Keep on going round the villages, preach to the people every day, and especially be most diligent in your vigilance to leave no newborn infants unbaptized. Pay the greatest attention everywhere to the instruction of the children in the day schools of the Christian doctrine, and take constant care to make the masters who are set over them do their duty with the greatest faithfulness. You will receive from Joam de Cruz 2000 fanams, a sum which he has collected to be applied to instructing the children. Ask, also, Father Joam de Lizana to give you the sum of money which you left with him, destined to the same purpose; and if anywhere you find it necessary, set up new schools or repair the old, taking all pains and care that in every single village and hamlet in the whole coast the children are constantly taught the elements of the Christian doctrine, and the prayers which they ought to know by heart. Do not fix your own dwelling place or even stay long anywhere, but constantly visit over and over again all the churches, as I used to do when I was in this country. And be quite certain that in this way of action you will gain great favour with God.

When I was at Munahpaud I learned the mischief that had been done to the church of that place, and I made an exact calculation of the sums necessary to repair it. Diego Rebello must be applied to for this money, in whose hands I have placed 2000 fanams, which the Rajah of Travancore gave me for building Christian churches in his states. Father Francis Coelho has already spent a part of this sum. He can tell you himself how much it is. Those other 2000 fanams in the hands of Joam de Cruz are to be spent, as long as they last, solely for masters and schools. And I seem to myself never to have said enough about one thing, and this it is which I wish you above all else to take care to do most constantly and most diligently—I mean the perpetual going round all the villages, one after another, never omitting to preach the word of God and to administer the sacraments, as you find the people, wherever you go, to need them; and I do not commit to your charge the laity alone, but the priests and clergy who have been ordained from among the Malabars. Look up these first of all, give them serious admonitions, and make use of any means which circumstances may require to make them live in piety and chastity, exercising their ministry for the glory of God, and giving wholesome examples of innocence and virtue to the people.

I forgot, as to Joam de Lizana, to tell you to deduct from the sum he has in his hands and which you are to ask him for, a hundred fanams which he lent me when you were at Punical, and which I spent on the ordinary service of the churches and catechetical lessons. You must therefore deduct this sum from the amount of the funds set apart for the expenses of the schools. I moreover enjoin you to avoid most scrupulously employing for any other purpose, however good, the money collected for the salaries of the catechists and teachers.

I am rather afraid you may be angry with me, as if I distrusted your memory, and so went on for ever thrusting on you the same advice over and over again. But you must forgive my anxiety, which may perhaps go beyond measure, and make me more careful than I need be in my overflowing desire to secure what I want, and take in good part that I again most urgently beg of you always to give the first place in your care to those two heads which I most earnestly commend to you, as matters which in my judgment are of the very highest moment. The first relates to your going perpetually round and round to visit the villages most assiduously, and without giving yourself any rest or stopping long anywhere; everywhere baptizing new-born infants, and instructing or providing for the instruction of the elder children who are capable of being taught. The second has reference to the sharp and careful vigilance to which I wish you to devote yourself in searching out the conduct of the native clerics of Malabar, and the example which they set the people; lest they not only incur eternal damnation themselves, but draw others also with them to hell. If you find anything wrong in them, put it down at once, for God's sake, and chastise them quickly and severely; for if we were to let the full powers which we have for this remain unused, like a sword in its scabbard, when occasion urged us to punish very serious offences against God, especially when there is cause of scandal to many, it would be imputed to us as a great crime hardly to be expiated by much punishment.

Do all you can to help Cosmo de Payva to rid his conscience of the burthen of the many thefts and acts of rapine by which he has so licentiously made the whole coast full of his deeds of violence, as also the exactions, the criminal acts and murders which were committed at Tuticorin on account of his unbridled avarice. Go and see him in private, and show him kindly how much it concerns his honour to make restitution of the money which he extorted from the poor wretches whom the Portuguese put to death. I would write to him myself if I had any hope that the fruit of my doing so would be any amendment in him. But I wish you to tell him in my name that I can never cease from the duty incumbent upon me, of making known to the King and to the Lord Governor of India, by letter or word of mouth, his most wicked crimes, that they may punish him as he deserves; and also of applying to Prince Don Henry, the President of the Holy Tribunal for Capital Questions in Religion,[22] that in virtue of his supreme authority *in foro ecclesiastico* he act against him according to law, as one who hinders the conversion of the heathen by barbarously persecuting the converts who have lately received the holy law and faith of Jesus Christ; and add at the end that there is only one way of closing my mouth and averting the severe punishments which are on the point of overtaking him. This way is a speedy and conspicuous repentance, showing itself in works which may satisfy the public scandal he has caused, by restoring at once all his ill acquired treasures, and giving the other public proofs, such as our Christian discipline exacts, that he sincerely repents and condemns his past crimes, and promises to lead an innocent life for the future.

If Joam d'Artiaga is still on the coast, it is my wish you should not allow him to reside there any longer; and in order to oblige him to go away, you will give strict charge to Cosmo de Payva not to remit any more money for his support, at least from any funds that would be charged to our account, because we do not consider it expedient that he should stay any longer in the country. Receive with all hospitality Vasco Fernandez, who will deliver this letter to you, for I hope from the goodness of God, which has already begun to shed on him singular graces, that some day he will make one of our Society. He is a young man of excellent conduct, and burning with great desires of serving God with generosity; and how right it is

[22] The Holy Office.

for us to help on and encourage such with all our might, I am sure you will understand of yourself, even if I do not tell you. I expect to receive full and careful letters from you, telling me at good length all particulars, how your health is, how you succeed in your work, whether the Christians whom you have the care of are making progress and how far, whether Cosmo de Payva has at all come to a better mind, and whether he has given back what he took away to the Christians whom he has robbed. May God our Lord be with you all, to give you all the aid that I desire from Him for myself! Farewell.

Your brother in Jesus Christ,

FRANCIS.

From Negapatam, April 7th, 1545.

This letter to Mancias—the last which remains to us of those addressed to him by Francis Xavier, and perhaps the last that was actually so addressed—is remarkable on many accounts. It was written after the abandonment of the expedition against Jafanapatam, of which, however, Xavier seems to have been so reluctant to give up all hopes that he speaks as if it were still undecided. We find him saying, in the letter immediately following this, that he had been prevented from returning to the Fishery Coast or Travancore from Negapatam by the unfavourable winds, and that he had taken the impossibility of sailing westward as an intimation from above, and determined to visit Meliapor, or the city of St. Thomas, to seek for light from heaven at the shrine of the first Apostle of India. He says nothing to Mancias about the causes of the failure of the expedition, but we may guess that he did not think of returning to the parts in which Mancias was labouring, by the urgency of his instructions as to the carrying on of the work, and by his seizing the occasion which presented itself to write. We are told that Francis had embarked for Meliapor on Palm Sunday, March 29. After proceeding some distance, the vessel was caught by a storm, which forced it to take shelter under the lee of a projection of land, where it remained during Holy Week, which Francis passed on shore in prayer and the most rigorous fasting. They set sail again about Easter Day, but were again driven back by a tempest,[23] this time to Negapatam, whence the letter was written on Easter Tuesday. The week spent in prayer and contemplation of the Passion of our Lord had not, as we see, revealed to Francis any clear knowledge of his future destination, and, as he tells the Fathers at Goa to whom the next letter is written, it did not come to him till he had been some time at Meliapor. There is great gravity and even severity about many of the directions. The letter is unlike those written to Mancias before he was a priest, and he is exhorted to look after the Malabar priests as well as the laity, and to take great care lest the former set a bad example and lead a life unworthy of their sacred calling. The passage about Cosmo de Payva is in the same strain of apostolical liberty with the letter to the King of Portugal already given. Joam d'Artiaga has again been giving trouble, and he is dismissed altogether from the mission.

The tempest which had driven back the ship in which Francis Xavier was sailing to Meliapor did not prevent his departure for that city. He made the journey overland on foot, and must have suffered great hardships and even dangers on the way: but he was now in one of those stages of his life when he was drawn specially to give himself to prayer and the most earnest seeking for light from God, and at such times he was most disposed to be alone and to embrace penance of every sort. He arrived at Meliapor in the course of April, and took up his quarters in the house of the Vicar (or parish priest), Gaspar Coelho, which was close to the church of St. Thomas.

The fame of the shrine of this Apostle, and the frequent miracles wrought there, are attested both by the historians of India and the biographers of Francis Xavier. According to old tradition, he had been martyred at Salamiua, a city out of the ruins of which Meliapor seems to have risen. Maffei[24] relates how the Apostle was said to have predicted that when

[23] Francis is said to have predicted this tempest, urging the captain to put back to port, before there were any signs of a storm.

[24] *Hist. Indic.* t. ii. p. 37.

the sea reached a certain stone cross which he had erected, which was then ten leagues from the shore, white men would come from the most distant parts of the earth to revive the religion which he had preached in India. The sea gained upon the land for centuries along that coast, and reached the stone at the time of the arrival of the Portuguese. Thus the ancient city had been in great part swallowed up. Meliapor, however, was the chief city and mart on the Coromandel Coast, and a place of great importance. One of the first orders issued to the Governor of India by King John of Portugal, on coming to the throne in 1521, had been to search for the relics of the Apostle and show them due honour. The constant and universal tradition of the country pointed out the spot. Maffei in another part of his history gives a detailed account of the discovery of the body of St. Thomas,[25] which was found with a staff, the lance which had been the instrument of his martyrdom, and a little vessel containing some blood. The relics were afterwards removed to Goa, but at the time of the visit of Francis Xavier they were still in the church at Meliapor. A fine church had been built by the Portuguese over the little chapel of wood which was said to have been built by the Apostle, and by the side of this, in a smaller chapel, the sacred body rested. Here it was, then, that Francis Xavier spent many a night in prayer, communing, as it were, with the first preacher of the Gospel in the Indies as to his own future course of labour for the salvation of the East. He stole out at night, across the little garden which separated the house from the church, as soon as he observed that the Vicar, who slept in the same room, was fast asleep. Here he is said to have been frequently molested and even beaten and bruised during his long vigil by the devil, and at other times to have been disturbed and annoyed by strange phantoms. He persevered through all, and obtained, as we see from the following letter, the divine illumination which he sought so earnestly and faithfully.

[25] *Hist. Indic.* t. viii. p. 157. The spot is now a suburb of Madras.

(XLVI.) *To the Fathers Diego de Borba and Paul of Camerino (at Goa).*

May the grace and charity of our Lord Jesus Christ always help and favour us! Amen.

The Jafanapatam expedition has just come to nought. So the Rajah, who had promised to become Christian, has not been reestablished in his dominions. An accident ruined the whole thing. A vessel of the King of Portugal's, returning from Pegu to the Indies with a full cargo, was driven ashore by a storm on the coast of the kingdom of Jafanapatam. The Rajah immediately seized the cargo. The Portuguese have been pleased to put off the war till they have recovered their property. Thus it is that what the Governor ordered has not been done. But it will be done yet, if so it please God.

I stayed several days at Negapatam, and then the wind, which was adverse to our return westward, prevented my setting out homeward. So I took this accident as a piece of advice, and betook myself to the city of St. Thomas. Then in the holy church of the Apostle I set myself to implore God, with continual prayer, to be pleased to make known to me His will, which I had fully made up my mind not to fail in accomplishing, for I was confident that He Who gives the will would give also strength to accomplish it.[26] And so here God in His infinite mercy has been pleased to remember me. With my soul flooded with an indescribable joy, I understood that God desired me to go to Malacca, and from thence to Macazar, where a great number of natives have lately become Christians, and there confirm these new converts in the faith which they have embraced.

I have had translated into their language, with short explanations, the elements and precepts of the Christian religion. It is quite right that those who have of their own accord become Christians should receive from us every kind of assistance, and that to be able to ask God to increase their faith and to

[26] *Qui dedit velle, daret etiam perficere.* (Orig.)

give them strength necessary to observe the divine law, they should have at hand prayers translated into their own language, the *Pater Noster*, the *Hail Mary*, and other prayers, and especially the formula of general confession. If they make use of it every day to confess their sins to God, it will take the place of sacramental confession until they have priests amongst them who know the language of Macazar.

Father Francis Mancias, with some Malabar priests, remains among the Christians of Comorin. Where they are my work is not wanted. The Fathers who have wintered at Mozambique, and others whom we expect from Europe this year, will accompany the Cingalese princes when they return to their own country. I hope much that God will give me great help for my voyage, since, as I have told you, He has condescended to let me know, with so much interior delight in my soul, what it is that most of all He requires of me, and I am so firmly resolved to accomplish what by His divine inspiration I have conceived, that if I were by any chance to leave it undone I should simply seem to myself to fight against God, and to have no right to hope for anything either in this life or after death. So if this year I can find no opportunity of going by a Portuguese ship, I shall not be afraid to trust myself to a Mussulman or heathen vessel sailing for Malacca. And I have so much confidence in God, for Whom alone I undertake this voyage, that even if there were to be no merchant vessel this year, and some open boat were to set out from hence to Malacca, I should not hesitate, relying on the help of God, to make the voyage in that. In truth, all my hope is fixed and rests in God. For His sake, therefore, I beg of you, my dearest brothers, not to cease to commend me, a poor sinner, to Him in your daily masses and continual prayers. I think I shall set out for Malacca towards the end of August, for the ships which are to sail thither wait for favourable weather, which generally comes about that season. I have asked the Governor of India for an order in writing to the Commandant of Malacca to provide me with a vessel and all other things necessary for the voyage to Macazar. I charge you of your charity to see that this order is made out and sent by the bearer of this letter. Send me at the same time a small Roman Breviary. Say a great many kind things in my name to Cosmo Añez, our very good friend and the most faithful of men. I do not write to him separately, because this letter is intended for all three of you.

If any members of the Society arrive who are foreigners and ignorant of the Portuguese language, they will have to learn it, otherwise there will be no one in these parts to understand what they say. I will write to you from Malacca, to tell you about the conversions already made and how the heathens are prepared, so that you may send us thither men fit to propagate our holy Christian faith among them, for you must make the house which is called after the holy faith justify its name. I will write to you more fully by the paramesses[27] which will sail in July. May our Lord bring us together in His blessed kingdom! for I know not whether we shall ever see each other again in this life.

FRANCIS.

The city of St. Thomas, May 8th, 1545.

Meliapor was a city of predilection to Francis Xavier. It was not by any means free from the scandals which prevailed at Goa and elsewhere. There were only about a hundred Portuguese families settled in the place, and the evil influences of the pagan corruption around them, as well as the enervating effects of the climate, had made large inroads on their Christian virtue. Nevertheless, the city won Francis' heart, for he found its people docile and ready for improvement, and no doubt the immense consolations which he received at the shrine of St. Thomas, after his future course had become clear to him, made him love the spot on which he had been so blessed. He spent four bright happy months at Meliapor. His days were given to labours for the spiritual good of the inhabitants, and his nights, except the short portion which he allotted to necessary rest, in prayer and contemplation. Some anecdotes of this time are given in the biographies. They all witness to the kind of magic which his presence exercised over the popula-

[27] native boats.

tion, especially the Portuguese, who, even when they were leading vicious lives, still preserved their faith, and were easily won by his sweet gay affability and the charm of his eminent holiness. All over the East he was already known as the holy Father, and so many of his wonderful sayings and predictions had come true that every one was convinced that neglect of his admonitions would be speedily followed by punishment from heaven. Once, as if forced by poverty, he asked a rich cavalier to give him a dinner. The man was living in open sin with a mistress to whom he was fanatically attached, and this lady was at table, and the walls were hung round with licentious paintings. Francis took no notice of anything, spoke to the lady as if she had been the cavalier's wife, talked pleasantly and at the same time seriously till dinner was over, and then took his leave with a thousand thanks to his host for having been so charitable as to feed him. The man's heart smote him as soon as Francis was gone, and when he thought of all that his guest's virginal modesty must have had to suffer during the repast, he was melted at the thought of so much charity. He was soon at the feet of Francis, asking him to hear his confession, and became a changed man for the rest of his life.[28] A certain Jerome Fernandez used to tell afterwards how he had been on a vessel which had been taken by pirates, and had only escaped by swimming ashore without anything but his clothes. He applied for alms to Francis, who put his hand into his purse and found nothing, and then, raising his eyes to heaven, and bidding him not despair, so great was the mercy of God, he took out of it a handful of gold fanams, and gave them to Fernandez. Another, a merchant, went to ask his blessing, as he was going on a distant voyage. Francis took his own rosary and gave it him, telling him that it would be of use to him if he had confidence in the prayers of the Blessed Virgin. The merchant was saved on a plank from a shipwreck

[28] Massei, l. ii. c. 7. Massei says he had not been to confession for fifteen years. Another penitent is mentioned by Bartoli, who had been away from the sacraments for twenty years, and was for a fortnight seen in the church daily, making his confession.

in which most of those with him were lost, calling on our Blessed Lady, and holding the rosary in his hands.

The story of Joam d'Eyro, a young merchant who gave his goods to the poor and became Francis' companion in his voyage to Malacca, is told by all the biographers of St. Francis, and is alluded to in the first letter which was written by the Saint after his arrival at that place. We may give it partly in the words of the English translation of Turselline, partly in those of Lucena, who had seen the sworn deposition. 'There was a certain young man, a merchant, called John d'Eyro, who came to Francis to confession, and hearing him discourse of divine matters, found there were certain other merchandize far richer than those with which he trafficked, and of which he had never heard before. Wherefore, giving over his former trading, and desirous to become a merchant of more precious wares, he entreated Francis to receive him for his companion.' [The writer means his companion in the Society.] 'He at first refused him absolutely (because, perhaps, he saw in him a secret inconstancy and intractable disposition), yet at last, by much entreaty, he obtained his desire, and so, settling his affairs, began to distribute his goods among the poor. But in executing of this his good purpose he was more forward than constant. For whilst he was busied about selling of his wares, he was vehemently solicited by the common enemy of mankind, who did so work upon him that having set his hand to the plough, on a sudden he began to look back, and sought again most greedily after those things which a little before he had contemned. Being thus wholly changed in mind, he packed up his merchandize in the most private way he could and conveyed them into a ship, intending to be gone. But although he deceived others, yet he could not deceive Francis, the which he most of all sought to do. Now having gotten all things together which he thought requisite, as he was about to take shipping, Xavier upon a sudden causeth him to be called unto him.'[29] He sent after him a lad called Antonio, says Lucena. The young merchant thought at first to brave it out. 'You

[29] Turselline, lib. ii. c. 17.

are wrong, my child,' he said, 'I am not the man you seek.' 'What,' said the boy, 'are you not called Joam d'Eyro?' 'Yes,' he said. 'Well, sir, Father Master Francis sent me to run quick, and find and call to him Joam d'Eyro.' There was a battle in the man's heart; but at last he determined to go, trusting in his own great secrecy, says the account, that Francis could not know what had happened; but he was undeceived as soon as he came into his presence. Francis said simply, 'You have sinned, Joam d'Eyro, you have sinned,' but so forcibly that Joam threw himself at his feet, saying, 'Yes, father, it is true, it is true, I have sinned.' 'Confession! confession! my child,' said Francis; and, adds Lucena, 'the same day he confessed, the same day he sold his ship that he had bought, the same day he gave the price of it and all the rest he had to the poor, the same day he ended with more grace, and rose to a better life by penance than he had lost by his fault, having gained besides, by the experience of his own weakness, a great advance in the knowledge and distrust of himself.'[30]

The time at last came for Francis to sail for Malacca, and we are told that so great had been the change wrought by his influence in the moral and religious state of the Portuguese, that there was no one left, when he set sail, who was known to be leading a bad and unchristian life. Francis left the people with blessings and predictions of happiness and prosperity, which were signally fulfilled, and they on their part showed so much grief at his going as to remind the Portuguese historian of the parting between St. Paul and his friends at Miletus. We find almost invariably that the sea voyages of Francis Xavier —which occupied a very large portion of the short period of years during which his Apostolate was carried on—are signalized each in turn by some miracle of charity or some anecdote of his gracious, affable, and playful sanctity. This voyage from Meliapor to Malacca has its story of this kind. A soldier was on board, very fond of cards, which were in great request to cheer the tedium of the passage. One day he was unlucky, and lost, first all his own money, and then a large sum, some

[30] *Vida da S. Francesco,* l. iii. c. 9.

hundreds of crowns, which had been committed to his care by a merchant at Meliapor, to be conveyed to a correspondent at Malacca. When all was lost, the poor man broke out into blasphemies against God, and then sank into a deep melancholy which brought him to the point of throwing himself into the sea. Francis was told of his danger; perhaps, as was so often his wont, he had been looking on at the game, talking with the players and bystanders. He took the man aside, and began to comfort him as well as he could, but it seemed impossible to make him resigned. Then Francis borrowed fifty reals of a friend, and brought them to him with a bright smile on his face, telling him to go and try his luck again. Before the play began, he took the pack of cards in his hands, turned them over once or twice, and then gave them to the players. This time the luck was all on the side of the soldier, who soon won back all that he had lost. He was going on with the game, when Francis forbad him to continue, and then taking him aside, spoke to him sweetly and gravely of the risk which he had run of throwing away his soul as well as his life. The man became truly penitent, and never touched cards again.

These anecdotes of Francis in his intercourse with his chance companions on his numerous voyages might probably have been multiplied almost indefinitely if there had been any one at hand to collect them at the time. We gather from them a picture of the Saint as individual and distinct in its features as that, for instance, which the mind forms to itself as it considers the several stories about St. Francis of Assisi, in his love for birds, animals, and the lower creation generally. The beauty, the simplicity, the exquisite gentleness, condescension, and charity of the picture assure us of its general truth, apart from the authority of the testimony on which each particular instance may rest. Amid all the wild roughness, the free license, and the reckless passions which had their play among the Portuguese mariners of the time, and the crowd of men of all races and creeds who were to be met with on board the merchant vessels of the Eastern seas, it was the fruit of no slight and feeble virtue to preserve purity, charity, meekness, justice, and temperance, without stain or flaw. A far more consummate sanctity must that have been which could mix so freely and easily with the crowd, and condescend so thoroughly to its ways and practices, and yet not only remain pure as the sunbeam that pierces the foulest dungeon, but be also a source of light and moral health and renovation to all around it.

We must suppose that Francis received, before sailing for Malacca, the letter for the Commandant of that place, which he had asked for from the Governor Sousa. If Sousa sent it to him, it was his last act as Governor in favour of Francis Xavier. About the end of August of this year a new Governor arrived, Joam de Castro, whose name became very famous in the annals of Portuguese India. Martin Alfonso de Sousa had been unsuccessful, at least he was unpopular with the Portuguese. He had lowered the pay of the soldiers, and at the same time opposed himself rigorously to the practice common among them of quitting the King's service to become traders. Other measures of his, which are mentioned by Faria y Sousa, seem to have had the same tendency to thrift, economy, carefulness in watching the interests of the revenue, and the like. He was also naturally severe and hot tempered. He is said to have so earnestly desired the arrival of his successor as to have adjured a friend of his, who was setting out for Portugal a few days before Joam de Castro arrived, and was hearing mass with him at the time, to tell the King to send him a successor, as he dared not govern India 'because men are so changed from truth and honour.' And he swore 'by that sacred Host, and by the true Body of Christ, which he saw therein with the eyes of faith,' that otherwise he would open the 'patents of succession'—sealed papers sent out by the King, with names of officers in them who were to succeed to the Governorship in case of a sudden vacancy—and resign the government to the first who should be named.[31] Don Joam de Castro brought with him three Fathers of the Society for the service of the mission.

[31] Faria y Sousa, *Asia Portuguesa*, t. ii, p. i. cap. xiv.

NOTES TO BOOK II.

(1.) *Daily Exercise of a Christian, drawn up by St. Francis Xavier.*

THERE are in the collection of the Letters of St. Francis Xavier several documents which are rather to be classed among his 'works,' than among his letters. It is much to be regretted that there are not more of these relics of his wonderful industry and diligence, for his own letters, and the writers of his time, mention several which do not seem now to exist. At least, they have never been published. There is so much to be learnt from his manner of setting forth even the simplest and most elementary truths, that it would be a pity to omit altogether the documents to which we refer; and we shall, therefore, place them here, where they may be considered as a commentary on what has been said in the text and his own letters as to his methods of practical instruction. The first document, which we find in the collection of F. Menchacha (*Epistolæ Sti. Francisci Xaverii*), is a rule of daily life for a Christian. It seems not to be intended so much for the Indian converts as for the Portuguese, as it clearly implies that the person following it can go every day to mass. It was the habit of St. Francis, as F. Poussines informs us, when he had won any body back from a bad life, to give him a method of living well and piously. This he used to teach to the ignorant *vivâ voce*, and to others he gave it in writing. There were thus many copies of it in existence, indeed he sometimes fixed it up in a public place, where people might copy it. We owe the copy which we possess to the zeal of Father Philippucci, an Italian Jesuit who had been miraculously healed by invoking St. Francis Xavier, and afterwards got leave to go and labour in India, whence he sent a large number of copies of letters of the Saint to Père Poussines. Philippucci obtained several copies of the instruction which follows, and comparing them together, selected the best text he could find, and translated it into Latin. (Philippucci lived at the end of the seventeenth century.) The title of the paper is given as follows:

To souls desirous of eternal salvation.

The Christian who is not satisfied to be one merely in name, but who would truly and practically act up to what he professes, should on awaking in the morning turn his mind to make three acts especially due to God and pleasing to Him. The first is the confession and adoration of the most Holy Trinity, the mystery of God one in Nature, three in Persons. The profession and confession of three divine Persons in one Essence is the distinctive mark of the Christian faith, and this we openly declare by making the sign of the cross and pronouncing at the same time the names of the Father, Son, and Holy Ghost, as the Church teaches her children to do, if only we accompany the movement of our hand and the sound of the tongue by devotion and attention of mind. The moment you awake, therefore, sign yourself on the forehead and the breast, and pronounce at the same time the solemn invocation of the Holy Trinity, with the deepest reverence of a devout mind, so to adore God the Father, Son, and Holy Ghost, One Eternal Almighty God Infinite in goodness.

The second duty is the exercise of the three theological virtues, thus to consecrate to our Creator the first fruits, as it were, of the day, and to gain to ourselves beforehand His favour which we so much need for everything. Repeat, therefore, the Creed, pronouncing each of the articles with your whole heart, and making an act of the strongest adhesion to all the dogmas it contains concerning the nature of God, the divine Persons, the Incarnation, life, death, and resurrection of Jesus Christ, the holy Church, and all the rest, saying in your heart as you give utterance to the words: O my God, Three Persons in one God, I believe in my heart all that the holy Roman Catholic and Apostolic Church believes and teaches concerning Thee; all that she believes and teaches concerning the Son of the eternal Father, Who for me was made man, suffered, died, and rose again, and Who reigns in Heaven with the Father and the Holy Spirit: and all the other articles of faith which this holy Church teaches and professes. I am ready to lose everything, to suffer all violence, and more than that, to pour forth my blood and my life, rather than allow this faith to be torn from me, or allow the least doubt as to any part of it. I am fully resolved to live and die in this profession, and if speech shall fail me when I come to my last hour, now at this moment, instead of then, I declare in words which express my whole heart that I acknowledge Thee, O Lord Jesus, for the Son of God, I believe in Thee, and I submit most humbly to Thee all my thoughts. Amen.

From Thee also, O Jesus Christ my Redeemer, and from Thy divine mercy, I hope that through Thy merits, assisted by Thy grace, I corresponding to this grace by good works, and fulfilling the precepts of Thy holy law, I shall one day come into the glory and happiness for which Thou hast been pleased to create and call me. Amen.

I love Thee also, O my God, above all things, and I hate and detest with my whole heart the sins by which I have offended Thee, because they are displeasing in Thy sight, Thou Who art supremely good and worthy to be loved; and as I acknowledge that I ought to love Thee with a love beyond all others, and strive to show Thee such love, so also I count Thee in my judgment infinitely above the worth of all things most fair and excellent, and I firmly and irrevocably resolve never to consent to offend Thee, or to do anything in any way which may displease Thy sovereign goodness and put me in danger of falling from Thy holy grace, in which I am most firmly determined to persevere to my last breath. Amen.

In the third place, in order to begin the day and the hours of light well, we must ask of God our Lord the assistance of His grace that we may observe exactly the ten commandments of His most holy law: for no one can arrive at eternal salvation except by observing them. Therefore, the precepts of the Decalogue should be repeated distinctly; and after having pronounced them slowly and attentively, these words should be added: God our Lord says that those who observe and practise these ten commandments will go into Paradise and there enjoy eternally supreme happiness. God our Lord says that those who do not observe and do not put in practice these ten commandments will go into hell, where they will be tormented eternally.

These two prayers should be added in order to obtain grace to observe the commandments of God:

I pray and beseech Thee, O Lord Jesus Christ, to grant me grace this day and during my whole life to observe perfectly the ten commandments.

I beg and entreat thee, holy Mary, my Sovereign Lady, intercede for me with thy most blessed Son Jesus Christ, and obtain from Him, to grant me this day and all my life grace faithfully to observe these ten commandments. Amen.

Afterwards should be said, with an attentive and devout heart, this prayer to God our Lord:

O Almighty God, Father of my soul, Creator of all things that are in the world, in Thee, my God and Lord, the source of all my good, I place my whole confidence; I hope, without any doubt, that I shall obtain eternal salvation from Thy grace through the infinite merits of the Passion and death of my Lord Jesus Christ, although the sins which I have committed from my tender years up to this day are very great indeed and very many. Thou, O Lord, hast created me, and given me body and soul and all that I have. Thou alone and none else hast formed me in Thy image and likeness. I return to Thee, O my God, endless thanks and praise, especially for the blessing Thou hast granted me of knowing the faith and the true laws of Jesus Christ Thy Son. Weigh in the balance, O Lord, my sins against the merits of the death and Passion of my Lord Jesus Christ, and not against my own slender merits, which are indeed none at all; and so I shall be free from the power of the enemy, and shall go and enjoy eternally the glory of Paradise. Amen.

Prayer to our most holy Lady.

O Mary, my Lady, the hope of Christians, and Queen of Angels and of all the saints who are with God in heaven; I commend myself to thee, my Lady, and to all the saints, now, as if I were at the hour of my death, to preserve me from the world, the flesh, and the devil, the enemies who plot against my soul, employing all their power, and hoping with deadly hate to thrust it down into hell. Hinder this, O most tender Mother, I pray and beseech thee. Amen.

Prayer to St. Michael the Archangel.

O my most excellent Patron, holy Archangel Michael, defend me against the devil at the hour of my death, when I shall stand before the judgment seat, giving to God an account of all my life. Amen.

Prayer to the holy Guardian Angel.

O Angel of God, who, by Divine appointment, art my guardian to watch over me in all my ways, be pleased this day to enlighten, preserve, rule, and govern me, whom the goodness of God has committed to thy charge.[1]

[1] O Angele Dei,
Qui custos es mei,
Me tibi commissum pietate supernâ
Illumina, custodi, rege, et guberna.

After this usual formulary (Angel of God, who art, &c.), should be added: I beseech thee, O holy and blessed Angel, to whose care and providence I am entrusted, be always at hand with help for me at the time of need. Bear my prayers into the sight of God our Lord, and let thy voice plead in His merciful ear, that by His mercy and through thy intercession, He may grant me the pardon of my past faults, a true knowledge of my present faults and a true contrition for them; and lastly, efficacious care to avoid those of which in future my frailty may be in danger, and that He may also grant me the grace to do good works and to persevere in so doing to the end of my life. Drive far away from me, by the virtue of Almighty God, all the temptations of Satan; and what I cannot merit by my own works, obtain by thine own gracious and powerful prayers to Him Who is the Lord of both of us, that no mixture of sin, no leaven of wickedness may have place in me. And if at any time thou seest me wander out of the right way and fall off to the crooked way of sin, use every means to bring me back again to seek my Saviour in the paths of justice. If thou seest me fall into tribulation and distress, then in thy kindly charity use all thy sweet offices with God to obtain from Him for me at once the help which I need. I beseech thee never to desert me, to protect me ever, visit me, help me, and defend me from all the vexations and assaults of evil spirits, watching over me night and day, at every hour and at every moment; direct me whither thou wouldst have me to go, and go with me and guard me. But above all things, O my guide and holy guardian, again and again I pray and beseech thee, bend all thy powers and redouble thy care for me at the time of my departure from this life, and permit me not to be terrified by the attacks or spectres of my enemies the devils. Let them find me shielded most efficaciously by thee, so that I fall not into despair, and leave me not before thou hast led me in unto the beatific sight of God our Lord; where with thee, with the most blessed Mother of God ever Virgin, and all the saints, we may enjoy for ever the glory of Paradise, which is to be given us through Jesus Christ our Lord, Who, with the Father and the Holy Spirit, lives and reigns for ever. Amen.

After having begun by these prayers, it is well for the faithful Christian, before giving himself up to the occupations of life, to meditate a certain space of time on the law of the Lord, which he may do profitably by renewing every morning the following exercise. Prostrate before God, let him go through and meditate separately the ten commandments of His law, according to this form. The first commandment of the divine law of my Lord and Creator is this: 'Thou shalt love and worship the Lord thy God with all thy heart,' &c. Then let him think over with himself and call to mind all the faults which, from his earliest years, he has committed against this precept during his whole life. Then, condemning and detesting them with his whole heart, let him implore God to pardon those faults, and make a firm resolution to avoid henceforth sins of this kind, and rather to incur the risk and loss of all his property, his health, and even his life, than commit anything contrary to a commandment so just and salutary.

Let him add two colloquies, in some such words as these. First to Jesus Christ let him say: I pray and beseech Thee, O Jesus my Lord, grant me to-day and all the days of my life, the abundance of Thy grace to observe this first precept of Thy holy law. Then to the blessed Mother of Jesus Christ: O my Lady, holy Mary, I beseech thee to pray for me to the blessed fruit of your womb, Jesus Christ my Lord, that this day and all the remaining days of my life He may mercifully supply to me abundant grace to perform fully all that is prescribed to me by this first commandment of His most holy law. In the same way let him go through the nine other precepts of the Decalogue.

This exercise, if gone through faithfully at the beginning of each day, is of the highest importance for securing eternal salvation. For as the Christian's whole hope and only way of arriving at the happiness to which he is called lies in his doing good works and avoiding evil works, of which the former are commanded and the latter forbidden by the ten precepts of the divine law, it is easy to see how much it will conduce to this end to consider exactly and distinctly each one of the divine precepts, and thus to have set before us as in a mirror the stains of our souls which must be removed, and how much is still lacking to us. From this springs true contrition, whereby we efface our old sins, and also that we guard ourselves beforehand against those faults into which we are in danger of falling on account of the treacherous occasions of daily life, and are able to weaken the power of bad associations and vicious habits, and daily acquire fresh strength from the firm and deliberate resolutions which we form, as also by imploring so continually the aid of God to resist the temptations to evil which may occur to us in all kinds of wickedness, every one of which falls under the ban of some one of the ten commandments of God, and consequently may be thought of with the greatest profit to our souls in this daily examination of those commandments, made in this consideration of them.

Here is also a remedy for that blindness of the spiritual eye so common in all those who live without reflection, who let themselves fall into sin without feeling it, and in whom long habit has so blunted the sting of conscience that they drink in iniquity like water, not knowing what they are doing, while they are preparing for themselves destruction at the end, and like gamesters, stake their eternal salvation or damnation on a chance throw. In this exercise care must be taken to dwell the longest time on those precepts as to which each one offends most often and most seriously; exciting a more lively sorrow for such sins in particular out of love for the Divine Majesty which they have offended, and gathering up all the strength of the soul to form an irrevocable resolution of abstaining from them henceforth, avoiding also the occasions of them, and taking all fit ways and means to root up the bad habit which carries us headlong into them, especially imploring the help of God's grace chiefly for this purpose.

After having gone through the ten commandments, the Christian should pronounce with the greatest attention these or the like words: I most firmly believe that if, which God forbid, death should surprise me before I had obtained the pardon of any grievous sin, committed against one of these ten divine commandments, immediately, and without any hope of a remission of the sentence, my poor soul would be damned and cast into the everlasting fire of hell, to be there tormented throughout eternity, without any redemption; also I am certain that if, as I desire and hope, when I yield my last breath, I am free from any mortal sin, and if I begin from this moment to correct in myself the bad habit of sinning against the ten divine commandments, then God our Lord will have compassion on my soul, and however great may have been the number of sins in my life, will lead me to eternal salvation, that is to say, to the glory of Paradise, after I have expiated the stains of my sins, by the trials and sufferings of this world patiently endured, or by the pains of Purgatory.

Every morning when he leaves his home the Christian's first steps should be to the church, and there let him be present at the holy sacrifice of the mass. While mass is being said, he may say within himself, or with his lips if he like better, these prayers, or others like them:

O Lord Jesus Christ, love of my heart, by the five wounds which Thy love for us inflicted on Thee on the Cross, help Thy servants whom Thou hast redeemed with Thy most precious Blood. Amen.

Lord Jesus Christ, most merciful Saviour of men, by the holy Cross which Thou hast consecrated by the touch of Thy most pure Body, and which Thou hast purpled with Thy most precious Blood; by the virtue of the Passion and the death which Thou didst suffer for me thereon, forgive me my sins as Thou didst forgive the thief crucified beside Thee; give me victory over the enemies of my soul; and by Thy grace bring the men who are against me to a true knowledge of Thy Divinity, and to true repentance of their sins. Amen.

When the most holy Body of the Lord is elevated and shown to the people, let him say:

I adore Thee, O Lord Jesus Christ, and I bless Thee for having ransomed the world and me by the holy Cross. Amen.

When the sacred chalice of the precious Blood of our Lord is elevated, let him say:

I adore Thee, O most sacred Blood of Jesus my Lord, shed upon the Cross to save sinners and me. Amen.

And as it is fitting that the Christian should be careful not only for his own salvation, but for that of others, I should advise every one to repeat this prayer for the conversion of infidels at the moment the priest consumes the sacred Body and Blood of Jesus Christ in consummating the sacrifice:

O Eternal God, Creator of all things, remember that the souls of infidels have been created by Thee out of nothing, and formed after Thine image and likeness. Behold, Lord, to the dishonour of Thy name, hell is peopled with them. Remember that Jesus Thy Son suffered for their salvation the most cruel death: permit not, I beseech Thee, O Lord, that Thy Son be any longer held in contempt by these infidels; but, appeased by the prayers of Thy chosen Saints, of the Church, the most holy Spouse of Thy Son, remember Thy mercy, forget their idolatry and infidelity, and grant that they may at length acknowledge our Lord Jesus Christ, Whom Thou hast sent, in Whom is our salvation, our life, our resurrection, by Whom we have been saved and set at liberty, and to Whom be all glory for ever and ever. Amen.

During the day the wear and tear of life and our promiscuous intercourse with men usually offer dangerous allurements to sin, especially to persons who by many sins in time past have contracted a habit of doing wrong. These last ought to recollect continually the shortness of this life, the nearness of death, the account they must render to God of all the actions of their life, the universal judgment when we shall appear before the inexorable judgment seat of Jesus Christ, the everlasting flames of the damned, and the eternal happiness of Paradise for which we were created, which is to be irreparably lost by any mortal sin. A person who is habitually filled with these thoughts, when he betakes himself to the daily occupations and recreations of life, will certainly fall far more rarely than others, and will rise again more easily after he has fallen: and he will generally be found ready and disposed to do that during his life which at the hour of death he would wish to have done. It will also be good for every one to be fully persuaded and thoroughly to understand that there is a great difference between sins of frailty, which are wrung as if by stealth, by the power of temptation or the unexpected snares of some false attraction, from persons otherwise well disposed to good, and the great sins of inveterate habit which have been long continued openly and shamelessly. The latter are incredibly greater than the former, the former more easily forgiven than the latter. So I should not be without hope that the repentance of persons whom a last illness might surprise in some fault of the first kind might profit them, but I should have great fears for people of the other sort, for such persons seem to me not so much to leave their sins as their sins to leave them; and it seems to me likely that there exists as it were an agreement between the divine mercy and justice of God, by which the indulgent kindness of His mercy may be allowed to cover those whose life has been once virtuously ordered, but who out of weakness and from the treachery of occasions of sin which they never sought may have been so unhappy as to fall into mortal sin, while those who, giving themselves an uninterrupted license in sin, are so bold as to carry on an open profession of wickedness to the very end of their life, will be sacrificed to the vengeance of the justice of God.

These things I especially commend to the thoughts of those who have hitherto found the holy war against sin a war of doubtful issue, and marked by successive alternations of fortune. As to those who are rather further advanced in the interior life and who have begun to taste how gracious is the Lord, I advise them often during the course of the day to raise their hearts to God, to make again and again acts of faith, of religion, of hope, and above all of pure and unmixed charity. It is a good thing to know by heart forms of these acts, taken from the psalms or sacred hymns, and to repeat them from time to time. They may also be expressed in common language, or even sung. Here is a metrical exercise of the love of God, without any mixture of our own interest, for the use of those who like it.

[Here follows the rhythm commonly known as the Act of Love or Contrition of St. Francis Xavier. There is a question whether it was not originally the composition of St. Ignatius; indeed, the Spanish sonnet is attributed to him by Father Menchacha, who thinks St. Francis made a shorter and more popular form of the same, perhaps in Portuguese. The Spanish runs thus:

No me mueve, mi Dios, para quererte
El cielo que me tienes prometido:
Ni me mueve el infierno tan temido
Para dexar por esso de ofenderte.

Tu me mueves, Señor; mueveme el verte
Clavado en essa cruz, y escarnecido;
Mueveme el ver tu cuerpo tan herido;
Muevenme tus afrentas, y tu muerte.

Muevesme al tu amor en tal manera,
Que aunque no hubiera cielo, yo te amara;
Y aunque no hubiera infierno, te temiera,

No me tienes que dar porque te quiera;
Que aunque quanto espero, no esperara,
Lo mismo que te quiero, te quisiera.

The common Latin version, which, as will be seen, though it gives the same thoughts, is not by any means a strict translation, is as follows:

O Deus, ego amo Te,
Nec amo Te, ut salves me,
Aut quia non amantes Te
Æterno punis igne,
Tu, Tu, mi Jesu, totum me
Amplexus es in cruce;
Tulisti clavos, lanceam,
Multamque ignominiam,
Innumeros dolores,
Sudores, et angores,
Ac mortem, et hæc propter me
Ac pro me peccatore.
Cur igitur non amem Te,
O Jesu amantissime?
Non ut in cœlo salves me,
Aut ne in æternum damnes me,
Nec præmii ullius spe;
Sed sicut Tu amasti me,
Sic amo et amabo Te,
Solum quia Rex meus es,
Et solum quia Deus es. Amen.

The following English translation is considered as the classical form of the rhythm in our language, and is attributed to Dryden:

'O God, Thou art the object of my love,
Not for the hopes of endless joys above,
Nor for the fear of endless pains below
Which those who love Thee not must undergo:
For me, and such as me, Thou once didst bear
The ignominious cross, the nails, the spear,
A thorny crown transpierced Thy sacred brow,
What bloody sweats from every member flow!
For me in torture Thou resign'st Thy breath,
Nailed to the cross, and sav'dst me by Thy death:
Say, can these sufferings fail my heart to move?
What but Thyself can now deserve my love?
Such as then was and is Thy love to me,
Such is, and shall be still, my love to Thee.
Thy love, O Jesus, may I ever sing,
O God of love, kind Parent, dearest King! Amen.'

We do not possess the common Portuguese form which was current in India when F. Philippucci made his collection of copies of letters and the like. If we may judge from the Latin version given us by Poussines and Menchacha, there were several thoughts in it which do not occur in the other forms; the latter part especially is very different. For this reason we subjoin it:

Ut Te colam, Deus meus,
Non me movet terror Tuæ
Manus vibrantis fulmina;
Nec horror ignis Tartari
Urentis æternum reos.
Tu me, Deus, per Te moves,
Tu, Christe, transfixus trahis,
Crux urget, incendit cruor,
Jesu, tuis plagis fluens.
Si cesset inferni metus,
Tollatur et spes gloriæ,
Ego tamen, mi Conditor,
Te, dotibus captus Tuis,
Te, numen admirans Tuum,
Sublime, sanctum, providum,
Amore inempto prosequar.
Te, Christe, Te Fili Dei,
Te Virgo proles Virginis,
Mansuete, fortis, innocens,
Dignate pro nobis mori,
Gratis merentem diligam.]

After the occupations of the day, when night, the time for rest, arrives, a Christian must never allow himself to trust his soul to sleep, which is the likeness of death, without being prepared as for death itself. For who can promise him that on the morrow he will awake in health of mind and body? If he is wise, he cannot doubt that most surely during the night which is about to begin many in this wide world will be overpowered by some accident while they sleep, and so pass from sleep to death. And since no one is able to guarantee him from being of the number, it would be unheard of folly to neglect those precautions, the irreparable omission of which may perhaps be matter for eternal sorrow. Therefore, let him kneel down before God, our sovereign Judge, and first give Him thanks for the great and innumerable blessings that He has given him during the course of his life, especially in the day that has just passed, as far as he knows them and can give thanks for them: then having first implored light from above to recognise his faults, let him set on the other side the evils he has committed, calling to mind and confessing with shame whatever sins, especially that day, he may have committed, against or beyond the law of God, in omission, deed, will, thought, or word.

Having thus collected his heap of sins, let him first condemn them in his own heart and abominate them with piercing sorrow, and then do away with them by the fire of the love of God, which alone has power that can destroy them, and by means of true contrition, conceived entirely out of perfect charity for God Who deserves infinite love, root out their remains and utterly blot them out, using all the force of his heart in this contrition; and then let him make a firm resolution never to consent to the like again, either for any hope of enjoyment or profit, or from the fear of any danger whatsoever. With these things in his mind let him repeat the ordinary form of confession of sins: *I confess to Almighty God*, &c. Let him also implore the help of God to perform what he has promised, making, for this purpose, prayers to Jesus Christ, to His most holy Mother, to the holy Guardian Angel, and to the Saints inhabitants of Heaven, like the prayers set down before.

Parents and the heads of families ought to take great care to accustom their children, both boys and girls, from their tenderest years to make these exercises daily morning and night, or others of the same kind, as far as the capacity of their age allows; and if they are not able to pray mentally, let them order them at least vocally, in the morning when they rise and before going to sleep at night, to pray to God on their knees, reciting three times the *Hail Mary*, according to the custom of the Church, as well as the Lord's Prayer and the holy Creed taking care to dwell rather more distinctly in thought on the Passion, death, and resurrection of Jesus Christ.

(2.) *Method of catechizing the Ignorant.*

A good deal has been said, both in the Letters and in the text (pp. 152, 166), about Francis Xavier's method of catechizing, or rather of holding a Catechetical Service, as it may be called. The following form is from the same source as the preceding Daily Exercise. It is addressed *To the Catechists of the Society of Jesus in India.*

I am going to lay before you, my dearest brothers, the form and method of teaching the elements of Christian doctrine to these ignorant nations which my own practice and its results have approved to me, hoping that if you observe the same you may find yourselves gathering satisfactory fruits for the glory of God our Lord and for the salvation of souls.

The people being assembled, whoever is to give the explanation of the Catechism should first make the sign of the cross, and then, with his head uncovered and his hands raised to heaven, he should pronounce in a clear and intelligible voice, with two boys ready to repeat it after him, the Lord's Prayer, he saying each word by itself, and the boys each word at once after him.

Then the catechist says to the congregation: 'Now, my brethren, let us make profession of our faith, and let us make acts of the chief and most excellent virtues, which are called theological, and which are faith, hope and charity.' Then he is to begin with faith, asking the people, 'Do you believe in One only true God, Almighty, Eternal, Immense, infinitely Wise?' All are to answer: 'Yes, Father, by the grace of God, we do believe.' The catechist must go on: 'Then all repeat together after me this prayer: O Lord Jesus Christ, Son of the living God, grant us grace most firmly to believe this article of our holy faith: let us add in order to obtain it a *Pater Noster*.' This prayer is to be said by all to themselves in secret. Then the teacher, raising his voice again, says: 'Now, then, all repeat after me: O holy Virgin Mary, Mother of God, obtain for us from God the grace to believe most firmly this article of our holy faith; and in order to obtain this favour from her, let us all say to ourselves, in her honour, the *Hail Mary*.' After all have secretly repeated it, the teacher continues: 'Do you believe, my brethren, that this true God is the One only God, One in Essence, and Three in Persons—

God the Father, God the Son, and God the Holy Ghost?' All are to answer: 'Yes, Father, by the grace of God we believe this.' Then the two prayers mentioned above are to be repeated, and the *Pater* and *Ave* said secretly by the people, each standing in his own place. Then the next question is to be put. 'Do you believe, my brethren, that this same God is the Creator of all things, that He is our Saviour and Glorifier?' And all answer: 'We truly believe this, Father, by the grace of God.' Then they say the two prayers, and the *Pater* and *Ave*. In this way all the other articles of the Creed are gone through, principally those which relate to the humanity of Jesus Christ our Lord; and this is the form in which the questions are put: 'Do you believe, my brethren, that the Second Person of the most holy Trinity, the only-begotten Son of God, conceived by the Holy Ghost, was made flesh in the womb of the most pure Virgin Mary, and was born of the same Mary our Lady, ever Virgin?' The people answer: 'Yes, Father, by the grace of God we believe it.' Then again is to come the repetition of the two prayers and the *Pater* and *Ave*, in the form prescribed above. The catechist goes on: 'Do you believe, my brethren, that this same Son of God, made man, was crucified, died, and was buried; that He descended into hell, and that He set free the souls of the holy fathers who were there expecting His holy coming?' They answer: 'Yes, we believe it, by the grace of God,' and add the usual prayers. The teacher asks again: 'Do you believe that this our Lord rose again the third day, and that He ascended into heaven, where He sits at the right hand of God the Father Almighty, from whence He will come again to judge the living and the dead; to examine and reward or punish, according to their merits, the good and wicked actions which they have done?' The people answer, that all this they perfectly believe, by the grace of God; and they add the usual prayers, with a *Pater* and an *Ave*. The catechist continues: 'Do you believe that there is a hell—that is to say, an eternal fire, where those who die out of the grace of God will be tormented everlastingly? That there is also a Paradise and an eternity of glory, which virtuous persons will enjoy who have ended their life in the same grace of God? Lastly, that there is a Purgatory, where souls satisfy for a certain time the justice of God, by undergoing the punishment of their sins, in case that having in their life done away with the guilt of them, they have yet not fully acquitted the debt of pain which they had incurred?' Then he should add: 'Do you believe in the seven Sacraments, in all the doctrine of the holy Gospels, and in all else that the holy Roman Church believes and professes?' The people answer: 'We believe all these truths, by the grace of God.' They add the two prayers, with a *Pater* and an *Ave*. The teacher goes on: 'Let us here offer to the Holy Spirit these seven *Paters* and *Aves* that we have just repeated, that He may be pleased to enrich our souls with His seven gifts, especially those which may help us to believe most firmly all that the holy Catholic faith teaches us.' After which he is to add: 'And now, my brethren, we have made profession of our holy faith.

'It now remains to make the acts of the two other virtues of which we spoke in the beginning, of hope and charity. Come, then, and say with me: O Jesus Christ, my God and my Lord, trusting in Thy divine mercy, I hope that by virtue of Thy merits, directed and assisted by Thy grace, corresponding myself to this grace by Christian works, and observing all Thy commandments, I shall arrive one day at the glory and happiness for which Thou hast created me.

'I love Thee, O my God, above all things, and with all my soul. I repent of having offended Thee, being what Thou art, most worthy of all praise, veneration, and service, because of the infinite love which I owe Thee, and because I esteem Thee far above everything else, however great; and I make the firm resolution never to do anything which may be contrary to Thy divine will, and put me in danger of losing Thy holy grace. Amen.'

Such should always be the opening service of the catechetical schools. After this the catechist should enter into a particular explanation of some one of the dogmas of our holy faith, of a sacrament, a virtue, or prayer, or some of those things which it is for the good of a Christian to understand; setting it forth in a continuous but plain discourse, adapted to the intelligence of the ignorant, explaining what he teaches, and at the end confirming it by relating some example. After this he should repeat the form of general confession for them, the children following him word for word; at the same time bidding all present to make, with all their heart and soul, an act of true contrition—that is to say, of sorrow for sin, formed from the pure love of God Whom they have offended. At the end he should tell them all to say three *Hail Marys*, the first for those present, and the two others for different intentions, as they may choose.

(3.) *St. Francis Xavier's Explanation of the Creed.*

It will be convenient to give in this place another document which remains to us of the same kind with the last. It is a long explanation of the Creed written by St. Francis for the people of the Moluccas. We have referred to it above (p. 168), and it may safely be assumed that it represents the ordinary manner in which Francis Xavier explained the articles of the Creed to the ignorant and to converts from heathenism. Theologians will be much struck with the refined and careful tone of the doctrine on certain more difficult points, as for instance, the salvation of the heathen, and the like.

Catechetical Explanation of the Creed for the Inhabitants of the Moluccas.

1. It delights Christians to hear and learn the manner and the order in which God made all things out of nothing, for the use and service of man. In the beginning He created the heavens and the earth, the Angels, the sun, the moon and the stars, the day and the night; plants and herbs of all kinds, roots and berries, and fruits of trees; the birds and animals which live upon the earth; the sea, the rivers, and lakes, and all things living in the waters. And after all these things had been created, He made, last of all, man, whom He formed after His own image and likeness.

2. The first man created by God was Adam, and the first woman Eve. Having formed and breathed into them both the breath of life, and having placed them in the terrestrial Paradise, He blessed them, betrothed them to one another, and united them in the bond of marriage, and commanding them so united to produce children, and fill the earth with inhabitants. Of this pair, Adam and Eve, we are all born; from them all nations everywhere have sprung. In this first type of our race we see an example of the unity of human marriage. For, as the God of all wisdom, the Author of nature, did not give Adam more than one wife, it is plain how contrary to the authority of God is the license in this matter which Mussulmans and idolaters and—what is still more wicked and deplorable—bad Christians also sometimes take, to have many women at once living with them; and even those who live with one concubine alone do not escape the condemnation from this primitive law; for God did not permit Adam and

Eve to beget children till they had first been united by the bond of lawful marriage by their Creator.

3. Therefore fornicators, inasmuch as they are rebels against God Who made them, must expect punishment fitted to their crime. Let those also who worship idols understand from this how great a crime they are guilty of; leaving and despising the one true God, the only true Creator of all things, they worship, in their fanatical error, mute idols and phantoms of hell; and though sound reason plainly shows us that we ought to seek the rule of our life from Him Who gave us the principle of life, they, in their sacrilegious folly, trust all their hopes and all their actions to witchcraft, the casting of lots, and the pretended foretellings of diviners. They pay to the devil—the implacable enemy of their salvation—the faith and veneration which they owe to God, the Author of all good things, from Whom they have received their soul, their body, all that they are, all their powers, and all that they possess. Impiety not more shameful and detestable in itself than fatal to the poor wretches who are guilty of it; for this senseless superstition excludes them from heaven, where a dwelling place of eternal rest full of all delights is prepared for souls who worship God—the blessed abode of that felicity for which the Creator, in His infinite goodness, made mankind.

4. How much wiser are real Christians! Faithful to God their Lord, they believe in Him and worship Him in spirit; and with all their mind and all the affections of their heart embrace Him, the one only true, supreme, and eternal Spirit, the Maker of heaven and earth; and they show this the religion of their heart by outward signs of devotion, by frequenting the sacred churches, where they see around the altars erected in honour of the living God images of Jesus Christ His Son, of the Virgin Mother of God, and of the Saints, God's servants, who, after a life passed faithfully in His service, reign with Him in the glory of Paradise.

5. In the midst of these solemn figures, which fill them with holy memories of the things and persons which they represent, kneeling on the ground, their hands raised to heaven, towards which they turn their eyes and hearts, they confess their belief in God, Whose dwelling place it is, in Whom alone they place all their happiness and consolation, by these words attributed to St. Peter: 'I believe in God, the Father Almighty, Creator of heaven and earth.' God created the Angels in heaven before He created man on earth. Now, the larger number of the Angels eagerly at once adored their God, rendering thanks, and glorifying Him for the

blessing of creation. Lucifer, on the other hand, and many Angels with him, refused to pay due adoration to their Creator; they said in their pride, Let us rise up, and make ourselves like unto God, Who reigns in the highest heavens. To punish this proud rebellion God cast Lucifer and the Angels who followed him out of heaven into hell.

6. Lucifer, thus cast down from heaven, saw Adam and Eve, the first of mankind, and was jealous of the grace in which God had created them; and to cause them to fall thence, he put into their hearts pride like to that which had made him fall from heaven. He met them in the earthly Paradise, and set before them the false hope of attaining honour equal to that of God, if they ate of the fruit forbidden by their Creator. Adam and Eve were lifted up in heart at the false representation that they would become like God, and, consenting to the temptation, ate of the fruit of the forbidden tree, and at once fell from the grace in which they had been created, and presently, as a punishment for their sin, God drove them out of the earthly Paradise. From that time they lived in banishment from the abode of bliss in a condition of toil and labour during nine hundred years, doing penance for the sin they had committed, the guilt of which was so beyond all expiation, that however great an amount of the most severe sufferings Adam and his children might pay, all would be insufficient to blot out the stain, and restore to them their former hope of gaining eternal happiness, which they had been deprived of, as a just punishment for the mad pride in which they had desired to become like God. So that, from that time, the gates of heaven remained closed to them by impenetrable barriers, which inexorably shut out Adam and his posterity from all access to that glory which he had irreparably lost, by committing a sin which involved the ruin both of himself and of all his children.

7. O Christians, what then will be our miserable fate? If so many Angels for one single sin of pride were driven headlong from heaven and cast into the depths of hell—if Adam and Eve for a like sin of pride lost the blessed possession of the earthly Paradise—what hope, what means have we, who are degraded by a great flood of sins of all kind, of ever rising out of the impurity which holds us fast, of washing away our stains and soaring to the highest heaven, where an abode of immortal blessedness has been prepared by God for immortal souls? Alas, all hope was lost; the damnation and eternal ruin of the human race were certain, without any way of escape being open, when St. Michael, our truest

friend, and the Angels who, like him, had remained dutiful and obedient and were in possession of the reward of their constancy, the most blissful enjoyment of eternal glory in the heavens, all together, taking compassion on the calamities of the human race, fell in humble supplication at the feet of God, and endeavoured to win from Him by prayers some remedy for the immense evils which, by the sin of Adam and Eve, had spread like a great flood over all their descendants; making their prayers in some such way as this:

8. 'O God of goodness, most merciful Lord and Father of all nations, now at last the time is come, the day so much expected from the beginning of ages has begun to shine, the day which Thou hast destined from all eternity and prepared, to show in it Thy mercy towards lost mankind. We see already the dawn of that day which is to open again the gates of Heaven to the children of Adam, once more restored to the grace of being Thine adopted sons; since now, from the holy Joachim and Anne, is born a daughter, that Virgin most holy above women, in whom is not the sin of Adam, Mary by name, whose virtues and holiness surpass incomparably in excellence all beings lower than God. And this Virgin being so pure and noble, it seems a work not unworthy of Thy infinite and most wise Omnipotence to form of her virginal blood, as it is easy to Thee, O Lord, to do, a human body, as of old, O Lord, Thou didst form the body of Adam, when so it seemed good to Thy holy will. And into this body, formed of the most pure substance of the Virgin, Thou canst also, Almighty Lord, at the same time create and infuse, uniting them by the most intimate union, some chosen and most beautiful soul, surpassing in holiness all the souls that Thou hast ever yet created or ever wilt create'—[Meantime God had resolved, in the secret counsels of the Holy Trinity, to join a Divine Person with our human nature in the womb of the Blessed Virgin Mary,]—'in order that of this Virgin, the most perfect of all others, should be born Jesus Christ, Thy Son, the Saviour of the universe. And thus, O Lord, will the Scriptures be accomplished, thus will the promises be faithfully fulfilled by which Thou hast bound Thyself to the prophets and patriarchs, Thy friends, who, relying upon them, are now waiting in Limbus Thy Son Jesus Christ, their Lord and their Redeemer.'

9. At this prayer of the holy Angels, the Most High, the sovereign Lord and Almighty God of all, touched by infinite compassion for our immense misery, most clearly known by Him, sent

from heaven the holy archangel Gabriel to the city of Nazareth, where the Virgin Mary dwelt; and this angel, as he had been ordered by Him Who sent him, said to her, 'Hail, Mary, full of grace, the Lord is with thee: blessed art thou among women; the Holy Ghost shall come upon thee, and the power of the Most High shall overshadow thee; and the Holy One Who shall be born of thee shall be called Jesus Christ, the Son of God.' On hearing these words of the Archangel, the most holy Virgin Mary answered: 'Behold the handmaid of the Lord, be it done unto me according to thy word.' At the very moment that the most holy Virgin gave her consent to what was proposed to her from God by the holy Archangel, God formed in the womb of the Virgin, out of her most pure blood, a human body, to which He most closely joined a soul created at the same instant; and then the Second Person of the holy Trinity, God the Son, became Incarnate in the womb of the Virgin Mary, uniting to His divine Person that soul and that body, both infinitely holy.

10. After this, nine full months having elapsed from the day in which the Son of God became Incarnate to that of His birth, Jesus Christ the Saviour of the whole world, true God and true man, was born of the Virgin Mary; and this is what St. Andrew professed in these words: 'I believe in Jesus Christ, the only Son of God our Lord;' to which St. John added at the same instant: 'Who was conceived by the Holy Ghost, born of the Virgin Mary.' Christ our Lord and Redeemer was born at Bethlehem, near Jerusalem. It was there that the Angels, and the Virgin His Mother, with St. Joseph and the Three Kings of the East, and many others besides, adored Him as their Sovereign Lord.

11. Meanwhile Herod, who was reigning in Jerusalem, fearing lest his kingdom, to which he was passionately attached, would be taken from him by this Child, desired to kill Him. But his cruel intention was baffled, Jesus was taken away in time. Joseph having been warned in a dream by an Angel, had fled from Bethlehem into Egypt, carrying with him Jesus Christ and the Virgin His Mother; and he remained there until Herod ended his life by a most wretched death. So great had been his barbarity, that he had slain in Bethlehem and round about all the children of two years old and under, thinking that Jesus Christ would be included in the massacre. That however was false, for Jesus was saved, as we have said, and He returned with the Virgin His Mother and St. Joseph into their own country and to the city of Nazareth, Joseph having been warned in Egypt by an Angel.

12. When Jesus had reached the age of twelve years He went up from Nazareth to Jerusalem to the Temple, where were the doctors of the law, and He explained to them the Scriptures of the prophets and the patriarchs, who had foretold the coming of the Son of God, teaching them with so wonderful a show of rare wisdom that all who heard Him wondered. From thence He went back to Nazareth, where He remained till He was about thirty years of age, when He went to the river Jordan, where St. John the Baptist was baptizing great numbers of persons who came to him, among whom John baptized Jesus Christ Himself in the waters of the Jordan. From thence Jesus withdrew to a desert mountain, where during forty days and forty nights He abstained from all meat and drink. On this mountain the devil, not knowing that Jesus Christ was the Son of God, strove to make Him fall into the three sins of gluttony, covetousness, and vainglory.

13. But, repelling all these temptations and victorious over the devil, Jesus quitted the mountain and descended into Galilee, where He converted great multitudes, cast out many devils from the bodies of men possessed by them, commanding them to depart thence, and even these obstinate and rebel spirits instantly obeyed Him; the people being justly filled with admiration, publishing everywhere the fame of His divine doctrine, set forth in discourses of infinite wisdom, and also of His wonder-working power, which was revealed by the healing of all sorts of sickness. Hence many were persuaded to give heed to the discourses of a Teacher of so much authority, and vied one with another in bringing to Him all the sick persons afflicted with whatever disease; and Jesus touching them with His most holy hands, did away with all their maladies, and sent them home, at once healed and filled with gratitude.

14. After this Jesus called twelve Apostles and seventy-two disciples, whom He took round with Him in His journeys from city to city and village to village, teaching the mysteries of the kingdom of God and preaching to the crowds who came together, confirming the truth of what He taught by numberless and great miracles; for in the sight of all the people, in the presence of His Apostles and disciples, He used to restore sight to the blind, speech to the dumb, hearing to the deaf, movement to the lame and to the paralytic; and the sight of these daily miracles confirmed His Apostles and disciples more and more in their faith in Jesus Christ, Who communicated to them so much power and wisdom that, though rude and illiterate fishermen, they preached

to the people, the divine doctrine of Jesus Christ, the Son of God, supplying in them the want of study and human learning. Moreover, by the invocation of His name, the Apostles themselves also wrought wonders, delivering men from different maladies and from the possession of evil spirits, and by these works, surpassing all human power, setting a seal to the truths which they announced as to the coming of the Son of God; so that though these truths were so new, they were proved and made abundantly credible by the witness of so many miraculous signs bearing the undoubted character of Divine testimony.

15. The great fame of Jesus and of His disciples having spread throughout Judea, came to the notice of the chief men of the nation, men full of a vain opinion of themselves, and of those especially who were called Pharisees, supercilious despisers of everything excellent, who used to be angry if any party or any sect except their own obtained even a slight renown for learning: and so it may easily be imagined what a bitter pang it must have been for these proud persons to find Jesus Christ, Who censured their doctrine, listened to with applause by the people, and so highly esteemed and considered in the enthusiasm of the multitude, that it seemed almost to be imminent that they themselves would be thrust out of the highest place in authority and reputation which they had so long held, and the new Teacher raised to their place with the handful of fishermen who formed his train. Moved, therefore, by the fury of hellish envy, they determined to put in motion all the artifices of calumny in order to take away both the reputation and the life of Jesus Christ.

16. With this intention they beset with artful words those who were at the head of affairs, and also persuaded Pilate, at that time governor of Judea, after having plied him with entreaties, suggestions of suspicion, and direct charges, to grant them the arrest of Jesus, which they clamoured for as necessary for the public peace. The foreign governor allowed himself to be so far gained over by the crafty machinations of these men; not that he was ignorant that their allegation of the public good was only a veil to cover their own envy, but either from weariness of resisting their importunate demands or from a desire to win favour with the more powerful of the people, he thought it worth while to purchase his own tranquillity or the favour of others at the cost of an illustrious man, who seemed quite of the same stamp as Elias and Jeremias among the ancients, or John the Baptist among men of that time, but whom he did not suppose superior to human nature. For if he had clearly

known that Jesus was the Son of God, it does not seem that any influence could have prevailed upon him to deliver Him to the fury of His envious enemies.

17. Jesus being thus taken prisoner by the authority of the government, His enemies out of their own malice went on further to insure themselves that He should be treated with all possible cruelty and ignominy by their own servants. He was dragged through the ways and principal places of the city, in the midst of a crowd who offered Him every sort of outrage, hurried with violence from one house to another before different tribunals, mocked, reviled, spit upon, and beaten with blows, and so at last brought before Pilate, with false witnesses against Him, amidst the furious clamours of the excited mob, who cried out for His death and for His death upon the cross. Nevertheless the judge hesitated, knowing the innocence of the accused; until they suggested to him that he would lose Cæsar's favour if he set free a man designated King of the Jews and Who would soon raise a revolt; and thus he was made to yield to the wishes of the accusers, and gave up Jesus. After he had caused Him to be inhumanly torn by scourges over His whole body from head to foot, he delivered Him up to be crucified by the Jews, who demanded this with savage clamour.

18. But before they crucified Him, the emissaries of the Pharisees, having dressed Him in mockery with the robes of a king, with a crown of thorns on His head, a reed for a sceptre in His hand, made sport of Him, bowing the knee before Him in ironical homage, and hailing Him King of the Jews, and then spitting in His face, striking Him on the cheek again and again, and snatching the reed from His right hand to strike Him with it on His head crowned with thorns. At last they nailed Him to a cross on Mount Calvary, near the city of Jerusalem. Thus Jesus Christ died upon the cross, in order to save sinful men; so that His most holy soul was truly separated from His most precious body at the moment that He expired upon the cross, and yet that both His soul and body, although disunited, never ceased each to remain joined to the divine Person. And as the spirit fled without ceasing to be united to the Divinity, so also the lifeless body, whether when it hung on the cross or was laid and buried in the tomb, always and everywhere had with it the inseparable company of the Divinity most closely joined to it, and was never separated from that Divinity.

19. Moreover, at the death of Jesus Christ the sun was darkened and lost its light, the whole earth trembled, the rocks were rent

and dashed against one another, the graves of the dead opened of themselves, and many bodies of the saints came forth, who showed themselves restored to life to many in the city of Jerusalem. At the sight of these prodigies, those who stood by Christ as He died were convinced, and cried out: Truly this man was the Son of God! All these things which we have just related are contained in the profession of the Apostle St. James, who added to the words expressed by the preceding Apostles: 'I believe in Jesus Christ, Who suffered under Pontius Pilate, was crucified, dead, and buried.' Jesus Christ was God, since He was the second Person of the most Holy Trinity; at the same time He was truly man, being the son of the Virgin Mary, and possessing a rational soul and a human body. In so much as He was man, He died really upon the cross while He was nailed to it. For death is nothing else but the separation of the soul from the body, in which and with which it has lived. And the most holy soul of Jesus Christ was separated from His body when He expired upon the cross.

20. And then that most sacred soul separated from His body, and remaining united to the Divinity of the Son of God, as it had always been since our Lord God created it, descended into Limbus. Limbus is a place beneath the earth in which were detained the souls of the holy fathers, prophets, patriarchs, and many others, assembled there waiting for the coming of the Son of God, by Whom they knew they should be delivered and transferred from this abode to Paradise. For from the beginning of the creation there have always lived in the world good men, who, as they had been friends of God, had freely professed the holy truths they understood and never dissembled what they believed before the wicked who opposed them. They reproved sinners, blaming severely the wickedness of any who rebelled shamelessly against God, the one Creator of all. But wicked and criminal men would not endure their censures: and so, by the inspiration and assistance of the devil, their sworn accomplice, under whose banners they were enrolled, they persecuted the good men, the friends of God, with every kind of evil deed, making them prisoners, banishing them, and vexing them with every kind of injury and insult.

21. Corresponding to this great difference between the lives of the good and the wicked was the very different condition of their souls when death had separated their souls from their bodies. All the souls who during their life had been virtuous went, when death had set them free from the bonds of the body, to the place just now mentioned, which I said was called Limbus, which being sunk far

down beneath the surface of the earth, is also called hell; not that there, as we understand when we speak of the place called simply and properly hell, there was any fire to torment them, or any other hurtful power to give them pain. Such punishments are reserved for the wicked, whilst the souls of the just, as became souls free from stain and dear to God, rested in the repose of a most blessed peace.

22. But below this abode of bliss is a lower region called Purgatory, because it is as a sort of cleansing place for purifying and making beautiful those souls who have ended their mortal life guiltless of heinous sin, in the grace of God, but who still have the lighter marks of venial faults, or who have not yet acquitted the debt incurred by mortal sins, which have been indeed retracted by salutary penance, but not so fully and perfectly as to get rid of the whole debt of the punishment due to their guilt. Here they continue to rub off, by the continued action of severe torments, the stains which still cling to them from the foul sin which of old encrusted them, until at length they have balanced the whole account as to guilt and as to pain which they were charged with, and got rid of all remains of either of these by means of suffering; and so their spirits have become clean even to extreme brightness, and are allowed freely to behold their inheritance, the delay of the possession of which for a certain just time they have had to bear as a punishment.

23. The last of these abodes beneath the earth is Hell properly so called, a most miserable abode of flames for ever inextinguishable, and of such unutterable and intolerable torments of every other kind, that if living men were only to apply themselves seriously each day for the space of one little hour, in picturing to themselves, even as imperfectly as the dimness of our present state permits, the nature of these torments, they would certainly feel greater horror of making themselves guilty of all the crime and wickedness by which they do not hesitate, almost in sport and with easy carelessness, to incur the sentence of having to endure these fearful torments throughout all eternity. There is Lucifer, prince of the spirits who rebelled against God. There are all the devils who followed his party, and were cast down thither with him from heaven. There are all those men who, from the beginning of the world, have breathed their last out of the grace of God and guilty of mortal sin. Those who have once been cast into these flames of hell suffer and groan there eternally and hopelessly, ever tormented by the keenest sense of immense and numberless pains, of

which they know for certain that they can never have, from any quarter at all, throughout an eternity of ages, any remedy or any relaxation or any consolation, however small.

24. O my brethren, what madness is this of ours, that we go on living so careless as we do of all fear of hell, while we are all the time preparing food for those undying flames by heaping upon our consciences the burthens of sin ever worse and worse! Is not this a plain sign that our faith is, I do not say small, but altogether none? We profess it indeed with our mouths, but our deeds and our life refute it far more cogently; for one who calls himself a Christian, and allows himself that license in sin which the Mussulmans and idolaters take, must certainly be thought a deceiver and liar when he says that he believes in the everlasting fires and punishments of hell reserved for those who violate God's law. The Church, whether of the faithful who are militant on earth, or of the Saints who reign with God triumphant in heaven, never prays for the dead who have been cast into the pit of hell; for she well knows they are shut out from Paradise for all eternity, that their hope is absolutely lost, their ruin irreparable. But the Church, both on earth and in heaven, aids with charitable prayers the souls who suffer in the pains of Purgatory, and is also full of care for the souls who are still in this world; she strives to obtain them grace from God, by means of which they may escape the utter misery of falling into the everlasting flames of hell.

25. Jesus Christ died on Friday, and His most holy soul, always united to the Divinity, descended into Limbus, and led from thence all the souls whom He found there awaiting His coming; and then on the third day, which was Sunday, He rose from the dead, reuniting His most holy soul to the body which it had quitted when He expired upon the cross. Presently, in His recovered life and in full possession of all the qualities of immortality, He appeared first to His most sacred Virgin Mother Mary, then to His Apostles and disciples, and others dear to Him, so that all that most bitter grief which they had suffered at His death was wiped away and abundantly compensated. He also offered, by means of His Apostles, pardon to His enemies and to those who had crucified Him, and granted it to all who consented to receive this grace. There were great numbers of these; for it turned out wonderfully that many of those who had obstinately refused to believe in Jesus Christ when He was alive, preaching, and confirming what He taught by great miracles, yet,—when He was no longer seen or heard, but believed, on the testimony of His

Apostles, to have risen from the dead,—these same put full faith in Him, placed all their hope in Him, and professed His religion and His worship, as the religion and the worship of God and the Saviour of men. And that what we have thus been putting forth is true, affirmed by St. Thomas in these words: 'I believe in Jesus Christ, who descended into hell, and the third day rose again from the dead.'

26. Jesus remained upon the earth after His resurrection from the dead for forty days, for two reasons, as far as we can understand. First, in order fully to convince His disciples of His resurrection, and secondly to teach them what they must do. They had been so disturbed by the most unexpected event of His death, they had been so swallowed up by sorrow on that account, that they were brought with the greatest difficulty to believe in His resurrection; nor was it enough for Him to appear to them once or twice; there was need of time, and the multiplication of the most manifest possible proofs of His really having returned to life by means of repeated meetings with Him. So our Lord, so full of condescension and kindness, that He might do this in a sweet gentle way, adapted to the infirmity of human nature, put off for forty days His triumphant entrance into heaven, and during this interval He instructed His disciples, in frequent discourses, what they were to believe, what they were to do, what they were afterwards to teach all nations, and what, after having convinced them of His doctrine, they were to enjoin on them to do, in order that they, and all those who should believe their preaching, might be able to reach the kingdom of heaven, and in due time follow Him there, whither He was to go before them.

27. Having fully gained both these ends, having entirely driven from the minds of His disciples all doubt concerning the death and resurrection of Himself, the true Son of God and Saviour of mankind, and having taught them sufficiently all things concerning the kingdom of God, that is, about founding the Church, the doctrine to be taught in it, the sacraments, and all other points of Christian discipline, which the Apostles were to institute throughout the whole world—then Jesus Christ, having no longer any reason to remain on earth, went forth with the Virgin Mary His Mother, the Apostles, and many others, to Mount Olivet, and there in the sight of them all ascended into the highest heavens, taking with Him the patriarchs set free from Limbus. Then opened wide the lofty gates of heaven, and all the Angels came forth to meet our Lord in His triumph, and made for Him a glorious

train up to the throne prepared for Him at the right hand of God the Father. Then He returned to the place whence He had come down to take upon Him our flesh in the holy womb of His Virgin Mother. There He sits now, the advocate of sinners, pleading our cause with His Father and disarming His lawful wrath, and sending us aid, by help of which we may be able to escape the danger of eternal damnation. And this is the meaning of the article of the Creed which is attributed to St. James the Less: 'I believe in Jesus Christ, Who ascended into heaven, and sitteth at the right hand of God the Father Almighty.'

28. But since this world, which had a beginning, must also have an end to close it; and that this its last scene may be as it ought to be, and in accordance with the divine Providence of its Creator, the intercourse of human society and the succession and change of different generations, propagating themselves far and wide, will not cease before a just judgment shall have been pronounced on the thoughts and words and actions of all men, allotting to each its due recompense. Jesus Christ, the supreme Judge, is to descend from heaven to pass this judgment on the causes of all men; and that this should certainly be was declared by Angels on the very day of His ascension from the earth. He will open His court, in which all men who have lived in any age and in every place will have to make appearance before the inexorable tribunal of the almighty allknowing Judge from Whom nothing is concealed, and will have to answer the questions, whether they have believed the dogmas proposed to them by the Church, and whether they have kept the commandments. Those who have done this will be admitted into the glory of Paradise; those who have refused to believe, as Mussulmans, Jews, and Gentiles, will be given up to everlasting fire, from which there will be no redemption; and those who have professed the faith, as bad Christians have done, but have neglected to obey the commandments of the Decalogue, those in like manner will be condemned by the irrevocable sentence of Jesus Christ to flames which are to burn for ever.

29. Before these things come to pass, and when the end of the world is at hand, all men then alive must die; for death is a debt of nature which every one must pay. Every man is born on the condition that one day he cease to live, and since not even Jesus Christ Himself, the Son of God, was exempted from this law, it is plain that it would be a rash and foolish hope in any one else to promise himself the privilege. But Jesus Christ

did not die for Himself, but for our sins, and He rose again by His own power, that by His own resurrection He might ratify our hope of one day rising again, and to make the bitter necessity of death more tolerable to good and pious men, His friends, by Himself sharing it to be our example. So, even if perchance there were to be found when the end of the world is at hand some saints perfect in all virtue, we must not think that they would pass to the happiness which they have hoped and merited without death. They also must taste of death, and then with the rest of men they will be restored to life, each one taking again the body which he had before, but that body transformed into a better condition by the attributes of beatitude; and so they will enter into the plenitude of their promised bliss.

30. When Jesus Christ shall thus descend from Heaven to hold the last judgment, all men from first to last who have before died shall rise again, all shall be judged by Him, good and wicked alike, but with an immense difference between them which can never be changed throughout eternity; the good passing on to everlasting joy, and the wicked to death and endless woe. This is the truth which St. Philip professed, saying, 'I believe in Jesus Christ, Who will come to judge the living and the dead.

31. And now, Christians, when we sign ourselves with the sign of the Cross, we profess our certain faith in the most Holy Trinity. This mystery of the Holy Trinity is this: we believe and adore One only God in Three Persons. The First Person is God the Father, Who is neither made, nor created, nor begotten; the Second Person is God the Son, Who is begotten of God the Father, not made, nor created; the Third Person is God the Holy Ghost, Who proceeds from the Father and the Son, but is neither made nor created. This we indicate every time that we sign ourselves, by making with the hand the form of a Cross. For we put the right hand to the forehead and we say, *In the name of the Father*, and thus we show that God the Father is neither made nor begotten. Then bringing the hand down to the lower part of the breast, and pronouncing these words, *And of the Son*, we signify God the Son, Who is begotten of God the Father, but not made, nor created. Finally, we touch with the hand the left shoulder, saying at the same time, *And of the Holy*, and then the right shoulder, saying the word *Ghost;* and thus we declare that the Holy Ghost proceeds from the Father and the Son.

32. This is the faith which every good Christian is bound to hold and to confess without any hesitation, believing, adoring,

and glorifying the Holy Ghost, consubstantial with the Father and the Son, and proceeding from them both; Who by His holy inspirations calls us back from sin, and moves our hearts to observe the ten commandments of the law of God our Lord, and the precepts of our holy Mother the Catholic Church; and Who prompts us on to practise the works of mercy both spiritual and corporal. This doctrine of the divinity of the Holy Ghost St. Bartholomew professed in these words, 'I believe in the Holy Ghost.'

33. All we who have embraced the Christian religion have resolved to observe its duties and keep its faith, and we ought not only to believe without doubt and as truths necessary to salvation all things concerning Christ our Lord, God and man, that the apostles, disciples, martyrs, and saints have believed; but at the same time we are also all bound by the same necessity to be perfectly convinced that He has instituted the Catholic Church upon the earth, the rulers of which are directed by the Holy Ghost; so that it is not permitted us in any way to doubt that what they prescribe as to be observed and what they teach as to be held is right and true. For in all things which by universal consent they decree to be done or avoided by all men,—as, for instance, in what after mature counsel they define concerning ancient dogmas, or controversies concerning these dogmas, which arise from time to time,—they have assistance of the Holy Spirit promised to them, by which they are not permitted to err. Therefore, the sacred canons of the Fathers, the decrees of the Councils, the universal edicts of the Supreme Pontiffs, which are set forth by the Cardinals, the Patriarchs, the Archbishops, the Bishops, and the other Prelates of the Church, ought to be received by us with humble veneration, certain faith, and ready obedience; and we ought to be firmly persuaded that these things are enjoined and taught by the authority and wisdom of our Lord Jesus Christ, Who continues to govern the Church, and guide it to its appointed end of eternal happiness by means of the ministers whom He has put in His own place. This is what the holy Apostle and Evangelist St. Matthew commended to us when he said, 'I believe in the holy Catholic Church.'

34. Another thing which we believe most certainly, if we do not bear falsely the name of Christian, is that the immense merits which Jesus Christ, by the heroic works performed during His mortal life, both by His actions and His sufferings, and His obedience to His Father, heaped up in store for the salvation of men,

are communicated to, and by a certain inward influx are profitable to, all true Christians who remain in the grace of God. So that as in the natural body, the members communicate to each other what each has of good, the vital strength spreading itself principally from the head over all the limbs, so in a mystical body such as is the Church, of which Jesus Christ is the Head, all the single members, that is to say, all the faithful universally, derive a secret sap of life by means of which they flourish and increase, from Jesus Christ, the only begotten Son of God, to Whom as their Head they are joined. For inward nourishment of heavenly food flows to them from Him, principally by the channels of the seven sacraments: these are, Baptism, Confirmation commonly called holy Chrism, the Eucharist, Penance, Extreme Unction, Orders, and Marriage. Those who receive these sacred mysteries with the due and fit dispositions, receive habitual grace, or the increase of this grace—a lifegiving quality of the soul which God has granted to men, unworthy in themselves of such a blessing, for the sake of the holy works which Jesus Christ performed during His earthly life. For because Jesus Christ, to obey His Father, endured so many ills, suffered of His own free will so many injuries and insults, the most bitter sorrows, the cross and death, He has merited any reward, however great, by this. But possessing of Himself all happiness, He needs no reward, and He transfers His right to such reward to us, and sets down as paid to Himself the profit that we gather therefrom. Hence the grace which is conferred upon us is the fruit of the merits of Jesus Christ, and is like an influence spread from the head over the members.

35. And as in the natural body it is not the head alone that gives nurture, strength, and life to the members which are subject to it, but also the members themselves produce these effects by secret influences on one another; so it is principally, but not altogether solely, from our share in the treasures which Jesus Christ has accumulated by His merits, what He did well and suffered patiently during His mortal life, that we are enriched. For Jesus Christ has willed that something should fall upon us and come to us from the store of favour with Him which has been acquired by His servants our brethren, by their virtuous actions and laborious endurance; so when they pray, grace is granted to us; when they suffer for us, or offer their former sufferings for us, we are set free from the penalty we owe to God's justice. Lastly, all their good works of every kind, as long as we remain in the grace of God and the unity of the body of the Church, profit us in various ways, their

superabundance being communicated to those united with them, and flowing over them with saving power.

36. We acknowledge also and confess that in God our Lord dwells power and authority to remit sins, that is to say, to efface the stain and remit the punishment of guilty actions, by which, abusing our gift of free will, we separate ourselves from God and rebel against Him; thus deservedly falling from His grace, to which He had before so kindly admitted us. We also confess and believe that this same power has been given and communicated by Jesus Christ our Lord to the priests of the Catholic Church, and that by the effect of this communication they now have authority to absolve from their sins whomsoever they find sufficiently disposed to be lawfully loosed, before God, from the bonds of their faults.

37. For this reason, those who feel themselves guilty of having offended God ought to labour earnestly to dispose themselves, showing due repentance for their faults, to obtain their pardon, and so secure the salvation of their soul. The cause is tried in the sacred tribunal which sinners approach, the priest being judge whether the penitent is worthy or not of the benefit of absolution; the accuser in this court is the same as the accused. The priest, as judge, takes cognizance of the cause, diligently considering everything as becomes so sublime an office. The penitent ought to make an entire and full confession of all mortal sins, unless time should be just wanting to go through all, as might happen in cases of extreme peril. When all sins are sufficiently known, and the priest pronounces the sentence of absolution, then the grace of God is poured afresh into the soul of the penitent, and by it are effaced the sins by which the soul had before been disfigured, and the certain remission of eternal punishment which had been incurred by these sins is granted to them. These two articles of Catholic doctrine are comprised in these words of St. Simon: 'I believe in the communion of saints and the forgiveness of sins.'

38. But as injustice would be done to the infinite goodness and justice of God, unless we believed firmly that God would never fail to reward abundantly those who serve Him faithfully by exact observance of His holy law, or, on the other hand, to visit with condign punishment the wicked despisers of His Godhead and the obstinate transgressors of His commandments; therefore we firmly believe that there will be a resurrection of the body, that is to say, that all men without exception, those who

have lived in times past, those who are alive to-day, or who shall live after us, will again come to life, and resume at the end of the world the same bodies which they had when they died, and will live thenceforth for ever therein either in torments or in glory. Because it is clearly necessary that God our Lord, in His most righteous and incorruptible justice, should, on the one hand, comfort with eternal joys the bodies of the Saints, who, during their mortal life, have made their senses and members subject to continual toil, even enduring, so as not to be separated from the love of God, many insults and blows from their persecutors, who have striven by all violence and savage cruelty to force them to offend God. For though what was virtuous and manly in this belonged to the soul, which remained constant in duty, yet the body also, having been deprived of many goods proportioned to it, having been pained, tormented, and oftentimes inhumanly torn to pieces on such occasions, is worthy, as well as the soul, of having its proper share in rest, pleasure, and glory.

39. On the other hand, it was equally proper that the bodies of those wicked men who, during their life, regardless of the divine law, have stained themselves with all licentiousness and every kind of vice, following their passions of gluttony or impurity in contempt of the commands of God, should be punished in their turn, and should, by having to bear for ever, against their will, fires that can never be quenched, expiate those pleasures on which they fed their appetites in the indulgence of unlawful lust, and thus, though too late, they should know how great an evil it is for a poor worthless creature to have dared to despise and provoke the supreme majesty of God, adorable above all. For these reasons, as I said, all mankind, the good and wicked alike, will rise again at that day of final Judgment, and their souls will put on again the same bodies which they received at their birth, and which they animated till the term of their death. They will be thenceforth united to them by a bond which will never be dissolved, and go with them, according to the merits of the life of each of mankind, either to heaven, to reign with Jesus Christ in the glory of Paradise, or to hell, to be with the devil in endless woe. This is what St. Jude confessed when he said, 'I believe in the resurrection of the body.'

40. But as our soul, which was created in the image and likeness of the Almighty God, inasmuch as it has a spiritual nature, is endowed with faculties which represent the divine perfections, that is to say, the will, the intelligence, and the memory, and as

such has from its creation been impelled by a certain innate desire inspired by its Creator, of uniting itself to Him of Whom it is the image, we cannot believe that so excellent a creation of God had this ever active instinct and longing given to it by its Creator for nothing. We ought rather to believe undoubtingly, as all Christians are persuaded, that by the divine assistance the human soul, unless it prevent this of itself, will hereafter have its desire satisfied, and will come even to the possession of that sovereign good which we call eternal life; and even before the resurrection of the body the souls which have died in the grace of God, and have been completely purified from all remains of sin, enter into possession of this life eternal, being admitted from that moment to the sight and the enjoyment of God.

41. Hereafter these souls, having again taken and united to themselves their bodies, in a state far better and more perfect, will enjoy that happiness, of which we are speaking, uninterruptedly for an unending eternity. All that endless space of time the souls of the Saints will enjoy with God in heaven, along with the choirs of numberless blessed Angels and jubilant and triumphant hosts of Saints from among men, the loving and beatific presence of God the Creator and Lord of all, Who will heap on every one of them all the blessings of heaven. The excellence of these blessings is so sublime, that however much in the mortal life we may strain ourselves in thought or by reasoning, we can never set before our minds any idea or picture of them which approaches even at a long distance the truth of what they are. So far transcending all our powers is the magnificence of God when it sheds its whole self on the Saints whom He loves! Nevertheless, the little which we can as it were stammer out concerning that ineffable felicity, abundantly suffices to show us how greatly we ought to desire it.

42. There then the Saints live happy and at rest in a glorious peace, with no complaint or offence of any one, with nothing to complain of in any one, loved and honoured by all there, all bearing to all the sweetest mutual love and veneration, abounding in all goods, I do not say which they need, but which they can possibly desire to make their enjoyment and glory perfect. They can feel no evil, nor be assailed by any, nor have the fear of any: and on the other hand, so great and so profuse is their most blessed abundance in all goods of every kind, as to surpass all their wishes, and to be enough for the enjoyment of endless ages. And all this blessedness is so certain and so securely guarded for them, that there can be no fear or risk of its being overturned or diminished

for ever. And this is what St. Matthias understood when he said, 'I believe in the life everlasting.'

(4.) *Other Writings of St. Francis Xavier.*

We find in a letter (which will be inserted in the second volume of this work) written in 1552, that Francis Xavier tells St. Ignatius that he has written a book in Japanese 'explaining the origin of the world and all the mysteries of the life of Christ.' It may perhaps have been a version of the explanation of the Creed which we have just given, with perhaps some special passages to meet the peculiar errors of the Japanese. This book, he adds, he has also written out 'in Chinese character,' meaning to take it with him to China. If this was not the same in substance as his explanation of the Creed written for the people of the Moluccas, it is lost to us. Orlandini also tells us (*Hist. Soc. Jesu*, l. xiv. n. 133) that Francis wrote a book at Cagoxima for the Japanese which contained a life of Christ, the penitential psalms, the litanies, and the order of the Church festivals. And in another place (n. 147) he tells us that some sermons were composed by Francis in Spanish, which the Japanese convert, who took the name of Paul of the Holy Faith, translated into Japanese. These also are lost, as far as is known, though it is impossible to say that they do not exist in Japan. We may add to our list two of his writings which are not lost. The first is the form of profession of faith which Francis taught his catechumens to learn by heart and to repeat before receiving baptism.

Profession of Faith.

O my God, I truly confess, as becomes a good Christian, the most Holy Trinity, Father, Son, and Holy Ghost, Three Persons in one God; and I firmly believe, without hesitation, whatever our Mother the Roman Church holds and believes, and so I promise that I will live and die in the holy Catholic faith of our Lord Jesus Christ, God and Man, Who died for us, and now, for and instead of the time at which I am to die, in case I be not then able to speak, I confess my Lord Jesus Christ with my whole heart.

The second is a Prayer to the Five Wounds of our Lord.

Prayer.

O Lord Jesus Christ, in Whose power all things are, and there is no one who can resist Thy will; Who didst vouchsafe to be born as man, to die, and to rise again: by the mystery of Thy most Sacred Body, and by Thy Five Wounds, and the shedding of Thy most precious Blood, have mercy upon us, according as Thou knowest what is necessary for our souls and bodies; deliver us from the temptations of the devil, and from all things by which Thou knowest us to be oppressed, and keep us safe and strengthen us in Thy service unto the end; give us time to do true penance, and give us the remission of all our sins when we die; make us also to love one another, our brethren, our sisters, our friends, and our enemies, and hereafter to rejoice for ever with all Thy Saints in Thy kingdom, Who, with the Father and the Holy Ghost, livest and reignest God for ever and ever. Amen.

A supposed Letter to Francis Mancias omitted at p. 211.

The letter mentioned in the note to p. 211 is almost certainly a sort of abridgment of other letters in the collection, if it should not rather be called a piece of patchwork made up by some copyist. F. Menchacha, *Prolegomena in S. Xaverium*, p. lxii., tells us that he inserts it 'instar cujusdam breviarii' of other letters. Such as it is, we subjoin it here. It is singular among the series to Mancias (if we except the first letter), in having the full formal salutation at the beginning.

To Francis Mancias.

May the grace and love of our Lord Jesus Christ always help and favour us! Amen.

I most earnestly beg of you, my dearest brother, to keep up a continual visitation of the coast where you are, going through the villages one by one, baptizing the newborn infants and instructing the rest. Assemble the men and women separately; make them all repeat the Catechism together; make them do the same frequently in private. Be on your guard against staying too long in one place, but go round the whole of the villages again and again, as I did when I was there, and as I do now where I am, though I have no interpreter. This fact will make it easy for you to imagine what kind of life I lead, and what sort of conversations I hold, when neither I nor the people here understand one another. However, I baptize the children, which does not require an interpreter, and I look to the wants of the poor, whose miseries and penury are manifest enough without one.

What I want you to do most particularly is to go on without ceasing baptizing the infants and instructing the children; for even if the grown up people and the fathers and mothers lose the happiness of heaven, at least the little ones, and the children who pass from this life before they have lost their baptismal innocence, will enjoy it.

As soon as the converts come back from the pearl fishery, visit the sick, if there are any, and provide them with what is necessary. At the same time let the children say the several prayers over them, and you yourself read the Gospel, just as you saw me do when I was in those parts.

I am now setting off for Cape Comorin, where I am taking twenty boats laden with provisions, to assist those poor converts who, terrified at the approach of the Badages, who are the fiercest possible enemies of all Christians, have left their villages and taken refuge on the little barren islands; and there they are now, exposed to all the heat of the sun, and the extremes of hunger and thirst. Some of them are even dying under their sufferings, and my heart is pierced through and through at their wretched lot. I beg of you, over and over again, go on praying for us. I am writing to the Patangatins and to the magistrates on your coast, to ask them to help these poor folk with their alms. I want you to take care that these alms are not extracted from the unwilling and the poor, but from willing and rich givers. Let the collection be made with all consideration of the inclination as well as of the powers of those who are canvassed for it. Farewell.

BOOK III.

FROM THE FIRST VOYAGE OF FRANCIS TO THE EASTERN ARCHIPELAGO TO HIS RETURN TO INDIA.

1545-1548.

CHAPTER I.

Francis at Malacca.

THE years spent by Francis Xavier in the peninsula of India itself, before sailing to the farther East, which was to be the scene of so many of his most glorious labours and most wonderful miracles, are quite exceptional as regards the number of his letters which remain to us. We must not expect in future anything like the almost daily chronicle with which, for a short space of time, the letters to Mancias have furnished us; and we must be content to take that series as giving us an insight into the affectionate charity and ingenious industry with which he helped on his subordinates, and looked after the interests of the converts under their charge, which we may be quite sure reveals to us what was ordinary in him, but of which we shall not hereafter be able to furnish so much unconscious evidence in his own words. The two years and a half (to speak roughly) which followed on his departure from the shrine of St. Thomas for Malacca and the Eastern Archipelago are, comparatively, barren indeed in correspondence; and although there are abundant facts, attested by authorities in which we can place the greatest confidence, preserved to us as to his life at this time, we cannot but lament that we shall have to rely so much more on the evidence of others than on his own accounts. These were years even unusually full of incident, of great successes, strange adventures, dangers, and escapes. They showed in the most striking way his wonderful power of winning souls, his influence on the public mind, his immense supernatural courage and confidence in God, his zeal and charity, and his miraculous gifts. Full of spiritual conquest themselves, they opened to him—as if in fulfilment of the promise implied in the Divine call which bade him leave India to help the new converts in Celebes—fresh fields of labour and enterprize for the glory of God, of which he had had no thought before. It is not too much to say that, at their close, his name filled the whole Eastern Archipelago as that of a great Saint and Apostle of God, gifted with the most marvellous miraculous powers, and that it seemed only natural to look forward for him to still grander achievements. In those days of ever fresh energy and wonder, when islands and countries, which had before loomed like shadows upon the bordering mist between the realms of knowledge and of imagination, were daily coming forth into the light, in all their fairy beauty and mythical richness, as the mariners and merchants of Portugal and Spain pushed their venturesome prows further and further into a mysterious and seemingly limitless world, a man had at last appeared in the East who would go, for the sake of the Gospel of Jesus Christ, wherever he could find a ship to take him, who feared nothing but that he might himself begin to fear, and who seemed to wield an imperial sway alike over the powers of nature and the hearts of his fellowmen.

Francis Xavier reached Malacca towards the end of September 1545. Malacca was then at the height of prosperity and pride. Originally a small town, it had gained immense importance from its convenient situation as a meetingplace for the merchandize of the two great divisions of the Eastern world—Arabia, Persia, India on the one hand; China, Japan, the Philippines, the Moluccas on the other; it was a port for Siam and Pegu, and fronted the great island of Sumatra on the south. At the time of the Portuguese conquest, under Alfonso Albuquerque, it is said that the town, which now seems almost confined to the neighbourhood of the river which divides it in two,[1] stretched along the seacoast for as much as a league. The Portuguese had gained possession of it more than thirty years before the visit of Francis Xavier; they had built a strong fortress, and appear also to have fortified the town itself, which became their chief seat in the regions beyond the Ganges—much what Singapore is to the English at the present day.

[1] Wallace, *Malay Archipelago*, vol. iv. p. 39.

In fact, Singapore has now succeeded to the place in mercantile importance once occupied by Malacca. The writers of the sixteenth and seventeenth centuries are loud in their praises of the beauty of its buildings, its soft luxurious climate, the happy mixture of moist mists and fresh breezes which temper the otherwise sultry atmosphere, and keep the land clothed with the verdure of perpetual spring, even under the torrid zone. Its inhabitants were, and indeed are, a motley population, the indigenous Malays predominating then, as the Chinese are said to predominate now. They had a character through the East for courtesy and refinement, but were conspicuous also, even among Oriental populations, for corruption and license of every kind. All the vices and miseries which Francis had found at Goa he was sure to find here, aggravated in the case of the Portuguese by the greater distance from Europe and from the seat of government; though, as there were no native communities of Christians to plunder or to protect, he would breathe freely at least from the annoyances of such men as Cosmo de Payva, and not have to exert himself to remedy the mischief caused by their tyranny.

The fame, of the 'holy Father' had been wafted over the Gulf of Bengal as it had before crossed the more narrow seas between Cape Comorin and Manaar, and the coming of Francis was expected and even known before he landed. It was never discovered how the news flew about, that the ship which hove in sight on that September day bore an Apostle on its deck, but so it was—the whole shore was crowded when he came to land, and young and old, men and women, were eager to catch the first sight of one of whom they had heard such wonderful things. The children in particular crowded round him, or were presented to him by their mothers, and it was noted that as he took them in his arms and placed his hand on their heads to bless them, he called them all by their right names. The general corruption of manners did not make the people the less vie with each other to do him honour, and to offer him a lodging in their houses; but, as usual, he took up his abode in the hospital, though after a time he seems to have left it to live in the house of some poor friends, close to a part of the wall which surrounded the city. The house stood on a high point over the shore, and was long considered to have been specially blessed in consequence of having harboured such a guest, and tales were told of persons who had fallen over the wall on to some rocks far below, and been taken up unhurt.[2]

The work at Macazar which Francis Xavier had specially had in view when he sailed from Meliapor had been anticipated when he arrived at Malacca. The Commandant there had already sent a ship to Celebes with a priest on board and several Portuguese laymen. Francis determined to await its return before proceeding further. Meantime he would give himself to the immense spiritual needs of Malacca itself. He began by very great austerities and continual prayers. He is said to have passed two or three days together without eating; his nights were spent in prayer, save a few short hours which he gave to necessary sleep. Two brothers, by name Pereira, watched him by night, and afterwards related how they had seen him immovable on his knees before a crucifix, his eyes swimming with tears, and his face burning like fire. The whole of the day, after he had said mass and recited his office, he gave to the exercises of charity of various kinds which he had already practised in Goa —visiting the sick in the hospital, the criminals in the prison, waiting on them, instructing them, giving them the sacraments, or hearing confessions and teaching in the churches; gathering the children together for the Catechism, teaching them pious songs, with which, as time went on, the houses and the streets began to ring; and going with them through the city at nightfall, calling on the people, by the sound of a bell, to pray for those in mortal sin, and for the suffering souls in Purgatory. He preached to the people on Sundays, but his instructions to the children were given daily, and he frequently found time for the slaves, who were in great numbers in the city.

Malacca was never thoroughly converted by Francis Xavier, though he spent more labour upon it, perhaps, than upon any other city in the East, and though it was the scene of some of

[2] See (*e.g.*) Massei, l. ii. cap. 8. He mentions two children and a woman.

his greatest and most famous miracles. He left it at last—as the Apostles were told to leave the cities which would not listen to them—shaking off the dust from his feet as a witness against it, ordering the priests of the Society to withdraw from it, and having prophesied calamities which were to befall it. But this was as yet future. For the time Malacca was notably improved. An abominable custom, which allowed fullgrown girls to go frolicking about the city in male attire and without any escort, and which naturally resulted in the ruin of many, was put an end to. The obscene songs which had resounded in the streets were changed for Christian hymns. Many great conversions took place, and the scandals which came from the open practice of concubinage were in several cases set right. But there were persons of influence, and even high ecclesiastics, who set the example of turning a deaf ear to the remonstrances and exhortations of Francis; and with this bad example to encourage them, the mass of the inhabitants treated him with respect, reverence, and admiration, and that was all. Nothing is more hardhearted than frivolous voluptuousness—the spirit of Herod and his Court, who would gladly have seen our Lord work a miracle to supply them with a new excitement, but before whom He, Who had so many words for the heathen Pilate, resolutely held His peace.

The accounts that remain to us of the four months which Francis spent at this time in Malacca, represent him as straining to the utmost the condescending charity of which we have already seen more than one example. He was to be found talking familiarly with rude soldiers, looking on at their games, interesting himself in their success or in their bad fortune. More than this, he put in practice all the devices which the extreme ingenuity of his zeal for souls could suggest to win scandalous sinners by degrees to a better life. He invited himself to the table, or accepted the invitations, of the men who were known to be living openly with the objects of their unlawful love, and, treating the poor victims of shame as if they had been virtuous ladies, he brought about in some cases their marriage and in other cases their dismissal. One rich and notorious sinner had as many as seven of these poor creatures living with him, and Francis managed to induce him to part first with one and then with another, until at length he brought him to his senses, made him dismiss the remainder with suitable portions, and then heard his general confession and reconciled him to God, determined to lead in future a life of virtue and piety.[3] Another remarkable conversion, of a different character, was that of a Jewish Rabbi, who was highly esteemed among his own people, and had distinguished himself by the abuse which he had poured upon Francis whenever his name was mentioned in his presence. Francis, hearing of this, made special prayers for him, and then, as he often did, went and asked the Rabbi to give him a dinner. The Jew, knowing the esteem in which Francis was held in Malacca, did not like to refuse him, but received him at first without any cordiality. Francis won him by his charming, bright, and humble conversation. He did not speak a word of controversy, but took his leave with great expressions of gratitude, his host accompanying him to the door, and refusing to let him go away without promising to come again. A friendship thus sprang up which ended in Francis convincing the Rabbi of the truth of the Christian religion, and his being solemnly baptized to the great joy of the city.

There was no lack of miracles to authenticate the mission of Francis, and to give force to his words at this time. Indeed miracles seem to have become almost matters of course, as if to make the obstinacy of those who could not be converted by his preaching more inexcusable. 'He wrought so many,' says

[3] It was at Malacca, after his return from the Moluccas, and consequently not precisely at the time of which we are speaking, that Francis is related to have converted one of these unhappy women in a still more wonderful manner. He had supped with a merchant in whose house she was living, with another companion like herself; and on being shown to his room, he asked to see the woman. Then he began to scourge himself on the shoulders with an iron chain, and, holding out another to the woman, bade her do for herself what he was doing for her. The merchant rushed in, and threw himself at the feet of Francis, crying out that he was the one who deserved such punishment; and both he and his two companions, who were well provided for in marriage, began to lead a thoroughly Christian life.

Bartoli, 'that in the account given of them afterwards, in the sworn testimonies of that time, the miraculous cures are not counted one by one, or many together, but all in a mass, it being said then that he healed all the sick people whom he touched, and that his hands were believed to be endowed by Heaven with universal virtue against every sort of malady.'[4] There was at least one very conspicuous miracle, the recalling to life of a girl who had been three days buried. She was the daughter of a lately baptized woman, and had died at a time when Francis happened to be away from the town. 'The mother,' says Bartoli, 'who had sought him everywhere when her child was lying ill, as soon as she heard of his return, took courage to think that he might be as able to raise her now she was dead as he would have been to heal her when she was sick; so she went at once to him, and throwing herself at his feet in floods of tears, began to say to him, exactly as Martha to our Saviour, that if he had been there, her daughter would not have died; but that nevertheless, if he were willing, he

[4] *Asia*, lib. ii. p. 104. He mentions, however, several particular instances. 1. Antonio Fernandez, a youth of fifteen, who was possessed by a devil, as well as sick of a mortal disease. His mother had recourse to an old Indian witch, whose incantations only made matters worse. At last, a pious woman of her acquaintance induced her to send for Francis Xavier, at whose approach the demoniac began to writhe and howl. Francis prayed by his side, read the Passion of our Lord, and applied a reliquary to the boy, who ceased from his contortions, and remained apparently senseless. Francis bade the mother give him some food at a certain time, when he would wake up and be able to take it, and bring him for nine mornings to the Church of our Lady del Monte, where he himself would say mass. The lad was quite cured the first morning. 2. Francesco Lopez Almeida, who was nearly in his agony, and was cured by Francis laying his hand on his head. 3. A brother of Rodrigo Diaz Pereira, who had been unable to take food for three days, and was cured on making his confession. 4. A child in convulsions, cured after the reading of 'a Gospel' over it. 5. He also mentions one of the remarkable predictions which are common in the life of St. Francis, as to the great danger which a certain vessel would incur, in which a merchant had embarked a valuable cargo. Francis, after praying a moment, told him to go, in God's name, with the ship, and on no account to throw the goods overboard. The ship, in the course of the voyage, got aground, and it seemed inevitable that the cargo should be sacrificed, but the merchant pleaded the prediction and order of Francis, and after a short time the sea rose enough to lift the ship off the shoal.

could make her return to life, that nothing was difficult to God, and that He would grant everything to his prayers. Francis marvelled to see so great faith in a woman who had not long ago been baptized, and as she seemed to him worthy of the grace which she asked, he lifted up his eyes to heaven and prayed God to grant her that consolation; then he turned to her and said resolutely that she was to go, that her daughter was alive. She, between hope and fear, did not disbelieve his word, but because he had not offered himself to come with her to the place where the dead child was, to raise her to life, she answered that she had been three days buried. "It matters not," said the Saint; "go and open the grave and you will find her alive." The woman made no more question, but with great faith and rejoicing ran to the church, and there, in the sight of many others who ran together with her at the miracle, caused the stone to be raised from the grave, and found the child alive.'[5]

Francis stayed at Malacca till January 1546. We must now give some letters which he wrote, before leaving, to Portugal and to Goa, which will almost explain themselves. The first is nearly repeated in the second, but we are inclined to think that the two are distinct, the first having been written soon after his arrival at Malacca, and the second in December. He probably repeated what he had already said on account of the uncertainty which existed as to the safety of letters sent to so great a distance.

(XLVII.) *To the Society in Portugal.*

May the grace and charity of our Lord Jesus Christ always help and favour us! Amen.

I wrote to you, dearest Brothers, from India that I was going to Macazar, where two kings have lately become Christians. On my way I went to the city of St. Thomas (where all the people, both Christians and heathens, affirm that the body of the most holy Apostle St. Thomas lies), intending

[5] *Asia*, lib. ii. p. 106.

to sail thence for Malacca. As I was waiting at that town for an opportunity of sailing, a certain merchant, by name Joam d'Eyro, was guided by an inspiration from above to join me as my companion. After spending some days with me, and getting to know a little about heavenly things, he began to perceive that there were certain traffics and wares far superior to his own, of the existence of which he had never up to that time had even a suspicion. So he left his old merchandize and gave up his trade altogether, and embraced evangelical poverty. We have lately both arrived at Malacca, which is more than five hundred leagues distant from Goa, and we are already on the look out for an opportunity of sailing on to Macazar. People who come here from that island tell us that the nation there is wonderfully fit and ready for the religion of Christ. They have no temples of gods, and no priests of any sort to urge the people to their worship. In fact, the sun is the only thing that they worship as a god, and they have no other religion at all. So I pray you over and over again, dearest brothers, for your love to Christ, to come hither many of you of the Society every year, for there is the greatest possible dearth of workers such as you. Be quite sure that for bringing these heathen to the flock of Christ, there is no need of great learning, but of great practice in virtue, and of great force of the Holy Ghost. May God of His goodness give us all that gift! Amen.

Malacca [September] 1545.

(XLVIII.) *To the Society in Portugal.*

May the grace and charity of our Lord Jesus Christ always help and favour us! Amen.

I wrote to you about my affairs at some length from India, before I set off on my voyage towards Macazar, where we have heard that two kings have become Christians. I have been waiting now for a month and a half at Malacca, looking out for a favourable occasion to sail for Macazar. We shall sail thither,

God willing, in about as much time more. Macazar is more than a thousand miles from Goa. Persons who have come here from thence tell us that the natives are very well fitted for the Gospel, so that a great number of Christians may be made in those parts. There are no temples of gods there, no priests of false religions; they worship the rising sun, and nothing else. On the other hand, the tribes are always at war with one another.

Since I have been at Malacca, which is a city on the sea, a famous and crowded mart for merchants, I have had no lack of holy occupations. On Sundays I preach to the people, though I admire my own sermons much less than those do who are so good as to listen to them. Every day for an hour, and sometimes more, I teach the children the usual prayers. I live in the hospital, I hear the confessions of the sick, say mass for them, and give them holy communion. I am so overwhelmed by the number of persons who come to confess, that I cannot satisfy them all by any means. I also employ a considerable time in translating the Catechism from the Latin into a language which the people of Macazar understand;[6] for it is very troublesome to be absolutely ignorant of the language of those one is living among. On my way from India, I went to the town of St. Thomas, where the natives affirm that the body of the Apostle is preserved. There are there more than a hundred Portuguese families. People visit the church, which is really very devotional, and all the inhabitants and neighbouring people agree in declaring that the body of the Apostle is laid in it.

Whilst I was waiting there for an opportunity of sailing to Malacca, I met with a merchant who had come there with a ship full of merchandize. This man, as soon as he got to have a little insight into spiritual things, easily understood that there were certain other wares far more precious than his own, which he himself had never before met with. So he gave up his ship and his merchandize, and became my companion

[6] This was the Malay language, which was generally understood throughout the Archipelago.

in my voyage to Macazar. His name is Joam d'Eyro; and he is now fully resolved to embrace poverty for his whole life and to serve our Lord Jesus Christ. He is thirty-five years of age, and has come to our Lord after serving in the ranks of the world all his life. He very much desires that you will pray for him and commend him to God.

At Malacca several letters were delivered to me, some from Rome and some from Lisbon, and it is quite incredible how much joy they gave me and still give. Every time I read them —and I read them often and often—the effect on me is that I fancy I am over there with you, or that you are here with me. If this is not allowed us in body, at least it is allowed us in spirit. The Fathers who have come with Joam de Castro have written to me here from Goa about their arrival. I am now going to write back to them, that two of them are to go to Cape Comorin to help Francis Mancias, whom I left there with three native priests instructing the Christians of Comorin. The third I order to remain at Goa to teach humanities to the youth in the College of Santa Fé. The ship by which this goes is hastening its departure, so I will not speak of the matters about which I wrote from India. Next year I will write some long letters about the people of Macazar, if God so will. One thing I beseech you, dearest brothers—to come out here as many of the Society as possible, every year. Here we want a great many of you, and for the conversion of the heathen we do not require much knowledge of theology, but a great practice of virtue. So I end, praying God that He will both show to us His holy will and give us the power to carry it out.

Malacca, November 10th, 1545.

(XLIX.) *To Father Simon Rodriguez.*

May the grace and charity of our Lord Jesus Christ always help and favour us! Amen.

I beg and implore you, by the heart of our Lord Jesus Christ, to send out here as many as possible of the Society: but all of them, whether preachers or others, let them be men of proved virtue. For the enticements to sin which offer themselves out here are very many. So, even if they are not excellent in learning, I pray you over and over again, let them anyhow be excellent in virtue; for in these parts men look up to virtue more than to learning, though the thing which carries all before it is virtue adorned by learning. The fortified cities and Portuguese garrisons in India require, as a general rule, learned men. We are very greatly indebted to the King of Portugal, our most excellent patron, and to the Portuguese who are in India, for their great benevolence and liberality to us. If we have any way at all of repaying them in kind for all their deserts to us, it is this one—as they are entangled in many great matters and enterprizes, to settle their minds and consciences for them, so that they may have clearly explained and laid open to them what they must do to be saved. May Christ our Lord, out of His goodness and mercy, hire many and good labourers into His vineyard, and bring us together again, wherever it may please Him, if not on earth, then at least in heaven. Amen.

Malacca, December 5th, 1545.

The letters which Francis Xavier mentions as having caused him so much delight must have furnished him with news of the progress of the Society up to the spring of the year in which he received them (1545). The annals of the Society for the previous year are full of the exertions of Peter Favre at Louvain and Cologne, and mention how he had been able to send a large band of recruits, mostly novices, and all men of literary culture, to Simon Rodriguez in Portugal, to add to the number of students in the rising College at Coimbra. They sailed from Antwerp with the Archbishop of Compostella, and were carried by a storm to Coruña, where one of them, Francis Strada, was asked to preach. He preached with so much vigour and unction, that one of the canons of Coruña renounced the world and joined the little band of Jesuit pilgrims on the spot. They went on to Compostella, and thence to Coimbra. The name of the canon was Joam Beira, and we find that he was thought fit to be sent almost at once to the Indies, forming one of the band of three Fathers, who were the first recruits who reached Goa after Father Paul of Camerino and Mancias. The state of the College of Coimbra was flourishing and full of the best hopes, and it was perhaps the news of this which made Francis write so joyously to the Society in Portugal.

He would have been still more delighted if he had known that his own letters were beginning to bear the fruit which he desired, and that they had made a conquest of one whom he must have known well at Paris, and who was soon to become one of the greatest supports of the Society in Europe. This was Jerome Nadal, whom Ignatius had in vain endeavoured to convert at Paris, where, using one of his many skilful devices to gain souls, he had led him aside one day, and read to him a letter which he had just written to his own nephew in Spain about renouncing the world, and providing for the salvation of his soul. Nadal saw his design, and producing a copy of the Gospel, which he carried with him, told Ignatius that he knew what to follow, but that as for him and his plans, he could not tell in what they would end. He went back to Majorca, his native island, and there lived for many years, well off and prosperous externally, but never feeling as if he were in his right place. Some holy souls with whom he was familiar taught him to give himself to prayer, and he had a design of collecting a little company of preachers, and devoting himself with them entirely to the good of souls. By chance, in the beginning of the year, a copy of one of Francis Xavier's letters from India was placed in his hand. It was that, if we may judge from the description[7] given of it by the anecdote, in which Francis describes his method of proceeding with the Christians of the Fishery Coast, and which contains so many burning words about the need of labourers in the great harvest

[7] See Orlandini, *Hist. Soc. Jesu*, l. v. c. 6. He says of the letter, 'ubi, post commemoratam ingentem inter Indos animorum messem, de confirmata Societate ab Apostolica Sede Franciscus plurimas Deo gratias agebat.' It may be remarked that Francis was aware of the confirmation of the Society before he left Portugal, but he could not have heard of the promulgation of the Bull until the first arrival of letters in India after he had been some time there.

which was so ripe to be gathered in in India.[8] Towards the end of the letter there was a passage in which Francis spoke of the delight which he felt in having at last heard of the solemn confirmation of the Society by the Pope. Nadal had never heard of the confirmation; indeed, he seems to have lost sight of Ignatius altogether. But the words of Francis Xavier brought back to his mind all that had passed at Paris, and how his confessor there had urged him to become one of the disciples of Ignatius. He went to Rome, and there, after a time, made the Exercises, in which he experienced the greatest possible difficulty in making up his mind, till at last the light broke in upon his soul, and he made a vow to enter the Society.

We hear nothing more of the Fathers who were expected when Francis left India, having, as he supposed, wintered at Mozambique, of whom the King had written in such high terms. The three whose arrival was announced in the letters received by Francis at Malacca came to India in the company of the new Governor, Joam de Castro, whose voyage out was unusually short. They arrived at the beginning of September, before Francis himself had reached Malacca. Either at this time, or by former letters, Francis had been appointed Superior of the Society in the East, and the letter in which he allots them their work is written in that capacity. But even as Superior he seems to prefer entreaty and request to the simple language of authority.

(L.) *To the Fathers Paul of Camerino, Joam Beira, and Antonio Criminale.*

May the grace and charity of our Lord Jesus Christ always help and favour us! Amen.

In a long letter that I sent you by the Commendatore[9] I gave you detailed information that I was all ready to start on my

[8] See above, pp. 155, 156.

[9] This was the letter given above (p. 298) from Meliapor. The 'Commendatore' must have been some officer who took the application from Francis to the Governor of India for letters of introduction to the Commandant at Malacca.

voyage towards Macazar; but we have had later news stating that affairs there are not in so good a state as we had thought, and so I have not gone there. I am now thinking of Amboyna, where there are already many Christians, and people say so much of the docility of the rest that the addition of great numbers more seems very likely. I will write to you from thence what I shall see of the state of the country on the spot, how the natives are disposed towards the faith, and of the fruit we may reasonably expect from labours to be spent amongst them. The experience I have already gained of the state of Cape Comorin and Goa, and that which, by the Divine blessing, I shall acquire of Amboyna and the Moluccas, when I have seen them, will enable me to write to you in which of these regions it appears that your industry may best employ itself, so as to be most profitable for the greater service of God.

For the present I beg of you two, my dearest Fathers Joam Beira and Antonio Criminale, as soon as you have read this letter, to get ready to go at once to Cape Comorin, where you will work with more usefulness to the service of God than at Goa, and you will take with you from Goa, if he is there, Fr. Francis Mancias; for he knows the country perfectly, and you will understand from him in what way you must live and work there. It is my particular desire that, if this letter finds Father Mancias at Goa, you both of you, with him as a third, set out together for Cape Comorin. I beg you in the name of God not to do otherwise; nor, whatever be the cause that stands in the way, let anything make you give up this journey, which is my positive wish, and I consider it as absolutely necessary. Father Nicolas Lancilotti will remain in the College of St. Paul, where he is to teach grammar, for which he has been sent from Portugal. As I am confident that in your great charity you will do what this letter prescribes and nothing else, I shall say no more on this point.

Now, my dearest Father Paul of Camerino, I pray you very much, for the love you have for Jesus Christ, to watch with the greatest care over the interest and preservation of the College. Above everything, I commend to you over and over again, to show prompt and perfect obedience to all those who have authority of any kind in it. Be sure that in no way can you do a thing more pleasant or sweeter to me than by entire obedience to them in all things. I declare, if I were myself where you are, I would do nothing, however small, contrary to or without the authority and pleasure of those who have the government of that holy College; I should make a point of obeying them most diligently in all that they should command me. I desire and hope that God may be pleased to breathe His holy inspiration into the very inmost core of your soul, that you may be entirely convinced that you can by nothing make yourself more pleasing to Him, or do more for His service and glory, than by denying your own will out of love for Him.

Write me word, I entreat you, about all of our fathers and brothers, especially Fr. Francis Mancias, by the vessel which will soon be sailing from Goa for the Moluccas. I am sure you will do this at good length and diligently, and I am already enjoying in hope and desire the pleasure which I shall have when I read the letter. I beg of you, my dearest brothers, to remember me constantly in your holy conversations with God and in your holy sacrifices. I feel peculiar need of this assistance from you, on account of the dangers I am about to incur, as I am going to sail to barbarous countries, infested by dangers of every kind. Simon Botelho, who is leaving this place for Goa, is very favourably disposed towards your holy house. He will give you a minute and full account of me and my affairs. He treats me as a great friend, and I have a great affection for him, for he is a truly good man, and one who sincerely loves God. I beg you to cultivate his friendship diligently. He has rendered me all the offices of a real friend, having sent me as a gift all that was necessary for the expenses and provision for the voyage I am undertaking, showing all the kindest possible proofs of most exquisite charity. May God, Who has the power, reward him in my stead, for I really feel how much I owe him.

May God our Lord, my dearest brothers in Jesus Christ,

bring us together in His holy glory, since in this life we have to live scattered in so many various places!

The least of your brothers in Jesus Christ,

FRANCIS.

From Malacca, December 16th, 1545.

The urgency with which Francis expresses his wish that the two Fathers from Portugal should proceed at once to the Fishery Coast must be explained by a fear which he may have had that efforts would be made to detain them at Goa. The letter is written in such terms as to enable them to plead that they had no choice in the matter left them by their Superior. The exhortation to Father Paul about obedience to the rulers of the College shows us that, in the very delicate position in which he was—for the College was not yet made over to the Society—he was often provoked to acts which might have embroiled him with the authorities. We shall hear more of this in the next letter to him.

CHAPTER II.

The Moluccas.

ST. FRANCIS XAVIER sailed from Malacca for the isles of the Eastern Archipelago on the 1st of January 1546. His immediate destination was the island of Amboyna, though the ship in which he sailed was bound for the island of Banda, somewhat to the southeast of Amboyna, and further from Malacca. He was now entering upon one of the most adventurous periods of his missionary life, sailing away almost beyond the reach of communications from India or Europe; for on his return he wrote to his friends at Rome, that a letter to the Moluccas from thence could not be answered, under the most favourable circumstances, in less than three years and three quarters. He had with him none of the Society, unless we count Joam d'Eyro, who still accompanied him: but he found Portuguese merchants and even settlers in most places which he visited, and his principal stay was in islands under the Portuguese crown, where there would be garrisons, churches, and priests, though not in any great numbers. It is not wonderful that our accounts of his proceedings during the year and a half on which we are now entering should be comparatively meagre, and somewhat confused. He wrote, as we shall see, very few letters that remain to us before his return to India in January 1548, and even the letters which have been preserved are written with all his usual reticence as to his own great conquests for religion, and are evidently, moreover, meant rather to give specimens of the work that could be done than a narrative of what had actually taken place. He gives indeed sufficient details and even notes of time to enable us to set before ourselves a kind of outline of his labours: but it is an outline which makes us long very much for more explicit delineation from himself, while the facts concerning him, which rest on evidence from others which there is no reason to question, are just enough to reveal to us how immense his activity must have been, how ubiquitous he seems to have made himself, how unsparing of himself he was, how many dangers he braved, and the wonderful success which attended him.

There is, as we have said, some uncertainty in the story when we try to arrange the facts which belong to this period of his life, and which are connected with the various places in that part of the Malay Archipelago which goes or went by the general name of the Moluccas.[1] His own language leads us to suppose that he used the name in a large sense to designate a tract of ocean sprinkled over with islands, but that he also looked on one country[2] as giving its name to the whole. Happily, the picture which the combined accounts furnish us, of his method of dealing with the people in this remote part of the world and of the traits of his character in which we are most interested, is not affected by our inability to trace his

[1] We have already noticed that Francis Xavier speaks of Molucco (Molucum) as a single place, at the same time that he speaks of it as a region, and also mentions the 'Molucca' islands. Strictly speaking, the Moluccas are the five islands which lie in a string from north to south along the western shores of the large island of Gilolo, to the east of Celebes. They are all small—Ternate, Tidor, Motir, Macian, and Batchian. But in a more general sense a great number of islands, some larger than these, are included in the Moluccas. Mr. Wallace allots them a space of ten degrees of latitude by eight of longitude, and they thus embrace the islands and groups between the Philippines and Timor, New Guinea and Celebes (*Malay Archipelago*, ii. 138). He counts among them Cerama and Bouro, as well as Gilolo, three very considerable islands. In the letters of St. Francis we shall find distances given, as to which we cannot depend on the accuracy of the copyists or translators, who had never been in that part of the world or seen a good map. He seems by *Molucco*, when used as the name of a single island, to mean Ternate: but Ternate is in sight of Gilolo, which some writers identify with the 'island of the Moors,' of which we shall hear so much; which, however, St. Francis is made to place at the distance of sixty leagues from 'Molucco.' We discuss elsewhere where this island—or islands—should be looked for.

[2] He uses the words *in continenti*.

footsteps everywhere, and give an exact account of each week of his time. As to this last point, we have enough from himself to mark the chief divisions of the period, and we must be content to follow former writers on the subject in placing the details which he does not mention where they most conveniently adapt themselves to those chief divisions. Francis Xavier never afterwards spent any time in the Moluccas, though he must have passed near them on his voyages to and from Japan and to the coast of China. When the evidence as to his actions came to be collected and his life to be written, on the testimony of persons who had been his companions or with whom he had met in the Moluccas, a number of beautiful anecdotes came to light, which relate to places which he had himself never mentioned, and works of charity or of preternatural power over which, as usual, his humility had drawn the veil of silence.

The history of Christianity in the Moluccas had hitherto been chequered by the action of the same conflicting causes which we have seen at work in India. Not many years before the arrival of Francis Xavier at Amboyna there had been a great movement towards the faith, and two kings in particular, one in the island 'of the Moor' (as to the exact site of which there must remain some doubt), and another in Ternate, had become Christians. The avarice, tyranny, and licentiousness of the Portuguese, added to their quarrels among themselves, had led to a general league against them and a massacre known as the Molucensian Vespers. Affairs had been in some measure restored, and religion greatly promoted, under the governorship of Antonio Galvan, one of those admirable men who occur from time to time in the history of Portuguese Asia; but a petition sent to King John III. by the native princes and people, to continue him in his authority as long as he lived, had not reached Lisbon till long after his successor had arrived, and affairs had fallen back into their former state, to the great detriment of religion. The history is too long to be related here, but what has been said may suffice to explain more than one passage in the letters of Francis Xavier.

The vessel in which he sailed from Malacca had a crew made up of Lascars and other heathens, many of them different in race and language one from another. The voyage lasted six weeks, and Francis found occupation enough for his charity and zeal in preaching to and instructing these wild mariners. The evidence of the Processes proves to us that on this occasion he had 'the gift of tongues' in the form in which it was imparted to the Apostles on the day of Pentecost, that is, that men of different languages understood him at the same time, each in their own dialect, and this miracle went far to make them docile to his teaching. He found Amboyna, as to Christianity, in the state which might have been expected from the history to which we have alluded. There were seven villages of native Christians, but the priest who had been their pastor had died or had been killed at the time of the general rising against the Portuguese, and the Christian natives were extremely ignorant, as well as strongly prejudiced against the Portuguese. They were also exposed to the depredations of the fierce islanders of the 'Moro' to the north, as well as to persecution from the Mussulmans in Amboyna itself. St. Francis was much touched, as we see by his letter, by the number of children whom he found unbaptized, and who died soon after they had been made heirs of the kingdom of heaven. He catechized the other children and the adults, and carried out as far as was practicable the method which we have seen him use in India and at Malacca. We are also told that he converted a number of heathens, and founded many churches on the island.

A great part of his time, however, was taken up by some unexpected visitors from Europe. The first voyage round the world had been made some years before by Magellan, who had sailed round South America for the express purpose of reaching the Moluccas from the western side, and of claiming them for the crown of Spain. He was then in the service of Charles V. The Moluccas were supposed to lie just on the line which separated the new part of the world allotted to Spain from that which was to belong to Portugal, and, in fact, the Philippines lie almost in the same longitude. Charles V. ultimately made over all his rights to them to Portugal, and thus the dispute was settled.[3] But other expeditions from 'New Spain' seem to have followed in the track of Magellan; and when Francis Xavier was at Amboyna, a fleet with Spaniards on board touched at the island, and remained for more than two months.

These Spaniards had been for some years in the Moluccas, endeavouring to establish themselves, now in one island, now in another, and claiming them as 'the possession of Castile,' notwithstanding the treaties. The Portuguese Commandant at Ternate had had considerable trouble with them. In 1544, Giordano de Freytas had made a truce with their commander, Ruy Lopez de Villalobos, for eight months, that he might get instructions from Goa. Discord broke out among the Spaniards, and many of them deserted to the Portuguese. In the course of the next year, 1545, Fernando de Sousa y Tavora, a Portuguese captain, was sent against them, and forced Villalobos and his men to come to terms. They were to be provided with all necessaries at Ternate until they could be conveyed to India, where they might either remain in the Portuguese service, or be sent to Spain, as they wished. This is the meaning of the Spanish fleet commanded by a Portuguese officer. Villalobos himself had died at Ternate. Fernando de Sousa y Tavora was conducting his dangerous captives—if such they

[3] Magellan sailed in 1519, and lost his life in one of the Philippine Isles, which he had discovered, in 1521. The first arrangement as to the discoveries in the New World had been made by Pope Alexander VI. who, in 1493, had decreed that a line should be drawn a hundred leagues west of the Azores. Portugal was to have all to the east, Castile and Aragon all to the west of that line. This did not satisfy John II. of Portugal, who thought the line too near the Azores; and by the treaty of Tordesillas, made in the next year, 1494, the line was removed two hundred and seventy leagues further west. Under this line the Portuguese claimed Brazil, when it was discovered. At the same time the Portuguese were limited eastwards by a line to be drawn one hundred and thirty-two degrees east of Paris, from north to south. It was supposed that the Moluccas were outside this line, but it just includes them. They were discovered in 1511. In 1529, as is said above, Charles V. sold all his claims on the Moluccas to Portugal for 370,000 gold ducats.

could be called—out of the region of the Moluccas, where they had been, and might still be, so mischievous. There were also two Portuguese vessels in port at the same time, and a contagious disease broke out among the crews of the fleets, which gave Francis a fresh occasion for the exercise of his fearless and indefatigable charity, while it at the same time disposed the mariners and soldiers to listen to his preaching. He devoted himself to hearing confessions, preaching, ministering to the sick, and reconciling persons at enmity—an office of charity of which we hear a good deal while he was among the Portuguese. Great fruits resulted from his exertions, and not the least of them was the extreme kindness and benevolence shown by the Portuguese merchants to the Spaniards in their distress, as they could hardly help looking upon them as intruders, who had already caused some trouble, and might hereafter cause more.[4]

This chance visit of the Spaniards gave Francis Xavier an occasion of gaining a very important recruit for the Society and for the heathen missions, to which his own heart was devoted. This was a priest of Valentia, Cosmo Torres, who had for many years felt a strong inward call to perfection, which he had never hitherto seen the way to fulfil. The first sight of Francis Xavier, his evident sanctity, and his extreme humility and charity, conquered him at once. He would have stayed with

[4] One of the anecdotes of this time might be used in a commentary on the text which tells us that 'God loves a cheerful giver.' A rich Portuguese merchant, Joam d'Arahujo, was frequently asked by St. Francis for wine for the sick. He always gave it, but with a certain difficulty. One day St. Francis sent another person to ask for him. Arahujo gave him the bottle, and told him not to come again; the wine he had, he wanted for himself. When Francis was told of the answer, his face kindled with zeal, and he said, 'Does Arahujo think that he will enjoy the wine he denies to Christ? He will die before he has consumed it, and this land of Amboyna is the last that he will see.' He warned Arahujo himself afterwards to prepare himself, for he had not long to live. Soon afterwards, Francis left Amboyna, and one day at Ternate, while he was saying mass, he begged the people to pray for Arahujo, who was just then dead at Amboyna. It turned out that the merchant had died at that very time. Joam d'Eyro, who had been left at Amboyna, wrote to Ternate to announce it, as well as another, named Carvaljo, who was present when Arahujo died.

him at Amboyna, as it appears, but he was either bound in some way to the Bishop of Goa, or at least was obliged to go and ask his leave to labour as a missionary. He went to Goa with the fleet, and there remained for a time working as a parish priest; but he soon made the Exercises and entered the Society. His name became very famous as a second father to the rising Church of Japan after the death of Francis.

It is evident, from the following letters, that Francis Xavier found great promise of success for apostolical labours in the Moluccas during these few months at Amboyna. He arrived in the island in the middle of February, and in May he is already writing for some of the Fathers to join him. We shall add to the letters written from Amboyna at this time others which give a general account, as far as we have it from himself, of his labours in the Moluccas.

(LI.) *To the Society at Goa.*

May the grace and charity of Jesus Christ our Lord be with us ever! Amen.

On the 1st of January 1546 we sailed from Malacca for the Moluccas. We landed at Amboyna on the 14th of February. This island is about ninety miles in circumference; it is well peopled with natives and foreigners. It contains six Christian towns or villages, which I visited one after another as soon as I landed, and where I baptized a great number of infants and children. Soon after, the fleet under the command of Fernando de Sousa touched at Amboyna, with Spaniards on board, who had come from New Spain to the Moluccas. The great number of vessels caused such a confluence of spiritual occupations, as it was necessary to hear confessions, to preach in public, to wait on the sick, and assist the dying, that time did not permit me to satisfy all duties. I have been able to form some idea of the character and disposition of the inhabitants, and I have come to hope that as soon as the lord of the island returns—he is a Portuguese of high rank, very devoted to religion, and now in command of the royal garrison at Molucco—I hope, I say, when he returns, that we shall gather in here abundant fruit of souls.

About four hundred miles from Amboyna is a country called the Land of the Moor, where many Christians are living in entire ignorance of the Christian law and worship. I am going to this country, in order to provide for the salvation of so many souls. I am persuaded that I ought, even at the peril of my life, to snatch their souls from destruction. I am resolved to meet any risk of death, even clear and plain, for I have placed all my hopes in Divine Providence, and I wish to obey those words of the Gospel, 'He that will save his life shall lose it, and he that shall lose his life for My sake shall find it.'[5] And believe me, my dearest brothers, that although the words of this sentence are in general very easy to understand, yet when the time comes when you have to make up your mind that you must lose your life for God, and incur the danger of death, then that saying, clear as light though it be, becomes so very obscure, that he alone can understand it to whom God, in His goodness, makes it plain. At such times indeed it is that one sees quite clearly how weak and frail human nature is. May God therefore, in His measureless mercy, so confirm and strengthen us in such dangers, and at such times, by His own might, that we may bravely undertake such risks and bear them to the end; and may He also remain with us always! Amen.

From Amboyna, May 8th, 1546.

(LII.) *To Father Paul of Camerino.*

May the grace and charity of our Lord Jesus Christ be with us always! Amen.

O my Paul! what I have so often entreated of you when I was with you, and have so often also begged of you by letter, that same thing I now most earnestly ask and pray,—that in

[5] Matt. xvi. 25. *Qui voluerit animam suam salvam facere, perdet eam, qui autem perdiderit animam suam propter Me, inveniet eam.* (Orig.)

all the affairs of the College you obey sedulously the Superiors. If I were in your place, I should have nothing more at heart than to do all they wished. I want you to believe me, and be convinced, that nothing is so safe, nothing so secures us from going wrong, as to desire to be always ruled by others, and to obey their commands from the heart. On the other hand, it is a perilous and hazardous thing to live as one's own master, casting off the authority of superiors. For even if you do a thing rightly when you depart from what is prescribed you, yet be sure, dearest brother, that there is more bad than good in it after all. You will therefore accurately obey in all things Father Diego de Borba, whose will agrees with the will of God, and be altogether under his power. If you will do this, you will do a thing pleasing not only to me, but also to God.

Send me two of our fathers who are now at Cape Comorin, particularly Joam Beira, and in their place substitute two of those who are lately arrived from Portugal. And I beseech those who are to be sent hither, that as, considering the multitude of stations and the magnitude of matters we have to attend to, we of the Society are too few, they make an effort to bring with them some men not of ours, who may serve and help us in teaching the Christian law and religious instruction to the villages in these islands. If they are not priests, at least let them be persons who have had rough handling from the world, the flesh, and the devil, and who desire to punish in themselves their own injuries and those of God. They must bring with them the sacred vessels and vestments for the holy sacrifice. But the chalices should be of tin; they will be safer than chalices of silver *a gente non sancta*—I mean the heathen among whom we are always living.

Some Spanish friars of St. Augustin are going from Amboyna to Goa; you may learn from them anything about me that you wish to know. I earnestly commend them to you, and beg you to help them in any way you can, showing them the highest marks of kindness and goodwill. They are excellent religious and very holy men. I am setting out for the Land of the Moor. May God abide with you; may He go with me, and, after this life, may He be pleased to transfer our souls to His own kingdom, where we shall attain and enjoy a great deal more peace and bliss than here!

From Amboyna, May 10th, 1546.

P.S.—Send the enclosed letter to our brothers at Comorin immediately, that they may have time to reach Goa, and sail for the Moluccas at the beginning of April next year.

(LIII.) *To the Fathers of the Society at Comorin, Antonio Criminale and Joam Beira.*

May the grace and charity of our Lord Jesus Christ be ever with us! Amen.

Last year, when I was at Malacca, I wrote you two letters to the same purpose, begging in the name of God you two, Joam Beira and Antonio Criminale, to set out without delay for Cape Comorin. I thought it well that you should go there to instruct and nourish those poor neophytes with Father Francis Mancias, whom I had left amongst these Christians with Joam de Lizana and three other native priests. And to make your act more meritorious, I commanded it formally in the name of your love of obedience. I doubt not that this letter reached you, and that you acted in obedience to it. I left Malacca on my way to Molucco the 1st of January, and on the 16th of February I landed on the island of Amboyna. I immediately went through all the Christian villages of the isle, and baptized all the newborn infants. About that time, D. Fernando de Sousa, with a fleet of Spaniards who had come from New Spain to the Moluccas, arrived at Amboyna. There were eight vessels, which gave me more occupation than I can describe. I had to be always hearing confessions, preaching on the Sundays, to bring many persons to make peace one with another, to visit and console the sick, and to assist and encourage the dying, so that I had no time free either during Lent or after it. I also got to know the disposition of the natives; and I hope, with the help of God, that when Giordano de Freytas, Governor of Molucca, and Sovereign Lord of Amboyna—a man very zealous for the propagation of religion—comes to fix his residence and home here, which is likely to be in less than a year from next November 1546, all the inhabitants will follow the faith of Jesus Christ. The island is about ninety miles in circumference. It contains a number of villages, of which seven are Christian. About four hundred miles from Amboyna, there is a country called 'of the Moor,'[6] where I am told there are a great number of Christians, but all utterly ignorant of the truths of religion. I am to go there very soon.

I am anxious that you should know this, that you may understand how much your work is needed in these countries. And though I am not ignorant that where you are you are not idle, yet as you are absolutely necessary here, I beg of you, in the name of Jesus Christ, you, Francis Mancias and Joam Beira, to come hither as soon as possible, and that this voyage may give you an opportunity of greater obedience and merit, I formally command it. If, by chance, either of you shall have quitted this mortal life, let another take his place at the choice of Father Antonio Criminale; but so that, in any case, one of you three remain with the native priests among the Christians of Comorin. If any of the Society arrive this year from Portugal to help our work, I entreat them, in the name of God, to proceed to Cape Comorin to instruct the Christians there. If there be any news from Portugal, write it to me, and give the letters from Portugal in charge to the Fathers who are to come hither. And that the new Fathers from Portugal may have greater merit by obedience, I command them, in virtue of my authority as Superior, to go to Cape Comorin.

And—as I perceive that this letter will hardly reach you before the beginning of March next year—one of the King's vessels will be going in May from Goa to the Moluccas, on board of which will be the King of Molucco, who some time

[6] *Regio est in continenti.* It does not seem to have been clear then whether it was an island or a continent.

ago was taken away as a prisoner; I wish you to come by that vessel. So as soon as you have read this letter, go at once from Cape Comorin back to Goa, and prepare yourselves, as I have said, to sail to Molucco. The people are hoping that the same vessel will bring their prince, whom they are always expecting. The Portuguese also think that the new Commandant of Molucco will be on board that vessel. If the King, of whom I speak, has received baptism at Goa, I have great hopes that a large number of his subjects will become Christians. But even if he should not have become a Christian, you may still render very great service here. Each of you should bring all that is necessary for the holy sacrifice; but let the chalices be in tin, in order to preserve them more easily from the greedy hands of the unholy race[7] among whom you will have to live. And now, as you are members of the Society of Jesus, and I have full confidence that you will execute all that I have asked you in the name of Jesus Christ, and that, for your love of obedience, I have commanded you, I shall add no more, except that you come without delay; for I am anxiously looking forward to your arrival. I feel sure that your coming, by the grace of God, will be well timed in itself, acceptable to Jesus Christ, and salutary to the people. I beg of you, my brothers, to bring with you some of the seminarists from Goa, who are priests, that they may be able to help you in teaching the Christian doctrine to these islands. Anyhow, let each one of you bring with him one companion at least, and if they are not priests or clerics, let them be at all events enemies of the world, the flesh, and the devil, and determined to have vengeance for the injuries they have received from them. May God, of His goodness bring us together in this life in His service, and, in the next, in His kingdom, where far greater rest and joy await us than we can have here.

FRANCIS.

From Amboyna, May 10th, 1546.

[7] *a gente non sancta.* (Orig.)

(LIV.) *To the Society at Rome.*

May the grace and love of Jesus Christ our Lord always help and favour us! Amen.

I wrote to you a year ago that two princes in the island of Macazar and a great number of their subjects had been led to the Christian religion. I thought this would be an opportunity for advancing the Gospel far and wide, and felt invited by the occasion of doing a good work for God; so I set out at once from Cape Comorin to go to Macazar as soon as I could. Macazar is more than two thousand seven hundred miles from Cape Comorin. Before embarking, I took diligent care that the Christians of Comorin should not be left without anything that was wanted for the rites of religion, and the cultivation of piety. I set over them five priests — Francis Mancias of the Society, three native priests, and Juan Lizana, a Spaniard by birth.[8] The Christian inhabitants of the island of Ceylon, at no great distance from Cape Comorin, are well instructed by two Franciscans and two secular priests. These two churches consequently had no need of my labours; and the other Christians, who reside in Portuguese settlements, are taught by the vicars of the Bishop of Goa. Seeing, then, that my work was not necessary in India, I went to Meliapor, which now bears the name of St. Thomas, in order to go from thence to Malacca. I there met with a merchant, who entreated me to hear his confession. After having made his confession duly, he was so strongly moved by Divine grace, that the next day he distributed to the poor the sum he got by the sale of his merchandize and his ship, and following Christ in His naked poverty, he joined himself to me as my companion.

Sailing from Meliapor, we came to Malacca, a much frequented city, belonging to the King of Portugal. There the Commandant told me that he had lately sent to Macazar a priest of great piety, with a considerable number of Portuguese, who were to protect the new Christians in case any trouble

[8] The text says Francis Lizana, but it seems a mistake.

should arise. So he told me to remain at Malacca till the ship which had taken them should return and bring news how things were. I followed the advice of the Commandant, and remained more than three months at Malacca. During this time there was no lack of opportunity for gaining merit. On feast days and Sundays I preached to the people in the chief church; the rest of the time I spent generally in hearing the confessions of the sick in the hospital where I lived, and relieving their miseries. I instructed new converts, and especially the children, in the elements of Christian doctrine; and I brought about reconciliations among the soldiers and the inhabitants, who had quarrels and feuds one with another. Every day after sunset I went about the city ringing a bell, to warn the inhabitants to wake up and pray for the mercy of God on the souls in Purgatory. A crowd of children from the catechetical school used to follow me as I repeated this call, and made a great stir in the city.

When I saw that the winds which would have been favourable to ships returning from Macazar had ceased to blow, and that nothing was to be heard of the priest and soldiers who had been sent there, I thought I ought not to wait any longer, and quitting Malacca I sailed for the Moluccas. The King of Portugal possesses a fort in the Moluccas called Ternate, in the most distant part of the Indies. About two hundred miles from this place, nearer to India, is Amboyna, an island about ninety-four miles round, with a large population, not only of natives, but of foreigners. The King of Portugal has given this island to a Portuguese nobleman illustrious by his virtue and piety, who, it is said, is intending in less than two years to settle there with his wife, his children, and all his household. Here there are altogether seven towns of Christians, all of which I went through and baptized all the newborn infants and the children not yet baptized. A great many of them died soon after their baptism, so that it was clear enough that their life had only been preserved by God until the entrance to eternal life should be opened to them. About the same time some Spaniards in eight ships came to the island, and remained about three months. All that time how I was distracted with occupations I can hardly tell you. I stirred all the crews up to a regular and virtuous life by sermons; I heard their confessions, I visited their sick, and encouraged them at the hour of death to leave this world with resignation and confidence in God; a very difficult thing for those who have been by no means obedient to His divine laws. The more daringly they have rolled in all sin and crime, the less hope and confidence in the mercy of God have they when they die. A good many also who were carrying on serious feuds with one another—a fault very widely spread among soldiers—were, with the help of God, brought to make peace. The fleet sailed from Amboyna for India, and I with my companion, Joam d'Eyro, of whom I have spoken to you, sailed in the opposite direction to the Moluccas.

Nearly two hundred miles beyond Molucco there is a region which is called 'Maurica.' Here, many years ago, a great number of the inhabitants became Christians, but having been totally neglected and left, as it were, orphans by the death of the priests who taught them, they have returned to their former barbarous and savage state. It is in every way a land full of perils, and especially to be dreaded by strangers on account of the great ferocity of the natives and the many kinds of poison which it is there common to give in what is eaten and drunk. The fear of this has deterred priests from abroad from going there to help the islanders. I have considered in what great necessity they are, with no one to instruct them or give them the sacraments, and I have come to think that I ought to provide for their salvation even at the risk of my life. I have resolved to go thither as soon as possible, and to offer my life to the risk. Truly, I have put all my confidence in God, and I wish as much as is in me to obey the precept of our Lord Jesus Christ: 'He that will save his life shall lose it; and he that shall lose his life for My sake shall find it.'[9] Words easy in thought, but not easy in practice. When the hour is come when life must be lost that you may find it in God; when danger of death is

[9] Matt. xvi. 25. *Qui voluerit animam suam salvam facere, perdet eam, qui autem perdiderit animam suam propter Me, inveniet eam.* (Orig.)

on you, and you see plainly that to obey God you must sacrifice life, then, I know not how, it comes to pass, that what before seemed a very clear precept is involved in incredible darkness. Not even the most learned men attain to the full force of these wonderful words, but those only whom God, the Teacher Who speaks to the soul, enlightens by a special favour. It is in such matters that we see clearly how great after all our weakness is, how frail and unstable is our human nature here. Many friends of mine prayed me earnestly not to go amongst so barbarous a people. But afterwards, when they saw that they gained nothing by prayers or tears, they brought me each what he thought the best possible antidote against poison of all sorts; but I have unrelentingly sent them all back, lest after burthening myself with medicines, I should have another burthen which I was before without, that of fear. I had put all my hope in the protection of Divine Providence, and I thought I ought to be on my guard, lest relying on human aid I should lose anything of my confidence in God. So I thanked them all, and earnestly entreated them to pray to God for me, for that no more certain remedy than that could possibly be found.

But I must return to my voyage to the Moluccas. We had a very bad time of it; many dangers from pirates, many more from tempests. The greatest of our perils was this, that we were in a very large vessel, and she was driven by the violence of a storm upon some shallows, and for three miles she went on with the bottom of the rudder perpetually grazing the sand. So that if she had come across any hidden rocks, or, what we were perpetually fearing, if the shallows had got still more shallow, we should certainly have been shipwrecked and she would have perished. I saw a great deal of weeping there, and a great deal of trouble and anxiety, for all were in expectation of momentary death. But God did not desire to destroy us, but rather to instruct us by the danger we ran, so that we might understand how poor our strength is when we have only our own forces or human protection to lean upon. For when you have found out how empty your hopes are, and, altogether ceasing to trust to human power, have placed all your hope on the

Lord of all, Who alone can easily defend you from any danger which you have come under for His sake, then indeed you will know by experience how God governs all things by His will and word, and that danger to life, however great, is to be despised in comparison with the heavenly joys which on such occasions and at such times it is His wont to impart. Not even death itself is any matter of fear to those who enjoy this divine sweetness. For although somehow it seems to be that when we have escaped dangers we can find no words to express how great they were, nevertheless there remains unfaded the extremely sweet memory of the benefit which God has bestowed. And this recollection is day and night a spur to us either to undertake willingly or to bear bravely to the end other toils for that best of masters, and makes us also have a very great veneration and love for Him all our life long, hoping that in His infinite goodness He will add to us always fresh courage and strength to work diligently and constantly for so good and kind a Lord.

When I was at Malacca, I fell in with a Portuguese merchant, lately come from the very rich kingdom of China. He told me that he had been asked by a Chinese—a good and honourable man, who had been a good deal in the city where the king dwells—whether Christians ate swine's flesh? and that he answered that Christians had no objection to swine's flesh, but that he should like to know why on earth he asked him such a question. Then the Chinaman said that there was a nation in the middle of China, shut in by mountains, whose manners and laws were very different indeed from those of the Chinese, and that this nation altogether abstained from swine's flesh, and, besides, kept many festival days in a very solemn manner. When the merchant told me this, I could not make a satisfactory conjecture whether these might be some of the Christians who unite the rites of the Hebrew law with the religion of Christ, as we know that the Ethiopians who live on the shores of the Red Sea do, or whether they were Jews, some of whom are scattered over all the world. I hear that all are agreed that they are not Mussulmans.

A great many merchants go from Malacca to China every year. I have charged many of them to find out with diligence what are the manners and rites and laws and institutions of this nation I speak of, so that by means of these marks I may find out what it is, and settle the question whether they are Jews or Christians. There are many who say that the Apostle St. Thomas penetrated as far as China, and that he made a great many Christians among that people. For before the Portuguese conquered India, the Greek Church used to send bishops there to take care of the Christians who were converted by St. Thomas and his disciples; and when the Portuguese first began to get possession of India, one of these Greek bishops of whom I speak is said to have affirmed, that he knew from other bishops whom he had found in India that St. Thomas had entered China, had gone through the cities, publishing the Gospel, and had converted many of the natives to Christ. As soon as I know anything certain, whether from what others find out, or from what I discover myself, I will let you know.[10]

Before I left Malacca, I heard that three of our Society had arrived at Goa, who wrote to me, and had my letters from Rome sent to me with theirs. When I read those letters, O, how I triumphed with joy at hearing about the affairs of the Society, just the things which I desired the most! As one of these three had come to be a master of grammar in the College of Santa Fé, and the other two to be employed wherever it seemed to me that they could be of the most use to religion, I wrote to them at once to leave the master at Goa, and that the others should go to Cape Comorin, and there join Francis Mancias in instructing the new converts. Now I have changed my mind, and am ordering them to come next year to the Moluccas, for I see in these parts a much greater opportunity of spreading the Christian religion.

Molucco is a region of small and almost numberless distinct islands, and it is not yet certain whether any part of it belongs to a continent. Generally, all the islands have many villages of inhabitants. The inhabitants would easily become

[10] This nation must have been the Jewish colony of Khai-Fong-Fou.

Christians, but for the want of people to preach to them. If we had somewhere here a house of the Society, the majority would be Christians. So I have made up my mind to bring it about that in these extreme parts of the world there should be a house somehow or other planted for our use: for I can already see in prospect how many nations that step would bring into the fold of Christ.

In this island of Amboyna the heathen are far more numerous than the Mussulmans, and there is a bitter hatred between the two; for the Mussulmans compel the natives either to become Mahometans or to be their slaves, and the heathen, hating even the name of Mahomet more than the yoke of slavery, repudiate altogether the superstition of the Mussulmans. If there were people here to teach them the true religion, they would join the fold of Christ without much difficulty, for they have much less objection to the name of Christ than to that of Mahomet. It is about seventy years since the plague of Mahometanism invaded this island: before that time all the inhabitants were heathen. The evil was introduced by some Mahometan cacizes (ministers of religion), who came from Mecca in Arabia, where the accursed body of Mahomet is honoured with great superstition, and drew a large multitude of people to their own sect. The native Mussulmans are altogether ignorant, and know nothing of the pestilential doctrine which they profess to follow, so that I am led to hope that they may be easily converted from the Mahometan religion.

I write all this to you at so much length that you may share my solicitude, and conceive, as is only right, an immense sorrow at the miserable loss of so many souls who are perishing daily, utterly destitute of aid. And those who desire to help them, don't let them delay; for even if they are not very well furnished with learning and other gifts, they will be quite fit for the work of which I speak, if they have made up their minds to come hither for the sake of Christ alone, to live with the people here, and breathe out their last in earnestly carrying out this resolution. If only a dozen would come out every year, so disposed, there would be an end altogether of this sect of Mahomet, and all would shortly be Christians. And what would result from this would be, that the majesty of God would not be insulted by so many atrocious and impious sins as is now the case at the hands of this nation, because they are ignorant of the true religion. For the inhabitants of this island are for the most part savage and barbarous men, remarkable for perfidy and wonderfully ungrateful.

There are also some islands in this part of the ocean the people of which eat human flesh, especially the flesh of their enemies who have been killed in battle. If any one of their own people dies by disease, they do not touch the rest of the body, but they cut off the hands and feet, and consider them great delicacies. And if we are to believe what is reported of them, they have even got to that excess of savagery, that when any one is preparing a specially elegant banquet, he asks his neighbour to give him his aged father, whom he kills and serves up to his neighbours to feast upon, and this request he makes on the understanding that he in turn promises to do the same for the man from whom he asks the boon, if ever he should wish to give a similar entertainment. And so great and so barbarous are the lusts to which they are subject, that they take up with all kinds of impurity. Within a month's time I intend to go to an island where, besides other unheard of crimes, each of the enormities I have mentioned is commonly committed, that is, they both eat the dead slain in battle and also give up their aged parents to one another to be banqueted on. The reason why I go there is that I understand they are willing to be converted from all their detestable wickedness to Christian piety.

The islands have a wonderful climate; they are full of large and dense trees, and have frequent rains to water them. They are defended on every side by steep rocks, and are so lofty and high that their inhabitants have no need of fortifications to repel hostile attacks. When war comes on, they think themselves quite safe enough if they can betake themselves to these rocks, the paths among which are so steep and so blocked up with stones that they never use horses, nor can use them. Moreover, there are frequent earthquakes among them, so great that mariners sailing by think that their ships have met with rocks. There is at the same time such a rumbling in the ground, that every one is frightened beyond all belief. Many of the islands send up fire to a great distance, and the flames burst out with a crash greater than that made by any brass gun, however large, when firing at full charge. Immense stones are sometimes cast up by the force and impetus of the fire. It would seem that as these men have no one to warn them about the punishment of the wicked, God has been pleased as it were to open to them the abode of hell, and give them some pictures of the fires in which sinners are to be for ever tormented, so that they may be admonished by that awful sight, and come to understand what punishments will await them unless they abandon their abominable vices and crimes.

All these islands differ among themselves in language, and indeed in some of them the inhabitants do not all use the same, but different villages have different dialects. However, all understand the Malay language, on account of the commerce. For this reason, when I was at Malacca I had the Creed, with an appropriate explanation, the form of general confession, the Lord's Prayer, the *Hail Mary*, and the ten commandments translated into the Malay tongue, that when I spoke to them about Divine truths they might better understand what I said. They have no literary monuments, and commonly do not know how to read or write; some few write in Malay words and Arabic letters. This is because the teachers of the Mahometan superstition, called Cacizes or Alfaquis, have lately taught, and are still teaching, some of the natives how to write. Before Mahometanism was introduced, there was absolutely no writing or reading among the natives.

In the island of Amboyna I have seen what no one would believe, and what has been unheard of till now; so perhaps it will be worth while to tell you. I saw a he-goat giving suck to his young kids with his own milk; he had one breast, which gave every day as much milk as would fill a basin. I saw i with my own eyes—for I would not believe it without seeing it. A respectable Portuguese has the goat, and is taking it away, meaning to carry it to Portugal.

But now to return to my intended voyage: I beseech you, my dearest fathers and brothers, by Jesus Christ the Lord of all things, by His most holy Mother, and the Saints of heaven who are in eternal glory, I pray and beg of you to remember me, and to pray God continually and most earnestly to be merciful to me. You see in how great need I am of protection. And I have often known that, in many dangers of soul and body, your prayers have been my saving. For my part, that I may not forget you, I carry about with me all your names, as they are written by your own hands as signatures to your letters to me, together with my solemn form of profession; and for the wonderful pleasure which I receive from that most delightful remembrance I give thanks first of all, as is right, to God, and then to you, my sweetest fathers and brothers, whom God has adorned with so many virtues. And as I have the confidence that some day I shall have far greater pleasure from the enjoyment of your company in life eternal, I now forbear to converse with you any longer for the present.

From Amboyna [May 1546].

The date of this last letter is not quite certain. It is given in the printed copies as May 1546, but the highest authority on the subject, F. Menchacha, thinks that it must have been sent from Amboyna a year later, after the return of Francis to that island from Ternate and the region of the Moor.[11] In that

[11] The internal evidence is contradictory; and therefore by no means conclusive either way. The chief reasons for postponing the date are, 1. that no other letter exists written in 1547 (but this argument may cut both ways, as it would tend to show that Francis was out of the way of opportunities till he returned to Malacca): 2. that the letter contains an account of the attempt made by his friends to prevent his going to the 'Isle of the Moor,' which attempt was made at Ternate after he had left Amboyna (but it is by no means certain that no attempt of the kind was made at Amboyna; and he most certainly contemplated going to 'Maurica' when he was there, and wrote about the dangers and his own apprehension of them to F. Paul of Camerino from Amboyna): 3. that he distinctly says (p. 376), that when the Spaniards sailed from Amboyna towards India, he set out with Joam d'Eyro in the contrary direction to Molucco (Ter-

case, we may probably suppose that it was written at different times, and finally sent off when Francis found himself again at Amboyna. If it was written, however, as seems to us more likely, before his voyage northwards from Amboyna to Ternate, it illustrates many of his characteristic traits of character: his diligence in gathering all possible information beforehand as to the places to which he was bound, his sanguine hopefulness as to the results of Apostolical labours, his zeal for the perishing souls of the poor heathen, and the like. In this case the danger which he mentions, when the ship in which he sailed was so nearly aground in shoal water, must have occurred on the voyage from Malacca to Amboyna. The ending of the letter, where he speaks of having carefully put together the signatures of all his brethren, and carrying them on his person, together with the formula of his solemn vows, gives us another touching proof of his intense love for the Society, and for all those with whom he was united therein.

In order to complete, as far as may be, Francis Xavier's own account of this period of his preaching, we shall place here the greater part of a letter which he wrote immediately after his return to India in January 1548.

---

nate). This is the only peremptory argument, but it depends on the translation of a single word. If *petiimus* ought to have been written *petimus* (I am going to), the argument is without force, and it is worthy of remark that the words, *ego cum Joanne Duro contrario cursu Moluccam petiimus*, are not strictly verified, because Joam d'Eyro was at first left at Amboyna. On the other hand, all the internal notes of time favour the supposition that the date as printed is right. 1. The expectation of the people of Amboyna that Giordano de Freytas would come and live among them, *intra biennium*, is expressed in the letter to Antonio Criminale and Joam Beira in the same way, *proximo anno a Novembri hujus anni* 1546: 2. the language about the 'Isles of the Moor' seems to imply that Francis had not yet gone there: 3. Francis speaks of his ordering the fathers to come to the Moluccas, in the present tense, *venire jubeo*. But this order was given in 1546, and obeyed in 1547: 4. the request, at the end, for prayers to help him in great dangers, agrees more with the prospect of a first voyage to Ternate and the Maurica, than with that of a return to Malacca and India. Moreover, when Francis was in Amboyna in 1547, being on his way westward, he would not be so likely to dispatch his letter from that island, as he would have had to take it with him to Malacca. Nor is there any mention in it of an intention to return homewards; whereas it is customary to him to speak of his immediate future.

(LV.) *To the Society at Rome.*

May the grace and charity of our Lord Jesus Christ always help and favour us! Amen.

In the year of our Lord 1546 I wrote to you a long letter about the Molucca islands, which are situated about sixty leagues from Amboyna. In that island of Amboyna, where the King of Portugal keeps up a garrison, a great number of Portuguese reside who frequent the Moluccas, which are exceedingly fertile in all sorts of spices. This is the only place where the clove grows, which we call commonly the girofle.[12] At Amboyna, which contains seven Christian villages, I stayed three months, and during that time I baptized a great number of children, whose salvation was in great danger from the want of any priest. The priest who had the charge of the mission died a long time ago. I had visited at leisure all the villages and baptized the children, when there arrived seven vessels, of which some were Spanish. These last came from New Spain, commonly called the West Indies, having been sent out by the Emperor Charles to discover new lands. They stayed at Amboyna about three months, and gave me plenty of occupation. I had to preach on Sundays and feast days, to hear many confessions every day, to appease differences, and to visit the sick. It was quite that kind of work, that, having to do with an unholy and quarrelsome set of people, I had very little hope of gaining so much fruit in the way of peace as I did. I give endless thanks to God, Who was so wonderfully good in pouring peace into the hearts of men who, I may almost say, make it a matter of profession to be never at peace either with God or man. After three months the Spaniards sailed for Portuguese India, and I lost no time in passing over to the Moluccas, where I spent another three months preaching on feast days, hearing confessions continually, and teaching the Catechism every day to children and converts. On Sundays and feast days, in the afternoon, I gave the converts a full explana

[12] cariophyllus, *Lat.*

tion of the Apostles' Creed; so that on these days I gave two instructions, one at the hour of mass to the Portuguese, the other in the afternoon to the converts.

I have very good reason to thank God for the fruits which came of this work. The converts took up the practice of singing hymns of the praises of God with so much ardour, that the native boys in the street, the young girls and the women in the houses, the labourers in the fields, the fishermen on the sea, instead of singing licentious and blasphemous songs, were always singing the elements of the Christian doctrine. And as all the songs had been put in the language of the country, they were understood equally well by the newly made Christians and the heathen. And, by the favour of God, the Portuguese in the country and the rest of the inhabitants, both Christian and heathen, took such an affection for me that I found favour in their eyes.[13] I passed from thence into the islands that are called 'of the Moor,' about sixty leagues from Molucco. There were here many Christian villages unattended to for a length of time, both on account of their great distance from India, and because the natives had put to death the only priest who was among them. In these islands I baptized a great number of children, and in the space of three months, for I remained that length of time, I visited all the Christian villages, and made them devoted to Christ and to myself. All these isles are full of dangers, on account of the feuds which rage among the inhabitants and their civil wars; the race is barbarous, totally ignorant of letters, devoid of any written monuments of the past, and without any notions of reading or writing. It is their practice to take away the lives of any whom they hate by poison, and in this way a great many are killed. The soil is rugged and destitute of productions which support life. There is no corn nor wine; the natives scarcely know what flesh meat is; they have no herds nor flocks, nothing but a few swine, which are rather objects of curiosity than food. Wild boars abound; good water is very rare; rice is plentiful; there are also trees in great

[13] *ut invenerim gratiam in oculis eorum.* (Orig.)

numbers from which they get a kind of bread and of wine, and others out of the woven bark of which the clothing which they all use is made. I have written all this to you, my dearest brothers, that you may know how much these islands overflow with heavenly joys. All these dangers and discomforts, when borne for the love of our Lord Jesus Christ, are treasuries filled full with heavenly consolations, so much so that one might think these islands were just the places where in a few years one might lose one's eyesight from weeping so abundantly the sweetest tears of joy. Nowhere do I remember either to have been so flooded with so much of limpid and perpetual spiritual delight, or to have borne so lightly all fatigue and bodily trouble, though I was going about islands begirt with enemies, inhabited by not the most trustworthy friends, and entirely destitute of anything that could help in sickness, or could defend and preserve life when endangered. In short, it seems as if these isles should rather be called the Islands of Divine Hope than of the Moor.

There is here a race of men, enemies to Christianity, called Javars. They believe that to kill any men they can get hold of is a sort of immortal life. And it often happens that when they have no strangers to kill, they kill their own wives and children. These Javars make great slaughter of the Christians. One of the islands is almost continually, throughout its length and breadth, shaken by earthquakes, and it sends up flames and ashes. The natives say that the violence of the subterranean fire is so great, that the strata of rocks on which a certain town is built are all on fire. What they say seems credible; for it often happens that large redhot stones, as big as the largest trees, are hurled into the air, and when there is a very strong wind such a quantity of ashes is sent up from the cavities that the men and women who are at work in the country come home so covered with ashes that you can hardly see their eyes or nose or face. You would think they were rather demons than human beings. This is what the natives tell me, for I have not seen it myself; during the whole of my stay there were no tornadoes. I also heard from them that during these violent winds the ashes are carried up into the air in such quantities that numbers of wild boars are blinded and suffocated by them, and that after the storm they find them dead in the fields.

They say, too, that during these tornadoes numbers of dead fish are found on the shores, killed in the same manner—the proof of this being that fishes who have drunk water in which ashes are sprinkled generally die. They asked me what it all meant. I told them this place was the abode of hell, into which all would be cast who worshipped idols. How severe the earthquakes are, you may judge from this—when I was saying mass on the feast of the Archangel St. Michael, the earth was so violently shaken that I was in great fear the altar itself would be upset. Perhaps St. Michael, by his heavenly power, was driving into the depths of hell all the wicked spirits of the country who were opposing the worship of the true God.

After having visited all the Christian villages, I returned to Molucco,[14] where I again spent three months more in preaching twice on feast days, in the morning to the Portuguese, and in the afternoon to the converts; hearing confessions every day, morning and evening, and teaching the Catechism besides. After having gone all through the Catechism, I explained on Sundays and feast days the articles of the Creed to the native Christians, taking one article day by day, and always speaking strongly against the worship of idols. On Wednesdays and Fridays I instructed the native wives of the Portuguese by themselves in the articles of the faith, the ten commandments, and the sacraments of confession and communion.

It was then the season of Lent, so that many of them approached the holy Eucharist, who had never done so before. During the six months I stayed at Molucco, both the Portuguese, their wives and children, and also the native Christians, made great progress in piety. After Lent I quitted Molucco and sailed towards Malacca, having received very great proofs of affection, not only from the Christians, but also from the heathen. I had no lack of work during the voyage. I met on a certain

[14] *i.e.* Ternate.

island with four Portuguese vessels, and I stayed twenty days with their crews. I preached to them three times, heard many confessions, and brought many to peace and concord among themselves. When I left Molucco, to avoid the lamentations of my friends and of the neophytes at my departure, I went on board suddenly at night. But that was not enough to keep my going away secret. In short, they caught me, and indeed this running away by night from the children whom I had begotten to Jesus Christ so affected me that I began greatly to fear lest my departure might have a bad effect on their salvation. So I enjoined them all to be diligent in carrying on the exercise of the Catechism in a certain church daily, and the converts to learn by heart a short explanation of the Creed, which I had given them. A pious priest, a very great friend of mine, took upon himself the charge of instructing them for two hours every day, and of speaking once a week to the native wives of the Portuguese on the articles of the faith, the sacraments of confession and the Eucharist.

When I was at Malacca I established the custom that at the beginning of night the souls in Purgatory, and the souls of the living who are in a state of worldly sin, should be recommended to the prayers of the pious in all the streets. This practice not only encouraged the good, but threw terror into the wicked. The city appointed a man for the purpose, to go round the town, with a lantern in one hand and a bell in the other, and calling out from time to time in a loud voice a strain of this sort, 'Pray for the souls of the faithful Christians who are suffering in Purgatory;' and then, 'Pray also for those who, lying under the burthen of mortal sin, take no pains to be delivered from it.'

The Mussulman king of Molucco is under the sovereignty of the King of Portugal, and thinks it an honour to be so. Whenever he names him, he calls him his Lord. He speaks Portuguese well. The Molucca region forms no part of the continent, but is entirely composed of islands. All the principal of these are under the dominion of the Mussulmans. The king himself is prevented from becoming Christian less by his

Mahometan religion than by his passions and the habits of a licentious life. Indeed, he has nothing of the Mahometan about him, except that he was circumcised when a child, and has been married a hundred times, and besides his hundred wives he has innumerable concubines.

The Mahometans in the Moluccas are very ignorant of the law of Mahomet. They have hardly any cacizes, and the few they have are very uninstructed and come from other countries. The king received me in the most friendly manner; so much so that the lords of his court did not like it at all. He sought my friendship, holding out hopes that he might one day embrace the Christian religion; he begged me not to keep at a distance from him because he professed Mahometanism, for he said Mahometans and Christians worshipped the same God, and a day would come when both would adopt one and the same religion. Every time I went to see him, he seemed highly delighted with my company; but I could never prevail upon him to become a Christian. All I got out of him was a promise from him that he would have one of his children baptized—he has a great number—on the understanding that this one becoming a Christian should have the sovereignty of the Mauric isles.

In 1546, when I was setting out for Molucco, I wrote from Amboyna to our brothers who had just arrived from Portugal, that in the next year some of them should sail to Malacca by one of the ships which go thither yearly from India. They did this, and three of our Society, of whom two are priests, Joam Beira and Ribera, arrived most opportunely at Malacca just as I landed on my return from Molucco. We spent a month together to my very great delight. I have not a doubt that they are quite the persons to render the greatest service to religion in the Moluccas. They set out for these islands in August, and the passage takes about two months. While they were at Malacca I made them acquainted with the manners of the country, and, from my own past experience, I gave them instructions how to deal with the people there. They are so far from India that we can only have letters from them once a year. I have also told them to write to Rome every year about the extension of the Christian religion in these countries, and the hopes that appear for the future, and they promised to do so.

I stayed four whole months at Malacca, waiting for a favourable season for the passage to India; the time was not without its spiritual occupation; and, as I could not alone satisfy the wants of all, I had to hear the complaints of some; but as their taking offence came from their repentance for sins, this did not afflict me, but rather gave me pleasure, as it was a proof of holy resolutions. I also spent much time in doing away with quarrels and enmities, which easily spring up amongst a fighting set like the Portuguese. After I had gone through the Catechism, I taught the children and the converts the explanation of the Creed in the common native tongue of the country, so that everybody might understand it. I had done the same in the Moluccas, in order that after their idolatrous superstition had been overthrown, I might lay firmly in their minds the foundations of the Christian religion. This instruction can quite well be given in a year, if only twenty words are learned each day, so as to be easily committed to memory by ignorant converts. Meanwhile you must often repeat the history of the coming of Christ, that it may plant itself and take root in their hearts as well as the explanation. It is only by this means that the people come to know the truth, and to look with abhorrence on the fables and witcheries held in renown by all heathen, ancient and modern.

I have diligently charged a certain priest here to supply my place, and to go through with them the same lessons in the forenoon. He has promised, and I hope by the favour of God that the work will hold on its course. When I left Malacca the principal inhabitants pressed me strongly to send them two of the Society to preach the Word of God to themselves, their wives, and the native Christians, and also instruct in my place their children, servants, and servant-girls in the Christian doctrine. They asked it with so much earnestness, that I think we ought by all means to satisfy their pious request in every way in our power, especially coming as it does from persons who have deserved very well of our Society.

We break off this letter for the present at this point, as the latter portion of it has reference to the great design on Japan, which began to occupy the thoughts of Francis Xavier from the time of his return to Malacca. What has been quoted of this letter, put by the side of that which precedes it, contains the only general sketch which we possess from his own hand of his labours in the Moluccas. We now proceed to supplement the statements of these letters from other authorities, whose accuracy cannot fairly be called in question. It is well to premise, that there is nothing to surprize us in the incompleteness of the statements of Francis Xavier himself; that he should leave out a great deal that would tend to his own praise is only natural in a man of his deep humility and saintly instincts. That he should omit all mention of the many deplorable proofs which he must have come across of the evil influence of some Portuguese here, as in India, on the cause of religion, is to be accounted for in many ways, among which we may mention the consideration already spoken of, that he must have been fully aware, as he has phrased it in an earlier letter, that what he wrote would pass through many hands and be submitted to many eyes. He could write boldly and openly enough to King John of Portugal, but there was no need to fill the houses of the Society and the minds of the Society's friends with attacks upon particular governors or commandants. But beyond all this, we must remember, that unless Francis Xavier had kept a careful daily journal of the expeditions which he seems to have made from Amboyna, from Ternate, and other places where he lingered longest, it would have been a real effort to him to recall all the islands which he had visited, and the particular circumstances connected with each visit. He speaks of going about from one to another, as if they were very numerous, and the letter which we have now before us —the only letter, as we think probable, which he wrote describing the Moluccas after having been among them—was written many months after his return to Amboyna, and some months after he had reached Malacca. Again, there was probably considerable sameness about the character of the people he met with, their reception of him, and his efforts for their benefit, just as there must have been much sameness about the more active portions of our Lord's public life, or as the characteristic features of any prolonged course of public elementary teaching in one place after another must necessarily be very much alike. The incidents which stand out in such a career are more novel to the people among whom the missioner, the apostolic preacher, or the wonderworking saint passes about, than to him, and their tongues are likely to be freer, as their minds are likely to be more pointedly struck, by just those doings or sayings which his own humility will conceal and easily forget. In this manner we account for the number of anecdotes of Francis Xavier, which undoubtedly belong to this time, for which his own letters might seem hardly to leave room, unless all the circumstances of the case are duly considered.

We have already spoken of some of his doings in Amboyna. Amboyna, as a short glance at a good map will show the reader, has a great many islets and islands in its neighbourhood. Francis went to visit several of these, the exact position of which it is not possible for us to identify, at least without the aid of other than modern maps. He went about, we are told, in a caracora—a native vessel, we may suppose, smaller than the prau in which Mr. Wallace made his voyage from Macazar to the Aru Islands.[15] A little to the north of Amboyna lies the large island of Ceram, which, from the names of some of the towns in it, we may conjecture to be the Baranura which is said to have been visited by St. Francis, and to have been the scene of one of the playful wonders which sometimes are to be found in the lives of the Saints, as in Scripture itself. We have the anecdote given in the *Relatio* (from the Processes) in the precise and simple words of an eyewitness, Fausto Rodriguez, who was an old man of eighty when he gave his evidence in the capital of the Philippines. They were sailing to Baranura when a sudden storm came on, and to appease it, Francis Xavier took from his neck a crucifix ('one finger long,'

[15] *Malay Archipelago*, ii. c. 28.

Rodriguez says, so it was the small crucifix that he wore on his heart), and dipped it into the sea, leaning over the boat's side. It chanced that it slipped from his hand into the sea, which accident so greatly afflicted Xavier that he gave great signs of grief. On the morrow they reached Baranura, in which is the town of Tamalo (Tamilan), to which the crew were bound; so the vessel was drawn to the shore and Xavier got out, and with one companion (Rodriguez himself) walked along the shore towards Tamalo. And when they had walked half a mile, and were now many miles away from where the crucifix had been lost, 'behold a sea crab runs out of the sea on to the shore with the aforesaid crucifix, holding it in his claws on either side, upright and lifted up, and so ran to Xavier and stopped in his sight. And Xavier flung himself on his knees, and the crab waited until he had taken the crucifix from its claws, and then ran back again into the sea whence it had come. And Xavier kissed and embraced the crucifix, and crossing his arms on his breast, lay prostrate on the ground in prayer for half an hour, and his companion, who was by his side, did the same, thanking the Lord Jesus Christ for so strange a miracle.'

Francis preached to the natives of Baranura, and after a week went on to another island (or city) which goes by the name of Rosalao, where his labours were entirely unfruitful, except in the conversion of a single convert, who afterwards became a soldier, and died from a wound received in battle with the name of Jesus in his mouth, as Francis Xavier had promised him should be the case.[16] In another little island called Ulate, also close to Amboyna, a great success awaited him, to compensate for the disappointment at Rosalao, which last place he had left solemnly shaking the dust off his shoes against it. Some enemies, it seems Mussulmans, were besieging the chief town, and the 'king,' or chief, was thinking of surrendering on account of the want of water. Francis passed through the besieging force, and promised him plenty of water if he would

[16] The Processes say that a number of Portuguese and natives gathered round to see him die, as the prophecy was well known.

allow him to raise a cross in honour of God. This was done in the presence of a great crowd, and then Francis knelt down and prayed, 'and there was a great rain.' The people were baptized, and the enemy went off in despair.

Francis Xavier now passed on to Ternate, which he calls 'Molucum' in his letter to the Society at Rome. Here he spent the three months of the summer of 1546, arriving there, we may suppose, early in June. Religion was in a bad state at Ternate. It had suffered much from the tyranny and bad example of the Portuguese, who allowed themselves every kind of license. The Soldan or King of Ternate was a bigoted Mussulman, who had reason to resent the harsh treatment he had met with from the Portuguese Commandant, Giordano de Freytas, who had sent him in chains some time before to Goa, on a mere suspicion of disloyalty. Joam de Castro found him at Goa when he himself entered on his governorship, and one of his first acts was to send him back with all honour to Ternate, condemning Freytas to pay all the costs and damage of his imprisonment, and appointing a new Commandant, Bernardino de Sousa y Tavora, instead of Freytas, who was called to Goa to give an account of himself. These acts of high justice were not uncommon in the Portuguese governors. Another King of the Moluccas, Tabarigio,—who is also described as King in Ternate, and seems to have been the elder brother of the other—had been in the same way sent to Goa a year or two before, and had been acquitted with all justice, but he had died a Christian at Goa before he could be restored, and he had left the Portuguese crown heir to his rights. The King of whom we are speaking —called Aeyro in the history—as St. Francis tells us, did not become a Christian, but he was friendly to the apostolical missionary, and like Herod 'heard him gladly,' though his own passions kept him in a bondage from which he was unable to free himself. That Francis should have acquired so much influence over him as he did is one of the strongest proofs which could be given of the wonderful power of his holiness, and the ineffable sweetness and simplicity in which it was clothed.

We shall find that Francis Xavier's efforts at conversion were not so fruitless in the case of another royal personage in Ternate; but it is right to speak first of the influence which he exercised over the Portuguese and those who were already Christians. We find in all the lives of apostolic men a reflection of the various shades of success and failure in different places which are to be observed in the preaching of our Lord and of the Apostles. Meliapor had responded to the teaching of Francis better than Malacca, Ulate better than Rosalao. Ternate was a place where he had very great success. He went to work, as was his wont, with penance and prayer, constant preaching, hearing confessions, catechizing, setting the children to sing the Christian doctrine, waking up the streets at night with calls to prayer for the souls in Purgatory and for men in mortal sin, and the like. He soon changed the face of the whole Christian population: scandals were removed, the sacraments frequented, feuds given up; the Confraternities of Mercy and of the Blessed Sacrament got rich with the number of offerings added to their funds by persons who had made unjust gains and were not able to make restitution to those whom they had defrauded. They had been very poor before, and now they were better furnished with money for charitable and pious purposes than any other such confraternities in the Indies. Gentile converts flowed in in numbers as the Christians became more worthy of the name which they bore, and a flourishing community of neophytes was formed, who were destined, not many years after this time, to show their constancy under great persecutions.

The converts seem to have been made both from Mahometanism and heathenism. There was one lord or chief of a village in the island who took the name of Francis, and was promised by the Saint that he should never abandon the faith. He stood firm, amid many strong temptations, when the time of persecution came. The most distinguished, however, of the converts was an ex-queen, Neachile, a daughter of the King of Tidor, and wife of a former King of Ternate. She was kept in close confinement by Aeyro, and she had suffered very much in her family through the Portuguese, who had brought ruin upon as many as three of her sons, who had been successively heirs to the throne. She was a clever acute woman, hating Christians, and thought to be very learned in the Mahometan doctrine. Francis Xavier visited her, and found her ready with a number of argumentative difficulties, which it took him some time to remove. In the end she was baptized, taking the name of Isabella, and finished her days in practices of piety and penance, a great example of patience, humility, and resignation.

The conversions at Ternate were probably helped on by some exercise of the preternatural power which ordinarily accompanied the labours of Francis Xavier; but we find but little mention of particular miracles. He had sailed from Amboyna in company with another vessel on board of which was a certain Joam Galvan, and this vessel had been separated from that in which Francis was by a storm. . Nothing was heard of Galvan, but his friends had not given him up when Francis, preaching in the church, suddenly recommended his soul to the prayers of the people. It turned out that the ship was lost, and Galvan drowned. But the standing miracle which seems to have broken down all opposition in Ternate was the heavenly character and charming sanctity of Francis himself, and we find evidence, both in his own direct statements and in the facts of the history, of the singular devoted affection with which he was commonly regarded. One part of this evidence lies in the earnest resistance made by his friends at Ternate, as well as at Amboyna, to his design of passing over to the 'Isles of the Moor' of which we are now to speak.

It seems as if St. Francis Xavier made it a rule to himself, to leave unvisited no neglected communities of native Christians within reach of which he came. He was always ready to labour for the revival of faith and manners among Europeans settled in the islands across which he came; and, again, he was ready and anxious, whenever opportunity presented itself, to preach to the heathen who had not yet received the word of God. But the congregations of natives who had been made Christians, especially those who had fallen back into ignorance from want of priests or other such causes, may be said to have exercised an irresistible attraction over his fervent heart. We have seen how devotedly he laboured for the Paravas on the Comorin Coast, and we shall have to see hereafter how strong a hold they retained upon his affections. They had been the firstfruits of his apostolical zeal; and whenever he heard of any nations in a position analogous to theirs, he seems to have deemed that it would be an abandonment of duty on his own part if he did not visit them and revive among them the religion which was dying out from no fault of theirs.

Early among the people of the Moluccas, the inhabitants of the Isles of the Moor,[17] in large numbers, had received Chris-

[17] It has already been hinted that there is considerable difficulty in identifying the 'Isle or Isles of the Moor,' though they are frequently mentioned in all the histories which relate to the affairs of the Moluccas. Lucena tells us that the name included several islands, and he mentions one called Batechina del Moro, which can be no other than Batchian. He also speaks of Morotoria, which may very well be Morty Island, to the north of Gilolo. The difficulty is in the distance from Molucco, or Ternate, which Francis puts in his letter (p. 386) at sixty leagues. Otherwise, we should say that Gilolo, or Almaheira, as it is properly called, was the chief island of the Moor, and that Morty and perhaps Batchian was also included in the general designation. The distance would suit the northern part of Celebes, where we find the name of Tolo, a place frequently said in the histories to be in the 'Isles of the Moor.' The probable solution of the difficulty seems to be this. St. Francis Xavier wrote his first account of the Isle or Isles of the Moor when he was at Amboyna in 1546, and could only know about them what he was told. The name 'Maurica,' 'of the Moor,' is clearly a name by which a large tract of sea or land would be designated, rather than one particular island. Then the navigators of those days had no very accurate ideas of distance. The Moluccas, as we have seen, were supposed to be further east than they actually are. There are also frequent instances of peninsulas and high portions of land being set down as separate islands; and, moreover, the whole of the Archipelago, including therein the Philippines as well as Japan, was but just emerging into the clear atmosphere of European knowledge. The most accurate account which exists of the Moluccas is to be found in the Dutch writer, Valentyn, who had been a 'minister' in Amboyna, Banda, and other islands. It is contained in his *Oud en Nieuw Oost-Indien* (Dordrechdt and Amsterdam, 1724), 5 vols. He gives a map of the Moluccas (vol. ii. part ii. p. 2), which seems to explain our difficulty. In this Gilolo is called Halmaheira, and the northeastern peninsula of the island is called Kust van Moro. Off it lies Morotay, or Morty, quite as far from Ternate as Ternate from Amboyna. But St. Francis says that the distance between the two last is 'sixty leagues.' Otherwise, Mr. Wallace's description of North Celebes (*Malay Archipelago*, i. c. 17) reminds us in many points of what St. Francis says of the natives of 'the Moor.'

tianity. One of their kings had become a convert; but the tyranny of the Portuguese, which seems to have been exercised more recklessly in those distant islands than in India itself, alienated the minds of the natives, brought about the general combination against the foreigners, of which mention has already been made, and Simon Vaz, one of the priests of the 'Isles of the Moor,' was murdered by those among whom he was labouring, his companion, Francis Alvarez, escaping covered with wounds. This happened in 1535, more than ten years before the arrival of Francis Xavier at Ternate. Since that time no priest had visited the islanders, and though there had been some apostacies—brought about, probably, by the influence of the native chiefs—the majority of the Christians remained such in name, though, from ignorance, in little more.

If Gilolo be the Isle of the Moor, or if it were supposed to consist of more than one island, so as to form with Morty and a number of small islets the group called by that general name, it must have been frequently gazed upon by Francis Xavier from the town of Ternate. But he would not need to have his eyes continually upon an island of which he had heard much, and the case of whose people was already stirring his heart to some generous enterprize in their favour. He has told us in both the letters last quoted, of the strong efforts made by his Portuguese friends to dissuade him from venturing on so inhospitable a soil, how he was threatened with certain death from the violence or treachery of the natives; and he has also intimated how his own nature shrank with fear from the certain danger which he seemed to be incurring. His language about the obscurity which comes over the meaning of the famous text about losing and finding life gives us a glimpse into his interior life, like that which is afforded afterwards by the words in which he speaks of the immense and ineffable consolations with which his soul was overwhelmed after he had made the venturesome passage, for which his friends,—like those of St. Paul when Agabus predicted his sufferings at Jerusalem, as Lucena says,—used so many efforts to frighten him.[18] We can hardly imagine that a heart so very quick, tender, and sympathetic as that of Francis Xavier can have been cold, phlegmatic, unimpressionable, when great danger was presented to it. On the contrary, there appear to be frequent indications in his letter that, without being less brave than the ordinary crowd of good and upright men, he was by no means indifferent to the risks of life and death, and that his calm heroic courage came rather from grace than from nature. These considerations make his own account of the discussion more interesting than ever. We see a supernatural instinct, also, in his refusal to arm himself with antidotes against the poisons which were so much in use among the people to whom he was going: it was the same instinct which made David decline the armour of Saul. He would trust to God, but to nothing else. It is said that the Commandant of Ternate forbade any one to furnish him with a boat to cross to the dreaded island: but this difficulty seems to have been overcome by the firmness of Francis himself.

When the ship in which he sailed to the dangerous island drew near the shore, it was seen that the people were ready to receive him with every mark of reverence and affection. The fame of the holy Father had reached even to those poor barbarians, and after a time he soon made himself as dear to them as to the other populations among which he had preached. He followed his usual method, baptizing the children, catechizing, preaching, teaching the boys and girls songs of the Christian doctrine, visiting the sick, and the like. Once he is said to have been in danger as he was preaching to a band of savages by the side of a deep river, and they took offence at the freedom with which he upbraided their predominant vices, and began to cast stones at him. He thrust a huge beam or trunk of a tree that was lying by into the water and leapt upon

[18] Lucena gives a long account of the attempt, and devotes a whole chapter to the reasons which Francis alleged in reply. It is quite in keeping with what was usual to the writers of his day, who seem sometimes to have put in speeches and arguments like ancient authors, where in modern times we should put a pictorial illustration.

it: an invisible hand guided him in safety to the other bank. Conversions became very numerous. The large city Tolo, of twenty-four thousand inhabitants, is said to have been entirely Christian when he left the island, and the number of small towns and hamlets where churches had been founded was very great. The island was volcanic, and subject to frequent earthquakes, and we have seen how Francis took occasion to instruct the natives concerning hell from the phenomena to which they were so accustomed.

No words can express better than those of Francis himself the wonderful consolations with which his soul was visited at this time. Nowhere had he had greater interior joy, and the gift of tears was so excessive in its sweetness and abundance that he might have lost his eyesight by perpetual weeping. He spent three months in this island or islands, which we may suppose to have been the September, October, and November of 1546. The whole sea in that part is as it were sown with islands. At the end of the seventeenth century the 'King' of Ternate claimed more than eighty as under his rule. We may well imagine that Francis visited many of these islands, though we have no record of his presence in them. In the Isles of the Moor, we are told, he left the Christians as well provided as he could with the teaching and repeating of the Christian doctrine organized, but, as it would seem, with no priest among them. He had already, however, determined that a house of the Society must be founded in the Moluccas, and was about to send some of his religious brethren at once to take up the work which he had begun. When the three months of which he speaks were over, he returned to Ternate, where he was received with immense joy, and remained till the end of Lent in the following year. He has given us his own account of his ordinary occupations during this time, of his attempt to get away by night to avoid the pain of parting with so many who had become tenderly attached to him, and of the arrangements which he made for the continuance of the exercises and services to which he had accustomed them.

We must most probably place at this time a remarkable

incident, which is mentioned on the sworn testimony of a number of witnesses in the Processes, and was selected as specially worthy of notice by the Roman theologians who drew up the *Relatio*, to which reference has already been made. The city of Tolo, it seems, soon after its conversion to Christianity, was assailed by the Mussulman 'King' of Gilolo, who, partly by persuasion and influence, partly by force, induced the inhabitants to throw off the kind of allegiance which bound them to the Portuguese, as well as their newly acquired religion. Some who stood firm were put to death, but the majority yielded: the churches and crosses were pulled down, and the Christian religion publicly insulted in every way. The news came to Ternate, the seat of the Portuguese Governor, while Francis was there, and he at once urged Bernardino de Sousa to revenge the insult offered alike to religion and to his sovereign. The *Relatio* speaks of endeavours first made by Francis to bring the people to their senses by persuasion and prayer, and he may perhaps have still been in the island at the time, or may have gone over on purpose. An expedition was organized, consisting of only twenty Portuguese and about four hundred Ternatese. Francis promised them success, and went with them. The town is described as placed on a height, in a position extremely strong by nature, which had also been carefully fortified. Iron spikes had been placed in the only path by which access was practicable. Francis knelt down and prayed, and then the mountain close by began to send forth smoke, cinders, and stones, which it had not been known to do before that time; an earthquake accompanied the eruption, which cast down a part of the fortifications, as well as many houses. The inhabitants fled to the woods, and soon came to supplicate Francis for pardon, and were forgiven and reconciled on duly doing penance and rebuilding the church, which had been destroyed. In later years we find the Christians of these islands very bravely suffering persecution, many becoming martyrs for the faith.[19]

[19] This incident of the 'victory' of Tolo, as it is called in some historians, i perfectly well authenticated by sworn testimony, collected in the Processes,

Francis remained at Ternate during the Lent of 1547, practising severe austerities, as well as all his usual works of charity and zeal for souls. Ternate, as we have said, was one of his places of success and consolation, and he parted from its people with the greatest regret at Easter. He seems to have sailed to Amboyna, but we may well suppose that he stopped here and there on the way. Soon after Easter, however, he was there, to find four Portuguese ships full of mariners and

---

and is mentioned in the Bull of the Canonization of St. Francis, as well as in the *Relatio* of the theologians. But it is placed at a different time from this by Bartoli, and Massei who always follows Bartoli. Bartoli puts it in 1552, the year of the death of Francis Xavier, at a time when it is indisputable that Francis was on his last voyage—that to the coast of China. In order to make this date agree with the history, he is obliged to suppose that Francis appeared miraculously at Ternate, where the expedition was fitted out, and that his presence during the whole time was either visionary, or owing to what is called 'bilocation.' There are certainly many instances of 'bilocation' in the lives of the Saints, and there is at least one well authenticated occasion in that of Francis Xavier, when he seemed to be with a party of sailors in a small boat, who had lost sight of the ship to which they belonged, and were lost for three days, while it is certain that he never left the ship. But in the present case there seems no need for any such hypothesis as that suggested by Bartoli and Massei, as the incident can very well have taken place at the time when Francis was in the Moluccas. There was certainly an attack on Tolo by the Portuguese forces in 1552 (though Tolo is not named in the annalists), and it was under the command of Bernardino de Sousa, who was also Governor of Ternate at the time of St. Francis' preaching in the island of 'the Moor.' Faria y Sousa gives an account of the expedition and of its success, which says nothing about an eruption or an earthquake, and in which the city is said to have surrendered after a siege, for want of water. The numbers of the expedition are also altogether different. The whole army consisted of 5000 men, of whom 180 were Portuguese. Bartoli was probably led into error by the name of Bernardino de Sousa; and this officer, we are expressly told, returned to Ternate in 1552 after a short interval, during which there was another governor. Lucena and Turselline place the incident at the present point of the life of Francis Xavier. The *Relatio* and the Bull of Canonization say nothing precisely as to its date, but the language of the *Relatio* is in favour of that which we have adopted. There is no mention either there or in the Bull of any bilocation, or of any visionary appearance. The account in Faria y Sousa of the later siege of Tolo is plain and straightforward enough. He is a writer who looks on everything from a 'secular' point of view, but he would certainly have mentioned the presence of Francis Xavier, if he had heard of it, as he is fond of introducing him when he can, as we shall see in the next chapter. His book, though tiresome in its dryness and curtness, is founded on a very large number of excellent authorities. The passage to which we refer in this note is to be found in *Asia Portuguesa*, t. ii. p. 2, c. 9.

soldiers, whose spiritual needs had to be attended to, and he had also to visit the Christian communities in the island.

He was at Malacca in July, and as the direct voyage between Malacca and Amboyna would take about six weeks, he would have been able to visit a few islands on his way westward, and it is perhaps at this time that we must place his short stay at Macazar itself, the conversions at which had been the original occasion of his leaving India for the further East. It is a characteristic of the lives of the Saints, that they so often seem to themselves to be called in a certain direction for a particular work, which, as it turns out, they are not to do, while another, which they had no thought of, takes its place. The fruits of Francis Xavier's expedition to the Moluccas were very great in themselves, and they led him on to further enterprizes for the glory of God. He had now laid the foundations in these islands on which others could build, and the history of Christianity in that part of the world, where the new Christians were soon put to the test by persecution, shows how solid those foundations were. He now hastened westwards, that he might look after the affairs of the Society in India itself, send missionaries to the Moluccas, and prepare the way for the establishment of a house of the Society, to be the centre of evangelical work in that teeming world of souls made after the image of God. There is evidence in the Processes that he visited Macazar at some time, and that he there baptized many converts, among whom were a king and his son. The Bull of Canonization mentions also several nations to whom he preached, among them the people of Java and Mindanao. The first mentioned island lay, like Macazar itself, on the direct route between Malacca and Amboyna. Mindanao is the most southern of the larger Philippines, and Francis may have gone in that direction while he was at Ternate. The number of places which claim his presence, and where there is good evidence that he preached and converted unbelievers, is altogether so great, that nothing short of the most marvellous activity on his part could have enabled him even to accomplish the distance from spot to spot within the intervals of time which are set down in his own letters.

CHAPTER III.

Four more Months in Malacca.

FRANCIS XAVIER arrived at Malacca, on his return from the Moluccas to India, in the middle of July 1547. He had been absent a year and a half, and could have had but very scanty intercourse with the Christian world which he had left behind him during that space of time. He was overjoyed on arriving at Malacca to find there three members of the Society—the first recruits whom he had seen face to face since he left Europe more than six years before. They were men entirely unknown to him, Joam Beira, the former canon of Coruña, whom we have already mentioned, Nuñez Ribeiro, a Portuguese priest, of whose antecedents we are told nothing, and a student, Nicolo Nuñez, not yet a priest. Francis had ordered Father Mancias to accompany Father Beira, but his former companion, with whose name and character we have become familiar, felt his courage fail him, and he preferred to remain where he was, among the Christians of the Comorin Coast. This disobedience cost him his dismissal from the Society by Francis Xavier. He seems to have remained in India, and probably laboured on as a secular priest.[1]

The three whom Francis found waiting for him at Malacca brought also good news concerning further supplies of Christian labourers from Europe: seven more of the Society, four of whom were priests, had arrived in the autumn of 1546 at Goa, and were already distributed along the Fishery Coast and in Travancore. There was news also from Europe, a bundle of letters we cannot doubt, which gave Francis intense pleasure after his long exile from the comparative nearness to home of

[1] He was one of the witnesses whose depositions are collected in the Processes, and died very piously at Cochin in 1565. (Léon Pagès.)

India and Cape Comorin. To make up for the silence of more than a whole year, he had probably two collections of letters to read about this time; for the Fathers would have brought the correspondence of 1546, and it is probable that that of 1547 reached him before he left Malacca. There was a great deal for him to hear about the progress of the Society, especially in Spain and Portugal. He would be told of Jerome Nadal's tardy but yet complete victory over the obstacles which had so long hindered him from entering religion, and of many other things which would have rejoiced his heart. Laynez and Salmeron had distinguished themselves equally for learning and for religious modesty at the revived Council of Trent. St. Ignatius had healed a difference between John King of Portugal and the Pope, and Le Jay, by the exertions of the same prudent father of the Society, had escaped a bishopric, which Ferdinand the King of the Romans had determined to force upon him. The Duke of Gandia, afterwards St. Francis Borgia, had procured from the Holy Father a solemn approbation of the book of the *Spiritual Exercises*, and had secretly promised to enter the Society himself as soon as he could rid himself of the multitude of secular business which his great position in the world forced upon his attention. But the piece of news which must have touched most tenderly the heart of Francis was that Peter Favre was dead. He had been sent to Spain for a certain time, and when the time was over—though he had already had a fever at Barcelona before embarking—he hastened to Rome. He had been asked for by John III. to go as Nuncio to Ethiopia, where there were some hopes, as has already been said, of bringing the Emperor back to Catholicity, and at the same time the Pope had asked that a third theologian of the Society might be sent to the Council of Trent, and St. Ignatius had intended that Favre should go. But Rome is often fatal, even to men of robust health, if they enter it in the dogdays. It was near the end of July when Favre arrived, and Orlandini tells us that Ignatius held a consultation of some fathers as to the prudence of allowing him to enter, and that he was overruled by them to permit this, against his own better judgment. The joy of being once more with Ignatius revived Favre for a time, but he soon fell ill, and died after a week, on the feast of St. Peter's Chair, the 1st of August 1546, just ten years before St. Ignatius, who died on the last of July 1556.[2]

For a full month Francis Xavier enjoyed the companionship of his new brethren, and gave them the fullest possible instructions as to the state of things in the islands to which they were to proceed, and the method to be followed in dealing with the inhabitants. Beira and Ribeiro were both excellent devoted men, and laboured with great fruit, the first in the Moluccas (properly so called), the other in Amboyna, where, about two years after the time of which we are speaking (August 1549), he died of poison administered to him by the natives. The missionaries sailed for their destined fields of work in the August of 1547. Francis remained, waiting for a ship to take him to Goa, and in the mean time practising his usual austere penances and carrying on the work of the Apostolate at Malacca. Malacca had soon to thank him for exertions of another kind. When we consider the distance between the Portuguese stations in the East, especially beyond the Ganges, when Malacca, Amboyna, Ternate, and perhaps one or two other places were their only strongholds—a distance to be reckoned by the difficulties of the navigation and the infrequency of communication between the several ports—it becomes rather a matter of surprize that they should have maintained their ground so constantly and with so much superiority over the hostile powers by which they were surrounded, than that they should have been often attacked, and sometimes brought to the verge of serious danger. The Mussulmans throughout the East were brave and warlike, and the native princes were rich and had abundant resources of men and materials. Even in India itself the Portuguese were often on the defensive, and had to exert their utmost force to maintain their position. The year before this, 1546, had witnessed the conclusion of the siege of Diu, which at one time had been in

[2] *Vita, P. Fabri*, t. i. cap. 22.

the greatest danger, and had at last been relieved by the Governor himself, who gained a brilliant victory over a numerous Mussulman army on St. Martin's Day, November 11th. But the garrison had at one time been almost overpowered, and the account of their brave resistance reads almost like a fable. The siege lasted more than nine months.[3]

It need not surprize us, therefore, to find that Malacca was in considerable danger at the time of this second stay of Francis

[3] See Faria y Sousa, *Asia Portuguesa*, t. ii. p. 2, cap. 1, 2, 3. At one time the fort was so badly off for provisions, that 'a crow taken upon the dead bodies was a dainty for the sick, and sold for five crowns.' At the same time the ammunition was almost spent. Another time, says the annalist, 'thirteen thousand of the enemy attacked the breach which they had made; only five soldiers resisted them, till Mascareñas (the Commandant) came with fifteen more.' At one time, when the garrison was reduced to two hundred men, Don Alvaro de Castro, the Governor's son, arrived with a reinforcement of four hundred more: but this accession of strength made them imprudent enough to attack a numerous army of besiegers in the open field, and they were driven back with the loss of sixty men, Don Alvaro himself being mortally wounded. In the final battle, which took place, as we have said, after the arrival of the Governor himself with reinforcements which raised the Portuguese army to between two and three thousand men, we are told 'the Portuguese were almost as good as lost, when Father Antonio del Casal, the Franciscan "Guardian," appeared running before them with a crucifix on the point of a lance raised on high, exhorting them all with religious words. They rallied themselves, and with a rapid charge *y catolico furor* covered the field with heads and arms, and legs and trunks, and dead. Rumecan' (the Mussulman Commander) 'fled, but returning to the fight with wonderful courage, forced the Portuguese to retire in very dangerous disorder. The Governor suppressed it less by words than by exposing himself to danger in such a manner as to displease his captains, old and young. At this time a stone broke an arm of the crucifix which the Custode held up on high. This was the turning point of the day, for the priest began to exhort the soldiers so powerfully, and the arm of the crucifix hanging from the nail, swinging about 'as if making signs to them to avenge the sacrilege,' inspired them with so much courage, that they attacked the enemy with irresistible violence, and drove them 'into the city' (the part of Diu outside the fort). It is curious to find the name of Cosmo de Payva among the officers who distinguished themselves on this occasion—he died fighting very bravely. Rumecan rallied again, and appeared on the field at the head of eight thousand men, but he was utterly defeated and slain. 'The enemy confessed,' adds Faria y Sousa, 'that while one of the battles of the siege lasted, they saw over the church of the place a beautiful Lady, clothed in white, who with her great brightness blinded them, and that in this day's battle they saw men whom they did not know in the field with lances, who did them the greatest harm.' This siege of Diu is a good specimen of the exploits which occur frequently in the *Asia Portuguesa*.

Xavier. At the extreme western tip of the Island of Sumatra there is still a petty state called Acheen or Atchen, the Soldan of which seems to have been a more important potentate in the time of which we are speaking than in our own. He was, and indeed is, master of a considerable territory in Sumatra; and his name frequently occurs in the annals of Portuguese India as that of a great enemy to everything Portuguese and Christian. 'In Malacca there was war with the implacable Acheen,' says Faria y Sousa (*Asia Portuguesa*, t. ii. p. 2, cap. 4). He sent an expedition of sixty ships and five thousand men against Malacca in the dead of night. The General was a 'valorous and daring Moor,' called the King of Pedir. Some were to land and surprize the fortifications, others were to set fire to the shipping in the harbour. It was the night of October 18. The men who were to surprize the castle came back again with some geese which they had captured, to show their King that they had at least landed; but these noisy birds aroused the city, says the chronicler, and he goes on to mention the geese which saved the Capitol, and to remark that no incident in the history of other nations is wanting in that of the Portuguese. But the harbour attack did not fail: all the ships except a few were burnt, the mariners being so much astonished and taken by surprize, that they stood looking on without as much as attempting to save them. The 'barbarians' sailed away in triumph, 'as though they had gotten a notable victory,' says Turselline, and happening to intercept a few fishermen, they cut off their noses, ears, and heels, and 'sent them to the Governor of Malacca with a letter written in their own blood, wherein most proudly and insolently they provoked him to battle. When the fishermen had given this letter to the Governor, he caused it to be publicly read before the soldiers, who were no less moved at the insolent brutishness of their enemies than at the miserable spectacle of their friends, who were thus mangled and disfigured by their wounds, and every one had his heart full of pity and indignation.'

Faria y Sousa tells us that there was a disposition on the part of the 'Capitan,' Simon de Melo, to make a joke of the challenge, which it was by no means convenient to accept. There was a very small force in the city, and—as he hints, by the neglect of those in authority—it would not have been easy to arm an expedition. The ships, moreover, had been nearly all burnt. 'Pitiable joke, indeed!' he says. 'But there was at Malacca then the great modern Apostle of Asia, St. Francis Xavier, who was not less zealous for the honour of our King than for the worship of our God, and he very earnestly disapproved the jest to the Capitan and the others, and urged them in some way or other to wipe out the injury.' They excused themselves, as there were but eight ships left, and these had been beached as rotten and unfit for service.

But Francis would not be put off. He was keenly sensible that, poor as was the support which the Portuguese gave to the cause of religion in many respects, still that cause was much bound up in the East with the prestige and power of Portugal. He had perhaps some of the old Spanish feeling about the Mussulmans—the feeling that made St. Ignatius, in the early days of his conversion, hesitate whether he ought not to have run a Moor through who vilified the blessed Mother of God. At all events he set to work. 'So much did that holy wrath of the great Xavier bring about,' says Faria y Sousa, 'that he prevailed, with his zealous discourses, upon some rich merchants so as to get these rotten vessels put into such a state that the soldiers and sailors might safely embark in them.' After all, there were only 180 Portuguese to go on board. Francis exhorted them, heard their confessions and gave them holy communion before they set out, and promised them a certain victory. He would have gone with them himself, but the people would not allow it. The armament set out to look for the enemy, who had waited out of sight; but disaster came at once, as the Commander's ship sank almost in the port itself. Francis revived the drooping courage of the soldiers and people by promising that they should have a reinforcement of two ships before night. The people were looking out from the heights all the afternoon, and it was already getting late when two sails were seen in the offing. They were the ships of a famous merchant of those days, one Diego Soarez de Melo, called the Gallego or Galician, and he intended to sail by Malacca, without stopping, from the Moluccas, in order not to pay the harbour duties. Francis had made his acquaintance on his own voyage to India, as Diego had fallen in with Martin Alfonso de Sousa between Mozambique and Goa, and been pardoned by him, says the annalist, because 'he pretended he could say much against Don Stephen,' that is, Don Estevan de Gama, the outgoing Governor whom Sousa was to succeed. The Gallego was then under sentence of death for some crime, and had taken to piracy. Francis went out to sea in a boat to intercept him, and persuaded him to join his galleys to the slender fleet which was to vindicate the honour of the Christian name against the infidels, and which he had christened the 'armament of Jesus.' The Gallego had with him sixty men, and his son Baltasar, a good officer.

The fleet sailed, under the command of Don Francisco Deça, a relation of Simon de Melo, and for several weeks nothing was heard of it at Malacca. A rumour was spread during this interval that the Portuguese had met with the enemy, and had been defeated and put to the sword. The people began to lose heart. The Capitan did not venture to show himself in public, as he was considered responsible for the loss of so many men, the husbands or sons or fathers of those who were left behind. Francis went on quietly at his usual occupations, only, on two occasions in each week on which he preached to the people in general, he always exhorted them, at the end of the sermon, to pray for the success of the expedition and the safety of those engaged in it. People began to murmur that the prayers had better be said for the souls of the departed than for the safety of the living. Some took to superstitious incantations to find out what had been the issue of the conflict, and these Francis sternly rebuked. Time went on, however, till the second Sunday in Advent (Dec. 4), and Francis preached to the people as usual at the principal mass. 'Being, therefore,' says Turselline, 'to conclude his sermon, upon the sudden he turned both himself and his speech unto the Crucifix, and by Divine instinct, and with great motion of body, breaking forth into a prophecy, he began by strange ejaculations to describe in words the first encounter of the two navies, to the admiration and astonishment of his auditors. Then, with an inflamed look and countenance and abundance of tears gushing out at his eyes, he cried out aloud, "O Jesu, God of my heart! I humbly beseech Thee by the last torments of Thy life that Thou wouldst not leave them whom Thou hast redeemed with Thy precious Blood!" Having uttered these and other such like words, which fear and confidence then suggested unto him, and growing weak and faint with the violent agitation of his body, he leaned awhile with his head upon the pulpit. Then, by and bye, as if he had awaked out of some ecstasy, lifting up his head he cries out on a sudden, with a cheerful and joyful countenance, "O ye Malacensians! cast off all sadness and rejoice, for now at last our fleet hath overthrown the enemy in battle without any bloodshed on our part, having lost but three men only; so little hath so noble a victory cost us! And in a most triumphant manner will they presently return home laden with spoils and pillage of the enemy, together with many ships which they have taken from them, and forthwith (he appointed a certain day) will they be safe with us. Come on, therefore, and in thanksgiving to God, the author of the victory, let us say together once *Pater* and *Ave* for the same, and repeat it again for those few of ours that be slain in the battle."' The same afternoon he preached to the wives of the Portuguese in another church, and told them the day on which tidings would arrive of the safety and victory of their husbands.

It was found afterwards that the decisive moment of the conflict had agreed exactly in time with the sort of ecstasy which had come over Francis in the pulpit on that Sunday. The enemy's fleet had sailed off about two hundred miles along the coast of the Chersonese on which Malacca lies, and had posted itself at a point on what was then and still is the coast of Siam, not far from Quedah, where they hoped to intercept a Portuguese fleet of merchantmen from Bengal and Pegu, every Christian on board which they meant to put to the sword. It was for this very country of Pegu that Diego the Gallego was bound when he thought to pass Malacca, and he would have run into the enemy's mouth if he had pursued his course. They had ravaged the country in the neighbourhood of Parles, a city not very far from the coast, and the King had taken to flight. The fleet lay in a sheet of water formed by a river of the same name with the city, which flowed thence in a large rapid stream into the sea.

The Portuguese fleet had instructions from Simon de Melo not to venture further along the coast than an island called Pulo Cambilam, which was either what is now called Pulo Penang, or somewhere near it, and which was the limit of the territory of Malacca. It is not very far from Quedah, and we must suppose the Acheenese fleet to have lain somewhat beyond that place. At all events the Portuguese could hear or see nothing of their enemies, and were turning reluctantly towards Malacca again, when a violent wind came on, blowing in their teeth with such force that they were obliged to cast anchor, and remained windbound for more than three weeks. This was considered a great marvel, as it was in the middle of the season of the southwestern monsoon, which would have taken them easily back to Malacca.[4] The delay caused by the adverse wind nearly exhausted the provisions of the armament, and as they could make no headway against the wind, they were obliged to turn their backs once more on Malacca and sail for a friendly port (Junçalao or Tenessari, says Lucena) on the Siamese coast to revictual. They did not get as far, and near Parles itself fell in with some fishermen who told them where their enemies lay. The Commander dressed himself as for a feast, had the ships' standards hoisted, ordered the men to regale themselves, and fired a general salute with his artillery, which was heard by the Acheenese, who at once prepared to descend the river to fight the Portuguese. Deça exhorted his men, reminding them that they were fighting for the cause of God, and that Francis Xavier had promised them a secure and full victory.

[4] See Lucena, lib. v. c. 13.

Between nine and ten on that Sunday morning the Acheenese fleet came down the river. The stream was full and rapid, and Deça had skilfully drawn up his little fleet—there were but eight ships—under the lee of a tongue of land which ran out into the stream, and made a small bay in which the water was comparatively still. This disposition, together with the utter want of judgment in the arrangements of the Acheenese commander, gave the Portuguese an easy and decisive victory, which may as well be related in the words of Turselline, with whom Lucena mainly agrees.

'In the mean time, the enemy's navy being set in battle array, came down the river with the stream, and the banks and shores on both sides sounded forth with horrible shoutings and confused noise of drums. The first squadron was led by the admiral of the barbarians' fleet, guarded on each side by four Turkish galleys. Then followed six other galleys, with nine ranks of ships' [he means ten rows of six ships each], 'and all abundantly appointed, not only with great ordnance, but also with plenty of small shot. The admiral, therefore, of the Portuguese, as soon as the first rank of the enemy was discovered, maketh towards them presently at unawares with three ships, commanding the rest to follow as they were ordered for the battle. Whereupon the barbarians, whether for want of skill or rather by God's ordinance, sailing on headlong with fury, discharged all their great shot against the Portuguese before they could so much as reach them, so as the bullets fell all into the water without doing any harm. But a Portuguese gunner, shooting a very great bullet out of the greatest ordnance, struck the admiral of the Acheenese so flat, that presently he sunk and drowned her, which was not only a presage of a future victory, but rather the conclusion of the combat itself. For the Turkish galleys, staying their course, left off the fight and began to help the captain and other principal men swimming to save themselves, which caused both their own and the fleet's whole overthrow. For the Turks had placed their galleys over thwart the river, and so had taken up a good part of the same, to receive in those that could swim unto them, not once thinking of the danger themselves were in, God had so besotted them. The six other galleys which followed the first squadron, coming down with the stream, ran upon the former which lay athwart, and all the rest of the nine ranks which came after fell against those which went before, and became so entangled one with another, and so dashed together, each one striving to get free from his fellow by force, that one would have thought there had been a battle among themselves. The Portuguese, perceiving manifestly that God's hand was in the business, failed not to follow the victory which was thus offered them from heaven. Wherefore presently calling out aloud upon the sovereign name of Jesus, they began to grapple with their enemies, and on every side to play upon them with their ordnance, lying there so entangled and burdened one by another that they were not able to stir. Thrice did they send out with all the violence they could the shot of all their great ordnance upon their ships, and no one shot was made in vain; nor was the enemy able to resist or make any use of their own artillery, being so thrust up together, and this without any loss to the Portuguese that assailed them. Now within a little while they had sunk nine of the enemy's ships and battered more to pieces, with no small slaughter of the barbarians.'[5]

In short, the barbarians were absolutely routed, and most of them threw away their arms, and tried to save themselves by swimming—a large number, however, being drowned in the rapid stream. All the ships were taken except those which were sunk, three hundred pieces of artillery, and an immense booty in armour, and other articles. A great number of the chief officers in the Acheenese fleet were killed, and the whole number of slain amounted to four thousand. Twenty-five ships were taken to Malacca by the victors, and the rest were set on fire. Two or three days after the battle, a messenger arrived at the city with the news of the victory, as Francis had foretold, and he was soon followed by the triumphant fleet.[6]

[5] Turselline, l. iii. c. 10, 11.

[6] There is some difficulty about the day of the victory. It seems certainly to have been on a Sunday, as Francis was preaching—probably Sunday Dec. 4.

The news had even been anticipated by intelligence from a certain King of Bintang—an island opposite Singapore—who had been hovering near Malacca with a large fleet, in expectation of the issue of the war. He had some claim, as it seems, to Malacca itself, and was nominally a friend to the Portuguese, though ready to declare against them whenever it suited his own interests. However, he heard of the destruction of the Acheenese fleet in time to retire in all haste with his fleet before he had given any sign of sinister intentions on Malacca. A day or two after, as we have said, the victors themselves appeared in triumph. 'Infinite, therefore,' says Turselline, 'was the joy which on a sudden surprized the Malacensians, when, so far beyond all expectation, they saw eight ships bring home twenty-five captives. As soon therefore as this victorious navy was arrived, the whole city (their great fear being now turned into excessive joy) went out to see and congratulate the same. And Francis himself, to whom a great part of that noble victory and triumph was due, goeth amongst the first, and, as soon as the general was landed, he embraceth him and the other principal captains of the navy, congratulating them for their fortunate success.'[7] And Lucena tells us how Francis bore in his hands a crucifix, and was followed reverently by the 'Capitan' and the chief men of the city, while salutes were fired in its honour on land and sea; and how he reminded the victors that their true general had been He in Whose honour they had fought, and Who had given them strength and valour to gain their victory.[8]

We may now resume the letter which was interrupted in the last chapter, written after the return of Francis to India, whither he sailed a few weeks after the victory over the Acheenese. It gives, as we shall see, the first account of a great scheme for the glory of God and the good of souls, which was now taking its place in his thoughts and prayers.

Faria y Sousa says it was on a Sunday, which was also a festival—that of St. Nicolas. But St. Nicolas' Day (Dec. 6) that year was on a Tuesday. It may have been that the first news of the victory was received on the Tuesday.

[7] Turselline, *Ib.*

[8] Lucena, *Vida*, l. v. c. 19.

(LV.) *To the Society at Rome.*

[CONTINUED.]

At Malacca, a Portuguese merchant, a man of great devotion and faith, told me a great many things about some very large islands which have lately been discovered. The country is called Japan. He told me that much more progress may be made there than in India in the propagation of the religion of Jesus Christ, because the whole nation in Japan surpasses others in its desire for knowledge. A certain Japanese came to me with this merchant. His name is Anger, and he had made up his mind to come and talk to me, from what he had heard from the people at Malacca. In Japan he had consulted some Portuguese merchants, his friends, and had laid open to them the wounds of his conscience, asking them for some remedy to heal his soul and appease God. These merchants had advised him to come to me at Malacca. He did as he was told, and embarked in their ship. But when he arrived at Malacca I was in the Moluccas. When he heard this, he set out for home with a sorrowful mind. He was already in sight of Japan when a storm came on suddenly, and an adverse wind drove the vessel after great danger back again to Malacca. He there heard of my return, and came to me most anxiously desiring to learn the Christian religion. He has some knowledge of Portuguese, so we conversed together without an interpreter.

If the rest of the Japanese have the same ardour for gaining knowledge that Anger has, then they surpass in genius all nations anywhere found. He was present at the explanation of the Catechism, and with the greatest accuracy wrote down in a book the articles of the Creed. Often, too, in the church, with all the people present, he repeated from memory the lessons he had learned, and asked many questions full of intelligence. In truth, he has a great thirst for knowledge—a thing which avails very much for a quick perception of truth. A week after his arrival at Malacca, he set out for India. I wished to get him to take the vessel in which I was to sail;

but, from his great familiarity with other Portuguese merchants, who were going to India, he did not like to leave such great friends, to whom he owed so much. I expect him at Cochin within ten days.

I asked this Anger, whom I have mentioned, whether he thought, in case I accompanied him to Japan, the inhabitants would become Christians. He replied, that his countrymen would not give assent instantly to everything they heard, but that they would be sure to ask a great number of questions as to the religion I was introducing; and that, above all, they would consider whether my actions agreed with my words. If I could do those two things—satisfy them by a consistent statement as to the questions they would ask, and give them no cause for finding fault with the goodness of my life—then, when the matter had been fully examined and taken cognizance of, the King, the whole nobility, and all the other grown up men would certainly join the flock of Christ—for theirs is a nation which follows the guidance of reason.

My friend the Portuguese merchant, who has been a long time in Japan, left me some very carefully drawn up papers, containing a description of the country, and the manners of the inhabitants, and other things—partly what he had himself seen, partly what he had learnt from good authority. I send you these notes herein inclosed. All the Portuguese merchants who come back from Japan assure me, that if I make this voyage, I shall spend my labour much better than in India, inasmuch as I shall have to do with a nation that is governed by reason. My mind seems to forebode, that in less than two years I or some one else of the Society shall go to Japan, though the voyage is very dangerous, both on account of the incredible storminess of those seas and the depredations of Chinese pirates—so that many vessels are lost from both of these causes.

So do you, my dearest fathers and brothers, pray to God for our safety in this voyage, in which many have perished. Meantime Anger will learn Portuguese thoroughly; he will become well acquainted with the resources of the Portuguese, the arts of Europe, and our manner of life; he will prepare himself duly for baptism, and will work for me in translating into Japanese the Catechism and a detailed explanation of the history of Christ, since he writes Japanese very well.

I have been in India a week today, and have not yet been able to see our brothers; so I can say nothing of the fruits that have been gathered in these countries during my absence. But I suppose that our brothers will themselves have written you an account of their affairs. In returning from Malacca to India I went through some great dangers: for three days and three nights the vessel was at the mercy of a tempest such as I never remember to have seen before. Many on board were already bewailing their certain death, and made vows that if, by the help of God, they escaped this peril, they would never again go upon the sea. The merchants were obliged to ransom their lives by the casting overboard all their goods. In the height of the storm I made supplication to God, calling in as intercessors on earth, in the first place, the men of our Society and its friends, then all Christians; hoping that by the Church, the Spouse of Jesus Christ, whose continual prayers even while she dwells on earth are heard in heaven, we should be most diligently commended to the Heavenly King. Then I implored the aid in order of all that are in heaven, and I especially invoked Peter Favre and all our brothers there, so as to use both living and dead intercessors to soften the anger of God. Lastly, I called upon all the choirs of Angels and all the different classes of the Saints one by one; and to obtain more easily the pardon of my numberless sins, I put myself under the patronage of the most Holy Mother of God, the Queen of heaven, who always obtains from her Son without trouble whatever she asks. Lastly, on putting all my hope in the infinite merits of Jesus Christ our Lord and Saviour, I enjoyed, surrounded as I was by so many and so powerful protectors, far greater pleasure while in danger in that horrible tempest than afterwards when I was delivered from the urgent peril. I am filled with confusion, that I, the most wicked of all mortals, should in that last moment of danger have shed so great a flood of tears out of heavenly joy. So then I prayed humbly to Jesus

Christ our Lord not to deliver me from this peril unless He reserved me for equal or even greater dangers by and bye for His service and glory. It has often happened that God has made known to me by an interior instinct how many bodily dangers and occasions of spiritual loss have been prevented by the prayers and holy sacrifices of my brothers, partly those who are still militant on earth, partly those already enjoying the rewards of heaven. My object in writing this, my dearest fathers and brothers in Jesus Christ, is that for so many and so great benefits which I have received, you should yourselves repay my debt, both to God and to yourselves, as I am quite unequal to repaying it.

When I once begin to speak or write of our Society, I know not how to stop; but the haste of the ships to depart obliges me against my will to leave off and close my letter. I cannot finish better than by making that old declaration: 'If ever I forget thee, O Society of Jesus, may my right hand be given to oblivion!'[9] so clearly have I seen how much I owe to all my brethren, and on how many accounts I am their debtor. God has been led by your prayers to grant me this very great boon, that according to my poor capacity I should understand how much I owe to our Society. In me there is no power or strength of mind which would make me at all able to take in the idea of such an accumulation of obligations; but, that I might in some measure escape the reproach of ingratitude, God in His goodness and mercy has imparted to me some amount, small though it be, of knowledge on this score. But let me make an end. I pray Jesus our Lord, that as He has brought us together in this miserable life by calling us all into His own Society, so He may hereafter bring us together in that eternal blessedness of His by calling us all into the society of those who reign in heaven—especially since in this life for the sake of Him we are so far scattered in body one from another.

If you ever send us any commands at any time, either while we are in the Moluccas or if we are to go to Japan, you must

[9] *Si oblitus unquam fuero tui Societas Jesu, oblivioni detur dextera mea.* (Orig.)

remember that no answer can reach you before three years and nine months are over. The reason is quite plain. Your letters arrive in India in the course of the ninth month after they are sent; then there is an interval of eight months more, that the ships may have favourable winds to proceed to Malacca; and in the going thither and returning thence, let them have the fairest possible voyage, twenty one months are spent. Then after all it takes eight months more for the letters to reach Rome, and that when the navigation is favoured by good winds and fair weather. Sometimes, on account of the unfavourable weather, more than a year is spent in the passage to Rome.

Cochin, January 21st, 1548.

The story of Anger (Han-Sir), the Japanese convert, is not quite fully told in the letter before us. In the heat of passion he had committed homicide in his own country, where human life neither was nor is of much account should passion or interest be concerned to sacrifice it. He was pursued either by the officers of justice, or, as what is known of Japanese manners makes us think probable, by the relatives of the man whom he had slain, and had taken refuge in a monastery of bonzes, expecting to find there not only protection from the avengers of blood, but also peace for his remorseful conscience. He found safety for a time, but was not secure against punishment; and his own conscience gave him no rest. His acquaintance with some Portuguese merchants led him to open his heart to one of them, Alfonso Vaz, who offered him all the help in his power, and suggested that he should secretly depart from Japan in one of the Portuguese ships. In India he would find persons who would assist him to set his soul in order and regain his peace of conscience. Vaz was not about to sail immediately himself, so he gave Anger a letter to another merchant, whose ship was to start sooner than his own. This was a certain Ferdinand Alvarez, but the Japanese took the letter by mistake to another Alvarez, George by name, who received Anger with great kindness, dissembled the mistake, and carried him off to Malacca, talking to him a great deal on the voyage about Francis Xavier, who was his great friend. Anger became extremely desirous to see Francis, whom he already looked upon as a man sent from heaven to heal the wounds of his soul; but when he arrived at Malacca, Francis had not returned from the Moluccas, and after waiting for some time, the Japanese gave up his intention of applying to him, and started on his voyage homewards. He was within sight of Japan when a tempest drove his ship back, and he was forced to land on the coast of China, and when he sailed again from China towards Japan, another storm forced him to put back into the port whence he started. Here he met again with Alfonso Vaz, who persuaded him to return to Malacca, and on his landing there, the first person he fell in with was his old friend Alvarez, who took him at once to Francis, who had arrived in the mean time from Amboyna. The rest of the history of Anger will be related in a future page.

It was now nearly time for Francis to sail for India. Before doing this, he had to part with the companion whom he had picked up at Meliapor, and who had remained faithfully with him during his adventures in the Eastern Archipelago. Joam d'Eyro had shown some instability of character, as we have seen, at the time of his conversion from a worldly life, and we may imagine that he would have given Francis trouble now and then during the time spent in the Moluccas. He was affiliated in some sort to the Society, as Francis speaks of him as his own companion and as vowed to the practice of evangelical poverty: but at the time when Francis left Europe there were not as yet any lay brothers, or temporal coadjutors, in the Society, nor do we know that that very important class of members formed a part of the original design of Ignatius. They were added, as well as the class of priests called 'spiritual coadjutors,' about the very time that Francis became acquainted with Joam d'Eyro, that is, in 1546. But though Joam d'Eyro may not have been, strictly speaking, a 'lay brother,' Francis considered him bound to the observance of poverty, especially in all that concerned the temporal assistance which he received from friends of Francis himself, and which he administered for the maintenance of both. Joam seems to have been desirous of rather more comfort than Francis thought good to allow, and he received money for the purpose 'more freely than discreetly,' says Turselline, 'under the colour of alms,' without telling his master, and Francis was much displeased, and 'he presently banished him for a time into an island near by, lying right against the harbour of Malacca, which had in former times been well stored with inhabitants, but was now left desolate. D'Eyro therefore, living there, saw upon a time in a certain church (whether awake or asleep is uncertain), the Mother of God sitting at the high altar upon a cushion, under a canopy richly adorned; with her he saw the child Jesus, Who endeavoured to allure D'Eyro, being much ashamed of his fault, by sweet means to come unto His mother. She at first, as though she had been angry, turned from him and put him away; then, after he had humbly entreated and beseeched her to pardon him, she at last received him, and admonishing him of certain faults, she left him suddenly, and, together with her child Jesus, mounted up to heaven. This vision was altogether secret, no mortal man knowing thereof but D'Eyro himself, nor had he spoken thereof to any. Being, therefore, after a while called back to Malacca, and making his confession to Xavier as his custom was, he said nothing of the vision. But Francis, knowing it by Divine revelation, asked him what that was which happened to him lately in a church of the island where he was? "To me?" quoth he; "I remember nothing." The father gently urged him to tell, but D'Eyro refused and utterly denied to have seen anything; and being in this manner often times asked . . he still answered to the same purpose. Then Francis, when he saw that he had to do with one of so obstinate a nature, began himself to recount everything in particular, as if he had been present.'[10] Joam d'Eyro was astounded, and became very penitent. Francis forgave him, and sent him to Goa in charge of some children whom he had brought from the Moluccas to be educated at the College: but it seems that Joam was not

[10] Turselline, l. ii. cap. 7.

to be his companion any longer. He afterwards became a Franciscan friar, and lived and died holily; and Lucena tells us that he had entered the order at the advice of his former master. The ship in which he sailed with the boys was in great danger during a storm near Ceylon, which Francis had foretold; and when all hope seemed to be lost, Joam d'Eyro comforted the crew and passengers by telling them how Francis had predicted their danger, but had also promised that they should escape it. The prophecy came true.

Francis himself embarked in another vessel, belonging to Garçia de Sousa, and which was bound for Cochin instead of Goa. He had determined to visit the Christians on the Comorin coast before proceeding further northward. This ship also had a terrible tempest to brave, and we have some account of it in the latter portion of the two letters last inserted in the text. A few details which he has omitted are preserved by others. He has said nothing about his own exertions in hearing the confessions of the passengers and in exhorting all to perfect resignation to the holy will of God. After he had done what he could in this way, he retired to a corner and became rapt in prayer. Francis Pereira went to seek some comfort from his conversation, but found him immovable before his crucifix, and was sufficiently consoled by the mere sight of him. At last, when the three days and nights were nearly spent, he arose, took a sounding rope from the steersman, and flung a portion of his robe into the sea with it, calling on God, the Father, the Son, and the Holy Ghost, to have pity on the crew and on himself. Then, as those who were present declared, there was suddenly a great calm. The writers of his life suppose that his meaning in dropping the portion of his robe into the sea was to plead before God that he was a member of the Society, of which he speaks so tenderly and lovingly at the end of the letter.[11] In a few days after the storm he landed safely at Cochin.

[11] See Massei, l. ii. c. 13.

THE LIFE AND LETTERS OF ST. FRANCIS XAVIER

THE LIFE AND LETTERS OF ST. FRANCIS XAVIER

HENRY JAMES COLERIDGE
(OF THE SOCIETY OF JESUS)

SECOND EDITION

IN TWO VOLUMES
VOL II

GYAN

Published by

GYAN

Gyan Publishing House
5, Ansari Road
Daryaganj, New Delhi-110002
Phone: 011-47034999, 9811692060
E-mail: books@gyanbooks.com

Distribution Network
gyanbooks.com
India, USA, Canada, UK, Australia, France

ISBN : 978-81-212-3709-3 (Set)
ISBN : 978-81-212-4998-0 (PB)
First Published, 1874

2nd Impression 2020

Printed at: Gyan Press, Delhi.

The Life and Letters of St. Francis Xavier
Author: Henry James Coleridge

THE LIFE AND LETTERS OF ST. FRANCIS XAVIER

BY

HENRY JAMES COLERIDGE

OF THE SOCIETY OF JESUS.

VOLUME THE SECOND.

LONDON:

BURNS AND OATES, PORTMAN STREET,

AND PATERNOSTER ROW.

1872.

To the Reader.

THIS Second Volume has been delayed by causes beyond my control, the effect of which I trust that the reader will forgive. Though it is considerably larger than its predecessor, I have been obliged to omit many documents illustrative of the text which would have made the work more complete. But it seemed better, if possible, to comprise the whole matter within two volumes—even though the second should exceed the size originally contemplated in this Series—than to extend the book to three. I could wish to have found room for several of the letters of the friends and companions of St. Francis, especially of Father Gaspar Baertz. Some quotations from them will be found at the end of M. Léon Pagès' French translation of the Letters. I regret also in particular having been forced to leave out the long letter referred to at pp. 305 and 386 from Joam Fernandez, which is full of interest in relation to the questions of the Japanese bonzes. I must content myself with publicly thanking the kind friends who took the pains to translate it for me from the Portuguese.

One cause for delay in the completion of the present volume arose from a circumstance which it may be worth while to make public. I was informed in the course of the autumn that a collection of manuscript letters of St. Francis Xavier was in existence in Portugal, many if not all of which had never been published. The same kind friends to whom I have already alluded were able to make inquiries as to this collection for me, and the result was to enable me to feel certain that the letters had been brought from the archives of the College of the Society at Goa in the last century, at the time of the suppression, but that they had all been already examined and translated by Father Phillippucci. There may doubtless still be existing letters of St. Francis which have never been printed, and he himself mentions several which have certainly been lost. The King of Portugal must have received many such. But I can see no ground for hoping that any considerable number will ever be recovered.

H. J. C.

London, Eve of St. Thomas the Apostle, 1872.

CONTENTS.

BOOK IV.

FROM THE RETURN OF FRANCIS TO INDIA TO HIS SAILING FOR JAPAN.

1548-1549.

CHAPTER I.

Francis revisiting the Paravas.

CHAPTER II.

Francis and Don Joam de Castro.

CHAPTER III.

Francis Xavier and his Religious Brethren.

CHAPTER IV.

Arrangement of the Missions in India.

CHAPTER V.

Francis starting for Japan.

[1] A duplicate of this letter was sent to the Society at Rome, with slight variations, which are indicated in the footnotes.

NOTES TO BOOK IV.

BOOK V.

FROM THE SAILING OF FRANCIS TO JAPAN TO HIS LAST RETURN TO INDIA.

1549-1552.

CHAPTER I.

Voyage to Japan and stay at Cagoxima.

CHAPTER II.

Firando, Amanguchi, and Meaco.

CHAPTER III.

The King of Boungo.

CHAPTER IV.

Voyage from Japan to India.

NOTES TO BOOK V.

BOOK VI.

From the last Return of Francis to India to his Death at San Chan.

1556.

CHAPTER I.

Last stay of Francis at Cochin and Goa.

CHAPTER II.

Francis and Don Alvaro d'Ataide.

CHAPTER III.

San Chan.

[1] A duplicate of this letter, dated July 22, is epitomized in a footnote, p. 539.

BOOK IV.

FROM THE RETURN OF FRANCIS TO INDIA TO HIS SAILING FOR JAPAN.

1548-1549.

CHAPTER I.

Francis revisiting the Paravas.

FRANCIS XAVIER landed at Cochin on the 13th of January 1548. It happened that the good old Bishop of Goa was on the spot, being engaged in a visitation of some of the widely separated towns in his immense diocese, and it must have been a wonderful consolation for both of them thus to meet unexpectedly after so long an interval. It was perhaps in consequence of the presence of the Bishop at Cochin that Francis wrote, almost immediately on his arrival, to the King of Portugal the letter which will presently be inserted. His last letter to the King had been written just three years before, and it was full, as we have seen, of most earnest exhortations as to the absolute necessity of the most rigorous measures to insure the propagation of Christianity in India and the protection of the converts. It would seem from the tone of the present letter that there were grave reasons for fearing, either that the King's will was not sufficiently determined, or that his mind was not sufficiently enlightened as to his duties in this respect. King John, indeed, may well be supposed not to have understood, and perhaps no one not on the spot could understand, the immense difficulties in the way of the progress of religion which were raised by the avarice and tyranny of the Portuguese, and the connivance and apathy of the governors. In fact, a glance at the annals of Portuguese India, which show us how one warlike enterprise after another occupied the attention and the energies of the viceroys and governors, is enough to make it at least intelligible that the minds of the highest officials of the Crown in India were too much turned in this direction to leave them time to watch minutely over the interests of the native converts or those who might become converts, who would thus be left to the tender mercies of subordinate commandants like Cosmo de Payva, who would prove themselves very serviceable officers in time of danger, and would thus be regarded with much favour at headquarters.

King John had not been deaf to the entreaties and exhortations of Francis, nor to the representations of the good Vicar Miguel Vaz, who, as we have seen, had undertaken the long voyage to Portugal with the purpose of pleading in person the cause of religion at the court. Miguel Vaz probably crossed in his voyage to Europe the path of Don Joam de Castro, the Governor of India, sent out in 1545 to supply the place of Martin Alfonso de Sousa. A long letter is extant from the King to Don Joam, written in March 1546, which may safely be considered as embodying the effects of the joint pleadings of Francis Xavier and Miguel Vaz upon the sovereign and his council. Many of the recommendations made by Francis were attended to. 'Governor, my friend,' the letter begins, 'the essential duty of Christian sovereigns, which is to watch over the interests of religion, and make their whole power serve to the maintenance of the faith, obliges me to communicate to you a profound grief which I have of late felt.' The King then states some of the causes of this grief. He has been told that idols are still publicly worshipped in many parts of his dominions, even in Goa itself, and in those places where the true faith ought to be most flourishing. He commands that the idols be sought for and broken in pieces wherever they may be found, and that most rigorous punishments be proclaimed against those who make or decorate them, who celebrate heathen games in their honour, or who protect and conceal the Brahmins, their ministers. Moreover, that the heathen may be attracted to conversion, not only by conviction of the truth and hope of eternal reward, but also by some temporal favours, the new Christians are for the future to enjoy all the liberties and immunities before enjoyed by Pagans. The King had been told that the natives are pressed into the service of his fleet. The Christians are henceforth to be freed from this obligation, except in the case of urgent necessity, and then they are to receive a fair indemnity for their labour. The abuse by which the Portuguese were in the habit of seizing and buying slaves very cheap, and then selling them at a large profit to Mussulman merchants and other heathens, is to be stopped by the Governor's diligence. An ancient law of the city of Goa allowed exorbitant usury; this is to be abrogated. A church, begun under the invocation of St. Joseph at Bazain, is to be finished and endowed. The preachers and missionaries to the heathen are to be supported by an annual grant of 3000 pardams, levied on the mosques in the Portuguese dominions. The new converts made by Miguel Vaz at Chaul are to have 300 large measures of rice every year, to be distributed by the Bishop. Some exactions practised on the Christians of St. Thomas by the Portuguese merchants at Cochin are to cease. The Rajah of Cochin is to leave off certain superstitious rites which he had been used to insist on in the sale of pepper, which were scandalous to the new Christians; and as to his persecution of the natives who have embraced the faith, the King of Portugal writes to him personally, but the Governor is also to insist on his abandonment of all such persecution. The people of Socotra are to be succoured against the Turkish cruisers, and Miguel Vaz is to be consulted as to the measures which are to be taken. The natives on the Fishery Coast are to be protected against those Portuguese officers who have been in the habit of imposing intolerable exactions upon them, which made them in fact fish for the pearls for their masters' profit and not their own; and if the Governor thinks that the coast can be sufficiently protected and the revenue received without the presence of any Portuguese vessels, these are to be recalled, and forbidden to frequent the coast in future, that the natives may be left to themselves in peace. Francis Xavier is especially to be consulted on these points, and also as to the policy of leaving the new converts altogether without any labour imposed on them as a matter of obligation to the Crown. As new converts from Paganism are frequently illtreated, and even despoiled of their goods by the heathen, Miguel Vaz is to be consulted as to the measures to be taken to grant them support and aid from the royal treasury, which assistance is to be distributed to them by the hands of their pastors. The fugitive prince from Ceylon is to be kindly received and supported at the royal expense, and his rights to the succession of the crown are to be carefully examined. But the Governor is not to wait for this to exact satisfaction from the Rajah of Jafanapatam for his detestable cruelty to his newly converted subjects, 'that all the sovereigns of India may know,' says the King, 'how dear justice is to us, and how much we have it at heart to protect all the oppressed.' Heathen artisans are not to be allowed to make images or pictures of Jesus Christ and the Saints. Churches are to be finished at Cochin, Coulan, and Calapour, and to be built at Naram and Coram, without regard to expense. Schools and places of meeting are to be built, whither heathens as well as Christians may come to hear sermons and be present at sacred functions. All idols are to be destroyed throughout Salsette and Bardez, and the minds of the heathen are to be prepared for this step. The letter, which is dated March 8, 1546, from Almeirim, concludes with some general recommendations as to the exemplary life of the missionaries, and the protection which is to be afforded to their neophytes.[1]

So much is necessarily left in this letter to the discretion of the Governor, that it may be doubted whether it would have been quite satisfactory to Miguel Vaz, who probably accompanied it on its journey to India, if he was not actually its official bearer. Joam de Castro was a fine specimen of the class of gallant Portuguese soldiers, who distinguished themselves in India and elsewhere in those, the heroic, days of the history of that now degenerate kingdom; but his government of the Indies was characterized rather by warlike exploits than by any great deeds for the advancement of the faith. He was thought to be guided more by secular policy than by considerations of the interests of religion. Francis Xavier must have learnt from the Bishop, when he met him at Cochin, that, as

[1] Léon Pagès, t. ii. p. 458.

to the affairs of Ceylon and the Fishery Coast in particular, those who looked more singly to the cause of Christianity were not at all satisfied with the proceedings of the Governor. But there was a piece of bad news which the Bishop would give Francis, which must have afflicted him still more deeply. Miguel Vaz had lately died, as it was said, with suspicion of poison, at Chaul, the very place mentioned in the King's letter to the Governor as the scene of his apostolical labours.[2] It appears that evil reports had been spread about, by which this good Bishop, whose right hand he had so long been, was blamed as having had some share in his death! We shall see that Francis Xavier thought enough of the mischief which such reports might occasion to contradict them formally and of his own knowledge to the King, whose ears they were sure to reach, all the more as it was evident that this zealous Bishop was not regarded with a friendly eye by some of the Portuguese officials, to whose tyranny and exactions he probably opposed himself. But the death of Miguel Vaz must have been a very severe blow, and the feeling of its severity may in part account for the very strong and urgent language in which Francis now writes to the King, just a week after his arrival in India, in order, no doubt, that it might reach Goa in time to be sent to Portugal by the ships which sailed that year. This letter, however, was the fruit of his own experience and reflections, as well as the report of the Bishop, and its language and recommendations must be considered as referring not only to India properly so called, but also to the settlements under the Portuguese Crown in the farther East, where Francis may probably have met with that jealousy and punctiliousness among officials, of which he complains as a serious hindrance to the advance of religion.

The letter, which was probably begun at Malacca, is as follows:

[2] Faria y Sousa, *Asia Portuguesa* (t. ii. p. 2, cap. 6) seems to hint that, though the blame was laid on some heathen converts lately received, the true culprits were Portuguese. 'Este murió de ponçona dada por Christianos nuevos [*Portugueses poderosos en Goa*] porque con poderes de Inquisidor tratava incorruptamente de la punicion de sus judaismos.'

(LVI.) *To John III. King of Portugal.*

Sire,

I believe and trust that your Highness will receive minute and distinct information as to what concerns religion and the worship and service of our Lord God in these parts of Malacca and the Moluccas, from the letters which I send to the Society in Europe. I have also sent with them answers to the letters which we have here received from you, Sire, whom we hold and acknowledge as the chief and the true protector of the whole of the Society of Jesus, and one who, by his love and benefits towards us, most amply fulfils the duties implied in such a title. As to the state of religion and the Christian people in India, the pious and religious men who are going from these parts to you, with the purpose of advancing the service of God, will most fully inform your Highness concerning them. Moreover, Father Joam de Villa Condé, a faithful minister of God, who has had much experience of what is going on in the island of Ceylon, is writing to your Highness concerning them certain things which it is of importance that he should tell you, and that you should know, for the relief both of your Highness's conscience and of his own. These matters he discusses at full length, clearly and with the utmost truthfulness, partly in his letter addressed to your Highness, partly in documents and remarks which he sends with that letter. He has communicated all to me. Your Highness would therefore do a thing worthy of that wisdom which you show in other matters, if you make a right use of information so trustworthy, and give as soon as possible any commands that it may seem necessary to issue in order to discharge your duty in this regard. Lastly, I believe also that my own brethren of the Society, as well as others, write regularly to your Highness, and give you particulars and minute information of the Christian communities at Cape Comorin, at Goa, and of the others in these countries of India which are in daily course of foundation and increase.

And now for what concerns myself in particular. I have

thought long and much, I have long deliberated in my own mind whether I should or should not write a letter to your Highness to set forth what, as I look round on all that goes on here, and give all my most attentive consideration, it seems to me ought to be done in order to spread our holy faith widely in these parts and establish the same firmly. I felt impelled on the one hand to make the attempt by my desire to serve God and promote His glory, and on the other hand I was deterred from being so bold by my want of hope that the effort would be worth the trouble, feeling no confidence that what I should propose would ever be carried into effect. And yet I seemed to myself not to have the power of keeping silence without neglecting my duty, since it was very evident that it was not without some counsel of God that I should have the grace of forming these conclusions so decidedly in my mind. Nor could I imagine any more probable reason why God should have been fain to let me see these things, except in order that I might communicate them to your Highness. And yet again I felt the fear lest, if I were to lay before you what gives me so much anxiety, this letter of mine might perchance accuse your Highness before God, and make more severe for you the terror and risk of that last judgment of His, by taking away from your Highness the excuse of ignorance.

I pray your Highness to believe how much pain all this has caused me. My own inmost conscience bore me witness that I looked or desired for nothing here but to wear myself out with work, and sacrifice my life itself in bringing about the salvation of souls in these regions of India, so to lessen as far as is in my power the weight of that duty which is incumbent on your Highness, and, by discharging a part of that obligation which has been committed to your charge, make the account of your Highness's conscience more easy, and give you greater security in that terrible hazard of the final judgment of God. And indeed your Highness's great love for our Society well deserves that I should wish to do this for your sake, and that I should think it well purchased at the cost of any exertion or trouble of my own. And to confess the truth, Sire, my mind has been wonderfully and very painfully torn and confused by these two heads of anxiety on such contrary grounds; fearing at one time lest I should fail in my own duty, fearing at another that I should increase your danger, I was drawn now to one and now to the other alternative. But at last I have come to make my decision in favour of one, and that one which bade me once for all do my duty and relieve my conscience by pouring out to your Highness the thoughts which I have so long kept back.

These, then, are the things which I have discovered from experience, long experience on the spot, in these regions of India, Malacca and the Moluccas, and which wound my soul and kill me with heart sickness. Let your Highness take for certain what I say, that in these parts, as elsewhere also, it is the general rule for many things to be omitted which it would be expedient for the service of God should be done, on account of certain rivalries which, though they are masked under an appearance of what deserves respect, are in truth vicious and hurtful. On account of these, the men who have the management of affairs out here are set against one another by secret and small causes of offence. One man says, 'This is my business, and I will not allow another to have the credit of it.' Another, on the other hand, says, 'I don't do this, and so I do not like you to do it.' Then comes another with a different complaint, 'I bear the burthen of the day and do the work, while the favour and the fruits of it go to others.' They get earnest and hot in their bickerings, and then each one works and writes for his own side, so as to gain his own advancement. Meanwhile time is wasted, occasions slip away, and the opportunity for promoting the honour of our Lord God is lost. And from just the same cause it often happens that occasions are neglected which would have brought much honour and great advantage to your Highness' interests in India.

I have been able to think of only one remedy for the evil, and if this remedy were applied, then, unless I am mistaken, many in these parts would become Christian, and those Christians who are now exposed to injustice because they have no favour with men in power, would become so dear and such objects of care to the magistrates, that no one, whether Portuguese or Indian, would dare to molest or plunder them. This remedy is, that your Highness signify, either by letters to the Governor and Commandants in India, or by word of mouth to those whom you send out hither to be at the head of affairs—signify to them, I say, clearly, and give them certainly to understand that, as to the increase of our holy faith, which is the thing which you desire above everything, you give that in charge to the Governor or the local commandant, rather than to the religious persons or to the priests who are in India; that you confide in the Governor or the Commandant before every one else; that from him you will exact an account of this matter; that to him you will impute the whole that is done in it, good or bad, and will repay it to him in reward or in punishment.

And that this declaration of your Highness might be the less liable to be explained away, I for my part should wish that in it you should particularly name every one of us who are working in these parts, and declare that it is not on any one of us, nor on all of us together, that you lay any part of the burthen and obligation which weighs upon your conscience, but upon him alone who by your authority has the power of Governor or Commandant in any place where there is any occasion of advancing the Christian religion; for that since God has bound your Highness by the strictest possible obligation of providing for the eternal salvation of the nations who are subject to you, that duty ought not to be delegated by your Highness to any but those who are the vicars of your own authority in these parts, and those who represent in the dignity of the magistracy the person of your Highness; and that if you shall find that by the negligence of any one of these persons it has come about that no great number have embraced the Christian faith under his government in the place confided to him, you will visit on his head the chastisement which may otherwise hang over your own on account of the neglect of so great an obligation, having beforehand given full and clear notice, that you have passed on the burthen of the whole of that most important duty, of taking care that the souls of the unbelievers who are subject to you be imbued with the Christian faith, to the shoulders of those who are your principal officers and ministers in these parts.

Therefore, Sire, whenever a Governor or Commandant writes to your Highness, let him state how the Christian religion goes on; how many, who, what sort of persons, have become believers from among the heathen; what hope or what means there may be of bringing others to the fold. Let him know that you will trust nothing but his own letters as to what is reported on these heads, and will not be content with any accounts from any other person whatever on these subjects. And if, in the province or place which any one has governed, our holy Church shall have been increased during the time of his command by but a small number of neophytes, while at the same time it is certain that great increase may be made at all times and everywhere, if only the Commandant desire it, then let your Highness seriously, and on your royal honour, declare in the diploma in which you institute such persons and confer authority upon them, that you will exact punishment from them for such neglect.

And I should very much wish your Highness to confirm this by oath, and openly pledge yourself, calling in solemn form upon the Holy Name of God, that any officer of yours through whose means it may have come to pass that the faith has not been propagated, shall, when he returns to Portugal, be fined of all his possessions, all his money and property be spent on works of mercy, and he himself be detained for many years in chains and severe imprisonment. And that they may be under no misunderstanding about it, nor flatter themselves that your threats will not be executed, I would have your Highness give them the clearest possible warning, both that most certainly and assuredly you will accept no excuses whatever that may be alleged on this matter, and that no way remains to them of avoiding severe punishment and of finding favour with your Highness, except that of making as many Christians as possible in the places and during the time of their command.

Why all this is necessary, Sire, I could prove by many arguments from experience, very well indeed known to me. But I am unable to dwell on these, that I may not be troublesome to your Highness, nor have to relate my own griefs, past and present, without any hope of making it worth the labour of doing so. I will only say this, that if the Governor or the Commandant, whoever he may be, were firmly convinced in his own mind that your Highness had said such things as I have been suggesting in perfect truth, and that your Highness would certainly act as you had declared and sworn that you would; then in a single year the whole island of Ceylon, many kings of the Malabar coast, and the whole of the peninsula of Comorin, length and breadth, would embrace the Christian religion. But as long as the Governor and Commandants of your places in India are not pressed by that fear of losing their rank and property unless they have made many Christians, do not let your Highness hope for any great success in the preaching of the Gospel in the Indies. And be quite sure that in that case there will neither be many who come to baptism, nor will those who have come advance much in religion; in short, that there is nothing that prevents every living soul in India from acknowledging our Lord as God, and of professing His holy doctrine, except the fact, that the Governors and Commandants who have neglected to take care of the matter have not been severely punished by your Highness.

And I say again that, as I hardly hope that it will ever be so, I am almost inclined to repent having written what I have, especially when I think that perhaps your Highness will receive a more inexorable judgment at the tribunal of God on account of the very fact that I have given you this warning. I know not whether at such a time the objection that your Highness may perhaps allege, that you are not bound to believe what I write, will be admitted; and I assure your Highness in the most perfect sincerity and entire truthfulness, that I would by no means have written what I have concerning the Governors or Commandants of these parts, if I had been able in any way to persuade myself that I could keep these things unsaid without sin.

I have not yet, Sire, fully made up my mind whether I shall go to Japan; but a great motive for my inclining to the plan of going to that country is added by this fact, that I am very much without hope that here in India I shall find that true and efficient support from the officials which is necessary in order to increase our holy faith and to preserve the Christians already made.

I entreat and conjure your Highness, by the love which you bear to our Lord God and the burning desire you have to do what is pleasing to Him, to grant to your faithful subjects here in India, and to me with them, this much of your wellknown royal favour, as to send hither next year a great many preachers of our Society; for I assure you, Sire, as a matter of the strictest truth, that your royal garrisons in India are in very great need of preachers, both on account of the Portuguese who dwell in the garrisons and of the newly-converted Christians who dwell in the towns and villages dependent on them. I speak from experience; and what I have seen and found myself makes me write this. When I was at Malacca and in the Moluccas I used to preach twice every Sunday or other holiday. I was obliged to do it, because I saw that both the soldiers and the people there were in need of being frequently fed with the word of God. So I used to give instruction from the pulpit at the morning mass to the Portuguese; in the afternoon I used to instruct their boys and girls, their slaves, and the free Christian natives, in discourses that each would understand, going through the explanation of the heads of Christian doctrine one by one. Then on a certain day in the week I used to preach a catechetical sermon on the Articles of the Creed and the Sacraments of Confession and Communion to a congregation consisting of the wives of the Portuguese, native, and half-bred. If this method of instruction were kept up vigorously everywhere and constantly, there would in a few years be a very great and profitable result from it to the service of God. At the same time, within the forts themselves, I used to preach the Christian doctrine daily to the children of both sexes of the Portuguese, as well as to their men and maid servants, and to the native Christians;

and this instruction produced as its fruit at once, that the idolatrous superstitions and magic incantations which used to be frequently practised among those ignorant converts were altogether abandoned.

I state all this minutely to your Highness, that your own wisdom may judge how great need we have of abundance of preachers in these parts, and what will follow naturally, that you may not forget to provide such an abundance as we want. For it is certain that if the great penury of such means of grace which is now felt is allowed to go on for the future, not only will those who have lately been converted to our holy faith not reverence it, but, as a general rule, not even the Portuguese themselves will be Christians farther than in name. I am very much afraid, Sire, that these desires of mine will not have their effect such as I wish them to have, and such as need requires; and knowing, as I do, the unhappy lot of India, I can hardly bring myself to any certain confidence that she will obtain the great good which I desire for her. It seems as if it were her natural lot, or rather, I should say, her congenital malady, not to be able to bear that any exactness in religion, or any excellence in the discharge of the duties of perfect virtue, should become a matter of common practice and flourish among the generality of her inhabitants.

On the 13th of January of the present year I arrived at Cochin from Malacca. There I found the Bishop, to see and converse with whom did me very great good, as I observed with what great charity he bears very severe bodily exertions, visiting one by one the garrison towns that he has in his diocese, and going also to see and labour among the Christians of St. Thomas. He certainly discharges his duties to the full as becomes that true and good pastor of souls which he shows himself to be by doing all this. For all these laudable works of his he gets exactly that reward from certain men in these parts which is the common recompense which the world is in the habit of meting out to the Saints. I was very much pleased, and indeed filled with a certain reverence, at seeing that holy man's patience under the trials to which he was exposed. I know well that a rumour is spread abroad in India against him by the children of the world—who, I believe, will even write to your Highness the evil suspicions which they entertain of him—which most unfoundedly asperses him on account of the death of Miguel Vaz. Now in this matter, Sire, I feel that I ought to bear this most true and sincere testimony in his favour; and I do so, that I may discharge a very serious duty. I affirm that I know for certain (though the way and manner in which I came to this knowledge cannot be told or written) I have it, I say, as a matter of entirely ascertained fact, that he can with no more justice be blamed for that matter than I myself, who was, at the time when it happened, in the Moluccas, and at an immense distance from this country.

I pray and beseech your Highness, by all the love you have for God, and all the desire you have to please Him, and to keep your own conscience pure from all contagion of stain, do nothing and order nothing in the matter which may give trouble to the good man I speak of; for if your Highness were to appear to give credit to this most calumnious falsehood, his detractors in India would gain authority and increase in confidence from your so doing.

Your Highness has appointed Pedro Gonsalvez, the Vicar General of Cochin, one of the dignitaries of your chapel royal, and has made his nephew one of the pages of honour in your palatial court. I count this as a favour done to myself; for the great obligations under which he has laid our Society force me to do this; so I assure your Highness that I and all of ours are particularly bound to you on this account. And this will less surprise your Highness, when I tell you that the house of the Bishop's Vicar at Cochin is the house of abode of the Society of Jesus. His goodness to us does not confine itself within the limits of any common hospitality or usual offices of friendship, but he goes so far in his liberality, that when he has spent upon our service whatever he has at hand, he borrows from others that he may spend on us still more. I beg your Highness, in the name of our whole Society, to order that the necessary letters may be sent from Portugal both to him and to his nephew, in order that their regular pensions may be paid them faithfully. Both uncle and nephew are well worthy of this favour; the Bishop's Vicar, because he watches for the eternal salvation of the faithful who are your Highness's subjects; and his nephew, because he is here serving as a soldier under your Highness's flag for his country and the commonwealth.

And now to end, I make this prayer: May our Lord God grant to your Highness to understand most thoroughly and intimately, and to put in execution also at once, all that at the moment of your death you would rejoice to have done.

Your Highness's useless servant,

Cochin, Jan. 20, 1548. FRANCIS.

We have two other letters of this same date, written to St. Ignatius and Simon Rodriguez respectively. The first shows the growing anxiety which Francis Xavier now felt about the government of the religious under his charge. Before his first departure for Malacca he had hardly begun to bear to any large extent the burthen of a religious Superior. Now, however, his subjects were multiplying on his hands; they were in most cases as yet unknown to him, their spheres of labour were widely scattered, and he himself could not linger long at any one place without abandoning the great schemes of farther apostolical conquests, which were now taking possession of his mind. Simon Rodriguez seems, perhaps of necessity, to have sent out labourers from Portugal, many of whom had not been long in the Society, and who were as yet hardly formed in the perfect spirit of the Institute. We shall now see with what exquisite charity and wisdom Francis devoted himself to this new work, which his position at the head of the Society in the East imposed upon him. His first impulse, we shall see, was to implore Ignatius to send out some one who might be a spiritual guide to himself as well as to his brethren. In other respects the contents of the two following letters require but little commentary.

(LVII.) *To the Reverend Father Ignatius of Loyola.*

May the grace and charity of our Lord God Jesus Christ always favour and help us! Amen.

God knows, my dearest Father, how greatly I long to see you in this life as well as in the next, that I may talk over with you a number of things which require help and remedy from you. No distance of place is an obstacle to obedience. I see that there are now many of our Society in these parts, and I see also that we are in great need of some good physician for our souls; and so, my best of Fathers, I pray and entreat you by our Lord Jesus, to look after us, your children here in India, as well as others, and send us some one of very great virtue and holiness, whose vigour and zeal may stir up my torpor and sluggishness. I am in great hopes, as you understand thoroughly, by God's assistance, the state and inclinations of our minds, that you will take diligent measures in order that the languor in virtue, which has crept over all of us here, may be strongly stirred up, and that we may be roused to the study of perfection.

This country wants from our Society nothing more urgently than preachers. Among those whom Master Simon has sent us there is not one, as far as I can hear, who is a preacher. Now the Portuguese out here in India, so strong is their friendship and goodwill towards us, desire in a wonderful degree to have some good preachers of our Society; so I conjure you, by God and His holy worship, to remember this just and pious request of theirs, and send hither some Fathers well fitted for that work, who may show the right path of salvation to those who have gone astray. Moreover, those of the Society whom you are going to send out for the work of carrying the Gospel as missionaries among the heathen population must be men of such approved goodness as to be able to go either with companions or without them wherever the interests of religion may call them, as, for instance, to the Moluccas, to China, to Japan. The mere description of China and Japan and of their inhabitants, which I enclose with this letter, will let you easily see what sort of men such work requires.

You would hardly believe how eagerly we are looking for the Indulgences from the Holy Father, the privilege for the high altar of the Church of our College, and the faculties for priests to administer the holy chrism instead of the Bishop; about all which I wrote to you in former years. As for the Lent, experience has taught me that there is no great need for any change to be made in that. The Portuguese inhabit places in India so very widely apart, that if the common good of all is to be considered, no change need be made. The winter season is by no means at the same time throughout all the Portuguese cities or towns; so that, considering what is good for all alike, it seems to me best that there should be no new law on the subject, although I see there are a good many who differ from me as to this.

I have not yet made up my mind whether, after a year and a half from this, I shall go myself to Japan, with one or two others of the Society, or whether I shall send two of ours there first. I have quite decided either to go or to send others, and as things are now, I incline to the plan of going myself. I pray God to give me a clear intimation of His will as to what is most pleasing to Him. I thought it best to choose one of the three of our Society who are gone to the Moluccas to be Superior of the rest, so I made choice of Joam Beira for the others to obey, as if he were yourself. They were very glad of it. I think of making the same arrangement as to the Comorin Promontory, and the other places where more than one of ours are placed. I beg that you by your own prayers and the prayers of those with whom you have influence may obtain the help of Heaven for us who are working in these barbarous regions; and that you may do this more earnestly, I pray the Eternal God to show you, by a light from Himself, how much need I am in of your help and guiding hand.

Cochin, Jan. 20, 1548.

(LVIII.) *To Master Simon Rodriguez.*

May the grace and charity of our Lord Jesus Christ always favour and help us! Amen.

I charge you, my dearest brother, for the love which you bear to Jesus Christ, to send us hither some preachers of the Society; men of that sort are most urgently wanted in India. Of all those whom you have hitherto sent I have seen none except Joam Beira, Father Ribero, and Niccolo Nunez the layman, who are in the Moluccas, and Adam Francis, who is here at Cochin. I have asked about the others, and people tell me that there is no one among them able to preach well. Another thing which I entreat you in the name of God is to be careful in choosing those whom you think of sending out hither to work for the conversion of the heathen. It is necessary that you choose men of proved goodness and tried virtue, men who for the space of some years have gained many and signal victories over themselves. They must also not be men of weak health, but strong; for the hard work in India requires not only the virtue of the soul but also the strength of the body. The King would gain great favour with God if he were to send to India as many preachers of our Society as possible, so ignorant and uninstructed is the whole race of the Indians. I write this to you on the strength of the experience I have now gained of all these parts.

However, if this affair of the propagation of the Christian religion among the heathen kingdoms seems to have its great difficulties, be careful not on that account to be frightened from carrying on the work which has been begun. In sooth, the first and greatest difficulty is in ourselves; so I consider that we should first take care of our own people, and then attend to the heathen. Now I beg you, do all you possibly can, for God's sake, that next year we may have some good preachers. I don't give you now any account of affairs in India, for it is only a week since I arrived from Malacca, and I have as yet not got much information about them. What I have found out is of a kind to make me sorry to know it. Our brethren, I believe, write at length to you about all their matters. Those of our Society whom you send out for the conversion of the heathen ought to be men who can be sent with safety either with companions or alone, wherever need may be, either to the Moluccas or to China, or to Japan, or to the kingdom of Pegu, or anywhere else. Among the people in any one of these places, even men who are not of great learning, provided they are endowed with remarkable virtue, will be able to do very good service for God.

If there is one thing which, for his very numerous and very great deserts at the hands of our Society, I should like to have the King of Portugal warned about, since it is his business beyond all to provide for the salvation first of his own people and those of the heathen who are in his dominions, I would desire that the King, both for the sake of the service of God and also to discharge a religious obligation of his own soul, should place in all the towns of India which are occupied by his garrisons good preachers, either of our Society or of the Franciscans or the Dominicans, who should be free and disengaged from other cares, to preach on the Gospel in the forenoon of the Sundays and festivals to the Portuguese, and in the afternoon should explain the Articles of the Faith to their servants and slave-girls as well as to the native converts, and should also once a week preach to the wives and children of the Portuguese on the Articles of the Creed and the Sacraments of Confession and Communion; for I have learnt by experience how great necessity there is out here for this kind of instruction.

If I thought that the King would not be averse to my most faithful and loving counsels, I would give him a most salutary bit of advice—for a quarter of an hour every day to meditate on that divine saying, 'What doth it profit a man if he gain the whole world but lose his own soul?' and to ask God to give him a thorough understanding of it, together with a strong interior feeling of its truth, and also to make that same sentence, 'What shall it profit a man if he gain the whole world,' and the rest, a kind of conclusion to all the prayers that he says. It is time now to tear away from the King the mistake under which he lies; for the hour is nearer than he thinks, when the King of kings and Ruler of rulers is to call him to Himself to give an account, with that terrible call—'Give an account of thy stewardship!' And so do you take care to bring about that he really sends out to India what is necessary for the propagation of the faith in that country.

From the experience which I have had, I can see only one way and one means for propagating religion in India—that the King should severely and by an edict declare to all the Governors of India that he trusts no one in India so much as those who with all their might strive to advance the limits of Christianity; that he orders and commands them to take in hand diligently to bring the island of Ceylon to the faith of Christ, and to increase the number of converts in the promontory of Comorin, and for this purpose to seek the succour of religious men everywhere, and to employ the priests of our Society and any others whom it may seem good to use for the increase of the worship of God. If the Governors should happen to show themselves negligent and inactive in this matter, let him strike terror into them, and declare by an oath (he will gain great favour with God by swearing this, and much more by fulfilling what he has sworn), that unless they free his soul from the religious obligation under which he lies, by propagating the Christian religion in India as much as possible, he will punish their want of zeal as soon as they return to Lisbon by the confiscation of their goods for public purposes and by long imprisonment. If the King issue such a decree to the Governors, and at the same time treat with severity those who do not attend to it, it is certain that a very large number will, by the help of God, become Christians; but that otherwise no great progress will be made.

You have now what I think on the matter. As to other things I will say nothing. I only say that if what I ask to be done be done, our wretched converts will be defended against injustice and plunder, and the other natives will without difficulty be brought into the fold of Christ. In the propagation of the faith of Christ among them, the work is really a mere mockery if the King's or Governor's authority is wanting to support us. Believe my word for it, for I have had more than enough experience in the matter. Why it is so I know well, but I need not say. I want to see two things in India; first, the Governors bound by the law I speak of, and second, good preachers in all the garrison towns of the Portuguese. Both these things would wonderfully advance the interests of religion at Goa and everywhere else in India.

May our Lord Jesus protect and keep us continually! Amen.

Cochin, Jan. 20.

As soon as Francis had finished these necessary letters, we can well understand with what affectionate interest and joy he would occupy himself in visiting his beloved Paravas on the Fishery Coast. It was now rather more than three years since he had left them. In the mean time they had suffered much, both from their inveterate enemies the Badages and from the tyranny and extortions of the Portuguese; but they had maintained their faith firmly, and shown much Christian fortitude and perseverance. Lucena[3] describes the joy with which Francis was received by his spiritual children; how, as he went round the villages which his watchful care had supplied with churches and priests, the people came forth to meet him in procession, singing the Christian doctrine as he had taught them, paving his pathway with their garments, or raising him on their shoulders and carrying him in triumph into the sanctuary. The faith of these neophytes had shone out in ways which remind us of the history of the primitive Church: some had cast out devils with the sign of the Cross, or cured the sick; others had endured tortures rather than deny our Lord; others had confuted Brahmins in dispute, or converted their fellow labourers or companions in slavery.[4] They had a great number of churches of their own, and were watched over by four Fathers of the Society, with three active priests and three lay brothers. Mancias was gone;

[3] *Vida*, l. v. cap. 24.

[4] See Lucena, l. c., and Massei, l. ii. cap. 13.

but his place was more than supplied by Antonio Criminale, an Italian of the diocese of Parma, a man of consummate virtue; Alonzo or Alfonso Cipriano, an old Castilian priest; and two others of the name of Enriquez, Francesco and Enrico, whether brothers or not we are not told. These two had been students in the University of Coimbra. Francesco had been won to the Society some three years before the time of which we are writing, after a sojourn of Pierre Lefèvre in the college in that city, during which a great impulse had been given to study as well as to piety. Three very distinguished men had been admitted to the Society by Pierre Lefèvre himself, Louis Gonsalvez, Antonio Gomez, and Emmanuel Sà; while as many as twenty others, among whom was Francesco Enriquez, already a priest, had made up their minds to the same step, though various circumstances had prevented their immediate admission. Enrico Enriquez seems to have been younger than his namesake. He was rich, as it is recorded of him that when he became a religious he distributed a very large sum of money to the poor.[5]

After a rapid tour through the several missions, Francis collected his small band of workers at Munahpaud, where they spent a fortnight together in a sort of retreat. They were all somewhat young in the Society, and Criminale alone among them had been more than a few months at the work among

[5] Antonio Criminale had reached India in 1545, in the fleet which brought Don Joam de Castro as Governor of the Indies in place of Martin Alfonso de Sousa. There were also two other priests, Joam Beira, already mentioned, and Niccolo Lancilotti, an Italian. Beira had gone first to Cape Comorin, and then, summoned by Francis, to Malacca and the Moluccas. Lancilotti remained at Goa. The next year no priests seem to have been sent; but in 1547 five fathers had arrived—the two Enriquez and Cipriano named above, Francesco Perez, Manuel de Morães, and Nunez Ribero. Perez remained at Goa, and Nunez Ribero was sent on at once with Beira to Malacca, where he met Francis Xavier on his return from the Moluccas, as related in the last chapter of the preceding book. His companion Niccolo Nunez was not yet a priest. The catalogue of the college of Coimbra mentions four others as lay brothers, who sailed with the fathers who arrived in 1547. As many as ten of the Society were sent in the year 1548, which we have now reached, four of whom were priests. We shall have to speak of several of them hereafter.

the Paravas, a work which, as we have seen, required much sagacity, prudence, and temper, as well as great zeal and industry. Francis took great pains to help and support them as much as possible. It may be supposed that Mancias had been left with some kind of authority over those who had joined or were to join him, and his defection left the Fathers of the Fishery Coast without any kind of immediate superior. A letter of Enrico Enriquez, written late in the year 1548 to St. Ignatius, states that they had elected Antonio Criminale, and that this choice had been confirmed by Francis. We do not know whether it had been made before his arrival from the East, or whether it was now made at his instigation.[6] After the retreat was over, Francis left them a long paper of instructions, which is generally included among his letters, and which, on that account, we insert here.

(LIX.) *To the Fathers of the Society of Jesus working among the Christians of the Comorin Coast.*

The thing which I wish to commend to you above everything else is that you should employ special diligence and watchfulness as to the baptism of little children, so as not to leave any lately born child not regenerated in the saving laver of Christ in any of the villages or farm settlements in which you are either at present labouring or shall hereafter have any charge. I consider that to be the chief and most salutary of all the forms of ministry in which you can be employed in these parts, and therefore I would have you never commit it to another, or trust for it to any one but yourselves. Make search and inquiry for yourselves, and baptize with your own hands all those whom you find in want of that most necessary Sacrament. I know that the royal officers who have authority over the natives have received orders, and also that the heads of families have been strictly charged to give information, and to fetch those who are to administer Baptism as soon as they see

[6] It is certain that St. Ignatius at one time entertained the notion of the election of the Superiors of each house by the members of that house. See Genelli's *Life of St. Ignatius*, (Eng. Trans.) p. 210.

their families increased by a new birth. But it is not well to rest upon this as a ground of security. The officials will have other things to do, and the fathers will forget. Meanwhile, the little ones will die without baptism. So you must go yourselves, make strict search and inquiry, asking from door to door whether, since you have been there, any woman has given birth to a child, and whether for any cause at all there is to be found there a soul which has not yet had the holy water poured upon it. You will very seldom make these inquiries without fruit. The people will bring you their babies, you must make them Christians at once and secure the salvation of their souls, which unless you use all this diligence will be in great danger of losing eternal happiness.

Trust my experience; all, of any moment, that we can do among this nation, all that is worth our labour, comes in the end to these two kinds of service, baptizing infants, and teaching the children who have any capacity for learning. So I would enjoin upon you to look after this second with as much diligence as the first, or even greater. I mean, that you take all most efficient care that the instruction of children goes on without intermission. I mean, that you are to take care that this is done by others, for it is quite clear that you cannot do it yourselves. You ought not to have a fixed and permanent home in any one single village, but to be always free and ready to pass to all spots, one after another, and watch over the increase of the Church in these parts by visiting and making a circuit over the whole country, which very much needs such vigilance. Thus you cannot find time for the attention necessary to the holding of schools everywhere, day after day. So you must appoint in each village or station fitting teachers and canacapoli, as we have already arranged, and these must assemble the children every day at a certain time and place, and teach and drive into them the elements of reading and of religion, and the prayers which all must know by heart. And that this may be done with greater exactness, you must never omit, whenever in your circuits you visit any particular village, to have all the children assembled, and to make them give an account, in the presence of their teachers, of what they have learnt, so as to put to the proof their diligence as well as that of their teachers, taking careful notice how much of the sacred prayers each one can recite without fault, and how far each one has got in learning and understanding the catechism. And you must give out that you will soon come back again to measure how far they shall have advanced beyond what they have now attained to, in proportion to the interval of time which will have elapsed, and that you will judge from that who has been working hard and who has been idle. The expectation of your visit will sharpen the industry both of the teachers and of the scholars.

You must see that on Sundays all the men are assembled in the church to recite the prayers, and make particular inquiry whether the Patangatins frequent these assemblies. In the places where you happen to be on such days, you will yourselves preside at these meetings, and after they have all recited the usual prayers from memory, you will shortly and clearly explain what they have been saying. Then you will speak against the vices which are dominant in the place, showing by clear instances and images, such as the ignorant can understand, how foul and mischievous they are, and then heaping up threats of the anger and vengeance of God, to terrify those who delay to amend their lives, and these threats should be not only of that distant and future anger of God which will rage against them after this life, but of His anger now hanging over them, and all but falling on them in diseases, plagues, early deaths, persecution from the heathen rajahs, who will despoil them, make slaves of them, put them to terrible kinds of torture; of the evils, in short, here and now, through which hardened sinners will have to pass on their way to the eternal punishment of hell. Make inquiry also in every place, whether there are any feuds or hatreds existing between people living there, and take great pains not only that the people are reconciled and lay aside all rancour from their hearts, but that they also make public profession of this, in order to do away with the public offence given. So the men between whom there has been notorious discord must in the assembly of the men (which, as I said, is to be held every Sunday), and the women likewise in the meeting of the women, which is to be held on Saturdays, must be made by you to call all the others there present to witness that they are sorry for the wrongs they have done and ask pardon for them; that they wish for the future to forget any that they have received, and that they have firmly made up their minds to show all the offices of Christian and brotherly charity to those whom before they held as enemies and objects of hate.

As soon as the translation into Malabar of the explanation of the Articles of the Faith, which I have charged Father Francis Coelho to provide, shall be finished, you must take diligent care that many copies of it, according to the number of the villages or hamlets, be written out and dispersed everywhere, and that it be read everywhere by some one who has a good voice and can be understood by all, to the people collected in their regular meetings, the men on Sundays, and the women on Saturdays. And wherever any one of you may happen to be on Sundays, let him add an instruction of his own to what has been read, explaining more clearly and distinctly any parts that may seem to have been less thoroughly understood by those whose minds are not very quick. Moreover, you must see that the alms and offerings due from people who have to pay what they have vowed after escaping from some danger of disease or misfortune, which are usually collected in these assemblies, of the men or of the women, be all distributed to the poor, and you must not allow even the very smallest particle of them to be spent on your own use.

Take care that it is clearly given out, every Sunday in the meeting of the men, and every Saturday in the meeting of the women, that as soon as ever any one of any condition soever is taken ill in any of their houses, they are at once to let you know, that you may be able to bring early help and administer all the holy rites which are necessary for providing duly for the soul at such a time. And give out, that if any one fails in this duty, and so any relation of his or any inmate of his house dies without the assistance of the sacraments, then without fail you will not permit him when he dies to be buried in the cemetery of the church with the sacred service. When you visit the sick, you will order that the holy Creed be recited by them if they are able, if not, by some one of those present, in their language; and ask the sick man at each article whether he most assuredly and most constantly believes what is being said? Then make him say the form of general confession, and the prayers which it is usual for all to know by heart, and after this, read the holy gospel over them.

When any one has died, you must go in procession from the church to the place where the corpse lies, with the Cross borne before you and the children with it, singing, as they go and return, the prayers which they have learnt in the school of Christian doctrine; when the dead body has been brought into the church, you will say the prescribed prayers, and again, according to custom, before the body is committed to the earth, and you must always make something in the way of a short sermon, appropriate to the occasion, to the crowd that is assembled for the funeral, admonishing them about the certainty of death, the uncertainty of life, how these thoughts ought to make them live a life of amendment, and not put off doing penance for sins, in which if they are caught by death, they will not be able to avoid eternal damnation; and how, on the other hand, if they persevere in the grace of God, they may justly hope, when they die, to pass into the joys of Paradise. You must charge them—the men on the Sundays, and the women on the Saturdays—to bring any sick children there may be to you into the church, that you may recite the gospel over them. That will have the effect of arousing and strengthening the faith both of fathers and mothers, and making them all love the Church and her sacred rites; and besides, it will be of great advantage to the life and health of the little creatures themselves.

Now as to lawsuits and disputes of right, which may spring up between the Christians. The first thing you must do is to work as gently and forcibly as you may, that both parties should talk their differences over together, and make the matter up in some fair and good manner between themselves. If there are any who cannot be induced to do this, and if the matter be not of great importance, then on Sundays, after the prayers have been said, you will put the affair into the hands of the Patangatius, who are the wardens of the church of the place, that they may hear both sides, and settle the cause. You must never, except as little as possible and on very rare occasions, allow yourself to be engaged in taking cognizance of such matters, for they would give you less leisure, and take away from the authority which is necessary for the discharge of the spiritual functions which are proper to our vocation. So, however much the contending parties may urge it upon you, offering to be bound by your arbitration, and asking you to hear them, excuse yourselves on the ground of more important duties, and prudently decline the expense of time which the hearing would cause you, as well as the odiousness of giving a judgment. Send the greater disputes to the Portuguese Commandant of that part of the country; or if the people concerned are very much more desirous to have a priest as arbiter, refer them in that case to Father Antonio Criminale.

Labour with all your might to gain for yourselves the love of the people. You will be far better able to help them if they love you than if they fear you. Never order a punishment for any one, or inflict one, before you have consulted on the whole matter with Father Antonio Criminale, and never, even with his consent, order any one to be apprehended or fined according to his deserts in any place where there is a Portuguese Commandant, without having informed him of the affair, and brought him to your own opinion by laying your reasons before him. When a man or woman has been convicted of carving idols, the fit punishment to be legally inflicted on such should be banishment from the place where the fault has been committed, and detention in another; but you must never send any one away on such an account without the assent of Father Criminale. When boys who are constant in attendance on catechetical schools deserve punishment, avoid giving it as much as may be without impairing discipline, for it is better to seem not to know, as you do, that they have done wrong as children of that age will, than by any severity, however just, to rouse in their tender minds a feeling of dislike to you. When they have taken an aversion to those who are to help and guide them as to their salvation, they will rush headlong into all excesses. You will generally get such children to be good far more easily by showing them a great deal of love than by any severity or violence.

Take diligent care never to speak hardly of the native Christians in the presence of the Portuguese; rather always defend them and take up their cause when they are accused, making excuses for them and commending them as much as you are able. You should ask the Portuguese to consider favourably what a bad education these poor creatures who are lately converted from idolatry to Christianity have had from their childhood upwards; how little time they have had free, during the short period since they embraced the faith—what with the many instances of the absence of priests, what with the invasions and alarms of invasions of the Badages—to give themselves seriously to the receiving the necessary instructions how to behave as Christians. Say that, if they take all these things wisely into account, not only ought they to be very indulgent in forgiving the defects of these uninstructed barbarians, but they may well wonder that they are not somewhat worse than they appear to be from the faults into which they fall, which are generally not of the most grievous kind.

You will be very kind to the Malabar priests, and provide for their good with all consideration, especially in matters belonging to religion, taking care that they accustom themselves to go regularly to confession, that they offer the holy sacrifice with all propriety and very often, and that they set a right example of holy living to the people. And when you have had to complain of them, or to reprehend them if they have been guilty in any way, especially take great care that no vestige of this which can be shown to others remain, especially in any letters which you may write to any one.

You must endeavour to gain the friendship of the Portuguese Commandant, showing him all observance and courtesy, and avoid any unfriendliness with him on any account whatsoever. Take the same pains in endeavouring to keep the good favour of all the Portuguese who are settled in these parts, showing no aversion to any one, and letting no one hate you, but rather endeavouring by all kindness, prudence, and true charity to be men of peace, even with those who hate peace. And if any of them are disposed of themselves to draw back from you, still keep a hold of them by offices of kindness and good will, so that even against their will they may come to feel and allow themselves to be loved by you, and so be afraid to let any difference they may have with you break out into an open rupture. At the same time, this does not mean that you are right to connive at the unjust oppression with which they may sometimes persecute the Christians. When you see anything of the kind, then by all means rebuke them, but do it gently and with every sign of love. If you make no way in this manner, then carry your complaint to the Commandant, and defend the right of the innocent victims of oppression with modesty, and as far as may be without losing your friendship with those against whom you plead. For the Commandant, I once more admonish you, on account of the importance of the matter, keep him at peace and well disposed with you at whatsoever cost, and let nothing be too much for you to be willing to sacrifice for the sake of avoiding the giving him offence and of retaining his goodwill.

Let your conversation with the Portuguese be always about sacred things, such as relate to the salvation of souls and to advancement in virtue. Speak to them in private as well as in public about Death, Judgment, the punishments of Hell and of Purgatory, urging them to frequent the sacraments of Penance and Communion, and to keep the Ten Commandments of God's law and all other things of that kind; for if in your dealings with them you never turn aside to other topics of conversation, one of two things will happen: either when they come to you they will enter on talk of the same sort—and this will do them very great good—or if they get tired of so much sad and serious conversation, they will leave off coming to see you, and leave you free for many good hours of time which are much needed for the urgent occupations of the manifold duties which you have to discharge.

Remember, when occasions offer themselves, to write to the fathers and brothers of our Society at Goa, telling them what may give them consolation and animate them to good deeds, concerning the fruits of your ministry and the issue of your endeavours for the glory of God. You must write also to the same effect to his lordship the Bishop, with all submission and reverence as to the prelate to whose authority and jurisdiction all these parts are subject. You must not go into any country or province, however much you may be urged by the rajahs and princes thereof, without the assent of Father Antonio Criminale and the Portuguese Commandant of the coast. If any of the rajahs invite you with extreme urgency, you must plead to them the obedience which you profess, making that your excuse, and urging that it renders it unlawful for you, without the command of your superiors, to leave the station at which you are placed. I once more admonish you, renewing my recommendation over and over again, to endeavour, wherever and with whomsoever you have to work, to make yourselves pleasing and amiable to men of all sorts, obliging all, and doing service to all and each, and never addressing any one except gently and modestly. This practical kindness, seasoned by courtesy of language, will win for you the love of all and open their hearts to you, and so afford you a great facility in gathering very glorious fruit of souls. May God grant you that blessing, and may He ever be with you all! Amen.

Yours wholly,

February 1548. FRANCIS.

When the circumstances of the case are considered, there is little to surprise us in the strong statement which occurs near the beginning of this letter, that the only kinds of ministry which were likely to be profitable in that country were the baptizing of infants and the instruction of children. It was not that Francis despaired of the adult population, which had just welcomed him so joyously and gratefully, and many members of which had during his absence given very remarkable proofs of the soundness and stability of their faith. But in any community, even in countries which have for centuries been Christian, the hope and security of the future lies in the young. A large portion of the human race dies in infancy; and thus the baptism of infants, so many of whom are never to grow to man's estate, is and has always been in effect one of the chief means by which the Church has peopled heaven through the merits of our crucified Lord, and its importance for the future glory of God is marked by the peculiar malignity with which the powers of evil in the world have always exerted themselves in so many various ways to hinder and prevent it. Again, the adults in the population were exposed to so many difficulties, both as to procuring instruction in the faith and as to the practice of the Christian law—partly from old habit and associations, partly from the influence of the luxurious and sensual paganism all around them, and, not least, from the scandal given to them by those who bore the name of Christian, as well as from the persecution, whether from heathens or Europeans, to which they were themselves exposed—that their want of a Christian training from their early years must have made their hold on the faith very precarious. In Christian countries the adult population is seldom sound unless it has been well and religiously educated; and here again we can trace the instinctive malice of the powers of evil in their resolute and unceasing efforts either to get hold of education for their own emissaries or to snatch it out of the hands of the Church. On the other hand, if the children were thoroughly grounded in the knowledge of Christian doctrine and the use of Christian sacraments, not even all the disadvantages of the position of the native Christians in India would be able to turn them from the observance of the law of God. When Francis Xavier wrote, he had but little prospect of seeing the field on which he had bestowed so much labour cultivated by a numerous and intelligent body of priests; and so long as the evangelical workers remained few in numbers, able only occasionally to visit place after place among the settlements without fixing themselves anywhere, the full development of the Christian life in all its manifold and beautiful variety and profusion, could not be expected.

One other passage in the foregoing letter deserves a word of comment, as we might otherwise fail to understand the careful provision made by Francis Xavier for the progress of the mission. The explanation of the Articles of the Faith, which he mentions as about to be translated into the Malabar tongue, was probably that long commentary on the Creed which has been printed in the preceding volume.[7] If the text of the letter above is correct, we gather from it that this translation was committed to Father Francis Coelho, one of the native priests who were still labouring with those of the Society in the mission. At the same time we are told that Francis gave a special commission to Father Francesco Enriquez to make a perfect grammar and vocabulary of the Malabar tongue, and thus at once to elevate, fix, and preserve it, and make it more useful as a means of communication among the tribes of different dialects, the tendency of which is to continual change and decay, and so to the isolation of one petty community from another. Father Enriquez obeyed, and within six months he had completely mastered the language, cast it into form, and arranged its vocabulary, and his facility in writing and speaking it had become a marvel to the natives themselves.

From Munahpaud Francis appears to have passed into Ceylon, where the interests of religion seem to have been in a critical state, the particular circumstances of which it is difficult to understand without more clear statements than have come down to us. The Cingalese princes mentioned in a former chapter seem to have been baptized at Goa, and installed in their kingdoms by the present governor, Don Joam de Castro; and either in consequence of their conversion or from other causes the Franciscans had sent a small band of missionaries into the island. Several places on the coast were occupied by these missionaries.[8] In the interior the King of Candy, who

[7] Notes to Book II. p. 321.

[8] Faria y Sousa, *Asia Portuguesa*, t. ii. p. 2, cap. 4, mentions Panaturè, Macù, Berberii, Galle, Beligam, all on the coast.

is supposed by Lucena[9] to have succeeded to the Christian prince, was well disposed to the faith, and only kept back from embracing it by the fear of a revolt among his subjects. He was thinking of putting himself under the protection of the Portuguese when Francis arrived,[10] and was received by him with extraordinary honours. The issue of his visit was that an embassy was prepared, which was to offer to the Governor of the Indies the alliance of the King of Candy, who demanded a strong garrison of Portuguese soldiers to secure him on his throne, and who was ready to become a Christian and pay tribute to the King of Portugal. Other accounts state that the Rajah of Jafanapatam himself was touched by the remonstrances of Francis, and promised to become Christian if the Portuguese would accept his alliance. It appears certain that it was in company with an embassy from one or other of these rajahs that Francis left the south of India about the end of February or the beginning of March, in order to seek the Governor of the Indies at Goa. He arrived at that city on March 20th, but found Joam de Castro absent.

[9] Lib. v. c. 26.

[10] When St. Francis arrived at Galle a Portuguese of the name of Miguel Fernandez was dangerously ill. Francis visited him, confessed him, and promised to say mass for him. After the mass was finished Miguel became perfectly well, and gave testimony to the fact when the processes were made.

CHAPTER II.

Francis and Don Joam de Castro.

THE Governor of the Indies, Don Joam de Castro, has already been more than once mentioned as a gallant and even heroic officer, and one whose brief period of authority had been signalized by great exploits and brilliant victories. The Portuguese historian of the Indies pauses before he passes on from his account of Don Joam's government to give us some characteristic notes concerning him. He was now in the prime of life, in his forty-eighth year. He was the son of a high officer of the Crown, and his mother was the daughter of one of the chief nobles of Portugal. When quite young, Joam had served in Tangier; and on returning home had received from the King an *encomienda* of five hundred crowns a year, which was his principal fortune for the rest of his life. Later on, he served under Charles V. in the expedition against Tunis, at which time he refused his share of some money distributed by the emperor to the Portuguese officers, saying that he served the King of Portugal, and looked to him for his reward. Another time he was in command of a Portuguese squadron sent to co-operate with some Spanish force for the relief of Ceuta. On the approach of the Moorish fleet, the Spaniards were for retiring, with the object, real or alleged, of concerting their measures; but Don Joam de Castro refused to stir, and the Moors, thinking the allied fleets were still united, withdrew themselves, leaving him the honour of having driven them off. Don Joam sailed to India in 1528 as captain of a ship in the fleet of Don Garcia de Noroña, who was going out as Viceroy. The King, who seems to have known his gallantry, offered Joam a grant of the captainship of Ormuz and a pension of a thousand ducats a year till he came into possession of the post. But he declined the position, saying he had not yet deserved such promotion, accepting at the same time the pension on account of his great poverty, and begging the King to remember him for the captaincy when he should have earned it. Noroña died in two years, and was succeeded by Estevan de Gama, the son of Vasco, and the immediate predecessor of Martin Alfonso de Sousa, as Governor of India. One of Estevan's expeditions took him up the Red Sea to Suez, on which occasion he went up to the famous monastery of St. Catharine on Mount Sinai, and knighted several of his followers, one of whom was Don Alvaro, son of Joam de Castro, who was also of the party. Joam seems to have returned to Portugal after the end of Estevan's government; and there the Infante Don Luis recommended him to King John as governor of India after Martin Alfonso. He was a man of letters as well as of arms, a classical scholar, and a good mathematician. When on the Red Sea, he got divers to go to the bottom for the sake of finding out what it is that gives its colour to the water, as Faria y Sousa tells us. He adds that Don Joam wrote a paper to prove that the water was red on account of the coral at the bottom, which opinion he himself combats, on the ground that coral is green until it comes up to the air, which hardens it and renders it red.[1] The same writer speaks highly of Don Joam's modesty as a governor, his condescension, and his integrity. Before sailing for India, he chanced to see a very fine suit of clothes in a tailor's shop, and was told that it had been ordered by one of his own sons, who was to sail with him. He took the tailor's scissors, and cut the suit into small pieces, telling the man to bid the youth who had ordered it provide himself with arms, and arms, and more arms.

If this anecdote was characteristic of the man, his government of India was quite in keeping with his character. He was always at war, and frequently exposing himself, even to rashness. We have already mentioned his great exploit of the relief of Diu and the defeat of the besiegers in November 1546. He had received the news of the severe wound of his son Don Alvaro—who had been knighted on Mount Sinai, and was per-

[1] *Asia Portuguesa*, t. ii. p. 2, cap. 5.

haps the young man who had ordered the fine suit of clothes in Lisbon—with heroic composure, going in procession to give thanks to God that Diu was still in the possession of the Portuguese. After his victory at Diu, he dispatched a messenger with the news to Goa, desiring, says Faria y Sousa, 'the city to lend him twenty thousand pardams for the use of the army, sending a lock of his whiskers in pawn for the money.' The city returned the pawn with respect, and sent him more money than he demanded, and the women their pendants, necklaces, bracelets, and other jewels. All was restored as it was sent, for the immediate need of the Governor had been already supplied by the capture of a rich ship of Cambaia, taken by Antonio Moniz Barreto on the coast of Mangalore. Brave and simple as he was, Don Joam was not free from the love of display, which may have been somewhat of a national failing. His arrival at Goa after the victory of Diu was splendidly celebrated. He was received with loud acclamations, and a splendid triumph prepared by the city, in imitation of those of Rome. 'The city gates and streets were hung with silk, the windows thronged with fine women; all places resounded with music and noise of cannon, and the sea was covered with vessels richly adorned. The Governor entered under a rich canopy, where, taking off his cap, they put on his head a crown of laurel, and a branch of it in his hand. Before him went the priest with the crucifix, as he carried it in the fight, and next to him the royal standard. Then Juzarcan (the Mussulman commander), his eyes fixed on the ground, perhaps that he might not see his prince's colours dragged and ours flying, and between them six hundred prisoners in chains. The remainder of the procession was made up of various pieces of artillery, and other sorts of arms placed in cars, forming most beautiful trophies. The Governor walked over leaves of gold and silver and rich silks, which their makers or owners had spread out before him.' The ladies, each one for that day taking the part of Aurora, bedewed him from their balconies with fragrant waters and scattered flowers on him. The description detains us long,' concludes the grim and curt annalist whom we are quoting; and he sums up and concludes the whole by a saying of 'our manlike queen, Doña Catalina, who, when the victory and triumph were related to her, said: In short, Don Joam conquered like a Christian, and triumphed like a heathen.'[2]

When Francis Xavier arrived at Goa, with the envoy of the King of Candy, of whom mention has already been made, Don Joam de Castro was at Bazain, some way to the north along the coast, engaged in military preparations and enterprises. The north-western coasts of India had been the scene of his operations in the year which had followed the relief of Diu, and he was soon to be engaged in organizing an expedition of which Aden was the object. It would appear that there was some reason to fear that the Governor was not disposed to take active measures for the simple furtherance of religion, or at least that influential members of the Council were likely to oppose such measures. The letter of the King of Portugal to the Governor, written after the complaints made by Miguel Vaz and Francis Xavier, though not strong enough to force an actively christianizing policy upon the Indian officials, was strong enough to rouse their enmity against the advocates of such a policy. There had already been occasions on which voices had been raised in the Council, saying that it did not much matter whether the Indian princes in alliance with the crown of Portugal became Christian or remained heathen. The Rajah of Tanore had sought baptism, and the Council, as we gather from Lucena, had refused to take his part in the quarrels with neighbouring princes which ensued.[3] The Governor himself had his hands full enough of warlike undertakings, and he was supposed not to favour the college of Santa Fè. It was necessary therefore for Francis Xavier to try the effect of a personal interview with Don Joam in the matter of the Rajah or King of Candy, whose cause he had espoused. Francis accordingly made a rapid excursion to Bazain, and was able at once to bring the Governor over to his own wishes. Antonio Moniz Barreto, already mentioned, one of the most dashing officers among the

[2] Faria y Sousa, *Asia Portuguesa*, t. ii. p. 2, cap. 3.
[3] See Lucena, *Vida*, l. vi. c. 2, 3.

Portuguese, was sent with two hundred men to garrison Candy and protect the Rajah. The issue of the enterprize, however, was unfortunate, on account of the treachery and inconstancy of the Cingalese prince. He was persuaded by another rajah that the Portuguese would seize his kingdom as soon as he declared himself a Christian, and he determined, in consequence, to massacre his new allies as soon as they arrived. Barreto had already landed, and was on his march inland, when he was informed of this treacherous design. It was dangerous to recede directly, so he made his men burn all their superfluous baggage, and then fought his way on bravely for three days, against a force of eight thousand men, till he arrived at a friendly territory without any loss.

Francis Xavier returned almost immediately to Goa, reaching that city early in April. His short visit to Bazain was not without its victory of apostolical zeal. His biographers tell us that he fell in there with a Portuguese noble, Rodrigo Secheira by name, whom, when in Malacca, he had found in the hospital, hiding himself in order to escape the hands of justice on account of a great crime which he had committed. It was probably a homicide, as Francis made his peace for him with his enemies, and also reconciled him to God by a general confession of his sins. But he exacted of him a promise to return to Europe. Secheira went as far as Goa on his way, and was there offered a lucrative post under the government at Bazain. He yielded to the temptation, and was soon immersed in his former vices. When Francis met him in a public place at Bazain, he had not been to confession for two years. Secheira came up to Francis with a smile on his face and an open hand, thinking to brave the matter off. Francis could be stern when he thought fit, and drew back as in horror. 'What, my son,' he cried, 'are you still in India? Is this the way you have kept your promise to God and to me?' And when Secheira began to excuse himself, he told him that whatever might be said about his not having returned to Europe, his having kept away from confession was inexcusable, and he could not have him for his friend as long as he was at enmity with God. Secheira was at once overcome, made his confession, and began a new mode of life under the direction of Francis.[4]

Joam de Castro was so charmed with Francis Xavier, that he exacted of him what was in some respects a considerable sacrifice, a promise to remain some months at Goa to assist him in regulating the affairs of his soul. It appears that the Governor returned to Goa about the same time with Francis. He seems already to have felt the approach of death, which was very soon to carry him off. He had already suffered from fever, and was also harassed by the misconduct or imprudence of some of his officers and soldiers. Aden, then as now a place of very great importance for any maritime power in the East, had been taken from the Turks by the petty Prince of Caxem, who, in fear of the common enemy, had put himself under the protection of the King of Portugal. There was a hope of a triumph more substantial even than that of Diu, but Aden was lost to the Portuguese by the timidity of Don Payo de Noroña, who was sent from Ormuz to help the new ally. Noroña was afraid of treachery, and retired to his vessel on the approach of a Turkish army, which took the place and put the prince to death. The Governor had sent his son, Don Alvaro, with a considerable force to assist him, but he arrived too late. Another object of the expedition was to eject the Turks from a fort which they had seized near Caxem itself, and here the Portuguese made the mistake, against the express will of their commander, Don Alvaro, of refusing all terms to the garrison, which was ready to treat, and even of detaining the envoys sent to make the proposals for surrender. The consequence was that the besieged made so desperate a resistance, that the fort was only taken at so great a loss of men to the Portuguese as to make their victory almost equivalent to a defeat.[5]

[4] He seems to have returned with him to Goa, and to have staid some time in the college with him, as it is of him that the story is told how he watched Francis during the night through a chink of the door of his room, and saw him spend the greater part of the time on his knees before a crucifix, after which he took a short sleep with his head on a stone, and then rose up to recite his office and say mass.

[5] Faria y Sousa, t. ii. p. 2, cap. 5, says that they killed five hundred men; but the number seems exaggerated.

This expedition to Aden is memorable in the life of Francis Xavier as having afforded him an opportunity of a conquest more truly glorious than that at which Don Alvaro aimed. It was on this occasion that he embarked on board one of the ships of the squadron without giving notice to any one, and with no other provision for the voyage than the breviary under his arm. He had made acquaintance in Goa with one of the class for whom he had so special a predilection—a rude rough soldier, of scandalous life, insolent temper, with the habits of almost every imaginable sin engrained, as it seemed, in his very nature, whose very language was so laden with blasphemies as to offend all who came across him. He had not been to the sacraments for eighteen years. Francis had poured forth numberless prayers for this poor sinner, had wept and done penance before God for his conversion. When the fleet was to sail he asked him to which ship he was to belong, and then, without more ado, took him by the arm, said how glad he was to find they were to be companions, and embarked along with him. Companions, indeed, they were, almost always chatting together and eating at the same mess. The soldier gamed as usual, and Francis stood by, always rejoicing over his successes and full of sorrow when he was unlucky. When the poor fellow broke out into blasphemies and indecent language, Francis seemed not to hear. The men were amazed at seeing his zeal so entirely kept under. It seemed as if the soldier had fascinated him. At last Francis took an opportunity to ask him in confidence how long it was since he had been to confession. The soldier coloured and sighed. His heart was already won. It was eighteen years, he said, since he had confessed, but the fault was not all his own. He had been to the Vicar-General of Goa to get rid of his sins, but the good priest had been so shocked at the tale which he heard, that he sent him away as if his soul could not hope for any share in divine grace. Francis took the side of the soldier. He said that great charity should be used to sinners, for whom our Blessed Redeemer had shed His blood, and that each one had his own burthen to bear, and so should be compassionate to others. At all events, he would make no difficulty himself as to giving his friend all the comfort in his power. If he had all the sins of the world on his conscience he would hear his confession willingly. He had full power to absolve him, and as for his penance, they would divide it between them, and the soldier should take as much of it as he liked for himself and no more. God in His infinite goodness desired his salvation, and asked of him nothing but a sincere repentance for having offended One Who loved him so much. The soldier was overcome, and begged Francis to help him in his confession. The fleet just then touched at some place on the coast, and several of those on board went ashore for a few hours. Francis and the soldier went into a grove near the beach, and were followed at a distance by some of the crew, curious to see what would happen. Francis sat down under a tree, and the soldier made his confession with many tears and sobs, striking his breast and giving every sign of sincere sorrow. After a time they were seen to part. Francis went farther into the wood, and after a time was followed by the soldier. It turned out that he had set his friend the light penance of a single *Pater* and *Ave*, but that he had withdrawn in order to bare his own shoulders, which he then began to scourge violently with an iron discipline, until the blood ran down freely. The soldier heard the noise, and ran after him; then, baring his own shoulders, he began himself to do penance for his sins, 'mingling his blood,' says the historian, 'with that of the Saint.' After this, the two friends parted, Francis to return to Goa, the soldier to fight under Don Alvaro, but not before he had received a number of rules for his future conduct from his friend, which he faithfully observed. On returning from Aden he became a religious, and was considered a model of penitence.[6]

The following letter—the only letter remaining to us of this spring and summer, the greater part of which was spent at

[6] See Massei, lib. ii. c. 14, p. 23 seq. Bartoli, *Asia*, lib. ii. p. 157. Lucena, lib. vi. c. 3. Conversions of this sort occur so frequently in the narratives of the life of St. Francis Xavier, that some readers may be tempted to think that they are various versions of the same anecdote. It must be remembered, however, that the occasions for such examples of charity must have been very frequent in his life. He spent a great part of his time on

Goa—introduces us to a friend of Francis Xavier, of whom we shall hear a good deal more in connection with the last great enterprise of his active life, the project of evangelizing China. Diego Pereira was probably about to sail from Cochin for Malacca and China, and Francis had intended to return to the Comorin coast if he had not been asked by Don Joam to remain at Goa. The Francesco Perez mentioned in the letter was one of the Fathers who had lately arrived from Portugal. He had been a student at Coimbra, who, four years before this time had been wòn to the Society, along with many others of the University, by the preaching of Francis Strada. His companion's name was Rocco Oliveira. We know nothing of his antecedents; but he appears to have come from Portugal with Perez and the rest in 1547. He turned out an excellent teacher at Malacca. They arrived there on the 28th of May, and Oliveira opened his school on the very day after their arrival. He had soon nearly 200 scholars. Perez also laboured with great success in the pulpit and confessional. Among other good works of his Lucena mentions the conversion of another Jew Rabbi, who had been born and bred in Rome itself, and had resisted all the influences of the Holy City.

---

shipboard, and he could hardly ever find himself on board a Portuguese ship without meeting several men such as the soldier described in the anecdote; and it is less probable that the various stories of such conversions should be repetitions of one and the same history, than that there should have been scores of instances of the same charity on his part of which we have heard nothing. For this reason it seems better not to depart from the statements made by writers like those quoted above, who had seen the documents on which the processes were founded. An anecdote very similar to that given above is related in the *Relatio* to which we have often referred, on the authority of a Portuguese soldier named Figueira, who was a comrade of the man converted. But in that case the number of years since he had been at confession is given as seven or more. Cochin is the place at which the vessel touched, and his confession was heard in a church which is named. Bartoli mentions a certain Leti as the witness in the case before us, the circumstances of which he gives as they are given above, and makes Cochin the place. Lucena names no place, but seems to think that the embarcation was from Bazain.

(LX.) *To Diego Pereira.*

May the grace and charity of our Lord Jesus Christ always help and favour us! Amen.

It would have been much more what I wish if I could have seen you before your departure for China, instead of having to write to you at a distance; but the Governor has desired me to come hither to Goa, and I am obliged to do as he wishes. I had a plan of visiting my brethren of the Society on the Comorin Promontory. It would indeed have been a joy to me if it had been allowed me to talk over with so true and faithful a friend as you a good many things which relate to my voyage to Japan which I hope to undertake in a year's time from this. I have heard from good authority that a rich harvest of souls can be reaped in those parts, and the Christian faith propagated far and wide. And now I charge you for the sake of the friendship between us to provide yourself before you go to China with a certain ware which is of infinite value, but which the merchants who go to Malacca and China generally don't seem to care for. The ware I mean is a good conscience, a thing which men of that sort know very little about. The merchants appear to persuade themselves that it will be all over with their fortune altogether if they look to the affairs of their souls and of their consciences.

Nevertheless I have good confidence that, by the assistance of God, my very dear friend Diego Pereira will take with him a very large supply of this merchandize of a good conscience, and that he will gain great riches thereby, though the rest of the merchants by their neglect of these things will be reduced to indigence. I shall certainly never leave off praying God to guide you in safety to China, to bring you back to us in safety and much increased and enriched in all the good things of the soul, far more than in those of worldly wealth. I am sending from this to Malacca two of our Society, one whose name is Francesco Perez, a priest who is to devote himself, according to my method, to preaching, hearing confessions, and instructing the children and the ignorant; and another who is not yet a priest, and who is to teach the children of the Portuguese to read, so that they may in future read pious and holy books rather than those law reports which circulate at Malacca, the reading of which makes the children Malacensians instead of Portuguese. May our Lord Jesus Christ be with you, as I wish Him to be with myself.

Goa, April 2. FRANCIS.

The last sentence of this letter is somewhat obscure, but it appears to mean that the children had hitherto had nothing to learn to read from except the public reports of the law courts, which no doubt had enough to occupy them in a great mart like Malacca frequented by merchants of so many different nations. Oliveira was to teach the children to read out of translations of the Lives of the Saints, or other good books, so that their young minds might not be filled with the quibbles and chicanery of men who were striving with all their might to overreach each other.

This summer of 1548 was a time of unusual repose in the life of Francis Xavier. The request of Don Joam de Castro that he would remain some months at Goa was equivalent to a command, and he was thus prevented from returning at once to his brethren who were labouring on the Fishery Coast. We are not even told that he occupied himself at Goa in any extraordinary work of preaching or catechizing, though we may be sure that he was not inactive in the confessional. We find pauses like this, of far longer duration, in the life of the great Apostle of the Gentiles, when God in His Providence seems to have withdrawn him for months together from the exercise of his active ministry, in order that he might rest and occupy himself in meditation, prayer, and contemplation. Even at such times, as when in prison at Cæsaræa or at Rome, St. Paul could not fail to make himself felt in his influence on his neighbours, or in his letters to distant churches, several of which, with a tender and glowing character of their own, were written in his captivity. Nor can we suppose that with Francis Xavier his period of rest was more than comparatively unoccupied. As the true test of holy activity is the gladness and readiness with which it falls back, when God so wills, upon the better portion of Mary sitting at the feet of our Lord, so also in apostolical men, their times of contemplation and close communion with God are the seedtimes and stages of preparation for future labours. In them these holy men seek out and have revealed to them the particular purposes of God for their more immediate future, and they store and strengthen themselves with the light and grace which are to guide and to sustain them in new enterprises for the glory of God, Who at such times is wont to overwhelm them with heavenly sweetness so as to grant them almost a foretaste of the joys of Paradise.

To these summer months belong a number of anecdotes of Francis Xavier which became current in Goa, and which have in many cases found their way into the Processes made for his canonization. He lived as retired a life as he could, spending great part of his days and nights in prayer, which he usually made in a 'coretto' or small 'tribune' adjoining the church, from which he could see the altar of the Blessed Sacrament. His eyes were often inflamed with tears or seemed to glance fire; his face was all aglow, sometimes he scarcely knew where he was or what he was doing, or to feel heat or cold in the intensity of his concentration upon God. Often he would open his robe and bare his breast to the air, or pour cold water upon it, as if he felt an insupportable fire within, and he was heard to cry out in the garden of the college, where he would pace up and down, 'No more, O Lord, no more!' At other times he was seen gently raised in the air, and his face seemed to send forth rays of light. He was wont out of devotion to the Blessed Sacrament to administer Holy Communion upon his knees instead of standing, and once he was seen to float in this attitude along the rail to give the sacred particles to the people. It is to this time that the story belongs, which tells how Francis was wont to hide himself in a corner of the campanile of the church, that he might make his prayer more secretly and out of reach of interruption, and how when, on a certain day, he had an appointment at a fixed hour at the Governor's palace, and had told a lad of the college to come and call him, the youth found him so entranced that, hour after hour, he came back to endeavour in vain to arouse him, until it was four in the afternoon before he succeeded in making him understand what he had to do. When the two went out at last on their errand, Francis roamed about here and there, unable to withdraw himself from the thought of God which so overpowered him, until at last he was forced to say, 'My son, let us go back, and visit the palace another day, for it is clear that God will have the whole of this day to Himself.' Another time he was crossing a piazza so absorbed in heavenly contemplation that he did not perceive a wild elephant running loose upon him, nor hear the shouts of the people who were warning him of the danger, which was only avoided by the sudden turn of the animal in another direction. Other wonders of a more usual kind are told of this time, how he had started up from the confessional on a sudden, and had run to a house in the neighbourhood where a poor man, in despair of finding a maintenance for his family, had begun to hang himself; how he had by a word delivered a lady who came to him in great anguish of mind from a troublesome temptation which she had long suffered; and how, with a poetic simplicity which reminds us of the anecdotes of St. Francis of Assisi, when a fine horse had been plunging and kicking savagely whenever an attempt was made to shoe it, he had gone up, stroked it, and tamed it. 'Brother horse,' he said, 'how is it that so beautiful as you are, you will let no one put shoes on you?' and the animal yielded to his words as the fierce wolf of Gubbio had yielded to his namesake.[7]

The month of June had hardly begun, when Francis Xavier had to discharge the last offices of Christian charity to his dying friend the Governor, Don Joam de Castro. He had already been ailing when he returned to Goa, and his heart had been afflicted by the failure of the attempt on Aden, and by the misconduct of the Portuguese at Chaul, in the blame of which his own son had a share. Faria y Sousa, who seems to lose no opportunity of a sour remark upon the great degeneracy which the immense temptations of their position in India brought on

[7] Massei (from Bartoli and the Processes), lib. ii. c. 14.

amongst the Portuguese, tells us that Don Joam was dying of a disease, which in his own time killed no man, though in old times it had killed thousands; 'for even diseases die,' says the old annalist. This disease was 'a keen sentiment of the miserable state in which he beheld India, without seeing any way to repair it,' and some few instances of misconduct just now mentioned. While he was in this state, a large fleet arrived from Portugal. It was the first which had been dispatched to the East since the news of the victory of Diu had arrived at Lisbon. The large number of seventeen ships had been fitted out to do especial honour to the occasion, and to the Governor, whose exploits were ringing in every ear throughout Portugal. 'It was the first time,' says Faria y Sousa, 'that any Governor of India had received honours from his King for any meritorious action.' He does not seem to think much of the honours bestowed on Don Joam. He was continued for three years in the government and raised to the rank of Viceroy, a title only exceptionally bestowed on the representative of the King in India. A sum of money was also given him over and above his salary, and his son, Don Alvaro, was made Capitan Major, or Admiral of the Indian Seas. Compliments and promises accompanied these honours. 'In those days,' says the chronicler, 'great deserts found rewards as niggardly as now great rewards find niggardly merits to earn them.'

But these rewards, such as they were, found Don Joam not in a state to enjoy them. He was dying fast—dying, as Faria y Sousa puts it, because he saw his country's fame at its last gasp. However that may be, he died like a Christian hero, and we can see, in what is told of his last days, the influence of the presence of Francis Xavier by his deathbed. Don Joam had been free in his letters to the King as to what he said about persons in India, and on his deathbed he asked their pardon for what he might have said against them. Finding himself unable to attend to public affairs, he nominated a council of government—the Bishop, the Governor of the city, the Chancellor, and two other officials. When he felt himself growing worse he called them to him, as well as the Superiors of the Dominicans and Franciscans, and Francis Xavier, and told them that though he neither expected nor desired to live, yet in the state in which he was it was necessary to be at some expense while he hung between life and death; that he had nothing of his own to provide himself with medicines and attendance, and that he begged them to order some part of the King's money to be applied for that purpose. Then he had a missal brought him, and raising his eyes to heaven, swore on it that he had never taken for his own use the money of the King or of any one else, and that he had never made any contract or bargain to increase his own property. He begged that notice of this declaration should be entered on the King's books. Soon after this, having received devoutly all the last sacraments of the Church, he expired in the arms of Francis Xavier. It was the sixth of June; he had been Governor for two years and eight months. 'They opened,' says Faria y Sousa, 'a private desk of his, and what they found therein was a discipline clotted with blood, and three reals. Such was his treasure. He was most devout to the holy Cross. They buried him in the church of St. Francis, and there were some demonstrations of sorrow for him—which, however, were remarkable chiefly because it is so rare to find in India any one who grieves for anything except for the disappointment of his own ambition or the failure of his own designs.'[8]

The mention of the devotion of Joam de Castro to the holy Cross reminds us of some facts concerning him stated by Lucena, which may serve to make the slight sketch here given of him more complete, as well as to illustrate some characteristics of the Portuguese settlers in India. Lucena tells us that during the governorship of Don Joam a discovery of a curious slab of white marble was made at Meliapor in digging for the foundations of a hermitage amid the ruins which marked the spot of the martyrdom of the Apostle St. Thomas. On one face of this slab was a cross in relief, with a bird like a dove over it, with its wings expanded, 'as the Holy Ghost is usually represented when descending on our Lord at His Baptism or our

[8] Faria y Sousa, t. ii. p. 2, cap. 5.

Lady at her Annunciation.' This cross was erected over the altar in the chapel which was built in the new sanctuary. As it was discovered during his governorship, Don Joam 'took it as a heavenly sign of great victories, which God would grant him for the honour and glory of the Cross;' and as in the year after the relief of Diu he obtained some wonderful successes at Salsette and in the neighbourhood, in which great numbers of Mussulmans had been slain with hardly any loss to the Portuguese, 'he considered that the Apostle St. Thomas had gained him these triumphs, especially as the chief rout of the enemy had taken place on his feast day, and as that was the first occasion on which, he himself having requested of his Highness that so it might be, the Portuguese began to invoke in India the name of the glorious St. Thomas along with that of Santiago at the outset of their battles against the infidels.' It was probably in this spring, perhaps during the weeks which Don Joam spent at Goa, before his death, in company with Francis Xavier, that the Governor, 'imitating the arch of Titus and the column of Trajan, decorated the walls and gates and entrances of the city of Goa, and the Government House,' and had an arch built of wrought stones which were brought from the mosque of Diu, with many cannon balls which the enemy had shot into the town on the top, and stone lions with shields bearing his arms on their breasts. The arch was against the wall of the Church of the Misericordia, and inside it was a representation of St. Thomas with his hand in the side of our Lord; and this was solemnly carried to its place with a grand procession, 'borne and accompanied by the Chapter of the See, the religious orders, the College, the Court, the civil authorities, and the soldiery and artillery, with salvos of cannon and musketry and vocal and instrumental music, and all other kinds of solemn and festive celebration; all which was to the great glory of the Saint, and the great consolation and spiritual delight of his great devotee, our Father Master Francis, out of respect and favour to whom Don Joam would have it that this noble triumphal procession of the sacred Apostle should start from the College.'[9]

[9] Lucena, *Vida*, l. vi. cap. 4.

CHAPTER III.

Francis Xavier and his Religious Brethren.

DON JOAM DE CASTRO died on the sixth of June, as has been said, and his death released Francis Xavier from any obligation to remain at Goa. Francis had intended to revisit his brethren who were labouring on the Fishery Coast and in Travancore as soon as possible. They were in continual danger, and most of them new to their work. But navigation was almost impossible till the beginning of September, and we find that Francis did not leave Goa till that time. The three months' interval was spent by him in his usual occupations, teaching the children and slaves the Catechism, preaching on Sundays and festivals, and putting himself at the service of any poor soul that was in need of spiritual charity.

The Governorship of India was a post never left unfilled. Whenever a Governor or Viceroy died in India, the 'patents of succession' were opened. After the decease of Don Joam, as the two officers whose names were first in order were absent from India, the government devolved upon the third, Don Garcia de Sà, a veteran of nearly seventy years of age, who had spent a great many years in India, and had very large experience both in civil and military matters. His reign was to be even shorter than that of Don Joam. He was a man of vigour and integrity, and began by putting in order many matters which had been left in a state of suspense during the later months of Don Joam's government. Whether the hard fighting of Don Joam had used up the munitions and armaments, or not, we are not told, but Garcia de Sà distinguished himself for the careful provision which he made in this respect, having good and strong galleys built, and furnishing all the Portuguese fortresses with artillery and ammunition, as well as gratifying the soldiers with an increase of pay. He was also a very equitable and just civil administrator. He was a good friend to Francis, and took some measures for the protection of his favourite converts on the Fishery Coast. Francis foretold his death privately to a friend in Malacca, Antonio de Sousa, two months before it happened. Garcia died in July 1549. It is mentioned of him that his integrity was so great, that though he had held considerable offices 'he was forced to give all he had to match two daughters, and yet the best part of their portions was their beauty, and that he was their father.'[1]

Francis also occupied himself during this interval in giving the Spiritual Exercises to several persons. The custom of 'making retreats' in common, according to which a number of persons go through the Exercises together, had not yet become prevalent, and, in the same way, the Exercises were usually extended, by those who made them, to the full space of thirty days. The Japanese Anger and his companions seem to have gone through the Exercises somewhat later than this; Cosmo Torres, already mentioned as having joined the Society, somewhat earlier. But these were all now at the College of Santa Fè, and would no doubt be objects of peculiar interest and care to Francis. It was during this time that they were formed by his fervent and gentle guidance, and that, in their turn, the Japanese strangers communicated to him so much knowledge about their country as served to kindle in him more ardently than ever the desire to go thither and preach the Gospel. We thus find what we may call the domestic circle in which Francis moved, enlarged and increased in interest. When he first came to India, he had but two companions, and he had never been able to live much with them from the time of the commencement of his apostolical labours. Now the little band of members of the Society of Jesus was being multiplied, and Francis had to govern them, form them, and encourage them. For the rest of his short life, this now became one of his chief occupations: even when in so distant a spot as Japan we shall find his thoughts occupied with them, and it is to his care for them

[1] Faria y Sousa, *Asia Portuguesa*, t. ii. p. 2, cap. 6.

that we owe some of the most wonderful and most characteristic of his letters.

The number of his religious subjects was almost doubled by the arrivals of the year 1548. On the third of September a ship from Lisbon, under the command of the admiral Joam de Mendoza, brought the first detachment of a reinforcement of ten of the Society, the remainder being on board another vessel of the fleet which arrived later. In all there were four Fathers, Gaspar Baertz, a Fleming, born at Goes in Zealand, Melchior Gonzalez, Balthazar Gago, and Antonio Gomez: the remaining six were either lay brothers, or scholastics not yet ordained—Joam Fernandez, Egidio Barreto, Paolo Vallez,[2] Francesco Fernandez, Manuel Vaz, and Luis Froes. Francis Xavier left Goa but a few days after the arrival of the first vessel, but he had time to make the acquaintance of Gaspar, who from this moment became one of his most useful and valued assistants in the work of preaching. His history was curious. He had studied philosophy and theology at Louvain, and had taken the degree of Master at the age of nineteen. After this, however, he became a soldier in the army of Charles V., and was wont in after life to reproach himself for what he considered his tepidity in the service of God by the recollection of the ardour with which, at the cost of so many risks and hardships and for so poor a reward, he had served an earthly king. It is not quite easy to trace him through the ten or eleven years of his life which passed between his leaving Louvain and his entrance into the Society; but he seems to have felt himself called to serve God for some time before the latter date, and either thought of or actually practised an eremitical life at Monserrato. Chance or business took him at last to Portugal, where he seems to have held some not very conspicuous office under the King's Treasurer, who one day lost his temper with him and even loaded him with blows; whereupon Gaspar took up his stick, and presented it to him, begging him to take it and beat him with it again whenever, without being in a passion, he

[2] Paolo Vallez is said by Orlandini to have been already a priest. *Hist. Soc.* l. viii. cap. 100.

thought that he deserved it, but imploring him also that when he thought fit to punish his servants he would not let his own passion be his counsellor. He entered the Society at Coimbra in 1546, and seems, like others, to have been moved to the step by the fervent preaching of Strada. While yet a novice, he showed on several trying occasions singular modesty and selfcontrol. It is probable that his learning was hardly known, as he could not speak Portuguese well, and had not been a student at Coimbra; at all events he concealed all his intellectual and acquired gifts so well, that he was thought stupid and uneducated, and was employed either in the kitchen or as keeper of the clothes of the community. One day the religious were accusing themselves of their faults in public to the Superior, Simon Rodriguez, and then Gaspar confessed that he had felt a strong temptation to desire to become a great preacher. Simon at once ordered him to get on a bench and preach to the community. After he had obeyed and blundered through an exhortation at which all were inclined to laugh, Simon asked him what he thought of his own sermon. Gaspar replied that, though he had got on so badly and might do worse other times, he did not give up the hope of being some day a preacher. Simon saw what was implied by his humility, simplicity, and sincerity. He ordered him to leave the employment of the lay brothers among whom he had worked, and to go over his studies again; then he had him ordained, and sent him out to preach.

Gaspar seemed to have received the gift of preaching along with his ordination, for he turned out at once so successful and powerful in the pulpit that his sermons became famous for the conversions which they produced, and he was in great request for what are technically called 'missions' throughout the country. We are told that whenever he arrived at a place to which he was sent, even if it were already evening and he had had no time to prepare himself, he used to go up into the pulpit and preach with all the fatigue and weariness of a long journey on foot to weigh him down. He was passing from one mission at Figuereiro to another at Pedroga when the order met him to embark for India. He went up into the pulpit at the lastnamed place, and preached one sermon with immense fervour and success, so that all the people were at his feet in an instant; he went on hearing their confessions all night, and until late in the forenoon of the following day; then he said mass, and went straight to Coimbra, whither he was summoned, and thence to Lisbon. On his voyage out to India he had displayed the same prodigies of charity, patience, and humility which had marked the outward voyage of Francis Xavier himself. He was always preaching, instructing, hearing confessions, or waiting on the sick, taking on himself all the lowest and most contemptible offices. The 'Capitan Major' himself, Joam de Mendoza, put himself under his direction, and a violent storm which fell on the ship in the passage from the Cape to Mozambique, and which frightened the most courageous and skilful among the sailors, gave him the opportunity of converting some most hardened and abandoned sinners, especially women, who were on board. The storm at length seemed to cease at his prayers. When at last the vessel reached Goa, the whole crew and all the passengers could speak of nothing but the virtues and sanctity of Master Gaspar.[3]

Another of the new band of Fathers had a reputation as a preacher hardly, if at all, inferior to that of Gaspar. This was Antonio Gomez, who had been longer in the Society, having been received into it at Coimbra during Pierre Lefevre's visit in 1545. He was thought one of the ablest men at Coimbra, and was Master in Philosophy and Doctor in Canon Law. When he entered religion, he distributed his large fortune to the poor.

[3] See Eus. Nieremberg, *Claros Varones de la Compania de Jesus*, t. i. p. 45, 46; Orlandini, *Hist. Soc.* lib. viii. c. 100-105; Bartoli, *Asia*, lib. v. p. 445 seq. Bartoli mentions Gaspar's having studied philosophy at Louvain, but does not speak of theology; Nieremberg speaks of both. It seems unlikely, though it is not impossible, that he would have been ordained and sent out as a missioner in less than two years after his entrance into the novitiate, unless he had already made his theological studies. The family name of 'Master Gaspar' was probably as we have given it, Baertz or Bartz being a common name in Holland. He is called Barzæus or Berzæus, Barzeo or Barzée, by the historians, according to the language in which they wrote.

Two years afterwards, we find him spoken of as a strenuous and successful preacher of missions in Portugal, where he went through the whole province 'Entre Douro e Minho' from town to town with a single companion, preaching two or three times a day in the open fields, lodging in the hospitals, living on food which he begged himself, watching by night to prepare what he was to preach by day, and edifying all by his zeal, charity, and indifference to all earthly goods and comforts. Each of them, says Orlandini, heard about fifty confessions every day.[4] Antonio was appointed by Simon Rodriguez to act as Superior to the rest, and even to govern after he had arrived at Goa. At the time when this arrangement was made no one in Portugal knew where Francis Xavier was, as he had not returned westwards from the Moluccas; but the appointment was unfortunate, and entailed a large amount of suffering and scandal on the Society in India. Gomez was in natural gifts and in education superior to Gaspar or any other of his companions, and no fault could be found with him on the score of zeal. But he was one of those instances which are for ever recurring in the history of the Church and of religious orders, of men with great and valuable gifts who are exalted before the time, without having grounded themselves in humility and solid virtue. Francis Xavier could hardly have been deceived as to the weak points in Gomez, though he speaks of him highly at first; never, however, with that warmth and tenderness which characterize his language to Gaspar and others. The appointment made by Simon Rodriguez was one which he had no right to make, yet it embarrassed Francis Xavier, as we shall see, who did not like either entirely to ignore or to acquiesce in it.

[4] *Hist. Soc. Jesu*, l. vii. cap. 67. He tells a characteristic story of one of these missions at Oporto. A bullfight was announced for one of the days of the mission. After the morning sermon Gonsalvez Vaz, Gomez' companion, gave out that he should preach that afternoon at the time named for the bullfight, that he invited all to come, and that he hoped to see who were the servants of God, and who of the world and the devil, by observing who came to church and who went to the bullfight. He meant to preach all the same, he said, even if he had only one old woman to hear him. The church was crowded long before the time of the sermon, and the bullfight deserted.

More than one of the companions of Gaspar and Antonio Gomez were men of mark and singular worth. One of the most conspicuous was Joam Fernandez, who never rose beyond the rank of a simple lay brother, and yet was of immense service to the young Church of Japan when he accompanied Francis Xavier thither. He was a rich young merchant of Cordova, trafficking in silks. Some business had taken him to Lisbon not more than fifteen months before the time of which we are speaking. A friend chanced to ask him to come to hear some service in the house of the Fathers; 'it would be the sweetest music he ever heard in his life.' Joam consented, and found himself present in a 'Congregation' of more than two hundred men, who met once a week for purposes of devotion and penance. One of the Fathers preached an exhortation, and then the lights were put out, and the members of the confraternity took the discipline together, amid groans and tears for their sins. Fernandez was a changed man at once; he resolved to give up the world, and become a religious. He asked to see Simon Rodriguez. Simon Rodriguez, doubting whether the rich young gallant before him would have the courage to persevere in the humble vocation of lay brother, which alone, on account of his want of higher education, was open to him, told him that he could only admit him after long and severe trials. But the first trial to which he was put was enough. He was asked whether he could bear to ride through the most frequented street of Lisbon, finely dressed as he was, upon a donkey's back with his face to the tail? Without hesitating a moment, he went through the ordeal leisurely and rejoicing. Simon then received him at once, in June 1547, and he was sent out to India in the following spring, where Francis Xavier discerned his merit, cultivated his soul with care, and took him, as we shall see, as his companion to Japan.

Melchior Gonzalez had been rather more than two years in the Society, before he sailed from Lisbon: his life was to be short, but he was to leave behind him the fame of an indefatigable and most devoted labourer. Balthazar Gago was another Portuguese recruit: he had a far longer life before him than Melchior, and he was to go to Japan, labour most successfully, and after nearly losing his life more than once, to return broken and relaxed in spirit to Goa and to Europe. Paolo Vallez, Luis Froes, and Francesco Fernandez, were all to become famous for their sufferings and labours for religion. Besides those mentioned in the list of recruits sent from Portugal, there was another, beside Cosmo Torres, who had joined the Society in Goa, on whom Francis Xavier's heart rested with particular affection. This was Alfonso de Castro, the son of rich and noble parents in Lisbon. He had known Francis Xavier and Simon Rodriguez on their first arrival in Portugal, and was one of the lads who were taught by them to go regularly to confession and communion once a week. He kept up these holy practices after the departure of Francis, and as he grew up to man's estate, the desire of serving God in religion became strong and engrossing in his heart. He knew that his parents would not consent to part with him, so he determined to go to India and ask Francis Xavier to admit him. He had a companion of his own age and of the same mind, and the two young men arranged with the captain of one of the vessels of the fleet which was to sail to Goa, got off in secret from the shore, and hid themselves in the hold. They were, however, tracked and discovered, and then Alfonso pleaded his cause so earnestly and resolutely, that his parents and friends had not the heart to hinder his departure. They provided him with what was necessary for the voyage, and then the two companions were allowed to depart in peace. Alfonso, as soon as the ship had sailed, distributed all his provisions and outfit to the poorest among the passengers, and lived during the voyage on alms, practising humility, charity, and other virtues in a way that gave the highest idea of his sanctity. On arriving at Goa, the two friends threw themselves at the feet of Francis, and were received into the Society. Alfonso's companion soon fell sick and died. Alfonso himself was cherished and carefully trained by Francis Xavier, who took him in the following year to Malacca, after he had been ordained priest, and then sent him to labour in the Moluccas, where he was soon to meet a glorious death.

Only a few days after the arrival of Gaspar and his companions, and before the arrival of the ship which conveyed the little band led by Antonio Gomez, Francis set off once more for the Comorin Coast. His old enemies the Badages had been as active as usual in molesting the new Christians. Some of the missionaries themselves appear to have been in great danger. Meanwhile, the newly arrived Fathers began to work with all the activity of long restrained fervour. Their first occupation seems to have been to give the Spiritual Exercises to a number of Gaspar's converts during the voyage. The 'Capitan Major' himself was one of them; another was an officer whose name is not recorded, sent out to take the command of one of the king's strongholds and settlements in the East; another was a doctor of canon and civil law; Diego Lobo, nephew of the Baron d'Alvito, was another; Luigi Mendez, four other young nobles, and a crowd of persons of inferior rank, are also mentioned.[5] Of these, Luigi Mendez alone, as far as Bartoli could discover, entered the Society. Gaspar soon began to preach. Indeed, on account of his great reputation and the high character given of him by those who had sailed with him, Francis ordered him to preach at once, before his own departure, on the Nativity of our Blessed Lady (Sept. 8th), in the church of the College. A great crowd assembled to listen to him; but his voice was so thin and weak that he was heard by only a very few. Francis bade him practise his voice in the church at night, and in a few days it was strong and clear enough for any use required of it. Gaspar spared neither his lungs nor himself. The College was badly furnished with teachers, so he took the class of grammar and of philosophy himself, and began also to give Scripture lectures in the book of Proverbs. He went on preaching also in the church. The second batch of Fathers, under Gomez, arrived the first week in October, after having been in considerable danger near Mozambique, to avert which, they had produced a relic of one of the companions of St. Ursula. Gomez, in the absence of Francis Xavier, seems to have assumed the command of the College: at least we find

[5] Bartoli, *Asia*, l. ii. p. 165.

Gaspar and others of the lately arrived Fathers acting in obedience to him. Gaspar was very successful in conversions. Among others, he converted a rich Brahmin, whom in the course of his visits to the prison he found detained there for some crime not mentioned. This conversion made a great noise, and was celebrated with public rejoicings. 'With the force of his spirit, says Gaspar's biographer, 'he soon so moved the city of Goa, that it did not know itself, although it had sometime had the benefit of the preaching of St. Francis Xavier. Gaspar preached daily to the nobility in the palace, to the slaves in the streets and public places, to the poor in the prisons, to the people in different churches, with an eloquence so new and so truly Christian, producing so many tears and such changes of life, that our people who had known him in Portugal were astonished. He kindled the fervour of the Portuguese, converted the heathen, edified and did good to all. It seemed as if he had an infused gift of speaking Portuguese, as he spoke it as if it were his native tongue, without even a foreign accent.'[6]

In the midst of all this fervour and religious renovation, a strange report spread through the city that Francis Xavier had been murdered by the Badages. The story was told with great particularity as to the circumstances of the tortures to which he had been subjected and the constancy with which he had borne them. The report served to bring out in public the universal opinion of his sanctity. Every one had something to say about his perfection and his works of charity, his fervour, his confidence in God under danger, his unwearied patience in suffering, his humility, his gentleness and sweetness to others, his unsparing severity to himself. Miracles that had hardly been heard of, secret prophecies which he had made and which had come true, and a thousand little acts of personal tenderness and instances of his prudence and wisdom in the guidance of souls, came to light now. A number of the Portuguese agreed to set out in order to redeem his sacred relics, as they considered them, from his murderers, and others set on foot an application to the king to ask for his canonization from the

[6] Nieremberg, *Claros Varones*, t. i. p. 47, 48.

Pope. The rumour was soon contradicted: while it lasted, it drew particular attention and veneration to the rest of the Fathers, and seems to have spurred on their religious zeal and spiritual activity, till the face of things at Goa was really changed for the better.

Scattered throughout the letters of this time which were sent home by the Fathers newly come to India, are notices of Francis which show the same instinctive appreciation of his marvellous and most attractive sanctity. 'I wish to tell you about Master Francis,' writes Enrico Enriquez to Ignatius Loyola in the October of this year. 'Give great thanks to God our Lord, with all of our Society. For what St. Paul says, that he became all things to all men, that he might gain all, this Master Francis tries as much as he can *et supra quod dici potest* to accomplish, and no pen can describe to your Reverence what a reputation he has in India, from which result much fruit and great praise to God our Lord, and all the people hold him for a great saint. He is never anywhere where he does not find superabundant occupations, so much so that a man thinks himself very well off if he can speak to him.' 'He is a true Father,' writes Manuel de Morães a few months later than this; 'no one, I think, can see him without great consolation, the very sight of him seems to move to devotion: he is a man of middle height, he always holds his face upwards, and his eyes are full of tears, his look is bright and joyous, his words few and exciting to devotion, you hear nothing from his mouth but "Jesus" and "O Most Holy Trinity." . . . And then he broke out, "O my brothers and companions, how much better is God to us than we thought of! Consider this and give great thanks and praise to God our Lord, that in so short a time as it is since our holy Society was confirmed, being only seven years, it has pleased Him to work in it all that we see, my dearest brothers: that some of us are in Rome, some in Valencia, others in Gandia, others in Coimbra, in the College of Santa Fè at Goa, and in Cape Comorin, and Socotra, and Malacca, and the Moluccas, and others, whither I am going, in Japan." These words he said,' continues Manuel, 'with so much devotion, that he moved all of us who were there to tears and devotion, only to hear his words so full of love and charity, said for an example to us and to make us all conceive greater fervour of spirit, and increased desires of suffering; and to this end, he related to us the trials and tribulations which he had suffered in the countries whence he came, in which he did such things and left behind him so great a fame of sanctity and virtue, that it is not just to write of it whilst he lives. So great is the esteem in which he is held all over India, both by great and small, that the man who is most his friend counts himself the most fortunate.' Another, Paolo Vallez, was sent on straight from Goa after his arrival with Antonio Gomez, and met with Francis at Cochin: 'Who can tell,' he says, 'the delight which my soul then received? I know not how to say it, except in poor words: this is truly a servant of God, and never was any like him! I do not say his speech, but his very look kindles in men such a desire to serve God as cannot be expressed. His mouth never ceased from saying, "Praised be Jesus Christ!" with so much love and fervour as to enrapture all whom he spoke unto.' Then he goes on to tell how Francis was never tired of asking about the fathers and brothers everywhere, especially Simon Rodriguez the Provincial of Portugal, but Father Ignatius above all, and also Father Strada. Melchior Gonzalez writes in the same strain. He was one of those who saw Francis at Goa before he left for Cape Comorin. 'Francis is all full of divine love, and seems to feel nothing else. It would be impossible to begin to describe his virtues; there would be no end to it—or to speak of his miracles and holy discourses. He is a man not old, and of good health, he drinks no manner of wine, and seems to feel no privation, because he is wrapt up in the wounds of his Lord. We may all say,' he adds, 'that we have among us a living martyr, and I think he will soon be really a martyr, for he seems to me to seek nothing else.'

Notwithstanding their frequent trials and sufferings, the state of the Christians on the Fishery Coast was, in many respects, flourishing. About this time we are told that there were fifty thousand Christians there, with a number of churches 'well built, and furnished with their altars, frontals, cloths, lamps which were always burning, in short, in everything the same as we have in Europe, only that those churches were more frequented by the Christian Paravas than ours by us.[7] In Travancore, on the other side of the Cape, things were worse for the time, and Francesco Enriquez was inclined to lose heart and go elsewhere. This brought him the following tender letter from Francis:

(LXI.) *To Father Francesco Enriquez.*

May the grace and charity of our Lord Jesus Christ ever favour and help us! Amen.

I would much rather, dearest brother, talk to you face to face than by letter, and so give you some little consolation for all the toils and discomforts and trials you are bearing for the sake of Christ. You do not ask for consolation of that kind which forms the delight of men of the world who give themselves to all the pleasures of this world that they may live in gaiety and enjoyments. We must needs feel a great compassion for the lot of such. The men whose part we should envy must be those of whom, as the Apostle says, the world was not worthy.[8] Do not grieve, my dear brother, that you make less progress than you could wish in your careful work among these new converts. As you tell me, the nation is addicted to idolatry, and the Rajah himself is hostile to our religion and bitterly persecutes Christians. Well, you do more good than you think, by regenerating in baptism for the kingdom of heaven the infants whom you so diligently seek out and collect. For if you choose to look around you in mind, you will find that of all people in India, whether white or black, very few reach heaven except those who die before they are fourteen years old, and so depart from this life with their baptismal innocence.

Do not you see, dearest brother, that you are doing more good where you are than you think? Surely we can see this in the case of the children whom you have baptized and who

[7] Lucena, *Vida*, l. vi. c. 6.

[8] Orig. *Dignus non erat mundus.*

are now enjoying the bliss of heaven, which they certainly would not be enjoying if you had left those parts and had not begotten them by baptism unto Christ. In truth the everlasting enemy of souls hates you very much and strongly desires that you should go out of the country as soon as possible, so that for the future no one may be called to the Kingdom of Heaven out of the realm of Travancore. It is one of his snares to hold out to us a hope of greater good for the service of God elsewhere; he tries to tempt and turn away those who are working usefully for God where they are at present; and so I am afraid that he may be attacking you with this artifice of his in order to drive you away from that part of the country.

But you should remember that during the eight months which you have now spent there, you have saved more souls by baptizing infants at the point of death than in all the years during which you have been in Portugal and in India; so do not think it wonderful that Satan should give you so much trouble as he does. He does it and fights for it that he may draw you out of that country into another where you may look after the salvation of very few instead of many. Now I will give you some news which I think will be very pleasant to you, that a great many of our Society have arrived since September from Portugal. When I left Goa I ordered them to come and help me here; now I am returning to Goa on a matter of business, which if I can accomplish as I desire, I am in good hopes that a great number will become Christians. I wish you to pray to God that although our sins hinder us from being good servants of His, yet He Himself, out of His infinite goodness and boundless charity towards men, may condescend to use our work, such as it is, for the propagation of religion.

Punical, Oct. 19, 1548.

It is not quite easy to trace Francis through each month of the interval between his departure from Goa in September 1548 and his final sailing for Malacca in the next year. He seems to have returned to Goa by Cochin before the end of October, but he certainly spent a good part of the winter at Cochin; in

February 1549 he went to the Governor in Bazain, and in March he was again in Goa.

At Cochin, where he is stated by some writers to have spent at least two months, he received to baptism the young Rajah of the Maldive Isles, who was seeking the aid of the Portuguese against a rebellion in his rather uninviting dominions. Christian though he became, the Portuguese authorities were not inclined to help him, and he lived to an old age in Cochin. He was a witness to one of Francis's miraculous elevations in the air while saying mass. We may now give the letters which remain to us belonging to this winter, reserving for the next chapter those which have more immediate reference to the arrangements made by Francis in India before his departure for Japan, the idea of which had been so long in his mind, and had gradually taken possession of him as that of the work which he was more immediately called on to undertake. The first letter was written from Goa during the visit mentioned as intended in the letter to Father Enriquez and before his departure for Cochin. This letter is a mere fragment, and we can only guess at its purport. It is addressed to a Father in Portugal, who had entered the Society in the spring of the year before this. His real name was Vasco Martinez; but when the foundation of the College at Coimbra was laid in April that year, it had been agreed, in honour of Ignatius Loyola, that the first person who joined the Society at Coimbra after the ceremony should take the name of Ignatius. Martinez bore the name most worthily. He seems to have written to Francis to ask him to use his influence about a foundation at Villa Viciosa, which does not appear to have come to anything. The Rocco Martinez mentioned at the end was probably the brother or cousin of the Ignatius to whom the letter is addressed.[9]

[9] The register of the College of Coimbra mentions a brother, whose name is not given, as having gone out to India with the rest in 1546. He might well be in the College at Goa at the time that this letter was written.

(LXII.) *To Father Ignatius Martinez, of the Society of Jesus.*

May the holy Name of Jesus be praised for ever! that we may love Him as we ought.

Although I have urgently advised in my general letter, . . . yet I write this to you privately that the greatest possible care may be taken about this business on account of its great importance, especially as everything at present seems to be in much confusion. I am writing to his lordship about the College of Villa Viciosa. God grant that it may be done just as I have told him it ought, for otherwise nothing much will be done at all. I am also writing to our Father Ignatius to explain the reasons for doubt which people will raise, for they are certainly not light matters. But God remains always the same; this is His cause, and He will Himself defend it.

Our brother Rocco Martinez is ill with a fever. We do not think it dangerous. He writes to you himself. The ships will only wait so short a time that I cannot write more, and all that is of most importance is contained in my general letter to all. If I could do anything by private letter, I certainly would very willingly.

May the holy Name of Jesus ever assist us!

Goa, Dec. 22, 1548.

The ships which brought the Fathers from Portugal this year must have conveyed the letters from Ignatius at Rome and Simon Rodriguez at Coimbra which Francis was always anxiously expecting. It seems that among the despatches from Ignatius there were letters to Antonio Criminale, Niccolo Lancilotti, Paul of Camerino, and Alfonsò Cipriano, promoting them, as it is called, to their final vows in the Society in the grade of spiritual coadjutors. Francis must have remained about two months at Goa before returning to Cochin, if, at least, we can depend implicitly on the date of the letter last printed. That he must have spent some time with the Fathers who had arrived since he left Goa in September, is probable on every account, and we may discern some fruits of his acquaintance with Antonio Gomez in the description which he gives to St. Ignatius, in the letter next to follow, of the sort of person required for the post of Rector of the College at Goa. We may notice also how especially Francis insists on the necessity of good practical judgment and prudence, and of the most delicate of all the virtues required in the missioner,—exquisite purity. We may reserve further remarks in explanation of this letter until after it has been put before the reader.

(LXIII.) *To the Rev. Father Master Ignatius of Loyola, General of the Society of Jesus, Rome.*

May the grace and charity of our Lord Christ always be with us! Amen.

My own and only Father in the Heart of Christ, I think that the many letters from this place which have lately been sent to Rome will inform you how prosperously the affairs of religion go on in these parts, through your prayers and the good bounty of God. But there seem to be certain things which I ought myself to speak about to you; so I will just touch on a few points relating to these parts of the world which are so distant from Rome. In the first place, the whole race of the Indians, as far as I have been able to see, is very barbarous; and it does not like to listen to anything that is not agreeable to its own manners and customs, which, as I say, are barbarous. It troubles itself very little to learn anything about divine things and things which concern salvation. Most of the Indians are of vicious disposition, and are averse to virtue. Their instability, levity, and inconstancy of mind are incredible; they have hardly any honesty, so inveterate are their habits of sin and cheating. We have hard work here, both in keeping the Christians up to the mark and in converting the heathen. And, as we are your children, it is fair that on this account you should take great care of us and help us continually by your prayers to God. You know very well what a hard business it is to teach people who neither have any knowledge of God nor follow reason, but think it a strange and intolerable thing to be told to give up their habits of sin, which have now gained all the force of nature by long possession.

This country, too, always tries the strength to live in, either on account of the great heats of the summer or of the excessive winds and rains of winter. In Socotra, the Moluccas, and Cape Comorin, the food and supplies are very poor, and the labour of body and mind very great indeed and beyond all belief, on account of the dispositions of the people you have to contend with. Then, also, the languages of these nations are not at all easy to learn; the dangers to life, both of body and soul, are many and very great. And yet, that all of our Society may give endless thanks to God, I am able with all truth to affirm that all your children of the Society out here in India have great care taken of them by God, so that we are by His mercy not only exempt from dangers of soul and body, but, what is a matter of great wonder to all, we are beloved and well regarded by all the Portuguese, private persons as well as officials and ecclesiastical superiors, and also by all the Indians, Christians and heathens alike.

Again, all the Indians, whether heathen or Mussulmans, as far as I have been able to make out hitherto, are very ignorant. So that those who are to go about in these parts for the purpose of propagating the Gospel, are not so much in need of learning as of virtue—above all of obedience, perseverance, patience, charity, and a very singular purity against numerous temptations to sin; and lastly, of an uncommon gift of counsel and prudence in the management of affairs, as well as strong health and vigour of body and mind, so as to bear labour and afflictions. I have said this, because I think it necessary that diligent examination should be made as to the virtues of the workers who may hereafter have to come to India. And if there are any of them whom you have not sufficiently proved in this respect, at least, I beseech you, let them be men in whom you may place great confidence. Such are the men who are wanted in India—men of singular purity and humility, with no appearance about them of pride or elation.

Any one whom you are to send to be Rector of the College at Goa, where he will rule the native students as well as our own people, must have, besides the other qualities which are necessary in Rectors, two recommendations in particular. In the first place, let him be conspicuous for singular obedience, so as to win by his obligingness and humility the good will of the government officials and ecclesiastical superiors. This is a place of all others where superiors of both kinds require the greatest possible degree of attention and obedience from those who are under them. If they see that we observe their wishes and obey their orders, they are wonderfully kind to us; but if they see any failing in this, they altogether turn against us. In the second place, he should be very easy and gentle; affable in behaviour and speech rather than grave or severe, so as both to desire and to be able to bind to himself in every way the hearts of all, and especially of the students and brethren whom he is to rule. On no account let him be a man who would rather be feared than loved, and who would take the line of keeping those of the Society who are committed to him under rule and subjection as if they were slaves. That kind ot sourness would make many leave us, and prevent any but a few from joining us.

For my part, I think that no force should ever be used, except perhaps that of love and charity, to keep any one against his wish in the Society, and I rather hold that those who dislike the institute of the Society should be sent away, even when they do not wish it; but, for those who are fit and proper subjects, they should be kept in it by the bonds of charity and made to increase in virtue and merits, especially since in these parts they have to bear so many sorrows for the sake of Christ our Lord. In truth, as it seems to me, the Society of Jesus is nothing but a society of love and concord, from which all sourness and all servile fear are altogether foreign and alien. I say all this, that you may pick out a man fit and adapted for the burthen of the post. He ought, in short, to be such a man as even in giving an order seems rather to desire to do what he is told than to command.

The experience which I have of these countries makes me think that I can affirm with truth, that there is no prospect of perpetuating our Society out here by means of the natives themselves, and that the Christian religion will hardly survive us who are now in the country; so that it is quite necessary that continual supplies of ours should be sent out from Europe. We have now some of the Society in all parts of India where there are Christians. Four are in the Moluccas, two at Malacca, six in the Comorin Promontory, two at Coulan, as many at Bazain, four at Socotra. The distances between these places are immense; for instance, the Moluccas are more than a thousand leagues from Goa, Malacca five hundred, Cape Comorin two hundred, Coulan one hundred and twenty, Bazain sixty, and Socotra three hundred.[10] In each place there is one of the Society who is Superior of the rest. As these Superiors are men of remarkable prudence and virtue, the others are very well content.

The Portuguese in these countries are masters only of the sea and of the coast. On the mainland they have only the towns in which they live. The natives themselves are so enormously addicted to vice as to be little adapted to receive the Christian religion. They so dislike it that it is most difficult to get them to hear us if we begin to preach about it, and they think it like death to be asked to become Christians. So for the present we devote ourselves to keeping the Christians whom we have. Certainly, if the Portuguese were more remarkable for their kindness to the new converts, a great number would become Christians; as it is, the heathen see that the converts are despised and looked down on by the Portuguese, and so, as is natural, they are unwilling to become converts themselves. For all these reasons there is no need for me to labour in these countries, and as I have learnt from good authorities that there

[10] The distances given by St. Francis are sometimes various, and must always be taken as merely rough statements. There may be some inaccuracy, also, in the transcription of the letters on these points.

is a country near China called Japan, the inhabitants of which are all heathen, quite untouched by Mussulmans or Jews, and very eager to learn what they do not know both in things divine and things natural, I have determined to go thither as soon as I can.

I undertake this voyage with great happiness in my soul, and with still greater hope, because I feel quite confident that the labour we may spend on that nation will produce solid and lasting fruit. In the College at Goa, which is called the College of Santa Fè, we have three Japanese students who came thither with me last year from Malacca. They tell us wonderful things about Japan. They are youths of very good virtue and extremely sharp wit; Paul in particular, who is sending you a letter of very good length. In the space of eight months he has learnt perfectly to read, write, and speak Portuguese. He is now making the Exercises, and with very good fruit. He is quite well instructed in the Christian doctrine. I have really a very good hope that by God's help there will be a large number made Christians in Japan. I have made up my mind first to go to the king of the country, and then to the universities and seats of learning, and, as I hope, with great gain of souls. As Paul tells me, the religions of Japan are said to have been introduced from Chinghinquo, a city beyond China and Cathay, a year and a half's journey from Japan. When I get to Japan I will write to tell you all about the manners and literature of the people and also about the religion and the doctrines of Chinghinquo. For in all the Chinese Empire and in all Cathay it is said that no other teaching flourishes except that which is handed down in this most famous university. So that when I have got well acquainted with their literature and the doctrine of this place of learning I will write to you about it all at good length. And I shall not fail also to write on the same subject to the University of Paris, that by means of the people there the rest of the universities of Europe may have information of these things. Of those of the Society here I think to take with me only one European, Cosmo Torres of Valentia, who has joined us out here, and besides those three Japanese youths whom I have mentioned. We shall set out, God willing, in next April.

Japan is more than thirteen hundred leagues distant from Goa. We must touch at Malacca and at China on our way. I cannot find words to tell you how much fruit of divine consolation and delight I enjoy in undertaking this business. It is well known that the voyage is exposed to very many and very great dangers from tempests, shoals, and pirates; so that the ship owners think it a great thing if one ship out of two hold her course to Japan. But I feel so moved and encouraged in my inmost heart, that I could never think of abandoning my plan of going to Japan, even if I knew for certain that I should have to undergo greater dangers than ever before in my whole life, so great is the hope of propagating the Christian religion which has arisen in me from what Paul the Japanese tells me, or rather from what God Himself puts in my heart. How fit and prepared the country is to receive the seed of the Gospel you will be able to understand from Paul's account of it, which I send you along with this letter.

In these parts of India there are as many as fifteen towns belonging to the Portuguese, in which many houses of the Society might be set on foot if the King would give something out of the public revenues for their commencement. I have said something about this to the King in my letter. I have also informed Simon Rodriguez of everything, and have also told him that it would be very much for the interests of religion if, with your leave, he were to come out here himself with as many as possible of the Society, and a great band of preachers, inasmuch as by his coming, which of course would have the King's favour, several Colleges of the Society might be founded. And to me, my Father, it does seem that the coming to India of Simon, who is so high in favour with the King, will be very seasonable. For he will come with authority from the King, either to found colleges or to assist the Christians—both those that are so already, and those that would be, if there were any one to show them favour. I wish that you would write to Simon what you wish to be done in the matter; for Antonio Gomez has told me that Simon has certainly made up his mind to come out to India with a great number of our people from Coimbra.

Both at Rome and elsewhere you have no lack of men of our Society who are not given to preaching or to literature, and who might be of great advantage to religion out here if only they had sufficient experience, and if they were furnished with the other virtues necessary for helping the heathen, but especially with remarkable purity; and if they had also considerable strength of body and mind, so as to bear the very great labours that have to be borne in these countries. So you must provide for us such workers according as seems good to you.

You would also do a thing well worth your while, and which would, as I hope, be pleasing to God, if you would send out to us all of the Society who are in India a letter full of spiritual precepts, as a sort of will and testament by means of which you impart to the least of your children who are at such a distance from the sight of you, the riches and treasures which you have received from God. Do it at your leisure; but I do beseech you some time or other grant us this favour. Enrico Enriquez, a Portuguese priest of our Society, a man of excellent virtue and good example, who is now in the Promontory of Comorin, writes and speaks the Malabar tongue very well indeed; and so he alone works with great profit as if he were a great many. His sermons and private conversations have made him a marvellous object of love and veneration to the native Christians. I beg of you to let such a man, so good, so laborious, so useful a worker in the vineyard of Christ, 'who bears the burthen and heat of the day,'[11] have the consolation of a letter from yourself.

There is a town called Cranganor, which belongs to the Portuguese, about twenty miles from Cochin, where Fra Vincenzo, of the most holy order of St. Francis, who is also *socius* to the Bishop of Goa, and a most true friend to our Society, has founded a really fine seminary, where quite as many as a hundred native students are maintained and formed in piety and learning. In his goodwill towards our Society Fra Vincenzo does not surpass the Bishop of Goa himself, who now has juris-

[11] *Qui portat pondus diei et æstus.* (Orig.)

diction over the whole of India, who is very devoted to us, and who desires to have your friendship; and so I should like you to write to him. But to return to Fra Vincenzo. He told me, out of the kindness which exists between us, that he wishes to intrust and hand over his seminary to our Society; and he has asked me again and again to inform you of his intention, and to provide a priest of the Society who may teach grammar to the students of this seminary, and preach to the inmates and to the people on Sundays and festivals. There is reason for this, because, besides the Portuguese inhabitants of the place, there are a great many Christians living in sixty villages in the neighbourhood, descended from those whom St. Thomas made Christians. The students of the seminary are of the highest nobility.

In this town there are two churches, one of St. Thomas, one of St. James. Fra Vincenzo, whom I have mentioned, hopes very much that you will get each of them a plenary indulgence once a year from the Holy Father, on the feasts of St. Thomas and St. James, and the seven days after each. This would be to increase the piety of the natives who are descended from the converts of St. Thomas, and are called Christians of St. Thomas. And besides these indulgences, he expects you to send him a priest to be a master and preacher in the town. These boons will bind him so closely to us, that he will be our own devoted friend in life and after death. He has committed this business to me very urgently. I can't tell you how he longs for the indulgences.

I will ask you one thing for myself: that some priest of ours may throughout the year say mass once a month for me at St. Pietro in Montorio, in the chapel where St. Peter the Apostle is said to have been crucified. I wish also that you would charge some one in the Gesù to write to us regularly and fully concerning the Colleges of the Society, the professed Fathers, their duties, and the work that the Society is doing and the fruit it is reaping. I have given orders at Goa that the letters from Rome be sent to Malacca, and that at Malacca they be copied and sent to me by many different hands to Japan.

And now, father of my soul, whom I venerate with all my

heart, I humbly pray you on my knees, for so it is that I write this letter, as if I had you here present to look upon, never to cease to implore God for me in your holy sacrifices and prayers, that as long as my life lasts He may give me the grace clearly to know and fully to carry out His own most holy Will. And I ask the rest of our brethren to be entreated to do the same for me.

Your least and useless son,

Cochin, Jan. 14, 1549. FRANCIS XAVIER.

The account of himself and of Japan referred to in this letter, as given by Anger, now called Paul of the Holy Faith, is still extant, as it was preserved both at Rome and at Coimbra, though we are not aware that the documents have ever been printed. In the letter to Ignatius Anger gives a short history of his adventures and of the manner of his conversion. The substance of this history has been related in a former chapter. The other document, about Japan, is long and interesting, and, together with the statements made by Portuguese merchants trading with that country, must have formed the foundation of all the knowledge possessed by Francis Xavier concerning it until he landed on its shores. The most curious statement in the letter which has just been inserted is that about the place or university called Chinghinquo—or, as it stands in the ordinary versions, Jenico—from which the religions of Japan, and, as Francis tells us in the companion letter to Simon Rodriguez, of China and Tartary also, are said to be derived. This mysterious university has puzzled most of the editors of the letters of Francis Xavier. The most reasonable explanation of the matter is, we think, to be found in the account of Japan drawn up from Anger's statements, and sent to Europe, to which we have just now referred. In that account Anger gives the story of the origin of the religion in a country (tierra) beyond China towards the west, called 'Chinguinquo or Chenguinco,' in which was born the holy prince Xaqua, whose history he then relates. This history is identical in all its main features with that of Sakya-mouni, the founder of Bhuddism, the more salient points of whose doctrine and whose five precepts are given in the document. The scene of Sakya-mouni's history lies about the Ganges, but it may be doubted whether Anger's statement was founded upon anything more than the dim knowledge which he had that the religion of his country had come from the West.

It may be observed also that Francis speaks in this, as in the following letter, of arrangements which he contemplated as if they were already made, considering, no doubt, the lapse of time which would intervene between the dispatch of his letter and its reception by Ignatius. No members of the Society were as yet at Socotra. The following letter is dated on the same day as the last. It must be remembered that Francis could only send letters at very long intervals, and that he probably wrote from time to time as he had leisure, and dated the letters when he was about to make up his packet. This next letter explains more fully his designs as to Socotra. The mention of Antonio Criminale reminds us that we have said but little hitherto about this distinguished Father, who was in a very short time from this to be the first of the Society to receive the crown of martyrdom in the Indies. He was still in the flower of youth—barely twenty-nine years of age. He was born in 1520, near Parma, and it was at that city that in 1540 he fell under the spell which the fervent and gentle spirit of Pierre Lefèvre threw over all who came near him. Lefèvre had been sent to Parma in company of Laynez, and had given the Exercises to a large number of persons, among whom was a good priest, Pezzani by name, a friend of the young Antonio, whom he brought to Pierre Lefèvre. Antonio made the Exercises, and put himself entirely under Pierre's direction. The next year he went to Rome alone and on foot, as a pilgrim, and was received by Ignatius into the house of the Society on probation. He was about to be admitted, when his mother died, and his father called him home. Ignatius advised him to go, and he so won on his father by his holy, devout, unworldly manners after his return, that in a few days he obtained his consent to his entering the Society; and he set out again on foot to beg his way to Rome, leaving behind him a wonderful increase of fervour and piety among his brothers and sisters. He was received into the Society in April 1542, and at once ordained subdeacon. Then he was sent, with six other young men, one of whom was the well-known Pedro Ribadineira, the sportive, boisterous boy, who was a sort of spoiled child to Ignatius, on a long pilgrimage, which was to lead some of them to Paris for their studies, others, among whom was Antonio, as far as Coimbra. He was ordained Priest in 1544, and came to India in 1545, with Don Joam de Castro, as has already been stated. Having been so much at Rome, he was well known to Ignatius, and this will explain the special mention made of him in the following letter. Moreover, Ignatius had just admitted him to his last vows, and we have still Antonio's letter of thanks to him for this favour, dated a few weeks before the letter of Francis Xavier, with which it was probably enclosed.

(LXIV.) *To the Rev. Father Master Ignatius of Loyola, General of the Society of Jesus, Rome.*

May the peace and charity of Christ our Lord be always with us! Amen.

My own and only Father in the Heart of Jesus Christ,—I have written to you three letters almost in the same words and at great length, which I have committed to the care of M. Simon. Antonio Criminale, with six others of the Society, is in the Promontory of Comorin. He is in truth, believe me, a holy man—a man made for work in these countries; and as you have many in Europe like him, I want you to send a good number of such out here. He is Superior of the others in the Comorin mission. He is wonderfully dear to the native Christians and to the heathen and Mussulmans, and I can hardly tell you how the fathers and brethren under him love him. Father Cipriano, who already suffers from old age, is to go to the island of Socotra; he is to leave at the end of January, and will take with him three of ours—one priest, the rest lay brothers. Socotra is an island about a hundred miles round, all its inhabitants are Christians, but such as have hardly anything Christian but the name, as many years ago they were deprived of Catholic priests. They say that they are descended from the Christians converted by St. Thomas the Apostle. I am in hopes that by the labours of Cipriano and the others they will come to better things. The island is very poor in crops and provisions; a rough place enough and full of troubles. And yet Cipriano, who is already sixty years old, is going there with great goodwill, full of confidence that he may do a good work for God there, and at the same time do penance for the faults of his youth. Although at first he alleged the excuse ot his declining age, which is not able to bear much labour, yet he directly afterwards declared that he would go without any difficulty at all if there were need. Niccolo Lancilotti, although an invalid, is now better, and is at Coulan, a town of a good salubrious air, about eighty miles from Cochin. He is there at the head of the foundation of a College.

And indeed a great many Colleges of the Society would be started in these parts if Master Simon (as I have already said in a letter to you) were to be sent out with great powers from the King, and bring with him a large number of the Society, of whom six or seven should be preachers, and many fit for hearing confessions, giving spiritual exercises, receiving heathen into the Church, and all of whom should be men of selfcommand and experience in affairs. I have also written to the King concerning Master Simon, that his Highness may send him with power not only to begin Colleges, but also to confer favours on the native Christians and the heathen, whom ever so little an amount of favour would make willing converts to Christianity.

I send you the Japanese characters. The Japanese write in a very different manner from other nations, beginning at the top of the page and writing straight downwards to the bottom. I asked Paul the Japanese why they did not write as we do? 'Why, rather,' said he, 'do not you write as we do? The head of a man is at the top and his feet at the bottom, and so it is proper that when men write it should be straight down from top to bottom.' I also send you an account of Japan, and of the manners of the natives, which Paul has given me. He is a very religious and trustworthy man. Two months hence I shall sail for Japan with Father Cosmo Torres, Paul, and two other Japanese, if God so will. When I am there I will write you an account of what their books contain, for I cannot get at this from Paul, who was a layman, and so never had any acquaintance with the literary monuments of Japan, which are in a sort of different language, like books written in Latin among ourselves. May Jesus our Lord teach us to do His will,[12] and after we have passed through the troubles of this life, bring us into His blessed and eternal home! Amen.

Cochin, Jan. 14, 1549.

The letter to the king, mentioned just above, must have been different from that which we are next to insert, which is written with even more than usual freedom and severity of language. Some persecution had probably been raging in Ceylon against the new Christians, and the inveterate evil of a conflict of interests and objects between the king's officers and the Franciscan missionaries had produced the usual result of the frustration of the work of the latter. We are not told whether the king spoken of was the Rajah of Candy, or the Rajah of Jafanapatam. The Franciscan Superior seems to have made up his mind to go to Europe himself to plead the cause of religion with the King. His name has already been mentioned in the letter of Francis to the King, written the year before this.

(LXV.) *To John III. King of Portugal.*

I do not write to your Highness all the calumnies, wrongs, and vexations with which the recent converts to our holy religion out here are harassed and oppressed. The Father Fra Joam of Villa da Conde, who is on his way to you, will give your Highness a full and most true account of everything of this sort, and will put the whole matter, as it were, before your

[12] *Doceat nos facere voluntatem suam.* (Orig.)

very eyes. He is a man to whom your Highness owes very many thanks for the great and innumerable labours which he has undergone in these countries of India in the service of God and of your Highness, to make more easy for you the account which the conscience and duty of your Highness exacts from you before God. But in measuring the deserts of Father Fra Joam, I would have your Highness take into consideration not only the exertions, the sufferings, the long watchings, and other bodily troubles, however many, great, and continuous they may have been, which he has had to undergo. All these things are mere child's play and sport when compared with the distress of mind, the terrible torments which have torn his soul to pieces, in seeing with his own eyes, and without any power to prevent it in any way, how the Commandants of your Highness's forts and the Procurator of your revenues savagely plunder and ravage and make a prey of these most miserable neophytes, these tender babes in the faith of Jesus Christ which they have only just adopted, and whom on that account these same Christian officers, who subject them to every vexation, ought rather to have cherished and to have loaded with every benefit. Believe me, Sire, this kind of heart pang is bitterest of all, far more than all the pains of the body; it is indeed, so to speak, a very dreadful kind of martyrdom, more terrible than any torture which tyrants can inflict, to be forced to keep still and be patient when you see destroyed in one moment, by the fault of others, all the good that had almost been brought to its final crown and consummation by most strenuous exertions and most painful perseverance of yourself and others, continued during a long space of time.

We have heard it reported here as certain, that the King of Ceylon is sending some very precious presents to your Highness, in return for the many great benefits which he daily receives from you. Now let your Highness understand as an undoubted fact, that in this man a most fierce and bitter enemy of Christ reigns in Ceylon, and, what it is almost a crime to say, is authorized and furnished with arms for injuring the cause of Christ and for oppressing our religion as much as he can, by no power on earth more than by the favour and the gifts he receives from your Highness. These things are as true as truth itself. Your Highness and others will not perhaps like to hear them, and I certainly write them with very great reluctance, especially as I fear that I shall have done so to no purpose; and when we who are here form our conjectures as to the future from the experience of the past, there is very great reason for us to fear that after this it will be as it has been hitherto, and that your Highness will show greater favour to that declared and bloody enemy of Jesus Christ of whom I speak than to the religious priests who are working for Christianity in Ceylon. When people see these things going on before their eyes, the clear evident facts sometimes prompt them to free speeches about you, which, Sire, with your good leave, I will here insert. They say that your Highness does not use your imperial power in India for the enlargement of the Kingdom of Christ, but only for the purpose of scraping together riches and securing for yourself, and those who belong to you, human and temporal advantages alone.

I pray your Highness to pardon me if I put things as they are, so clearly and without circumlocution; for I am compelled to do this by my sincere and true love for your Highness, and the desire which I have for your eternal salvation. I seem to myself to hear the sentence of God at the great Judgment Day giving out His decree, or rather declaring then to all what He has before decreed at your last moment, when you die; the stern necessity of which moment no one however powerful can avoid, no one, either by artifice of his own or the work of any one whatsoever, is able to escape. Nor, I beseech you, let your Highness think much of those commands, many and grave as they are, which you piously and with such fair show are in the habit of inserting in your royal letters to the Governor, the Commandants, and the other officials in India, ordering that before all things else care be taken for religion, and favour be shown to the Christians; for I, Sire, who am on the spot to see things as they really are here, am clearly convinced that no hope remains of any true and serious obedience being ever paid to these commands. And on this account it is one, and not the least, of the reasons why I intend to go to Japan, that I may fly away to those islands in the extreme East, and there labour for God with greater usefulness than has been possible to me hitherto.

Father Fra Joam takes with him, in order to be communicated to your Highness, certain statements concerning the unhappy Christians of the Comorin Coast. I beg your Highness to have some pity upon them, and not to think it too much trouble to be a father to them; for they are indeed fatherless, on account of the late death of Miguel Vaz, in whom they have lost a most excellent and a most true father.

It is now five and forty years that a certain Armenian Bishop, by name Abuna Jacob, has served God and your Highness in this country. He is a man who is about as dear to God on account of his virtue and holiness as he is neglected and despised by your Highness, and in general by all who have any power in India. God thus rewards his great deserts Himself, and does not think us worthy of the honour of being the instruments whom He uses to console His servants. The Franciscan Fathers alone take care of him, and show him kindness to which nothing can be added. But for this, the good old man would long ago have breathed out his soul, worn out by affliction. Allow me, Sire, to advise what I think would be well. I would very much recommend your Highness to order a letter to be written in your name to this good Bishop in kind and honourable terms, and to let an order which may be shown to the Governors and Procurators, your officers, be inserted in the same letter, enjoining on them, and especially on the Commandant of Cochin, to show him honour, give him hospitality, and treat him with favour and attention, especially whenever he asks for or is in need of anything. While I have been writing this I have seemed to myself to be serving and doing a favour, not so much to that pious Bishop as to your Highness. For at present, from the charity of the Franciscan Fathers, he wants for nothing, while your Highness is very greatly in want of the goodwill and intercession of a man very acceptable to God as he is, and this benefit you will be able to earn by such an act of kindness as I mention. This Bishop very greatly deserves such treatment on this account if on no other—that he has spent much labour in attending to the Christians of St. Thomas, and now in his all but decrepit old age he conforms himself most obediently to all the rites and customs of our holy Mother the Roman Church. I know that your Highness is in the habit of writing to the Franciscan Fathers, and this letter to the Armenian Bishop might be inserted in the same packet; and I would urge your Highness to write it full of all manner of expressions of your favour, esteem and affection for him.

And now may God our Lord impress deeply on the mind of your Highness a clear knowledge of His most holy will, and may He at the same time supply you with strength and give you His holy assistance, that you may fully and perfectly execute the same in such wise as your Highness would rejoice to have done in the final hour of death, when, Sire, you will have to give to God an account of all your life up to that time! That moment, which will decide on your eternity, will come more quickly than your Highness thinks, and so it is well to take measures in good time that you may go to meet it well prepared. Kingdoms and reigns pass away, and after them will succeed a new and most unexpected aspect of affairs, such as never yet came into the mind of your Highness, not even in thought or in the first beginnings of suspicion. For you will see yourself despoiled by death of your kingdom, cast out from all your possessions, and thrust forth into other realms, far different from these—realms of terror and darkness, into which it will be a very hard and a very bitter lot to be banished after having been torn away from those others of your own: more especially if—what God avert!—you were to be sentenced to remain outside Paradise, and to be denied all hope of ever entering there.

Your Highness's useless servant,

Cochin, Jan. 26, 1549. FRANCIS.

The next letter which remains to us seems probably made up of more than one despatched to Simon Rodriguez by the same ship which took the letters to the King and to Ignatius. At least, the copy of the letter preserved in the College at Coimbra ends with the paragraph at p. 90 about Fra Vincenzo and Cranganor. We shall speak in the next chapter of the final arrangements made by Francis as to the posts and employments of the members of the Society before he left India, and need here only repeat the remark that neither the mission of Cipriano to Socotra, nor that of Antonio Gomez to Ormuz, of which place we now hear for the first time in these letters, really took effect. The rest of the letter needs no explanation.

(LXVI.) *To Master Simon Rodriguez.*

I can find no words, my dearest Brother Simon, enough to express the amount of joy which the arrival of Antonio Gomez and the others who came with him caused me. I must tell you that they are making great progress in piety, and that by the good example of their lives, by the sermons they preach, by the confessions they hear, by the meditations they give, and by their private conversations, they advance the interests of religion wonderfully, and every one is exceedingly pleased with them. There is indeed much need of such excellent men of our Society out here, especially in the city of Ormuz and in the town of Diu, places which want good preachers much more than Goa itself, so great is the number of Portuguese who are there living in a way altogether degenerate from Christian rules and laws. So, in order to meet the necessity, I have determined to send to Ormuz Antonio Gomez, a man highly gifted with powers of preaching and doing other kinds of work of our Society. Master Gaspar will remain in the College of Santa Fè.

You will most certainly gain great favour with God if you come out to India with as many as may be of the Society, bringing seven or eight good preachers with you, and other men of much experience and moderation. There is no such great need of much learning for the conversion of the heathen, for the people in these countries are very barbarous and ignorant, so that men even of moderate learning may do very serviceable work for God out here, provided they are men of great virtue and strength. In all the towns in India where we could place a preacher of our Society with another priest to help him in hearing confessions and doing the other functions of our Society, it would be possible to have a house of the Society for the sake of educating the children of the Portuguese and of the natives.

I have written to our Father Ignatius to give you leave to come, and also to the King to send you to India with a large company of our Society and with great authority from himself. If this shall come about, you may believe me that your coming will be of much greater advantage to religion than you think. Another thing about which I have written to the King, is to get him to provide for the children of the Portuguese whose parents have lost their lives in his service and left their children orphans and poor. For no one thinks of paying them the salaries and sustenance which are owing to their parents. So that it would not be out of the way to found some colleges in India where orphans of this sort might not only be supported, but also educated. And as the King is bound also to look after the welfare of the natives, it would be for the interests of religion to give orders that the children of native Christians in certain places should have the Catechism taught them. So I am writing to his Highness to assign, if it seems good to him, about five thousand gold pieces out of the revenue of Bazain for the opening of a house of this kind. I hope confidently that the King, with the good help of God, will do all these things by means of your coming out.

I have lately heard of the country of Japan, which lies beyond China more than six hundred miles. They tell us that the inhabitants are very clever, very desirous of learning not only religious truth, but also the natural truths which are a part of education. The Portuguese who have come back from Japan tell us this, and indeed it is proved well enough by certain Japanese themselves, who last year came with me from Malacca to India, and have lately been made Christians at Goa, in the College of Santa Fè. You will be able to see this well enough yourself from the account of Japanese matters which we have sent you, which we got from Paul the Japanese, who is called Paul of the Holy Faith, a man really of very excellent virtue and perfect truthfulness. He is writing to you about himself and his affairs, and the benefits which God has bestowed upon him. So in the month of April next I intend to go to Japan with Cosmo Torres, a priest of our Society; for I am persuaded that the Christian religion will be propagated in those parts far and wide; add to this, that here I am doing nothing, and am not wanted, since, on account of our brethren who have come out this year, my work is by no means necessary to the Indians, more especially as in a short time you are either coming out yourself, or going to send out some one else in your place with a large body of our Society. I do hope very much that you will come yourself. I also think that just at your arrival I shall have reached Japan, and you will set things in good order here according to what I say in these letters, and then if God, as I hope, gives me a favourable opportunity of doing some good work in Japan, we shall see one another again at Goa.

Then as time goes on, a great many of our Society, by the good help of God, will penetrate into China, and from China into that famous University of Chinghinquo, which lies beyond China and Cathay. For Paul tells me that all the Chinese, the Japanese, and the Tartars get their religion from the city of Chinghinquo. The religion of Japan is contained in certain recondite books which the common people know nothing of, just as Latin books are not known to them among ourselves. For this reason Paul, who is a private person and knows nothing at all about the literature, says he has nothing to tell us about the religious doctrines of the country. When I get there, if God so wills, I will write to you at full length what these sacred books of theirs contain. My plan is, as soon as I arrive in Japan, to go to the king himself and the principal seats of learning, which are to be found in the royal cities; and when I have made myself well acquainted with all these matters, I intend to write what I have found out, not only to India, but to the Universities of

Portugal, of Italy, and above all of Paris, and admonish them, while they are devoting themselves heart and soul to learned studies, not to think themselves so free and disengaged from responsibility as to take no trouble at all about the ignorance of the heathen and the loss of their immortal souls.

Pedro Gonsalvi, the Vicar of Cochin, who is a very great friend of our Society, is writing to commend to you some affairs of his own. I pray and beseech you not to fail to do all that you can in his case, both as regards the King and as regards the benefits which he asks for the Christians who form his people. You may be quite sure that he is a true and genuine friend of the Society; he takes into his own house with the utmost kindness all of ours who have to be at Cochin. Another thing—I want you to get eight or ten casks of wine for the Fathers at Goa, and those who are dispersed over the whole East, to be used at mass. Wine is very necessary out here; but it is not only very dear but also extremely scarce. Our Fathers at Malacca, at Cape Comorin, at Socotra, and in the Moluccas have no wine for the holy Sacrifice except what is brought from India. The Bishop of Goa and the Franciscan Fathers have wine furnished them at the public expense from Portugal; and in the same way the King ought to assign a quantity of wine to the College of Santa Fè, whence it may be sent to the other Fathers.

Father Cipriano is to go this year to the island of Socotra with one priest and two lay brothers. In that island there is a certain Mussulman lord who has gained supreme power by violence and rules against all the laws of justice and right. He cruelly oppresses and persecutes the Christian inhabitants; he takes their children from them and makes them Mahometans, besides overwhelming the parents themselves with infinite ills and troubles. I wish you very much to urge the King, in his great desire to protect religion, to do something at last in the way of looking after these Christians. He can do it without any expense and with no trouble, if he will give orders to his fleet on its way to the Indian seas to put down the Mussulmans, who are really weak. The inhabitants have had all their arms taken from them, and are oppressed by the yoke of a very severe bondage; and so they hate the very name of the Mussulmans. So I pray you, by Jesus Christ our Lord, to interfere in favour of the liberty of those Socotrians, since they are really in a state of such unjust slavery. The whole aspect of the island is really wretched. Some years ago, when I was on my way to these parts, the lot of the inhabitants moved my pity very much, so cruelly are they persecuted by the Arabs, who have the command of the seas. The whole matter, as I say, can be settled with no expense, at the simple command of the King. Alfonso Souza, who was formerly Governor of India, can give abundant testimony to what I say, as he has seen all these things with his own eyes.

I have sent Manuel Vaz[13] back to Goa, thinking it not best to let him return to Portugal. After seeing Antonio Gomez at Goa, I have thought it better to make Master Gaspar Rector of the College; so that Antonio may be freed from all care, and be able to give himself entirely to preaching, hearing the confessions of the people, and giving the Spiritual Exercises. He has much more facility for these things than for government, especially as Gaspar is very good in bearing the burthen of the administration of the house. Give orders, I beseech you, that every year some of the Society are sent out hither after you, and let most of them be priests. Write also to Rome and to all places where the Society exists, that they may send to Coimbra some priests of great experience and noted virtue, who, not being highly gifted with learning or powers of speaking so as to be fit for preaching, or not being very useful in Europe for the work which is done in our Colleges, will be of great use out here in the conversion of the heathen. For although they may do a certain amount of good where they are, yet their industry will certainly be much more fruitful in good out here. If there are any besides who have completed their

[13] The text has Michael, or Miguel, but it is a mistake, founded on the similarity of the name of the late Vicar. Manuel Vaz was a lay brother, who seems to have lost his vocation. He had come to India the year before this.

course at Coimbra, I think you should send them hither to us for the same reason. I entreat you, do not permit it to happen that any year should pass without our having a supply of the Society sent out. Those who are now at the College of Goa have not yet sufficient experience, learning, and virtue for the conversion of the heathen.

At Bazain the King, at the request of Miguel Vaz, who was formerly the Vicar General of India, allotted three thousand gold pieces for the building of a house in which the children of the native Christians were to be instructed. It is thought here that the King wished the administration of that house to be committed to our Society; for eight or nine of our Society, and six Franciscans, came out with Miguel from Portugal. But Miguel landed the Franciscans at Bazain, and gave to them, to distribute and dispense, the money which the King at the request of the Governor Joam de Castro had assigned for the conversion of the heathen. I went lately to Bazain to arrange some affairs for the Christians of the Moluccas, and had some conversation with the Franciscans. They are reduced to a very small number, and again and again begged me to send thither some one of the Society who might provide necessaries for the converts out of the money so assigned, and might also administer the Seminary; so I left Melchior Gonsalvez there with a companion.

Now that Miguel Vaz and Fra Diego de Borba are lately dead, the management of the College at Goa has come to Cosmo Joam, who, having undertaken the care of the revenues and of the completion of the building, found himself so much occupied by business of the King's, that since the arrival of Antonio Gomez he has made over the charge of the College altogether to the Society. It is now the proper time that the cession should be confirmed by royal authority. I would have you get a diploma issued, and bring it with you to India.

There is a town of the King's called Cranganor, fifteen miles from Cochin. There there is a fine College, which was built by Fra Vincenzo, the companion of the Bishop, where as many as a hundred youths, children of the native Christians, who are called Christians of St. Thomas, are educated; for there are sixty villages of these Christians of St. Thomas around the town, and from them the students I speak of are derived. If you ask what sort of a place it is, it looks really very handsome, whether as regards the site or the elevation of the building itself. Fra Vincenzo has done a wonderful work in these parts. He is extremely friendly to me and to our whole Society. He assures me that he is taking measures to leave the administration of the College in our hands when he dies. He is very urgent in asking for a priest of our Society, well versed in grammar, to teach the pupils and to preach to the people on festival days. We must do as he wishes; and I beseech you to send out such a priest as he wants who may do just as he tells him in everything.

At Cranganor there are two churches; one of St. Thomas, which is very piously frequented by the Christians of St. Thomas, and another of St. James, adjoining the College. Fra Vincenzo wishes very much that Indulgences should be obtained for both these churches, to be a consolation for these Christians and to increase piety. So I beg you very much to procure, either through our people at Rome or through the Pontifical Nuncio at Lisbon, a yearly plenary Indulgence for each, beginning from the Vigil of St. James and the Vigil of St. Thomas respectively, and lasting for the eight following days. I would have this Indulgence offered only to those who may have duly approached the Sacraments of Penance and holy Communion, and then piously and devoutly visited these churches at Cranganor. If you will manage these two petitions which I have made to you in the name of Fra Vincenzo, and if at the same time you send him a kind and obliging letter, you may be sure that you will bind him to yourself and to the Society for ever. I also beg of you again and again to write in the same way to the Bishop, who is a very great lover of our Society.

I have written to the King to ask him to make a certain priest, Estevan Luis Buralho by name, a chaplain of his Highness. I have done this not so much for his own sake as because he has some sisters who are orphans and poor, and if their brother is looked upon with honour as having a post in the King's Court he will easily be able to find husbands for his sisters. In making marriages out here there is a great desire for connection with men of good family who are in favour with the King; so if you manage this, you will have safely provided for three orphan girls. The mother of this priest is married again to Gonsalvo Fernando Concinati, and her son desires to gain favour at Court in order to make his stepfather also a good friend to himself and his sisters. He desires therefore that the King should make this stepfather one of his own honorary Chamberlains, without salary, and he persuades himself that if he becomes one of the Court in this way, he will treat himself and his sisters with the love of a father.

The Franciscans are all our best possible friends, but particularly the Guardiano Antonio Casali. He will finish his turn of Superior in two years, and wishes very much to return to Portugal; so I beg of you to get him letters and faculties from the King, enabling him to go back as soon as his time is over, for he is now in his fifth year out here, working for God and the King.

Father Niccolo Lancilotti, whom I have sent to Coulan for the sake of his health, is getting better every day. He is a man just exactly made to please the people there. There is now a talk of establishing a College there, for the instruction first of the children of the Portuguese, and in the second place of the Christians of Comorin and of St. Thomas. The people of the town are not very numerous, and are badly off, so that they cannot even begin a seminary of themselves. I have written about the business to the King, showing him of what great advantage to religion such a College would be. Please to get the King to send orders to the Governor of India and to his own Procurator to build the house at the public expense, and to build it large in size, so that many orphans both of Portuguese and native parents may be supported there. Coulan is a place where all things are very plentiful and very cheap, so that at no great expense a very large number of students might be supported.

If you come hither yourself, my dearest brother Simon, your coming will certainly be very greatly for the benefit of the Christian religion and also for your own delight, but this is all provided that you come armed with authority from the King both to advance the worship of God and relieve the native Christians. So I admonish you again, to come richly supported by the King and the Queen that you may keep the commandants and royal treasurers to their duty; that will be the one way for you to do service to India and the worship of Christ greater than any one would ever expect.

I have received joyful news from Malacca, as to the good work done by Francesco Perez and Rocco Oliveira for religion. You will learn all from their own letters. We have also the best of news from the Moluccas. Joam Beira and his companions are working under great hardships and in perpetual danger of life, to the great increase of the Christain faith. The report spread about concerning the murder of Beira seems, to me at least, to have nothing in it. Only a little before the time named he wrote me a most diligent account of all that he was doing, all his trials and dangers. After the ships left Ternate his companions wintered for three months at Amboyna. Meanwhile Joam Beira came to Ternate from the Maurica to the commandant, to ask him to send a force of Portuguese to help the Christians there. On his return thither from Ternate, it is said that something very sad happened to him, but I can find nothing about it either in any letters that have come or upon any good authority. However, I can affirm for certain, that those who love God and their neighbour are tried out there, like gold in the furnace. I do not know whether anywhere else in the whole Christian world those who serve God and work for the salvation of souls have so many labours and so many and so great dangers of death to try their virtue, as in that land of the Maurica. I wish you to pray God for those of ours who have gone there, and for those who are to go, for I have determined shortly to send two or three of our Society. It is my opinion that those islands of the Moor will give many martyrs to our Society, and they will soon have to be called not islands of the Moor but islands of Martyrdom. So those of ours who desire to give their lives for Christ may be of good heart and rejoice, for they have now a training place of martyrdom ready to their hands where they may satisfy their desire.

The voyage to Japan and China, as all people warn me, is very full of sufferings and dangers. I have as yet had no experience of it, but when I have made it—I shall sail, as I think, in about two months and a half from this—I will write you word all about that and everything else. So when you come to India, with the goodwill of God, next year, as I suppose, you will receive letters from me from Japan. Nuñez Ribera is at Amboyna, in a very safe town where there are a great many Christians; I understand from his letters that he is working with very good fruit. The two of ours who are in the Comorin Promontory are of great service to religion. You will be able to understand this well enough from their own letters which I send on to you, in which they tell you fully all that they are doing. It has pleased God to call our dear and very sweet brother Adam Francesco out of this life to Himself, to give him the reward of his many and great labours here. His death answered to his life, and that, as far as I have heard from others and as I saw myself, was rich in holiness. He was a very pious man, and had a great and burning zeal for bringing heathen to the flock of Christ. I commend myself to his prayers far more than I commend him in mine to God, for I hold it for certain that he is now enjoying the bliss for which he was born.

I am now on my way to Goa, to prepare myself a good time for my voyage to Japan next April. I shall go from Goa to Cambaia to the Governor of India, who is now at Bazain, that he may make arrangements for the interests of the Christians in the Moluccas, and provide for those of our Society whom I am soon going to send thither. One of these will be a preacher who may remain in the royal town, and preside over the commencement of a college where the children of the Christians of the Mauricas and of the Portuguese may be taught. Another house will also be begun there, where the orphan children of Portuguese, as well as with the Japanese whom by God's favour I shall send there, will be taught the Christian religion. And as our people in India are beloved and acceptable not only to the Bishop and his clergy, but also to the religious and all others, Christians and heathen alike, I am strongly induced to hope that our Society may be spread far and wide in these countries.

So do you, my dearest brother Simon, make it your business to come out hither as soon as possible with great forces of our Society, partly preachers, partly also workers in other ways. Only avoid one thing—not to bring many young men, for out here we want men of from thirty up to forty years of age; men moreover adorned with all other virtues, but especially with humility, meekness, patience, and above all, purity. You know my old bad habit, that when I write to you I can never leave off. Well, this of itself ought to be enough to make you see what pleasure I take in such an occupation, but especially when I have set myself down to write after having been challenged to do so by letters from you. So now I will end, though it is hard to know where to stop. But I do hope that some day or other we shall see one another again, in China or in Japan, or at all events in heaven, where, as I hope we have alike been called by the singular bounty and gift of God into a share of His celestial kingdom, we shall enjoy God the everlasting Fountain of all good things for ever and for ever! Amen.

Cochin, Jan. 28, 1549.

The next letters, the last sent to Europe at this time which remain to us, are letters of recommendation; but Francis breaks out, as of old, about what was nearest to his own heart, when writing to his most familiar friend, Simon Rodriguez. The merchants who arrived at Cochin from Malacca just at the same time of the year as Francis himself of the year before, had brought him the good news from Malacca of the progress of religion, which is mentioned in the letter last printed.

(LXVII.) *To Master Simon Rodriguez.*

May the grace and love of Christ our Lord also help and favour us! Amen.

Do not be surprised that I write to you so often. There are a great many here who are going to Portugal, and ask me for letters to take to you; and I am very glad to seize every opportunity of talking with you, and indeed I am so bold as to trust that what I feel so much fruit to my own soul in writing will not be read by you without pleasure, on account of the love that is between us.

The persons who will deliver to you this letter are two honourable and good men, excellent Christians, inhabitants of the city of Malacca, where they have their house and families. Their reason for their voyage is, that they have to discharge certain duties and obligations to which they were bound. They will tell you a great deal about the city of Malacca, about the labours of our Fathers there, and about the fruit which results from those labours. All these things they are perfectly well acquainted with, as being eye witnesses of all.

They take with them also letters from Father Francis Perez, in which I imagine he has done as he promised to do, that is, given a long, clear, and minute account of the results with which the functions proper to our Institute are there carried on. They will also tell you about the affairs of China and Japan, for they have been a long time at a place which lies so conveniently for traffic with those parts and countries that the people there know best of all what goes on in them. They say that all my friends and acquaintances wonder at me very much for trusting myself to so long and dangerous a voyage. I wonder much more at their little faith. Our Lord God has in His power the tempests of the Chinese and Japanese seas, which they say are as violent as any others anywhere in the whole world. To His power all the winds are subject, all the rocks and the whirlpools and the quicksands and shoals, which they say are to be found in those seas in such great numbers, so dangerous, so sadly famous for the shipwrecks they have caused. He also holds in His sway all the pirates of whose numberless hordes they tell us, and who are exceedingly savage and are wont to put to death with exquisite tortures all whom they take prisoners, and especially all Portuguese. And as this our Lord God has all these things under His dominion, I fear nothing from any of them. I only fear God Himself, lest He should decree some just chastisement upon me on account of my negligence in His service, and because I am by fault of my own unfit and useless for the work of advancing the Kingdom and Name of His Son Jesus Christ among the nations who know them not. Except this, I fear nothing, and I count as naught all those other causes of fear, dangers, labours, and the like, which my timid friends vie with one another in pressing upon me as so very formidable. I laugh at them all in full security, and the simple fear of God alone extinguishes in me all fear of His creatures; for I know that they can hurt no one, except those to whom and as far as their Creator allows them to be causes of trouble.

But to return to our two friends. I pray you for all the regard you have for the love and service of our Lord God, that for the few days during which they are to be at Lisbon you take care of them tenderly, see that they are provided with a convenient lodging, and help them in all things according to your ability and their requirements. And when you have heard all the many things that they will have to tell you about India, and you send them back with their business all finished, then be careful to give them long and accurate letters to carry to us, informing us all about all the fathers and brothers of our Society who are in Italy, France, the Low Countries, Germany, Castile, and Aragon, and in particular about that blessed College of Coimbra which is so dear to me. These letters you should direct, I think, to our Fathers at Malacca. The original will be given to them by these two citizens of Malacca on their return home, and will be kept there, and copies of them will be sent to us from the port of Malacca—whence many ships sail yearly for China and Japan—by such a number of ways, that they will reach us by some one of them at least which will escape all accidents. May our Lord God bring us together in His holy glory in Paradise! Amen.

Your most devoted and loving brother in Christ,

Feb. 1, 1549. FRANCIS.

The other letter of introduction shows us a little more of the manner in which Francis was always trying to lead those who applied to him for any favour to look after the concerns of their soul as well as their temporal interests. It also gives the first hint of what afterwards exercised an important influence on his schemes and movements—an increased vigilance and severity on the part of the Chinese government as to the exclusion of foreigners, especially Portuguese, from their ports.

(LXVIII.) *To Master Simon Rodriguez.*

May the grace and love of Christ our Lord always help and favour us! Amen.

The person who will deliver this letter to you is a man with whom I have a certain amount of acquaintance. He is going to Portugal in order to ask the King for a reward for some service which he has done to the state, and has urgently pressed me to give him letters of recommendation to you as to that business. Now I am quite aware, and I have not concealed from my friend himself, that it would be much more profitable to employ himself in another branch of the art of petitioning—applying, that is, to God, and obtaining from Him the pardon of his sins—than to go supplicating from a mortal king an earthly reward for his merits and good deeds. But it was not possible to persuade him, at least here, to give up his hopes and intentions. I am of opinion that when he lands in Portugal you should try whether the change of scene has changed his mind in this respect; and if perchance the evils and dangers of the voyage have made him more amenable to heavenly admonitions, then persuade him rather to stay in Portugal as a monk than to come out here again as a soldier. If you succeed, you will have done the poor wretch a very great kindness, and have made gain of a soul that was lost. But if his mind be still fixed on transitory things, and he be not able to rise to such a height of philosophy as I mention, then by all means let him have your help in obtaining his just demands, and use your influence, as far as you may, that out of the rewards which he has earned by long service as a soldier he may have at least so much given him as may be enough for him to live on at home. And I beg you again and again, for the love of God, to attempt to get this done for His sake.

After I had written all the letters which I had determined to send to Portugal by the hand of Pedro Fernandez, who has discharged in these countries of India the office of Vicar to the Bishop, some ships arrived here from Malacca, bringing certain news that the Chinese ports are unfavourable and hostile to the Portuguese. This, however, will not frighten me from attempting the voyage to Japan, which I mean by the help of God to undertake, as I have already told you that I have made up my mind to do. There is nothing more fruitful of good to the soul in this life of misery than to live in the midst of great dangers of death, the true and only cause for braving which has been the simple love of God and of pleasing Him, and the sincere desire to extend our holy religion. Believe me, it is sweeter for a man to live in labours of this sort, than to pass his time in peace and leisure without them. May our Lord God unite us in His holy glory! Amen.

Your most loving brother in Christ,

Cochin, Jan. 25, 1549. FRANCIS.

The six weeks or two months which Francis Xavier spent at Cochin at this time were not without their activity. Indeed, Francis was there at the special invitation of his good friend Pedro Gonzalvez, of whom we have found him speak so highly in his letters, and whose great desire was that his own people should for some time have the benefit of his apostolical zeal. He preached in the churches, instructed children, and visited the sick, as usual, and was as successful as was his wont in the conversion of sinners and in the reform of manners. Two miracles of this time have been specially recorded. In the first instance it was a child of four years of age, who had been many weeks ill of a fever, and was given over by the doctors. The parents, without making any direct petition to Francis, brought him in to see the child. Francis made the sign of the Cross over him and recited a Gospel, and the child at once opened its eyes, gave signs of joy, and was found to be entirely cured. The other instance was of that knowledge of the interior state and conscience of another, which is one of the gifts sometimes communicated to the saints. Francis met opposite the church of St. Antony at Cochin an acquaintance of his, a man of bad life, who at the very moment was meditating the execution of some profligate design. The man came up and kissed his hand, and was received with great kindness. Then Francis changed his look, became very grave, and asked him how he was. 'As well as possible, thank God,' was the reply. 'Well enough as to the body,' said Francis, 'but how as to the soul?' And then he went on to tell his friend all that he had been devising in his most secret thoughts. No one knew it but the man himself, and he was at once struck with contrition, made his confession, and gave up his evil life.[14]

[14] Massei, *Vita di S. Francesco*, l. ii. c. 14, p. 246.

CHAPTER IV.

Arrangement of the Missions in India.

THE letters written by Francis Xavier after his return to Malacca from the Moluccas in 1547, show us how firm a hold the idea of an expedition to Japan had taken on his mind, almost from the first moment when he had met the Japanese Anger and his Portuguese friends. His was the heart and soul of an Apostle; and as St. Paul longed for Rome, or Spain, or even still more distant countries, while he was yet in Asia Minor, or Greece, or his prison at Cæsaræa, so the tidings that told Francis of new islands where the Gospel had never been preached, seemed almost to put upon his conscience the duty of devoting himself to the work of carrying among them the name of Jesus Christ. Moreover, he had done for India, for Malacca, and for the islands of the Eastern Archipelago, that which was particularly his own work—the work of laying foundations and of beginning that system of preaching, teaching, catechizing, and training the people which we see him following everywhere. It called for all his devotion, energy, firmness, and prudence to initiate a system which required so much unostentatious labour on the part of the missioner, and which, if it could but be perpetuated, would certainly, as far as human measures could secure such a result, have made the growth of the new Christian populations to maturity and strength certain. But the system could be administered by men who could never have founded it, and it was the mission of Francis Xavier to found it in as many places as possible rather than to remain fixed in any one place after founding it. The labourers who were to carry on his work had now been supplied him from Europe, if not in numbers as large as he had desired, if not such in quality as his sanguine imagination had represented them to him when his 'prophetic mind'[1] pictured to itself Antonio Araoz or even Simon Rodriguez himself coming out to India at the head of a large band of followers, at least sufficiently for the purpose of working on the foundation which he himself had laid. With India, Malacca, and the Moluccas so well manned as they now were, or were soon to be, with priests of this Society, Francis might feel what St. Paul expressed when he wrote to the Romans from Corinth, that he had 'now no more place in these countries.'[2] Nor can we doubt that he was also strongly influenced by the disappointment with which he was met in every attempt to convert the natives of India on a larger scale than had hitherto been accomplished, and to penetrate into the interior of the great peninsula itself, partly on account of the misconduct and bad example of the Portuguese, partly on account of the avarice and tyranny of their superior officers, partly also on account of that hatred to the Christian name that was only too natural in nations which could not help looking upon it as identical with the name of Portuguese.

The expedition to Japan, which presented itself to his mind with so many attractive features to recommend it, was therefore an enterprise which Francis might have concluded to undertake on grounds of simple reason. The Japanese were intelligent, noble, manly, liberal, anxious to learn and ready to be convinced of the truth. The field was open, and free from many of the obstacles which were felt so fatally in India and elsewhere. There were no Cosmo de Payvas, no rapacious slave robbers, no Portuguese settlers who might outdo the heathen themselves in licentiousness and fraud, no Jews or Mussulmans to dispute for the possible converts with the Christian preacher, or to add their own errors, vices, and dishonesties to the native corruptions of the manners and tenets of the pagans. Danger itself, the many forms of 'peril' which St. Paul enumerates, 'perils of waters, perils of robbers, perils in the wilderness, perils in the sea,'[3] had become attractive to Francis Xavier, since his experience in the Moluccas of the immense and most wonderful consolation with which God, who can never be outdone

[1] See vol. i. p. 99. [2] Romans xv. 23. [3] 2 Cor. xi. 26.

in generosity, is wont, by way of compensation, to overwhelm those who brave all things for His sake. And yet it is most certain, that neither the reasonableness nor the attractiveness of the enterprise decided Francis Xavier to undertake it. As he had waited so long at Meliapor and elsewhere, before embarking on what he then thought was to be a voyage to Macazar, in order to gain a clear light and conviction that it was the will of God that he should at that time go thither and nowhere else, so during all the months which elapsed between his return to India from the East and his second departure for Malacca, he was studying and praying and seeking in every possible way to ascertain the particular direction of the Holy Ghost as to the voyage to Japan. This accounts for whatever appears like hesitation or indecision in him at this time, though all the while he was laying his plans and making his arrangements for the long absence which the voyage was sure to entail upon him. Even up to the very last, after he had written, as we have seen in the preceding chapter, to Ignatius and Simon Rodriguez about the certainty of his departure, even while he was at Malacca itself making his final arrangements, he was still commending the matter with all earnestness to God in humble prayer for light.

Japan, which in our time has been almost revealed anew to the civilized world, whose ambassadors and students we have seen in our streets, whose works of art and ingenuity are filling us with admiration, while we are looking with intense interest on the new social and political developments of which it is being made the scene, had been first discovered by Europeans, seven years before the time of which we are writing, almost at the same moment when Francis Xavier put his foot on the shores of India. The famous adventurer, Fernand Mendez Pinto, has told us, in some amusing chapters of his history, how he arrived with some other Portuguese in the ship of a corsair at the isle of Tanixooma, the first land of Japan, as he says, and how he was nearly losing his life, because the son of the King of Boungo wounded himself and almost blew his thumb off by attempting to fire off the 'arquebuse' of the stranger who was lying asleep.[4] It appears that about the same time that Mendez Pinto and his companions landed at Tanixooma, three other Portuguese had been driven by a storm into the port of Cagoxima, in the kingdom of Satsouma—that is, into the very home of Anger, the Japanese fugitive whom St. Francis Xaxier fell in with, five years later, at Malacca. These first chance visits of the Portuguese were soon followed by the establishment of a considerable traffic, and the way was thus paved for the introduction of Christianity. But it was a singularly favourable circumstance that Anger and his companions should in the first instance have come to India and been instructed in the faith. Francis was thus enabled to enter Japan with devoted friends and disciples at his side, to whom the customs and language of the country were perfectly familiar. His daily intercourse with them at Goa and on the voyage must have furnished him with an unusual store of knowledge concerning the new nation to which he was about to preach, and we see from the detailed description given of Japan in the papers drawn up by Anger, or from his dictation, that he and his companions fully deserved the credit for intelligence and quickness which is given to them in the letters of Francis.[5]

Before the departure of Francis for Japan could be thought of, it was necessary that he should arrange the affairs of the Society in India, which he was to leave behind him for an almost indefinite period, and with which he could only hope to hold very rare communications. The first few letters which we have remaining to us of the spring of 1549, after the dispatch of the vessels to Europe, show us how much this care pre-occupied the mind of Francis Xavier. He had already discovered those defects in the character of Antonio Gomez which made it likely that he would be a bad and unfortunate Superior at Goa, especially if left to himself without Francis to guide him. On the other hand, Francis was very desirous of sending a thoroughly active, and zealous, and prudent missionary to Ormuz,

[4] Mendez Pinto, t. ii. ch. 132 (French Translation). See also Charlevoix, *Hist. du Japon*, t. i. p. 178.

[5] We give this account of Japan in the Notes to this Book.

the far famed emporium at the mouth of the Persian Gulf, and before he left Cochin for Goa he seems, from the letters last inserted, to have intended to send Gomez to this post, placing Gaspar Baertz in his place as Rector of Goa. We are told that on his arrival, this plan, which would have saved a great deal of misery at Goa, was changed, on account of the resolute humility of Gaspar, who implored so earnestly that he might not be set to rule his brethren, that Francis had not the heart to resist him. It is possible that Francis also saw danger in the alteration which he had contemplated, of sending Gomez by himself to Ormuz. At all events, the plan was changed, and Gaspar Baertz was sent to the lonely and difficult post where he soon won for himself the fame of an apostle.

Ormuz, or Hormos as it is called by Messer Marco Polo, stood in his time on the Kirmanian coast at the mouth of the Persian Gulf, but having been laid waste by the Tartars, the city was soon afterwards transferred to the island, five miles out at sea, which was so famous as a mart in the time of which we are writing. It had nothing but its position to recommend it, and since the town on the island was demolished in the 17th century by Shah Abbas, it has been valuable only as supplying salt in great abundance. When Francis Xavier sent Gaspar to be its Apostle, there was a fine city on the island of some thirty or forty thousand inhabitants. It had two large harbours, sheltered from every wind, and was a sort of Venice in the East—a place where the merchants of Arabia, Persia, Armenia, India, China, and of the eastern coast of Africa, met with those of Europe. It is one of the hottest places in the world, and by nature one of the worst supplied even with the ordinary conveniences of life. It had hardly any fresh water, and all that was not imported was of bad quality. Scarcely any grass or trees would grow on the parched salt soil. A missionary who stayed there some time, as Bartoli tells us, 'used to say that this island had worse upon it than the curse pronounced on all the earth in punishment of Adam's disobedience, that it should bring forth thorns and briars, because in this place not even these could grow. An old report said that once the island had been set burning by subterranean fire for seven years together, and that on this account its hills remained heaps of cinders, just whitened at the top. No birds or animals are seen there all the year round,' he adds, 'but every morning a dew falls which congeals into grains, has a very sweet taste, and is called "manna."' Against all these natural disadvantages the wealth and luxury of its inhabitants had striven so successfully as to make the city of Ormuz one of the wonders of the East. A proverb said that if the world were a ring, Ormuz would be the gem set in it. It was a city of fine streets and palaces, the houses were ingeniously contrived to shield off the intense heat of the sun, and the cool breezes, which happily blew daily, were conducted by a contrivance of pipes through every room. The roofs were flat, and the inhabitants slept in the open air upon them, in large vessels full of water, with their heads only projecting.[6] With all the heat, the climate is not unhealthy, and diseases are rare, says Bartoli, following other writers; he attributes the good health of the inhabitants to their perpetual perspirations. Ormuz seems to have been independent under its own king, when the great Albuquerque conquered it, assisting a deposed king to regain his throne, building a fortress, and making it tributary to the crown of Portugal. This was its political condition at the time of which we write.

Its moral state was enormously and infamously bad. It was the home of the foulest sensuality, and of all the most corrupted forms of every religion in the East. The Christians were

[6] Marco Polo, t. i. p. 102 (Col. Yule's edition, 1872), speaking of this country about Hormos,—the ancient Ormuz, on the mainland, says, 'The residents avoid living in the cities, for the heat in summer is so great that it would kill them, hence they go out to sleep at their gardens in the country, where there are streams and plenty of water. For all that, they would not escape but for one thing, which I will mention. The fact is, as you see, that in summer a wind often blows across the sands which encompass the place so intolerably that it would kill everybody were it not that, when they perceive that wind coming, they plunge into water up to the neck, and so abide till the wind has ceased.' On this Col. Yule remarks (p. 112), 'The custom of lying in water is mentioned also by Sir John Mandeville, and it was adopted by the Portuguese when they occupied Insular Hormuz, as P. della Valle and Linschoten relate. The custom is still common during great heats in Sind and Mekran.'

as bad as the rest in the extreme licence of their lives. There were a few priests, but they were a disgrace to the Christian name. A zealous bishop had once lived there, and soon wore himself to death. Mahometanism was in great power, and possessed a very magnificent mosque. The Arabs and Persians had introduced and made common the most detestable forms of vice. Ormuz was said to be a Babel for its confusion of tongues, and for its moral abominations to match the cities of the Plain. A lawful marriage was a rare exception. Foreigners, soldiers, and merchants, threw off all restraint in the indulgence of their passions. The children of Christian fathers and Jewish, heathen, or Mussulman women were brought up in the religion of their mothers. The riches of the place attracted every possible luxury to enhance the general licence. Avarice was made a science: it was studied and practised, not for gain, but for its own sake, and for the pleasure of cheating. Evil had become good, and it was thought good trade to break promises and think nothing of engagements, and the most extortionate forms of usury were common and avowed. One of the successors of Master Gaspar at Ormuz said, that if a council of devils were to assemble to draw up formulas of robbery, they would never invent so many and so specious ways of defrauding as he saw contrived and practised every day by the merchants of Ormuz, who were called all over the East the 'Doctors of Usury.' He added, that if the famous Doctor Martin Navarrus—Francis Xavier's uncle—were to come out thither, he would have to begin his studies again, and take his degree of Doctor a second time, so much would he have to learn about exchanges and contracts of which he had never heard. In the midst of all this licence and dishonesty, human life was of little value, and assassins were easily to be found for a certain sum to make away with any one who had given offence to another in immoral intrigues or in money transactions.[7]

Francis Xavier would gladly have given himself to this stronghold of Satan. He used to say, we are told, that it would

[7] This account of Ormuz is mainly taken from Bartoli, *Asia*, t. i. l. 5, pp. 442 seq.

not surprise him if the whole island were some day to be submerged for the wickedness which reigned there. And in truth, at the present day, it is more of a desert than Babylon or Tyre. But Francis was called by God to Japan. It was against his practice to send any one of those under him to a place where he had not himself preached and laboured, but Ormuz was bad enough to make him depart for once from this rule. It remained to send some one in whom he could thoroughly confide, and to instruct him fully and minutely as to the plan on which he was to work, leaving him at the same time all the discretion which the circumstances of the case required. Francis had soon discerned the great worth of Gaspar Baertz, and though he had wished to place him at the head of the College at Goa, in many respects the most important post in India, he determined to send this his best worker to Ormuz, in the same spirit in which he had himself been given to the Indian missions by Ignatius.

The instructions given by Francis to Gaspar are almost the most precious part of all that remains to us of their writer. At first sight they might seem to find their place by the side of his rules for the daily exercise of Christian virtues, or of his long explanation of the Creed given in the preceding volume. But they are not simple instructions—interesting as such would always be to us if they came from the pen of Francis Xavier. The reader will find Francis insisting much, in the paper which we are next to insert, on the necessity of a study and familiar knowledge of mankind for the Christian preachers and apostles, on the indispensable need of experience and acquaintance with the human heart acquired by constant and observant intercourse, if any really great effect is to be produced in gaining souls to God. He is almost severe—at least he seems to have felt that what he had said needed some counterbalancing—against the mere study of books, however good and authoritative, as a preparation for the apostolic life and ministry. We may be sure, then, that in his instructions to Gaspar Baertz he has drawn largely on his own experience. It is his own method of dealing with men which he urges on his disciple.

We may therefore take a large part of the following treatise, as it may almost be called, as a sort of unconscious contribution to our knowledge of Francis Xavier given us by his own hand. In many points this is obvious upon the very face of his instructions. The immense importance which he attaches to the care of the missionary's own conscience as his first and most essential duty, the continual practice of works of humility and charity, which he recommends, the prudence on which he insists as necessary in all dealings with men, the attentive humble consideration to be paid to the Bishop's Vicar and the priests of the place, and also to the Governor of Ormuz, the practice of preaching on board ship and on the Sundays and festivals when the place of destination has been reached, the labours which are to be undertaken for the conversion of the heathen, the custom of going round the streets by night to solicit prayers for the holy souls,—these and several other points which are salient in his instructions to Gaspar we already know to belong to the daily practical life of Francis Xavier himself. This being the case, it is easy to see that in other matters he is also relating his own experience and recommending the method pursued by himself. We learn thus what was the staple of his sermons, how he dealt with penitents in the confessional, how he behaved himself with the rough lawless class of sinners, the merchants, the soldiers, the seamen, or again with the officers of the revenue and the rich but good-natured voluptuaries who were thrown across his path or drawn to him by that irresistible attractiveness which was his special gift, the dowry of his holiness and of his close loving imitation of Him who was the friend of publicans and sinners. Ormuz, wicked as it was, perhaps pre-eminent in wickedness, must yet have been a place not different in kind as to its inhabitants or their vices from Malacca, or Ternate, or even Cochin or Goa itself: and we may learn more than we already know of Francis Xavier, in his familiar intercourse with the many men which he reclaimed to God at those places, by these directions which he gives to Gaspar as to the stray sheep at Ormuz. Above all, we may be sure that in the heroic charity which he recommends in the confessional, when he says that timid souls who cannot for shame reveal their sins are to be encouraged, by their confessor's revealing even to them the worst sins of his own former life, we have a lesson which he would never have given if he had not practised it himself. The same may be said as to the manner in which novices and postulants are to be dealt with, and the universal rules of prudence, sweetness, and the careful study of men's characters before attempting to do them good, which are here inculcated.

If the letter of instruction to Master Gaspar be read in the light of these considerations, we shall come to understand its value, not only as embodying spiritual counsels of the most exquisite and refined wisdom, but as adding largely to our acquaintance with the character of Francis himself.

So long a document as that which we are now to insert could not, of course, have been written all at once, and we find that, although there is a tolerably clear sequence and arrangement in several parts, the writer has now and then gone back to points on which he has touched before. The letter runs as follows:

(LXIX.) *To Father Gaspar Baertz, going to Ormuz.*

Above all things be mindful of yourself, and of discharging faithfully what you owe first to God, and then to your own conscience; for by means of these two duties you will find yourself become most capable of serving your neighbours and of gaining souls. Take care always to incline, even beyond moderation, to the practice of the most abject employments. By exercising yourself in them, you will acquire humility, and daily advance in that virtue. For this reason I would have you not leave to any other, but yourself take charge of, the teaching the ignorant those prayers, which every Christian ought to have by heart: an employment certainly by no means ostentatious. Have yourself the patience to make the children and slaves of the Portuguese repeat them word by word after you. Do the same thing to the children of the native Christians. Those who behold you thus diligently employed will never suspect you of any arrogance—they will be edified by your modesty; and as modest persons easily attract the esteem of others, they will judge you more fit to instruct themselves in those mysteries of the Christian religion of which they are ignorant.

You must frequently visit the poor in the hospitals and poorhouses, and from time to time exhort them to confess themselves, and to communicate; giving them to understand that confession is the remedy for past sins, and holy communion a preservative against relapses—that both of them destroy the causes of the miseries which they now suffer, and which they fear for the future, by reason that the ills they suffer are only the punishment of their offences. On this account, when they are willing to confess, you shall hear their confessions with all the leisure you can afford them. After this care taken of their souls, do what you can to help the poor creatures in what they want for their bodies; recommend them with all diligence and affection to the administrators of the establishment in which they are, or else procure them from others who can help them the relief which they need.

You must also visit and preach to the prisoners, and exhort them earnestly to make a general confession of their lives. They have more need than others to be stirred up to this, because many or most people of that sort have never made an exact confession since they were born. After this, ask the Brotherhood of Mercy to have pity on those poor wretches, and to labour with the judges to look into their causes and to provide daily food for the most necessitous, who oftentimes have not wherewithal to subsist. You must be of all the service you can to the Brotherhood of Mercy, showing yourself devoted to it, promoting it, commending it, and most readily working in every way in your power to help it.

If in that great port of Ormuz you have to hear the confession of any rich merchants whom you find to have the possession of ill-gotten goods on their consciences, and who are bound and willing to restore them, but yet cannot make restitution to the persons who have been injured, either because they are dead, or because of themselves they know not who or where they are, even though they force upon you the money for restitution, remit the whole thereof into the hands of the Brotherhood of Mercy, even though you may think of some necessitous persons on whom such charity might be well employed. Thus you will not expose yourself to be deceived by the insidious tricks of wicked men, who affect an air of innocence and poverty; men full to the throat of imposture and wickedness, but who cannot so easily deceive the Brotherhood of Mercy, to whom it will be much safer and more seemly for you to transfer the invidious and perplexing office of making all due inquiries; thus the alms will reach those who are truly poor, and the greedy lying of these avaricious impostors will be defeated. And besides, you will gain the more leisure for those functions which in a more especial manner belong to your state of life, which is devoted to the assistance of souls: otherwise this frequent and manifold care of the distribution of alms would deprive you of no small part of the leisure which you will need so much. In fine, by this means you will prevent the complaints and suspicions of men, who from their own common badness, would be ready to think evil of you, as if, under the pretence of serving others, you were cunningly playing a game for yourself, and withdrawing for your own use a part of the money entrusted to you to give away, thus cheating the necessities of the poor and practising a wicked theft upon them.

In dealing with those whom in the various intercourse of life you come across, whether in spiritual or secular things, whether at home or abroad, whether it be in the way of speech or of company, whether their familiarity or friendship with you be only ordinary or of the highest degree, always bear yourself as if you had it in your mind that they might one day become your enemies instead of your friends. By this management of yourself, you will never let them be aware of any act or word of yours which, if they were to bring out at any time when in a passion, might make you blush for it as an exposure of yourself, or be sorry for it on account of mischief it might cause to your work and business. This perpetual watchfulness and care is made necessary for us on account of the wickedness of this corrupt world, whose children are continually observing the children of light with mistrustful and malignant eyes. And the same care is due also for the sake of your own spiritual advancement, which will make great progress if you regulate all your words and actions by continual and most attentive prudence.

By this same precaution you will guard the inconstant minds of your friends against the danger of change. In any case you will prepare for yourself in their minds many things which will be your defenders, for they will remember the uprightness of your conduct, and they will conceive a reverence for you which will put them to confusion if ever they become your enemies. This consideration of the instability of men will also make you look more to God, despise yourself more, and cling to God, Who is ever present to us, with extreme humility and great sweetness of soul: practises which if we omit, we find a number of things stealing upon us which hurt the eyes of people who see us, and gradually alienate from us their goodwill. The examen, which we call particular, will do a great deal as to keeping up this carefulness. Take care never to fail to make it twice a day, or once at least, according to our common method, whatsoever business you have upon your hands.

Before all things, devote your first and principal care to cleansing your own conscience and keeping it without stain. Let your diligence in preserving or in cleansing the consciences of others come after this of your own; for how can a man be of use to others who takes no care for himself? Preach to the people as frequently as ever you can; for the usefulness of preaching spreads far and wide everywhere; and amongst all evangelical employments there is none from which greater fruit for the service of God and the good of men can be expected.

In your sermons beware of admitting any doubtful propositions as to which there is difficulty, because doctors are divided. For the subjects of sermons should be chosen from clear and unquestionable truths, which tend to the regulation of manners and the reprehension of vices. Set forth the enormity of sin, enlarge on the atrocity of the offence to God's infinite Majesty which is committed by the sinner. Imprint in souls a lively horror of that sentence which shall be thundered out against guilty sinners at the last judgment. Represent with all the colours of your eloquence those most bitter pains which the damned are eternally to suffer in hell. In fine, threaten them with death, and especially with sudden and unexpected death, those particularly who neglect the service of God, and who, having their conscience loaded with many most grievous sins, think nothing of sleeping on in supine negligence in such a condition. You are to mingle with all these considerations the remembrance of the cross, the wounds, and death of Christ, by which He vouchsafed to atone for our sins; but you are to do this in as moving, pathetical a manner as possible, by figures and colloquies proper to excite emotions in the mind, such as cause in our hearts a deep sorrow for our sins, on account of the offence done to God thereby, even so as to draw tears from the eyes of your audience, who are then to be led to make resolutions of cleansing their consciences as soon as possible by confession, and of celebrating their reconciliation to God by due reception of the holy communion. This is the one true idea which I wish you would propose to yourself for preaching profitably.

When you reprove vices in the pulpit be careful never to speak against or attack any person by name, especially those who are officers or magistrates. If they do anything which you disapprove, and of which you think convenient to admonish them, make them a visit, and speak to them in private; or when they come of themselves to confession, whisper to them in the secret tribunal of penance, what you have to say to them. But altogether avoid the speaking against them openly; for they are a sort of people who are commonly difficult and irritable, and they are so far from amending upon such public admonitions that they are stung by them, and become furious, like bulls under a gadfly, and rush headlong to perdition.

Moreover, before you take upon you to give even private admonitions take care that you know them a little first, and have some familiarity with the people whom you wish to correct, so to prepare your way: and then make your admonition either more gentle or more strong in tone according to the measure of your favour or authority with the friend you are reproving, so as to be more free and severe with one who is more bound to you, and more sparing and cautious with one with whom you are less familiar. Take care always to temper the sternness of your reproof with the serenity of your air, a smiling countenance, and gentle glances, and much more by the civility of well-mannered words, and the sincere protestation of your love, which is the only thing which forces on you that unpleasant but necessary attempt to deliver a friend from the stain which disfigures him. It is good also to add marks of submissive reverence to the pleasingness of your discourse, with tender embraces, and all other fitting marks of the sincere goodwill and unquestionable respect which you have for the person of him whom you are correcting. These things are the honey and preserves which are mixed with and which season the bitterness of the dose, unpleasant in itself, and which will turn out of no use if it be administered without some such condiment to men whose stomachs are likely to be turned by it. For if a harsh voice, a rigid countenance, or threatening aspect and a lowering brow should be added to the natural disagreeableness of so unpleasant a matter as a reprehension, I am very much afraid that men of such fastidious delicacy and sensitive ears will not be able to restrain their bile. They have power at their back, they are accustomed to adulation; and it is more likely, in such cases that they will shake off all restraint and moderation, and send their inopportune censor about his business, with a good deal of abuse into the bargain.

For what concerns confession, how you are to advise others, and they to practise it, this is the method which I judge the fittest for these quarters of the world, where the licence of sin is very great, and the use of penance very rare. Whenever you find a person who wishes to unburthen in confession a conscience laden with a long accumulation of sin, exhort him in the first place to take two or three days of preparation, to examine his conscience thoroughly, to go back to the first recollections of his childhood, then through all the various stages of age and occupation which he has passed through in all his life up to this time, making up the account of all his sins of deed, word, or thought, and if his memory require it, writing it down and reading it over. When he is thus prepared, you can hear his confession, after which it will generally be well that you should not give him absolution at once, but persuade him to think it over for two or three days, to withdraw his mind from his ordinary occupations, and by means of meditations adapted to excite him to sorrow for his sins, out of love to God Whom he has offended, to prepare himself to gain greater fruit from his sacramental absolution. During those three days you shall exercise your penitent in some of the meditations of the first week of the Exercises, giving him the points, and teaching him the method of meditation and of prayer, and you shall counsel him also to help himself, by means of some voluntary penance, for example, of fasting or disciplining himself, to conceive in his inmost heart a true detestation for his offences, and even shed tears of repentance.

Besides this, you must take care, if the penitents have unjust possession of anything belonging to others, that they make restitution in this interval of time; or if they have injured the reputation of any one, that they retract what they have said; or if they are engaged in unlawful attachments and have been living in sin, cause them to break off those criminal engagements, and remove at once the occasions of their crime. However solemnly and seriously they may promise to do these things at a future time, it is not safe to trust them without the actual performance of their engagement. Let them perform beforehand what they declare that they will do. There is not any time more proper to exact from sinners these duties, the performance of which is as necessary as it is difficult. For when once their fervour and excitement of mind have grown cold, and their familiar enticements have begun to drag them back with fatal persuasiveness to the sins to which they have long been accustomed and which they have but just left off for the time, it will be in vain to ask them to keep their promise. Before, therefore, you send them away absolved from all their sins, insist by all means on their anticipating these dangers. Otherwise, so frail is human nature, you will have to bewail to no purpose their speedy relapse towards the precipice, from the slippery declivity of which you have not far enough removed them.

In dealing with sinners in the sacred tribunal of penance, take heed lest by any hasty severity you frighten away those who have begun to discover the wounds of their souls to you. How enormous soever their sins may be, hear them, not only with patience, but with mildness; help out their bashfulness when they find it difficult to confess, testifying to them your compassion, and seeming not to be surprised at what you hear, as having heard in confession sins much more grievous and foul than theirs. And lest they should despair of pardon for their faults speak to them of the treasures of the infinite mercies of God. Sometimes when they have confessed some crime with great trouble of mind, hint to them that their sin is not altogether so great as they may think; that by God's assistance you can heal even more mortal wounds of the soul; bid them go on without any apprehension, and make no difficulty of telling all. It is necessary to use this motherly indulgence, so to speak, in order to assist these poor souls in bringing forth their sins, for in truth it is a most painful labour which they undergo in bringing to birth the spirit of salvation, until at last they have emptied the whole terrible sink of their conscience.

You will find some of them whom the weakness either of their age or sex will make them feel more ashamed as to revealing to you the foul lusts with which they have stained themselves. When you perceive that, meet them more than half way, telling them that they are neither the only nor the first persons who have fallen into such foul sins, that you have met with far worse sins of that kind than those can be which they want the confidence to tell you. Impute a great part of their offence to the violence of the temptation, the seductiveness of the occasion, and the concupiscence innate in all men. More than this, I tell you that in dealing with such persons, we must sometimes go so far and so low, in order to loosen the chains of this miserable shame in these unhappy persons whose tongues the devil has by his cunning tied up, as of our own accord to indicate in general the sins of our own past lives, so to elicit from these guilty souls the confession of the sin which they will otherwise hide, to their irreparable loss. For what can a true and fervent charity refuse to pay for the safety of those souls who have been redeemed with the blood of Jesus Christ? But to understand when this is proper to be done, how far to proceed, and with what precautions, is what the guidance of the Spirit and your experience must teach you at the time in each particular conjuncture.

You will sometimes meet with men—and I would that they may be few—who doubt of the power and efficacy of the holy sacraments, and especially as to the Presence of the Body of Christ in the Eucharist. This comes from their not frequenting those sacred mysteries, from their continual intercourse with pagans, Mahometans, and heretics, or from the bad example given them by some Christians, and even (which I speak with shame and sorrow) by some of our own priestly order; for when they see some priests, whose life is not more holy than that of the common multitude, still go rashly and almost as a pastime to the altar, they imagine that it is in vain that we teach that Jesus Christ is present in the holy sacrifice of the mass, for that if He were there present, He would never suffer such impure hands to touch Him with impunity.

The way you should take to set these people right is as follows. First establish yourself in their friendship by courteous speeches and kind manners, and then endeavour by familiar questions to elicit their private thoughts. If you find in them the errors I have mentioned, then search out their causes, occasions, and beginnings. You will thus understand where to apply your remedy, and then do this with all diligence and vigour, alleging whatever, as the occasion suggests, may seem to be of use; take great pains to prove clearly the truth of that sacred dogma, and never leave off till you have conquered, and till they protest that they are most firmly persuaded with a faith certain beyond all doubt that the Body and Blood of Christ our Lord and Redeemer are most truly present under the species of bread and wine duly consecrated. After that it will not be difficult to lead them to cleanse their souls in good faith by confession, and to receive more frequently the sacred banquet of the table of God with due devotion.

When in the sacred tribunal of penance you have heard all that your penitents have prepared themselves to confess of their sins, do not at once think that all is done, and that you have no further duty to discharge. You must go on further to inquire, and by means of questions to rake out the faults which ought to be known and to be remedied, but which escape the penitents themselves on account of their ignorance. Ask them what profits they make, how, and whence? what is the system that they follow in barter, in loans, and in the whole matter of security for contracts? You will generally find that everything is defiled with usurious contracts, and that those very persons have got together the greater part of their money by sheer rapine, who nevertheless asserted themselves so confidently to be pure from all contagion of unjust gain; having, as they said, the true testimony of a conscience that reprehends them in nothing. Indeed, some persons' consciences have become so hardened that they have either no sense at all, or very little sense, of the presence of even vast heaps of robberies which they have gathered into their bosom.

Use this method with particular diligence towards the king's ministers, commandants, treasurers, the receivers, and other officers and farmers of the revenue, whensoever they present themselves before you in the sacred tribunal—in short, with all who, under any title and right whatever, have anything to do with the charge and handling of the public money and dues. Interrogate all these people by what means they grow rich on the discharge and income of their offices. If they are shy of telling you, search and scent it out in every way, and the most mildly that you can. You will not have been long on the hunt before you come on sure tracks which will lead you to the very dens and lairs of their frauds and monopolies, through which an inconsiderable number of men divert to their own private hordes emoluments belonging to the public. They buy up commodities with the king's money, and at once sell them again with an enormous percentage for themselves, raising the price to an immense rate, which has to be defrayed out of the pockets of those who are under a necessity from their business of coming into the market as purchasers of that merchandise. Too often, also, they torture creditors of the treasury with long delays and cunning shifts, that they may be driven to compound with those sharks of the state by remitting a part of their due claim, while the others pocket the remainder, which they call the fruits of their industry, being in reality the booty gained by their most unprincipled robbery.

When you have squeezed out of them the confession of these monopolies and the like, drawing them out by many and cautious questions, you will be more easily able to settle how much of other persons' property they are in possession of, and how much they ought to make restitution of to those they have defrauded, in order to be reconciled to God, than if you should ask them in general whether they remember to have defrauded any one. For to this question they will immediately answer that their memory upbraids them with nothing. For custom is to them in the place of law; and what they see done before them every day, they persuade themselves may be practised without sin. For customs bad in themselves seem to these men to acquire authority and prescription from the fact that they are commonly practised. You should admit of no such law; but should declare seriously to such people, that if they will heal the wounds of their conscience, they must restore and altogether give up their unjust possessions, which they have acquired by bad faith. And at the same time point out to them what these wrongly acquired possessions are, using the knowledge gained by their own confessions.

Remember to be especially obedient and docile in all things to the Vicar of the Bishop. When you are arrived at Ormuz, you must go to wait on him, and falling on your knees before him, you should humbly kiss his hand. Neither preach, nor hear confessions, nor teach the Christian doctrine, nor exercise any other employment of our Institute without his permission. Never have any contention with him for any cause whatsoever, or differ from him. On the contrary, endeavour by all submission, and all possible services, to gain his close friendship in such sort that he may let himself be persuaded by you to go through the meditations of our Spiritual Exercises under your direction; if not all, at least those of the first week. In the same way cultivate the goodwill of all the other priests by every kind of good office and goodwill, and avoid like the face of a serpent every occasion whatsoever of dissension and conflict with them. Pay them all the greatest reverence and the most particular marks of respect, so as to win for yourself their love in return. From which it will naturally arise that they may be inclined to trust to you the care of their souls, and accept without dislike an invitation to make the Spiritual Exercises, if not for the whole month as we do, at least by retiring from the world in their homes during a certain number of days, during which you may visit them daily, and explain to them the subject of their meditations, taking them from those of the first week.

Pay a great respect and obedience to the commandant, and make it apparent, by the most profound submission, how cordially you respect him. Beware of any difference with him, on whatsoever occasion; even though you should clearly see that he fails in his duty in matters of the highest importance. Only when you perceive that your attentions have won for you his favour and good graces, be so bold as to visit him; and after you have duly declared, in the first place, your love for him, and the concern you have for his honour and safety, then, with all modesty and gentleness of countenance, speak of the deep sorrow which affects your heart to see his soul in danger and his reputation damaged by reports of discreditable doings of his noised about in the world. Then you shall make known to him the discourses of the people concerning him, which will probably be put in writing, and go to a far greater distance than he would be willing they should, if he bethinks him not in time of giving satisfaction to the public. Nevertheless do not take this office upon you before you are well satisfied that his disposition to you is such that it appears solidly probable to you that he will take in good part your admonition, and that it will do him real good.

You must be much less ready to yield to the requests which many will make to you, that you should act as their ambassador in carrying their complaints to the commandant. Refuse as firmly as you can such an office, giving as an excuse your continued occupation in preaching, teaching, hearing confessions, and in the study and thought which are required as preparation for these duties. These things will leave you no time for the laborious and tedious business of frequenting the antechamber of the great, and spending idle hours in their halls to await the rare moments of obtaining a difficult admission to their presence. You may add that even if you had the time, and if access to an audience was always open to you, you do not well know what would be the use of your interference, for if the commandant be such as they themselves charge him with being, it would be vain to hope that a man who is touched neither by respect to God nor by a due regard to his duty—as they themselves assert—would make any account of you if you were to suggest better things to him.

The whole time that remains to you after you have discharged your necessary duties should be spent in the conversion of the heathen to the Christian religion. In choosing between different employments and ministrations, take care always to consider that those the usefulness of which is clearly of wider range are to be placed before others. This rule will teach you never to prefer the hearing of a confession to preaching in public, never to omit the catechetical instruction fixed at a certain hour every day for the sake of exhorting any single person in private, or attending to any similar work which will benefit only one. During the hour which precedes the appointed time for the catechetical instruction you or your companion should go through the piazza and streets of the city, inviting all with a loud voice to come and hear the explanation of the sacred doctrine.

You must write from time to time to the College at Goa, to tell them what are the ministrations fitted to promote the glory of God you are exercising, what order you follow in them, and what fruit results from them in souls, God prospering your own weak efforts. Take pains that these statements are carefully made, so that our people at Goa may be able to send them to Europe, where they will be a sort of specimen of our work in these parts, and of the favour of God Who condescends to grant some success to the trifling labours of this least Society of ours. Let nothing get into the letter which may give just offence to any one, nothing that may not appear likely to induce the readers at the very first sight of it to praise God and do Him service. You must also frequently write letters on the same subjects (with all due caution as to the person whom you address) to his Lordship the Bishop and to Cosmo Añez; imparting to each the happy news of the fruit which by the blessing of God results from the labours devoted to souls in those parts.

As soon as you arrive at Ormuz, I would have you go privately to visit the best and most truthful men you can find there, who have also the greatest experience of the manners of the place and of its commerce. Inquire diligently of them what are the dominant vices there, what are the prevalent kinds of fraud in the matter of contracts and loans, and so on. When you have found out these things plainly and certainly, you will be able to prepare for ready use arguments and remarks fitted either to open the eyes or to rebuke the obstinacy of persons who may come to you, whether in familiar intercourse or in sacramental confession, as to the palliated practice of usury, or of dishonestly gainful contracts, or of any other form or shape of the manifold and various wickednesses which are in vogue in that mart of Ormuz which is so full of merchants of every nation.

Every night go round the streets of the city, recommending to the prayers of the living the souls of the dead who are suffering for their sins in Purgatory. Use few words in doing this, but let them be well chosen for moving the compassion of the hearers, and begetting in them some religious feelings. Add some words also to try and rouse them all to pray for souls stained with mortal sin, and to obtain grace for them from God to emerge from so wretched a state. At the end of each exhortation give out the recitation of *Our Father* and *Hail Mary*, and say the first words of each yourself aloud.

Let it be a matter to which you pay continual and unrelaxed attention, to show yourself to all those with whom you have to do with a kind and calm countenance, getting rid of every sign of severity, overbearingness, arrogance, suspicion, sourness, anger, and threatening. Otherwise, if the people who come to you find that you are set against them by these signs of evil disposition, they will certainly be checked and will turn away from you, without giving you that confidence which is requisite in order that being with you may do them good. You ought much rather to put on an appearance of courteous affability, using the gentlest and most winning smiles, and the like, whenever you have to reprove any one in private on account of some fault of his which requires admonition. At such times you ought to take the greatest pains in every way, that your countenance and look may both breathe all charity and kindliness, through which alone you must give out that you are impelled to make the man whom you reprove your debtor for the great benefit of wiping away a stain which defiles him, and that it is not any aversion or feeling of dislike that makes you break out in reproaches against him.

If there are any priests, clerics, or laymen who desire to enter the Society and to make the Spiritual Exercises, and whom you think proper persons to do so, you can send them to Goa with a letter stating who they are and what they want. Or even if at Ormuz itself you think that they can profitably help you, you may then admit them to live with you, and put them to the proof, as far as may be, with the usual 'experiments' of the noviceship.

On Sundays and festivals you should preach at two in the afternoon or a little after, either in the chapel of the Confraternity of Mercy, or in the church, explaining the articles of the Creed to the men and maidservants and the free Christians and the children of both sexes of the Portuguese. Before this, send your companion through the streets of the city with a bell, and besides ringing it, let him give out an invitation to admonish all to assemble to hear the explanation of the Christian doctrine—unless, indeed, you prefer yourself to make this announcement in the streets. Take with you to the place where the sermon is to be the summary of Christian doctrine and the explanation of the articles of the Creed, as well as the rule I have drawn up for passing daily life in a Christian and holy manner, in which is set down the manner and method in which Christians who are desirous of eternal life are to worship and invoke God every day, how they are to guard themselves against falling into sin, and to do all those things which conduce to the certain gaining of the end of our being, the grace and happiness which we all desire.

Give a copy of this rule to those who come to confession to you, giving them as their penance for a certain number of days to do what is there prescribed. They will thus gain a habit, and custom will make them easily continue of themselves what they have at first taken up at the injunction of their spiritual father. For they will have found out how useful a thing it is, and will be attracted by its pleasantness, for that form suggests short exercises of devotion, which are very good: and we have found by experience that many who have begun to use it after their confessions, have continued to do so to the great profit of their souls. For this cause I think it best that you not only should give it to those who have been to confession to you, but that you should communicate and commend it to any others who are taking some pains about their own salvation, even though they are the penitents of other priests. And as I see that you cannot easily have copies enough of that paper to distribute so largely, I would advise you to post it up in some public place —suppose, the church of our Lady of Mercy—written out on a board, so that any one who wants to use it may be able to write it out for himself.

When you have judged any to be fit to help the Society, and have duly admitted them into it, you must give them the Exercises for a month, according to our custom, and after this prove them by trials of such a kind as that there may be no appearance in them of any ridiculous exposure to the laughter of the public. You may tell them, for instance, to wait on the sick in the hospitals, and to shrink from no offices, however humble and disagreeable, which belong to such a place, and to attendance upon them in their cure. You may bid them also go to the prisoners in the gaols, and devote themselves with all the sedulity of religious charity to the consolation and recreation of those poor souls. And you may let them practise in public any other similar duties which unite our own humiliation to the work of doing good to others.

But do not either order or permit them to make sights of themselves to the public in such ways as would cause men to think them mad. I don't wish the low mob to laugh at them and to take pleasure in the mimic, and, as it were, theatrical exposure of such men to ridicule. The people are to be reminded by the sight of them of their own duties, and to see in them laudable examples of what is right. It will be so if they never appear in public except in a dress or guise that belongs to some good work, as when they have satchels on their shoulders and go from door to door to beg for the indigent, or when in the sight of all they carry the contributions which they have collected to the asylum of the poor. These are the sort of victories over self and over the world which they should gain; and the people when it sees them should be moved to good, and the poor should enjoy the benefit of what they do.

But even to these trials, which are very disagreeable to nature, you must not expose them all indiscriminately. Find out first what each man's courage is, and what he can do without trouble. All men have not equal strength—difference of disposition, of education, of progress in virtue, causes a great difference among novices, and this difference must be the first thing to be taken into account by any one who has to rule them, so that he may settle what sort of exercise suits each, that is, in what each may be tried in such a way that it may be fairly hoped that he will make profit of the trial, according to the measure of God's grace communicated to him. Unless the Master of Novices has the gift of discernment, it will easily happen that some will be burthened beyond their strength, and so will despond, look back, and go away, while the same men, if they had had a more experienced guide, might hereafter have made great progress in religious virtue.

There is another evil in this illadvised enjoining of mortification which exceeds the power and condition of novices who are as yet tender babes in the spiritual course—for it causes in them an aversion to their master, and takes from them all confidence in opening to him their inmost hearts. But you, or any other who has to train young souls to religion, must provide, with all possible care, that when they feel in their minds the suggestions either of depraved nature or of the evil spirit, calling them away from the right path, they should declare them as soon as they arise, and be perfectly ingenuous in confessing them. Unless they do this, they will never free themselves from these snares, they will never make their way through these insidious obstacles to the height of perfection. On the contrary, these first seeds of evil which they have unhappily taken in and fostered by their imprudent silence about them, will gradually grow up into more troublesome disquietudes, until at last they will make them become weary of holy discipline, and force their poor conquered minds to look back to the place from which they came, shake off the yoke of Christ, and rush again into their old free way of living.

If, either from their own confessions or from any other signs, you find any to be violently disposed to vainglory, to indulgence of the desires of the senses, or to any other faults, you may use the following useful way of suggesting to them a remedy which may suit their danger. Tell them to take a certain time to get together arguments of every sort, which they may think most efficacious to use to some one who is either puffed up by arrogance, or given to self-indulgence, or under the influence of any other disease of the soul under which they may be themselves suffering, so as either to put him right if he has already gone wrong, or to guard him if he is in danger of doing so. Point out yourself the books or the passages, and be a guide to them in finding matter which may serve their purpose. When they have made their collection, order them to make sermons out of it, as if they were to have to preach them either in the church or in the street, or to the convalescent in the hospital, or to the prisoners in the gaol. Then make them actually preach these sermons. We may well hope that they themselves will, of their own accord, use the remedies which they have prescribed to others, and that these antidotes against what poisons the soul will sooner exert their power on the minds of the preachers, to which they have been so thoroughly applied by the deep study and careful thought which they have spent on the subject, than on the hearers, who only casually take cognizance of the thoughts of others put before them without any preparation on their part. No doubt they will be ashamed to fall into a fault from which they have taken so much pains to deliver other people.

You may, with due proportion, use a similar device to cure certain sinners of almost desperate perversity. These men say they cannot command themselves, so as to put away from themselves the occasions of their sins, or to restore the property of others which they possess in bad faith. So, of their own will, they remain in a sinful conscience, deprived of the sacrament of absolution, and quite aware that they are justly denied it. And yet the disgrace of the sort of voluntary excommunication in which they know themselves to be involved, to the scandal of the public, makes them sometimes feel wearied of their iniquity, and also from time to time, conceive some fears of the danger of eternal damnation in which they live.

First of all make these men friendly to you by significations of kindness, and then suggest to them in their good sense to think over what they would say to a friend who was struggling with the same difficulties, in order to cause him to rise up out of the mire and leap out of the ditch into which he had fallen. Ask them pleasantly to make a sort of school exercise of the matter, and to take the trouble in familiar talk with you to see what their own wits will be able to do in inventing arguments to be used in persuasion of this head. Hear what they have to say, and approve of it, and then gently retort upon them what they adduce, and beseech them for the sake of the friendship which is between you to do the same kind office to themselves which they have done to others, and to take to their own hearts and apply to their own wounds the medicine which they think to have so much saving power in removing the diseases of their friends. God has created their souls to praise Himself, and so to gain their own happiness, and when He sees them rushing to destruction down the precipitous paths of vice, He gives them in His mercy this care for the salvation of others as a sort of handle by which they may be drawn back from death. They ought first to have true charity for themselves in proportion to the love which they bear to others; and He lets this last remain, so that they may be turned back thereby to take the necessary care for their own salvation which they have neglected so miserably. This same artifice is not to be dispensed with by us, whom it becomes as long as life remains and as the opportunity of doing so is not taken away, to leave nothing untried in the way of bringing souls back to the service of their Creator, and prevent their eternal loss.

There will sometimes come to you in the confessional men who are engaged in impure attachments, or who are full to overflowing with booty which they have gained by rapine, over which they gloat with greedy devotion. As to getting them to send their mistresses away from their houses, or to restore to others what they have been despoiled of by their unjust practices, you cannot bring them to this either by love or reverence to God, of which they have absolutely nothing left, or by the fear of death or of hell, to all sense of which they are hardened. There is only one way of terrifying such persons, and that is by threatening them with the infliction of the only ills they are afraid of—the ills of this life. To such men therefore you should declare, that shortly, unless they make haste to appease the wrath of God, they will find themselves overwhelmed by calamities, their goods lost by shipwrecks, the authorities prosecuting them, by calumnious lawsuits, tribunals condemning them, by long sufferings in prison, incurable diseases in the midst of the greatest poverty and destitution, their miseries mitigated by no consolation, infamy which will brand them and their posterity with an indelible stain, and the public hatred and execration of all, such as they remember well were the lot of such and such persons whom you may name, well known to them, and who deserved such evils no more than they do. Tell them that no one can despise God with impunity, and that His wrath is all the more irrevocably let loose on men in proportion as He has more patiently waited for their repentance. The image of such calamities may well strike them with a first impulse of the fear of God, which may be the beginning of wiser thoughts, instead of the madness in which they have hitherto been involved.

Whenever you are preparing yourself to talk with any one concerning the things which belong to the worship of God and the salvation of the soul, put in practice this precaution—not to say a word before you have divined and discovered by any sign you can note what is the interior state of the man's mind. I mean whether he is quiet or under the influence of some strong passion—whether he is ready to follow the right path when it is shown him, or whether he is in error with his eyes open, irrevocably wedded to low cares and objects, to which he has been hitherto in the habit of postponing his religious duties, and seems likely to do the same for the future; whether he is the subject of temptations from the devil, or whether he is left to himself and his own nature—in fine, whether he is disposed to listen to an admonition, or whether he is rough and irritable to the touch, so that it may be feared that he will break out into a rage if he be handled too incautiously.

When you have got some presumptive knowledge on these points, you must adapt your address to the person accordingly. Speak gently to the angry, quietly to the troubled, use some appropriate artifice to insinuate your business into the mind of the preoccupied; be more free and expansive with well-disposed persons, who are likely to be docile and easily led to anything that is good. At the same time, never be foolishly fawning to any one, never stop short at mere compliments, always skilfully mix up some wholesome medicine in what you give to the sick man, however much he may turn from it, so that by degrees he may be disposed to a better state. When any one is all on fire with excitement from a keen sense of recent injury, then do you also blame the deed of which he complains. If it be bad in itself, then use what reasonings you can to persuade him that the doer has fallen out of imprudence, and not sinned through malice. When you see that your man listens to you, and is not altogether displeased, you may add that God has perhaps permitted this in order to punish him for some similar offence which he has himself committed. Then ask him familiarly, whether he remembers ever to have injured any one in word or deed? Whether, at least, in his youth he was not somewhat illtempered with his parents, disobedient to his teachers, quarrelsome with his companions, and may not have given some one or other just cause to complain of him? And when he acknowledges this, tell him that he must think it fair that he is now paid off in kind. For now he has offered him by God a very precious opportunity of wiping out his former fault. If, on the other hand, his complaint be not just, take him in hand gently and gradually, pull to pieces the false arguments by which he persuades himself of what is so far from being the case. Then increase your boldness little by little, show him a little gentle anger, as he really deserves, and then, at last, when you feel you can do it safely, give him a more severe scolding. These artifices, by the blessing of God, sometimes charm away the illhumours of men so overwhelmed with troubles, and dissolve the sort of spell by which they have been bound, so as to leave them free and able to do what is right. When you have thus made your way easy, you must go on with confidence, and bring your work to the greatest perfection in your power, spending yourself to the utmost in your desire to do honour to God, and win for Him the love and reverence of the souls which He has created to love and to praise Him.

The injunction which I have given above—namely, that you should find out from men who are well acquainted with the matter what are the commercial frauds most common at Ormuz—I would not have confined either to that place in particular, or to those specific heads of which I spoke. Wherever you are, even if it be only in passing and on a journey, always make it a point to try to find out as exactly as possible from good men who know the ways of common life, not only what are the prevalent crimes or customary tricks of cheating in such places, but the whole manners of the people there, the opinions and prejudices of the populace, what the nation is intent upon, what are the peculiar customs of the country, the mode of government, the method of the courts, the forms of suits, the quibbles of lawyers, and whatever has any sort of bearing upon the character of the state or of civil society there. Believe my experience, nothing of all this is useless for the physician of souls to know, in order that he may at once understand their diseases, may easily provide remedies, and may always have at command a power of readily and quickly meeting all necessities.

This will teach you what to dwell upon most frequently in your sermons, and what to insist on urgently with your penitents. This knowledge will arm and prepare you for your promiscuous conversations with men, and you will be so fortified by it, as never to be amazed at anything as new, never to be put into a ferment at any unforeseen occurrence: it will make you feel at home in all the variety of questions that will arise one after another, it will make you dexterous in the multiplied business you will have to transact with men of all sorts, and also give you authority with all. When men of the world are admonished of anything by religious persons, they generally despise them, because they think that they have no experience of affairs. But if they find that any one is quite as well versed as they are and has as much experience as themselves in the common usages of civil life, they will hold such a one in admiration, trust themselves to him, and will not hesitate when he urges them even to do violence to themselves, and to carry out whatever he advises them, even though it be arduous. So you see what great fruit may come from such knowledge, and therefore you must now consider that it is your business to labour in acquiring it as much as in old days you laboured to learn philosophy or theology. And it must be sought, not from dead books written on paper or parchment, but from living books—that is, from men who have had experience in affairs, and who know well the manners of the people. With this knowledge you will do more good than if you poured forth upon the crowd whole libraries of speculations.

Wherever this learning of which I speak has won for you any kind of authority or consideration with some, remember that the first proof of your authority must be to arrange and bring about without fail that they make an examination of all the sins of their whole life, and then confess them in the sacrament of penance, and after this endeavour to excite themselves to a true detestation of these sins in a retreat and by meditations adapted to them, drawing from them reasons for such detestation from the majesty of God and the love which all His creatures owe to Him. You may be sure that this is the foundation of everything good, this is the principal thing, to which all others must be postponed.

In the next place take pains to extricate them from the entanglement of legal disputes, which are the seedplots of hatreds and calumnies. Persuade them therefore to put an end to their lawsuits by the arbitration of friends, and so save a great deal of money, of trouble, and of reputation. If they ask you to be arbiter, do not refuse. You can find time for the matter conveniently both for them and for yourself on Sundays or days otherwise free from the transaction of business, when you can hear one after another the complaints or demands of the intending litigants, and propose some middle plan of compromise, on which it may be much better for them to agree than to run the daily risk of falling from their condition and making a sad shipwreck of their honour, with all the expense, the weary delay, the great hazards which they would run through the falsehoods of bribed witnesses, the deceits of impostors, the numberless snares of the gentlemen of the law, the labyrinthine mazes of cavilling pleadings, the heat and bustle of the tribunals, the perpetual restless battle of alternate recriminations, which will roll on backwards and forwards like the tides of the Euripus. If you dwell on these things you will deliver your friends who are thinking of entering their causes in the courts from the itch for litigation, and it will be still more easy, in the case of persons who have already become acquainted with the air of the lawcourts and been wearied by the tumultuous contests of the tribunals, to make them entertain the advice of abandoning of their own accord suits which they have begun.

I know this will not please the attorneys and advocates and other forensic leeches of various denominations, who get great gains out of the number and length of lawsuits. When such persons complain of you on this account, you can partly despise their complaint, partly you should attack in your own way any of them whom you can reach, making them afraid to practice their mischievous tricks of protracting causes by interminable delays, and warning them of the urgent danger in which they lie of losing eternal happiness. And, that they may look well to an affair of so much moment, you can invite them to a few days of retreat to be spent in pious meditations.

You are to remain at Ormuz until you receive letters from me ordering you to go somewhere else. Write to me by the ships which go to Malacca, directing your packet to Francesco Perez. I wish you in these letters to tell me precisely and in particular whatever of moment has resulted from your labours. Francesco Perez will take care that they are sent on from Malacca to me in Japan, if it shall please God to send me thither for the service of His Divine Majesty. If for the space of three years you get no letter from me, nevertheless remain all that time at Ormuz, however much you may be invited or called elsewhere by any other person, for for the next three years I think it well for the glory of God you should remain there, and I give you a direct order so to do.

After the three years have elapsed, if no letter from me reaches you, you must still remain at Ormuz until the Rector of the College of Santa Fè bids you leave it. So you should then write to him at great length what you have up to that time done at Ormuz, what fruit you have gathered by the help of God, what you expect in future; tell him also the distinct command which I gave you when I went away as to your remaining there for three years, even although during that time you might have been called away by the Rector at Goa. For the rest, you may assure him that since the time fixed by me has expired, you are now entirely at his command, and ready to do at once whatever he may order you. At the same time lay before him any thing which, after you have weighed all before God, may seem to you worthy of consideration in deciding what is best either as to the opportuneness or as to the necessity of your remaining any longer in that post. When he answers this letter, do whatever he commands you without any excuse or delay. What I have told you as to sending your letter to me from Ormuz to Malacca, do not understand as if it would be enough to do that once a year only. I wish you never to let a single ship sail from thence to Malacca without a letter from you to me, directed, as I have said, to the care of Francesco Perez.

When on board the ship in which you are to embark for Ormuz, I beseech you to take great care of the layman who is given to you as companion. Persuade him to go to confession, and when you have brought him by your exhortations to a better life, take diligent precaution that he may not go astray again. On board ship you must preach on the Sundays, and on other days when you think it well so to do. I leave all that matter to your own discretion, so as to decide, when you have considered all circumstances, what is expedient for the moment. In your sermons make no display of erudition or of memory, reciting a great number of passages as proofs, or authorities from the old Fathers. Let a few of these, well chosen, be enough. Let a great part of your discourse be taken up with graphic descriptions of the interior condition and disorder of souls in a state of sin. Let your sermon set before their eyes, and let them see in it plainly as in a mirror, their own restless devices, their cunning artifices, their most vain hopes and imaginations, all the deceitful designs which they entertain in their souls. Add also the miserable ends to which all these things lead, unravel the sophisms of the captious suggestions made to them by their deadly enemy the devil, show them the way to extricate themselves from his toils, and heap upon them motives of fear to terrify them if they do not do this.

The truth is, that men listen attentively to those things above all which reach their inmost conscience. Sublime speculations, perplexed questions, scholastic controversies, soar not only above the intelligence of those who are creeping along on the ground, but also above their interest. They make a great deal of empty thunder and vanish away without any fruit. You must show men clearly to themselves, if you wish to have them hanging upon the words of your mouth. But to set forth what their own interior feelings are, you must first know them; and the only way to know them is to be much in their company, to study them, observe them, pray with them. So turn over and over again these living books; it is from these that you will gain everything—how to teach them with efficacy, how easily to act on and affect and turn and move sinners whither it behoves them to be moved for their souls' salvation.

Do not however neglect the study of dead books on account of this. Holy Scripture, the Fathers of the Church, the sacred Canons, ascetical books, and those which treat of moral subjects, duties, rights, and their distinctions—all these must be diligently consulted at proper times. It is in them that we find how to remedy temptations, the arguments by which to persuade, the motives of heroic affections, and examples of all that is praiseworthy taken from the lives of the Saints. But after all, these things have no warmth or life, and are of little avail, unless the minds of the audience are first opened so as to admit them into their own depths. And the certain key thus to open them is that picture and representation of each one's interior state of which I have spoken, skilfully drawn by a preacher who has full knowledge of the ways of men, and set in a good light before the eyes of everybody.

Since the King in his munificence has ordered that what

is necessary for your support at Ormuz should be provided at the expense of his treasury, you should avail yourself of this favour from our excellent Sovereign, and accept from his officials alone the means of which you are in need. What others offer you, even of their own accord, reject; for it is of signal importance for the authority and liberty of one who has the charge of souls to be under no obligation on the score of the supply of his food, which is in fact to owe his life and breath, to any one of those whom it is his duty to direct in the way of salvation, and to correct and pull up whenever they go astray. The common saying is very true as to gifts of this kind: 'He that takes, is taken;' for he loses all confidence as to finding fault with or using his right of censure with a man towards whom he has allowed himself to take up the humble position of a dependent, and thus bound himself to him by the reverence due to a patron. Hence it is that we are sometimes in such difficulties as to finding words in which to reprove people who feed us when they deserve reproof; or, if sometimes our zeal and sense of duty impose on us to do violence to our shyness in this respect, yet still we do not gain much good, for the people look down as with a kind of superciliousness as if they were our masters, and had lawfully purchased that position, as they think, at the cost of the benefits which they have conferred upon us.

This is true in general of all—but more particularly is it true of certain persons, concerning whom I think it necessary to put you on your guard. There are men who are deeply plunged in vice, and who will yet affect familiarity with you, and will even vie with one another in seeking to win your friendship by kind offices. It is not that they have any desire of profiting from your conversation and discourse so as to amend their own wicked ways, for they have made up their minds to abide in them to the last. It is that they wish to stop your mouth and tie your tongue, for their own consciousness of guilt warns them to be afraid of your censure. I think you should not altogether repel these persons, nor entirely reject their good offices. Do not refuse even their invitations to dinner, or their presents, if they are slight and of little value, such as water, fresh fruits, and the like, to reject which is commonly considered among the Portuguese in the East as an insult to those who offer them. Let them see plainly, and even declare to them freely, that you accept their presents only on the condition that they are ready to take in good part admonitions and exhortations from you; that you also will promise to come and sup with them on the express understanding that they will prepare themselves on your invitation to make confession of their sins and approach the Eucharistic Banquet in Holy Communion. And those little presents of food and dainties which I said had better not be refused for fear of injuring your friendship, send as soon as ever you have received them to the sick in the hospitals or to the prisoners in the gaols or to other indigent persons. The people will see and approve of and applaud the use which you make of the presents that you receive, and will absolve you from all suspicion of liking delicacies or of seeking favours which may turn to your own profit.

As to where you are to live, you must decide when you get to Ormuz, considering the state of things which you find there, making your choice to live either in the public hospital, or in the house of the Confraternity of Mercy, or in a small house near the church, as shall seem most expedient. If it shall happen that I call you to come to Japan, write at once to the Rector of the College here, in two or three different ways by the ships which sail to Goa from Ormuz, asking him to provide some one of ours who may be fit to help and console the people of the lastnamed city, and to send him as soon as possible to take your place at that post.

Finally; I earnestly commend to you to take care of yourself beyond everything else. Never cease to remember that you are a member of the Society of Jesus. In all the particular occasions of doing work of various kinds which will present themselves at Ormuz, your own practice and experience on the spot will teach you what is most for the service of our Lord God. There is no better or surer teacher of prudence than experience. Be careful diligently to commend me to Him Who is the Lord of both of us in your own daily prayers, and let those whom you direct in the service of God do the same. And let my last charge in this long exhortation be this—at least once a week read over carefully the whole of this paper, lest at any time you should fall into some forgetfulness of the things which are enjoined to you therein. May God our Lord accompany you on your voyage and lead you safe to your destination: and may He also abide with us who remain here! Farewell.

Goa, March 1549. FRANCIS.

Gaspar Baertz seems to have left Goa for his mission at Ormuz towards the end of March, not long before Francis himself started for Cochin, whence he was finally to embark for Malacca. In the course of the winter two new priests of the Society had been ordained by the Bishop of Goa; Manuel de Morães and Alfonso de Castro, both of whom have been already mentioned. Manuel had been destined by Francis Xavier to accompany Cipriano on the mission to Socotra, and went to Cochin from Goa to meet his colleague; but at the last moment Francis changed his mind, gave up the idea of Socotra for the present, and sent Cipriano to Meliapor, determining to take Manuel with him to Malacca, and thence to send him to the Moluccas. Manuel sang his first mass at Goa soon after his ordination; Alfonso de Castro seems to have wished to make a longer preparation, and embarked without having yet offered the holy sacrifice.

The arrangement to be made at Goa, now that Gaspar Baertz was out of the question as Rector of the College there, appears to have cost Francis Xavier much anxiety. We have already seen that he had had to urge obedience and submission to the secular Superiors of the College on Father Paul of Camerino.[8] This difficulty no longer existed; and Father Paul was a man of very great virtue, humble, simple, sanctified, laborious, and a great lover of poverty and abjection of every kind. He had never left Goa since his arrival, and was to labour there until his death, eleven years after the date at which we have now arrived. His chief work was the unostentatious

[8] See Letters l. and lii. (vol. i. pp. 360-370).

hard drudgery of attending to the young native scholars of the College, to whose spiritual and bodily welfare he was devoted, and whom he succeeded in forming to sober Christian virtue and to great zeal for the Catholic faith. He was a man of comparatively little learning, and, it would seem, no talent for preaching; and his offer of himself to Ignatius, before leaving Rome, as a helper and even servant to the Fathers who were to be sent by the Pope to India, may perhaps have been one of the incidents which suggested the institution in the Society of the 'grade' of Spiritual Coadjutor. Father Paul was quite in his element in the continual labours of humility and charity to which he had devoted himself, his constancy in which won him the esteem and veneration of all who knew him. We are told in particular of his devotion to the sick, especially the poor creatures, slaves and others, who were to be found lying in the streets, turned out of doors by their masters—these he used to carry himself to the hospital, and wait upon with a charity which moved those who saw it to intense fervour.[9] Paul was hardly a man for government, and yet Francis Xavier had already discerned in Antonio Gomez the defects which might render him positively mischievous. Yet Antonio had been appointed Rector, as we have seen, by Simon Rodriguez. He was a Portuguese, and as such acceptable to the Fathers his fellow countrymen scattered over India, and he seems also to have stood very high in the favour of the Governor. It is probable that, if Simon had never made the appointment, Francis Xavier would have kept Antonio in a subordinate place; as it was, he hit upon a middle course, which need not have involved any inconveniences if it had not been for the character of the two men who by it were placed almost side by side. This middle course was to continue Antonio Gomez in the Rectorship of the College, but at the same time to make Father Paul the Superior of the whole Society in India in the absence of Francis himself, and therefore Superior also to Gomez.

The following letter was probably written to serve as a record

[9] The fullest account of Father Paul is to be found in Bartoli, *Asia*, lxvii. p. 734 seq.

of this arrangement, and we may discern in its earnest exhortations to peace and harmony the anxiety which Francis felt as to what might happen when his back was turned, and when he was too far off to remedy any trouble, even by letter. The exhortations of which we speak are addressed to Father Paul, but it is not difficult to see that they were meant more for Antonio Gomez than for him.

(LXX.) *To Father Paul of Camerino.*

As I am on the point of departing for Japan, I beseech and entreat you, the Superior of the College of Goa, by all the desire you have to please our Lord God, and by the love which you feel towards our Father Ignatius and the whole of the Society of Jesus, first and above all things endeavour, by very great humility, very attentive circumspection, by always taking pains most maturely and rightly to make up your judgment in everything, to live in tranquillity, concord and love with Antonio Gomez and with all our brethren who are scattered in various places in India. From the intimate knowledge which I have of all the workers of the Society of Jesus who are at present serving God and the Church throughout these countries, I am easily led to think that they do not need a Superior to guide them in the way of the service of God, but still, that they may not lose the opportunity of earning merit by means of obedience, and because the order of right discipline so requires, I think it convenient that some one should be set over them to whom they are to be subject. And so, relying on your modesty, prudence, and knowledge, I have thought it the best thing to do to put you over them as their Superior and guide, to whose authority, with the limitations which I shall presently point out, all are to be subject, whether of our Society or the extern students at Goa or elsewhere, who have hitherto been accustomed to obey the orders and authority of the Rector of the College of Santa Fè. You then will exercise authority over them, until such time as some legitimate revocation of the same shall be duly signified to you.

And now here are the restrictions which I wish to place upon that authority, for certain just causes. In the first place, I command that Antonio Gomez is to have full and absolute rule, with perfect right, over the extern students of the College, whether Portuguese or natives. I also appoint that he shall have the free administration of the revenues, and all the money of the College, to demand and receive it from those who owe it, and to spend it on what is necessary for the house as shall seem good to him. So you must not interfere in any way with his doing this, nor demand any account from him of it. Everything also that relates to the dismissal or admission of students, whether Portuguese or Indians, by him, you must leave to his cognizance and judgment, approving as good whatever he may decide, and never interposing your own authority as to anything of the sort. If you have any difference of opinion with him as to anything of these, give your advice or make your request to him, but never prescribe anything in a matter of this kind in virtue of obedience. Moreover, I commit to him alone the punishments to be inflicted on boys of either kind, as well as the whole arrangement of the domestic discipline, and the distribution of all offices, and the appointment or choice or rejection of the servants of the College. And I order that he shall discharge all these duties in his own way, without any questioning or contradiction from you or any one else.

And here, once more, because the matter is so important, I beseech you, and, by the obedience which you have freely promised to our Father Ignatius, by virtue of which I command you what I now write, I adjure you, and entreat you in every most efficacious way in my power, that there never come between you and Antonio Gomez any discord or disunion, any verbal altercation, any beginning or appearance of quarrel, but rather the truest brothership proved by signs from each of you that your wills are perfectly united, and that you have the greatest love for one another; that you are with one heart bent upon promoting, each one on his own part, with the utmost diligence, the common good of the whole household. And this union of aim should be always manifesting and declaring itself, so as to cut away every occasion of offence and murmuring whether within or without the College.

Whenever any of our brethern who are working for the benefit of the people of the Promontory of Comorin, by continually visiting their villages, may write to you, as Niccolo from Coulan, or Cipriano from Meliapor, or Melchior Gonzalez from Bazain, Francesco Perez from Malacca, or Joam Beira and his companions from the Moluccas, to ask for your help with the Governor or the Bishop whose favour may happen to be needful to them by reason of some business, or to beg of you for any other kind of help or service, spiritual or bodily, whatever it may be, of which they chance to be in need, then leave everything else and devote yourself to the carrying out their requests with the utmost diligence and charity. And speak to Antonio Gomez, that he may at once strenuously and with open hand do whatever lies in him to do in that regard. And when you write to those most laborious and harassed workers, who are bearing in the sun and dust the burthen and heat of the day at their own extreme cost and sweat, take care that you never let the smallest drop whatsoever of sourness find its way into your letter, but let it, on the contrary, breathe the most exquisite love and sweetness. Let all savour or shadow of reproach, or complaint, or all mention of anything that may offend them or make them sad, be utterly absent from what you write. Supply them at once attentively and liberally with all they ask for as necessary for their support, their clothing, for the keeping up or restoring their health; for you must have deep compassion on the great and continual labours which they undergo, working with all their might in the service of God, and which they bear up under day and night without any admixture of human consolation.

This I would say most especially of those who have the care of the Christian congregations in the Comorin Promontory and in the Moluccas, for these men are most truly weighed down by the overwhelming burthen of a most heavy cross. So, for God's sake, lest they should break down under the weight, be most careful, with the utmost solicitude of which you are capable, that they never ask in vain or ask twice over for anything that you understand them to want, either for the comfort of the soul or for supplies for the body; for if these last fail them, it is certain that their souls also will grow faint and give way. They are in the ranks of the fight, you are safe in the camp, which you have to guard; and I am so decided in my judgment that this duty of yours to help them in every way is so just and ought to be so entirely put before every other, that I do not hesitate to adjure you, in the name of God and of our Father Ignatius, to strive with all your might to leave nothing undone on your part in the way of the most extreme diligence in discharging it with the utmost alacrity, and giving them abundantly, and more than abundantly, what they demand.

And as to what regards yourself more particularly, my dear brother, I beseech you again and again to go on increasing in virtue by continual progress, letting your wholesome example be like a shining light before the eyes of all, as hitherto indeed you have always done. Never let an occasion of writing to me pass by. I shall expect from you long and full letters, telling me a number of pleasant things about yourself, about the whole community, about your mutual concord, about the inseparable charity between you and Antonio Gomez, about each of our fathers and brothers who are working in the Comorin Promontory; about Cipriano, who is living at Meliapor, about those of the Society who have landed from the ships which are to come this year from Portugal, who they are, how many of them have a good talent of preaching to the people, who are priests, who are lay brothers. I require you to be particular in telling me which belong to these two classes, their number and kind, their names, their qualities, their strength, and the virtues which they possess; all must be written out at length. There are at least two certain ways by which you can keep up this correspondence with me. Twice every year a King's ship leaves Goa: in September for Banda, in April for the Moluccas. Each of them touches at Malacca on its way, and there is our brother Francesco Perez, who will receive the letters directed to me, and will take care to send them to me in Japan, by opportunities which will not fail him. And please take care to read over the paper which I leave behind me for you once every week, and to refresh your memory, not only of my commands, but also of me myself, in my absence; and I write this to be a spur to you to make you commend me to God in your prayers, and to have me recommended in the prayers of the brethren at Goa, and of all your devout penitents, male and female.

I have charged Antonio Gomez, that if any preachers come out from Portugal, he is to send some of them to our stations up and down India—Cochin, for instance, where there is so much want of a good preacher of our Society—also to the parts about Cambaia, or suppose, the city of Diu. I recommend the same matter to you also; so if the ships that are to come out this year bring any good supply of men of our Society who are good at preaching, arrange with Gomez about distributing them conveniently, so that by one or other of you they be without fail sent to the places I have mentioned. And as I am afraid that the many occupations which your manifold duties of government involve will not easily leave you any free leisure for writing diligently and minutely to me all these things which I desire to know, I think you should commit this as a business to our good Dominic, or to some other of the Portuguese in the house, and order him carefully to collect and make notes of all things that are worth knowing, the news of which from time to time may come to Goa by various hands, concerning our Fathers who are scattered in the various missions or stations, and particularly about Gaspar, who is at Ormuz. Just before the regular time for the departure of the ships for Malacca you can collect what he has written, and put it up in a packet directed to me, and add in your own hand anything that you may happen to have to inform me about in private.

As you have never yet had the opportunity of seeing with your own eyes the work that is going on in the various missions which depend upon this College, or what is the state of the places in which our Fathers are labouring, and as you have had no experience of the sort of life they lead in the Comorin Coast, at Meliapor, at Coulan, in the Moluccas, at Malacca, and at Ormuz, I would never have you by an absolute command bid any one of those who are working there come to you. For it may happen that on account of your ignorance of what is going on in those places you might by so doing give a fatal blow to some good work already begun, and there might be some matters on which great exertions have been spent, and which have thus been brought very near a prosperous issue after having had long to wait for it, which might be altogether thrown into confusion by your calling away those engaged in the work at an inopportune moment, and mischief might be done to the cause of the salvation of souls and of God's glory which it would be very difficult to repair. This is the reason why I am writing as I am at this moment to Father Antonio Criminale, not himself to leave his post at the summons of any one whatsoever, and not to permit any one of his fellow workers in teaching religion to the Christians of Comorin to leave his station, whoever it may be who recalls him, unless, looking at the circumstances on the spot, he thinks it can be done without any inconvenience. I give the same orders to the others who are on the same stations, neither themselves to leave work which they have begun, nor to permit their companions in labour to be taken away from their work and go elsewhere, for to do this would be to spoil great hopes and to lose precious opportunities of enlarging the kingdom of Christ, by retiring at an improper time and at a moment when to do so is greatly injurious to the interests of God's service. So it will be more prudent for you never to interpose your authority in these matters or to give in virtue of obedience a command as to which you are not sufficiently certain whether it is expedient that it should be carried out or not.

However, though I particularly forbid that any one of ours who is labouring in the missions should be ordered by you to come to Goa, unless you have first inquired as to their opinion in the matter and ascertained their consent, yet, on the other hand, if any of them from urgent causes come to you without your orders, I bid you receive them very kindly, treat them with special charity, and attend to their wants with all goodwill, whether it be that they want some bodily remedies or relief, or whether their souls are out of order, and they have come either of their own accord, by reason of their own danger, or by the persuasion or bidding of their companions who may feel some brotherly anxiety about them, to seek some spiritual medicine, confession or correction, or a few days of retreat. All these good offices you are to show them with all fatherly charity, taking care that they do not perish, or get any hurt to their souls. And now, my dearest Brother Paul, I do most urgently entreat you to observe all these things which I have said in this letter.

Entirely yours,

April 1549. FRANCIS.

We find in the foregoing letter an enumeration of the stations of the several Fathers in India, which records the final arrangements made by Francis before sailing for Malacca. Niccolo Lancilotti was at Coulan, Melchior Gonzalez at Bazain, and Cipriano at Meliapor. Antonio Criminale was still the Superior of the Fathers on the Comorin Coast and in Travancore. The strict prohibitions issued by Francis against the removal of any of these missionaries from their post must have very much curtailed the powers, which would otherwise have been exercised by the Superior at Goa. We have seen the severe injunction laid on Gaspar Baertz with regard to Ormuz. The disposal of the Fathers who might arrive from Portugal after the departure of Francis is left to some extent to Antonio Gomez, who is apparently associated with Paul of Camerino in the government of these new subjects. We shall observe something of the same sort further on. It is probably to be accounted for by the fact that not only was Gomez a Portuguese, while Paul of Camerino was an Italian, but that Gomez, as has been said, had been appointed Superior by Simon Rodriguez, and it was probable therefore that the new comers, who were likely to be Portuguese themselves, would be addressed to him. Francis was therefore obliged to provide against any clash of authority in the way indicated, and he may well be supposed to have half foreseen the difficulties to which Master Simon's unfortunate appointment might ultimately lead. But he had now done what he could to secure the good conduct of the affairs of the Society at Goa, and provided by earnest injunctions the largest and most charitable succour possible for the hardworked missionaries throughout India in any need that might come upon them. Here, again, we may be sure that the rules which he gives to Father Paul were but the expression of his own overflowing lovingheartedness whenever he had the opportunity of assisting his brethren. The time was now come for him to sail again eastwards, and on the 25th of April he embarked at Cochin[10] for Malacca, taking with him, as has already been said, Father Cosmo Torres, Joam Fernandez, Anger otherwise Paul of the Holy Faith, and the other Japanese, Emmanuel, a Chinese student of the College of Santa Fè, as well as Alfonso de Castro, Manuel de Morães, and a brother, Francesco Gonzalez. The three last were destined for the Moluccas. During the few days that the party spent at Cochin, Alfonso de Castro so won upon all who saw him and heard him preach, that the inhabitants petitioned Francis to leave him with them to found a college of the Society. But Francis was inexorable. Alfonso was destined to win a crown of martyrdom in the Moluccas.

[10] It was on this voyage to Cochin that the anecdote occurred which is mentioned vol. i. pp. 111, 112, of Don Diego di Noroña, who was at first scandalized by the familiar manner in which Francis conversed with the sailors, soldiers, and others who were on board with him.

CHAPTER V.

Francis starting for Japan.

THE voyage of Francis Xavier and his little band of companions from Cochin to Malacca was prosperous, though Lucena speaks of one storm in the course of the passage, when the captain was so alarmed at the danger which threatened his heavily-laden vessel that he had given the order to throw some of his cargo overboard, but was prevented by the intercession of Francis, who assured him that the wind would fall, and that they would sight the land before night. All came about as he had said. But this incident probably belongs to a later voyage to the same place. This voyage, however, had its memorable conversion. A man of noble birth was one of the passengers, and he was accompanied by a woman with whom he was living in a scandalous manner. Francis, as usual, made himself the intimate and affectionate friend of this poor sinner, and paid him so much attention, without taking the least notice of the well-known profligacy of his life, that, as Lucena tells us, those on board the vessel were inclined to say of him as the Pharisee said of our Lord, that if he had been a prophet he would have known what sort of a person his chosen companion was. When they disembarked at Malacca the victory was won. 'Sir, it is now time!' said Francis. The man was at his feet in a moment, he made his confession, provided for the poor woman, and began to lead a good life.

Francis was received with great joy at Malacca. He had not been at that city since a short time after the great defeat of the Acheenese fleet; and besides, the zeal and charity of Francesco Perez and Rocco Oliveira had produced a great change for the better in the population. They came to meet him at the port, singing the canticles of the Christian doctrine which he had taught them.

Francis himself, in a letter which we shall presently insert, gives an account of the extraordinary fervour and almost superhuman exertions of Father Francesco Perez and his companion. The humility, poverty, and mortification in which they lived, preached as powerfully as the words which the Father uttered in the pulpit, and they had already received several applications from men who desired to be admitted to the Society. As they had no power to receive postulants, they could only give the applicants the Spiritual Exercises, and practise them in some of the trials which were usual in such cases. The most conspicuous of these recruits was a young Portuguese of noble family, nineteen years of age, Joam Bravo by name. He had probably come out to India to seek his fortune either as a soldier or a merchant, and had chanced to sail to Malacca from Goa in the King's ship, bound for the Moluccas, commanded by a relation of his own, Don Diego Sousa, in which ship Francesco Perez and his companion had been conveyed. Bravo was attracted to thoughts of a more perfect life, and to the Society, by observing the holy, mortified lives of Perez and Oliveira. After making the Exercises, he would have returned at once to Goa to seek his admission from the hands of Francis Xavier, but that the arrival of the Father at Malacca was known to be so close at hand that he might have crossed him on his way. Bravo, therefore, waited. Meanwhile, he struggled vigorously to conquer himself in all possible ways, waiting on Perez and the other as their servant, attending the sick in the hospital, going about the city to beg for food and alms: a greater humiliation to him than it might have been to others, as he was well known and had many noble relatives who laughed at him and reproached him. Francis Xavier received him into the Society, and took the pains to give him a carefully drawn paper of instruction, which is happily preserved to us. Joam Bravo afterwards became a very eminent Father in the Society, and spent his life in the Indies.

The time passed by Francis at Malacca before embarking for Japan was rather more than three weeks, as we are told that he arrived on the last day of May. Before proceeding further with our narrative, we may here insert some of the letters written during this interval of preparation. The first is to the King, in which Francis formally announces his intention of sailing, without fail, to Japan. It is pleasant to find him speaking so gratefully of the assistance afforded to him by the Governor of Malacca, Don Pedro de Silva, who remained always a firm friend to Francis Xavier. He was the third son of the great Vasco de Gama, the discoverer of the route to India by the Cape of Good Hope. On his return to Portugal Vasco was made a Count, and also created Lord High Admiral; and we shall find Francis speaking of him under these titles. His eldest son was Estevan de Gama, of whom we have already heard, as Governor of India before Martin Alfonso de Sousa. The second son was Cristoval, the famous captain in the Portuguese invasion of Abyssinia in 1541. Pedro was the third son. The fourth will appear later on in our history in colours as dark as those in which his three brothers are painted are bright. He was the Don Alvaro d'Ataide, the 'Capitan' of Malacca in 1552, who opposed to the utmost the embassy to China, on which Francis Xavier had reckoned to secure him an entrance into that country.

(LXXI.) *To John III. King of Portugal.*

Sire,—I had often heard and deeply considered the many and marvellous things which various persons—and those good judges in the matter, as having been themselves on the spot—report concerning a remarkable disposition which is observed in the island of Japan for the reception of our holy religion. Upon this I thought that I ought strongly and urgently to beseech our Lord God to vouchsafe to let me feel some interior movement in my heart which might signify to me whether it were His holy will that I should go thither, and also to give me strength to accomplish what He might command me. It has pleased His Divine Majesty to grant my prayer. For I feel the most intimate certainty and conviction in my mind, that it is expedient for the service of God that I should go to

Japan. This has given me a ready and vigorous confidence, and I have put an end to all delay in the matter by sailing from India, that I may follow the undoubted call of God, Who urges me on to this voyage by frequent and strong interior impulses.

We have now got as far as the port of Malacca on our way to Japan. There are two of our Society with me, and three Japanese Christians, lately converted, but very good. After having been fully instructed in the mysteries and doctrines of the life and teaching of our Lord Jesus Christ, they were baptized at Goa in the College of Santa Fè. They have learned to read and write in our manner, they recite the prayers of the Church, and make meditation at regular hours. What moves and affects them most of all is the consideration of the labours and sufferings of Christ, and the remembrance of His cross and death. They often meditate upon these things with very deep and strong sentiments and very tender affections. They have exercised their minds with very great attentiveness in the ascetic meditations of Father Ignatius, and have carried away from them most remarkable fruits in the clearer knowledge of God. They frequent of their own accord the sacraments of confession and communion, and they feel urged to join us in this voyage to their own country by great desires of leading their own people to the religion of Christ.

We, the six whom I have mentioned, arrived at Malacca on the last day of May of this year 1549. The Commandant of the fortress of Malacca has received us with the usual kindness. He at once offered us most readily all the favour and assistance that could be expected from him towards the carrying out and promoting this expedition of ours,—undertaken, as it is, with great hopes of serving God and pleasing your Highness: and his sedulous carefulness in all good offices has gone far even beyond the courtesy of his words. He has put himself to so much pains in seeking for us a comfortable ship, and providing us with every other convenience for going whither we are bound with all safety and ease, as to fulfil most abundantly all the liberal and kind promises which he made to us on the first day of our landing here. Nothing could exceed his extreme courtesy in readily and with full goodwill offering to us whatever was in his own power to give; and as for what had to be obtained for us from others, by canvassing, influence, and request, he has exerted himself so much in bringing people round to us by every effort in his power, and doing all he can to make them well disposed to us, and he so has worked in our cause in a way that has shown us signally his very tender charity towards us, that we feel ourselves quite unable ever to reward his goodness to us as it deserves. If he had been our own brother we could not have expected from him any greater or more efficient kindness. So that I pray and beseech you, Sire, that, for the love which you have for God our Lord, your Highness will condescend to repay in our stead the very great debt we owe to Don Pedro de Silva on this account. He has commanded that we should be largely supplied with whatever is necessary for us, not only for our support during the voyage from this place to Japan, but also for our expenses and sustenance during a considerable stay in that country, as well as for the building of a chapel in which we may offer the holy sacrifice of the mass to God. For this particular purpose he has given us thirty measures of the best pepper picked out of the whole quantity that was then at Malacca. He has also given us many beautiful and very costly presents to ofer to the King of Japan, that he may be favourably inclined to us by means of them, and so be more easy in admitting us into his kingdom and tolerating us there.

I tell your Highness all these particulars, that you may understand what benefits and honours I receive from your faithful subjects in the Indies. I really believe, Sire, that I shall speak the simple truth when I say that no one ever came to India who has received so much honour and favour from the Portuguese who reside there as has been shown by them to me. The whole of this I owe to your Highness, and to your frequent and efficient recommendations of me to those who are the administrators of your Highness's royal power throughout the countries of the Indies. And as among them Don Pedro de Silva, the Commandant of your fortress of Malacca, has been signally eminent in assisting me, paying me honour, and making me presents, and has bound me to him by a series of benefits which my own want of means and power forbid me from ever returning in kind as they deserve, I beg your Highness to allow me to find in your liberality the means of supplying the deficiency caused by my poverty. I shall gain all I want if your Highness will vouchsafe for my sake to show large and bountiful favour to this good officer, and to others who have made me so deeply their debtors, and thus repay back to them that which I owe to them without having the means of rewarding them.

May our Lord God of His infinite goodness and mercy fully and thoroughly enlighten the mind of your Highness with the clear knowledge of His holy will, and give you moreover the grace perfectly to execute what you know to be pleasing to Him, exactly as you would rejoice to have done at the moment of your death, when you will be placed before the judgment seat of God to give an account of all that you have done throughout your whole life. Most strongly do I again and again beseech you, Sire, not to be slow about at once doing, in preparation for that last trial and decisive moment, everything that can now be done in the way of dispatch and anticipation. For at the time of our last sickness, and when death is at hand and draws nigh, then the wretched mind of the sick person is so fixed upon what it has to suffer for the moment, the anguish, the bitter and numberless sorrows which then press upon it, as by no means to have time to attend to other cares or thoughts except those which that terrible scene, which then for the first time presents itself to the soul, strikes home to it —thoughts very sad indeed and very tormenting, though to no profit, the images of which no one can form for himself unless he has had experience of them.

Your Highness's useless servant,

FRANCIS.

Malacca, on the Feast of Corpus Christi, 1549.

The next letter, written at the same time, is to the Fathers at Goa.

(LXXII.) *To Fathers Paul of Camerino, Antonio Gomez, and Balthasar Gago.*

May the grace and charity of our Lord Jesus Christ be ever in our souls! Amen.

I write these few lines to you hurriedly, for I am quite sure that you will not fail to be pleased to hear how our voyage has fared, and about our arrival at Malacca. We sailed from Cochin on April 25th, having first experienced there an incredible amount of kindness at the hands of the Franciscan Fathers. They received us with the greatest show of charity, and there was certainly no room for any suspicion that it was not sincere. We owe them very much on that account, and shall always acknowledge that we owe it. Our run to Malacca took us not quite forty days. We arrived there strong and vigorous, both myselt and Father Cosmo Torres and the rest; no one was ill, no one had even sea-sickness, or even the slightest tendency to internal derangement. The weather during the whole voyage was very fair. No danger or even alarm from the Acheenese pirates. Such prosperity did it please our Lord God to grant to that our voyage, to Whom we one and all pay very great praises and thanksgiving on that account, and we beg also that you will do the same for us. We disembarked at this port of Malacca on the last day in May.

The Commandant and the whole city, from the highest to the lowest, received me with great marks of joy and goodwill. On our first interview I commended to the kindness of the Commandant the voyage we intend to make to Japan. He at once in the most ample manner offered all that was in his power, and then carried out in deed with very great diligence what he had promised. He has shown so much kindness and activity that he has wonderfully bound us and all our Society to him thereby. In all the pains which he took about our business his very great love to us was conspicuous. Indeed, for our sole sake and at his own expense he was willing to fit out and send a Portuguese ship to Japan, and he would have done it also, if he had been able to find a vessel fit for the purpose. When this plan became impossible, he bethought him of a Chinese vessel of the form which they call a junk. The captain of this is a Chinese, by name Ladro, and though an idolater, he has a home and family at Malacca. This man promised that he would take us straight to Japan, but the Commandant did not think that it was safe to trust too lightly to the word of a heathen, so he exacted a contract, by which the man pledged as the security for the promise he had made his wife and his whole household property, on condition that unless it be shown by letters in our own handwriting which he brings back from Japan that he has taken us thither straight according to the agreement, his wife whom he leaves at Malacca and all that he possessed in the Portuguese dominions should become confiscated to the royal treasury. Besides this, the Commandant has furnished us in the most provident liberal manner with all things that we require for the voyage as far as Japan, and for establishing a home there for ourselves. He has also spent two hundred gold pieces upon presents for the King of Japan, to make him favour us and our preaching. We sail to Japan in a straight course, without making any delay at all in the ports of China. We trust that God will prosper our voyage, and bring us in safety to that country where His holy Name may be glorified, being made known by us first of all to those blind nations.

On Trinity Sunday Alfonso duly offered his first mass to God, with solemn music and all full ceremonies, having a deacon and subdeacon to assist him. A great number of clerics in surplices came in solemn procession to the house of the Confraternity of Mercy, where we were lodged, and conducted the new priest, whom we also followed, to the principal church of the town, and after the mass was over they brought us back to the same place. He was assisted in this function by the Vicar of the Bishop and our Father Francesco Perez, Father Cosmo Torres doing the part of deacon. The same day I preached a sermon to the people, who were wonderfully delighted and deeply moved to reverence at so grand a ceremony, having never seen a first mass offered to God with so much ceremony so carefully observed.

I expect to receive from you a letter, lengthy and diligent, telling me clearly and particularly both all about the general state of the whole College, and how each one of the fathers and brothers who are living there are, how he is in health, what he is doing, what progress he makes, how industriously and how fruitfully he is labouring. You will grudge me a thing which produces the sweetest possible fruit in my soul, if you cheat me of any part of this information which I desire so much. Besides this, I desire to know how many of our Society have landed from the ships which have come from Portugal, of what quality they are, how many of them are priests, or clerics, or lay brothers, whether any of them have a gift for preaching, and how great a gift, and what other good endowments they possess. I should like this subject of itself to fill two or three sheets of large paper. Lastly, tell me about all our brothers in the Comorin Coast, those who are at Coulan, Meliapor, Ormuz, and Bazain; write so as I may know everything as if I had it there before my own eyes. This letter I wish one of you two, Father Paul or Father Antonio, to write to me, and besides that, I wish you to tell each one of our fathers and brothers who are living with you, that I beg them very much not to think it too much trouble to write to me letters of their own telling me the state of their souls. Such is my special affection to each one that it will be a delight to me to hear what are the heavenly gifts by which each one is refreshed by God, what are his peace and joy of mind, what the alacrity with which he presses on to perfection by his service to God our Lord. I should wish also that some one of the native students—suppose Diego of Mozambique—should write to me in the name of all, and do not let our people wait till I extract from them letters in return by sending them letters of my own to begin with, for though I have quite charity enough for this, yet I have not leisure enough, as all may easily see. I wish this letter to be communicated to them all, and they each one to receive it as written to himself by name. All these letters which I speak of are to be sent, as I have before told you, to Malacca to Francesco Perez, who will take care to send them on straight to me in Japan.

Remember yourselves, and take care, I beseech you, that all our Fathers and brothers remember also, earnestly to commend to God in their daily intercessions and prayers, the Commandant of Malacca as if he were myself. The benefits he has conferred upon us and upon the whole Society are so splendid, that we are altogether unable to repay him, unless we obtain help from the almighty beneficence of God our Lord to make up for our poverty and weakness, and so free us from the very disgraceful stain of ungrateful hearts. The letters from Lisbon or Coimbra or Rome from Father Simon or others which you will receive directed to me, I have already told you to send to Malacca by the ship which leaves Goa for Banda; but if they do not come to hand in time for that, then let them at least be put on board the King's ship which is to be sent in April to Ternate, and by the same means and occasion do not forget to inform our Fathers in the Moluccas of all that has happened worth mentioning in Europe and in the Indies.

But if you shall see in the bundle of letters for me from Europe any that have the royal seal upon them, as to these I give you this particular order. You must unseal those copies of them which come to you by the first ship, and read them, then make them up again into a packet and send them to Malacca. I wish these letters to be read first by you two, Father Paul and Father Antonio, for this reason—because I think there will be in them some mention of two matters of business for the full execution of which in my absence you will have of necessity to do something. A long time ago I wrote to the King about Donna Isabella, formerly Queen of Ternate, the mother of the King who reigned there before the present King. When I was there this lady became a Christian by my ministry. I also wrote about Balthasar Veloz, a near connection of the King of the Moluccas whose sister he has married; a man full of great love to our Society, who is very diligent and very useful indeed in working for the conversion of the heathen to our

Lord. The King is always so kind to me that I have reason to hope that he will answer me on these two heads, and indeed I expect that very probably certain royal diplomas which I have endeavoured to obtain in favour of both these persons who have deserved so well of religion will be sent along with these letters to me. If it turns out that I am not deceived in this, then I again and again entreat you to forward these diplomas, with the greatest care, to the charge of our Fathers at Ternate by the royal ship which leaves Goa for the Moluccas in April.

But if the King's letters say nothing about this, and if there is not to be discovered in the whole packet any letter from the King directed to both or at least to one of these two persons, then I beseech you Father Paul and Father Antonio to go at once to call on the Lord Governor and pray him very earnestly to let examination be made whether in the packet of letters from the King to himself which has just arrived, there be found orders as to an annual pension to be paid to Queen Isabella; or as to a certain honour or exemption granted to Balthasar Veloz by favour of his highness. And if these are found, then prevail upon the Governor both to do of his own accord everything else that may be necessary to give a full practical effect to the liberality of the King, and also to intrust the diplomas to you, who will take care that they be delivered to those whom they concern. That which relates to the Queen Isabella it will be enough for you to commit to our Fathers who are stationed at Ternate; as for that which is for Balthasar Veloz, I think you should address that yourselves in a special packet with letters from you, filled with every kind of expression of gratitude and desire to serve him, taking great care to let him see that by doing benefits to those of ours who are within his reach, he binds to himself all the members of the Society in every place to a return of goodwill, which will always show itself by efficient service whenever occasion arrives.

And now, Father Antonio Gomez, I urge upon you in the strongest and most urgent manner I can, to show with all diligence to the Reverend Fathers of the Order of St. Francis and

St. Dominic—I had almost said, not only reverend, but to be honoured by us as the blessed in Heaven are honoured—the highest possible charity, the most humble veneration and the most obsequious devotion in every thing, not only paying exquisite respect to them as a body, but also proving to them each singly, as you have to deal with him, your true and most sincere love by means of every kind of courtesy and attention. And make it a rule that every kind of dissension with them, every beginning or appearance whatsoever of rivalry or jealousy, is to be avoided by you and by all of ours as you would avoid a wild beast or a venomous serpent. And as to this matter consider this—that in order to prevent feuds, and in order to extinguish in their very birth the enviousness and the suspicions which are the seeds of discord, nothing can serve more efficaciously than that every one of our Society should show the utmost modesty at all times, modesty not at all put on or false, but founded on that intimate lowliness of heart which induces of itself to all external humility. And I would have you by no means keep shut up in your own minds these your thoughts and affections towards those most honourable religious of those illustrious Orders, but show them in action, visiting them courteously from time to time, and as far as may be upon any occasions which you may take advantage of, or even which you look out for, winning their goodwill by all kinds of honour and attention; and let the public itself see this, so that those who desire to see priests contending with one another, may understand at once that they must hope for no spectacle of the sort from you or on account of you. Moreover you must make it a study to win to yourselves the very populace itself and every human being of whatever kind where you are, and cause all to bear you goodwill, for their own sake. For that is the only way for you to be able to help them for the salvation of their souls. And the principal means and hope of gaining this kind of popularity—popularity not sought for the sake of gain, but in the cause of religion—lies in this, that in all your words and deeds and gestures you show in your daily conversation the perfectly modest composure of a mind that despises itself, true fraternal love amongst yourselves, and towards all others in general the most unfeigned charity, ever ready to show itself in acts.

This last matter, I mean as far as relates to love among our own people for one another, I wish you, Father Paul, who are the Superior of the rest, to consider as particularly addressed to yourself. Take it in good part that I pray you here again once more, and that I beseech you to leave nothing undone that can make you an object of love to our brethren who are under your rule, and to think it a much more important thing that they love you with all their heart than that they obey your very nod. What follows now is for all of ours in India. I now give them warning that they should be prepared in mind and ready at a signal, if perchance I should find that there is greater opportunity of working with ease and profit in Japan than where they are, and should call them to come in large numbers to the richer harvest there. I quite expect that I can hardly fail very soon to summon some of them thither, and that the rest will have to follow after no long interval, as soon as the first successes have given us a pledge for further hope.

All of you take the most constant care that the Bishop may always have towards you the most lively goodwill and the most hearty favour. I would not have you content yourselves with mere signs of honour and barren declaration of veneration as the proofs of your devotion to his service—you must go beyond even all manifestations of the most submissive reverence to him, and as far as he may permit you, take upon yourselves a share of his labours, and by very readily putting on your own shoulders a part of that immense weight of work which is so heavy upon him, of his care of all the Churches, in as far as he may desire to let you bear the burthen for him, relieve the grey hairs of that excellent old man and father, the supreme ruler of what belongs to the Christian religion in these parts. You must accomplish to the very utmost all his commands, and execute his desires even if they are only hinted to you by a nod, and in this matter I would have you make no limit at all to your obedience to him, except only that which is the utmost limit of your whole strength strained as far as is possible to you with all the exertions you are capable of.

In the next place, I must communicate to you the anxiety which torments me, that, as far as our moderate powers allow, we should repay the great debt which we owe to our excellent and most liberal King for the great benefits with which he so unceasingly honours us, and also to the Portuguese in India for the very great love with which they treat us. It is easy to see that it is not in our power to return their good favour in any other way than by prudently and constantly applying ourselves, by means of the ecclesiastical ministrations of our Institute, to the work of securing the eternal salvation of the Portuguese wherever they are, either passing from place to place or fixed as residents. This work especially requires good preachers, and it has been long a pain to me that such preachers are sadly wanted in many settlements of the Portuguese, which are now numerous enough and are in great need of such helps. Even if we had not a duty of gratitude to make us supply such a need, we should be obliged to it by a feeling of common charity.

Now this want is felt more especially in Cochin and Bazain. For this reason I feel obliged, Father Antonio Gomez, to order you in virtue of holy obedience, that when the preachers who are expected very soon from Portugal arrive, you send one of them at once to Bazain and another to Cochin, even if there come no more than two, and there should be no one left for the College at Goa. For you yourself can go on doing that work as you have done hitherto; and see that you make no delay at all about this. Besides that my own formed opinion and certain judgment make me give this order, I have also pledged myself as to this to his lordship the Bishop, to whom I now write that I have ordered that it should be so done, every other consideration being postponed. May God our Lord in His infinite mercy thoroughly impress upon our minds a clear knowledge of His own most holy will, and at the same time furnish us continually with strength to obey it, with all that utmost and full perfection with which we should rejoice to have obeyed it at the moment of our death.

I explained to you in the letters which I wrote from Cochin how necessary it is that a house should be given to the Society at Coulan, to which our fathers who are labouring in the instruction of the Christians along the Comorin Coast may betake themselves, and from which they may start from time to time, and in which there may also be set up a school for the boys of those countries; to which also our missionaries who break down under the immense fatigue of that work they have to do, whose strength gives way from time to time and who contract very serious diseases, may be taken and receive all due care. So, my brother Antonio Gomez, arrange with the Governor and with the Chief Treasurer to find some way of bringing about this good work, which will not bear delay, by sending as soon as may be to Father Niccolo at Coulan some money or some other means by which he may be able at once to set in operation so very urgent a business.

What I am now going to add concerns you, Father Balthasar Gago, for I want your help in a certain business. I have already charged Father Paul and Father Antonio to send me information about our domestic affairs, under which name I may include all that relates to the persons, the houses, and the acts of our fathers and brothers of the Society in India. But it is necessary also, or at least very useful, that I should have intelligence of what goes on in distant parts and what is done by externs. This business I have set apart for you, confiding very much in your charity towards me, so I pray you take the trouble for me to look through the letters and despatches concerning European affairs which are brought to India, and also to make inquiries of persons who come out hither, and then from what you have read and heard make a selection for me, under these heads which I mention. What is the condition of our Society at Rome? How much has the College at Coimbra increased? Whether in either place any, and how many, of ours offer themselves to be sent out to help us here? Does the business of the mission to Æthiopia go on well, or is it abandoned? Has the Patriarch who was to have been sent out here been as yet named? How soon is it said that he will sail? What is our good Father Simon thinking of, or what is he doing? What are the reverend fathers of the Franciscan and Dominican orders undertaking in India? What is the fruit which results from their labours for souls? Have they had supplies of their own brethren sent out to them from Europe, especially of preachers? I wish also that you would particularly tell him whether our good friend Cosmo Añez is well and flourishing? With what good success does our Lord God prosper his home and family? And then at the end tell me what I delight to hear about yourself, your health, your progress in the spiritual life, the desires you feel of doing great things and suffering hard things for the glory of Christ. And although I know that you will do all this of your own accord and very willingly for my sake, because you are so good and kind, nevertheless I add, in order that you may not be deprived of the merit of obedience, that I distinctly order you to do it. And lastly, I inform you that you must be ready and prepared, and look for a signal from me that you are to start, for I shall call you out here sooner than you think.

Once again I address myself to you, Father Antonio Gomez, charging you most urgently, that if our fathers on the Comorin Mission should bring to you their requests or complaints, or those of the Christians whom they have to look after, who are sometimes wretchedly oppressed by violence and injustice, from the Commandant, you exert yourself strenuously to help him, leaving every other business aside for this, in which you should get Ruy Gonzalez to help you; as he is the Patron and father to those poor people, and has much influence with the Governor, he will be both able and willing to collect them powerfully.

And now it remains that I should beg the prayers of all of you to strengthen our great weakness in this perilous, doubtful, long, and laborious voyage of ours to Japan. I beseech you therefore all alike, as many as live in the College of Goa, to have the kindness to implore in your daily prayers and sacrifices the special help of God for Father Cosmo Torres, for Joam Fernandez, for Paul the Japanese, and his two companions, Manuel the Chinese, and Amador, and lastly for myself.

We are told here a great many things about Japan which fill us with the greatest hope that our voyage thither will lead to results which will abundantly repay the labour. They say that you can see there far and wide the fields white with the harvest, that many of the people are wearied with their ancestral superstitions, that many are desirous to hear about the law of Christ, the reputation of which has reached them with very great commendations; they show us letters also of some merchants dealing in the kingdom of Siam, who testify that some Japanese had landed there and had been heard to say that their countrymen wished to see some European priests come amongst them to teach them the true doctrine concerning God. Such are our hopes, and we are eager to fly to the spot where they may become true, our hearts full of spirit and of that confidence which is a sort of augury and presage, and which finds nothing too great to promise to itself in the way of success. But may God grant that our own sins may not intercept the rich streams of gifts of grace and heavenly succours, without an abundant torrent of which all labour for the conversion of the heathen is in vain! Farewell. Your most devoted brother in Christ,

Malacca, Feast of Corpus Christi, 1549. FRANCIS.

It is evident that Francis Xavier was anxious to start as soon as possible for Japan. He was already aware of what he afterwards mentions in his letters, that to reach Japan that year he must leave Malacca in June. We may attribute to the shortness of the interval which he had at his disposal the inability of the Commandant of Malacca to find a Portuguese ship in which he might embark. We are told by the historian of the life of St. Francis that many Portuguese merchants came forward to offer their vessels for this purpose. It was thought that the presence of the Apostle on board any ship would secure her safety from the great dangers of all kinds by which the navigation to Japan was beset. But the ships were not ready for sea: repairs were wanting to one, another had not completed her cargo, another was not yet manned. For some reason or other, every Christian ship was at this moment unavailable. Paul of the Holy Faith is said to have made a pungent remark on this occasion. 'All this happened,' he said, 'by a singular providence of God. If the Japanese his countrymen had seen on the one hand Master Francis preaching the holy law of God, and at the same time and place had also seen, on the other, the Christian merchants doing things contrary to the same law, they would have formed their judgment of it rather from the deeds of the merchants than from the words of the preacher, and would have told Master Francis, how could it be that the Christians looked forward to the good things of heaven after death, if they lived now as if there were no goods but those of this world? He thanked God,' he said, 'that no European entered Japan along with Francis.'

The mention of the Bishop's Vicar in the foregoing letter introduces us naturally to what the biographers of Francis Xavier tell us of another great triumph of his charity which was gained during this stay at Malacca. It has already been said that the city was never altogether converted by his preaching, and it was to be the scene of his last and most terrible disappointment. It would appear that one reason at least for the comparative stubbornness of a part of the population was to be found in that which is the greatest affliction that can befall a Christian community—the bad example and the negligence of the chief of the clergy. The Vicar of Ormuz, to whom Gaspar Baertz was instructed to pay so much submission and charitable attention, was a man whose life was a scandal to religion. Alfonso Martinez, who had been Vicar at Malacca for thirty years, was another instance of a lax and negligent ecclesiastic, though we are not told whether his life had been positively bad in the ordinary sense of the term. He had always been a friend to Francis Xavier, who, on his arrival at Malacca this time, found him dangerously ill, and what was far worse, in a state of despair as to the salvation of his soul. He had lived all those years in a state of carelessness, and now that his last hour seemed to be approaching, he passed from indifference to melancholy, and from melancholy, as we have said, to despair. In vain did his friends try to rouse him to confidence in the mercy of God: he replied only by howls and groans, declaring that for him the time of mercy was past. At last, when he was told that Francis had arrived, it seemed as if a ray of hope had pierced the gloom of his heart, and he endeavoured to rise from his bed and dress himself that he might go to meet his dear friend. But he fainted away from weakness on making the effort. Francis was soon at his side, exhorting him to confession in his own loving and forcible manner. But at first he was unsuccessful: a fresh access of despair fell on the poor soul which had so long neglected its duties, and Francis seemed to plead in vain. At last he turned to God in ardent prayer, and bound himself by vow to offer a large number of masses, in honour of the most holy Trinity, our Blessed Lady, the Angels, the Saints, and for the holy Souls of Purgatory. Martinez was softened, made his confession with great contrition, received the last sacraments, and expired peacefully in the arms of Francis Xavier. The Vicar mentioned as assisting at the first mass of Alfonso de Castro may probably have been the successor of Martinez, as we are not told that the latter held his office down to the time of his death.

The remainder of the letter which has last been inserted is remarkable, even among the letters of Francis Xavier, as an evidence of the thoughtful and tender anxiety with which his heart lingered over the brethren whom he had just left behind him in India. He had not long parted from them, and we cannot suppose that he had not given them, before leaving Goa, many of the injunctions, about writing to him both as to the external affairs of their mission and the state of their own consciences, which are here repeated. Even the little boys of the college are to let him know how they are. He would gladly write to each one of his brothers, but one letter must do for all. Again, all must pray much for the King, and for Pedro de Silva the good Commandant of Malacca. Great care is to be taken about keeping up the best relations with the Bishop and with the members, all and each, of other religious orders in Goa.

Then his mind runs off to the Queen Isabella of the Moluccas, and to Balthasar Veloz, for both of whom he has asked certain favours from the King, which the fathers at Goa are to see, if possible, secured to them without delay. Then again, he is not content with the letters which he hopes to receive from Fathers Paul and Antonio Gomez, the Superiors at Goa: he must have Father Balthasar Gago epitomize for him all the news which arrives from Europe, and all matters in India external to the immediate affairs of the Society. On the other hand, Francis says but little in this letter of his own expectations as to Japan, and we might suppose that it was written before the arrival of the good news as to the embassy from a Japanese prince asking for instructions in Christianity which came to cheer him before he left Malacca; unless indeed, as was likely, some other letter was written to Goa at this time, which has not been preserved.

Alfonso de Castro and his companions were to sail for the Moluccas, but perhaps would leave Malacca after Francis himself. Our next letter seems to have been sent to Joam Beira at the same time.

(LXXIII.) *To Joam Beira.*

May the grace and love of Jesus Christ our Lord always help and favour us! Amen.

The Fathers who are now leaving this for your parts will tell you with all fulness all about our brethren who are dispersed in various places in India, and who are everywhere, by the grace of God, labouring usefully for the propagation of the kingdom of Christ, as well as about those who are working in Portugal, and what fruit results from the labours of all. As I am sure of this, I can spare myself the trouble, by no means light, of writing at great length to you what you will hear much more conveniently and leisurely from them, who are fully furnished with all the information on these subjects, and will give it you in familiar conversation by word of mouth. As for myself, I have to tell you that I have now made up my mind and determined to sail to Japan, since I have learnt from competent sources that the natives there appear to be admirably disposed to receive the preaching of the doctrine of the Gospel in such a way as to give hope of great fruit.

We go together, six in number, three Europeans and three Japanese. These last are very honest men and very good Christians. They were baptized at Goa, and learnt, in the College of Santa Fè, to read and write in our language. Each of them has made the Exercises for a whole month, with very great fruit to his soul, and up to this time they have gone on adding to this fruit by daily and by no means small advances. They are all impelled to return to their country by their great longing to communicate to their friends and families the treasure which they have found for themselves, and of leading their fellow countrymen away from foolish superstitions and reconciling them to Christ, the only light and salvation of the world. It is said that some of the great people in Japan are thinking of sending an embassy to the King of Portugal, to ask him to send them some priests who may preach to them the law of Christ. We all go in very high spirits and confidence, hoping that some remarkable fruit will come from our voyage, the almighty power of our Lord God helping in His mercy our own weak efforts. I am now pretty well aware how much good can be done in these parts; and if, when I reach those islands at the end of the world, I come to think clearly that more return for our labours may be justly expected there, I mean to call you all to join me, and transplant you to work in places where a larger harvest may be reaped. So you must prepare your hearts and work up your zeal even now, that nothing may prevent you from obeying me without delay, as soon as you receive my letters calling you away to Japan.

Father Alfonso is to go to you, and his station is to be at the fortress of Ternate, where he is to preach both to the Portuguese and their slaves and servant-girls, and also to the free native Christians. He is also to explain the Christian doctrine every day, as I used to do when I was there; and once a week he is to explain the articles of the Creed and the Ten Commandments to the wives of the Portuguese assembled in a separate congregation, and to teach them also the way of properly and profitably frequenting the sacraments of penance and holy communion. When I called to mind what I saw there when I was on the spot, it seemed to me expedient that Father Alfonso should stay at least a year at Ternate, and even for a longer time, if it seemed useful to you, forming your judgment from experience of the present. He is a clever and able person; and after he has fully discharged his ministry for the good of souls, I think he will still not lack leisure, industry, and influence for the transacting of any business of yours, or of the Christians in the islands in which you are stationed at various places for the purpose of instructing them, providing you in due time, from the mart there, with whatever you may want, and, as often as it may be necessary, gaining the favour of the Prince of Ternate, or of the Portuguese Commandant or Treasurer, on behalf of you or your friends.

Manuel de Morães and Francesco Gonzalez are on their way to you, to be under your authority at the Moluccas. You have great reason to rejoice that these two, as well as Alfonso, whom I have already spoken of, are sent to you. They have all of them those gifts from which you may well expect great assistance. I am looking for letters from you telling me that you have been gathering in a rich harvest into the garners of the Church where you are. Would that they might tell me that the King's son had become a Christian! I knew, when I left, that he was thinking of something of the kind. As to the islanders of the Moor, what will they tell me? Will it be that there is a sign of hope that they are about to return to a better mind, and make peace with us? As for your people at the Moluccas, I wish to know whether they show any inclination or disposition to believe the preaching of the Gospel. Also as to the neighbouring countries, if any good news of the same kind should reach you concerning them, I beseech you do not cheat me of it. How glad I should be to hear from you that a door was opened to the Gospel at Macazar; that Tolles or Celebes seemed not averse to the Gospel! Do not fail to tell me how the Prince of Ternate behaves with regard to the Christians; whether he shows any, and how much, favour to the ministers of the Gospel and the whole affairs of religion. Tell me everything of this kind fully, so that one may be able to judge in what proportion the fruit corresponds to the labour spent in that part of the world, and whether it is expedient to send further supplies to increase the number of our workers there. Take care to inform our Father Ignatius at Rome, and Father Simon Rodriguez at Lisbon, as to how many idolaters have become Christians where you are, what progress the converts have made, what sort of constancy they show under persecution, what are the number of sermons delivered and sacraments administered, what profit in souls results from the sacred administrations of the priests, and how assiduous and strenuous they are in their ministrations. And also any other tidings of the same sort, which may be published in Europe and rouse the minds of those who hear them to give praise to God.

But in writings of the kind I speak of two things must be carefully observed: first, to make a selection of what you insert, leaving out whatever may give offence by casting reflections upon any one, and whatever it may cause unpleasantness to mention, and also to be prudent in adapting your whole style and tone to the gravity becoming an ecclesiastic; so that your accounts may be such as may be passed from hand to hand, made public, and communicated to externs as well as to ours, as soon as they arrive in Europe. For you must know and consider that such descriptions of what is being done in such remote parts of the world are much sought for and eagerly read throughout Spain, Italy, and elsewhere. So that it is very proper that we should take very peculiar care and caution as to what we write to be sent thither, in order that our letters, which will certainly fall into the hands not only of friends but also of persons not very favourable to us, sometimes even of those that have some jealousy or hostility to us, may, if it is possible, give satisfaction to all, and stir up all to give thanks to, and congratulate with, God and the Holy Church, and, at all events, never afford any legitimate cause to any one of offence or sinister interpretation. I would also have you write circular letters to the same purpose to all our brethren throughout India, to give them the good news of the happy success of what you are doing for the glory of God.

When you have occasion to ask anything of the Lord Governor or his lordship the Bishop, write privately to Antonio Gomez, and ask him to manage the business for you by a private interview. Ask him also for what you may want for the support and clothing of our fathers and brothers. I have told him to be at your service for things of that kind, and to take care that all the supplies which you let him know that you are in need of be duly forwarded to you by the ship which is usually sent every year from Goa to Ternate. Lastly, you must take care to keep me informed, by letters by no means perfunctory, but going fully into detail, as to all that may happen, good or bad, concerning your own labours, the issue of the preaching of the Gospel, domestic discipline, and the progress in virtue of all of ours; all which letters, as well as those which I have already enjoined upon you, you must duly seal up and send to Father F. Perez at Malacca, to whom I have given in charge to avail himself diligently of the many opportunities which that crowded mart affords of ships sailing in every direction, so that the letters may be faithfully forwarded, and the correspondence between us, which is so necessary for the government of the Society, may be carried on.

If any of our Society should wilfully fall into a fault for which he ought to be expelled from it (and, as you know, an obstinate refusal to obey would be among the chief of such faults), then, according to the arrangements which I have made with his lordship the Bishop, and which I communicated to you last year, you will order such a one in virtue of holy obedience and under pain of excommunication to present himself as soon as possible to his lordship, by whose authority he must hereafter be guided, because the Society will no longer acknowledge him as her child. And what I have thus ordered you, you must clearly let each one of those whom you have with you know so to have been enjoined upon you, that every one may understand at what peril he may commit such a fault. And let no one flatter himself that, however much he may fail in his resolution to gain perfection, and however slow and obstinate he may be, that he may nevertheless consider it certain that he will remain and persevere in the Society.

May God bring us together in His holy glory! for as for this life, our pilgrimage lies in such different directions that it does not seem very likely that we shall at any time meet. Farewell.

Malacca, June 20, 1549.

P.S. A fear occurs to my mind, when I think of the occupations you have where you are, whether you have leisure enough to write the letters which I have spoken of to our Father Master Ignatius, Master Simon, to all our brethren in India, as well as about your own affairs to Goa. So I suggest to you the means of making the work shorter, which I now state. You will have, as I have said, our good Alfonso at Ternate. I think that you should order to be sent to him from all the stations of ours throughout the Moluccas accounts, however hastily made up, as long as they are true and exact, of all that is done, stating what kind of ministerial functions our priests are discharging, with how much exertion, and what fruit of souls; whether they are exposed to any persecutions, of what sort and from whom, how much constancy they show in resisting them, and what victories and successes they gain by the aid of God. They should state also what are the dispositions and conditions of mind among the heathen in those parts, and what hope there is for the future from them. And as Alfonso is not only prudent, but also fluent, with a good style and hand, he, out of the accounts sent to him, will make up letters in the name of you all such as it is well to send to Europe and India. Moreover, he will manage any business you may have, partly with the Commandant at Ternate, partly by means of Antonio Gomez at Goa. He will leave to you one only concern of which you cannot at all put off the burthen on to the shoulders of another,—the business, namely, of writing to me, as I by all means desire, and as it is necessary that you should write, as to the state, the spiritual progress, the talents, the virtues, or the imperfections of each one of ours who are fighting out there under your leadership.

It is said here that you have been killed in the Isles of the Moor; but these rumours can be traced to no authority. We do not mean to give ear to such evil reports; and we hope, on the other hand, that by the good favour of God our Lord you will live many years yet to work in His service. If, however, contrary to what we believe and desire, then I give orders that all of our Society who are at present in the Moluccas, or shall hereafter arrive there, are to obey Father Alfonso. As to this matter, I here subjoin an order, which is to be duly promulgated, as follows: 'Father Ribera and Niccolo Nuñez, if Father Beira should die, are to obey Father Alfonso. Manuel de Morãez and Francesco Gonzalez, who are in the Moluccas, I order you in virtue of holy obedience, that if Joam Beira should have happened to die, you acknowledge Alfonso de Castro as Superior, and obey him. But if, as I think most probable, and as I hope is the case, Joam Beira is still alive, I desire and command both of you to obey him exactly as your lawful Superior.'

FRANCIS.

The date of these last letters shows that the term of the short stay made by Francis and his companions in Malacca was nearly expired when he wrote them. The Feast of Corpus Christi fell that year on the 20th of June, and Francis was to sail on the 24th. Yet the number of letters which remain to us, dated before his departure—though it is probable that some which he wrote at the time have not been preserved—shows us how much he must have been occupied with his correspondence during the last half week. We may, however, well suppose, as has been already said, that he began his letters long before he finished and dated them. The next two letters in the collection are addressed, the one to the Society at Rome, the other to the Society at Coimbra. They are almost absolutely identical in their contents, and it seems at first sight more probable that Francis only wrote one, which was copied at Coimbra in a somewhat shorter form, and thus forwarded in copy to Rome, than that he wrote both the letters, as they remain to us, in full. But, on the other hand, it was undoubtedly his custom to write the same letters twice or three times over, and we cannot think that the collectors would give us the letters twice over unless two separate copies had been made by Francis himself. We shall give the copy which seems to have been made last of the two, as it is somewhat fuller than the other.

We find mention in this letter of the desire of one of the princes of Japan to become a Christian, and of his sending an envoy to the Governor of the Indies to obtain teachers. The story about the Portuguese merchants who were put into an old haunted house by the Japanese is highly characteristic both of the times and of the country, which has retained even down to our time that jealousy of foreigners which shows itself in excluding them as far as possible from unrestrained intercourse with the population and from residence amongst them. We may defer any remarks on the remainder of the letter until after its insertion.

(LXXIV.) *To the Fathers and Brothers of the College of Coimbra.*

May the grace and love of Christ our Lord always help and favour us! Amen.

I wrote to you at full length last January, and besides this, I feel confident that all our brethren who are scattered about in these parts, each one from his own station, has done the same, according to my orders to them, telling you what rich and happy fruit of souls this vineyard of the Indies produces, and how prosperously the Christian religion increases in growth, not only in the royal garrisons, but also in the other towns which belong to the heathen.

I came hither from India last April, in order to embark at this port of Malacca for Japan. I have two of our Society with me—one a priest, the other a lay brother—and also three Japanese converts whom I have first had well instructed in fundamental knowledge of the mysteries of our Lord Christ and of the Catholic Faith, and then baptized at Goa. They were instructed in the elements of the Christian doctrine in our College of Santa Fè, where they also learned to read and write in our language. They also made the Spiritual Exercises for a month with very great attention and extreme desire to profit from them. Nor was God wanting on His part to meet this goodwill of theirs which He had Himself prepared, for He gave them very deep feelings as to the immense benefits which they had received from the great liberality of Him their Creator, which they then gratefully thought over for the first time in their lives, blaming themselves for and weeping over their former blindness as to acknowledging the same. This made them feel such burning affections of the love of God in return, of devotion, and other like virtues, that all of us who used to live with them at that time would have thought ourselves very well off indeed if we had been affected in like manner.[1]

They are now using with much care the proficiency which they have gained of reading and writing after our manner, in acquainting themselves with writings, generally those which explain the mysteries of our Lord, and in reciting at a certain hour every day the Psalms and other prayers of the Church. I asked them once, when they were doing this, what part of such volumes they felt the greatest delight in reading aloud, and they answered me that it was the history of the sufferings and

[1] This sentence is a little varied in the copy of the letter addressed to Rome:

'After duly receiving baptism, they exercised themselves with great diligence and equal fruit in meditation on the truths relating to man and to God. But by the singular goodness of God they were so strongly roused to the knowledge of His heavenly bounties towards them, and they were loaded with divine grace to such a degree, that we may well wish that all of you might share in the great blessings which God, so to say, heaped upon them with a full hand.'

death of Christ.[2] What confirms what they said is, that we have observed them give all signs of tender compassion at any chance mention or remembrance of the pains and death of the Lord Jesus; and not only this, but turn to the thought of themselves, go back to it from time to time, and that they are invariably very deeply moved at that consideration. All the time that they were making that month of retreat at Goa, we used to see that they were visited by wonderful joy and heavenly sweetness, and often melted into calm and happy tears.

Before they were put under the training of the Spiritual Exercises, we had kept them for several months at learning by heart the articles of the Christian faith and the mysteries of the life of Christ, and in making their minds familiar with the cause of the Incarnation of the Son of God in the womb of the Blessed Virgin Mary, and the whole plan of the redemption of mankind. I have often asked them, which of all the sacraments of the Christian law seemed to them of most salutary use? and they always answered that, on account of their usefulness and universality of application, which extended to every kind and circumstance of condition and place, they gave the first rank of all principally to two sacraments, those of holy Penance and of holy Communion. They used to add, that all the doctrines of the Christian religion appeared to them to hold together so aptly among themselves, that they thought that no one of sound judgment could help approving of them if ever he came to know them. I have heard one of these men, who is called Paul of the Holy Faith, sighing deeply and exclaiming, 'O unhappy people of Japan, who adore the creatures which God has made in order that they may be your servants!' I said to him, 'Paul, why do you talk so?' He answered, 'I pity my poor fellow countrymen, who give divine honour to the sun and moon, whereas those stars are servants to those who acknowledge the Lord Jesus, and by His command they give

[2] The Roman letter goes on as follows:

'They therefore make this their chief reading and meditation. As long as they were making the exercises they received so much heavenly joy from them, and so many pious tears, that the effect remained for many months.'

light to men by day and by night, that they may use that light to understand the glory of Jesus Christ the Son of God.'

But to return to our voyage. We arrived at this city of Malacca, three of the Society with three Japanese, on the 31st of May of the year 1549. We were met as soon as we landed by consistent statements of many persons at once, who vied one with another in telling us wonderful news as to the very excellent hope that might be entertained of the great likelihood of success for the preaching of the Gospel in Japan. Their authority consisted in some letters which they showed us, lately received from some Portuguese merchants their friends who were trading in that country. In one of these letters it was stated that a certain Prince in these islands of Japan, a man of great wealth and power, wished to become a Christian, and had already sent an ambassador to the Governor of India to ask in his name that some teachers of the Christian religion might be sent to Japan, by whom he might be instructed in the faith.

There were some other letters directed to me personally, which informed me that some Portuguese merchants on landing at a certain city in Japan, and seeking for a place of abode where they might lodge, had had assigned to them by the petty Prince of the district some buildings which had been left without inhabitants, because experience had proved that they were much infested by ghosts. The Portuguese entered them without knowing anything of this inconvenience, which the Japanese very cunningly said nothing about. For some nights they were continually surprised to find that when they lay down to rest the clothes and coverings of their beds were pulled off, without their being able to see any one. At last a servant of their party was frightened out of his wits in the dead of the night at the appearance of a terrible spectre, and cried out so loud in betrayal of his fright that he woke them all up. They leapt up from their beds, seized their weapons, and ran to the poor fellow who was shouting, as if they were going to repel a night attack made by thieves. But they found the door fastened and the servant safe and alone. They asked him why he had made such a noise, and he could give no account of it, except that he had seen a most terrible appearance, which, however, had vanished when he had made the sign of the Cross. After this the same servant set up a great many figures of the Cross in various places about the building and at the doors of the rooms. Meanwhile, the neighbours, who knew all about it, came to ask how the strangers found themselves in the haunted house, and they were full of wonder at their remaining there so long without hurt. And as it chanced that they had heard the servant shout out in the night and the noise made by the others in running to his assistance with their weapons, they asked the next day, what had been the reason of their panic that night? The Portuguese then stated what had happened to them, and the Japanese confessed that the building had for a long time been considered as infested by a certain evil spirit. As that kind of plague is common in those parts, they asked the Portuguese, if they had any remedy at hand which would cure it, to be so kind as to say so and communicate it to them. The Portuguese answered that nothing was more efficacious for the driving away of malicious spirits than the sign of the Cross. Soon what had happened and what they had said got to be spread abroad widely, and crosses made of paper, or wood, or any such substance, were to be seen at the doors of nearly all the houses in the town; the natives, who were often wont to suffer great molestation from the visits of hellish ghosts, making use with great eagerness of the defence which had been made known to them against such assaults.

The same letter, addressed to me, also added, that the Japanese nation appeared to be extremely well disposed to receive the preaching of the Gospel. It is very circumspect and prudent, judging of things by motives of reason, and also wonderfully curious to learn anything new that is brought to it. For this reason I for my part have conceived a great hope, relying on the assistance of God, that very considerable fruit will result among some of the Japanese, perhaps in all of them, and that a great number of those wandering souls will join themselves to the fold of the holy Church, unless indeed our own sins hinder our Lord God from vouchsafing to use us as the instruments of His glory. Still, I did not all at once act upon these fair auspices which seemed to invite me to the expedition. Since then, I have long and carefully deliberated in my own mind, looking out and searching by all possible indications for some sign of the will of God in this matter.

However, when once I had clearly recognised in myself the intimation and conviction that it was altogether the desire of God, and that it was a matter which His service required, that I should go to Japan, I gave myself up to the plan so entirely and irrevocably, that it seemed to me that if I were now to desist from what I had begun, I should be more wicked and more detestable than the very idolaters of Japan. I am confirmed in my purpose because I see that the enemy of the human race is setting a great many devices in motion in order to make me give up the thought of it, and this makes it by no means obscure that he dreads no small defeat and destruction to his own interests if it is carried out. He may make whatever disturbance and opposition he will, and we shall go on all the same in perfect carelessness as to the empty bugbears he may raise. We have got ready all that is wanting for the celebration of the Holy and Unbloody Sacrifice, with which we intend to offer the Sacred Host, and so take possession of those countries and nations in the name of Christ our King. What may be the success attending our first beginnings, you will fully learn next year, if God wills, by letters which you will then receive from me.

I have already made up my mind, as soon as ever I disembark, to go to the King of all Japan himself, wherever he may be, and lay before him the message which I have for him from the Supreme Emperor of all nations, our Lord Jesus Christ. I am told that the King has always with him a large band of men of letters, who are full of confidence in their own genius, learning, and eloquence. I do not fear much, relying on God, from the opposition of all their learning; for what good learning can people have who do not know Jesus Christ?[3] And as

[3] The letter to Rome continues thus:

'But he who looks to nothing else but the grace of God, the preaching of the Gospel, the salvation of souls, what shall he refuse, what shall he

we care for and seek for nothing else but the glory of God and the manifestation of Jesus Christ unto the salvation of souls, what kind of loss or danger can there be of which we ought to be so very much afraid? It is true that we are defenceless and unarmed, yet it is easy for God both to shield us from all harm in the midst of the hostile armies not only of the large nation we are going to, but also of the devils who are so much irritated against us, and also to help us to be conquerors. And if anything else please Him, we do not count it bitter, whatever it may be that is according to His will. In such case as this, it is victory even to fall, provided that the body alone fall, and the mind remain unconquered.[4] There is only one kind of wound at all that is to be feared, and that is when the mind is wounded by giving consent to sin. But as God our Lord is wont to give to all sufficient grace to serve Him and to abstain from sin, we trust in the divine mercy that this grace will by no means be denied to us. All that is good or bad in us consists in our using well or using ill the grace of God, and we rest with very great confidence, first on the merits of our holy Mother the Church, the Spouse of Jesus Christ our Lord, and then specially on the merits of all who belong to the Society of Jesus, and of all the faithful of both sexes who are serving God under their advice or direction; so that, with all these embracing us under their patronage and assisting us by their prayers, we hope to be able to co-operate faithfully with and make good use of the grace which God our Lord will offer us in due time.

It is a great comfort to us to know that God, who judges the inmost feelings of the human heart, sees clearly with what wish, with what aim, with what prayer, and in search of what it is that we are moved to undertake this voyage to Japan. Our

fear? For if we shall find ourselves not only in the land of barbarians, but even in the realm of devils, yet no barbarism, no rage of demons will be able to hurt us, except by the permission and concession of Almighty God.'

[4] Letter to Rome:

'One thing alone we fear, least we offend God Himself; and if we avoid offending Him, we promise ourselves certain victory over our enemies, He favouring us.'

own consciences tell us that in that expedition we seek and desire nothing else at all, save only that we may lead the souls of men, created in the image of God, to the knowledge of their Creator, that the Supreme Author of all things may be praised as He deserves by the creatures whom He has made in His own likeness, and the frontiers of the empire of our holy Mother Church, the Spouse of Christ, may be advanced and her realm enlarged. And so we go glowing with vigorous confidence, and we venture to presume and reckon on as a thing certain and as if our hope had received a pledge of its fulfilment, that this voyage of ours to Japan will unfailingly issue in happy and joyful success. There are two things which support me against all the threats and preparations of the devil, who is already threatening hostilities and letting us know clearly enough that he means war to the knife, in order to frighten us from our course. The first of these is, as I have just said, the conviction that God knows with perfect clearness the rectitude of my intentions in undertaking the voyage. The second is, the most certain knowledge of the entire and absolute dominion of the will of God over all created things, so that no one of them can do anything at all except by the permission of God. And that this law binds the devils themselves, and that, however much they may wish to hurt any one, they cannot do so unless they first obtain leave from God, is clearly seen in the history of Job. The sacred Scripture bears witness, that his most savage enemy Satan could not in the slightest degree harm that holy man without the assent and pleasure of God.

I say all this because it is a matter of the greatest certainty that the passage from Malacca to Japan which we have made up our minds to attempt is beset with very urgent and imminent danger of death of a dreadful kind. There will be all the extreme violence of most furious storms, there will be danger that cannot be detected beforehand from hidden rocks and quicksands, there will also be the risk of fierce attacks from the pirates who infest those seas. The fear of these perils is by no means a vain fear, as is proved by the number of examples increasing with the number of those who make the venture, in which persons who have attempted this voyage have been shipwrecked or reduced to slavery. It is commonly said here that it is a matter of experience, and which cannot by any human means be avoided, that out of all the ships which sail from this or any other neighbouring port for Japan, one in every three is lost by one of the three causes of destruction which I have mentioned—storms, rocks or shoals, and pirates.

I have often, in thinking of these things, had the fear come into my mind, lest most of the learned men of our Society, when they are sent out here to preach the Gospel, and come to experience for themselves the severe labours that are requisite, and the very great risk that there is to body and life, which, from the very condition of the enterprise we have in hand and the state of affairs as they are here, we are obliged to expose to continual danger, might have a kind of scruple about it, as if we were committing the fault of rashness, and as if all this were in some way to tempt God, which the sacred Scriptures speak of so severely. But when I have thought over the whole matter at full leisure, I did not find it difficult to get rid of the objection, and to lay aside all fear. For I am confident that the fatherly Providence of God over our Society will in His own sweet way bring about, that all those noble gifts of learning and eloquence which the men I speak of have brought to our Society, may be so tempered by our training and the holy discipline of religious life, as to be always under the control of the Holy Spirit, Who will animate these men as He does the other members of the Society.[5] Unless this were to happen, I for my part should have great fears for them, nor should I be able to feel at rest, having before my mind continually what I remember to have heard our blessed Father Ignatius say, that the true children of the Society of Jesus ought to make great exertions in order to conquer themselves, and to seek out means of driving away from their minds those terrors of things that appear formidable,

[5] The letter to Rome has it thus:

'But when I have recollected myself, I cease to fear, since I am confident that the spirit of the Lord which dwells in the learning and learned men of our Society would moderate all this, otherwise learning would bring much more hurt than advantage.'

which hinder men from putting their full hope and entire confidence in God. For though a lively hope and faith of that sort be a gratuitous gift of God, which He bestows on those on whom it pleases Him to bestow it, nevertheless for the most part He gives it to those who keep a stern hold over themselves, and who leave nothing undone by means of which they may obtain the full subjugation of all their feelings, out of their love for God, to considerations of His divine service and glory.

There is, believe me, a wide difference between those who trust in God while they are nevertheless furnished with all things which are necessary for the support and convenience of life, and those who do the same in extreme destitution and entire want of all the supports of life, into which state they have thrown themselves of their own accord for the sake of imitating Christ. And it follows from this that there is also a great difference between those who place their trust and hope and confidence in God without being in danger of death, and those who trust in God and hope in Him, and at the same time of their own accord and free will expose themselves, in order to give Him pleasure, to evident danger of death, while they have it in their own full power and choice either to avoid such or to encounter them. And to my mind it seems that a man who in this way has made his choice to live in continual danger of death, out of the mere desire to serve God, and casting aside all other motives or aims, will very soon feel a great weariness of this present life and a great desire for death, that he may thereby be graciously removed unto a better life, and may reign with God in heaven; since this life, as we call it, is rather one long death and a state of exile from that glory, for the enjoyment of which we are intended by our Creator.

Our good brothers and companions, the Japanese who are going with us to Japan, tell us that the ministers of religion there will be scandalized if they see us eat flesh or fish. We go therefore with our minds determined whatever may be the severity of the diet which it may be necessary for us to use, to take away all occasion of such offence. Those who come from

Japan tell us that there is in that country a great multitude of men of that sort, who lead what looks like a kind of religious life, and practise severe asceticism. They say that these men have very great authority with the people, so that high and low alike all hang upon their nod, and are ready to do any service at their command. I tell you this that in your prudence you may form an idea what great and fierce battles are ready for us in Japan, and that in your charity you may strive to obtain for us from Him Who is the Lord of all of us, by means of your daily sacrifices and prayers, the aid that is necessary in order to conquer such bitter foes. And I hope that in this way we shall be kept up by the merits and prayers of all the sons of the holy Society of Jesus.

They say that we shall set sail either on the feast of St. John Baptist of this year 1549, or on the night before. We have settled to sail straight for Japan, and for a distance of about two hundred leagues to run along the coast of the celebrated kingdom of China, never disembarking or approaching the shore, until we reach Japan. The sailors say that this may be on about the tenth or fifteenth of the following month.[6] And when this happens, by God's favour, you must expect long and full letters from me, in which I shall inform you of the position and character of the country, the nature of the people who inhabit it, their disposition, manners, laws, superstitions, errors, studies, universities, and learning—of the exercises which are practised in acquiring it, and the method by which it is taught.

Our good Paul gave me great pleasure once, telling me about a certain monastery in his country, where there are a number of members of the community who devote themselves to literature. He said that there was one who was their superior, a certain old man who appeared to excel all the rest in wisdom, and who from time to time makes an address to all the community assembled together. Then he bade each one of them by himself meditate for the space of an hour on some prescribed subject, such as this or another like it—what the soul might seem likely to say to the body at the last moment of their

[6] *i.e.* (as in the letter to Rome) 'the middle of August.'

separation?[7] what it will think, when it has been set free from its connection with matter, and finds itself in the severe pains of hell, or of the fire of Purgatory under the earth? for even these men seem to have got hold of some kind of knowledge of these things. When the hour has been spent in consideration on this subject, the teacher I speak of is wont to question his disciples one by one, as to what each one has found out in his meditation, and to praise them more or less, according to the merit of what they produce, or even, if any one brings up something which is quite unworthy of notice, he gives him a scolding. He told me also that these cenobites are in the habit of preaching to the people about once a fortnight, that they have a large audience of men and women, and are listened to with much attention and emotion, that often a good part of the audience, especially the women, are moved to tears, particularly when, as is often done, the orator displays a painted representation of the torments of hell. So Paul told me, speaking of what he had seen.

I asked him, whether he remembered any sentence which he had carried away from those sermons? He answered that one of these preachers whom he was listening to had once said that a wicked man or a bad woman was worse than the devil, because what the devil could not do by himself, he did by the means of bad men and women, as is seen in thefts, in false witness,[8] and in other crimes, which are brought about at the persuasion of the devil, and by the actions of bad men following that persuasion. All who tell us what they have seen of the Japanese agree in one thing, that they are a nation with an exceeding eagerness for knowledge. I shall tell you at full length what my own practice and experience among them may teach me. May God our Lord through His infinite mercy unite us in His

[7] This sentence is rather differently given in the letter to Rome:

'As for example, when death at the last breath stops the voice, if the power of speaking were then given to the soul departing from the body, in what words would it address its body at that moment of separation? Also if there were to be any one who had been recalled from hell to life, what would he seem likely to say to others?

[8] The Roman letter has 'perjury.'

glory! for in this life I do not well know when or how we can hope to see one another. However, obedience could bring even that about, for obedience finds it easy, whenever it pleases, to arrange things which appear in themselves to be most difficult.

The useless servant of all my brethren of the Society of the Name of Jesus,

Malacca, June 22, 1549. FRANCIS.

It cannot surprise us if we find in the account given by Francis Xavier of the institutions of Japan features which are not prominent in the Japan of the present day, or at least in the very partial descriptions which have come to us, chiefly from the pens of diplomatists and political representatives of European powers, who have seen almost nothing of the country, except the modern capital, Yeddo. This remark applies more particularly to some passages in the letters which will be given in the next chapter, with regard to the universities or academies of Japan, and the communities of religious persons of both sexes, the names of which, it is only natural to suppose, may have become altogether transformed in the successive stages through which they have reached us since they were taken down from the lips of Anger—or, as he was probably called in Japan, Han-Siro—by Francis or his companions. The passages about the dangers of the voyage, the sources of his own confidence, and his consciousness of his own purity of intention, are probably the simple outpourings to his distant but much-loved friends, so few of whom, comparatively, he had ever seen in the flesh, of the thoughts and feelings of which his mind was full; but they were not without their usefulness to those to whom they were addressed, especially at Coimbra, to which he had come to look as the nursery of the future missioners of India and Japan. The same may be said of the doubt which Francis speaks of, more fully in the letter sent to Coimbra, than in the copy of the same which was addressed to Rome, as to the view which learned theologians might take of the peril to which the missioners exposed their lives on such voyages as that which he was now about to undertake. He was perhaps thinking that he might have to call on some of those who had already arrived in India, or were on their way thither, to follow him to Japan, and he may well have wished that they should begin at once to practise that perpetual abnegation and self-conquest which alone could fit them to brave the dangers, both physical and moral, which awaited them in the enterprise. As to the concluding paragraphs of the letter, in which Paul of the Holy Faith is quoted as to the interior practices of the monasteries of bonzes, and as to the preaching to the people of some of the cenobites, there is nothing in these statements inconsistent with what is witnessed to by travellers both of earlier and later dates. Preaching was the great means for propagating his religion employed by Sakya-mouni. The cenobite systems of Buddhism, as well as the other religions existing by its side in Japan, have probably decreased in internal strength and vigour, as well as in external influence, since the time when Han-Siro took refuge in a monastery of bonzes, after committing a homicide; but even in the present day the practices of which he gave report to Francis Xavier are not unknown.

We have already said that the letter on which we are now commenting was written twice over, and addressed to the Society at Rome, as well as to the College at Coimbra. These letters, however, by no means exhausted the activity of Francis Xavier during this short stay at Malacca, busy as he must have been about the arrangements for his voyage, and occupied as he could never fail to be, in a city where he was so well known, with works of charity and religious zeal. The next letter in our series is dated the same day with the foregoing. It seems at first sight to be a simple expression of the hearty admiration and joy of the writer at the labours and success of Francesco Perez and his associate; but we find as we proceed that Francis is to impose a command on Gomez and Paul of Camerino to send fresh labourers to the mission at Malacca, and that his commendation of Perez, the missioner already there, is intended to introduce the order almost as if it were a petition. There is a remarkable buoyancy and glow of hearty joy through all his writings at this time.

(LXXV.) *To Father Paul of Camerino and Father Antonio Gomez, at Goa.*

May the grace and peace of our Lord Jesus Christ be always in our souls! Amen.

As soon as I landed here I was struck with greater wonder than I can easily find words to express, at seeing with my own eyes the immense harvest which in this city of Malacca, as in some large field of rich corn, is gathered into the barn of Christ by the labour and industry of the single evangelical workman Father Francesco Perez. Every Sunday and feastday he preaches in the morning to the Portuguese in the largest church in the city. In the afternoon in the same place he diligently expounds the articles of the holy Creed to the less instructed free men or to the slaves of both sexes. Once in the week in the church of our Lady the Mother of God he preaches to a large congregation of the wives both of the Portuguese and of the native Christians a sermon adapted to their capacity and condition. And besides all this, every single day he teaches and explains in the most laborious manner the elements of the Christian doctrine to a very large crowd of boys in the church of the Confraternity of Mercy. Besides these things, which might certainly be enough abundantly to occupy a single man, it would not be easy to count the number of penitents whose confessions he alone hears.

Here then is a worker in the Lord's vineyard who is certainly no sluggard or idler. We see him exerting himself so unweariedly and so continuously that he has to cheat himself of the time necessary for eating and sleeping. I certainly hope that he will never hear from our Lord that reproach in the holy parable: 'Why stand ye here all the day idle?' for, in truth, no one can ever find him at any hour either of the day or night when he is not intent on the work of extricating souls from the snare of sin, and making them advance in the service of God our Lord, Who made them. When he preaches there is such a concourse that the largest churches will not hold the congregation. In familiar intercourse he is wonderfully courteous and affable, so as to attract at once all whom he comes across, and he is singularly popular with all, high and low alike. He is the beloved favourite of the Commandant and also of all the inhabitants, and is commonly honoured with the reputation of a truly apostolical man, very dear to God on account of his insatiable desire to gain souls to Him.

I confess to you, my brothers, that when I saw all this I was ashamed of myself, when I beheld with my own eyes how great a store of rich spoils was being continually added, by the help of God, to the treasuries of the Church by this one man of weak constitution and continual ill health. The consciousness of my own sluggishness smote me in my inmost heart with a feeling of shame and confusion. Just consider—the multitude of men who are continually being roused to the serious amendment of their lives by the private or public discourses of Francesco Perez is so great, that they would keep at least six priests well practised at hearing confessions well occupied all day long, with nothing else to do. And yet this same man, in addition to all these occupations, discharges fully and well all the duties of domestic chaplain, as it is called, in the Confraternity of Mercy, and you know how constant and manifold those duties are. What can I say to this, except confess once more, that I and those like me ought to be covered with shame, that we who are in health and strength do but little, while the weak and the invalids are enriching themselves with the spoil of so many souls snatched from the jaws of hell?

Then there is Rocco Oliveira, the companion of Father Perez, who also works as strenuously and as usefully as the Father. He is master of a numerous school of boys. Some of them he teaches to read and write our language, to others he teaches Latin grammar. He has been so long at this that many of them have now finished their schooling, and have gone home again, having got through the whole course of which they are capable, and at home they show by the simplicity of their manners and the good examples they give in every respect, to the great joy and thankfulness of their parents, how great the difference is between boys well taught and boys untaught. They read with ease, and understand as far as is necessary the common summaries of the Christian doctrine; they recite the prayers of the Church from book, and this so modestly that all who see them are provoked thereby to give praises and thanks to God, for they carry themselves with as much recollection and composure of countenance as the novices of religious orders at home. No one can ever hear an oath or an improper word from them, not even of the lightest kind, such as is more easily pardoned. Among other edifying things of this kind which our good Rocco has established, is one which is very highly approved of—he often brings out his schoolboys in a long procession, answering one to another by twos and twos, with their eyes fixed on the ground, their walk grave and slow, singing the litanies, or other sacred chants of the same kind. These processions, which are very pleasant sights, are in great demand among the people, especially for the purpose of adding dignity to funerals, whenever one of the Christians here happens to die. The elder lads take the bier of the deceased man on their shoulders, and carry it to the place of burial. There is not one of them who does not know perfectly the *Our Father*, the *Hail Mary*, and the Creed, as well as some other Christian forms of prayer, and who cannot repeat them at any moment without mistake. They all know how to serve mass reverently, and all hear it every day. They meet at school early in the morning, and after midday, after hearing the explanation of the Christian doctrine which Perez repeats every day, they go to school again, when Oliveira teaches them. After they have heard and repeated their lessons, and gone through the rest of their school work, they kneel down, and in a loud voice recite, all together, their holy prayers. When I see all this my mind is filled with incomparable consolation. Pray God, I beseech you, to preserve the good that has already been gained, to promote what has been begun, to crown with increase these first fruits, to the praise and glory of His holy Name, and to the more perfect service of His own divine Majesty.

Alfonso is going to the Moluccas, where he alone will have

to do what the two whom I have been speaking of, Perez and Oliveira, do here. It is with difficulty that I can move him hence, because, as I trust you will understand well enough from what I have just said, his work here was very necessary. But as that which is most urgent has to be attended to first of all, you must now assist this station of Malacca as soon as possible by sending it the aid which it so eagerly craves. So send to this place without delay a priest of ours, who is well versed in settling cases of conscience, that he may relieve Francesco Perez, who is oppressed by such a number of different kinds of work, of at least some part of the burthen of hearing confessions every day. There is no other Portuguese settlement in India that can easily compete with Malacca in its need of good confessors. There is here an incredible confluence from all parts, on occasion of the various traffic, of a multitude of Europeans and Indians alike. All the former and a great number of the latter profess the Christian religion, and on account of the frailty of our human nature they have great need of the remedy of sacramental penance, and, if they do not find priests to administer it to them at the convenient moment, they live in very great and most urgent danger of losing the eternal salvation of their souls. So if within the year 1549 any priests of our Society arrive from Portugal, it will be easy for you to send to this place some one of own your community (whose place the newly arrived fathers may supply) by the ship which sails from Goa to Malacca in the month of April in next year, 1550. I say the month of April, for though I know there is another ship which usually sails thither from Goa in the month of September, I am still unwilling that the supply of a priest, which is so much needed for the city, should be put off to the later time of passage.

See, moreover, whether you have in the community any one of our brethren who, though he be a layman, has still so much education as to be able to teach boys to read and write. I should very much desire that such a person should be assigned as companion to the priest whom I have already appointed to come out here, that he may to some extent supply the place of Rocco Oliveira, who must of necessity go to Goa next year, to receive there the priesthood, and when he has been ordained, to return as soon as possible to Malacca. So, now that I am about to set sail for Japan I leave this order, that in the year 1550 Rocco Oliveira is to be sent to Goa by the ship which regularly sails for that port in the month of November, together with our novice Joam Bravo, whom I desire to study grammar there. It is therefore my decided will, and so I command you, Father Paul of Camerino and Antonio Gomez, in virtue of holy obedience, to send to Malacca in the month of April next year, or if some unforeseen cause which cannot in any way be evaded should prevent this, then as soon as you possibly can, the two whom I have spoken of, a priest able to hear confessions, and another of the Society fit to direct the school.

I am writing to Father Niccolo to be Superior of and to watch over ours who are at Meliapor, and also those who are living on the Comorin Coast and at Coulan. In the same way I am ordering the missioners of Comorin to obey Father Niccolo, and to have recourse to him about their own affairs, as often as either for themselves they need assistance, or for the Christians of whom they have charge they require favour and patronage, writing to him at Coulan or at Cochin, for on account of business he is always passing to and fro from one of these places to the other. I have also given order to Father Niccolo, to ask from Goa for whatever he may be informed that the people at Comorin have need of. And I desire you, Father Antonio Gomez, to carry out at once whatever he requests, and I charge and enjoin you as earnestly as is possible to let yourself omit in that regard nothing which belongs to the very height of diligence and the most devoted charity. Father Niccolo is to be subject to Father Paul, as when I quitted India I remember to have left him orders to be. The pupils of the College of Goa, whether Portuguese or natives, are to be governed as Father Antonio Gomez wills. Antonio Gomez himself, as I have already ordered, must be subject to Father Paul of Camerino, who is also to be Superior of those who are stationed at Bazain and at Ormuz, so far as I have given orders and explained distinctly to them. And I command both of you to take great pains that everything in India goes on in this order and discipline, and also to inform me of all that passes. Farewell.

Your most affectionate brother in Christ,

Malacca, June 22, 1549. FRANCIS.

The mention of Niccolo Lancilotti, who was stationed at Coulan, and who is in this letter appointed local Superior of the missioners on the Comorin Coast and at Meliapor, is so far surprising, as it seems to supersede the former appointment of Father Antonio Criminale in the latter capacity, at least as regards the labourers near Cape Comorin. Lancilotti has already been mentioned in the letters more than once as an invalid, whose health was gradually recovering itself under the comparatively salubrious air of Coulan, where he was posted. He felt his own want of strength keenly, if we may judge from a letter which he wrote to Ignatius Loyola,[8] in which he speaks of himself as an unfruitful tree, only encumbering the ground, while his brethren, strong and vigorous men, were doing so much on every side of him for the service of God. This inactivity and unfruitfulness, however, were by no means barren in results. He was usually the only priest at Coulan, and so had alone to bear the burthen of preaching to the Portuguese, instructing the heathen and intending converts, and keeping up the faith of those already converted. He had soon the care of the seminary projected, as we have seen, by Francis Xavier,[9] and which was founded and maintained at the King's expence, in accordance with the suggestion of the Saint. In the care of the boys, for whose benefit the seminary was instituted, he showed great devotion and singular prudence: his pupils turned out more like religious novices than secular youths. He was also noted for remarkable gifts in the way of direction and government, was much valued by the fathers in India on that account, and highly trusted by St. Ignatius. It would seem that Francis Xavier had already discovered these rare qualities in the invalid missioner

[8] Quoted by Bartoli, *Asia*, l. vii. p. 728.

[9] See the Letter to Simon Rodriguez, *ante*, p. 91.

at Coulan. It is remarkable also that Antonio Criminale was already dead when Francis wrote the letter which we have last inserted. It seems hardly possible that he could have known this, though there might perhaps have been time for this news to reach him before he left Malacca; but it appears incredible that Francis, whose own perpetual prayer it seems to have been that he might have the grace to suffer martyrdom for the cause of Jesus Christ, should not have made any mention of the glorious death of his religious brother, if the tidings had reached him at this time.

Criminale had, in fact, laid down his life like a good shepherd for his flock. The little island or peninsula of Remanancor, lying close to the land at the northeastern extremity of the Fishery Coast, seems to have been famous for a pagan shrine, served by Brahmins, and resorted to by pilgrims from all parts of southern and central India. Near this spot was a Portuguese fort, at a place called Beadala, already mentioned in one of the letters of Francis Xavier.[10] The Commandant of this had dug a trench across the narrow tongue of land which connected the pagoda with the coast, apparently by way of bravado and insult to the natives. The challenge was taken up, however, much to the cost of the Portuguese themselves, by the old enemies of everything Christian along the coast, the uncontrollable Badages. An army of six thousand men marched upon the fort, or rather on a much easier prey, the Christian population in the neighbourhood. The Portuguese garrison, numbering only forty men, embarked and made off, notwithstanding the earnest entreaties of Antonio Criminale, who happened to be on the spot, and who urged them to endeavour to come to some arrangement with the enemy. Several Portuguese were wounded in their flight, and five died. The alarm and misery of the unfortunate Christians thus abandoned to their fate can easily be imagined. The Father, urged to seek his own safety with the Portuguese, refused, and remained to share the fate of such of his poor flock as could not escape by sea. The accounts of his martyrdom are remarkable. As the Badages

[10] Letter xxxi. vol. i. p. 225.

approached, he threw himself on his knees, his arms extended in the form of a cross, and his eyes raised to heaven. First one party and then another passed him, and struck by some sudden respect, left him unhurt; but before he could make his way to the church, he was wounded, stripped, and left lying with a lance through his body. He detached the lance, and went on slowly crawling to the church, when another party of the Badages fell on him and dispatched him. He was only in his thirtieth year, and was the first of a long series of members of the Society who obtained the crown of martyrdom in the Indies.

We have still three more letters remaining to us, written by Francis Xavier during this short period of expectation at Malacca; and if those which have already been inserted tell us so much of his zeal for souls, his simplicity of intention, his intrepidity in the face of danger, and his tender care for his religious brethren, the three which follow next in order reflect other features of his character, without some consideration of which our estimate of him would be incomplete. The first letter, which is addressed to the same fathers at Goa as the last, shows his inexhaustible charity under a new and pleasant form. It is written with that peculiar liveliness of which we have seen instances in his letters to Le Jay and Laynez from Lisbon[11]—instances which make us regret that we have fewer letters of this kind, addressed familiarly to friends without any fear of their being shown to others. We can almost picture to ourselves the rough, honest, truthful cavalier to whom Francis suggests, not only that it is time for him to settle down after so many adventurous wanderings, but also that he should marry a certain virtuous and worthy young lady, an orphan at Goa, whom her future husband had never seen. We can imagine the commendations which Francis would bestow upon her in order to win his friend to promise on the spot to marry her. Then there is a different and scarcely less picturesque sketch presented to us—the good dame besieging the doors and parlours of the College of Santa Fè with daily attentions, sending in clothes or food as she guesses that the fathers or brothers may be in need, always ready to take

[11] Letter ix. vol. i. p. 95.

in a poor girl rescued from evil ways, to help a family in sudden distress, to nurse the sick, or to assist in the instruction of a convert. Such she used to be: but now misfortune has fallen upon her. She is a widow, and her only child, a fine marriageable girl, good, simple, modest, and attractive withal, is an orphan, with but slender dowry, except that her father held an office under the crown—for which he probably had to pay—and in the patent which conferred it a clause has been inserted, by virtue of which she may take it with her as a marriage portion to any one who may win her for his wife. There is a little difficulty in the way of the arrangement contemplated by Francis, as the office in question is rather beneath the dignity of his friend, whom he proposes as husband to the orphan girl, and he accordingly furnishes Antonio and Paul with excellent reasons, by means of which the Governor, Don Garcia da Sà, or—as Francis had already predicted his speedy death—his successor, may be persuaded to let the office be sold, and the money thus raised applied to swell the scanty portion of the intended bride.

(LXXVI.) *To Father Paul of Camerino and Father Antonio Gomez.*

May the grace and love of our Lord Jesus Christ be always with us to help and favour us! Amen.

Since I wrote to you at such great length, something has happened which has made me think it well to say a few words to you once more. You must understand that I have fallen in here with an old friend of mine. I have very few so dear to me. His name is Cristoval Carvalho. He is unmarried, singularly virtuous, rich, of good family, altogether highly accomplished, and of good parts. In the desire which I profess of helping on every one to salvation, I began to urge on my friend, for the sake of the affection between us, and to implore him for the love of God, to make up his mind to give up the rattling, desultory, wandering sort of life which he has been leading, so full of danger to his property and even to his life, and, what is of much more importance, exposing him to the greatest peril of losing his eternal salvation. How long was he to go on passing from place to place, a stranger everywhere, never more than a chance guest wherever he happens to be? would he never have a home of his own to be quiet in? would he never find an unoccupied moment to recollect his thoughts and put his conscience in order? and so on. Well, on all this he showed himself by no means inclined to despise my benevolent exhortations. Indeed, he confessed that he was beginning to feel somewhat bored by his perpetual wanderings. He had been afloat long enough, and was now looking with a yearning heart for the port and fixed anchorage of a settled life. In fact, he was minded to plant his home somewhere or other; to collect under a rooftree of his own the ample means which he had gained by traffic of so many kinds, in which he had been prosperous enough, and there apply his wealth, which he had no occasion to go on increasing, in whatever way might be required by calls of charity and religion, and of gratitude to God Who had given it to him, as well as by the repose which was suitable to his years, which have now got on to the point at which decline begins, and by the care of his bodily health.

While we were talking of all this, there came most happily into my mind the remembrance of that good lady, whose maternal love for our Society, evidenced as it is by diligent and daily services, has made us dub her with the title of our 'Mother.' So I proposed to Carvalho to marry the daughter of this good dame. I spoke, as I could with all truth, of the good disposition, the virtue, the high character of the girl. My man was by no means deaf to what I said; indeed, he was much moved by the very sincere praises which I gave to that good maiden and her qualities. In short, he promised that he would marry her. Now, I have no doubt at all, that he will be as good as his word; he has always been a man of such truthfulness, and besides, the unfailing and staunch friendship which he has always kept up with me is another security. Especially too, as he quite sees that the step will be a very excellent, useful, and honourable one for himself—one that will enable him to lead a peaceful, happy, and tranquil life. So I have not hesitated to communicate the whole matter to our Mother, in a letter which I have written to her, as if it was quite sure to come off, if she consents to it; and I cannot doubt that she will do so, and think it a great happiness to gain so splendid an alliance with such a man as Cristoval, good as well as rich.

The affair is, as you see, in good train; but nevertheless there are many obstacles that intervene to prevent the execution of such plans, and in this case I see clearly that the affair will not be easily managed, unless you take it up and urge it with all your might. So I pray and entreat you both to remember the great devotion to us which that good Mother of ours has shown; her acts of daily liberality to us; her immense charity and goodwill; and then to consider that God now offers you a very precious occasion of repaying all her benefits to us by a return and recompense prompted by our gratitude to her, which is indeed only one favour against many, but which still will be so important in itself as to weigh in the scale as if it were a whole host of acts of kindness. So pray exert yourself to the utmost, both working yourselves, and also asking and using the credit and efforts of the first Treasurer,[12] to the same end, in order that that afflicted family may not lose the benefit of this most happy opportunity. Do, I pray you, all that you can, that, now that Divine Providence, in its care for the lonely state of that most honourable widow, and for the bereaved condition of her orphaned daughter, as good and innocent a girl as any in the world, offers this means of relief to each, they may each have the full benefit of it.

I don't think you will have much trouble in bringing Cristoval Carvalho to the necessary point. I know well his constancy and faithfulness, and I can't fear for a moment that he will recall his word, or refuse to accomplish what he has promised me. As for the Treasurer, in order to get him to do what he can, it will be enough to allege, as you may with perfect truth, that the matter is one which he may most properly use his au-

[12] Probably Francis' friend Cosmo Añez.

thority to bring about, for it belongs, above all things else, to the praise and service of our Lord God. And in the next place it is one in which he ought to feel the highest concern, because upon it depends the good estate and the safety, the whole interests of the peace and hopes, of a family which has been left under his charge, of a lady of the highest character, who is his own relative, and of a young maiden who is really one in a thousand in point of worth, who looks to him as her guardian for help and patronage. I am in high hopes that when you say this to that good and prudent man, the Treasurer, God will, in His goodness, aid you, so that you may easily persuade him to what we desire.

And now you know very well that our Mother has in her possession a royal rescript, duly signed and sealed, granting her power to transfer the office under the crown which her husband, Diego Froez (to whose soul may God give glory !), held while he was alive, with all its emoluments, to any one to whom she may choose to give her daughter in marriage, and thus, in fact, to make the post a part of her dowry. This being so, it will be necessary to get the Governor to allow the office to be assigned to some one else, who will pay a sum of money for it, which may be applied to the completion of the girl's dowry. The reason why this is necessary, is that Cristoval Carvalho is too high in rank and too rich not to think it beneath him to have anything to do with that employment, especially as, as I have said, he is tired of troubles and of business, and what he so looks for in his married life is ease and repose from his past labours. I feared from the first that this might be the difficulty in the matter—that perhaps people would be found at Goa to contend that such a rescript should be observed to the letter, exactly as it stands in the text, that thus what his Highness had written should be stuck to against his own intention, and against the manifest equity of the case, and to strive, by this false allegation, to prevent the King's benevolence from taking effect, and to shut this orphan maiden and her widowed mother out of their fortune. If anything of this kind should oppose itself, I beg of you to act on the other side, exert yourselves to the utmost, and use all the energy in your power, by yourselves, by means of the Treasurer, and by means of any one else whose credit and intercession may seem likely to be of any avail, in order to bring the Governor and the King's officials, in whose power the matter lies, to put this benignant interpretation on the will of his Highness in granting this privilege. Every one can surely see that the King simply intended that the daughter of Diego Froez should have the advantage of the reward owing to her father. He could not have intended that, if it should chance that she should come to be married to a man who was not fit to administer her father's office, this poor young lady should be mulcted of a large part of what her father has left behind him. I do hope confidently that God, Who is the Defender of the widow and the Father of the fatherless, will help you to win this most equitable suit. And I am so earnest in desiring you to take it up and urge it so strongly, that I really think that you cannot, without incurring the guilt and shameful stain of ingratitude, which would fall in disgrace upon the whole of the Society, omit any possible industry or diligence in this matter of so much importance to our good mother, until you succeed in getting rid of all obstacles and bringing to a happy conclusion this marriage, which I am sure God approves; that so provision may be made for the good condition, comfort, and dignity of a lady who has conferred such singular obligations upon us, and of that virtuous modest maiden, her daughter.

You will find Carvalho himself very easy to manage, and docile in all that may be required of him. As I said, he has promised me, and he is a man of stainless faith, but more than this, he has let me see well that he thinks very highly of such a connection as that I am speaking of, and he has the greatest hopes of finding that this marriage will give him the rest he wants, the tranquil happiness for what remains of this life, which he so much longs for. And now I think I have said enough to explain this desire of mine, and unless I am mistaken, to make you approve it. I shall consider it a most joyful piece of news and a great favour to myself, if I hear from you that I have gained my point. May God unite us in His glory! for whether we shall ever see one another again in this life is at present very uncertain. Farewell.

Your brother in Christ,

Malacca, Eve of St. John Baptist, 1549. FRANCIS.

The next letter, written at the same time, is on quite a different subject—the excellent qualities of one of the King's officials at Malacca. He seems to have been auditor of the revenue, and as such to have had need of great integrity and uprightness in deciding questions which came before him. Francis pleads earnestly with the King for some greater reward than his friend has as yet reaped in the salary or perquisites of his office.

(LXXVII.) *To John III. King of Portugal.*

Since your Highness, in your royal letters from Portugal, has commanded me to give you a written report of those who in these regions of India faithfully and diligently discharge the duty committed to them, I would have your Highness know that Duarte Barreto, who has lately been managing the affairs of your realm at Malacca, has in the discharge of his office left nothing undone which could have been looked for from a man of skill, industry and faithfulness. He has taken care of the interests of the revenue, he has done good service to the merchants, by deciding the cases before him justly without respect to persons, and he has moreover conducted himself in all respects in such a manner, that his administration as magistrate has done honour to your Highness among the natives in this part of the world, for men have taken him as a specimen, and have commonly thought that you are in the habit of sending to them as officials of your kingdom men whom you know to be very well furnished with those virtues which you most highly approve, and which you yourself possess in abundance.

For my part, I consider that the glory of kings and princes who have widely extended dominions is concerned in this, that they commit those parts of their dominions, which they cannot administer themselves, to men to whom it may be honourable for themselves to be thought like, men of whom the people may think, when they have seen them and had experience of their honesty, gravity and justice, and learnt to honour and value those virtues in them, that they behold and have before them, in the deputies sent to live among them by their sovereign, an express portrait of the noble and honourable qualities of their absent sovereign himself. Duarte Barreto belongs beyond all others to that most excellent number and kind of ministers, who make their supreme happiness consist in rendering perfect service to their King. On this account he is a man who deserves that your Highness should deign to advance him in substance and in dignity, and whose very distinguished services you should think it well to seek occasion to remunerate. In order to act as he has done, he has had to undergo a great deal of labour, and, as there are abundance of bad characters out here, to take up a good many quarrels and fight many battles.

The appointment at Malacca, of which I spoke, cannot well be considered as an adequate reward for his sedulous diligence during so many years. In the first place, it has happened by some chance that it brought him in very little; and in the second place, he was not able to hold it for the full term; and so he has left this place a poor man. Be good enough, therefore, Sire, to make some provision for him, as a man who in truth has well earned any favour, however great, from your Highness. I pray that God may add many years to the prosperous and happy life of your Highness, and that He may grant you in His clemency to know in this life His most holy will, and mercifully supply you with abundant strength of soul to think and act and feel as you would rejoice to have done in your last moment.

Your Highness's useless servant,

Malacca, June 23, 1549. FRANCIS.

One letter more remains to us, which from the particular manner in which it is dated seems to have been the very last work of Francis Xavier before embarking for Japan. The little church of Our Lady of the Mount, near Malacca, was near the favourite abode of Francis when at that place, mentioned in the preceding volume.[13] It was there that he was saying mass at the time when the insolent challenge of the Acheenese Commander to Don Simon de Melo arrived, which led to the organization of the Christian armament, whose signal victory over the barbarians was announced by Francis in the pulpit at the moment at which it took place.[14] There then, the night before he sailed, with his mind full of Japan and of the dangers of the voyage he was so soon to have, Francis must have stolen away from the countless friends who would be anxious to see him and force on him their offerings or good wishes at so critical a moment, and spent a part of his few remaining hours in quietly drawing up a rule of life for Joam Bravo, the newly admitted brother of whom mention has already been made. The next evening, 'about sunset,' says Mendez Pinto, who was at Malacca at the time, 'he embarked in a small junk belonging to a Chinese corsair called Necoda, and then the next morning set sail and departed.' He was soon to be alone with his few companions amid the strange crew of superstitious idolaters in whose company he was to suffer so much, as we shall see when we come to speak of his voyage. The admiring crowds, the friendly generous merchants, Don Pedro de Silva, the son of the great Vasco de Gama, who had shown him so much kindness, Perez and Oliveira with their troops of penitents and happy Christian children streaming along the streets in procession, all were soon to be as far from him as if he had left them behind in another world. And in the far distance beyond Malacca, there were others, still dearer and subjects of greater anxiety or affection from whom he was separating himself, with great likelihood of never meeting them again—his beloved children on the Comorin Coast, the missioners to whom he had entrusted them, Niccolo at Coulan, Cipriani at Meliapor, Antonio Criminale, as he may have thought, among the pearl fishers, and then his old companion Paul at Goa, Antonio Gomez, the subject of many an earnest prayer, and his chosen

[13] Vol. i. p. 348. [14] Vol. i. p. 412.

disciple Gaspar Baertz at Ormuz, for whose benefit he had poured out so much of his own carefully stored experience of men, and of the means of leading them out of the mazes of sin and reconciling them to God. And far beyond these again there lay Italy and Rome, and Lisbon and Coimbra, each with their little knot of friends for whom his heart yearned, as it seems, all the more intensely as the time since they had parted grew longer and longer, without making their associations and memories less fresh within him. There was Simon his peculiar friend and brother, there also that father of his soul, whose name seems to force itself upon his pen even in this last paper which he drew up, which describes so simply and plainly that daily rule of life which, in principle, was the great security for the unity of spirit between the widely scattered members of the Society, and those maxims of selfknowledge and selfconquest which he himself had learned so many years ago when he first became the disciple and child of Ignatius.

(LXXVIII.) *To Joam Bravo.*

My dearest brother,—I should wish you to follow with the greatest constancy every day the following order for your religious life. In the morning, as soon as you are awake, meditate on a mystery of the life of Christ, beginning from His holy Nativity and going on in continuous order to His triumphal Ascension into heaven. You have the matter for these meditations arranged in order in the book of the Spiritual Exercises. You must spend at least half an hour in this holy meditation, with the same attention and devotion of mind, and all the observances and rules which you remember that you used when you went through the exercises of your month's retreat. You must go on every day to a new meditation, so that when, for instance, on Monday you have contemplated the Nativity of Christ, on Tuesday you must consider His Circumcision, and so on in order, until by the end of the month you have gone through all the actions of the Lord Jesus and come to the end of all, that is, the glorious Ascension. After this you should begin again, and go through the same round from the first, proceeding from one mystery to another that comes next to it, and so spend another month in going over the same steps as before. At the end of each of these exercises you must renew the vows which you have once made, especially those chief vows of poverty, chastity, and obedience, making them, I say, over again, and offering them to God, reviving and rekindling the same deep fervour with which you made them the first time. Besides other fruits that you will gain, you will by this repetition of your vows blunt the assaults of concupiscence and of our infernal enemy, both of which will be always inciting you to evil things, and for this reason I think you should never omit this renewal.

After you have dined and rested a little afterwards, you must repeat your morning's meditation, and spend half an hour upon it, considering again the same mystery, and you must add again at the end the renewal of your vows. This must be a fixed and immutable rule for you, always kept up amid all the variety of your actions during the day, and no avocation or occupation must be so important to you as to prevent you from giving a full hour every day to this pious meditation of the most holy life of Christ our Lord. And in this matter the division which I have arranged for you will be convenient, so that you may put aside half an hour out of the morning, and half an hour out of the afternoon for this purpose. It seems to me that the most free space for the last will be the time towards evening when Father Francesco Perez, with whom you live, holds his catechetical school : that will be a time when you will be at lesiure to attend to your afternoon prayer.

At night, before you go to sleep, you must examine your conscience, enquiring into the thoughts, words, and deeds of the whole day, and also whether you have left out anything of what you ought to have done. Examine all these things as if you were presently going to cleanse your soul in sacramental confession to a priest, and then conceive deep contrition for what you have done amiss, or for what you have omitted, out of regard to God, Whom you have offended thereby, and Whom you love above all things, and then pray Jesus Christ earnestly to prosper you, and promise amendment. After all this, recite the *Pater* and *Ave*, and compose yourself to rest in such a way that sleep may steal upon you with your thoughts fixed on divine things, and your mind preparing itself to spend the next day in greater holiness.

When you wake the next morning, raise your thoughts at once to heaven, and while you are putting on your clothes and washing your hands and face, call to mind the faults into which you fell the day before, and ask of our Lord grace to avoid them that day. Then make your morning meditation, as you have done the day before, and in the same way go through your other duties in order. Be so constant in this method of life, as never to think it lawful for you to give up the least part of it, except when hindered by illness, and whenever as long as you are well and strong, you shall, under pretext of any intervening cause whatever, either have put off or not fully performed any of these things presented to you, make it a matter of conscience and confess your fault before the Fathers, asking of your own accord to have punishment given you for your negligence in either omitting, or doing in a perfunctory way, a thing which has been so urgently enjoined upon you by your Superior.

For the rest, whatever you may have to do, wherever you may go, in whatever you may be engaged, whether occupation or relaxation, always be on the alert and endeavour strenuously to exert all your strength in striving to conquer yourself in everything, break your desires, embrace what your feelings shrink from, and especially to beat down your innate appetite for praise and superior excellence, and spare no pains at all until pride be torn out by the roots, and you are able to bear willingly to be put down below everything and even to rejoice to be despised. Be sure of this, that without this submissiveness, without this command over the evil movements of the soul, you will do no good either to yourself or to others, nor will you be able to please God or to persevere in the Society of Jesus.

Obey the Father with whom you live in all things, and execute with the greatest alacrity whatever he may order you, however disagreeable it may be; never resist him, never make for any cause whatever any exception to what he orders, and listen to what he says and bend yourself entirely to his word as your director in all things, exactly as if our Father Ignatius were present and were to command the same things. Whatever temptations, of whatever sort or manner, you find yourself assailed by, tell them at once with the greatest candour to your Superior, and persuade yourself, as of a matter of the greatest certainty, that there is no other way to avoid yielding to them; and besides this advantage, there is another great gain for the soul attached to this openness in confessing the secret movements of the heart. For by that means we gain great favour with God, a sort of favour which brings with it a pledge of great reward hereafter, on account of the generally troublesome victory which we win over our natural feeling of shame. Yes, and a great blow is inflicted thereby on the hopes and insiduous machinations of our hellish foe, whose principal power to hurt us lies in his remaining concealed, and who is disarmed if he be dragged into light, and then it turns out that all his perverse expectations are dashed to the ground, and he is made a laughingstock of those whom he was plotting against, and who are safe and secure against him. Farewell.

Most cordially and affectionately yours,

FRANCIS.

In the Chapel of our Blessed Lady of the Mount, near Malacca, the night before the Feast of the Nativity of St. John the Baptist, 1549; just about to set sail for Japan.

NOTES TO BOOK IV.

(1.) *Account of Japan sent to Father Ignatius Loyola at Rome, drawn from the statements of Anger (Han-Siro), the Japanese Convert.*

In his letter to Ignatius Loyola, St. Francis mentions the account of Japan given by his convert Paul of the holy Faith. We find this document, with another similar account, written by Jorge Alvarez (a Portuguese merchant), in the volume of letters preserved in the College of Coimbra. The first we give in a close translation:

Information respecting the island of Japan, given by Paul, formerly called Han-Siro, recently converted to our holy Faith, a native of the said island.

Northwards from China, and further east, the Portuguese merchants discovered an island called Japan, in the same latitude as Italy: it measures (according to the account given me) 600 leagues from east to west, and 300 in width. From that island came, in the month of April last, a man of great intelligence and sagacity named Angero, bringing with him two servants. Among other things, he asked information concerning our holy Faith, and having been instructed therein, after a short space of time he became a Christian, taking the name of Paul. He remained with us in this our College of St. Paul of the holy Faith, in Goa, where he learned to read and write Portuguese, and translated into his own language a short summary of the doctrines and practices essential to our holy religion. This man gave himself to prayer and contemplation, calling on and sighing for our Lord Jesus Christ; his goodness is so great that it cannot be easily told. Whilst a catechumen he gave, at our request, an account of the customs and laws of his country; but since he was not initiated in the sects as some of his countrymen who are held to be learned, and he only knew the common language, on this account he related things only according to the current popular opinion. This information I transmit to you as he told it to us, intending to write all more certainly by and by, and how our Father Master Francis has by that time been there, and has himself made personal acquaintance with the inhabitants and the writings of that country.

In the first place, he informed us that the whole island of Japan is subject to one king; under him there are great lords, like our dukes and counts; their number amounts altogether to about fourteen in all Japan; and when one of them dies, his eldest son inherits the entire estate, the younger sons having some castle allotted them for their maintenance, on condition that they maintain obedience to the head of the family, so as not to divide the estate. The least of these nobles, he says, can send into the field 10,000 men, others 15,000, others 20,000 or 30,000. The chief ruler or king is called Voo; he is of a more noble race than the rest, and can only marry in his own family. He has jurisdiction in things spiritual as well as temporal, and over both seculars and religious, these last being very numerous in this country; indeed, his authority seems like that of the Pope amongst us. Though he has authority over all, he never makes war or puts any to death; all such things he leaves to another among them, who is like the Emperor, and is called Goxo, and with whom rests all the government, and who rules the island. He is under the obedience of the aforenamed Voo, and when he visits him, he kneels and bends his head on his thigh; and, though he has a great court of lords, captains, and soldiers, who superintend matters connected with carrying on war and justice, if the Goxo should do any evil, the Voo can cause him to be deprived of his kingdom and beheaded. The less obey the greater very much, on account of the stern justice they use. All crimes are by them punished with the same severity. The Voo lives as follows: he takes a wife of his own family, and when the moon begins to wane he begins to fast and to separate from his wife, and give himself to meditation and prayer for fifteen days, eating very little, and being dressed in white the whole time, and wearing a large crown upon his head, until the moon changes: but when she begins to increase, he at once begins to lead a life of pleasure with his wife, goes to hunt, and enjoys many other amusements. If his wife dies before he is thirty he may marry again, but not after that age; and the rest of his life he must keep perpetual chastity, and live like a religious, and at no time may he have intercourse with any woman but his wife.

Besides the great lords, the nation has other gentlemen, merchants and officials of every grade, as amongst ourselves. Generally no one has more than one wife. If she prove unfaithful, and the husband can surprise her with her paramour, he is authorised to kill them both; if he kill only one, public justice proceeds against the other, and puts him to death; but if he kill neither, it is considered a disgrace to him. When a wife is believed guilty of adultery, yet cannot be taken in the act, she is sent home to her father's house, and then the husband does not lose his honour, but may marry again, she herself being for ever dishonoured and not allowed to remarry. It is thought infamous for one who lives with his wife to have intercourse with another woman. The nobles send their sons to the monasteries to be educated as soon as they are eight years old, and they remain there until they are nineteen or twenty, learning reading, writing, and religion; as soon as they come out they marry, and apply themselves to politics.

There are in these islands three sorts of religious, who have monasteries like our friars, some within the cities, and some without: those in the cities do not marry, live on alms, and shave their heads and beards. They wear long habits with wide sleeves, almost like our friars; in winter they cover their heads, but the rest of the year they are always uncovered; they eat together like friars, and fast many times in the year. These religious eat no animal food, in order to afflict their bodies and extirpate all sinful desires, and this abstinence is common to all the religious. They rise in the middle of the night to say prayers, which they chant for about half an hour, and then sleep till dawn, when they again arise, and say other prayers; they also recite prayers at sunrise, at midday, and in the evening; at this last time they sound a bell, and all the people fall on their knees to pray, as we do at home. These religious pray in a language not understood by the common people, just as our priests do in Latin.

These religious preach frequently to the people; their sermons are well attended, and they move both themselves and their hearers to tears. They preach that there is one Supreme God, Creator of all things; and that there is a Purgatory, Paradise, and Hell, and that all souls, alike good and bad, go to Purgatory, and then separate, the good for the place where God is, the bad for the abode of the devil, who, they say, is sent by God into the world in order to chastise evildoers. These religious lead a very virtuous life, except that they are stained by an abominable sin connected with the boys they have to teach in their monasteries, although they teach the people that this is a great sin, and praise chastity. They wear long black robes from head to foot, and are very learned. Each house has a Superior, whom all obey, and they receive only virtuous persons to become priests. There is another sort of priests, whose members dress in gray; these likewise do not marry. They have religious houses for women, like nuns. It is said that they have intercourse together, but that the birth of children is prevented by certain drugs. All the houses of these religious men have nuns' houses by their side. They are persons of little learning; they pray in the same manner with those before mentioned, and sometimes they fast. There is also another sort of religious, who go clothed in black robes and do much penance. They go to prayer three times a day, at morning, at evening, and at midnight. All the houses of prayer of these religious are alike, and contain images made of wood and gilt. There are also pictures painted on the walls. All adore one God, whom they call Dinicho in their language, or sometimes Cogi. The second order of gray religious mentioned above, when they make prayer in their choir, make it together with the nuns, the friars on one side, the nuns on the other, chanting alternately, at midnight as at other times.

This excellent man also narrated to us the history of a man who is esteemed a saint among them, as we say. He said that there lived once in a land beyond China, called Chenguinquo, a king named Sanbon, whose wife was called Illagabuni. One night this king dreamt that a son was to be born to him, who should be a very great man and regarded as a god in all those lands. This dream he told to his wife, who nine months later had a son, whom they called Xaqua, at whose birth two huge winged serpents were seen to float over the palace, descend to where the child was without doing him any harm, and presently disappear. When Xaqua was nineteen years old, his father wished him to marry; but he, impressed with the miseries of this life, fled by night to the mountains, where for the space of six years he lived a life of solitary penance. At the end of this time he reappeared amongst his countrymen, and began to preach with great fervour and eloquence to all those people. His reputation for sanctity soon spread, and he acquired unbounded influence, so that he remodelled the laws of the country, and taught the people how to adore God. It is said that Xaqua made 8000 converts, some of whom carried his doctrines into China, preaching his laws and religion; that they converted China and the kingdom of Chenguinquo, making the people destroy the idols and pagodas; and that they were established in China and Chenguinquo, and thence came to Japan, making the people do the same; and even now fragments ofancient statues are found there, as they are found at Rome.

This Xaqua taught that there is one God, Creator of all things; and exhorted his followers to accept five precepts: 1. not to kill; 2. not to steal; 3. not to commit fornication; 4. not to be passionate for things that cannot be remedied; 5. to forgive injuries. He also wrote many books full of much virtue and very useful, wherein he taught the manners which men ought to observe, each according to his state.

He prescribed frequent fasts, and taught that penance is highly pleasing to God, and of great necessity for the salvation of sinners: he urged religious to be diligent in visiting the sick and exhorting them to make their wills; and when they see the sick person to be in danger of death, they are to preach to him of the goods of the other life, and tell him not to be pained about present things, since all is vanity. And when the sick man dies, the said religious are to come in procession, chanting, and take the body to the cloister of their monastery, always asking God to pardon his sins; and they are to bury all poor and rich without any difference, nor receive anything for this as a reward, he being held a bad man who would receive it, though it is true that he exhorted them, if the family of the dead offered some alms, to take them.

This good man also affirmed that in Japan they do penance in this way, fasting and observing chastity a hundred days continuously, and then retiring into a wood situated on the side of a mountain, in which live some austere anchorites and in which many fearful sounds and horrible cries are heard, and strange fires seen. The penitents remained here seventy-five days, eating only as much rice as could be contained in the palms of the hands, and drinking water. At the end of the time they all united, and went to a desert beyond the forest, sometimes more than 1000 at once, and kneeling before a pagoda each one confessed aloud the sins of his whole life, all the others being silent and very attentive, and after this each one swore on the idol to keep the confessions of the others secret. All the time they never sleep nor undress, they wear a coarse rough dress, are tightly girt, have their heads uncovered, and never sit. Each day they walk five or six leagues in the neighbourhood of the forest, all together as in procession, and at certain fixed places they rest a long time and light a large fire and warm themselves. There is a master who guides all their prayers and penances, and if any one sleeps at this time of rest, the master beats him; and if any one falls ill and cannot go on, they leave him alone, and he dies abandoned, while the others continue their march. But if any one die before the others, they all help to bury him, and leave in writing on a post the name of the dead man and where he comes from. And these pilgrims carry a tablet on which is their name and that of their home.

Paul also says that these pilgrims often see many monstrous phantasms and diabolical illusions, the devils often presenting themselves amongst them, so that a hundred persons seemed two hundred, each person having as it were his own double by his side; and the master seeing that some had not the tablet with their name, would bid his penitents be quiet and pray earnestly to Dinicho their god to deliver them from such company; and on this prayer the devils would disappear, and leave the penitents to finish their exercises in peace, at the end of which they were found weak, worn, and disfigured by their friends who come to revest them in their ordinary apparel and conduct them home.

Paul told us also that there are in Japan many sorcerers and enchanters; however, they are little esteemed by wise and prudent men; there are also very great astrologers, who foretell events to come. The natives write chronicles of their history, much as we do ourselves, and they resemble us also in their manners and subtlety of invention. Indeed, the author of our present information gives tokens of a mental power which many of us might envy; nor is his cleverness of an unpractical kind, being shown in action as well as in speech. He appears much shocked at the vices which he cannot but perceive amongst Christians. He thinks that all the Japanese will become Christians, because it is written in their law and in their books that all laws are to be one, and they expect a more perfect law than their own, and he cannot imagine one more perfect than ours. He says he is very happy in having received so great a blessing from God, in that he has been taken as the instrument to introduce Christian people into Japan, who may preach this holy law; and although he is married, he offers himself to go to Japan and stay with the fathers who go there two years more, until some good beginning of a Christian community is made there, and until the fathers know the language.

He says that the climate is very healthy, and that hurricanes and earthquakes are of frequent occurrence. The fruits and metals are much the same as those of Europe; also the animals and birds, which are both very numerous; there are few poisonous serpents. No wine is made from grapes, but a fermented liquor is distilled from rice, as from barley in Flanders; there are wild vines in the woods which bear grapes. The people eat rice with meat and fish as in India. Wheat is plentiful; it is not made into bread, but used for pastry and the like, rice being used as a substitute for bread. The flesh of wild fowls is eaten, but not that of chickens; indeed no domestic animal is used as an article of food. He says that in this country there is a duke who has on his banner a sign like a cross, and none but his own family can bear it. The whole nation pray on beads as we do; those who can read use little books, and those who pray on beads say on each bead a prayer twice as long as the *Pater noster.* These strings of beads, or rosaries, have one hundred and eight beads. They say that their learned men teach that each man has one hundred and eight sorts of sin, and that he must say a prayer against each of these. This prayer is in a tongue not understood by the people, as Latin with us. When they get up in the morning, they say nine words, raising the fingers of the right hand, to defend themselves against the devil. The religious make profession and vows of chastity, poverty, and obedience, and practise this in humility before they are received into religion.

The climate of Japan resembles that of Italy, and the natives are much like the Italians in height. They are discreet, magnanimous, and lovers of virtue and letters, honouring learned men very much. Their customs of government in peace and war are like ours. Justice is very expeditious. A man is allowed to kill his own slave for an insult or injury. The supreme dignity of the Voo, who is like the Pope, descends to his eldest son or to his nearest relation by the father's side. So it is with the other princes. The Goxo intervenes if these quarrel among themselves; and if any one is contumacious or disobedient, he makes war on him and takes away his realm and cuts off his head; yet the dignity is not taken out of the family, but descends to his next heir. They use prayers, alms, pilgrimages, and fasts for the remission of sins of the living and the dead many times in the year, eating, when they fast, at the same hours that we do. In a mountain in the island there are 5000 religious, very rich, with many servants, well housed and clothed. They observe chastity so much that no woman is allowed to enter the monastery, nor anything female. Women after childbirth are fifteen days without any one touching them, and do not go to church for forty days. Poor women who have many children kill the youngest that they may not grow up to suffer poverty, and this is not punished.

He said also that 1600 years ago or more, the idols were destroyed in the kingdom of Jenico (Chenguinquo), by which you go to Japan, passing by China and Tartary, and also in this island, by means of the doctrine of Xaqua. When he preached about hell, he said that souls were tormented therein by the demons with divers torments, the damned being in perpetual flames, and other similar pains. He said there was a Purgatory, where the souls which have not done sufficient penance in this life for their sins are detained until they are purified, and that in Paradise are the angels, who are contemplating the majesty of God. They believe that the angels are defenders of men, and for this reason they carry with them images of the angels, who, they say, are spirits made of other substance and elements than ours. They use many prayers in praise of God, and practise contemplation, especially the religious. They assemble round the altar when they chant, and they ring bells to assemble the people for the sermons, and sacrifices, and other common prayers; and when any one dies they assemble to bury him or to burn him, with many lighted candles. All their laws and scriptures and prayers are in a language which is not the common tongue, as Latin with us. We asked this good man whether they practised sacrifices; and he said that some of the priests, especially the prelate, in certain vestments, come into the church, and in presence of the people they burn certain scents, like incense—aloe-wood sticks, and certain odoriferous leaves—upon a stone like an altar, chanting certain prayers. The churches of this people have the same privilege as ours, so that the officers of justice cannot seize or take any one from them, save only for theft. They have in their temples many images of saints (men and women) painted, of large size, with crowns and glory like ours; and they venerate the saints as we venerate ours; and although they adore one God, Creator of all things, yet they pray to the saints to intercede with God for them.

This nation eats all kinds of food, and does not practise circumcision; so that it would appear that the Gospel had been preached in the country, and that on account of sins the light of faith had been obscured, and that then some heretic like Mahomet had taken it away altogether. While I was writing this paper there came to me an Armenian Bishop, who has been more than forty years in these parts, who said that he had read that the Armenians had preached in China in the beginning of the primitive Church. Nevertheless, it would be very well that the light of the holy faith and of the doctrine of the Gospel should be once more made to shine upon these nations; and although from Rome to Japan there are 8000 leagues of journey, yet to those who love God and the salvation of souls all the toils and dangers of the world are pleasures. If God will, our Father Master Francis, together with Paul (the author of this information), and two men of Japan who are already Christians, and three others, fathers or brothers of our Society, will, if God so please, sail to Japan this next April, and in two years your Reverence will have information of the good which we may hope to do in that country by the grace of Jesus Christ our Lord, *Qui est benedictus in sæcula sæculorum.* Amen.

Cochin, beginning of January 1549. *Laus Deo.*

(2.) *Account of Japan by Jorge Alvarez.*

This notice is contemporaneous with the foregoing. We can only find room for an abridged account of it.

The writer, who appears to be the captain of a ship, begins by enumerating the principal ports of Japan, and goes on to give a brief account of the country. He describes it as beautiful and fertile, abounding in vegetable productions of every kind, these being for the most part the same as those indigenous to Portugal. The natives obtain three crops every year. They use horses for all agricultural purposes, as there are scarcely any oxen to be met with; and indeed very few domestic animals of any kind. Game is abundant, and eagerly sought after as an article of food. The common people ensnare their prey by means of nets; the upper classes employ falcons, the highest nobles being permitted to use eagles. Deer are always shot with arrows. Fish of every kind abound both in the sea and in the rivers.

There are hot springs in several places. One stream is remarkable for being intensly cold at its source, and becoming lower down just as hot; it makes its way through a bed of mud to the sea. In this mud the poorer inhabitants scoop hollows, which fill with tepid water; in these they bathe themselves at sunrise and sunset. The women have a custom of dipping their heads three times under the water, some of which they carry away with them in wooden vessels, sprinkling it with their fingers through the streets as they return home, and on the floors of their houses, reciting at the same time certain words, 'which,' says the writer, 'I could not understand, though I feel certain they were rather a devotional exercise than a mere ordinary custom, as not all the women practised this.'

Japan is frequently visited by earthquakes. It is surrounded by numerous volcanic islands of various dimensions, which smoke all the year round, and not unfrequently emit fire. Hurricanes are of common occurrence at the time of full moon; but in the month of September there always comes one hurricane more furious than the rest and of longer duration; while it prevails, ships are frequently carried a long distance inland. These tempests, however, give warning of their approach, being invariably preceded by a fine rain, so that the natives are enabled to adopt measures for insuring their personal safety. The houses are low and firmly built for the sake of security, with straw-thatched roofs fastened on by means of large stones. They are divided into rooms and anterooms: locks and bolts appear to be unknown. Each house is surrounded by an enclosure, which serves the purpose of a kitchen garden; and every abode is provided with a separate water supply; also with an oven, a loom, a wooden mill for grinding rice, and a stone mill for grinding corn. The stock of poultry belonging to each family is confined to a single cock and hen.

The natives are for the most part of middling height, hardy, well made and fair complexioned. The nobles wear their beards cut short, after the manner of the Moors, the lower orders wearing theirs long; all appear to shave their cheeks and the crown of the head, leaving the hair long behind. They keep their heads constantly uncovered, the old men alone wearing, in cold weather, a silken cap. The men wear an undergarment of flax, reaching to the knees, with sleeves as far as the elbows; the lower part of the arm being always bare. Over this shirt is worn a sort of jacket, made of unbleached flax and somewhat elaborately adorned with various devices, coloured in white, gray, black, and blue, so as to distinguish the wearers. The costume is completed by pantaloons of ample dimensions, open at the sides and fastened in at the waist by a leathern belt; and in muddy weather a sort of half boot is added to protect the foot.

The Japanese seem upon the whole to have made a pleasing impression upon our sea captain, to judge from the account he now proceeds to furnish us with, and which we will give in his own words. 'This people is very proud, and easily offended: all, old and young, use cutlasses and other arms, which they are allowed to wear from the age of eight years. They are almost all skilled in the use of arrows, and carry large bows, like the English. They protect their bodies by means of coats of mail and iron, close fitting, and painted. They are not a covetous race, but on the contrary liberal, and very hospitable to strangers, with whom they seem eager to make friends, and from whom they seek to gain information about other countries, although unable to do so to any great extent, owing to their ignorance of the proper questions to be asked. They are very particular about having their hospitality returned; those who came on board our ships were most anxious to gratify their curiosity in every respect. Theft they hold in peculiar abhorrence, even the least dishonesty being punished with death: whenever they hear of a thief being at large, the chiefs sally forth to hunt him down, and it is regarded as a great honour to be the first to discover and kill him.'

We have next a few details respecting the food of the inhabitants, and the manner in which it is partaken of. They eat three times a day, and always very sparingly, eating but very little meat, and never the flesh of any domestic animal. Their food appears to consist chiefly of various kinds of grain, as rice, millet, and the like; they seldom, if ever, make bread. Arrack, made from rice, is the universal beverage; but drunkenness is apparently unknown, for as soon as any one feels himself getting out of his own control, he ceases his potations, and betakes himself to sleep. The Japanese eat sitting crosslegged on the ground, like the Moors, and use sticks like the Chinese: they eat out of earthenware bowls, painted black outside and red within. Cold water is never drunk, either in summer or in winter. There are many inns in Japan, where travellers can obtain refreshments, and pass the night also, should they be so minded.

No one can have more than one wife; the women are married by their parents, and great is the vexation if any match is not approved of by those in authority. Should any wife prove idle or faithless, her husband may send her home, if she have not already borne him children; but after she has had children he may put her to death at once for either of these faults, without himself incurring any penalty. The result of such stringent regulations is that the women jealously guard the honour of their husbands, and are willing to live quietly and attend to their houses. There are no prisons, as every one is expected to execute justice in his own home. The rich men and nobles are allowed to possess slaves; but these latter have so much liberty that if they do not desire to remain with their master, they have only to inform him of their wish, for in this case he is obliged to find them another owner; or if he fail to do so, they are free to escape from him if they can; if they run away without any warning, they are liable to be put to death. The Japanese have a special liking for coloured people, Caffres being their chief favourites: to see them they travel considerable distances, and they treat them with all possible distinction.

They are much attached to the person of their king, the highest nobles considering it an honour to have their sons employed about the court; every one is expected to enter the presence of royalty upon his hands and knees. Even among equals guests are received kneeling, the entertainers remaining in their humble posture until the new comers are seated. All persons, of whatever rank, who chance to meet the King out of doors, remain bent double until he has passed, and when persons of the lower orders encounter their superiors, they remove their shoes and bow down in very lowly guise. They are accustomed to speak almost in whispers, and 'despise us foreigners,' remarks our informant, 'on account of our loud talking.' They sit round in a circle in their houses, even at meal times: they are fond of music, their principal instruments being drums and fifes; they have fixed rules of entertainment, but are no lovers of games. They are good horsemen, their horses being numerous and small; the princes and nobles have very fine horses, which they breed themselves.

The abodes of the chiefs are strongholds situated on an isolated hill, always about two leagues distant from the coast. The hill made choice of must not be rocky, and must possess a supply of water; when the dwellings are erected, the earth excavated to form the gangways is used to construct a wall, which encircles the whole group of buildings and is raised to a height greater than that of any of them, in order that they may be protected from the hurricanes. The dwelling of the chief is distinguished by its central position and greater height. 'I myself,' says the writer, 'visited the fortress of the king; it contained nineteen separate houses, but no less than forty-seven gates opening into as many passages or streets. The enclosure encircling it was composed of sandstone; the walls, of which the width was greater than the height, were of solid earth, strengthened by palisades; the entrance into this stronghold is high up and difficult of access, it is so narrow that horsemen can only enter in single file. In fact I have never seen any fortress, even of stone, which appeared more impregnable.' The natives have in their houses idols, to which they pray as soon as they are up in the morning with their beads in their hands; and at the close of their devotions they pass them three times rapidly through their fingers, accompanying this action with a threefold prayer—for preservation from evil, for temporal blessings, and for deliverance from their enemies. Some persons, in expiation of some crime committed in early life, or through the effect of some great sorrow, take vows of poverty and chastity, leaving their wives if they have any, dividing their goods between their idols and the poor. The women are comely, with fair skins and pleasing manners; they do all the work of the house, as weaving, cooking, and the like. Good wives are held in much esteem by their husbands; indeed they altogether rule them and go hither and thither as they list, without ever thinking of asking leave of their lords. The women wear a long garment reaching from the neck to the feet, fastened in at the waist; over this they wear petticoats, like European women, and like them too they much admire long and thick hair, and spend a great deal of time and care on dressing their heads. They shave the forehead to a considerable height, are very devout, and go constantly to the temples to pray and recite their rosaries.

These Japanese have two kinds of temples. One kind adjoins the dwellings of the priests or bonzes, who live in community, each, however, having his own cell where he sleeps and studies. They all rise in the night and say office together, the oldest reading out, the others responding. Towards evening they sound bells, which they strike with hammers of iron or copper; they also use gongs, borrowed from the Chinese, as are all the sacred writings they possess, and many of their religious rites as well. From time to time they say their beads, like the laity. They live on vegetable food, and are much thought of both by small and great, so that even the king is to a certain extent subject to them. The least able members of the community are sometimes sent out to beg in the streets and villages, or made to employ themselves in helping the aged women who do their housework. Their houses of prayer are well kept; the idols being gilt, and having heads like those of the Caffres, with pierced ears like the Malays; these temples are surrounded by trees, and afford sanctuary for a certain number of days to every class of criminal, excepting only thieves. Some of the idols resemble Christian martyrs and confessors, as St. Stephen and St. Lawrence; they are represented as shaven. Round the sides of the temples are arranged cushions, on which the bonzes sit to pray; the central space being appropriated to the people who kneel there, men and women together, and invoke the martyrs with uplifted hands.

Then we have farther details concerning these bonzes, which we will give in the writer's own words:

'The bonzes are all shaved with razors; they have rooms built at a short distance from their monasteries, where they go twice a day to perform their ablutions. They heat the necessary water at stoves erected for the purpose, the wood for the fires being given them for the love of God. They wear wide shirts like those of laymen, and over these a black habit reaching to the feet; they have stoles round their necks and wear caps like women, and no trousers. They are exceedingly anxious to hear about our religion and are much amused with our images, which they place on their heads; they seem to wish to visit our country. There are orders of black and gray friars; all practise community of goods. They can read and write Chinese, but not speak it, and are thus constrained to carry on communications with the

Chinese by means of writing, as these latter cannot speak Japanese. They celebrate the obsequies of the dead, and also pray for the sick in the following manner. All the fathers assemble in the temple, where they sit in order, the oldest nearest to the altar, and so on, the youngest being in the middle; they have a large trumpet, and after one of the oldest fathers has recited prayers, they blow this trumpet, and all respond in unison or in harmony. The ceremonies last from daybreak until midday; during this time food is brought to the bonzes by those who have engaged their services and who make a point of being present with their relations.

'These orders include women as well as men; the women live in houses apart and take vows of chastity, any breach of which is severely punished; they have no peculiar dress. Many members of the highest families enter these orders, some married women even leaving their husbands in order to do so.

'There is also another order for men; they have different and smaller idols, which are shut up in tabernacles and only brought out on festivals. These idols are kept in houses built in groves at some distance from any habitation, and are regarded with much veneration. The priests who serve these temples dress like the laity, and carry arms; on their heads they wear square caps, reminding one of the sail of a ship, and a small cape reaching below the beard. They are much given to witchcraft, and wear their beads round their necks, by which mark they may be known: they admit women to play a part in their worship, but are none the less obliged to observe strict chastity. They have no connection with the other sort of bonzes, but resemble them in possessing no sacred books of their own, and in using the same kind of bells.'

Their manner of conducting funeral obsequies is told as follows: 'Four or five fathers repair to the temple, taking with them an old woman; as in the former case, those at whose request the ceremonies are performed supply the officiating minister with food and wine. One of the priests opens the tabernacle, and having taken out a drum, a pair of castanets, a hoop with bells, and a woman's gown and coloured scarf, he closes it again. The woman proceeds to put on the dress and fasten the scarf around her; then she performs upon the various instruments, singing and dancing, while the bonzes join in the chorus for the space of half an hour; at the end of which time they again eat and drink, and thus the ceremony ends. I have seen one of these idols; they are ugly and ill made. As far as our discoveries have at present extended, there appears to be but one language in use throughout the country.'

[We need hardly enter into the many questions which might be raised by a comparison of these accounts of Japan, which are obviously written in the most perfect good faith, with the present state of the country, in many respects, no doubt, greatly different from its state in the sixteenth century. The first account, taken down from the lips of Han-Siro, afterwards Paul of the holy Faith, is clearly the work of a religious of the College at Goa, and may be somewhat coloured by the desire which such an enquirer would naturally feel to discover as many resemblances to Christianity as possible in the religion of the country to which so much attention was then drawn within the walls of the College. These resemblances extended, in the mind of the writer, not only to external rites, but also to many religious doctrines. The merchant, Jorge Alvarez, whose name appears in the travels of Mendez Pinto, takes a more simply external view of the Japanese than the writer in the College. Both of them seem to speak more highly of the morals of the Japanese in general than modern travellers would speak. A great number of details in each account would be recognized as answering to what is found in the present day by readers familiar with late books about Japan, but it would be a task beyond our present purpose to attempt to point these out. The accounts must be taken as interesting in themselves, because they are among the earliest statements concerning Japan which can have reached Europe in the sixteenth century, and interesting also for our present purpose, because they show us what Francis Xavier had heard about this country and its inhabitants before he himself landed on its shores.]

BOOK V.

FROM THE SAILING OF FRANCIS FOR JAPAN TO HIS LAST RETURN TO INDIA.

1549-1552.

CHAPTER I.

Voyage to Japan and stay at Cagoxima.

SOME of the biographers of Francis Xavier have introduced their account of his labours in Japan by a long description of the country, its history and natural characteristics, its population, and its political and religious institutions. Japan was as much of a new world to their readers as Mexico or Peru to the contemporaries of Cortes or Pizarro. In our time, as has been already said, Japan has become once more, at least partially, open to Europeans, and there is hardly a country in the East which has attracted so much attention, or about which so much has been written. It is true that the modern accounts of Japan and the Japanese are slight, superficial, and partial; we have been told very little that was not known in the seventeenth century concerning the country itself, as distinguished from its capital and the few ports which the late treaties have opened to Western visitors, and the more substantial parts of such knowledge as has been laid before us seem rather to have been derived from Charlevoix or Kaempfer, than from the personal investigations of the writers of our time. We may, however, presume that enough is generally known about Japan in our day, to excuse us from the task of attempting a new description, unsatisfactory as such an account must always be, when it is not based upon a personal acquaintance with the country.

The story of the seven weeks' voyage between Malacca and Cagoxima is told by Francis himself in the first part of a long letter which he had an opportunity of sending, with others, to the Fathers of the Society at Goa, after he had been between two and three months in Japan. The accommodation on board the small junk must have been of the most inconvenient kind, and though the vessel was of course decked, there were probably no cabins, no means of shelter, or privacy, or protection against sun and sea. The crew was composed of superstitious pagans, who might, humanly speaking, at any moment have taken it into their heads to throw the Christians overboard, and who must have had many temptations to illtreat them. This does not seem to have prevented Francis Xavier from remonstrating with them on their idolatrous practices, though they disregarded his words entirely. The physical sufferings of the voyage were thus the lightest part of what he had to bear. On the other hand, the navigation was prosperous, and the greatest danger which the missionaries ran was the risk of delay in some port of China, which would have deferred for many months their arrival in Japan.

The following letter (which we must divide, in order to give the account of the voyage by itself, before speaking of what passed when it was over) must have been written from time to time between the Feast of the Assumption—on which day St. Francis Xavier and his companions reached the harbour of Cagoxima—and the beginning of November, when it was dispatched to India. It is remarkable for the comparatively large space occupied by reflections and exhortations. This shows us how much and how practically Francis Xavier was already thinking of summoning some of his religious brethren to join him in Japan. Indeed it was accompanied by another letter, in which three Fathers were actually summoned thither. We also see how interior perfection was the one quality which he desired above all others in his assistants, and how anxious he was to lose no opportunity of doing what was in his power to form in them the true apostolical spirit. The letter is spoken of by himself as a letter on 'the interior feelings of the mind,' and he desires it to be sent round and read in all the missions of the Society in India. It must therefore be considered as an exhortation as well as a narrative.

(LXXIX.) *To the Society at Goa.*

May the grace and charity of Christ our Lord always help and favour us!

I wrote to you at great length from Malacca about our voyage thither after we left India, and about all that happened there as long as we remained. Now for the rest. We arrived in Japan, by the favouring help of Almighty God, on August the 15th, having set out from Malacca on the Feast of St. John Baptist at evening. We sailed on board the ship of a heathen merchant, a Chinaman, who promised the Commandant at Malacca that he would carry us to Japan. By the goodness of God we had very favourable winds. However, as perfidy so often rules barbarians like him, our captain at one time changed his intention, and began to give up keeping to his course towards Japan, and loiter about the islands that came in the way, for the sake of wasting time.

There were two things in this which we found especially hard to bear. The first was that God had given a most favourable wind, and yet we were not using it, whereas if it failed, we should not have been able to hold on our course to Japan, but should have been obliged to winter on the coast of China, and, of necessity, wait over again for a favourable season and state of weather. The other was that the captain and sailors were always, against our will and in spite of all our efforts to prevent them, offering abominable worship to an idol which they had with them on the poop, and consulting the devil from time to time, whether it would be advantageous or not to sail to Japan? They would also ask him whether we should be able to hold on our course with favourable weather? and as they told us, the result of the lots was at one time good, at another unfavourable.

When we had sailed three hundred miles, we put in to a certain island, and there made ready our rigging and equipment for the very severe storms of the Chinese sea. Thereupon our sailors offered many superstitious sacrifices to the idol, and fell again to casting lots, asking the devil whether we should have good winds? By chance the lot so fell as to promise us a very favourable wind, so that we were not to stay any longer where we were. So without delay we heaved up our anchor and set sail in high spirits; they relying on their idol, which they worshipped with great devotion, burning candles and sticks of aloe-wood on the poop; and we trusting in the God Who rules heaven and earth and sea, and in Jesus Christ His Son, for the sake of propagating Whose religion we were on our way to Japan. But while we were thus on our way, these pagans took it into their heads to ask the devil whether their ship would return safely to Malacca from Japan? The lots declared that she would reach Japan, but would not return to Malacca. Hereupon the pagans came to a stand, and at last made up their minds to give up for the present the voyage to Japan, to winter in China, and to put off going to Japan till the next year. What do you imagine we thought and felt during that part of the voyage, while the devil was being consulted by his own worshippers as to our voyage to Japan, and the captain of the ship managed the whole business just as the devil willed and chose? Well, as we were sailing on slowly, on a single day and night, off a port in Cochin China, belonging to the Chinese,[1] two very serious things happened to us.

It was the Feast of St. Mary Magdalene about vesper time, and as the sea was swelling, and the water became rougher on account of the wind, the ship being anchored off a shoal, Emmanuel the Chinese, one of our companions, fell head foremost, as the vessel rolled, into the sink of the ship, which was open. We all thought he was killed, for he had fallen from a great height, and the sink was full of water. However, by the goodness of God he escaped death. He stuck some time in the pump, with his head downwards, and up to his middle in water, and at last with great difficulty and exertion we got him out, badly wounded on the head. He lay a long time without coming to himself, but by God's great mercy he was at length restored to health. Just as we had begun to attend to his cure,

[1] Probably Touron: Léon Pagès, t. ii. p. 142.

there comes another roll of the ship, and the daughter of the captain was cast overboard into the sea. The violence of the storm was so great that our efforts to help her were all in vain, and she sank in the waves in the sight of her father and of all of us, close to the ship. There was so much wailing and groaning all that day and the night which followed, that everything seemed very mournful and miserable, whether from the grief of the barbarians, or the danger in which we were. For the pagans turned at once to appeasing their idol with sacrifices and ceremonies; they spent the whole day and night, without taking any rest, in killing birds and placing dishes before the idol. And when the captain asked why it was that his daughter had perished? the lots told him that if our friend Emmanuel had been killed in the sink, his girl would not have come to harm. You see what great danger we were in, as our life depended on the answer given by the devil and on the will of his servants.

What would have become of us, if God had permitted that most bitter enemy of ours to deal with us according to his own desires? For my part, when I saw such great and open insults offered to Christ our Lord by those abominable rites, and yet could in no way hinder them, I prayed many times to God, that before we were lost in that tempest, He would deliver those men whom He had created in His own image from their very great and impious errors, or, if He was to permit them to remain in these same errors, at least that He would allot very severe torments to the common enemy of man who was the author of all those superstitions, every time that he incited the captain to consult him by lots or to worship him as God.

On the same day on which these troubles happened and during the night which followed, it befell me, by the good gift of God, to feel and experience a great many things concerning the very great frights which the devil, when by God's permission he has the power given him, is wont to inflict upon timid men exposed to danger, as well as concerning the means of defence which we ought to use in such a case and at such a time against the assaults of the enemy. It would not be at all useless for you to know them, but for brevity's sake I pass them by. The sum of it all, and the most certain safeguard, is this, to have the greatest presence of mind and courage against the enemy, utterly distrusting yourself, and entirely relying upon God, so as to have all your strength and all your hopes placed in Him, and by no means in the world to allow yourself to seem to fear or to doubt of your victory, with a patron such as He is and One so great for your defender. It very often came into my mind that if God had really increased at my prayer the punishment and pain of the devil, then it was very likely that the latter might vent his rage and hate upon me, for he very often threatened me and gave me to understand that the time was come when he would avenge on me the increase of his pain.

But the devil can never hurt any one at all, except as far as God Himself permits it: so that at such times we ought much rather to fear having any distrust in God, than to fear the assaults of our enemy. For God does permit our foe to harass and vex those who are led by their own timidity not to trust in their Creator, who do not seek for strength in Him, and do not place their hopes on Him. This plague of timidity makes many men who have begun to serve God lead a sad and anxious life, in that they bear the sweet yoke and cross of Christ and yet do not advance bravely and constantly. Timidity causes us this evil, a very great, a very fatal and mischievous evil—that having begun to lean only on your own weakness, when there is need for far greater strength and for resources such as God alone can give, your courage fails in difficult matters, so that you do not make good use of the help of Heaven, which invites you to have a good hope of victory. On the other hand, presumptuous men,—who are led by their selfconfidence to rely more than is right on their own strength, and who despise lesser conflicts with temptation, although they have never trained themselves in these to victory,—these are even more weak than timid men when great dangers and sorrows beset them. For their undertakings have turned out in a way so entirely contrary to their expectations that they lose all heart and are dejected in small matters as well as in great. So that they go into conflicts of this kind with so much repugnance and so much fear, as to run a great risk of their salvation, or at all events of losing all tranquillity. For they do not acknowledge their own weakness, and thus they consider the cross of Christ too heavy to be borne, and their life must of necessity be anxious and bitter.

For how can we expect it to be with us, dearest brothers, at our last moments, unless we have practised ourselves in having a good hope and in confidence in God during our lives? At that time we shall certainly find ourselves surrounded by far greater dangers, temptations, and sufferings both of mind and body than ever before. For this reason it is right that those who have a desire to serve God should take great pains in little matters, and lower themselves and empty themselves as much as possible, so that they may have an utter distrust of themselves, and an immense trust in God, and thus they may become accustomed, when great dangers of life or death or great trials present themselves, to have great hope in the goodness and mercy of God. And this they will gain, if they conquer themselves in things, however little they may be, to which they have an aversion, and if they devote themselves altogether to the study of Christian humility, and so are entirely free from self-confidence, while they raise up their hearts to placing the very highest confidence in God.

For in truth no man is really timid and weak who knowingly leans upon the assistance of God. However many may be the hindrances to perseverance and perfection of virtue which the enemy of us all may place in your path, yet after all you will run a far greater risk in great difficulties and troubles if you distrust the aid of God, than if you confront the perils which our deadly foe raises against you. Would that pious men, in the place of those fears and terrors which the devil uses in endeavouring to deter them from the service of God, would substitute the fear they ought to feel of God their Creator in case they should chance to give up what they have begun for Him. Would that they would once for all make up their minds that it will be far worse for them to neglect the will of our Divine Master than to brave what is in truth the impotence of the devil! O good

God! if they would do this, how full of sweetness would their life be, and what progress would they make in virtue, taught by their own experience the knowledge that of themselves they can do nothing, but on the other hand that they can do all things with God to help them! And how, too, would our foe be broken down and perplexed, seeing himself conquered by those whom he more than once before had overcome!

But now to return to our voyage. As soon as the tempest had relented, we raised anchor and set sail, resuming with many tears the course which we had interrupted. In a few days we reached a port of China, called Canton, and then the sailors and the captain himself thought that they would winter there. We opposed their decision, partly by prayers, partly by threats that we should complain of their breach of faith to the Commandant at Malacca. So God in His goodness put it into their minds not to stay longer in the island of Canton, but to weigh anchor and sail for Tchin-tcheon. God was also so good as to give us a continually favourable wind, and in a few days we drew near to this second port on the Chinese coast, Tchin-tcheon. They were just about to enter the port with the intention of spending the winter there, because the season for sailing to Japan was nearly past, when on a sudden a boat puts out to us in a great hurry, telling us that the harbour is invested by pirates, and that it will be all over with us if we come any nearer. This bit of news frightened the captain, who moreover saw that the brigantines of the pirates were not more than four miles distant from us; and so, to avoid that immediate danger, he determined to shun that port. But now the wind was adverse to a return to Canton and favourable to sailing to Japan, and so we held our course thither against the will of the captain, the sailors, and the devil himself. So by the guidance of God we came at last to this country, which we had so much longed for, on the very day of the Feast of our Blessed Lady's Assumption 1549. We could not make another port, and so we put into Cagoxima, which is the native place of Paul of the holy Faith. We were most kindly received there both by Paul's relations and connections and also by the rest of the people of the place.

[Cagoxima, the port at which Francis Xavier and his companions landed, lies on an arm of the sea which deeply indents the coast of the southern and most westerly of the islands of which Japan is made up. It has not, unfortunately for its inhabitants, escaped, like so many other of the cities of the country, the notice of the foreign visitors of Japan in our own time. It chanced that a relative of its ruler, the Prince of Satsouma, was the daimio who thought himself insulted by an English party in the streets of Yeddo in 1860, and as in the fray that ensued an Englishman was murdered, the strange logic of international law made it appear necessary that Cagoxima should be bombarded and set on fire some months after the accident. Its great distance from Meaco, the seat of the Dairi's government, made it seem an unfortunate necessity for Francis Xavier to land there; but it is probable that the misfortune was in truth a great advantage. Certainly, as Francis informs us in his letter, the people and the prince alike received him at first very well. Paul of the holy Faith was welcomed by his family and friends; and when he proceeded, some days after his landing, to pay his respects to the local prince of Satsouma, a few miles off, he was very graciously and kindly received. The prince particularly admired a Madonna with the Holy Infant, a picture which had been brought from India, and which Paul took with him to show at court. The prince's mother was charmed with it, and desired to have a copy made for herself. Paul talked a great deal with them both of India, the power of the Portuguese, and the Christian religion, and the princess asked him to let her have the chief heads of his new faith in writing. From this time Paul was actively employed either in translating the Creed and Catechism into Japanese, or in spreading the knowledge of the Christian religion among his own family and friends, a very large number of whom he ultimately succeeded in converting.

Meanwhile, Francis was preparing himself for his arduous enterprise very quietly and intently; practising great humility, praying a great deal by day as well as by night, offering up constant austerities to aid his prayers, and learning the elements of the language with all the docility, and far more than the patience, of a child. He soon got to know the Commandments and Creed in Japanese, and was able to give a short explanation of both. Paul's help was invaluable to him. In this way six weeks passed on. When St. Michael's Day came, Francis chose it for his first open advance, a visit to the Prince of Satsouma. The Prince received him hononrably, and a few days later gave him leave to preach the Christian law, which he allowed any of his subjects to embrace if they chose.

The first step was thus gained; but the public preaching was not long to continue unmolested. Francis had, in the meanwhile, done his best to secure another advantage. He had visited and even cultivated the bonzes. They were the teachers of the people, held in extraordinary veneration among them notwithstanding the wellknown impurity of their lives, and if, as was hardly possible, they could have been gained over, or induced to remain tolerant of the new religion, the most powerful impediment to its spread would have been removed. The letter before us hints at the cause, or rather at some of the many causes, on account of which the influence of the bonzes was sure to be thrown into the scale against the Christian teaching. It was not only that their occupation would be gone if the people were converted, but their habitual practice of impurity of the most unnatural kind, which they were even ready openly to defend, and which by reason of their sanction passed as a thing not forbidden by the natural law, was certain to steel their hearts against the arguments and evidences adduced in support of the truth.

It must be remembered, in reading the statements in this and other passages of this letter of St. Francis Xavier in which he speaks of the bonzes, and generally of the religion of the Japanese, that his acquaintance with the details of the forms of falsehood against which he had to contend was necessarily imperfect and superficial. The writers of the century following the time of his preaching tell us many details about the religious state of the couutry of which he could hardly have been aware. He looked upon it from outside, as a foreign Catholic looks, for example, upon the Protestantism of Great Britain or Germany, with no intimate knowledge even of the nomenclature of the various sects into which the heterogeneous mass is really divided, and much less with any idea of the immense variety of forms of opinion and practice which exist side by side in any Christian country which has renounced unity and thrown aside dogma and Catholic tradition. Such a man would see no difference between a Ritualist and a Plymouth brother, he would imagine that the influence of Oxford and Cambridge would be paramount in the Free Kirk of Scotland and among the Welsh Methodists, and might suppose the Wesleyan meeting houses which he might see by the roadside to be under the jurisdiction of the Archbishop of Canterbury. In reality, of course, no latitude of syncretism which prevails among Christians can be like that which, in a country like Japan, would mingle into a whole, the incoherence of which would not at once be detected from without, the old native paganism of the worship of the Kamis, with the more splendid, and in many respects less corrupt, superstitions of Buddhism, with the doctrine of Confucius, imported from China, and with the other elements of which the popular religion was made up. It is most probable that the people themselves knew but little of the theoretical and doctrinal differences between the various religions which invited their devotion and imposed on their credulity.

The reason for these remarks will be obvious to any one who has made himself acquainted with the accounts of the several religions of Japan given by the later authors already named. The description given by Francis Xavier of the old bonze called Ningh-sit with whom he had so much conversation, as it seems, with Paul for his interpreter, would seem to point to a member of the Buddhist hierarchy. Yet this same old man is said to have been doubtful about the immortality of the soul; a statement which would naturally imply that he was an official of the Sintos, that is of the adherents of the older paganism of the Kamis, which seems to have been the indigenous religion of the race. But there were originally no priests, properly so called, in the religion of the Kamis. The shrines were attended by secular persons, who wore a particular dress when occupied in religious rites, and who held aloof from the common people at all times, as possessing themselves something of a sacred character. Thus what bore the appearance of a priesthood was developed, even in the religion of the Kamis, though the 'bonzes' were properly Buddhist ecclesiastics. In the same way, the religion of the Kamis came to have, what it had not originally, its external pomp of worship, processions, litanies, offerings, and images supposed to be miraculous. The fundamental idea of Buddhism required these things quite as little as that of the earlier of the Eastern religions. They grew up around it because they are, in reality, the expression of the natural instincts of humanity in presence of what it supposes to be divine truth and power. The monastic and religious system, again, is more congenial to Buddhism than to the Kami religion: and yet we find among the latter both religious men and religious women, the Kanousis and the Bikunis. It is therefore hardly worth while to inquire whether the Ningh-sit mentioned in the letter before us were really a Buddhist 'bonze,' or a Sintoist. In the former case, we should have to suppose what is so often found among the official adherents of a false and imperfect religion, that is, that scepticism as to one of the fundamental doctrines of his own creed had invaded his mind. Indeed, it is remarkable all through the slight but very significant and interesting accounts which have come down to us of the disputes waged by Francis Xavier with the bonzes and learned men of Japan, that the question so often turned, not upon what may be called the more positive and distinctive parts of the Christian faith, the Incarnation, the Atonement, and the like, but upon matters which touch the natural law, the doctrines of natural religion, the Providence and the justice of God.

After these general remarks on the false religions with which Francis Xavier was now confronted as the Apostle of Christianity, we may continue the letter of which a part has already been given.]

(LXXIX.) *Continued.*

We shall write to you about Japan just as far as we get acquainted with it, and what we ourselves have learnt. In the first place, the nation with which we have had to do here surpasses in goodness any of the nations lately discovered. I really think that among barbarous nations there can be none that has more natural goodness than the Japanese. They are of a kindly disposition, not at all given to cheating, wonderfully desirous of honour and rank. Honour with them is placed above everything else. There are a great many poor among them, but poverty is not a disgrace to any one. There is one thing among them of which I hardly know whether it is practised anywhere among Christians. The nobles, however poor they may be, receive the same honour from the rest as if they were rich; nor can any noble, however poor and needy, be induced to contract marriage with even the richest plebeian. They think that by coming down to ally themselves with plebeians they lose a great deal of dignity and estimation, and thus it is that they despise riches in comparison with dignity. They have a great many observances of courtesy among themselves. They are very fond of arms and weapons, and rely upon them very much. The highest and lowest alike always wear their swords and daggers—even boys of fourteen years of age. They never bear an insult either in word or deed.

The common people pay very great respect to the nobles, and these in their turn think it a great honour to themselves to wait on the Kings and Princes and obey their word. They seem to me to do this rather from their desire of honour than out of fear, lest by not behaving thus they should lose anything of their own dignity. They are sparing and frugal in eating, but not in drink. The wine they drink is made of rice, for here there is no other. They abhor dice and gaming as things highly disgraceful, because gamesters are greedy of other men's goods, and their desire of gain leads them on to the desire of stealing. They seldom swear, but when they do, they swear by the sun. Most of them can read, and this is a great help to them for the easy understanding of our usual prayers and the chief points of our holy religion. They have not more than one wife. There are few thieves among them, and this is on account of the severity of the punishments inflicted for theft, as all thieves are put to death. So there is no kind of theft which they do not hate in a remarkable degree. They are wonderfully inclined to all that is good and honest, and have an extreme eagerness to learn.

They listen with great avidity to discourse about God and Divine things, especially when they can well understand what you say. Of all nations I have ever seen I cannot remember ever to have found any, either Christian or heathen, so averse to theft. They do not worship any gods under the form of beasts. Most of them venerate certain ancient men, who, as far as I have been able to ascertain, used to live after the fashion of the old philosophers; most of them worship the sun, some the moon. They listen willingly to things consonant to nature and reason; and although they are not themselves free from crimes and wicked practices, yet, if you show them that their sin is contrary to reason, they readily acknowledge its guilt and obey the law of reason.

I find the common secular people here less impure and more obedient to reason than their priests, whom they call bonzes. These men are so given up to the most abominable kind of lust as to make open profession of it. This plague is indeed so common to all here, men and women alike, that the mere custom of it has taken away all their hatred and horror of the crime. We often speak against this detestable form of wickedness, and when we show them how wicked and how hateful to God the people are who commit such great impurities, we find that others listen to us with favour and are well disposed, but the bonzes themselves, when we admonish them to abstain from such filthy lusts, try to turn the edge of what we object to in them by laughter and jokes. However severely we reprehend them, they are utterly hardened to all shame, as if their turpitude had gone so far that they no longer feel it at all.

There is a sect of these bonzes who have a dress externally not very unlike our own monks. They wear a habit of an ashen colour, with their heads and beards always shaven—it seems as if they were shaven every third or fourth day. Their discipline and rule of life are very lax. There are communities of women of the same sect, with whom they live promiscuously; so they have a bad name among the people, who do not approve of their great intercourse with the women. They say that when these women find themselves with child, they use medicines to procure abortion. And, as far as I can judge from the community which is here, I do not think the people have too bad an opinion of them. These bonzes hate and are at variance with some others, who dress rather like the clergy among ourselves.[5]

[5] The following passage from Kaempfer (*History of Japan* ap. Pinkerton, *Voyages*, &c., t. vii. p. 788) will perhaps explain this passage on the 'bonzes' and religious women here spoken of:

'Multitudes of beggars crowd the roads to all parts of the empire, but particularly on the so much frequented Tokaido.' [The Tokaido, or royal road from Nagasaki to Yeddo, was made by the famous Taicosama, the persecutor of Christianity, many years after the time of Francis Xavier.] 'Among them are many lusty young fellows, who shave their heads. This custom of shaving the head hath been originally introduced by Sotoktais, a zealous propagator of the Fotoge, or doctrine of the foreign pagan worship' [by this, Kaempfer means Buddhism], 'and was kept up ever since. For being vigorously opposed in the propagation of his doctrine by one Moria, he commanded all that had embraced his worship to shave part of their heads, to be thereby distinguished from the adherents of Moria; and he likewise ordered that their male children should have their whole head shaved, after the manner of their priests, and by virtue of this solely enjoy the privilege of begging.

'To this shaved begging tribe belongs a certain remarkable religious order of young girls called Bikuni, which is to say as much as nuns. They live under the protection of the nunneries at Kamakura and Meaco, to whom they pay a certain sum a year, which they get by begging, as an acknowledgment of their authority. Some pay besides a sort of tribute or contribution to the Khumano temples at Isja. Their chief abode is in the neighbourhood of Khumano, from whence they are called Khumano no Bikuni, of the nuns of Khumano, for distinction's sake from other religious nuns. They are, in my opinion, by much the handsomest girls we saw in Japan. The daughters of poor parents, if they be handsome and agreeable, apply for and easily obtain this privilege of begging in the habit of nuns, knowing that beauty is one of the most persuasive inducements to travellers to let them feel the effects of their generosity. The jammabos, or

There are two things here which altogether astonish me. One is, that the most abominable sins are thought nothing of—and this has come about by the fault of their ancestors, who were corrupted by this plague of impurity themselves, and have left to their posterity the example of such foul lust. And it is very true that the daily habit of vice of this kind quite depraves

---

begging mountain priests . . . frequently incorporate their own daughters into this religious order, and take their wives from among these bikunis.'

Kaempfer goes on to speak of the manners of these bikunis as not wanting in external modesty, though he says that they are free with any traveller who encourages them, and that they are really neither poor nor virtuous. Then he goes on to speak of the 'mountain priests.' 'They have their head, or general of their order, residing at Meaco, to whom they are obliged to pay a certain sum of money every year, and in return obtain from him a higher dignity, with some additional ornament whereby they are known among themselves. They commonly live in the neighbourhood of some famous Kami temple, and accost travellers in the name of the Kami which is worshipped there, making a short discourse of his holiness and miracles, with a loud coarse voice: meanwhile, to make the noise still louder, they rattle their long staffs, loaded at the upper end with iron rings, to take up the charity money which is given them; and last of all they blow a trumpet made of a large shell. . . . In some places they accost travellers in company with a troop of Bikunis, and with their rattling, singing, trumpeting, chattering, and crying, make such a horrid frightful noise, as would make one mad or deaf.'

If modern travellers are to be trusted, the Japanese are no longer so truthful and so averse to cheating as Francis Xavier states them to be. But they may naturally feel on the defensive with foreigners who force themselves upon them, as has been the case of late years. The other statements in the text, as to the practice of abortion, and the rivalries and feuds between different religious communities, are abundantly confirmed by other writers. Taicosama (Fidé-Yosi) interfered by force to put an end to the rivalries spoken of.

'Each one of the thousand divinities of the Buddhist mythology,' says M. Humbert, 'had made room for itself in Japan, and had its temples, its statues, its monastic confraternities. Bonzes, religious men, nuns, abounded throughout the empire, principally in the centre and southern part of Nippon. Each convent vied with its neighbour in industrious arts to obtain the greatest following. But gradually the rivalry became so outrageous, that jealousy, bitterness, hatred, poisoned the mutual relations of certain powerful and ambitious orders. Invectives were followed by acts. The imperial police threw itself across the first encounters of tonsured heads; but it was soon unable to oppose a barrier to the torrent. Bands of furious monks, in frocks and cassocks, armed with sticks, pikes, and flails, rushed at night on the property of the confraternity which gave them umbrage, ravaging all that they came across, ill-treating, killing or dispersing the

human nature, just as continued carelessness and sloth in the practice of virtue gradually undermine all pursuit of perfection of life. The other thing is, that though the bonzes lead more depraved lives than the rest, and though all know this, they are still held in so much honour by them. The bonzes have besides many other errors; but that I may not detain you about them, I may say that the more learned any one among them is, the more shamefully does he err.

I have often conversed with some of them who are more learned than the rest, and especially with the bonze who in this place is respected and honoured by all, both on account of his reputation for learning and high place in their priesthood, and also on account of his great age, for he is already eighty. He is a sort of bishop among them, and is called Ningh-sit, which in the Japanese language means 'Heart of Truth.' Happy man, if the name really fitted him! I have had many talks with him, and have found him uncertain and doubtful whether our soul be immortal, or whether it perishes at the same time as the body; and he was not consistent with himself, at one time affirming this, and at another denying it. I am very much afraid that the rest of these men of letters are much like him. You would hardly believe how singularly fond he is of me; and indeed both the bonzes and all the others are delighted with our company. What they wonder at above all is that we have come the whole way from Portugal to Japan, a voyage of more than six thousand leagues, for no other purpose than to deal with them about divine things, to set forth the Christian faith, and show them in their errors the way of eternal salvation. They all declare that it must have been God Himself Who gave us this mind.

One thing which I very much wish you to know, in order

conventual victims of their attack, and retiring only after having set fire to the four corners of the "bonzery." Sooner or later, however, the aggressors were assailed in their turn at unawares, and underwent the same treatment. Six times in the course of the twelfth century the monks of the convent on the Yéïsan burnt the 'bonzery' of Djensjósi: twice the monks of this latter reduced to cinders the convent of the Yéïsan,' &c. &c. *Japon Illustré*, t. i. p. 276.

that you may give great thanks to God is, that this island is well fitted and prepared to receive the Gospel. If we all knew the language, I do not doubt but that a great many Japanese would become Christians. God grant that we may soon acquire it well! as we have already for some time begun to understand it. In these six weeks, by God's favour, we have got so far that we already give explanations in Japanese of the Ten Commandments. Now my chief reason for writing all this so fully to you is, that you may rejoice and give thanks to God our Lord, for that new regions are thus laid open, in which your own industry may some day find a large field for exertion, and that you may in the mean while furnish yourselves with solid virtues and a great desire of suffering many things for Christ. And what I could wish to sink deep into your hearts and always remain there is this, that a ready and entire will to practise humility and lowliness, a will by which you devote yourself and your life to the glory of God, is a sacrifice more pleasing and acceptable to Him than even a great number of very important services rendered without a will of that kind.

Do you therefore be ready, for perhaps in less than two years I shall write and summon many of you to Japan. In the mean while meditate upon and cultivate humility with all diligence; conquer yourselves in all those things from which our depraved nature shrinks; and make it your constant work by God's grace to know yourselves thoroughly. Self-knowledge is the nurse of confidence in God, and the motive of Christian humility. It is from distrust of ourselves that confidence in God is born, true and genuine confidence. This will be the way for you to gain that true interior lowliness of mind, which in all places, and especially here, is far more necessary than you think. I warn you also not to let the good opinion which men have of you be too much of a pleasure to you, unless perhaps in order that you may be the more ashamed of yourselves on that account. It is that which leads people to neglect themselves, and this negligence in many cases upsets as by a kind of trick all that lowliness of which I speak, and puts arrogance in its place. And thus so many do not see for a long time how much they have lost, and gradually lose all care for piety and all tranquillity of mind, and thus are always troubled and anxious, finding no comfort either from without or within themselves.

I do therefore pray and beseech you to cast away all confidence in your own powers, in human wisdom and reputation, and keep all your hopes and thoughts continually fixed on God alone. If you do this, then I shall consider that you are sufficiently armed and prepared against all the troubles which may beset you either in the mind or in body. For God lifts up and strengthens the humble, those especially who in the practice of even humble and abject offices keep their eyes, as on a mirror, on their own weakness, and conquer themselves nobly in such practices. These are the persons who in the greatest labours and sufferings will show virtue and constancy, and neither Satan and his ministers, nor the storms of the sea, nor savage and barbarous nations, nor anything else, will be able to separate them from the love of Christ.[4]

For they know for certain, from their confidence and hope in God, that nothing can ever have power to hurt them without His permission, that all things are ruled and governed by God's decree and counsel; they are shielded by the guardianship of God, and there is nothing that they can fear, save this one thing alone, lest they may offend Him. If sometimes it be that by the permission of their heavenly Lord they are harassed and vexed by the devil or by men, or by anything else, then they feel sure that their virtue is being put to the proof, or their vices or faults are being punished and expiated, and that thus they are either gaining an increase of merit or of humility. And so they give God all due thanks for these great benefits, and, that they may not be wanting in gratitude to those who furnish them with matter for the exercise of virtue and for gaining reward, they pray with all their hearts to God for peace and pardon for them. Such as these I trust you, by God's help, will become.

For my part, I know a man who, when he had got the habit of placing all his hope and confidence in God, even in the very

[4] Latin, '*Poterit eos separare a caritate Christi.*' Rom. viii. 39.

midst of dangers, was in a wonderful way laden with heavenly gifts, which it would be long to give an account of. And as we must suppose that the trials already passed are lighter than those which are to come upon us, I pray and adjure by Jesus Christ those who are hereafter to come to Japan, that they prepare themselves for the hardest things, and break down and tame their own desires, which are the hindrances to such great good. Take heed to yourselves, dearest brothers, for there are many now tormented in hell, who after having by their discourses opened the way to heavenly bliss to many, yet have themselves at last come to those eternal punishments, because they have been inflated by the false and deceitful idea of their own excellence, and so have wanted this humility of heart. But there is no one at all in hell of the number of those, who, when afflicted by the sufferings of this life, have made it their business to fortify their souls with that interior humility of which I speak.

Always keep in mind that saying of our heavenly Master 'What does it profit a man if he gain the whole world, but suffer loss of his own soul?'[5] Take heed lest you have any confidence in yourselves, and because you are older than others in the Society, therefore prefer yourselves to those who have come later. I should feel much greater joy of heart if (as I hope may be the case) I should hear that any elder one among ours was very often thinking within himself how little progress he had made, after spending so many years in the Society; how much time he has lost, not only in remaining still but even in going back—since in the way of perfection not to make progress is to recede.[6] Those who dwell on such thoughts are sure to feel ashamed and to reproach themselves with their indolence and sinfulness, and so, roused up by the spirit rather of interior than of exterior humiliation, gain courage and strength to make up for their losses. And so they become examples to those with whom they live, both novices and the rest.

Come therefore,—practise yourselves, all of you, assiduously

[5] Orig. Latin, *Quid prodest homini si universum mundum lucretur animæ vero suæ detrimentum patiatur?'* Matt. xvi. 29.

[6] Orig. Latin, *In via perfectionis non progredi regredi est.*

in these meditations, when you feel the desire of being conspicuous soldiers in the armies of Christ our Lord. And believe me, that those who may come here will have their virtue well tried, and whatever extreme diligence you may have used in acquiring virtue of any kind, you will find none that you have not use for. I do not mean by all this to make out that it is difficult and arduous to serve God, for we know that His yoke is easy and sweet. For if you seek God in truth,[7] and enter vigorously the path which leads to Him, you will certainly find so much delight proceed from His service, as will easily mitigate and soften whatever sharpness or bitterness there is in conquering yourself. O good God! men do not understand what great and pure pleasure they forfeit because they do not resist vigorously enough the assaults of the devil—a thing which deprives our poor weak hearts not only of acquaintance with all the goodness of God, but also of the consolations of this miserable life—especially when such a life, without any of the sweetness which comes from God, is continual death rather than life.

I fear that the devil should beset some of you, putting before you certain very great and wonderful exploits which you may achieve for the service of God in other places and occupations. What would he do, I wonder, if he got you into a position more open to his assaults? All his plans have this aim, to make you solicitous and anxious, so as to be no good either to yourselves or to others among whom you work. And so he whispers to you: 'What are you doing? Do you not see that in your attempts here you are spending your work in vain?' This is a thought which tempts most of those who have given themselves to the service of God, and I urgently pray you over and over again to resist it bravely and constantly, for in truth this evil is so pernicious to piety and perfection in virtue, that it makes us not only run slowly in the course which we have begun, but also proceed as far as we do with great trouble and anguish of mind. So let each one of you, wherever he may be, study to help first himself and then others in this, and let him make up his mind that he can nowhere do more service-

[7] Orig. Latin, *Si quæras Deum in veritate.*

able work for God than in the place which has been assigned him by his Superiors. And at the same time trust, that when the fit time comes, God will put it into the minds of those who govern you to send you to that particular place above all others where your work will be most fruitful. In this way you will be happy and ready, and make great progress in virtue, and spend all your time well; and time is a thing the value of which is very great indeed—though many do not know it—since of all our idle time so accurate an account has to be given to God. But men who are anxious and uncertain in mind neither make any progress where they wish to be, because they are not there, nor, where they are, do they do good to themselves or others, because their thoughts are elsewhere.

I would have all of you that are living in the College of Santa Fè exercise yourselves long and much in the knowledge of your own weakness, and fully open your faults to men who can help you by counsel and other assistance, such as your confessors, and other men of experience in the community. The reason for this is, that when you are sent to these parts you may be able to take care of yourselves and of others, by means of the experience and knowledge which you have gained from those who guide your lives. You may assure yourselves that you will be attacked by new kinds of temptation when you are sent out in pairs or even singly, and find yourselves by sea or by land surrounded by danger from storms or from savage men, —dangers of which you have before never even thought. So that if there be any who have not much and for long practised themselves in taming the evil motions of their hearts and in making themselves acquainted with the snares of our most crafty enemy, I leave to their own judgments to consider how great the danger will be in which they will find themselves when they are confronting and attacking the world which lies all in darkness and iniquity.[8] And who will be able to escape the assaults of the enemy except those who have made much way in humility?

There is also another anxiety which worries me, namely,

[8] Latin, *Qui totus positus est in maligno.* 1 John v. 19.

lest the devil, transforming himself into an angel of light,[9] should deceive some of you by his tricks, setting before your mind the great obligations to God under which you live, and all the miseries out of which He has delivered you by calling you into the Society of His Son, and so lead you into a vain confidence and security, so that you ask to be sent out here before the time, reasoning with yourselves in this manner, that if already in so short a space of time God has bestowed on you at Goa so many great benefits, He will certainly give you many more and much greater when you are sent out hither for the conversion of the heathen. And when the devil has cast this thought into your minds, he may easily persuade you that you are doing nothing where you are.

But this attack of the enemy may be repelled in two ways. First, if you consider that there are many wicked men who, if they were to wash off the filth, so to speak, of their former life, and were to be placed in that same school of virtue in which you are, would not only change their manner of living, but would also, to your very great shame, surpass you in virtue and diligence. I say this to put you in mind of what is the truth, that is, that the reason why you abstain from more serious faults is that where you are there are no occasions of offending God, and many of enjoying Him. Persons who do not know whence this very great blessing proceeds are apt to attribute it to their own virtue, and so neglect things that seem small while they are in themselves great, while the persons who despise them so foolishly are small indeed, and themselves worthy of all contempt. In the second place, you must take diligent care to refer all your desires and judgments to your Superiors, having perfect confidence that it will turn out that God will give them in His goodness that mind and purpose in governing you which will be more profitable to your true interests.

Moreover, take care never to ask anything of them with importunity. Some do this, and urge their Superiors so much that they extort from them what they desire, however hurtful it may be; and if it be denied them, they complain openly that

[9] Latin, *Transfigurans se in angelum lucis.*

their life is unpleasant and bitter. Poor men! they do not understand that all that bitterness and trouble arise and are increased from this,—that after having once given and devoted their will to God, they neglect their vow, and endeavour to turn their will the other way and regain it for themselves. The more they try to follow their own will, just so much in proportion is their life more anxious and their mind more disturbed. There are many of these men who are so much their own masters that they hardly ever obey their Superiors willingly—except when they are commanded to do what they themselves wish.

For God's sake take care not to be of this class. In all matters at home, carry out with the greatest care what your Superiors put upon you to do, and by the help of God, avoid the suggestions of the devil, who tries to persuade you that you can gain more profit in some other office, that so you may not well discharge the business which is given you to manage. This is a kind of artifice with which he is wont to assail those who are employed in letters and education.

I implore you again and again, for the sake of Jesus Christ, endeavour in all humble and abject duties to win great victories over the devil. And in doing what you are set to do, take even much more pains to resist the temptations which belong to the duty, than in making great bodily exertion and labour to discharge what is ordered you. For there are some who satisfy their duty exteriorly, but not internally, because they take no pains at all to keep under the evil movements of the soul, and to get rid of the impediments to the discharge of the duty which the devil puts in the way in order to retard them in the way of virtue. These men generally lead a sad and anxious life, and make no progress in piety and virtue. Let no one deceive himself. No one can ever excel in great things who does not first excel in small.

There are a great many errors of a number of persons to be met with in this matter, but those who chiefly fall into such faults are men who, under the guise of piety and of the desire of converting souls, take measures to escape from the light cross—for light it is—of obedience in order to take up another far heavier. Miserable men! they do not consider that one who cannot bear a slight burthen will much less be able to bear a great one. Those who with but little virtue and little power of obedience are eager to undertake great things, as soon as they find themselves oppressed by the weight of these matters, condemn their own folly and cast off the burthen altogether. Even of those who will come from the College of Coimbra to India, I fear there may be some who, as soon as they see themselves in danger in those terrible storms of the ocean, may wish themselves rather in the College than in the ship. So it is—there is a certain kind of pious fervour which waxes cold even in the voyage to India.

Again, others, if they have kept their ardour till they have arrived, yet, when they go about through the countries of the heathen and begin to be oppressed by troubles in one place and to be exposed to danger in another, then, unless virtue has taken deep root in their hearts, they easily give way, and so at last that fire of zeal which they brought with them is extinguished, and the same men who when in Portugal were all in love with India, now that they are in India feel a great longing for Portugal. The same thing may come over some of you who are accustomed to the blessings and conveniences of the College, and have conceived a great and ardent zeal and are very eager to be sent forth to become hunters of souls. When they are in the midst of this conflict which they had so much desired, and when their ardour has cooled down a little, perhaps it may be that they will not be able to live, for the wish they have to be in the College again. Do not you see, then, what is the final issue of these sudden and premature fruits of charity, and how dangerous great attempts are, unless our strength corresponds to them?

I do not, however, say this in order to repress your noble impulses to piety, or to deter your ardent minds from difficult enterprizes, so that you may not show yourselves excellent workers in the propagation of the Christian religion, and leave to your successors illustrious examples of virtue and holiness.

I only say it in order that you may endeavour to be great even in small things, and learn clearly from your temptations and conflicts with the devil what your own strength is, and then altogether place your entire hope, confidence, and security in God alone. If you do this with constancy and perseverance, I have no doubt that you will daily increase in submissiveness and in piety, and will by and by gather in a very large number of the heathen to the fold of Christ, and all this with great agreeableness and tranquillity of mind, in whatever part of the world it may be that you have to work.

For it may well be expected that men who have learnt what are the troubles and diseases of their own minds, and who take great care to heal them, should also charitably attend to the wounds of others, and help them in their dangers even at the risk of their own life. For men who make it their study to find out and cure their own evil affections find no trouble in discovering and curing those of others. So also those who are moved by the sufferings of Christ our Lord find it easy to move others to the same feelings. And I do not see how you can communicate any emotion to another, unless the same be first thoroughly impressed and burnt in upon yourself.

But now let me at last return to the narrative we began about affairs in Japan, from which we have been digressing. In the native place of Paul of the holy Faith, in whom we have found a true and genuine friend, the governor of the city, the chief citizens, and indeed the whole place, have received us very kindly. Everybody came with great wonderment to visit the new priests from Portugal. They are not displeased with Paul for having become a Christian, but rather respect him for it, and all his kindred and others who have any relationship to him congratulate him on having gone to India, and having seen things which no others of his countrymen have ever seen. The Prince of this place was six leagues away from Cagoxima, and when Paul went to pay his respects to him, he was very glad of his return, and showed him much honour, asking himself also a great many things about the manners, the power, and the resources of the Portuguese. When Paul told him all about them, he seemed to be very highly delighted with what he heard.

Paul had taken with him a very fine picture of our Blessed Lady with the Child Jesus sitting in her lap, which we had brought from India. When the Prince saw the picture which Paul had brought he was quite struck with wonder; he at once fell on his knees and venerated it in the most pious manner, and ordered all who were present to do the same. After this his mother saw it and gazed upon it, and was filled with wonderful admiration and delight, and a few days after when Paul had returned to Cagoxima, she sent a man—and a very good person he was—to see about getting a copy of it taken somehow or other. However, there were no means of doing the thing at Cagoxima, and so the matter went no further. The same lady sent us a request by the same hand, that we would give her in writing the chief points of the Christian religion. So Paul devoted some days to this work, and wrote out in his own native language a great many things concerning Christian mysteries and laws.

You may take my word for it, and also give God great thanks, that a very wide field is here opened to you for your well roused piety to spend its energies in. If we knew the Japanese language, we should long ere this have been at work at this large uncultivated field with great fruit of souls. Paul indeed has diligently preached the Gospel day and night to some relations and friends, and has thus brought to the faith of Christ his wife and daughter, as well as many kinsmen and intimate friends. And, as far as things have gone as yet, those who become Christians do not find themselves commonly blamed for what they have done. As the Japanese for the most part know how to read, they soon learn our prayers by heart.

May God grant that in order to explain His divine truths we may master the language as soon as possible, for then at length we shall be able to do some good work for religion! At present we are like so many dumb statues in the midst of the people. They talk about us and discuss us a good deal among themselves, and we are able to say nothing all the time, not knowing their language. We are making ourselves children over again in learning the elements of it. Would that we may match the simplicity and candour of children! At all events we are at present making ourselves like them, both in learning the tongue of the country and in meditating on their simplicity.

We owe indeed a great debt to God for this, for bringing us into these heathen countries, where we may forget ourselves altogether. Everything here being in the hands of heathen and of enemies to the true religion, we have no one but God to hope in, no one but Him to have recourse to for protection. At home in Europe, where the religion of our Lord Christ flourishes, it somehow or other happens that the people we have to deal with, and created things, such as the love of our parents, our country, our relations, the intercourse we have with our friends, the conveniences of life, the remedies against disease, and the like, are so many hindrances to our fixing and placing our whole and entire hopes on God alone. But here, where we are so far from our home, among barbarians, utterly destitute of all human defence and resources, it is a matter of necessity for us to rely only on our confidence in God. And the thought of the very great benefits thus conferred on us by God is a source of no common shame and self reproach to us.

For we almost see with our bodily eyes the goodness of God towards us. So that whereas, having come to these parts out of a desire to extend our divine religion, we thought that we were doing something worthy of reward from God, we now clearly see that it was indeed a very special blessing which God conferred on us that we came. He, by bringing us to Japan, has set us altogether free from that love of human things, which was a snare and net to us, so that we had not had much hope in God. I beg you to help me to give thanks to our Divine Lord for such great favours, that I may not fall into the fault of ingratitude; a fault which turns aside the flowing source of God's bountiful goodness, and hinders him who has been ungrateful for lesser gifts from receiving others still greater.

And moreover we think we ought not to hide from you other blessings also which we find granted to us by God out here, in order that you may join us in giving endless thanks to God the Giver. In other places the food is plentiful, and thus it excites the appetites and fosters them, to the detriment of frugality and temperance. Hence there commonly follow many serious evils either to soul or body. Intemperate persons suffer, on the one hand, many things and painful things from their doctors, and, on the other hand, make their life a troublesome one or perhaps even bring it to its end. And when they are under treatment they find their medicines much more disagreeable than they have ever found their good meals pleasurable. The troubles caused by their medicines are followed perhaps by other sufferings which are very far more severe; for they are often obliged to trust their very lives to the doctors, and these make a great many mistakes and apply a number of useless methods of cure before they hit upon what really heals the disease.

For this reason I consider it a great benefit God has done us, in bringing us to this place where we are, which is altogether destitute of delicacies, and where, however much we may wish, we can give our bodies no indulgences at all. People here never kill fowls or eat them. The common food is vegetables and rice; wheat, fish, apples, and other fruits are considered luxuries. Thus it is that on account of their temperance most people here enjoy very good health: you see a great many old people about. This in itself is enough to prove that our nature, which otherwise might seem to be quite insatiable, is really contented with little. For ourselves, we are in excellent bodily health: may God give us the same health in our souls!

There is also another thing, which I am almost compelled to mention to you. God seems to be holding before our eyes a certain great blessing, and I wish you to help us by your prayers and sacrifices to obtain it from Him. There are a great number of bonzes in Japan, who are very much looked up to by the people, although their vices are very well known by all. The reason why they are held in so much honour seems to be their singular abstinence as to food, for their laws forbid them to take any flesh or fish, or wine, they live on vegetables, apples, and rice alone, and they take food only once a day. These bonzes, as I said, are numerous. Their monasteries have but small revenues, but on account of their great frugality, and also because those of them in particular who dress like our clerics, keep at a great distance from all familiarity with women, which is a great crime with them, and devote themselves rather with all diligence to the expounding of certain histories or rather fables of their superstitions, they receive great veneration from their countrymen. Now the Christian truth is opposed in the highest degree to their bad tenets and errors, and so there is a chance that as soon as we begin to preach the Gospel and refute the lies which they teach, we shall have them all attacking us with great hostility.

We have indeed only one thing in view, which is to bring the Japanese to the knowledge and faith of Jesus Christ our Lord, and we trust that we shall accomplish this by the help of Him whom we serve. And it does not seem that we have any danger to fear from the people itself, unless perhaps it be roused against us by the bonzes. Not even with them shall we enter into any conflict rashly, but at the same time we shall not be wanting in what is due to the glory of God and the salvation of souls. We know well enough that they cannot hurt us unless God permit it. But if it should be so that we lay down our life in so pious and good a cause we shall certainly count that among God's greatest benefits to us, and we shall be grateful to our enemies themselves, for bringing us to the end of this continual death which is now our life and to the entrance of that life which is blessed and eternal. We are determined not to desist from proclaiming the truth by any threats or terrors of theirs. If God bids us rather lose our own life than give up the salvation of their souls, we are determined to obey His command, with His own good assistance and supplied by Him with strength and courage, for the sake of drawing the Japanese out of all the darkness of their superstitions into the light of the Gospel. I have very great hope that the help of God will not be wanting to us in such a matter, since we entirely distrust our own strength, and have placed all our hopes in the might and supreme power of Christ our Lord, and in the patronage of His most holy Mother, of all the Angels, and especially of the Archangel Michael the Prince of the militant Church. We also place much hope in that Archangel under whose protection and guard the country of Japan is placed, and to him and to the other Angels, guardians of men, we daily commend ourselves and our undertaking, that they may not cease to implore God for the conversion and salvation of the Japanese who are under their care. Moreover we continually implore the aid of all the blessed in heaven, in this horrible danger and loss of souls, and we supplicate for the preservation of so many images of God, pleading the merits of all these powerful intercessors to their Creator. And we do not doubt that whatever fault we may commit by negligence or carelessness in this very supplication for the aid of the heavenly host, is made up for by those blessed allies of ours, who offer with the greatest eagerness and diligence to the most Holy Trinity these poor desires of ours to do what is pleasing to God.

The protection of so many and so mighty defenders encourages us far more to hope for victory, than do the great and frequent snares and threats of the devil deter us from this conflict. We should certainly do the most foolish thing in the world, if we were to rely on our own power or wisdom. But God in His good Providence allows so many terrors, sorrows, and dangers to be put in our way by our enemy, that He may break down our spirit, give us lowly hearts, and train us to submissiveness of mind and humility, so that we may never in future feel any trust in our own prudence, but all entire trust in His Divine Protection. And in this He shows at once very clearly His own goodness and how much He remembers us, for He continually sends us internal teachings that we may learn how entirely nothing is what we can do in our own strength, suffering our minds often to be molested by small troubles and dangers, in order that we may never trust in ourselves, and so wait on the support and aid of our most loving Father. For if people undertake anything with self confidence, they often find trifling hindrances more troublesome and more difficult to overcome, than even very great dangers and calamities prove to be to those who distrust themselves entirely, and have placed upon God all their reliance.

It is a great matter for our consolation that you should not be ignorant of any serious care or anxiety that besets us, so that you may help us either by your sacrifices or by your prayers. God knows our many and great faults, and we are very fearful that the fair wind of His Divine help may never carry our endeavours to their desired end, unless there be some great improvement in our life and manners. For this purpose we must use the prayers of all the members of our Society and of all that love it, that by their means we may be presented to the universal Church the Spouse of our Lord Jesus Christ, and we trust that she will communicate to us her innumerable merits and commend us to her Spouse and to our Father Jesus Christ, and to His most holy Mother. And so They in their turn will obtain of the Eternal Father, the Source and Author of all goods, that He may always keep us in the path of duty, and, overpowering our faults by His own infinite goodness, may continue ever to heap upon us His heavenly gifts. For in truth for His sake alone it is that we have come to this strange country—and of this He is my best witness, Who sees clearly all our minds and intentions—and from a desire of delivering the souls of men from the long established bondage of the devil, who aims at being worshipped as God on earth, since he could not attain to that in heaven, whence he has been cast down, and so vents his hatred upon men and among them upon these miserable Japanese.

But now we must give you an account of our stay at Cagoxima. We put into that port because the wind was adverse to our sailing to Meaco, which is the largest city in Japan, and most famous as the residence of the King and the Princes. It is said that after four months are passed the favourable season for a voyage to Meaco will return, and then with the good help of God we shall sail thither. The distance from Cagoxima is three hundred leagues. We hear wonderful stories about the size of Meaco: they say that it consists of more than ninety thousand dwellings. There is a very famous University there, as well as five chief colleges of students, and more than two hundred monasteries of bonzes, and of others who are like cœnobites, called Legioxi, as well as of women of the same kind, who are called Hamacutis.

Besides this of Meaco, there are in Japan five other principal academies, at Coya, at Negu, at Fisso, and at Homia. These are situated round Meaco, with short distances between them, and each is frequented by about three thousand five hundred scholars. Besides these there is the Academy at Bandou, much the largest and most famous in all Japan, and at a great distance from Meaco. Bandou is a large territory, ruled by six minor princes, one of whom is more powerful than the others and is obeyed by them, being himself subject to the King of Japan, who is called the Great King of Meaco. The things that are given out as to the greatness and celebrity of these universities and cities are so wonderful as to make us think of seeing them first with our own eyes and ascertaining the truth, and then when we have discovered and know how things really are, of writing an account of them to you.[10]

They say that there are several lesser academies besides

[10] It is of course almost impossible to identify the names of the places, or of the orders of religious persons, as given in the versions of Francis Xavier's letters. The 'academies' which he names above may probably have been monasteries of bonzes of different sects, in which learning was especially cultivated. We have sometimes felt tempted to think that the long residence of Francis at Paris and the immense debt which he felt to the University there, made him ready to see universities everywhere. As to Japan, however, there seems no doubt that there were numerous seats of learning. Meaco itself was almost a city of 'bonzeries,' in many of which letters were highly cultivated. The names mentioned in the text may some day be recognized. It is curious that in the abridged copy of this letter sent to Coimbra, of which we shall speak hereafter, the name Frenojama is inserted in the list of 'academies.' Frenojama was certainly the name of a seat of learning, as it is mentioned as such in the speeches of the bonzes with whom Francis Xavier disputed before the King of Boungo (see chap. iii. of this book). Bandau or Bandou, which Francis seems to have thought to be a separate island, was the name of a tract of country in the more northern part of the large island of Nippon (the chief island of Japan), and seems to have included the neighbourhood of Yeddo itself. It is mentioned as conquered by the Cambacundono in 1589. Charlevoix, *Hist. du Japon*, t. i. p. 538.

those which we have mentioned. If we see that the minds of all these natives are fit and prepared for Evangelical cultivation, perhaps we shall write to all the chief universities of Christendom, to relieve ourselves of a certain religious scruple which we feel by casting it upon them, in that they might so very easily, with the power of all their virtue and learning, prevent such immense loss, and bring numberless heathen to the knowledge and worship of their Creator and their Saviour. We shall write to their members, as to our Superiors and parents, to look upon us as their younger brethren, and at the same time explain what joyful and abundant harvests of souls may be reaped here by means of them. Therefore we shall ask them again and again, that if any of them cannot come hither themselves, at all events they may countenance those who may have devoted themselves in this way to the glory of God and the salvation of souls, and will find awaiting them here greater and more solid consolation of soul than at home. And if the matter shall be of sufficient importance to require it, we shall also not hesitate to inform the Holy Father himself concerning it, since those who are prepared to come to the worship of Christ, the bosom of the Church, and the obedience of the Supreme Pontiff, must be a part of the charge of him who is the Vicar of Christ, the Father of all nations, and the Pastor of all Christians. And we shall also diligently invite all the pious religious orders so dear to God, who are burning with the desire of extending the Christian kingdom, to come out at once and slake that heavenly thirst for souls which they feel in these islands of Japan, as well as in the country of China, which is far larger than this, and which it is said that it is easy to enter from hence without any fear of hurt from the natives, if you have the public guarantee of the King of Japan, whom we hope, if so it please God, to find well disposed towards us, and whose friendship also we hope to use for that purpose. For the King of Japan is a friend of the King of China, and on account of the friendship between them he is said to have with him a ring and seal, in order that he may give to his subjects who are going to China a public passport signed by the royal seal. It is said that a good many

Japanese ships sail to China, with a voyage of ten or twelve days. We are in great hopes that if God gives us only ten years of life, we shall see many great results produced, partly by those who may come out hither to us, partly by those here whom they may bring to the knowledge and practice of the true religion. Within the course of next year, the fiftieth of this century, we shall write to you more at full length concerning the state of things at Meaco and at the universities, as far as relates to Christian interests. This very year two bonzes, who have been educated in the Universities of Meaco and Bandou, and several other Japanese with them, are going to India to learn the mysteries of our religion.

On St. Michael's day we had an interview with the Prince of Cagoxima. He received us very honourably, and advised us to keep with the greatest diligence the precepts of our Christian law. If he come to see that it is true and good, the devil will burst with rage. A few days after, however. he gave leave to all who are in his dominions and under his power to embrace the Christian religion if they will. These bits of good news I have wrapped up in the last sheet of my letter, that you may the more rejoice and give thanks to God. This winter we shall spend, I think, in explaining the articles of the Creed at considerable length in the Japanese language, with the intention of having the explanation printed, so that as we cannot ourselves be present everywhere to help everybody, the Christian religion may be spread in as many places as possible, as most of the Japanese are able to read what we shall print, and our good Paul will most faithfully render into his native language all that may seem necessary for salvation.

Now therefore that so large a field is laid open for your virtue to work in, it is time for you to prove to God and the inhabitants of heaven how strongly you are impelled to piety and devotion. To do this you must manifest the most thorough humility of mind in your life and exterior, and leave all care of your own reputation to God. He of His own accord will win for you esteem and authority among men, or if He does not do this, it will be for your sake that He does it not, because He sees that there is danger lest you should attribute to yourselves what belongs to Him. There is one thought which is a great consolation to me—that I persuade myself that you always remark so many faults in your own souls for you to reprehend, that you have a great hatred for all arrogance, and that at the same time you have the highest desire for absolute and consummate virtue, so as not to leave room for anything on account of which others may blame you. In this way you will come to look on the praise of men as a cross, inasmuch as it reminds you of your own faults.

But now I will at last make an end of my letter, although indeed there could never be an end of my showing you how much I regard you, all and each. If the hearts of those who love one another with the love of God could be seen, then, dear brethren, you would certainly see your own images imprinted on my heart. And indeed, perhaps, if you were to use it as a mirror you would not be able to recognize yourselves therein, because I have a very high respect for your virtue, and you, on the other hand, have a great contempt for your own weakness, and on account of your remarkable humility you would never recognize yourselves in my heart, although there would be your images imprinted thereon for you to see. I beseech you, brethren, regard one another with true and genuine love, and never let any feeling of offence spring up among you at any time; turn with all diligence those noble desires, which you feel of working and suffering for Christ, to the study of mutual love and to the removal of all offence if any should chance to arise. You know well that divine saying of Christ our Lord, 'In this shall men know that you are My disciples, if you have love one for another.'[10]

May our Lord Christ show what His holy Will is, and give us out of His great goodness strength perfectly to accomplish it! Yours wholly in Christ,

Cagoxima, Nov. 11, 1549. FRANCIS.

[10] Latin, *In hoc cognoscent omnes quod discipuli mei estis, si dilectionem habueritis inter vos.* St. John, xiii. 35.

We are not told by what means this letter with the others which follow was dispatched to India: but we know that Portuguese ships were frequenting the Japanese ports, especially one or two at no great distance from Cagoxima, and we may conclude that the Domenico Diaz, mentioned in the letter below to Don Pedro de Silva, was either the captain of one of these vessels or a Portuguese who had accompanied Francis in this or another voyage, and who was leaving Japan by one of these ships. Up to the time at which the letters were written, all had gone on fairly as to the propagation of the Gospel in Japan: though we can see that Francis was anticipating opposition, and even persecution which might imperil his life and that of his companions. We need not therefore speak of the change of affairs at Cagoxima till we come to the next chapter. The letter which has last been inserted was accompanied by a long despatch, in most respects a duplicate of that of which we are speaking, to the Society at Coimbra.[11] This duplicate, however, leaves out the part of the letter more particularly intended for the members of the Society in India, all of whom it would almost seem as if Francis thought of transplanting in due time to Japan. Francis also sent the following formal letter, ordering three of the Indian subjects to join him as soon as possible, though it could not be in less than a year and a half or two years. Gaspar Baertz and Balthasar Gago are already known to us. The third, Diego Carvalhez, is a new name, nor does the register kept at Coimbra of the fathers and brothers dispatched from Portugal to the Indies tell us anything about him. It is probable that the omission of his name is to be accounted for by the fact that he was a Spaniard, and was not sent to India from Coimbra. At least there was a Diego Carvalhez who entered the Society at Alcala in 1547. He had belonged to the household of Pedro Ortiz, of whom mention has already been made,[12] and who befriended the Society in its first years in Spain. Pedro had taken into his own house near Alcala a number of students of the Society who had fallen dangerously ill, and more than one of his household had sought admission

[11] See the Notes to this book. [12] Vol. i. p. 45, 49.

into it in consequence of the edification which they had received from its members when on their sickbeds. Diego, who entered in 1547, seems to have been sent out to India before he was ordained priest, as we find Francis arranging for his ordination before he was sent to Japan.[12]

(LXXX.) *To the Fathers Gaspar Baertz, Balthasar Gago, and Diego Carvalhez.*

May the grace and love of Jesus Christ our Lord always help and favour us! Amen.

As I find that where I am in these kingdoms of Japan things are well disposed for a very considerable advancement of our holy Faith, and as my memory recalls to me that you have long been animated by burning desires to promote the glory of God by helping your neighbours to find salvation for their souls—I have come to conceive the confident hope from this knowledge which I have of you, that by the help of our Lord God you will not be wanting in virtue and interior humility, by the aid and protection of which you may be able to accomplish what you desire, and at last arrive at the fulfilment of what you have so long prayed for. I command you therefore, in virtue of holy obedience, in order that you may have the greater merit, that unless any one of you be hindered by his state of health, you, Master Gaspar, Balthasar Gago, and Diego Carvalhez, come to Japan, to the city of Meaco, whither I am soon to go, and where I hope to meet you. And you, Balthasar Gago and Diego Carvalhez, all through the journey are to obey Master Gaspar, in whose prudence and humility I trust and confide that he will discharge the office of Superior with the attention and diligence which are meet. And as I am perfectly certain that as soon as you see this letter you will come hither without any delay, your piety, of which I have seen so many proofs, so persuading me, and the perfect mind in which you are as to readiness to obey, even with danger of death, for the

[12] He is said by Léon Pagès to have died soon after the letter summoning him to Japan arrived. See Orlandini, *Hist. Soc. Jesu*, vii. 49.

love of Him Who first was made obedient for us even unto death; therefore I shall add nothing to what I have already said as to you and your journey hither, hoping that God will bring you on your way and that I shall soon see you here safe and sound. Written with his own hand, by your most loving brother in Christ,

Cagoxima, Nov. 11, 1549. FRANCIS.

The next letter, also sent at the same time, shows that his labours in Japan did not make Francis unmindful of the wants of India.

(LXXXI.) *To the Society at Goa.*

May the grace and charity of our Lord Jesus Christ always help and favour us! Amen.

If you have me so much in remembrance as I have you, we shall both find it easier to bear the longing we feel to see one another in the body, as we are nearly always present to one another in the mind. I commend to you, as urgently as I possibly can, the garrisons of the Portuguese throughout India, which are without priests of ours. I do this on account of the extreme benefit and obligations conferred on all of us who are in India by the King of Portugal. If the preachers of the Society from Lisbon have arrived at Goa, you will provide for these garrisons by their means; if it is not so, then you will supply them with others of the Society who by their virtue and humility may help the Portuguese, hearing confessions, holding discourses, training children and servants in Christian piety, rousing others to a good life by means of pious meditations, and discharging the other offices of our Society. Indeed good men are always preaching to the bad by the example of their life, and in this way they often do more good than others who preach in the pulpit—for there is far more power to move men in deeds than in words.

If you have in the College at Goa persons of our Society who are fit to teach the Christian doctrine to the young in all the churches in the city, I think you should send them at the accustomed hours, so as to teach the Catechism every day, and on Sundays and Festivals to add an exhortation apposite to the part of the Catechism which has been explained, and at the same time to tell some of the remarkable doings of some Saint. The Rector of the College should do the same in the largest church of the town. If there are besides in the house other preachers who are fit to teach the children the rudiments of Christian doctrine, I shall be very much pleased if they so teach them, and if by the fragrance and example of their virtues they rouse others to the pursuit of piety. But let all use the common vernacular as spoken among the Portuguese, and which the native Christians and slaves generally use. This is also what I used to do when I was at Goa—for that kind of speech flows more easily into the ears and minds of the audience. And let me know from time to time what is being done in this respect.

I most earnestly exhort you to attend first of all to yourselves. That is the principal thing. 'For he who is bad to himself, to whom is he good?'[12] How can any one take care of others who neglects himself? How will any one be attentive and diligent in other persons' concerns, who is careless as to his own? As for the pupils of the College, take care that the larger number of them be Japanese or Chinese; teach them good manners and to read and write; practise them particularly in Portuguese, that they may serve as interpreters here, where they will be of great use. I really think that there is no part of the world where greater fruits of souls can be gathered than in Japan and China. Two Japanese bonzes, who have given up their sacrilegious priesthood and have been converted to Christianity, will arrive at the College at Goa this year. Take care to treat them courteously and kindly, just as I used to treat Paul of the holy Faith, the Japanese, when I was with you. The character of the Japanese is such that nothing in the world can bend or guide them, except kindness and benevolence. You will send me the three Fathers I have demanded. The letter about interior dispositions of mind, which

[13] Latin, *Qui enim sibi nequam est, cui bonus erit?*

I have placed in the same packet with this, I should like to have sent round to the other houses of the Society in India and read aloud there. May Christ our Lord in His goodness and mercy unite us all in His eternal joys! Amen.

Cagoxima, Nov. 5, 1549. FRANCIS.

The next letter is very characteristic of its writer. We have already seen how far Francis Xavier was from putting full confidence in Antonio Gomez, whom he had yet felt almost obliged to leave in a post of so much power and responsibility as that of Rector of the College at Goa. It may at first sight seem strange that he should address him as the Superior who had the management of the Fathers in India, and was to be looked to to carry out the orders as to the dispatch of some of these to Japan, given in the foregoing letter. As a matter of fact, Antonio Gomez was already upsetting the College of Santa Fè, and had almost entirely set aside the authority of the good and simple Father Paul. The proper place to speak of all that had passed at Goa will be when we come to the return of Francis Xavier from Japan; but the letter on which we are now occupied needs for its full illustration some such knowledge of the character of the person to whom it is written as is contained in this simple statement of fact. Francis probably thought it best to address his letter to Antonio, adding the saving clause that it was also for Father Paul,—who was, after all, to give the final command which was to dispatch the missionaries to Japan, —both on account of the fact already mentioned, that Antonio was a Portuguese, and was looked upon as a representative of Simon Rodriguez, and also because he thus secured the execution of his own orders more certainly than if the letter had been addressed to Paul alone. But we cannot read it at all carefully without seeing that Francis measured Antonio with perfect sagacity. Cosmo Torres was wishing for him in Japan at once —perhaps Antonio might have been ambitious of so glorious a field of labour for himself. His faults were not want of energy or of self devotion, but of judgment, of humility, of charity, and gentleness in dealing with men. His character would have been a noble one, and capable of the greatest services, if he could have given up his own ideas and his own ways: in short, if he could have schooled his heart and soul in those lessons of humility, self distrust, and obedience on which Francis insisted so much in his instructions to the missionaries. Francis would have him wait, ripen, attend first to his own perfection, and thus become a fit instrument of the glory of God. His letter is full of charity, and at the same time not without its note of sternness, especially in the passage in which he warns Antonio against disobedience.

One of its chief purposes, however, is connected with a different subject. He is most anxious to secure a ready means of conveyance for the successive bands of missionaries whom his ardent soul already saw on their way over the dangerous seas which lay between India and Cagoxima. He has an expedient ready at hand for this object, and so he has carefully made a list of the sorts of merchandize the sale of which was sure to be profitable in Japan, and Gomez is to flaunt this list in the eyes of the governor and of the officials of the revenue, in order to get them to take the necessary steps for establishing, as we should now say, commercial relations between the Portuguese crown and the empire of Japan, a step which would lead to a considerable enrichment of the royal treasury and, no doubt, to large gains on the part of the officials themselves. If the arrangements which he proposes can be carried out, there will be a 'royal ship' sent every year from Goa to Osaka, the port of Meaco, the Venice of Japan, as it has often been called. But if this cannot be, at least the governor may give the commission of opening the Japanese trade, with a monopoly of the market, to one of his own friends, who will be quite ready, in view of the large return held out to his hopes, to equip a ship at his own expense, in which case, as Francis puts it, there will be no fear of a rotten or unseaworthy vessel being sent. We shall find that the subject is again broached in the next letter, to Don Pedro de Silva, the 'Capitan' of Malacca. The careful precautions on which Francis insists in order to prevent the ships which may be dispatched to Japan from turning aside to the nearer ports on the Chinese coast, may remind us of the danger which he had himself undergone of losing many months on his voyage to Japan by the same sort of lingering.

(LXXXII.) *To Father Antonio Gomez, of the Society of Jesus.*

May the grace and love of Christ our Lord be always with us to help and favour us! Amen.

As the letter which I wrote the day before yesterday (common to all of you of the Society of Jesus who are living at Goa) is so long and deals so much in detail with everything, there is hardly anything left for me to write to you in particular except this one: that you are continually present to our mind and memory. Nor does my heart ever cease from ardently wishing for your soul more grace and spiritual progress than perhaps you desire for yourself. I should wish indeed that you should take care of all our brethren scattered over India, whom I have committed to your charge; but be sure that above all others I recommend to you yourself, and that I have no greater desire, and consider nothing to be of greater importance, than that you should apply all your efforts to be always advancing and urging on to better things your own soul. And if I came to know that in this business you relaxed even the least point from the extreme of vigilance, I should not think you by any means fit to have committed to you the salvation of others, or indeed any affair at all of serious importance. But if, as I rather incline to think and as I pray God that He may grant, you are strenuously and vigorously continuing to press on with relentless speed to the great end ever kept before your mind, of bringing about the greater glory of God by your own perfection, getting rid of all obstacles whatsoever, and if I come to know this for certain, then I should by no means be without hope that the time may come when I may call you out hither, to send you to Meaco or Bandou, that is into the very strongholds and headquarters of the superstitions of Japan, where you may find abundant means to fulfil the holy desires which you have conceived.

Be careful not to omit to write to me fully and at good length about all our brethren who live scattered about India, as well as those who are in Portugal and at Rome, telling me what each one is doing, and with what fruitfulness they are labouring in the vineyard of the Lord. I have great hopes of much fruit to my soul and of exceeding consolation in reading these letters of yours, and I pray you not to cheat me of this, and not to spare either paper or pains in doing it: especially as I, who, as you well know, have no great abundance of leisure at my disposal, have taken the trouble to inform you in a letter so lengthy as that which I made up yesterday of all that I think can be pleasant or useful for you to know. So I expect and request that you on your part will repay my diligence gratefully and in kind. I wish you to be careful and sedulous in arranging that the Fathers whom I send for from Goa to Japan should get themselves free at once, laying everything aside, and be ready at the appointed time. I wish you also to use in urging this matter the authority over such concerns which I have conferred upon you. You know the way of doing this efficaciously as well as kindly, adapting yourself to the capacity and character of each person.

Father Cosmo Torres, who is very fond of you, is writing to you, and in the vehemence of his affection for you is desiring for you a great many things, which I fear are not quite good for you just at present. No, let what is at present unripe come to maturity, and let us wait for the opportune moment, which will arrive in due time. Meanwhile, be assured of this, that I intend you for greater and nobler things than either you or this good Father who is so devoted to you desires. It will hardly fail to come about, that before three years are over you will have letters from me calling you out hither to go to one of the most famous universities of these kingdoms, where perhaps you will enjoy far greater showers of Divine consolations than you imagine, and will gather a very much more copious harvest of souls than any that you reap, however large it may be, from your labours in cultivating the Indian mission. But about this at another time. What is now urgent is this. I was fearing that perhaps some rather tender affection might steal over you towards some one of those of the Society whom I am calling out hither, and so, under some specious pretext or other, you might think it lawful to make an exception and keep such a one with you, substituting another in his place. Now I tell you again and again, beware of attempting anything of the kind. Be quite sure that if, which God forbid, you were to do such a thing, you would grievously sin against your particular duty in a matter of the greatest importance, against the explicit command of your Superior, and would become guilty of a fault which God would punish by no means lightly. For your own sake, as well as on other accounts, I desire to prevent this; and so I order you, in virtue of holy obedience, to send off at once every single one and all of those to whom I am writing by name and summoning them hither, leaving out no one and changing no one on any pretext whatever, and to take care that they may be ready for the voyage when the time comes for the ships which are bound for these parts to set sail. By the ships which sail from Goa for Ormuz—usually not before March—send thither a copy of my longer letter written on the day before yesterday, and at the same time the letter which I am writing to Master Gaspar in particular, bidding him come to us as soon as possible, so that he may have it early, and may be able to get himself ready to come out hither in good time before the April of the next year, availing himself of the vessels which usually sail to the East about that month. For we ourselves left Goa for our voyage hither in that same month of April.

If it should happen that any one of those whom I send for should die, then arrange about substituting another for him with Father Paul. And when you have both agreed in approving of some one for this purpose, then order him on my part in virtue of holy obedience to come out with the others. For I think it good to lay this precept of taking the voyage, by virtue of the authority which I possess, on each of them, that they may not lose the reward of obedience. It seems to me expedient that they should bring with them two lay helpers, or at least one. These lay brothers, besides being industrious and hardworking men for the duties of domestic service, however humble they may be, must also be men of tried virtue, as to whom we may be safely confident that they will be secure from falling into sin, whatever occasions may present themselves. This is so important a matter that I repeat my commands. You must choose, I say, for this work men whose constancy in good has been perfectly proved by trial; men whose innocence may be safely exposed even to the most attractive seductions of temptation, for such are very abundant in this country, which presents so many most dangerous snares and pitfalls as to be in truth the ruin of those who do not walk cautiously, and who are deficient either in attention so as to avoid, or in courage so as to break through, the nets to catch souls which are most insidiously set on every side.

While these Fathers are making their preparations for departure, I should like you at full leisure to deal with the Governor and get him to write a letter to the King of Japan, adding also some presents, to be given to him together with the letter. This will have much weight in recommending the preaching of the Gospel to these nations. When besides its innate power from above it is assisted by these external vouchers also, I have good reason to hope for it very great success, so much that I believe that in a short time a flourishing Church of Christ will be formed in Japan by the conversion of very large numbers. Moreover, as we must win every one by his own bait, and as people who are accustomed to calculations of temporal profits are not so much moved by what is shown them as to spiritual gains, you must take care diligently to explain to the guardians of the royal revenue at Goa, that they have now a very uncommon opportunity of opening a new source of income from Japan which will be of great advantage and value to his Highness. It would be easy to obtain permission for a house in the maritime city of Osaka, the chief emporium of all Japan, to be publicly assigned to the officials of the King of Portugal, as well as storehouses for European goods. These could be exchanged at a high profit for silver and gold of the best quality, large quantities of which are brought to Osaka from the mines of the country, which are very productive; a factory and exchange would be set up, all to the great benefit of the royal revenue of Portugal. Unless this hope be set before them, I am very much afraid—and I should like much that my suspicion should turn out vain and false—that the people who manage the King's interests at Goa will not easily be induced to send a large vessel to Japan in his Highness's name, for the single and simple purpose of conveying preachers of the Gospel to that country. We shall be very glad indeed that Christ should be made known, even though it be as it were by a bye blow. We shall consider it a gain, if the Kingdom of Heaven be taken account for even as a sort of appendix to a search for wealth of this world, the ministers of religion who are necessary for the salvation of souls being safely conveyed to a spot where a ripe harvest invites them, on a ship principally destined to establish the relations of human commerce. If however, on account, perhaps, of the present state of India, affairs should not be yet far enough advanced for the sending of an ambassador and a ship in the name of the King or of the Governor, he might still do a great favour to some one of his own kinsmen or acquaintance by granting him leave to make the embassy on his own account with the monopoly of trade with Japan, which would be of immense profit. Unless I am mistaken, such a person would very willingly fit out at his private expense a good merchant vessel for this voyage, as he might look with great probability, indeed with a sort of certainty, for very large gain from such a venture.

You can tell well enough what rich merchants there now are at Goa, and what is the fortune and the ambition of each of them. Get some one of them, and that you may tempt his palate with a foretaste of the gains to be gathered in Japan—which happen now to be so serviceable to religion—set before him, and indeed before any of them whom you think it may be of use thus to tempt, the catalogue which I send herewith of the goods which could be at once sold here for a great price, of which there is abundance in India. The thing to be done would be to put a large quantity of these goods on board a ship to be dispatched hither, and if the owner were unwilling to run the risk himself, he might give the command to another, whom he could trust as his agent; and we will exert ourselves to the utmost to help on the rapid sale of the merchandize thus sent, and, from the knowledge we have at present, we are able to promise that great profit is open to any one who would undertake the speculation. Well, if you set all these things properly before the right people, there is sure to be some one roused by the promise of money to be so gained, so as to be ready to make any agreement that may be insisted on as the price of such expectations. Then there will be no danger lest an unseaworthy ship should be chosen. They will take care that the vessel to which they mean to commit so large a part of their property be the best furnished that can be found, and they will spare no pains and no expense. Thus we shall gain on our side, that is, the preachers of the Gospel will be taken on board the same vessel, and be sent where there is so much need of them with the greatest possible security.

You have now my ideas as to the way of procuring a convenient passage for our brethren from your parts to these islands. As to this, I will add a bit of advice gathered from our own experience. Any one who wants to reach this safely and quickly, must sail from Goa in April and from Malacca in June. So you must take care that the ship which is to come here have all its freight and plenty of provisions on board, and leave Goa and Malacca at the dates I have mentioned, nor let its commanders let themselves be induced, by any consideration whatsoever, to turn aside from their course on the way to any port of China, under any pretext at all either of a profitable market for their goods or of taking in supplies, which they must be abundantly furnished with from other sources. Don't let them even disembark on any of the islands which lie in their course for the sake of trading, except indeed under urgent necessity of watering, which must be done with the greatest haste and expedition. Let them be assured, let them trust our experience, that any one who wants to avoid the most serious danger ought to sail on a straight course, and without stopping anywhere at all, from Malacca to Japan; and any one who does otherwise will run a good chance not only of a most prejudicial and tedious delay, but of incurring danger to life. And as to the amount of time which he will lose, to speak of nothing else, you can guess from a comparison of the result of taking the two courses respectively. The direct course from Goa to Japan, when the ship sails with the utmost slowness, takes four months and a half. If you turn aside to China, your ship will hardly reach Japan within seventeen months after it has left Malacca.

And as I know how much power avarice has over the minds of merchants, when it sets before them the attraction of a good prospect ready at hand, to make them disregard all promises and adopt sudden resolutions, I should think it worth while to scheme a little so as to take away the material cause for any trafficking in Chinese ports, and that you should take care that the vessel does not carry more pepper than what the merchants know can be well got rid of in the Japanese trade. If they are aware that they have on board so large a quantity of that staple that they can afford to get rid of their superabundance in the Chinese ports, and still have plenty to sell to the Japanese, then it will be hardly possible to restrain them, when they are so near the marts of China, from following the dictates of their own avarice and interrupting their course, however much the season may be against such a measure, however much the sailors may exclaim. So, when the ship which is to bring out the Fathers is being laden, you should get from the proper authorities an order that not more than eighty bags of pepper be put on board. That is about the quantity which can be quickly sold at Osaka at a very high profit.

There is also another precaution which I should like to be taken in order so much the more efficaciously to restrain the avidity of the merchant captains. Ask his Excellency the Governor, who will make no difficulty to granting you such a favour, to order an express clause to be added to the rescript in which he commits to the commander of the vessel which is to come hither the charge of taking out our Fathers to Japan, in which it may be stated that he expressly forbids him to land at any port in China for the sake of trafficking. For as the last moment of favourable weather for those who wish to reach Japan from China is fixed at the first of August, so that unless on that day they sail with the regular winds, which blow for about a month after that, the people acquainted with nautical matters say that there is no hope of getting to Japan that year, it is manifest that merchants sailing from Malacca near the end of June will not be ready for the voyage across to Japan at the beginning of August if they entangle themselves in business in the Chinese ports, which would imply a delay which would lose them the opportunity of the run to Japan, and force them to wait again, till the next year comes round, for what they called the monsoon, that is, wind and weather favourable for the voyage across, which will not recur till that stated time. And as this would be a severe injury to the preaching of the Gospel, which is above all other things dear to the King, the Governor could give full notice that if any one does this he will incur the penalty inflicted on those who knowingly oppose the King's command, since he has only received the commission to convey the Fathers to Japan under the expressly stipulated condition of sailing thither straight without turning aside, otherwise the King would have intended them to be intrusted to another ship and another captain.

Send to the Fathers who are at Cape Comorin a written copy of the long letter which I wrote to you on the third of this month. As soon as we have any certain hope from Meaco, I will at once write to you fully, as also to our brethren at Coimbra, and our Fathers at Rome. If Diego Carvalhez has not as yet been ordained priest, you must ask his lordship the Bishop to ordain him. Manage to make Ruiz Gonzalez your friend, and show him all possible kindness, for it is of importance to us to have his goodwill, since the Comorin Christians are under his charge, so that the Fathers of our Society who are looking after the religious affairs of the Promontory are daily in need of his favour in many ways. I want to hear from you about Melchior Gonzalez, about the College at Bazain, the Franciscans who before held it, whether any friars of that Order have lately come from Portugal, whether the College which has once been given up to our Society is still governed by ours, and whether it is expected that it will be so perpetually. So take care to inform me fully about all these things in your first letter. Tell me also about Father Niccolo, what fruit follows from his labours at Coulan, and whether he diligently presses on the affair which I so earnestly commended to him as a thing so highly necessary for teaching the children of the Comorin Christians to read and write, and for the help of our Fathers who are sent to those parts. I again and again beg of you never to fail to help those Fathers as to anything that they are in need of; rather be yourself on the watch for them, anticipate their requests and even their desires, on all occasions making application to the Governor and the Treasurer, so that all that is necessary may be supplied them, and even, when there is urgent need, and no more ready way of assisting them presents itself, providing for them in the mean time out of the home funds of the College. I desire also to hear from your letters whether the preachers of our Society who are expected from Portugal have yet arrived at Goa, how many they are, and with what gifts each of them is endowed. When they are distributed, you must consider before all other places the city of Cochin, for I know how much it is in need of the work of a good preacher. All these things that I write to you are to be considered as written to Father Paul also, to whom you will communicate them, and to whom it will belong to assign to the preachers the places to which they are to be sent, and to send them thither by his authority.

Two Japanese bonzes are going to India from hence, who have been brought up in the Universities of Meaco and Bandou. Take care to be attentive to them in all things, with every mark of goodwill. The Japanese character is won by love and kindness. Take care by all ways in your power to be in very good favour with his lordship the Bishop and also with his Vicar, showing them the highest love mingled with great veneration, serving them at a nod, and obeying them in all things. They are our superiors, and whatever we have to settle with them will be arranged incomparably more quickly and easily by obedience and humility. I beg of you again not to omit any particle of extreme diligence in dispatching to this country at the appointed time the Fathers whom I am calling hither. If God prospers our designs and helps our labours, you will some day receive from me letters which I shall write from Meaco before a year is over. May our Lord heap upon you all as much grace here and as much glory in Paradise as I desire for myself!

Cagoxima, Nov. 5, 1549.

The above has been dictated by me, and what follows I add with my own hand. For the love of our Lord God I beseech you take most diligent pains to make yourself beloved by all and every one of our brethren. You will gain this if you console those who are with you with good and gentle words, and those who are at a distance with frequent and kind letters. I should very much wish you to have a fixed place and time for continually explaining the Christian doctrine to the ignorant, and I should wish you to do this in the cathedral church, and that in the same place you should on Sundays and feast-days preach to the people in the morning, and in the afternoon explain the articles of the Faith to the slaves and to the children of the Christians in the language which they understand, as I used to do when at Goa. I desire this, that you may give an example to others. I also pray you most earnestly, write to me minutely about the interior state of your soul. You know how much I should rejoice, if I should learn from this manifestation the things which I so anxiously and solicitously desire as to your progress towards perfection! Among the many bits of extremely happy news which I might receive, I should count it among the first of all if I were to hear from the concordant witness of many that you were very much beloved by all the brethren of our Society, whether those who are under the same roof with you, or those who are occupied elsewhere, far off or near, in other houses or in the missions. If I hear that they are all dear to you, that will be very pleasant, but it will only give me half the joy I want. In order that it may be full and complete, I must be persuaded both that you have a most tender affection for all of them, and also that you in return are extremely loved by them. Farewell.

Yours in the Lord,
FRANCIS.

We have already spoken of Don Pedro de Silva, the Commandant of Malacca, to whom Francis Xavier professed himself so deeply indebted for his assistance as to his voyage to Japan. His first batch of letters sent from that country is closed by one in which he thanks Don Pedro with all the effusion of his affectionate heart, and at the same time seeks to interest him in his own plan for the establishment of a regular commercial intercourse between the Portuguese authorities and the newly opened empire. He also recommends to him some Japanese who were to visit Malacca.

(LXXXIII.) *To Don Pedro de Silva, Commandant of Malacca.*

We have at length reached Japan, sir, borne thither not more by favourable winds than by your good offices to us. For, next after the benevolent Providence of God, the prosperity of our voyage has been secured most of all, as we gratefully acknowledge, by the extreme kindness and liberality shown by you to us when we were making our preparations for departure. You provided us in the most loving manner not only with abundance of stores for the voyage, but with the best vessel of all that were to be had at the time, and with everything of the same sort that could be useful to us. You cut, by means of the continual favour shown us by one in so eminent a position of authority, all the knots and delays which presented themselves in the business; and not only this, but to crown all your goodness, you added many precious gifts, by means of which we might win for ourselves that goodwill from the princes of this country which is so necessary to us.

With these presents in charge, we arrived, by the help of God, on the 15th of August, the happy and auspicious day of the feast of our Blessed Lady's Assumption, at Cagoxima, the native place of Paul of the holy Faith. On his account we were received with all goodwill by the chief magistrate, the prefect, and all the people of the place. That same Paul, our faithful companion, began immediately to show his zeal for the religion which he had so unfeignedly embraced. He spent his whole days and nights in setting the Christian doctrine before his parents, kinsmen, friends, of all age and class, persuading them of its truth, and this with so much effect that now, when I am writing, he has made Christians of his mother and wife, his male and female relations, and whole cousinhood of both sexes, besides a large number of his other friends and former acquaintances.

The soil of this country, as far as I have hitherto been able to perceive, is now so well and happily disposed to receive the seed of heavenly doctrine, that we have the best right to expect a plentiful harvest of souls if only cultivation be not wanting. The nation is one with which reason prevails over passion very generally. They commit many sins, but the sins they commit do not establish a prescription against the authority of right reason, because they generally sin through ignorance ; so that it is easy to see that they will amend if they be taught. Thus even bad customs leave to reason its empire in some sort unimpaired, since they are not followed openly against its decree, but rather insinuate themselves in an irregular and underhand manner, as it were, without establishing themselves in possession. Thus it is that this nation has not much accustomed itself to indulge in full licence of following vice against the vain reclamation of reason, as is the case elsewhere, where men sin knowing what they are about, and with unblushing malice.

We should by this time have already gone to Meaco, where the Emperor of Japan and the chief princes of the nation live, if we had had seasonable winds to allow of the voyage. We are told that after four months from this time the regular setting in of the winds which will take us thither is expected. Then, if God so grant, we shall sail to Meaco. There are many and wonderful reports about that city, the royal capital of Japan, which I shall entirely believe when I have seen it for myself. They say that the number of houses in it is reckoned at ninety thousand. Two Portuguese who have been there, one of whom is still in Japan, say that the city of Meaco seems to them larger than Lisbon. The houses are all of timber, built up with woodwork and floors one above the other, as in our country. If it please God, in the next year from this I will tell you all about these matters in a long letter drawn from my own experience. My mind is filled with much hope, that by the good favour of Jesus Christ a large part of Japan will embrace our holy religion, on account of the authority which reason, when it is clearly understood, exercises over the nation.

And a good part of this great fruit which we expect as so very probable will be set down to your liberality and kindness, by which, partly by your words and your own exertions, partly by the efficacious orders which you issued when it was necessary, and also by the giving those beautiful presents out of your abundance with which we might win the favour of the King of Japan, you delivered our plan of preaching the law of Christ in this kingdom from infinite difficulties, which we ourselves should have been too weak to overcome. This makes me trust that, by the help of God, you will finish and bring to the glory of full and complete success the work which your father, the Lord Conde Almirante,[12] so long ago began; and that you will have all the greater merit with God, in that your father gained for the King of Portugal by the opening up or the frequentation of the route by sea to these nations of the East, hardly any other fruit than the advantage of temporal gain; whereas you, with far higher fortune, by so kindly assisting our voyage hitherwards, have brought about the eternal benefit of the extension of the kingdom of Christ and the spreading of the

[12] Vasco de Gama.

glory of God. I write this that you may understand how much you are bound to God for choosing you for so great a work, and for casting deep into your mind the seed of that most praiseworthy design of enlarging the frontiers of our holy religion in these parts of the world. Nor, believe me, will a man who seeks first the kingdom of God ever want abundance of opportunities of human prosperity. For, unless I am mistaken, this expedition of ours to Japan promises to produce rich results to the King and to his realm, the interests of which you devote yourself to with so much faithfulness and diligence.

Osaka is a maritime city, the chief seat of trade in Japan, two days' journey from Meaco. With God's help, it will be easy to obtain that right of domicile in that city should be given to the consuls of the King of Portugal, as well as power to build storehouses where they might keep merchandize from India and Europe, until they might be exchanged at leisure with the precious metals of the country of Japan, with manufactures and produce, but especially with silver and gold, which are brought for sale from nearly all parts of these islands in great quantity to that port, which is the richest that they have. In order that such commerce, which would be very profitable on both sides, may be the more easily established, I shall try to persuade the King of Japan to send an ambassador to India, who might see how great an abundance there is there of things most useful for the convenience of life, yet of which Japan is destitute, and on his return might arouse his countrymen to the desire of such things, and so render them more inclined to agree to conditions of mutual traffic. The result may be, that without difficulty an agreement may be made between the Governor of India and the King of Japan, both as to other regulations of commerce, and also particularly as to the establishment at Osaka of a factory and register of the Portuguese revenue.

I have great confidence in our Lord Jesus, that before two years are over I shall write to you that we have at Meaco a church dedicated in honour of our most holy Lady the Mother of God, that henceforth those who sail for these islands may be able, in the terrible storms of the Chinese Archipelago, to invoke the Blessed Madonna of Meaco. Now if you could trust me so far as to allow me to take the office of your agent in these parts, I would venture to promise that I will manage, whatever portion of your property or money you should like to commit to me in such capacity, to return you the same increased by an interest of more than a hundredfold, and with your profit quite secure from all dangers of shipwreck or sea voyage. This would be an amount of good fortune in traffic as to which there is no risk, such that no Captain of Malacca before you has ever made money more safely or more productively. Would you like to know of what kind of this most rapid and profitable investment I am speaking? I will tell you without circumlocution. Make up your mind, I beseech you, to give us something to divide among the poor Christians of this country—those who are and those who are to be. This money so invested, I promise you, on the security of Christ Himself, will be returned to you in heaven multiplied a hundredfold, without being exposed to the uncertainties of winds and waves, or to the arms and snares of pirates. While I have been writing this I have been rather afraid that I might not find your mind at present ready to run the hazard of this investment which is to have its profit in hope. And yet nothing can be safer. I know, however, that you Commandants of Malacca have such lofty notions, that although you are generally sufficiently alive to chances of gain in other ways, you usually neglect this most certain method of quick and large returns.

The corsair who commanded our vessel died here at Cagoxima. He did his work for us, on the whole, as we wished, throughout the voyage, and yet we were not able to repay him by good offices either when we came to port or when he died. He himself chose to die in his own superstitions; he did not even leave to us the power of rewarding him by that kindness which we can after their death do to other friends who die in the profession of the Christian faith, in commending their souls to God, since the poor fellow by his own hand cast his soul into hell, where there is no redemption.

Many Japanese are on their way hence to you. They have been induced to do this by what they have heard our friend Paul relate of the wonders of the power and virtue of the Portuguese. I pray and beseech you, by all that you owe to God and your own noble condition, receive them with all honour and liberality, and let them be lodged splendidly and comfortably with gentlemen of Portugal of wealth and high character, who have received injunctions from yourself to show them all kindness. This will do much, believe me, towards drawing them on to embrace the Christian religion, if they find by their own experience that Paul's account of the Portuguese is true.

Domenico Diaz, to whom I give in charge my letter, to be delivered to you, is a very great friend of mine, as dear to me as I am dear to him. His kindness and goodness to us has been proved by me by continual services during our unbroken companionship in this long voyage. You will do me a special favour if you would discharge for me, since I cannot do so myself, the debt of kindness which I acknowledge that I owe to a man who has deserved very much at my hands. May our Lord God lengthen your life to many years, and take you back in health and prosperity to Portugal, as you and your lady wife desire! Farewell.

Your friend, with all my soul,

Cagoxima, Nov. 5, 1549. FRANCIS.

The arrival of this letter, together with that of the Japanese recommended by it to the good offices of the Capitan of Malacca, was made the occasion of public demonstrations of joy. Don Pedro had the royal standard hoisted on the fortress, the guns fired a salute. and a grand procession was organized to go to the Church of our Lady del Monte to give thanks for the good news which seemed to promise the conversion of Japan. Magistrates and soldiers joined the Vicar General and clergy in this procession. The streets were hung with colours, and lighted up at night. The Vicar sang high mass in presence of all the authorities. Soon after this, the Japanese strangers were baptized, Don Pedro de Silva himself standing as their godfather.

CHAPTER II.

Firando, Amanguchi, and Meaco.

THE letters which have been inserted in the last chapter must have been sent to India by some Portuguese merchants trading on the coast at one of the ports not far from Cagoxima, if not at that place. It appears that the Prince of Satsouma had not been altogether uninfluenced by their presence in the kind reception which he accorded to Francis Xavier, and in the permission which he had given him to preach the Christian law in his dominions. The Japanese princes seem to have been eager to gain the advantages of trade with Portugal for their own ports, and the prince looked for this temporal advantage in his toleration of the new priests from Europe. He was soon disappointed, and this downfal of his expectations prefaced the way for the change of his policy in regard to Francis Xavier. The port of Cagoxima does not seem to be well sheltered,[1] and was in this respect much inferior for the purpose of the Portuguese ships to that of Firando or Firado, on an island of the same name, some fifty or sixty miles north of Nagasaki, which, at the time of which we are writing, had not yet been founded. Firando is said to be difficult of access on account

[1] The 'bombardment' of Cagoxima by an English force in 1867 was occasioned by a storm, which came on in the bay while the squadron which had been sent to demand satisfaction was lying there, after having seized some steamers belonging to the Prince of Satsouma. He had made no resistance, but when the storm arose, 'not doubting,' says M. Humbert (*Japon Illustré*, t. ii. p. 391), 'that the gods who were the protectors of the Great Niphon had of themselves aroused from the bottom of the sea the dragon of tempests, with whose aid he could not fail to annihilate the barbarians,' ordered the batteries of the port to open upon the ships in their distress. This caused the action, which ended in the burning of the captured ships, a number of junks, the docks, workshops, and powder magazines, and a part of the town itself.

of rocks and shoals, but a safe harbour when it is once entered.[2] It chanced that the Portuguese merchants discovered the superiority of Firando just at the time of Francis Xavier's early sojourn at Cagoxima, and the change which they made in simple provision for the safety of their vessels brought on the storm which must have been for some time gathering over the missioners in the dominion of Satsouma.

We do not know the exact moment, after the leave given by the prince for the public preaching of the Gospel and for his subjects to embrace Christianity, at which this change of affairs took place. Some time probably elapsed after Francis Xavier dispatched his letter. Meanwhile he had been preaching freely; he had, as we have seen, had many friendly interviews with a chief of bonzes, the Tunda, as he is said to have been called, of one of the Buddhist monasteries in the neighbourhood. Francis Xavier does not tell us himself of other incidents which attended his preaching, which have come to us on the testimony of eyewitnesses. No reader of his life will be surprised to find that now again his apostolate was illustrated by miracles. The most famous of these could not have been the first, for it was wrought in favour of the only daughter of a nobleman whom, in his agony of bereavement after her death, the new converts urged to recommend his case to the God of the Christians, and to have recourse to the prayers of the great teacher of the Portuguese. The father went to Francis Xavier, and threw himself at his feet; but sorrow choked his utterance, and he could say nothing. Francis retired for a few moments with Joam Fernandez into the little oratory in which he said mass, and after a short, fervent prayer, came back to the poor suppliant and told him to go, that his prayers were heard. He said nothing more, and the nobleman was grieved and hurt. In this frame of mind he went homewards, and was met, first by a servant, who told him that his daughter was alive, and then by the girl herself, who ran to him and threw herself on his neck. She said that as soon as she had breathed her last, two horrible demons had seized her and were about

[2] Humbert, *Japon Illustré*, t. i. p. 17.

to cast her into hell, when two men of venerable aspect came and rescued her, and the next moment she found herself safe and well. The father took her to the house where Francis Xavier and Fernandez were staying, and as soon as she saw them, she cried out that they were the two who had delivered her. Both father and child were at once instructed and baptized. Another miracle, different in character, is recorded of this time. A Japanese had been insulting and jeering at Francis, who turned to him and said gently, 'God preserve your mouth, friend!' The man was struck at once with a horrible and noisome cancerous disease in his mouth. These and other miracles served to increase the credit of the missioners, and it seemed likely that large numbers would become Christians at Cagoxima.

The change was not long in coming. The bonzes, who had hitherto at least listened to the new doctrines, and two of whom had even become converts, took the alarm, and went to the prince, threatening him with calamities of all kinds if he allowed the worship of the ancient gods of their country to be scorned. It may be questioned how far their influence might have weighed with him, but for the chance coincidence of their remonstrance with the abandonment of Cagoxima as a mart by the Portuguese. The prince was incensed at what he considered ingratitude, withdrew his permission as to the teaching of the Christian law, and forbad any one, under pain of death, to become Christian.

It does not appear that this edict of the Prince of Satsouma was followed by any active measures of persecution: but the whole attitude of the people changed with regard to the Christian teaching. For many months Francis Xavier confined himself to the careful instruction of the neophytes who had already been gained, chiefly the family and friends of Paul of the holy Faith, who were able to assemble from time to time for prayer and worship, to studying the language of Japan, and to translation into that tongue of the summary of the Christian doctrine and of the mysteries of our Lord's life, of which mention has already been made. The rest of his time was spent in prayer and in the exercises of penance. This was the laying of the foundation of that famous Church of Japan which was to give an almost unexampled instance of heroic fortitude and constancy under persecution. The converts became more and more firm in the faith, and seem from the first to have been possessed with the spirit which afterwards animated so many thousands of Japanese martyrs. They were singularly devoted to their new faith and its teachers.[3]

Meanwhile the months passed on, and there was as yet no favourable opportunity of proceeding to Meaco. This is explained by a passage in a letter written by Father Cosmo Torres, the companion of Francis Xavier at this time, who states that the Prince of Satsouma had promised to find them a ship for Meaco, but that afterwards he advised them to delay until the wars raging at that time around the capital might be over. Perhaps the prince's interest in the voyage had cooled down, but the wars were no fiction. At the beginning of September 1550 Francis determined to pass to Firando. The same reason which had turned away from him the favour of the Prince of Satsouma might secure him that of the less important and powerful

[3] We have at this time a considerable gap in the account of the residence of Francis at Cagoxima. It is very possible that this city was his ordinary place of abode, but it is not necessary to suppose that he made no excursions to places in the neighbourhood, and there are certainly notices of his activity elsewhere for which it is difficult to find a more convenient time than this. Thus he is said to have been walking once by the sea-shore, where some fishermen were dragging in their nets, which, to their great affliction, were empty. Francis blessed the nets with the sign of the Cross, and bade them cast them again into the sea. This time the nets were found full to abundance, and that part of the sea remained afterwards remarkably productive. Another anecdote speaks of a town which was visited by a severe pestilence, which was delivered by his prayers. The conversion of a large number of the people was the consequence. He also cured a deformed child, taking him in his own arms, healed a leper and gave sight to a blind man by making the sign of the Cross over him, and wrought several other miracles recorded in the Processes, which are not assigned to any place or time. See Massei, l. iii. c. 7, who quotes the evidence of Martino Lupo from the Processes, and the *Resumo Historico* (Goa 1861), by Felippe Neri Xavier, an exceedingly useful little work, on account of the number of its references to scarce books about the East, and its stores of local information. We regret not to have known of it until the present chapter was passing through the press.

lord of Firando,[4] and he might find there some Portuguese merchants who might give him news of India and perhaps even letters from Europe. The Christians of Cagoxima were in deep affliction at losing him. Paul of the holy Faith was set over them as a sort of head.

Francis travelled on foot, carrying himself the little bundle in which was contained all that was necessary for the celebration of mass. He took with him his European companions, Cosmo Torres and Joam Fernandez, a convert named Bernard, the prophet of Cagoxima, and another Japanese. He had not gone many miles on his road when he was invited by one of the great lords of the country, whose name is given as Ekandono or Eshandono, to visit him in one of the great castles which are described by travellers in Japan.[5] Ekandono had heard wonders of the 'bonze' from the west who had been teaching a new religion at Cagoxima, and was eager to see and hear him. Francis preached with great earnestness and power, and was able to

[4] Francis speaks, however, of Firando as belonging to the kingdom of which Amanguchi was the capital.

[5] 'The castles of the Japanese nobility are built either on great rivers or upon hills and rising grounds. They take in a vast deal of room, and consist commonly of three different fortresses or enclosures, which either cover and defend, or, if possible, encompass one another. Every enclosure is surrounded and defended by a clean deep ditch, and a thick strong wall built of stone or earth, with strong gates. . . . The principal or innermost castle or enclosure is called *sonmas*, that is the true or chief castle. It is the residence of the prince or lord who is in possession of it, and as such it is distinguished from others by a square, large, white tower, three or four stories high, with a small roof encompassing each story, like a crown or garland. In the second, called *ninmas*, that is the second castle, are lodged the gentlemen of the prince's bedchamber, his stewards, secretaries, and other chief officers, who are to give a more constant attendance about his person. The empty spaces are cultivated, and either turned into gardens or sown with rice. The third and outwardmost is called *sotogamei*, that is the outwardmost defence, as also *ninnomas*, that is the third castle. It is the abode of a numerous train of soldiers, courtiers, domestics, and other people, everybody being permitted to come into it. The white walls, bastions, gates, each of which hath two or more stories built over it, and above all, the beautiful tower of the innermost castle, are extremely pleasant to behold at a distance.' Kaempfer's *Hist. of Japan* (Pinkerton), p. 772. A similar description is given by M. Humbert, *Japon Illustré*, t. i. p. 33, and an engraving, p. 27.

baptize seventeen persons before he left the castle. Among these, though in secret, was the lady of the house and her eldest son. Ekandono himself was doubtfully inclined, but allowed of their baptism. Francis left them a copy of the Japanese explanation of the Christian doctrine, and carefully regulated the exercises of piety and manner of life of the little community.

Neither Francis nor either of his two companions mention this incident,—indeed, his own account of his work during that year is unusually concise, as we shall see. But this little Christian community was found many years afterwards (in 1562), in a state of innocence and fervour, which shows the blessing which rested upon the work of Francis Xaxier, as well as the instructions which he gave and the system which he established in order as far as possible to secure the perseverance of converts under such circumstances. In the year last mentioned, Father Luis d'Almeyda was sent to visit the Christians in Firando, Cagoxima, and Boungo—a kingdom in the neighbourhood of Satsouma of which we shall have more to say presently. On his way he was told to call at the castle of Ekandono, and his letter gives a description of it which seems to justify the wonder with which it filled him. It had, he says, ten distinct bulwarks or walls connected by drawbridges, 'so high that the head swims when you look down,' and a very deep ditch : all was said to have been cut out of the rock by sheer work, but Father Luis thought it could hardly be the work of man. In the centre of these outer fortifications rose the principal castle, where the visitor was received with much joy, especially by the lady of the nobleman who owned the castle, and fourteen others whom Francis had baptized himself. They came round him, he says, 'asking for news of Father Francis, and of the progress of Christianity in other parts of Japan, rejoicing much in the good tidings which I gave them, for it was many years since they had seen Father or Brother of the Society. He that after God kept them in the faith was an honoured old man, a sort of "majorduomo" of the castle, whom all loved very much on account of his virtue.' He and the lady related many miracles which God had wrought since Father Master Francis went away, for he had left them some devout prayers and litanies written by his own hand (which the lady kept as relics), and these they used to apply to sick persons and so heal them. One of these sick had been Ekandono himself, whose life had at one time been in danger, and who had been at once cured. Once a week the Christians all met to take the discipline together with a discipline which Francis had left behind; but the old man considered it so precious that he would not let any one give himself more than three strokes with it, lest it should be worn out. Almeyda baptized some children, two of whom were lads, sons of Ekandono, whom he found perfectly prepared for baptism by the instructions of the old man, whom, on returning a week or two after, he found just dead. He preached several times, and converted some of the heathen in the fortress, one of whom was so very clever, that he wrote down at once all the instructions which Almeyda gave him, and made a book of them. He and the eldest son were left in charge of the rest. On Sundays and feastdays they all met, and a chapter of the book about the Christian doctrine was read, about which they talked for an hour. They frequently assembled for prayers. The Christian doctrine was taught constantly, and the harmony and fervour among them was truly wonderful. Ekandono himself told the Father that he was only prevented from becoming a Christian by fear of the prince.[6]

Firando was the scene of a sort of triumph for Francis Xavier. A Portuguese ship was trading there; the captain received Francis with a salvo of artillery, and conducted him with all honour to the prince, who gave him leave to preach freely. Conversions were now very numerous. In a few days there were more Christians made than had been gained in

[6] Massei mentions a still more striking instance of the long time during which the memory of Francis Xavier's preaching was kept up without the presence of missionaries, in the case of a place called Canadabè, thirteen leagues from Cagoxima, where fifty-five years after his visit—which was probably made at this time—a number of Christians were found, among whom was the daughter of the chief nobleman, who was baptized, when a little girl, by Francis, and had since consecrated herself to God by a vow of chastity. Massei, l. iii. cap. i. p. 294.

Cagoxima during the whole year. But Francis determined to press on to Meaco, or at least to other parts of the country, as if to explore it in the interests of the faith. He left Cosmo Torres at Firando, to continue the work already begun, and took with him Joam Fernandez and his two Japanese converts. 'You may well imagine, my fathers and brothers,' writes Cosmo Torres to the Society at Goa, 'how I felt at being left and separated from his company, knowing the great dangers and toils which they would incur, for they left Firando at the end of October, when the great snows and frosts of this country begin. But as to Father Francis, for the great fire of the love of God which is in him for the manifestation of the holy Catholic faith, neither the frosts, nor the snows, nor the fear of the unknown race, could hinder him from undertaking this most dangerous journey. When they had to go by water, over certain parts of the sea there were many pirates, and on account of these they had to hide themselves below the decks of the boats in order not to be recognized; and when they travelled by land they went as servants of certain gentlemen on horseback, and had to run at a gallop to keep up and not lose their way. When they came by night to the inns, dead with cold and hunger and wet through, they found no sort of comfort there.' He goes on to speak of their sufferings from the deep snow or from rough roads and thickets, and from the stones thrown at them by the boys and rabble, and the like. 'With all this they never ceased preaching and confessing our holy Catholic faith . . . and you may see,' he adds, 'what beginnings our Father Master Francis has made in this country, and us who followed him he encouraged more by deeds than by words; and however much we toiled and suffered we were always ashamed in comparison to his labours, the which, not to be over long, I do not relate minutely and in particular—the insults, and the hunger, and the cold which he endured, going about that country for four months, always on foot, and often unshod, for the great streams that there are.'

This description hardly applies in its fulness except to the long journey which we shall presently have to speak of from

Amanguchi to Meaco; but the picture of the fervour and love of suffering shown by Francis at this time would apply to the whole of his stay in Japan. From Firando he embarked for Facata, a port on the southern and smaller of the great islands of which Japan consists, off the western coast of which the island of Firando lies, and from thence sailed again to Simonoseki,[7] the port of Amanguchi, the capital of a considerable state on the larger island of Niphon. Amanguchi was at that time one of the largest and most populous cities of Japan, the mart through which the commerce between the other islands passed, and the capital of one of the most fertile provinces of Niphon. It was a very wicked place, infamous beyond measure, on the same account as Ormuz. Its condition moved the zeal of Francis Xavier. He began to preach in the streets and public places, though without moving more than the curiosity of the crowd. His preaching, however, led to invitations to come and explain his doctrine in private houses, to which he willingly consented. He disputed with the utmost freedom and courage. On these occasions he practised in a signal manner that fearlessness of all human things which he recommended in his letters. Joam Fernandez related afterwards how Francis, usually so humble and meek in demeanour, confronted the pride and arrogance of the rich and noble Japanese who used to interrogate him, bearing himself in a most lofty and dignified manner, as became the ambassador of the God of Truth. At times, Joam himself had to answer them in the same bold uncompromising manner, and he confessed that while he did so he sometimes expected to see the sword of his questioner flash from the scabbard, to make the heads of both Francis and himself roll in the dust. Francis encouraged him by telling

[7] Simonoseki, like Cagoxima, has become unfortunately famous in the history of the lately renewed intercourse between Japan and the European nations, as the scene of an act of violence on the part of the stronger parties in that intercourse. Simonoseki is in a position of very great importance, commanding the strait named after it, which separates the greater island of Niphon from the second, Ximo. The strait is the passage from the west nto the inland sea of Japan, on which a number of ports, among others Osaka, lie, and through which is one of the routes to Yeddo itself. Its bateries have been destroyed by an allied squadron.

him that the only way to dominate those lofty spirits was to fear nothing at all that they could do. In truth, it appears that he won, at all events, their respect by his demeanour; though the bonzes heaped insults upon him, and the common people ran after him, abusing him, turning him into ridicule, and pelting him with stones and filth. At last, his presence and way of proceeding in the city came to the ears of the prince, who sent for him and asked him why he had come to Amanguchi. Francis made him a long harangue. After setting forth the chief points of the Christian doctrine, he began to inveigh against the vices of the nobles, who had received from God greater blessings than others; and then he went on to reproach the prince himself for his indulgence in unnatural vices, giving scandal to all his people, and preparing for himself a sentence of eternal damnation from the Supreme King of all, before whom the greatest monarch of the world is but a worm. The prince listened attentively, and let him go unhurt.[8]

Francis continued preaching in Amanguchi for several weeks, but without any effect. Very few became Christians. He left the city at the beginning of December 1550, and began, with Fernandez and the two Japanese converts, that toilsome and apparently fruitless journey to Meaco which has already been mentioned in the extract given from the letter of Cosmo Torres. The country was overrun by armed bands, belonging to the forces employed in a civil war then going on; there were abundance of robbers besides, and at certain passes and ferries money had to be paid by travellers. It was either on this account—that he might pass free as a servant—or because of a divergence from the road, which was necessary on account of robbers, and that he might be able to regain the road without fail, that Francis offered himself as a servant to one of a company of merchants, who made him carry his baggage, running at the same time by the side of his horse. Not far from Meaco, he fell severely ill, but soon recovered, and pursued his way. Meaco he himself describes as an immense city, but with a

[8] Francis is said on this occasion to have signally confuted a bonze of great reputation.

great part of it in ruins on account of the civil war. He was unable to obtain an audience either of the Dairi or Cubosama, the spiritual and temporal heads respectively of the empire. We are told by his biographers that a large sum of money was asked as the price of admission, and that he was altogether unable to raise it. He preached in the streets, but the people either were too preoccupied with the war which was going on to attend to him, or listened merely out of curiosity. He laid the foundations of the future Church of Meaco by his sufferings rather than by his successes. Ten years later, that Church was to begin to flourish. It is probable, however, that Francis learnt by this visit to the capital much as to the state of things in Japan which he had not before suspected. He may have seen that even if the Dairi or Mikado gave him leave to preach, his authority would not practically extend far beyond the walls of his own residence; that Japan was not a kingdom like Spain or Portugal, in which the sovereign was everything, and his word absolute law even to the extremity of his dominions. There was a significant contrast between the apparently secure tenure and exercise of power which he observed in the petty princes of Satsouma and Naugato—the kingdom of which Amanguchi was the capital—and the titular magnificence of the Mikado—great as was still his authority when supported by the Cubosama—which could not preserve his own capital from the ruinous effects of war. On leaving Meaco, Francis Xavier seems to have determined to adopt a somewhat different line of conduct from that which he had hitherto thought of. He would make his advances at the courts of the local sovereigns, and he would lay aside for that purpose, not indeed his humility, meekness, poverty, and mortification, but something of that outwardly despicable appearance, which in itself he held so dear, but which he knew how to lay aside in order to serve the cause of Him for whose sake he loved it.

The journey to Meaco, therefore, was not entirely unfruitful even of other results than the sufferings and humiliations to which it had exposed Francis Xavier. He had baptized a few dying children, whom he had found exposed by the roadside, and he had reaped a plentiful harvest, as we have said, of personal sufferings; in some cases even his life had been in danger, as he had been assailed by the crowds to whom he could not forbear from speaking of the Gospel, and more than once was wounded by arrows and almost stoned to death. He seems to have returned from Meaco by sea, taking boat probably at Osaka, and this may account for his returning to Firando rather than to Amanguchi. At Amanguchi, however, he made up his mind to begin his new career of preaching. He took with him the letters and presents from the Governor of the Indies, the Bishop of Goa, and the Captain of Malacca, which had been originally intended for the Mikado himself. He dressed himself in a manner more becoming the Envoy of Portugal, and, with his companions as attendants, demanded an audience of the Prince or King of Naugato. He was very well received by the King, who was charmed with the presents—among which Cosmo Torres tells us were a 'manicordio e relox,' a musical instrument of some sort, and a watch, with other more costly articles. Oxindono, as he was called, was unwilling not to show all courtesy to the representative of the secular and religious authorities of that half unknown power in India and the Eastern Archipelago which had so strangely risen up of late years, to interest and alarm the various countries at whose ports its ships were so continually presenting themselves, laden with strange merchandize of the most costly sorts, and whose prowess in arms seemed quite on a par with its spirit of mercantile adventure. The next day an edict was placarded in the city of Amanguchi, allowing of the preaching of the Christian religion, and an empty 'bonzery' or monastery was assigned for the residence of the new teachers. A large present of gold and silver, which Oxindono sent to them, had previously been refused by Francis.

We have now reached a point in the history of Francis Xavier's stay in Japan at which we may again use his own words. The following letter is remarkable for its comparative brevity, and for the absence of all reflections and exhortations. It seems almost as if it were merely the draft of a letter, summing up the events of the last year very shortly, and written at a time when Francis was uncertain whether he might find a means of sending it to India. There are no personal appeals or injunctions. Another hypothesis may be that it was written after he had had some incomplete tidings as to the state of things at Goa which required his presence, and which made him unable to pour himself out with his usual freedom when writing to his religious brethren.

(LXXXIV.) *To the Society at Goa.*

Last year, dearest brethren, I wrote to you from Cagoxima concerning our voyage, our arrival in Japan, and what had been done in the interests of Christianity up to that time. Now I will relate what God has done by our means since last year. On our arrival at the native place of our good Paul, we were received very kindly indeed by his relations and friends. They all of them became Christians, being led by what Paul told them; and that they might be thoroughly confirmed in the truth of our religion, we remained in that place a whole year and more. In that time more than a hundred were gathered into the fold of Christ. The rest might have done so if they had been willing, without giving any offence to their kinsfolk or relations. But the bonzes admonished the prince (who is very powerful, the lord of several towns), that if he allowed his people to embrace the Christian religion, his whole dominion would be destroyed, and the ancestral gods of the country, which they call pagodas, would come to be despised by the natives. For the law of God was contrary to the law of Japan, and it would therefore result that any who embraced that law would repudiate the holy founders of the ancient law of their forefathers, which could not be done without great ruin to the town and realm. Let him look, therefore, with reverence on those most holy men who had been the legislators of Japan, and, considering that the law of God was opposed and hostile to the law of his fathers, let him issue an edict forbidding, under penalty of death, that any one in future should become a

Christian. The prince was moved by this discourse of the bonzes, and issued the edict as they had requested.

The interval after this was spent in instructing our converts, in learning Japanese, and in translating into that tongue the chief heads of the Christian faith. We used to dwell shortly on the history of the creation of the world, as seemed useful for the men we had to deal with; as, for instance, that God was the Maker and Creator of the universe, a truth which they were entirely ignorant of, and the other truths necessary for salvation, but principally the truth that God had taken on Himself the nature of man. On this account we translated diligently all the great mysteries of the life of Christ until His Ascension into heaven, and also the account of the last judgment. We have now translated this book, for such it was, into Japanese with great labour, and have written it in our own characters. Out of this we read what I have mentioned to those who came to the faith of Christ, that the converts may know how to worship God and Jesus Christ with piety and to their souls' health. And when we went on to expound these things in our discourses, the Christians delighted in them very much, as seeing how true the things were which we had taught them. The Japanese are certainly of remarkably good dispositions, and follow reason wonderfully. They see clearly that their ancestral law is false and the law of God true, but they are deterred by fear of their prince from submitting to the Christian religion.

When the year came to an end, seeing the lord of the town to be opposed to all extension of our religion, we determined to pass to another place. We therefore bade farewell to our converts; they loved us so much that they shed many tears, and giving us great thanks for having shown them the way of eternal salvation at the cost of so much labour of our own, were very sorrowful at our departure. We left with them Paul, their own townsman, who is an excellent Christian, to finish their instruction in the precepts of religion. We then went to another town, where the lord of the place received us very kindly; there we remained a few days, and made about a hundred Christians. None of us knew Japanese; nevertheless, by reading the semi-Japanese volume mentioned, and talking to the people, we brought many of them to the worship of Christ.

I charged Cosmo Torres with the care of these converts, and went on with Joam Fernandez to Amanguchi, the seat of a very wealthy king, as he is thought among the Japanese. The city contains more than ten thousand households; all the houses are of wood. We found many here, both of the common people and of the nobility, very desirous to become acquainted with the Christian law. We thought it best to preach twice a day in the streets and cross roads, reading out parts of our book, and then speaking to the people about the Christian religion. Some of the noblemen also invited us to their houses, that they might hear about our religion with more convenience. They promised of their own accord, that if they came to think it better than their own, they would unhesitatingly embrace it. Many of them heard what we had to say about the law of God very willingly; some, on the other hand, were angry at it, and even went so far as to laugh at what we said. So, wherever we went through the streets of the city, we were followed by a small crowd of boys of the lowest dregs of the populace, laughing at us and mocking us with some such words as these: 'There go the men who tell us that we must embrace the law of God in order to be saved, because we cannot be rescued from destruction except by the Maker of all things and by His Son! There go the men who declare that it is wicked to have more than one wife!' In the same way they made a joke and play of the other articles of our religion.

We had spent some days in this office of preaching, when the king, who was then in the city, sent for us and we went to him. He asked us wherever did we come from? why had we come to Japan? And we answered that we were Europeans sent thither for the sake of preaching the law of God, since no one could be safe and secure unless he purely and piously worship God and His Son Jesus Christ, the Redeemer and Saviour of all nations. Then the king commanded us to explain to him the law of God. So we read to him a good part of our volume; and although we went on reading for an hour or more, he listened to us diligently and attentively as long as we were reading, and then he sent us away. We remained many days in that city, and preached to the people in the streets and at the cross roads. Many of them listened to the wonderful deeds of Christ with avidity, and when we came to His most bitter death, they were unable to restrain their tears. Nevertheless, very few actually became Christians.

Finding, therefore, that the fruit of our labours was small, we went on to Meaco, the most famous city in all Japan. We spent two months on the road, and passed through many dangers, because we had to go through countries in which war was raging. I say nothing of the cold of those parts, nor of the roads so infested by frequent robberies. When we arrived at Meaco, we waited for some days that we might obtain leave to approach the king, and ask of him to give us permission to publish the divine law in his kingdom. But we found all ways of access to him altogether closed. And as we discovered that the edicts of the king were generally thought little of among the princes and rulers, we laid aside our design of obtaining from him any such license, and I determined to sound and try the minds and dispositions of the people themselves, so as to find out how disposed that city was to receive the worship of Christ. But as the people were under arms, and under the pressure of a severe war, I judged that the time was most inopportune for the preaching of the Gospel. Meaco was formerly a very large city; but now, on account of the perpetual calamities it has undergone in war, it is a great part in ruins and waste. At one time, as they say, it contained one hundred and eighty thousand dwellings. It seems to me very likely that it was so, for the wall which encircles it shows that the city was very extensive indeed. Now, although a great part of it is in ruins, it yet contains more than a hundred thousand houses.

When we found that the city of Meaco was neither at peace nor prepared to receive the Gospel, we returned to Amanguchi, and we presented to the king there the letters and presents which had been sent as signs of friendship by the Governor of India and the Bishop of Goa. The king was very much delighted both with the letters and with the presents, and that he might reward us, he offered us a great amount of gold and silver. These gifts we sent back, and then asked him that, if he desired to make some acceptable present to the strangers who had come to his city, he would give us leave to announce the law of God to his people: saying that nothing could possibly be more pleasing to us than such a gift. This he granted us with the greatest goodwill.

He accordingly affixed edicts in the most crowded places of the city, declaring that it was pleasing to him that the law of Heaven should be announced in his dominions; and that it was lawful for any, who desired, to embrace it. At the same time, he assigned an empty monastery for us to inhabit. A great many used to come to us to this place for the sake of hearing about the new religion. We used to preach twice a day, and after the sermon there was always a good long dispute concerning religion. Thus we were continually occupied either in preaching or in answering questions. Many bonzes were often present at the sermons, and a great number of others, both of the common people and of the nobility. The house was always full of men,—so full, that at times some were shut out for want of space. Those who asked us questions pressed them so well home, that the answers we gave enabled them thoroughly to understand the falsehood of their own laws and founders, and the truth of the Christian law. After disputes and questionings for many days, they at last began to give in and betake themselves to the faith of Christ.

The first of all to do this were those who in the discussions and questions had shown themselves our most strenuous adversaries. Many of these were persons of good birth, who, when they had embraced Christianity, became our friends with an amount of warmth which I can find no words to describe. And these new Christians told us with the greatest faithfulness the mysteries, or rather the absurdities, of the Japanese religion. As I said at first, there are as many as nine sects in Japan, and they are very different one from another in their teaching and ordinances. When we got to know the opinions of these sects, we began to look up arguments by which to refute them. So we used to press hard by daily questions and arguments the sorcerer bonzes and other enemies of the Christian law, and we did this so efficiently, that at last they did not venture to open their mouths against us when we attacked and refuted them.

When the Christians saw the bonzes convicted and silenced they were of course full of joy, and were daily more and more confirmed in the faith of our Lord. On the other hand, the heathen, who were present at these discussions, were greatly shaken in their own religion, seeing the systems of their forefathers giving way. The bonzes were much displeased at this, and when they were present at the sermons and saw that a great number became Christians daily, they began to accuse them severely for leaving their ancestral religion to follow a new faith. But the others answered that they embraced the Christian law because they had made up their minds that it was more in accordance with nature than their own, and because they found that we satisfied their questions while the bonzes did not.

The Japanese are very curious by nature, and as desirous of learning as any people ever were. So they go on perpetually telling other people about their questions and our answers. They desire very much to hear novelties, especially about religion. Even before our arrival we are told that they were perpetually disputing among themselves, each one contending that his own sect was the best. But after they had heard what we had to say, they left off their disputes about their own rules of life and religions, and all began to contend about the Christian faith. It is really very wonderful that in so large a city as Amanguchi in every house and in every place men should be talking constantly about the law of God. But if I were to go into the history of all their questionings, I should have to write on for ever.

The Japanese have a very high opinion of the wisdom of the Chinese, whether as to the mysteries of religion or as to manners and civil institutions. They used to make that a principal point against us, that if things were as we preached, how was it that the Chinese knew nothing about them? After many disputations and interrogatories, the people of Amanguchi began to join the Church of Christ, some from the lower orders and some from the nobility. In the space of two months quite as many as five hundred have become Christians. Their number is daily being added to; so that there is great cause for joy, and for thanking God that there are so many who embrace the Christian faith, and who tell us all the deceptions of the bonzes, and the mysteries contained in their books and taught by their sects. For those who have become Christians used to belong, one to one sect, another to another; the most learned of each of them explained to us the institutions and rules of his own way of belief. If I had not had the work of these converts to help me, I should not have been able to become sufficiently acquainted with, and so to attack, these abominable religions of Japan. It is quite incredible how much the Christians love us. They are always coming to our house to ask whether we have anything at all which we wish them to do for us. All the Japanese appear naturally very obliging; certainly the Christians among them are so very good to us that it would be impossible to exceed their extreme kindness and attentiveness.

May God in His mercy repay them with His favour, and give us all His heavenly bliss! Amen.

Amanguchi [July 1551].

The incidents which are but slightly sketched in the foregoing letter are dwelt upon much more fully in other letters which were not dispatched by Francis to Europe until after his return to India. We must here, therefore, to some extent, anticipate what might otherwise have to be said by way of commentary on those letters. It is clear that after his interview with the Prince of Naugato, the position of Francis was greatly changed in the eyes of the people. He now reaped the harvest which he had sown some months before at Amanguchi in the midst of humiliation and ill success. He preached frequently and copiously; and after the sermon, as he tells us, there was a dispute concerning religion that sometimes lasted for several hours. From his later letters we gather that he was hardly left time to recite his breviary, or to take his food or rest, on account of the throng of persons who came to the monastery which had been allotted to him as a residence, in order to ask questions and propose difficulties concerning religion. We have here two facts which must have taxed his energies to the utmost, and the companions and witnesses of his labours tell us that now, as on former occasions—perhaps even in Japan, for there is nothing to limit their evidence to his sojourn at Amanguchi alone—Francis Xavier was assisted by the peculiar gift of apostolic men like himself: his sermons were not those of a foreigner who had scarcely learnt the language of the country in which he was speaking, but he spoke freely, flowingly, elegantly, as if he had lived in Japan all his life. There is evidence also that at this time he preached fluently in Chinese to the merchants of China who traded in the port of Simonoseki.

Another wonderful form of the same gift is also mentioned in the accounts of Francis while at Amanguchi, which reminds us of the manifestation of miraculous power on the day of Pentecost, when the Apostles spoke in one language and were understood in several, persons from so many different parts of the world hearing their words each one as if spoken in the language of his own country. When several questions were put to Francis at the same time by different persons in the crowd, he made one answer which satisfied all. In after years, when other missioners succeeded him in Japan, the people complained that they did not answer their questions as immediately as the first teacher of Christianity they had seen.

Everything that we hear about the Japanese at this time shows how foreigners were struck with the extraordinary inquisitiveness with which their active intelligent minds flew upon the theological and philosophical questions raised by the introduction of a new religion. We have seen how Francis himself thought it a matter of wonder that the whole city should be talking of the law of God. It was not the languid critical curiosity which St. Paul found among the idle speculators at Athens. Japan was a new soil for the seed of divine truth to fall upon: it had not as yet rejected the faith, and amid the mass of corruption and error which it presented to the eyes of its Apostle there were singular elements of good, which he seems to attribute to the natural uprightness and reasonableness of the national character. The Japanese, as he describes them, were a sturdy honest race, not effeminate, not frivolous, not childish. False religions had long overlaid the remains of primeval truth which had been handed down from the earliest fathers of mankind; the religious and devotional instincts which are innate in man had been attracted by fabulous deities, behind whose imaginary powers lurked the indefatigable enemies of the human race; and the natural law itself had, in more than one of its most immediate developments, become obscure and hidden in their minds. Thus inhuman cruelty was the rule as to children, who, either before or after they were born, were murdered by their parents without its being considered a crime. Suicide was in some cases even honourable. Unnatural lusts reigned throughout the whole of society. Francis Xavier, as we have seen, was perfectly conscious of this; and yet in the true spirit of that large and noble theology which he had so eagerly studied in Paris, and which came to be now so serviceable to him in a land which no European had heard of when he was a student, he could excuse much of what he saw on the plea of ignorance, and he rested his hopes of the conversion of many on the ground that they did not knowingly sin against reason, heinous as were the crimes which they committed. This account of their state is quite consistent with the serious earnestness with which these Japanese at Amanguchi applied themselves to theological discussions; and it made the work of missioners a real battle, a continual conflict of reason and argument, in which hot answers, exaggerated statements, or illogical syllogisms, were sure to bring confusion even upon the advocates and defenders of truth.

This was something Francis had never met with since he left Paris, and his mind was evidently deeply impressed, not only with the necessity of immense interior humility and mortification in those who were to combat for the faith, in order to secure the assistance of God, but also of trained intellect and capacity in wielding the weapons of theological argument, that the human part of the means of warfare might not be wanting. The Japanese were hungry for truth: they had minds that could see the difficulties which revelation presents, especially when it is historically considered; and the men who were to feed them with truth must be able to stand up against questionings, some of which, coming straight from the unsatisfied cravings of the human mind, breathed all the subtlety of the scholastic disputations with which he had been familiar when he first made the acquaintance of Ignatius. In India there was nothing of this. If Francis could have penetrated, as Robert de' Nobili afterwards penetrated, the more refined and recondite teaching ot the Brahmins, he might have found something more intellectual to cope with than he ever found. To him the Indians were a soft, vicious, ignorant, barbarous race, with little mind and no strength of character. If we can imagine a barbarous and hideous Corinth, India was like such a Corinth to Francis when he went there to do the work of St. Paul. If the Athens of St. Paul had been the Athens of the days of Socrates, young, vigorous, fresh, not more blooming with every artistic beauty than glowing in every vein with the purest and most active intellectual life, then Japan might be compared to such an Athens when Francis Xavier became prematurely grey in disputing with her children.

We shall see how strongly Francis Xavier speaks in his letters to Ignatius Loyola and Simon Rodriguez of the necessity of sending only picked men to deal with the active intelligent society on which he had come, as it were, by surprise. Another great element of difficulty in the way of the Gospel preachers must have been more obvious to him from the first —the opposition which was sure to arise from the powerful order of bonzes, under which name, as has already been said, he includes the ministers of all those different religions and sects which divided the Japanese among themselves to such an extent, that controversy was no new employment to them when Christianity appeared to draw the attention of all and the animosity of many on itself. When he wrote the letter which we have last inserted, he seems to have made some progress towards the intelligence of the different sects of this nation. It would seem that the 'concertation' concerning religion, which he speaks of as ordinarily taking place after his sermons, was not a simple answering of questions and objections on his own part, but that he and his companions carried the war into the country of the enemy by asking of their opponents explanations of recognized facts, such as the existence of the world, and the like, and that they were glad also to ascertain from others the common answers given by the bonzes and learned men on such matters. The records of the College of Coimbra contain a very long paper, which professes to be a translation in Portuguese of an account given to Francis Xavier by Joam Fernandez of the questions discussed between Cosmo Torres and himself on the one hand, and a number of Japanese interrogators on the other, after Francis himself had left Amanguchi. The questions turn on all sorts of points,—the nature of God, creation, the difference between men and beasts, the nature and immortality of the soul, the devils and angels, the way of sanctity, what happens after death, hell, Paradise, and the like. Joam himself was the 'chief speaker' on these occasions, as he had learnt the language faster than Father Cosmo, and he most faithfully recounts the various objections and difficulties, ending by commending himself through Francis to the prayers of all the good brethren and fathers at Malacca and Goa, in the hope that they would soon come out and take up the controversy themselves.

Francis mentions in his subsequent letters the difficulty which had most weight upon the minds of his first converts at Amanguchi—the objection, namely, that, if no one could be saved without the observance of the law of God, it appeared strange that so good a God should have deferred till that time the publication of His law in Japan. Francis tells us first, in general, that he answered the difficulty so as to remove all scruple from their minds; and, a little later in the same letter, he mentions how he had shown them that God never left men without His law written in their hearts, or the witness of their consciences, and that thus salvation was possible for them; as also, that if they were lost, it would have been by their own fault. The whole range of the controversy, as far as we can gather it, or imagine it with any certainty, is most interesting; and Francis Xavier was thus, in fact, called upon to make his 'Apology for Christianity' as the earlier fathers had been called on to make the same to the heathen philosophers and emperors before whom they pleaded. In doing this he began a work which in China and India, as well as in other countries, was taken up by members of the Society in subsequent years, and which will only be duly appreciated and recognized when, if ever, the good Providence of God may reward the many labours spent and the many lives laid down in those countries for the sake of the Gospel by making those magnificent regions of Eastern Asia the homes of great and flourishing Churches of Jesus Christ.

We could hardly expect not to find these busy prosperous months of preaching at Amanguchi illustrated by the miracles which so constantly accompanied the apostolic labours of Francis Xavier. The two Japanese converts already mentioned gave their testimony that he had healed many sick persons by the sign of the Cross or by holy water. Other prodigies are recorded. The most conspicuous prodigy of this time, however, was, in general, the holy mortified lives of the ambassadors of Christ, and in particular the meekness of Joam Fernandez, who, when a man approached him one day as he was preaching as if to whisper something into his ear, and then spat in his face, gently wiped away the spittle with his handkerchief, and went on with his sermon. It is said that this instance of humility and serenity brought about the most remarkable conversion of the time, that of a young doctor of great reputation for learning, who was about to enter among the bonzes. He was baptized by Francis Xavier, taking the name of Laurence, and was soon afterwards received into the Society. His name became famous in the annals of the infant Church of Japan.

CHAPTER III.

The King of Boungo.

THE letter of Francis Xavier to the Society at Goa which was last inserted does not speak of any intention on his part of returning to India. It is, however, likely that as soon as he found the serious nature of the intellectual work before the missioners who were to attempt the conversion of Japan, he became aware of the necessity of selecting carefully the men to whom the task was to be committed. Japan was by far the most promising as well as the most arduous field of labour which he had as yet met with; and Francis Xavier was not a man who would spare any pains to meet all the difficult requirements of the work before him. Freed from many of the drawbacks which shackled the ministrations of the missioners in India, he found himself in presence of a nation of reasoners dominated, as to religious matters, by a strong and organized hierarchy of bonzes, in high credit with the people on account of their supposed learning, of the prestige of centuries, of the immense influence which the popular superstitions gave them, and of the external sanctity of their lives, though this last element of their reputation was not free from flaw and suspicion. Such a race of men were sure to bring very great power into the field against Christianity, which would destroy the sources of their wealth and influence by the same blow which shattered their fabulous creed. He had relied hitherto, as we have seen from his letters, on the men whom he had left behind him in India, or whom he had sent to the Moluccas, to be the future missioners of Japan. But after his experience at Cagoxima, Firando, and Amanguchi, he felt that he must seek for greater learning, greater readiness in theological disputation, if not for greater sanctity and selfdevotion, than he had as yet at his command in the men who were to continue his work; and on this account it is by no means improbable that he would have returned to India to seek such among the fathers who must have arrived from Portugal during his absence, even if there had been no imperative reason for the westward voyage in the circumstances of the Society over which he was bound to watch. It is certain that after he had been two years in Japan, he began to think it necessary once more to turn his eyes towards Malacca and Goa.

Religion had now made very considerable advances in Amanguchi. Francis was very cautious in admitting converts until they had been well instructed and proved, and yet we find, either at the date of which we are speaking or a little later, the Christians in the city numbering as many as three thousand souls. The bonzes lost their young disciples in troops, and the instruction given to the converts was so solid and at the same time so intelligible, that laymen and even women were found able to meet the ministers of their former religion in argument, and easily confute their sophistries and fables. On the other hand, whenever, to regain their credit, they attempted to meet Francis himself on the ground of argument, they found themselves confounded, silenced, and made ridiculous. They betook themselves, therefore, to endeavours to influence the King or Prince of Naugato by the fear of the calamities with which the just anger of the native gods of Japan would be sure to visit him and his states if the new religion were any longer tolerated. Oxindono could not revoke his edicts: he had accepted Francis as an envoy bearing presents from the Governor of India, and it is probable that he would have feared alienating the Portuguese merchants, to conciliate whom seems to have been generally an object among the petty kings of Japan at this time. But he secretly persecuted the converts, confiscating their goods, and the like—a measure, however, which only increased their fervour; and Francis Xavier was able to bear them witness that there was no one of them who was not ready to lose all that he had, and even his life itself, for the sake of his faith. This spirit of martyrdom was characteristic of the Japanese Christians from the very beginning; and it testifies to the thorough instruction given to them by the missioners, as well as to the influence of the apostolic sanctity and greatness of soul which were conspicuous in their first great teacher. Meanwhile the bonzes of Amanguchi were serving the cause of the Gospel in another way—by spreading over the country a number of libellous charges against the new preachers and their doctrine, and thereby turning the public attention forcibly upon them.

It must have been about the end of August 1551 that Francis learnt that a Portuguese ship was staying at Figi, the port of Fucheo, capital of the kingdom of Boungo, of which incidental mention has already been made. The kingdom of Boungo lies on the northeastern coast of the large island of Ximo or, as it is called in modern maps, Kiou Siou,—the same part of the Japanese group in which Satsouma and its capital Caxogima are placed. The King himself appears to have sent to inform Francis of the arrival of the Europeans and to beg him to visit him. Mendez Pinto, who was one of the Portuguese merchants belonging to the ship, reckons the distance from Figi to the point of Kiou Siou opposite to Simonoseki as about sixty leagues. The captain of the party, Duarte (Edward) Gama, was charged with some letters to Francis, from which he could learn how much his presence was required in India. As soon as Francis Xavier heard of their arrival, he sent a Christian convert to them with the following letter:

(LXXXV.) *To the Merchants at the Port of Figi.*

The direction of this letter will not, as is usual, bear the names of you to whom it is addressed, and you will be the less surprised at this when you learn, what is the truth, that the very reason why I write is to know your names. I pray you to be so kind as to tell me who you are? what is the name of the ship which has brought you hither? did you leave everything at peace and quiet at Malacca when you set sail? I beg of you to be so good as to write us a short answer informing us of these things. Meanwhile, I beseech you not to take it amiss if I suggest to you to steal a little spare time from the occupation of your business in order to spend it upon the examination of your consciences. Believe me, that, after all, is the one merchandize by far the most profitable of all merchandizes, and the profit which comes from it comes very much quicker, and is much more abundant, than that which is the fruit of the exchange of the wares of Europe with the skins or silks of China, although it be true that the profit of that lastnamed trade is cent per cent, as much as the capital itself. I was thinking, if it so pleased God, of making an excursion hence to salute you, as soon as I receive your answer. May our Lord God in His immense clemency keep us all with His divine Hand ever over us, and preserve us, by His grace, in this life, constant and firm in the service of His Supreme Majesty! Amen.

Your brother in Christ,

Amanguchi, Sept. 1, 1551. FRANCIS.[1]

[1] Mendez Pinto, who gives a narration of all that passed while he belonged to the party of merchants at Figi, as well as during the subsequent voyage of Francis Xavier, quotes the letter rather differently from the text that we have followed, which was found at Macao by Father Philippucci. The latter part of the letter is much the same in both versions, and it is quite possible that Mendez Pinto's copy may be correct, the beginning of the original having been perhaps torn off as a relic before the time of Father Philippucci's visit. Mendez Pinto gives it as follows:

'May the love and grace of Jesus Christ, our true God and Saviour, dwell always in your hearts, through His holy mercy! Amen.

'By some letters of advice which the merchants of this city have received, they have been informed of your happy arrival in this country. But inasmuch as the news has not seemed to me so true as I desire in my soul that it may be, I have thought well to assure myself thereof truly by means of the Christian whom I send to you. Wherefore I pray you very urgently to let me know by him whence you at present come, also from what port you have set sail, and at what time you reckon upon returning to China, for I would much wish, if such were the good pleasure of God, to endeavour as far as is possible to me to pass this year from hence to India. You will also oblige me greatly if it please you to let me know your names and that of your ship by the same means, and also of the captain who commands it, giving me also certain tidings whether all is in peace and tranquillity at Malacca.' [Then follows the exhortation to devote some time to the regulation of their conscience.] *Voyages de Mendez Pinto*, t. iii. c. 208.

This letter of Francis Xavier caused great joy to the Portuguese. Such was his reputation all over the East, so much in particular had his open affable charity endeared him to the seafaring class, among whom much of his time was necessarily spent, that we are told that his arrival anywhere was welcomed joyously by merchants and sailors, who always showed him special marks of reverence and love. The merchants immediately sent him news from India and Malacca—probably the letters which had been confided to them by Francesco Perez—and informed him that they were to sail in about a month for China; that there were three on board who were bound for Goa at the beginning of the next year, and that one of their company was Diego Pereira, his own intimate friend. Francis immediately set out with three Japanese Christians, one of whom, it appears, was the young doctor, Laurence, having first summoned Father Cosmo Torres to join Joam Fernandez in charge of the Christians of Amanguchi. After journeying on foot to within a few miles of Figi, he fell ill, his feet were swollen, and he had a violent headache; so he sent on the Japanese to inform the merchants of his approach. The Portuguese at once set out to meet him, riding themselves and leading a horse for him to mount if he would. 'Having set out,' says Mendez Pinto, 'we had hardly gone a little more than a quarter of a league when we met him coming in the company of two Christians, whom within a month he had converted to the faith, men of the highest quality in the kingdom. For this reason the King of Amanguchi, availing himself of their conversion as of a specious pretext, had confiscated the income they had of two thousand taels, which are worth three thousand ducats. Now, inasmuch as we were all in our holiday dress, and mounted on good horses, we were quite struck with confusion to meet him in so sorry a plight; for besides that he was on foot, he carried on his shoulders a bundle in which were all the things necessary for saying mass. It is true that the two Christians who followed him relieved him from time to time, and helped him to carry this burthen. To say the truth, the thing astonished us and saddened us much. But because he would never accept any of our horses, we were obliged to accompany him on foot, although it was against his will; and this served for a great example to the two new converts. When we arrived at the river of Figi, where the ship was at anchor, he was received with all the show of joy that it was possible for us to offer him, insomuch that all the artillery was fired off four several times, consisting of sixty-three "berches," falconnets, and other pieces, so that the noise was very great, on account of the hollow rocks which were thereabout. But the king, who at that time was at the city, astonished at so extraordinary a thing and at hearing us fire in this way, imagined that we were fighting some squadrons of corsairs which were reported in the city to be upon the coasts, and sent at once in great haste a man of quality to ask us what it was. He addressed himself to Duarte de Gama, and gave him the king's message, with some offer of aid agreeable to the occasion. But the captain answered him, in words full of courtesy, thanking him kindly for his offers, that we were rejoicing at the arrival of Father Francis, because he was a holy man, for whom the King of Portugal, our master, had great respect. The gentleman was no less astonished at what he heard than at what he saw. "I must confess to you," he said to Duarte de Gama, "that I shall go back in great confusion, and not knowing what answer to give to my king; for our bonzes have assured him that this man of whom you speak to me is not a saint, as you say, but that it is certainly true that they have sometimes seen him talking to the devil, with whom he has a secret understanding; and that for the rest, he does by witchcraft some marvellous things, whereat ignorant persons are astonished; and that he is so miserable and so poor, that the very vermin with which he is covered have pity on him, and will not eat his flesh. So that I have considerable fear that they will lose all the credit which they have with the king when he knows the contrary of what they say, and that he will never more see them or listen to them; for it seems most likely indeed that a man whom you prize so much, and whom you receive with so much rejoicing and honour, is in truth such a one as you say, and not such as the bonzes have pictured him to the king." '

The messenger returned to the King of Boungo, who immediately sent a young noble of his own family with a letter to the 'father bonze of Chimahicogim'—the Japanese name for Portugal—begging him to come and see him. Mendez Pinto gives the letter in full, and there is no reason for supposing that his version is not, in the main, authentic. The young noble who bore it came down the river in a sort of state barge, well attended, and was received with a salute of fifteen cannon, which pleased him greatly. It was determined that Francis should proceed to Fucheo, up the river, on the morrow. The Portuguese captain and his friends insisted on being allowed to escort him with every possible mark of honour; and although Francis resisted out of humility, he had to give way, probably thinking that it was important for the interests of religion that an impression should be made on the King and on his subjects.[2]

The description of the progress of Francis Xavier to make his visit to the King of Boungo is a perfectly characteristic bit of Mendez Pinto's narrative, and illustrates also that love of display which was as inherent in the character of the Portuguese as was loyalty to their King and to their faith. Every one, says Mendez, did his best on the occasion. 'We embarked in the shallop of the ship, and in two pinnaces (manchuas), which had their standards and their banners of silk, on board which also there were trumpets and hautboys, which sounded alternately—a novelty which seemed so great to the people of the country, and astonished them so much, that when we arrived at the quay, we had a difficulty in landing, for the great number of people who had crowded together there. There met us the Quamsyandono, Captain of Canafama, and by the express order of the King he had a litter with him in which he wished to place the Father. But he would not accept of it on account of his respect for us, and walked straight to the palace accompanied by a number of nobles and thirty of us Portuguese. There were also our servants, in number as many as ourselves,

[2] Mendez Pinto, t. iii. c. 209-213 (for all related in this chapter).

all finely dressed, and having gold chains round their necks. Father Francis had a full cassock of black camlet, a surplice over it, and a stole of green velvet brocaded with gold. In his suite walked our captain with a baton in his hand, as major-duomo, and there followed him five of the most honourable and richest of the merchants, who, as if they had been the Father's servants, carried with much ceremony certain things in their hands, as for example, one carried a book in a cover of white satin' (this book was the translation of the 'Catechetical Instruction'), 'another some slippers of black velvet which we happened to have with us, another a Bengal cane with a gold enchasing, another a picture of our Blessed Lady wrapped in a scarf of violet damask, and another a parasol to be held over a person when walking; and in this order and array we passed through the nine principal streets of the city, where there was so great a crowd that every place was full of people to the very roofs of the houses.'

Mendez goes on to relate how, when they arrived at the court of the palace, they found a hundred men drawn up, armed with darts and lances and scimitars richly adorned. They next came to a long gallery, and here the merchants knelt before the Father, and each presented to him the article which he had been carrying, filling the Japanese nobles who were looking on with admiration at the dignity and majesty of the person to whom they thus paid homage. Then they came to a great hall in which were a number of gentlemen clothed in satin and damask of divers colours, with short swords covered with plates of gold. Here a child of between six and seven years of age, led by an old man, approached the Father, and made him a little speech, praying that his arrival at the King's palace might be as pleasant to both of them as the rain which God sends from heaven when the ricefields suffer from drought. Some sentences of this kind passed between Francis and the child, who seemed to speak with an intelligence far beyond his years, and then they went on through another chamber, where a number of 'lords of the kingdom rose up to make their *gromenares* to the Father, as they call their compliments,' putting their heads thrice to the ground; then through another long gallery, bordered by orange trees, to another hall where the King's brother received the visitors; and at last, after an almost endless series of rooms, they arrived in the presence chamber of the King, who advanced five or six steps to meet Francis, would not let him kneel to him, but, on the contrary, paid to him himself the respectful salutation of the *gromenare*.

We must, however, forbear from giving the full narrative of this remarkable interview. The King received Francis with the utmost respect, made him sit by his own side, and provoked a bonze who was present to rebuke him severely and to break out into a long and passionate eulogium on his own order. The King at last lost patience, and ordered him out of the room. The bonze departed, calling down the anger of heaven upon such kings. Then the King made Francis Xavier sit at the same table with himself, and also entertained the Portuguese visitors. Francis knelt to kiss his scimitar, a sign of great respect in Japan, and prayed that the God of heaven might reward him for his goodness by giving him His own grace, that he might make profession of His holy law as His true servant, and come after death to enjoy His presence eternally. The interview ended with great expressions of amity on both sides.

This Civan, King of Boungo, whose name meets us continually in the early annals of the Church of Japan, was a young man of about twenty-two years of age, brave, intelligent, and just. His reputation was very high among the princes of Japan. His life was stained by some great impurities, of that abominable kind which was so prevalent in his country. Except this great blot, his character was untarnished. He is said, a few years before this time, to have interfered with his father in favour of some Portuguese merchants, whose ship with her rich cargo the King was advised by some of his counsellors to seize. Civan defended the strangers out of compassion and a natural love of justice. They found out their danger after it was over, and also discovered to whom they had owed their safety. Some of them conversed with the young prince about the Christian religion. He had also heard of Francis Xavier, at the time of his preaching at Amanguchi, and was well disposed to receive him for his own sake, and not alone on motives of policy.[3]

This interview between Civan and Francis Xavier removed all difficulty as to the public preaching of Christianity in the kingdom of Boungo. Francis began immediately, and his efforts were eminently successful. Converts came to him daily. A great sensation was produced by the conversion of a certain Saqay Gyran, a learned bonze of Canafama, who, after disputing a good deal in public with Francis, gave way one day in the presence of a large audience, and made a public profession of his faith in Jesus Christ. Francis was so continually occupied with the Japanese that the Portuguese complained. They could only see him late at night and in the early morning, when he was at their service to hear their confessions. He told them, however, that they must never wait for him at meal times, as the food in which he delighted was to be occupied in restoring souls to their Redeemer. He was still very cautious in admitting new converts to baptism until he had fully instructed them, and he kept many waiting rather than expose them too soon to the trials which were sure to fall upon them. He had long conferences with Civan, and though he did not succeed in making him a Christian, he prepared him for conversion by inducing him to amend his life. The prince dismissed one who was the object of an impure attachment to him. He had before been niggardly in dealing with the poor, on account of the false teaching of the bonzes, who held that poverty was a sin; he now became a great almsgiver, and he even issued an edict against the prevalent custom which shocked so much the tender heart of Francis, by which infants were frequently put to death

[3] Charlevoix, *Hist. du Japon*, l. i. § 8, p. 213, says that this prince was the same mentioned by Fernand Mendez Pinto in the passage already referred to (see *ante*, p. 103) as having met with a severe accident when trying to fire off an arquebuse. The age there mentioned would certainly suit Civan; but the prince is named by Mendez Pinto as Arichandono, and is said to have been the second son of the King of Boungo. If he were the same as Civan, it seems strange that Mendez Pinto should not say so, as he might himself have been recognized and welcomed by the prince.

either in their mothers' womb or as soon as they were born. The bonzes were furious, and decried and calumniated Francis Xavier to the utmost of their power; but to no effect, on account of the cordial support afforded to him by Civan.

Meanwhile, a sudden and terrible danger threatened Father Cosmo Torres and his companion Joam Fernandez at Amanguchi. After the departure of Francis, as we learn from a letter written to him by Joam, the Japanese bonzes and others, who had learnt to be afraid of the powerful words with which he had been wont to silence their objections, thronged around Father Cosmo, hoping to find him less of a master in argument. We have already mentioned the long list of questions which Joam faithfully transmitted to Francis Xavier. The bonzes of Amanguchi are said to have been so confounded with their ill success in argument with Joam and Father Cosmo, and their inability also to move Oxindono to take any active steps against the missioners, that they incited a sudden revolt against the prince on the part of one of his great lords, which took him by complete surprise. Whether the bonzes were at the bottom of the movement or not, Oxindono lost heart, and perhaps over estimated the danger. He acted like a true Japanese: he shut himself up in his palace, had it set on fire, stabbed his son with his own hand, and then cut himself open. The confusion which followed was a perilous time for the new Christians and still more so for their teachers, but it seems to have been soon over. There was a short interval of plunder and massacre, but no Christians suffered. The missioners were sought for, but they were safe. The wife of a chief noble forced some bonzes, who depended upon her gifts, to receive the two strangers for a time; and then, for still greater security, she concealed them in her own palace.[4] The storm soon passed away, and when order was restored the nobles of the kingdom of Naugato met to elect a new sovereign, and fixed upon the brother of the King of Boungo, who was already predisposed to favour the Christians. It must have been about this time that Francis deter-

[4] This lady was the wife of Nectandono, and is mentioned, with her husband, in the letter of Francis to Europe (below, p. 341).

mined to build a small church for the use of the Christians at Amanguchi. He borrowed the necessary money from the Portuguese merchants at Fucheo.

The time was now approaching when the Portuguese ship must sail for the coast of China, whither the captain was bound to convey the merchants who had embarked in his vessel. Francis went to take leave of the king, and had a long and earnest conversation with him on the topics which had been discussed between them in their frequent conferences. He spoke particularly of the uncertainty and shortness of life; he bade him think of the handful of dust and ashes which was now all that remained of so many great kings and emperors of whom the history of Japan told him, and urged him, before it was too late, to provide for his own soul. His words were not to bear their fruit for many years. Civan was withheld by considerations of policy and prudence, perhaps also by the fascination of passion not altogether put away. Francis Xavier was on the point of leaving him, when an attendant announced that the famous bonze Fucarandono was outside desiring to speak with his Highness. Fucarandono was one of the great lights of the country: he had attained a grade in the hierarchical system of the Buddhists which but few reached, and had been for thirty years a teacher in one of their most renowned seats of learning. He was then the superior of a monastery called Mias Gimaa, some few leagues from Fucheo, and had been requested by his brethren at that place to come and help them in their contest with the European teacher. The name of Fucarandono appeared to disconcert the king, who was afraid, from his very great reputation, that he might prove too difficult an adversary even for Francis. Francis begged that he might be asked to come in, and Fucarandono entered.

The accounts of the various conferences and disputes between Francis Xavier and this famous bonze, which are given at considerable length by many of the biographers of the former, appear to be originally derived from the narrative of Mendez Pinto, from which we have already quoted. As Mendez was very unlikely to invent arguments of the kind, and as he candidly confesses that he does not always remember the answers given by the Father to the objections and questions urged upon him, we may feel more secure in accepting his statements than if they had come to us from the pen of some theological writer of the sixteenth or seventeenth centuries, in which it was not considered unlawful even for historians to follow the example of writers such as Thucydides, Livy, or Tacitus, and put speeches of their own into the mouths of the persons concerned in some actual scene. Mendez, like many travellers in regions unknown to the men of their own day, was once thought a great romancer, but the verdict of modern criticism is more favourable to him than that of some of his own contemporaries. But if he has ever yielded to the temptation of telling 'travellers' tales' in his most amusing book, it has been on subjects very different in character from that of these conferences at which he was present; and we may fairly accept his narrative as giving us a most interesting insight into the sort of points as to which the controversy was waged, in which moreover he is entirely consistent with Francis Xavier's own statements.

After the first compliments, which were ceremoniously paid on both sides, the King asked the bonze why he had come. Fucarandono replied that he had come to see and take leave of the Father of Chenchico[5] before he left. He then asked Francis, says Mendez, whether he remembered him? 'Certainly not, for I have never seen you before,' said the Father. It seems to have been a part of the doctrine concerning the transmigration of souls held by these bonzes that it was a reward of virtue to remember what had passed in a former stage of existence, and a mark of weakness or wickedness to forget it. This was probably the reason why Fucarandono began on this point. He then asked Francis whether he had any more of the stuff which he had sold him at Frenojama fifteen hundred years ago, when he had sold him fifty 'picos' of silk? Francis asked

[5] Here again we have the name Chenchico, which has given us much trouble on account of Francis Xavier's statement about the University of 'Jenico' or Chinghinquo (see *ante*, p. 75), from which the religions of China, Tartary, and Japan were derived. We are inclined to conjecture that the word must simply be a name for the 'West.'

him quietly how old he was? Fucarandono replied that he was fifty-two. 'How then is it possible that fifteen hundred years ago you were a merchant, and that I sold merchandize to you? And if it is true what you bonzes preach publicly, that Japan was only peopled six hundred years ago, how can you have traded at Frenojama fifteen hundred years ago, since you would have us believe that at that time the country was a desert?'

The bonze, rather disconcerted, went on to lay down his doctrine about the eternity of the world, the endless number of lives through which all human souls pass, and the like, as well as on the blessing of a good memory. All this the Father, says Mendez Pinto, refuted thrice over with words so clear, reasons so evident, and comparisons so apt and natural, that the bonze was struck with confusion, 'of which reasons,' he adds, 'I shall not speak here in order to avoid prolixity, and much more because I avow that my wit is not capable of understanding them.' Fucarandono then went on with the general subject, and afterwards asked Francis Xavier why he forbade the unnatural lusts so common in Japan. Here again Mendez tells us that the Father reasoned so clearly and so forcibly as to carry with him the approval of those who were present, whereupon the bonze became furious, and broke out into outrageous language. The bystanders interfered, and the prince himself—whose dinner time had arrived—told him abruptly to leave the room, and that if he had not been a bonze he would have had his head cut off.

This dismissal of Fucarandono, however, entailed grave consequences, which enable us to understand more completely the position of the King towards the bonzes, and the danger to which even he was exposed in favouring the Christian teachers. The bonzes broke out into open hostility to the Court, and if they had been able to find, as at Amanguchi, one or more powerful lords to take up their quarrel, the danger which Cosmo de Torres and Joam Fernandez had incurred would have been repeated in the case of Francis Xavier. As it was, the bonzes put Fucheo under a sort of interdict. They shut up their temples, refused to offer any sacrifices for the people, and even declined alms, as if heaven was irrevocably offended by the toleration of the new preaching. The people began to move, and the King was obliged to act with great prudence. The Portuguese, brave as they naturally were, took the alarm, and all went on board their ship. It must be remembered that their departure was already fixed upon; still, there can be no doubt that they thought themselves and Francis in great danger. He had retired to a poor hut with a few native Christians, and was there quietly waiting the issue of the affair. Duarte de Gama, the captain, went to find him and urge him at once to take refuge on board the vessel. We have seen more than once how Francis had spoken of the blessedness of dying for the faith and the name of Jesus Christ; how it had been remarked of him that he seemed always to have martyrdom in his heart and on his lips. The moment of which we are speaking was perhaps that moment in his life at which he seemed to be nearer to the fulfilment of his desire than at any other. He told the captain that he knew that he was unworthy of the great favour of being put to death for such a cause. He begged him to excuse him to the merchants on whose part he came, that for the present he could not follow their advice, as by so doing he should give great scandal to the new converts to the faith, and give them a very bad example, by which the devil and his adherents would profit. He begged Duarte, therefore, to set sail in all freedom in order to discharge his engagements to his passengers; but for himself he was obliged to do otherwise out of regard to his merciful God, Who in order to save him had Himself died upon a cross.

There was no resisting the appeal implied in these words. The captain went back to the ship, and offered to make it over with all its cargo to the passengers in quittance of his engagement; they might take it and go—he would remain with the Father, and never abandon him. His resolution was contagious. The merchants all resolved to wait, whatever happened. The ship, which had left her moorings in preparation for sailing, returned to her former place, and the Christians were as much encouraged as the bonzes were mortified at seeing the readiness with which rich men of the world like the merchants were willing to risk their property and lives in the service of Francis Xavier.

The decision of the Portuguese merchants had a great effect on the enemies of Christianity. The tumult caused by the bonzes seems to have subsided as rapidly as it had arisen, and they themselves were driven to new measures, more in accordance with reason and right in their opposition to Francis. It is to this that we owe the account of one of the most curious scenes in his life, the details of which are, however, very imperfectly given to us by the friendly chronicler, Mendez Pinto. The biographers of Francis, and the historian of the Church of Japan, have endeavoured to fill up the gaps in the narrative of the Portuguese adventurer, and something may be gathered from the statements made by Francis himself in his letters to Europe. Except, however, this last source of information, the accounts given by Bartoli, Charlevoix, and others, of the conferences of which we are about to speak, must be considered rather as representing what probably took place than what is certainly recorded.

The conferences in question were the result of a renewed attempt on the part of the bonzes to silence and confute the Christian preacher. That they should have adopted this policy may be taken as an evidence of the truth of what Francis Xavier so often asserted about the Japanese, both as to their extraordinary love of discussion and as to their general readiness to bend to the decision of reason. We have no cause for supposing that there were not among the bonzes, as among the rest of the Japanese, many who were sincerely in search of truth, and eagerly desirous to submit to it at any cost to themselves, though they had a more direct interest than any other class in the population in the maintenance of the national religion, and perhaps also, as Francis Xavier says, were frequently more impure in their lives than those whom they taught. Their influence over the people was undoubtedly very great, while at the same time the whole conduct of the King of Boungo and his lords seems to show that the aristocracy were ready enough to see them turned to ridicule and reduced to silence, and were not afraid to act violently against them. But in any parallel case, as in theirs, we should probably find more reasonableness and goodness of intention than we might at first sight suspect. From whatever motive, however, the bonzes had proposed that the dispute between their great champion Fucarandono and Francis Xavier should be renewed. The King at once assented, and as the Portuguese ship could not delay long, the conference began immediately.

On the first day, to all appearance, some attempt was made to intimidate the King, or at least his foreign guests. Fucarandono appeared at the palace gates escorted by three thousand bonzes, all of whom desired to be present at the disputation. The King, however, refused admittance to all but four with Fucarandono himself. Francis came at the same time, escorted by the Portuguese merchants and their captain, who had resolved to show him, if possible, still more honour on this occasion than when they had accompanied him on his first visit of ceremony to the palace. They were gorgeously dressed with chains of gold, and they waited on him as his servants, kneeling to him when he spoke to them, and carrying in their hands their caps garnished with pearls. The bonzes, says Mendez, were filled alike with displeasure and astonishment. Certain rules of the discussions had been agreed upon at the request of Francis, in order that they might not degenerate into mere conversation, or be interrupted by violence and outrageous language. These rules were, that they should speak with moderation and without abusive language; that the disputants should accept the decision of the bystanders as to what was reasonable; that at the end of the disputation judgment should be given by a majority of voices; that the bonzes should not directly nor indirectly hinder those who wished to become Christians; that when a contradiction arose in the argument, appointed judges should decide upon it; and lastly, that what was proved by actual reason and accepted by the common judgment of men should be acknowledged as true.

The disputes lasted five days, and we have, as has been said, but very imperfect reports of what took place, especially of the answers and arguments alleged by Francis Xavier himself. It is, however, not difficult to gather a general idea of the line which the controversy took. The first disputation was opened by Fucarandono in a tone less haughty and more gentle than that which he had before used. The King had asked the general question, Why the bonzes objected to the preaching of the new law? Fucarandono stated the objections very naturally. The new law was altogether contrary to theirs, and tended to the discredit of the service of the old gods of the country; the precepts of the foreign teacher condemned things which had always been permitted by their old Cubocamas; he gave out publicly everywhere that the salvation of men was only to be found in the doctrine which he himself preached; and that the 'holy Fatoquins, Xaca, Amida, Gizon, and Canom, were enduring perpetual torments in a profound pit in the house of smoke, handed over by the justice of God to the old serpent of the abode of night.' Francis desired that the objections to his teaching might be put one by one, so that he might answer them in the same way. This was agreed to, and Fucarandono asked him 'Why he spoke against the gods?'

Mendez Pinto sums up the answer given by Francis in a few lines, and then tells us that all who heard him, except the bonzes themselves, were so convinced of the reasonableness of what he said, that Fucarandono was not allowed even to reply upon his answer. We can only gather from this that Francis Xavier enlarged upon the nature and attributes of God as they may be known, according to the doctrine of Scripture, from the visible creation, and from our experience of providence and conscience; that from this he went on to argue that these attributes could only belong to one Supreme Author and Creator of all things, and that therefore Xaca, Amida, and the rest could not have any right to the divine character. The controversy, as so often happens, was then turned to a very different subject, though one which, no doubt, was of great practical importance to the bonzes who were arguing against Christianity. They were in the habit of giving 'letters of credit' on heaven, by means of which, for the payment of a certain sum of money, the mourning relatives of deceased persons enriched in the next world those whom they had lost in proportion to their offerings. Francis was asked why he objected to these 'cochumiacos,' as Mendez calls them. The question obviously opened the whole subject of heavenly rewards and of the means by which they are gained; and Mendez tells us that Francis Xavier spoke of good works wrought in faith and charity, of the Incarnation and Passion of our Lord, of redemption through His death, of baptism and perseverance; and also that he turned his argument against portions of the doctrine of the bonzes, the unreasonableness of which might easily be understood by any one, such as their denying salvation to women, their condemning all the poor to reprobation, and the evident worldly interest which they had in keeping up such a system as that of their letters of credit. Here again Mendez tells us that the audience were altogether on the side of the Christian argument.

This seems to have been the last point discussed during the first of these solemn disputations, over which the King himself presided, and at which a great crowd of nobles was always present. Of the following days we have even less of a detailed account in the narrative of Mendez Pinto. He tells us that some of the things which they put to Francis Xavier were very subtle and high, such as the human mind could not have imagined, while others were childish and easy things which any one could have answered. Sometimes they related to the most important subjects, and at others to the most trivial. He mentions a few as specimens, and they are very interesting to us. Before going to the disputation Francis used to beg the prayers of the Portuguese, both, as he said, on account of the weakness of his own mind, and also because the devil spoke by the mouth of these enemies of the law of God. Mendez mentions the following difficulties. The first was the resumption of a point which had been touched on before, the doctrine of the bonzes concerning poverty. 'God was the enemy of the poor,' they said, 'since He refused to them the good things which He gave to the rich. This was an evident mark that He did not love them.' This it was not difficult for Francis to refute, and the Portuguese reporter tells us that the bonze who argued this point was obliged to acknowledge his defeat. Another took his place with an ingenious piece of frivolity, which perhaps appeared to his companions as a miracle of cleverness. 'The Father,' he said, 'had certainly come a great distance to teach the Japanese; but to what profit if his doctrine were false? There are, according to what he tells us, two Paradises,—one in heaven, one on earth, and one only can be enjoyed by any one. Now, Paradise is not the place of labour, but the place of repose. But man evidently has his Paradise here on earth. Kings, princes, great men, rich men, all rest in the enjoyment of their dignities, their wealth, their power; even the poor have their natural enjoyments. The creatures whose lot it is here to labour are the poor animals, beasts of burthen, and the like; their life is passed in toil and affliction, and the Paradise of the next world must be for them, and not for men, who are so prone to sin.'

This was intended, it would seem, to be an absurd conclusion deduced from what Francis Xavier taught about the blessings of the next world being the reward of sufferings endured here. Another objection of the bonzes was meant to meet his doctrine about the creation of all things by God—a doctrine entirely new to the Japanese—and the consequent dependence of everything upon Him. If God was to be so much honoured and thanked for having created all things, as the Father said, then Amida must have still greater honour for having preserved them. For they might have been good at the beginning, but they soon became degenerate and corrupt through sin, so that all would have fallen to nothing, but that Amida was born of them. They said, says Mendez Pinto, that Amida was born eight hundred times, in order to give perfection of being to the eight hundred species of things which exist in the world. This statement looks like a mistake on the part of Mendez. It was Buddha, and not Amida, who was said to have been eighty thousand times born, in order to give substance and perfection to the eighty thousand species of the world. This argument appears to have produced a quarrel among the bonzes themselves, who, as Mendez tells us, were on the point of coming to blows in the presence of the King and the whole audience.

There is a family likeness about these objections, as well as a great air of probability. On the following day, the King came himself to invite Francis Xavier to the dispute, speaking of it as a kind of sport like hawking, and telling him that there were still two birds left for him to deal with. It would seem that the bonzes had prepared a long paper, full of objections of the same sort as those which have just been mentioned; but the King interfered, saying that the Portuguese could not be kept waiting from their homeward voyage for ever, and that the bonzes must cut the matter short. They then requested that they might simply ask Francis some very good things which they desired much to learn of him, and that there need be no disputation. Certainly the last conferences turned on more important and fundamental objections than those before urged—objections which will always be found in serious and thoughtful minds to whom the Christian doctrine of the universe is presented, if they have not some high and reverential ideas concerning the nature and attributes of God, and His position and rights with regard to His creatures and the government of the universe which He has made for His own glory.

The bonzes, says Mendez, came to the Father and begged him to forgive them the past, and then asked him their new questions. It astonished them, they said, if God foresaw things past as well as future, by reason of His infinite knowledge, how it was that He did not when creating the angels foresee the disorder which Lucifer and the rest would cause by their disobedience, so as to prevent the necessity of His divine justice having to condemn them to perpetual punishments. If He foresaw that, what could be the explanation why His divine mercy did not prevent an evil from which so many other evils would follow, so many offences against the Divine Majesty? But if to justify Him it is said that He did not see it, then what the Father taught concerning Him was false. Francis answered their difficulty, declaring to them 'very largely,' says the reporter, what was the truth in this matter; but they contradicted him with reasonings so subtle, that he turned to Duarte de Gama, who was by his side, and said, 'See! what these people say does not come from themselves, but from the devil who instructs them on this subject; nevertheless the confidence which I have in God makes me hope that He will answer for me.' The bonzes seem to have got hot upon the answers which Francis gave, as the King rebuked them for their violence, and told them to listen to reason, and not bark like so many dogs; at which the nobles present began to smile, much to the disgust of the Japanese disputants. Mendez relates next how Fucarandono went back after this to objections of a more frivolous character. He had heard Francis invoke God under the name *Dius* or *Deus*, and it seems that *diusa* in Japanese means a lie. In the same way the Japanese word *sancte* means something foul or profane. The objection was therefore urged on Francis that he called the Creator and Lord of all things a lie, and that in the Litanies of the Saints, which he used to recite with the Christians after mass, he called the Saints by a bad name. After hearing the explanation given by Francis, the King himself advised him to use another word, *Beate* instead of *Sancte.*

Later on the dispute went back to more serious and fundamental difficulties. The bonzes raised the question about God's foreknowledge of the sin of Adam and its consequences. Why did He not prevent it? Again, they objected to the great delay which had taken place in bringing about the healing of the sins of the world by means of the Incarnation. If God was to send His Son to redeem the descendants of Adam after his fall, why did He not show more diligence in succouring so extreme a need? And, they added, if it were replied that the delay was in order that men might learn the enormity and hideousness of sin, this was not enough to excuse God from a want of care and attention in waiting so long. All these difficulties, says Mendez, the Father answered with reasons so clear and pertinent that it was impossible to reply to him. The conference ended by the King rebuking the bonzes again for their want of reasonableness. The Christian law, he said, was founded upon reason, and those who opposed it ought not to be so unable to meet it upon that ground. He took the Father by the hand, and, followed by all his Court, led him to the house where he usually abode with the Christians around him, the bonzes threatening meanwhile the vengeance of Heaven upon a king who allowed himself to be so easily misled by a sorcerer and worthless adventurer.

This is what is actually known to have passed in their celebrated conferences. Several of the points raised in them are mentioned by Francis Xavier himself in the letter which we shall presently insert, though he seems to be speaking of the questionings addressed to him while at Amanguchi. The mixture of ingenious trifling with the serious difficulties which have been so often urged in every age and in every part of the world against the government of God in relation to His permission of evil, the delay of redemption, and the partial distribution of saving truth, is very remarkable and very characteristic. Mendez Pinto's narrative has every note of faithfulness and sincerity. The answers attributed to St. Francis Xavier by so many of his biographers do not rest on exactly the same authority as the questions of the bonzes as here given; but they are perfectly in harmony with his own statements, as well, of course, as with Catholic theology. Here, at the farthest end of the known world, he found the benefit of those long years of intellectual and theological training which he had spent in the University of Paris. The Japanese bonzes were intelligent and clever; but the force of their objections did not lie in the ability of those by whom they were urged. It lay partly in the nature of the subjects to which they referred, inasmuch as the plan of God in the government of His creatures is a scheme which human intelligence can never entirely comprehend, though faith and reason alike enable us to see that that scheme contains nothing that is unjust or unmerciful or in any way inconsistent with the character of God as He has revealed Himself to us. It lay partly also in the fact that the whole idea of God as a Creator, and, consequently, as absolute Lord over His creatures, who have no rights before Him except such as result from His own ineffable holiness and the essential conditions of the nature which He has given them, was an entirely new thought even to the wisest of the Japanese, as well as in the constant tendency of human nature in its present condition to exalt itself and make itself the centre and arbiter of the world. And whenever even Christian minds are untrained in true thoughts and reflections concerning the dominion and the nature of God, and in the practice of that humility which is the natural attitude of a creature in respect to its Creator, there will be a danger of their not seeing at once the answers to such difficulties as those now mentioned which are given by our Lord and His Apostles. More than this: after all has been said that Scripture and Catholic theology teach us to say with regard to the government and providence of God, there will always remain that inadequacy in our conceptions of both which leaves us much to adore without attempting fully to explain it, in that reverential spirit which made St. Paul exclaim after unravelling one great difficulty of this kind, the reprobation of the Jews: 'O the depth of the riches of the wisdom and of the knowledge of God! How incomprehensible are His judgments, and His ways how unsearchable!'[5]

Francis Xavier embarked with the Portuguese immediately after the close of these conferences. He first took an affectionate and solemn farewell of the King, exhorting him once more to think most seriously over the danger of delay in embracing the religion of the truth of which he appeared to be convinced. We know from the letters of Francis Xavier how he could rebuke the good King of Portugal, on whose support, humanly speaking, the whole of the Indian missions depended, and he would certainly not be likely to be less freespoken in the presence of the young King of Boungo. After his farewell, and a tender parting from the new Christians, Francis set sail on Nov. 20, 1551. He took with him the two Japanese Christians, Bernard and Matthias, who had already been for some time his companions, as well as an envoy from the King of Boungo to

[5] Rom. xi. 33.

the Governor of the Indies, asking for the Portuguese alliance, and for Fathers of the Society to teach Christianity to his people.

The following letter was not written till the January of the following year, after Francis had arrived in India. But it sums up so completely the history of his sojourn in Japan that it will be better to insert it here, rather than defer it till after the account of his homeward voyage.

(LXXXVI.) *To the Society in Europe.*

May the grace and charity of our Lord Jesus Christ be ever with us! Amen.

By the favour of God we all arrived at Japan in perfect health on the 15th of August 1549. We landed at Cagoxima, the native place of our companions. We were received in the most friendly way by all the people of the city, especially the relations of Paul, the Japanese convert, all of whom had the blessing to receive the light of truth from heaven, and by Paul's persuasion became Christians. During our stay at Cagoxima the people appeared to be wonderfully delighted with the doctrines of the divine law, so entirely new to their ears.

Japan is a very large empire entirely composed of islands. One language is spoken throughout, not very difficult to learn. This country was discovered by the Portuguese eight or nine years ago. The Japanese are very ambitious of honours and distinctions, and think themselves superior to all nations in military glory and valour. They prize and honour all that has to do with war, and all such things, and there is nothing of which they are so proud as of weapons adorned with gold and silver. They always wear swords and daggers both in and out of the house, and when they go to sleep they hang them at the bed's head. In short, they value arms more than any people I have ever seen. They are excellent archers, and usually fight on foot, though there is no lack of horses in the country. They are very polite to each other, but not to foreigners, whom they utterly despise. They spend their means on arms, bodily adornment, and on a number of attendants, and do not in the least care to save money. They are, in short, a very warlike people and engaged in continual wars among themselves; the most powerful in arms bearing the most extensive sway. They have all one sovereign, although for one hundred and fifty years past the princes have ceased to obey him, and this is the cause of their perpetual feuds.

In these countries there is a great number, both of men and of women, who profess a religious rule of life; they are called bonzes and bonzesses. There are two sorts of bonzes—the one wear a grey dress, the others a black one. There is great rivalry between them, the grey monks being set against the black ones, and accusing them of ignorance and bad morals. There are also two kinds of bonzesses—some wearing the grey dress, some the black; they are subject to the bonzes of their own rule and colour. The number of these bonzes and bonzesses in Japan is immense, and almost incredible to those who have not seen it for themselves. I have heard on testimony worthy of belief that there is a sovereign in whose dominions there are eight hundred convents containing thirty persons at least, bonzes or bonzesses; there is an infinite number containing four, or six, or eight persons each; and I am inclined to believe it, as far as my own observation goes. The system of the sects prevailing in Japan is derived from China, an empire which occupies the opposite continent. The Japanese have thence received written traditions concerning the founders of the different sects, who are said to have lived for two or even three thousand years in voluntary penances in complete solitude. The principal of these are Xaca and Amida.

There are altogether nine rules for both men and women, all differing in their laws and precepts; each one is free to apply himself to that which he likes best. Hence it follows that under the same roof the husband, wife, and children belong to different sects; and generally speaking this custom occasions no disorder, every one being at liberty to live according to his own persuasion. Nevertheless disputes and controversies often exist among them, each person endeavouring to prove his own rule superior to the others, and sometimes they have been known to come to blows on the subject.

All of these sects observe a wonderful silence about the creation of the world and of souls. They all speak of abodes of the virtuous and of the wicked; but not one gives any explanation of the nature of the place assigned to the good, nor by whose power it is that the souls of the wicked are cast down to hell. They confine themselves to holding up the example of the founders of the sects, who they say, for the redemption of an infinite number of human beings who do not expiate their sins by any suffering, have tormented themselves by unheard of severities, lasting for an immense length of time.

At the same time they assert that all persons who, without having done penance for their sins, have invoked the fathers and founders of their sects, will be exempt from all suffering; but that this is only the case when they invoke them with perfect confidence, and place all their trust in them. They are convinced that the intercession of these holy persons can actually snatch them out of hell. But the sects of which I speak tell numberless fables and prodigies concerning their founders, which are too long to relate. Some of them set forth 300, others 500 precepts; but they all agree in this, that there are five principal and essential precepts which it is indispensable to keep. The first is not to kill, and not to eat anything which has been killed; the second is not to steal; the third not to commit adultery; the fourth not to lie; the fifth to abstain from wine. These laws are common to all the sects. At the same time, the bonzes and the bonzesses, when preaching to the people about these laws, persuade them that profane persons, occupied with worldly business, are unable themselves to observe these five precepts; but that they themselves are ready to make satisfaction for all the evil or inconvenience which may happen to them in consequence of breaking them, on condition of the people giving them convents, yearly revenues, and money for all necessary uses: in short, of paying them every kind of honour and homage. These conditions being fulfilled by the people, they engage to observe the whole law in their stead. The rich and noble of the country therefore, in order to enjoy a greater licence of sinning, give the bonzes everything they want. Hence the Japanese hold them in great veneration, as every one believes that by their prayers souls are delivered from hell, the bonzes having taken upon themselves to make satisfaction as to these laws for the whole people.

On certain days the bonzes preach publicly. The sum of all their discourses is that none of the people will be condemned to hell, whatever may be the number of their past and present crimes, for the founders of their sects will take them out of the midst of those flames, if perchance they are condemned to them, especially if the bonzes who have made satisfaction for them constitute themselves their intercessors. And indeed the bonzes boast greatly to the people of their own holiness, on the ground of their obedience to the five laws. At the same time, they also say that the poor who are unable to show kindness to the bonzes have no hope of escaping hell. And they say women are as badly off if they neglect the five precepts. For they say that each woman, on account of her monthly courses, is covered with more sins than all men put together, and that thus so foul a creature can hardly be saved. They go on to say that there is some hope even for women of escaping from the prison of hell, if they give a great deal more than the men to the bonzes. They further declare that persons who in their lifetime have given money to the bonzes will after their death receive ten times as much in the same coin, for the necessities of their new life; and there are numbers of men and women who entrust considerable sums to the bonzes, in order to receive tenfold in the next world, and the bonzes give them a security in notes, which they write. The ignorant people have no hesitation in believing in this multiplied interest on funds thus invested. The notes of the bonzes are carefully preserved, and people about to die order them to be buried with them, in the belief that the devil will fly at sight of them. The bonzes have thousands of other impostures which I cannot speak of without pain. One thing is very amusing, that though they take money from everybody by way of alms, they themselves never give anything to any one. I omit, for the sake of brevity, the infinite number of ways they have of getting money given to them. But I cannot help grieving and feeling indignant at all the tribute the people pay to men like these, and all the honour in which they hold them.

But to return to what we did in Japan. In the first place, we landed, as I told you, at Cagoxima, Paul's native place, where by his constant instructions he converted all his family to Jesus Christ, and where, but for the opposition of the bonzes, he would easily have converted the whole town also. The bonzes persuaded the King, whose authority extends over a good part of the country, that if he was to sanction the introduction of the divine law into his dominions, the result would be infallibly the ruin, not only of his entire kingdom, but also of the worship of the gods and of the institutions of his ancestors; and that he ought for the future to forbid any one becoming a Christian, on pain of death.

After the lapse of a year, seeing this prince openly opposed to the progress of the Gospel, we bade farewell to our neophytes at Cagoxima, and to Paul, in whose care we left them, and went on thence to a town in the kingdom of Amanguchi. Here a great number of persons having become converts to the Christian religion, I gave them Father Cosmo Torres to instruct them. I myself went on with Joam Fernandez to Amanguchi, the capital of the kingdom, an immense city containing more than ten thousand houses. Here we preached the Gospel to the people in the public streets, to the princes and nobles in their own residences. Many heard us eagerly, others with reluctance. We did not always escape unhurt, having many insults offered us by the boys and the crowds in the streets. The king of the country summoned us to his presence, and, having asked the reason of our coming, invited us of his own accord to explain the law of God to him; he listened to us with deep attention for a whole hour while we spoke to him of religion.

But as we saw but little fruit of our zeal and labours at Amanguchi, we went to Meaco, the metropolis of all Japan, and the seat of empire. This journey took two months, and after going through infinite fatigue and danger, we reached Meaco at last. It is said that Meaco formerly contained 180,000 families; now, through the calamities of war, it only contains rather more than 100,000. In this city we could get no admittance to the sovereign; and as we saw that the minds of the inhabitants were too much disturbed by the great troubles caused by the war to be inclined for discourses on religion, we at once returned to Amanguchi.

The King was made favourable to us by the letters and presents sent by the Bishop and the Governors from India and Malacca, and we obtained from him without difficulty the publication of edicts declaring his approval of the promulgation of the divine law in the cities of his dominions, and permitting such of his subjects as pleased to embrace it. When he had done us this favour he also assigned a monastery to us for a residence. Here by means of daily sermons and disputes with the bonzes, the sorcerers, and other such men, we converted to the religion of Jesus Christ a great number of persons, several of whom were nobles. Amongst them we found some able to inform us, and we made it our business to gain acquaintance with the various sects and opinions of Japan, and so know how to refute them by arguments and proofs prepared for the purpose.

The bonzes seeing themselves betrayed by their own adherents and conquered in public disputes, were in the greatest trouble and bursting with indignation, especially because the new converts openly declared that they were induced to profess the Christian religion by perceiving that the bonzes, who were the teachers of the religion of their fathers, could not defend it.

The Japanese doctrines teach absolutely nothing concerning the creation of the world, of the sun, the moon, the stars, the heavens, the earth, sea, and the rest, and do not believe that they have any origin but themselves. The people were greatly astonished on hearing it said that there is one sole Author and common Father of souls, by whom they were created. This astonishment was caused by the fact that in their religious traditions there is nowhere any mention of a Creator of the universe. If there existed one single First Cause of all things, surely, they said, the Chinese, from whom they derive their religion, must have known it. For the Japanese give the Chinese the pre-eminence in wisdom and prudence in everything relating either to religion or to political government. They asked us a multitude of questions concerning this First Cause of all things; whether He were good or bad, whether the same First Cause were the origin of good and of evil. We replied that there exists one only First Cause, and He supremely good, without any admixture of evil.

This did not satisfy them; they considered the devils to be evil by nature, and the enemies of the human race; God therefore, if He were good, could never have done such a thing as create beings so evil. To these arguments we replied that the devils were created good by God, but became evil by their own fault, and that in consequence they were subject to eternal punishment and torment. Then they objected that God, Who was so severe in punishing, was not at all merciful. Again, how could He, if He created the human race in the manner we taught, allow men sent into the world to worship Him to be tempted and persecuted by the devil? In like manner, if God were good, He ought not to have made man so weak and so prone to sin, but free from all evil. Again, it could not be a good God, they said, Who had created that horrible prison of hell, and be for ever without pity for those who suffer therein the most fearful torments for all eternity. Lastly, if He were good, He would not have imposed on men those difficult laws of the ten commandments. Their religious traditions, on the contrary, taught that all who should invoke the authors of their religion would be delivered even from the torments of hell.

They were quite unable to digest the idea that men could be cast into hell without any hope of deliverance. They said, therefore, that their doctrines rested, more than ours, on clemency and mercy. In the end, by God's favour, we succeeded in solving all their questions, so as to leave no doubt remaining in their mind. The Japanese are led by reason in everything more than any other people, and in general they are all so insatiable of information and so importunate in their questions, that there is no end either to their arguments with us, or to their talking over our answers among themselves. They did not know that the world is round, they knew nothing of the course of the sun and stars, so that when they asked us and we explained to them these and other like things, such as the causes of comets, of the lightning, and of rain, they listened to us most eagerly, and appeared delighted to hear us, regarding us with profound respect as extremely learned persons. This idea of our great knowledge opened the way for sowing the seed of religion in their minds.

Only one of the nine sects prevailing in Japan teaches that souls are mortal, but this sect is considered detestable by the followers of the rest. Its adherents are extremely vicious and corrupt, and cannot endure to hear hell mentioned.

In the course of two months, after numerous conferences, we baptized about five hundred persons at Amanguchi, and every day, by the mercy of God, others are added to the number. The converts are very zealous in exposing to us the tricks and frauds of the bonzes and sects of Japan; they show so diligently great affection and respect towards us that we have great confidence that they are true and solid Christians.

Before their baptism the converts of Amanguchi were greatly troubled and pained by a hateful and annoying scruple—that God did not appear to them merciful and good, because He had never made Himself known to the Japanese before our arrival, especially if it were true that those who had not worshipped God as we preached were doomed to suffer everlasting punishment in hell. It seemed to them that He had forgotten and as it were neglected the salvation of all their ancestors in permitting them to be deprived of the knowledge of saving truths, and thus to rush headlong on eternal death. It was this painful thought which, more than anything else, kept them back from the religion of the true God. But by the divine mercy all their error and scruple was taken away. We began by proving to them that the divine law is the most ancient of all. Before receiving their institutions from the Chinese, the Japanese knew by the teaching of nature that it was wicked to kill, to steal, to swear falsely, and to commit the other sins enumerated in the ten commandments, a proof of this being the remorse of conscience to which any one guilty of one of these crimes was certain to be a prey. We showed them that reason itself teaches us to avoid evil and to do good, and that this is so deeply implanted in the hearts of men, that all have the knowledge of the divine law from nature and from God the Author of nature before they receive any external instruction on the subject. If any doubts were entertained on the matter, an experiment might be made in the person of a man without any instruction, living in absolute solitude, and in entire ignorance of the laws of his country. Such a man, ignorant of and a stranger to all human teaching, if he were asked whether it were or were not criminal to kill, to steal, or to commit the other actions forbidden by the law of God, and whether it were right to abstain from such actions, then, I say, this man, so fundamentally without all human education, would most certainly reply in such a manner as to show that he was by no means without knowledge of the divine law. Whence then must he be supposed to have received this knowledge, but from God Himself, the Author of nature? And if this knowledge is seen among barbarians, what must be the case with civilized and polished nations? This being so, it necessarily follow that before any laws were made by men the divine law existed innate in the hearts of all men. The converts were so satisfied with this reasoning, as to see no further difficulty; so that this net having been broken, they received from us with a glad heart the sweet yoke of our Lord.

But our greatest enemies are the bonzes, because we expose their falsehoods. As I have said, they used to make the people believe that it is impossible for persons in general to keep those five commandments which I mentioned, and that, therefore, they would observe them for the people, on condition of the people giving them maintenance and honour. They give their word that if any one has to go down into hell he will be delivered by their intervention and labour. We, on the contrary, proved to the people that in hell there is no redemption,[6] and that no one can be rescued from it by the bonzes and bonzesses. Convinced by our arguments, the people complained that the bonzes had deceived them. At last, by the help of God, the bonzes themselves were forced to confess the truth that they could not save any one from the punishment of hell by their prayers, but that unless they gave out that they had this power, they would infallibly be reduced to die of hunger.

And indeed, soon after this, the bonzes, as the assistance they received from their disciples gradually failed, experienced great difficulties as to their maintenance, and had to live in a state of degradation. We have had such sharp disputes with them on the subject of hell, that it does not seem likely that they will ever be reconciled to us. A great number have already left their rule and returned to secular life; and these men expose to us the frauds and tricks of the bonzes who live in the convents. Thus (at Amanguchi, at least) the credit of the bonzes and bonzesses diminishes much every day. The Christians have assured me that of a hundred convents which there used to be there, a great part will soon cease to exist, being deprived of the alms of the inhabitants.

Formerly the bonzes and bonzesses who had broken one of their five precepts were punished with death by the princes and nobles of the places where they lived, whether they were found guilty of offences against morals, or theft, or of falsehood, or whether they had committed homicide, or caused the death of any living creature, or eaten flesh of such, or drunk wine. But at present this discipline is entirely relaxed and corrupted; the greater number drink wine, eat meat secretly, make a trade of lies, openly indulge in fornication, and commonly have boys living with them, whom they corrupt in the flower of their youth. This they themselves profess, and they declare it to be no sin, and the people on their authority indulge in the same abominable crime. They commonly say that if it is lawful for the bonzes, why not for secular people? Besides this, they keep a number of women in their monasteries, who they say

[6] Lat. Orig. *In inferno nullam esse redemptionem.*

are the wives of the men who till their farms. This gives great scandal to the people, who look with suspicion on the great intercourse the bonzes have with the women. The bonzes also visit the bonzesses at all hours, for purposes of business, and receive visits from them in the same way. The people look on this with an evil eye. They say there is a certain herb which the bonzesses eat that they may not become pregnant. For my part, it does not astonish me that the bonzes are covered with so many and so great sins. They are a set of men who have the devil in the place of God, and it is a matter of necessity that they should commit crimes innumerable and abominable.

All the Japanese use a long rosary of beads in their prayers, invoking the founder of their sect at each bead. The different sects recite their series of prayers, some more frequently, others more seldom. The principal founders of the religions, as we have mentioned, are Xaca and Amida. The grey bonzes and bonzesses and most of the people chiefly venerate Amida; the rest of the people do not leave Amida out, but render most honour to Xaca. I have carefully inquired whether this Xaca and Amida were persons celebrated for their wisdom, and have begged the Christians to give me an account of their lives in writing. At last I have discovered from their books that they were not men at all, for they are said to have lived a thousand or even two thousand years. Xaca was born eighty thousand times over; and many other such things are handed down by tradition about them which can never have happened. So that I conclude that they were not men, but mere inventions or portents of the devil.

I earnestly beg all who read this letter of mine, by the zeal they have for the propagation of the worship of God, to pray that our Lord Jesus Christ will give us the victory over these two demons Xaca and Amida, and over the others like them, especially since at present their credit is waxing weak at Amanguchi, not without the special providence of God. A principal nobleman of this kingdom and his wife, a person of great merit, have shown us so much affection, that their efforts have never been wanting to us in spreading our divine religion; but although they both know its truth, they can neither of them be induced to embrace it. Their reason is that they have built at their own expense a great many monasteries for bonzes, and assigned them revenues in order that the bonzes may constantly pray to Amida to preserve them from the calamities and miseries of this life, and bring them one day to that happiness which he himself enjoys.

These two gave a hundred reasons besides for not becoming Christians; but the principal was that having always been great worshippers of Xaca and Amida, and having given for their sakes large gifts to the bonzes, and built a great number of monasteries, they would, if they were to pass over to the Christian religion, lose the accumulated good of so many years of devotion, and all the fruit of their past life. They are convinced that all the money they have given to the bonzes in the names of Xaca and Amida will be returned to them with large interest after their death, together with an abundant recompense of their worship and devotion. So, not to lose these advantages, they steadily refuse to be converted to Jesus Christ.

The Japanese believe that in the abode of the blessed there will be splendid banquets and all the good things of life in plenty and elegance, so that the more pleasing a person has been to Xaca and Amida, the higher he will be in greatest glory. All these stories make up the mysteries and fables of the bonzes, who, with the object of destroying the effects of our preaching, used to preach themselves in their own temples, and most shamefully revile both us and our God in the midst of a vast multitude of hearers. The God of the Christians, they said, is something unknown and unheard of; He can only be the greatest and most abominable of devils. We were the disciples of this demon, so that every one should take care not to embrace the faith of Jesus Christ, for that no sooner should He be adored as God than Japan will perish. They also made a captious interpretation of the name of God, saying that it is the same as 'Diusa,' which in their language means a lie; 'so let them look to themselves, and be diligently on their guard against us.'

Such and many other such impious calumnies they uttered against God, Who nevertheless, in His infinite mercy and clemency, turned all to His own glory and to the good of souls. In fact their false charges against us increased our authority with the people, and the number of our Lord's worshippers was daily swelled. The people saw clearly, and said openly that the jealousy of the bonzes was the cause of their accusations against us.

I have tried long and diligently in this country to discover from all indications whether the Japanese have ever had the knowledge of Jesus Christ, and I have at last found from their books and conversations that they have never heard anything at all of Him. At Cagoxima, where we remained a year, I noticed that the prince and his relations had a white cross in the armorial bearings of their family, but that they were entirely ignorant of the name of Jesus Christ.

When I was at Amanguchi with Father Cosmo Torres and Joam Fernandez, the King of Boungo, one of the most powerful of the country, wrote to ask me to go to him; a Portuguese vessel had come into his harbour, and he wished to talk with me on certain subjects. So, both to find out how he was affected towards our holy religion, and to pay a visit to the Portuguese, I set out at once for Boungo, leaving Cosmo and Joam with the Christians. The King gave me a most gracious reception, and it was a great pleasure to me to meet with the Portuguese. While I was at Boungo the devil stirred up a great war at Amanguchi. A powerful nobleman declared war against the King, drove him from his capital, and stripped him of his dominions. The latter seeing no way of escape, and not choosing to fall alive into the hands of a furious adversary, so lately his subject and servant, plunged a dagger into his bowels, and killed himself, at the same time causing his son who was with him to be put to death, and ordering both bodies to be burned, that the enemy might find no remains to insult. All was done as he ordered. You may judge from the letters written to me by our brethren at Amanguchi, which I send you, how great was the peril they incurred in that war. After the King's death, the nobles and grandees of the kingdom having successfully ended the war, and seeing that the state of Amanguchi could not stand without a sovereign, sent ambassadors to the King of Boungo, begging him to send his own brother to Amanguchi, whom they would make king. The King of course complied with their request, and so his brother became King of Amanguchi. The King of Boungo commands numerous and very warlike troops, and as things go with Japanese kings, has vast dominions to govern. He has a great liking for the Portuguese. No sooner was he informed of the power and character of the King of Portugal than he wrote to him asking to be admitted into the number of his friends, and sending him a rich suit of armour as a token of friendship. He has also sent an envoy to the Viceroy of India, offering him with many compliments his friendship, alliance, and good offices; this messenger, who came to India with me, has been most honourably and liberally received by the Viceroy. Before I left Japan, the King of Boungo promised the Portuguese and myself to take Cosmo Torres and Joam Fernandez under his protection. The sovereign elect of Amanguchi bound himself in the same way, when he enters into the possession of his kingdom.

During our residence in Japan, that is to say for two years and a half, we lived at the expense of the munificent King of Portugal. His Highness had ordered more than a thousand gold crowns to be given to us as alms for our journey to Japan. It is incredible how much this excellent monarch has favoured us, and how much he has spent and daily continues to spend on our colleges and residences, and for the supply of all our necessities.

I had been some time at Boungo, when the opportune presence of the Portuguese vessel invited me to give up the idea of returning to Amanguchi; and I made up my mind to sail from Boungo for India, in order, after so long a separation, to revisit our fathers and brothers, and to provide members of the Society fitted for the work of cultivating the Japanese mission, as well as other necessary things quite wanting out there. I reached Cochin on the 24th January, and I was received in the kindest manner by the Governor. Next April some fathers will be sent to Japan from India, and the King of Boungo's ambassador will return home in their company. I have very great hopes that, by the favour of Jesus Christ, there will be a plentiful harvest in these countries; for a nation so ingenious, moderate, so desirous of instruction, so much guided by right reason and so well adorned with other eminent qualities, ought to be, as it were, a rich and fertile field from whence copious and joyful results may be expected.

The university of Bandou, situated in an island of Japan, which has given its name to its country, is the most famous of all; and a great number of bonzes are constantly going thither to study their own laws. These precepts are derived from China and are written in Chinese characters, which are different from the Japanese. There are two kinds of writing in Japan, one used by men and the other by women; and for the most part both men and women, especially of the nobility and the commercial class, have a literary education. The bonzes, or bonzesses, in their monasteries teach letters to the girls and boys, though rich and noble persons entrust the education of their children to private tutors.

The bonzes are persons of acute mind, and are very fond of studying, especially what relates to the future; they are fond of considering what will happen to them, what will be their end, and all questions of this nature. There were some of the bonzes who, in the course of their meditations, had come to believe that there was no way of saving souls in their system. They argued in this way: It is necessary above all things that there should exist a single origin of all things; now, in their books there is not a word on the subject, for there is a wonderful silence in them all as to the creation of the universe; and therefore if any of their predecessors were acquainted with this first principle—a thing not confirmed by any authority, written or traditional—they must have kept the knowledge to themselves and hid it from their descendants.

Now, men of this sort were wonderfully delighted with the

divine law. One of them embraced the faith of Jesus Christ at Amanguchi, after being many years in the university of Bandou, where he had a flourishing reputation for learning. Before we came to Japan he had thought of becoming a bonze; afterwards he changed his mind and married. The reason he assigned for this change was, that he had seen the falsehood and emptiness of the Japanese religions, and therefore did not believe in them at all, but he was bound to pay his homage to the Author and Creator of the universe. Our Christians were overjoyed at his accession, for he was and was thought to be the most learned man of the city.

Later on, if God wills, fresh members of the Society will be sent to Japan every year, and a house of the Society will be established at Amanguchi, where the fathers will learn the language of the country, and acquaint themselves with the doctrines and rules of the different sects. By these means the good and learned members of the Society who are to come hither from Portugal to aid the university of Bandou, will find brothers there acquainted with the language and the religions of Japan. This will be an immense advantage to the European fathers to whose lot this mission may fall.

At present Cosmo Torres and Joam Fernandez are entirely occupied in teaching the mysteries of our religion, and in preaching to the people on the wonderful deeds of our Lord. Many of their hearers are so affected by the history of the life of Jesus Christ, that they cannot hear the account of His passion and death without weeping and tears. Cosmo writes the sermons in our language, and Fernandez, who knows that of the country well enough, translates them into Japanese. Through their labours the Christians are advancing greatly in piety. The converts, who used formerly to recite that series of prayers on their beads, invoking each the founder of his own sect on the several beads, have now learnt how to worship Jesus Christ, and are being formed in piety, and change their old superstitions into prayers in the honour of God.

They are so attentive and anxious for information in matters of this sort, that when taught to make the sign of the Cross, they insist on understanding what is the meaning of the words, '*In the name of the Father, and of the Son, and of the Holy Ghost*'—why, as the right hand is lifted to the head, we say, '*In the name of the Father;*' why, when it is lowered to the breast, we add, '*And of the Son;*' and why, lastly, when it is moved from the left to the right shoulder, we say, '*And of the Holy Ghost.*' They are delighted with the explanation of all these things. When they are taught to say, '*Kyrie eleison, Christe eleison,*' they want to know the meaning of the words. And in saying our Lady's rosary, after the Angelical Salutation, at each small bead they repeat the names of Jesus and Mary as an invocation. They learn all these, as well as the other prayers and the Creed, by degrees, out of a written copy.

One of the things that most of all pains and torments these Japanese is, that we teach them that the prison of hell is irrevocably shut, so that there is no egress therefrom. For they grieve over the fate of their departed children, of their parents and relatives, and they often show their grief by their tears. So they ask us if there is any hope, any way to free them by prayer from that eternal misery, and I am obliged to answer that there is absolutely none. Their grief at this affects and torments them wonderfully; they almost pine away with sorrow. But there is this good thing about their trouble,—it makes one hope that they will all be the more laborious for their own salvation, lest they, like their forefathers, should be condemned to everlasting punishment. They often ask if God cannot take their fathers out of hell, and why their punishment must never have an end. We gave them a satisfactory answer, but they did not cease to grieve over the misfortune of their relatives; and I can hardly restrain my tears sometimes at seeing men so dear to my heart suffer such intense pain about a thing which is already done with and can never be undone.

Opposite to Japan lies China, an immense empire, enjoying profound peace, and which, as the Portuguese merchants tell us, is superior to all Christian states in the practice of justice and equity. The Chinese whom I have seen in Japan and elsewhere, and whom I got to know, are white in colour, like the Japanese, are acute, and eager to learn. Their intellect is superior even to the Japanese. Their country abounds in plenty of all things, and very many cities of great extent cover its surface. The cities are very populous; the houses ornamented with stone roofings, and very elegant. All reports say that the empire is rich in every sort of produce, but especially in silk. I find, from the Chinese themselves, that amongst them may be found many people of many different nations and religions, and, as far as I could gather from what they said, I suspect that among them are Jews and Mahometans.

Nothing leads me to suppose that there are Christians there. I hope to go there during this year, 1552, and penetrate even to the Emperor himself. China is that sort of kingdom, that if the seed of the Gospel is once sown, it may be propagated far and wide. And moreover, if the Chinese accept the Christian faith, the Japanese would give up the doctrines which the Chinese have taught them. Japan is separated from Liampou (which is a principal town in China) by a distance of about 300 miles of sea. I am beginning to have great hopes that God will soon provide free entrance to China, not only to our Society, but to religious of all Orders, that a large field may be laid open to pious and holy men of all sorts, in which there may be great room for devotion and zeal, in recalling men who are now lost to the way of truth and salvation. I again and again beg all who have a zeal for the spreading of the Christian faith to help by their holy sacrifices and prayers these poor efforts of mine, that I may throw open an ample field to their pious labours.

I have nothing to say concerning India: the brothers there are charged to render you an account of what is going on there. I have just returned hither from Japan, bringing back a sufficient amount of bodily strength, but hardly any strength in virtue and spirit; but I place all my confidence in the goodness of God and the infinite merits of our Lord Jesus Christ, that I may bring to its accomplishment, as I have designed it, this most irksome voyage to China. My hair has become quite white, but I am as active and robust as I ever was in my life.

The labours which are undergone for the conversion of a people so rational, so desirous to know the truth and be saved, result in very sweet fruit to the soul. Even at Amanguchi, when the King allowed us to preach the faith and a vast concourse of people gathered round us, I had so much joy and vigour and delight of heart, as I never experienced in my life before. I saw how by means of our ministry the spirit of the bonzes was broken down by God, and the most glorious victory over most formidable enemies was gained. I delighted also to see the joy of our neophytes at the defeat of the bonzes, and their evident zeal to attack the pagans and draw them to baptism, as well as their exultation when the battle was won, as they talked over their victories among themselves, when the superstitions of the heathen were put to flight. These things made me so overflow with joy, that I lost all sense of suffering.

Would to God that these divine consolations which God so graciously gives us in the midst of our labours might not only be related by me, but also some experience of them be sent to our European Universities, to be tasted as well as heard of! Then many of those young men given up to study would turn all their cares and desires to the conversion of infidels, if they could once taste the delight of the heavenly sweetness which comes from such labours, and if the world knew and was aware how well the souls of the Japanese are prepared to receive the Gospel, I am sure that many learned men would finish their studies, canons, priests, and prelates even, would abandon their rich livings, to change an existence full of bitterness and anxiety for so sweet and pleasant a life. And to gain this happiness they would not hesitate to set sail even to Japan.

As I arrived at Cochin at the time the ships were about to depart, and as the great number of friends who have come to salute me have frequently interrupted me in the midst of my letter, I have written in great haste and with much disturbance. So now I will end—though I know not how to end when I am writing to my dearest fathers and brothers, and about my joys in Japan too, the greatness of which I could never express, however much I might wish to do so. I end my letter then, begging and imploring God to vouchsafe to unite us some day in the bliss of heaven. Amen.

The least of your brothers in Jesus Christ,

Cochin, 29th January 1552. FRANCIS.

It would be tedious, as we have already said, to attempt to compare all the statements made by Francis Xavier in his account of Japan with later information on the same subject. What we can discover as to the names of the national deities as they sounded in his ears, illustrates sufficiently the confusion which the great mixture of religions in the country had thrown not only into the accounts given to strangers, but probably over the minds of the people themselves. Xaca must be taken to represent Sakya-mouni, or Buddha. Amida seems to be the personification of the old Japanese idea of a supreme divinity, represented under nine different forms which symbolized his essential perfections.[7] If we go back to the names as given in the disputes with Fucarandono, we find Gizon and Canom placed side by side with Xaca and Amida. Gizon may perhaps be Izanami, the goddess whose mirror plays so important a part in the worship of the Kamis, and Canom the subordinate deity who has the most frequented temple in Yeddo, as also the famous temple at Kioto of the 33,333 idols.[8]

Before we take final leave of Japan in this volume, we may mention for the last time the good Paul of the holy Faith. We have a short letter from him written to the College at Goa in 1549, at the time when everything seemed favourable at Cagoxima, and sent with the first letters of Francis Xavier from that city. Paul simply asks for prayers and relates the conversion of his kinsfolk. He begs that his friends in India will intercede for them that they may persevere, 'since it is not enough for our salvation to begin to serve God, but we must persevere unto the end. Though we are far apart in body, it seems to me that we

[7] See Humbert, *Japon Illustré*, t. i. p. 264.

[8] Ibid. t. i. p. 150 and 265. Sir Rutherford Alcock speaks of the temple of 'Quanwon' at Asaska, the suburb of Yeddo. The idol there has thirty-six arms, to express the power of the supposed deity. *Capital of the Tycoon*, ii. 307.

are always united in spirit, and in body also we shall be united in the day of judgment, when we shall all live again—may God grant that it be to reign with Jesus Christ!' Mendez Pinto tells us that Paul was obliged to go into exile by the persecutions of the bonzes some months after Francis Xavier left him, that he went to China and was murdered by robbers near Liampou. But the Christians over whom he had been set in charge remained firm and constant under all trials, not the least of which was the entire want of priests and religious teachers. They had been thoroughly instructed, and possessed the summary of Christian doctrine which Francis had left them. Many years after this, when they came to be visited for the first time by a priest, they were found to have kept up their faith and religion in great purity. This statement will surprise no one who is familiar with the annals of Catholic missions, and the fact which it records is typical of the history of the Church of Japan. It is now believed that when in our time Japan was partially opened to Europeans so many generations after the great persecution of Christianity which seemed to have drowned it in blood, and when no Catholic priest had been in the country for more than two centuries, there were still communities of Christians who had kept up their practice of the Gospel law, the Catholic Creed, and the administration of baptism. And even the renewed persecution of the present day will not, as we may confidently hope in God's mercy, avail to stamp out in this noble, intelligent, and faithful race the remains of the religion of Jesus Christ, so long ago painfully planted in the soil of Japan by the modern Apostle of the East.

CHAPTER IV.

Voyage from Japan to India.

WE have already seen that the voyages of Francis Xavier were generally marked by some extraordinary victory of his charity, or some indication of the prophetic gifts with which he was from time to time endowed. This homeward voyage from Japan, in the last weeks of 1551, became more famous in the East than any other of which we have spoken; and in this case we happen to have abundance of the most unexceptionable testimony as to the efficacy of his prayers and the blessing which his presence seemed to cause to all who were in his company. The vessel in which he embarked at the port of Figi was bound for Canton, or rather for the island of San Chan, which was the station where the Portuguese traffic with Canton was carried on. Mendez Pinto, whom we shall find more at home on nautical subjects than on the theological questions discussed between Francis Xavier and the bonzes in the presence of the King of Boungo, was, as has been said, one of the Portuguese passengers on board the ship in which Francis embarked. Mendez tells us how at first they hugged the Japanese coast for some time, and then struck across the open sea in the direction of China. After a week, however, the moon changed, and the weather changed in consequence. A violent storm fell on the vessel, and she was obliged to put about and run before the wind in a north-north-westerly direction 'through an unknown sea which no one had ever yet navigated,' as Mendez says. For five days they were at the mercy of the storm, and saw neither sun nor star, and the helmsman lost all reckoning.[1] On the second day of the five something had to be done to clear the deck of all

[1] Mendez says that they were running towards Papua, Celebes, or Mindanao, which hardly seem to lie in a northern or north-westerly direction from their course, and are sufficiently widely apart one from another.

encumbrances,[2] and the ship's boat was secured at the stern, fastened by two strong cables, with fifteen men in her. Night came on, and they were unable to get on board the ship again. Francis Xavier was the life of the whole party during the storm, working himself in clearing the decks, encouraging and comforting the rest. 'After God,' says Mendez, 'he alone was the captain who encouraged us, and made us take breath so as not to sink under the labours and abandon ourselves entirely to chance, as some wished to do if he had not hindered them.' About midnight loud cries to God for mercy were heard from the boat: the ropes by which she was held to the ship had given way, and she was left behind in a moment. The captain's nephew, a lad whom he loved most tenderly, was with the party in the boat, and his uncle endeavoured to get the ship round in order to seek for the boat. The result was the imminent danger of the vessel herself; she lay across the waves, was deluged by the heavy seas, and was almost swamped. At the moment of greatest peril Francis was on his knees in the captain's cabin, and he called aloud on Jesus Christ, the Love of his soul, to succour them, for the sake of the five wounds which He had suffered on the Cross. The ship righted and got once more before the wind, but the boat was lost to sight. Francis Xavier, however, bade them to be of good cheer, as within three days 'the daughter would come back to the mother' —by which words, say the Auditors of the Rota, who have summed up the evidence from the sworn witnesses examined in the Processes, he signified darkly that the boat would return to the ship. He is said to have been especially anxious to save two Mussulmans, who were in the boat with the rest. When daylight came, nothing could be discerned from the ship but the sea covered with foam. The rest of the story we may give chiefly in Mendez Pinto's own words, though

[2] 'Il fut resolu de rompre toutes les œuvres du chapiteau jusqu'au tillac, afin que pas ce moyen le navire fut plus a son aise, et qu'il fut mieux obeye au gouvernail.' Mendez Pinto (French translation, t. iii. p. 422). Some writers understand the 'chapiteau' to be the forecastle. It appears that the object was to cut away all the upperworks, which might have retained any heavy seas which flooded the deck.

his account has often to be completed by that of other eyewitnesses.

'It was a little more than an hour after daylight, when the blessed Father Xavier, who had retired to the captain's cabin, came on deck, where were the master, the pilot, and seven other Portuguese. After having given good-day to all with a joyous and serene countenance, he asked them if they did not see the boat approaching, to which answer was made No; and then he asked the master pilot to send one of the sailors aloft to see if he could not discover it. At the same time one of those present said, "It will appear when we have lost another like it." On which the Father answered him: "O, Pedro Velho" —such was his name—"O, Pedro Velho, how little faith you have! What! think you that anything is impossible to our Lord? For me, I have so much confidence in Him and in His most sacred Mother the Blessed Virgin Mary, to whom I have promised that I will say three masses in her blessed house of the Mount at Malacca, that I hope that they will prevent the souls which are in that boat from perishing." At which words Pedro Velho was so confounded and astonished that he said nothing more. However, the master pilot, to satisfy the request which the Father had just made him, went up himself with another sailor to the top, when, after having looked round on every side for nearly half an hour, they made their report that nothing appeared. On which the Father answered, "Come down then, since there is nothing more to be done;" and having called me to the forecastle[3] where he then was, very sad as far as we all could judge, he told me that I would oblige him if I warmed a little water for him that he might drink it, as he had a weakness of stomach. But I was so unhappy that my sins hindered me from doing him this good turn, because the day before, when the hurricane came on, they had thrown the stove overboard to lighten the deck. Then he complained to me that he had a great pain in his head, on account of the sickness which came on him from time to time; and I answered him: "It cannot be otherwise than that your Reverence should

[3] 'Chapiteau.' Mendez Pinto.

be so indisposed, because for three nights you have not slept and you have not eaten a single morsel," for one of the servants of Duarte de Gama had so told me. "I assure you," replied the Father, "that I am sorry for the unhappiness of this young man, to see him so disconsolate; for all the last night, after the boat was lost, he never ceased weeping for the loss of Alonzo Calvo his nephew, who is in it with the rest of his companions." Seeing, then, that the Father was yawning every moment, I said to him, "Your Reverence would do well, meseems, to retire awhile into my little cabin, for perhaps you might get some rest;" an offer which he accepted, saying, "So be it, then, for the love of God." Thereon he begged me much to send a Chinese servant whom I had to shut the door after him, and not to stir, in order that he might open it for him when he called; and this he said to me about six or seven o'clock. After having retired into my cabin, he remained there all day until sunset, and as I once happened to call my servant who was at the door, as I said, to ask him to give me a little water, I inquired of him also whether the Father was asleep? "He has not slept at all," he answered, "and he is still on his knees on the couch weeping, with his head down." On which I told him to go back and sit at the door, and go to him as soon as he called him. In this way the Father remained unceasingly engaged in prayer until sunset, and then at last left the cabin, and came to where all the Portuguese were sitting down on the deck under the bulwarks, on account of the great rockings and rollings of the ship.

'After having saluted them, the Father asked of the pilot if the boat was to be seen? To which the other answered that naturally it was impossible but that it had been lost amid such high seas; and that even supposing that it pleased God to save it by a miracle, it was more than fifty leagues off. "So it seems naturally," said the Father; "but I should be very glad, since nothing could be lost by that, if you would go up aloft again, or send some sailor up, who might cast his eyes over the whole surface of the sea." The pilot told him that he would very willingly go; and he went up with the master's mate, more to satisfy the desire of the Father than from any thought he had of being reasonably able to discover what he wished. They were both up there a good long time, and at last they affirmed that they had seen nothing at all over the whole sea. This grieved the Father very much, as all could judge, so that he bent his head upon the bulwark, and was for some time sighing as if he would fain shed tears. Then after he had taken a little breath, as if to try to rest under the sadness which he felt, he raised his hands to heaven and said, with tears in his eyes, "O, Jesus Christ, my true God and Lord, by the merits of Thy sacred death and passion, I pray Thee to have pity on us, and to save the souls of the faithful who are gone astray in that boat!"

'Then he leant his head again upon the bulwark and remained so for the space of two or three *Credos*, as if he were asleep; and then a little boy, who was seated up in the shrouds, began to cry, "Miracle! miracle! here is our boat!" All those of the ship came running at these words, and at that same moment they saw the boat on the sea, not farther than a gunshot off, a little more or less; insomuch that astonished at a thing so new and extraordinary, they began all in a throng to weep like children, so that they could not hear one another in the ship for the loud cries that they made. They all came to the Father to throw themselves at his feet; but he would not permit it, and retired into the cabin of the captain and shut himself up inside that no one might speak to him. All those who were in the boat were immediately received into the ship, with all the rejoicing and happiness which was natural in such a case. And therefore I forbear now to relate here the particulars of this welcome, because it is a thing which can better be imagined than written. And so after the little time was over which remained before it was full night, which came about half an hour afterwards, the Father sent a little boy for the pilot, and told him to praise God who had done these marvels, and that he should at once get the ship ready, because the bad weather would soon end. So at once all was done to satisfy the Father's desire with all possible diligence, and at the same time were performed the devotions which he enjoined; and it followed that before the great yard was hoisted and the sails set, the hurricane ceased entirely, so that we found a good wind from the north, and continued our voyage to the joy and contentment of every one.'[4]

This is what Mendez Pinto tells us of this famous miracle. His memory was doubtless accurate as far as it went, but he seems to have omitted one or two circumstances which other witnesses have recorded. The first of these is that Francis Xavier, when he came on deck after his many hours of prayer in the cabin, insisted on sail being shortened, in order to slacken the speed at which the vessel was running before the wind. The large sail was therefore lowered, and the crew as well as the Father had to suffer the severe tossing of the vessel which was the consequence for some considerable time. The other accounts[5] tell us that at last the men got impatient, the master gave orders to hoist the sail, but Francis would not allow it, that he bent his head down on the yard and wept and sobbed, as Mendez tells us in the text. Another circumstance omitted by Mendez is that when the boat appeared in sight, it was seen to come straight on the ship as if steered by an invisible hand, notwithstanding the roughness of the sea, and that when it touched the side, it stopped as of itself. Finally, a number of witnesses swore that when the party from the boat came on board, they declared that they had had Father Francis with them all the time, that he had been their only support and guide and comfort, and that his presence had inspired them with so much courage and serenity that they had been free from all alarm. It is certain that the two Mussulmans were converted by the miracle, and received baptism.[6]

[4] Mendez Pinto, t. iii. p. 430.

[5] Summed up by Bartoli, *Asia*, t. i. p. 277.

[6] The evidence for this celebrated miracle is epitomized in the *Relatio*, to which we have before referred. The *Relatio* tells the story in the first instance (without adding the circumstance of the bilocation of Francis) on the authority of Duarte Gama ('vir nobilis et regiæ domûs patritius'), Galeotto Pereira ('regiæ domûs patritius'), Antonio Martinez, a sea captain, Antonio Diaz, the man who went aloft to look out—all of whom were present and gave their testimony juridically. There were forty-eight other witnesses *de auditu*, many of whom had heard eyewitnesses tell the story. After proving that the fact was miraculous, the *Relatio* goes on to say, 'Many of the witnesses and writers add that Xavier appeared to those who were in the boat,

The ship arrived soon after at San Chan, but it was much shattered by the storm, and moreover was to spend the winter in a port of Siam instead of sailing straight for Malacca. But two other Portuguese ships were still at San Chan, having waited for a fortnight for a favourable wind to take them to Malacca. One of them was the ship of Diego Pereira, the intimate friend of Francis Xavier. Pereira offered him a passage to Malacca; and Francis at once embarked, taking an affectionate leave of the good Portuguese merchants who had been of so much support to him in his difficulties in the kingdom of Boungo. It was noted that as soon as he set foot on Pereira's ship the wind became favourable. They sailed for Malacca immediately. During this voyage it was that Francis matured his plan for an attempt to introduce Christianity into China. The letter which was inserted at the end of the last chapter shows how much his thoughts were now turned in this direction. He was bent upon furnishing the Japanese mission with learned as well as pious workmen, men who could defend their religion intellectually and meet the subtle difficulties suggested by the bonzes, as well as preach to the people by example as much as by word of mouth. Meanwhile, he would himself cut at the root, as it were, of the Japanese objections by bringing about, if it were possible, the conversion of that great, intelligent, cultivated, and peaceful empire which seems to have attracted his imagination from the first moment that he heard of its influence over the rest of the Eastern nations. The boldness with which Francis Xavier always aimed at accomplishing his work thoroughly, even though to do so involved the most arduous enterprize, as well as the temporary suspension of his own activity on what happened for the moment to be the frontier, so to speak, of the advancing kingdom of the faith, is thoroughly characteristic of him, and is one of the numberless points in which we find his spirit so identical with that of the father of his soul, St. Ignatius.

tossed about by the waves, and in the utmost danger, and that when they were taken up into the ship they told the sailors and passengers that Xavier had been all the time with them in the boat, and had kept her up in the midst of the seas, and that they were filled with astonishment when they found that at the same time he had been in the ship.'

We shall find that Ignatius soon after this time was intending to recal Francis himself from the East for a time necessarily by no means short, on account of the immense distance which he would have had to travel, in order that his presence in Europe might secure the more perfect organization of the attempts for the conversion of the Indies and the countries lying beyond them. So Francis Xavier himself was now anxious to leave Japan for a time to other labourers, and direct his own efforts to China. He found a sympathetic friend in Diego Pereira, with whom he now held long talks while the ship was moving with a favourable wind along the coast of the country which the heart of the Apostle was now yearning to invade. Pereira seems not to have been of noble birth, but he had risen by his skill and industry to the possession of large wealth, and was devoted to Francis and his schemes for the advancement of the Gospel. We have seen how Francis had suggested in the case of Japan that an ambassador should be sent by the Governor of the Indies in the name of the King of Portugal, who might negotiate for commercial relations as well as help on the introduction of Christian preachers. He had also suggested that if the state of affairs in India forbade the dispatch of a regular embassy, the commission might be handed over to some friend of the Governor's, who might be willing to undertake the expedition at his own expense, looking for his reward to the great commercial gains which he might make thereby. Francis conceived a plan exactly like to this for the opening of relations with China. The Governor or Viceroy of India might be asked to send an ambassador to the Court of China, and in the train of this ambassador Francis himself would go, and thus find a way to begin the preaching of the Gospel under the licence of the Emperor himself. He was ready, indeed, to enter China in any possible way, even if his fate was only to share the imprisonment of a number of Portuguese merchants who had been seized in this country, the coasts of which were most severely guarded against all foreigners. But it would be far better, far more likely to secure success as to the free preaching of the Christian law, if he could go as the companion of the envoy of a king whose name was so formidable all over the East as the King of Portugal.

Diego Pereira entered heartily into the plans of Francis, and offered his ship and his fortune to carry them out, if he could be named ambassador of the Portuguese crown to China. It was arranged between them that Francis should obtain the appointment from the Governor of India, and as Pereira had to leave Malacca immediately after arriving there for a mercantile voyage to Sonda, he was to give the Father letters to his agent at Goa to prepare all the costly donatives which in those days were necessary for embassies in the East, and to defray liberally all the other expenses of such an undertaking. Meanwhile, the vessel, called the Santa Croce, was not to escape the danger which we find so constantly haunting the voyages of Francis Xavier. She was caught by a typhoon before reaching Singapore, and was for a time in great peril. Francis retired for a few moments to pray alone; then he came on deck, raised his hands and solemnly blessed the vessel. 'The Santa Croce,' he said, 'shall never perish at sea, but only on the shore where she was built, where she shall fall to pieces of herself. Would to heaven that so it was to be with the other ship which sailed with us from San Chan!' In a few minutes the danger was over, but the ship had not proceeded far on its route before she came to a part of the sea where planks, merchandize, portions of wreck, and dead bodies were floating. The other ship had gone to pieces in the storm from which she had escaped.[7]

[7] Massei here quotes the evidence of Domenico Caldeira in the Processes, which seems to refer to this ship. He says that on his return from Japan Francis had already put his bundle containing the sacred vestments and other necessaries for the celebration of mass on board a ship which was bound directly for India. Pereira's ship was only bound for Malacca, and there was much doubt whether they would arrive there in time to catch another ship for India. But the captain was heard to speak of the voyage in blasphemous language—'he would get to India, God willing or not.' Francis remonstrated with him, and asked him to say rather that he would reach India, if so it pleased God. He then told Caldeira to take his baggage out of the ship and to embark it in another, which must have been the Santa Croce. When he saw the wreck of the other covering the waters, he pointed out to his companions the danger which they would all have run if they had remained on board her.

The prediction here mentioned about this famous ship, the Santa Croce, is one of those selected by the Auditors of the Rota out of the many similar prophecies witnessed to in the Processes afterwards made for the canonization of Francis Xavier. 'The ship,' says the *Relatio*, 'survived Father Francis for twenty years, and old as it was, rotten and shattered by the waves during so many voyages and storms, it always escaped safely. The sailors and merchants, trusting to the aforesaid prediction, used eagerly to embark their merchandize therein, and sailed from place to place without any fear of shipwreck or loss. Whenever it came into port, the ship was received with salutes and shouts of joy, and all India called it the 'ship of the holy Father.' At last it was sold to a certain captain of Diu, who after many voyages took it into the port of Cochin, and it was there hauled ashore in order to be repaired, on which it fell to pieces, and nothing but a heap of timbers remained of it.' Diego Pereira himself was one of the witnesses who are quoted in evidence both of the prediction and of its accomplishment.[8]

[8] There are several anecdotes about this ship, as was only to be expected. Massei, l. iii. p. 378, tells some of them. The Santa Croce once sailed from Malacca to Cochin laden almost to the water's edge, and after sailing about twenty-four miles, began to leak. The people on board fired guns of distress, as she was sailing with a fleet of merchantmen, but no one would consent to relieve her of part of the cargo. The captain turned back to Malacca, and was received with shouts of scorn and hisses, for having doubted of the promise of Francis Xavier. He turned back, then and there, and arrived safe at Cochin. Another story is that a certain Jorge Nuñez took a plank of the old ship after she went to pieces, and worked it into a small vessel of his own, which also enjoyed a sort of charmed existence amid the storms and perils of the Indian seas. Francis Xavier also made a prediction similar to that of which we are speaking as to Francesco d'Aghiar, the steersman of the ship of Duarte Gama, in which he came from Japan, and which experienced the terrible storm just now related. Francis promised D'Aghiar that he should never perish by water, and that no ship which he navigated should perish in any storm at sea. D'Aghiar after this used to sail in the most rotten vessels, without the least fear, and was always free from danger. A story is told in which his ship, a very poor one, escaped alone of a large fleet, and another of his singing cheerily in the midst of a very dangerous storm, answering, when interrogated as to his extraordinary confidence, that he feared nothing in any ship whatever, on account of the promise made by Master Francis. Bartoli, p. 278.

Malacca, to which port Francis was now drawing near, had suffered severe calamity since he had left it. We may remember the apparent anxiety with which he had inquired about Malacca in his short letter to the Portuguese merchant at Figi. Some of his biographers tell us that before leaving Japan he had urged Duarte de Gama to hasten his departure in order to succour the place: and it seems certain that a rumour that some great misfortune had befallen it was current at San Chan before the Santa Croce sailed, so that Diego Pereira had hesitated as to venturing to make for that port. His fears were relieved by Francis, who told him that the danger was over, and that he should find a single ship, that of his relative Antonio Pereira, not yet departed for India. What had happened was this. Malacca, as we have seen, was an exposed station, with no Portuguese settlement or garrison within easy reach; and, on the other hand, in the near neighbourhood of several very powerful native or Mussulman states, the rulers of which were always on the watch, ready to seize an opportunity of swooping down on so important and yet so unprotected a position. We have already mentioned the King or Rajah of Bintang, who, but for the Portuguese conquests, would have been the sovereign of Malacca. This potentate, at the head of an army of ten thousand men, with two hundred ships, swollen by contingents from a number of the Mussulman states and from Java itself, laid siege to Malacca in the summer of 1551. The Portuguese garrison in all numbered about three hundred men, and after much hard fighting they were obliged to retire into the citadel, leaving a great part of the city at the mercy of the enemy, who ravaged it with fire and sword. The siege of the fortress lasted for nearly three months, during which Francesco Perez was continually exposing himself, crucifix in hand, at the head of the defenders, who were reduced at last to great straits for food, especially for water. The enemy at one time gained an important position, which seemed to involve imminent danger to the fortress itself, and more than once attempted to carry it by assault, though they were repulsed with great loss. At last Fernandez de Carvalho, who had opportunely arrived with a squadron of three ships earlier in the siege, made an unexpected attack on the besiegers, a part of whom had withdrawn on account of a rumour purposely spread abroad by the Portuguese of a descent to be made on their own territory, and succeeded in dislodging them from their positions, and putting them to flight. Two thousand of the enemy were killed, and they left behind them their artillery and stores; but a third part of the defenders had lost their lives, while the invaders had carried off, before their final defeat, an immense booty in property and slaves. The misfortunes of Malacca did not cease with the siege, as the enemy had poisoned a well before retiring, and a number of the inhabitants who had taken refuge in the fortress lost their lives from drinking the water.[9]

The siege had ended while Francis was still in Japan. When the Santa Croce arrived off Singapore (where at that time there seems to have been no settlement, though the straits seem to have been a sort of rendezvous for ships), a light vessel was found there bound for Malacca, by means of which Francis forwarded the following hurried note, to secure himself an immediate passage to India.

(LXXXVII.) *To the Society at Malacca.*

May the grace and love of Jesus Christ our Lord be ever with us to help us and favour us! Amen.

To-day is the fortieth day since we left Japan, where the Christian religion, by the favour of God, is advancing in a wonderful way. I have left all of the Society whom I brought with me safe and sound, by the goodness of God, at Amanguchi (a large city, the capital of a kingdom), that they may take care of the people there, many of whom have already become Christians, and many more are daily becoming such.

[9] See Bartoli, *Asia*, t. i. pp. 279, 280. Faria y Sousa (*Asia Portuguesa*) tells the story somewhat differently from Bartoli, and we have followed him in several particulars.

Other things I will explain when I see you; but get ready, I beseech you, for me, some of the things necessary for the voyage to India, and provide that one of the ships bound for India may await our arrival. For it is of great importance for the glory of Christ our Lord and the salvation of souls, that I should go on at once to India from Malacca. Send Joam Bravo with your answer to my message hither to me as soon as possible. I will tell you by and by all about Japanese affairs, which I know for certain it will be most pleasant and delightful for you to hear about. But enough for the present. May God be with us all! Amen.

From the Straits of Singapore, Dec. 30, 1551.

Francis Xavier was received at Malacca with great joy. The survivors of the siege came to tell him that if he had been on the spot the calamity would not have happened. Don Pedro de Silva, still 'Capitan,' as it appears, welcomed him affectionately. The Japanese envoy whom he had with him was entertained with as much splendour as the circumstances would permit. Francis communicated to Don Pedro, and also to his brother, Don Alvaro d'Ataide,[10] who seems to have been at the time in Malacca, his designs as to the embassy to China and his intention of proposing Diego Pereira for that undertaking to the Viceroy, Don Alfonso de Noroña, who had arrived in India in 1550. As far as we can gather, no kind of opposition was given by either of the brothers.

Francis sailed almost immediately for Cochin. He arrived

[10] There is some uncertainty as to the time at which Don Alvaro succeeded his brother as 'Capitan' of Malacca. Pedro was certainly in command at the time of the siege. Alvaro came out from Portugal in the fleet which brought Don Alfonso de Noroña in 1550. He is said by some to have been at Malacca at the time of which we are speaking, and to have agreed with his brother in supporting the embassy suggested by Francis. On the other hand, Don Pedro did not leave Malacca till after Francis Xavier, and seems even to have been there when he returned a few months later. And Faria y Sousa (*Asia Portuguesa*, t. ii. p. 2, cap. 10), a little after this date, speaks of a dispute between the two brothers, Don Alvaro endeavouring to enter on his office before his brother's term had expired. It is quite certain that he did not succeed as 'Capitan' till after Francis Xavier's short visit at the beginning of 1552.

in time to catch the Portuguese ships which were to sail for Europe, and his first occupation was to write hastily to Ignatius Loyola and Simon Rodriguez and the Society in Europe as to the needs of the mission of Japan. The two following letters, therefore, really belong to this part of our subject, though they were written after Francis had returned to India. We have already given the long letter to the Society, dispatched at the same time.

The opening of the letter to Ignatius needs a word of commentary. Francis Xavier had hitherto been Superior of all the members of the Society working in the Indies, but the Indian mission had not been made a separate 'Province' until 1549, after his departure for Japan. Some of the difficulty which Francis had felt as to the appointment of Antonio Gomez, of which we have more than once spoken, may have come from the fact that India was then to some extent under the Province of Portugal. In 1549 Ignatius Loyola had erected India into a Province, and had made Francis Xavier its Provincial Superior. The 'patents' by which the appointment was formally signified to him seem to have accompanied the letter from Ignatius to which he alludes so tenderly in the opening sentences of his own letter which we now insert. At the same time he received another document, communicating to him all the privileges of the General of the Society, except that of admitting fathers to the profession of the four vows.

(LXXXVIII.) *To my holy Father in Jesus Christ, Ignatius at Rome.*

May the grace and love of our Lord Jesus Christ ever help and assist us! Amen.

O, my true Father! I have just received at Malacca, on my return from Japan, the letter of your holy charity. The news which I hoped for, and which it has given me, of the life and good health of one so dear and so venerated, have filled my soul with a joy known to God alone. I have read there many words breathing all your sweetness and piety; I have reread them many times for the comfort and the good of my soul. I go over them again in my mind, feeding on them, so to speak, continually; especially those last words which are, as it were, the seal of charity, and which conclude your letter, 'Yours entirely, so that no length of time will ever be able to make me forget you, Ignatius.' I have read these words with tears of delight, and as I write them I weep at the blessed remembrance of past days, and of the sincere and holy love with which you have always enfolded me, and which still follows me. I consider that God was pleased to deliver me from all those great toils and dangers in Japan, chiefly because your prayers and fatherly intercession in my behalf induced Him to favour me.

No words can express all that I owe to the Japanese. It is by their means alone that our Lord, by an interior illumination, has penetrated me with a knowledge of my countless sins. Up to this time, wandering outside of myself, I was ignorant of the abyss of miseries which were concealed in my conscience; until, in the labours and trials of that country, the eyes of my soul have been at last opened and the Divine Goodness has allowed me to see clearly, and touch as it were, by living experience and sensible impression, how very much I require another person to be given to me, to exercise the most sedulous care over me. Consider therefore what your holy charity is doing in putting under my guidance so many holy souls of the fathers and brothers of the Society residing in these countries. Nothing but the Divine Mercy has made me sensible in a manner transcending all evidence how ill prepared I am with the most necessary qualities for this ministry of direction. I ought rather to have hoped to be placed under the care and authority of my brothers, than to be charged with directing them.

Your holy charity adds that you greatly desire to see me once again before the close of this life. Our Lord, who reads the depths of my soul, knows the keen and sweet emotion of tender love which this affectionate expression of your precious love has roused in my inmost heart. And as often as I turn over these words in my mind (which is very often) unbidden tears fill my eyes, and break forth gently and irresistibly at this one sweetest image on which my heart dwells, that it is possible I may again clasp you in my arms: a thing difficult enough to bring about, as I see, but nothing is impossible to holy obedience.

In the name of the passionate zeal for the service and glory of our Lord God with which you are animated, I ask one favour of you, which if I were in your presence I would implore before your holy feet on my knees: it is that you would send here some man thoroughly well known and approved by your holy charity to be made Rector of the College of Goa. Such a man chosen by yourself, and so to say formed by your hands, is very much required by that College.

With regard to Japan, the reason why I am convinced that you should send there persons of great excellence and eminent both for virtue and learning, to be sent to the universities of that empire, is this. There are many there, unlearned though prudent men, who possess good judgment, and when they are convicted of their errors they take refuge in the answer that there are a multitude of learned persons in their country also who have devoted their lives to deep research, and to the reading of all kinds of books. These learned ones, they say, deny the truths which we maintain, and must have their arguments confuted and be gained over to us, in order that others who rely on their authority may be themselves converted. Therefore letters and science are indispensable.

The most remarkable strength of soul and patience, and indeed all virtues in perfection, are absolutely necessary for those who are preparing for such great conflicts. They will come, a few poor foreigners, to match themselves against the whole glory and reputation of a haughty people relying on its pride in itself and its institutions, entirely ruled by the bonzes, the first personages in the country as to dignity and esteem. Their boldness will expose them to a thousand sufferings when the hornets they have irritated shall fly upon them. They will find that they cannot do with impunity what is the first and most necessary thing to be done,—to tear to pieces the sophistries of the bonzes, to confound their falsehoods, to expose the unworthy and secret artifices with which they suck the purses of the credulous people.

From my experience when on the spot, I can well imagine how the mad fury of these false priests will break out on seeing before them a man who is able to deny to their face the power of which they boast, to snatch by their secret rites from the flames of hell souls already condemned to them; and if their ridiculous pretensions are publicly convicted of falsehood, their chief source of gain will cease to exist. And when their shameful and unnatural crimes, the detestable obscenity of which is in their eyes a matter of joke, perhaps even a subject of praise, are branded with just and severe reprobation, then it is only natural that these raging boars, pierced by the spear in their filthy mire, will run in fury and madness on the men who have cast pearls before them. As I have before said, the preachers of the truth on these and other like subjects in this country cannot fail to be violently attacked and severely tried, and they will surely be tasked to the utmost to 'possess their souls in patience,' to use the words of the Gospel; and this patience they must acquire by practice, and be powerfully armed therewith before they expose themselves to such dangers. I am writing to Father Simon, or in case of his absence to the Rector of the College of Coimbra, to send no one for the Japanese universities who has not been seen, examined, and approved by your holy charity.

I cannot repeat too often that our brothers will have to endure conflicts and trials beyond all common expectation. Visited constantly and most unseasonably, they will not have a moment of the day (often not of the night) free from importunate inquirers; questions will follow one upon another incessantly; the nobles will send for them, and it will be impossible to refuse to go to them. These distractions will rob them of time for daily prayer, meditation, recollection of the soul in God, and other spiritual exercises of the kind. They will not have time to celebrate mass at least for some days after they first show themselves, on account of the crowd of visitors; they will barely have leisure for accomplishing the obligation of Office, or for necessary food and sleep. One of the faults of this people is without any shame to take up the time of foreigners, especially people who come from a distance, whom they generally treat contemptuously and make game of them wantonly, even when they are harmless and in no way troublesome. But if these foreigners venture to attack and blame openly what the common people reverence and admire, if they lift up their voice against the different sects of false religions, if they satirize and strike with the censor's rod the public crimes of the nation, and do it thoroughly and earnestly, if they declare obstinately that no one who has gone down into the fires of hell can be delivered from them by any sacrifice or almsgiving or rites performed by their living relations and friends; then they will certainly have to undergo a violent tempest of ill will; even the wisest of the natives will be exasperated at their thinking so hardly as to the souls of persons, dear to them, who are already dead; they will, for the most part, despise the new religion as imperfect and impotent, as confessing at once to inability of applying any remedy to souls already condemned. People's minds here are filled with cares and questions as to this point, because the literature and the old traditions of the country abound in stories of hell and do not say anything about Purgatory.

Now all this being so, it is self evident that what we want here are powerful intellects, practised in dialectics, gifted with a popular eloquence, quick to follow error in its shiftings and even to anticipate them, able to snatch the mask from lies which plausibly bear the semblance of reality, to unravel sophistical arguments, and to show the incoherence and mutual contradiction of false doctrines. As a matter of fact, these bonzes are wonderfully ashamed and confused if the want of harmony and even the self contradiction of their dogmas are brought to light, or when they are so caught in the bonds of an invincible argument that they cannot escape from it. To these intellectual gifts must be added bodily strength—capable of resisting the severest cold of winter. Bandou, the chief Japanese university, is situated in the most northern part of these islands, and the others are not far off. It is found out here that natives of a colder climate are distinguished beyond others for skill and genius. As to the food, rice is almost the only thing to eat, though there is a little wheat and a few vegetables, greens, and other things of that sort, dry and not very wholesome. The only wine is made from rice (the making is an art); it is very scarce, and so extremely dear. But the most troublesome trial of all is the continual anxiety caused by daily perils.

Old men are unsuited for the work in this country; they would not have the necessary strength for the labours which are indispensable. Neither are young men desirable, except those in whom the defect of age is supplied by great virtues, proved openly by severe trials; otherwise they would rather ruin themselves than be of use to others. All kinds of temptations and occasions of sin abound in Japan. Added to this, men's minds are more delicate here than anywhere else, and are easily scandalized by the very slightest appearance of an imperfect example in persons who claim to teach others. I am writing all these particulars as minutely as they are here set down to Master Simon, or if he should be absent, to the Rector of Coimbra.

I should be most glad if your holy charity would be so good as to write to Coimbra desiring that the missionaries intended for Japan may be first sent to you at Rome. I have often thought that Belgians or Germans, acquainted with Portuguese or Spanish, would be well fitted for this destination. The men of both these countries bear fatigue well, and are prepared by their temperament and education to bear the cold of Bandou. It has seemed to me as very probable that there must be a great many fathers, natives of these two countries, in the different Colleges of Spain and Italy, where perhaps they are not so very useful, not being masters of the native elegances of the language of the country. If they were transplanted to Japan, they would do very efficient service there, and gain the reward of great fruit of souls. I have thought it also my duty to suggest to your holy charity, if this idea pleases you, to order that more strict prudence be exercised in the choice of persons to be sent from the Spanish and Portuguese Colleges to live in India. It would be better that only two fathers should sail yearly for India, provided they were persons such as this country requires; in the first place sufficiently advanced in spiritual perfection, and then possessing the eloquence and learning indispensable for preaching and hearing confessions. These also I should wish by your order to make a pilgrimage to Rome before sailing hither; for those trials of journeys help to form them, show them the extent of their strength, inure them to labour, and strengthen them to endure future perils by the remembrance of the past dangers which they have safely escaped. Lastly, we shall gain this also: that they will not be new to the fatigues of missionary labours, as we find men to be who come hither from their own homes carried quietly on board ship, without having any practice at all in going about the country as pilgrims.

Besides this, there are here so many inducements to self indulgence, such strong and seducing allurements, not only to sloth and idleness, but even to wickedness, that it seems right that the virtue of those who are to be exposed to these spiritual dangers should first be proved by most careful trials; lest unhappily unsuitable persons should creep in among our missioners, who instead of the comfort we might have expected from their arrival and residence amongst us, would occasion us the most grievous trouble, and do things in consequence of which we are obliged to dismiss them from the Society. Let your holy charity see, I beseech you, whether it will be well yourself to admonish Master Simon on this point.

No one of those of ours now at Amanguchi, or of those at present in India and intended to go to Japan, God willing, next year or in some following year, seems to me fitted to be sent to the Japanese universities. But they will spend their time in studying the language, and in learning the doctrines of the different sects, so that when the fathers whom we expect come from Europe, sent as from your own bosom, they may make use of the others as faithful helpers and interpreters in disputing with the bonzes. I hope very confidently that the Church of

Amanguchi will grow and develope very largely. It already has a great many Christians; and many among them are excellent: new converts are being instructed and baptized every day. I live in the firm hope that our Lord will preserve to us Father Cosmo Torres and Joam Fernandez, and not suffer them to be put to death by the idolaters—first, because they seem to have already escaped the first and most instant dangers, and the fury of the bonzes, excessively irritated in their earliest attacks, appears to have softened with time and to be gradually waning; also because there are so many Christians there, several of them of distinguished rank and power, who watch very zealously day and night over the safety of our missioners. Joam Fernandez, though a simple layman, is most useful on account of the fluency he has acquired in the Japanese language, and of the aptness and clearness with which he translates whatever Father Cosmo suggests to him. At present he is entirely occupied in explaining all the mysteries of Jesus Christ to the people in daily instructions.

As I perceive in the Japanese a happy disposition for approving the Christian religion when sufficiently explained to them, and for persevering with constancy therein when they have received it, as well as handing it on to their posterity, I think that even the greatest labour would be well employed in cultivating them. As to this thought, I find much strength and consolation in the hope I place in your holy charity, which bids me ask that you will send some fathers of great sanctity whom we may fitly oppose to the teachers of the superstitions of Japan. One of the principal motives to induce you to do so, is the superiority, which is very evident to me, of the Japanese nation over all the others at present discovered in these parts. I do not think that there is any other nation living under its own laws and not subject to the King of Portugal as to which we may hope that the Christian religion will take root and remain firm and lasting. As far as I know, the Japanese nation is the single and only nation of them all which seems likely to preserve unshaken and for ever the profession of Christian holiness if once it embraces it; but this will doubtless not be without great sufferings and heroic conflicts on the part of the preachers of the Gospel.

China, an immense empire, enjoying profound peace, regulated by a number of very wise laws, is governed by a single sovereign whose will is absolute. It is a most opulent empire, abounding in everything necessary for human life. A narrow strait separates it from Japan. Its people are remarkable for intelligence, and employ themselves in study, chiefly of laws and human jurisprudence, and also of political science. The ambition of the greater part of the people is to gain a deep knowledge on this subject. The faces of the natives are pale and beardless, and their eyes are small. They have generally kind open dispositions, and are lovers of peace, which flourishes and is firmly established among them, without any fear of wars. Unless some new obstacles should arise and alter my plans, I hope to sail for China in this year 1552, whither I am attracted by the hope of being able to do good work in furthering greatly the service of God to the benefit of both the Chinese and Japanese nations. As soon as the Japanese learn that the Chinese have embraced the faith of Jesus Christ, there is reason to hope that the obstinacy with which they are attached to their own false sects will be lessened. So I am full of confidence that by the labours of our Society, the Chinese and Japanese will abandon their idolatrous superstitions and adore Jesus Christ, the Saviour of all nations.

I may tell you by the way of a singular and strange thing which is observed as to the mutual intercourse of these two nations. Their languages are different, so that people who speak the one do not understand the other. But an educated Japanese can read and understand what a Chinese writes, only, when he reads it aloud, what he says is unintelligible to the writer himself if he be there. For the Chinese letters are not like the characters we use, which express the various sounds of the human voice, but they represent the things themselves, and so are innumerable. And those people in Japan who affect to be learned learn the signification of these letters, that is the objects which they designate, not the word or name which they represent. And in order to make elementary instruction easier and the labour of teachers lighter, they have hit upon this compendious method. They set forth on a board the Chinese letters, putting upon each a picture of the thing which they signify—as, for example, they put a representation of a man upon the character which is fixed on to signify a man, and so on. So the Japanese, when they read, have the representation to guide them, and in their minds they think of the thing which the Chinese who has written the character had in his mind; but when they come to read aloud what is before them, they utter the Japanese words which signify the thing. The Chinese hear them, and do not know in the least what they mean. And so in turn, if a Chinese reads to a Japanese the same writing, the latter will not understand a word of what he says.[11]

We have written a book in the Japanese language explaining the origin of the world, and all the mysteries of the life of Jesus Christ. We have transcribed this book into Chinese characters, and intend to carry this copy with us when we go into China, so that while we are learning the language of the country we may be able to show the Chinese a sample of the truths we bring to them written in characters which they know. I pray and beseech your holy charity, in the name of your love for God and your zeal for His service, yourself to recommend me earnestly to God in your daily prayers and holy sacrifices, and make the rest of the Society do the same. I ardently solicit (and your holy charity will be my interpreter and mediator in this matter) that the suffrages of all the fathers, especially the professed, and their powerful intercession with our common Lord, may be procured for me. These prayers, in union with the merits of the whole militant Church, and with the prayers

[11] On this adoption by the Japanese of the Chinese characters, see Sir Rutherford Alcock, *Capital of the Tycoon*, i. 167. There is a better account in M. Humbert, *Japon Illustré*, t. ii. p. 33 seq. The same excellent work curiously confirms the statement made a little above about the arms of the Prince of Satsouma. These are figured in M. Humbert's book, t. i. p. 392, as a broad circular hoop of black with two equally broad transverse bands crossing the white circle in the middle. The cross is therefore there, but in black.

of all the blessed who in their lifetime were of our Society, and the petitions of the whole of the Church triumphant, may obtain for me from our Lord God the grace clearly to know in this life what His holy Will desires of me, and the assistance and strength necessary for accomplishing in all fulness and perfection whatever it may be His order or command that I should do.

The least of your sons, and the farthest from your presence,

Cochin, Jan. 29, 1552. FRANCIS.

The next letter, to Simon Rodriguez, accompanied that to Ignatius.

(LXXXIX.) *To Master Simon Rodriguez.*

May the grace and love of Jesus Christ our Lord always help and favour us!

I am anxious to inform you of different matters relating to Japan, so as to give you a notion what kind of labourers are required for that country. Men, in the first place, of tried experience, proved by suffering and dangers, should be chosen, in order to win the people to the true faith. At Bandou, and in the other universities, great conflicts and great persecution await them from the bonzes. So I say they will be violently assailed, and to such a point, that there may be risk, lest in seeking to save others they lose themselves, unless they possess great strength of soul and confidence in God. They will have to endure very severe cold, Bandou being much further north than Amanguchi; they will also have to put up with want of food, there being almost nothing to eat but rice and vegetables, and a few like things. For such an undertaking, as you see, it is self evident that men of great virtue and of good physical constitution are required.

I think it would be advisable to send some Belgians and Germans, who are accustomed to cold and bodily suffering, and being away from their native country, and not knowing the language, can do no great work in preaching in Portugal or elsewhere. You have many such in Italy, Spain, and France. I should wish them also to be well practised in argumentative conclusions, in solving captious objections, so as to be sufficiently learned publicly to confound the bonzes, whose authority is of greatest weight in the universities—in fact to make them contradict themselves openly. I shall send some of our people hence to Amanguchi to learn the Japanese language, and get some idea of the doctrines and errors of the nation, so that other more eminent subjects of the Society sent hither may find them able companions and interpreters, and then go to attack the universities, and that, even though not sufficiently acquainted with the language of the nation, these fathers may dispute themselves with the bonzes by means of interpreters, until they themselves know Japanese. I beg you to let our blessed Father Ignatius know about the men whom you are going to send to the Japanese universities.

A great concourse of men go from all parts of Japan to the university of Bandou, to gain learning. When they return to their country, they teach their fellow-countrymen what they have acquired. I am told that Bandou is a very large and well populated town; its inhabitants are famous for their noble blood, but also for military prowess, although many of gentle and peaceful nature are to be found. I entreat you to take care to send us brothers of proved virtue and modesty for this place.

To give some idea of the difficulties which those destined for Japan will encounter when they appear in the universities, they will be continually assailed with questions and disputes one after another, they will be the sport of the people, mocked and laughed at by every one. They will have no leisure time for meditation or the contemplation of divine truths, none for saying mass, especially at Bandou and Meaco, scarcely even the necessary time for reciting the Divine Office. The missionaries' dwelling will be constantly thronged with a crowd of natives—sometimes visitors, sometimes inquirers, sometimes people sent by the nobles, to invite them to a visit without ever admitting any excuse.

In fact so many importunate people come at every instant

that barely a moment can be found for bodily needs, for taking a little sleep or food. Satan will lay snares for them in wonderful ways, and our brethren deprived of their hours of divine meditation and office, and above all of the fruits of the most Holy Eucharist, if they have added to this the persecution of the bonzes, the excessive inconvenience of the cold, the insufficiency and difficulty about food, and the absolute hopeless absence of all human consolation and aid,—these, I say, who have to undergo so many and such great miseries, must be endowed with singular virtue.

You must, then, be very careful in the choice of subjects to be sent to Japan. Old men are not suitable because they are wanting in strength, and young men are not because they lack experience. Believe me, the zeal and virtue of those who enroll themselves for Japan will be indeed abundantly tried, and more than enough; but, on the other hand, they will be filled in a marvellous way with heavenly consolations if they bear their trials and fatigues courageously, and use the grace and help of God, which are given most largely in the greatest difficulties, to win the victory over our everlasting enemy.

I again implore you, my dearest Brother, to send to India such subjects as, although few in number, may be of great service; as there are at present in Europe so many houses of the Society, two at least might be chosen every year from each house gifted with a natural talent for preaching, and who might render even still greater service by their example than their words. India is indeed of all countries the one where such subjects are the most necessary. I would have you charge the fathers who are sent, to admit no one into the Society amongst their fellow travellers. If a certain number of subjects are received in India, to be applied later on to Humanities, it ought only to be those who are possessed with a good foundation of learning and virtue and come to us merely to finish their studies. You send away a great number of subjects from the colleges in Europe; and we would rather have them here than receive out here into our number men who only know how to read and write.

Most desirable it would be if no one were to come from Portugal to India before finishing his studies, and no one be received into the Society here excepting subjects required for domestic purposes. Studies out here are a very slow concern; those who undertake studies here must wait a great many years before they will be fit to preach, hear confessions, and be of use to the Society and people of the country.

O my Simon! may God unite us in the heavenly country, since for His sake we live so far apart on earth! However, what if we are to meet again in the kingdom of China? I earnestly beg of you to ask our Lord to give me the grace to open the gates of China to others, for I am fit for nothing myself. You must treat the affair concerning the Fishery Coast (which Enrico Enriquez has written to you about), I mean about the Commandant, with his Highness; it is very important for the good of religion.

Cochin, Jan. 30, 1552. FRANCIS.

The last paragraph appears to refer to a topic unfortunately by no means new in the letters of Francis Xavier—the exactions and vexations which the Christian converts on the Fishery Coast had to suffer at the hands of the Portuguese officials. We may well suppose that the memorial as to the Commandant or 'Captain' of the Fishery Coast, to which reference is made, is a document which has come to light in our time, and was first printed by M. Léon Pagès at the end of the second volume of his translation of the letters. The complaints of the Christians therein contained are, at all events, of the same character with those alluded to by Francis Xavier, who seems to have forwarded some document of the sort drawn up by Enrico Enriquez. The pearl fishers say that the Captain makes them pay him a certain tribute on account of their fisheries, even when they do not fish, and also to fish in a way which they do not like. They ask to be allowed to pay the dues only on the fishing which they actually make, and not to be compelled to fish against their will, 'for such,' they say, 'is the right which the Governor Garcia de Sà conceded to them;'

and they ask his Highness that this order may be carried out. Again, the Captain exacts a tax from them on the fish which they catch, and on which they live. This is an entirely new impost, and they demand to be relieved from it. Again, the Captain exacts dues from them on the cowries which they trade with to Africa, and makes them sell to him for a third part of the price which foreign traders offer for them. This abuse also they beg may be forbidden for the future. Again, the Captain and his friends used to claim a monopoly of the sale of rice, and to sell it to the natives at an arbitrary price, forcing them to take it whether they would or no, and then prosecuting them until they had paid him. In the same way the Portuguese official put dues upon their coasting trade, on which the transport of their provisions depended, their boats being not allowed to sail except under his licence. Further, he moved them about arbitrarily from village to village, never leaving them fixed for long in the same place, and exacting certain fees whenever they were thus transplanted. On all these points they appeal to the justice of his Highness for relief, and they also ask that fugitives from neighbouring territories, who may be driven out by tyranny or persecution, may be welcomed and allowed to live in peace in the settlements of the Fishery Coast, in order that by this means they may be encouraged to place themselves under the protection of his Highness, and that the number of converts to Christianity may be increased. The memorial concludes by saying that all these things have been already ordered by Garcia de Sà the Governor, and have also been made the subject of petition by Ruy Gomez de Camynha, a resident at Goa, who holds the office of procurator of their interests.[12] And the Christians pray that his Highness

[12] We are inclined to think that the Ruy Gomez mentioned here is the person whose name is written Ruy Gonzalez in the letter to Antonio Gomez and others inserted above (p. 163). The office mentioned is the same as that named here. It is evident that the translations of letters like those of Francis Xavier are sure to be less accurate in the proper names than in other matters, and in the transcripts—perhaps even in the originals—the names Gonzalez and Gomez would both be represented in the same abridged form, the first and the two last letters alone being given.

will grant their requests as a special favour, in which the interests of the service of God and the increase of the faith are concerned.[13]

It would not be easy to draw a more complete picture of official tyranny and exaction than that which is given, as it were, in outline in this document. The Christians were evidently looked upon by the Captain of the Fishery Coast as a race of slaves, with no rights and no friends, out of whom he and his friends were simply to squeeze what they could. The mention in the document of Garcia de Sà as a former governor of the Indies, fixes the date of these complaints at the year 1552, though it is just possible that they may have been drawn up between the time at which Francis returned from Japan and his last departure for India in the following April. It is therefore certain that neither the orders of the King, in his letter to Joam de Castro, nor the injunctions of the governor who succeeded Joam, had been able to effect any change for the better in the conduct of the Portuguese officials at a distance from the capital, and the strong language used in some of the letters of Francis Xavier to the King is abundantly justified.[14]

[13] See Léon Pagès, t. ii. p. 523 seq.

[14] M. Léon Pagès prints, at the end of the document to which reference has been made above, a short letter from Francis himself, which appears to be appended to the memorial. If there is no uncertainty as to the connection between the two papers, we must of course suppose the shortest, which is from Francis himself, to have been drawn up at this time. This hypothesis, however, is not altogether free from difficulties drawn from internal evidence, as the note is addressed to a Vicar General who seems to be either going to Portugal or to be about to write to the King, and mentions as a very desirable thing the coming of Simon Rodriguez to India armed with certain power from his Highness. This, although not incompatible with the later date of 1552, seems more naturally to belong to the year 1549. It appears to us, therefore, uncertain at what date the letter should be fixed. It was as follows:

Memorial for the Vicar General of the things regarding which he should treat with the King, for the good of the Christians in India.

Your Reverence should remind the King to send a great number of preachers of the Society of Jesus into these countries, and secondly into the garrisons in India. There is a great want of preachers, as your Reverence well knows.

What a service would his Highness render to God, if he sent to these countries of India Simon, with a great many members of the Society of Jesus! Indeed, his coming would produce great fruits among the souls of the Portuguese in India, and make many Christians in Japan, which is peopled with infidels. At the same time it would be a great favour from his Highness if Master Simon were invested with civil jurisdiction over all the Christians of this country, so that no one else should have authority over them except those appointed by Father Master Simon, besides those persons designated by his Highness to occupy these offices. Indeed the captains invested with this jurisdiction over the Christians of the country, only use it to commit wrong and to seize property from the legitimate owners against their will, thus scandalizing the Christians of the country, and preventing the conversion of unbelievers, because of the ill treatment which the latter see inflicted upon those who are already Christians.

In the event of Master Simon's not coming, your Grace may obtain from the King that he should confer on the Bishop this civil jurisdiction over the Christians of the country, and that none shall have jurisdiction nor authority over them, save those appointed by the Bishop or by his Highness. And these officials will remain in their employment so long as they fulfil their duty: so that the Bishop can dispose of these officials, and invest other persons with their appointments when the first do not fulfil their duty.

[One line is almost entirely effaced.]

NOTES TO BOOK V.

(1.) *Letter to the Society at Coimbra from Cagoxima, November 5th,* 1549.

A LETTER is extant from Francis Xavier to the Society at Coimbra, under the same date as the long letter already given (p. 227 seq.) addressed to the Society at Goa. It seems probable that both letters were written by Francis himself, rather than that the letter to Coimbra was an abridgment sent on from India—especially as the letter to Goa contains so much of exhortation and instruction for the fathers and brothers immediately subject to Francis himself. It is not, however, worth while to reproduce the letter to Coimbra in full, as it is in substance, as has been already said, a simple repetition of the narrative parts of the longer letter to India. It consists, in Father Menchacha's version, of eight paragraphs or sections. The first contains the account of the voyage towards Japan, as far as the accident by which the daughter of the corsair was drowned. In the passage which follows, as to the incident of the answer given by the idol, that if the Christian Emmanuel had died the girl would have escaped, Francis leaves out the curious statement about his own prayer that the devil's torments might be increased, and says, 'I took to earnest prayer, and asked God very often that before we were swallowed up by the waves, He would deliver those men made by Him after His own image and likeness from their false and erroneous opinions and impious superstitions; for it is a foul sight and a thing altogether intolerable that the perpetual enemy of the human race itself should be adored in the place of God by men who are made to praise God.' The second paragraph relates succinctly the rest of the voyage and the reception of Francis and the others at Cagoxima. The third, which is very long, gives in abridgment what is said in the former letter as to the characteristics and manners of the Japanese, the bonzes, their unnatural impurities, the different orders of religious, the bad lives of the bonzes, who live with women of their own order, the wonder which Francis felt at the way in which the most abominable sins were thought nothing of, and at the credit in which the bonzes were, notwithstanding their vices. It ends with a short account of his intercourse with Ningh-sit. The fourth paragraph sums up a few of his thoughts about the opening of a great field of labour, and the necessity of great selfdiscipline, patience, and submission, as a preparation for it, which occupy so large a space in the letter to India. It is curious that it has the following sentence: 'It will, perhaps, very probably turn out that I may call a number of you out hither within the next two years.' The fifth paragraph takes up the story of their residence at Cagoxima, Paul's visit to the Prince of Satsouma, and what passed about the picture of our Blessed Lady. It also mentions their need of the language, the way in which their position makes them trust entirely to God, and the benefit of the great scarcity and simplicity of food in Japan. The next paragraph sums up very briefly the anticipations of Francis as to the opposition of the bonzes, and his own readiness to sacrifice his life for the salvation of the Japanese. The seventh paragraph is an abridgment of what is said in the former letter as to his journey to Meaco, and as to the Japanese universities (in the list of which the name Frenojama is inserted), and as to his intention of writing to Europe when he has found out how things are in these universities. Where he speaks of inviting members of other religious orders, he adds, 'if they come out even in the greatest numbers, there will still be room left for the endeavours and labours of more.' He then mentions the conversion of the two bonzes, who are going to India, and his own visit to the Prince of Satsouma, as well as the edict of toleration issued by that prince. The last paragraph of the letter is a sort of condensation of the exhortations to humility and mutual charity which occur at the end of the letter to Goa.

(2.) *The Evidence as to the possession of the gift of tongues by Francis Xavier.*

The *Relatio super sanctitate et miraculis Francisci Xaverii*, to which reference has been made in the Preface to the first volume of this work, as well as elsewhere, is too long a document for us to analyze in the present volume, which already threatens to exceed its destined limits. We may, however, give at least one specimen of its chapters, and the mention of the exercise of the 'gift of tongues' by Francis at Amanguchi may serve as the occasion for the insertion of a short epitome of the argument as summarily represented by the Auditors of the Rota in their chapter on this subject.

The chapter begins by asserting, as from the evidence collected in the Processes, that Francis Xavier had this gift, which he exercised in two ways. First, he spoke the languages (which he had never learnt) of natives to whom he went to preach the Gospel as freely and elegantly as if he had been born and educated in the midst of those nations; and in the second place, it not unfrequently happened that men of different nations heard him at the same time, each in his own language. This happened elsewhere, and particularly in the port of Jafanapatam, and was considered as a great miracle, which made people venerate him, and also converted many.

The fact asserted being thus divided into two parts, fourteen witnesses are referred to who prove both parts at once. One of them, Emmanuel Fernandez, an old man of eighty at the time of his examination at Cochin, said that he knew Father Francis on the Fishery Coast, and in the port of Jafanapatam on the Coromandel Coast he had seen Francis preaching to the natives in their own tongue, and that all marvelled that he spoke so well, though he had just come there, and their language was very difficult to learn. And in the same town and port there were persons of divers nations and various tongues, and in a certain sermon which the said Father delivered in the presence of this witness, all affirmed that they heard him, each as if he were speaking in their proper and natural language. Emmanuel himself was witness that as soon as he came into a region he could speak any tongue, and this was considered a great miracle, and many were converted thereby. Another witness testifies to have heard of the miracle from persons who were present at Jafanapatam when Francis preached as mentioned above, and also to the common opinion and fame which prevailed concerning this matter, and how it was commonly said along the whole Fishery Coast that as soon as he had come there he had preached in the language of the Paravas as if he had been born there. Another, examined at Lisbon, testifies to the public report, and that he had heard himself from persons worthy of credit of the possession of the gift of tongues by Francis Xavier, so that when he spoke in one language he was heard by people of different nations in the native language of each. Several other witnesses are enumerated for this. Then a witness whose examination was taken at Bazain, Rodrigo Diaz Pereira, one of the King's nobles (Aulæ Regiæ Patritius), states that he sailed with Father Francis in the same ship to Banda, that is, to one of the Moluccas, and had seen many heathen converted to the faith by the labours and preaching of the Father, and that he used to preach the faith to them in their own language. Another witness follows who deposes to the same from common report. Another says that he heard from his uncle Gaspar de Cerqueiros Abreu, commander of the 'Japanese expedition,' that he had often heard Father Francis preaching in Japan or to the Chinese, and that while he understood him in his own native Portuguese, all the others who were present understood him each in his own language, though they were of other nations. Another witness, examined at Goa, declares that he had heard from persons worthy of credit, and particularly from four brothers who had been companions of Francis when in India, that when he first went to Japan and knew little or nothing of the language, yet though he preached without an interpreter, partly in Spanish, partly in Latin, partly in Portuguese, with a few Japanese words mixed up, he was understood by all as if he had spoken in the native language of each, and that the same happened in the Isles of the Moor and on the Fishery Coast. Another bears witness that it was notorious and testified by persons who had heard Francis's sermons, that in the places on the Comorin Promontory and the Fishery Coast he used to preach in the native language so perfectly and easily that it seemed, as it were, his own by birth, and that all understood the exhortations which he made in public, nor was there any one who did not, on account of the appropriateness of the language which he used, and so it was commonly said that the whole people would have become Christian if he had not gone on so soon to other parts. Another witness says that those who were Xavier's companions and heard his sermons affirmed that he spoke in the idiom or language of all the men whom he went among in India, as one who really had the gift of tongues, speaking to the people of Malabar or the Moluccas without an interpreter, and preaching with as much ease in the Molucca dialect as in Portuguese, being himself from Navarre.

The auditors of the Rota then proceed to show how wonderful this gift must have been, quoting the promise made by our Lord as to the signs which shall follow those who believe, and also the words of St. Paul that tongues are a sign, not to believers, but to unbelievers. As to the sign, it is proved in this case by the evidence which establishes that it was held for a great miracle, and that many were converted by it; and hence it is clear that they must have been certainly aware that Francis Xavier could not have learnt the languages, and they would not otherwise have marvelled at his being able to speak them. They illustrate this from the case of the Jews, who marvelled how our Lord knew 'letters,' never having learnt them, and they say that St. Chrysostom states that this was miracle enough to have converted them. Then they mention a calculation that the languages of the nations among which Francis preached were at least thirty in number, very difficult to acquire, and such as no one even with long study can perfectly master so as to speak elegantly and fluently. On the other hand, Francis Xavier was only ten years and a half in the East, two and more of which were spent in Japan. Again, the writers remark that to speak a language elegantly and to speak it easily are different things, as also to speak it simply without great elegance; but the two first named habits require very long practice and are acquired with great difficulty, whereas Francis Xavier had no time even to have practised speaking in the languages, which he used nevertheless to speak as soon as he arrived in any place where they were spoken. They argue also, from his great occupation in other things and from there being no places where these languages were taught, that he could not have acquired them naturally. The auditors then prove that the second form of the gift—the speaking in one language and being understood in many—was a real instance of the gift of tongues and also was held as a miracle, from the account of the gift as it was given to the Apostles on the day of Pentecost. They also quote St. Cyprian (*Serm. de Sp. Sto.*) on this subject, and also Bozius *de Signis Ecclesiæ.* They end by arguing that it was highly probable that Francis Xavier would have had this gift, inasmuch as it had been given to the Apostles to enable them to be of use to those to whom they were sent, and the power of being understood by many of different languages at the same time seemed necessary to them, so also as this servant of God was sent to the East for the salvation of its peoples, it seems to follow that as in other respects he had received the spirit of the Apostles, so also in this respect he should be like unto them.

(3.) *Disputes at Amanguchi between Cosmo Torres and the Bonzes.*

We had prepared a translation of the letter of Joam Fernandez to Francis Xavier, giving an account of the questions proposed at Amanguchi to Father Torres, and of the father's answers. But want of space compels us to sacrifice this interesting document, with many others. It seems to have been used by the author of the *Histoire de l'Eglise de Japon,* and we may refer to the English translation (1705), t. i. p. 120 seq.

BOOK VI.

FROM THE LAST RETURN OF FRANCIS TO INDIA TO HIS DEATH AT SAN CHAN.

CHAPTER I.

Last Stay of Francis at Cochin and Goa.

RAPID and active as were the movements of Francis Xavier at all times of his life, when he had once come to a decision as to the course which it was the will of God that he should immediately pursue, the swiftness, energy, and industry which characterized him from the time that he had grown prematurely grey under his labours and privations in Japan seem wonderful even in him. It may well have astonished the Portuguese mariners of the time that he should have reached Cochin within very little more than two months after his departure from Fucheo. Except during the five days of terrible tempest which gave him the occasion to display so many features of Christian charity in the voyage from Japan to San Chan, the winds and seas seem almost to have been at his command. He stayed, as we have seen, but a few days at Malacca. Francesco Perez and Joam Bravo would tell him of the news from India, which showed him how greatly his presence was required there; and indeed, if he met at Malacca the letter from Ignatius appointing him Provincial Superior, he would have needed no other spur to hasten his steps towards the country where so many of his subjects were awaiting his direction. He made his arrangements with Diego Pereira for the expedition to China with great dispatch, and their arrangements required that he should be once more at Malacca before the summer was far advanced. He had thus not many weeks to spare before he must be again on his way to the furthest East.

He had been absent from India not far short of three years—a long time from the active, bustling, and changeful existence of the Portuguese settlers in Asia. He had left Don Garcia de Sà Governor of the Indies. Garcia de Sà had died about the time that Francis had reached Cagoxima, and had been succeeded by Jorge Cabral, a gallant officer, who, as Faria y Sousa tells us, hesitated to accept the charge, expecting to be soon superseded by the arrival of a new Governor sent direct from Portugal.[1] In fact, before the end of the following year, 1550, Don Alfonso de Noroña arrived from Europe with the title of Viceroy to take the government from his hands, much to the loss of India, if we may judge from the tone of the Portuguese chronicler. The new Viceroy was the son of the Marquis de Villa Reale, and must have known Francis Xavier when in Portugal. At all events, he was sure to do his best to help him in all that concerned the advancement of the faith, as far as his own powers extended.[2]

In many respects, though not in all, the news which Francis might have learnt at Malacca and at Cochin concerning the Society in India was such as might fairly rejoice his heart. His religious brethren had been generally labouring with great success and edification to all, while the troubles which he was called upon to remedy were in the main the work of one or two men at the most. The general results of the Indian mission were so satisfactory, there had been so great and so fruitful a display of charitable selfdevotion and religious zeal, that about a year before Francis left Japan, his friend the Bishop of Goa had written to St. Ignatius at Rome, thanking him for the services rendered by his children, and speaking of them in terms of the highest praise. We have already mentioned the heroic death of Antonio Criminale, which took place while Francis was waiting at Malacca to embark on his Japanese voyage. Another member of the Society had been martyred on the day on which he landed at Cagoxima. This was Nuñez Ribero, whom he had sent to the Moluccas in 1548. We have seen in

[1] Jorge Cabral was Capitan at Bazain at the time of the death of Garcia de Sà, when the patents of succession were opened, appointing him to the Governorship. Faria y Sousa (t. ii. p. 2, c. 7) gives a long argument between Cabral and his wife Doña Lucrecia Fiallo, who seems to have persuaded her husband to accept the office, 'non siempre son danosas las mugeres,' says the historian.

[2] Lucena (*Vida*, l. ix. c. 18) calls him 'antigo divoto do Padre M. Francesco.'

what strong language Francis had spoken of the immense hardships which were to be endured in the mission of the Moluccas, and of his expectation that those islands would soon be the scenes of martyrdom. The story of Nuñez Ribero reads like a commentary on the words of Francis. He laboured with the most boundless charity, both for the Portuguese sailors of the ships which had to wait a certain time at Amboyna, where he was stationed, and afterwards for the natives. He gave away everything, even his own most necessary clothing. He lived in a state of privation which made the external conditions of his existence almost those of the savages to whom he was devoting himself. His life was more than once in danger from violence, and once he had nearly lost it after a shipwreck for want of food and shelter. He was at last poisoned at the instigation of some Mussulmans.

We are, however, forced to conjecture that the mission of the Moluccas was not entirely prosperous, in the truest sense of the term. We find that two of those whom Francis had sent thither from Malacca, when he himself was about to start for Japan, had in some way misconducted themselves—probably they had committed some grave breach of obedience. These two were Manuel de Morães and Francesco Gonzalez. We also find that Joam Beira himself was afterwards obliged to sail for India, in order, as it seems, to transact some business of importance to his mission with the Viceroy at Goa. At this time, therefore, the young priest Alfonso de Castro was alone at his post in those dangerous isles.

Ormuz, at the mouth of the Persian Gulf, had been the scene of the heroic labours and glorious sacrifices of Gaspar Baertz, who had shown the true apostolic spirit, and carried out most perfectly the instructions which Francis Xavier had given him.[3] Gaspar was now at Goa, awaiting the time at which he had been ordered to sail for Japan, and Father Joam Gonzalez

[3] Father Gaspar's work at Ormuz could not be done justice to in less than a separate chapter. It fills fifty pages of Bartoli's first volume of *Asia*. It is one of the many collateral subjects which want of space compels us to abandon.

Rodriguez had taken his place at Ormuz. The most conspicuous conversion in India had been that of the Rajah of Tanore, already mentioned, which had been mainly due to the zeal and skill of Antonio Gomez. The movement towards a reform of manners among the Portuguese, which had been begun by Francis himself, and urged on by the Fathers who had arrived from Portugal in 1548 with Antonio, had been continued, and it was now a rare thing for any one to venture on a voyage, whether for commercial or military purposes, without first reconciling himself to God by the reception of the sacraments. The King of Portugal had been so well pleased with the labours of the Society, as formally to commit to the care of its members all the seminaries of various kinds which he had founded throughout India, and was more than ever bent on providing in Portugal for an abundant supply of missioners for the East.

There was much, therefore, of good tidings to greet Francis on his return from Japan. But the picture was not altogether without its dark side. At Cochin itself, where he was received with all demonstrations of joy and reverence, there were many hearts sore with indignation against others of the Society. When Francis had last visited Cochin, the inhabitants had entreated him to leave them Alfonso de Castro, that he might begin the foundation of a college for the benefit of the town. Francis had been unable to grant the request, but it seems to have been renewed, as to the foundation of a college, in his absence, to the Fathers Paul and Antonio Gomez; and as the latter had already usurped that fulness of authority in India from which Francis had so carefully excluded him, he had gone to Cochin himself to make arrangements in the matter. A church dedicated to our Lady the Mother of God had been made over to him by the Confraternity to whom it belonged; but after a time the donors repented of their gift, and asked for the church back again. Gomez acted with a high hand. The Governor, Jorge Cabral, was his devoted friend, and when the complaints and murmurs became louder on his refusal to surrender the church, Gomez was not afraid to use his influence with the secular authorities, and have the chief movers on the part of the Confraternity cast into prison. Such an act of violence was unheard of in India, and was entirely contrary to the spirit of the Society. The first act of Francis Xavier was to set this trouble right. He begged the Vicar and the local magistrates to meet him, and assembled also the members of the Confraternity. Then he came before them with the keys of the church in his hands, and throwing himself on his knees, protested that he made no claim, nor would accept anything at all, except what their pure bounty chose to bestow upon him, and at the same time he asked pardon in the humblest manner for what had been done in his absence. The whole company was moved to tears. The Confraternity immediately assembled in formal council, and made a solemn and irrevocable donation of the church to the Society.

Francis next punished the two refractory members of the Society who had returned from the Moluccas, Manuel de Morães and Francesco Gonzalez, who seem to have been waiting at Cochin, were sent on to Goa at the same time with the following letter.

(XC.) *To Father Paul of Camerino.*

May the grace and love of our Lord Jesus Christ always help and favour us! Amen.

Father Paul,—Manuel de Morães and Francesco Gonzalez are leaving this to go to you. As soon as they arrive and you have read this letter, you must go to his Lordship the Bishop at his palace, and tell him that you give back and restore to his authority the first mentioned father, who on account of his priestly character is specially subject to him, being no longer under the obedience of any religious society, inasmuch as I have informed you by letter that he is duly released from his vows and dismissed from the Society. Let his Lordship therefore make use of this subject, gifted with considerable talents for the ecclesiastical ministry, entirely as he pleases, with full right, since the Society has cut him off from her own body, and given him back to his Lordship's authority with full liberty; you must then tell Moráes himself that you dismiss him from the Society having received orders to do so from me. You must also send away Francesco Gonzalez, and tell him too that henceforth he must consider himself independent of us. You must not allow these two to live at the College any longer, or to have any intercourse with our brothers, even of acquaintance and conversation. It is very painful to me that they have done things which oblige me to come to this extreme decision, and what is more grievous still, I very much fear that they are not the only subjects to whom I must show the same severity. God our Lord knows how pierced to the heart with anguish I am in writing you this letter.

I had hoped on returning hither to enjoy a little repose from the many toils I have undergone elsewhere, but now, instead of consolations, I find more distressing troubles: suits undertaken out of wrongheaded excitement, quarrels, public differences, which cause offence to the people, and the like. These things are not indeed what I recommended when absent. As far as I see, many obey imperfectly or not at all. May God be praised for ever, and in all things!

You must write to Melchior Gonzalez, who is at Bazain, telling him to go at once to Goa, for I order him to do so. You must receive Balthasar Nuñez into the house, and keep him there until my arrival. Do not receive a youth named Thomas Gonzalez, who is starting for Goa, until I come. Tell him, however, in the mean time, that if he wishes to serve God in the Society he must go to the Hospital, and there wait on the sick until I arrive, which, by God's grace, I hope will be soon. Go and visit the Bishop from me, and kiss his hand in my name. Tell him that I long above all things to present myself to his illustrious Lordship, hoping to receive sweet fruit and consolation to my soul from his most delightful company, and that I hope then to express by word of mouth how obliged I am to him for all his favours and kindnesses, which have been too great for me ever to repay or even sufficiently to estimate. I have a great longing to see again our brothers at Goa, and especially our fathers, from whose conversation I expect no little consolation. Adieu.

Yours entirely in Jesus Christ,

Cochin, Feb. 4, 1552. FRANCIS.

Early in February, Francis himself arrived at Goa. A large numbers of fathers and other members of the Society were awaiting him at the College of Santa Fè, for several had been admitted in his absence by Father Paul of Camerino; others had come to Goa, as Gaspar Baertz, in consequence of letters from himself, or from some other cause, and no less than twelve had arrived from Portugal in the preceding year. Francis on landing proceeded first to the hospitals of the city to visit the sick—his general custom when he returned from a distance—and thence to the monasteries of other religious orders. After this he went on to Santa Fè, where he was received with tears of joy and devotion. After embracing the fathers and brothers collected at the door, he asked if they had any one in the house who was sick. He was told that there was one, whose life was despaired of by the doctors. He went up at once to the sick man's cell, laid his hand upon his head, read a Gospel over him, and gave him his blessing. The sick man, who had heard of his arrival, and had been praying to see him, recovered almost immediately, and lived for many years afterwards.

The majority of those assembled at Santa Fè had never seen the grey-haired man of five and forty whom they received with so much reverence. We may gather from what Francis wrote to St. Ignatius about reserve in admitting novices in India, that there had been somewhat too much of freedom used in this respect by the good Father Paul of Camerino, and, indeed, one of the first things done by Francis Xavier on this visit to Goa, was to send away a number of novices whom he judged useless for the Society. Some of those, however, who had entered the order at Goa during his absence were noted for their services in after time. These were Simon de Vera and Fernand de Osorio, both of whom died in the Moluccas after very great labours in the cause of religion. Another, Pedro de

Alcaçeva, was to become famous for the care with which he brought home to India the body of Francis Xavier himself, as well as for many years of most faithful ministrations to the young boys of the College. Simon Rodriguez had sent thirteen from Lisbon, many of whom afterwards rendered glorious services to religion. Melchior Nuñez Barreto, a priest, was the Superior of all on the voyage. He had two brothers in the Society, one of whom was Joam Nuñez Barreto, the Patriarch of Ethiopia. Melchior had been eight years in the Society when he left Portugal, having entered religion on the same day on which he had received the cap of Doctor in the University of Coimbra. We shall find Francis selecting him at once for an important post at Bazain. The same may be said of Father Antonio Eredia, who was at first appointed by Francis to be the Rector at Cochin, and afterwards transferred to a still more laborious work at Ormuz, where he displayed the same heroic charity which Gaspar Baertz had learnt from the instructions and examples of Francis himself. There was another Father Manuel de Morães or Moralez, to take the place of him whom Francis had just dismissed. The number was made up by Gonsalvo Rodriguez, Cristoval de Costa, Melchior Diaz, and Alexio Madeira, all of whom seem to have been priests. The rest were brothers, though some of them were afterwards ordained. One Brother, Jorge Nuñez, lost his life during the voyage, having caught a dangerous disease while attending on the sick.

The College of Santa Fè, as has been already hinted, had been seriously injured by the Rector, Antonio Gomez, and Francis found the city full of complaints on that score. Antonio seems to have brought from Europe his own ideas about the proper management of a College, drawn from the University of Paris and the College of Coimbra. We have seen that Francis Xavier had thought it best to leave the arrangement of the College entirely in his hands. Antonio used his power without any moderation, and his manner was as haughty and peremptory as his measures were violent. First the order of time and the domestic arrangements were changed; then a severe accuracy and perfection of regularity were exacted, under pain of sharp punishments, of the lads of the Seminary, as if they had been the novices of a religious order, rather than children but recently acquainted with the elements of the Christian faith. Disorders and discontent broke out among their ranks; complaints were made to persons outside the College; some boys ran away, or tried to scale the walls by night. At last Antonio Gomez dismissed the entire number of boys who remained, and filled the College with children of the Portuguese. The whole city was scandalized; but Antonio was strong in the support of the existing Governor, Jorge Cabral, and for the time nothing could be done. Father Paul of Camerino, forbidden by Francis Xavier himself to interfere with Gomez in the management of the College, could do nothing, and Gomez had even practically usurped the power which belonged of right to Paul himself, and assumed the government of the whole Society in India.[4]

Gomez seems to have had other faults, at which the biographers of Francis only hint. He was a hot-brained man, given to prophecies and fanciful prognostications, some of which he was obliged publicly to apologize for. His great favour with Jorge Cabral, certain unpopular acts of whom were attributed to his counsels, brought about a strong set of popular feeling against him when the new Viceroy had been installed, and

[4] Bartoli (*Asia*, t. i. p. 321, 322) tells the story in a somewhat different way, saying that Gomez had begun his innovations, as well as claimed authority even to coerce by force any who resisted his will, before Francis Xavier left India for Japan in 1549. He says that Francis then deposed him, but that Gomez, strongly supported by some official personages, who hoped by his means to recover the favour of the king which they had forfeited, managed to get himself retained in Goa, and even confirmed in his authority in the College. It is always hazardous to differ from Bartoli, who, besides being an accurate writer, had access to documents—which, however, he seldom quotes—which may not be accessible to us. Still it appears that the letters of Francis, which are our best guide in such matters, do not lead us to suppose any violent outbreak on the part of Gomez before the date when Francis left India in 1549. And Bartoli, in the places to which we have referred, speaks of the Governor Jorge Cabral as the great support of the innovating Rector. Jorge Cabral did not succeed as Governor, till after Francis Xavier left for Japan. It is, however, quite possible that Bartoli may be right, as his account is not absolutely inconsistent with the letters to which we refer.

when the late Governor was on his way to Portugal, and so could not himself bear the odium which, rightly or wrongly, he had incurred. Gomez, however, had still very powerful friends at Goa. When Francis arrived, he at once deprived him of all authority, making Gaspar Baertz Rector of the College. He then dismissed the Portuguese lads, who had supplanted the native boys as the inhabitants of Santa Fè. Gomez appears to have been foolish enough to endeavour to screen himself from punishment by the intercession of his friends outside. The Viceroy himself is said to have been interested in protecting him. Francis Xavier was not likely to yield an inch to such influences. He determined to send Gomez away to Diu, with peremptory orders not to move from the place without leave. Every effort was made that he might be allowed to remain in Goa, but Francis was absolutely inflexible, and even now made up his mind, unless he saw great amendment, to dismiss him from the Society. He gave him, however, a chance, as we have said, sending him to Diu, far to the north, and he may perhaps have thought it better that he should be sent to Europe before his dismissal. It seems that he afterwards determined that he should be dismissed in India. Antonio's end was very miserable. He set sail, after his dismissal, for Portugal, with some idea, as it would seem, of appealing to Ignatius Loyola; but the ship in which he sailed was wrecked, and he lost his life.

The letters of the fathers from India of this date speak of the joy and devotion caused in all hearts by the presence and conversation of Francis Xavier. Melchior Nuñez speaks of him as a man who though living upon earth seemed to have his conversation in heaven; of his immense charity and zeal for souls, which made him ready to do anything in the world to serve them; of his great confidence in all dangers and trials; and of his joyous affable conversation, while at the same time he was so recollected that it seemed as if he was in continual prayer. 'His great desires for the honour of God fill me with astonishment,' says Melchior, 'as also his wonderful patience in bearing with the defects of others, his humility and condescension.' He adds that Father Gaspar was very like Francis in his confidence and affability. Francis undertook many works for the glory of God in the city, and also paid great attention, as we are told, to the religious community under his charge, frequently assembling them, and speaking to them on spiritual subjects, the love of their vocation, the practice of self-knowledge and self-abasement, as well as of all other virtues, but especially of obedience. We shall have to insert presently some of the instructions which, as these letters tell us, he wrote for the fathers who were going to a distance.

In truth, we now find ourselves, as in the case of the time spent by Francis Xavier among the Paravas and in Travancor, at a period of his life the narrative of which might be very short except for the abundance of the letters and instructions which remain to us from his pen. He seems to have remained at Goa till the time came for him to sail for Cochin, there to embark for Malacca, and the intervening weeks are marked by very few incidents. But he was now, more than at any time of his life, chiefly occupied with the arrangement of the province confided to his care by St. Ignatius. The Provincial Superiors of the Society are usually fixed within the limits of their government, and find little time to devote themselves to external works for the advancement of religion. Francis Xavier, however, had to provide for the administration of his province during what might perhaps be as long an absence as that which had been ended by his return from Japan. The Society had suffered much during that last absence, and it was his duty, as well as his anxiety, to provide against the recurrence of such troubles. The extraordinary circumstances of the case, under which he had to discharge the functions of an Apostle as well as of a religious Superior, abundantly account for all that he did, and we shall see that Ignatius Loyola himself considered —while he was as yet ignorant of the fact—that if he had gone to China he had done what he was prompted to do by the Holy Ghost. Afterwards, when Melchior Nuñez was Provincial, and left India for Japan, Ignatius did not approve it. We must look on it as a Providential blessing, that Francis Xavier was called to a distance so soon after entering more formally than before on the regular duties of a Superior. We have thus gained what we might otherwise have lost, the detailed instructions in writing which he gave to more than one of his religious subjects at this time. Put by the side of his long instruction to Gaspar Baertz, already inserted, and with certain passages of his letters, these instructions may be said almost to form a code for the guidance of religious workers and religious Superiors. They are among the purest effusions of his loving and tender heart, of his heavenly wisdom, of his wonderful experience of men, and they show us in a particular manner the identity of his spirit as to all matters relating to religious life with that of St. Ignatius himself. At the time when Francis left Europe, the rules of the Society were unwritten, except as to its great principles, and the system of government, necessarily the result of experience growing into form as the order developed, was as yet in its infancy, except, again, as to its principles. Yet we find the most perfect harmony between the instincts of Francis Xavier as expressed in these instructions, and the system of Ignatius as unfolded in the Constitutions.

These considerations may excuse us if we arrange the letters and documents of this time not quite in their chronological order, though we shall depart but little in this respect from the ordinary arrangement. But it may be well to group together the letters to the same persons, or to the same class of persons. We shall begin with a short series of letters addressed to the father lately mentioned, Melchior Nuñez, whom Francis sent to take charge of the mission and College at Bazain. The College, of which mention has already been made,[5] seems now to have been handed over to the Society, and to have had considerable revenues attached to it for charitable and missionary purposes. The first part of the letter which now follows is the formal document by which Melchior is appointed Superior.

[5] (pp. 89, 275.)

(XCI.) *To Father Melchior Nuñez Barreto.*

I, Francis, knowing well, Father Melchior Nuñez, your virtue and prudence, and confiding therein, command that this whole house of Bazain be subject to you, and by my authority I order you to take in hand the government of this entire community, and the receipt and administration of the revenues belonging to this house assigned for the maintenance of the members of our Society who are dispersed in different parts. I command that from the day you duly enter upon the possession of this government which I commit to you, not only all the fathers and brothers residing at Bazain shall recognize you as their Rector, and obey you absolutely as such, but also the members of the Society who may come thither occasionally on their way to Diu; or elsewhere, as long as they remain, are to be subject to your authority, unless it be shown by a paper in my own handwriting that I, or that the Rector of the house of Santa Fè at Goa, have exempted them. During my absence you will obey the said Rector as you would obey our Father Ignatius. This is my deliberate order, and as a signification and proof of this my will, I sign this paper with my own hand.

Goa, College of St. Paul, Feb. 29, 1552. FRANCIS.

I will add here the advice and orders which I should wish you to follow in the fulfilment of your office.

I will begin by the care of the revenues, which the King and the Governors of India in his name have generously granted to the Society, not only for the wants of our members at Bazain, but also for those here at Goa and the residences depending upon it. In the first place, I wish you diligently to find out from Melchior Gonzalez, who has now for a long time been charged with collecting and spending these revenues, exactly how much of such money he has received, what has been actually paid, what remains to his account; and you must give me an exact report in writing of what you thus discover, as I am anxious to know it. Tell me also with perfect exactness precisely the sum in specie that the same Father Gonzalez may hand over to you when you enter on your office.

Next, in disposing of these sums, you ought to have great consideration for the needs of our brethren here, and of the house of Goa, which is burthened with debt, as well as the residences of Cochin, Coulan, and Comorin, which all receive, or rather expect to receive, their support from Goa. Our unfortunate brethren there ask for aid oftener than they receive it, and for the most part are forced to battle for a length of time with destitution, my intimate knowledge of which makes me very miserable. Although his Highness amongst his many charities has granted them certain pensions, yet these are generally not paid, on account of the embarrassments of the treasury, pensions on which are but niggardly discharged in this country. So I consider it just that you should spend, out of the annual rents you have received or are to receive at Bazain, just what mere necessity requires for the food and clothing of your own community, without going beyond such necessity; and I beg of you, in the name of God's service and of charity, to bear in mind that it is not right that you and yours, because you are at the source of our supplies, should enjoy a superabundance, whilst our brethren, who bear the burthen and heat of the day, and who have just as much right to what comes from that source, being far off, are forced to grow old before the time in misery and squalor. I beg of you therefore to cut things down even to the quick, so as to be able to have a considerable sum over and above your own wants to pass on to those charged with the administration of the College of Goa, who may employ it in aiding our brethren of Cape Comorin, Coulan, and Cochin, who are spreading the kingdom of Jesus Christ with infinite labour and suffering; so that if any thought of building where you are should rise in your mind, beware of doing so without seeing an actual and absolute necessity.

Moreover, with regard to the daily expenses of yourself and of our brethren and the pupils of the Seminary, use such frugality as may allow the expenditure to be as small as possible. But understand that I do not by this enjoin on you to be parsimonious in an odious and unbecoming degree. I even forbid you positively to retrench anything from the real necessities of the house and its inmates; all I ask is, that considering and pitying the extreme distress under which the evangelical labourers (especially on the Coast of Comorin) are suffering, you should, out of charity, limit yourself to what is absolutely required, until at least there is some provision made for the wants of this much afflicted Church. I say, with the tears in my eyes, that many children die there unbaptized, simply because funds are wanting to enable our priests to exist in the poorest manner. If they were on the spot, and able to be going about incessantly, as they ought, everywhere round those most unfortunate settlements, they would always be in time to regenerate the children to Christ before their death.

With regard to the way of collecting your rents, this is what I thought of advising: it does not seem suitable that you should collect them yourself, or by any of ours. You must use the services of one or more of your lay friends, making them, as it were, your procurators for this business. In the first place, make your choice of good pious men, regular in their religious duties, for the purpose—men who, in common life, are considered just and upright, and show their piety by frequenting the sacraments of Confession and Communion. It would even be advisable to give these persons some meditations to make, out of those of the First Week of the Spiritual Exercises. I am, in the next place, desirous that wealthy people with some property of their own should be made choice of for this matter, if there be any such to choose from. My reason for preferring them to a poorer class is chiefly that a great part of income of this sort has to be gathered from people of small means, such as artisans, who barely live by the daily work of their hands; most of them are unable to pay at the given time, and if the collectors do not allow the payment to stand over, the poor men are prosecuted at great loss to themselves; but they will easily get indulgence from wealthy men, especially if they are virtuous and inclined to be merciful; and such men can easily advance the money out of their own substance, looking to receive it in due time, while men of smaller means are inexorable, exacting the rigour of the law, taking pledges, and seizing the property of their unfortunate debtors if they have not ready money at hand to pay at the given time.

But, above all, for the ardent longing you have to obey and be pleasing to God our Lord, I beg and entreat of you to give no one any offence or just cause of complaint. You will do as I wish if the people see that you are always modest, humble, quite removed from all kind of pretension. So you ought to begin your government, by giving proofs to the world of your profound abasement, fulfilling openly the most humble employments in the hospitals and prisons, ministering to the poor, teaching the ignorant people and young children. These works please all, and will endear you at once to the people, and when they have conceived an affection for you they will not easily be inclined to interpret badly your words and actions. Be careful, however, after having made a good beginning, not to let yourself grow weary, out of confidence in your past successes. But go on generously, making it your aim to become more and more perfect, and let the people see that this is your determination. If your industry slackens, you cannot remain where you were in favour and grace; you will sink to a lower level than that from whence you rose, since in these matters if any one ceases to advance, he is carried backwards even against his will.

The next letter to Nuñez is a few weeks later. He was a very successful missioner at Bazain, labouring indefatigably for the improvement of the Christians and the conversion of the heathen, and spending a large part of the night in prayer, and in the day preparing his sermons. He preached, we are told, twice on Sundays and feasts, and four times during the week besides; his sermons produced great conversions, and he had often, on leaving the pulpit, to devote the rest of the day to hearing the confessions of those who were brought to repentance by what he had said. We find Francis commending his method of preparation and preaching, which he must have submitted to him by letter, and also acquiescing in his difficulties about appropriating the revenues of his College, which seems to have been liberally endowed by the King, to the needs of other houses. This is a sufficient commentary on the two letters which follow.

(XCII.) *To Father Melchior Nuñez.*

I beg you most earnestly and desire of you that, for the love which you bear to Jesus Christ, and for the desire which you have for the glory of God, you make it your study everywhere to be 'a good savour' of Christ, and set yourself as an example of all virtues to the city in which you are, and avoid altogether giving any offence to the people. You will succeed in what I say, if moderation and Christian humility shine out in all you do. So at the beginning you must exercise yourself diligently in humble and abject offices, and then the people of the town will be won to you in this manner, and will take whatever you do in good part; much more, of course, if they see that you persevere in the cause with daily increased ardour. Wherefore I earnestly pray you not to forget your own progress in virtue: for you are well aware that one who does not make progress in virtue, goes backwards.

I again, then, ask of you and beg of you for the sake of God, let your example excite the people to piety. If you are well furnished with humility of mind and with prudence, I do not doubt that you will both reap good results from your labours and become a really good preacher. Humility and prudence are the parents and teachers of many great deeds. You must visit very often the hospitals and the prisons. These offices of Christian humility, besides that they are pleasing to God and helpful to men, have also the effect of making people esteem highly those who practise them and respect them much, even though they have not the office of preachers nor any facility of preaching.

You must diligently gain to yourself and keep as diligently the love of the Commandant, the Vicar, the clergy, the Brethren of Mercy, the King's magistrates, and indeed the whole city. This general regard is of great moment to enable missioners to turn in the right direction the wills of men, both by preaching and by hearing confessions, and paying visits. It is my great desire that in your work of cherishing and increasing this new

Christian community, you should be aided by the authority and assistance of the Commandant, the Vicar, and the Brethren of the Confraternity of Mercy. Take pains, therefore, that whatever increase may accrue to the worship of God by means of you be all attributed to their exertions. Thus it will be that they will give more help to your endeavours, and hinder them less. You will also gain another thing—that in your difficulties and contentions you will have many more friends and protectors, and fewer adversaries, or rather none at all. For who will venture to attack you, when you are known to be covered by the protection of men of such position? So if at any time you are writing to the King of Portugal about the propagation of the faith, you must make honourable and grateful mention of their remarkable zeal for Christian interests, and if you think well you may show them your letters, and by all means ask the King to let them know that their good offices towards us and towards religion have been very pleasing to his Highness, and to speak in the letters in approbation of their zeal in such a way, as to attribute to them chiefly, after God, all the increase that has been made in the divine worship and the Christian religion.

You must never write to the King except about matters relating to religion, and to the conversion of the heathen. As to all other matters, you ought to write to the Society in Portugal. In order to avoid giving offence to people, I should wish you not to collect the revenues of the College and of the new converts, either in person or through any other of the Society, if this can be avoided, but rather by means of some pious man fit for the commission. For I do not suppose it would be difficult to find some wealthy person to act as agent, so that he may neither manage the business at any risk to our income, nor be too vexatious in his exaction from the poor. Such a man you should instruct in meditation on divine truths, then lead him on to frequent the sacraments, and then, with his own goodwill desire, set over the business of which I speak. May God in His goodness unite us in Heaven!

Goa, April.

(XCIII.) *To Father Melchior Nuñez, at Bazain.*

May the grace and love of Jesus Christ our Lord be ever with us to help and favour us! Amen.

A namesake of yours, Melchior Gonzalez, has given me your letter, which I have read with no small pleasure. May God give you the grace to scatter a 'good odour' on Society where you are, now that there is so much feeling of offence against us among the people there. I pray and conjure you with all the earnestness I can, by all the desire which you have to serve and please God our Lord, take the most efficacious means in your power to concilitate people to yourself and to the Society, and to leave nothing undone, however difficult, that comes in your way to do to this end. If you are humble and prudent, I am in great hopes that by God's help you will gain great fruit there. I send to you from this Francesco Enriquez, that he may stay at Tana with Manuel. Osorio may remain with you for household duties, and Barreto to teach reading and writing; you yourself, meanwhile, being occupied in spiritual ministrations, and in conversing piously and holily with men of all sorts, as well as in explaining the Christian doctrine and in preaching.

As for your sermons, I have been very much pleased with what you write to me as to your system of preparation, as to the form and whole method which you have determined to follow in them. I think you should keep to this method, and practise yourself in the manner you suggest as often as possible, for I hope in good confidence that the favour of God will not be wanting to you, that if you are humble you will turn out a great preacher. Send Francesco Lopez to this College by the first ship which sails hitherwards from you. Take care often to read over the written instructions I have given you as to the way of carrying on the advancement of the Gospel where you are. You will learn many other things from you own practice and the experience of events, if you are humble and prudent, if you carefully watch what occurs, considering and comparing all with the advice and orders which you have received from hence. Francesco Enriquez is to live at Tana, whither he is now sent, under your authority. I should wish you to give him an order of obedience most diligently to avoid giving offence to any one, and to show himself meek and signally patient on all occasions. You must also inquire from others, by means of watchers whom you can trust, whether he or any one else of ours give to anybody a just cause of offence. If you find that it is so, meet the matter at once without delay, applying some fitting remedy to the evil. Thus it is that I would have you watch first over yourself, and then over others. But if you should find any one of ours guilty of a serious sin which goes so far as to give public scandal, and to irritate the people against us not altogether without reason, then at once dismiss him from the Society; for I now from this moment consider as dismissed those whom you may dismiss. For I have so much confidence in your prudence, that I am certain that no one will be sent away by you except for just cause.

As to the annual income of your College, take care that it is spent rather in the building up of spiritual temples than of those which are sensible and material. Of this second class of sacred buildings, which have to be raised up of wood or stone, you must spend money upon none, except such as are absolutely necessary, such as you cannot refuse to build without the very gravest public inconvenience. If any plans of building are set before you with no other recommendation than that they will improve the splendour of decoration or present a more stately outside, decline them on the ground that it is requisite to postpone them to more urgent calls, and they can well be put off to more convenient times. Whatever you may have over and above from your income, spend, as I told you, in educating native boys in wholesome knowledge and good manners. For these are spiritual temples in which God is better honoured than in others, since when these boys have grown up to be men, they will by means of their good example, and by spreading the teaching which has been given them, be instruments for God of matters which most greatly concern His glory and the salvation of men.

A few days ago I sent you from hence Paul of Guzerat, who has been a pupil of this College for many years. He is a good speaker in the language of the people, and is sufficiently furnished with learning to teach the elements of the faith to the Christian natives. He would also be able to preach usefully to the people, if some of ours who are not so ready as he is in the vernacular would supply, as occasion requires, his lack of fuller erudition, by putting his arguments in proper shape and giving him matter for his sermons.

I quite approve of what you say in your letter about the revenue of the College, that you think we should faithfully take care that it be spent according to the intention of the King, as signified in the document of its foundation. That is just what I also wish by all means to be done, both because it is an obligation of justice to do so, and in order that the people may not be scandalized, seeing—which God forbid—that this is neglected. But after you have abundantly provided for the needs of all the poor who are at Bazain, according to the prescription of the royal diploma, then, if there is any surplus, there can be no doubt that it would be rightly spent, and spent not against the King's will, in contributing to the aid of the poor boys we have here, especially those who are natives of Bazain, and those who may hereafter be useful there, as we see in the instance of this Paul of Guzerat. So if out of the collection of clothes which is usually distributed every year from the funds of your College to the poor at Bazain you have any bundles of stuff which are not wanted by the people there, you may send them to us, if at least this can be done without any complaint or offence on the part of any one. For we have here a seminary full of lads, for whose clothing the arrival of such a present would be very convenient—on the condition, however, as I said, that nothing at all be taken away from any of the poor at Bazain, who have the first right to the benefit of this bounty of his Highness. You must see, therefore, that the wants and desires of all these are faithfully satisfied, in order that our consciences may be free from burthen and for the greater service of God. If, when this obligation has been fulfilled, no crumbs remain for you to scatter in this direction, then we will make up our minds to bear contentedly the absence of such aid.

For the rest, apply yourself entirely to the exercise of preaching and of hearing confessions, visiting and consoling the sick in the hospital, and the prisoners in the gaol, and in other like works of charity to your neighbour, being always ready to run to all duties of the kind as often as you are invited to them by the managers of the Confraternity of Mercy, whose special business they are. If you practise such ministrations with charity and humility, the result will be, by the good gift of God, that you will have favour and authority with the citizens, and however little natural eloquence you may possess, yet that little which you are able to bring to bear will do much, because it will be strengthened by the companionship of zeal and modesty, and by means of it you will produce a great movement among the minds of the people, and gather in very rich fruits. Only take care—and this I press upon your attention again and again—take care to keep up the closest union and friendship with the Bishop's Vicar and the other priests in the place, with the Commandant, the magistrates, and the King's officials, and conduct yourself prudently, kindly, humbly, and with thorough goodwill towards the whole population. Believe me, the best hope of success in preaching is not to be placed in exquisite learning, or elegant diction, or in display, or in a sort of scenic exhibition of eloquence. The head and sum of the art lies in being approved of by those whom you address, and in pleasing them, and in gaining the keys of their hearts before you knock at the doors of their ears. If your audience love you, you will persuade them to do whatever you will, and you will easily win a great many souls to God if you never alienate any one from yourself.

Next September, at which time I hope to be at Malacca, let me find full and copious letters to meet me there from you, informing me distinctly and minutely of the fruit of your ministrations. You should write also to the fathers of this College, and of course much oftener, on account of your near neighbourhood and of the multitude of persons who pass from the one place to the other. May our Lord God bring us together in the glory of Paradise! Amen.

Your brother in Christ,

Goa, April 3, 1552. FRANCIS.

We may place next in order a letter addressed to the father who had been sent to Ormuz to take the place of Gaspar Baertz. We know but little of him, and even his name is variously given. He seems either to have been admitted into the Society in India by Father Paul, or to have come from Spain, and not from Portugal in the usual way. It would appear that he had shown himself at Ormuz rather as a disciple of Antonio Gomez in some of his less mischievous characteristics than a follower of Master Gaspar. He was likely to give offence and go wrong unless he was corrected betimes. Francis Xavier, therefore, speaks to him with the utmost plainness, and even threatens him with dismissal from the Society, while at the same time he assures him that he believes him to be strong enough in virtue not to take the reprehension badly. We are glad to know that this Joam Gonzalez Rodriguez lived to serve the cause of religion with great earnestness and success.

(XCIV.) *To Father Joam Gonzalez Rodriguez.*

God our Lord knows how much I should have preferred to converse with you face to face rather than write to you from a distance. There are many things which can be treated much more quickly and more effectually by word of mouth than by letters, always so slow in themselves, and silent in the event of an unforeseen objection. I was delighted to hear what I did of you from persons who had recently left you, but I should have felt rather more joy if I had received from their hands a letter from you, telling me of the fruits of your labours at Ormuz, or, to speak more modestly, the fruits which God has vouchsafed to produce through you, as also those which He would produce if He could trust you more fully, but which He is compelled not to bring about, in consequence of the opposition He meets with from the faults and imperfections by which you oppose His desires. These obstacles on your part hinder Him from manifesting Himself by you. You ought to accuse yourself unceasingly of this impediment to grace, and to grieve in humiliation and penance that by your own fault you are not a fitting instrument in the hand of God for the great and glorious works which He had prepared. Hence there is an immense loss, for which you alone are to blame, both of glory, which would have gone back to God were it not for you, and of spiritual fruit in the souls under your charge, from falling on which divine graces and blessings very great and without number are hindered, simply because you are not what you ought to be. Dwell therefore diligently on the thought of the very severe account which will be required of you at the day of the last great judgment of all the good things which God was desirous of bestowing and was ready to give, but which you have hindered Him from giving.

One thing I command you absolutely—to be very obedient to the Bishop's Vicar, so as neither to preach, nor hear confessions, nor celebrate mass without his approbation and consent; and never forget that this is not my advice only, but my order. You are forbidden (in virtue of holy obedience) to disagree with the Vicar Episcopal from any cause whatever, or even to have any quarrel with him. Labour with all zeal at those occupations which you can discharge in peace and harmony with him. I am confident, on account of what I think of his virtue and charity, that if he sees you humble and obedient, he will be more ready to grant you liberally the faculties which you require than you will be to ask for them. You must show great veneration and respect to the other priests; carefully avoid ever showing a low opinion of any, or giving the slightest offence by contemptuous conduct. Make all your friends, and give them the example of perfect obedience to the Vicar Episcopal—that so the whole people may learn to emulate the priests in paying that full and entire obedience to the Vicar which is due. I would have you think so much of the fruit of such an example as to be convinced that by showing others this humility you will do them much more good than by a hundred sermons. Be careful to avoid all singularity, showing yourself off to the world, and seeking to catch popular favour; rather let it be seen that you turn with horror from all aiming at fame and vainglory. A great many members of our Society have suffered very much from this ostentation and vain desire to appear singularly perfect. I have sent away several from the Society since my return from Japan, because I found them infected with this fault amongst others. Take heed to yourself to be diligent to avoid committing such a fault, which might lead to your being dismissed also. In order to live in the Society with those sentiments of humility which are suitable to it, bear in mind how much more necessary the Society is to you than you to the Society. Watch then, always, never to forget yourself; if any one forgets himself, can one hope that he will be mindful of others? I write these lines inspired by my real and tender love towards you, and because I hear frequent little bits of bad news that you are observed to be less humble, less inclined to obey, than is needful for the example which you should give to the people of Ormuz.

I have begged Master Gaspar to write to you, because he knows the town and inhabitants of Ormuz by great experience, gained by the long sojourn he has made there; and I hoped that he could give you good and useful advice touching your conduct in that place as suits the interest of the greater service of our Lord God. You ought then to have the same respectful feeling as to his letters that you have as to mine. I say more, —I command you to comply with the advice his letters contain, as if I had written them myself, and to obey the orders they may contain. I wish you not to let yourself be entangled in cases of marriage, nor ever to absolve, without the counsel and consent of the Vicar Episcopal, those who have contracted clandestine alliances; and I command you thus in virtue of holy obedience. When Master Gaspar went to Ormuz, I gave him in writing certain rules to follow when there. I hear he left you a copy of these instructions at Ormuz. I beg you to read it over every week, so that you may always have fresh in your memory the precepts therein collected, and that your actions may be guided thereby. I feel sure that this will help you to walk according to a sure method in the service of God.

So much am I convinced that the interest of God's greater service requires you to show perfect obedience and submission to the Vicar, that I order you, by virtue of holy obedience, as soon as you receives this letter so enjoining you, to go and kneel down before him, and humbly implore him to forgive you all the acts of disobedience and other faults besides by which you have grieved him up to this time. You must then kiss his hand, declaring that in so doing you do what I have ordered you to do. At the same time let him tell you what he wishes you to do, and you must obey his orders scrupulously. That this perfect unity between you and the Vicar Episcopal may not be of short duration, but remain good and firm always, you must visit him once a week and kiss his hand, as a pledge both of your submission and obedience to him. Take care never to fail in this duty, even if your nature rebels, and though you are obliged to do violence to your judgment and inclination in performing it. For all this must be done, in order to confound the malice of the devil, the father of discord and disobedience.

Be careful in preaching never to attack or wound any one, directly or by allusion, nor to put forth opinions and doctrines with too much refinement or speculation in them, or such as to show off learning. Leave all quibbles and affectation of that kind, and speak of the sins which are most commonly committed in the town; attack them with an ardent zeal for the divine glory, but with a modesty equal to your zeal. Do not reprove in your sermons even public sinners, known to be such, and taking no pains to hide their sins. Seek them in private, and give them fraternal advice.

In all your conduct consider this, that it will give me more pleasure to hear that you have obtained the very smallest result, even such as that expressed by this line, ————————, which does not cross the whole page, without trouble or giving offence to any one, than that you had obtained an immense result, such as may hardly be represented by a line stretching across the whole page, thus:

---

if this great success has to be wrung forth by noise and contention, amid the complaints of many who consider themselves hurt, or even of a single such person. And so persuaded am I that this is a matter of supreme importance, and so that on this depends all hope and means of really procuring the advancement of souls for the greater glory of God, I earnestly beg you to let all this advice sink into your heart, and to practise it, performing all your duties, especially your sacred duties, with calm and love and every sign of charity, with no violence or angry aggression or contention with those opposed to you.

I wish you to write to me at good length, telling me in minute detail the results which God has vouchsafed to work, by your means, in the city of Ormuz. Let me know distinctly how far you are living in a friendly manner with the Vicar, how well you get on with the other priests, how respectful you are towards them, and how they in return show you affection; and lastly, how much favour you are in with the people, or whether, on the contrary, there be any uncomfortable reports or complaints current against you. Send your letter to Goa; for though I have settled to be leaving in three weeks, I will tell the fathers of the College to take care to send it on to China, whither I am going. I shall long to receive it, and I shall hope for great delight from its telling me the good news which I wish to hear.

With God's grace, the affairs of Japan prosper wonderfully. Cosmo Torres and Joam Fernandez remain there, devoting themselves to the instruction of the very numerous natives who have embraced Christianity, and who are every day embracing it. Both understand the language of the country, and by the constant use of this necessary instrument are reaping very abundant fruits. Some of ours will go this year to help them, and share their labours, which are so vast that I cannot express them in writing. They surpass beyond comparison all those (wonderful as they may be) which the other members of the Society undergo in this country. I tell you this that you may endeavour continually to obtain for them the Divine assistance in your daily prayers and sacrifices. When you write to the College of Goa, do not omit to add to the same packet a letter addressed by yourself to his Lordship the Bishop—short, indeed, but expressing in the most marked manner your very profound veneration and devoted submission to him, and give him therein an account of all that you have done at Ormuz. You owe him this, both because he is our superior and also because he is full of the greatest charity towards us, and favours us greatly in every way in his power.

I have written to you with so much freedom because you are a man of no common virtue and perfection; one who thinks it a favour to be admonished, and would rather be reprehended usefully than be fed with empty flattery and adulation, because his judgment and good sense make him able to distinguish between wholesome bitters and poisonous sweets. I should have used blandishments and expressions meant to please, if I had thought I was addressing a weak-minded and feeble person; but I have trusted to your strength and solidity, and have not hesitated to throw aside all dissembling, and let you see without disguise into my inmost thoughts. Thank God, I beg of you, for having made you such that I have been able, without imprudence, to put before you the simple truth without any condiment. The wisdom which you have acquired in so high a degree by means of long continued progress renders it easy for you to disdain the flattery which would seduce you to evil, and makes you prefer rather to be scolded, than to be praised to your hurt and insincerely by people who fear to offend your weakness and foolishness. It is well for children and beginners, but it would be an insult to practised soldiers in God's service to think that they required pampering with the milk of children or the soft indulgence due to nurselings. Believe me, I have not taken up my pen to write to you so simply and crudely without first imploring the light of the Holy Spirit. I have felt His inspiration moving me to write in all confidence in that way which suits men who are perfect, and who have passed beyond the weaknesses of beginners and of those who are but little advanced in their career. As, by the mercy of God, we shall soon see one another in the glory of Paradise, I will not add a word more, save to beg you never to forget with what great love for you, as God is my witness, I have written this letter, and so to receive it with equal tenderness of reciprocal affection. In reading it, look to that same thing on which my eyes were fixed as I wrote it; that is to say, the greater glory of God our Lord, and the greater good of your soul, so very dear to me. Farewell.

Your brother in Christ,

College of Santa Fè, at Goa, March 22, 1552. FRANCIS.

You must show this letter to the lord Vicar of the Bishop.

It seems natural to place immediately after this letter of charitable reproof, the edge of which is taken off by the great display of affection which accompanies it, another letter of the same kind, in which some of the expressions and arguments of the former are reproduced. This letter is to Father Alfonso Cipriani, the pious old Castilian, who entered the Society and came out to India as an old man, and whom, after the design to send him as missioner to Socotra had fallen through, Francis had appointed to labour at Meliapor. Cipriani had known Ignatius, as it seems, at Barcelona before the latter went to Paris, and had renewed his familiarity with him at Rome, where he had also become acquainted with many of the first fathers of the Society. He was a man of indefatigable zeal and mortification, and burning with desire to advance the kingdom of God. Some letters of his to Ignatius exist, written while he was at Meliapor, where he laboured for twelve years, until his death in 1559, when he was about seventy years of age. He speaks in these letters of the extremely bad moral state of Meliapor, especially of the Portuguese and 'old' Christians, who seem now to have fallen off from the fervour which had been kindled in them at the time of the visit of Francis Xavier. He declares that Francis went to Japan and China, driven by the injury done to all apostolical work by the scandalous lives of the Christians; and he says that he himself loses four where he gains one, and that the Indians used it as an argument against the Christian preachers, that their fellow Christians, who were supposed to believe in and to hope for eternal good, showed themselves so reckless in their pursuit of temporal pleasures and possessions as to hesitate at no iniquity for the sake of securing them. As for Meliapor, he says that he expected to see the judgment of God descend upon it; and in truth he lived to see it visited by terrible chastisements.

Such was Alfonso Cipriani—ready enough to complain even in violent language against the vices and moral miseries around him, but resolute and patient withal in cultivating the field of labour allotted to him under all possible disadvantages. He was held in great reverence by the people, even when they did not listen to his reproofs, and he is said to have suddenly become a very powerful preacher in the exercise of his zeal. Unfortunately, the scandal given to the people had to be laid at the door of some civil authorities in Meliapor, and even at that of the Bishop's Vicar himself. Cipriani was not a man to hold his tongue when his heart was full, and he spoke from the pulpit against the guilty parties. It would seem from the letter of Francis Xavier, that there was also a quarrel between the Vicar and Father Alfonso, in which the latter had gone to law with his ecclesiastical Superior.[4] This is enough to render the following sharp but most loving reprehension intelligible:

(xcv.) *To Father Alfonso Cipriani.*

Very ill indeed have you understood the directions which I gave you to be followed in Meliapor. You show clearly what little good has remained to you,—that you have profited very

[4] Bartoli, *Asia*, tom. i. p. 729, gives a long account of Father Cipriani (or Cipriano, it is uncertain which), who was thought to enjoy some supernatural gifts besides his great virtues. But he does not mention the legal proceedings, which seem, however, implied in the letter of Francis.

little,—from your intercourse with our blessed Father Ignatius. I blame you exceedingly for having also taken proceedings by legal writs and actions of lawyers against the Vicar. Ah, this is always the way in which you yield to your violent nature, pulling down with the left hand whatever you build with the right. You must know that I have been displeased beyond belief by the rudeness and discourtesy with which I hear that you have behaved at Meliapor. If the Vicar does not act as he ought, most certainly he will not be taught better by such reproofs from you, especially when they are pressed upon him so imprudently as has been the case now. You have been so long accustomed never to cross your own will in the very least degree that wherever you are you offend every one, and give very clear proofs of your intractable and churlish disposition to all who have to deal with you. God grant that one day—even if late—you may repent of these imprudent acts!

I entreat you, by your love for God our Lord, to learn to control that hard and stubborn mind of yours, and to make up by good works in the future for the faults you have hitherto committed. And do not flatter yourself by ascribing these savage movements of passion to natural severity of character. This is no fault of disposition, but of extreme negligence and culpable disregard of your greatest duties, which you owe to your own conscience and to your neighbours,—those of obedience, moderation, and charity. If you do not believe this on my word, you may assure yourself that you will see it most clearly at the hour of your death. I earnestly entreat you, in the name of our blessed Father Ignatius, to learn—during these few days remaining to you before that last hour—to learn and to practise self possession, meekness, patience, modesty, and submission. Understand that all things are brought about by humility. If you cannot do as much as you wish, do what you can accomplish in quietness and goodness. In these parts of India there is no gaining anything by violence; and the good which might undoubtedly be done by patience, submissiveness, and moderation is stifled in its very birth by foolish outbursts of anger, quarrelsomeness, and violent passion. Good that is done without offence or disturbance, even though in itself not greater than this little line ——, is much better and greater than good gained in another way, though it appears ever so much larger, so as to be expressed by a line which reaches across the whole page.

I greatly fear that all I have now said may not be sufficient to bring you back into the right path; but I know, and I wish you too to know, and I tell you beforehand for certain, that when you come to pass from this life to the next you will suffer very sharp stings of conscience for this bad and indiscreet conduct of yours.

Francesco Gonzalez Fernandez seems to me like you in everything—harsh, irritable, and impatient; you are both made after the same type, and are in the habit of giving the specious names of zeal and religion to the outbreaks of your unbridled passions. That speech of yours certainly has a very grand sound: 'What? can we endure in silence to see injury done to God's glory, and obstacles placed in the way of saving souls?' How then? do you repair that injury, or do you heap fresh mischief upon it, by the storm and tumult of detestable quarrels? I repeat it—you will never obtain from the Vicar by threats and contentions what you cannot obtain by modesty and humility.

By that piety and obedience which you both acknowledge that you owe, and will not deny that you wish to pay, to our Father Ignatius, I beseech both of you, immediately after reading this letter, to go to the Vicar, and, prostrate on the ground before him, each of you humbly to ask his pardon for everything which you have done not pleasing to him; then kiss his hand; and if you wish to give me a very great consolation, let me hear that you have both humbled yourselves so far as of your own accord to kiss his feet; by which you will seal by so much surer a proof your repentance for past faults, and your promise that you will be modest for the future, and do nothing contrary to his will while you are at Meliapor. Believe me that to have done this will be a very great comfort to you at the hour of death. Put your confidence in our Lord God, and do not doubt that if your moderation is known to all men, you will easily obtain whatever you ask which is for the glory of God and the salvation of souls.

The manifest error of you two, and of all like you, consists in this: you think that the mere name of the Society of Jesus gives you a sort of hereditary right to great consideration from every one, before you have gained it by great and remarkable proofs of the lowliest humility. Doubtless you remember the great veneration shown by all, both high and low, to our Father Ignatius; and you think it just that you should be treated by all with the same respect yourselves, although you have given no proof at all of those virtues by which he merited such consideration. What you should have done was first to imitate the good works of our Father, and try to win those more excellent graces of his which moved our Lord God to give him such favour in the sight of all men; for that is a vain and foolish confidence of yours which leads you, who have given little or no public proof of eminent virtue, to expect that these fruits of respect and popular favour, which are the reward of very great self abasement, will fall to your lot who are so forgetful of religious humility, as even to be angry if people do not pay you this respect, and show themselves in all things obedient and submissive to your will.

I well know that you will be eloquent in excusing these errors, and that you would assure me that if I were with you, I should not consider that there is any fault in all this, since you only engaged in this suit from a motive of pure love of God, and zeal for the salvation of souls. But now from this time forth I give you warning and desire you to be fully convinced, that you will only waste your breath in excusing this fault, however skilfully, to me; and you may rest assured that in my opinion your cause will be certainly lost, and I add besides that by trying to defend an action which cannot be approved you would cause me great displeasure, in addition to your fault; and I must confess, on the contrary, that nothing would be more delightful to me than to hear that you have freely acknowledged and condemned the fault you have committed in all this.

No—let the past, which is beyond recall, be corrected, as far as possible, by penitence, and let every precaution be taken in providing for the future. For the rest, I beg you above all things to take great and continual pains that there may be no more suits or contentions with the Vicar, the priests, the Governor, or any magistrates whatever, no matter how evident and public their faults may be. I would rather that you should apply a gentle remedy, as far as you can in conscience do so; abstain from all remedies which cause disturbances, and are worse than the disease itself, and do not risk losing by anger and violence all the fruit which you might bring to maturity by humility and meekness.

So far this letter has been written at my dictation; in what follows you will recognize my hand and heart. O Cipriani! if you knew with what love I write those words to you, you would surely remember me night and day, and it may be that you would not be able to restrain your tears in thinking of the most tender and ardent charity burning with which I take you to my heart. O, would to Heaven that the hidden secrets of our hearts could be revealed in this life! then, believe me, my brother Cipriani, you would clearly see how deeply your name is engraved in the inmost depths of my soul. Farewell.

Yours wholly, so that I never can forget you,

April 1552. FRANCIS.

The next letter is an instruction to Father Antonio Eredia, one of those who had last arrived from Portugal, to whom Francis at this time intrusted the mission at Cochin.

(XCVI.) *To Father Antonio Eredia.*

Here are the instructions which I prescribe to you to follow in Cochin. First of all, endeavour as far as in you lies, by all industry, and with all your might, to gain to yourself the love of all the people, of the priests, the religious, and more especially the brothers and managers of the Church of our Lady the Mother of God; using the utmost diligence, and employing all ways and means, to convince them that your only desire is to further their wishes, and to do your part in increasing the devotion and veneration of the people towards that holy temple of the Mother of God. Visit them, therefore, frequently with all courtesy, and in your spiritual necessities, doubts, and troubles, have recourse to them, and consult them with confidence.

Make known to the Brothers of Mercy the corporal necessities of the poor who ask your help, pleading the cause of the sufferers before them, and obtaining from that Confraternity the assistance which you are unable to afford yourself owing to our want of means, which you must not conceal. Explain also to the poor, that what you give them is not out of your purse, but that it comes from the liberality of the Confraternity of Mercy. When on such occasions they come to you to make known the penury under which they are, you should take the opportunity of explaining to them that other need of which they are less sensible, and which they take less pains to relieve—of spiritual help for the soul: help which, if they desired it, they could always have abundantly and at hand; exhorting them earnestly not to neglect this, but to turn their thoughts to God, to adore and pray to Him, and to obtain His mercy by having recourse to the sacraments of Penance and the Eucharist: show them that you are ready to help them in this, and assure them that when they have performed this first duty, you will not fail to obtain them help for their other temporal wants as to food and money in the manner already mentioned.

In your promiscuous intercourse with persons of all conditions, take great pains that your behaviour be such that all equally may see in you a modesty free from pride. Never speak to any one except kindly and respectfully, showing carefully to both priests and seculars the degree of regard due to each, and remembering the words of St. Gregory, that humility begets love, and pride begets hatred. If any fruit should follow your labours, be careful not to desire any praise for yourself, and if it should be given to you, not to appropriate it, but to attribute it all to those who have advised and assisted you, gratefully and frankly acknowledging that they are the principal authors of those good works. If you desire the good name and credit of our Society to flourish, and if this is the end of your efforts, you must be firmly convinced that you will only help to and attain your object by giving great proof in your intercourse with every one of humility and modesty altogether removed from all appearance of pride. For seeing you truly humble, people will suppose that the other members of the Society whom they do not see are like you who are present before them, and will then form a true idea of the religious of the Society of Jesus, and regard our Institute with that approval and affection which every one readily gives to those who despise themselves.

This is the only way to spread abroad a good opinion of our Society, as you will more easily perceive by remembering that those who were the first to make this Order famous by the labours which they undertook for the honour of the Church, did so indeed by the practice of every virtue, but more especially by showing themselves everywhere the brightest examples of the contempt of human glory, and of true humility, which they regarded as the foundation of the other virtues. By imitating them you will show yourself worthy of bearing the name, and will promote the reputation of the Society. In any other way you would go astray, and you would be the means of destroying the work which they have built up.

Remember, above all things, that influence with the people, and the favour and applause of the multitude, are the gift of God alone, Who gives it to those only whom He sees to be so well fortified in solid virtue that He may fairly trust them to make good use of so powerful a talent for their own salvation and for that of those to whose advantage they devote themselves. On the other hand, those whom God sees disposed to usurp the credit of any success that may attend their ministration, and to make a boast of it, He is wont to deprive of their gift, not giving them popularity, and not allowing them to be borne along by the fair wind of public favour, lest His gifts should be despised, being ascribed to human efforts, and lest the ignorant multitude, incapable of distinguishing between saints and imperfect persons, should attribute the honour due to true apostolic labourers to tepid men, careless in God's service and decked out by undeserved and false praises with a fallacious appearance of exquisite virtue. Pray, therefore, continually and fervently, that our Lord God may give you grace to know and feel in the inmost depths of your soul of how many and great hindrances to the spread of the Gospel you have been the cause, and how your faults had prevented God from making Himself known as He would wish to the people intrusted to you, and whom you have so ill cared for: since through your own defects you are wanting in the influence essential and fitted to convince them of necessary truths; and that because you have not merited that heavenly gift by the requisite fervour and fidelity.

When, at the hour appointed for us by our Society for the daily examen of conscience, you go through all your actions for the purpose of discovering your faults, do not fail to examine yourself very strictly on your manner of preaching the word of God from the pulpit, of administering the Sacrament of Penance in the sacred tribunal, and lastly, on your familiar conversations and daily intercourse with all classes of persons. Look very closely into what you have from negligence omitted to do, or what you have done badly, and resolve seriously on the necessary amendment, which you must then carry out with great fidelity. For if as soon as you have perceived your fault you strive to correct it, our merciful Lord will not fail to accompany your repentance with His voluntary gifts, and to turn even your past errors to your great profit by loading you with His graces.

I do not, however, wish you to place, as many do, your hope of winning the affection of the people in human arts, or to take cunning measures for getting yourself liked and spoken well of by the multitude, so as to act and speak in a way that flatters and pleases them. Such arts are utterly unworthy of a preacher of the Gospel; and besides that they take with them as an inseparable companion that most dangerous craving for the empty praise of the people, are also injurious to Christ our

Lord, whose honour they ought to seek and look to before everything else. And such preachers prefer their own credit, seeking their own fame as the first thing; and when once they have obtained it, as if they have obtained all that they want, they relax that fervent zeal which they ought to have, to do their utmost to promote the greater glory of God by a real conversion of souls.

I charge you to weigh what I have said most attentively in your mind, and to flood and penetrate its inmost recesses with these good sentiments: and if, in meditating on divine things, our most merciful God should favour you, as is His wont, with some heavenly illumination, do not let it escape from your mind, but note it down in some little book to assist your memory. Believe me, that a great part of the real spiritual profit of God's servants consists in such observation, and in carefully recalling to mind pieces of knowledge of this sort given to them in mental prayer and meditation. And if any one who has from time to time been favoured with these flashes of divine light writes down the truths revealed by them, he will read them over again after a while, with a very great increase of affection and advantage—that is to say, when he has himself experienced what he had set down in writing. He will then recall to mind those beautiful thoughts, and taste again those keen feelings which had passed from his memory; or at least he will gain from their clearer consideration the salutary vigour which will enable him to labour fervently, and to think wisely according to the needs of his present circumstances. Great indeed is the difference of savour and spiritual sweetness in ordinary readers of those things written by the saints when fresh from their conversations with God, and in those who read again in them what they have themselves experienced and made their own! But it is certain that the reading of such things is of small profit to those who have not this sort of memory and interior of them.

I advise you, therefore, strongly to make a little journal, and to note down carefully in it the secret illuminations with which God has enlightened your mind in your daily meditations. Value them very highly, and esteem yourself unworthy of them, humbling yourself, as you ought, all the more deeply because of these labours with which He exalts you.

Take great and practical pains to acquire a good number of wise and faithful friends, even among seculars, who are sharp sighted enough to observe the faults you commit in preaching, in hearing confessions, and in all other such functions, and also free enough to point them out to you with all sincerity; so that, knowing your defects by these means, you may correct them properly, and avoid them for the future.

In the administration of the Sacrament of Penance avoid a perfunctory haste, and show a patient attention to your business, so as to urge on your penitents to greater and more certain progress; and if, in this way, you should have to do with persons requiring and capable of receiving spiritual help, and who are also in tolerably easy circumstances, so that they are both desirous and able to give some time to the affairs of their souls,—then, after hearing their confession, persuade them to wait for a few days, and to employ the time in conceiving a real hatred of their sins, and sorrow for having offended a God infinite in power, and supreme in all that attracts love. To this end, you should set them to meditate on death, judgment, and the pains suffered by the lost in hell; by means of which meditations they will understand in what fearful evils they have entangled themselves by sin, and conceive so great a hatred and disgust of their past transgressions, that they will shed real tears of penitence from a contrite heart, and make a purpose of amendment, such that it may be reasonably hoped that they will sin no more in future.

Especially is this method to be observed with those who are living in occasions of sin, and among hindrances to good works, and who, therefore, considering the frailty of human nature, cannot be safely believed when they promise amendment of life, without some pledge of security. Such are persons who have been at enmity, and have not yet been reconciled to their enemies: those who have not yet so abandoned intercourse with the objects of criminal attachments as to be considered safe from falling when they find themselves on the slippery ground of the recurrence of dangerous occasions: lastly, those who are in possession of the property of another, and have hitherto sought pretexts for delaying restitution. You should engage all such persons, after confession, in pious exercises suited to their state, and not give them absolution till you consider that they have made satisfaction, and on dismissing them exhort them to come frequently in future to the sacred tribunal of Penance.

As often as you should happen to hear the confessions of persons who, knowing that they are in possession of money unlawfully acquired, bring it to you, to be given at your discretion to the poor, the owners not being to be found, you must not use the very smallest part of it for yourself or for the College, however pressing may be your penury: nor may you even distribute it to needy persons or families at your own discretion: but hand over the whole sum to the Prefects of the Confraternity of Mercy, to be bestowed as they think best. By this means the door will be closed against suspicions, which, besides being dishonourable to you, would lessen the respect in which the promotion of God's glory demands that you should be held.

In familiar interviews and conversations with persons of whatsoever condition, to promote whose spiritual good is your daily labour, behave always with such prudence and circumspection that in talking with them, however much you may trust to their intimacy with you, no word may pass your lips for which you could be justly blamed if they should ever be estranged from you: a thing which is possible, and which you ought to suppose certain. This is a most important caution, not only for your good but also for that of those under your charge.

When persons who have made their confession with manifest signs of penitence beg for absolution, you ought not to give it till they have made the requisite satisfaction, especially as to three kinds of sin: *i. e.* enmities, attachments, and unjust possession of the goods of another. Bid them first be publicly reconciled to their enemies, put away every occasion of sinning against purity, and restore ill-gotten gains to the rightful owners; then let them do whatever else may be necessary for greater security. Do not let them think promises enough, but insist on their fulfilment: for with these people, who are as ready and liberal in making promises as they are slow and backward in keeping them, one should always make bargains with the earnest money in hand. Endeavour as much as is possible, with the help of God, to defend and increase the good odour and the good name of the Society by great humility, holiness, zeal for souls, and labours undertaken on their behalf: for they who gained for our Society the celebrity which it enjoys did so, with the blessing of God, in the way I have pointed out. I pray that He may be with you always. Amen.

Your brother in Christ,

Goa, April 2, 1552. FRANCIS.

The next letter explains itself. Andrew Carvalhez must have been admitted to the Society in India, and consequently needed an introduction to Simon Rodriguez in Portugal, when about to return thither for his health.

(XCVII.) *To Father Simon Rodriguez, of the Society of Jesus.*

May the grace and love of Jesus Christ our Lord ever help and favour us! Amen.

Very soon I shall write to you at length touching the affairs of the Society in this country, but I must send this short letter separately for a particular reason. It concerns Andrew Carvalhez, who will be the bearer of it. I think it necessary to send back to you this excellent young man on account of his health. He was getting on very badly in India, and at his age and with his temperament the doctors hoped that his native air might restore his strength, which is exhausted by illness, and make him once more as strong as ever. On returning from abroad, I found by the concordant testimony of all here that he is equal in intellectual gifts, in progress of studies, and in endowments of grace to any one of ours out here. Our older fathers hope much from this youth because of the virtues which God our Lord has already given him, and which in His mercy He will cause to increase. I think it is as they say, and willingly make you a partner in my joy, desiring and praying that this brother may grow into thousands of thousands,[4] and produce for the Society the fruit we expect. I beg of you, therefore, by your love and devotion towards God our Lord, my dearest Brother Simon, to receive Andrew Carvalhez in Portugal with all the love and charity with which I and he also hope that you will receive and tend him. As to the news in these parts, I will write to you copiously and minutely, by the help of God, before setting sail for Cochin. My departure will, I think, take place in a fortnight. May God our Lord unite us in the glory of Paradise, for when in this life we shall be able to meet and embrace I certainly do not see! Be sure of one thing, my sweetest Brother Simon,—that I carry everywhere your image very deeply engraven on my heart, and that this image makes you ever present to my thoughts. The desire to see you with my bodily eyes, with which I so long felt almost to impatience, has become less hard for me to bear because of the consolation which I have in beholding continually in my heart your much loved person. Farewell.

Yours in Christ,

Goa, March 27, 1552. FRANCIS.

We next come to a series of letters written to Gaspar Baertz, who was to take the place of Francis Xavier as the Superior in India during his absence, as well as to fill that of Rector of the College of Goa, unless some one should arrive from Europe sent by Ignatius himself for that purpose. We may place at the beginning of this series a spiritual instruction, which contains advice to Gaspar simply as a preacher, and makes no mention of the rectorship or government of others. Like so

[4] Lat. orig. *crescat in mille millia.* Gen. xxiv. 60.

much of what he wrote to the same admirable religious, every word seems to come with intense feeling from the very heart of Francis.

(XCVIII.) *To Father Gaspar Baertz.*

You ask me, my dear Gaspar, that as I am continually recommending humility, and as you yourself understand the great value and importance of that virtue, to go farther, and suggest to you some method of practising it. It is a subject which I take great pleasure in speaking of, both because I would do much to gratify you, and still more because I hear something of the applause of your sermons which sounds in your ears; and I sometimes fear (love is always full of anxiety and fears), that perceiving how much you please every one, you may begin not to be displeased with yourself. In this letter, therefore, I will set down what occurs to my mind as likely, if I mistake not, to be of use to you as a sort of talismanic antidote, to hinder the bad effect of the pleasant poison of vainglory, which creeps secretly into unwary souls, borne by the flattering breath of popular applause.

Be careful, above all things, to make the very favour which your preaching finds with the people an occasion of continually greater and greater humiliation: understanding clearly, and acknowledging, that in this there is nothing of your own; and faithfully giving the entire praise to God, as the sole Author of whatever ability you may possess, and whatever profit your hearers may derive from it. Farther, you should confess that for all this fruit of your labours you are a debtor to the people: for, in truth, you may and should believe that our Lord God, moved by the devotion of these good folk thirstily craving to learn what concerns religion and the salvation of souls, bestowed on you, though unworthy of such a favour, the skill and power to instruct them properly, so that they may profit according to their desire. You, therefore, are merely the minister of the bounty of another, which is in no way attributable to you, since all luminous intelligence and vigorous action in you, all docility and sensibility in your hearers, are gifts granted by God, not to your merits, but to those of the Church and the pious people to whom you preach. And this should be a motive for your loving the people, and feeling under the greatest obligation to them, because our Lord has, for their sakes, communicated to you eloquence and learning: which if you claim for your own, and ascribe to your merits, you would be guilty of injustice and ingratitude, unworthily forgetting from Whom and for whose sake you have received these gifts.

Besides this, you may well consider that any really valuable fruits resulting from your labours ought to be attributed to the prayers and suffrages of the members of the Society, who, fighting for God in different parts of the world, implore the divine assistance on the endeavours of their brethren fighting elsewhere: and because they do so with exceeding charity and humility, our Lord God deigns to grant their prayers by sometimes using the sons of the Society as the instruments of His glory and of the salvation of souls. If you get this thought well fixed in your mind, you will certainly never let yourself be tickled by the acclamations and praises of those who admire the eloquence of your sermons: but the more highly you are exalted, the more you will abase yourself; knowing most surely that you will one day have to give a very strict account of this talent which has been intrusted to you, with danger to yourself, for the good of others, in the exercise of which talent you will be able to see nothing altogether your own, except very many faults of imprudence, negligence, and ingratitude to God who gave it to you, to the people for whose good He gave it, and lastly to your mother, the Society of Jesus, whose prayers have prevailed with our most gracious Lord to bless your labours with some success.

It will also be useful to compare the abundance of the harvest reaped with the far greater abundance which there would have been had it not been hindered by your fault. You should therefore most fervently and urgently implore God to grant your mind a ray of heavenly illumination, which may shine therein so clearly as to show you how continually your defects and daily falls place great obstacles in the way of the goodness of God, so as to hinder it from attaining its end through the fault and imperfection of the instruments He employs; thus forbearing to reveal Himself more clearly, and to bring about those great things which He had intended to do by your means for His glory and the salvation of men. And when these sentiments are firmly impressed upon your mind, I should like you to manifest them to God, who reads the heart, rather than to declare them in words to men. They will be, as it were, goads with which to drive away vainglory, and being pricked by them you will be attentive to yourself and recollected, and not only be preserved from an indolent security, but rather forced to set a guard over yourself, watching most carefully on every side that you may not sin by imprudence. never stumble and fall, never be a scandal to the people either in public conduct or private intercourse. For, as I have said, it is right that you should regard them with gratitude and respect as the cause of the grace granted to you by God.

In the next place, when you meditate on all these things, I earnestly advise you to write down, as a help to your memory, those heavenly lights which our merciful God so often gives to the soul which draws near to Him, and with which He will also enlighten yours when you strive to know His will in meditation, for they are more deeply impressed on the mind by the very act and occupation of writing them down. And should it happen, as it usually does, that in course of time these things are either less vividly remembered or entirely forgotten, they will come with fresh life to the mind by reading them over; the original thoughts themselves will be revived by recourse to these records, and as though you had again discovered the mine from which you originally got them, you will dig deeper into its veins, and what was before the loftiest height to which your thoughts had risen will serve as the foundation of a new and still nobler spiritual edifice. For thus does the Divine Wisdom, which by a simple instinct of free mercy loves to communicate itself to men, rejoice to lead those who watch for its guidance from light to light, and out of twilight, by ever brightening rays, and through splendours ever increasing, into the full glory of the noon. And as God is wont to give His choicest favours in greatest and most constant plenty to those who seek in meditation for ways of depressing still more and more their own vileness, do not doubt that by perseverance in this holy practice of humility and of an intimate knowledge of your faults you will be enriched with still greater advances, not only as to your own perfection, but also to the procuring of the salvation of others; and you will know by experience this most certain truth, which is not understood by all, that it is only in his sincere self contempt that the whole hope lies that a preacher of the Gospel will gain real and great fruit in souls, and that that cannot be abundant or solid fruit which destroys him who reaps it, aiming at the good of others at the cost of ruin to himself.

O, then, for the love of God, by all that you owe to our Father Ignatius and the whole Society of Jesus (and you well know how much you are indebted to both), I pray and entreat you again, and once more again, as earnestly and forcibly as I can, persevere constantly in these practices of self abasement. For should you interrupt them (which God forbid!), I should fear that you would lose your soul (may God avert such a calamity!): as you cannot deny that you have either heard from others of, or yourself seen, many persons who, not being well grounded in humility, have, after having preached to others, become themselves reprobate. I warn you again and again, beware lest you should increase their number! Never let these most miserable instances, which you have yourself known, pass from your memory. Recall them frequently to your mind, bringing leisurely before it the sad mournful images of so many on whose words, as they preached from the sacred pulpit, far greater crowds hung than now listen to you; who preached more gracefully, more eloquently, more admirably than you, by whose sermons many more persons were convinced and converted from idolatry and from sin than you have brought to a better life: and nevertheless (unhappy men!), after God had made use of them as instruments to snatch multitudes from the tyranny of the devil and from the brink of hell, and to bring them into the Kingdom of Christ and to the blessedness of Heaven, their own lot was that most wretched one, themselves to be thrust down by a most just condemnation into everlasting flames, for that they arrogantly attributed to themselves the glory which was due to God alone—for that they caught at the breath of popular favour and empty applause—for that, puffed up by the praise of men, their hearts swelled with self conceit: and that thus, towering with haughtiness and arrogance, they became the marks of the thunderbolts of Heaven, which are hurled against the proud.

Let those, therefore, who witness these terrible warnings be struck with a holy fear, and form themselves in humility. Let each look to himself, and carefully examine his own purposes and desires. Whoever fairly balances what he has received and what he has returned will certainly see that he has no cause for boasting, but abundant cause for fear and humiliation: for in this great business of the salvation of souls, however successfully it may have been conducted, what is there that we can justly ascribe to ourselves, or congratulate and honour ourselves upon? O no, there is nothing---nothing whatever of our own: except the many faults of imprudence and disloyalty which we have mixed with our good beginnings. This is our share: for the conversion of souls is the work of God, who loves to magnify the wonderfulness of His goodness by the weakness of the instruments He uses: thus choosing us, the meanest of His servants and most worthy of all contempt, to manifest the glory of His Name to men.

Lastly, take care that it never enters your mind to compare yourself with other members of the Society whose labours make less show, and in consequence to despise them as obscure, and incapable of great things. You ought, on the contrary, to be firmly convinced that the origin of your distinction is precisely the lowliness and hiddenness of those who discharge mean offices in the house: for it is certain that these humble brothers of yours, who are engaged in mean employments for His glory, obtain for you from Him whom they so devoutly serve the strength and power which make you so distinguished; and you are more deeply indebted to them than they to you. If you are inwardly penetrated with this conviction you will never despise them, but will heartily love them and venerate them, putting yourself far below them, to the great advantage of your own soul.

Your brother in Christ,

FRANCIS.

The following three papers, though commonly reckoned among the letters of Francis Xavier, are in reality formal documents, conferring on Gaspar the Rectorship, of which mention has already been made.

In the name of our Lord Jesus Christ! Amen.

1. I, Francis, the unworthy Superior of the Society of Jesus in this province of India, relying, Master Gaspar, on your humility, virtue, prudence, and other gifts, which make you a sufficiently fit person to rule others, command you in virtue of holy obedience to assume the government of this College of Santa Fè at Goa, and to be the Superior thereof with the name and power of Rector. I also order that all the Portuguese fathers and brethren of the Society of Jesus, who are on this side of the Cape of Good Hope, and beyond this at Malacca, the Moluccas, Japan, and anywhere in these regions, be under your authority. Those also who hereafter may come from Portugal, or from any other part of Europe, to these provinces or houses to be placed under my rule, I will that all of them be subject to your authority, unless our Father Ignatius should send here any one nominated to be Rector of this College of Goa. I have asked him by letter, setting forth at full length the reasons why it appears necessary that he should do so, to send hither some one of large experience in whom he has great confidence, to be Superior of this College, and to rule all ours who are in the surrounding missions or stations dependent thereupon. If, therefore, any one of our Society should arrive at Goa with a commission duly signed which he can show from our Father Ignatius, or any one else who is General Superior of the Society of Jesus, for the purpose of undertaking the government of this house and of the missions which are under it, I then command you in virtue of holy obedience, and I leave the order for you here in writing, at once to yield your place to such a person, give into his hand without any delay the management of the College and all attached to it, and make yourself his subject, and obey him in all things.

But if any one coming from Portugal were to say that he was

sent for this purpose, and yet did not show his letters signed by our Father Ignatius or any else, Superior General of the Society of Jesus for the time being, I forbid you to acknowledge him as Rector, or to transfer to him the government which I have intrusted to you. But if he seem a man fitted to govern, and you yourself require such assistance, then you may delegate to him your authority, and commit to him as vicar your power, revocable at pleasure, always saving your own right and superior dominion, to which he no less while he rules in your place than the rest who obey him and you must be subject. For it is my decided will, and by the power given to me, I order that you, Master Gaspar, and you alone, until the General of the Society arrange otherwise, shall govern this College of Goa with authority supreme next after mine, and be the ruler, as I have said, of all ours who dwell in these regions. And I command all of them, in virtue of holy obedience, to be subject to you, Master Gaspar, the Rector of the College of Goa, in order that there may be no room for the inconveniences which might otherwise follow, and which to our great disturbance have, as we know, followed on former occasions.

And if any one should be refractory against this my appointment, which has been made after mature deliberation, and is now declared to all, or if he should endeavour to elude it by any cavil or by any arbitrary interpretation, either giving himself out as Rector, or refusing to you all due obedience, I command you, by virtue of holy obedience, to dismiss that person from the Society, with whatever excellent gifts in this respect he may be endowed; for he lacks the most important gifts of all, humility and obedience.

What I have said about your substituting some one as vicar to yourself, I have put in that you may be more free sometimes to make excursions from Goa, to visit the Colleges at Cochin, Bazain, and Coulan, and the mission of Cape Comorin. Experience has taught me that great fruit to ours who are living in those places, and a great return in the way of the service and glory of God our Lord, comes from such visitations of Colleges and residences. I think, therefore, that you should often make them; but in such a way and at such times that the College of Goa may lose as little as possible from your absence.

In order that no one of ours may perhaps think that these things which I have thus far enjoined are of light moment, and so may venture to disregard them or think too little of them, I again bid you and command you by the authority which I possess, that, if any one of ours fail to obey you as if you were myself, you dismiss him at once from the Society; and do not let the thought trouble you for a moment, that perhaps it may seem as if by and by the Society might be sorry to have lost any such person on account of his distinguished gifts of eloquence, learning, or any other talent. Refractory persons of this kind will always bring to our Order much more harm than advantage. Those who consult our best interests most justly care little for small gains which have to be purchased by very great mischief, which may very well be set in the balance against the wonder or even the offence and murmuring caused among the people, who are likely enough to blame us for the dismissal of workers whose fair outside is a cloak for hidden faults. Therefore never hesitate or doubt for a moment boldly to cut off from our body limbs that do it harm; and be at your ease, on my authority, as to what people will say or their empty fears. Another thing of the same kind—I forbid you also, by virtue of my authority, never to readmit on any account into our Society any one whom I have dismissed before I go to China; and, moreover, send an order through all places subject to your government that no one of our Society anywhere is to admit such persons under his roof even as a guest.

The revenues already assigned to the Colleges—the extraordinary gifts which the King sometimes makes, and all the dues and resources of this community, whatever they are, which belong to it by the liberal concessions of our lord the King or of the Governors who are here his representatives—all these you must collect and exact with great attention and care, either by yourself or by other fit persons whom you appoint so to do. Take great care that they be fully and entirely collected and faithfully spent in food and other necessary things for the fathers and brothers of the Society who live in this house, or who are sent from it to other places; for unless they are helped from hence with all necessary supplies for the body, they are quite unable to devote themselves as is requisite to the work for souls for the sake of which they are sent out. And whatever over and above inevitable expenses remains of the annual income of the house must be put aside for the purpose of getting rid of debts. The rest must be spent on living and other such purposes, but only necessary purposes, for ours who live both in the College and in the residences thereto attached, as well as of the boys whom the natives send us to educate, and the orphans of the country.

Signed, as a proof that this is my true order,

FRANCIS.

Given in this College of Santa Fè, April 7, 1552.

2. After what has been written above, three other things appear to me worthy to be particularly recommended to you. I command you, Master Gaspar, Rector of this College of Santa Fè, in virtue of holy obedience, not to go for the space of three years complete outside the island of Goa, unless within that space of three years some one of ours should arrive duly sent by the Superior General of the whole Society of Jesus, with letters witnessing thereto, to assume the government of this same College. As soon as such a one arrives, and you have resigned to him the government of this College, then you are released from this my precept, and, if the new Rector, to whom you as well as others will be subject, sends you, you may freely go whithersoever he bids you. I again charge and order, in virtue of holy obedience, all those who in these regions of India acknowledge me as their Superior, to obey you also, Master Gaspar, and to be subject to your government. And if any one refuses to obey you, you will just show him this letter of mine, in which I order all who are my subjects to show themselves as obedient and submissive to you as to me, if I were there present, and then, if he persist in his contumacy, dismiss him from the Society and have nothing more to do with him.

I again charge and command, in virtue of holy obedience, all and every one of the Society of Jesus placed under my authority, that if any one should arrive hither, chosen by our Father Ignatius, or any other General Superior of the Society of Jesus, as Rector of this College, and duly appointed as such—which will be seen by letters signed by our Father himself—that all at once acknowledge him as their legitimate Superior, and make themselves subject to him and obey him as they would me if I were present. But if any one refuse to do this, then I beg and charge the Rector aforesaid, unless the General Superior has otherwise ordered, to dismiss such disobedient person from the Society. And that there may be no doubt as to this my full and deliberate will in making these orders, I here sign this paper with my own hand.

Goa, April 7, 1552. FRANCIS.

3. Whereas the Supreme Pontiffs have granted certain faculties and privileges to the Society of Jesus to be communicated by the Superiors General, and whereas our Father Ignatius has sent me copies of the rescripts in which their concessions are enumerated, and has also given me power to impart to those of ours who I think will make good use of these favours, the enjoyment of these

Pontifical concessions, either by myself, or by others, I, thinking that you, Master Gaspar, Rector of this College of Goa, and those who are under your authority, will by this communication of these faculties be more fully empowered to gain so much greater return of good in the souls of those among whom you work, do therefore communicate the same fully to you, and, relying on your well approved prudence, I also commit to you to be in my stead, so that you may dispense and impart all the privileges of every kind granted to us by the bulls of the Popes to those to whom, and in as far as you shall judge to be expedient to the greater service of our Lord God to impart them.

FRANCIS.

Goa, April 7, 1552.

The following document is of the same character with the preceding.

In the name of our Lord Jesus Christ.

Considering with myself the shortness of our life and the great uncertainty of the day and hour to each person of death, which is most certain to come to all men, fearing also lest this house may incur some disturbance if it were necessary for it to choose for itself a Rector in the place of Master Gaspar, if he were to be taken away by death before our Father General has appointed a Rector to this College, I have thought that it was my duty to anticipate as far as I can, before I leave for China, the inconveniences which might arise from such an unforeseen event, by settling at once something certain and naming the person who in the mean time, until it shall be known from Rome that anything has been settled by the General of the Society, is to govern this community, as well as the other stations of the Society from the Cape of Good Hope to the extreme East, and whom all of ours, priests, clerics, and lay brothers, must obey in all things as their Superior.

If therefore anything, as I said, should happen in the course of nature to Master Gaspar, let Manuel de Morales be Rector of the house, and if he be absent at the time, let him be fetched at once, to come hither and take possession of the government. And from that time let all the fathers and brothers, both at Goa and elsewhere, begin to obey him as the lawful Rector of all. But until he arrive, let Father Paul be Rector in his place, who will resign the government to Father Manuel de Morales as soon as he shall come hither, and from that time put himself subject to the said Father Manuel, as the rest. And if before he become Rector, or after he has begun to be Rector, the said Manuel de

Morales be carried off by death, then let Master Melchior Nuñez be Rector, whom I now appoint and desire to be acknowledged by all as Rector with the same right, if perchance it should please God to transfer Father Gaspar Baertz and Father Manuel de Morales from this life to the joys of Paradise before our Father General of the Society of Jesus has appointed a Rector to this College.

These things I have thought well thus to decree, both in order to obviate other evils which might arise, and also to avoid the necessity of collecting into one assembly all the fathers who are occupied in preaching the Gospel in various and very widely separated places throughout India, who I do not think can be called away from the stations and ministrations in which they are working without grave inconvenience to the souls of those under their charge, and equal detriment to the service of God. For these reasons I command and enjoin, in virtue of holy obedience, all the Fathers of the Society of Jesus who are in India, to put into execution what is prescribed in this paper; and since I so decree and order of set purpose and after mature deliberation, to the greater glory and service of God our Lord, in order that no one who sees this paper may doubt about my will, I have signed it with my own hand the 7th of April 1552. FRANCIS.

The next letter is sometimes called an instruction as to 'the manner for avoiding all offence to men,' addressed to the same Father, Gaspar Baertz. It is confined, however, to two chief heads, each requiring consummate prudence—that of dealing with disputes between husbands and wives, and that of attacks made upon the religious of the Society by members of other orders.

(XCIX.) *To Father Gaspar Baertz, Rector of the College at Goa.*

As to the manner and method to be followed in intercourse with men so as to avoid all offences, I have thought it right to give you these precepts, which I much wish you to put in practice, and to require of all members of the Society under your authority. None belonging to us should converse with women, whatever may be their age, rank, or condition, except in a public place, such as the church. They should not visit them in their own home unless they are in danger and extreme necessity, or on account of an illness which threatens death, for meeting which in a Christian way they require to be prepared by the confession of their sins. Even then they should not be visited save in the presence of their husbands or relations; but if they have no relations at hand, let it be before respectable persons of the neighbourhood, but never without witnesses, such as, in case of need, could give their testimony to what they have seen. If, then, it should happen that a woman who has no husband and has lost her parents has to be visited in her own house, no member of our Society should enter unless accompanied by a respectable man, known as such both among the relations and acquaintances of the woman, and among the neighbours and inhabitants of the city or village, so as to prevent all suspicion and to cut short gossip. But they should not be visited, even with these precautions and this company, except in the case I have named, of extreme danger and of very serious illness. And whenever a woman who is not in danger of death may seem able, either then with some exertion, or after a short time, to go out of her house, she should be waited for at the church.

On this point, again, it is necessary to be careful, even with those who are most seriously ill, not to multiply the visits of any beyond what is required by urgent necessity. And altogether you must be severe in this matter, cutting things, as we say, down to the quick, so as to suppress and make as rare as possible for our brethren all communication with that sex, these interviews being of little profit and of very great danger, the uncertain hope of a generally moderate benefit to the divine service being only too often purchased with the doubtful chances of losing innocence and fair fame. I also do not wish our fathers to employ too much time and leisure in instructing even the mothers of families who frequent our churches, however great inclinations they may seem to have to good. The reason for my judgment is that women are generally inconstant in their purposes and full of talk in their conferences;

the result is a great loss of time in intercourse with them, and but very little fruit of any sure or solid advantage.

How far better it is to give more time to their husbands, and to take pains in instructing and exciting them to all noble deeds! Men, it is certain, are naturally more able to take in good advice when given; more constant in their resolutions to follow it. What you accomplish with them is solid and permanent. If they have promised a thing, they will fulfil it. If they are won over to God, they will set in order their wives and families. They should be your chief objects; and the labourers of the Society ought to spend more time and more diligence in cultivating them, for where the seed is sown more thoroughly the harvest is more abundant. This prudence, believe me, is a great destroyer of gossip, nonsense, trifling, and small piques, so insist strongly on its invariable practice by all under your charge. If any quarrel should exist between husband and wife, and charity suggests that ours should interfere to make peace, let these arbiters of conciliation be sure that for the success of their work, it is far more important to listen patiently to, and admonish diligently, the husband than the wife.

Let them set to work on the husbands, and leading them dexterously away from the subject of the moment, persuade them to purify their soul at once by a general confession, for which they may prepare themselves by a short retreat and by meditation on some of the subjects of the first week of the Exercises. After our father shall have heard the husband's confession of all the sins of his life, let him gently lead him to consent that sacramental absolution shall be deferred for a few days, during which he may exercise himself in holy meditations and works of penance, and in serious deliberations as to future amendment of life. When in these sentiments, and with strong resolutions to give himself up entirely to God's service, he will easily be persuaded to follow advice for the purpose of securing internal peace with his wife. The source of evil once checked, and the causes of resentment removed, you will be surprised to see that in applying a remedy to one person you have cured two at once.

Should it happen that when one of ours is occupied in a matter of this kind, the wife comes to him apart and says she has great desires of serving God, but that an impediment to this lies in the necessity of living with her husband, as being bad and dissolute, and of disorderly habits, and that she has legitimate reasons for separating from him, such as she believes could be proved judicially and would suffice to obtain legal authority for a separation—as to all these reasons, and more which such persons are wont so cleverly to bring forward, you must take care not to be moved thereby to approve of this thought of divorce. You should remain firm in advising them to stop with their husbands. These tender longings for religion soon grow languid in that inconstant sex, and later on they will condemn their own design and your advice. Supposing them to be constant, still the danger to the husband and the public scandal which is almost inseparable from such cases are evils too serious to be overbalanced by the fruit of the devotional advantage of a single soul, who wishes in married life to anticipate the benefits of widowhood. Again, in these cases, carefully avoid blaming the husband before others, even when it is clear that he alone is to blame. See him alone, and gently exhort him to make a general confession, and then take occasion, from his own self-accusation, to scold him, but mildly, and so as to make him understand you are sorry for his own sake for the injury he has done to himself by his fault, rather than that you are moved by the accusations of his wife, who has complained of him. Consider it a thing above all things to be avoided that the husband should feel or suspect that you rather favour the wife most and care more for her interests, for such an opinion would give a most severe blow to all hope of success. Therefore, however much the fault may be the husband's, never let him even hear you say so; but when you have led him to make the avowal to you himself, then you may, without difficulty, blame him for that of which he accuses himself. But even then your sentence must be free from all bitterness. Therefore, censure what he himself confesses with sorrow, so as to show him that you rather grieve with him than are angry with him.

Let love, kindness, and charity towards the sinner be conspicuous in your words and countenance. Everywhere men require to be treated with gentleness, but nowhere more than in India. They are as touchy as glass to offence, any violence makes them recoil and break; to gentleness they bend, you can turn them as you will. You will obtain everything here by prayer and affectionate manners, nothing by threats or severity. Again I repeat this advice; take heed again and again. If a husband and wife take you as umpire, and plead their cause in person or by advocates in your presence, never let yourself blame the man before others, however nearly his fault may be brought home to him. The passionate minds of women eagerly take hold of such words, and are incredibly inflated thereby. They are always on the look-out for opportunities of humbling their husbands, and when they seem to feel that the cause is going in their own favour, if hints of an inclination to their side are allowed to fall from no other than the religious men chosen by themselves as arbitrators, they openly triumph, and let themselves loose with greater freedom for the future in complaints, accusations against their husbands, and excuses of themselves, heaped one on another without end, all to be poured with that mad loquacity of theirs into the ears of the imprudent priests who have encouraged them.

I go so far in thinking that the husband should not be blamed in the wife's presence, that I even think that the priest should not appear to believe the wife's defence when she relates the domestic quarrels, pleading her own cause and trying to persuade him that no part of the blame is to be imputed to her. Even if her statement be probable and true, it is well that she should not be excused by him who presides at the reconciliation. He should rather warn her seriously of the paramount duty imposed on the wife of honouring her husband and bearing with his ways. This is the law, let him add, which God Himself has laid down for all women, and which in general they unconsciously transgress, led astray by emotions of anger or other passions, too confident of their own innocence, and excessively indulgent to themselves, and so they give their husbands cause for anger, while they ought rather soothe them and conciliate them by their patience, submission, and obedience. They should therefore accuse themselves, even when their conscience seems to acquit them. At the same time they should earnestly endeavour to love and practise serenity of soul, indulgence, obedience, humility, so as to live in submission to their husbands, as the Apostolical Epistles teach Christian women.

After having thus cleared themselves with the husbands, against all suspicion of favouring the wives, our brethren must in turn be careful not to offend the wives, by whom they might be suspected of unjust partiality for the husbands. They must not seem to believe in the shame cast by the latter on their wives. But they should observe an equal balance, not letting the scale fall to either side, reserving an ear for the accused, as the saying is, condemning no one unheard, and take the defence always into consideration as well as the accusation. Thus administering their office they will not only avoid offending either party, which would compromise the termination of the matter, but will also approach nearer the truth. In fact, with disputes of this kind, both parties are generally in fault, one more, the other less; each in their turn have a share in the fault, so the quietest way is to reprove them both, not entirely absolving either, receiving with hesitation and caution what each alleges in self-justification. This is a simpler method of gaining the end of reconciliation, and at the same time shuts the door against the murmurers and discourses of reckless tongues.

After all, when any one finds that he has tried all he can in vain in these matters, let him send the parties whom he despairs of reconciling either to his Lordship the Bishop, or to his Vicar: and let him do this without exasperating either, or speaking to either harshly. For our human weakness is prone to break out into complaint against those from whom any one seeks what he thinks fair and does not get it. So that unless the unsuccessful mediator be very prudent, he may let a sharp word or two escape him which may touch one or both of the litigants, as being averse to reconciliation or unjust. He will get nothing by this but the hatred of the one whom he has hit, or perhaps the contempt of both parties, who will see the imprudence of their chosen arbitrator, and acknowledge too late their mistake in choosing him. So that in order that you may not lose the friendship of one or both of the dissentients, as well as your own time and toil, endeavour by all show of patient kindness, and by prudently complimentary language, to send them both away at peace and goodwill at least with yourself.

And, as a general rule, I entreat you to be always recollected and self possessed in your intercourse with all kinds of men. Never forget that we are held up as a spectacle before this perverse world, that we are always watched by the assiduous and inquisitive eyes of envy, and of malice always inclined to evil judgment, ready to seize every occasion of thinking and talking ill of us, both from men's own inclinations, and from the instigation of the evil spirit our restless and watchful enemy: and be convinced that of all the steps of imprudence that is the most fatal which, besides present evil, plants the seed of future mischief. We seem to ourselves to be hurried on by pure zeal for the Divine glory, and yet with our intention directed good, we fall, and careless of acts and words, so long as we are urging on the work of religion, we do and say what we shall afterwards blush or grieve for under a burning sense of the serious evils which have resulted, which we should have foreseen by circumspection or provided against by moderation, yet which have been allowed to take place by our rashness, and furnish us with abundant matter for useless and tardy repentance.

Dread especially giving yourself up to the anger which may be provoked by a thousand occasions, at the sight of so many crimes, but which yet causes the headlong fall of over zealous men unless they step very carefully on this slippery ground, unless they restrain their tongue from bitter speeches, by the bridle of a modest gentleness: without which all the keenness of reproof will evaporate in emptiness. How many persons have ever been improved by excited reprehension from a man white with passion? Never reproach those who must be corrected except with calmness; let no anger appear in the few words in which you address yourself to the cure of people who have themselves fallen through excitement, otherwise you would give an example of the evil rather than a remedy. The generality of men ascribe all anger to vice: they are so far from being ready to believe that divine charity alone kindles the zeal of religious persons who are intemperately violent against sinners, that they look upon this violence as a proof that these persons are just like other men, and that they let themselves be carried away hither and thither by their own vehement passions as much as the commonest of the people.

With religious of other orders, and in general with all priests who for any reason may dispute with you, you will always show yourself full of deference and humility according to the precept of the Apostle, giving 'place to wrath' and agitation if any sign of it should appear in them, and do this not only in cases where your own conscience reproaches you, but also where you clearly know that you are innocent and they in fault: nor even then desire any greater revenge on those who trouble you unjustly than a humble silence, which modestly refrains from vindication of its rights, when you perceive that all you could allege would be in vain, because their ears are closed against you by prejudice and anger. Retire into your own hearts at such times, and sigh over the condition of these people hastening to their own fall by violating right and justice; upon whom God will sooner or later take vengeance more sharply and severely than you or they suspect. Therefore pour forth your prayers for them continually before God, touched at the sight of their weakness and thoughtlessness: above all things avoid giving way to the trouble you feel, revenging yourselves on them beforehand in thought or silent desire of evil you might wish them, or in conversation or word before others, exposing their injustice much less by any actions which in turn do them hurt.

Regard all those feelings which flesh and blood, with the depraved instincts of our nature, rouse in the imperfect, as infinitely dangerous and injurious to you, unless you banish them. Be certain, without any doubt at all, that God is wont to shed profusely His most precious graces and blessings upon those who, for the love of Him, patiently suffer heavy charges without any wish for revenge, and who overcome by the sweetness of divine charity all inclination to return the injury. Then it is that God, so full of mercy, feels, so to speak, obliged to compensate abundantly for that of which they have been deprived by injustice; to load with honours and benefits those whom calumny disfigures and violence despoils, while their tranquil and peaceful souls remain unmoved by indignation, however great may be the wantonness of the assault. He will take peculiar care to inflict in His own good time the shame and confusion they have merited upon the authors of the mischief, who so unjustly oppose you, who disturb your pious enterprizes. But He will not do all this if you take any part yourselves in the matter, and either by angry feelings in your wounded heart, or complaints put into words, or by doing anything in your power to put your persecutors to pain, endeavour yourselves to inflict vengeance upon them.

If it should happen, from which may God preserve us! that a dispute should arise between you and any other religious, be careful above all things to avoid disputing with them before the Governor or Commandant, or in presence of any secular whatever. Laymen are wonderfully scandalized at hearing and seeing such outbreaks in men who are consecrated to God. If these religious have declaimed against you from the pulpit, or have defamed you in public conversation, you will apply to his Lordship the Bishop, and you will beg him, if he thinks fit, to call them before him, and after having heard the cause before the two parties, to decide what may seem expedient to make up the quarrel, and put an end to a scandal so mischievous to the people. You will tell his lordship that I myself beg him to attend to this work himself, and put an end in good time to any divisions of this nature, lest they should be brought before secular magistrates, or in any way get abroad among the people, which should be avoided if possible.

For the rest, even should these religious have declaimed against you in the pulpit, I absolutely forbid your making in your turn your apology and defence of your own rights from the same place. Let it suffice for you, as I have said, to place the matter before the Bishop, and to prevail on him to summon your adversaries, listen to them in your presence, and after taking thorough cognizance of everything to terminate the business in some way or other, checking by his wisdom and authority the scandals which might arise, and which would cause immense harm among the people. On this point, you should observe that the honour of the Society does not consist in energetically defending our rights before the people, in winning our cause by arguments before men, or in gaining the applause of our audience at an unbecoming time and place. The whole affair stands or falls by the judgment of God. If God should disapprove of what we do, the false favour of the world would not efface our real stain before God. Let us look to this beyond all else, that we be at one with God as to our line of duty, that we act by His inspiration, that we truly rejoice that we are approved by Him. Now God would never approve of our prolonging our disputes to the great disturbance of the public. He desires His own to give place to wrath, to appease tumults, to live in calmness, to be peaceable even with those who hate peace.[8]

Not only do I earnestly advise you to behave thus under such circumstances, but I prescribe and command it by my authority. I repeat it, you must not plead your own cause, even when publicly attacked, but have recourse to his Lordship the Bishop, and stand by his decision, earnestly imploring him not to hesitate in restoring peace in the land where the enemy has sown discord.

Finally, above all, I commend to you yourself: be careful always to remember that you are a member of the Society of Jesus. This thought will suggest to you on all occasions what you ought to do. Farewell.

Goa, April 15, 1552. FRANCIS.

[8] Ps. cxix. 7.

We come next to what is in fact a long instruction on the method of government to be pursued by a Superior of the Society, both as regards the internal discipline of his house and his relations with others abroad. Here again we have, as in the instruction given to the same Father Gaspar when going to Ormuz, the results of the careful thought, prayer, and experience of Francis Xavier as to some of the most important duties which can fall to the lot of a religious. We need not dwell on the evident carefulness and consideration of all possible circumstances and issues with which this document is drawn up, nor the forethought as to future arrangements which it displays.

(c.) *To Father Gaspar Baertz.*

In order that you may be able to discharge worthily, to your own spiritual advantage as well as that of others, the government of the College at Goa and of our brethren in those parts which I have intrusted to you, I think it right, just as I am starting on a very distant journey, to leave you the following precepts in writing, which I entreat you to read very frequently during my absence, keeping them constantly present to your memory. For I think that these suggestions will be a useful guide and counsel to you in all your administration of such matters, so as to direct you profitably towards that end which is our sole aim, the greater glory of God.

Above all things, strive to keep your mind firmly established in the consciousness of your own abasement, according to those precepts which, at your request, I have already given you on this subject. Recall them by daily meditation, dwelling on them so that they may sink deeply into your soul, that thus the points I suggested, and the other lights on the subject with which God in His mercy may favour you in meditation, may be indelibly engraved upon your mind. Behave with great modesty, affability, and indulgence towards those fathers who reside with you, as well as those who live elsewhere under your authority, with no severity or sternness, except to those who might take unfair advantage of your meekness or humility. In the latter case, looking to their good alone, and not that you may support your authority, or punish them for despising it, let them feel your power just so far as is necessary, in order that by moderately chastising them you may raise them from their fall by needful correction, and that the scandal given to our brothers who have witnessed the fault may be removed by the wholesome example of its repression.

Let every fault against obedience committed by the fathers or brothers be visited by some penance. In this matter no exception is to be made for priests over clerics and lay brothers. Should any one under you treat you with pride, and if, puffed up by a vain opinion of himself, he should meet your orders with a lofty brow and arrogance and haughtiness, be stern with him, showing him the severity of a master rather than kindness and affability. Impose public penances for daily faults on these rather than on others; above all, be careful that they do not see any weakness in you, or that you fear them, and so will allow other faults to pass unpunished, but especially those against authority. Nothing confirms contumacious subjects in their boldness and prompts them to rebellion more than any proof they may have seen of weakness on the part of their superiors. If they perceive them to be anxious and timid, hesitating to impose punishment upon subjects who refuse the respect and obedience due to their superiors, there is no end to their inflation, which reaches even insolent audacity. The success of their conduct encourages them to persevere therein, and the evil will continually increase, each step being fraught with great mischief to the common peace. You must therefore carry out with great exactness what I prescribe, not allowing any personal consideration or fear of the opinion or observations of the world to prevent you from doing as you ought.

Among inferiors there are some who, without being self willed, sometimes neglect the commands of their superiors through weakness and forgetfulness, without any contempt for these orders, but from indolence and carelessness. You should correct these more gently, softening the severity of reproof by a kind countenance and deportment, while, as a penance for their fault, inflicting only a slight punishment. If among the lay brothers you observe any who set themselves above their rank, with some appearance of arrogance, be most careful to humble them, setting them to the meanest offices in the house; and as long as you notice in them this vain opinion of themselves, treat them in a grave, severe, or as it might seem, a contemptuous manner. This coldness will cure their inflation; and if it brings about more humility on their part, you can relax your disdainful manner, and when they are reduced to due modesty, you will instantly soften the severity of your aspect, as if to thank and rejoice with them; in order that, by a comparison of the different effects of different conduct, they may learn what is best, and at the same time disabuse themselves of a terrible mistake, by which such persons sometimes delude themselves, fancying they are necessary to the Society. The Society however does not want proud people; and this, if they are wise, they will learn from the severity shown them by their superior as long as they claim too much for themselves.

Take care never to admit into the Society any subjects lacking industry, of poor judgment, limited intelligence, or indifferent strength, men not fit to manage anything well. Nor, again, those whom you may suspect to be inclined towards the religious life rather by weariness of their own indigence, than by zeal for God's service. To those whom either you or Father de Morales may admit, I wish that you yourself should give the month's retreat, and in this duty do not let any one else take your place. During the whole of this time you will watch them with scrupulous attention, studying them until you know them thoroughly. After the Exercises, put them to humble occupations, for example, the care of the sick in the public hospitals, domestic work in the kitchen, or other lowly offices of the same kind. Whilst they are making the Exercises, you will make them render you a most exact account of the efforts they have made to acquit themselves well of the usual meditations according to the prescribed method. If you find that they do this with sloth and tepidity, you may either send them back whence they came, relieving the Society at once of a useless weight, or, if you have a ray of hope as to their amendment, you may withdraw them for a few days from the practice of these holy meditations, taking away from them, as a punishment, a privilege of which their negligence has rendered them unworthy, so that this humiliation may cover them with confusion, and lead them to desire more earnestly to return to this course with their companions, and persevere with them for the required space.

As to the making vows you will observe the following plan. First, you will tell all the persons whom you may have received to probation, not to bind themselves by any engagement before God, without having first communicated with you, and obtained your consent. Insist on this chiefly at the beginning of the Exercises. Those who have been sufficiently tried, and who are to make the vows in due form, these may bind themselves in precise terms to poverty, chastity, and obedience. But warn them beforehand that this engagement on their part, and the obligation of the vows, only bind them by virtue of that act of religion while they remain in the Society. That if (from which God preserve them) they are excluded from it on account of any fault, by the Rector, or by any one who has power from him, they will remain entirely released from all obligation of such vows. Let them make their vows in your presence, pronouncing the form given to you in writing, the words of which express their oblation of themselves. You will also prescribe to them beforehand the other rules to be observed, one of which should be that they read aloud the formula of the vows at mass, when the priest is going to administer communion, and then at once receive the Blessed Sacrament. This rule, which makes the obligation of their vows depend on their remaining in the Society, is the more indispensable in this country of the Indies, because there are here fewer monasteries belonging to other religious orders, into which subjects might pass who, having made their profession in our Order, are found to be unfit for it. Therefore, that the Society may be free to rid herself of hurtful members, without which power she cannot exist, it is most expedient to declare to those who take the vows, that the engagement they contract by these religious vows is dissolved by their legitimate dismissal from the Society by the Superiors thereof.

You will write to our brethren who live in different parts of this country, forbidding any of them, in any place, to receive a person into the Society without consulting you, and warning them that such admission is invalid, because they do not possess the legitimate power for it. If, therefore, subjects present themselves to them, whom they consider suitable, they should write to you what are the talents and qualities which they possess for working for the service of God in the Society. When you have answered that you do not object to enroll these persons in the Society, there is nothing to prevent their receiving a certain hope that they may obtain their wish, so they may be sent to you at Goa, or, if you prefer it, you will desire that one of our brothers, who is capable of it, may give them where they are the month's retreat, and that then they may begin to be put to the interior trials of our Institute. Still, as a general rule, it seems to me preferable, when there is no insuperable obstacle, that they should be summoned to this College, where I think they can be examined with greater facility and certitude. Notwithstanding, I leave the matter altogether to you; and in this and all other matters you will always act truly and simply in whatever way seems to you to lead most directly to the greater service of God.

You will carefully exhort all the superiors of houses or dwellings of the Society in this country,—whether those where our brethren are charged with the direct care of souls, being the only directors of vacant churches deprived of their ordinary pastors, or those who are working as auxiliaries to the ordinary priests of the place,—to write every year to our blessed Father Ignatius, and accurately and at full length, explaining to him in detail whatever good God vouchsafes to work by their means, in those places and among those people where they are employed. But let them carefully avoid inserting in these accounts anything which could offend any one who might read them. Let them leave out faults which cannot be remedied, which it is no use to speak of, and which cause a scandal; the telling of which might occasion in the readers a useless sorrow, and bring on the writers a just charge of imprudence. Let them be content to say what it is well should be known, and what is worthy of mention; the propagation of God's kingdom, the triumphs of grace, the idolaters converted to the religion of Jesus Christ, and the guilty reclaimed from the path of their iniquities. And let them add any hopes that may appear of further and immediate progress. They should also send letters to all the members of the Society in Europe, with the same contents and composed in the same way, informing them, for the honour of God and their mutual consolation, of the success of their labours, without any offensive allusion or every illtimed complaint, any indiscreet revelation of what ought to be kept in silence. Some of these letters may be addressed to the Society at Coimbra, who will have them conveyed throughout Spain. The others, to ours at Rome, and to the fathers and brothers of the Society dispersed in all the countries of Europe. You will yourself write privately to the Rector of the College at Coimbra, as to the state and success of your College at Goa, telling such things as you think may please him: but in the style of your letters do not think of his judgment, but remember that a great number of people belonging to every class will judge of your language, for letters of this kind are eagerly sought and widely spread. Your modesty and prudence will both make you dread and avoid censure from them. And you should endeavour that your reports of events in India may satisfy public curiosity, so as not only to give no offence, but also to do good no the readers.

I think you should also carefully write to inform our blessed Father Ignatius, how important it is for the extension of God's glory here in the Indies, and for the greater spiritual benefit of souls, that he should obtain from the Pope spiritual favours for our brethren in these countries, such as plenary indulgences offered to those who have worthily approached the Sacraments of Penance and Holy Eucharist. It would be necessary that these opportunities held out to the people of obtaining these sacred benefits should recur several times in the year, that is, on the most solemn feasts, and that they should not be offered in one short space of time for every place at once. Since there is here but a small number of priests, especially of such as are capable of skilfully deciding cases of conscience, where there is a great number of penitents, a sufficiently long time is necessary for them to open all the secrets of their soul and to accomplish due satisfaction. The fathers also, after imparting to one town or place the advantages of the Papal Indulgence, should have leisure to proceed to another for the same purpose.

Remind our Father also to take care that, if possible, the grants of these favours should be sent to us in due form with the necessary signatures and seals affixed for the authentication in the regular way, so as to be shown to the suspicious. In these countries some people can with difficulty be persuaded to receive as certain indults of this kind, unless there are incontestable proofs and guarantees. It would also be useful that these diplomas should express formally in so many words the Pope's intention that the benefit and fruit of these graces should extend to all the faithful of every sex, age, and condition, settlers, natives, or travellers who are found, for whatever reason it may be, beyond the Cape of Good Hope as far as the extreme East.

You will more easily induce our Father Ignatius to consent to take this trouble, if you give him, as you can with truth, a magnificent account of the spiritual fruits, really great and marvellous, which the Jubilee that he previously dispatched us from Rome produced here. This Jubilee was limited to a short space of time and fettered by restrictions, and yet it produced such great good. You can argue what still greater advantages we may hope for from plenary Indulgences rightly allotted, granted for a period of several years, and recurring with the solemnity of certain feasts. In this matter I would have you put forth all your powers of persuasion, using the most strenuous efforts, so that Father Ignatius may feel that he should do his utmost in obtaining us these graces. You will add that I also join with the utmost energy in your solicitations, and that I shall esteem it a singular favour to myself, if he yields to my entreaties, and vouchsafes to obtain for these people so precious an opportunity of spiritual advantages. You will also write to Master Simon, or to the Rector of the College at Coimbra, begging that they will themselves treat of this matter with the King, explaining to him the immense fruits which must infallibly result from the promulgation of these Indulgences, so as to prevail on his Highness to help us by writing to Rome, or rather settle the matter at once by his high influence and favour with the Pontiff, arranging that these indults be consigned to Father Ignatius, addressed to the College of the Society of Jesus at Goa, so as to be given out at the discretion of the Fathers of this College. The consequence will be that the people, won by the favours which these fathers have obtained and will dispense to them, will regard them with greater honour and respect, so that their labours will be more acceptable, and so more profitable to all sorts of people.

When people seek admittance to the Society, do not, I advise you, hasten to receive them, however fit, at too early an age; reject absolutely those that you know belong to any of those classes which our Father Ignatius has by name excluded for ever from entrance into our Order. One of these is, as you know, to be of Jewish extraction. Be careful also not to admit any one unless he is eminently gifted with the qualities suitable to some one of the special ministrations of our Institute. If they are uneducated, I absolutely forbid their being received among the spiritual workers, however great may be their ability, and when a number of persons who are unexceptionable offer themselves, avoid accepting too many. Choose a few amongst a great number, the worthiest among the worthy, taking into consideration at the same time the number of our residences and offices, and also the ordinary casualties, so that there may be enough to send where necessity calls, to supply the places of those who fail by sickness or death, and yet not more than are wanted, so as to be doing nothing and burthening the house.

You must be careful never to allow any of ours to be raised to the priesthood if he is not sufficiently learned, and unless the innocence of his life be thoroughly proved to you by the experience of several years. Father Ignatius has forbidden this most expressly. Even had he kept silence, the thing speaks for itself, and the sad remembrance of those serious annoyances which have occurred to us from this source should be enough to make us avoid it. Do not be deceived by the hope of perfection in religion which may be remarkable in an ignorant man, as though that compensated for the defect of knowledge. These hopes are often proved fallacious by experience. Circumstances cause the mask to be dropped, and such persons show themselves what they really are. I wish, therefore, that you should be lynxeyed in penetrating the secret depths of souls, so as not to be misled at once by a few tears shed in prayer, or by the sighs wrung from some of these in holy meditations. Wait until real experience has convinced you that these subjects practise an active control over the depraved inclinations of nature, over anger, ambition, selfwill, and that they have a perpetual horror for every kind of vainglory, before you make up your mind that they deserve the credit of a sanctity perfect in every respect, and, so to speak, consummated.

The order of charity requires us to give our care first to persons of our own community, and then to externs. See, then, in the first place, that you fulfil the duties of a genuine father towards our own people, to the native children and orphans who are pupils of this house, providing carefully all that they want either for soul or body. When this duty is accomplished you can expend whatever remains of time and strength in the service of others. I command you this in the name of our Father Ignatius, and I advise it with all the earnestness that I can command. Indeed, I am deeply assured that this counsel is of the utmost importance. It seems to me that those who desire only to please men and who are satisfied with a vain appearance, without caring for a moment to be pleasing in the sight of God, Who pierces the depths of the soul, are no worse than those who, taking no heed of complaints at home, seek the favour of the town, falsely thinking that they have fulfilled their duty, whilst they are neglecting its first and principal obligation, in order to devote all their energies in the most preposterous manner to secondary and accessory works. Those who do this are in the most complete error, and lest you should be of the number I desire you recall this advice of mine daily to your memory.

I see that the office which is intrusted to you is so manifold and full of detail that it is evident that you can never discharge alone all its duties yourself. As it is necessary that you should use deputies who will take charge of a number of particular matters for you, I wish you to have two rules as to this. First, in any function only to employ those who you know are competent to fill it. Secondly, to watch vigilantly over all, to demand frequently an account of what they have done, and if they have committed any fault not to let it pass unpunished. Consider that you are placed on high to watch over all, and according as in this duty you have been either strict and indefatigable, or careless and negligent, so you will have provided well or badly for your inferiors, and either have fulfilled your duty, or have rendered yourself guilty of bad administration of your power.

The greater part of this care of yours should be given to those functions which are of the widest utility. You should, therefore, attend first and principally to the sermons addressed to the people by ours, to the hearing of confessions, to their familiar conversation and intercourse with those without. Finally, to the handling of charitable works. The preachers you must form to a true idea of their function, and approve or correct them as is needed. Confessors you will admonish and instruct, seeing how they do their business. Then, as far as may be, see that the familiar intercourse of the brothers with people of various conditions shall be fruitful and religious, by giving advice beforehand or by examination afterwards, so as to procure in every point the perfection suitable to our Institute.

Take care to keep yourself informed by certain and frequent intelligence as to the state and doings of our brothers who are going about to preach, or those who are dispersed in the various residences about there. Write to them frequently, and carefully explain the most minute details. Desire them in turn to write to you often and at full length. Attend diligently to this correspondence. Study at leisure the letters you have received. Think over your own before writing them, and consider, what is really the case, that a great part of your duty consists in this diligence. You will also inquire of any strangers who arrive from places where ours reside, how they go on, in what respect they are held, what they may have heard people say of them, and the like.

Write to me at Malacca most fully about all the affairs of the College; about each of the fathers sent out to preach the Gospel; about the country where each is; with what ardour, with what success they are working: be careful not to do this in a summary way. Enter into everything and descend to the most minute particulars. Say also what is the political condition of these countries, for of this also it is well we should be informed. Do not forget to give an account of what other religious bodies are doing for the glory of God and the salvation of souls. Add the last news from Portugal; what report or letters tell us of our brethren at Coimbra, at Rome, and all over Europe. As to the letters directed to me which may reach you, especially those from Master Simon and from our friends at Rome, you will take care if there are, as is usual, several copies of them, to address one to Malacca to Father Francesco Perez; for I will tell him to get it transcribed and to send me copies by more than one way. If you have only received one copy, you will open the letter, have it transcribed by a trustworthy secretary, and keeping the original, send the copy to Father Perez. Remember to do this every year. You must insist that the fathers living at Bazain, Cochin, Coulan, on the Comorin Coast, and at Meliapor, write to me once every year carefully and at length. I can by no means allow this duty to be neglected either by you or them.

I desire most earnestly that you and all our fathers should show yourselves full of obedience and submission to his Lordship the Bishop. Take special care never to cause him, under any circumstance, the least annoyance; on the contrary, study in all things to serve and please so kind and indulgent a Father, who for so many reasons deserves that we should show our filial devotion to him in every way. You will tell the fathers who live away from Goa to write sometimes to show their veneration to the Bishop, and to inform him briefly of the spiritual fruit which, by the help of God, they reap from their labours. They should add all they can say with truth in praise of the Bishop's Vicars in the places where they are residing, carefully praising whatever they are doing for the public good. Let them give liberal praise to all that is done by the other religious and priests for the good of the Church, by preaching or other sacred functions. If they have nothing favourable to say let them hold their tongues, and not consider it their business to lay before the Bishop any complaints against his Vicars or the other evangelical labourers. There will never be wanting people to do this. Should they find it necessary to treat with the Bishop upon any other business, I would not have them put it into these letters, which I wish to be designed to give consolation and refreshment to this good Father. If they have business of this kind, let them write about that at another time.

Admonish, in my name, all of ours to show everywhere a great obedience to the Bishop's Vicars, telling them how painful it would be to me to hear from any quarter that there had been any sort of difference between the Vicars and the Fathers of the Society, who labour in places under them. Add that in the letters they write to me I wish them to say what good understanding they have with the Vicars. Further, it would be an immense pleasure if they could get the Vicars to write to me testifying to the value and the abundance of the fruit gathered by our fathers who are employed in their districts. I now again enjoin you, on account of the importance of the matter, take care that our fathers, especially where there are Portuguese garrisons, whose mission is there, live in perfect union with the Vicars, and that they never on any account enter into any difference with them. In order that this recommendation may have more weight with them, mention particularly in your letters that, before setting sail for China, I left you in this College an order to expel from the Society any belonging to us who should offend against the Vicars, or who should in any way have been at variance with them.

After my departure, apply to the Bishop, if he thinks fit, to write regarding the Jubilee to those parts where the fathers of the Society are, desiring them to promulgate it, that those spiritual fruits of which it gives promise may come to light. This Jubilee has been extended to the whole of the present year 1552, that the benefit of it may be enjoyed without difficulty by all in the Portuguese settlements throughout the Indies with a great dearth of opportunities for cleansing their souls by confession. This delay will allow of their being all attended to in order, by sending our fathers to different places, according to requirement. It was that motive which made me ask for an extension to the whole year of the faculty of acquiring so signal a grace.

Should it happen that among the fathers who come from Portugal this year there are some gifted with an unusual talent for preaching, I think you had better send one with a lay brother to Diu, giving him the instructions which I formally wrote for the fathers at Ormuz. There are, as you know, two of them; for I gave you a number of precepts when you went there for the first time, and I added some others for him who succeeded you in your mission. I know that some copies of each remain. You will let them who go to Diu have a copy, earnestly advising them to read it frequently, and to fulfil it to the letter. If among our brethren who are expected to arrive from Portugal by the next vessels there should be one, I do not say of very great experience in preaching, or giving fair hopes of producing great effects in the pulpit, but not unlearned, one who seems likely from his strength of mind and body to be able to endure great labours, you will send him to Malacca by the fleet which starts from Goa by the April monsoon, so that from Malacca he may sail for Japan by the first opportunity, and then work together with Cosmo Torres. But see that he takes with him a small sum of money, collected when here as an alms to serve for maintenance for him and the others, for evangelical workmen in that country as yet reap no fruit but hard work. They have abundance of good to do and evil to suffer, but nothing on which to live or give their bodies any comfort. Exert yourself, therefore, to assist them in these two points, using, I beg of you, your utmost zeal and efforts; and specially strive also to obtain from God, by the prayers and sacrifices of yourself and others, that He will deign to show favour to those going thither both amid the innumerable perils of that vast and dangerous ocean, as well as living there amid the miseries and trials which are to be found in Japan.

If all the fathers brought by the fleet expected from Portugal this year should be equally excellent in eloquence and learning, so that there should be none amongst them who does not seem likely in the gift of speech to surpass our brother Antonio Eredia, who now fills the office of preacher at Cochin, I would have you send one of these fathers immediately to Cochin to replace Eredia, carrying him your orders that he should repair to Japan. But before making this decision, consider carefully whether it is really probable that this father will acquit himself of the preaching at Cochin with more fruit and advantage than Eredia; for if this is not certain, and if it seems prudent to suppose that the newly arrived is only equal and not superior to Eredia, I see no reason for making any change. Therefore, leaving Eredia where he is, you should, I think, send the last arrived preacher to Japan.

I give you much the same orders regarding Melchior Nuñez, who is now Superior of the College at Bazain, fulfilling the office of preacher in the same town. I wish, I say, if the Portuguese vessels bring a good number of eminent preachers, that one might be sent to succeed Nuñez; a man capable of producing great effect among the people, stirring up souls by his discourse, and at the same time able to manage with the necessary prudence and discernment the domestic administration and the disposal of the funds which his highness has granted the Society at Bazain for the support of evangelical labourers. In this case let Melchior Nuñez, set free from the administration of Bazain, sail by the April monsoon to Malacca, and hence to Japan. From my knowledge of Melchior Nuñez's eminent qualities, too good for the work at Bazain, I should be glad that such a man, set free from that charge, and replaced by a competent successor, could be transferred thither. The great learning which he possesses in so high a degree will make him much more useful there than at Bazain. If this were done it would be useless to remove Eredia from Cochin for other reasons, but especially because the great poverty of Japan does not, for the present at least, require more than one additional labourer. Whatever happens, leave no stone unturned, as they say, omit no effort or exertion to dispatch at least one of ours to Japan this year to share the labours of Cosmo Torres.

Both you and all ours of the College at Goa must preserve true friendship with the reverend fathers and friars of the Orders of St. Francis and St. Dominic, keeping this friendship alive by all the kind offices of religious charity in your power. You will beware, as far as in your power, not to give any of these religious a ground of quarrel. If the dissension begins on their side, and break out in the pulpits, I implore you, in God's name, to abstain from answering them before the people. Let them say what their zeal may inspire: but do you practise in silence the virtues of charity and obedience. I expressly forbid you to prolong the discussion noisily under any pretext at all; however much you are injured, however unjustly you may seem to be calumniated, I will not have you utter a word in public, such as might give your hearers the least idea of your vexation and of your sense of injury. Nothing can be enough to balance the scandal that conflicts of this nature cause among the people.

If, however, it should seem to you that thus to allow the declamations of your adversaries to be repeated with impunity were to cause scandal as well as offence against God, while this people, in uncertainty as to which they should believe of the two parties, should incur danger to their souls, you should place the matter before the Bishop, begging him to summon before him your public traducers, and after having heard their accusations in your presence, and listened to your defence, to terminate the difference by his own decision, so as to restore peace and compose those quarrels which disturb the congregation. For we, as well as these fathers, aim only at one sole object, which is the increase of the worship of God, and the progress of souls in the way of salvation. By thus invoking the authority of the Bishop between you, you will, as far as you are concerned, take sufficient precaution that the Divine Majesty may not be offended, and that the simple faith of the people be not offended by such discussions; and when friendship has been restored between you and those fathers, your efforts should be directed towards keeping up and increasing the union; you will sometimes visit them, and show them all the good offices of religious charity.

You must, by every proof of goodwill, make friends of the parish priests in the town, and the Superiors of the churches, under whatever title, in order to please them; you will, if in your power, do all they may ask of you, preaching in their churches as often as they ask you; and upon every occasion when you meet them, both your actions and words should abundantly prove your entire devotion towards them.

Never let either yourself or any of ours be entangled in worldly business under any pretext whatever. When such requests are made to you, reply that, after the ministration of God's Word and the Sacraments, there remains to you hardly the space of time necessary for prayer and study, for preparing yourselves for the holy functions of public preaching, and for deciding cases of conscience in confession. Without inverting the order of charity, you cannot postpone the care of souls and the service of God to the pursuit of earthly advantage or low temporal gains. Thus you must rid yourselves of all troubles of this nature; unless you do this, you will cause great harm to yourself and to the Society. Be sure that this is the door which gives the world entrance into religious houses, to the immense ruin both of religion and of religious.

In intercourse with persons who visit you, prudently consider what are the views of each. Some come for the sake of their spiritual progress, others in hope of temporal advantage. We even see people sometimes with whom the sacrament of Penance is an opportunity of seeking gain, who approach the ears of God's minister to recite the secret miseries of their poverty, and to reveal their indigence rather than their sins. I exhort you to avoid persons of this sort with great care; and, that you may not leave them longer in error, tell them at once that you cannot assist them either by giving them money or by gaining them favour with men. Cut short summarily all interviews with these people, for they are full of talk; and if you give ear to them, they will take a deal of your time, to no purpose. Such people have lost all sense of spiritual losses; their whole mind is simply bent on the desire for the material help of which they are in need. Dismiss people of this kind, whatever their sex, condition, or position, with a few words. Keep them at a distance, as drones who would rob your stores of honey. Their thoughts are all of this earth, and if they get possession of a person, they will much sooner draw him down from heavenly thoughts and make him give up the salutary helping of souls, by their importunate demands for corporal assistance, than will he, with all his effort, raise them out of that mire of low cares in which they are fast stuck.

I urge this advice on you the more earnestly because I am sure it is most absolutely necessary for you. Do not consider a moment the complaints and murmurs which may be made against you by these speculators, who seek worldly advantage out of religion—who will attempt perhaps to avenge themselves by accusations against you for your firmness in not yielding to their desires as they wished. Let them feel that you entertain not the slightest fear or anxiety as to their opinion or resentment; let them never detect in you any softness or apprehension at their empty talk. That would show you are not sufficiently detached from the world; as if you could deliberate whether you should please and make yourself agreeable to it, or to Jesus Christ, to whom you are bound by your vows; which would seem a sort of abandonment of the ranks of the Lord's army—a disgraceful apostacy from your purpose of irrevocably pursuing what is most perfect.

In the care of the boys of the seminary who are the children of natives, or orphans, you must diligently see that they want nothing, either as to food, clothes, or remedies, when sick. Watch very carefully that they receive a solid and regular instruction, both in the elements of Christian doctrine and in letters, according to the intelligence of each. Remember that the intention of the founders, who erected this College with the King's money, and the repeated and precise orders of his Highness, are to the effect that in the seminary of Goa native children should be trained in good habits and in a liberal education. Be careful therefore to discharge in all these points the duty which has devolved upon you. You know well what the complaints of old were. Avoid carefully exposing yourself and the Society to similar accusations.

Every time vessels sail for Portugal you must write to his Highness short and careful letters, informing him of all the spiritual fruits which have been gathered at Goa and in the other parts of India by the labours of the Society. For this purpose you must collect an account beforehand of all that has been done in different parts; and you must take the chief points, and so form an account such as you may hope it will please his Highness and his court to read. In other letters you must recommend to the King the material affairs of the College, telling him what it wants, in order to bear the expenses which fall upon it. State the sum to which the secure revenues of the year amount, and the extraordinary gifts, and when they come in. It is important that these details should be stated with precision, because I understand that the King sometimes bids that certain extraordinary receipts should be assigned by the officers of finance to the College of Goa; and I do not know whether the fidelity of the ministers has always corresponded to his Highness's liberality. The King, hearing from you all that you have received, will take care that if anything less than what he ordered has been paid, it shall be made up to you. You will add that the fathers who are sent from this College to preach the Gospel in different parts, on their arrival at the mission intrusted to them, are frequently prevented, by the want of the merest necessaries, from rightly discharging their duty; and then you can suggest that it seems to you worthy of his Highness's piety and munificence that he should deign to send a rescript, duly attested and sealed, commanding that in all Portuguese garrisons where there are stations of the Society our fathers should receive out of the royal treasury and stores both food and such other subsidies as may be necessary. His Highness should also order another rescript to be dispatched, commanding the Captain at Malacca to send to our fathers residing at Japan a sufficient sum for their maintenance, drawn from the royal treasury. In fact they can expect little or no help from the natives, on account of the barrenness of the country and the poverty of the inhabitants, which results from it. Write yourself to Master Simon, or the Rector of the College of Lisbon, most urgently recommending to them these three matters: the income of the College of Goa, the support of the fathers who dwell in Portuguese garrisons, and the support of the mission of Japan, that they may themselves speak to his highness on these matters, and promote them by continual pressure.

I remind you again, and I beg you to remember that the letters which you send—to the King especially—should be written with prudence and deliberation, for they are seen and judged by a great number of people. Adieu.

Goa, April 1552. FRANCIS.

The next letter is a kind of companion to the foregoing, relating more particularly to the management of temporal concerns and the particular circumstances of the College at Goa, which appears to have been mismanaged by Antonio Gomez in financial as well as in more important respects. Francis repeats, as we shall see, the warning against an indulgence in the too common taste for overbuilding which he had given to Melchior Nuñez, and dwells with great urgency on the necessity of relieving the missioners among the heathen in every possible way.

(CI.) *To Father Gaspar Baertz.*

With regard to the temporal administration of this house which is intrusted to you, I have thought it right to advise you as follows separately and more distinctly.

You will collect carefully, and having gathered them together, keep by you the charters and title-deeds, wherein the foundation and property of the College are set forth, such as the rescripts of our lord the King assigning to this College the revenues taken from the pagodas; the donations and other grants named in his Highness's letters signed and sealed in due form, and attested and confirmed by the former Governors of India; in short, all the authentic documents and original papers. In your intercourse with the secular procurator of the house and with Cosmo Añez—who in everything that concerns the revenues of the College has great authority, because of the importance of his office, as well as the fullest experience—have as frequent and as familiar interviews and dealings with them in the way of all friendly offices as may be required by the interest of the College. Spend as much time and be as intimate with them as may be necessary in order to put on a firm footing the revenues of the College, which are now in a shaky state, and on which we find we cannot depend; for a great part of those annual sums which previously belonged to the priests of the pagodas and are now allotted to the support of the missioners, is never paid, the persons bound obstinately refusing payment, and in many other instances the clear rights of the College have come to naught by unjust violence and a hardy refusal of satisfaction. You should, therefore, urge upon Cosmo and the others to arrange some efficacious remedy for these abuses.

I used to think it would be well—you will judge whether it is so or not—that letters should be obtained from the ecclesiastical authorities, in which threat of anathema should be proclaimed in the usual solemn form against all who refuse to pay the income due to this College, or in any way keep back property belonging to it; this threat to be carried out, if in a fixed time they have not restored what they possess unjustly, and set their conscience right by returning their unlawful spoils to the legitimate owners. But these and other measures of the same nature, which might be taken amiss by the people—such as to arrest and imprison the farmers of the revenue who neglect to pay the pension charged upon it—must be carried out by externs, so as to bring less odium on the Society.

All the funds of the house should be in your own hands, under lock and key; you alone should put in and take out; you alone should disburse, to the persons employed by you, the sums you think necessary towards the expenses of our brethren, the pupils, and the preachers labouring at a distance for religion. Poor men! they most commonly suffer extreme misery from the want of the absolute necessaries of life; and what is the worst, they are obliged to give up great undertakings, to the immense prejudice of the souls under their care, sinking under the pressure of want, after waiting long in vain for promised assistance. I pray you to provide against such misfortunes by a fair and prudent distribution of the college revenues, which you will, as is reasonable, first employ for the necessities of the house, for our own brothers and the externs in it; then send part to our people at Cape Comorin and in the Isles of the Moor, who are languishing in the most grievous want; to those also at the Moluccas and Japan, that they may be enabled to live at least poorly; for without some help they will be obliged to leave undone most important works, and to sacrifice vast hopes, to the great injury of God's kingdom. I have mentioned those who live away from Portuguese settlements, and in the midst of natives, because their condition is in this way the hardest. Those who reside in the King's garrisons, or in other places of settlement or resort for Europeans, will never be allowed to want, nor to give up their labours for the salvation of souls for want of maintenance—misfortunes which may well befall those who dwell away amid barbarous populations, partly hostile and partly in misery themselves. These labourers will die of hunger if they do not receive assistance from their brothers at a distance.

Above all things, I greatly desire that you should attend carefully to pay off the debts contracted by the College; for it is wrong to retain the property of another when we can restore it—a fault which seriously offends God and soils the conscience, as well as being a scandal to the people. For this reason, I urge it again and again on you, let there be no neglect, but use all your energies and efforts not to delay the fulfilment of so urgent and just a duty. In order to be able to do this, do not undertake any new buildings, nor even finish those that are begun. True, our dwelling is confined, but that which is most necessary should be done first. When the debts are paid, you can by degrees raise your walls and put on your roof.

And in general see that you take infinitely less care of those edifices which are raised with stone and mortar than of the spiritual temples of God; these temples are your brethren and the pupils intrusted to your faithful care, whom you should feed, watch over, and especially urge on to advance in virtue; this is the sovereign duty committed to your zeal. I know that there are some buildings which cannot be deferred, such as the wall round the garden of your house, and the shutting up of entrances, if there be any left but the principal door. For the shutting up of religious houses by a perfect and complete enclosure concerns the discipline and good name of the house to such an extent, that labour for that purpose upon it cannot be legitimately delayed. Such things, then, must be carried out at once, and at any cost.

Then I wish to warn you against any tenderness, or bashfulness in refusing, which may come over you when a crowd of poor externs beg you to assist them from the College funds, or when farmers of the revenue come and ask you to remit a part of your pension, alleging a thousand pretexts, and urging their own penury. Others will come to you in the confessional, and pour out the history of their family needs, their want of food for themselves and their families, and will implore you to supply their wants. I sympathize with them myself, but I forbid you to be softened by such cases beyond what reason and God permit. To give an alms with the property of others is a robbery. Now, in order that when you hear such requests you may cast upon me all the invidiousness of refusal, from this moment I tie your hands, and in virtue of my authority command you in so many words to tell all these petitioners that this house is overloaded with debt, and is hardly able for the daily support of the brethren and of the pupils. It has also other burthens: it has to support the fathers who preach the Gospel at a distance; it ought to supply the public hospital, and many other such works. For these reasons, I have ordered you in formal terms, and under obedience—which you cannot transgress without offending God—to give nothing to any one from the College revenues, for all that might thus be withdrawn would be taken from the wants of our house, to which all that we receive of the entire annual income does not suffice. But avoid particularly that expensive kind of penitents who in the Sacrament of Penance seek their temporal advantage and the nourishment of their bodies rather than spiritual remedies. I advise you to get rid of them with a few concise words. These people are much more sensitive to the wounds of fortune than to those of the conscience, and their philosophy is quite of the earth; they are entirely occupied with the hope of coaxing out a little money, and are deaf if you speak to them of their spiritual progress. If you do not send them away, you will yourself be distracted and called off from the more important things.

Many Portuguese heads of families ask that the College lands should be given them to farm. Is this for the interest of the College? I doubt it; and I fear that these concessions, if they are often made, will some day be a serious injury to the community. Examine the question prudently; take full counsel with the procurator and friends of your house, and resolve, upon whatever may seem best. This College owes some debts, but it has still more owing to it. I wish that you should know to a letter who your creditors are, and the sums owing to them; and make the same inquiry as to your debtors. Make careful lists of each. I allow you, however, to be less scrupulous in finding out what rights you have against others than in ascertaining and settling as soon as possible what others have a right to claim from you. You should set about this most earnestly; and when persons ask gifts of you, you can give this reply,—that you are in debt, and are bent upon discharging your debts as soon as possible; that you are bound to employ for this all the means that remain after the necessary expenses of so numerous a community; that nothing, in fact, is left to be distributed in any way, as you would like, among those to whom you would wish well, and whose poverty you compassionate, since everything is expended upon the food, clothing, and medical treatment of the members of the community, the guests, seminary pupils, and the sick in the hospital; without speaking of the necessary buildings, and other countless sources of expense. This should be no specious pretence or excuse; you should do as you say, watch night and day to stint a little from the daily expenses, as far as may be, thus to pay your creditors. Experience should teach you economy; what you have found advantageous be careful to repeat, and avoid all that you have discovered to be disadvantageous or of little use.

Study carefully the people to whom you intrust anything, for seldom do we meet with faithful agents. As far as you can, prefer those who are in the habit of going to confession to you at least once a month, and who at the same time go to communion. I wish that a great part of the substance of the letters that you are to send me at Malacca in the month of September, and which Francis Perez will take care of, should be these two heads: first, what is owing to you; second, what is owing by you. Add all about your domestic affairs, the fruit of your work and that of the other brothers; whether, and how far, the inhabitants of Goa have profited by your preaching and other ministrations; what news has come from Portugal, and what is going on as to peace or war; all that concerns our fathers living away. Write all these matters to me in a full and circumstantial manner; employ a secretary whose writing is correct and easily read. Choose as the collector of your revenues some honourable and rich merchant, generally one amongst those who is most highly thought of in the town; especially avoid choosing a poor person, lest we incur lawsuits. Consider whether it would not be cheaper to get two slaves to wash the clothes instead of sending them out to be washed. Also, whether it would not be desirable to keep a brother who perfectly understands the cultivation of vegetables for the care of our garden, rather than employing an extern. I see a good deal is spent on the food and salary of the gardener and of the two negroes who work under him. This charge could be given to one of our lay brothers, giving for his assistance two slaves, purchased for this purpose. In this and other such matters reflect carefully what is best, inquiring into them yourself, and taking the advice of experienced strangers who fear God and who take an interest in the College.

Out of the payment which Alvarez Alfonso owed us, 500 pardams have been remitted; this gives you still greater right to insist on the speedy payment of the 500 which he still owes. Don't be prodigal with funds which are not your own. Remember the hunger and privations endured by our brothers who, in the houses dependent on ours, are melting under the heat and burthen of the day. Remember the others at Japan, at the Moluccas, and at Cape Comorin, who are exposed without consolation to the severest trials.

I request you to send to Cioran[9] on Sundays Dom Augustin, the secular priest, giving him a fair stipend. I disapprove of either of our brothers residing there, and you must call home the one who is there now.

As to those who may be received into this house, you must

[9] Cioran or Choran was an island a few miles from Goa, on which there was a little property belonging to the Colleges with a church dedicated to our Lady. The text refers to the arrangements for serving this church by means of a secular priest, instead of one of the fathers.

seek to know, during their first probation, what mode of life they have led in the world, what trade they have practised or know, so that you may understand what function, or duty, or office in the house can be securely confided to them. From time to time tell Manuel de Morales to preach to the people in the cathedral, giving him warning and preparing him beforehand, that he may acquit himself worthily in that pulpit. You can also, if you think fit, share this work with him, taking it week about. Think of this, and decide on what seems best to you. Do not forget my orders about Balthasar Nuñez, and since it seems to me of the utmost importance, I command you under holy obedience to carry them out fully, making him go through the spiritual Exercises and putting him to the lowest offices within the house, not out of doors. I commend to you most earnestly the Japanese who are here. You must see that they sail for Portugal in a safe and comfortable vessel. It appears to me well that you should yourself give the Exercises to the brothers who are on probation for entering the Society, and then, after having thus learnt deeply to know them, keep those whom you may think suitable to the Society, send ing away those whom you find unfit. Never allow yourself to be persuaded by any entreaty, or the intercessions of any number of friends, to accept a subject not possessing the qualities necessary for usefulness to the Society.

Find competent persons to attend as far as is required to the farm situated in the Isle of Cioran, with the rural labourers and workmen there. You cannot see to this either yourself or through any of ours. I have already advised you to send Dom Augustin there every Sunday. As for other things required there, intrust them to chosen persons worthy of confidence. As soon as Francesco Lopez arrives at this house, tell him to make the Exercises, hear his general confession yourself, and put him to work in the kitchen, or at some humble occupation of that nature. Return to Matthew, as soon as he asks for them, 36 pardams which he lent me at Japan. Fix a day for Alvarez Alfonso to pay his debt to us, and let it be kept to: it may be after Easter. FRANCIS.

The fathers and brothers of the Society, in whatever part of the Indies they may be, must not write any letter to Portugal, either to his Highness or to any one out of the Society, without their sending such letters open to this College. The letters must all be put into one packet here and addressed to his highness, or into another directed to Master Simon, or to the Rector of St. Anthony at Lisbon.

April 1552. FRANCIS.

Another paper left with Father Gaspar Baertz related to Antonio Gomez and Andrew Carvalhez, the letter of whom we have seen already commended by Francis to Simon Rodriguez. There seems to have been some reluctance on his part to return to Portugal. As to Antonio Gomez, the paper shows that Francis had finally determined to cut him off from the Society, and provides for the execution of this intention.

(CII.) *To Father Gaspar Baertz.*

I command you, in virtue of holy obedience, to do as follows after I am gone as to two of our Society. If during the course of this year Antonio Gomez leaves the residence at Diu where he now is, and goes elsewhere, under any pretext or circumstance whatever, then open the first paper I leave and do what I prescribe therein, sending a copy or this, which I have written, to the said Antonio Gomez, and keeping the original by you; and in a letter of your own to him you will intimate to Gomez the orders which I give him in the said paper which I leave closed in your hands.

After the vessels going to Portugal have set sail and put to sea, even if until then Antonio Gomez has remained quietly in the residence at Diu, you will open the second letter, which I now leave sealed, and send him a copy of this also. You will show the original to the lord Bishop, and you will beg him to be good enough to certify the conformity of the copy with the original. With this attestation of the lord Bishop, you will send the copy to Gomez, and you will beg the Bishop for the future to write to him as his own subject and of his own authority to order him to go or to act as he shall himself decide. Still it would, in my opinion, be better that he should be allowed to remain at Diu.

If Andrew Carvalhez, whom for good reasons I had ordered to return to Portugal, should deliberately not come to Goa at the right time, and let the ships sail without him, I order you to expel him at once from the Society, and I formally forbid you to allow him, for any reason whatever, to be raised to the holy orders of the Diaconate or Priesthood in India, even if the Bishop should come to Cochin this year. And if the same Andrew Carvalhez should come to Goa contrary to the orders I have given him, you will not receive him into the College, as being no longer one of ourselves. For if, contrary to my orders, he should come to Goa, I mean him from that moment to be excluded from the Society. You will signify this to him in due form, and you will send him away. At the same time you will, in my name, implore the lord Bishop, with most earnest entreaties, not to admit him to the Diaconate or Priesthood.

April 1552. FRANCIS.

One more letter to Father Gaspar Baertz remains to be inserted here. It is a sort of memorandum, summing up in brief the chief heads of advice and instruction which Francis had given him, and as such might seem almost superfluous in our collection. Still it has one or two touches of its own, and we therefore place it by the side of the others.

(CIII.) *To Father Baertz.*

These last counsels I repeat and sum up on the eve of my long and doubtful voyage, as if, dear Gaspar, I could never sufficiently forearm you. You will understand that I do so on account of the extreme solicitude caused by my love for you, and so will take in good part my repeated charges. Above all things, take care for yourself, and watch over your own soul.

You know how true it is: 'He that is evil to himself, to whom will he be good?' Always show sincere charity and amiable modesty to the fathers and brothers under you; banish severity and austerity of manner except towards those who you feel will abuse your kindness. To such you may put out a little sharpness for their own good, not to revenge yourself, especially if it appears that selfesteem has made them proud. For it is to their interest, for their own sake and our neighbours', to put down their pride. But those who have only sinned through ignorance or weakness, you can often forgive with advantage to themselves, and without hurting discipline; to the arrogant, indulgence is poison: it makes them wonderfully insolent and ready to upset everything, if they find their rector wanting in vigour and courage.

To admit many indiscriminately into the Society is not a help, but a burthen to it; a small number of energetic subjects gifted with superior spiritual or corporal powers would be worth a whole host of others. Do not burthen yourself with a number of useless subjects, but reinforce the body with men of real value. Constantly exercise those who are recently admitted in profound selfabnegation, and in a thorough mortification of their corrupt inclinations. Set them also to humble avocations outside, to begging from door to door for the poor, to serving the sick in public hospitals, and to all works of this kind, which are generally held in esteem. But, according to my opinion, you should never order them to make a public spectacle of themselves by actions or dress that would make them ridiculous. It often happens that these extraordinary actions cause in the beholders a surprise which borders on scandal, and in those even who have held themselves up to the contempt of the world, a secret sense of pride, as though they had performed something heroic. Take care rather to make them practise mortifications, the good effects of which are well known: such as to make them confess, in presence of their brothers, the faults they have committed in the duties prescribed to them, and to perform the penance after receiving it. Thus the mind is humbled in a salutary manner, and zeal is quickened. But all these trials should not be employed until a previous knowledge has been gained of the disposition and strength of subjects; for all measures do not equally suit all persons; what is profitable to one is hurtful to another. The prudence of a director consists in prescribing to each what suits his nature.

You will not let any member of the Society be raised to the priesthood unless he be distinguished by profound knowledge and eminent virtue, tested during several years. Those who are ordained priests without this careful caution will never be what the Institute nor the expectations of men require. And would to God we had seen fewer examples of the results of such negligence! You should exert yourself to improve strangers as well as our own brothers; but in order, remembering that towards persons in the house you are discharging a debt, while to strangers you are doing good gratuitously. Due order requires us first to satisfy justice, and only afterwards to bestow our care on others. God will hold you responsible for our brothers whom He has intrusted to you. The good you do to others is in addition to your duty, and is only meritorious in one who does not lavish it until after having entirely satisfied all necessary claims. Those are guilty who neglect the principal work and expend their zeal on accessory labours, like a man who, being depraved in his own interior, should content himself by merely imposing on men by exterior virtue, and who would thus heap God's anger upon his own head. Such also would be a man who does nothing at home, but in public puts on an air of strenuous activity, through a foolish and fatal ambition. The more widely he scatters his activity, the more greatly will he err. Avoid then this fault, and give your utmost pains, first to what is most important, and in the next place, to what is secondary.

As to the way of helping our neighbour, the more general it is, the more perfect. So let the most important of offices in your eyes be preaching, public instruction in the elements of the Christian religion, and hearing confessions. In hearing confessions examine attentively in what disposition the persons have approached you; for there are some who seek their own interest under the appearance of piety; they pretend to come and seek remedies for their conscience, when they really have in view to get help for their material existence. In these persons generally I have detected the most imperfect sense of spiritual miseries; your words are scattered to the winds if they refer to the cultivation of the soul and the hope of a future life. These people are attached to earth, and so they will remain; they altogether savour of earthly things. Send such people off without delay, and have no fear as to their complaints, nor any hope ever to come to an understanding with them. Your efforts and aims run in contrary directions—they are of the world, and you belong to the Kingdom of Jesus Christ. Ought not a soldier of Jesus Christ to blush at dreading the murmurs of the profane vulgar? Should he not be insensible to the judgments of those who prefer earth to Heaven? Follow our Lord to Whom you are vowed, and despise the complaints of men who belong to the opposite camp. I say more: be careful that these men should never see in you any fear of their hostile talk. Bear yourself boldly, so that all may understand that you neither value the praise of these men, nor fear their blame.

April 1552. FRANCIS.

But few incidents remain to be placed by the side of this long series of letters written by Francis Xavier during his last stay at Goa. We are told that at this time he received an offer of a College for the Society at Chaul, one of the spots occupied by the Portuguese on the coast. Chaul was to the north, about one hundred and twenty miles from Goa. Francis refused the offer. He had only thirty subjects in India, and he did not wish to multiply Colleges too much, especially when the Portuguese were a mere garrison.

The affair of the Chinese embassy, on which so much of the hopes of Francis for the future depended, encountered no obstacle at Goa. The Viceroy willingly gave the patents which constituted Diego Pereira ambassador of Portugal to the Chinese Court, and he added strong letters to the Commandant of Malacca, ordering him to favour the expedition in every possible manner. Diego had given Francis letters of credit on his agent in Goa for thirty thousand ducats, and these went to prepare the embassage on a magnificent scale, in the purchase of rich presents to be made to the Chinese Emperor in the name of the King of Portugal, as well for the other necessary expenses. The royal treasury also contributed to the outlay, and as we learn from a letter which Francis wrote on the eve of his departure from India, large sums were raised among pious and charitable persons for the general purposes of the voyage, which included also among its objects the liberation of a number of Portuguese captives from the prisons in China. Everything seemed to promise well, and we do not find any note of anticipation or dread of failure either in the letters of Francis himself or in any other record of the time.

The following letters to St. Ignatius, to Simon Rodriguez, and to the King of Portugal were written at Goa during the week before Francis finally left that city. They were sent at the same time with the two Japanese converts, whom Francis mentions, whom he had determined to send to Europe, that they might be able to take back to their own countrymen some intelligence as to the grandeur of Europe and of Rome. A lay brother, Andrea Fernandez, accompanied them. He was sent by Francis Xavier to confer with Ignatius by word of mouth ; and it is perhaps on this account that the letters do not contain more details as to the arrangements in India and what had happened in the Society since Francis returned from Japan. Ignatius had desired that some confidential person should be sent to him from India, in order that he might be more fully informed of the state of the Society than was possible by letter, and that the person sent might plead the cause of the Indian missions authoritatively and intelligently at Lisbon and at Rome. This order from Ignatius had arrived while Francis was in Japan, and Antonio Gomez had appointed Father Melchior Gonzalez to go to Europe. But Gomez felt unwilling to deprive India of so active a worker, and recalled the order at the last moment. Francis Xavier, however, carried it out, sending Andrea Fernandez, who performed the task admirably, and returned in due time with a large company of fathers.

The mention of the Jubilee in the letter to Ignatius needs a word of comment. In 1550, the year of Jubilee at Rome, Ignatius had obtained from the Pope the faculty to communicate the spiritual advantages which were to be gained, in the ordinary course, only by visiting the shrines at Rome during that year, to the Superiors of the Society in the Indies, and other countries subject to the crown of Portugal, with leave to publish the Indulgences and to fix the conditions which the faithful were to fulfil instead of the visit to the Roman basilicas. The Jubilee was kept in India in 1551, and with very great fruit. Francis hints at some little want of formality in the papers by which the faculty was conveyed. It is probable that the committal of the publishing the Indulgences to the priests of the Society may have caused some jealous questionings as to the strict legality of their powers. Francis also procured the extension of the time to the whole of 1552.

(CIV.) *To my Father in Christ, St. Ignatius.*

May the grace and love of Jesus Christ our Lord always help and favour us! Amen.

Last January I wrote to you about my return from Japan to India, about the great number of heathen who have there been converted to Christ, about the hard work done by Cosmo Torres and Joam Fernandez, whom I have left at Amanguchi, and who diligently instruct the Christians,—those who already are such and those who are daily being received. In a few days two of our Society are going to Amanguchi, who are partly to help Torres by their labours, partly to be taught the Japanese language, so that when fathers of approved virtue arrive there from Portugal, who are to go to the Japanese universities, they may have ready these others as faithful interpreters whom they may use. Already by the goodness of God a house of the Society is established at Amanguchi—all that distance from

Rome; for it is more than 4200 miles from Goa and 6000 leagues from Rome. After six days, if God approves, we shall go—three of the Society, two of whom are priests—to the kingdom of China.

This kingdom, which is very large, lies opposite Japan.[*] It is crowded to a very great degree with men of sharp wits and much learning. As far as I have been able to find out, studies flourish there, and in proportion as a man is more learned, in that same degree does he surpass the rest in rank and influence. It is well enough ascertained that the religions which exist in Japan have been brought from China. We go full of hope and confidence in God, and we trust that the name of Christ will at last make its way into China. I beg of you not to cease praying for those of ours who are in Japan, and for those also who are going to China. When, by the favour of God, we have arrived in China, I will write to you fully as to our reaching it, and as to our hope of propagating religion there.

I have made Gaspar, the Belgian, Rector of the College at Goa. He is a man of approved virtue, and laden with heavenly gifts, a very good preacher, singularly beloved by our own people and the whole city. I have ordered both fathers and brothers in these parts to obey him. So I go to China with a joyful heart, and free from all anxiety about affairs at home. If perchance while I am absent God should call Gaspar out of this life, I have left with him a paper signed by myself in which a rector is appointed in his place by me. The great distance between China and Goa has warned me to do this.

I have also thought it for the interests of religion to order, before my departure for China, that next year a certain person, one of our Society, should be sent from this to Portugal, and from Portugal to Rome, with letters for you, that you may hear what he will tell you—how very much these countries require men practised and proved in the toils and dangers of life. Men of that sort do a great work in the extension of the worship of God, but the rest, even if they are learned, do very little indeed if they are but poorly experienced in labours and trials. From what I have seen in Japan, two things are quite necessary, both for all who are to labour for the salvation of the Japanese, and especially for ours who are to go to Japanese universities. These two things are, first, a great experience, gained by having passed through many troubles and dangers, and by great self knowledge. For in Japan they will have to bear more severe frosts, more inconveniences in the way of want of means, and other like matters, than anywhere in Europe; added to which there will be vexations and ridicule from the natives, who think that foreigners are hardly men, and especially from the bonzes, who persecute the preachers of the law of God most bitterly; though it is true that in all these sufferings God makes Himself wonderfully sweet to us.

It does not seem as if it would be safe to take the vestments and other things necessary for saying holy mass to the Japanese universities, on account of the distance of the journey and the robbers who infest the roads. As therefore in all these trials and hardships the consolation of the Holy Sacrifice and Communion must be wanting, it is easy to see how much virtue and strength of soul the men must have who may be sent to these seats of learning. Secondly, they must be well furnished with cleverness and knowledge, in order to give easy and apposite answers to the questionings of the Japanese. It is of great importance that they should be well learned in philosophy, especially in dialectics, that they may be able to refute and convict the obstinate argumentation of the Japanese—I mean to show them their own inconsistencies, and that they contradict themselves. I should like them also to know some astronomy, for the Japanese are wonderfully desirous of knowing all about the wanings and eclipses of the sun and moon, why the moon so often grows larger and smaller; or again, whence comes the rain, the snow, the hail, what comets are, and what are the causes of thunder, lightning, and the like. It is incredible how far the explanation of such things goes towards conciliating their good will. These things I wanted you to know about Japanese affairs and manners, since when you want to choose the men who are to be sent, the first thing is to know the customs of the place to which you are to send them.

It has often occurred to me to think that Belgian or German fathers would do very well for the missions in Japan, inasmuch as they can bear cold and toil, especially also as in Italy and Spain they can have no field for preaching, being ignorant of the language of the country. For although they must not be altogether without Spanish or Portuguese, in order that they may understand our own people in Japan, still they can learn that language in the course of their journey to India and Japan, which will take them at least two years.

There is one thing which I much wish you to know: we want out here some principal man of the Society, a man who knows well and loves much our Institute, a man who has had of old much intercourse with yourself. Such a man is indispensable to this College at Goa, and to all of the Society scattered out here in so many different places, if at least they are to be brought into conformity to the laws and constitutions of our Institute. It is not necessary that he should be a preacher; even if he had no gift of that kind, he would be of use and advantage to us. I pray and beseech you by Jesus Christ, appoint some one chosen by yourself as Rector of this College. Even if he be not so wonderfully learned, yet any one whom your judgment has chosen will be the proper man whom this house requires. The fathers and brothers out here are in wonderful expectation of such a ruler, one who has been long and much with you. If he were to bring with him Indulgences for eight days, by which the people may be invited on certain feasts to go to the sacraments of confession and communion, he would do a thing very pleasing to them, and very advantageous to the worship of God.

It can hardly be told how many people have been saved by the Jubilee which you sent out. All such Indulgences I would have you send to us, contained in Pontifical rescripts, duly and authentically sealed, with the seals attached. There are people here who question such Pontifical graces if any of these formalities are wanting. Some tried to find fault even with the Jubilee which you sent, saying that it was not attested, nor ratified by the Pope's authority, because it had not the usual marks. However, by God's approval, it obtained its proper force and authority.

It concerns the interests of God that the priests of our Society who are to come out here should first be diligently proved. We want here well tried priests. I have written to warn Father Simon, or if he is absent, the Rector of the College of Coimbra, not to send us fathers who are of no use in Portugal; for they will be of no more use in India. But it would be much better if you were to give an order that no priest at all of the Society were to go to India until he had made a pilgrimage to Rome, and been there approved by the Father General.

It would be very very pleasing to me if you would order some one of ours to give me an account of all the fathers who came to Rome with us, as well as of the rest. He should also write to us diligently and fully about the increase of the Society, the number of our colleges, houses, and professed fathers, the distinguished men who have been enrolled in the Society, the men noted for learning and erudition who have joined. A letter such as that would give us a great deal of relief and consolation among the great labours by land and by sea which we have to bear in Japan and China. May God bring us together in the happiness of the blessed in heaven, and in this life also, if it be for His glory! If that were enjoined me, it could be done easily by the power of obedience. People all tell me that I could get to Jerusalem from China. If I find this to be true, I will let you know how many leagues of journey there are, and how many months it would take.

The least of your sons, and the furthest exiled from you,

April 9, 1552, Goa. FRANCIS.

This letter was accompanied by two to Simon Rodriguez. The first and most important urges him, among other things, to use all his influence, both with Ignatius and with the King, to bring about what Francis so much desired at this time—that select men of great virtue and learning should be sent to India and Japan, and that the Society in India should have the advantage of the presence of a Superior at Goa who had lived long with Ignatius himself, and who was well acquainted with the Constitutions and practices of the order. The journey of Simon to Rome in 1550,[10] to which allusion is made in the letters, was undertaken partly with a view to the formation and promulgation of the Constitutions, which Ignatius had been long occupied in composing, and which he now desired to lay before the fathers assembled in a General Congregation. They were unanimously approved, but the prudence of Ignatius would not allow him to publish them at once, till they had been gradually introduced and tested by experience.

(CV.) *To Father Simon Rodriguez, in Portugal.*

May the grace and charity of our Lord Jesus Christ always help and favour us! Amen.

On my return from Japan to the Indies, I wrote to you from Cochin on Japanese affairs. Now I want to inform you of my departure for China, which will take place a week hence. I take with me three members of the Society, two priests and one lay brother. We are starting full of confidence in the loving goodness of God, in good hope of advancing the religion of Jesus Christ. I will tell you about our voyage, upon our arrival at Malacca.

Two members of the Society are being sent to Japan this year, to learn the Japanese language; so that any fathers of eminent virtue and experience coming from Lisbon to Goa may find in Japan members of the Society acquainted with Japanese. The letter will set forth to the Japanese intelligently and clearly the Christian doctrines and other instructions which they receive from the European fathers. This will be a great help to those fathers who are destined to attack the Japanese universities, so as to bend the whole nation to the delightful yoke of Jesus Christ.

You have reason to return thanks to our Lord Jesus

[10] The Congregation was held at the end of 1550 and beginning of 1551, see Genelli, *Life of St. Ignatius* (Engl. trans.) pt. ii. ch. i. p. 212.

Christ that we have here several of the Society, both fathers and brothers, who have rendered, and who daily render, great services to the Christian religion by preaching, hearing confessions, the reconciliation of differences, and other works of piety. My soul has received ineffable consolations on this account. I have appointed, as Rector to the College at Goa, Father Gaspar, whom I highly value for the perfection of his humility and obedience. He has a wonderful talent in the pulpit every time he preaches, which is very often; the church resounds with the weeping and groaning of the people. Thanks be to God, the only Giver of good things.

The brother who brings you this letter has been sent to explain to you by word of mouth how greatly not only Japan and the Chinese Empire—if, as I hope, by God's help, the Gospel should find entrance there—but India itself requires fathers of our Society, men of thorough experience, of high virtue and faithfulness, and of singular strength of mind and body. Such, above all, should be the subjects destined for Japan, China, the Moluccas, and Ormuz.

The fathers who come hither into these parts to help on the salvation of souls must be gifted with these two qualities. First, they should be inured to fatigue; the more any one has of this the more useful will he be, both to himself and others. Secondly, they must have sufficient learning for preaching, hearing confessions, and giving crushing answers to the numberless questions of the Japanese and Chinese bonzes. The priests who would be of no use in Europe would be useless here. On this account I have thought it well to send you this Brother Fernandez, to treat of these matters with you, and to choose on your advice fit men, before he goes to our Father Ignatius at Rome.

I am making the same statement to our Father, and I ask him first to send an experienced and approved father of the Society, one that is familiar with himself and thoroughly acquainted with our Institute, to be Rector of the College at Goa, and have under him all our people dispersed in the East, and to teach and explain to the others the laws and constitutions of the

Society and of our method of life. I also ask our father to send out to the Indies fathers of great experience, even without deep learning and without particular powers of preaching, who may easily resolve and satisfy the questions of the Japanese and Chinese bonzes.

It will be a great thing for the interests of religion that next year he should send, besides a Rector for the College, four or five well experienced priests of the Society, who if not preachers, should at least be capable of bearing fatigue. There must, I think, be many such in Italy and Spain among those who have finished their studies and are now working for souls. Such subjects are very much required in these parts. Young men, who have only just left the shelter of college, and who as yet have been untried and unproved by the labours and troubles of life, might very easily do no good to others and perish themselves, for they can have no experience of the trials to be undergone in Japan.

I have said that there we have to suffer the extreme of cold. And there are so few helps and appliances for keeping out the cold, that there is not even a bed to sleep on. There are great difficulties also about food. There are continual and violent attacks from the bonzes and the people, many temptations to sin, much derision and insolence from the populace. Finally, in my eyes the most grievous trial of all, among the Japanese universities, the long distances do not allow of our carrying the articles necessary for the Holy Sacrifice, and so one has to suffer the privation of that heavenly Food, which 'strengthens the heart of man,'[11] and which is the only consolation for every trouble. This is the greatest misery we have in these parts. At Amanguchi, where the Society has a residence, mass can be celebrated; but at the universities, whither our fathers from Amanguchi must go, it is not so. It would be impossible to carry the sacred vessels for the Holy Sacrifice without danger along roads infested by robbers. I should sadly fear therefore that if any subjects were sent to the mission of Japan, who were not fortified with virtue sufficient to resist the

[11] Ps. ciii. 15.

weight of such extreme trials, that they would be almost infallibly ruined.

I think that for enduring the excessive cold and other trials of these countries the Belgian or German priests of the Society would be very fit; having had years of such experience, these subjects seem suitable above all for Japan and China. But I doubt not that, as this is a thing which serves to His glory and the salvation of souls, God will afford you the means of effecting it, and of sending out as fit subjects as possible for these countries. Again and again I entreat you, select persons who have been practised in labour and danger, so that, with God's help, they may triumph over all these miseries and sufferings. Those whose virtue has never shown itself in trial and persecution are never rightly trusted with any great commission.

I beg you to speak to the King, if it seems good, and get him to write to our Father Ignatius, to ask for some experienced fathers for the Japanese mission, as well as a man of eminent virtue and prudence to be at the head of this College and of the Society in the Indies. In these countries the Society is wonderfully scattered and dispersed abroad. It has to work in Persia, Cambaïa, Malabar, on the Fishery Coast, to Malacca, the Moluccas, the Isles of the Moor, and the archipelago of Japan. All these places are immensely distant from Goa. Since our fathers and brothers dwell in such remote and widely separated regions, the Rector of the Society at Goa, if he is to provide for their necessities, watch over their safety, and remedy their infirmities, ought certainly to be a man of great experience and exalted virtue.

It seems to me the best thing that the bearer of this letter should take to Father Ignatius your letter and his Highness's at the same time as mine, for I have written about the matter to our Father. It appears to me that the subjects I wish for could be taken without inconvenience from houses of the Society in Europe. Fathers of little talent for preaching are not much wanted there. The subjects that we receive into the Society here are only useful for business and household work. There is scarcely one sufficiently educated to be fit to be a priest. I tell you this that you may understand that some priests should be sent to us every year.

O, Simon, my dearest brother, do you see how great the work is that we have in hand? And if God wills that the light of the Gospel should be carried to so judicious and docile a people, you too will do well, I think, to come yourself to China, to slake your thirst for the salvation of souls. If, by the help of God, I penetrate there, I will write to you about the character of the people, and the hopes there are of planting the Gospel among them. I feel such an ardent wish to see you again before I die, that I am always thinking to myself how I may have my wish; and I may have it, perhaps, if China were opened to us. Meanwhile I again and again most earnestly entreat you to send us next year such fathers as I have described; you can hardly imagine how necessary they are, but I wish you to trust my experience. I have desired Father Gaspar to write diligently to you about all that goes on here of the benefits done to souls.

Since I hope to write to you at length from Malacca, I will only add one thing. I am expecting a good long letter from you about your journey to Rome, and as to the things done and decreed in that holy assembly. There is nothing in the world about which I desire more to be informed, having been unable, in punishment of my sins, to be there myself. If, as I much fear, on account of your occupations, you cannot yourself give me all these details, I beg you to commit the matter to some one who accompanied you in the journey. I shall be most sincerely grateful.

I also wish you to arrange that the Rector of the College at Coimbra should let me know by letter the names of all the fathers and brothers under his direction, their virtues, their learning, and their dispositions. And as I fear that the pressure of his duties may not leave him the leisure for such a thing, I beg him to see that it is done by some one else who is acquainted with the subject, that I may not be ignorant of the ardent zeal to suffer for Jesus Christ which animates my brothers. Certainly they have some reason to remember me, since last year I went all over Japan for their sakes; and now I am going to China to prepare for them a way to come and convert those nations, that this immense field once laid open, their great piety and virtue, incited by the fire of divine love, may have ample room to work.

May God please to join and unite us in the company of the Saints, and in this world too, if it should be for His service!

Goa, 7th April 1552. FRANCIS.

I beg you to send the brother who bears this letter to Rome without delay, so that next year he may return to us accompanied by many fathers. For if the Christian religion gain admission into China, and if my life lasts, in three or four years I intend to return to the Indies, so as to take with me some of our fathers and brothers as companions in so glorious an enterprize, and then I shall return thither to pass the rest of my days and end my life in Japan or China.

The postscript to this letter shows what might have already been conjectured from the previous letter to Ignatius, that Francis Xavier meant China or Japan—probably the former—to be the chief field of his future labours. He would open that country to Christianity, as he had opened Japan; then he would return to India for reinforcements, and taking with him some of the fathers whom by that time Simon and Ignatius would have sent out to him, he would return to China, possibly to make his way backwards along the overland track, which had been travelled by a number of European adventurers in the previous centuries, to Asia Minor, Jerusalem, and Rome. Such was his dream—we shall see how far it was fulfilled. The next letter recommends the two Japanese converts to the special care of Simon: the mention of the warning to be addressed to Charles V. not to permit Spanish fleets from New Spain to attempt intercourse with, or the conquest of, Japan, is extremely curious. It almost seems as if Francis had some presage in his mind of the mischief which was to result from the collision of Spain and Portugal in the extreme East.

(CVI.) *To Father Simon Rodriguez in Portugal.*

May the grace and love of Jesus Christ our Lord always help and favour us! Amen.

Matthew and Bernard, two Japanese, have followed me to the Indies, with the intention of repairing to Portugal and Italy, and particularly Rome itself, to see the Christian religion in all its majesty, and then to return to their country to recount to their fellow citizens what they have found and seen. I commend them to you as earnestly as I can commend any one in the world. Take care that they may come back with their desires fully and happily satisfied; for their testimony will win high authority for us and for the Christian name.

The Japanese despise other nations in comparison with themselves; this has prevented their entering into commercial relations with any other people until the arrival of the Portuguese about eight or nine years ago. The Spaniards call these islands the 'Silver Isles;' and some Portuguese in Japan told me that the Spaniards in going to the Moluccas sail by Japan; that if any one of their vessels attempted to touch there it would inevitably be lost, and that the Japanese give as a reason that the sea of Japan, on the side towards New Spain, is filled with shoals, so that vessels are stranded and lost.

I write this that you may bring about that their Highnesses the King and Queen may write to warn Charles the Emperor and King of Spain not to send his fleets from New Spain to take possession of the Silver Isles; his vessels would, as things are now, all be lost. Even if they got there safely, if they were to try to take possession by force, they would have to do with a people as warlike as they are greedy for pillage, and who seem able enough to capture even a large hostile fleet. Besides, the country is so barren and waste that foreign armies would be easily vanquished by famine alone. There are also such frightful storms around these islands, that Spanish vessels without a friendly port for shelter would certainly be lost.

I repeat that the Japanese have such a love for weapons

of war, that the mere desire to pillage the Spaniards' arms would, judging from their character and habits, be enough to make them massacre the Spaniards to a man. I wrote all this long ago to his Highness, but perhaps his occupations may have effaced the whole thing from his mind. So in order to satisfy my conscience on the matter, I beg you to remind him of them. It would be deplorable to hear that numerous fleets from New Spain, bound for the Silver Isles, had perished at sea. With the exception of Japan, there are no isles in this part of the East which contain silver mines.

Again I urge you to receive the two Japanese in such a way that they may learn a great many wonderful things about our churches, our universities, and the other marvels of Europe, to tell to their people at home. I am confident that they will be astonished at the wealth and power of Christians. Bernard, and Matthew also, have lived much with me at Japan. They are poor, but full of faith. They attached themselves to me in Japan, and they followed me on my return to the Indies, with the intention of going to Portugal, and thence to Rome. Japanese of noble rank feel no desire to visit foreign countries, though some of our neophytes, men of honourable position, think of going to Jerusalem, to visit the place of our Lord's birth and passion. Matthew and Bernard are among the first of these, but whether, after seeing Rome, they will go on to Jerusalem, I do not know.

I should have liked to send two of the learned bonzes to Portugal, so as to give you a specimen of Japanese intellects, as sharp and sensible as any in the world; but they being noble, and at ease, will not consent to leave their country even for a time. I tried to bring other neophytes with me, who abandoned the idea for fear of the difficulties of a sea voyage, especially for such a great distance.

I beg you then to send these, Matthew and Bernard, on to Rome, that they may come back with some of our fathers; and testify to their countrymen as to the immense distance existing between the greatness of Christians and of the Japanese. May God grant, if it is for His service, that some day we may see one another again in China, or if not there, at any rate in the Kingdom of Heaven, where I mean to enjoy with still greater pleasure the fruits of your sweet and tender friendship, which I have so long been without.

Goa, April 9, 1552. FRANCIS.

The letter to the King, written at this time, the last letter addressed to him by Francis Xavier which has been preserved to us, needs no comment.

(CVII.) *To John III., King of Portugal.*

On my return from Japan this year I wrote to your Highness from Cochin, giving my letter to the vessels that were sailing for Portugal. I then gave an account of the present state of religion at Japan and of how fit and favourably disposed the Japanese nation is to embrace the religion of Jesus Christ. I added that the King of Boungo is an admirer of your royal virtues, and sends you a magnificent cuirass in token of his friendship. I said that two members of our Society will soon start for the town of Amanguchi in Japan, where we have already a residence and church, and where two of ours of great goodness and faithfulness are engaged in instructing neophytes. May God grant that by means of your Highness's most admirable munificence the Christian religion may be widely propagated in these countries also! I said too that I had resolved on going to China, because we see signs which justify great hopes of spreading the Christian faith there.

In five days I shall leave Goa for Malacca, on the way to China, with a brother of our Society, and also with Diego Pereira, ambassador to the Emperor of that country. We are taking this Sovereign rich presents, bought by Diego Pereira, partly with your Highness's funds, partly with his own. But we carry him another present, such as perhaps within the memory of man no king has ever offered to another king,—I speak of the Gospel of Jesus Christ. If the Emperor of China understands its full value, he will certainly prefer it above all his treasures, however great they may be. I have a hope that God will cast a look of mercy upon this large empire and nation; that He will open the eyes of those men created after His own image to the knowledge of their Creator, and of Jesus Christ the common Saviour of all.

Three of us altogether of the Society start with Pereira for China, in order to set at liberty the Portuguese who are in captivity there, to obtain the alliance of the Emperor of China for the Portuguese, and lastly to wage war with the devil and his followers. We shall inform the Sovereign first, and then his subjects, in the name of the King of Heaven, that henceforth they must no longer worship the devil, but God, the Creator of men, and Jesus, their Redeemer and Lord. It may seem a bold undertaking to go to an unbelieving nation and a very powerful Sovereign in order to reprove them and to preach the truth to them,—a thing in our time full enough of danger even with Christian kings and princes, not to speak of barbarians. But what fills us with confidence is that the design has been inspired by God Himself, who is the aim and end of all my thoughts, and He has filled us with the happiest hopes, so that trusting to God's mercy, we doubt nothing as to His divine power, which is infinitely higher than the power of the Chinese King, and of all the kings of the world.

As the matter is altogether in the hand and power of God, there is no cause for fear or doubt. We certainly ought to fear nothing, except to offend God and so incur the punishment due to the wicked. Therefore it seems a greater extreme of audacity for men, who see most clearly their own sins and crimes, to take up the preaching of His law, than to go to foreign nations to reprove and teach the truth to most powerful kings. That which increases still more my hope and confidence is the thought that for so great a work as the offering of gospel light and truth to a barbarous nation, blinded by vice and superstition, belonging, if I may use the expression, to a lifferent universe, God has chosen men so utterly without skill and without virtue as ourselves. So what is necessary is, that since it has so pleased God to order it, in answer to the prayers and alms of your Highness, I should have a will ready to correspond to all this courage and confidence, which God in His goodness has given me, in preaching His holy law.

I have asked various graces of your Highness in favour of those who here rule your realm; all have been granted liberally on your part. I return you, for them all infinite thanks. And now I ask you another favour in the name of all true Christians; Portuguese and Indian, and in the name even of the heathens, particularly of the Japanese and Chinese. I ask with all the urgency I may that in your admirable zeal for the worship of God and the salvation of souls, you will deign to have sent to us this year as many priests as possible: men of capacity, who at home and abroad have worked for the salvation of souls with great credit for virtue and piety—such subjects, in fact, as India requires. For men without experience of ordinary life, whatever may be their learning and knowledge, are of no great use in these countries. Therefore, most excellent Sire, I again and again implore you, by your singular charity towards God and towards men, the images of God, deign to write very carefully to Rome to Master Ignatius, the Father of our Society, to send to the Indies a good number of priests, prepared to bear much suffering both of body and soul, even if they be deficient in eloquence for preaching, because such men are required for the Indian missions, especially for those of Japan and China.

With these fathers let him send a Rector for this residence and College, a man of tried and known virtue whom we can trust, and who perfectly knows our rules and Institute; for such a man is very necessary here. You may be sure that such priests will be of great use in the Indies, Japan, and China; and these countries require men capable of bearing severe and frequent combats. They should therefore possess solid virtue and sufficient learning to reply to all the difficulties which may be proposed to them by some of the most subtle people in the world, that is to say, the Japanese and Chinese. In order to make the difficulties presented by these countries better understood, I have thought it best to send a brother to Father Simon in Portugal and to Father Ignatius at Rome, with letters from me.

It remains that for the glory of our Lord Jesus Christ and the salvation of souls, your Highness should deign to write to Father Ignatius to instigate his zeal, already so ardent, that he may satisfy abundantly and at once the interests of divine glory and of your piety, by sending us at least six such men as I desire, as well as the Rector whom I have described. I am sure they will be very efficacious for the glory of God and the salvation of these nations.

I place such confidence in your Highness's great goodness, that I doubt not you will add to all your other singular benefits this last, which will be the filling up and crown of the rest.

From your Highness's useless servant,

Goa, April 10, 1552. FRANCIS.

The time was now come for Francis to take leave of Goa. It is said that on parting from his friends he let them see that he knew that, as St. Paul said to the priests of Ephesus, 'they should see his face no more.' One of the penitents of Francis, Doña Catalina de Chiaves, began to weep when he told her that this was his last visit, and to comfort her, he added that she should see him again before she died. She survived him for some years, and shortly before her death he appeared to her and filled her with joy.

But nowhere was his departure felt so deeply as in the College of Santa Fè. The letter from Goa, to which we have already referred, after speaking of the instructions which he wrote for the fathers who were going to a distance, mentions how he used to exhort the inmates of the College to the service of God and to desires of greater perfection, 'as one who was taking his leave as if he should never see or converse with them again, giving us spiritual conferences in which were many doctrines precious and helpful to the soul. . . . And when the time of his departure was coming, he used at night to give spiritual conferences to the brothers, which much consoled them; and the last things which he commended to us after his last discourse with many tears, were constancy in our first vocation, most profound humility, which arises in all from knowledge of self, and above all things holy obedience and promptitude in following it out. This large charge he repeated many times, as of a virtue much beloved by God and very necessary in the Society. He made Provincial of the parts of Asia Master Gaspar, to whom he gave all his power, and made him Rector of the College of Goa, to provide from thence for all other parts. And then he put himself on his knees before him and offered him obedience on his own part and on the part of all who were absent, giving us an example of that obedience of which he had just been speaking; and all the fathers and brothers did the same with great consolation and joy, because such a pastor had been given them. And having done these things, Father Master Francis departed with his companions on the Maundy Thursday, after the function was over.'[12] These last words put before us a touching picture. There is no function in all the range of the offices of the Church more tender and loving than that of Maundy Thursday, when the altar puts on again its white festive dress for a short time; when the *Gloria in Excelsis* rings through the sanctuary still haunted by the mournful strains of the *Tenebræ* of the evening before; when but one mass is sung, and so all the faithful, priests as well as laymen, crowd to the altar rail to receive the Blessed Sacrament on the day of its first institution from the hands of the Superior of the church. Francis himself would probably say the mass and give communion to all his brethren, to the students of the college, to the throngs of the faithful to whom he was so dear. Then he would bear in solemn procession, while the *Pange lingua* was being sung, the consecrated host which was to be consumed on the following morning of Good Friday to the altar of the Sepulchre, there amid lights and flowers to be adored without ceasing until the time came for

[12] 'A quinta feira de Endoenças, acabado officio.'

the ceremony of the next day. He would kneel awhile to adore his Lord on the altar, and then depart, with his heart full of love and thankfulness, never to return alive.

Francis spent a few days at Cochin, as usual in his voyages to and from Goa. He was overwhelmed with news about the state of affairs on the Fishery Coast. The labours and sufferings of the missionaries there were little known, on account of their being usually alone; but Francis had experienced these himself, and we have seen how anxious he was that all possible assistance should be secured to them. One of them was just dead—Paolo Valle, of whom he speaks in the next letter, which was written at this time from Cochin to Gaspar Baertz. Paolo had been taken prisoner by the Badages, and detained by them for a month, suffering the greatest privations and outrages. At last the Christians managed to rescue him, but they were pursued, and only saved themselves and the father by taking to their boats. Paolo was almost worn to death; a low fever attacked him, and after lingering for three months, he died on the 1st of March in this year. We subjoin the letter to which we have just referred.

(CVIII.) *To Father Gaspar Baertz.*

May the grace and love of Jesus Christ our Lord help and favour us! Amen.

Since my arrival at Cochin I have received many letters from Coulan and Cape Comorin. All these letters inform me of the extreme misery of our brethren who serve religion in these parts, in lack of all resources corporal and spiritual. From Cape Comorin they announce the death of Father Paul, a man of great perfection in virtue. There now only remains Father Enrico Enriquez, and throughout the country there is no other priest of our Society. He begs most earnestly that a companion should be sent to help him in the administration of the Sacraments, for he is not equal to it alone on account of the number of the Christians and the long distances. Think whether you can manage to set free Father Antonio Vaz and Brother Antonio Diaz, whom you could send, after winter, to the Coast of Comorin, where they are in such miserable need of workers. Should it seem to you that Antonio Vaz is little suited, or if he seems necessary where he is, think about Francesco Lopez, whom I have lately sent to Bazain. As far as I can now judge, I should be very glad to know that one of these brethren were sent to Cape Comorin with Antonio Diaz, or some other lay brother of tried virtue whom you could securely send as companion with any priest who may go to that mission. In the name of all your love for God, I entreat you to use your utmost zeal in this matter, for it is of the greatest importance.

Father Niccolo, at Coulan, is beset by grave difficulties and is reduced to extreme poverty, being destitute of provision for fifty native children of the house and two or three Portuguese besides; especially as youths from the Coast of Comorin who get ill are often sent to him to be taken care of; and as the College of Coulan is but poorly endowed, Father Niccolo asks with much justice to have some present help from the royal grants formerly bestowed on the College, which have not been duly paid—in fact, these grants are seldom paid the year that they are due. Speak, I pray you, to the Viceroy, that he may receive the back payments now that they are so necessary to him, since he has not before been paid all that the King assigned him; and if the Viceroy thinks fit, let him send a royal command to the Commandant of Coulan, to pay at once a hundred pardams to the College, which may somewhat relieve the present misery of that house. I implore you for the love of our Lord God, take care that on the first opportunity of sailing after the winter a priest of the Society, with a lay brother, may embark for Comorin, as I have said, and that they may pass by Coulan, and there, in virtue of the royal order of which they are the bearers, receive from the Commandant the sum of a hundred pardams to be given to Father Niccolo.

Make a list of the sums due from the King to the College at Goa, and exert yourself with his majesty's ministers, especially the Viceroy, to procure such letters and orders as may seem necessary for obtaining a full settlement. Use the same precautions for the house at Ormuz and at Bazain. Especially take great care to avoid managing these affairs too gently or timidly; they should be carried on in an energetic and almost obstinate manner. The whole race of receivers and revenue people, who under whatever title dispense the King's funds, is a hard set, and the most legitimate requisitions, if proffered gently and bashfully, are eluded by them; they will give nothing but what is dragged from them. Therefore they should be approached with no softness of mien but with a confident speech, nor should delays be easily granted: they have unlimited devices for rendering these delays eternal; and as they only boast among themselves when they succeed, to treat them with moderation is to violate our duty; you must dun them importunately and recklessly, and do not hesitate almost to altercate and quarrel with them until their promises have passed into action. Otherwise you will scarcely ever prevent large sums out of the King's treasury, destined by his majesty's pious wishes for the use and necessities of religion, from being intercepted and appropriated by avaricious and perverse ministers, to the immense and irreparable injury of religion and the salvation of souls. You must think justifiable any way that secures success in so highly important an affair.

Employ every effort for discharging the debts of your house as soon as possible. I wish that in the letters you dispatch by the vessels that sail for Malacca next September, you should send me a list of the liabilities of the College at Goa, and that every time you write to me you should let me know what is owing to you, and what you yourself owe. It will be very useful to know both at once, and to compare the two. When the revenues due to the College are received from those who have to pay them, tax farmers or other debtors, be on your guard against a foolish unjust compassion, so as to allow them to retain a portion, which, as we know, has happened several times in preceding years through most criminal negligence, on which account, and nothing else, at Cape Comorin, Coulan, and at Cochin, a great number of pious works undertaken for the good of souls, which would have prospered had they been continued, have been interrupted for want of the assistance expected from Goa. This assistance could not be sent, on account of most unreasonable concessions made to the people indebted by the collectors of the revenues of the College at Goa, upon which all the other houses depend. On this account you should yourself watch, and use all the means at your disposal for preventing any weakness of the procurator as to exacting the full debt, indulging the avarice of men to the danger of his own conscience and God's service.

It will be necessary for you to assist Father Antonio Eredia. On the very first opportunity when winter is over, you will take care to send him to Cochin 250 or 300 pardams. This sum is just now quite indispensable for him to complete the enclosure of the buildings, and to carry on various other works of absolute necessity, without which a community could not be kept together or exist. For until now, it has been a miserable and most difficult undertaking to lodge decently our brethren and visitors in the house at Cochin. In reading this letter, do not imagine that while I am thus engrossed regarding the College at Cochin, I lose sight of the embarrassments of Goa; believe me, they are present to me, I know and remember them. But comparing all the circumstances, I think the most indispensable duty is to help those among our brothers who are in the greatest distress. I have therefore reduced the sum I ask for to what I have named to you, and which is strictly necessary for them. They want much more, but we must put one inconvenience against another; do you guide yourself by the promptings of a prudent charity, and having first provided for the wants of the inhabitants of your house, whether Portuguese or natives, then extend your protection to those at Cochin, Coulan, and Comorin.

I beg you to calculate exactly what Alvarez Alfonso owes to this College. Find out also the value of those sums which, through mistaken kindness, the receivers of our revenues have remitted to him in past years. How they settled it with their consciences I know not. I should be very anxious if I thought I had to render an account, as they will have to do, of this foolish indulgence, the deplorable result of which has been to cause the utter lack of means for the propagation of God's kingdom, and support of evangelical labourers on the coast of Comorin, Coulan, and Cochin. Insist upon his paying all he owes, so that you may spend it first for the necessities of your house and then for the places dependent on it, which I have just named. How necessary it is that temporal means should not be neglected, you have an instance in my present journey, which is of immense interest for God's glory, and which I should not have had the means of undertaking had you not exercised your utmost zeal in collecting alms at Ormuz, which alms have been my chief resource. What would have happened had your zeal flagged? We must have given up everything, and allowed to vanish, just as it seemed within our grasp, so splendid an opportunity of extending God's kingdom. And would this opportunity ever have returned? But enough on this subject.

If some fathers from Portugal reach you this year, remember to use your best efforts to surmount all obstacles; and contrive that next year one of them at least shall sail for Japan, as companion there to Cosmo Torres, according to my instructions left you in writing: I now only remind you of it. I wish you to give a lay brother of the Society as companion to this father; be careful also that both are abundantly furnished with means for the journey. After the expenses of the voyage something must be left to provide for their maintenance at Japan, for the country is fertile to us in labour and spiritual fruits, but sterile in money and resources of every kind. I beg you, as you love me, take this matter to heart. For I desire most ardently, and consider it of the first importance, that another priest of the Society should be sent as soon as possible to assist Cosmo Torres.

If the hope I speak of from Portugal should fail, because in the expected vessels no father is found who is capable of this mission, still, I pray you, see whether in any other way you can obtain the same object. For instance, if a subject should present himself for entrance into the Society who was already a priest, or capable of receiving holy orders, whom you would have no difficulty in preparing for them, and whom, after the trial of a short novitiate, you might, on account of the emergency, judge fit to send to Japan,—if you meet with a subject of this kind, or if you find at your disposal one of the fathers of whom I have spoken, I will take care that the opportunity is not wanting for his journey from Malacca to Japan. I will see to this in my own journey by begging the Captain of Malacca graciously to further the plans of whichever of our brothers may arrive from Goa, on the way to Japan.

In considering as to the admission of subjects who seek an entrance into the Society, you will study very carefully the qualities of soul and body with which they may be gifted; and you must never burthen the Society with subjects useless at home and abroad. After having received subjects for the novitiate, if, when you have profoundly studied their character, you discover that they are void of gifts of soul and faculties of body, according to the measure necessary for their utility in the Society, hasten to send them home again. Regarding the novices that you employ in the house upon such offices as require frequent intercourse with strangers, and freely going backwards and forwards, such as the duties of purveyor, dispenser, and others of like nature, watch over them diligently, and observe most carefully what example they give outside as to sobriety, self restraint, and modesty; notice with what fidelity they manage their business, and expend the money intrusted to them, and whether they render an exact and scrupulous account of their receipts and outlays; for you know how dangerous is the administration of such offices, and how imprudent it is to commit them to persons who are not firmly established in great self command, faithfulness, and sanctity of life—virtues which form at the same time their safeguard and our guarantee against all danger of a fall on their part. Indeed, their fall would be at once a supreme dishonour to the Society, and a great scandal to our neighbours.

As for Balthasar Nuñez and the lay brother who has come from Bazain with Melchior Gonzalez, take care to exercise them long and seriously in the most humble duties of the house, for instance, in the kitchen and other employments of the same nature; and do not allow them to go out. If in the course of these trials you discover that they are unsuitable to the Society, you will send them away to look after their own business. When Francesco Lopez returns from Bazain, you should give him the Exercises at leisure, and also break him in by the humblest labours of the house. Pay constant attention and the most active vigilance to the improvement and spiritual progress of these three subjects. This advice of mine is not unfounded: I have reason to fear that these three persons are not such as I could wish, or such as they ought to be for the glory of God and their own perfection.

Be equally watchful over the others, and proportion the degree of your attention to the character of each, occupying yourself incessantly in fortifying, encouraging, and improving them. When, as I have ordered, you send a priest and a lay brother to Cape Comorin, you will send also by them one of the chalices which I have left you. My reason is, that I remember that a few years ago a Christian belonging to this Coast of Comorin sent a sum of money to Goa, to be spent in the purchase of a chalice. The managers of the College received this money, and used it for the necessities of their house, and up to this time have never sent the chalice. Let it be sent now, and this obligation cancelled. The other chalice which remains can be given next year to the father who sails for Japan, for there is only one chalice there.

When you write to me at Malacca, do not be sparing of your time or paper, and do not hurry as though it were a duty fulfilled by task. Give a full and particular account of everything, with the smallest details. I have hopes of great spiritual consolation from the perusal of your letters; for they will inform me of all I wish to know regarding all my brothers, who in your College are fighting in the cause of God, and in the surrounding residences. Employ a secretary who writes a good and legible hand. You will direct the packet to Francesco Perez, at Malacca; but it is absolutely necessary you should send me your letters in the month of September, by the vessel which then sails for Banda. Francesco Perez will diligently take care to convey them to me in China.

You will write to our good Cipriani, who resides at Meliapor, telling him he should live in perfect harmony with all the world, especially with the Bishop's Vicar and all the priests in that residence; and you had better express yourself to him with precision and without circumlocution, and distinctly inform him that I have left you in writing a formal command to expel from the Society those subjects who are disobedient to the Superior or Rector of this College; you will add that, on account of this order, no personal consideration of any one at all will prevent your fulfilling what is commanded in so absolute a manner. Make this statement to him *ad terrorem*, and that he may watch over himself, and understand that such a threat extends even to him.

Estevan Luis Buralho, who has reached the diaconate in holy orders, is coming to your town. I love this young man very much, and I hope that by the grace of God he will by and by become a good religious. Do all that he asks of you in my name, and speak to the Bishop in his favour as often as he asks you or requires. It is not only the hope I entertain which has attached me to him; it is also a duty of gratitude which compels me to do all I can in order to repay favours he has rendered me in a thousand cases, serving and assisting me upon every opportunity, as often as I asked him. I confide to you the payment of my debt of gratitude, and I trust you will discharge it perfectly and energetically.

May our Lord sanctify you, and call you to His glory! Adieu.

Cochin, April 24, 1552.

Father Antonio Eredia here has a book which is useful to him, but which will be far more necessary to me where I am going. This book is *Constantinus*,[13] which I find I must deprive

[13] *Constantinus* was the name of the author of a Greek-Latin Lexicon of that century.

him of, and take it to China. I remember having seen here two other copies, one in the possession of Francesco Lopez, the other in the hands of Father Manuel de Morales. I beg you to send one of these two as soon as possible to Father Antonio Eredia, for he has the greatest need of this book. Exert yourself zealously with the Bishop, to induce him to summon to his presence a priest of Malabar named Antonio Ferrano, and to order this priest, under threat of anathema, to appear on a certain day before his tribunal at Goa; for Ferrano puts obstacles to the preaching of the Gospel in the place where he is, and proves himself a public adversary and dangerous enemy to the fathers who labour for the increase of religion on the Coast of Comorin.

Entirely yours in Jesus Christ,
FRANCIS.

The day after this letter was written, Francis Xavier took his final leave of India. He had with him Father Balthasar Gago and four lay brothers, Duarte Silva, Pedro Alcaçeva, Alvaro Ferreira, and Francesco Gonzalez. He had also with him a young Chinese named Antonio, who had been educated at the College of Santa Fè. He was to serve Francis as interpreter, but it turned out, as might have been expected, that the few years which he had spent at Goa had made him almost forget his native tongue.

CHAPTER II.

Francis and Don Alvaro d'Ataide.

WE have seen with what a joyous buoyant heart Francis Xavier had embarked in 1549 for Japan. The expedition to China, to which he was now looking forward, was certainly fraught with fewer dangers, and seemed far less likely to be thwarted in its course or unsuccessful in its issue than that former voyage. China was a peaceful, civilized empire, as famous for justice and equity as for its tranquillity and power. There might be some difficulty at the ports, perhaps; but when it became known that an Envoy of the great King of the West had been sent to treat with the Emperor, it was not to be expected that any lack of courtesy would bar the onward path of the friendly mission. Francis himself was in the vigour of life and strength. The white hairs of age had come before their time to his head, but he was still in the prime of his years, his heart full of great plans, the execution of which could not overtask the powers which had hitherto made his preaching so efficacious, and given him a sort of empire over all whom he had come across. His influence was firmly established over whatever was Christian in the East; he had never been unable to obtain what he asked from the Portuguese authorities; and the ineffable charm of his humility and charity made merchants, and sailors, and soldiers, the rich and the poor, we may almost say the good and the bad alike, eager to befriend him and to serve him. No one seems to have doubted that he would return from China, as he had returned from the Moluccas and from Japan, with the glory of success to enhance the prestige which he already possessed all over the East. If any one had been asked to predict how his designs were to fail, he would have thought of accidents by sea or land, tempests and hurricanes, the audacity of pirates, or the impenetrable jealousy of Chinese officials, and would never have conceived it possible that a Christian and Portuguese hand would be raised to bring about the frustration of his hopes.

Francis Xavier, however, knew that he was certain to meet with opposition, because he was engaged in a great design for God's glory. It was afterwards known that even when he was first speaking of the matter with Diego Pereira on his voyage from San Chan, he had predicted that they would certainly have great trouble. Now, when he landed at Malacca on this last voyage from Goa, he instantly begged his religious brethren to pray for the Chinese expedition, as he felt instinctively that the devil was preparing to thwart it. Francis had parted with Diego Pereira at the beginning of the year at Malacca. Diego had had to take his ship, the famous Santa Croce, to Sonda, and to return to Malacca in time to meet Francis when he came back from India with the diplomas and letters constituting his friend the Envoy to China, as well as with the rich presents and other necessaries for the expedition. Don Pedro de Silva was now no longer 'Capitan;' his brother Don Alvaro was on the point of entering on his government, which meanwhile was administered by another official. Alvaro was proud and illconditioned, as we may gather from his having endeavoured to oust Pedro before his period of Captaincy had elapsed. He was probably also poor, and anxious to make money while in authority at Malacca. We are not told whether he had at first entertained the notion that he himself, and not Diego Pereira, was the proper person to represent the Portuguese Crown in the embassy to China. But he had a secret grudge against Diego Pereira, who, before sailing for Sonda, had refused to lend him a sum of ten thousand ducats. It is only a matter of conjecture whether Francis Xavier was aware of this; but he had armed himself against any possible difficulty on the part of Don Alvaro in two ways—first, by procuring for him some favours from the Viceroy, who conferred on him, at the request of Francis, the 'Capitanato' of the sea, a naval command, independent of the Captaincy of the fortress, and involving not only power but emolument, and certain other privileges not specified; and secondly, by procuring the stringent orders, which have been already mentioned, from the Viceroy, enjoining on Don Alvaro and all other officers of the Crown to further to the utmost of their power the intended Embassy, and threatening them with severe punishment in case of disobedience. With these precautions Francis may have felt that he had little to fear in the way of human opposition to his designs—which yet was to come, as it were, from a hand which he had armed himself, for it was the power of the 'Capitan of the sea' which was to be used against him.

The voyage was prosperous. It is probably here that we must place the anecdote referred to in a former page,[1] when, near the Nicobar islands, the weather became so bad, and the ship seemed to be in so much danger, that the captain was giving the order to throw overboard the cargo; but Francis Xavier interfered, promising that the wind would soon fall and they should come in sight of land. When the prophecy came true, all were rejoicing and congratulating themselves, but Francis was sighing and sorrowful. 'Pray for Malacca,' he said; 'it is infected by the plague.' It was true. On arriving at Malacca, where Francis was received, as usual, with immense joy, they found the plague raging. The ship's crew was attacked, and forty soon died.

Francis devoted himself at once to the service of the plague stricken, as if he had come to Malacca for no other purpose. As the hospital was full to overflowing, he gave up to them a part of the residence of the Society, and provided rooms in other houses where fifty or sixty were received at a time. He was always ready to hear the confessions of the sick, and to assist the dying. It was the common opinion, that to die in his arms was to be secure of salvation—so efficacious and encouraging were the exhortations and suggestions with which he aided the poor sufferers to leave this world for the presence of God. He went about the city begging alms for the poor:

[1] p. 148.

he carried the sick to the hospitals himself, and then waited upon them as a servant. Among the sick was Don Alvaro himself, and Francis attended him with particular affection and diligence, saying mass for many days in the room in which he lay ill. It seemed as if he had gained his heart. Don Alvaro had not as yet given a single sign of opposition; on the contrary, he had spoken of the Embassy as likely to produce great public good. But, for the moment, the minds of all were too full of the plague and its ravages to attend to other subjects.[2]

Diego Pereira returned to Malacca after Francis had been some time on the spot. Francis sent to warn him before he landed, not to assume any pomp or state as ambassador, but to appear in the city as simply and modestly as possible. His arrival forced Don Alvaro to raise his mask, at least partially. The 'Captaincy of the sea' gave him some authority over the vessels which put into the port, and he availed himself of this —it was the first exercise of his authority—to seize the rudder of Pereira's vessel, which he had placed in front of his own palace. His excuse was that he understood that an attack was impending from the Gial, the warlike and hostile tribes in Java, which had furnished a large contingent to the army which had besieged Malacca the year before. This pretext, however, was soon taken from Don Alvaro. A Portuguese ship arrived from the Archipelago with the news that the tribes in question were at war among themselves, and so had no time to think of an attack on Malacca. The 'Capitan' was therefore forced to bring to light the malignant project which he had long ago conceived.

'As this quarrel,' says Mendez Pinto, who was at Malacca at the time, 'was founded upon hatred and avarice, the devil set fire thereto more and more; whence it came that after the

[2] Massei, p. 3, cap. 10, p. 298, mentions here two miracles which are found in the Processes. In the first case Francis detected a sin that a lad had committed by the torn and dirty state of a 'cotta' he had on. In the second case he raised from the dead the only son of a devout woman. The lad had sucked the point of a poisoned arrow. His name was Francis, and he afterwards became a frate of the Franciscan Order.

Father had laboured thereat for twenty-six days, with much diligence, the Capitan would never grant to the Father what he asked him, nor permit Diego Pereira to take him to China, as was ordered expressly in the patents of the Viceroy, besides that he spent large sums upon that design. And the better to colour his malice he was ever giving new explanations to the patents of the Viceroy, throwing out by way of raillery that this Diego Pereira whom the Viceroy meant to speak of was a gentleman who was living in Portugal, and not that other whom the Father presented to him, who had been the simple valet of Gonzales Contino, and was not a man of quality enough to be sent as ambassador to as great a monarch as was the King of China. This is how this affair passed, and by reason of it some of the most honourable of the place, moved by a pious zeal for the honour of God, and seeing that things were getting worse and worse, and that the Capitan would not listen to reason, nor consider what was represented to him, assembled together one morning, and besought him not to incur the fault of a thing which would do such great mischief to the honour of God, and for which he would have to give a very strict account in the next life. Moreover let him think what all the people would spread abroad concerning him, if he would really hinder so holy a man as Father Xavier from going to preach the law of God to those Gentiles, without considering that it thereby appeared as if our Lord Jesus Christ would use His service to open in that country a door to the Gospel for the salvation of souls. But the Capitan, instead of being moved by these words, only answered that he was old enough not to need counsel; that if the Father was willing to take so much pains for God, let him go to Brazil or to Monomotapa, where there were unbelievers as well as in China. For the rest, he had sworn that as long as he was Capitan, Diego Pereira should never go either as merchant or ambassador, and if God asked him to give account for this he would do so. He added to this that the voyage which Diego Pereira wished to make to China under the shadow of the Father, in order to gain a hundred thousand ducats of profit, belonged properly to no one but himself, as recompense for the services of his father, the Conde Almirante, and not to a servant of Gonzales Contino, whom Father Francis without reason wished to support in so bad a design. Saying this, he dismissed them. Then the Superintendent of the Finances, the Factor (Fazor), and the officers of the customs, seeing the extravagant answer which the Capitan had given, went all together one morning to tender a representation (requête) in the name of the King, saying that there was an ordinance made by preceding Governors, which expressly enjoined that on no account was hindrance to be opposed to the departure of any vessel that wished to set sail, provided that it undertook to return and pay the dues; and that according to this ordinance, Diego Pereira had put in a memorial to them, in which he set forth in writing that he bound himself to give to the King, of the profits of his ship, thirty thousand ducats for the necessities of the fortress, of which he paid the half down, and gave security for the rest against his return. That being so, they prayed the Capitan not to hinder the voyage, protesting that if he made it fruitless without cause, as was the case, the King would seize this money from the goods of the Capitan himself. He answered that if Diego Pereira bound himself to pay the King thirty thousand ducats, in consideration of the representation which they made, he for his part bound himself to give them thirty thousand cuts with the staff of a halberd there before him; and saying this, he ran to a rack of pegs to take it down and do what he said, which made them get to the door very fast.'[3]

Mendez then speaks of the marvellous patience of Francis Xavier under all this storm. 'He never made any other answer when he heard these things, but to cast his eyes to heaven and say, "Blessed be Jesus Christ!" words which he uttered with the same ardour with which they rose from his heart, not without sometimes shedding tears in abundance. And it was said publicly in Malacca, that if the good father desired, as it very much appeared that he did, to be martyred for the love of God, this persecution was to him in place of a great martyrdom. And, without falsehood, I must avow that as often as I call to

[3] Mendez Pinto, *Voyages*, t. iii. p. 435 seq.

mind how I have seen with my eyes the great honours which the King of Boungo, Gentile though he was, paid to the blessed Father in Japan, only because he had heard say that he was a man who imparted knowledge of the law of God, as I have heretofore related, and the evil treatment which I afterwards saw inflicted on him in Malacca, I am quite beside myself with astonishment, and believe in truth that there is no good Christian who must not be equally astonished.'[4]

Things went so far in resistance to Don Alvaro, that Francesco Alvarez, the officer actually holding the government, though not the Captaincy of the sea, gave orders that the rudder of the Santa Croce should be removed from his house by force; and it was only when Don Alvaro prepared a body of armed men to oppose the execution of this order, that Francis Xavier interposed, saying that material force must not be used for an enterprize for the glory of God. He was already offering prayers, masses, and penances continually for the conversion of Don Alvaro. He had used the good offices of Don Pedro de Silva, who seems not yet to have left Malacca, but in vain—they were as useless as his own entreaties.

It was then that, for the first time since he had left Portugal, Francis Xavier made public the character of Apostolic Nuncio with which he had been invested by the Pope at the request of the King. When he landed in India he had informed the Bishop of the briefs which he possessed, but from that time he had kept silence on the subject, and had never acted on his power. He now communicated the briefs to the Vicar of Malacca, Joam Suarez, and begged him to inform Don Alvaro of the danger he was in, inasmuch as all who impeded a Nuncio Apostolic in carrying out his mission were solemnly excommunicated by the Pope. He would not ask for any fresh excommunication to be launched against Don Alvaro, but he would not allow it to be passed over in silence that he was already excommunicated by the Church and the Roman Pontiff, if he persisted in his opposition to the voyage to China.[5] It appears

[4] Mendez Pinto, *Voyages*, t. iii. p. 435 seq.

[5] See below, letter to Father Gaspar Baertz, p. 528.

that the Vicar was not as hearty in the matter as Francis could have wished. He was worshipping the rising sun in currying favour with Don Alvaro, and the power of the Portuguese Commandants was so unlimited on the spot and during the tenure of their office, that we can understand without justifying the weakness of Joam Suarez. However, the excommunication was formally intimated to Don Alvaro. The Vicar took with him Francesco Perez, the Superior of the College, and the Auditor General Francesco Alvarez, already mentioned, and went to the Capitan. He explained the case, reading to him the document furnished him by Francis Xavier, and told him that he was excommunicate unless he gave way. He urged him as his pastor, entreated of him as his friend, and implored him as his servant, not to impose on him the obligation of publicly declaring him excommunicated. After the Vicar had finished, Francesco Alvarez read the order of the Viceroy as to the Embassy, and pointed out especially, for the second time, that the possible case of his resistance was there declared to be one of the gravest crimes,[6] and liable to most severe punishment.

Don Alvaro was not to be turned from his purpose by any entreaties or by any threats. He treated the Pontifical briefs with the same disrespect as the order of the Viceroy; indeed, he went so far as to accuse Francis Xavier of having forged the former. To the disgrace of Malacca, it must be said that there were not wanting people to take his part against Francis, who was insulted in the streets and unable at last to set foot outside the College. He preserved his usual serenity and gentleness of manner, and not a word of complaint escaped his lips. He spent whole nights before the Blessed Sacrament in the church, praying for Don Alvaro, and offered up mass frequently for his conversion. But there is a power in obstinate malice and envious spite which God sometimes does not choose to break, and which no power but His can bend. Don Alvaro remained unshaken. At last he consented—perhaps it was a sort of com-

[6] 'segunda vez lhe tournon a notifiar *a pena do caso major.*' *Resumo Historico*, ii. 167. The document drawn up for the Vicar of Malacca is quoted in full in this work.

promise with his conscience, by which he persuaded himself that he might escape the guilt of hindering an Apostolic Nuncio in his mission—to allow Francis to go to San Chan in the Santa Croce without Diego Pereira. There would be no embassy, but the missioner would be allowed to proceed on his path. Alvaro even seized the ship and the merchandize, leaving only a small part to Pereira, and he put on board along with a portion of Pereira's crew some people of his own. These last were either privately instructed, or disposed by the example of their master, to show little respect and kindness to Francis and his companions. Pereira seems to have behaved nobly; he readily sacrificed his goods to his enemy, and at the same time his people were ordered to attend carefully to all the wants and requests of Francis and his companions, and to furnish him with any money or merchandize he should desire, as the means of securing a landing on the coast of China. This seems to be the proper place for inserting the touching letter which Francis addressed to Pereira at this time.

(CIX.) *To Diego Pereira.*

May the grace and charity of our Lord Jesus Christ always help and favour us! Amen.

Since it has come about, from the greatness of my faults, that God has not been pleased to employ both of us for the expedition to China, the whole blame must be laid upon my sins; they have been so many and so great as to have stood in the way not only of myself, but of you, your interests and money, which you had spent on the preparations for this embassy. However, God is witness of my goodwill for His service and for you; and were it not for the sincerity of that goodwill, the grief which I feel at this moment would be greatly keener than it is. I am now going on board ship, where I shall wait until it is time to set sail, so as to be out of sight of your people, who are always coming to me in tears, and who complain that the failure of the embassy is a fatal blow to them. May God forgive him on whom lies the responsibility of so many and such great misfortunes!

I only ask one thing of you, and that is, not to come to see me, and so add to my sorrow by the sight of your grief and misfortune. Yet I am confident that this calamity will turn to your advantage; for I doubt not that the King, to whom I have made the request by letter, will worthily reward your admirable zeal for the religion of Jesus Christ. I have ceased to have any dealings with the Commandant, who has not hesitated to oppose a voyage which would have done so much for the spreading the Christian religion. May God forgive the man! I grieve for his lot, for he will have to suffer a far severer punishment than he can ever have imagined. May our Lord preserve your health, and direct, guide, and accompany my present endeavours! Amen.

From our house at Malacca, on the point of embarking in your ship.

June 25, 1552. FRANCIS.

The last words of this letter allude to the fact that Francis took up his abode in the ship for some time before he sailed. We have two other letters of this time, which show the thoughtful charity and noble gratitude of the writer. The first is about a case in which a man had to be persuaded to avoid scandal for the future by marrying a lady with whom he had been living.

The other letter from Malacca is about a sum of money which Francis had borrowed from Don Pedro de Silva. Don Pedro was soon to start for India, and Francis is most anxious that the money should be ready for him the moment that he landed.

(CX.) *To Master Gaspar Baertz of the Society of Jesus, Rector of the College of Goa.*

May the grace and love of our Lord Jesus Christ always help and favour us! Amen.

Master Gaspar, I am writing to his Lordship the Bishop on an important matter concerning a friend of mine. His name is Alvaro Gentili. Considerations concerning his duty and eternal salvation require him at once to contract a lawful marriage with a woman with whom he has lived unlawfully, and who has borne him children. He still hesitates, however, and requires a final push to make him accomplish this necessary business. I have observed that his mind is much occupied with esteem and reverence for his lordship; and I doubt not that if the supreme influence of so venerable a personage be added to the many reasons which I have put before him to bring him to do what is right, and to my constant entreaties, he will break off all delay and do what God requires of him. I beg of you, then, to talk over this matter with the Bishop, and to induce him—which you will easily do—to be so kind as to write to Alvaro Gentili, exhorting him seriously, and if necessary commanding him, to do at once what his personal honour, his station in life, and the position of his children, require, by publicly marrying their mother. I suspect there is another reason which makes still more necessary the exhortation I am begging you to get the Bishop to make to Alvaro Gentili. From his ambiguous answers about the matter which is so obviously advantageous to him, I have come to think that he is himself desirous of this marriage, but that he is deterred by his consciousness of some concealed canonical impediment, such as we know often to exist secretly in matrimonial cases. However, if such a thing does exist, he has not mentioned it to me. I merely suspect it, from my experience in similar cases. I have told my suspicions to his Lordship the Bishop, so that, having this information, he may have more ready at hand the effectual remedy for this poor soul, by being so good, in virtue of the authority he possesses, to remove the impediment, and so get rid of all obstacles to the remedy which the affair requires. I beg of you to be diligent and urgent in this business with the Bishop, and do not fail to write by the vessels which sail from Goa to Malacca in April (which is the proper time for favourable winds) to my friend Alvaro Gentili, of whom I speak, informing him of what you have either already done with the Bishop in his business, in consequence of what he has told you, or of what you hope to be able to accomplish with regard to the impediment, if any such exists, and if our friend will consent to declare it frankly to you himself. In this way I think it will be well to meet Alvaro's hesitation half way, as he seems to hang back from some secret motive of delay, which he will have less hesitation in acknowledging if you can give him hopes that he may be released by ecclesiastical authority from any difficulties of this nature. Once more I commend to you all this business with all the earnestness and efficacy I am capable of. May God unite us in the glory of His Paradise! Adieu.

Yours entirely in Jesus Christ,

Malacca, July 13, 1552. FRANCIS.

(CXI.) *To Father Gaspar Baertz.*

May the grace and love of Jesus Christ our Lord always help and favour us! Amen.

You must know, Master Gaspar, that I am indebted to D. Pedro de Silva far more than I shall ever be able to repay, even by the most energetic efforts. Indeed, when he was in command at the fortress of Malacca he showed me such favour in everything concerning the service of God, that I cannot remember any one who has helped me with so much true kindness since I came to India. I had come to Malacca, to pass from thence to Japan. D. Pedro, within two days, by his energetic diligence, procured me for this voyage the best ship that was to be had at the time, nor could I under the circumstances expect a better. Besides this, he gave me presents in kind, to the value of 200 crowns, bought with his own money, as an offering to the Sovereign of Japan, for the purpose of winning his favour, which was so needful, for the propagation of the faith of Jesus Christ. Would that God had permitted that D. Pedro de Silva should be Governor of Malacca this year also, then D. Diego Pereira's embassy to the Chinese empire, on which we had fixed our hopes so much for a great extension of our holy faith, would certainly have had a more favourable issue. How differently his own brother, D. Alvaro, has acted towards me, in taking from me the means of sailing for China, and depriving me of the vessel placed at my disposal by the Governor! May God forgive him! But I greatly fear that the Divine Majesty, so grievously insulted by his injustice, will visit him with a far severer punishment than he expects or imagines.

But to return to his brother Don Pedro, so different from him. He has lately lent me, in the most obliging manner, 300 gold crowns, of which I stood in need at the present moment, for paying off an old debt contracted in Japan. When I was in that country I thought it absolutely necessary to have a church built in the town of Amanguchi, and for this purpose I borrowed 300 gold crowns from some Portuguese merchants who were trading there, and spent the money on that work. The time for paying my debt had passed, and my creditors came to call upon me to redeem my word. Don Pedro came forward to assist my poverty with the most ready kindness, lending me the money just as I wanted it, and almost as a free gift. As soon therefore as he sets foot in Goa, I desire and order you to hasten to pay to him this sum of 300 crowns. You will draw it from the rents and revenues of the College, or from the pension of 2000 gold crowns granted by the King out of his treasury to the house of Santa Fè at Goa, not only for the benefit of the inmates of that house, but for the aid of the various missions and establishments for the propagation of the Gospel in different countries of the East, of which the Japanese mission is one of the most useful.

Take care that there be no delay in discharging this debt. Go and see Don Pedro immediately you know of his arrival, and give him his money with every expression of gratitude. I should be much distressed if by any delay of yours in performing so pressing a duty—one which I so earnestly enjoined on you, and which ought to come before all others—Don Pedro were obliged to jog your memory, and to ask you for payment. That would be very bitter news for me, and I am sure you will save me that pain, by executing most promptly, and in spite of all difficulties, this order of mine; and if you were—I do not say to neglect it, for that I cannot fear from you—but to let anything at all stand in the way as a pretext for not fulfilling it, I should consider that my most serious orders have little weight in your eyes.

May our Lord God unite us in the glory of Paradise! Farewell.

Yours entirely in Jesus Christ,

Malacca, July 16, 1552. FRANCIS.

The memory of the last days spent by Francis at Malacca was afterwards treasured by those who had been most frequently with him, as that of a time full of instances of his charity, his serene firmness, and the supernatural gifts with which he was so richly endowed. Several prophetical declarations which he made at this time were afterwards remembered. One of his promises to Diego Pereira was, that neither he nor his children should ever want, and the fulfilment of this prophecy was remarkable. Diego himself, as was to be expected, was amply recompensed by the King of Portugal for all his sacrifices. Many years after, a son of his, Francesco Pereira, fell into poverty, and one day had no provisions in his house. 'There passed by that house,' says Massei, 'a youth of very fair aspect, selling bread and fruit and many other kinds of provision, and Francesco went to the door and took in abundance what was enough for himself and all his family. But not finding in his purse any money to make payment, he took a robe of his wife's to give as a pledge instead. But the youth, with words of graceful kindness very far above the condition which seemed to be his, refused all, and left in great courtesy the best part of what he was carrying, and so disappeared. Francesco could never find him again, for all the great pains which he took thereto, and so it was thought that he was an angel sent by God to fulfil the promises made by His servant.'[7]

Another celebrated prophecy related to Don Alvaro him-

[7] Massei, p. iii. cap. x. p. 405.

self. Francis declared that before he finished his government, God would strike him in his substance, his reputation, and his person, in such a way as to make those who should hear it tremble. It was not difficult to predict that Alvaro would incur the inevitable lot of the persecutors of the Church and of the servants of God; but Francis Xavier's words foretold almost the particulars of the chastisement which God was sure, sooner or later, to inflict. It was also remembered by Francesco Perez and the other members of the Society at Malacca, that one day while in company with Francis — it seems to have been just before his departure, when he was taking leave of them — they had seen him suddenly throw himself on a bed and remain for some time, to all appearance, senseless. Then he rose up 'all wearied, and like a man who had dreamt very painful things,' and exclaimed, 'God forgive you! God forgive you!' naming one of the principal members of the Society in Europe. It was long afterwards known that at that time there had been great troubles in the Society in Portugal, on account of the person named.[8]

We must place at this time the last interview which passed between the good Father Joam Beira and Francis Xavier. Joam was on his way to India, in order to secure the taking of some measures against the King of Ternate, who was behaving in a hostile manner to the Portuguese and to Christianity. He had much to say to Francis, and appears to have opened to him some very sweet lights and inspirations which he had received in prayer. We shall find Francis presently referring to these. Another dear brother whom he was to part from for ever was Francesco Perez. He had caught the plague himself in his service of the sick, and lay at the door of death. When

[8] The person was no other than Simon Rodriguez himself. He had governed in Portugal with immense popularity, but not quite in accordance with the constitutions which Ignatius had been drawing up. It therefore became necessary to transfer him to another sphere of labour, in Spain, which was done with the consent of the King. The troubles were caused by the unwillingness of many of the Portuguese subjects to obey the new Superiors both of the College of Coimbra and the Province; and it was thought that Simon, in a visit he paid to Coimbra, had not done all that he might have done to calm the agitation.

Francis Xavier went to take leave of him, he showed signs of sadness, as he had hoped to die in the arms of his spiritual father. He begged that he would not forsake him. Francis told him that there was no need for him to wait in order to help him to die. He was to recover, and live many years labouring for God. A few days after the departure of Francis Xavier, Perez recovered, and lived to fulfil the prediction for seven and twenty years.[9]

At length the day came for the Santa Croce to sail. Francis once more left the ship, and went up to his favourite shrine of our Lady del Monte. There he remained in prayer until sunset, while a crowd gathered around to see him for the last time. At last he was told that the anchor was weighed, and that sail was being set. He went down the hill to the shore, accompanied by numberless friends weeping and entreating him not to risk himself in so perilous an undertaking as that of an attempt to enter China. He said he was going whither God called him, and consoled them with loving admonitions and warnings. Before he reached the strand, the Vicar General, Joam Suarez, came to take leave of him. He seems to have been a timid man, wishing to do his duty and at the same time stand well with Don Alvaro and others like him. He asked Francis whether he had taken leave of the 'Capitan'? would it not be better? and might not people think that he had been moved by human feeling if he left without saluting Don Alvaro? Francis answered with firmness and dignity. He and Don Alvaro would meet no more in this life; they would see one another again in the Valley of Jehoshaphat on the day of the terrible judgment, when Jesus Christ, the Son of God, would come to judge the living and the dead, and they would both stand there before Him, and Alvaro would have to give an account of what he had done in preventing him

[9] Another prophecy of this time related to Gaspar Mendez di Vasconcello, whom Diego Pereira had intended to send on board the Santa Croce to look after his merchandize. Francis told him that Mendez would not go, as he was to stay at Malacca and die shortly. Mendez at the time was in full health, but he fell ill before the ship left, and died four days after she had set sail.

from going to preach to the unbelievers the faith of Jesus Christ, the Son of God, who had died on the Cross for sinners. Very soon, indeed, would Don Alvaro feel the beginning of the chastisements for his sins; chastisements which would fall on his honour, his property, and his person; and as for his soul, might Jesus Christ our Lord God have mercy thereon! They came then to the open door of a church which looked upon the sea, and there Francis knelt down and prayed aloud to Jesus Christ, the Love of his soul, by the sorrows of His most holy death and passion, by the precious wounds which He was always presenting for us to His Eternal Father, and the merits thereof, to have pity on and to save the soul of Don Alvaro, that he might find mercy and pardon before the Lord. He bent himself down to the ground, and prayed in silence for a while; then he rose up, took off his shoes, and beat them against one another and against a rock by the shore, that he might cast off from his feet the very dust of Malacca. The people were stupefied, but the Vicar spoke a last word, 'How? is this parting for ever? for I surely hope in our Lord that you will soon come back to us with much peace!' 'As it pleases the mercy of God!' Francis answered, and mounted the side of the boat which was to take him to the ship.

CHAPTER III.

San Chan.

THE Santa Croce was not long in reaching Singapore, and there she must have remained for two or three days, since we have some letters dated thence by Francis Xavier, which he sent back by some vessel bound for Malacca. In them he speaks more freely than in the few short notes which he had written at Malacca. It is probable that he feared that his letters might be intercepted. Indeed we are told that Don Alvaro actually seized a bundle of his correspondence with Europe, expecting to find therein some attacks upon himself, but there was nothing. Nevertheless, Francis had written to the King to commend Diego Pereira to his notice, and it could hardly be but that he must have said something about the manner in which the embassy to China had been defeated. These letters have not been preserved to us; indeed, we have no letters to Europe later than those written before Francis left India for the last time.

The letters from Singapore require but little commentary. Francis is most anxious that the Bishop of Goa should be got to send to Malacca the formula declaring that Don Alvaro d'Ataide has incurred the penalty of excommunication by his conduct in the matter of the Chinese mission. We may consider this as sufficient proof that the Vicar, Joam Suarez, had not been bold enough in this respect to satisfy Francis: and indeed, we find a confirmation of this in one of the subsequent letters to Diego Pereira. Suarez perhaps objected that he had not seen the bulls appointing Francis to be Nuncio Apostolic. The bulls were at Goa. Or again, he may have pleaded that as Francis himself was allowed to proceed, and Pereira alone was detained, it could not be said that the Nuncio had been hindered in his mission. The want of courage which Suarez then manifested may have been a real support to Don Alvaro, and may have had a share in making Francis form the resolution, which we shall soon see him putting into words, to withdraw the members of the Society altogether from Malacca. The following letter explains very clearly the exact line taken by Francis in dealing with Don Alvaro. He did not ask that he should be excommunicated; but that as he had already incurred the penalty of excommunication, by virtue of the Pope's bulls, the ecclesiastical authorities should declare that such was the case.

(CXII.) *To Father Gaspar Baertz, Rector of the College at Goa.*

May the grace and love of our Lord Jesus Christ always help and favour us! Amen.

You will hardly believe, dear Master Gaspar, what trials were in store for me at Malacca. I cannot write them to you myself; I have desired Francis Perez to give you an account of them. You may believe what he writes, incredible as it may seem. I am going to the islands of China, which lie near the city of Canton, destitute of all human help, but protected, as I hope, by that of God. I am in hopes that pagans will open to me the way of entering the Chinese continent, since Christians have closed it against me, fearless of the sentence of the Church and of the anger of God which they have incurred. You will, then, use all diligence that his Lordship the Bishop may send to his Vicar in Malacca the formula of excommunication, by virtue of which the Governor of Malacca and the other persons who have caused the failure of a plan so useful to the Christian religion, may be publicly and by name declared to be cut off from the Sacraments of the Church.

I desire that it may be expressed in this decree that I have been sent to India by his Holiness Paul III. as Apostolical Legate, the bulls conferring which authority on me have been verified by the prelate himself. My reason for acting in this way is that in future no one may oppose the propagation of the Christian religion and the designs of pious men for that purpose. I would never ask of an ecclesiastical superior to exclude any one from the communion of the faithful; but I will do all in my power to let the world know that men who have already incurred excommunication by the decrees and bulls of the holy Pontiffs are so excluded. I will never consent in any way to connivance as to not publishing their miserable condition; that the publishing it may one day bring them to themselves, and lead them to seek a remedy for the wounds of their souls, and also that they may not have the audacity in future to delay any member of the Society who may be going in the interests of religion to the Moluccas, to China, or to Japan. So use every means that this edict may arrive at its destination.

Of the four of the Society whom I brought with me, I have sent three to Japan—Balthasar Gago, Duarte de Silva, and Pedro de Alcaçeva. They are in a good ship, and their weather hitherto has been good. I pray God to bring them safely to Amanguchi, where Cosmo Torres and Joam Fernandez are at present. I have kept with me one of ours and Antony the Chinese. Both are seriously ill, to my great annoyance and their own. Thanks be to God! Remember to send another of ours to Japan next year. He must be a priest, and also a man of learning. The subjects for Japan and China ought always to be learned and well read. If you have not a priest, send another, some clever man able to learn the Japanese language. At the same time, you should get by way of alms for our brethren in Japan a certain sum, either out of the treasury or from the Confraternity of Mercy, or from other pious persons, in order to help to some degree the penury and want in which those poor sufferers live.

Send F. Joam Beira without delay back to the Moluccas, where his presence is so necessary, together, if possible, with a priest of the Society, a man well furnished not so much with learning as with virtue; for in the Moluccas goodness of life is required more than learning. So the fathers who are sent thither later ought to be more approved and tried.

I again enjoin you to observe diligently the injunctions which I left with you; in the first place, those which regard the salvation of your soul, and your own perfection; in the second place, those relating to the administration of the Society. Should it happen, which God forbid, that I am not able to penetrate into China, I shall return to Goa, if I am alive, in the month of January next year. Meanwhile be sure to write me full details of everything concerning the affairs of India and Portugal; send me news of the Bishop, of the Franciscans and Dominicans; offer respectful greetings to all of them in my name, and beg them not to fail to recommend me to our common Lord in their holy sacrifices and prayers. Ask the same favour of the spiritual friends of our Society. Indeed, we who are living in China or Japan need a more than ordinary protection from God. May He in His mercy bring us to our heavenly country, where we shall certainly enjoy a far more tranquil life than in this place of exile! Amen.

Straits of Singapore, July 20, 1552. FRANCIS.

The next letter is to Joam Beira, who, as has already been said, was on his way to Goa. Its contents need no further commentary than the facts already stated.

(CXIII.) *To Father Joam Beira.*

May the grace and love of Jesus Christ our Lord always help and favour us! Amen.

Joam Beira, by all the love which you have for God's service, I order and implore you not to communicate to any one in the world the interior feelings which God has communicated to you; I mean those gleams of knowledge with which your soul has been enlightened from Heaven, on matters not involving the spiritual progress and salvation of the Christians of the Moluccas and the Islands of the Moor, or of others whose direction has been committed to you. As to matters concerning the advantage and spiritual progress of the Christians, you will discuss them with the Lord Viceroy, and do your utmost to obtain from him the orders and letters patent which you may judge necessary for those objects. And if you think you will succeed more easily by means of the authority and influence of the Lord Bishop, then go to him to present your request, and entreat him to induce the Lord Viceroy to extend the royal protection to the Church of the Moluccas, and to grant in favour of that Church the proper orders and rescripts in order to defend it from the injustice and plots of the King of the Moluccas, whom you consider hostile thereto.

Try to settle this business at Goa as quickly as possible, that you may be ready to return as soon as possible. I should like you to be ready to avail yourself of the ships which sail in May from Goa to the Moluccas, that you should take some of our priests with you. If there should be no priests at your disposal, you could bring some of our brothers who have had some education, and are destined for the priesthood, or even simple laymen. These last, if they are well disposed and intelligent, are more easily guided because of their greater humility, and so they are, I think, to be preferred for the maintenance of peace and union among our brothers of that residence. Settle too with Father M. Gaspar that at least one priest or one layman of the Society shall be sent regularly every year to the Moluccas. Pray do not let anything prevent your starting for the Moluccas in May; you are ardently desired there, as your absence is sensibly prejudicial to the interests of religion.

Take this letter with you to Goa, that it may be read, if necessary, to our brethren who are in authority there. I feel sure that when they know my intentions, they will not oppose your return in virtue of this order; but be careful not to reveal to anybody in Goa the things which you told me at our private conference in the church at Malacca. I am writing to Father Gaspar, urging him to help in every way, and to facilitate the speedy settlement of the affairs for which you have made this voyage, so that you may get through your business and be at liberty to seize the first opportunity of returning to the place from whence you came. But be sure not to start without the Viceroy's letters patent, drawn up in correct form, and revoking in so many words the privileges granted to the King of the Moluccas by Don Joam de Castro, because that King shows such flagrant bad faith as to fulfilling what he had promised in return, in not granting the advantages stipulated in favour of the Christians and the Portuguese. In short, his conduct is in direct contradiction to his words and engagements.

May God reunite us in the glory of Paradise!

Your brother in Jesus Christ,

Straits of Singapore, July 21, 1552. FRANCIS.

The two following letters relate mainly to a Japanese whom Francis had picked up, and whom he hoped to turn into a useful interpreter for the fathers who might in the course of the next year proceed to Japan.

(CXIV.) *To Father Master Gaspar Baertz.*

May the grace and love of Jesus Christ our Lord always help and favour us! Amen.

Master Gaspar,—Antony the Japanese is now sailing for Japan with Balthasar Gago and Pedro de Alcaçeva, to act as their interpreter till they reach Amanguchi. At my request John the Japanese has consented to render the same service to the Father, or the brother, not yet a priest, as the case may be, who is to be sent to Japan next year, and he will accompany him to Amanguchi. I beg you, in the name of God, to obtain for this good convert, who is in a very destitute state, an alms to the sum of about 30 pardams, and to buy with it for him such articles as he will know can be readily and profitably sold in Japan. This little capital will enable him, for the future, to live in a quiet way in his own country on his earnings. I was obliged to give him hopes of this advantage, to induce him to return to his native land, which he was obliged by extreme poverty to leave. But to inspire him with more zeal, so that he may serve our brother, who is soon to start, with fidelity and attachment, I think that, besides the gift I have just mentioned, which you will get for him from the Confraternity of Mercy, or from some rich and charitable person, you ought to receive him into your house, to feed him, and to attach him closely to the Society by great charity. As I hope that what I have said will be enough to show you how just my request is, and how much I have it at heart, so I will add nothing to this expression of my wishes, feeling sure that they will be faithfully followed.

May our Lord God bring us together in the glory of his Paradise!

Straits of Singapore, July 22, 1552.

Master Gaspar,—I think that the sum collected by way of alms which you are to send to Japan for the relief of our brothers, who are employed in that new vineyard of Jesus Christ, ought to be entirely converted into gold coin of the highest and best standard; you had better therefore take the opinion of experienced persons in choosing from the different gold coins, and keep, for this purpose, those which are acknowledged to be of the purest metal. I have heard it said that the Venetian gold was the most esteemed on this account. Ascertain by the opinion of persons acquainted with the subject, whether there is money to be found of the same standard. In Japan gold is exchanged to great advantage if it is of the best specific weight and standard, for the purest metal is in request for the enchasing of weapons, which is almost the only use to which gold is put in that country. Let our brother who is to be sent to Japan next year, that is to say in 1553, be trained to very great patience, for he will require an invincible patience to withstand the countless trials, first of the voyage, and then of the living, and abode. See also that he takes enough Portuguese cloth for himself and for the brothers whom he will find in the country, that they may be protected from the extreme cold of the winters, which are there far more severe than anywhere else.

Your most loving brother in Jesus Christ,

FRANCIS.

(cxv.) *To John the Japanese.*

John the Japanese, my son,—I am writing to Father M. Gaspar, to procure for you from the liberality of pious persons at Goa the sum requisite for getting for you such articles as may be sold with profit in Japan, for I do not wish you to return to your country as destitute as you left it. You will go hence to Goa with Father Joam Beira, by the vessels which sail at stated times from Malacca to India. On your arrival give the letter which I send to you, with this one, to Father Gaspar, the Rector of the College at Goa; it concerns you. Be careful to serve the fathers who are to come from Goa to Japan with zeal and fidelity till you all reach Amanguchi. I exhort you to confess all your sins frequently to a priest, with great sorrow for having offended God, and a firm purpose of amendment. I also wish you often to receive the Holy Eucharist with the deepest reverence and desire of fortifying yourself against the danger of losing the grace of God. To avoid this great evil, ask often for the Divine assistance, and when you are exposed to occasions of sin, strive with all your strength to remain steadfast in the service of God; remember that if you commit sin, you will have to suffer for it very severely in this world, or the next. You must therefore fear the falling into sin as the most terrible of misfortunes, by which you incur the eternal punishment of hell. When you are in Japan do not fail to greet Mark and Paul affectionately for me. May God make you holy and happy, and bring you to the glory of His Paradise!

Straits of Singapore, July 22, 1552.

Say from me to Father Francis Perez, showing him this letter, that when you are setting sail for India, he is to write to Cochin to Father Antonia Eredia, charging him in my name to collect some alms for you in that town, either from the Confraternity of Mercy, or from persons who are under his spiritual direction. Let the said Father F. Perez know that I shall be very glad if, in expectation of your return from India, he will collect at a favourable opportunity and keep for your use, a little money to be given to you on your arrival from Goa and departure to Japan; give him this letter to read, that he may know of my wish. He will help you more or less according to his ability, and if anything should prevent your taking letters from Perez to Eredia, you can show this letter, when you reach Cochin, to Eredia, rector of the college in that town. It will be sufficient to inform him of my intentions on your behalf, and he will do all in his power to raise something for your assistance. Once more I charge you to take every care of the fathers who will go with you to Japan, and to obey and serve them with perfect fidelity.

I add this with my own hand: My son John, serve the fathers, who will go with you to Japan with the utmost care, and accompany them to Amanguchi.

Your friend from the bottom of my heart,

FRANCIS.

On the outer fold of the letter is written 'To my son John.' On another: 'John my son, Joam Bravo will read this letter to you.'

The letter to Diego Pereira (of which we have another short epitome, which was probably sent in duplicate) shows all that extreme and affectionate consideration with which Francis now regarded him.

(CXVI.) *To Diego Pereira.*

Señor,—Having so lately seen you who are so very dear to me, and so tenderly loved, I cannot help being torn by a longing regret, and by the thought and picture of the danger in which I have left you, exposed daily to mortal contagion under a sky where the air is poison, and infected by the breath of so many plague stricken sufferers. This anxiety brings you constantly to my thoughts, and pierces my heart with bitter fear, lest something should happen to you, as is the lot of man, far different from your deserts and my prayers for you. In this ship, all your people, knowing your wishes, treat me with great kindness and honour, supplying me with everything necessary in abundance, not only for myself, who am in good health, but also for my companions who were sick, as you know, when we left. But all these sick, by the Divine mercy—for we know that even when God's hand is raised to strike us, He is merciful, and, coming from His hand, even ills have the virtue of graces—all these sick, by the Divine goodness, are daily getting worse. How sick at heart I am, and what bitter anguish consumes me, is known only to the Lord, Who consoles and afflicts us according to His good pleasure, Whose providence dispenses both joys and sorrows in an admirable manner; to Whom be praise and glory from all creatures in heaven and on earth for ever !'

I send you, Señor, the letters which I have addressed to his Highness and to the Viceroy of India, open, and with the seal detached, in order that you may be able to read them, and then close them up. Indeed I could have wished, for your sake, that my letter to the King could be taken to Portugal this very year by some confidential friend of yours, who could present it to the King, obtain and bring back the royal decree; for I am not rash, I think, in taking for granted that this decree will be what it is important to us both that it should be, and you know how necessary it is that it should reach us quickly. You can show this letter to Don Pedro—it will doubtless be a pleasure to him to see how I have spoken of him to his Highness. You will have observed that I have made two copies of the letter, one sealed, the other open, to be closed by you after you have read it. You will send them in different dispatches, and by different ships. I think, if you see no objection, that one of the two might be intrusted to Don Pedro himself, as he is going to the King. I should like the other to be given to the care of some one chosen by you—some very trustworthy friend whom you consider will handle most faithfully and prudently a matter so nearly affecting your fortune and honour. But I leave the whole thing to your will and wisdom.

I do most earnestly entreat you, Señor, to be careful of your life, your health, and also of your temporal condition; first of all, keep out of the way of contagion and of all dangerous communication with persons attacked by the pestilence, or with those who serve them; in the next place, be careful of your fortune, and do nothing imprudent—regulate all things with circumspection and mature judgment; do not, while accepting the good offices of those who profess friendship to you, confide too readily in any one, or go further than is safe with him till experience has shown you his true sentiments; lest, as is often the case, a false appearance of goodwill should have been assumed for the purpose of imposing on you.

Above all things, Señor, I conjure of you and beg it of you as a special favour, that the more you are pressed by adversity, the more you will turn to God in your heart. This is the only way by which you can gain consolation and courage, now that troubles and storms have fallen on you. In the name of your filial love to God, and of the comfort which you take pleasure in giving me, I entreat and beg of you as a favour, for which I shall be your debtor, that now that your heart is tossed by storms from the keen sense of your great affliction, caused by the recent injustice which has been done you so undeservedly, you will set apart some time to compose yourself, and after cleansing your soul by sacramental confession, go to the sacred banquet of the Body of our Lord in holy Communion, and so submitting every feeling of your soul to the providence of God, accept as good what He has been pleased to permit; hoping at the same time, as I do myself, not only that this violent storm will not injure you, but that it may be for the whole of your life an abundant and fruitful source even of temporal advantage and of public honour.

I keep, and shall take with me to China, Francesco de Villa; both because I stand in the greatest need of his services, and that I consider that no one is more capable of looking after your affairs on board, and of helping Thomas Scandelho, your agent. When, by God's help, we are on Chinese soil, we will send him back to Malacca by the first ship that sails. And if it is not God's will to open China to us, and I am refused an entrance there, I shall avail myself of the first opportunity to reëmbark for Malacca, and return to that town from the Chinese shores; should I happen to arrive there before the sailing of the vessels which are returning to Portugal, I would go to India in one of them.

I have been thinking that it would be well, Señor, if you wrote yourself to the King at full length, and minutely dwelling on all the advantages which could not fail to accrue to the Portuguese interests from the establishment of commerce with China, and if a residence were obtained for the King's officers in the port of Canton. I should like you to write on the same subject, and as carefully, to the Viceroy of India. For I am writing myself to the King in the same tone, as you may see by the letters which I send open. You will read and seal them, making them into a single packet with yours, which will contain similar information, and you will address it thus: 'To our Lord the King, from Father Master Francis.' Be careful, above all things, that the person to whom you intrust the delivering the despatches into the King's own hands is thoroughly attached to us—a man of sufficient authority and management, and also one whom you know to have important reasons obliging him soon to return to India, so that we may be sure that he will come by the first ship returning from Portugal to Goa, and thus enable us to have our business finished at once.

If our Lord God deigns to open the way for me into the Chinese empire, do not fail, Señor, as soon as you know that it is so, to write to me often, and by every opportunity; for however I may fare, it will give me the greatest consolation to have news of the health and doings of one so dear to me.

May our Lord grant you as much consolation in this life and glory in the next as I desire for myself! Farewell.

Straits of Singapore, August 1, 1552.

The Bishop's Vicar at Malacca has begged me to write on his behalf to his Highness. I am complying with his wish, although I have been told that, in the affair of our Embassy to China, he did not accomplish all that was in his power for our service, or rather for the service of all; and that he sacrificed the interests of God and of the propagation of our holy religion to the favour of Don Alvaro, the Captain of Malacca, to whom he wished to show himself devoted, for the sake of some worldly advantages which he hopes to purchase by his flattery. It is indeed a great mistake in which any one lives, who neglects God, from Whom all good comes, and hopes to gain what he wants or desires by means of men. Indeed it is my way to revenge myself on those who have offended me by loading them with all the benefits in my power; for God will infallibly send them the punishment they have deserved: and you will see, Señor, by very remarkable instances, that God will punish very severely all who have opposed me when I was labouring in His service. But in truth, Señor, I declare to you, that at this moment I feel a deep compassion for these men, and I tremble lest far heavier punishments than they expect should be hanging over their heads. Be so kind, Señor, as to give into the Vicar's own hands the letter in which I recommend him to the King, so that he may send it with his own.

If God brings me into the empire of China, as I hope from His mercy, I shall inform the Portuguese who are there of all that they owe you. I shall tell them of all your efforts, all your expenditure, the object of which was their help and consolation; lastly, according to your desire, I will salute them all in your name: and as you intend to continue to help them, I will lead them to hope that if in any way you are able, through God's help, to overcome the obstacles which have hitherto hindered your pious intention, you will be with them within the next year. I beg you, Señor, for your own sake, often to visit our fathers at Malacca; I feel sure that their society and conversation will alleviate the mental sufferings which agitate and distress you. Once more farewell.

Your very true friend, FRANCIS.[1]

[1] The duplicate of this letter, referred to above, is much shorter, and is dated July 22d. It consists of three paragraphs in Father Menchacha's edition. The first mentions, very briefly, the fear Francis expresses on account of the danger in which he has left his friend, the kindness shown

The voyage from Singapore to San Chan—the last voyage of Francis Xavier—was made memorable by several prodigies, and we find incidents of this kind crowded into the few last months of his life, as if he was to be magnified before men, after having incurred so severe a disappointment at Malacca. After leaving Singapore, the vessel was becalmed for fourteen days. There were in all five hundred souls on board, and the fresh water was soon consumed. No land was to be seen. The ship lay motionless on the sea, the torrid summer's sun streaming fiercely down upon it from a cloudless sky. Boats were sent out to search for some island that was thought to be not far off, but after they had ventured as far as they could go with safety, they returned without any results.[2] In this terrible strait, the captain and crew—they were in great part Don Alvaro's people, and so hostile to Francis—remembered that they had the 'holy Father' on board, the power of whose charity and miracles had rung through the whole East. They went to Francis, and besought him to help them in their need. Francis placed a crucifix before them, and bade them all kneel with him and sing the Litanies of the Saints. Then he retired for a short time into his own little cabin to pray, after which he came forth and bade them be of good courage. He had a boat lowered, and went into it with a child. He told the child to take some of the sea water and taste it. It was salt. Then he bade him try

---

to him on board the ship by Pereira's people, as also to his companions who are so ill that their sickness daily grows worse, the desire of Francis that Pereira will frequent the sacraments and visit the fathers at Malacca, and his hope that all will turn to his honour and profit. The second paragraph, without mentioning the Bishop's Vicar, speaks of the great mistake made by those who seek the advancement of their interests from men and not from God, as also of the best way of vengeance, that of trying to do good to those who have injured us. Francis then speaks of his intention of telling the Portuguese in China what they owe to Diego Pereira. In the last paragraph he begs Pereira to let him have news of him. If he does not reach China, he will perhaps return to Malacca, and thence to India. He sends with this letter a letter of his own to the Viceroy, which Diego must send on by a faithful messenger, and write himself also to the King and the Viceroy in the sense mentioned above.

[2] Bartoli says they were near Formosa, but could not get to land. *Asia*, t. i. p. 338.

again. This time it was sweet. On this Francis went on deck and ordered the crew to fill all the barrels and vessels they had with the sea water. They obeyed him, but when they tasted the water it was still salt. Then Francis Xavier blessed the water in all the vessels with the sign of the holy Cross, and it was found to be sweeter and fresher than the water of Bangan, as the sailors said. Bangan was the name of a spring at Goa, the water of which was highly prized. There was enough water, after abundantly supplying all present needs, for the people on board to keep some of it as a treasure, and in this way it became famous over the East, being often used for cures and the like, as if it were the water of some miraculous well.[3]

The calm ceased, and the Santa Croce was able to pursue her course to San Chan. The remainder of the voyage was full of wonders, which, as we have said, seem crowded to an unusual degree into these last weeks of the life of St. Francis. A Mussulman lost his child, a boy of five years old, who fell overboard at a time when the ship was running fast before the wind, and when it was impossible even to make an attempt to save him. The poor father was in despair for three days, till he chanced to come across Francis Xavier on the deck. It seems that Francis had not heard of the accident. He asked the father whether he would believe on Jesus Christ if his child were restored to him? The man declared that he would, and after a few hours he met his child as bright and joyous as ever,

[3] This miracle is one of those which were specially selected from the Processes by the Auditors of the Rota as being beyond all doubt and cavil. They tell the story much as it is told in the text, which is mainly taken from Bartoli (*Asia*, t. i. p. 338, 339), except that they leave out the incident of the little boy in the boat who first tasted the water. The eyewitnesses, whose names are given, and who swore to the truth of the facts at Cochin, are two whose names occur in the letters of St. Francis at this time,—Domenico Caldeira, who was ninety-eight years old when he was examined; and Joam Botelho, who was eighty-five. Botelho was one of those who drew the water out of the sea at the order of Francis, and tasted it before it was blessed, finding it salt, and then again after it was blessed, when it was sweet. There were a great many other witnesses who had heard the story from eyewitnesses perfectly worthy of credit, but these two seem to have been the only survivors within reach of the persons actually present.

running to him on the deck. He kept his promise, and was baptized with all his family. The ship put into Tchin-tcheon, the same port at which Francis had touched on his voyage to Japan three years before, and the marvels related by the crew and passengers drew universal attention to the holy Father. He preached to people of all nations, and baptized sixty Mussulmans. While he was administering baptism on the deck of the vessel, the bystanders remarked that he seemed to be of almost gigantic stature, so that he could reach forward to pour the sacred water of regeneration upon the heads of those who were kneeling behind the rest at a distance from him. When they had left Tchin-tcheon and proceeded on their voyage, they ran past San Chan without knowing it. Francis warned the crew of the fact, but they would not believe him. After a time, however, they lay to and sent a boat to look for the island. It was missing for some days, and they began to give it up, till Francis told them that it would soon return with some fresh provisions on board, sent as a present by the Portugese merchants already on the island. All came about as he had said, and the ship reached its destination.

The little island of San Chan, which has been made so famous to Christians as the resting place, for a short time, of the body of St. Francis Xavier, is described as half wild and barren, covered with brushwood, haunted by tigers, and inhabited by a poor and simple population. As the Portuguese ships were not admitted to Canton, San Chan was a rendezvous for them as well as for the junks of the Chinese traders, who exchanged goods with them. The Portuguese were not allowed to settle even here; but they ran up huts of wood and branches during the few months of their stay in the island. Life at San Chan during this time was wild, jovial, and even licentious. Occasions of self indulgence abounded, money was plentiful, the restraints imposed upon the Portuguese even in India were wanting, and religion was but little more thought of by many Christians than by the pagans. There were gaming and drinking, as well as other kinds of debauchery; and even those who did not go headlong into a course of vice, gave themselves up to enjoyment. The Portuguese, as always, received Francis with great joy. They built for him in a couple of days a little chapel, with a hut attached to it. Here he said mass daily and administered the sacraments, spending the rest of his time in teaching children, making up quarrels, and other such offices of charity. One of the gifts, the exercise of which characterizes this last stage of his life, was that of the knowledge of the future. Among a number of instances which were recorded afterwards, there is one which so beautifully expresses his generous grateful charity, as well as the relations in which he stood to the rich Portuguese merchants, that it can hardly be passed over. We have already incidentally heard of Pedro Velho, a merchant who was among those who had shown Francis so much respect and kindness while in the kingdom of Boungo, and who was reproved by him during the passage from Japan to San Chan for his want of faith. He was now trading at San Chan with a large sum of ready money, such as it seems to have been necessary for the merchants to carry with them in those days, and his chest was always readily opened on application from Francis Xavier. It seems that he was on very familiar terms with Francis, who used to exhort him to do penance by taking the discipline, and when he refused, alleging the tenderness of his skin, Francis would go and inflict the penance on himself. One day Francis was in want of a sum of three hundred ducats for a good girl, to whom he wished to give the money as a portion, in order to save her from the temptations to which her youth and beauty might otherwise expose her. He went to Velho, who was playing chess with another merchant. 'Ah, Father Francis,' said he, 'this is a bad time to come and ask me for money, when I am doing my best to get some of my neighbour's.' 'All times are good for doing good, Pedro,' said Francis; 'and now you have your purse in your hand, you can give more easily.' 'I must get rid of you,' said Velho, pretending to be in a pet. 'Here is the key of my chest; go and take whatever you want.' The chest contained a sum equal to forty-five thousand scudi. Francis took the money which he required, and gave back the key with many thanks. When his game was over, Velho thought he would go and see what Father Francis had taken; but he found that his money bags were as full as before. Nothing seemed to have been touched. He went to Francis to complain that he had played him an unfriendly trick. Francis assured him that he had taken as much as he wanted. 'Little or much,' said Velho, 'I find nothing gone; and when I gave you my key, my intention was that we should go shares in the whole money, and that you should take your half; God forgive your Reverence!' The good man spoke with his whole heart in his face: he had really meant as he said. Francis's countenance lighted up as with a heavenly fire, as was his wont when he uttered his numberless prophecies and revelations. 'Pedro,' he said, 'your offering has been accepted by our Lord, who weighs the most secret intentions of the will. He will pay you in due time. And now I promise you on His part, that never while you live shall you want what is becoming to your station. You will have times when you may be in danger of poverty, but you will always have good friends to succour you; and besides this you shall not die without first knowing the hour of your death.' Francis afterwards told him that he should know death was at hand, and prepare for it, when the wine tasted sour in his mouth.

Pedro Velho became a changed man from that day. He had lived hitherto as an honest but easygoing merchant, enjoying life, though keeping away from grievous sin; now he became almost a religious in his care as to the perfection of his daily actions, and in the restraint which he put upon his senses. He lived for many years, and was always saved from want, when his fortune had been bad, by the kindness of his friends. He gave a good part of his substance to the poor, and had many masses celebrated for his soul. At last one day at Macao, at an entertainment in the house of a friend, he asked for a cup of wine, and found that it tasted sour. He asked another friend to taste it, and this one found it sweet and good. Then Velho knew that the time was come for the prediction of Francis Xavier to be fulfilled. He arranged his affairs, prepared his soul for death, and went about bidding his friends goodbye as if he were going on a voyage, only asking them to come to the church and be present at his funeral. He had the requiem mass sung, laying himself on a bier with burning candles around him. The last absolution was given by the priest, and when his servants went up to lift off the pall with which their master had covered himself, Pedro Velho was cold and motionless: he had died during the mass.[4]

Francis reached San Chan in the last week of August 1552. He had not been long on the island before he fell ill of a fever, which kept him to his bed for a fortnight. Towards the end of October he wrote the letters which are next inserted, and which show the state in which his prospects as to China were at the time.

(CXVII.) *To Diego Pereira.*

God in His most bountiful mercy has brought us and your shiper, Señor, safely in this port of San Chan. You will receive information, from those who are able to give it, of the state and conditions of trade, and of the actual and future results which commerce may offer. I, who am unlearned in these matters, deem it more prudent to say nothing. I will only write to you concerning my own affairs. I am daily expecting a merchant, who has undertaken to take me to Canton. I have agreed to give him as his price twenty piculs of pepper; the picul is a weight peculiar to the country, and is equal to 120 Portuguese pounds. May this affair succeed, as I hope it will, for the service and greater glory of our Lord God!

If there is one man in the whole of this undertaking who deserves reward from Divine Providence, it is undoubtedly you; and you will have the whole credit of it. With the ut-

[4] This prophecy is selected by the Auditors of the Rota in their *Relatio.* They place it, however, at Macao, where there was no settlement till some years after this time. The historians who had seen the Processes place the fulfilment of the prophecy at Macao, and this perhaps explains the difficulty. The witnesses for the truth of the prophecy and its fulfilment are very numerous, including the son-in-law and two daughters of Pedro Velho himself.

most generosity, you have advanced the expenses for my journey and that of my companions as far as this island, as well as the price to be paid, as I said, for my conveyance to the Chinese continent and the province of Canton. Thomas Scandelho, your agent, accomplishes faithfully your orders, and gives me all I ask. May God reward him for his great charity, and for the continual acts of kindness which he performs on all possible occasions!

The Chinese merchant, whom I expect to conduct me to the territory of Canton, is well known to Manuel de Chaves, having kept him at his own house at Canton for several days, when he escaped from prison. This makes me feel confident that he will not be unfaithful to his word; and I have moreover discovered, in my dealings with him in this port of San Chan, that he thinks a good deal of the 120 measures of pepper, as I said. I hope, through means of Manuel de Chaves (whom I expect to find at Canton at liberty, and preparing to return to India) to write to you at length about the issue of the affair of our passage, and the reception I meet with at Canton.

If (which God forbid!) this Chinese merchant were not to keep his word, and no means remained of going this year to the continent of China, I am undecided what to do. I am not certain whether I should go back to India, or to the King of Siam, whs, they tell me, is preparing a solemn embassy to the Chinese Emperor, and possibly I might find some place or other in its train. If I return to India, I see no hope of success as long as Alvaro de Gama rules at Malacca. We should obtain nothing just or favourable there, and nothing would go well with regard to the expedition to China, unless God, who is all powerful, does by His supreme might some, thing which we do not at all expect. I do not write my inmost thoughts on this subject; I only say one word—that I fear very much that God will punish Don Alvaro more severely than he dreams of, if, indeed, his punishment has not already begun.

I wrote to you a long letter from the Straits of Singapore, and I feel confident that my letter has reached you safely, for

I gave it into the hands of Manuel de Fonseca, a servant of Antonio Pegado, who is very trustworthy. I have nothing farther, then, to say touching my affairs, excepting that I have just recovered from an attack of fever which had lasted a fortnight. If the voyage to China comes about, you will receive ample news by the letters I shall send from Canton by Manuel de Chaves, with others, full of particulars for the King. If circumstances were to hinder me from going on this voyage, Diego Vaz, of Aragon, offers kindly to take me with him; he proposes going to Siam, and he has just bought a Chinese junk for the purpose. I am inclined to this plan, because by occasion of the Siamese embassy I think I see that access to China and Canton is possible, and from thence I might write to you by Manuel de Chaves. This idea pleases me so much, that I almost lean towards the voyage to Siam. I beg you, therefore, if you find a favourable opportunity for sending letters to Siam, to take the trouble to do so, and let me know what you have resolved to do since I left, and in what state your affairs are—whether your embassy seems likely to come off at least next year, for then I would wait for you at Comaï,[5] or in some other port belonging to Canton. May God deign to grant it! With what delight we should embrace at finding one another on the soil of China, the object of our most earnest desires! If God wills otherwise, and if we are not to meet again in this life, may He, the most loving Lord of us and of the whole world, deign in His infinite mercy to allow us to meet some day in the glory of His Paradise, where we shall be for ever happy together! Farewell.

San Chan, October 21, 1552.

Francesco de Villa renders you all possible service on board ship. I ought to testify his deep gratitude towards you. He declares publicly that he owes his estate and fortune to you, and that he is indebted to you for the bread that he has to eat. He will return to you with Manuel de Chaves, and will

[5] It was, according to all appearance, the anchorage of Ke-moi, in a small island opposite Amoy, depending on the province of Fo-kiew. Léon Pagès.

beg to be excused for having come hither without having had your leave. If there is a fault in the matter, it must be imputed to me. Once more farewell.

Your true friend from his heart,

FRANCIS.

(CXVIII.) *To Francesco Perez of the Society of Jesus.*

Francesco Perez, I command you in virtue of holy obedience, as soon as you have read this letter, to leave Malacca and get ready as soon as possible to embark for India in one of the vessels which will sail by the next monsoon. If this letter reaches you after the ship have left, go by the vessel which sails by Coromandel to Cochin, where you must remain, employing yourself in preaching, confessing, and teaching the Catechism, as you did at Malacca, observing the order and method which I recommended and put down on paper when I left Malacca for Japan. If the difference of place demands a change, follow the rule which I gave in writing to Antonio Eredia, whom you are to succeed in the care and government of the College at Cochin. At the same time I order Eredia himself, or any other father, who since my departure may for any cause have been placed at the head of the house at Cochin, to go to Goa as soon as he has seen this letter, which you will show him, and there hold himself in readiness till he be sent to Japan. The day you enter the College of Cochin the Superior will give up his authority, and you must take his place, governing the house with the powers of Rector, depending, however, to the degree I have prescribed, on the Rector of the College of St. Paul at Goa. At Cochin, in accordance with the Institute of the Society, and with the talents which have been given you, you will employ your whole strength in procuring the glory of our Lord God, and in helping both our brothers and externs to advance in the ways of salvation and perfection. And although I am convinced that you will perform these things or any others greater and more in number, without hesitation, and at the mere sign of my will, still in order to add to your merits

I make use of the authority with which I am invested, and command you and Eredia also, or whoever may be Rector of the house at Cochin, in the name of obedience to do all that I have said in this letter. The Rector will immediately resign the government of the house and proceed to Goa by the first opportunity, and you will take his place. You will have under your authority not only all our brothers, both priests and laymen, who are now at Cochin, but those also who may come there at any time, whatever may be their rank and station and dignity, with the exception of any one whom the Rector of Goa from certain causes may perhaps desire to be exempt from your authority. And let all know that I command this in virtue of obedience. Do not you then fail to leave Malacca at once, and to go and take the government of the College at Cochin, both which things I order you to do.

Port of San Chan, October 21, 1552. FRANCIS.

(CXIX.) *To Francesco Perez of the Society of Jesus.*

May the grace and love of Jesus Christ our Lord always help and favour us! Amen.

By the grace of God we have reached the port of San Chan, 120 miles from Canton. On disembarking I had a hut made, in which I offered the Holy Sacrifice every day till I fell ill. I suffered altogether for a fortnight from the fever, and now by God's goodness I am restored to health. I do not want for holy occupations. I hear confessions, appease quarrels, and do other things of that sort. A great number of Chinese merchants from Canton come to this island for the sake of commerce, and the Portuguese have often dealt with them diligently to procure my passage to Canton; but they have all flatly refused, declaring that it would be at great risk to their lives and property if the governor of that town should hear of it, and it was impossible to persuade them to receive us on board their junks.

However, doubtless by God's arrangement, we have met with a honest Canton merchant, who has come to an agreement with me for 200 gold pieces. He promises to take us in a little vessel, which is to carry no one else but his own sons and a few faithful slaves; so that if the governor of the town ever gets to hear of the affair, he will not be able to find out from the crew who it was who took us to Canton. He has also promised that we shall be in his house for three or four days, with our books and baggage; and then very early one morning he is to take us to the gate of the town and put us on the road leading to the government house. I shall go straight to the governor, telling him that I am come to announce the divine and heavenly law to the Emperor of China, and then I shall produce the Bishop of Goa's letters addressed to that monarch. All the Chinese merchants are always glad to see us, and say they shall be very glad if the matter is accomplished.

I am aware, as all tell me, of the twofold danger of this enterprise. It is possible that the Chinese merchant after receiving the gold may leave us in a desert island, or throw us into the sea to conceal his crime; and again, if we reach Canton, the governor may put us to all kinds of unheard of tortures, or make slaves of us for life. It is a capital crime for a foreigner to enter any part of China without a passport. But there are other dangers besides, greater and more unknown, all of which I cannot enumerate to you, but I will mention a few of them.

The first, then, is mistrust of God's goodness and providence; especially when I have only come to this country in obedience to God, and from pure love of Him, to declare to the Chinese nation the most holy law of God, and to preach to them His only Son Jesus Christ, the Author of our salvation. Since He in His mercy has given us this mind, to doubt of His help and protection in the midst of the dangers which are before us would be a greater and more real danger than any that could be brought on us by His enemies. For neither the devils nor their satellites and servants can hurt us, without the permission of Almighty God. If God is our defender, how easily will He dispel all perils! And besides, we shall follow the precept of the Lord Jesus, '*He that loveth his life shall lose it, and he that hateth his life in this world keepeth it unto life eternal;'*[6] words which are in accordance with those other words of Jesus Christ, '*No man putting his hand to the plough and looking back is fit for the kingdom of God.*'[7] As, then, we see that these spiritual dangers are more serious and more certain than any perils of the body, we prefer to face those of this life rather than incur everlasting death. In truth we have resolved and are positively determined to enter China. May God only prosper our footsteps for the spreading of His Faith; and then let the devils and their army do their worst! I care not for them. '*If God be for us, who shall be against us?*'[8]

I hope that the ships which are sailing soon for India will bring you letters from me, announcing my entry into the city of Canton. My companions are perpetually sick. The Chinese lad I brought here to act as my interpreter has, I find, forgotten his native tongue; but I have found another well acquainted not only with the language, but with the literature of his country, who has offered of his own accord to accompany me in my voyage. May God reward him for it in this life, and after death! I beg you to pray that God will keep him firm in his intention and purpose.

All the good Chinese who know us take pleasure in our company, and earnestly desire that we may penetrate into China. They have already got an idea that the books which they see us carrying everywhere contain better doctrine than theirs; and though it is possible that it may only be from their love of novelty, they would like to see us enter their country. Notwithstanding, as I told you, these Chinese refuse altogether to take us there themselves. I am daily expecting the merchant with whom I made the agreement. God grant that he may not fail me! Should that misfortune happen, I know not what I should do, whether I shall return to India, or go to Siam, to join the embassy which the King of Siam is said to be shortly about to send to the Emperor of China. I will let you know

[6] Lat. orig. *Qui amat animam suam in hoc mundo perdet eam, et qui odit animam suam in hoc mundo in vitam æternam custodit eam.* S. John xii. 25.

[7] *Qui ponit manum suam ad aratrum et respicit retro, non est aptus regno Dei.* S. Luke ix. 62.

[8] *Si enim Deus pro nobis, quis contra nos?* Rom. viii. 31.

what we shall do by a ship that sails for Malacca after a few days. May Jesus Christ our Lord grant us His help and guidance, that we may one day come to the possession of the glory of heaven!

The least of your brothers in Jesus Christ,

Island of San Chan, October 22, 1552. FRANCIS.

(CXX.) *To Father Gaspar Baertz.*

May the grace and love of Jesus Christ our Lord always help and favour us! Amen.

I do not know whether it was from Malacca or from the Straits of Singapore that I wrote to tell you what had happened to me. God has brought us safe and sound to San Chan, a Chinese island about 120 miles from Canton. Here I am in daily expectation of a Chinese merchant with whom (in consequence of severe edicts forbidding the entrance of a foreigner without a government passport) I have agreed for 200 pardams to be taken to Canton. May God permit this plan to come about! I have heard that the Emperor of China has been sending persons into different countries to learn their manners, institutions, and laws. So there is reason to hope (and this the Chinese themselves tell me) that the King will not despise the Christian religion, or reject it at once. If God grants me life, and deigns to make use of us for His work, I will let you know about it. For the present, I charge you to watch over your soul, for in truth if you do not I can have no hope of you.

Remember to read again and again and observe very strictly the rules which I left with you, especially those as to self humiliation, in which I recommended you to exercise yourself every day. Fear above all things lest, in looking round on all that God is pleased to do by means of you and our brothers, you should learn to forget your own soul. My great love for you all makes me wish very much that you would consider very seriously within yourselves how many things, through your fault, God has not done. I would rather see you occupied with this thought than with that of the great works of which you are the instrument. The first thought would cause you to feel shame and humility, by making you sensible of your imperfections and miseries; the latter might be the means of your running into danger of pride and presumption, trusting in good deeds with which you have nothing to do, and in wonders of grace which are the work of God alone. Pray consider how many persons this pernicious error has led into danger, and how fatal it would be to the whole Society if such a contagion should ever spread in it.

I also charge you to receive very few subjects into the Society; choose those who are capable of devoting themselves to literary studies, or of attending to the work of the house. I assure you it would be better to buy slaves—yes, slaves—for domestic employments, than to admit into the Society persons unfit for it. If any of those whom I have sent away are at Goa, be sure not to receive them back on any pretence, for they are not suited to our Institute. If any one of them should completely reform his life, and give sufficient proof of it, by public penances, voluntarily accepted and long persevered in, so as to have made in your judgment full satisfaction, you may send him to Portugal to the Superior of the Society there, with a recommendation from you; for I am satisfied that none of these persons are fitted for India.

And should any member of the Society, priest or layman, be guilty of any serious fault, which has given scandal to others, send him away instantly, and do not allow yourself to be persuaded by any one to receive him back, unless perchance his sense of guilt, his repentance, and voluntary penance, have been such as to save him from this calamity. Otherwise, on no account receive him; not if the Viceroy and the whole of India were to ask you to do so. I remind you also to send to the Moluccas and Japan none but well tried brothers, of great virtue and experience; these are the kind of workmen wanted in these countries.

Recommend me very much to all the fathers and brothers of our Society, and to all our friends. Greet the Dominican and Franciscan Fathers from me, and beg them not to cease to intercede for me with God in their prayers and holy sacrifices.

May God direct us continually, and call us some day to the enjoyment of His everlasting bliss in heaven!

The least of your brothers in Jesus Christ,

San Chan, October 25, 1552. FRANCIS.

The plan which Francis mentions in these letters, according to which he was to be landed on the Chinese shore, and after three or four days left to shift for himself with the mandarin who governed at Canton, was necessarily alarming to the Portuguese merchants. The year before this, one of their ships had been driven ashore on the Chinese coast. It had been mercilessly confiscated, and the whole crew thrown into prison. The Manuel de Chaves whom Francis mentions was probably the captain or owner of this ill-fated vessel. Indeed, the Chinese prisons were full of Portuguese, the liberation of whom had been made one of the main objects of the projected embassy of Pereira. If Francis were to give himself up to the mandarin after landing, the Chinese merchant might escape, as Francis had pledged himself by an oath not to reveal his name to the authorities. But the latter were very likely to make his appearance an excuse for a descent on San Chan with an armed force, which might seize whatever ships and merchants it could find there, and thus punish what was looked upon as an invasion. This accounts for the strong opposition which we are told was made by the Portuguese to the design which Francis had conceived, which, however, he would certainly have executed, if the Chinese merchant had not played him false. His intention to carry out at all costs the heavenly inspiration which had guided him to the coasts of China is an instance of what frequently meets us in the lives of the Saints.

The servants of God are strongly and unmistakably prompted to undertake some great work for His glory, and then in His inscrutable providence He does not permit the execution of the design, giving them the merit of the intention, and of the faithfulness and perseverance with which they have followed it out against the greatest difficulties and dangers. China was not yet to open her gates to the Gospel of Jesus Christ. The magnificence and sound policy of the attempt remain the same, for if it had been given to Francis Xavier to found a flourishing Church in that great Empire, the Christianization of the extreme east of Asia would have been secured. It was such a design as only an Apostle could conceive; its failure entailed a long series of calamities, and the loss of a precious opportunity which has never recurred. The power of Portugal was already beginning to wane, and the European influence in the East was at no distant date to be transferred to Holland and to England, Protestant powers, the first of whom made no scruple of letting her envoys trample on the Cross for the sake of securing a footing in Japan, while the latter has at least never thought it unwise to sacrifice the interests of Christianity to those of commerce or political power. Again, it would have been a bad example to future missioners if Francis Xavier had abandoned his design on China merely because he could not enter its ports as a member of a Portuguese embassy. These thoughts may not have been in his mind: but he at least intimates that he was guided by that true instinct of sanctity which bids the servants of God never look back when they have put their hand to the plough, never to yield to the obstacles of various kinds which the devil raises against them, but to make such opposition a fresh motive for their perseverance, an additional reason for implicit trust in the power of the God whose cause they have in hand, and Who is wont to bring about the mightiest results by the weakest instruments and when all human hope of success has faded away.

Francis calmed the alarm of his Portuguese friends by promising not to land on the Chinese coast till their ships were safe on the high seas on their way to Malacca. The appointed day for the coming of the Chinese merchant was the 19th of November. Before that time, all the ships except the Santa Croce had left San Chan. They took with them the last set of letters which remain to us from the hand of Francis.

(CXXI.) *To Father Francis Perez of the Society of Jesus.*

May the grace and love of Jesus Christ our Lord always help and favour us! Amen.

As Gaspar Mendez's ship was weighing anchor, I gave Francesco Sanchez, one of the passengers, a letter for you, which I hope has reached you; and I beg you to take to heart the orders which it contains, and which I here repeat, and to give all heed and attention to carry them out. I have been expecting for a week the merchant who is to take me secretly to the city of Canton. I have the fullest confidence in his return, unless some hindrance should occur beyond the power of man to overcome, and I rely on the great value of the reward which I have promised him, and which he highly appreciates himself; for the quantity of pepper which I have agreed to have delivered to him, if he conveys me safe and sound to Canton, will easily obtain for him a profit of more than 350 gold pieces of our money. I have to thank my very dear friend Diego Pereira for the means of buying my passage to China at so high a price, and he has of his own accord, and with great generosity, placed at my disposal this large quantity of very valuable merchandize. May God reward him! as I cannot, for I shall owe him a debt, I can never repay all my life. I beg you all to use your most zealous endeavours to render signal services to this excellent man in every part of India where it is possible to serve, support, or assist him, whenever any of you may have the opportunity; to embrace eagerly every means of doing him kindness, without sparing your utmost pains. The most earnest efforts of our united body will never be enough to repay only this last sacrifice which he has made at so great a cost to himself, one so beneficial to the propagation of our holy faith, in order to introduce us into the empire of China, hitherto impenetrably closed against the Gospel. By this means the Society of Jesus will obtain the object of all its constant prayers—the power of spreading the kingdom of Jesus Christ and bringing into the Church the many nations of that immense empire: and as results are rightly attributed to their origin, it will really owe all these blessings to the generosity of one single man, Diego Pereira, who out of his own fortune has provided the funds so necessary for my voyage, that is to say for the beginning of this great work.

Pray inquire of him whether he has hopes of surmounting the obstacles in the way of his embassy, and if he is coming to Canton next year. I desire this as greatly, as I expect it little. God grant that my small hopes may be contradicted by a more fortunate issue than I look for! God forgive the man who is the cause of so great a misfortune! I greatly fear that before long a terrible vengeance from the God he has offended will overtake him, and it may be that he is even now about to experience its first effects. I am writing to Pereira himself, so that if he obtains a more favourable result than I dare hope for he may be good enough, on sailing for China, to take with him some of our Society, whom Father Gaspar will send to him from Goa, if he has notice given him some time beforehand. I have told him this by letter. But if, as I think most likely, Pereira, despairing of the success of his mission, should pass by Malacca, and direct his course towards Sunda, then it will no longer be necessary for the priest who would have gone with him to China to sail from Goa to Malacca in May. You should give notice of this, as I have told you in good time, to Father Gaspar, the Rector of the College at Goa; and I wish you to be clearly informed of Pereira's intentions before your departure for Malacca. I have dismissed Ferreira from the Society, as he was not fitted for it; when therefore you arrive at Cochin, and have taken the management of the College, I command you, in virtue of obedience, not to receive him into the house. Do all you can to urge him to enter the Franciscan or Dominican Order: and if you succeed, ask those fathers to grant him admission. Write also to Father Gaspar Baertz at Goa; saying, that by virtue of my authority I absolutely forbid his receiving Ferreira into the community or under the College roof; only let him do all he can to help him as to his admission into the Order of St. Francis or St. Dominic.

If by God's grace I am able to reach Canton, I will do all

in my power that you may hear of it from me next year, by letters which I will send you to India, which I will dispatch, if possible, so as to catch the vessel sailing to Coromandel. I shall use for this Pereira's ship on its return to Malacca; I only pray it may reach Malacca in time. If all this can be successfully arranged, you will be able to hear at Cochin during March of my arrival at Canton. With this view, it may be well, when you leave Malacca, to ask Vincent Viegas to be good enough, as soon as he hears that Pereira's vessel has returned from the Chinese coast, to ask for and take charge of any letters from me which it may bring, and to send them to Cochin by way of Coromandel. And that these letters may not be left at Coromandel, especially if, as I think will be the case, there is no immediate opportunity of sending them further by sea, you will do well to beg Diego Pereira himself beforehand to send you my letters to Cochin, together with his own, so as to be forwarded, in case of necessity, overland from Coromandel.

With regard to your departure for Malacca. A day or so before you start, I think you should ask Vincent Viegas to take charge of our house in the city, and of the little chapel in the suburb attached to it dedicated to Our Lady the Mother of God. Ask him, then, to allow you to commit these two houses of the Society to his care and custody. And lest, in the course of time, either he himself, or any other in his name, should think of acquiring any right of property in these two places, you must put in his hand the copy of the deed of gift, by which the Bishop has made over these two buildings in regular legal form to the Society of Jesus in perpetuity; and at the same time you must get Vincent to give you an acknowledgment, declaring that he takes these two houses under his charge and protection simply as a trust, and for their preservation, and that he is ready to restore them to the Society when required to do so. You must take with you the original of the Lord Bishop's deed of gift and diploma, that they may be sent in the safest way from Cochin to Goa, to be kept in the latter town in the archives of St. Paul.

I most positively order you to adhere resolutely to your determination of leaving Malacca, and I expressly forbid your being you to let yourself be persuaded to remain there by any entreaties however pressing, or by deceitful promises from any one. You must not continue wasting your labours, which, as things are, may be far better employed elsewhere, on a town so ungrateful and unworthy of your help, as has for some time been the case. If you think well, you can leave with Vincent Viegas, the good priest I have mentioned to you, our Brother Bernard, who can occupy himself as he has hitherto done, in teaching children the rudiments of grammar and the elementary prayers, as well as the Catechism. But in this matter I leave all to your discretion; you will settle as seems best to you, either to take him or to leave him. I should not like Ferreira, who has been dismissed from the Society, to sail for India in the same ship with you: do your best that he may embark in another. If there is none to be found, or if he refuses to part from you, and begs you earnestly to take him with you, you may consent to do so, on the express condition that he must solemnly promise to enter some other religious order. After he has entered into this formal engagement, you can receive him, and charitably do all you can to help to confirm him in his resolution.

The interpreter who consented, as I told you, to come with me to China has been frightened, and given up the idea. He remains here, having abandoned me; we are determined to run all risks, relying on God's help. There are three of us—Antony of the holy Faith (a Chinese educated at our college), Cristoval, and myself. Pray much to God for us, for we are going to expose ourselves to the almost certain danger of the most dreadful slavery. But our consolation is in this thought with which we are deeply penetrated,—that it is infinitely preferable to be a captive in chains for the pure love of God than to purchase the most delightful liberty by basely and ungratefully deserting the sufferings and the Cross of Jesus Christ. Should it happen that the Chinese merchant, on whom depend our hopes of going to Canton, should change his mind through fear or any other reason, and break his word, I have resolved in this last case to sail for the kingdom of Siam, for which voyage I have a favourable opportunity. In fact, I have heard that a ship was being fitted out there for Canton, and if I can get on board, by God's protection I hope before the end of the year to land on the shore which is the object of so many prayers to me. Salute very heartily all our friends for me, and especially Vincent Viegas, and beg them to commend me to our Lord. May He remain with you, and accompany me! May He bring us all to the glory of Paradise! Farewell.

Your brother in Jesus Christ,

Port of San Chan, November 12, 1552. FRANCIS.[9]

(CXXII.) *To Diego Pereira.*

I have nothing, Señor, to write to you at present, except to repeat over and over again the assurance (which however often it were expressed, would be always inadequate to my obligation) of my gratitude for the daily and hourly kindness which your affection and charity are constantly lavishing on me without end or measure; you have, even in your absence, thought of means of exercising these virtues through your servants and representatives, who assist and do me services in all ways and at all times. Among them is Thomas Scandelho, your agent, who supplies me so affectionately and generously with everything I ask for, that it is easy to see that he knows and shares the extreme tenderness and goodness which you entertain for me, not only always ready, but always eager and anxious to give me even more than I ask and more than I want. May our Lord God reward you, for He alone can! I am unable to pay my debt to

[9] Father Menchacha gives another letter here, which is obviously a duplicate of that to Francesco Perez (October 22). It is addressed to Francesco Perez and Antonio Eredia, and formally orders the first to go at once to Cochin and assume the Rectorship there, and the second, or any one who may be in his place, to surrender his post to Perez, and go to Goa, there to prepare for the voyage to Japan as soon as Father Gaspar Baertz orders it.

you, and must owe it for the rest of my life; but though I can never pay the principal, I will not fail, at any rate while I live, to pay you as it were a daily instalment, and interest according to my ability, by continually praying our Lord God to preserve you from all evil, and never to suffer you in this life to be deprived of His grace, but to keep you always flourishing both in body and mind through all accidents of health and unfavourable chances of fortune, always constant in the faith, diligent in the duties of holy religion and divine worship, so that He may one day crown your merits, and receive your soul to the glory of His Paradise. And as in spite of my endeavours I can never satisfy myself as to this, I call on all my brothers the fathers of the Society of Jesus, who are serving the holy Church in different places in India, to be my helpers and assistants: certainly all would have performed this duty of their own accord; nevertheless I have, so to speak, added spurs to their willingness by ordering them to show you all the offices of most friendly goodwill as an eminent patron of our Society, and commend you to God in their daily prayers and sacrifices as a mainstay of the Christian religion in this country, on whom rests the chief hope of seeing the holy law of Jesus Christ, the Son of God, preached in the empire of China, and of spreading His glory to the ends of the earth. Indeed our Lord Himself, Who knows so well your ardent zeal for His service, Who so truly values your labours so profitable for the extension of His kingdom, could not fail, independently of the prayers of His servants, to encircle you and your interests with His constant favour and protection, and to further the accomplishment of your desires to this holy end of helping the preaching of the Gospel and the calling wandering souls to the faith of Jesus Christ. If, Señor, the affair of your embassy to the Sovereign of China intrusted to you by the Viceroy of India should be at length successfully arranged next year, I beg of you to deal with Francesco Perez (whom I have ordered to set sail for Goa) so that he may procure from Father Gaspar Baertz, the Rector of the College of Goa, a priest of our Society, whom you may take with you when you embark for China. I should wish the valuable vestments which, as you know, we had prepared for that expedition, to be given to him to bring them with him. When our project failed, I left them at Malacca in the care of Francesco Perez; that father will deliver them to you on seeing this letter, which will sufficiently acquaint him with my intentions. I will send the chalice, a part of the same set, which I brought with me, by Thomas Scandelho, so that you may, if you think well, give them all to the father who is to accompany you on your embassy.

I would go to Malacca with your people, if I could hope that you would start for China next year. Now, I am following a more probable hope of going there this very year, which rests on a merchant of Canton; and if (which God forbid!) he should fail me, I have now made up my mind to accompany an Aragonese named Diego Vaz, who, as I told you, is going to the kingdom of Siam. From thence, I rely on being able easily to reach Canton next year by a Chinese junk. Thus should it happen that your embassy really starts next year, I hope that we shall meet again, God knows with what consolation, at Comaï or at Canton. Pray write to me, if you have an opportunity, to the kingdom of Siam, saying what you have decided, for under any circumstances I shall much like to know the state of your affairs from yourself. As to the particulars of my agreement with the Chinese merchant who is to take me into the city of Canton, I do not give them to you yet: it will be more convenient and satisfactory to do so when the matter is over. You may look for them in letters which I hope to send you by Manuel de Chaves. If our fathers at Malacca, Goa, or elsewhere, can render you any services towards the favourable conclusion of your embassy, do not fear using them; you will find Francesco Perez, Gaspar Baertz, and all the others, wherever they are, eager at the first expression of your wishes to serve you with all their power; they know perfectly how much I have this at heart. But—and this is the chief point in their eyes—they are firmly convinced that this matter concerns, above all, the glory of our Lord God, and the release of a vast number of

clamation of the terrible anathema which he has so rashly brought upon himself will fill him with terror at the thought of so great a calamity, and inspire him with some sentiments of penitence, which may be the beginning of his salvation, and might excite in him a salutary desire of meriting by due satisfaction the lawful absolution of the Church at the hands of her competent ministers.

The other reason which moves me to take this step is my wish to hinder for the future any such audacious attempt of wicked persons, which would be so hurtful to the preaching of the Gospel. For I see by experience that the apostolic labourers of our Society will often find opportunities of embarking at the different Indian ports for Japan, the Moluccas, or other countries, to preach the law of Jesus Christ, and that the officers, invested in such places with the authority of royal governors, may be tempted by avarice, jealousy, or other bad passions, to thwart and insult them, by causing the failure of their plans, as has happened to myself. In order, therefore, that these officers may not imagine that such crimes will remain unpunished, this bad example must be made infamous by its terrible issue, and must be branded with so much ignominy that those persons whom the fear of God does not influence may be made to shrink from its imitation by the disgrace before men, the dishonoured name, the mark of shame burnt in on his forehead, which will render this poor man so utterly infamous for ever. I am convinced that some of these persons let themselves go with more audacity to such wickedness partly from forgetting the severe punishments attached to this kind of crime, through the sordid cares in which their souls are plunged, and partly often through their disgraceful ignorance of the discipline of the Church, in which they are wonderfully uninstructed. It is necessary to put visibly and palpably before them an example of the Church's severity inflicted on a person of note, that by this salutary warning they may be held back when instigated to perpetrate a deed so injurious to religion; and that perceiving the danger they incur in this way of sin, they may restrain their licentiousness by fear.

The letter of the Bishop, or of his Vicar General, declaring the Commandant of Malacca separated from the Sacraments of the Church and under anathema, should be taken to Malacca by Joam Beira, or by any other of our brothers who are going there to embark for Japan. At Malacca he must place it in the hands of the Bishop's Vicar. In order that this latter may not put off carrying his orders into effect, you must obtain the Bishop's promise to write, or to order his Vicar General to write in his name, a special letter to the Bishop's Vicar at Malacca, charging him under pain of anathema not to delay publishing in the Church the excommunication incurred by Don Alvaro. As for yourselves, beware in the name of God of neglecting this order of mine, and so of committing the great sin of violating obedience. Let me hear before the end of the year how diligent you have been in this, and what has been the issue of this affair.

With regard to myself, I have written this letter in the midst of preparations and anxieties relating to my passage from this island to the Chinese continent. The voyage will be most painful under my present straitened circumstances; it is full of a thousand dangers, of very doubtful issue, and full of terrors. How it will turn out I know not, but I have a firm confidence, and a strong inward assurance, that however things may go, the result will be good. If—which God forbid!—my hopes of the Canton merchant captain, whom I expect every moment, should fail, I am determined, as I told you, to go by sea to Siam, whence there is some expectation of being able to get to China. Should this hope too come to nothing, through some accident, then I shall return to India. But my mind presages that I shall not be driven to this last resolution, and I persist in believing that my first hopes will be fulfilled, and that I shall have my prayer and place my foot at last on Chinese ground.

One truth has been proved to me by the clearest evidence, and I tell it you confidently, and wish you to be fully convinced of it. The devil has an unspeakable dread of the Society of Jesus entering China, and every effort in this direction seems to wound the very apple of his eye; it makes him rage with impotent fury, and lash himself up, and boil over with passion. Take my most certain word for it, in this port of San Chan, where fresh obstacles to our passage to China are raised every hour, he keeps contriving them in swarms, one after another, as though he thought the first nothing, and that new ones were always needed; and if I were to describe them by letter, or by work of mouth, I should never end. I perceive most clearly that the war cry has sounded in the camp of hell, and the spirits of darkness, all in consternation, are arrayed against us as if to defend their last entrenchments. But let it be no less certain to you, that I am confident, relying on the unfailing help and grace and favour of our Lord God, that Jesus Christ, our Saviour and Redeemer, will expose to the scorn of the whole world the enemy of mankind, disappointing his wishes and making his vain hope void; and the glory of the Divine Majesty will shine all the more brightly because the instrument of these wonders will be one so mean, because that by means of me, the least and the vilest of men, He will overthrow that insolent spirit, so bold in his pride, and expose him to the most shameful defeat and universal derision.

It is to you especially, Master Gaspar, that I now particularly address myself. I most earnestly beg of you not to fail to fulfil exactly and completely everything which I commanded you on my departure, whether by word of mouth or by writing, in the form of instructions. Be careful to forget nothing, nor to neglect carrying it out at the proper time: as if supposing me perhaps dead, you might imagine yourself free and independent and no longer under obedience to me. I remember a case of this kind when certain persons fell into this error in consequence of my long absence. In truth I shall not die before the time appointed by God; long indeed it is that life has been a burthen to me, and to die my prayer; but it is idle for men to speculate curiously as to the hour of my decease, which is settled beforehand in the eternal decrees, and which the foolish opinions of men cannot hasten or retard. This counsel is given to fortify you against the temptation of trusting too much to your own judgment; as you may remember a time when you allowed yourself to follow your own opinion irrespective of my instructions. Whether you did the best thing in the world on that occasion, or whether you made a mistake, God knows; but I should not like by any chance on my return next year to find in India anything that I should have to punish.

And pray pay particular attention to what I am about to add. Be very severe, I would almost say be most fastidious, in choosing persons to be received into the Society. The few who have stood the sharp test, as I may say, of the first examen should then go through all the successive experiments of the novitiate at home. Indeed I have seen in certain persons, who had passed through the first beginnings, things which made me mistrust the judgment of those who could have admitted them. They were persons who, as experience shows, ought to be excluded from our Society, from consideration of our own good character and tranquillity. It was impossible for me not to make an example of this sort in the person of Alvaro Ferreira,[10] whom I have struck off the list of our brothers. Should he come to you, be sure not to receive him into your house, but you may give him the help of your advice and influence to enable him to enter another religious Order. But you must absolutely refuse to receive him back into our Society, however pressingly he may entreat you; and you must understand that you are forbidden this by the obedience which you owe me; for after mature deliberation, and by my authority, I order you not to receive into our house Alvaro Ferreira, whom I know to be in no way suited to the ways of our Society.

Should it happen that when this letter reaches Goa another than Gaspar Baertz is Rector, let him, whoever he may be, understand that the directions I have given to Gaspar apply equally to him.

Port of San Chan, November 13, 1552. FRANCIS.

[10] A Captain Alvaro Ferreira was martyred at Achen in 1565, with four other Portuguese, because they would not abandon the faith of Jesus Christ. Perhaps he may have been the same religious who was not able to remain in the Society, but to whom God afforded the opportunity of confessing the faith, and gave the grace of martyrdom. Léon Pagès.

A few days after these last letters were written, Francis Xavier was again struck by the fever. It was Sunday the 20th of November, after he had said mass. The mandarins at Canton had stopped the supplies of food on which the sojourners at San Chan mainly depended. There was thus a scarcity of provisions on the island, and Francis suffered real privation, the people of Don Alvaro, of whom the greater part of the crew of the Santa Croce was composed, still showing him but scanty kindness, out of fear of displeasing their master. At the same time the day passed on which the Chinese merchant had promised to appear. The interpreter on whom Francis had reckoned had already given up the design for want of courage. No hopes remained; and the fever came to bid him prepare to meet his Lord. He had long known that his death was at hand: he had taken leave of his friends, even in India, as if he were never to see them more. While at San Chan, he had once been in company with six others, Portuguese merchants. Francis had said to them that they must look after their souls: 'within a year,' he said, 'the greater number of us will be dead.' Five of the seven, besides himself, died within the year.

When the fever first attacked him, Francis had come on board the Santa Croce as to a kind of hospital: but the motion of the ship made it difficult for him to keep his thoughts fixed on God, and he begged to be taken ashore. He was apparently lying on the ground in the open air, when Jorge Alvarez, the same, as it seems, whose account of Japan we have printed above, could not bear to see him so abandoned, and took him into his own hut. It gave him hardly any shelter from the cold wind and rain, but it was something. On the Tuesday, the good Jorge thought it would be well to bleed the patient. Francis knew that this could but be a fresh torment, but he consented, and the operation was repeated a second time. His nerves were lacerated, and he fainted under the pain.

Then there came on a great nausea, so that he could not eat even a few almonds, which the captain of the ship sent him as a present. So he went on suffering through the week; lying in the wretched cabin, gazing up to heaven through a small window in the side, and talking with the tenderest devotion to a little crucifix which he held in his hand. On the Monday week after his illness had begun, he became delirious for a time: his wanderings were all about his expedition to China. After this he lost his speech, but on the Wednesday he regained it, and his mind no longer wandered. He begged that the vestments and sacred vessels which he had used for mass, as well as his manuscript of the Christian doctrine in Chinese letters, and the rest, might be taken on board the ship. Antonio, the Chinese lad from the College, and Cristoval, the other mentioned in his last letter, were his only attendants. Antonio related afterwards how on one of these days, Francis had fixed his eyes on Cristovel, and began to weep, saying, 'O miseravel, O miseravel!' Some months after the poor boy fell into a habit of sin, and died suddenly and miserably. This was Francis's last prediction. He spoke a good deal in ejaculations, but chiefly in Latin, so the lad could only remember what was not new to him, such as his favourite exclamations, '*O Sanctissima Trinitas*,' '*Jesu Fili David miserere mei*,' and '*Monstra te esse matrem*.' So the fever went on, and he grew weaker and weaker. He could take nothing for some days before the end came. At last, on the Friday, the 2d of December, about two in the afternoon, he fixed his eyes lovingly upon his crucifix, his face lighted up with joy, sweet tears poured from his eyes, and he breathed his last, repeating the words of the *Te Deum*, '*In te Domine speravi, non confundar in æternum!*'

The body of Francis Xavier remained unburied till the Sunday after his death. Some of the Portuguese belonging to the ship were touched at the sight of his corpse; but it does not seem that the majority showed any great devotion. The fear of Don Alvaro was strong upon them. The good pilot, however, Francesco d'Aghiar, was there, and he did what was in his power in honour of the Saint whose companion he had often been. Jorge Alvarez, also, had a coffin made, in which the body was placed, clothed in the priestly vestments: but it was thought well to cover it, and fill the coffin, with quick lime, in order that the flesh might be consumed, and the bones taken to India. Late on the Sunday evening the coffin was lowered into a grave dug on the top of a low spur of hill, close to the shore. There was a level space on the summit, and here they planted a wooden cross, at the foot of which was the grave, with two mounds of stones, one at the head and the other at the feet. No one followed Francis to the grave but Antonio the Chinese, two mulattos who bore the coffin, and Francesco d'Aghiar.

It is possible that the utter abandonment and destitution in which Francis had died to some extent encouraged the Portuguese in their neglect. One of Don Alvaro's men wrote to him at Malacca saying that Master Francis had died, and had done no miracle in his death; that he had been buried at San Chan like any one else, and that they meant to bring his body to Malacca when they set sail, that the people there might not say that they were not as good Christians as themselves. Meanwhile time went on, and after the middle of February the time came for the ship to depart. Antonio the Chinese asked the captain to have examination made as to the state of the bones of Francis Xavier. But when the coffin was opened, and the lime removed, the body was found entire, fresh, the flesh soft and succulent, the veins full of blood. The Portuguese who made the examination tried to cut off a small piece from near the left knee, and found that blood flowed freely. Even the vestments were unhurt by the lime. The prodigy at once converted the indifference of the Portuguese into veneration and devotion. The men of the crew crowded round, weeping, and begging pardon for their neglect and coldness. The body was taken as it was, in the coffin, on board the Santa Croce, which set sail immediately, and after a perfectly prosperous voyage, reached Malacca on the 22d of March 1553.

It was late in the evening, but the news of the arrival flew through the city. There were none of the Society there. Francesco Perez and his companions had punctually obeyed the order of Francis as to leaving Malacca. Some priests were sent on board that same evening by the Vicar; they examined the body, and testified to its wonderful preservation. The next day a solemn procession was organized, and the body was carried to the Church of our Lady del Monte, the shrine which we have more than once mentioned as so much beloved by Francis. The clergy, the nobles, the people, even, it was remarked, the heathen and Mussulmans themselves, all thronged with torches and candles to honour one whom they regarded as their Apostle. The plague had been still raging at the time when the Santa Croce came into the harbour—while the sacred body was being carried through the streets it ceased all of a sudden. The city also had been suffering from want of provisions, and a supply came in just at this moment.

Don Alvaro d'Ataide alone was indifferent to the arrival of the body of Francis Xavier. He was at play with one of his officers when the procession passed. He went to the window, made a scornful remark on the devotion and simplicity of the people, and resumed his game. We may as well add here the sequel of his history. A little more than a year after the time of which we are writing, Don Antonio de Noroña, a son of the Viceroy, was sent as Capitan to supersede Don Alvaro, against whom a number of charges had already been, and were afterwards, made. One of these charges rested on his disobedience to the Viceroy's orders. Don Alvaro was put in prison, and his goods confiscated. Such severity was exercised against those of his party, that a number fled from Malacca, and took refuge in the Mussulman states. Don Alvaro was sent to Portugal. He had already a sort of leprosy creeping over his body, and while in prison at home a bad abscess broke out in his neck, and his whole body became so corrupt that no one could be found to go near him and wait upon him. In this state the poor man died; helped, as may be trusted, by the prayers for the salvation of his soul of the Saint who had predicted so accurately the inevitable temporal chastisement which his public opposition to the Church had brought upon him.

The body of Francis Xavier was buried in the doorway leading to the sacristy; but it was taken out the coffin, and covered with earth. The grave is said to have been too short; certainly a wound was made on the shoulder, whence blood flowed fresh and fragrant. So things remained till August, when Joam

Beira arrived at Malacca with two companions, on his way back to his mission at the Moluccas. He could not bear to leave Malacca without seeing the body. Diego Pereira and some other devout friends of the Saint disinterred it secretly. It was found perfect and fresh as before, emitting the most exquisite fragrance. A cloth spread over the face was stained with blood, and there was a wound in the side, from stones which had fallen in when the earth was pressed down. Diego Pereira now had a magnificent coffin made, in which the body was laid, the head resting on an embroidered cushion, and the whole covered by a coverlet of cloth of gold. It was put in a secure place, and Joam Beira left one of his companions, a lay brother, Manuel Tavora, to take charge of the corpse until it could be moved from Malacca. Soon after Pedro d'Alcaçeva arrived, on his way back from Japan, and it was by him that the transfer to Goa was finally arranged.

The two brothers set out late in 1553, on board an old unseaworthy vessel, the worst, it was said, that was then navigating the Eastern seas. More than once on the voyage she was saved in a preternatural manner. Once she got aground on a shoal, and once she ran against a rock. The last time the danger was so imminent, that the crew gathered round the sacred body in the cabin, imploring the intercession of Francis as if he had been alive among them. In January the vessel arrived at Cochin, where the body was venerated by Francesco Perez and a crowd of others. It touched at Baticala on its way northwards, where a lady who was desperately ill heard of the arrival of the body, and declared that she should recover if she could see it. She was taken on board the ship, and was immediately healed. The captain seems to have put into Baticala on account of adverse winds from the north; and he despaired of reaching Goa before Holy Week, which that year fell very early. He went on in a boat to Goa, to announce the approach of the treasure which his ship contained. The Viceroy immediately equipped one of the large swift galleys of the country, and sent the Superior of the College of Santa Fè, with two other religious and some choristers and orphans, to escort the body at once to Goa. Gaspar Baertz was already dead—he had been long ailing, and had finally broken down on a Sunday in the October before, while he was explaining in the pulpit of the Cathedral the Gospel of the day:[11] 'The kingdom of heaven is like unto a king, who would take account of his servants.' He had died on the 19th of October, having just sent for Melchior Nuñez, who, according to the orders of Francis Xavier, was to succeed him; for Manuel de Morales, whom Francis had put first in the order of succession, had worn himself out in Ceylon, and though ordered to Goa for his health, had died there two months before Gaspar himself.

The galley to which the body of St. Francis was now transferred left Baticala amid salvos of artillery from the ships lying there, and the chanting of the *Benedictus Dominus Deus Israel* by the youths sent from the College, and reached the harbour of Goa on the Thursday in Passion Week, March 15th. The galley anchored opposite a church of our Lady at Rebandar, about half a league from Goa itself; and as it was night, a message was sent on to the Fathers of the College to be ready to meet the body when it arrived at the quay the next morning. It was taken into the church, where Melchior Nuñez said mass very early the next morning; and almost before they had time to arrange for the start to Goa, six large boats arrived with Diego Pereira and a number of other Portuguese gentlemen and merchants on board, with torches in their hands, come to do honour to the Saint whom they had known and loved. Before they reached the quay, the number of these boats had swollen to twenty. On the quay was the Viceroy with his Court, the Council, the Envoys of allied Asiatic princes, and a crowd of nobles and people, the Chapter, the Brethren of Mercy, and the religious community of the College. The orphans carried in front a large crucifix veiled (for it was Passion Week), and once more the sweet strains of the *Benedictus* rang through the air. The procession through the streets was impressively touching, 'so much,' says an eyewitness, 'that in all that assembly of Christians tears and sobbings were so universal, that

[11] The 21st Sunday after Pentecost.

the mere sight thereof was enough to make a sinner become truly converted.' The procession marched from the gate of the city straight up the great street, which from one end to the other was richly hung with tapestries and silken cloths, the windows crowded with ladies, while below the doors were filled with vessels of incense and fragrant scents. Flowers were showered in the path, all the forts fired their cannon, the church bells rang joyously. So it went up to the College of St. Paul, 'and although that day was the Friday of Lazarus,[12] the College nevertheless made great festival, all the altars were richly apparelled. There were quantities of lamps and candelabras and crosses of silver, and the like. The sacred body having arrived in the church was placed near the High Altar, and a solemn Mass was sung with concert of voices and instruments, conformable to the solemnity of so great a feast.[13]

Others relate how many wonderful cures were wrought upon the sick as the body was borne through the streets. Among the persons healed was Doña Juaña Pereira, probably one of Diego's family, who recovered at once from an illness of three months; and also a child which lay at the point of death with a blessed candle lighted in its hand. The body lay in the sanctuary with the face, hands, and feet uncovered, in order to satisfy the devotion of the people, whom it was difficult to keep from it. That day the mass of the Holy Cross was sung by the Chapter, and on the Saturday the mass of our Lady, by the Franciscan friars. On Sunday the body was placed in a cavity made in the wall of the sanctuary, near the gospel end of the altar.

The ships which came that spring from Portugal brought a letter from St. Ignatius, written at the end of the preceding June, in answer to that of St. Francis Xavier of January 29th, 1552. St. Ignatius begins by rejoicing over the good news as to the opening of Japan and China to the preaching of the

[12] Friday in Passion Week.

[13] Mendez Pinto, t. iii. p. 455 seq.

[14] See *Resumo Historico*, cap. 75. The account of the burial and translation given above is condensed from Bartoli and Massei.

Gospel. Then he goes on to say that he regards as a wise measure what Francis has mentioned as possible, his sending to Japan and China Gaspar Baertz and others; and if he has himself gone to China, as he has spoken of as probable if the affairs of India permit, that also he regards as good, being persuaded that it is the Eternal Wisdom Who guides him. But, he adds, as far as his own lights go, he thinks Francis will do more for God by remaining in India and sending others, as he then may be able to make his work felt in more countries than one. Still further, he says, considering the greater glory of God and the greater good of souls in India, and the dependence of India on Portugal, he has made up his mind to order him by holy obedience to return to Portugal on the first favourable opportunity; and so he commands him in the name of Jesus Christ, though his return to Europe be in order to his going back again as soon as possible to India. Moreover, in order that when people oppose his departure he may be able to make them understand the reasons for the determination, Ignatius adds certain heads—the good effect which the presence of Francis may produce on the King, as to the progress of the faith in India, Guinea, and Brazil, the need which the Holy See has to be thoroughly informed as to the state of affairs in India, the necessity that Francis should come to choose and form for himself subjects in Portugal and Rome, and the good which he might do in the affair of the mission to Ethiopia. As for his subjects in India, he could govern them meantime as well from Portugal as from China or Japan. Such was the provision made by Ignatius for that long desired meeting, of which both he and Francis Xavier had spoken so tenderly in their letters—a meeting the enjoyment of which was only to be granted to them in the kingdom of heaven.

The body of St. Francis Xavier still rests at Goa, in the church which formerly belonged to the religious of the Society which he loved so much, and which one of the successors of his friend, King John III., was persuaded by a despotic minister to persecute so savagely. His work lived after him, and is living still,—although it would be difficult to say whether the ignorant opposition of heathen barbarity or the more culpable malice of enemies calling themselves Christians has done the most to mar the fulfilment of his glorious designs for the conversion of the East.

We may trust that India has not been allowed to retain him without a special intention of the good Providence of God in favour of the nations for whom he laboured so devotedly. We may hope that the presence of his relics on those distant shores may be an earnest that the day is to come when the darkness which has hitherto covered the largest, the richest, the most populous of the world's continents may be rolled back, when the early dreams of Ignatius and his companions about the East may be more than fulfilled, and the countless churches of Christian Asia may form the brightest gems in the diadem of the Spouse of Christ. Two glorious names, that of St. Thomas their ancient, and that of St. Francis their modern, Apostle, will then receive preeminent honour from myriads of rejoicing believers, whose grateful praises will faintly reflect the reward decreed to them above, where 'they that are learned shall shine as the brightness of the firmament, and they that instruct many to justice as stars for all eternity.'[15]

[15] Dan. xii. 3.

THE END.